A Comprehensive Dictionary
of the Middle East

Also by Dilip Hiro

Non-Fiction

Non-Fiction
Iran Under the Ayatollahs (2013)
After Empire: The Birth of a Multipolar World (2012)
Apocalyptic Realm: Jihadists in South Asia (2012)
Inside Central Asia: A Political and Cultural History of Uzbekistan, Turkmenistan,
Kazakhstan, Kyrgyzstan, Tajikistan, Turkey and Iran (2011)
Jihad on Two Fronts: South Asia's Unfolding Drama (2011)
Babur Nama (2007)
Blood of the Earth: The Battle for the World's Vanishing Oil Resources (2006)
Iran Today (2006)
The Iranian Labyrinth: Journeys through Theocratic Iran and its Furies (2005)
Iraq: A Report from the Inside (2003)
Secrets and Lies: Operation Iraqi Freedom and After (2003)
The Rough Guide History of India (2002)
Iraq: In the Eye of the Storm (2002)
War Without End: The Rise of Islamist Terrorism and Global Response (2002)
India: The Rough Guide Chronicle (2002)
Neighbors, Not Friends: Iraq and Iran After the Gulf Wars (2001)
Sharing the Promised Land: A Tale of Israelis and Palestinians (1999)
Dictionary of the Middle East (1996)
The Middle East (1996)
Between Marx and Muhammad: The Changing Face of Central Asia (1995)
Lebanon: Fire and Embers: A History of the Lebanese Civil War (1993)
Desert Shield to Desert Storm: The Second Gulf War (1992)
Black British, White British: A History of Race Relations in Britain (1991)
The Longest War: The Iran-Iraq Military Conflict (1991)
Holy Wars: The Rise of Islamic Fundamentalism (1989)
Iran: The Revolution Within (1988)
Inside the Middle East (1982)
Inside India Today (1977)
The Untouchables of India (1975)
Black British, White British (1973)
The Indian Family in Britain (1969)

Fiction

Three Plays (1985)
Interior, Exchange, Exterior (Poems, 1980)
Apply, Apply, No Reply & A Clean Break (Two Plays, 1978)
To Anchor a Cloud (Play, 1972)
A Triangular View (Novel, 1969)

A COMPREHENSIVE DICTIONARY OF THE MIDDLE EAST

Dilip Hiro

OLIVE
BRANCH
PRESS

An imprint of Interlink Publishing Group, Inc.
www.interlinkbooks.com

First published in 2013 by

OLIVE BRANCH PRESS
An imprint of Interlink Publishing Group, Inc.
46 Crosby Street, Northampton, Massachusetts 01060
www.interlinkbooks.com

Library of Congress Cataloging-in-Publication Data

Hiro, Dilip.
A comprehensive dictionary of the Middle East / by Dilip Hiro.
p. cm.
ISBN 978-1-56656-904-0
1. Middle East—Dictionaries. I. Title.
DS43.H57 2013
956.003—dc23
2013000294

Printed and bound in the United States of America

Cover image copyright © Monysasi | Dreamstime.com

To request our complete 52-page full-color catalog, please call us toll free at 1-800-238-LINK, visit our website at www.interlinkbooks.com, or write to Interlink Publishing, 46 Crosby Street, Northampton, MA 01060
e-mail: info@interlinkbooks.com

Contents

List of Maps

Using this Guide

Abbreviations Used

9/11	September 11, 2001	Gen.	General
abbr.	abbreviation	GDP	Gross Domestic Product
A.D.	Anno Domini (L., Year of	GMT	Greenwich Mean Time
	the Lord); used for the	i.e.	id est (L., that is)
	first millennium only)	km	kilometer
A.H.	After Hijra	lit.	literally
aka	Also known as	lt.	lieutenant
b.	born	m	meter
B.C.	Before Christ	pl.	plural
brig.	brigadier	pop.	population
ca	circa	q.v.	quod vide (L., which see)
col.	colonel	r.	regina/rex/elected leader
cu	cubic	sing.	singular
d.	died	sq.	square
der.	derivative	St.	Saint
est.	estimated	U.K.	United Kingdom
EUR	Euro	UN	United Nations
fig.	figuratively	U.S./USA	United States of America
ft.	feet		

Alphabetical Order

The alphabetic order does not take into account spaces, hyphens, or the Arabic definite article "al"/"el."

In the Arab Middle East (a) the current rulers of Jordan and Saudi Arabia, and the past rulers of Egypt and Iraq are called kings; (b) the ruler of Oman, sultan; (c) the ruler of North Yemen, imam; and (d) the rest, emirs. For (a), (b), and (c), see the first name of the ruler, and for (d) the family name. For the king of Iran, see the family name.

Alternative Spellings

The spelling given in the headword is preferable to the alternative(s) mentioned later.

Cross-References

The cross-reference noted by [*q.v.*] means that further information about the subject is available under the word(s) after which it appears.

No cross-reference is used for the countries of the Middle East, except for Palestine and Transjordan.

Index

It covers the list of entries and sub-entries in alphabetical order.

Preface

The best way to use this reference work is to look up the term(s) first in the Index.

This general-purpose dictionary pertains to the Middle East, a region covering Bahrain, Egypt, Iran, Iraq, Israel, Jordan, Kuwait, Lebanon, Oman, the Palestinian Territories, Qatar, Saudi Arabia, Syria, the United Arab Emirates, and Yemen. The reason for this selection is given under the entry: Middle East.

The dictionary covers the following subjects: Arab-Israeli wars, Arab Spring, biographies, Christianity and Christian sects, civil wars, country profiles, ethnic groups, geography, government, Gulf wars, history and historical places, hostages, international agreements and treaties, Islam and Islamic sects, Judaism and Jewish sects, languages, literature and writers, military and military leaders, miscellaneous, non-conventional biological-chemical-nuclear weapons, oil and gas, personalities, the peace process, politics, political ideologies, religious ideologies and ideologues, regional conflicts, regional organizations, terrorism, tourist designations, and the United Nations.

I have included only those personalities who made an impact on the politics, military, religion, or literature of a country or the region, and who reached adulthood around the turn of the 20th century or later. Likewise, I have included only those international agreements, protocols, or treaties that were signed, or initialed, in the 20th century or later. In the case of political, religious, or politico-religious parties and personalities, I have paid as much attention to those in power, now or in the past, as to those in opposition.

Since standard ways of transliterating Arabic and Hebrew words require acutes, graves, ogoneks, and so on, and these are not used by the English-language news agencies or newspapers, I have opted for the spellings current in the English-language print media. Within this context I have been consistent—using, for instance, Halacha, not Halakha; Muslim, not Moslem; and Quran, not Koran.

Dilip Hiro
London, January 2013

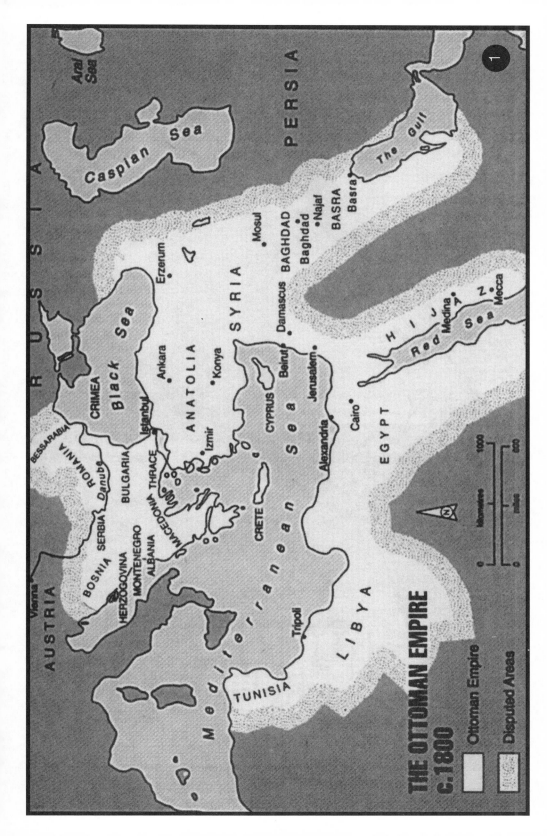

THE OTTOMAN EMPIRE
c.1800

Ottoman Empire

Disputed Areas

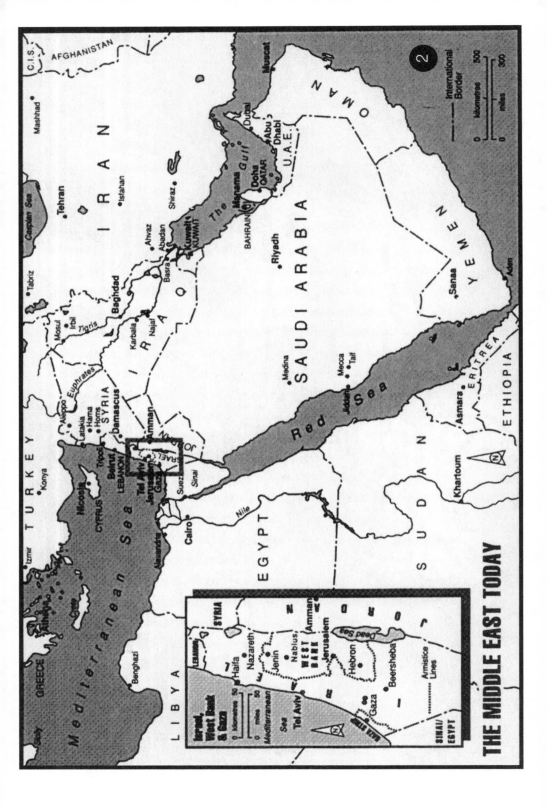

THE MIDDLE EAST TODAY

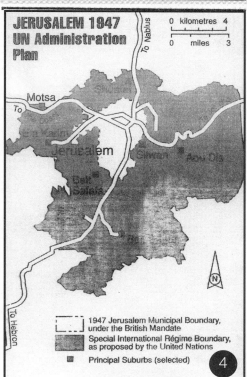

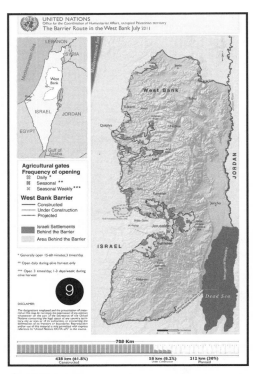

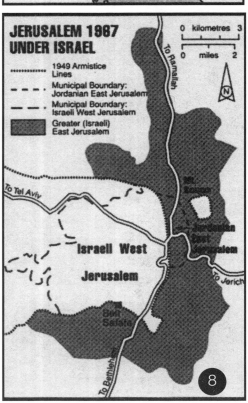

(Maps 9 & 10 courtesy of United Nations Office for the Coordination of Humanitarian Affairs occupied Palestinian territory. To view the full details and most up-to-date versions visit http://www.ochaopt.org)

A

aal (Arabic: *of a family or clan*): The term aal is used for Arab families or clans of distinction.

Aal Saud *(Arabic: House of Saud)*: see House of Saud.

Abadan: *Iranian city* Population: 415,000 (2011 est.) Situated on an island of the same name in the Shatt al-Arab [*q.v.*], also known as Arvand Rud [*q.v.*], Abadan is called after its eighth-century founder, Abbad. It thrived as a port during the rule of the Abbasid dynasty (751 A.D.–1258). But with the silt from the Shatt al-Arab expanding the delta gradually inwards, its commercial importance declined. With the Shatt al-Arab emerging as the boundary between the Persian and Ottoman Empires in the mid-17th century, Abadan became a disputed territory. It was not until 1847 that Iran succeeded in acquiring it.

Soon after petroleum was discovered in the area in 1908, it became the site of an oil refinery owned by the Anglo-Persian Oil Company. In 1937, pressured by Iran and Britain, Iraq conceded to the thalweg principle that the median line of the deepest channel for the four miles of the Shatt al-Arab opposite Abadan should delineate the international boundary. With the Iranian economy booming in the early-to-mid-1970s due to high oil prices, Abadan prospered. The city participated in the revolutionary movement that overthrew the regime of Muhammad Reza Shah Pahlavi

[*q.v.*] in 1979. It suffered heavily in the Iran-Iraq War (1980–88) [*q.v.*], when its oil facilities were destroyed. It has since been rebuilt.

Abbas, Mahmoud (1935–): *Palestinian politician; prime minister of Palestinian Authority [q.v.], 2003; president of Palestinian Authority, 2004–* Born of middle-class parents in Safad, Palestine [*q.v.*], he and his family fled to Syria during the 1948–1949 Arab-Israeli War [*q.v.*]. Abbas graduated in law at Damascus University, and then earned a doctorate in history at the Patrice Lumumba Peoples' Friendship University, Moscow. His doctoral thesis was published later in Arabic, titled *The Other Side: the Secret Relationship between Nazism and Zionism* (Arabic: *al-Wajh al-Akhar: al-Alaqat as Sirriya bayna an Naziya wa as Sihyuniya*).

In 1965 he was one of the founder members of Fatah [*q.v.*]. Three years later, he was elected a member of the Palestine National Council [*q.v.*]. As a moderate voice in the Palestinian leadership, he became a target for assassination by the Abu Nidal group [*q.v.*] in 1974 in Beirut [*q.v.*]. He was the chief initiator of secret contacts with leftist Jewish groups of Israel.

Elected to the executive committee of the Palestine Liberation Organization [*q.v.*] in 1980, he was appointed as head of the PLO's department for national and international relations. In his book *The Road to Oslo*, published in 1994, he described the clandestine contacts in 1992 between the PLO, then a banned organization in Israel, and the leaders of the Labor [*q.v.*] and Likud [*q.v.*] parties. After Israel legalized the PLO in January 1993, the PLO chairman Yasser Arafat [*q.v.*]

put Abbas in charge of the clandestine talks with Israel, which were held in Norway, where the Palestinian delegation was led by Ahmad Qurei.

On 13 Sept 1993, as the counterpart of Israeli foreign minister Shimon Peres [q.v.], he signed the Declaration of Principles on Palestinian Self-Rule at the White House ceremony in Washington in the presence of U.S. President Bill Clinton (r. 1993–2001), Israeli Prime Minister Yitzhak Rabin [q.v.], and Arafat. In 1994 he moved to Gaza [q.v.]. Two years later he was elected secretary-general of the PLO's executive committee, thus becoming Arafat's deputy in the PLO.

Lacking in charisma, he had little popular support. He was widely considered as too accommodating toward Israel. His description of the two-year-old al-Aqsa Intifada of 2000 [q.v.] as a disaster that had resulted in the Palestinian Authority [q.v.] losing all it had built up summarized his viewpoint.

Appointed the first prime minister of the Palestinian Authority in March 2003 by President Arafat, he resigned six months later when Arafat refused to transfer authority over security forces to him. After Arafat's death in November 2004, he was elected chairman of the PLO. As the candidate of Fatah, he won the presidential election in January 2005 with 62.5 percent of the vote, well ahead of his nearest rival, Mustafa Barghouti, an independent, at 28.5 percent. In the parliamentary election in 2006, Fatah lost to Hamas [q.v.], which emerged as the majority party. In early 2007, a unity government of Hamas and Fatah under Prime Minister Ismail Haniya [q.v.] was formed. After the

Hamas takeover of Gaza [q.v.] in June, Abbas declared a state of emergency and appointed Salam Fayyad [q.v.] as prime minister.

In May 2008, Abbas said he would step down if his peace talks with Israeli Prime Minister Ehud Olmert [q.v.] did not result in an agreement in principle within six months. But he did not keep his word. In January 2009 he unilaterally extended his presidential tenure by a year in order to align the next presidential and parliamentary elections. But he continued in office after that date. The promised elections were not held.

His peace negotiations with Benjamin Netanyahu [q.v.], who succeeded Olmert in March, proved sterile. It was only at the urging of U.S. President Barack Obama (r. 2009–) that the two leaders met at the White House in early September 2010. But three weeks later, when—following the expiry of Israel's partial moratorium on constructing Jewish colonies in the occupied West Bank [q.v.]—Israel resumed construction, the peace talks collapsed again. Abbas had said earlier that he would not negotiate while construction in the West Bank continued.

After the ouster of Egyptian President Hosni Mubarak [q.v.], in February 2011, foreign minister Nabil al-Araby [q.v.], acting as a genuinely honest broker, succeeded in reconciling Abbas and Hamas [q.v.] leaders in May. They agreed to work together to end the Israeli occupation. Hamas backed Abbas's attempt at the United Nations in September to win recognition of Palestine [q.v.] as a member state. It failed.

In early February 2012 Abbas signed an agreement with Hamas

leader Khaled Mashaal [*q.v.*] to form an interim unity government with him as president and prime minister as a prelude to holding parliamentary and presidential elections.

Abdul Aziz bin Abdul Rahman al-Saud (1879–1953): *founder and king of Saudi Arabia, 1932–53* Also known as Bin Saud of Saudi Arabia. Born in Diraiya, central Arabia, Abdul Aziz grew up in Kuwait, where his ruling al-Saud family was exiled following its defeat in 1891. In 1902 he regained Diraiya and neighboring Riyadh [*q.v.*] from the rival Rashid clan, which was allied with the Ottoman Empire. After consolidating his domain, he captured the eastern Hasa region in 1913. Two years later in the midst of World War I, Britain, the leading European power in the region, recognized him as ruler of an independent Najd and Hasa. In 1920 he conquered the Asir region on the Red Sea. The next year he defeated his rival, Muhammad bin Rashid, who was based in Shammar. After he had added more territories to his domain in 1922, he called himself the Sultan of Najd and its Dependencies.

He couched his campaigns in Islamic terms, as a struggle to punish either religious dissenters or those who had strayed from true Islam as encapsulated by Wahhabism [*q.v.*]. He also made it a point to marry into the family of the defeated tribal chief, thus consolidating his control of the captured territory. In the process he acquired 17 wives and sired 45 sons and 215 daughters. Among his spouses the most important were Hussah bint Ahmad al-Sudeiri, mother of seven sons, known as the Sudeiri Seven, including Fahd [*q.v.*], Sultan, Nayef [*q.v.*], and Salman; Jawrah bint Musaid al-Jiluwi, mother of Khalid [*q.v.*]; Asi al-Shuraim, mother of Abdullah [*q.v.*]; and Tarfa bint Abdullah al-Shaikh, mother of Faisal [*q.v.*].

In 1924 Abdul Aziz defeated Sharif Hussein bin Ali al-Hashem in Hijaz [*q.v.*] and deposed him. Having declared himself King of Hijaz and Sultan of Najd and its Dependencies in January 1926 (later King of Hijaz and Najd and its Dependencies), he sought international recognition. The following year Britain recognized him as King of Hijaz and Najd and its Dependencies. In 1929 he came into conflict with the militant section of the Ikhwan [*q.v.*], the armed wing of Wahhabis, which had so far been his fighting force. Assisted by the British, then controlling Kuwait and Iraq, he crushed the Ikhwan rebellion. In September 1932 he combined his two domains, combining 77 percent of 1.12 million sq. mi./3.1 million sq. km of the Arabian Peninsula [*q.v.*], into one—the Kingdom of Saudi Arabia—and called himself King of Saudi Arabia. He made his eldest son, Saud [*q.v.*], crown prince, and Faisal the next in line.

He faced an economic crisis caused by a severe drop in the tax paid by the pilgrims to Mecca [*q.v.*] following a decline in their numbers due to global depression. It was against this background that he granted an oil concession to the Standard Oil Company of California in 1933 for £50,000 as an advance against future royalties on oil production. Modest commercial extraction, which started in 1938, was interrupted by World War II, in which he remained neutral until March

1945. Despite its growing links with U.S. petroleum corporations, Saudi Arabia failed to gain Washington's recognition until Abdul Aziz met U.S. President Franklin Roosevelt (r. 1933–1945) aboard a U.S. warship in the Great Bitter Lake of the Suez Canal [q.v.] in February 1945. The next month he was instrumental in getting the Arab League [q.v.] established in Cairo [q.v.]. His regional policy was conservative, committed to maintaining the status quo and shunning any dramatic moves toward the creation of larger Arab states through merger or confederation.

As a domineering and militarily successful tribal chief, he behaved like an autocrat in domestic affairs. When he acquired the title King of Hijaz he announced the establishment of a 24-member Consultative Council, consisting of clergy, lay notables and merchants in line with an injunction of the Quran [q.v.], which requires the governor to consult the governed. The Council played an insignificant role for a while and then became extinct. Following a dramatic increase in oil output after World War II, the economic boom overstretched the rudimentary institutions of the state, supervised by Abdul Aziz and some of his close aides. It undermined the traditional, spartan Wahhabi lifestyle of the House of Saud [q.v.]. Yet it was not until October 1953—a month before his death—that he issued a decree appointing a council of ministers as an advisory body.

Abdul Ghani, Abdul Aziz (1939–2011): *Yemeni politician; North Yemeni prime minister, 1975–80, 1983–90, 1994–97* Born into a Shafii Sunni [q.v.]

family in the Hujariya region of North Yemen, Abdul Ghani went to a teacher training college in Aden [q.v.], South Yemen. He then obtained an economics degree from Colorado College, Colorado Springs, in the United States. After his return to Aden he taught economics. When South Yemen became independent under a leftist regime in late 1967, he left for North Yemen, where he was appointed minister of economy and health. In 1971, after the formal end of an eight-year civil war in North Yemen [q.v.], he became governor of the Central Bank.

His absence from the country during the civil conflict; his Shafii origins, which set him apart from the fractious Zaidi Shia [q.v.] military officers and tribal leaders; and his technocratic background stood him in good stead. Following the coup by Colonel Ibrahim Hamdi [q.v.] in June 1974, he was nominated to the ruling Military Command Council. In January 1975 Hamdi appointed him prime minister, a position he continued to hold, along with the membership of the ruling Presidential Council—despite the assassination of Hamdi and his successor, Ahmad Hussein Ghashmi [q.v.]—until October 1980, when he was made vice-president by President Ali Abdullah Saleh [q.v.]. He took on the additional job of premier in November 1983 and stayed in that position until the unification of North and South Yemen in May 1990.

As a representative of Shafiis, who were slightly more numerous than Zaidis in North Yemen, he was assured of high office. In the five-strong Presidential Council for united Yemen that followed, he was one of the three

North Yemeni members. He retained
his position when the first popularly
elected parliament of united Yemen
chose members of the new Presidential Council in October 1993. His
main area of expertise remained finance, industry, and economic development. He supported Saleh in the
civil war [q.v.] that erupted in May
1994, and was appointed prime minister after it ended in July. Following the
1997 parliamentary election, he was
replaced as prime minister by Faraj
Said Ghanim. Later that year, on the
formation of the 59-member nominated Consultative (Shura) Council,
decreed by the president, Abdul
Ghani was appointed its chairman.
He held that position until his death
from injuries sustained in a rocket attack on the presidential compound in
June 2011.

Abdul Maguid, Ahmad Esmat (1923–):
*Egyptian diplomat and politician; secre-
tary-general of the Arab League, 1991–
2001* Born into a middle-class family
in Alexandria [q.v.], Abdul Maguid
trained as a lawyer at universities in
his native city and Paris. He joined the
Foreign Service when he was 27. As a
career diplomat he rose steadily up the
hierarchical ladder, becoming ambassador to France in 1970. When Anwar
Sadat [q.v.] became president later
that year, he named him deputy foreign minister. From 1972 to 1983 he
served as his country's chief representative at the United Nations. The following year he became foreign
minister and deputy premier. In May
1991, following the expulsion of Iraq
from occupied Kuwait, in which
Egypt played an important role, he
was unanimously elected secretary-

general of the Arab League [q.v.], the
event signifying the restoration of
Egypt as leader of the Arab world
after 12 years of ostracizing after its
unilateral peace treaty with Israel in
1979 [q.v.]. In 2001, he was succeeded
by Amr Moussa [q.v.].

Abdul Rahman, Omar (1938–): *Egyptian Islamist leader* Born into a poor
peasant family in Gamaliya village,
Daqaliya district, in the Nile [q.v.]
delta, Abdul Rahman went blind in
infancy as a result of diabetes. After
his education in local religious schools
he joined al-Azhar University [q.v.] in
1955. He obtained a doctorate in literature in 1965 and became a lecturer in
Islamic studies at al-Azhar's branch at
Fahyum in the Nile delta.

As the prayer leader of the mosque
in the nearby village of Fedmeen, he
delivered sermons that were critical of
the government of President Abdul
Gamal Nasser [q.v.] and its ideology
of Arab socialism [q.v.]. Following
Egypt's defeat in the June 1967 Arab-
Israeli War [q.v.], he became more
daring in his attacks on Nasser and
Arab socialism. He was arrested in
1968 and expelled from al-Azhar. On
his release he criticized the official
policies on religious trusts [q.v.] and
Islam [q.v.]. After the death of Nasser
in September 1970 he was arrested
because of his call to the faithful not
to pray for the soul of Nasser, whom
he considered an atheist. He was released as part of the general amnesty
President Anwar Sadat [q.v.] granted
following his coup against Ali Sabri
[q.v.] in May 1971.

After a brief stint as a lecturer on Islamic affairs at the University of Asyut
in southern Egypt, he took up a job of a

teacher of Islamic studies in Saudi Arabia. He stayed in touch with Islamist activists in Egypt during his annual holidays there. On his return home in 1978 he became a professor of Islamic studies at the University of Asyut.

He attacked Sadat for the Camp David Accords [q.v.] and economic liberalization which, according to him, had led to moral and material corruption. After Sadat's assassination in October 1981 he was one of the 24 suspects who were arrested. He was accused of issuing a fatwa (a religious decree) for Sadat's assassination. But he was released, along with another suspect, due to lack of evidence.

Denied reinstatement as a professor at Asyut University, he settled in Fahyum. He continued his attacks on the regime, now headed by President Hosni Mubarak [q.v.]. He was arrested in 1984 for delivering a subversive sermon, but was found not guilty. He urged his followers to join the Afghan Mujahedin who, financed and trained by Saudi Arabia, America and Pakistan, were conducting a jihad [q.v.] against the Soviet-backed regime in Afghanistan. Among those who followed his exhortation was his son Ahmad. Addressing meetings throughout the country, he demanded that Egypt should be run exclusively according to the Sharia [q.v.]. His speeches inspired both al-Gamaat al-Islamiya [q.v.] and al-Jihad al-Islami [q.v.]. The government put him under house arrest in Fahyum and prevented him from speaking in public. In response he issued a fatwa allowing the faithful to capture weapons from the security forces in order to wage a jihad against the secular regime of President Mubarak.

In 1989 he was allowed to go on the hajj [q.v.] pilgrimage in Saudi Arabia]. But instead of Mecca [q.v.], he arrived in Khartoum, the capital of Sudan, where a pro-Islamic military junta had seized power on 30 June 1989. Fearing retribution from Egypt, the Sudanese leaders refused him asylum. Abdul Rahman toured a few European capitals before visiting Pakistan and Afghanistan, where his two sons had reportedly joined the Ittihad-e Islami (Arabic: Islamic Alliance), a pro-Saudi Afghan mujahedin group, which, along with other such factions, was funded and trained by the U.S. Central Intelligence Agency (CIA) working in conjunction with Pakistan's Inter Service Intelligence.

In late 1989 Abdul Rahman received a tourist visa from the U.S. embassy in Khartoum, where he had arrived from Pakistan, even though he was on the prohibited list. In America he ran a mosque in Brooklyn, which gained popularity among the Egyptian, Sudanese, and Yemeni immigrants. He obtained an immigrant visa, and moved to the adjoining state of New Jersey. From there his followers sent thousands of tapes of his sermons to Egypt. Following the bombing of the World Trade Center in New York in February 1993 and the aborting of a plan to bomb the United Nations and other targets some weeks later, Abdul Rahman was arrested as a suspect. He was found guilty in October 1995, and sentenced to life imprisonment for seditious conspiracy for a bombing plot. In early 1999, from his high security jail in the U.S., he endorsed the unilateral cease-fire declared by al-Gamaat al-Islamiya in Egypt.

Abdullah bin Abdul Aziz al-Saud

(1923–): *Saudi king and prime minister,*
2005– Son of Abdul Aziz al-Saud
[*q.v.*] and Asi al-Shuraim of the
Rashid clan, which was defeated by
Abdul Aziz in 1921, Abdullah was
born and educated in Riyadh [*q.v.*].
He started his career as governor of
Mecca [*q.v.*] and became deputy defense minister and commander of the
National Guard [*q.v.*] in 1963. When
Khalid bin Abdul Aziz [*q.v.*] acceded
to the throne in 1975 he appointed
Abdullah second deputy premier. As
commander of the National Guard,
the most cohesive and reliable armed
force in the kingdom, Abdullah was
influential. He belonged to the inner-
most circle of senior Saudi princes.

He headed the traditionalist-na-
tionalist trend within the royal family,
which was at odds with the modernist,
pro-American faction led by Crown
Prince Fahd bin Abdul Aziz [*q.v.*], especially over the pace of economic development. He advocated a
pan-Arabist policy and cultivated
friendly relations with Syria among
others. He attempted to conciliate
Syria and Iraq and bring the Lebanese
Civil War (1975–90) [*q.v.*] to an end,
but in vain.

When Fahd became king and
prime minister in 1982, he named
Abdullah crown prince and first
deputy premier. During the Gulf crisis
of 1990–91, unlike the defense minister, Prince Sultan bin Abdul Aziz, Abdullah was reluctant to invite U.S.
forces to Saudi Arabia. But he was
overruled by King Fahd. He continued
to command the National Guard. He
was distressed when a bomb at the
National Guard training center in
Riyadh in November 1995 killed

seven people, including five American
officers. Later that month, following a
stroke, Fahd passed on his powers to
Abdullah. Though, on recovery, Faisal
nominally retrieved these powers three
months later, there was less of Fahd's
imprint on the administration during
the subsequent years as Abdullah became the de facto ruler.

He tried to defuse internal tensions
by conciliating political and religious
dissidents at home and abroad. Yet he
failed to address the long-running
contentious subject of the continued
presence of U.S. troops on Saudi soil.
The issue came to the fore in June
1996, when a huge explosion outside
the Khobar Towers, a multistory residential block for the U.S. military personnel near the Dhahran air base,
killed 19 American servicemen.

Abdullah continued the earlier policy of aiding the Taliban (Persian: Religious Students), a faction of
hard-line Islamic fundamentalists
[*q.v.*] in Afghanistan, created largely
by Pakistan in late 1994, culminating
in the recognition of the Taliban government in May 1997. In the region
he mended fences with Iran [*q.v.*], especially after the election of Muhammad Khatami [*q.v.*] as president in
August 1997. In early 1998 he refused
to allow the Pentagon to use Saudi
bases to strike Iraq because of its failure to cooperate unconditionally with
UN weapons inspectors. In July 2000
he advised Palestinian leader Yasser
Arafat [*q.v.*] not to compromise on
the future status of Jerusalem [*q.v.*] by
conceding the sovereignty of the
Dome of the Rock/Haram al-Sharif
[*q.v.*] to Israel in his talks with Israeli
Prime Minister Ehud Barak [*q.v.*] at
Camp David in Maryland, U.S.A.

Following the attacks on three American targets by hijacked aircraft on 11 September 2001, Abdullah violated the quota of the Organization of Petroleum Exporting Countries [q.v.] by increasing oil output by 500,000 barrels per day (bpd), and shipped an extra 700,000 bpd in Saudi tankers to America, thus lowering the oil price from $28 to $20 within weeks. Yet Washington's relations with Riyadh soured when it emerged that 15 of the 19 hijackers of 9/11 were Saudi nationals.

In early 2005, yielding to the George W. Bush administration's drive for democracy in the Greater Middle East, Abdullah ordered municipal elections in cities, with the voting right limited to male adults.

Later that year, following King Fahd's death, Abdullah ascended the throne. He became the fully-fledged prime minister and head of the Military Service Council while retaining his command of the National Guard. He was also chairman of the Supreme Economic Council and president of the High Council for Petroleum and Minerals. A keen horseman, he had the distinction of founding the Equestrian Club in Riyadh. One of the richest persons in the world, his net worth was put at $25 billion in 2008 by *Forbes* magazine.

To overcome the challenge to the kingdom by militant Islamists, his government carried out a series of crackdowns involving simultaneous raids by security forces, wide-scale detentions, torture, and public beheadings. Under his watch, the judicial system was reorganized and the royal succession codified. In 2012, the expanded Princess Noura bint Abdul Rahman University for Women, the renamed Riyadh University for Women, became the largest higher education institution of its kind in the kingdom.

Abdullah became the first Saudi ruler to receive Russian president Vladimir Putin in Riyadh in 2007. He strengthened economic ties with China. Despite his warm relations with President Bush, he failed in his efforts to further the Israeli-Palestinian peace process. But he succeeded in winning the approval of the Saudi and other Islamic scholars to hold interfaith dialogue with Christian and Jewish leaders at a conference in Madrid, Spain, in July 2008. According to the documents leaked in 2010 by WikiLeaks [q.v.], a non-profit media organization formed to publish secret files of public interest, Abdullah repeatedly urged the U.S. to "cut off the head of the snake," meaning bomb Iran's nuclear facilities, while there was still time.

At the beginning of the Arab Spring [q.v.], Abdullah gave refuge to ousted Tunisian President Zine al-Abidine Ben Ali in mid-January. Two weeks later he admonished U.S. President Barack Obama (r. 2009–) for being too hasty to urge Egyptian President Hosni Mubarak [q.v.] to step down. Later he offered asylum to Mubarak, who declined it. In mid-March he sent tanks and 1,000 troops to Bahrain [q.v.] to help quell pro-democracy protests. He was the prime mover behind the $20 billion aid package to Bahrain and Oman [q.v.], divided equally between them, to help their rulers to create jobs over the next 10 years. Wedded to the status quo, he initially stood by the Syrian regime of

President Bashar Assad [*q.v.*] as it repressed the protestors demanding political reform. But in August he reversed this policy, withdrew the Saudi ambassador from Damascus, and then spearheaded an anti-Syria campaign at the Arab League [*q.v.*] and the United Nations. At home, he pledged to spend $130 billion to increase social benefits, reduce unemployment, and provide housing for his rapidly growing subjects, as well as bolster the security forces and religious police.

Abdullah I bin Hussein al-Hashem

(1882–1951): *Emir of Transjordan 1921–46; King of Jordan 1946–51* Son of Sharif Hussein bin Ali al-Hashem of Hijaz [*q.v.*], Abdullah was educated in Istanbul, where his father was kept under surveillance from 1891 until the coup by the Young Turks in 1908. From 1912 to 1914 he represented Mecca [*q.v.*] in the Ottoman parliament. During World War I, he participated in the anti-Ottoman Arab revolt led by his father, in June 1916. When Sharif Hussein declared himself King of Hijaz in 1917, Abdullah became his foreign minister.

The disintegration of the Ottoman Empire in 1918 strengthened the hands of Sharif Hussein and his sons. In the summer of 1920, Abdullah assembled an army with the aim of expelling the French troops then occupying Syria. He entered the British-mandated territory east of the Jordan River [*q.v.*], called Transjordan [*q.v.*], in January 1921 and set up a government in Amman [*q.v.*] two months later. In July London offered to recognize Abdullah's rule in Transjordan if he accepted the British

mandate over it and Palestine [*q.v.*] (awarded to Britain by the League of Nations a year earlier) and renounced his plan to capture Syria. He consented provided the clauses of the mandate about the founding of a National Home for the Jews [*q.v.*] were not applied to the Emirate of Transjordan. This was agreed, and endorsed later by the League of Nations.

In April 1923 Britain announced that it would recognize Transjordan as an autonomous emirate under Emir Abdullah's rule if a constitutional regime was established there and a preferential treaty with London signed. He agreed, and declared Transjordan "independent." But it was only in April 1928 that he proclaimed a constitution, which stipulated that legal and administrative authority should be exercised by the ruler through a legislative council. The resulting nominated body was powerless. He then signed the Anglo-Transjordanian Treaty with Britain [*q.v.*]. At home, it was not until 1939 that he transformed the council into a cabinet and gave it some authority.

In 1941 he dispatched his Arab Legion troops, commanded by British officers, to Iraq to aid Britain in crushing the forces of Rashid Ali Gailani [*q.v.*]. When London recognized the independence of Transjordan in May 1946, he changed its name to the Hashemite Kingdom of Jordan and called himself king. The subsequent revising of the 1923 Anglo-Transjordan Treaty [*q.v.*] happened in March 1948.

To extend his realm to Palestine, then being colonized by the Zionists [*q.v.*], Abdullah reached a clandestine, unwritten understanding with Zionist leaders not to oppose the partitioning of Palestine and the emergence of a Jewish state, if they let him take over the Arab part of Palestine. But the secret leaked, and the other constituents of the Arab League [*q.v.*] resolved to thwart the plan. In his clandestine meetings with Golda Meir [*q.v.*], a Zionist leader, in November 1947 and early May 1948, he explained his inability to stick to his agreement. This coincided with London's advice to him to seize control of the Arab segment of Palestine in alliance with other Arab countries rather than through a deal with the Zionist leaders.

After the Arab League's decision to dispatch troops to capture Palestine on the eve of the British departure on 14 May 1948, Abdullah became commander-in-chief of the forces from Egypt, Iraq, Jordan, Lebanon, and Syria. His Arab Legion captured substantial parts of Arab Palestine while not attacking the zones allocated to the Jews in the UN partition plan of November 1947. In Jerusalem [*q.v.*], which was earmarked for international control, the Arab Legion seized the eastern part. In December, 2,000 Arab Palestinian delegates in Jericho [*q.v.*] acclaimed Abdullah as "King of all Palestine," which meant most of what could be saved from the Israelis.

He began to transform his military occupation of Arab Palestine into annexation, presenting his action as a response to orchestrated calls by local Palestinian notables to that effect. His move alarmed other Arab leaders. As before, he entered into a clandestine dialogue with the Zionist leaders in April 1949 to settle the sticky points about a truce between Jordan and Is-

rael. The talks culminated in a draft non-aggression pact between the two countries in early 1950. Once again the secret leaked. When pressured by fellow Arab leaders to scuttle his unilateral peace plan with Israel he agreed, provided they let him annex Arab Palestine. They did so. Formal annexation followed in April and changed the character of Abdullah's realm. It now contained a large body of politicized Palestinians, who felt betrayed. Most of them considered him a traitor and a lackey of the British, who had made underhand deals with the Zionists at the expense of Arab interests. In July 1951, Shukri Ashu, a young Palestinian, assassinated Abdullah as he entered al-Aqsa mosque in East Jerusalem [*q.v.*] for Friday prayers.

Abdullah II bin Hussein al-Hashem

(b. 1962–): *Jordanian king 1999–* Born to King Hussein [*q.v.*] and Muna Gardiner, he was named the crown prince on birth. But fearing his assassination, which would put an infant on the throne, King Hussein amended the constitution and named his younger brother Hassan as the crown prince. After attending prestigious private schools in Britain, Abdullah graduated from Sandhurst Military Academy. He then obtained a graduate degree in international relations from Oxford University in 1984, and followed it up with a year of studies at Georgetown University in Washington.

Pursuing a military career, he became a brigadier general in 1994. Four years later he was given command of the Jordanian Special Forces and promoted to major general. Suffering from terminal lymphatic cancer, and dissatisfied with the way Prince Hassan had conducted state affairs in his absence, King Hussein revoked the amendment designating Hassan as crown prince two weeks before his death on 7 February 1999, and named Abdullah the crown prince.

As a result, Abdullah acceded to the throne with no experience in civil administration, politics, or diplomacy. Following the counsel of the senior advisers he inherited, he continued his father's friendly relations with Israel [*q.v.*]. Dependent on the supply of Iraqi oil, he maintained cordial relations with Iraq [*q.v.*], ruled by President Saddam Hussein [*q.v.*], and expressed distress at the continued suffering of Iraqis because of the UN economic sanctions. After the installation of Bashar Assad [*q.v.*] as Syrian president in 2000, he improved ties with Syria [*q.v.*].

By presiding over the Arab League summit in Amman [*q.v.*] in March 2001, he became chairman of the Arab League for a year. It was in that role that he visited Washington in the aftermath of the terrorist attacks on the U.S. in September. The bill on free trade with Jordan, which had been languishing in U.S. Congress for three years, was passed in three weeks. The move helped Abdullah to advance economic liberalization in Jordan.

Political liberalization, however, remained a distant dream. A 2006 survey by the Jordan University's Center for Strategic Studies found that more than three-quarters of respondents believed they would be punished if they attempted to demonstrate peacefully in public.

Following 9/11, Abdullah promised Jordan's unequivocal backing for President George W. Bush's "war on terrorism." On the eve of the Anglo-American invasion of Iraq in March 2003 [*q.v.*], he allowed the Pentagon to operate from bases in Jordan. He continued his father's policy of countering the rise of Islamic fundamentalists [*q.v.*] in his kingdom. He maintained cordial relations with Israel while emphasizing the need for the establishment of an independent Palestine [*q.v.*]. According to the documents leaked in 2010 by WikiLeaks, a non-profit media organization formed to publish secret files of public interest, he urged Washington to bomb Iran's nuclear facilities.

Due to his economic liberalization policy, the annual GDP growth averaged 7 percent. Yet in November 2009 he dissolved parliament halfway through its four-year mandate and then cancelled the general election. When the election was held in November 2010, it was boycotted by the opposition. The turnout was low.

Responding to the onset of the Arab Spring [*q.v.*] in 2011, Abdullah replaced his prime minister twice, first in February and then in October, with his choice falling on Awm Shawkat al-Khasawneh, a former judge of the International Court of Justice. In June he promised British-style parliamentary government, but it was not until February 2012 that he spelled it out: fair elections, a law guaranteeing the broadest representation, a parliament based on political parties, and governments drawn from that parliament. Yielding to the pressure of the Islamic Action Front [*q.v.*], the leading opposition party, he became the first Arab leader to openly call on Syrian President Assad to step down. Yet when his

Prime Minister al-Khasawneh, acting independently, reached out to the IAF, he replaced him with Fayez al-Tarawneh, a former premier, known to be a yes-man, in April 2012. In general the protest movement remained quiescent chiefly because of the citizens' fear of bringing about the bloodshed that was then scarring neighboring Syria.

Abu Ammar: (Arabic: *father of construction*); *see* Arafat, Yasser.

Abu Dhabi: *city and emirate in the United Arab Emirates* [*q.v.*].

Abu Dhabi city: *capital of United Arab Emirates and Abu Dhabi emirate* Population Abu Dhabi: 970,000 (2010 est.). Located on the offshore island of the same name, Abu Dhabi (Arabic: *father of gazelle*) was founded by members of the Aal bu Falah clan of the Bani Yas tribe in 1761. A quarter of a century later they transferred their base from the al-Jiwa oasis to Abu Dhabi. In the early 20th century its 6,000-odd inhabitants were dependent on pearl fishing and petty trading for their livelihood. It was not until the discovery and extraction of petroleum in the Abu Dhabi emirate in the early 1960s that its capital began to expand. After the installation of Shaikh Zaid bin Sultan al-Nahyan [*q.v.*] as emir in 1966, ambitious plans to modernize Abu Dhabi were undertaken. Within a decade it had been turned into a modern city with offices, hotels, light industry, and an international airport. With the formation of a confederation of seven emirates, called the United Arab Emirates [*q.v.*], in 1971, Abu Dhabi was selected as its capital.

Oil wealth has turned it into an affluent metropolis, more Westernized than Arab, with the world's leading corporations locating their regional headquarters there. At the same time economic diversification has transformed the city into an important center for financial services and a tourist destination. In 2007 it topped the per capita income league table for cities in the world. In the same year it became the center for the awarding of the International Prize for Arabic Fiction managed in association with the Booker Prize Foundation in London.

In 2009, Abu Dhabi city was selected as the headquarters of the newly established International Renewable Energy Agency. Its suburb of Masdar is set to become the globe's first carbon-free settlement by 2025.

Abu Dhabi Emirate: Area 26,000 sq. mi./67,350 sq. km; population 1.80 million (2010 est.); *see* United Arab Emirates.

Abu Iyad: *see* Khalaf, Salah.

Abu Jihad: *see* Wazir, Khalil.

Abu Mazen: *see* Abbas, Mahmoud.

Abu Musa Island: *an offshore island in the Gulf* Population: 2,130 (2011) On the eve of the independence of the Trucial emirate of Sharjah [*q.v.*] in 1971, Muhammad Reza Shah Pahlavi [*q.v.*] of Iran pressed his claim to three islands at the mouth of the Gulf [*q.v.*], including Abu Musa. After Iranian troops had landed there, Britain, the erstwhile imperial power in the region, mediated. As a result, Sharjah and Iran agreed that both flags would fly on the island, and that Iran would pay Sharjah an annual subsidy of £1.5 million until oil had been discovered in the emirate. In 1973, oil was discovered in a field off the Island of Abu Musa. Due to the territorial dispute with Iran, Sharjah received only half of the oil revenue. In 1984, during the eight-year-long Iran-Iraq War [*q.v.*], Iran stopped paying Sharjah. In September 1991 Sharjah protested that Iran had exceeded the privileges it had been allowed under the 1971 agreement. But its efforts to secure the involvement of the United Nations did not get far. In 1994 the Gulf Cooperation Council [*q.v.*] took up the matter, and urged Iran to agree to refer the issue of its occupation of Abu Musa and Greater and Lesser Tumb Islands [*q.v.*] to the International Court of Justice. Tehran argues that its sovereignty over Abu Musa island was not open to negotiations. The issue remains unresolved.

Abu Nidal: *see* al-Banna, Sabri.

Acre: *Israeli town* Population: 46,300 (2011 est.), two-thirds Jewish, one-third Arab; also known as Akko. The commercial importance of Acre, a port on the Bay of Acre, dates back to the 15th century B.C. when it was renowned for its glass-making and purple-dyeing industries. King Ptolemy II of Egypt (r. 283–246 B.C.) changed its name from Accho to Ptolemais. When the Arabs captured it in 638 A.D. they called it Akka. Conquered by the crusaders (1104–1187), it was renamed St. Jean d'Acre. When the Knights of St. John acquired it in 1191 they made it the capital of Palestine [*q.v.*]. Its surrender to

the Saracens in 1291 heralded the decline of the Latin Kingdom of Jerusalem and the Crusades. It fell under the Ottomans (1517–1918), with a brief interregnum under Egypt (1832–1840). It formed part of the Palestine that was formally placed under the British Mandate in 1922. The 1947 UN partition plan for Palestine assigned Acre, then an Arab settlement of 12,000, to the Arabs. But in the war that ensued, the Zionist [*q.v.*] forces seized it, and incorporated it into Israel.

Five-day-long inter-ethnic violence erupted in October 2008 when an Israeli Arab [*q.v.*] violated the no-traffic protocol in a Jewish neighborhood during Yom Kippur [*q.v.*].

The town's tourist offerings include the old town wall, an outstanding mosque built by Ahmad al-Jazzar in the late 18th century, and a stunning view of the Bay of Haifa.

A.D.: *Abbreviation of Anno Domini* (Latin: *Year of the Lord*) Since "the Lord" refers to Jesus Christ, Anno Domini supposedly begins with his birth. But, by most estimates, the actual starting point of the Years of the Lord was between 4 B.C. and 8 B.C.

Adonis: *see* Asbar, Ali Ahmad Said.

Aflaq, Michel (1910–89): *Syrian political thinker and politician* Born into a Greek Orthodox [*q.v.*] family in Damascus [*q.v.*], Aflaq received his higher education at the University of the Sorbonne, Paris, where he came under leftist influence. Back in Damascus in 1934 he taught history at a prestigious secondary school. Together with Salah al-Din Bitar [*q.v.*], a fellow teacher, in 1940 he established a study circle called the Movement of Arab Renaissance (Arabic: *Baath*). They published pamphlets in which they expounded revolutionary, socialist Arab nationalism, committed to achieving Arab unity as the first step. In 1942 Aflaq devoted himself full-time to politics.

Once the mandate power, France, had left Syria in April 1946, Afkaq and Bitar secured a license for their group, now called the Party of Arab Renaissance. They decided to merge their faction with that of Zaki Arsuzi [*q.v.*]. Out of this, in April 1947, emerged the Arab Baath Party [*q.v.*] in Damascus. Aflaq was elected senior member of the executive committee of four. In August 1949, following a military coup by Col. Sami Hinnawi, Aflaq was appointed education minister. But when he failed to win a seat in the general election held three months later, he resigned.

In late 1952 he fled to Lebanon to escape arrest by the dictatorial regime of Col. Adib Shishkali [*q.v.*]. The next year he merged his group with Akram Hourani's Arab Socialist Party [*q.v.*] to form the Arab Baath Socialist Party [*q.v.*]. He remained the new party's secretary-general as well as its chief ideologue.

After the Baath Party seized power in Syria in March 1963, it failed to maintain unity, with its moderate "civilian" faction opposed by its radical "military" faction. When the military wing prevailed over its rival, Aflaq, who was associated with the moderates, left for Lebanon. He retained his position as secretary-general of the National (i.e., All-Arab) Command of the Baath. The next year he flew to Brazil.

Following the successful coup in July 1968 by the Baath Party in Iraq [*q.v.*], owing allegiance to his faction within the National Command, Aflaq was invited by Iraq to return and resume his leadership. He accepted the offer. But in September 1970, when the Iraqi government failed to assist Palestinian commandos in their fight with the Jordanian troops, Aflaq showed his displeasure by leaving Baghdad [*q.v.*] for Beirut [*q.v.*].

His estrangement lasted until 1974 when he returned to Baghdad to head the party's National Command. He enjoyed high status and much reverence in Iraq. However, while the Iraqi regime regularly published his articles and tracts, it did not let him determine state policies and practices. During the Iran-Iraq War (1980–88) [*q.v.*], Aflaq was the butt of many attacks by Iran, anxious to depict Iraq, guided by a Christian [*q.v.*], as a state that had deviated from Islam. Significantly, after his death in 1989 the Iraqi media claimed that Aflaq had converted to Islam [*q.v.*] before his demise.

Agudat Israel (Hebrew: *Union of Israel*): Israeli political party and international organization of ultra-Orthodox Jews [*q.v.*], Agudat Israel was formed in Katowice, Poland, in 1912, largely by the ultra-Orthodox Jews of Germany, Poland, and Ukraine, to address Jewish problems from a religious perspective. A member had to accept the supremacy of the Torah [*q.v.*] in Jewish life. Its adherents in Palestine [*q.v.*] boycotted the quasi-governmental organs of the Yishuv [*q.v.*]. They did so primarily because the creation of Israel through human endeavor—

such as the one by Zionist [*q.v.*] pioneers in Palestine—was against their belief that Israel, as a "peoplehood," would be redeemed by the messiah [*q.v.*], and secondarily because they were against women's suffrage. They considered that Jews [*q.v.*] were a religious, not an ethnic, entity, and believed that Jewish problems could be solved only by the Torah.

When its members in Palestine accepted funds from the Jewish National Fund [*q.v.*] to set up kibbutzim [*q.v.*] and theological institutions, it split, with the dissenters forming the Neturei Karta [*q.v.*] in 1935. By World War II, Agudat claimed a world membership of 500,000 mainly ultra-Orthodox Jews. In 1947 its Central World Council set up international centers in New York, London, and Jerusalem [*q.v.*].

Once Israel was founded in 1948, Agudat decided to participate in the state's affairs. On the eve of the first general election in 1949, it combined with Poale Agudat Israel [*q.v.*] to form the Agudat bloc, which in turn allied with the Mizrahi bloc—Mizrahi [*q.v.*] and Poale HaMizrahi [*q.v.*]—to constitute the United Religious Front [*q.v.*]. It won 16 seats and joined the government to run inter alia the religious affairs ministry. The Agudat bloc entered the 1951 election separately, and won five seats. It joined the government, but quit in protest against the passing of a law prescribing conscription for women. While existing separately, Agudat parties stayed in opposition during the era of the Labor-dominated [*q.v.*] governments, which ended in 1977. Later they merged, winning four seats in 1981 and two seats in 1984. On the

eve of the 1988 election they combined with two small religious groups to form the United Torah Judaism [*q.v.*].

A.H.: *Abbreviation of After Hijra* (Arabic: *Migration*) Islamic [*q.v.*] era began with the migration of the Prophet Muhammad from Mecca [*q.v.*] to Medina [*q.v.*] on 15 July 622 A.D. [*q.v.*].

Ahdut HaAvodah: (Hebrew: *The Unity of Labor*): *Zionist political party in Palestine* [*q.v.*] Originating in the split in Poale Zion [*q.v.*], caused by the increased cooperation between socialist pioneers and the financial institutions of the World Zionist Organization [*q.v.*], the right wing, nationalist faction of Poale Zion merged with the followers of Berle Katznelson, committed to founding workers' institutions, to establish Ahdut HaAvodah in March 1919. It played an important role in the establishment of Haganah [*q.v.*] and Histadrut [*q.v.*]. It was instrumental in getting *Davar* (Hebrew: *Word*), the daily newspaper of Histadrut, started in 1925 under the editorship of Katznelson.

In the spring of 1929 Ahdut HaAvodah and HaPoale HaTzair concluded a merger agreement and produced a common platform. A large majority of 2,500 Ahdut HaAvodah members ratified the amalgamation. In January 1930 a joint conference, representing 5,650 members, established Mapai [*q.v.*].

Ahdut HaAvodah-Poale Zion (Hebrew: *The Unity of Labor-Workers of Zion*) Zionist political party in Palestine and Israel, Ahdut HaAvodah-Poale Zion was the result of the merger in April 1946 of the Tanua LeAhdut HaAvodah [*q.v.*] and the remnants of the Poale Zion [*q.v.*]. It was popularly known as Ahdut HaAvodah. In early 1948 it combined with HaShomer HaTzair to establish Mapam [*q.v.*].

Protesting at Mapam's tilt toward the Soviet bloc, which was seen as pursuing an anti-Zionist policy, Ahdut HaAvodah adherents decided in 1954 to acquire a separate identity. The party won 10 parliamentary seats in 1955, seven in 1959, and eight in 1961. It became a junior partner in the Mapai-led [*q.v.*] coalition from 1955 onwards. On the eve of the 1965 election it signed an agreement for a *maarach* (Hebrew: alignment) with Mapai, the resulting bloc winning 45 seats out of 120. The maarach widened in 1968 to include Rafi, and finally resulted in the merger of the three constituent parties into the *Mifleget HaAvodah HaYisraelit* (Hebrew: *The Israeli Labor Party*) [*q.v.*].

Ahmad bin Yahya (1895–62): *ruler of North Yemen, 1948–62* The eldest son of Imam Yahya of the Hamid al-Din branch of the Rassi dynasty, which for centuries had governed the northern and eastern highlands of Yemen, inhabited by Zaidi (Shia) [*q.v.*] tribes and latterly under the suzerainty of the Ottoman Turks, which ended in 1918. Bearing the title *Saif al-Islam* (Arabic: *Sword of Islam*), Ahmad assisted his father militarily as the latter tried to recreate the historical Greater Yemen by extending his realm to the Shafii (Sunni) [*q.v.*] region to the south. In the 1920s and 1930s he led campaigns to suppress tribal revolts.

Following an abortive coup in February 1948, which resulted in the murder of his father, Ahmad assumed supreme power. Like his predecessors, he was elected imam [*q.v.*] (religious leader) by Zaidi chieftains, and was called Imam Ahmad bin Yahya.

Ahmad pursued his father's ambition to recreate Greater Yemen by annexing the British protectorate of Aden. When London frustrated his plans, he turned militantly anti-British and befriended Egypt's pan-Arabist [*q.v.*] president, Gamal Abdul Nasser [*q.v.*]. In April 1956 he signed a mutual defense pact with Egypt which provided for a unified military command. He offered to join the United Arab Republic (UAR) [*q.v.*], the union of Egypt and Syria, soon after its formation in early 1958. The resulting loose federation of the UAR and North Yemen was named the Union of Arab States. By then Ahmad had concluded friendship treaties with the Soviet Union and the People's Republic of China.

At home he continued his father's despotic style of government, much facilitated by his program of modernizing the military. In August 1955 he crushed a coup attempt by a group of officers and two of his three brothers. After the breakup of the UAR in September 1961, he cut his ties with Nasser and began to attack him. Nasser retaliated by allowing the North Yemeni dissidents use of Cairo Radio for anti-Ahmad propaganda. Suffering from ill health, he passed on much of his authority to his eldest son, Muhammad al-Badr [*q.v.*], before his death in September 1962, which triggered a military coup and ended the 1,064-year rule of the Rassi dynasty.

Ahmadinejad, Mahmoud (1956–):
Iranian politician; president 2005–
Born in the household of barber
Ahmad Sabaghian and his wife
Khanum, in Aradan, a village 80
mi./130 km southeast of Tehran
[*q.v.*], he was the fourth of seven children. In 1960, his father migrated to
Tehran where he changed his surname
to Ahmadinejad, meaning descendants of Ahmad, and became a blacksmith. A brilliant student, Mahmoud
ranked 132nd among the nearly
400,000 who took the university entrance examination. He enrolled as a
civil engineering student at the Iran
University of Science and Technology
(IUST). He participated in the anti-
Shah movement. On the eve of the
revolution in early 1979, the whole
family fled to a provincial town to
avoid his arrest.

At the outbreak of the Iran-Iraq
War in 1980 he joined the Baseej
militia (official title, *Niruyeh Muqawa-
matt Baseej*, Resistance Force Mobilization), which served as an auxiliary
to the military. In 1986 he enrolled for
a master's degree in civil engineering
at the IUST. After obtaining it, he became a lecturer at the IUST. He went
on to serve as an advisor to the governor-general of Kurdistan province for
two years. In 1993 he was appointed
governor-general of Ardebil province
until he was sacked by President
Muhammad Khatami [*q.v.*] in 1997.
Later that year he got his doctorate in
transport and traffic engineering and
planning, and returned to teaching.

After the second municipal election
in Tehran in early 2003, won by the
conservative Alliance of the Builders
of Islamic Iran, he was elected mayor.
Refusing to accept the mayor's salary,

he lived austerely. He laid roads, gave
interest-free loans to the needy, and
put religious emphasis on the cultural
centers established by his predecessors.

In the first run for the presidency in
2005, he surprisingly came second,
beating the far better-known former
parliamentary speaker Mahdi Karrubi
by a slim 2 percent. Karrubi's complaints about vote-rigging in Isfahan
[*q.v.*] were ignored by the Supreme
Leader Ayatollah Ali Khamanei
[*q.v.*]. In the second vote, he defeated
Ali Akbar Hashmi Rafsanjani [*q.v.*]
by 62 percent to 38 percent.

On assuming the presidency in August, he refused to move to the official
residence in Saadabad Palace in upscale north Tehran. Instead he settled
for living in one of the buildings in the
well-guarded Pastor Square complex
of the government in south Tehran.

As a social-religious conservative,
he reversed liberalization in Iranians'
social-cultural life introduced during
the eight-year presidency of his predecessor, Khatami. There was also a
crackdown on the reformist groups at
universities. His policy was backed by
Khamanei, a diehard conservative.

Untutored in economic affairs, instead of investing cash from the record
high oil prices, he consumed it in raising pensions and salaries and giving
cheap loans. On the other hand, by
using the everyday language of the
people and touring each of the 31
provincial capitals, addressing rallies
there and collecting petitions from citizens, he widened his popular base.
He also rallied the nation on the issue
of Iran's right to enrich uranium for
peaceful purposes.

Over-confident of his public
standing, the government allowed

three 90-minute TV debates between him and each of his three challengers on the eve of the presidential election in June 2009. This gave an unprecedented opportunity for opposition views to be aired before an audience of 50 million. It dramatically enhanced the chances of reformist Mir Hussein Mousavi [*q.v.*], a former prime minister during the 1980–1988 Iran-Iraq War [*q.v.*].

At 84 percent, the voter turnout was the second highest in the Republic's history. It meant that more of the upper-middle and upper class Iranians—often secular—went out to vote than before. This favored Mousavi. So the official result, announced posthaste, giving 62.5 percent of the ballots to Ahmadinejad to Mousavi's 33.9 percent, stunned most Iranian and foreign analysts. Whereas the United States and the 27-member European Union doubted the veracity of the election result, Russia, China, India, Brazil, and most Muslim states, including Turkey, congratulated Ahmadinejad on his reelection. There were massive protest demonstrations against the widely suspected poll-rigging. The violence with which the security forces quashed them killed 69 protestors.

The reelected Ahmadinejad continued his hardline policies domestically. Despite the strong showing by Mousavi, he made no concessions to the reformist camp.

Islamic Iran's generally hostile policy toward the U.S. going back to the time of the revolution continued under his presidency. In response to Washington's success in getting the UN Security Council to impose a series of sanctions against Iran on the nuclear issue from 2008 onwards,

Ahmadinejad, supported by Khamanei, hardened his stance. He strengthened ties with China, Russia, Brazil, and Venezuela.

His policy on the nuclear issue was backed by the reformist opposition. In the final analysis, authority in this matter rested with the Supreme National Security Council, charged with formulating policies on defense and national security. Chaired by the president, it consisted of 18 civilian officials and military commanders, including two representatives of the Supreme Leader. Its decisions had to be ratified by the Leader before they were implemented.

Ahmadinejad's statements on the Holocaust have been interpreted differently—from his description of it as "a myth" to "there is a need for a group of dispassionate scholars to sift all the evidence and reach a conclusion." Equally, his declaration in Persian that the "occupying Zionist regime" should "vanish from the pages of time" has often been translated as "Israel should be wiped off the map."

Under his presidency, Iran continued to support Hizbollah [*q.v.*] and Hamas [*q.v.*] politically and financially. In September 2010, he criticized Palestinian Authority president Mahmoud Abbas [*q.v.*] for reviving direct talks with Israel, and urged Palestinians to continue armed resistance against the occupation by Israel.

In December, his government's removal of subsidies on petroleum products and agricultural produce led respectively to two-fold and sevenfold increase in the price of bread and gasoline. It decided to distribute the expected annual savings of $60 billion by making monthly payments of $43 to each citizen who applied for it, thus compensating large, lower-income families. In its report in June 2011, the International Monetary Fund praised Iran's economic policies because these hugely lessened the government's burden and lowered domestic energy consumption, thus leaving more petroleum for export.

Politically, Ahmadinejad tried to strengthen the presidency at the expense of the clerical establishment. The resulting strain in his relations with Khamanei became public in 2011. The parliamentary election in March 2012, seen as the test of strength between the two camps, showed Khamanei to be the predominant force. However, his views on the Arab Spring [q.v.] chimed with those of Khamanei, both leaders describing it as the Islamic Awakening [q.v.] in the Arab world.

Ahmadinejad became the first Iranian president to visit Iraq administered by a Shia-dominated government. His relations with Afghanistan and Pakistan were cordial. He exchanged state visits with President Hugo Chavez of Venezuela, and cultivated warm relations with Brazil.

al-Ahmar, Abdullah Hussein (1919–2007): *Yemeni politician* Son of Shaikh Hussein bin Nasser al-Ahmar, head of the Hashid tribal confederation, who was executed in 1959 for his part in a failed coup against Imam Ahmad bin Yahya [q.v.], Ahmar succeeded his father. When civil war erupted in September 1962 soon after Imam Ahmad's death, he sided with the republicans. He was appointed governor of the Hajjah district northwest of the capital, Sanaa [q.v.].

In the republican camp he allied with conservative politicians and opposed radical military officers, especially President Abdullah Sallal [q.v.], a general who dominated the regime. His opposition to the participation of Egyptian forces in the conflict made him popular with Saudi Arabia, which backed the royalist camp. In September 1966, when Sallal attempted to arrest Ahmar in Sanaa, the latter fled to his tribal base and took up arms against the central authority. Once the Egyptian troops had withdrawn from North Yemen after Egypt's defeat in the June 1967 Arab-Israel War [q.v.], he returned to the capital with his forces. As one of the plotters to depose Sallal in November 1967, he was a leading architect of the "Third Force" government led by President Abdul Rahman al-Iryani [q.v.]. He won over most of the tribal leaders to the republican side and, assisted by Saudi Arabia, helped to conciliate the warring sides. The civil strife ended in 1970 with the formal abolition of the monarchy.

After the promulgation of a new constitution in December 1970, stipulating a Consultative Assembly, partly elected and partly nominated, Ahmar was elected its chairman. After Col. Ibrahim Hamdi [q.v.] carried out a bloodless coup in June 1974 he compelled Ahmar to resign, and disbanded the Assembly. The new constitution, promulgated by the Military Command Council, led by Hamdi, provided for a fully nominated Constituent People's Assembly (CPA) to act as a consultative body. Since Hamdi did not appoint Ahmar to the CPA, the two fell out. In April 1977 Ahmar led a rebellion against Sanaa in the north, which was crushed by Hamdi.

Following Hamdi's assassination in October and the accession to power of Ahmad Hussein Ghashmi [*q.v.*], Ahmar's relations with the center improved. He was appointed to the CPA. The succession to the presidency of Ali Abdullah Saleh [*q.v.*] after the assassination of Ghashmi in mid-1978 saw further enhancement of Ahmar's political standing. But his continued close links with Saudi Arabia, his opposition to the improvement of ties between North Yemen and the Soviet Union, and his disapproval of unity between North and South Yemen inhibited any further rise in his influence.

With Saleh proving more durable than anybody had foreseen, the situation in the tribal areas stabilized by the mid-1980s, and Ahmar settled down in the role of an elder statesman. After the unification of the two Yemens in May 1990, he founded the Yemeni Islah Group [*q.v.*], with an Islamist program. In the first multiparty parliamentary election, held under universal suffrage in united Yemen in October 1993, the Islah Group won 62 of the 310 seats and Ahmar was elected Speaker. In the 1994 Yemeni civil war [*q.v.*], he actively sided with the government. Following the 1997 general election, in which the Islah secured 53 seats, he retained his post of Speaker. With the tenure of the parliament extended to six years, Ahmar's status remained unchanged until 2003. The subsequent parliament reelected him speaker.

After his death in December 2007, President Saleh announced a three-day mourning period and praised him as "one of Yemen's permanent political fixtures."

Ahvaz: *Iranian city* Population: 1.43 million (2008 est.) The history of Ahvaz, situated on the banks of the Karun River, dates back to the Achaemenian Empire (539–330 B.C.). Ahvaz declined after that period but was revived by Sassanian King Ardeshir (r. 224–41 A.D.), who dammed the river and called the settlement Hormuz Ardeshir. In c. 275, near Ahvaz arose Gunde Shapur University in c. 275 A.D., the greatest place of learning in its time. (Today, the city's university carries the historical name). Following its capture in 637 A.D., the Arab conquerors changed its name to Suq al-Ahvaz, the last word being the plural of Huzi/Khuzi, the local tribe.

Situated in the midst of fertile land that was particularly suitable for prized sugarcane, the city continued its prosperous existence throughout the Umayyad (661–750 A.D.) and Abbasid (751–1258 A.D.) Empires, and after. But when the local dam broke in the mid-19th century the future of the city was doomed. It was saved later in the century by official plans to develop a new town across the river to complement the old settlement.

With the discovery of petroleum in the region in 1908, Ahvaz, being the capital of the oil-rich Khuzistan province, received a boost. Its prosperity continued for the next seven decades. As the center of the oil industry it played a crucial role in the revolutionary movement that toppled the monarchy in Iran in 1979. In the Iran-Iraq War (1980–88) [*q.v.*] it became a front-line city and suffered some damage. It is now one of the largest urban centers in Iran. In 2011 it was one of the 10 most polluted cities in the world.

Aigptios: *see* Coptic Church and Copts.

al (Arabic: *the*): The Arabic definite article *al* is frequently used with proper nouns, especially places and people, as well as adjectives. For instance, Basra is written as al-Basra [*q.v.*] in Arabic [*q.v.*], and Nur al-Din Attasi [*q.v.*] as Nur al-Din al-Attasi.

Alawis (Arabic: *followers of Ali*): *Islamic sect* Also known as Alawites. The term Alawi came into vogue in Syria during the French mandate (1920–46), replacing the earlier terms: Nusairi and Ansariya. According to some scholars, Nusairi is a derivative of the first theologian of the sect, Muhammad bin Nusair, who in 245 A.H./857 A.D. proclaimed himself *bab* (gate) to the 10th Shia [*q.v.*] Imam Ali Naqi and of his son, Muhammad, who died before him. And Ansariya is derived from the name of the mountain range where they lived.

Alawis are an offshoot of the Twelver Shias [*q.v.*], sharing their belief that Imam Ali, cousin and son-in-law of the Prophet Muhammad, was the legitimate heir but was deprived of his status by the first three caliphs. They portray Ali as a bearer of divine essence, and hold him in higher esteem than any of the earlier prophets mentioned in the Quran [*q.v.*], including Adam, Noah, Moses, and Jesus. They follow certain rituals derived from Christianity [*q.v.*], including the celebration of Christmas [*q.v.*]

and Epiphany [*q.v.*], and from Zoroastrianism [*q.v.*], including Nawruz [*q.v.*]. Taqi al-Din bin Taimiya (1263–1328), an orthodox Sunni [*q.v.*] Syrian theologian, described them as more dangerous than Christians and urged a jihad [*q.v.*] against them.

The seven pillars of the Alawi sect include not only the five pillars of the Sunni sect—*shahada* (Islamic credo), *salat* (five prayers), *zaka*t [*q.v.*] (alms), *hajj* [*q.v.*] (pilgrimage to Mecca [*q.v.*]) and *sawm* (fasting during Ramadan [*q.v.*])—but also jihad (holy struggle) and *waliya* (devotion to the Imam Ali family and hatred of their adversaries). They share their annual festivals with Shias, including Eid al-Fitr [*q.v.*], Eid al-Adha [*q.v.*], and Ashura [*q.v.*].

In 1974, Imam Musa al-Sadr [*q.v.*], an eminent Twelver Shia theologian based in Lebanon, ruled that Alawis were part of the Shia school of Islam.

Of the four million Alawis, almost three million live in Syria, another million in Turkey, and 100,000 in Lebanon. In Syria they are mostly settled as peasants, chiefly in the mountainous region around the port city of Latakia [*q.v.*]. They account for a large majority of the country's professional soldiers. The best known Alawi politician is Syrian President Bashar Assad [*q.v.*].

Aleppo: *Syrian city* Population: 2.98 million (2011 est.) The importance of Aleppo, with a history stretching back to ca 2000 B.C., stems from the strategic position it occupied on the caravan route connecting the eastern Mediterranean region with the lands further east. It was part of the Achaemenian Empire (539–330

B.C.), and it continued to prosper during the later Roman and Byzantine periods. It fell to Muslim [*q.v.*] Arabs [*q.v.*] in 637 A.D., and retained its commercial importance during the subsequent Islamic empires, from the Umayyads, who build the Great Mosque in 715 A.D., to the Ottoman Turks (1517–1918).

Under the Ottomans it emerged as the principal trading center in their Arab empire. With the decline of caravan transport, local entrepreneurs took to industry, especially leather, textile printing, and silk manufacture. By the early 20th century Aleppo had emerged as a rival to Damascus [*q.v.*]. Besides the Great Mosque, the citadel, constructed in the 13th century, is a chief tourist attraction. Aleppo is now the largest city of Syria.

During the anti-regime protest as part of the Arab Spring [q.v.], the city remained comparatively calm until mid-2012. It then witnessed a long battle between armed rebels and security forces and suffered heavy losses in lives and property, including the burning down of much of the historic Old City.

Alexandria: *Egyptian city* Population: 4.59 million (2011 est.) Founded by Alexander the Great in 332 B.C., Alexandria was the capital of Ptolemies (323–30 B.C.). In 306 B.C. it became the site of the Bibliotheca Alexandrina, a library with 700,000 items, which was destroyed by fire in 47 B.C. As a major port it rivaled and then outstripped ancient Carthage to become the largest city in the Mediterranean region. It emerged as the leading center of Hellenic and Jewish arts and sciences. Later, in 30

B.C., it formed part of the Roman Empire and was its most populous provincial capital, with 300,000 free citizens. After Muslim [*q.v.*] Arabs [*q.v.*] captured it in 642 A.D., they transferred the capital to al-Fustat near Cairo [*q.v.*]. It became the second-largest city of Egypt, a position it has maintained.

It is the headquarters of the Greek Orthodox [*q.v.*] patriarchate. A highly developed port, it is an important industrial center. Its main tourist offerings include the Hadrianic catacombs and Pompey's Pillar.

In 2002 it became the site of a newly constructed library, named after its ancient predecessor, Bibliotheca Alexandrina, capable of holding four million volumes. At first, though possessing only a quarter-million books, it became the largest and the most advanced library in the Arab world.

The Arab Spring [*q.v.*] in Egypt had its origin in the killing of the 28-year-old Khaled Saeed in Alexandria by two policemen in June 2010 which led to the setting up of a Facebook page, "We are all Khaled Saeed," and the subsequent silent protest that resulted in the conviction of the guilty police officers. This episode would prove to be the preamble to the vast protest demonstrations in Cairo [*q.v.*] in January 2011.

Algiers Accord (1975): *see* Iran-Iraq Treaty of International Boundaries and Neighborliness (1975)/Treaty of Frontier and Good Neighborly Relations (Iran-Iraq, 1975).

Ali, Salim Rubai (1935–78): *South Yemeni politician; president 1969–78* Born into a middle-class family in

Zinjibar near Aden [*q.v.*], Ali trained as a teacher. Later he studied law and became involved in a militantly anti-imperialist movement, the National Liberation Front (NLF) [*q.v.*]. In October 1963 he led a guerrilla campaign against the British in the Rafdan Mountains. The British left four years later after handing over power to the NLF. Accused of factionalism by the NLF leadership, Ali chose to go into self-exile. But he continued to conspire.

In June 1969 President Qahtan al-Shaabi [*q.v.*], a moderate, was ousted by the leftists within the NLF and replaced by a presidential council of five (later reduced to three), headed by Ali, who was elected to the NLF central committee and politburo. The new regime purged the party and government of moderates. It carried out rapid socioeconomic changes at home and followed radical foreign policies.

By the mid-1970s, however, Ali began showing signs of pragmatism, especially concerning Saudi Arabia, which had been deeply hostile to socialist South Yemen. This put him at odds with the radical, pro-Moscow faction led by Abdul Fattah Ismail [*q.v.*], secretary-general of the NLF. The rivalry between the two intensified and became entangled with relations between North and South Yemen. The assassination of North Yemeni President Ibrahim Hamdi [*q.v.*] on the eve of his visit to Aden [*q.v.*] in October 1977 made matters worse. The differences between Ali and Ismail hardened around the structure of the proposed Yemeni Socialist Party [*q.v.*], developmental strategy, and foreign relations, particularly with Saudi Arabia.

The break between the two rivals came in June 1978. A special emissary of Ali, dispatched to his North Yemeni counterpart, Ahmad Hussein Ghashmi [*q.v.*], succeeded in killing both the president and himself with explosives hidden in his briefcase. One version had it that Ali had sent his envoy to secure Ghashmi's assistance in a planned coup, but his adversaries had got wind of it and had replaced his emissary with their own. Just as this drama was unfolding in Sanaa [*q.v.*], the two adversaries clashed in Aden. While Ali used the army to overcome his opponents, Ismail deployed the party's People's Militia. Ali lost, and was executed.

Alignment Bloc (Israel*)*: *see* Labor Alignment (Israel).

Allawi, Iyad Muhammad (1945–): *Iraqi politician; interim prime minister, 2004–2005* Born to a wealthy Shia [*q.v.*] merchant family in Baghdad, he was educated at the elite Baghdad College, a Roman Catholic [*q.v.*] Jesuit high school run by an American organization. After graduating as a physician in Baghdad, he pursued higher medical studies in London. There he headed the Iraqi students' association affiliated to the Baath Socialist Party [*q.v.*]. Unhappy at the rise of Saddam Hussein [*q.v.*] in the Baath Party in Iraq, he resigned from it in 1975, and began plotting against Saddam Hussein in collusion with some Iraqi generals. In 1978 the attempt by a henchman of Saddam to assassinate him failed.

During the 1980s, in association with dissident Iraqi army officers, Allawi began plotting to overthrow

President Saddam Hussein. In 1990 he became one of the three founders of the Iraqi National Accord [*q.v.*] funded by Saudi Arabia's intelligence agency, Istikhabart. It established links with U.S. Central Intelligence Agency and focused on recruiting disaffected Baathist military officers and others.

The joint INA-CIA plan to mount a coup against Saddam Hussein in June 1996 failed when the Iraqi intelligence operatives succeeded in infiltrating the INA's cells within Iraq. Of the 130 military officers detained after the coup's failure, 30 were executed. The government confiscated the assets of the Allawi family.

After the passage of Iraq Liberation Act in October 1998, Washington recognized the INA, now led exclusively by Allawi, as a group eligible for U.S. assistance. During the administration of U.S. President George W. Bush (r. 2001–2009), the INA and Allawi became the favorites of the CIA and the state department. They participated in the Iraqi Open Opposition conference in London in late 2002.

Following the Anglo-American invasion of Iraq [*q.v.*] in March 2003, Allawi was appointed a member of the Interim Iraqi Governing Council (IGC) by the United States. He focused on running the IGC's security committee charged with reforming the army, police, and intelligence services. But his opposition to purging Baathists from official positions was ignored by the U.S. consul, Paul Bremer, the administrator of the Coalition Provisional Authority of Iraq.

Appointed acting prime minister by Washington in June 2004, Allawi headed an interim cabinet until April 2005. His government quickly earned the odium of widespread corruption, collaboration with America, and a heavy-handed security policy implemented by Allawi. He closed the bureau of the Al-Jazeera satellite TV channel, and appointed Ibrahim Janabi, a former Iraqi intelligence officer, as the chief media regulator. He strongly backed the Pentagon's controversial offensives to seize control of the rebellious Sunni [*q.v.*] city of Falluja and the Shia holy place of Najaf [*q.v.*] from the militia of Muqtada al-Sadr [*q.v.*]. However, his attempt to issue an emergency ordinance authorizing him to declare martial law, impose curfews, and detain suspects was overruled by Washington.

On the eve of the December 2005 parliamentary election, Allawi's INA formed an alliance with other secular groups to form the Iraqi National List (INL). With only 25 seats in a house of 275, the INL emerged as the distant third. Yet it found a place in the coalition government of Nouri al-Maliki [*q.v.*]. But Allawi declined a cabinet post. He spent most of his time in Amman [*q.v.*]. Instructed by him, INL ministers quit the government in 2007.

In early 2009, he formed al-Iraqiya List [*q.v.*] (Iraqi National Movement), an alliance that included Iraq's Sunni Vice President Tariq al-Hashemi. During the run-up to the general election in March, he visited all the neighboring Sunni-majority countries, with the Saudi government barely disguising its support for him. In the election al-Iraqiya won two more seats than the 89 its rival Maliki-led State of Law alliance did. After failing to gain the backing of the majority of legislators to form a cabinet, Allawi agreed to support the national unity government of Maliki when he was promised the presidency of the proposed National Council for Higher Strategic Policy (NCHSP). Even after the parliament had amended the constitution to incorporate the NCHSP, it remained a paper organization. Allawi resigned its presidency in October 2011.

A.M.: *Abbreviation of Anno Mundi* (Latin: *Year of the World*) This pertains to the Jewish era that began with the estimated date of creation, according to Genesis in the Old Testament [*q.v.*]: 3760 B.C. Jews [*q.v.*] use this dating system. *See also* Jewish calendar.

Amal (Arabic: acronym of *Afwaj al-Muqawama al-Lubnaniya*, The Lebanese Resistance Detachments): *Lebanese militia* Amal was formed in July 1975, a few months after the outbreak of civil war in Lebanon, as the armed wing of the Movement of the Disinherited, which had been established in February 1973 by a radical Shia leader, Imam Musa al-Sadr [*q.v.*]. It was popularly known as *Amal* (Arabic: *Hope*). After the "disappearance" of al-Sadr in August 1978 during his visit to Libya, Amal came under the leadership of Shaikh Muhammad Mahdi Shams al-Din and Hussein Husseini, who forged strong links with Iran after the Islamic revolution there in early 1979. It gained many recruits from the 300,000 Shia emigrants from southern Lebanon who had abandoned their homes as a result of Israeli bombings.

By spring of 1982 the leadership of Amal had passed on to Shams al-Din

and Nabih Berri [*q.v.*], a layman Shia leader. Since Berri was close to Syria, Amal increasingly became a fixture of the policies being pursued by Damascus, especially in the ongoing civil strife. The victory of the pro-Syrian camp in the Lebanon Civil War [*q.v.*] in October 1990 improved the status of Amal. Once the government decided to dissolve all irregular forces, 2,800 militia of Amal, which once had 14,000 men under arms, were absorbed into the regular Lebanese army in September 1991.

It continued to function as a political party, and ran in parliamentary elections, with its leader Berri being elected parliamentary speaker. In the 2000 general election, it allied with Hizbollah [*q.v.*], and together they won all of the 23 seats in the governorate of South Lebanon. In the 2005 parliamentary election, the Amal-Hizbollah alliance secured 35 seats, with Hizbollah gaining 14. As part of March 8 Alliance [*q.v.*] in the June 2009 general election, Amal won 13 seats out of the total of 57, with Hizbollah securing another 13.

American hostage crisis in Tehran (1979–81): *see* Hostage-taking and hostages.

American University in Beirut: From the 1830s onward Christian missionaries from the United States started establishing schools and colleges in Lebanon. After securing a charter from the state of New York in 1863 and raising funds in the United States and Britain, Daniel Bliss of the American Protestant Mission opened the Syrian Protestant College in Beirut [*q.v.*] in 1866. Despite its name the college was non-sectarian. It soon acquired a school of medicine. In 1882 English replaced Arabic as the language of instruction. Following the end of the Ottoman rule in 1918 and the arrival of the French as victors, the trustees changed its name to the American University in Beirut (AUB) in 1920.

Education in the arts and sciences, imparted by the AUB to a student body drawn from all over the Arab world, helped create a class of Arab intellectuals with a wide perspective. The AUB thus performed a significant role in producing political leaders and stimulating Arab political and intellectual activity. Throughout the 1975–90 Civil War [q.v.] (during which—in 1984—its president, Dr. Malcolm Kerr, was killed), it continued to function while its hospital provided much-needed services. After the conflict its research program focused on the reconstruction of Lebanon. Between 1870 and June 2011, it awarded 82,032 degrees and diplomas.

American University in Cairo: Established in 1919, the American University in Cairo (AUC) was financed by U.S. citizens interested in furthering education in the Middle East. Charles Watson, its founding president, was born of missionary parents and grew up in the Egyptian city of Asyut. It provides American liberal arts and professional education in English to predominantly Egyptian students.

In 1928, female students were accepted and by 1994 their ratio had climbed to 50 percent. Incorporated in the United States, the AUC operates within the framework of the cultural relations agreement signed between

Egypt and the United States in 1962, which was renewed in 1975. Despite the best intentions of its founders, the AUC has remained an exclusive institution because of its small student body and high tuition fees. Its student body of about 5,000 students in 2007 was less than 0.5 percent of the national total.

In 2008, the AUC moved from its eight-acre downtown campus to a newly built 280-acre campus in the upscale suburb of New Cairo, with a plan to raise the student body to 5,500.

To mark the first anniversary of the ousting of President Hosni Mubarak [q.v.] on 11 February 2011, AUC students screened films of military and police brutality and demanded that the Supreme Council of the Armed Forces should cede power to the interim government.

Amichai, Yehuda (1924–2000): *Israeli poet and novelist* Born Yehuda Pfeuffer to a businessman father in Wurzberg, Germany, Amichai moved to Palestine [q.v.] along with his parents in 1936. After graduating from a religious high school in Jerusalem [q.v.], he enrolled in the British army in 1942. After World War II he joined the Palmah [q.v.] and fought in the 1948–49 Arab-Israeli War [q.v.]. He joined the Hebrew University in Jerusalem in 1949 and started writing poetry.

Much influenced by W. H. Auden (d. 1973), a left-wing British poet famed for his personal poetry written in a casual tone, Amichai combined everyday Hebrew [q.v.] with the language used in the Old Testament [q.v.] and the Jewish prayer books. An iconoclast, he derided the spartan way of life preached by the pioneering Zionist [*q.v.*] leaders, especially David Ben-Gurion [*q.v.*], during the first decades of Israel and unashamedly aspired to bourgeois comforts. In 1962 his *Poems (1948–62)* became a best-seller.

By continuing to harness the flat idiom of daily life with images from the Hebrew Bible [*q.v.*] and Jewish liturgy, he transformed the rhythm and vocabulary of Hebrew poetry. His work, distinguished by its depth and virtuosity, was read widely. By the time he was 70 he had published 11 volumes of poetry in Hebrew; two novels, including *Not of This Time, Not of This Place* (1963); and several short stories. His later poetry is criticized as being thematically unadventurous and covering old ground. His works were translated into 25 languages. The titles translated into English include *Love Poems, More Love Poems, Poems of Jerusalem, Open-Eyed Landscape, Great Tranquility: Questions and Answers, The World is a Room and Other Stories,* and *Yehuda Amichai: A Life of Poetry 1948–94.*

After the 1967 Arab-Israeli War [*q.v.*] he became an advocate of peace with the Palestinians and a supporter of the Peace Now [*q.v.*] movement. He won the Israel Prize for literature in 1982.

Amman: *capital of Jordan* Population: 2.85 million (2011 est.) The origins of Amman, a city of hills, lie in distant antiquity, around 4000 B.C. Both its present and biblical names are derived from Ammon, the capital of the Ammonites, its full title being *Rabba' Ir Bene Ammon* (Hebrew: *Great City of Ammon's Sons*). It is the site of the battle in which Uriah met his death

(the battle having been ordered by his supreme commander, King David), enabling his wife, Bathsheba, to marry King David.

Having captured the settlement, Egyptian King Ptolemy II Philadelphius (r. 283–246 B.C.) called it Philadelphia. This name survived the arrival of the Greeks, Romans, and Byzantines, and the city thrived under the Romans. After conquering it in 635 A.D., the Muslim [*q.v.*] Arabs [*q.v.*] renamed it Amman. It began to decline, and by the early 13th century was reduced to ruins.

When faced with the problem of re-settling the Circassian [*q.v.*] refugees from the Caucasian region of Tsarist Russia, Ottoman Sultan Abdul Hamid II (r. 1876–1909) hit upon the idea of directing them to the virtually defunct Amman in 1878. The revived Amman was still a village when Abdullah bin Hussein al-Hashem [*q.v.*] camped there with his troops in 1921 on his way to Syria. Two years later it became the capital of Transjordan [*q.v.*].

From then onwards it began to expand—a process accelerated by the influx of Palestinian refugees after the 1948–49 Palestine War [*q.v.*] and again after the June 1967 Arab-Israeli War [*q.v.*]. In September 1970 the city became the center of an armed conflict between Palestinian guerillas and the Jordanian army.

On the whole Amman has benefited greatly by the enterprise of its Palestinian residents, and has become the financial, commercial, communications, political, and educational center of Jordan. Among its tourist offerings are a Roman amphitheatre and the old citadel.

Anaiza tribal federation: (Also spelled Anaza.) Anaiza is one of the 25 major tribal federations in the Arabian Peninsula [*q.v.*]. It is considered noble because of its claim to lineal descent from Yaarab, the eponymous father of all Arabs. Its origins can be traced back to the 15th century and the territory around the town of Diraiya in the Najd region [*q.v.*]. The House of Saud [*q.v.*] belongs to the Masalikh clan of the Ruwalla tribe of the Anaiza federation. The ruling al-Sabah clan [*q.v.*] of Kuwait is part of the Amarat tribe of the Anaiza federation. *See also* Tribalism.

Anglo-American Commission on Palestine (1946): After World War II, the American Congress and president pressured Britain to scrap its 1939 White Paper—limiting annual Jewish immigration to Palestine to 15,000—and conceded the Zionist demand to admit 100,000 Jewish refugees camped in Cyprus into Palestine [*q.v.*]. In response Britain agreed to the appointment of a joint Anglo-American commission to study the Palestine problem. In its report, published in April 1946, the Commission proposed that Britain should continue its Mandate, that 100,000 Jewish refugees be let into Palestine, and that all illegal militias—primarily the 65,000-strong Zionist irregulars, armed with weapons from wartime munitions factories—be disbanded. Britain agreed to continue the Mandate only if the United States shared the responsibility. It refused. While the U.S. urged immediate admission of the Jewish refugees into Palestine, Britain made this conditional on the disarming of the Zionist militias

whose violent activities were increasingly threatening British life and property in Palestine.

Anglo-American invasion of Iraq, 2003: *see* Gulf War III

Anglo-Bahraini Agreement (1914): In order to ensure supplies of oil—the fuel adopted by the British navy in 1913—Britain imposed an agreement on Bahrain whereby the latter was barred from giving petroleum concessions to non-British companies without London's prior permission.

Anglo-Egyptian Treaty (1936): The outbreak of the Italian-Ethiopian War in 1935 made Britain, the dominant foreign power in Egypt, amenable to redefining Anglo-Egyptian ties. The result was the signing of an Anglo-Egyptian treaty in 1936, valid for 20 years. It gave Britain the exclusive right to equip and train the Egyptian military. While it required Egypt to expand its transport and communications facilities and make them available to the British forces, it entitled Britain to build as many new air bases as it wished. It signified a formal end to the posting of British troops outside the Suez Canal [*q.v.*] zone, subject to Egypt building up its defense capabilities sufficiently. British troops were to be stationed specifically to guard the Suez Canal until such time that the two signatories agreed that Egypt could do the job alone. Britain retained the right to take over all defense and communications facilities in the event of war.

The treaty disappointed Egyptian nationalists. In the 1950 general election the nationalist Wafd [*q.v.*] won decisively. Reflecting the popular mood, which sought to avenge the humiliation suffered by the Arabs [q.v.] in the Palestine War (1948–49) [q.v.], the Wafd government pressed Britain to withdraw its troops from Egypt. When London stonewalled, Cairo unilaterally abrogated the 1936 Treaty in October 1951. The ensuing official non-cooperation, reinforced by popular guerrilla actions, made the British base in the Suez Canal zone virtually inoperative. The tussle between London and Cairo paved the way for the overthrow of the Egyptian monarchy in less than a year. The new regime was anxious to see the departure of the 70,000 British troops occupying 300 sq. mi./777 sq. km of the Egyptian territory. It signed an agreement with London in October 1954 for a British withdrawal by the end of the year.

Anglo-Iraqi Treaty (1930): When oil was discovered in Iraq in 1927, Britain, the Mandate power, decided to redefine its relations with Iraq. In September 1929 it agreed to sponsor Iraq's membership of the League of Nations. A year later a 25-year treaty was signed, to be implemented after Iraq had become a member of the League of Nations as an independent state. It required Iraq to formulate a common foreign policy with Britain and allow the stationing of British forces on its soil, in exchange for a British guarantee to protect it against foreign attack. London ended its Mandate over Iraq in October 1932. A major upheaval in 1941 in Iraq, involving a coup by Rashid Ali Gailani [q.v.] and its suppression, confirmed the supremacy of Britain over Iraq's nationalist forces.

When faced with the popular Iraqi demand for full independence after World War II, Britain renegotiated the terms of the 1930 treaty. It presented the new document (initialed by both sides in the British port city of Portsmouth in January 1948—the Portsmouth Agreement—valid for 20 years) as signifying an alliance between two equals. However, because it did not include British troop withdrawal from Iraq, it went down badly with the Iraqi public. Large-scale demonstrations in Baghdad [q.v.] against the Portsmouth Agreement brought down the government and aborted the new draft treaty, thus implicitly confirming the annulment of the earlier treaty.

Anglo-Jordanian Treaty (1948): After Transjordan [q.v.] had acquired independence in May 1946 its ruler, Abdullah bin Hussein al-Hashem [q.v.], assumed the title of king and changed the name of his realm from the Emirate of Transjordan to the Hashemite Kingdom of Jordan. This necessitated revision of the 1928 Anglo-Transjordanian Treaty. A revised version, valid for 20 years, was signed in March 1948. It incorporated the principle of mutual assistance in the event of war, and allowed Britain to use military bases in Jordan for an annual subsidy of £12 million to the king. In December 1955 Amman [q.v.] witnessed massive demonstrations against the treaty. This was followed by a call by parliament, elected in October 1956, for its abrogation. In January 1957 Egypt, Syria, and Saudi Arabia together offered to replace the British subsidy for at least 10 years. The Jordanian monarch, Hussein bin Talal al-Hashem [*q.v.*], approached London to end the treaty. This was done in March 1957.

Anglo-Kuwaiti Agreement (1913): In order to ensure supplies of oil—the fuel adopted by the British navy in 1913—Britain imposed an agreement on Kuwait that barred the latter from giving oil concessions to non-British companies without London's prior permission.

Anglo-Omani Agreement (1925): In order to ensure supplies of petroleum—the fuel adopted by the British navy in 1913—Britain imposed an agreement on Oman whereby the latter was barred from giving oil concessions to non-British companies without London's prior permission.

Anglo-Ottoman Convention (1913): In July 1913 Britain signed an Anglo-Ottoman Convention with Ottoman Sultan Muhammad VI (r. 1909–23). Among other things, it recognized Kuwait as "an autonomous *caza* [Arabic: *administrative unit*] of the [Ottoman] Empire" under Shaikh Mubarak I al-Sabah, who had the status of an Ottoman *qaimmaqam* (Arabic: *district governor*). Mubarak's autonomy was recognized within an inner (red) circle of 40 mi./103 km radius, centered on Kuwait port, which included not only the islands of Warba and Bubiyan but also Mashian, Failakah, Auhah, and Kabbar. Beyond that, in a segment of land with a radius of 140 mi./362 km, centered on Kuwait port, marking the outer (green) boundary defined by the Convention, Mubarak was authorized only to collect tributes from the tribes.

However, the outbreak of World War I in 1914, when the Ottomans sided with the Germans, invalidated the Convention and allowed London to announce that Kuwait was an "independent shaikhdom under British protection."

Anglo-Persian Agreement (1919): After World War I, the government of Persia (now Iran) was in such dire financial straits that only British subsidies could keep it afloat. This encouraged Britain's foreign minister, Lord Curzon, to realize his dream of turning Persia into a British protectorate. He concluded a secret agreement with the Persian government in 1919 that gave Britain enormous political, economic, and military control over Persia. When the terms of the agreement were disclosed on the eve of a debate in the Persian parliament, there was furor not only in Persia but also in the United States and Bolshevik Russia. The parliament refused to ratify it.

Anglo-Qatari Agreement (1916): According to this treaty, Britain guaranteed the territorial integrity of Qatar while Qatar agreed not to cede any mineral rights to a third party without Britain's prior consent.

Anglo-Transjordanian Treaty (1928): In April 1923 Britain announced that it would recognize Transjordan as an autonomous emirate under the rule of Emir Abdullah bin Hussein al-Hashem [*q.v.*] if a constitutional regime was established there and a preferential treaty with London signed, requiring him to formulate a common foreign policy with Britain, and allow the stationing of British forces on its soil in exchange for a British guarantee to protect Transjordan against foreign attack. He agreed, and declared Transjordan "independent." But such a treaty was signed only in February 1928.

Anglo-Yemeni Treaty (1934): Following World War I, Imam Yahya Hamid al-Din (r. 1918–48) dispatched his forces to capture several border areas that London considered part of its Western Aden protectorate. Periodic efforts to negotiate a deal failed until 1934, when a 40-year Anglo-Yemeni Treaty of Peace and Friendship was signed in Sanaa [*q.v.*]. It accepted North Yemen's southern frontier as the status quo until future negotiations produced a final settlement.

Ansariyas: *see* Alawis.

Antiochene rite: *see* West Syriac rite.

anti-Semitism: *prejudice against Jews* [*q.v.*] As the Jews are blamed for killing Jesus Christ, who was born a Jew, Christians [*q.v.*] have harbored feelings against Jews since the inception of Christianity. This has resulted in periodic persecution of Jews, often involving expulsion, in Christian countries, where Jews came to be confined to specific areas— ghettoes. The earliest ghettoes were in 11th-century Italy. They existed until the late 19th century in Austria, Bavaria, Germany, Italy, and Russia. Restrictions on the trades that Jews could pursue led more and more of them to resort to money lending, thus providing the popular prejudice with an economic dimension.

After the emancipation of Jews in the late 19th century, pseudoscientific theories were advanced to prove the racial inferiority of Jews. In order to divert popular disaffection, political demagogues and certain governments (Russia being a prime example) blamed Jews for the ills of society. A forged document entitled *Protocols of the Wise Men of Zion* appeared in 1903 in Tsarist Russia. The tract claimed to reproduce the minutes of world Jewish leaders in the late 19th century outlining their plans to bring about the moral decay of non-Jewish societies, and to control global economies and media with the aim of dominating the planet.

Hatred of Jews, a Semitic race, reached its peak in Nazi Germany (1933–45), based on the theory of the superiority of the Aryan race, and resulted in the extermination of nearly six million Jews in Europe, a genocide commonly described as the Holocaust.

Antonius, George (1892–1942): *Lebanese writer and thinker* Born into a Greek Orthodox [*q.v.*] family in Lebanon and educated in Egypt, Antonius settled in Palestine [*q.v.*] in 1921 after taking up a job with the education department there. Nine years later he joined the New York-based Institute of Current World Affairs headed by Charles Crane, cochairman of a U.S. commission on the Middle East [*q.v.*] in 1919.

A lucid writer and an eloquent speaker, he became a leading spokesman of Palestinian Arabs [*q.v.*]. He testified before the (British) Peel Commission (1937) on Palestine, and acted as an adviser to the Arab delegates to the Round Table Conference on Palestine in London in 1939.

The Arab Awakening, his book on Arab nationalism [*q.v.*], published in 1938, established him as an original thinker. He traced the roots of Arab renaissance to a nascent movement in Beirut in the 1880s, composed largely of Arab Christians [*q.v.*] educated in the Protestant [*q.v.*] and Roman Catholic [*q.v.*] mission schools and colleges of Lebanon. In Palestinian politics he allied himself with radical Haajj Muhammad Amin al-Husseini [*q.v.*].

Aoun, Michel (1935–): *Lebanese military officer and politician* Born to Maronite [*q.v.*] parents, Aoun graduated from Lebanon's Military Academy as an artillery officer. He underwent further training in France during 1958–59. He rose steadily in the army, which became increasingly fractured along religious lines as the Lebanese Civil War [*q.v.*], starting in 1975, dragged on for many years. His second period of training was in the United States from 1978 to 1980. Four years later President Amin Gemayel [*q.v.*] promoted him to brigadier-general and appointed him military chief of staff.

In the absence of a properly elected president to follow him, Gemayel called on Aoun to form a temporary military government. When he appointed five military officers as cabinet ministers, the three Muslim commanders refused to serve. By declaring a "war of liberation" against Syria in March 1989, he further alienated the Muslim [*q.v.*] population and militias. The resulting blockade of the limited area controlled by him made his position tenuous. He rejected the National Reconciliation Charter [*q.v.*], which had been adopted by an overwhelming majority of the Lebanese lawmakers meeting in Taif, Saudi Arabia, in October 1989. He ignored the election in November of Rene Muawad as president and later (following Muawad's assassination) of Elias Hrawi [*q.v.*], as well as President Hrawi's dismissal of him. He continued to occupy the presidential palace in Baabda, a suburb of Beirut.

His clashes with the Lebanese Forces [*q.v.*], a Maronite [*q.v.*] militia, undercut his standing among Christians and further reduced his area of control. In October 1990 his troops collapsed when attacked by the joint forces of his Lebanese opponents and Syria. He took refuge in the French embassy. In August 1991 he left for France after the Lebanese government had granted him conditional amnesty.

He returned to Lebanon in May 2005 after the Syrian troops had withdrawn from the country, and formed the Free Patriotic Movement. The party participated in the subsequent general election as part of the March 8 Alliance [*q.v.*] and won 15 seats, with Aoun in the lead. In early 2006 he signed a memorandum of understanding with Hizbollah [*q.v.*]. Later that year he and his party participated in the massive protest demonstrations calling for the resignation of Prime Minister Fouad Sinoria [*q.v.*]. In 2008, the reconstituted cabinet included five ministers affiliated with the Free Patriotic Movement. In the May 2009 election his party won 18 seats and attracted nine parliamentary deputies from other groups. In the new national unity cabinet led by Saad Hariri [*q.v.*], the Free Patriotic Movement secured five ministries.

When Hariri's government fell in early 2011, Aoun's group joined the government formed by Najib Mikati [*q.v.*] in June. Two months later he described the unrest in Syria as "minor incidents confined to one or two neighborhoods in Homs [*q.v.*]."

Aql, Said (1911–): *Lebanese writer* Born into a Maronite [*q.v.*] family in Zahle, Aql soon established himself as an outstanding poet with extraordinary lyrical powers. His use of symbols set a new trend in Arabic poetry, as did his (later) practice of using colloquial language instead of classical Arabic, a traditional practice in the Arab world. An intellectual, he believed that Lebanese identity was rooted in its distant Phoenician past and had little to do with Islam [*q.v.*] or Arabism [*q.v.*]. He went on to develop a version of the Latin alphabet that he claimed was more suitable to the "Lebanese" language.

His ideas appealed to Maronite intellectuals who, during the period between the two world wars, were intent on giving shape to a Lebanese identity distinct from Syria and the Muslim-dominated Arab hinterland. With the tide of Arab nationalism [*q.v.*] rising after World War II, his particularist thesis lost ground. But the later arrival of a large number of Palestinians in Lebanon revived his ideology among Maronites, especially the ultranationalist militia, the Guardians of the Cedars [*q.v.*].

Since the publication of his first book, a stage play, in 1935, he has published many works of drama, poetry, and essays as well as song lyrics in literary Arabic [*q.v.*], Lebanese Arabic, or French.

al-Aqsa Intifada: *see* Second Intifada

Arab Baath Party (Syria): Michel Aflaq [*q.v.*] and Salah al-Din Bitar [*q.v.*] established a study circle in Damascus [*q.v.*] in 1940, called the Movement of Arab Baath (Arabic: *Renaissance*). They published pamphlets in which they expounded revolutionary, socialist Arab nationalism [*q.v.*], and were committed to achieving Arab unity as the first step. Once the Mandate power, France, had left Syria in April 1946, they secured a license for their group, now called the Party of Arab Baath. They decided to merge their faction with the one led by Zaki Arsuzi [*q.v.*]. Out of this, in April 1947, emerged the Arab Baath Party in Damascus. Aflaq was elected senior member in the executive committee of four.

The party's basic principles were described as the unity and freedom of the Arab nation within its homeland, and a belief in the special mission of the Arab nation, the mission being to end colonialism and promote humanitarianism. To achieve this, the party had to be nationalist, populist, socialist, and revolutionary. While the party rejected the concept of class conflict, it favored land reform; public ownership of natural resources, transport, and large-scale industry and financial institutions; trade unions of workers and peasants; the co-option of workers into management; and acceptance of "non-exploitative" private ownership and inheritance. It stood for a representative and constitutional form of government, as well as freedom of speech and association within the bounds of Arab nationalism.

Arab Baath Socialist Party: *see* Baath Socialist Party.

Arab Cooperation Council (1989–90): *a regional Arab organization* Consisting of Egypt, Iraq, Jordan, and North Yemen, the Arab Cooperation Council (ACC) was formed in Baghdad [*q.v.*] in February 1989. It brought together those Arab countries outside the Gulf Cooperation Council [*q.v.*] that had aided Iraq during its war with Iran from 1980 to 1988 [*q.v.*]. However, the ACC decided on cooperation only in economic and non-military fields. The fourth ACC summit in Amman [*q.v.*] in February 1990 decided to work toward ending Jewish emigration from the Soviet bloc to the occupied Palestinian and Arab territories. In April the ACC urged the comprehensive removal of all weapons of mass destruction in the Middle East. Iraq's invasion of Kuwait in August 1990 resulted in the disintegration of the ACC, with Egypt allying with the United States to forge an anti-Iraq alliance.

Arab Democratic Party (Israel): *Israeli political party* Formed in 1988 in Nazareth [*q.v.*], the Arab Democratic Party (ADP) aimed to unify Israeli Arabs [*q.v.*] behind a three-point program: recognition of the Palestinian people's right to self-determination, recognition of the Palestine Liberation Organization (PLO) [*q.v.*] as their sole representative, and the withdrawal of Israel from all the Occupied Arab Territories [*q.v.*]. It won one seat in the 1988 election and two in 1992. On the eve of the 1996 election, it merged with another group to form the United Arab List [*q.v.*], which secured four seats.

Arab Deterrent Force: *Arab League peacekeeping force in Lebanon, October 1976 to July 1982* The Arab League [*q.v.*] summit of October 1976 ordered the deployment, for an initial period of six months, of a peacekeeping force—called the Arab Deterrent Force (ADF)—to maintain the cease-fire in the Lebanese Civil War [*q.v.*], which erupted in April 1975. Its 30,100 troops were drawn from Syria (25,000), Saudi Arabia (2,000), Sudan (1,000), South Yemen (1,000), Libya (600), and the United Arab Emirates (500). It was to function under the Lebanese president. Libya soon withdrew its contingent. The ADF's mandate was renewed every six months.

The ADF became embroiled in skirmishes with Maronite [*q.v.*] militias. By the middle of 1979, with the departure of the Sudanese, Saudi, South Yemeni, and UAE troops, the ADF had become a purely Syrian force. In April 1980 it clashed with the leading Maronite militia near Zahle, which induced Israel's intervention. The ADF won.

In late June 1982, during the Israeli invasion of Lebanon [*q.v.*], the Arab League foreign ministers failed to extend the ADF's tenure, which was due to expire shortly. But the Lebanese government did not formally ask Syria, the only country providing ADF troops, to withdraw its soldiers, partly because it did not wish to put the Syrian forces on a par with Israel's by demanding their pull-back. The ADF's mandate ended in July 1982. Later the Lebanese authorities separately formalized the presence of the Syrian troops in Lebanon.

Arab East: Arab East is the term applied to the Arabic-speaking Middle East [*q.v.*], excluding Arab North Africa (Algeria, Libya, Mauritania, Morocco, and Tunisia) and Djibouti, Somalia, and Sudan. It includes Bahrain, Egypt, Iraq, Jordan, Kuwait, Lebanon, the Occupied Arab Territories [*q.v.*], Oman, Qatar, Saudi Arabia, Syria, the United Arab Emirates, and Yemen.

Arab/Arabian Gulf: *see* the Gulf.

Arab Higher Committee (Palestine): The killing of Shaikh Izz al-Din Qassam [*q.v.*], a popular Arab leader, by the British in Palestine [*q.v.*] in an encounter in November 1935, and the discovery of an arms cache in a cement consignment for a Jewish builder in Jaffa [*q.v.*] led the different Arab factions to form the Arab Higher Committee (AHC) in early 1936 under the leadership of Haajj Muhammad Amin al-Husseini [*q.v.*]. The AHC rejected the British proposal for a legislative council, with 14 Arabs and eight Jewish members, because of the over-representation of the Jewish minority. It called on its followers to stage a general strike on 1 April 1936. The strike, which developed into a wide-scale Arab rebellion, lasted until 12 October.

A month later, a British royal commission headed by Lord Peel visited Palestine. In July 1937 the Peel Commission recommended partition. When the AHC rejected this, the British banned the committee in October. Its leader, al-Husseini, fled to Lebanon. From there he continued to guide the AHC, which revived the Arab rebellion in 1938. It lasted until the spring of 1939.

Following the British White Paper of May 1939, which restricted Jewish immigration to 15,000 a year, the AHC was legalized. During the summer of 1946 the British tried to find common ground between the AHC and the Jewish Agency for Palestine [*q.v.*], but failed. The AHC, led by al-Husseini, continued as representative of the Arab Palestinians [*q.v.*] during the subsequent events. In 1958 al-Husseini proposed that the AHC should join the recently formed United Arab Republic [*q.v.*]. Egyptian President Gamal Abdul Nasser [*q.v.*] accepted this in principle, but postponed action until after Palestine had been liberated. With the formation of the Palestine Liberation Organization [*q.v.*] in 1964, the AHC became redundant.

Arab-Israeli War I (1948–49): *14 May 1948 to 7 January 1949* Often called the Palestine War, and (by Israelis) the War of Independence (Israel) [*q.v.*].

Background: In November 1947 the Arabs in Palestine [*q.v.*] rejected the United Nations (U.N.) partition plan, contained in the UN General Assembly Resolution 181, which gave the Jews [*q.v.*], owning 6 percent of the land, 53.5 percent of Palestine [*q.v.*]. At that time the Arab [*q.v.*] population was about 1,200,000, the Jewish almost 650,000. In early 1948 the British advanced their date of departure to 15 May from 1 October, specified by the U.N. On 14 May the Yishuv [*q.v.*] National Council's 13-member People's Administration declared the establishment of Israel [*q.v.*]. Following an Arab League [*q.v.*] decision, Egypt, Iraq, Jordan,

Lebanon, and Syria, along with Arab Palestinian fighters, resolved to attack Israel. The overall commander of the Arab forces was King Abdullah bin Hussein.

OPPOSING FORCES: The 26,000 Arab troops comprised 7,000 Egyptians, 4,000 Iraqis, 5,000 Jordanians, 2,000 Lebanese, 4,000 Palestinian irregulars, and 4,000 Syrians. Of these only Jordan's Arab Legion, commanded by British General John Glubb [q.v.], was professionally led. The Lebanese and Syrian troops were former territorial militiamen. The Egyptian and Iraqi forces were badly led and were equipped with poor British-supplied arms. By the end of the first phase of the war in mid-June the total number of Arab troops had increased to 35,000.

The Israeli force consisted of 30,000 fully mobilized Haganah [q.v.] soldiers (about two-thirds of whom were World War II veterans), supported by 32,000 reserves, 15,000 armed Jewish settlement police, and 32,000 home guards. By the end of the first phase of the war in mid-June 1948, the Israeli combat force had doubled to 60,000.

EVENTS: The armed conflict, which started on 14 May 1948, went through four phases: 14 May to 11 June; 9 to 18 July; 15 October to 6 November; and 21 November 1948 to 7 January 1949. The total combat period was four months.

14 May to 11 June: In the north the Syrian and Lebanese forces, assisted by Palestinian irregulars, captured much of north-central Galilee. In the central sector Jordan's Arab Legion occupied most of southern and eastern Jerusalem [q.v.], including the Old

City, and held on to the Jerusalem–Tel Aviv [q.v.] road. In the southern sector the Egyptian army, helped by Palestinian irregulars, overran Gaza [q.v.] and then captured Ashdod. The other Egyptian column seized Beersheba and Hebron [q.v.], and linked up with the Arab Legion in Bethlehem [q.v.]. A UN cease-fire came into effect on 11 June.

9 to 18 July: In the northern sector the Israelis spread out from Haifa [q.v.]. In the center they captured Lydda (Lod), Ramle, and the neighboring airport. The second UN ceasefire went into force on 18 July and lasted until 15 October, except in the south. At the end of this truce the Israeli forces were 90,000 strong.

15 October to 6 November: In the north the Israelis captured the Hula valley and occupied a strip of southern Lebanon. In the central sector they broadened the Tel Aviv–Jerusalem axis. By capturing Beersheba in the south, they separated the Egyptian troops in Hebron and Faluja. The Egyptians evacuated Ashdod and Majdal to consolidate their positions in the Asluj-Gaza region. A UN truce went into effect on the southern front on 6 November. In the north and center, ceasefires took place on 30 November.

21 November 1948 to 7 January 1949: In the south the Egyptians initially enlarged their area around Gaza and Asluj, but later their overall position deteriorated. On 1 December, 2,000 Arab Palestinian delegates in Jericho [q.v.] proclaimed Abdullah bin Hussein "King of all Palestine," which meant most of what could be saved from the Israelis. The final truce between them and the Israelis came on 7 January 1949.

HUMAN LOSSES: Arab Palestinians: 16,000 dead, including those killed during January to mid-May 1948; other Arabs: 2,500 dead; Jews: 6,000 dead.

ARMISTICE AGREEMENTS: Following negotiations between the warring parties on the Greek island of Rhodes, Israel concluded armistice agreements with Egypt on 24 February 1949, Lebanon on 23 March 1949, Jordan on 3 April 1949, and Syria on 20 July 1949. Iraq, which lacked common borders with Israel, signed no such agreement with Israel.

These agreements divided up the territory allocated by the UN to the Arabs in Palestine (area 10,435 sq. mi./27,026 sq. km) among Egypt, Israel, and Jordan. Egypt retained control of the Gaza Strip [*q.v.*], measuring 146 sq. mi./378 sq. km, as an Egyptian-administered territory. Having acquired extra 2,220 sq. mi./5,750 sq. km above the 5,600 sq. mi./14,500 sq. km allocated to it by the UN partition plan, Israel annexed them. Thus the Jews, who formed nearly a third of the population of Palestine on the eve of the war, seized 75 percent of the country instead of the 54 percent allocated to them by the UN. Controlling 2,297 sq. mi./5,949 sq. km of Palestine, King Abdullah annexed them, subject to final settlement. Jerusalem, earmarked for international administration by the UN, was divided between Israel and Jordan, with Jordanian East Jerusalem measuring 2.5 sq. mi./6.5 sq. km. As for Lebanon and Syria, the international borders of Palestine became the armistice lines between them and Israel.

Arab-Israeli War II (1956): *see* Suez War (1956).

Arab-Israeli War III (1967): *5 to 10 June 1967* Often called the June 1967 War or the Six-Day War.

BACKGROUND: Taking seriously Israel's threat to overthrow it, the nine-month-old radical Baathist regime in Syria signed a defense treaty with Egypt in November 1966. In early 1967 Israel attempted to cultivate disputed Arab land in the Syrian-Israeli demilitarized zone, thus triggering a confrontation. A month later Syria informed Egypt's president Gamal Abdul Nasser [*q.v.*] of Israeli troop concentration along its border. Promising to aid Syria on 16 May, Nasser dispatched Egyptian troops to eastern Sinai [*q.v.*]. Two days later, he asked for a partial withdrawal of the UN Emergency Force (UNEF) [*q.v.*], which had been patrolling the truce lines since the end of the 1956 Suez War [*q.v.*] on the Egyptian side. Since the UN could not agree to withdraw partially from the areas where the Egyptian and Israeli forces were in direct confrontation, its secretary-general, U Thant, offered to withdraw all of the UNEF. Egypt agreed.

Having stationed Egyptian troops at the tip of the Tiran Straits [*q.v.*] in Sharm al-Shaikh on 22 May, Nasser blockaded the straits, thus closing off the Israeli port of Eilat. This raised the temperature in the region. Reflecting the popular mood, King Hussein of Jordan [*q.v.*], hitherto hostile to Nasser, rushed to Cairo [*q.v.*] on 30 May to conclude a mutual defense pact and place his forces under Egyptian command. Earlier Israel had told its superpower ally the United States that it would go to war if one or more of the following events occurred: the departure of UNEF; the blockading of the Tiran Straits; the signing of a Jordanian-Egyptian defense pact; or the dispatch of Iraqi forces to Jordan. By the end of May, all but one of these eventualities had come to pass.

Opposing forces: (Weapons) Combat aircraft: Israel 260; Egypt 434, Iraq 110, Jordan 28, Syria 90. Tanks: Israel 1,100; Egypt 1,200, Iraq 200, Jordan 287, Syria 750.

Events: Early in the morning of 5 June Israel mounted preemptive air and ground assaults. It attacked all 17 Egyptian airfields and destroyed three-fifths of Egypt's warplanes, consisting of 365 fighters and 69 bombers on the ground. Egypt also lost 550 tanks in Sinai [*q.v.*]. Later in the day Israel struck at the Jordanian and Syrian air forces on the ground, destroying more than two-thirds of their combat aircraft. It rejected the UN Security Council's call for an immediate cease-fire on 6 June.

On the Egyptian front, Israel captured the Gaza Strip [*q.v.*] on 6 June, the day Egypt decided to withdraw its 80,000 soldiers and 1000 tanks from the Sinai Peninsula. Having occupied most of the peninsula by 8 June, Israel reached the Suez Canal [*q.v.*] the following day. On the Jordanian front the Israelis had captured East Jerusalem [*q.v.*], Bethlehem [*q.v.*], Hebron [*q.v.*], Jenin, and Nablus [*q.v.*] by 7 June. The Israelis then accepted a UN-sponsored cease-fire on this front. The Syrian front witnessed artillery duels on the first four days. The Israelis violated the UN-sponsored truce on the fifth day (9 June) by launching an offensive to capture

the Golan Heights [*q.v.*]. It had achieved this aim by the evening of the sixth day (10 June) when the final cease-fire came into effect. In the naval battle the Israelis captured Sharm al-Shaikh on 7 June, thus ending the blockade of the Straits of Tiran.

Human losses: Egyptians: 11,500 dead, the majority dying of thirst in the Sinai desert, 15,000 injured. Jordanians (military): 2,000 dead, 5,000 injured; (civilians of Palestinian origin) 4,000 dead; 1,000 injured. Syrians: 700 dead, 3,500 injured. Israelis: 778 dead, 2,558 injured.

Weapon losses: Egypt: 264 aircraft, 700 tanks. Jordan: 22 aircraft, 125 tanks. Syria: 58 aircraft, 105 tanks. Israel: 40 aircraft, 100 tanks.

Arab-Israeli War IV (1973): *6 to 25 October 1973* Often called the October 1973 War, the Ramadan War (by Arabs [*q.v.*]), or the Yom Kippur War (by Israelis).

Background: Unlike previous armed conflicts, when Israel had taken the initiative, this time Egypt and Syria mounted pre-planned attacks on Israeli forces, but only those in the Occupied Arab Territories [*q.v.*], with the aim of regaining the Egyptian or Syrian land they had lost in the June 1967 War [*q.v.*]. They did so after having tired of peaceful attempts to recover their lands. The Arab move, which came on the eve of the Yom Kippur [*q.v.*] holiday in Israel, took the Israelis completely by surprise.

Events: *6–8 October:* The Egyptian Second Army crossed the Suez Canal [*q.v.*] at Kantara and Ismailia in the central sector, and the Third Army did likewise at Port Suez in the south. On the Golan Heights [*q.v.*] front the Syrians captured Mount Hermon and made gains at Khushniya.

8 October: The United States began an arms airlift using the planes of the Israeli airline, El Al.

9 October: Israeli military was fully mobilized. The Soviet Union began to airlift arms to Egypt and Syria, the latter receiving two-thirds of the shipments.

10–12 October: Israel counter-attacked on the Golan Heights front, and advanced east of the armistice line north of Qunaitra to Saasa.

11 October: Egypt mounted an offensive to relieve the Syrians.

13 October: Washington began using U.S. aircraft to ship weapons to Israel.

15 October: An Israeli offensive along the Suez succeeded in creating a wedge between the two Egyptians armies north of the Great Bitter Lake of the Suez, and established a bridgehead near Deversoir on the western bank.

15–19 October: Repeated Arab attempts to regain Syrian territory on the Golan Heights were frustrated by the Israelis.

16 October: An Arab oil embargo [*q.v.*] was imposed on the military backers of Israel.

19 October: Having expanded the bridgehead, the Israelis pushed southwards on Egyptian soil in order to surround the Egyptian Third Army along the eastern bank.

21 October: Henry Kissinger, U.S. secretary of state, arrived in Moscow to negotiate a deal with Soviet leaders. By then the United States had airlifted 20,000 tons of weapons to Israel, plus 40 Phantom bombers, 48 A4 Skyhawk ground attack jets, and 12 C-130 transporters. (By the end of the airlift on 15 November, 33,500 tons of U.S. arms had been shipped to Israel, while Soviet arms shipments to Egypt and Syria amounted to 15,000 tons.)

22 October: Following Kissinger's successful talks in Moscow, a truce, specified by UN Security Council Resolution 338 [*q.v.*], went into effect at 18.52 GMT. But soon after, Israel broke the cease-fire on the Golan front and regained Mount Herman.

23–24 October: Violating the truce on the Suez front, the Israelis rushed to Adabiya in the Gulf of Suez to encircle the Egyptian Third Army. But their attempts to seize Port Suez failed.

24 October: Moscow put on alert seven airborne divisions for airlifting to Egypt if the Israelis went ahead with their attempt to surround the Egyptian Third Army.

25 October: Washington put its military on "precautionary alert" because of Moscow's possible intervention in the war. UN Security Council Resolution 340, renewing its cease-fire call, went into effect, marking a formal end to the hostilities.

During the 20-day conflict, as signatories to the Joint Defense and Economic Cooperation Treaty of the Arab League [*q.v.*], nine Arab states (Algeria, Iraq, Jordan, Kuwait, Libya, Morocco, Saudi Arabia, Sudan, and Tunisia) dispatched 50,000 troops and air units to Egypt and Syria, including 30,000 Iraqi troops sent to Syria.

HUMAN LOSSES: Egyptians: 9,000 dead, 15,000 injured. Syrians: 3,500 dead, 9,000 injured. Israelis: 2,552 dead, 6,027 injured.

WEAPON LOSSES: Egypt: 300 aircraft. Syria: 160 aircraft. Egypt and Syria combined: 1,800 tanks. Israel: 114 aircraft, 800-plus tanks.

Arab Jews: *Jews originating in Arab countries. See also* Oriental Jews and Sephardim.

Arab League: *a collective of independent Arab states. Official title: League of Arab States* (Arabic: *Jamiat ad Duwal al-Arabiyya)* In early 1942, faced with the prospect of Germany conquering North Africa, including Egypt, Britain tried to sway popular Arab opinion toward the Allies by publicly favoring the idea of unity of the Arab world, extending from the Atlantic to the Persian Gulf [*q.v.*]. After countering the German threat in North Africa in World War II, London acted behind the scenes to bring about a preliminary Arab conference in the Egyptian city of Alexandria [*q.v.*] in September–October 1944. It was attended by the official representatives of Egypt, Iraq, Lebanon, North Yemen, Saudi Arabia, Syria, and Transjordan, as well as a Palestinian observer on behalf of Arab Palestinians. Their decision to form the League of Arab States—a cooperative of independent Arab countries—was ratified on 22 March 1945 in Cairo [*q.v.*] with the signing of an appropriate pact. Its objectives were to coordinate and reinforce political, economic, and cultural policies of its member states, and mediate disputes among them or between them and others. Its Charter combined the concept of a common Arab homeland with respect for the sovereignty of the individual member states.

The first secretary-general of the Arab League, headquartered in Cairo, was Abdul Rahman Azzam, an Egyptian diplomat. With more and more Arabic-speaking countries

becoming independent, membership in the League expanded to include Libya (1953), Sudan (1956), Morocco (1958), Tunisia (1958), Kuwait (1961), Algeria (1962), South Yemen (1967), Bahrain (1971), Oman (1971), Qatar (1971), the United Arab Emirates (1971), Mauritania (1973), Somalia (1974), the Palestine Liberation Organization (1974), and Djibouti (1977). With the union of North and South Yemen in May 1990, membership declined to 21. Then, with the admission of Comros Island in 1996, the total rose to 22.

In 1950 the Arab League members signed a Joint Defense and Economic Cooperation Treaty (JDECT) [*q.v.*], primarily to provide protection to member-states against Israel. Four years later the Egyptian president, Gamal Abdul Nasser [*q.v.*], opposed Iraq's plan to join a Western-sponsored defense Organization, arguing that such an arrangement by a JDECT member would link all JDECT affiliates to the West. Under the provisions of this treaty, in the October 1973 Arab-Israeli War [*q.v.*] nine Arab League members dispatched troops and air units to Egypt and Syria and engaged in hostilities with Israel. However, in May 1982, when Iraqi President Saddam Hussein [*q.v.*] tried to invoke the treaty to secure military aid from Arab League members, he failed. This happened because Iraq was not engaged in war with Israel; Iraq had started the armed conflict by invading Iran in September 1980; and such leading members of the Arab League as Syria and Libya had lined up with Iran.

Since 1948 the Arab League has been enforcing an economic boycott of

Israel from its office based in Damascus [*q.v.*]. Following its recognition by the United Nations in 1958 as a regional body, the Arab League has been acting inter alia as the UN's Arab region educational, scientific, and cultural organization. It has been instrumental in creating an Arab postal union, an Arab union of wireless communication and telecommunication, a nationality code, and an Arab cultural treaty. It is the headquarters of 17 Arab trade unions, including the union of iron and steel workers, and physicians and veterinarians. It now has 11 specialized ministerial councils and 17 permanent technical committees.

After Egypt signed a unilateral peace treaty with Israel in March 1979, an Arab League summit suspended its membership and moved the League headquarters to Tunis. Egypt was readmitted to the League in May 1989, and the headquarters were returned to Cairo in October 1990. Seven months later Esmat Abdul Maguid [*q.v.*], the erstwhile foreign minister of Egypt, was unanimously elected secretary-general of the Arab League.

Following the Oslo Accord I of 1993 [*q.v.*], Tunisia and Israel agreed to base economic liaison officers in each other's capitals. In 1994 the six-member Gulf Cooperation Council [*q.v.*] decided to end secondary and tertiary boycotts of Israel. The secondary and tertiary boycotts apply respectively to an Arab League ban on trading with companies that deal directly with Israel and those that trade with such companies.

In 2001, Maguid was succeeded by Amr Moussa [*q.v.*] as the Arab League's secretary-general. On 24 March 2003, the Arab League foreign ministers demanded—by 21 votes to one (Kuwait)—the immediate and unconditional withdrawal of the American and British troops from Iraq. Washington and London ignored the call.

Since 2003, the following countries have been granted observer status: Brazil, Eritrea, India, and Venezuela.

The cumulative arrears of member states crossed the $100 million mark in 2004. This led to the cancellation of nearly 200 projects and left many League employees unpaid for months.

In 2010, Arab League member states, occupying an area of 13,953,041 sq. km/5,394,250 sq. mi., had a total population of 360 million, and a cumulative GDP of $1,903,301 million.

In mid-March 2011, by a majority vote, the Arab League asked the 15-member UN Security Council to impose a no-flight zone over Libya in order to halt the killing of civilians. Following the Security Council's resolution to that effect, leading members of the North Atlantic Treaty Organization (NATO) unleashed a bombing campaign against the regime of Colonel Muammar Gaddafi. Moussa condemned the broad scope of NATO bombing but to no avail.

As protest against the rule of President Bashar Assad escalated from March 2011, and the regime became ruthless in suppressing protest, the Arab League suspended Syria's membership in November because of its regime's violence against civilians. The League's approach to the UN Security Council to act resulted in a resolution calling for "a Syrian-led political transition" in Syria in February 2012. It won the support of 13 members but was vetoed by Russia and China.

Arab League Summits: Until 1963 League members were normally represented by their foreign ministers at the meetings of the Arab League Council of Ministers. But from 1964 member states started meeting at the head-of-state level. The list of the ordinary summit meetings follows:

FIRST SUMMIT: 13–17 January 1964 in Cairo [*q.v.*]. It resolved to "struggle against the robbery of the waters of Jordan by Israel."

SECOND SUMMIT: 5–11 September 1964 in Alexandria [*q.v.*]. It welcomed the establishment of the Palestine Liberation Organization (PLO) [*q.v.*] to "liberate Palestine from Zionist imperialism."

THIRD SUMMIT: 13–17 September 1965 in Casablanca. It renounced "intra-Arab hostile propaganda."

FOURTH SUMMIT: 29 August–1 September 1967 in Khartoum. Held in the wake of the June 1967 Arab-Israeli War [*q.v.*], it reaffirmed Palestinians' rights in their own country, and declared: "No negotiations with Israel, no treaty, no recognition of Israel."

FIFTH SUMMIT: December 1969 in Rabat. It called for the mobilization of all Arab states against Israel.

SIXTH SUMMIT: November 1973 in Algiers. Held in the wake of the October 1973 Arab-Israeli War [*q.v.*], it set down strict conditions for talks with Israel.

SEVENTH SUMMIT: 30 October–2 November 1974 in Rabat. It declared the PLO as "the sole and legitimate representative of the Palestinian people" with "the right to establish the independent state of Palestine on any liberated territory."

EIGHTH SUMMIT: 25–26 October 1976 in Cairo. This widely attended summit backed the idea of an Arab Deterrent Force to de-escalate the Lebanese Civil War [*q.v.*].

NINTH SUMMIT: 2–5 November 1978 in Baghdad [*q.v.*]. It condemned the Camp David Accords [*q.v.*] of September 1978 between Egypt and Israel, and decided that pan-Arab sanctions against Egypt, including suspension of its League membership and severance of diplomatic relations, would go into effect when it signed a peace treaty with Israel.

TENTH SUMMIT: 22–25 November 1979 in Tunis. It deliberated over continued Israeli occupation of southern Lebanon following Israel's invasion of Lebanon in March 1978 [*q.v.*].

ELEVENTH SUMMIT: 21–22 November 1980 in Amman [*q.v.*]. It adopted a strategy for joint Arab economic action, dealing with pan-Arab development until 2000.

TWELFTH SUMMIT: in Fez, Morocco. It is recorded as having taken place in two phases: on 25 November 1981 and on 6–9 September 1982. On 25 November, following sharp disagreement over a peace plan drafted by Saudi Crown Prince Fahd [*q.v.*], which implied de facto recognition of Israel, the meeting was suspended after five hours without a joint communiqué. Reconvening on 6 September 1982 in Fez, the summit adopted a peace plan similar to the one submitted by Fahd, now Saudi king. It demanded the withdrawal of Israel from the Arab territories occupied in 1967; the dismantling of Jewish settlements in these areas; Palestinian self-determination under the PLO, resulting in a Palestinian state in the West Bank [*q.v.*] and Gaza Strip [*q.v.*], with East Jerusalem [*q.v.*] as its capital; interim UN supervision of the West Bank and Gaza; and the guaranteeing of peace for all the states in the region by the UN Security Council.

THIRTEENTH SUMMIT: March 2001 in Amman. It was held in the aftermath of the election of hawkish Ariel Sharon [*q.v.*] as the Israeli prime minister. It decided to appoint Amr Mousa [*q.v.*] the League's new secretary-general.

FOURTEENTH SUMMIT: March 2002 in Beirut. It adopted a peace plan of Saudi Crown Prince Abdullah [*q.v.*], offering Israel total peace with all the League members in exchange for its total withdrawal from all of the Occupied Arab Territories [*q.v.*], the establishment of an independent Palestine state, and the granting of the right to return to the Palestinian refugees. It rejected exploitation of war on terrorism to threaten any Arab country and use of force against Iraq.

FIFTEENTH SUMMIT: 1 March 2003 in Sharm al-Shaikh, Egypt: It warned that serious threats to Iraq (by America) could lead to a military conflict with grave consequences for the region and the peace of the Arab world. On March 24, the League demanded—by 21 votes to one (Kuwait)—the immediate and unconditional removal of American and British troops from Iraq.

SIXTEENTH SUMMIT: 22–23 May 2004 in Tunis. It declared that the Arab states were committed to democracy, equality, freedom of expression, and rights for women.

SEVENTEENTH SUMMIT: 22–23 March 2005 in Algiers. This conference coincided with the 60th anniversary of the founding of the Arab League. It reaffirmed its commitment to the Saudi peace plan adopted in 2002.

EIGHTEENTH SUMMIT: 28–30 March 2006 in Khartoum. It focused on Arab-African cooperation.

NINETEENTH SUMMIT: 27–28 March 2007 in Riyadh. The Summit called on its members to recognize the recently formed Palestinian unity government of Fatah [*q.v.*] and Hamas [*q.v.*], and cooperate with it. It condemned the political, economic, and military siege imposed by Israel on the Palestinian Territories [*q.v.*].

TWENTIETH SUMMIT: 29–30 March 2008 in Damascus. Noting the continuing sectarian and other violence in Iraq, the Summit called for maintaining Iraq's territorial integrity, achieving sectarian and ethnic reconciliation, and ending the presence of foreign troops.

TWENTY-FIRST SUMMIT: 28–30 March 2009 in Doha [*q.v.*]. The Summit condemned Israel's war on Gaza [*q.v.*]. It expressed solidarity with Sudan facing threats to its security, stability, and territorial integrity, and supporting Qatar's peace efforts within the framework of the Arab-African Ministerial Committee. Iran attended the meeting as an observer.

TWENTY-SECOND SUMMIT: 30 March-1 April 2010 in Sirte, Libya. Palestinian Authority [*q.v.*] president Mahmoud Abbas [*q.v.*] rejected demand by Syria and Libya to formally pull out of peace negotiations with Israel.

In 1970, the Arab League started holding emergency summits.

FIRST EMERGENCY SUMMIT: 27–28 September 1970 in Cairo. Egyptian president Gamal Abdul Nasser [*q.v.*] succeeded in achieving a cease-fire between Jordan and the PLO.

SECOND EMERGENCY SUMMIT: 17–28 October 1976 in Riyadh. It approved the formation of the Arab Deterrent Force for peacekeeping in the Lebanese Civil War.

THIRD EMERGENCY SUMMIT: 7–9 September 1985 in Casablanca. Boycotted by Algeria, Lebanon, Libya, South Yemen, and Syria, it failed to back the agreement between the PLO and Jordan envisaging talks with Israel on Palestinian rights.

FOURTH EMERGENCY SUMMIT: 8–12 November 1987 in Amman. It endorsed UN Security Council Resolution 598 of July 1987 [*q.v.*] on a cease-fire in the Iran-Iraq War [*q.v.*], and criticized Iran for prevaricating over its acceptance of the resolution. It also declared that the resumption of diplomatic links with Egypt was an issue to be decided by individual members.

FIFTH EMERGENCY SUMMIT: 7–9 June 1988 in Algiers. It decided to fund the PLO to continue the six-month-old Palestinian uprising, called Intifada [*q.v.*], in the Israeli-occupied territories.

SIXTH EMERGENCY SUMMIT: 23–26 June 1989 in Casablanca. It decided to readmit Egypt to the Arab League. It also set up a Tripartite Committee of the heads of state of Algeria, Morocco, and Saudi Arabia to secure a cease-fire in the Lebanese Civil War and restore constitutional government in Lebanon.

SEVENTH EMERGENCY SUMMIT: 28–30 March 1990 in Baghdad. It condemned the recent large increase in the migration of Soviet Jews to Israel.

EIGHTH EMERGENCY SUMMIT: 9–10 August 1990 in Cairo. Twelve members out of the 20 present condemned Iraq for its invasion and annexation of Kuwait, and accepted the request of Saudi Arabia and other Gulf states to dispatch troops to assist their armed forces.

NINTH EMERGENCY SUMMIT: 22–23 January 1996 in Cairo. The Summit declared that the waters of the Euphrates and Tigris rivers be shared equitably between Iraq, Syria, and Turkey.

TENTH EMERGENCY SUMMIT: 21–22 October 2000 in Cairo. This summit was convened to debate the Second Intifada [*q.v.*] of the Palestinians against the Israeli occupation. Iraq was invited, thus signaling the end of the Arab League's boycott of Iraq due to its invasion of Kuwait. It called on its members to freeze their ties with Israel. It set up two funds to help the Palestinians struggling against the Israeli occupation.

Arab nationalism: Nationalism in the Arab world was defined in opposition to foreign rule, first by Ottoman Turkey and then by Britain and France. In the 19th century, Egyptians were in the forefront in rebelling against their Ottoman masters. The Ottoman sultan's recognition of Muhammad Ali as viceroy of Egypt in 1805 signified the special place the Ottomans were prepared to assign Egypt. In time Cairo [*q.v.*] became a haven for non-Egyptian Arab intellectuals who clashed with their Ottoman rulers. The relative freedom that Cairo afforded helped to engender Arab nationalism as well as pan-Islamism [*q.v.*].

With the supplanting of Ottoman power by that of Britain in the wake of the opening of the Suez Canal [*q.v.*] in 1869, Arab nationalism grew in opposition to British influence. It reached a peak in 1882, when Col. Ahmad Arabi Pasha attempted militarily to end British interference in Egyptian affairs. He failed. The result was British occupation of Egypt, which provided a powerful foil to nationalists.

Elsewhere, especially in the Levant [*q.v.*], the educational institutions established by American and French missionaries in the 1860s provided fertile soil for the growth of Arab political revival, resulting in such secret associations as al-Ahd (Arabic: *The Covenant*) and al-Fatat (Arabic: *The Young Woman*). When the Ottoman regime suppressed these groups, their members fled to (post-1882) Egypt. But little of importance occurred until World War I. During that conflict anti-Ottoman feelings, harnessed by the British, escalated into the Arab Revolt of 1916, which was led by Hussein bin Ali al-Hashem of Hijaz. After the war the Arabs felt let down by the victorious Britain and France, which carved up the Arab world in their spheres of influence according to the secret Sykes-Picot Pact [*q.v.*].

Arab nationalism in Egypt revolved around the Wafd [*q.v.*]. Elsewhere it centered on the Hashemite dynasty [*q.v.*], whose members ruled Iraq and Transjordan. But the close relationship between London and King Faisal II [*q.v.*]—illustrated by the latter's restoration by the British after they had crushed the successful nationalist coup in 1941—disappointed Arab nationalists. The behavior of another

Hashemite, King Abdullah of Transjordan [*q.v.*], before and during the 1948–49 Palestine War [*q.v.*] further disappointed Arab nationalists.

By then the establishment of the Arab League [*q.v.*] in 1945 had provided a regional perspective to Arab nationalism. Its base in Cairo set the scene for the merging of Egyptian nationalism with a larger Arab nationalism. This happened after the overthrow of the decadent monarchy in Egypt in 1952 by nationalist republican officers led by Gamal Abdul Nasser [*q.v.*].

As the decade progressed, and especially after 1956, when Egypt finally secured the withdrawal of British troops from its soil after 74 years, Nasser came to symbolize Arab nationalism in its widest sense. But Nasserism [*q.v.*], which was associated more with the leader than with an ideology, faced competition from Baathism [*q.v.*], which had emerged as a well-defined ideology in Syria. In 1990 Arab nationalism received a severe blow when Iraq, a proponent of Baathism, invaded and annexed Kuwait—the first instance since the founding of the Arab League of a member-state acting so aggressively toward another.

Arab Nationalist Movement: *pan-Arab political party* The Arab Nationalist Movement (ANM) came into being in 1952 as a result of the merger of two groups, composed chiefly of the students and staff of the American University in Beirut [*q.v.*]. George Habash [*q.v.*], Nayif Hawatmeh [*q.v.*], and Ahmad Khatib [*q.v.*] were among the founders of the ANM, whose main slogan was: "Unity [of

Arabs], Liberation [of Palestine], Revenge [against the Zionist state]."
While they increasingly saw the need to revolutionize the Arab world in order to confront the modern Jewish state of Israel, they placed much hope in the Egyptian military coup of 1952, especially as a vehicle to effect Arab unity. The ANM applauded the formation of the United Arab Republic [q.v.] in 1958, and was disappointed when it broke up three years later. The subsequent failure of any of the three leading republics—Egypt, Syria, and Iraq—to unify left the ANM disappointed with both Nasserites [q.v.] and Baathists [q.v.].

Since the liberation of Palestine was its top priority, in the mid-1960s the ANM set up a Palestinian section with its own armed wing and began guerrilla actions against Israel.

In the rest of the Arab world it did well in those regions where Nasserism and Baathism were comparatively weak, the main example being the Arabian Peninsula [q.v.]. It was the ANM's South Yemeni branch that first issued a call for armed action in 1959 to frustrate the British plan to set up a Federation of South Arabia, composed of the Aden Colony, the Eastern Protectorate States, and the Western Protectorate States. Four years later the ANM played an important role in welding together the various nationalist groups active in South Yemen when they held a congress in the North Yemeni capital of Sanaa [q.v.], and fostered the emergence of the National Front for the Liberation of South Yemen [q.v.], which decided to achieve independence through an armed struggle. It succeeded in 1967.

In adjoining Oman, in early 1962 the ANM's Dhofari supporters cooperated with the members of the leftist Dhofari Liberation Front (DFL) to secure an independent Dhofar. The outbreak of an insurrection in South Yemen in 1963 encouraged the ANM's Dhofari section to merge with the leftist DFL and start a guerrilla campaign in Dhofar, which continued for a decade.

The Arab defeat in the June 1967 Arab-Israeli War [q.v.] finally destroyed the ANM's confidence in the Egyptian and Syrian regimes, and led to the pan-Arab body being divided into individual sections in different countries.

Arab Nationalist Movement, Palestine: In December 1967 the Palestinian section of the Arab Nationalist Movement, along with its armed affiliates, combined with the Syria-based Palestine Liberation Front to form the Popular Front for the Liberation of Palestine [q.v.].

Arab Nationalist Movement, Saudi Arabia: Starting as a clandestine group in Dhahran in 1964, the Arab Nationalist Movement graduated into something bigger in early 1966. During the next three years the party built up a base among military officers, oil workers, civil servants, and teachers. Its planned coup in June 1969 was foiled only hours before its scheduled implementation. The subsequent arrest of 200 conspirators, followed by scores of executions, destroyed the party.

Arab socialism: Originating as Egyptian socialism, the term was transformed to Arab socialism when Egypt and Syria merged in 1958 to form the United Arab Republic (UAR) [*q.v.*]. Its leading proponent was Egyptian President Gamal Abdul Nasser [*q.v.*]. He first imbibed the virtues of socialism through his friendship with Josip Tito of Yugoslavia and Jawaharlal Nehru of India, whom he first met at the non-aligned nations' conference in Bandung, Indonesia, in April 1955. The 1956 Egyptian constitution provided for a National Union which, though composed of all political tendencies, stood for abolition of feudalism and exploitation, and the reorientation of private property for the higher interests of society. It stipulated that workers must be taken into management.

Following the breakup of the UAR in September 1961, Nasser accelerated his campaign against the urban rich in Egypt. A series of decrees introduced progressive income tax and the nationalization of insurance, banking, and major industrial and commercial companies. During the winter of 1961–62 Nasser drafted a 30,000-word Charter of National Action. After debating the document in Cairo in May 1962, the National Congress of the Popular Forces—consisting of trade unions, professional syndicates, and other voluntary groups—adopted it. The charter combined its belief in "scientific socialism" and the "struggle against exploitation and in favor of equal opportunities" with the aim of achieving the unity of "all the working forces of the people," including national capitalists. It argued that political and social democracy were indivisible, and that, to assure freedom of choice in politics, a citizen must be freed of exploitation of all kinds and

given equal opportunity to enjoy a fair share of the national wealth. The body that was to implement the changes was to be called the Arab Socialist Union [*q.v.*], composed of an alliance of five segments of the workforce: peasants, workers, intellectuals, soldiers, and national capitalists.

Declaring that his regime had ended the exploitation that had existed in the monarchical era, Nasser stressed that relations between different socioeconomic classes must now be peaceful. This differentiated Arab socialism from Marxist socialism, with its belief in ongoing conflict in a society with different classes. Also, objecting to attaching an ethnic or a nationality label to socialism, the Marxists in Egypt preferred to subscribe to the concept of an Egyptian path to socialism.

Arab Socialist Party (Syria): The Arab Socialist Party (ASP) was founded by Akram Hourani, a lawyer from Hama [*q.v.*], in January 1950. By participating in the anti-French armed struggle after World War II, he had gained popularity with the officer corps of independent Syria. Following his advice, the government decided to disregard the social background of the applicants to the country's only armed forces academy, in Homs [*q.v.*]. Since a military career was the only way a son of a poor or middle-income peasant could raise his social status, the academy attracted many applicants from these social classes. Given the party's commitment to ending feudalism and distributing state land to the landless, and its leadership of peasant agitation, it soon enjoyed a considerable following among young cadets and officers. Sharing their opposition to the dictatorial regime of Col. Adib Shishkali [*q.v.*], the leaders of the ASP and the Baath Party [*q.v.*] decided in September 1953 to form the Arab Baath Socialist Party [*q.v.*], and did so six months later.

Arab Socialist Union (Egypt): In May 1962 a National Congress of the Popular Forces, attended by trade unions, professional syndicates, and other voluntary groups, adopted the Charter of National Action. Besides explaining Arab socialism [*q.v.*], it specified the political structure upon which it was to be built. The body that was to implement the National Charter was to be called the Arab Socialist Union (ASU). It was perceived as an alliance of five segments of the workforce: peasants, workers, intellectuals, soldiers, and national capitalists. The ASU was established in November 1962. It had a pyramidal structure, with units of 20 at village, workplace, or neighborhood level forming the base, the executive committee led by the republic's president at the apex, and district and provincial committees in between. The ASU's legislative branch was called the National Assembly. In it, as in all other elected bodies of the ASU, 50 percent of the seats were given to workers and peasants (meaning those owning less than 26 acres/10.6 hectares).

In practice, the original intent of ensuring greater participation in the government by the masses was not realized, and the ASU's exceptionally broad base and lack of cohesion inhibited it from becoming an active political agency to effect a socialist transformation of society. Within the ASU, elections were held only for the provincial committees. Therefore, instead of emerging as a popular body to guide the state's executive arm, the ASU became subordinate to the state, assisting civil and military bureaucracies to implement official policies decided by President Gamal Abdul Nasser [*q.v.*], his advisers, and the cabinet (many of whose members sat on the ASU's executive committee). It became common knowledge that the best way to secure the cooperation of the increasingly powerful civil servants was by achieving an important position in the ASU, whose membership soared to six million in four years. As a result a mutually supportive triad of rich farmers, state bureaucrats, and urban professionals grew up and monopolized power.

Following the creation of the ASU's central committee in July 1965, Nasser appointed Ali Sabri [*q.v.*], the leftist prime minister, as the ASU's secretary-general, with a mandate to transform the organization into a cadre-based party. Soon the ASU's district and provincial committees were manned by salaried functionaries drawn from civil servants, business managers, teachers, lawyers, landowners, and factory floor managers, and trained at one of the three institutes of socialist studies. Sabri established the Socialist Youth Organization (SYO) as an auxiliary to the ASU, but with its own cadre, and soon built up its strength to 20,000. But after Egypt's defeat in the June 1967 Arab-Israeli War [*q.v.*], Nasser moderated his socialist leanings. He decided to reestablish the consensus that had existed before the creation of ASU and SYO cadres. In October he dissolved the

SYO, and in June 1968 he changed the ASU's structure back to the one prevalent in the pre-Sabri days.

In the wake of Nasser's death in September 1970 there was a revival of the debate on the ASU's role. President Anwar Sadat [*q.v.*] made it subservient to the state executive. After the October 1973 Arab-Israeli War [*q.v.*] parliament made ASU membership voluntary for participants in a political or trade union election. The debate on whether the ASU should be divided into five parts, each one representing a different social class within the "working forces," led to a decision by an official commission to form three forums within the ASU. Following the parliamentary election of October–November 1976, the ASU lost its political role, but it remained the sole owner of all major newspaper publishing companies and retained its authority to issue a license for a new publication. In August 1978 Sadat's invitation to Mustafa Khalil, the ASU secretary-general, to head his newly announced National Democratic Party [*q.v.*] formally ended the ASU.

Arab Spring: *grass roots pro-democracy movement in the Arab world*; also known as Arab Revolutions (Arabic: *al-thawrat al-Arabiyya*) Arab Spring stands for a series of demonstrations and protests in the Middle East [*q.v.*] and North Africa for democracy, which started peacefully but in some cases escalated to recurrent bloody clashes, and even to civil war, as in Libya. The movement originated with the self-immolation by Muhammad Bouazizi, a computer science graduate making a precarious living as a fruit vendor, in the Tunisian town of Sidi Bouzid on 17 December 2010. By spring of 2012 it had resulted in the ouster of autocratic Tunisian President Zine el Abidine Ben Ali and Egyptian President Hosni Mubarak [*q.v.*], Colonel Muammar Gaddafi of Libya and Yemeni President Ali Abdullah Saleh [*q.v.*] under varying circumstances. Taking their cue from the United States, the senior generals in Tunisia as well as in Egypt withdrew their support from the chief executive, paving the way for his downfall. In Libya it was the military intervention by the North Atlantic Treaty Organization that brought about the overthrow of the Gaddafi regime and his death. In Yemen, defying popular pressure, Saleh succeeded in blocking his departure by unconstitutional means and handed over power only after his deputy Abd Rabbu Mansour al-Hadi had won the specially arranged presidential election. Due to the exceptionally complex ethnic and religious composition of Syria, and the steadfast Russian backing for Syrian President Bashar Assad [*q.v.*], the Arab Spring seemed to have encountered an almost insurmountable barrier.

TUNISIA: In Tunisia, Bouazizi's dramatic act shocked the public at large. Protest demonstrations against the corrupt, dictatorial Ben Ali followed throughout the country. The government's brutal means failed to quash the popular unrest. On 14 January 2011, the violent skirmishes between protestors, pouring out of mosques after Friday prayers, and security forces became so bloody that Ben Ali lost the confidence of the military high command. This compelled him and his family to flee to the Saudi city of Jeddah [*q.v.*], where they were given refuge by Saudi King Abdullah [*q.v.*].

EGYPT: Ben Ali's overthrow acted as a catalyst in Egypt, where discontent against Mubarak's regime had been brewing since 2006 against the background of rocketing prices and declining living standards. A call for one-day nationwide strike on 6 April 2008 to protest high inflation and political repression under the emergency laws imposed since 1981 was disseminated by Facebook, blogs, Twitter, and mobile phone text messaging, with a "General Strike in Egypt" Facebook group gaining 54,000 members. The government responded by arresting and convicting a dozen cyberspace activists, all of them based in Egypt. But two years later it faced a challenge mounted from outside Egypt.

The appearance in cyberspace of the deformed face and battered head of 28-year-old Khaled Saeed, killed by two policemen in Alexandria [*q.v.*] on 6 June 2010, shocked many Egyptians, including Wael Ghonim, who ran Google's marketing department for the Middle East and North Africa from Dubai [*q.v.*]. He set up a Facebook site titled "We are all Khaled Saeed" without giving his identity by using the innocuous word "admin."

Within a few weeks, his page attracted almost 222,000 members. They focused on getting the guilty policemen punished while demanding the lifting of the emergency laws that facilitated police brutality. To stay within the emergency law, "admin." advised silent protest mounted by people dressed in black reading the Quran [*q.v.*] or the Bible [*q.v.*] while standing in a line in a street. The gov-

ernment did not know how to stop the source of the protest, which succeeded in seeing the offending police officers were sentenced to seven years' imprisonment. Thus the cyber protestors had their first success.

Unsurprisingly, following the overthrow of Ben Ali on 14 January, the "We are all Khaled Saeed" Facebook page became a rallying point for the protest on 25 January. Yet it was only on the following Friday, 28 January, that peaceful demonstrations in the Tahrir Square of Cairo [*q.v.*] gathered momentum after the weekly Muslim congregational prayers.

At this point the Mubarak government withdrew the riot police and sent army troops to Tahrir Square, the epicenter of the civil uprising. Violent clashes between protestors and the security forces broke out as Mubarak combined his promise on 2 February not to enter the next presidential election in 2013 with his appointment of Omar Suleiman, his intelligence chief, as vice president, a post he had deliberately left vacant. Demonstrators were not satisfied. On Friday, 4 February, labeled "Day of Departure," an ever-larger gathering of protestors demanded Mubarak's immediate resignation as the economic life of the nation started ebbing.

Behind the scenes Egyptian defense minister Field Marshall Muhammad Hussein Tantawi was in daily contact with his counterpart in Washington, Robert Gates, who stressed U.S. President Barack Obama's advice not to use military force to disband the over one million demonstrators who had set up tents in Tahrir Square. Before 25 January, several senior generals on the Supreme Council of Armed

Forces (SCAF) privately disapproved of Hosni Mubarak grooming his businessman son, Gamal, to succeed him, thus breaking the monopoly over power that the military had enjoyed since 1952. The burgeoning popular protest coupled with Obama's withdrawal of support for Mubarak led the fence-sitting generals to join the anti-Mubarak camp.

On 10 February, claiming that a national dialogue on political reform was in progress, Mubarak transferred power to Vice President Suleiman, but refused to step down. But the next day he bowed to the popular will backed by the SCAF. By the time he resigned after 18 days of civil uprising, and retired to the presidential palace in the sea resort of Sharm al-Shaikh, 846 protestors were dead and 12,000 were arrested.

After assuming power, the SCF accepted the amendments to the constitution proposed by its appointed committee. These were designed to prepare Egypt for free and fair parliamentary and presidential elections. Once the amended constitution was approved in a referendum on 25 March by a large majority on a turnover of 91 percent, the country's revolution entered a new phase.

At his trial in August, a bed-ridden Mubarak denied charges of killing protestors and abuse of power. Following massive protest at the slow progress toward democracy, Tantawi promised a presidential poll in June 2012. The SCAF appointed Kamal Ganzouri, a former prime minister, as head of a national salvation cabinet.

Staggered elections to the People's Assembly started in late November and continued until early January 2012. The Democratic Alliance, led by the Freedom and Justice Party [q.v.], won 235 of the 508-member People's Assembly, with the Islamist Bloc [q.v.] headed by the al-Nour Party [q.v.] gaining 127 seats. In the 180-member Consultative Council elections that followed, the FJP-led Democratic Alliance gained 105 seats and the al-Nour-led Islamist Bloc [q.v.] gained 45.

In the first round for the presidential poll on 23–24 May there were 12 candidates. Since none of them received 50 percent plus one vote, there was a second round on 16–17 June between the Freedom and Justice Party's Muhammad Morsi [q.v.] and Ahmed Shafiq [q.v.], the last prime minister of Hosni Mubarak, who was given a life sentence on 2 June for his part in the killing of protestors during the 2011 upheaval. Shafiq lost to Morsi by 48.3 percent of the vote to 51.7 percent.

Two days before the presidential election the Supreme Constitutional Court ruled that some of the articles on which the bicameral parliament was formed were unconstitutional. The SCAF dissolved both houses of parliament and re-assumed legislative powers.

In August President Morsi forced the 75-year-old Tantawi, head of the armed forces, and 64-year-old Sami Anan, the Army chief of staff, to resign, thereby ending the dual power structure. In October, Morsi granted pardon to all the protestors detained and tried in the civil protest movement between 25 January 2011 and 30 June 2012, the day he assumed the presidency, which marked the official end of the Arab Spring in Egypt.

Libya: By then, buoyed by Mubarak's downfall, the opposition to

Gaddafi in Libya had taken up arms. Making a deceptive use of the UN Security Council resolution in March authorizing a no-fly zone to protect civilians from the Gaddafi regime's attacks, NATO intervened directly into the Libyan civil war. Yet it took another six months to see the regime in Tripoli toppled.

BAHRAIN: The eastward advance of the Arab Spring wave hit Bahrain, where the predominantly Shia [*q.v.*] opposition had been agitating for political reform since 2009. Like their counterparts in Cairo's Tahrir Square, the protestors in the Pearl Square of Manama [*q.v.*] during February-March 2011, were peaceful. That did not stop the ruler Shaikh Hamad bin Isa II [*q.v.*] from declaring martial law and letting loose the security forces who shot 30 demonstrators dead. His violent response was capped by the arrival of the largely Saudi contingent of 1,000 soldiers under the banner of the Gulf Cooperaton Council [*q.v.*] in mid-March. Aware of the stationing of the U.S. Fifth Fleet in Bahrain, the Obama White House did nothing more than issue mild criticism of the ruler's crackdown.

KUWAIT: Like Bahrain, Kuwait had an earlier history of popular dissension with the rule of Shaikh Sabah IV al-Ahmad al-Jaber al-Sabah [*q.v.*], centered on widespread corruption and nepotism. With its parliament enjoying the most power of any elected body in the Gulf monarchies, the opposition lawmakers had been publicly critical of the ruling family. The Arab Spring arrived when there was rising tension between the parliament and the Sabah-dominated cabinet amidst allegation of corruption at the highest level of government. Demonstrations, attracting tens of thousands, occurred with increasing frequency. In November the protestors broker into the parliament house. The cabinet led since 2006 by the ruler's nephew, Nasser Muhammad al-Ahmad al-Sabah, resigned. The emir dissolved the parliament and ordered a fresh election in which the opposition won more than two-thirds of the seats.

However, given the bountiful oil reserves of the emirate, and the close links of the royal family with the U.S. buttressed by Kuwait's defense pact with Washington, there was no prospect of the al-Sabah clan losing its hold over the country.

That too was the case with the royal family of Saudi Arabia for the same reasons that applied to its Kuwaiti counterpart.

SAUDI ARABIA: Encouraged by the events in Egypt, web activists in the Saudi kingdom declared Friday, 11 March, as the first day for mass protests demanding constitutional monarchy and a democratic government. But a heavy-handed police action combined with a religious ruling against demonstrations kept most of the potential protestors off the streets—except in the major Shia city of Qatif in the Eastern Province. There, peaceful demonstrators, shouting "One people, not two—the people of Qatif and Bahrain!" demanded the release of Shia prisoners. The next Friday, 18 March, King Abdullah [*q.v.*] made a rare televised speech. He thanked his subjects for not staging large pro-democracy protests, and offered $93 billion in benefits to underprivileged Saudi citizens and for strengthening of the security and religious police forces. This was in addition to the $37 billion he had announced a month earlier to ease social pressures.

Significantly, King Abdullah was instrumental in co-opting Qatar and Kuwait to provide $10 billion in aid to Bahrain and Oman. The promised handout helped Sultan Qaboos [q.v.] of Oman, whose hydrocarbon resources were puny compared to those of Saudi Arabia, Kuwait, and Qatar.

OMAN: Inspired by the peaceful demonstrations in Bahrain, in mid-February 2011, the protestors in Muscat demanded higher salaries, an end to corruption, less official control of the media, and an equitable distribution of oil wealth. Those who staged a sit-in outside the Consultative (Shura) Council building in Muscat [q.v.] on 1 March demanded that the council be given real powers of legislation. Protest in the industrial port of Sohar at the end of February turned violent, with a shopping mall set ablaze. The police firings killed two demonstrators. When protest spread to a few oilfields, Qaboos appointed a committee to draft proposals for boosting the power of the Consultative Council. He reshuffled the cabinet, firing unpopular ministers, and abolished the ministry of national economy, known to be corrupt. After raising the salaries in the public sector, he mandated an increase in the minimum wage in the private sector from $364 a month to $520. He doubled social security benefits.

No such concessions came from the rulers of the United Arab Emirates

UNITED ARAB EMIRATES: The Arab Spring arrived in the UAE against the background of collapse in real estate

values in the confederation caused by the 2008–2009 virtual global credit freeze. The government moved quickly to block a website popular with those UAE nationals who called for a constitutional monarchy and an elected parliament with full legislative powers.

They arrested five dissident intellectuals, charging them with threatening state security and undermining public order. At the end of a seven-month detention they were sentenced to two years' imprisonment which was commuted by UAE President Shaikh Khalifa bin Zayid al-Nahyan [q.v.].

YEMEN: In contrast to the sparsely inhabited UAE, Oman, and Bahrain, Yemen has a population of 25 million and the lowest GDP per capita in the Arabia Peninsula. As a republic with a directly elected president and parliament, it had acquired a multiparty system. Yet Ali Abdullah Saleh [q.v.] had contrived to remain president since 1978, initially of North Yemen which contained four-fifths of the population of the united Yemen.

Therefore, the republic was vulnerable to the winds of the Arab Spring. But unlike Tunisia and Egypt, the military high command in Yemen split, and Saleh refused to step down except in a manner that had a legal stamp. So the crisis lasted for a year, during which 2,000 people were killed, many of them as a result of fighting between loyal and dissident troops.

The GCC mediators led by the Saudis, who coordinated their strategy with Washington, played the crucial role in resolving the crisis, which had enabled al-Qaida in the Arabian Peninsula [q.v.] to establish itself in three southern provinces. In other words, the Yemen imbroglio was unraveled within the U.S.-led camp.

Syria: Such a strategy could not be deployed in Syria because the U.S. lacked any leverage there, diplomatic or military. Alone among the Arab capitals, Damascus remained attached to Moscow. Having witnessed NATO's duplicitous use of the UN Security Council resolution on a no-fly zone, imposed to protect civilians, to intervene directly into the Libyan civil war, Russia and China vetoed a resolution on Syria at the Security Council in October 2011 and again in February 2012.

Thus, in Syria the Arab Spring got entangled into rivalry between the U.S.-led bloc and the Sino-Russian diplomatic alliance. Having lost the friendship of Libya under Gaddafi, Moscow was keen to retain its close diplomatic and military ties with Syria, where it has a naval base in Tartous.

Internally, the one-third of the Syrian population that was not Sunni Muslim [q.v.] was apprehensive of its future shorn of the protection offered to it by the secular Baath Socialist Party [q.v.]. Among Sunnis the influential business class, which had done well under the Baathist rule, was also reluctant to rock the boat.

As in Egypt, the Syrian opposition made use of social networking media to organize demonstrations and keep the outside world informed. Initially, the protestors' demands were modest: release of political prisoners and an end to the 48-year-old state of emergency. But with the government reacting harshly, the opposition demanded Assad's immediate resignation. Assured of the loyalty of the predominantly Alawi [q.v.] military high command, Assad resorted to using tanks and heavy weapons to regain control of the areas taken over by the armed opposition.

At the same time, Assad made concessions, starting with the lifting of emergency in April 2011, followed by the constitutional end to the Baath Party's monopoly over power, and held elections first at the local level in December 2011 and then for the national parliament in May 2012.

Though periodically calling on Assad to step down, Western leaders from President Obama down were privately concerned about the influence the Syrian Muslim Brotherhood [q.v.] exerted even in the Western-backed Syrian National Council [q.v.], whose leadership was dominated by Westernized Syrian intellectuals settled in Europe—not to mention the Free Syrian Army, rife with Brotherhood militants. There was also the question of rebuilding a fractured Syria after the overthrow of the Assad regime. The experience of Iraq during and after the war in 2003 was salutary.

Another complicating factor was the irreconcilable division within the opposition. It was split three ways. At home it was represented by the National Coordination Committee for Democratic Change [q.v.]. Opposed to violence, it was prepared to negotiate with the regime. The Syrian National Council too was against violence, but it actively lobbied for an invasion of Syria by the Western powers along with Saudi Arabia and Qatar. By contrast the 10,000-strong Free Syrian Army, composed almost exclusively of militant Sunnis, was all out for an armed confrontation with the Assad regime. On their part, the Western powers and the Western-backed Syrian opposition refused to recognize that armed protestors and other militants were killing security forces.

Before the United Nations-brokered ceasefire between the government and its opponents came into force on 12 April 2012, more than 9,000 civilians and armed rebels and 2,600 security personnel had been killed.

It seemed the Assad regime had the backing of one-third of Syrians, most of them belonging to religious and ethnic minorities. Another third, consisting almost exclusively of Sunni Muslims, supported the insurrection. The rest, including many middle-class Sunni urbanites, the beneficiaries of the regime's economic liberalization, did not like either camp but were apprehensive of the alternative.

With the ceasefire unraveling, and Sunni and Alawi villages resorting to violent attacks on one another, Syria slipped into a civil war in July. By now the initial civil movement for democracy in Syria had morphed into a struggle between regional and global powers—with Iran, Iraq, Russia, and China siding with the regime, and Turkey, Saudi Arabia, Qatar, and the Western nations opposing it.

The situation worsened in mid-July after the killing of the defense minister and his deputy during a meeting by a bomb triggered by remote control. In a concerted move, the rebels gained control of parts of Damascus and Aleppo. The International Committee of the Red Cross ruled that Syria was in the midst of a civil war. Backed by Russia and Iran, Assad re-

iterated his resolve to defeat the rebels. Due to lack of popular support in the city neighborhoods they had captured, the rebels were often unable to consolidate their gains. The government mounted periodic offensives to regain the lost territory. The stalemate at the UN Security Council continued. Annan decided to step down as the UN-Arab League envoy for Syria at the end of August and was replaced by Lakhdar Ibrahimi.

As the size and importance of the Syrian and foreign jihadists rose in the war, the Western powers and Turkey decided not to supply anti-aircraft missiles to the rebels who continued to be vulnerable to the regime's air strikes. Western leaders feared that such weapons would end up with Islamist extremists and make Western aircraft vulnerable once Syria had gone off the boil. By early September, the conflict had claimed the lives of nearly 20,000 civilians and armed rebels and 8,000 members of the security forces. The ongoing battles in Aleppo, Damascus, and Homs [q.v.] raised the death toll steadily.

LEBANON: The intractable crisis in Syria made the Lebanese President Najib Mikati [q.v.] maintain strict neutrality in any comments he chose to make on the events in Lebanon's most important neighbor. That was not the case with the leaders of the pro-Syria 8 March Alliance [q.v.] and the anti-Syria 14 March Alliance [q.v.]

JORDAN: Unlike Mikati, in August Jordanian King Abdullah II bin Hussein [q.v.] called on Assad to step down. He did so to placate the Islamic Action Front [q.v.], the political wing of the Muslim Brotherhood.

In early 2011, the Arab Spring in Jordan took the form of demonstrations by the IAF and leftists as well as the educated, unemployed people. The participants made economic and political demands, and complained about corruption. In response the monarch replaced his prime minister twice, first in February and then in October, with his choice falling on Awm Shawkat al-Khasawneh, a former judge of the International Court of Justice. Though he promised British-style parliamentary government in June, it was not until February 2012 that he spelled out the modalities: fair elections, a law guaranteeing the broadest representation, a parliament based on political parties, and governments drawn from that parliament. When al-Khasawneh, acting independently, reached out to the IAF as part of the promised political reform, he was replaced by a yes-man of the Palace, Fayez al-Tarawneh, in April 2012.

The pro-democracy opposition has been careful not to agitate against the king because that would open the fault lines between East Bank tribesmen and Jordanian citizens of the Palestinian origin, leading to a civil war. The bloodshed in Syria witnessed by Jordanians on their TV sets is another factor to keep the protest quiescent. Lastly, there is the unique element at work here: Jordanians fear that if their country disintegrated, outsiders would try to convert it into a Palestinian state.

Not surprisingly, Syria's strategic location in the Middle East makes all parties apprehensive of the prospect of chaos that would follow Assad's downfall.

Arab West: Arab West is the term applied to all the countries of Arab North Africa: Algeria, Libya, Mauritania, Morocco, and Tunisia. It is separated from the Arab East [*q.v.*] by the Libyan Desert.

Arabia: *see* Arabian Peninsula.

Arabian Peninsula: Area, about 1.12 million sq. mi./2.91 million sq. km; population 67.16 million (2011 est.). Peninsula, southwest Asia; between the Red Sea and the Gulf of Aqaba to the west, the Persian/Arabian Gulf [*q.v.*] and the Gulf of Oman to the east, and the Arabian Sea and the Gulf of Aden to the south. It is divided into Bahrain, Kuwait, Oman, Qatar, Saudi Arabia, the United Arab Emirates, and Yemen. Surrounded on three sides by mountains, the treeless peninsular plateau slopes eastwards toward the Persian Gulf, a region rich in petroleum [*q.v.*].

Most of the inhabitants of the region are to be found on the coastal plains. They have maintained contact with the rest of Asia, stretching as far as the Philippines, and with the eastern coast of Africa. The history of these peoples goes back to antiquity, when Arabia was divided between the realms of Sheba and Maain. Besides those settled on the coast or in the interior oases, there are nomads and others who transport goods between the Indian subcontinent and the Mediterranean.

They came under the sway of the freshly proclaimed religion, Islam [*q.v.*], in the second and third decades of the seventh century. United by this monotheistic faith, the Arabian tribes soon conquered adjoining territories.

But after the Caliphate was moved in 661 A.D. from Medina [*q.v.*], the burial place of Prophet Muhammad, the founder of Islam, to Damascus [*q.v.*], Arabia lost its primacy in the Islamic Empire. Later, in 1517, it became part of the Ottoman Empire, and remained so for four centuries. In the mid-18th century its central Najd region [*q.v.*] came under the influence of Wahhabism [*q.v.*]. One of its followers, Abdul Aziz bin Abdul Rahman al-Saud [*q.v.*], built up his kingdom, Saudi Arabia, in the wake of the collapse of the Ottoman Empire in World War I, which covered four-fifths of the Peninsula.

Arabic language: Arabic belongs to the family of Semitic languages [*q.v.*], its sisters being Hebrew [*q.v.*] and Aramaic, and is written from right to left. It has been a written language at least since the early fourth century A.D. It has a two-part word structure, the root consisting mostly of three consonants and providing the basic meaning; and the pattern, consisting of vowels, giving grammatical meaning to the word. Prefixes and suffixes serve the functions of the definite article, pronouns, and prepositions. For example jihad [*q.v.*] and mujahid (one who conducts jihad) have the common root, jhd. Since the Quran [*q.v.*] is written in Arabic, it is the religious language of all Muslims [*q.v.*]. It is also the language of Arabs [*q.v.*], irrespective of their religious affiliation. The language as written in the Quran is known as Classical Arabic, and links all the countries of the Arab world, from the Persian Gulf to the Atlantic. But the spoken language varies from region to region and there are five major groups of dialects: those found in Iraq, the Arabian Peninsula, Syria, Egypt, and North Africa.

Arabism: *See* pan-Arabism.

Arabs: Arabs, who claim descent from Ismail/Ishmael, son of the prophet Abraham by Hagar, appear frequently in the Bible [*q.v.*] as Ishmaelites. In the Old Testament [*q.v.*], the Second Book of Chronicles (17:11) alludes to "some Arabs" bringing 7,700 sheep and 7,700 goats as presents to King Jehosophat of Judah (r. ca 870 B.C. to ca 851 B.C.), the term describing nomadic people from the eastern bank of the Jordan River [*q.v.*]. An inscription of King Shalmaneser III of Assyria in the eighth century B.C. refers to "Gindibu the Aribi" as a member of the group of rebelling notables whom he had defeated. Later inscriptions in Assyria and Babylon are full of allusions to Aribi or Arab, a term used for nomads inhabiting the northern and central Arabian Peninsula [*q.v.*]. During the rise of the Greek and Roman civilizations the term came to include the inhabitants of the whole peninsula.

The word *Arab* is a derivative either of a Semitic root linked to nomadism, or of "abhar," meaning to pass or move. Nomadic Arabs worshipped nature—rocks, water springs, trees—or idols, and this continued until the arrival of Islam [*q.v.*] in the mid-seventh century. The Arabs settled in the oases came under the influence of such pre-Islamic religions as Judaism [*q.v.*] and Zoroastrianism [*q.v.*]. Later Islam took hold in the world of Arabs, who became its leading proselytizers. In modern times an Arab means someone who speaks Arabic [*q.v.*]. In 2010 there were an estimated 360 million Arabs living in 22 member-states of the Arab League [*q.v.*].

al-Araby, Nabil (1935–) (Also spelled el Arabi) *Egyptian lawyer and diplomat, foreign minister 2011, and Arab League [q.v.] secretary-general, 2011–* Born into a middle-class household in Cairo [*q.v.*], Araby obtained a law degree from Cairo University in 1955. After working for a law firm for a decade, he pursued postgraduate studies in law at New York University and secured a doctorate in judicial science in 1971.

Two years later he joined the foreign ministry. He was the legal adviser to the Egyptian delegation to the UN Middle East peace conference from 1973 to 1975. For the next six years he served as director of the legal and treaties department of the ministry of foreign affairs. He was part of the Egyptian delegation at the Middle East peace talks at the U.S. presidential retreat of Camp David in 1978. For the next three years he was Egypt's deputy permanent representative to the United Nations. He served as ambassador to India from 1982 to 1984 before returning to his previous post at the foreign ministry. In that capacity he led the Egyptian side in its dispute with Israel on the demarcation of the border at Taba. Egypt won the case in 1988.

Araby acted as an arbitrator at the International Chamber of Commerce International Court of Arbitration in Paris in a dispute concerning the Suez Canal from 1989 to 1992. From 1991 he was Egypt's permanent representative to the UN for the next eight years. Then he served as a member of the International Court of Justice from 2001 to 2006. On his return home he was appointed director of Regional Cairo Center for International Commercial Arbitration.

During the pro-democracy demonstrations in Cairo in January–February 2011, Araby was a member of 30-strong group of high-profile Egyptians which, acting as a liaison between protestors and the authorities, insisted on the resignation of President Hosni Mubarak [*q.v.*].

After Mubarak's ouster he criticized the absence of separation of powers in Egypt, lack of judicial independence, and the failure of the past regime to uphold Egypt's interests in its dealings with Israel. Following his appointment as foreign minister in the first post-Mubarak government in March, he opened the Rafah border crossing with the Gaza Strip [*q.v.*], brokered reconciliation between Hamas [*q.v.*] and Fatah [*q.v.*] on the basis of power-sharing until fresh elections, and improved relations with Iran.

In July he replaced Amr Moussa [*q.v.*] as the secretary-general of the Arab League [*q.v.*]. He played an active role in highlighting the repression of the protestors in Syria by President Bashar Assad [*q.v.*]. But in February 2012 his efforts to have the UN Security Council adopt a resolution requiring transition of power in Syria failed.

Arafat, Yasser (1929–2004): *Palestinian politician; chairman of Palestine Liberation Organization, 1969–2004; president of Palestinian Authority, 1994–2004* Born Mahmoud Abdul Rahman Abdul Rauf Arafat al-Qudwa, nicknamed Yasser (lit. carefree), to a merchant father who was originally from Khan Yunis in the Gaza Strip [*q.v.*] but later ran a shop in Jerusalem [*q.v.*]. Arafat was born in Cairo [*q.v.*] during his father's temporary residence there. Both he and his parents were in the Gaza Strip [*q.v.*] at the time of the 1948–49 Palestine War [*q.v.*]. He graduated as a civil engineer in 1955 from Cairo University, where he was chairman of the local Palestinian Students Union. The union was based in the Gaza Strip, then under Egyptian control. During the Suez War [*q.v.*] he worked as an engineer with the Egyptian army. He then took up a civil engineering job in Kuwait.

Along with Salah Khalaf [*q.v.*] and Khalil Wazir [*q.v.*], fellow Palestinians from Gaza, he formed a clandestine group called Fatah [*q.v.*] in 1958. Five years later it was allowed to open an office in Algiers, capital of the revolutionary state of Algeria, to train commandos. This was in line with the Fatah strategy of employing popular revolutionary violence to liberate the Palestinian homeland. In 1964 in Baathist-run Damascus [*q.v.*], guided by Arafat, Fatah decided to launch guerrilla actions against Israel from Syria. The first operation was mounted on 1 January 1965. After the June 1967 Arab-Israeli War [*q.v.*] he met Egyptian President Gamal Abdul Nasser [*q.v.*], who pledged support but no funds.

In March 1968 Fatah commandos engaged Israelis in a battle in the Jordanian border town of Karameh, which increased the popularity of Fatah and Arafat, known as Abu Ammar. Four months later Fatah ended its boycott of the Palestine National Council (PNC) [*q.v.*] of the Palestine Liberation Organization [*q.v.*]. Fatah delegates attended the fifth session of the PNC in Cairo in July 1968. With an estimated guerrilla force of 15,000, Fatah emerged as the PLO's largest constituent. The PNC elected Arafat chairman of the PLO's executive committee at its sixth session in early 1969.

Arafat, who had emerged as an arbiter between the leftist and rightist factions within Fatah, now extended his mediation skills to hold together a motley assortment of Palestinian groups—some Marxist-Leninist, some pan-Arabist, some funded by leading Arab states, and all possessing militias. He stuck to two basic positions: no single Arab regime should be allowed to co-opt the PLO; and all sociopolitical ideologies committed to the liberation of Palestine [*q.v.*] must be accommodated. After the expulsion of the PLO from Amman [*q.v.*] in the wake of Palestinian battles with Jordanian forces in 1970–71, the PLO headquarters moved to Beirut [*q.v.*]. Here the PLO, under his leadership and financed by private and governmental contributions, channeled through the Palestine National Fund [*q.v.*], began to set up "a state within a state."

Following the Arab summit's decision in late October 1974 to recognize the PLO as the sole legitimate representative of the Palestinian people, Arafat's status rose. The next month he addressed the General Assembly of the United Nations (where the PLO had been accorded observer status) in the course of its debate on the Palestinian issue.

By now the PNC had adopted the idea of establishing a homeland on the

West Bank [*q.v.*] and the Gaza Strip as a step toward the final goal of liberating all of Palestine. Pro-Soviet groups affiliated to the PLO played an important role in getting this line adopted by the PNC. Ever since Arafat's visit to Moscow in July 1968, as part of an Egyptian delegation led by Nasser, the Soviet Union had taken a keen interest in Arafat and the PLO, and backed its guerrilla activities as a lawful expression of the Palestinian people's right to self-defense in the face of continued military occupation by Israel. In the Lebanese Civil War [*q.v.*], which erupted in April 1975, Arafat and other Palestinian leaders sided with the leftist Lebanese National Movement [*q.v.*] to fight the right-wing Lebanese Forces [*q.v.*]. His vehement opposition to Egypt's U.S.-inspired effort to reach unilateral peace with Israel in 1977–78 turned him politically leftwards.

At Fatah's fourth congress in May 1980 it was decided to intensify the armed struggle against the Jewish state. Israel reciprocated by compelling Arafat to remove the PLO headquarters and troops from Beirut after besieging that city in August 1982 during its invasion of Lebanon [*q.v.*]. He moved the PLO administrative staff to Tunis and dispersed the Palestinian fighters to several Arab states.

Following a series of meetings with King Hussein of Jordan [*q.v.*], in February 1985 he agreed to joint Palestinian-Jordanian moves toward a peace settlement with Israel and the formation of a Palestine-Jordan confederation after the founding of an independent Palestine. But he failed to win the backing of the majority of PLO constituents. In April 1987 his agreement with King Hussein was annulled, and the unity of the PLO was restored. His flirtation with King Hussein and Egypt's President Hosni Mubarak [*q.v.*] soured his relations with President Hafiz Assad [*q.v.*] of Syria, who wanted the PLO to coordinate its policies with him.

In November 1988 the PNC, meeting in Algiers, proclaimed the State of Palestine, with Arafat as its president, a status that was formally recognized by 91 of the 110 states that had accorded recognition to the PLO. His disavowal of terrorism against Israel, and his declaration that the State of Palestine, consisting of the Gaza Strip, the West Bank, and East Jerusalem [*q.v.*], would coexist peacefully with Israel, were endorsed by the PNC. The following month, addressing a special session of the UN General Assembly in Geneva, he repeated his earlier declarations. This led to open contacts between the PLO and the United States, albeit at a low level. But when he failed to condemn an unsuccessful Palestinian raid on an Israeli military target (which according to a PNC statement was still a legitimate activity), the U.S. suspended its talks with the PLO in June 1990.

This, and the rapidly increasing migration of Soviet Jews into Israel, led Arafat to ally himself with the radical leader of Iraq, President Saddam Hussein [*q.v.*]. He sided with the Iraqi leader during the crisis that followed Iraq's invasion and occupation of Kuwait in August 1990. This alienated him from the rulers of the rich Gulf States and resulted in the stoppage of their subventions to the PLO. It also distanced him from the presidents of

Egypt and Syria, who joined the anti-Iraq alliance to counter the Iraqi aggression. Following Iraq's defeat in February 1991 he tried to regain his lost popularity, an uphill task. Deprived of the advice and friendship of his longtime comrades Khalil Wazir (assassinated in April 1988) and Salah Khalaf (assassinated in January 1991), he felt increasingly isolated.

During the preliminary talks leading up to a Middle East peace conference under the joint auspices of the United States and the Soviet Union in October 1991, he agreed to Israel's demand that the Jordanian delegation should consist of an equal number of Jordanians and Palestinians acceptable to Israel.

When the bilateral negotiations that followed proved sterile, Arafat, through his well-trusted aides, set up a clandestine channel to conduct secret talks with Israel in Norway. The resulting accord was signed in the presence of Arafat and Israeli Prime Minister Yitzhak Rabin [q.v.] by Mahmoud Abbas [q.v.] and Shimon Peres [q.v.] in Washington on 13 September 1993, which became known as Oslo Accord I [q.v.]. It required Israel to vacate the Gaza Strip and the West Bank town of Jericho [q.v.] as a first step toward granting Palestinian autonomy in the Occupied Territories [q.v.].

In July 1994 Arafat moved to Gaza to administer the Gaza Strip and Jericho as president of the Palestinian Authority (PA) [q.v.]. He shared the 1994 Nobel Prize for Peace with Rabin and Peres.

In September 1995 he signed an autonomy agreement on the West Bank with Israel, which became known as Oslo Accord II [q.v.]. It divided the West Bank into A/B/C zones: A (3 percent of the territory, covering seven major cities, including Hebron), full PA civil control with external security under Israel; B, joint control (24 percent of the territory, covering 465 villages), where Israel had the power to intervene at its own discretion to maintain overall security; and the rest as C (73 percent of the territory), under full Israeli control.

But, with the assassination of Rabin two months later, followed by the defeat of Peres by hard-liner Benjamin Netanyahu [q.v.] in the prime ministerial contest in May 1996, the Oslo Accords began to unravel, especially after Netanyahu refused initially to meet Arafat. The reluctant signing of the Wye River Memorandum [q.v.] in October 1998, with Israel agreeing to hand over 1 percent of the West Bank to the A area and another 12 percent to the B area (maintaining full control over 60 percent of the West Bank), did little to reverse the trend.

The situation improved with the election of Ehud Barak [q.v.] as Israel's prime minister in May 1999. But Arafat's summit meeting with Barak, chaired by U.S. President Bill Clinton at the presidential retreat of Camp David in July 2000 to reach the final settlement between Israel and the Palestinians, failed primarily over the issue of the status of the Noble Sanctuary [q.v.] in Jerusalem's Old City, with Barak insisting on Israeli sovereignty over the third-holiest shrine of Islam [q.v.]. Barak's defeat by the hawkish Ariel Sharon [q.v.] in February 2001 against the background of the Second Intifada [q.v.] of the Palestinians, opened a grim chapter for Arafat, who would come to be shunned by the newly elected U.S. President George W. Bush.

As violence between the two sides escalated, Sharon systematically destroyed the Palestinian Authority's administrative and economic infrastructure—an enterprise that got a further boost when in June 2002 Bush publicly called on the Palestinians to change their leadership. Bush's subsequent statement that he envisioned an independent State of Palestine existing side by side with Israel in mutual security did little to raise Arafat's stature.

In November 2004, he died of an undiagnosed disease in a hospital near Paris after falling seriously ill in Ramallah [q.v.], the de facto headquarters of the Palestinian Authority since 2001.

Arbil: *see* Irbil.

Arif, **Abdul Rahman** (1916–2007): *Iraqi military leader; president, 1966–68* Born into a middle-class family in Baghdad, Arif enrolled at the local military academy and became an officer. A nationalist and an opponent of the pro-Western stance of the monarchical regime, he joined the Free Officers group that overthrew the royalist regime in July 1958.

When his younger brother, Abdul Salam Arif [q.v.], clashed with Abdul Karim Qasim [q.v.], who headed the republican regime, Arif's career came under a shadow. Abdul Salam's fall ended Arif's future prospects in the military. The situation changed abruptly in the wake of Baathist [q.v.] coup and the assassination of Qasim in February 1963 when Abdul Salam

Arif assumed supreme power. Arif became the acting chief of staff.

Following the accidental death of Abdul Salam Arif in April 1966, Arif emerged as the presidential choice of the ruling Revolutionary Command Council. By continuing the overall policies of his dead sibling, he provided continuity. While maintaining friendly relations with Egypt under its radical president, Abdul Gamal Nasser [q.v.], he preserved Iraq's independent stance. He continued his brother's autocratic style of government, but lacked his charisma and astuteness.

Though he kept Iraq out of direct confrontation with Israel during the June 1967 Arab-Israeli War [q.v.], the negative impact of the Arab debacle rubbed off on his government. The opposition felt emboldened to demonstrate in the streets, demanding free elections. This paved the way for the disaffected Baathist officers, led by Ahmad Hassan Bakr [q.v.] and the military intelligence chief, Abdul Rahman Nayif, to overthrow Arif in July 1969. He was forced into exile in Turkey.

A decade later, when Saddam Hussein [q.v.] became president, Arif was allowed to return home. After Saddam Hussein's overthrow in 2003, he moved to Amman [q.v.], where he died.

Arif, **Abdul Salam** (1920–66): *Iraqi military and political leader; president, 1963–66* Born into a middle-class family in Baghdad, Arif enrolled at the military academy and became an officer. His experience in the Palestine War (1948–49) [q.v.], in which the Iraqi troops performed poorly, turned him against the pro-Western regime of King Faisal II [q.v.]. He played a leading role in organizing the Free Officers group that ended the monarchy in July 1958. During the coup he led the contingent that seized the capital.

In the subsequent republican regime he emerged as second only to Abdul Karim Qasim [q.v.], serving as deputy chief of staff, deputy premier, and interior minister. But he soon clashed with Qasim, who disagreed with his plan to lead Iraq into a union with the United Arab Republic [q.v.], consisting of Egypt and Syria. He lost all his jobs in September and found himself behind bars. Accused of conspiracy to kill Qasim and mount a coup, he was found guilty and given capital punishment. But his sentence was commuted by Qasim, who ordered his release in 1961. This time his conspiring, conducted in alliance with Baathist [q.v.] officers, culminated in the termination of Qasim's regime in February 1963. He became president, but without much power. However, finding the Baathists at odds with one another, he got rid of them and assumed full authority in November.

An admirer of Egypt's President Abdul Gamal Nasser [q.v.], Arif emulated his policy of enlarging the public sector by carrying out progressive nationalization. He embarked on a plan to unite Iraq and Egypt, starting with economic and military coordination and a joint presidential council. He tackled the long-running Kurdish [q.v.] problem and was on the verge of signing an accord with the Kurdish insurgents when he was killed in an air crash in April 1966.

Arlosoroff, Chaim (1899–1933): *Israeli politician* Born in Romny, Ukraine, Arlosaroff moved with his family to Germany in 1905. He obtained a doctorate in economics at Berlin University. At the age of 19 he joined HaPoale HaTzair [q.v.], and two years later started editing the party's newspaper. At 24 he secured a seat on the executive council of the World Zionist Organization (WZO) [q.v.].

In 1924 he migrated to Palestine [q.v.] where he became secretary of HaPoale HaTzair within two years. Following the merger of HaPoel HaTzair and Ahdut HaAvodah [q.v.] to form Mapai [q.v.], he emerged as one of its main spokesmen. At the WZO's congress in 1931, he won a seat on the executive committee of the Jewish Agency [q.v.], and became head of its political department, dealing with international affairs. He maintained good relations with the British Mandate and sought accommodation with the Arabs [q.v.] in Palestine.

Following Adolf Hitler's ascent to power in Germany in January 1933, Arlosaroff helped German Jews to migrate to Palestine by striking a deal with the German government, which allowed Jews to depart with most of their property. This was denounced strongly by the right-wing Zionist Revisionists [q.v.] and their extremist faction in Palestine, Brit Habriyonim.

In June 1933 Arlosaroff was killed during a stroll along the Tel Aviv [q.v.] seashore. Three suspects, all members of Brit Habriyonim, were arrested and tried by a British Mandate court. Two were released for lack of evidence, but the third, Abraham Stavsky, was given a death sentence.

He appealed and was acquitted due to insufficient evidence. Arlosoroff's murder split the Yishuv [*q.v.*] into two hostile camps, with leftist Zionists blaming the Revisionists, and the latter blaming the Arabs for the killing. The controversy simmered on. In 1982 the Likud-led [*q.v.*] government of Israel instituted an inquiry. The report of the commission, published in June 1985, was inconclusive.

Armenian: *an ancient Indo-European people, originating from the Lake Van region in eastern Turkey* Armenians claim to be the descendants of Haik, a descendant of Noah, and call themselves Hayq (plural of Hay). In the sixth century B.C. they became part of the Persian Empire and were called Armina. Later, in 189 B.C., the Armenians established an independent kingdom, which fell to the Romans in 69 B.C.

Around 300 A.D. they became the first nation to adopt Christianity [*q.v.*], thanks to the efforts of St. Gregory the Illuminator, and since then religion has played an important role in their lives.

After a history rich in vicissitudes, interspersed with independent Armenian kingdoms, they became subjects of the Ottoman Empire in the 16th century. As a result of a continual struggle between the Tsarist, Persian, and Ottoman Empires, the Armenian-majority areas fell under different rulers. Between 1894 and 1915 Armenians suffered persecution and massacre under the Ottomans. In World War I, when the Ottoman Empire was arrayed against an alliance consisting of Tsarist Russia, its government considered the Armenians to be pro-Russian "fifth-columnists." It decided to expel some 1.75 million Armenians from Turkey into Greater Syria [*q.v.*] and Palestine [*q.v.*]. Roughly a third managed to escape expulsion. Of the rest, an estimated 50 percent perished because of starvation or Turkish violence en route. Most of those who survived settled in North America, Western Europe, or the Trans-Caucasian region of the former Soviet Union, which included the Armenian Soviet Socialist Republic.

In the Middle East today, substantial Armenian communities exist in Lebanon and Iran. They belong either to the Armenian Orthodox Church [*q.v.*] or the Armenian Catholic Church [*q.v.*].

Armenian Catholic Church: *part of the Roman Catholic Church [q.v.], but performing an Eastern rite* The Armenian Catholic Church was established in 1742 by Abraham Artzivian, the Armenian Catholic Bishop of Aleppo [*q.v.*], after he was elected patriarch of Sis, the capital of Cilicia (now in Turkey).

Its liturgical language is Classical Armenian. Following the Ottoman persecution of Armenians during World War I, the Church was reorganized. In 1932 the head of the Church, called the Patriarch of the Catholic Armenians and Katholikos of Cilicia, moved the Church's headquarters to the convent built in 1749 in the village of Bzoummar, 36 km/22 miles northeast of Beirut [*q.v.*]. In 2008 there were about 12,000 adherents in the Beirut diocese, and 10,000 in the Isfahan [*q.v.*] diocese. The Church had 376,000 followers worldwide.

Armenian language: *a member of the western branch of the Indo-European languages* Though Armenian had become the dominant language in the Lake Van region of eastern Turkey by the seventh century B.C., it did not acquire an alphabet until the fourth century A.D.

Armenian Orthodox Church: Also called the Armenian Apostolic Church or the Armenian Apostolic (Orthodox) Church. The Armenian Orthodox Church split from the Eastern Orthodox Church [*q.v.*] in the fourh century and in 506 A.D. adopted the Monophysite doctrine: that is, the belief that Christ had a human and a divine nature, united in one person. Its liturgical language is Classical Armenian. Its worldwide adherents are estimated at eight million.

After transferring to different sites, the headquarters of the Church, called the Catholicos of all Armenians, was returned in 1441 to Echmiadzin in present-day Armenia. While Echmiadzin continued to be the site of the Catholicos of all Armenians, the Catholicos of Sis was moved to Antelias, Lebanon, in 1930.

The church's estimated one million adherents are scattered throughout not only Lebanon, Syria, Kuwait, Iran, and Cyprus, but also North America.

Arvand Rud *(Persian, Arvand River)*: *See* Shatt al-Arab.

Asbar, Ali Ahmad Said (1930–): *Syrian poet and essayist domiciled in Lebanon* Born into an Alawi [*q.v.*] family in Qassabin, a village near Latakia [*q.v.*], Asbar obtained a philosophy degree from Damascus Uni-

versity in 1954, with special interest in Sufism [*q.v.*]. A staunch member of the Syrian Social Nationalist Party [*q.v.*], whose leader, Antun Saada [*q.v.*], named him Adonis, he received a year-long jail sentence for his subversive politics. In 1956 he escaped to Beirut [*q.v.*], where he combined further studies with journalism and literary writing, mainly poetry and literary criticism. He cofounded and coedited *Shiar* (Arabic: *Poetry*), a literary magazine, from 1956 to 1963.

Influenced by the classical Shia [*q.v.*] poets he had studied as part of his Alawi upbringing, he started out as a conventional poet, publishing two volumes of verses in the conventional Arabic ode (*qasida*) style. But by the late 1950s he had begun to experiment with the prose poem *(qasidat al-nathr)*, infusing it with density and tension, metaphoric representation, and rhythms. His volume *Mihyar of Damascene: His Songs* (1961) broke fresh ground in its diction, syntax, and imagery. Instead of using traditional images he employed a complex set— including the Tammuzian symbols of Adonis and Baal, biblical figures and symbols, and such myths as that of the Phoenix—to portray revolutionary change in a mystical light. He broke with traditional diction and style and employed a totally new syntax that was authoritative yet original. Considering classical Arabic as too intellectual and cerebral for writing about modern urban life, he grappled with the roots of the words and explored their untapped potential through various rhythms, producing a language as robust as its classical counterpart. The complexity and creative exoticism of Asbar's poetry, and its association with modernity, made it doubly attractive to a generation of young poets. He condemned the present servility and repression in the Arab world and lamented the past, scarred by foreign invasions and inertia. Alluding to the Phoenix, he put his hopes in the future.

His challenge to the traditions of language and poetry ran in tandem with his propensity for protest and defiance and his sociopolitical vision of liberation from the status quo. The humiliation and pain caused by the Arab defeat in the June 1967 Arab-Israeli War [*q.v.*] created a social environment that made both his political views and his poetry attractive. The resurgent hope and pride epitomized by the rise of the Palestinian resistance movement in the late 1960s tied up with his thesis: like Tammuz, the god of revival in the Babylonian religion, who is associated with Greek Adonis, the legendary Phoenix is reborn out of the ashes of the fire that consumes it. His response to the Arab defeat in 1967 came in the form of a long poem, *This Is My Name* (1970).

By the time he published *Introduction to Arab Poetry* (1971), marking the birth of post-modernist poetry in Arabic, the movement for radicalizing linguistic structures, coining new words, and experimenting with fresh metaphors had taken root. He had also established his own literary journal, *Mawaqif* (Arabic: *Attitudes*) (1968–78). In *The Shock of Modernity* (1978) and *Manifesto of Modernity* (1980) he summarized his literary views, stating that "there is no trace of memory in my poetry in the cultural sense, neither on the level of heritage nor on the personal level."

When Lebanon plunged into a long, bloody civil war in 1975 [*q.v.*], he moved to Damascus [*q.v.*] where he became a visiting professor at Damascus University. In 1980, he departed for Paris, where he has kept up his writing and supplemented it with teaching. His views on Arabic have mellowed. In 1984 he stated that a rediscovery of "language is a rediscovery of Arabic's modern potential connotative possibilities, forgotten meanings and latent metaphorical dimensions." The only language in which he realized he could write was the terse, elevated language of classical Arabic poetry—disassembled, modulated, and revolutionized by him, yet possessing the aura of the old poetry and its rhetorical hold on readers and listeners.

In June 2011, amid the bloody repression of the Syrian protestors, he addressed an open letter to President Bashar Assad [*q.v.*], calling on him to step down. At the same time he condemned the use of violence either by the Syrian opposition or other Arab countries.

He is the author of more than 20 books in Arabic. The ones translated into English include *The Fixed and the Changing* (1974), *The Book of Siege* (1982), *Sufism and Surrealism* (1995), and *If Only the Sea Could Sleep* (2002). He is the winner of the Bjorson Prize (2007) and the Goethe Prize (2011).

Ashkenazim: (Hebrew: *plural of Ashkenaz, derivative of Ashk'naz, meaning Germany*): Literally, the term applies to all those from Germany; but in practice, from the ninth century onward, it increasingly meant German Jews [*q.v.*] and their descendants, including those who had left the German lands. They are different from the Jews originating in Spain and Portugal, called Sephardim [*q.v.*], in their pronunciation of Hebrew [*q.v.*], their prayer rituals, and their mother tongue, Yiddish [*q.v.*]. Until the late 15th century Ashkenazim and Sephardim were almost equal in number. But by the late 1920s, about 90 percent of the 16.5 million Jews worldwide were Ashkenazim, a term now applied to Jews of northern or central European origin. Following the Holocaust during World War II, which resulted in the death of six million Jews, the remaining 9.5 million Ashkenazim constituted 82 percent of the global Jewish population of 11.5 million. At the founding of Israel in 1948, Ashkenazim made up 80 percent of its Jewish population.

However, because of the large intake of the Jews from the Arab states and the higher birth rate among them, and Sephardim, the proportion of Ashkenazim in the Israeli Jewish population fell below 50 percent by the mid-1960s. Later, due to the large-scale influx of Soviet Jews, which started in 1990 on the eve of the Soviet Union's disintegration and continued until 1994, the proportion of Ashkenazim rose sharply, and they became the majority. In 2009, however, at 2.8 million they were 50 percent of the total Jewish population of 5.58 million.

Since 2003 their chief rabbi has been Yona Metzger.

Ashura: (Arabic: *Tenth, meaning 10th of Muharram*): *a fasting day for Muslims*
In Islam [*q.v.*] it is the day when Allah created Adam and Eve, paradise and hell, the pen, and life and death. Tradition has it that Prophet Muhammad fasted on this day.

Ashura: (Arabic: *Tenth, meaning 10th of Muharram*): *an annual ritual of Shias*
Ashura is the final day of the dramatic events of 1–10 Muharram 61 A.H. [*q.v.*] (8–17 May 681 A.D.) in Islamic history. The narrative of this period is told annually by professional reciters in the mosques and meeting halls of Shias [*q.v.*], and is mounted as the second act of a passion play of Islam [*q.v.*], accompanied by frenzied grief and tears, wailing, and self-flagellation in public by the faithful on the final day.

The narrative runs as follows. After the death in April 680 A.D. of Muwaiya bin Abu Sufian—the Umayyad governor of Syria who had challenged Ali bin Abu Talib, a cousin and son-in-law of the Prophet Muhammad, for the caliphate—his son, Yazid, became the caliph. Hussein, the oldest surviving son of Ali, then living in Medina [*q.v.*], staked his claim to the caliphate on the ground that it belonged to the House of the Prophet, of which he was the most senior member, and that Yazid was a usurper. His stance won him swift and fervent messages of support from the Iraqi town of Kufa [*q.v.*], a stronghold of Ali's partisans. This news reached Yazid who rushed a trusted aide, Ubaidullah bin Ziyad, to Kufa, who succeeded in neutralizing the anti-Yazid forces in the town.

By then the unsuspecting Hussein, accompanied by his family and 72 retainers, was well on his way to Kufa. On 1 Muharram 61 A.H. (8 May 681 A.D.), Hussein's entourage was intercepted near Karbala [q.v.], some 30 mi./48 km from Kufa, by Yazid's soldiers. For the next eight days their commander tried to obtain Hussein's unconditional surrender. But Hussein, believing in his right to the caliphate, resolved to do battle and perish rather than surrender or retreat. He also reckoned that his martyrdom would revitalize the claim of the House of the Prophet to the caliphate. On the morning of 10 Muharram, Hussein led his small band of partisans to confront Yazid's 4,000 heavily armed troops. His warriors fell one by one, and he was the last to die.

This heroic tragedy of a man of charisma and piety tells the faithful that the true believer should not shirk from challenging the established order if it has become unjust and oppressive, despite slender chances of overthrowing it.

Assad, Bashar (1965–): *Syrian military and political leader; president, 2000–* Born into the Alawi [q.v.] household of Hafiz Assad [q.v.], in Damascus [q.v.], he did his baccalaureate in 1982. He graduated as a physician, specializing in ophthalmology, and began practicing as an ophthalmologist at a military hospital outside Damascus in 1988. Four years later he went to London to specialize in ophthalmology. In 1994 he returned home after the death of his elder brother Basil in a car accident.

As the head of the Syrian Computer Society, he initiated a computerization program. After passing the General Staff course in 1997, he was promoted to Lt. Colonel. He was put in charge of Syria's relations with Lebanon. Following the death of his father, Hafiz, on 10 June 2000, he was promoted to lieutenant general, and named commander-in-chief. Once the constitutional age requirement for president was lowered from 40 to 34 he was elected president on 10 July 2000.

In foreign affairs, he maintained his father's freshly initiated policy of mending fences with Iraq, which culminated in the reopening of the oil pipeline between the two neighbors in late 2000, with 200,000 barrels of Iraqi oil flowing daily into Syria. He stuck to the earlier Syrian position that Israel had to withdraw from all of the Golan Heights [q.v.] in return for total peace and normalization of relations.

At home, when 99 leading intellectuals demanded an end to the 37-year-old martial law, his government announced that the emergency laws had been suspended. His freeing of 600 political prisoners still left 1,500 politicians incarcerated. His political liberalization led to the demand that the Baath Socialist Party's [q.v.] monopoly over power, guaranteed by the constitution, be ended. This was unacceptable to the old guard in the party and the military and intelligence services. So he slowed down the pace of political reform.

In the wake of the 11 September 2001 attacks on the U.S. by al-Qaida [q.v.], Assad's government offered intelligence to Washington, thus thawing Syria's relations with the sole superpower. But since it continued to support Lebanon's Hizbollah [q.v.] and allowed Hamas [q.v.] and other radical Palestinian parties to maintain their offices in Damascus, America retained Syria on its list of the countries that sponsor international terrorism. Assad maintained Syria's long-standing alliance with Iran.

He opposed the Anglo-American invasion of Iraq in March 2003 [*q.v.*], and later allowed the exiled Iraqis to help conduct resistance against the Anglo-American occupation of Iraq. In September 2004 the UN Security Council passed Resolution 1559 by nine votes (the minimum needed) with six abstentions, requiring Syria to withdraw all its troops from Lebanon.

Assad's relations with the U.S. soured after the assassination of Lebanese Prime Minister Rafiq Hariri [*q.v.*] in February 2005, followed by the accusations of Syria's involvement in the killing. Pressured by the Western powers and the UN, he withdrew the last of the Syrian troops in Lebanon on the eve of the Lebanese general election in May. In August 2006 he described the performance of the Hizbollah in its war with Israel as "successful resistance."

He was reelected president in 2007 with 97 percent vote. In April 2008 he revealed that he had been discussing the future of the Golan Heights and a peace treaty with Israel for a year, with Turkey acting as a mediator. But following Israel's war in Gaza [*q.v.*] in 2008–2009, Turkey gave up its role.

He improved relations with Russia as well as major countries in South America, particularly Brazil and Venezuela. He described the push for the Israeli-Palestinian peace by U.S. President Barack Obama (r. 2009–) as "weak."

Following his meeting with Malcolm Hoenlein, executive vice chairman of the Conference of Presidents of Major American Jewish

Organizations, in December 2010, Assad approved the renovation of 11 synagogues across Syria.

The Arab Spring [*q.v.*] movement in 2011 started with the modest demands of the release of political prisoners and the lifting of the emergency laws dating back to 1963. Assad responded harshly. The killing of three protestors in the southern city of Deraa on 18 March opened a new chapter. However, a month later, he ended the emergency rule. But as the anti-regime resistance intensified in the Sunni-dominated cities of Hama [*q.v.*] and Homs [*q.v.*], with the calls for his removal from office, Assad resorted to brutal repression, using heavy weapons against civilian areas. This in turn led to the formation of the irregular Free Syrian Army [*q.v.*], composed of army defectors and armed civilians. Assured of the loyalty of the mainly Alawi top officers of the military and intelligence agencies, he tried to quell the unrest with increasing force while making half-hearted moves to reform the political system.

In January 2012, by a majority vote, the Arab League [*q.v.*] urged him to step down and hand over power to a deputy. He rejected the call. The next month he held a referendum on the reformed constitution, which abrogated the Baath Party's monopoly on power. It won 89.4 percent support on voter turnout of 57 percent. At the end of the first year of the civilian resistance in mid-March 2012, over 7,500 civilians and nearly 2,100 security personnel had been killed.

Pressured by Russia, Assad accepted the six-point peace plan of Kofi Annan, the UN-Arab League envoy, to resolve the conflict in Syria, which called for a Syrian-led solution to the conflict. The brief ceasefire in April ended in late May when the Free Syrian Army mounted a countrywide offensive, which led Assad to reaffirm his resolve to crush the armed rebellion. With the rebels launching offensives in Damascus and Aleppo in mid-July, the pressure on Assad's forces grew. But the backing for his regime by Russia and Iran remained intact, with Iraq adding its support. Assad calculated that the continuation of the civil war would lead to the Syrian and foreign jihadists rising to the fore in the rebel camp which would cool the ardor of the West and Turkey to fund and arm the insurgents. He was therefore disinclined to compromise.

Assad, Hafiz (1930–2000): *Syrian military and political leader; president, 1971–2000* Born Hafiz Wahhash in the family of a notable in Qurdaha, an Alawi [*q.v.*] village near Latakia [*q.v.*], Assad enrolled at the Homs [*q.v.*] military academy in 1951 and graduated as an air force pilot four years later. He underwent additional training in Egypt. Soon after the formation of the United Arab Republic [*q.v.*] in early 1958, he took a further flying course in the Soviet Union.

The dissolution of all Syrian parties, including the Baath Socialist Party [*q.v.*], of which Assad had been a longtime member, left him disgruntled. In early 1960, while serving in Egypt, he became one of the five founders of the clandestine Military Committee. After the secession of Syria from the UAR in September 1961 the Military Committee became active. It was the main force behind

the Baathist coup in March 1963. Six months later Assad was elected to the regional (i.e., Syrian) high command of the Baath Party. His de facto status as commander of the air force was formalized in December 1964, when he was promoted to major-general.

In May 1965 he was elected to the national (i.e., all-Arab) high command of the party. In the growing discord between the moderate civilian and the radical military factions of the ruling party, Assad was firmly with the latter. His faction mounted a successful coup in February 1966, and he became defense minister. He then developed an Arab nationalist perspective, concentrating on winning a military contest with Israel, whereas his rival, Salah Jadid [*q.v.*], pursuing a socialist path, urged a revolutionary transformation of Syrian society. The high command of the Baath failed to resolve the conflict. Assad used his status as defense minister to consolidate his position in the military to challenge Jadid. This came in February 1969, and ended with Assad in the ascendancy in the party high command and the government.

Deferring to advice from Cairo and Moscow, he refrained from monopolizing power, and inter alia retained Nur al-Din Attasi [*q.v.*], a Jadid ally, as president. But because Jadid continued to dominate the party machine, the tussle between him and Assad was not fully resolved. The final clash came in November 1970 during the national congress of the Baath in Damascus [*q.v.*]. Assad gained full control, purging and arresting his adversaries. He assumed the additional offices of prime minister and secretary-general of the Baath, leaving the presidency to his nominee, Ahmad Khatib. Under his guidance the new party high command nominated a 173-strong People's Assembly to draft a constitution.

In February 1971 the People's Assembly ratified the party high command's nomination of Assd as president, and this decision was confirmed in a referendum in March, winning 99.2 percent support. When in January 1973 the draft constitution described Syria as a "democratic, popular, socialist state," an influential group of Muslim clerics attacked the document as "secular and atheistic," and demanded insertion of an article proclaiming Islam [*q.v.*] as the state religion. Assad temporized by persuading the People's Assembly to amend the constitution to specify that the president must be Muslim. But the clergy did not think this sufficient. To pacify them, Assad declared that the October 1973 Arab-Israeli War [*q.v.*] was a jihad [*q.v.*] against the enemies of Islam. In early 1974 he went on an umra [*q.v.*] to Mecca [*q.v.*], and this established him as a true believer. He was reelected president in 1978, 1985, and 1992.

Assad put Syria on a firm institutional path, with elections to the People's Assembly held every four years. The Assembly was dominated by the Baath-led National Progressive Front [*q.v.*], formed in 1972, which included pan-Arabists [*q.v.*], Socialists, and Communists [*q.v.*]. The real power lay with the high command of the Baath, which was led by Assad. Complementing it was the intelligence network that permeated all important segments of society and government. The major opposition force, the Mus-

lim Brotherhood [*q.v.*], remained outlawed.

Assad's intervention in the Lebanese Civil War [*q.v.*] in mid-1976 to bolster the Christian [*q.v.*] camp revived the Islamist forces, who started a campaign of assassination and terrorism. This graduated into near-insurrection in Aleppo [*q.v.*] and Hama [*q.v.*] in March 1980, and reached a peak with an assassination attempt on Assad in June. In response, he went all out to crush the Islamists, who retreated and consolidated their position. Their violent activities resumed and culminated in an insurrection in Hama in February 1982. Assad hit back with unprecedented force and regained control. Signs of fission within the ruling elite surfaced when Assad suffered a heart attack in November 1983. His younger brother, Rifaat, tried to seize power but failed.

He finally overcame this crisis, which threatened to turn into civil war, in March 1984, the month in which he successfully aborted the Lebanese-Israeli peace treaty [*q.v.*] that Lebanon, cajoled by the United States, had initialed in May 1983 in the aftermath of the Israeli invasion of Lebanon [*q.v.*] in June 1982. His involvement in the Lebanese civil strife was based on the doctrine that a special relationship existed between Lebanon and Syria, and that the defection of Lebanon to the U.S.-Israel camp would present extreme danger to Syrian security. He continued his Lebanese involvement until finally, in October 1990, the pro-Syrian side won.

His relations with Egypt fluctuated. Initially he strengthened his ties with Egypt, coordinating the war against

Israel in October 1973. But he became disillusioned with Egyptian President Anwar Sadat [*q.v.*] when the latter began to pursue policies that were to culminate in Egypt's bilateral peace treaty with Israel in 1979. Assad made Syria the centerpiece of the Steadfastness Front [*q.v.*], which included the Palestine Liberation Organization [*q.v.*], and opposed readmission of Egypt into the Arab League [*q.v.*], from which it had been expelled in 1979. He signed a Friendship Treaty with the Soviet Union in 1980.

Reflecting the divisions within the national (i.e., pan-Arab) command of the Baath Party, with Michel Aflaq [*q.v.*] operating from Baghdad [*q.v.*], he remained cool toward the Baathist regime in Iraq [*q.v.*], led first by Ahmad Hassan Bakr [*q.v.*] and then Saddam Hussein [*q.v.*]. There was a rapprochement with Iraq in 1978, but this proved transient. With Assad siding with Iran in the Iran-Iraq War (1980–88) [*q.v.*], relations between Syria and Iraq soured. Following Saddam Hussein's invasion and occupation of Kuwait in August 1990, he tried to persuade the Iraqi leader to withdraw from Kuwait. When that failed he joined the anti-Iraq coalition led by the United States, and sent troops to assist Saudi Arabia's defense.

On assuming power Assad committed himself to divest Israel of the territorial gains it made in the Arab countries in the June 1967 Arab-Israeli War [*q.v.*]. However, his forces failed to retake the Golan Heights [*q.v.*] during the October 1973 War. Following a disengagement agreement with Israel, he ensured that no guerrilla attacks were launched on Israel from Syria. Following Egypt's

defection from the Arab camp in 1979, he embarked upon a plan to achieve strategic parity with Israel, a costly proposition. At the same time he tried to maintain a unified camp among Israel's Arab neighbors by thwarting any attempts at additional bilateral deals involving Israel. His success in Lebanon encouraged him to frustrate any such plans by Jordan's King Hussein [*q.v.*].

Considering the Palestinians an important part of any alliance to deal with Israel, Assad wished to become a mentor of the PLO chairman, Yasser Arafat [*q.v.*]. But the latter's resolve to maintain the PLO's independence led to frosty relations between the two leaders. By inciting a revolt against Arafat's leadership within Fatah [*q.v.*] in 1983, Assad managed to weaken his position.

With the decline of the Soviet Union as a superpower from 1989 onwards, Assad had to lower his sights when it came to tackling the issue of Israel. In October 1991 he agreed to participate in the Middle East peace conference, which was meant to lead to bilateral talks between Israel and its Arab enemies. He ensured that the conference was held on the basis of UN Security Council Resolutions 242 and 338 [*q.v.*], calling on Israel to withdraw from the territories it occupied during the 1967 War. In the Syrian-Israeli talks he insisted that Israel must promise to vacate the Golan Heights in return for total peace with Syria before details of a peace treaty could be fleshed out. He succeeded in getting the U.S. to play an active role in the Syrian-Israeli negotiations.

In late 1995, once Syria and Israel had agreed to a 10-point framework, its representatives held talks at an American venue in early 1996. But, when suicide bombings by radical Islamist Palestinians killed 50 Israelis in late February–early March, Israeli Prime Minister Shimon Peres [*q.v.*] demanded that Syria condemn the attacks. Assad replied that these explosions had nothing to do with Syria. Peres unilaterally terminated the negotiations with Damascus. The talks remained suspended during the three years when Benjamin Netanyahu [*q.v.*] was Israel's prime minister. They resumed after the election of Ehud Barak [*q.v.*] as Netanyahu's successor. In September 1999, U.S. Secretary of State Madeleine Albright backed Assad's demand for total withdrawal from the Golan. Three months later Barak met Syrian foreign minister Faruq al-Shaara in Washington. In March 2000 U.S. President Bill Clinton presented Barak's proposals to Assad in Geneva. These included Israel's retaining sovereignty over a narrow strip on the northeastern shore of Lake Tiberias to safeguard its water resources. Assad offered to give Israel access to the strip but not sovereignty. The talks broke down. Elsewhere, in 1997 he began repairing his relations with Iraq.

In the 1999 presidential referendum, he secured 99.98 percent of the valid votes, a shade lower than the figure of 99.99 percent in the referendum of 1992. During the last days of his rule, marked by his failing health, he released 225 political prisoners. Overall, his long rule was marked by his consistency and tenacity. A distant and authoritarian personality, he combined realism with a cool, calculating disposition.

Assembly of Experts, Iran (1979):
After the proclamation of the Islamic Republic of Iran in April 1979, its leader, Ayatollah Ruhollah Khomeini [*q.v.*], decreed the election of a 73-member Assembly of Experts—each member representing about half a million people—to review the draft constitution prepared by the government. Elected in August on universal suffrage, the Assembly, consisting of religious and lay members, was dominated by the ruling Islamic Republican Party [*q.v.*]. It approved a constitution of 175 articles, which was ratified in a referendum in December 1979. Articles 107 and 108 empowered the clerical members of the Council of Guardians [*q.v.*] to decide the qualifications of the experts and the size of their assembly, which was authorized to choose the (supreme) leader or leadership council of three or five members.

Assembly of Experts, Iran (1983–):
Elections to the 82-strong Assembly of Experts, each representing about half a million people, were held in December 1982, with the Assembly convening in 1983. Only Muslim clerics were allowed to run for election. Seen as a permanent constitutional body, the Assembly met once or twice a year in Qom [*q.v.*], away from the glare of the media. In November 1985 one of its members, Ahmad Barikban, leaked its earlier decision to name Ayatollah Hussein Ali Montazeri [*q.v.*] as the future (supreme) Leader (Persian: *Rahbar*). But in early 1989 irreconcilable differences emerged between Montazeri and the (supreme) Leader, Ayatollah Ruhollah Khomeini [*q.v.*].

Montazeri resigned as the successor-designate in March. The Constitutional Review Council, which Khomeini appointed in April, was hard at work when Khomeini fell seriously ill and died on 3 June 1989. During an eight-hour session, the Assembly of Experts rejected the alternative of a (supreme) leadership council and instead voted President Ali Khamanei [q.v.] as the (supreme) Leader.

After Khamanei took office he decreed elections for a fresh Assembly of Experts, which was given tenure of eight years by the revised constitution. The new Assembly with an increased membership of 86 was elected in October 1990 and met in 1991. It elected Ayatollah Ali Mishkni its Chairman. It endorsed Khamanei as the Leader for eight years, and set up a sub-committee to monitor his performance. This sub-committee submits its confidential report to the Assembly which meets only twice a year.

On the eve of the election for the Fourth Assembly in October 1998, the Guardians Council [q.v.] ruled that a lay person could stand for election provided he was found to be an expert on Islam according to its test. However, no non-cleric passed this test.

The Fifth Assembly, elected in December 2006, met in February 2007. The voter turnout of 60 percent exceeded the previous figures. The Assembly reelected Mishkni as its Chairman. After his death in July, Ali Akbar Hashemi Rafsanjani [q.v.] succeeded him by defeating the hardliner Ayatollah Ahmad Jannati by 41 to 30 votes. Rafsanjani got reelected in March 2009 by defeating Ayatollah

Muhammad Yazdi, former chief justice, by 51 votes to 26.

In the aftermath of the protest about the alleged rigging of the presidential election in June, which led to the reelection of Mahmoud Ahmadinejad [q.v.], Rafsanjani reportedly consulted some Assembly member regarding convening an emergency session but did not find much support for the idea.

In March 2011, Rafsanjani did not offer his candidacy for chairmanship which went, unanimously, to 80-year-old Ayatollah Muhammad Reza Mahdavi-Kani, a leader of the conservative Association of Combatant Clergy [q.v.].

Association of Combatant Clergy

(Iran): (Persian: *Jame-e Ruhaniyat-e Mobarez-e*) Popularly known as *Jame*, its nucleus was formed in 1976 when the clerical followers of Ayatollah Ruhollah Khomeini [q.v.] began meeting clandestinely in Tehran [q.v.] to exchange socio-political information. It arranged the smuggling of Khaomein's speeches on cassettes from the Iraqi city of Najaf [q.v.] into Iran [q.v.]. Its founders included Ayatollahs Murtaza Motahhari (assassinated in 1979) and Muhammad Beheshti (assassinated in 1981) and Hojatalislams Ali Akbar Hashemi Rafsanjani [q.v.] and Ali Khamanei [q.v.]. As the Islamic revolutionary movement built up in 1977–78, it became more active and began gradually to surface. It played a vital role in establishing local Revolutionary Komitehs (Committees) [q.v.].

After the revolution it became the new order's main instrument to transform the traditional religious infrastructure into a religio-political apparatus of the state. As the political arm of the clergy, it actively backed the ruling Islamic Republican Party [*q.v.*] in elections and referendums. Since engaging in everyday politics had hitherto been seen by traditional clerics as an extremist activity, the Jame acquired an aura of radicalism. After Beheshti's assassination in 1981, Ayatollah Hussein Ali Montazeri [*q.v.*] became its leader. He took a radical stance on many issues. In 1982, when Montazeri stepped down due to pressure of work, its leadership went to Muhammad Reza Mahdavi-Kani. As a leading member of the Guardians Council [*q.v.*], he declared land reform and foreign trade nationalization bills to be un-Islamic, which alienated those who were committed to bringing about economic reform. They departed to form the Society of Combatant Clerics [*q.v.*] in 1988, leaving the Jame as a distinctly conservative body. In the subsequent parliamentary elections the Jame formed an alliance with other conservative organizations.

Assyrian Christians: *see* Nestorian Christians.

Aswan High Dam (Egypt): Successor to the Aswan Dam, the Aswan High Dam on the Nile is 1.24 mi./2 km long and 176 ft./30 m deep. It was the centerpiece of the economic plan of Egyptian President Gamal Abdul Nasser [*q.v.*], and was designed to transform the country's cotton-based economy into something more robust and varied by irrigating two million acres of land and boosting electric supplies several-fold. In February

1956 the World Bank for Reconstruction and Development (WBRD) agreed to lend Egypt $20 million if the United States and Britain provided it with credits of $70 million to meet the hard-currency costs of constructing the dam.

Ignoring warnings from Washington, Nasser continued to direct his foreign policies along a nonaligned path. In April 1956 he recognized the seven-year-old People's Republic of China, thus angering the United States, which wanted the new Communist republic to remain isolated. On 19 July the United States informed Egypt that it had decided against providing aid for the Aswan High Dam because it considered the Egyptian economy too fragile to support such an ambitious project. Britain followed suit. A week later, addressing a rally in Alexandria [*q.v.*], Nasser declared that the Universal Suez Maritime Canal Company [*q.v.*], headquartered in Paris, would be nationalized forthwith, and the management of the waterway would be assigned to an Egyptian Canal Authority, adding that foreign currency revenues from the Suez Canal [*q.v.*] would be used to finance the High Dam's construction.

The Soviet Union declared that nationalization of the Suez Canal was within Egypt's legal rights. It stepped in to buy Egyptian cotton, which accounted for 85 percent of the country's exports. It also signed an agreement with Egypt to provide the latter with low-interest loans, amounting to $130 million, and the services of 5,000 Soviet technicians. Construction work on the project started in 1960. By the time the Soviet leader,

Nikita Khrushchev, had inaugurated the first stage of the High Dam in May 1964, Egypt's electricity output had trebled. When its final phase was completed in January 1971, the Aswan High Dam had the capacity to hold back from the tail-end of the Nile's autumn flood some 5 billion cu m of water. Since then it has increased the irrigated farm land by almost 500 percent.

The resulting Lake Nasser, measuring 2,030 sq. mi./5,250 sq. km, became one of the largest reservoirs on the planet. It caused a fivefold increase in agricultural land. It produces 2.1 gigawatts of electricity, equaling the total capacity of Egypt's power plants before 1967, and enabling most villages to be electrified for the first time. Since then this proportion has come down to 15 percent.

Atef, Muhammad (1944–2001): (Also known as Abu Hafs, Abu Khadija, Tayseer Abdullah) Born Muhammad Sobhi abu Sitta in a poor, religious family in Menoufia, Egypt [*q.v.*], Atef grew up to be a tall man of 6'6" (1.98 m). A devout Muslim [*q.v.*], he trained as a police officer and rose through the ranks during the 1970s. He joined the clandestine al-Jihad group [*q.v.*] soon after its founding in 1978. When the expected Islamist insurrection against the government failed to materialize in the wake of the assassination of President Anwar Sadat [*q.v.*] in October 1981, he became restless.

In 1983 he went to Pakistan to participate in the jihad against the Soviets in Afghanistan. Here he came into close contact with Osama bin Laden [*q.v.*], who found his police background useful in training Arabic-speaking mujahedin. He was one of the founders of al-Qaida [*q.v.*], which emerged from *Maktab al-Khidmat* (Persian: *Bureau of Service* [to non-Afghan Mujahedin]), established in 1984. When bin Laden returned to Saudi Arabia [*q.v.*] in 1990, Atef stayed behind in Afghanistan.

The next year he joined bin Laden in Khartoum, Sudan, where al-Qaida began to function as an umbrella organization to coordinate the activities of extremist Islamist groups worldwide. He was a member of the policy-making Shura Council of 12, and head of the military committee. He acquired the *nom de guerre* of Abu Hafs (Arabic: *Father of lion*).

In 1992–1993, he supervised the military training of the tribes in neighboring Somalia opposed to the UN intervention there. He aided and abetted the attacks on the American troops within the UN force, as a consequence of which 18 American soldiers were killed while hunting for Somali warlord Muhammad Farah Aideed, and which left nearly 500 Somalis dead.

He accompanied bin Laden on his return to Afghanistan in 1996, and took charge of training fresh al-Qaida recruits in the camps run by the organization. After the suicide bombings of the U.S. embassies in Nairobi and Dar as Salam in August 1998, which killed 227 people, a U.S. federal grand jury returned a 238-count indictment (covering 227 murders and 11 other charges) against Atef and 16 others, charging them with leading a terrorist conspiracy from 1989 to present, working in concert with other terrorist groups to build weapons and attack American military installations. Washington announced $5 million reward for information leading to Atef's arrest.

In January 2001 he caught media attention with the video of the wedding of his daughter Khadija to Muhammad, 18-year-old son of Osama bin Laden. Following the terrorist attacks on the U.S. in September, Washington froze his assets along with those of 11 others.

Soon after the evacuation of Kabul by the Taliban on 12–13 November, Atef was killed in an air strike by U.S. warplanes.

Attasi, Nur al-Din (1929–92): *Syrian politician; president 1966–70* Born into a landlord family of the Attasi clan, based in the countryside around Homs [*q.v.*], Attasi acquired a medical degree from Damascus University in 1955. He joined the Baath Socialist Party [*q.v.*] as a youth. As a qualified doctor, he volunteered to work with the Algerian National Liberation Front. Following the Baathist coup of March 1963, he became a member of the ruling National Council for the Revolutionary Command. He was interior minister during 1963–64, then deputy prime minister during 1964–65.

In the internecine fighting within the Baath Party he sided with the radical Military Committee, which included Hafiz Assad [*q.v.*] and Salah Jadid [*q.v.*], both Alawis [*q.v.*]. After the Military Committee had captured power in February 1966, Assad and Jadid emerged as the real leaders. Aware that their Alawi origin was a political liability in a predominantly Sunni [*q.v.*] society, they used Attasi,

a Sunni, as a front man. He became president of Syria as well as the secretary-general of the regional (i.e., Syrian) and national (i.e., pan-Arab) high commands of the Baath Party. In 1968 he also headed the government. But his real authority was limited.

As rivalry between Assad and Jadid sharpened, he inclined toward Jadid. Following the first skirmish between the two contenders in February 1969, which showed Assad to be the stronger party, he retained his positions as part of a compromise. But when Assad finally won in November 1970 he dismissed Attasi as president, premier, and secretary-general of the Baath Party, and jailed him. His trial release 10 years later, when the Assad regime faced a severe Islamist challenge, ended when he failed to cooperate with the authorities. However, his subsequent house arrest soon ended when he agreed to refrain from politics.

Azerbaijan (Iran): The name Azerbaijan is derived from Atropates (Greek: *protected by fire*), a lieutenant of Alexander of Macedonia, who, following his commander's victory over the Persian Empire in 328 B.C., founded an independent kingdom in the region. In Iran today Azerbaijan embraces the provinces of East Azerbaijan (population, 4 million, 2011 est.) and West Azerbaijan (population, 3.3 million in 2011 est.). The Aras River separates Iranian Azerbaijan from the Trans-Caucasian Democratic Republic of Azerbaijan (DRA). It is a chiefly mountainous region with fertile lowlands.

Settled by the Medes before the eighth century B.C., it became a province of the Persian Empire. Its town of Orumiyeh was the reputed birthplace of Zoroaster, the founder of Zoroastrianism [q.v.]. After a long spell as an independent kingdom after 328 B.C., it again became part of the Persian Empire in the third century A.D. Following the victory of the Muslim Arabs [q.v.] over the Persians in 637 A.D., the region fell under the Islamic caliphate, and its population was converted to Islam [q.v.]. During the 11th–12th centuries it was ruled by the Seljuk Turks and in the 14th century by Tamerlane. From the early 17th to the early 19th century it was governed by the Persian shahs. In 1828, following his defeat by the Russians, the shah ceded all territory west of the Caspian Sea and north of the Aras River to Tsarist Russia. He organized the remainder as a province named Azerbaijan. In 1938 Reza Shah Pahlavi [q.v.] divided it into East Azerbaijan (capital, Orumiyeh) and West Azerbaijan (capital, Tabriz [q.v.]).

Following the entry of the Soviet Union into World War II in June 1941, its troops occupied these provinces of Iran, which was neutral in the conflict. In December 1945 the Democratic Party of Azerbaijan proclaimed the National Government of Azerbaijan, with Azeri [q.v.] as the official language. A year later, after the Soviet troops had withdrawn, this government surrendered to the Iranian troops sent by Tehran.

Both East and West Azerbaijan are populated primarily by Azeris [q.v.] who are largely Shia [q.v.], and secondarily by Kurds [q.v.] and Armenians [q.v.]. Like the majority Persian-speakers in Iran, they participated in the revolutionary movement that toppled Muhammad Reza Shah Pahlavi [q.v.] and ushered in an Islamic republic. Following the breakup of the Soviet Union in 1991, and the emergence of the Democratic Republic of Azerbaijan (DRA), contact between these provinces and the DRA increased sharply. However, predictions that, inspired by nationalism, the Azeris in Iran would secede and combine with the DRA to form Greater Azerbaijan proved ill-founded.

Azeri language: Also known as Azerbaijani language, it belongs to the southwest Turkic group of languages and is akin to Turkmen [q.v.] and modern Turkish of Turkey. Written in the Arabic script, it developed as a literary language in the first quarter of the 19th century. In Iran, during the rule of the Pahlavi dynasty (1921–79) [q.v.], its use was suppressed. Azeri-speaking Iranians make up about 17 percent of the national population. In the Soviet Republic of Azerbaijan (1920–91), the Arabic script used for Azeri was changed to Latin in 1922, and then to Cyrillic in 1939. After the founding of the Democratic Republic of Azerbaijan in 1992, the government decided to revert to Latin.

Azeris: Also known as Azeri-Turks, these Turkic people speak a language that is akin to modern Turkish. In Iran they are the predominant majority in the provinces of East and West Azerbaijan [q.v.], with a combined population of 6.5 million, according to the 2006 census.

al-Azhar University: (Arabic: *Resplendent*): *Islamic University in Cairo* Established in 977 A.D. in the al-Azhar mosque in Cairo [q.v.] by the Fatimid caliphate (969 A.D.–1171), the al-Azhar University is the oldest institution of its kind in the world, and the leading center for higher Islamic learning. It later became a model for European universities, based on the principle of combining a place of prayer with that of higher learning, and having students live on the premises. The gown worn by the teachers of classical universities of Europe today is a variation of the dress used by the religious teachers at the al-Azhar, who sat on chairs by a column while students squatted on the floor in front of them.

The traditional teaching practice continues, as does the stress on teaching the Sharia [q.v.], theology, and Arabic [q.v.]. The university imparts instruction in the four schools of Sunni Islam [q.v.]. In the last quarter of the 19th century philosophy was added to the curriculum.

But it was not until two years after President Gamal Abdul Nasser [q.v.] had nationalized the university that a major reform of the curriculum was carried out. As a result, several non-traditional disciplines such as social sciences were introduced, and a hospital and medical faculty added. A supplementary campus was set up at Nasr City. But even the non-religious faculties stress the study of Islam [q.v.].

Women were admitted in 1962, but they continue to be instructed separately from men. The university attracts students from all over the world. But it does not admit Shias [q.v.] as students despite the fact that it was established by a Fatimid caliph who was a Shia. In 2010, the al-Azhar's 12 colleges in Cairo, eight in Asyut and

20 more in other cities had 293,425 students on their rolls.

Its rector is recognized as the highest Islamic authority in Egypt. Following the 11 September 2001 attacks on the United States, its rector Muhammad Sayyid Tantaoui declared that their perpetrators were heretics.

After the ouster of President Hosni Mubarak [q.v.] in Februqary 2011, Shaikh Ismail Shaheen, deputy head of the al-Azhar University, called on the ruling Supreme Council of the Armed Forces (SCAF) to hand over authority to a civilian government. But a year later he opposed the call for civil disobedience and a general strike to compel the SCAF to do so immediately.

Aziz, Tariq (1936–): *Iraqi politician* Born Mikhail Yahunna of a Chaldean Catholic [q.v.] family in Mosul [q.v.], Aziz obtained a postgraduate degree from Baghdad University in the early 1950s. He joined the clandestine Baath Party [q.v.] soon after it was established in Iraq in 1950. After the overthrow of the monarchy in July 1958, he joined the *al-Jumhuriya* (Arabic: *the Republic*) as a journalist. Following the Baathist coup in March 1963 he became editor of the party's mouthpiece, *al-Jamahir* (Arabic: *the Peoples*). Despite the ups and downs experienced by the Baath Party during the next five years, he remained loyal to the party. When it seized power for the second time in July 1968 it was better organized and led. It established a daily newspaper, *al-Thawra* (Arabic: *the Revolution*), in 1969, and Aziz was appointed editor.

Like many other young party members, he was attracted to Saddam

Hussein [*q.v.*], the youthful leader. With Saddam's star rising, he moved closer to the center of power. In 1972 he was appointed to the highest ruling body, the Revolutionary Command Council. Two years later he was elected to the national (i.e., pan-Arab) high command of the Baath Party and was made minister of information. In 1977 he was elected to the regional (i.e., Iraqi) high command of the Baath, a position of greater import than a cabinet post. Saddam Hussein became president in July 1979 and appointed Aziz deputy prime minister. In April 1980 he was the target of an unsuccessful assassination attempt by Islamic militants. In January 1981 he took up the additional job of foreign minister.

During the Iran-Iraq War (1980–88) [*q.v.*] Tehran used Aziz's high office in Iraq as proof that the Iraqi regime was run by infidels. During the war he was active in maintaining cordial relations not only with the Soviet Union, the traditional ally of Iraq, but also with France and, from 1984 onwards, the United States. In the course of the Gulf crisis—triggered by the Iraqi invasion of Kuwait in August 1990 and culminating in a war between Iraq and the U.S.-led coalition in January 1991—he emerged as the chief spokesman and negotiator for Iraq in the media and around the negotiating table. His fluency in English and experience as foreign minister proved useful assets to President Saddam Hussein. In March 1991 he reverted to being deputy premier, and was Iraq's top negotiator in its dealings with the United Nations, including the UN Special Commission (Unscom) on disarming Iraq [*q.v.*].

His repeated efforts to have the United Nations lift sanctions against Iraq failed in the absence of a clean bill of health from Unscom, a precondition for ending the sanctions, as stated in the UN Security Council Resolution 687 of April 1991 [*q.v.*]. However, as the roving ambassador of Saddam Hussein, he succeeded in improving Iraq's relation with the rest of the Arab world as well as China, France, and Russia.

Following the Anglo-American invasion of Iraq in 2003 [*q.v.*], Aziz went underground, but soon surrendered to the occupying American authorities, who imprisoned him. They held him captive in Camp Cropper near the Baghdad airport.

In March 2009 the Iraqi High Tribunal found him guilty of crimes against humanity and sentenced him to 15 years in jail. In August the Tribunal sentenced him to seven years in prison for forcibly displacing Kurds. In January 2010 he suffered a stroke. Nine months later the Tribunal handed him capital punishment for persecuting the Islamic parties. But, with the Iraqi President Jalal Talabani [*q.v.*] refusing to sign the execution order, he remained imprisoned.

Azzam, Abdullah (1941-89): *Palestinian Islamist ideologue* Born in Jenin, Palestine [*q.v.*], Azzam and his parents fled to Jordan [*q.v.*] during the 1948–49 Arab-Israeli War [*q.v.*]. After graduating in Islamic theology from Damascus University in 1966, he fought in the June 1967 Arab-Israeli War [*q.v.*]. He then pursued further religious education at al-Azhar University [*q.v.*], and obtained a doctorate in *fiqh* [*q.v.*], Islamic jurisprudence, in

1973. After teaching the Sharia [*q.v.*] briefly at Jordan University, Amman [*q.v.*], he moved to Saudi Arabia to lecture at the King Abdul Aziz University in Jiddah [*q.v.*]. His taped lectures became popular among pious young Saudis such as Osama bin Laden [*q.v.*]. Azzam held that jihad [*q.v.*] was compulsory for a true Muslim, and that only by engaging in jihad would the faithful be able to revive the Islamic umma [*q.v.*] under a caliph as a prelude to restoring the glory of Islam [*q.v.*].

Attracted by the anti-Soviet jihad in Afghanistan that got going in 1980, Azzam traveled to Pakistan, where he became a lecturer in Islamic studies at Islamic University in Islamabad. Once the scheme of recruiting Arab [*q.v.*] volunteers for the jihad, called mujahedin, initiated by bin Laden, had become established in the early 1980s, he moved to Peshawar, the base of bin Laden. Later bin Laden, who treated Azzam as his mentor, extended this program to non-Arab Muslims [*q.v.*].

In 1984 Azzam set up the *Maktab al-Khidmat* (Persian: *Bureau of Service [to the Mujahedin]*) primarily as a reception center for the newly arrived recruits. During his worldwide travels to raise funds for the Maktab, he visited the al-Khifa Refugee Center in Brooklyn, N.Y.—in pursuance of the official U.S. policy of encouraging American Muslims to join the anti-Soviet jihad in Afghanistan—in 1987. By then the Maktab started providing social welfare to the widows and orphans of the non-Afghan mujahedin.

Once the Soviets withdrew completely from Afghanistan in February 1989, Azzam claimed victory for the jihad. Seven months later a car bomb killed him and his two sons as they were entering their mosque for the Friday prayer. This shattered bin Laden, who then resolved to continue running Maktab al-Khidmat under the new title of al-Qaida [*q.v.*] but with a more ambitious aim of creating an international network of those who had participated in the anti-Soviet jihad.

B

Baalbek: *Lebanese town* Population: 82,600 (2010 est.) Baalbeck is the site of an ancient city dedicated to the worship of Baal or Bel, the sun god, its name in Greek being Heliopolis, Sun City. Its recorded history goes back to the time when Alexander the Great (r. 336–323 B.C.) conquered Greater Syria [*q.v.*] in 332 B.C. After Alexander's death Baalbek came under the rule of the Ptolemies, Seleucids, and Romans, when it thrived. It became part of the Islamic caliphate in 637 A.D., and this continued under different dynasties until the dissolution of the Ottoman Empire in 1918. Major excavations around the turn of the 20th century revealed two Roman temple complexes: one dedicated to Jupiter, Venus, and Mercury; and the other to Bacchus.

Baath Party: *see* Baath Socialist Party.

Baath Socialist Party: *pan–Arab political party* Also known as Arab Baath Socialist Party, it emerged in March 1954 in Damascus [*q.v.*] from the amalgamation of the Arab Baath Party [*q.v.*] and the Arab Socialist

Party [*q.v.*]. The party's basic principles were unity and freedom of the Arab nation within its homeland, and a belief in the special mission of the Arab nation to end colonialism and promote humanitarianism. To achieve these ends, the party had to be nationalist, populist, socialist, and revolutionary. While the party rejected the concept of class conflict, it favored land reform; public ownership of natural resources, transport, large-scale industry, and financial institutions; trade unions of workers and peasants; the co-option of workers into management; and acceptance of non-exploitative private ownership and inheritance. It stood for a representative and constitutional form of government, and freedom of speech and association within the bounds of Arab nationalism [*q.v.*].

According to the Baath Socialist Party, Arabs [*q.v.*] formed a single nation currently divided into various regions (countries). Therefore, the party was headed by a National Command that covered the whole Arab world and served as the central executive authority. Under it were certain Regional Commands in those Arab states where the party was strong enough to justify the establishment of one. Below the Regional Commands were branches. These were composed of sections made up of divisions, each of which consisted of a few three-member cells. Until 1966 the National Command was based in Damascus. Following a split in it later that year, the breakaway group established itself first in Beirut [*q.v.*] and then, after the Baathist coup in Iraq in July 1968, in Baghdad [*q.v.*]. With the overthrow of the Baathist regime by the Anglo-

American troops in 2003, the party ceased to exist.

Baath Socialist Party (Iraq): The Baath Socialist Party in Iraq, which started secretly as the Arab Baath Party [*q.v.*] in 1950, had 208 members in 1954. It held its first (clandestine) regional congress in late 1955, when it decided to cooperate with other nationalist groups. It played only a marginal role in the anti-royalist military coup in 1958. Despite being suppressed by the new ruler, Abdul Karim Qasim [*q.v.*], the party expanded. By the time the Baathists, joined by non-Baathist sympathizers, overthrew Qasim in February 1963, the party had about 1,000 active members and 15,000 sympathizers. Once in power, Baathist leaders fell out among themselves, allowing the non-Baathist Abdul Salam Arif [*q.v.*] to usurp power in November.

The failure of Iraqi President Abdul Rahman Arif [*q.v.*] to participate fully in the June 1967 Arab-Israeli War [*q.v.*] was used by the Baathists to build up their popular support. In mid-July 1968 an alliance of Baathist leaders and non-Baathist military officers overthrew Arif, and a fortnight later the Baathists elbowed out the non-Baathist conspirators and seized total power. By then the party had 5,000 active members.

The governing five-member Revolutionary Command Council (RCC), headed by President Ahmad Hassan Bakr [*q.v.*], institutionalized the interweaving of the party with state institutions, and with secular society at large. The interim constitution of July 1970 formalized the party's supremacy by stating that the RCC, the highest state body, had the right to select its new members from the regional (i.e., national) leadership of the Baath. The party tightened its grip over the armed forces, police, and intelligence. Once Saddam Hussein [*q.v.*], who had earlier built up the party's militia, had acquired a seat on the RCC in November 1969, he busied himself with restructuring and strengthening the party. To broaden the popular base of the regime, the RCC sponsored the formation of the National Progressive and Patriotic Front [*q.v.*] in July 1973, with the Baath in the lead.

Iraq's war with Iran (1980–88) [*q.v.*] brought about a marked change in the Baath. In the name of increasing production, the importance of Baathist socialism was minimized and the private sector was encouraged to grow at the expense of the public sector. The concept of pan-Arabism [*q.v.*] was made subservient to the idea of Iraqi nationalism, which was used as the prime force to motivate citizens to join the war effort. During the Kuwait crisis of 1990–91 the party machine was put to full use to shore up support for the regime. After Iraq's defeat in the Second Gulf War (1991) [*q.v.*] that followed, the regime came to rely heavily on the loyalty and tenacity of the party's ranks and leaders. As UN economic sanctions against Iraq drastically lowered living standards, the government ensured the loyalty of party cadres by singling them out for economic perks. In the parliamentary elections of 1980, 1984, 1989, 1996, and 2000, the Baath won 183, 188, 138, 169, and 142 seats respectively out of 250. In 1996 and 2000, when Baghdad lacked control of the Kurdish Autonomous Region,

President Saddam Hussein nominated the 30 seats allocated to the region.

After the 2003 Gulf War [*q.v.*], the U.S.-led Coalition Provisional Authority (CPA) outlawed the Baath Party and sacked all its members employed in the public sector jobs after dissolving the security forces and intelligence services of Iraq. Its leaders went underground. Operating either at home or from abroad, they actively assisted or participated in resistance against foreign occupation. Many of the middle rank Iraqi Baathists took refuge in Syria where they made peace with their erstwhile rivals. The post-CPA government that followed from 2004 onward carried out a thoroughgoing de-Baathification of society.

Baath Socialist Party (Jordan): Jordan's Baath Socialist Party evolved out of the Arab Baath Party [*q.v.*], which, founded secretly in 1948, received a boost from the incorporation of the West Bank [*q.v.*] into the Hashemite Kingdom of Jordan in 1950. It was part of the nationalist-leftist alliance, led by Suleiman Nabulsi [*q.v.*], which emerged as the leading parliamentary group in the 1956 election. Its leaders and a large majority of its members came from the urban educated class, with teachers and students forming its backbone. Later, despite a ban on all political activity in 1957, the Baath continued to exist clandestinely. From 1958 to 1961 it was helped by the United Arab Republic (UAR) [*q.v.*] to mount anti-monarchist agitation. After the collapse of the UAR, the Syrian Baathists [*q.v.*] lent support to their Jordanian counterparts once they seized power in 1963. The loss of the

West Bank to Israel in the June 1967 Arab-Israeli War [*q.v.*] resulted in a dramatic weakening of the party in Jordan, from which it failed to recover.

Baath Socialist Party (Lebanon): Lebanon's Baath Socialist Party, which started as the Arab Baath Party [*q.v.*] in 1948, was hobbled by the enforcement of a law, passed in 1949, that banned parties linked to extraterritorial organizations. Yet in the tolerant climate created by the speedy end to the 1958 Lebanese Civil War [*q.v.*], the party was able to host the fourth national (i.e., pan-Arab) congress of the Baath Socialist Party in Beirut [*q.v.*] in 1959. It did so again in 1968 for the pro-Iraqi faction of the Baath. After the ban on groups with extraterritorial ties had been officially lifted in 1970, the party was able to function legally.

During the Lebanese Civil War [*q.v.*] from April 1975 onward Syria fostered its faction of the Lebanese Baath, which set up its own militia. In July 1987 it joined the Unification and Liberation Front of seven nationalist and progressive parties. Two years later the party, led by Abdullah Amin, joined the Lebanese National Front of 14 Lebanese and four Lebanon-based Palestinian groups with a program to scrap the confessional system, end the Israeli presence, and defeat the forces of Gen. Michel Aoun [*q.v.*]. In the national unity government, formed in December 1990, Amin was given a post. He continued to lead the pro-Syrian group.

As part of the 8 March Alliance [*q.v.*], the Baath Party won one seat in the 2005 general election and two in the 2009 election.

Baath Socialist Party (North Yemen): Pioneering Baath Socialist Party cells were formed in North Yemen in 1955–56. After the end of the Yemeni Civil War [*q.v.*] in 1970, North Yemen began to receive substantial aid from the Baath-ruled Iraq, and this enabled the Iraqi Baathists [*q.v.*] to foster the party in North Yemen. President Ibrahim Hamdi [*q.v.*] allowed centrist and leftist groups, such as the Baath, to function semi-clandestinely (while maintaining the official ban on political parties) to help him counterbalance the pro-Saudi conservatives. In 1976 the Baath Party merged with the Democratic Party of Popular Unity, a leftist group, and the Revolutionary Democratic Party, consisting of former members of the Arab Nationalist Movement [*q.v.*], to establish the National Democratic Front [*q.v.*].

Baath Socialist Party (South Yemen): The first Baath Socialist Party cells were formed in South Yemen in 1955–56. After independence in 1967 the party was free to function openly. With South Yemen becoming a recipient of aid from the Baathist government of Iraq, the Baath's future seemed assured. But later, as the ruling National Liberation Front [*q.v.*] proceeded with its plans to bring all parties under the umbrella of the United Political Organization-National Front as a prelude to forming the Yemeni Socialist Party [*q.v.*] in 1978, Baath leaders reluctantly dissolved the group.

Baath Socialist Party (Syria): Syria's Arab Baath Party [*q.v.*], an urban-based group, turned militant by absorbing the predominantly peasant membership of the Arab Socialist Party [*q.v.*] and becoming the Arab Baath Socialist Party [*q.v.*]. However, after the founding of the United Arab Republic (UAR) [*q.v.*] in 1958, UAR President Gamal Abdul Nasser [*q.v.*] suppressed the Baath in Syria. A coup by Syrian military officers against Nasser's regime in 1961 resulted in Syria seceding from the UAR. This ran counter to the Baath Party's pan-Arabism [*q.v.*].

After the party had captured power in March 1963 it became divided into two factions: an anti-Marxist, chiefly civilian wing headed by Michel Aflaq [*q.v.*], and a radical, primarily military wing led by Gen. Salah Jadid [*q.v.*]. The conflict between them was not resolved until early 1966 when the radicals seized total power and drove Aflaq into exile. What contributed greatly to their victory was the military support of Gen. Hafiz Assad [*q.v.*], the air force commander.

Following Syria's defeat in the June 1967 Arab-Israeli War [*q.v.*], once again two factions emerged within the party. The political wing, led by Jadid, stressed combining economic development with a people's war to liberate the occupied Golan Heights [*q.v.*]. The military faction, led by Assad, favored sticking with conventional warfare, and ending Syria's isolation by moderating its internal and external policies. Using his position as the defense minister, Assad curbed the political wing's influence in the military but he failed to wrest control of the party from the Jadid faction.

When, in September 1970, Assad refused to provide air support to the Palestine Liberation Organization [*q.v.*] in its fight with the Jordanian army, a schism developed in the party and the government. A fortnight-long congress of the party in Damascus in November failed to resolve the conflict. When the gathering ended Assad mounted a bloodless coup and arrested top party and military leaders. He then took measures to moderate the party's policies and leadership. In March 1972 he made it share power with other groups in the National Progressive Front (NPF) [*q.v.*].

Assad's intervention in the Lebanese Civil War [*q.v.*] in June 1976 on the side of the right-wing Maronites [*q.v.*] led to quiet rumblings in the Party. Aware of this, he tried to explain his stance to the nation. Aware too of the rising corruption within the party, Assad called a special congress in late 1979 to address the problem. It replaced two-thirds of the regional (i.e., national) command of the party, and appointed a commission to ensure that no party member used his position for personal gain. During the armed struggle by the opposition Muslim Brotherhood [*q.v.*] in 1980–82 the party rallied round the regime. When Assad sided with Saudi Arabia and America during the Kuwait crisis of 1990–91 there were murmurs of disapproval among party ranks. But these died down as Assad consolidated Syria's position in Lebanon after the end of the civil war there in October 1990. In the 1994 general election the Baath Party, a member of the National Progressive Front, gained less than half of the 250 parliamentary seats. In the 1998 parliamentary election the party won 135 seats.

Under the presidency of Bashar Assad [*q.v.*], the Baath Party secured

134 seats in the general election of 2003, followed by 135 four years later. Because of the political unrest that arose as part of the Arab Spring [*q.v.*], the parliamentary election due in May 2011 was postponed to February 2012. It took place in May and was held under the new constitution in which the Baath-led NPF no longer enjoyed monopoly on power. The new Parties Law gave citizens the right to establish a political party outside the NPF so long as it was not based on religion, ethnicity, or tribal affiliation. Three new parties were licensed, followed by the licensing of the opposition Popular Front for Change and Liberation (PFCL). The official turnout for the parliamentary election was 51 percent. As expected, the Baath Socialist Party retained 134 seats, with the PFCL scoring a derisory five seats.

During the rule of Bashar Assad, party membership, almost mandatory for securing a job in government or a public sector enterprise, rose from 1.7 million to nearly 2 million in the spring of 2011. As a result of the civil protest followed by an armed rebellion, leading to a substantial dislocation of the population and a decline in the GDP, the number of party members fell.

Baathism and Baathists: *see* Baath Socialist Party.

Babis: *religious sect* The origin of Babis goes back to 20 May 1844, the day when Ali Muhammad Shirazi (1819–1850)—a native of Shiraz [*q.v.*] who studied theology at the Shia [*q.v.*] centers of Najaf [*q.v.*] and Karbala [*q.v.*]—declared himself to be the *bab*

(gate) to the Hidden Imam, the last of the 12 Imams of Twelver Shias [*q.v.*]. In his sermons he advanced a progressive concept of prophets, arguing that each prophet brought a new message superseding the previous one. Proclaiming himself a prophet, he published a new scripture, *Bayan* (Persian: *Declaration*), which contained laws superseding many in the Quran [*q.v.*]. This turned Muslim [*q.v.*] clergy against him. His followers, Babis, broke away from Islam [*q.v.*] in 1848. He was executed on 9 July 1850 in Tabriz [*q.v.*] for challenging a basic Islamic tenet that Muhammad was the last prophet of Allah. During the next few years the Iranian government suppressed the Babi movement, which later evolved into the Bahai movement [*q.v.*].

Babylon: *Iraqi town* Population: 25,000 (2010 est.); Greek variant of Babilu, Akkadian, meaning Gateway of gods. One of the oldest places in the world and a leading city in ancient times, Babylon—situated by the Euphrates River [*q.v.*], which has since changed course—was the capital of Babylonia nearly four millenniums ago during the reign of Hammurabi (1792–50 B.C.), and retained that position for about a thousand years. Most of its ruins—situated near the Iraqi town of Hilleh and first excavated by German archeologists from 1899 to 1914—have been restored to an approximation of what existed at the height of the city's prosperity under King Nebuchadnezzar (r. 605–562 B.C.). At that time it was the planet's largest settlement, covering 2500 acres/1000 hectares.

To immortalize himself Nebuchadnezzar ordered that each of the bricks laid to erect temples and such other buildings as the Ishtar Gate, the Temple of Marduk, the ziggurat, popularly called the Tower of Babel, which was the city's name in Arabic [*q.v.*] and Hebrew [*q.v.*], should carry the following words in cuneiform writing: "Nebuchadnezzar, King of Babylonia, son of Nabopolassar, King of Babylonia, am I." After it fell to the Persians under Cyrus the Great in 539 B.C., it continued to be the leading city of the world. It surrendered to Alexander of Macedonia in 331 B.C.; and it was here, his planned capital, that he died eight years later in Nebuchadnezzar's palace.

Reconstruction of the ancient city began during the presidency of Saddam Hussein [*q.v.*], and included the 26-centuries-old Lion of Babylon, a black rock sculpture. Many of the newly baked bricks carried the inscription: "Built by Saddam Hussein son of Nebuchadnezzar to glorify Iraq." After the 1991 Gulf War [*q.v.*], a presidential palace was constructed atop a neighboring hill. A plan to build a cable car line over Babylon was interrupted by the Anglo-American invasion of Iraq [*q.v.*] in 2003. The occupying American forces built a military base, leveling sections of the ancient site to build a landing area for helicopters and parking lots for heavy vehicles. Also, in the chaos that followed the invasion, some antiquities were lost due to looting. It was only in May 2009 that the restored Babylon was opened to tourists again.

al-Badr, Muhammad (1926–96): *ruler of North Yemen, 1962* As the eldest son of Imam Ahmad ibn Yahya [*q.v.*], Badr assisted his father in administer-

ing North Yemen and fulfilling specific assignments. In 1955, when Imam Ahmad faced an armed revolt by two of his brothers, Badr mobilized the Bakil and Hashid tribal confederations and saved his father's throne. He was named crown prince. He encouraged his father to sign a friendship and trade treaty with the Soviet Union. In 1956 he undertook a tour of the Soviet bloc countries, and this led to a series of friendship and commercial agreements between North Yemen and several Communist states. During his father's trip abroad for medical treatment in 1960, Badr introduced some of the reforms promised by him, only to see them rescinded on his father's return.

After succeeding his father on 18 September 1962, Badr tried to reduce growing opposition by granting an immediate amnesty to political detainees. But eight days later the commander of the royal guard, Brigadier-General Abdullah Sallal [*q.v.*], staged a coup against him. He managed to flee to the north where he rallied the tribes against the new regime in Sanaa [*q.v.*]. The resulting civil war [*q.v.*] lasted until 1970. Since the rapprochement between the royalist and republican camps, brokered by Saudi Arabia, was based on the acceptance of a republic in North Yemen, Badr went into self-exile in Britain.

Baghdad: *capital of Iraq* Population: 6.15 million (2011 est.). Baghdad is a derivative of the Persian [*q.v.*] compound Bag "garden" + dad "given," meaning "Given garden." Situated by the Tigris River [*q.v.*], Baghdad has attracted traders and travelers since the Sumerian age (ca fifth millennium B.C.). Its recorded history, however, dates back to 763 A.D., when it was founded by the second Abbasid caliph, Mansour (r. 754–75 A.D.), who made it his capital. It reached its pinnacle of prosperity as a commercial center under Caliph Haroon al-Rashid (r. 786–809 A.D.), a condition well captured in many episodes of the classic *The Thousand and One Nights*. The city suffered a setback in 836 A.D. when the Abbasid capital was moved to Samarra [*q.v.*]. This lasted until 892 A.D. Baghdad suffered severely from the invasion of the Mongols in 1258, which ended the Abbasid rule. It faced a similar fate twice more—in 1400 under Tamerlane and in 1524 under Shah Ismail of Persia. When it came under Ottoman suzerainty in 1638 its population was less than 15,000.

After the collapse of the Ottoman Empire in 1918, and the subsequent creation of Iraq by the amalgamation of Mesopotamia [*q.v.*] and the province of Mosul [*q.v.*], Baghdad was made the Iraqi capital. Since then the petroleum wealth of the country has had an invigorating effect on the city. Besides commerce, it developed industry, transport, and financial services. Funded by a dramatic rise in oil revenues in the mid-1970s, modernization gathered pace. During the Iran-Iraq War (1980–88) [*q.v.*], Baghdad was an intermittent target of Iranian aerial bombing and ground-to-ground missile attacks. During the six-week Second Gulf War (1990–91) [*q.v.*], it suffered considerable damage. Most was repaired within a decade.

A more extensive destruction came during the Anglo-American invasion of 2003 [*q.v.*], due to the continuous aerial attacks on the city, followed by the arson and looting of almost all public buildings by mobs. Due to the intersectarian violence between Sunnis [*q.v.*] and Shias [*q.v.*], which reached a peak in 2007, concrete walls were built to separate neighborhoods. Since then the security situation has improved.

Among its tourist offerings are the Mustansiriya Law College and the Abbasid Palace, built in the second quarter of the 13th century, and the Museum of Antiquities with its unique collection of relics from the Mesopotamian civilization.

Baghdad Pact (1955): *see* Central Treaty Organization

Bahais: *religious faith* The founder of the Bahai faith was Hussein Ali (1817–1892), a Shia [*q.v.*] native of Tehran [*q.v.*] and half-brother of Sobh-e Azal, the chosen successor of Ali Muhammad Shirazi, the founder of Babism [*q.v.*]. A few years after Shirazi's execution in 1850, Hussein Ali became the leader of the exiled Babi community of Baghdad [*q.v.*]. In 1863 he declared himself Baha Ullah/Bahaollah (Arabic: *Glory of Allah*), a manifestation of God, whose arrival had been predicted by his predecessor, Shirazi, the Bab. As almost all Babis followed Baha Ullah, they came to be called Bahais.

Baha Ullah authored major works, including *The Most Holy Book* and *The Book of Certitude*, setting out the laws and explaining the nature of God and religion, as well as numerous meditations, prayers, sermons, and letters. His eldest son, Abdul Baha (1844–1921), buried in Haifa [*q.v.*], is regarded by Bahais to be the infallible interpreter of Baha Ullah's teachings.

By the time of Baha Ullah's death in 1892 in Acre [q.v.], Bahaism had evolved as a pacifist faith without clergy, its beliefs including unity of all religions, equality of sexes, and spartan living. Its temples are open to people of all religions, and Bahais are encouraged to open temples and build schools, hospitals, and orphanages around them. Bahaism requires its followers to be monogamous, fast for 19 days in a year, and offer daily prayers. The Bahai community governs itself through elected bodies, starting at the local level and graduating to the global, with the Universal House of Justice, based in Haifa, at the top, administering the Bahai commonwealth. The Bahai calendar, which commences on the day of the spring equinox, consists of 19 months with 19 days each, plus four intercalary days.

Among other things, Baha Ullah said that a religion continuously evolves. Since this ran counter to the traditional view of Islam [q.v.] as the last, most perfect, revealed Word of Allah, transcribed as the Quran [q.v.], the clergy in Iran declared Bahaism heretical. Nonetheless it attracted an increasing number of followers. Responding to a campaign against them in the early 1930s, Reza Shah Pahlavi [q.v.] closed down Bahai schools. During the anti-Bahai campaign in 1955 Tehran's governor personally seized the local Bahai spiritual center. But the Shah resisted demands to outlaw Bahaism and purge the government of Bahais, estimated to be 10,000 to one million strong. When the Universal House of Justice in Haifa complained to the United Nations on human rights grounds, the Iranian representative at the UN claimed there were no Bahais in Iran. Yielding to the pressure of the Islamic revolutionary movement (1977–78), Muhammad Reza Shah Pahlavi [q.v.] forced his court minister, Amir Abbas Hoveida [q.v.], to resign, and dismissed his own Bahai physician as well as four Bahai generals.

After the founding of the Islamic republic in Iran in 1979, Bahais faced persecution and closure of their temples. Most of them left, and those who remained limited themselves to prayers at home. In 2010, there were an estimated 300,000 Bahais.

Outside the Middle East, Bahai centers exist in the United States, Germany, India, Uganda, Australia, and Panama. According to the Bahai World Center, in 2010 there were 7.7 million Bahais globally, with 1.8 million in India.

Bahain:

OFFICIAL NAME: Kingdom of Bahrain

CAPITAL: Manama [q.v.]

AREA: 273 sq. mi./707 sq. km

POPULATION: 1,234,571 (2011 census): Citizens 47.5 percent; Noncitizens 52.5 percent.

GROSS DOMESTIC PRODUCT (nominal): U.S. $26.484 billion (2011 est.); per capita, $23,465

GROSS DOMESTIC PRODUCT (Purchasing Power Parity): U.S. $31 billion (2011 est.); per capita, $27,000

NATIONAL CURRENCY: Bahraini Dinar (BHD) 1 BHD=U.S. $2.65 = £1.68 = € 2.01 (2011)

FORM OF GOVERNMENT: constitutional monarchy; cabinet nominated by the ruler.

OFFICIAL LANGUAGE: Arabic [*q.v.*]

OFFICIAL RELIGION: Islam [*q.v.*]

ADMINISTRATIVE REGIONS: Bahrain is divided into five governorates.

CONSTITUTION: The ruler of Bahrain became a sovereign in August 1971 with the abrogation of Bahrain's 1892 treaty with Britain, allowing the latter to conduct its external affairs and defense. The constitution, drafted by a partly elected constituent assembly, specified a National Assembly of 42, with 30 deputies to be elected on a limited franchise. The first Assembly, elected in December 1973, was dissolved in August 1975 and the constitution suspended. A quarter-century later, the Supreme National Committee (SNC) appointed by the ruler, recommended a transition to a two-chamber parliament with four-year tenure—to be called the National Assembly—consisting of the 40-member lower house of the Council of Representatives (Arabic: *Majlis an Nuwab*) elected on universal suffrage, and the 40-member upper house of the Consultative Council (Arabic*: Majlis al-Shura*), nominated by the ruler. In legislative terms, the two chambers were a par. But a joint session of the National Assembly was to be chaired by the speaker of the Consultative Council. The SNC's proposal was endorsed by a popular referendum in February 2001, and a new constitution was promulgated in 2002.

CONSULTATIVE COUNCIL: Established in 1992, the fully nominated Consultative Council, with tenure of four years, was an advisory body, lacking legislative powers. Its initial size of 30 members was raised to 40 in the new constitution of 2002.

ETHNIC COMPOSITION: (2011) Bahraini and other Arabs 51.4 percent, Asians 45.6 percent, other 3 percent.

EXECUTIVE AUTHORITY: Executive authority rests with the ruler, called the Emir. As head of a council of ministers appointed by the Emir, the prime minister is in charge of running the day-to-day administration. Four-fifths of the 25-strong cabinet belongs to the ruling family.

High officials:

Head of state Shaikh Hamad ibn Isa II al-Khalifa, [*q.v.*] 1999–

Crown prince Shaikh Salman ibn Hamad al-Khalifa, [*q.v.*] 1999–

Prime minister: Shaikh Khalifa ibn Salman al-Khalifa, 1971 –

Speaker of the Consultative Council: Ali bin Saleh al-Saleh, 2010–

President of the Council of Representatives: Khalifa bin Ahmad al-Dhahrani, 2010–

HISTORY (SINCE CA 1900): The al-Khalifa dynasty, which has ruled the 33-island archipelago of Bahrain since 1783, signed a series of treaties with Britain in 1861, 1880, and 1892, turning Bahrain into a British protectorate and the base of British residency in the Persian Gulf [*q.v.*]. In 1932 Bahrain became the first Gulf territory to discover oil. The oil workers' efforts to gain trade union rights in the late 1930s failed.

Bahrainis showed their rising political consciousness by staging anti-British demonstrations during the 1956 Suez War [*q.v.*], when Britain, France, and Israel together attacked Egypt. After the accession of Shaikh Isa II al-Khalifa [*q.v.*] in 1961 there were demonstrations for political reform. But this protest and an oil workers' strike in 1965 were in vain. It was not until 1970 that the ruler compromised by appointing a 12-member advisory Council of State. As the British prepared to leave in 1971, he transformed the council into a cabinet and charged it with framing a constitution.

Britain transferred its Royal Navy base HMS *Juffiar* in Manama to the Pentagon after the ruler had agreed to lease it to the United States. The Pentagon renamed the facility as first the Administrative Support Unit Bahrain, and then the Naval Support Activity Bahrain. In the coming decades it would become home to the U.S. Naval Forces Central Command and the U.S. Fifth Fleet, and the primary base in the region for the naval and marine activities in support of Washington's wars in Iraq and Afghanistan.

Severe rioting and strikes in March and September 1972 led Shaikh Isa to concede a 42-member constituent assembly, half-elected and half-nominated, to draft a constitution. These elections were held on a limited franchise in December 1972. The constituent assembly submitted a constitution to the Emir in June 1973. He approved it. Elections to the National Assembly were held on a limited franchise in December, but the Emir dissolved the parliament and suspended the constitution in August 1975.

With 70 percent of its nationals being Shia [*q.v.*], Bahrain was most affected by the Islamic revolution in Shia-majority Iran in 1979. When the Islamic opposition demanded that Bahrain be declared an Islamic republic, Shaikh Isa II, a Sunni [*q.v.*], reacted with a heavy hand. In 1981

Bahrain became a founder-member of the Gulf Cooperation Council [*q.v.*]. Early the next year the government arrested 60 people on the charge of plotting a coup. In the Iran-Iraq War [*q.v.*] Bahrain sided with Iraq. During the Kuwait crisis (1990–91) Bahrain took a firm pro-Kuwaiti line.

After the 1991 Gulf War [*q.v.*], Bahrain signed a 10-year defense agreement with the U.S. Domestically, to meet the rising demand for reform, the Emir appointed a 30-member advisory council in late 1992 which held its inaugural session in January 1993. This proved insufficient, and in December 1994 widespread anti-regime demonstrations broke out, with protestors belonging to liberal, leftist, and Islamist factions calling for the restoration of the dissolved parliament. Government repression followed, but violent protest, inspired partly by the Islamic Liberation Front of Bahrain and the London-based Bahrain Freedom Movement, revived in March, leading to large-scale arrests and curfews. By April 1995 the disturbances and the state action had led to the deaths of 16 people and 1,600 arrests. In July the ruler agreed to let Washington base its Fifth Fleet in Bahrain.

His decision in September 1996 to enlarge the Consultative Council, and let half of its 40 members be elected indirectly through professional and cultural organizations, did not satisfy the opposition demanding a return to the 1973 constitution. The number of people killed in arson attacks and bombings rose to 30. In 1998 the State Security Court imposed heavy sentences on convicted political dissidents.

The situation changed in March 1999 when Crown Prince Shaikh Hamad became the ruler after the death of his father. He lifted the 25-year-old state of emergency, reshuffled the cabinet, and released over 300 political detainees. When, in July, the State Security Court sentenced the leading oppositionist, Shaikh Abdul Amir al-Jamri, to 10 years' imprisonment, the new ruler pardoned him. But, in December, while promising to hold local elections on the basis of universal suffrage, he failed to mention the timetable.

A year later, the Supreme National Committee, appointed by him, drafted a National Action Charter, which recommended a constitutional monarchy and a bicameral parliament. A referendum, held in February 2001, endorsed the National Action Charter. Shaikh Hamad declared Bahrain to be a constitutional monarchy. During that year, Shaikh Hamad renewed the defense agreement with the U.S. for 10 years. In 2002, he secretly extended that agreement by another five years, a fact that became known only in September 2011.

In the 2002 election to the 40-member Council of Representatives, boycotted by the main opposition groups, 21 seats were won by secularists or moderate Islamists [q.v.] or pro-government independents. The participation of the religious parties in the 2006 general election altered the political environment. Due to its close links with the Ulema Council of the Shia school, al-Wefaq won 17 of the 18 seats it ran for. On the Sunni side their two parties together garnered 13 seats. So three-quarters of the 40 elected members of parliament (MPs)

belonged to religious parties. With that the influence of clerics in politics rose. The most prominent among them was Shaikh Isa Qasim, who had returned from exile in Iran in 1990. He became the spiritual guide of al-Wefaq and the leading authority on such issues as codification of personal law and participating in or boycotting elections.

In 2008, Bahrain was named the world's fastest growing financial center by the City of London's Global Financial Centers Index. Bahrain's banking and financial services sector, particularly Islamic banking, have benefited from the regional boom.

Starting in late 2009, Shias in rural areas staged regular protests, demanding the release of dozens of political prisoners. Inspired by the events of the Arab Spring [q.v.] in Tunisia and Egypt, from 14 February 2011 onward Shias started demonstrating against discrimination in housing, education, and employment, and their exclusion from command positions in the military and security forces. King Hamad responded with a crackdown in which 30 demonstrators were killed. After bloody clashes, protestors occupied the Pearl Square, where they stayed in tents. In mid-March the monarch declared a state of emergency, which empowered the security forces to dissolve any organization they considered a danger to the state. With the direct involvement of 1,100 Saudi soldiers, the monarch crushed the protest, with the security forces demolishing the 300-ft. sculpture topped by a giant pearl at the center of the Pearl Square. Over 1,400 people were arrested and more than 4,000 were sacked from their jobs. The National Security Courts handed out stiff jail sentences to protestors. The U.S. issued tempered criticisms of the crackdown but did not press for political reform. On 1 June the ruler lifted the state of emergency.

He appointed a five-member Bahrain Independent Commission of Inquiry (BICI) of internationally reputed jurists and legal experts. In its report in November it concluded that the government had used excessive force and that there were many instances of torture of the detainees. It recommended reorganization of the National Security Agency (NSA). A subsequent royal decree termed the NSA an intelligence-gathering agency without powers of law enforcement and arrest.

In January 2012 King Hamad announced amending the constitution to authorize the Parliament to approve cabinets proposed by him and to question and remove cabinet ministers. The opposition leaders said Parliament would still not have the power to question or dismiss Prime Minister Shaikh Khalifa ibn Salman al-Khalifa, who had been in office since 1971. Overall, in their view, the amendments did not meet the aspirations of the people who took to the streets periodically for months to demand democratic transformation.

LEGISLATURE: With the introduction in 2002 of a bicameral National Assembly—the elected lower house called Council of Representatives and the fully-appointed Consultative Council on a par with it—the legislative powers reverted to it. Four major opposition parties, religious and secular, boycotted the 2002 election because they objected to the ruler placing the fully nominated Consultative Council on a par with the Council of Representatives. In that election a majority of the seats went to pro-government, liberal, and leftist members.

On the eve of the 2006 election, al-Wefaq National Islamic Society, a Shia [q.v.] Islamist group and al-Amal al-Islami, a radical Shia Islamist faction, formed an alliance. This led two Sunni [q.v.] Islamist groups—the Salafi [q.v.] al-Asalah (Arabic: *of noble descent*) and al-Minbar Islamic Society—to follow suit. Also, the leftist National Democratic Action, known as Waad, ended its boycott. The voter turnout was 72 percent, far above the 56 percent for the 2002 election. The result was: al-Wefaq National Islamic Society, 17; al-Minbar, 7; al-Asalah, 6; National Democratic, 1; pro-government, 9. With one exception, all the sitting liberal and leftist members lost their seats. (al-Wefaq, led by Shaikh Ali Salman, is also known as the Islamic National Accord Association.) The result of the general election held in October 2010 was: al-Wefaq National Islamic Society, 18; al-Asalah, 3; al-Minbar Islamic Society, 2; and Independents, 17.

Following the killing of seven protestors demanding political reform in demonstrations starting on 14 February 2011, the 18 Wefaq members resigned their parliamentary seats. When elections to these 18 seats were held in September–October, Wefaq boycotted the election. Four seats were uncontested. For the remaining 14 seats, the voter turnout was 17 percent, and these were won by pro-government candidates.

RELIGIOUS COMPOSITION (2011 est.): Muslim, 81 percent; Christian, 9 percent; Hindu, 9 percent; other, 1 percent.

Bahrain Freedom Movement:

Bahraini opposition group known in Arabic as Movement for Free Islamic Bahrain (Arabic, *Harkat al-Ahrar al-Bahrain al-Islamiya*) Based in London, the Bahrain Freedom Movement (BFM) actively helped trigger and sustain Bahrain's five-year-long intifada (1994–99) which was backed by the country's liberals, leftists, and Islamists [*q.v.*]. They demanded that the suspended 1973 constitution be restored and its elected parliament revived. The Bahrain Freedom Movement was led by Saeed Shehabi, a member of Bahrain's al-Wefaq Islamic National Society [*q.v.*]. Following political reform by King Hamad [*q.v.*] after his accession, which resulted in amnesty to opposition activists, many BFM members returned home. Among those who did not was Shehabi. He resigned from al-Wefaq when it decided to participate in the 2006 general election. The BFM maintains the Voice of Bahrain website, which was blocked for several years by the Bahraini government.

Bahrain National Liberation Front: *see* Popular Bloc (Bahrain).

Bakdash, Khalid (1912–95): *Syrian politician* Born into a Kurdish [*q.v.*] family in Damascus [*q.v.*], Bakdash obtained a law degree at Damascus University. Politically active while in his teens, he became the secretary-general of the Communist Party of Syria and Lebanon [*q.v.*] in 1936. He was jailed by the French Mandate. On his release he traveled to Moscow and enrolled at the Communist International College. After Syrian independence in 1946 he returned to Damascus. By the early 1950s he and Akram Hourani were acknowledged to be among the country's most able politicians. In 1954 he gained a seat in parliament, and became the first parliamentary deputy in the Arab world elected based on universal suffrage.

During the preliminary talks between Egypt and Syria on unity in 1957, Bakdash proposed a federal tie. When this was rejected, he and other Communist leaders, anticipating the dissolution of all political parties in Syria, went into self-exile in Prague, Czechoslovakia. He called for Syria's secession from the United Arab Republic [*q.v.*]. But when this happened in September 1961 the new Syrian rulers refused to allow him or any other Communist leader to return home. The Baathists [*q.v.*], who seized power in March 1963, maintained a similar stance, although the radical Baathists' victory in February 1966 changed the situation somewhat. When Bakdash returned to Damascus in the autumn the regime reluctantly accepted his presence on the condition that he would not hold meetings or make speeches.

In 1968 he was replaced as secretary-general of the Communist Party of Syria [*q.v.*]. Four years later President Hafiz Assad [*q.v.*] implemented Bakdash's proposal to create a broad-based National Progressive Front [*q.v.*]. With his election as the party's secretary-general in 1974, he resumed his position as the Arab world's most senior Communist leader. In 1986, he disagreed with the deputy general secretary Yusuf Faisal when the latter backed the reformist policies of Mikhail Gorbachev, the first secretary of the Communist Party of the Soviet Union. Faisal left to lead a breakaway Communist Party.

After Bakdash's death his widow, Wisal Farha, was elected the main party's general secretary.

Bakhtiar, Shahpur (1914–91): *Iranian politician; prime minister, 1979* Born into a family belonging to the powerful Bakhtiari tribe, Bakhtiar finished his higher education at Paris University in 1940 with a doctorate in international law and political science. He enrolled in the French army to fight Nazi Germany. On returning to Iran in 1946 he took up a job with the Labor ministry and served for two years. He joined the Iran Party, a secular nationalist group, which in 1949 combined with two other organizations to form the National Front [*q.v.*], led by Muhammad Mussadiq [*q.v.*]. He became deputy minister of Labor in the Mussadiq government from 1951 to 1952.

After the downfall of Mussadiq in August 1953 and the suspension of normal political activity, Bakhtiar turned to practicing law. This brought him into conflict with the regime, especially after the establishment of the secret police, Savak, in 1957. He was detained briefly in 1961.

As the anti-government protest gathered pace in the autumn of 1977, he and Karim Sanjabi, another lawyer, revived the National Front. Rattled by the rising revolutionary movement, Muhammad Reza Shah Pahlavi [*q.v.*], anxious to co-opt a politician not associated with his regime but acceptable to the United States, turned to Bakhtiar. On 29 December 1978 he agreed to form a government on the (unwritten) condition that the Shah would go abroad for holiday and that on his return he would act as a constitutional monarch. He tried to reach a compromise with Ayatollah Ruhollah Khomeini [*q.v.*], then in Paris, but the latter declared his government illegal. To gain popular support, Bakhtiar released all political prisoners and promised to disband Savak. But he failed in his gamble, and the National Front expelled him. When on 11 February 1979 military leaders declared themselves neutral in the standoff between Bakhtiar and Khomeini, now heading a parallel government in Iran, he went underground before escaping to Paris.

He was the mastermind behind a failed coup attempt in July 1980 against the Islamic regime in Iran. He then cooperated with Iraqi President Saddam Hussein [*q.v.*] as the latter prepared for an invasion of Iran in September. He founded the monarchist National Resistance Movement in 1982, and remained a loyal supporter of the young pretender, Reza Cyrus Pahlavi. After an unsuccessful attempt on his life in 1980, Bakhtiar was given official protection by the French government. Despite this, he and his male secretary were assassinated in August 1991. One of the assassins, Ali Vakili Rad, was arrested in Switzerland in 1992, tried in France, and sentenced to life imprisonment in 1994. He was freed in 2010 in exchange for the release of Clotilde Reiss, a French researcher, arrested a year earlier in Tehran [*q.v.*] on charges of spying.

Bakr, Ahmad Hassan (1912–82): *Iraqi officer and politician; president, 1968–79* Born into the al-Tikriti clan from Tikrit, Bakr enrolled into the army in 1938 and graduated from the Baghdad Military Academy four years later.

He secretly joined the Baath Party [*q.v.*] in 1956 when he was a colonel. He was a leader of the Free Officers Organization, which staged the republican coup in July 1958. A pan-Arabist [*q.v.*], he wanted a union between Iraq and Egypt and sided with Abdul Salam Arif [*q.v.*] against Abdul Karim Qasim [*q.v.*]. With Qasim emerging as the sole leader, Bakr lost his army post. He played an important part in the Baathist coup against Qasim in February 1963 and became prime minister, securing a promotion to major-general. At the sixth national congress of the Baath Party in October, he was elected to the national command. After the dismissal of his Baathist government by President Abdul Salam Arif in November, he continued as deputy premier for a few months.

His elevation to secretary-general of the Baath regional command in 1965 ended the internecine party divisions. This allowed the party and its military adherents to concentrate on regaining power. In mid-July 1968 Bakr headed the group of Baathist and non-Baathist officers that overthrew President Abdul Rahman Arif [*q.v.*] and made him president. A fortnight later he ousted his erstwhile non-Baathist ally, Premier Colonel Abdul Razzaq Nayif. Besides being the new prime minister, Bakr was chairman of the ruling Revolutionary Command Council (RCC) and the military chief of staff. In 1969 he became field-marshal.

In conjunction with Saddam Hussein [*q.v.*], a close relative, he focused on widening his power base in the officer corps. In the internecine party divisions, he tried to play a mediating role which, given his seniority, suited

him. He reached an accord with rebellious Kurds [*q.v.*] in 1970, and three years later he inaugurated a broad-based National Progressive and Patriotic Front [*q.v.*]. But his strategy for countering the growing discontent among Shias [*q.v.*] by conciliating Shia dissidents and adjusting party ideology to the rising tide of Islamic revival did not prevail. Saddam Hussein, the rising star, overruled it.

The sudden move by Egyptian President Anwar Sadat [*q.v.*] in late 1977 to make unilateral peace with Israel led the regimes of Bakr and President Hafiz Assad [*q.v.*] of Syria to bury the hatchet. A visit by Assad to Baghdad [*q.v.*] in October 1978 set the scene for the unification of their republics. Sensing that Saddam Hussein was not genuinely interested in a union, Bakr sent a secret message to Assad during his visit to Baghdad in mid-June 1979 to expedite the unity negotiations. Informed of Bakr's move, Saddam Hussein acted against him swiftly. A month later, on the eve of the 11th anniversary of the Baathist revolution, Saddam Hussein secured Bakr's resignation from all his governmental and party posts on "health grounds." He spent his last years under house arrest in ignominy.

Balfour Declaration (1917): Balfour Declaration is the title given to an important policy statement on Palestine [*q.v.*] by Britain in November 1917 in the form of a letter from the British foreign secretary, Arthur James (later Lord) Balfour, in the coalition government of Prime Minister David Lloyd George, to a prominent British Zionist [*q.v.*] leader, Lord Rothschild (born Lionel Walter):

Foreign Office
2nd November 1917
Dear Lord Rothschild:

I have much pleasure in conveying to you on behalf of His Majesty's Government the following declaration of our sympathy with Jewish Zionist aspirations which has been submitted to, and approved by, the Cabinet. "His Majesty's Government view with favor the establishment in Palestine of a National Home for the Jewish people, and will use their best endeavors to facilitate the achievement of this object, it being clearly understood that nothing shall be done which may prejudice the civil and religious rights of existing non-Jewish communities in Palestine, or the rights and political status enjoyed by Jews in any other country." I should be grateful if you would bring this declaration to the knowledge of the Zionist Federation.

Yours sincerely,
(Arthur James Balfour)

The Balfour Declaration applied to Palestine, which then lacked geographical or political existence with defined borders. In the Ottoman Empire, Palestine was scattered over the *sanjak* (Turkish: *county or district*) of Jerusalem and the *vilaya*t (Turkish: *province*) of Beirut, Jerusalem [*q.v.*] and its suburbs being ruled directly from Istanbul.

The Balfour Declaration arose out of the convergence of Britain's imperial aims with Zionist aspirations, which came to the fore during World War I (June 1914–November 1918), when Britain was pitted against the Central Powers, consisting of Germany, Austria-Hungary, Bulgaria, and the Ottoman Empire. The January 1915 Ottoman offensive against the Suez Canal [*q.v.*] across the Sinai Peninsula [*q.v.*] made London realize the strategic importance of Palestine in defending the Suez Canal, Britain's lifeline to its Indian Empire, and resulted in its resolve to control Palestine after winning the war.

In a memorandum to the cabinet in March 1915, Sir Herbert Samuel (later appointed British High Commissioner for Palestine), a Zionist, proposed establishing a Jewish homeland in Palestine as a cornerstone of the British policy in the Middle East. Until then the world Jewry, concentrated in Germany, Austria-Hungary, and the United States had by and large remained neutral in the war. With the U.S. joining the conflict in April 1917 on the Allied side, the role of the American Jewry became important. In order to gain its active cooperation the pro-Zionists in the British government, led by Prime Minister Lloyd George and Foreign Minister Balfour, in September 1917 proposed backing the Zionist cause, but failed to win cabinet approval. They then sought the advice of U.S. President Woodrow Wilson, known to be a pro-Zionist. Wilson replied that the time was inopportune for anything more than a statement of general sympathy for the Zionists. The next month, responding to Zionist pleas and rumors of Germany's wooing the Zionist movement, Lloyd George and Balfour again broached the subject with Wilson. After some hesitation he approved a draft statement which, after minor editing, was issued by Balfour on 2 November 1917 in the form of a letter to Lord Rothschild. Endorsed by the chief Allied Powers, it was included in the San Remo Agreement of 1920 [*q.v.*] and incorporated into the British Mandate over Palestine authorized by the League of Nations in July 1922.

Baluchis: *nomadic community with a tribal structure* Baluchis are to be found in present-day Iran, Pakistan, and Afghanistan. Their recorded history goes back to the 10th century A.D. Adherents of Sunni Islam [*q.v.*], they are now a settled community in Iran, concentrated in the Sistan and Baluchistan province and forming 2.5 percent of the national population. After the Islamic revolution in 1979, their demand that the Sunni codes of the Islamic law [*q.v.*] be recognized on a par with the Shia [*q.v.*] code was accepted by the Assembly of Experts [*q.v.*] charged with drafting the constitution.

Bani-Sadr, Abol Hassan (1933–): *Iranian politician; president, 1980–81* Born into a religious family in Hamadan, Bani-Sadr pursued his university education in Tehran [*q.v.*], specializing in economics, sociology, and the Sharia [*q.v.*]. He was sympathetic to the National Front [*q.v.*]. For participating in an anti-government demonstration in June 1963, he served a four-month jail sentence. He won a scholarship to Sorbonne University in Paris. After gaining a doctorate in sociology and economics, he stayed on in the French capital.

During a visit to Najaf [*q.v.*], Iraq, in 1972 for his father's funeral he had a meeting with Ayatollah Ruhollah Khomeini [*q.v.*]. He then strengthened his ties with the Islamic Student Society in Paris. When Khomeini arrived in Paris in early October 1978 from Iraq, Bani-Sadr became a member of the Ayatollah's inner circle of advisers. On his return home with Khomeini six months later, he emerged as Iran's chief architect of economic policies. Through his newspaper, *Inqilab-e Islami* (Persian: *Islamic Revolution*), he urged radical policies and was glad to see the government of Mahdi Bazargan [*q.v.*] fall in early November 1979.

In the new cabinet he became minister of economy and finance. As a member of the Assembly of Experts [*q.v.*], he succeeded in getting a bill of rights incorporated into the constitution. By winning 75 percent of the vote in the presidential election in January 1980, albeit with Khomeini's backing, Bani-Sadr enhanced his stature. Khomeini appointed him commander-in-chief of the military.

With the outbreak of hostilities with Iraq in September 1980, his handling of the war came under the critical scrutiny of leaders of the Islamic Republican Party [*q.v.*], the majority party in parliament, which was at odds with him. He also clashed with Premier Muhammad Ali Rajai [*q.v.*], who had been foisted on him by parliament. Initially Khomeini tried to mediate between the two sides, but as Bani-Sadr began to court the Mujahedin-e Khalq [*q.v.*], a party detested by the Ayatollah, he turned against Bani-Sadr. On 20 June 1981 the Iranian parliament found him incompetent and Khomeini dismissed him as president. He went underground and then, along with Masoud Rajavi [*q.v.*], the Mujahedin-e Khalq chief, escaped to France.

The National Resistance Council (NRC) [*q.v.*], formed by Bani-Sadr and Rajavi, masterminded a successful campaign of assassination and terror. But when Rajavi began to collaborate with Iraq, which was still engaged in a bloody war with Iran, Bani-Sadr broke with Rajavi in April 1984 and quit the NRC. He continued his political activities, independently from Versailles, near Paris. He was a vocal critic of the disputed presidential election of June 2009. He argued that the spontaneous uprising had cost the regime its political legitimacy, and then its religious legitimacy when, following Ayatollah Ali Khamanei's [*q.v.*] dire threats to the protestors, the government had carried out a bloody crackdown.

In *The Economics of Divine Unity*, published before the revolution, Bani-Sadr offered an exposition of Islamic economics. Rejecting capitalism and Soviet socialism, he argued that Islamic teachings were a means to a just and equitable society. In 1991, he encapsulated his later political experiences in *My Turn to Speak: Iran, the Revolution and Secret Deals with the U.S.*

al-Banna, Hassan (1906–49): *Egyptian Islamic leader* Born into a religious family in the Nile delta town of Muhammadiya, Banna graduated from Cairo Teachers College. He became a primary school teacher in Ismailiya, capital of the British-occupied Suez Canal [*q.v.*] Zone. An avid reader of *al-Manar* (Arabic: *The Lighthouse*), edited by Muhammad Rashid Rida, he was much influenced by the writings of this Islamic thinker. In 1928 he established *al-Ikhwan al-Muslimin*, the Muslim Brotherhood [*q.v.*], as a youth club, its main stress being on moral and social reform through communication, information, and propaganda. It then turned into a political-religious movement, which argued that Islam [*q.v.*] was a total ideology, offering an all-pervasive system to regulate every detail of the political, economic, social, and cultural life of believers. Based in Cairo [*q.v.*] since 1933, and led by the charismatic, spartan Banna, the Brotherhood spawned 500 branches by 1940, drawing its support from students, civil servants, artisans, petty traders, and middle-income peasants. After World War II, as the anti-British struggle escalated in Egypt, the popularity of the Brotherhood, with its strong anti-imperialist credentials, soared. In 1946, Banna claimed a Brotherhood membership of 500,000.

He held the Egyptian political establishment solely responsible for the Arab debacle in the 1948 Palestine War [*q.v.*]. The Brotherhood's secret cells started to engage in terrorist and subversive activities. Prime Minister Mahmoud Fahmi Nuqrashi retaliated by banning the Brotherhood in December 1948. Three weeks later Nuqrashi was assassinated by a Brotherhood militant. This led to further repression of the organization. On 12 February 1949 Banna was killed by the government's secret service agents in Cairo. He left behind his memoirs as well as numerous published speeches and articles.

al-Banna, Sabri (1937–2002): *Palestinian leader* Born into a prosperous, plantation-owning family in Jaffa [*q.v.*], Banna and his family fled to the al-Bureij refugee camp in the Gaza Strip [*q.v.*] after the establishment of Israel in May 1948. They then moved to the West Bank [*q.v.*] city of Nablus [*q.v.*]. While working as an electrician's assistant, Banna joined the Baath Party of Jordan [*q.v.*] in 1955. After the failed coup in 1957 against the regime of King Hussein [*q.v.*], the Baath Party was suppressed. Banna moved to Riyadh [*q.v.*], where he established an electrical business and joined a secret Fatah [*q.v.*] cell. In 1967 he was expelled from Saudi Arabia for participating in a demonstration following the Arab defeat in the Six-Day War [*q.v.*].

His trading company in Amman [*q.v.*] became a useful conduit for Fatah. In 1969, when he was a member of the Fatah Revolutionary Council, Banna was appointed Fatah's representative in Sudan. In July 1970 he was transferred to Baghdad [*q.v.*] as Fatah's envoy. There he began to echo the views of the Iraqi regime rather than represent Fatah's interests. Soon he started to work for the Iraqi secret service. Following his criticism of the decision of the Palestine National Council [*q.v.*] in mid-1974 to set up a "national authority" on any "liberated" territory in Palestine [*q.v.*], Banna was expelled from Fatah. In November he was found guilty by a Fatah court, based in Beirut [*q.v.*], of plotting to kill a Fatah leader, Mahmoud Abbas (*nom de guerre*: Abu Mazin) [*q.v.*], and was sentenced to death in absentia.

Encouraged by Iraq, he set up his own group—Fatah: The Revolutionary Council [*q.v.*]. The group was generously funded by Iraq, which used it to settle scores with Syria in 1976–77. Banna's Baghdad-based activities ended in 1983 when, in order to qualify for aid from Washington for the Iran-Iraq War [*q.v.*], Iraqi President Saddam Hussein [*q.v.*] expelled him and his men to show that Iraq was distancing itself from international terrorism.

Banna was then hired by Syria, which used his group as part of its coercive attempt to dissuade King Hussein of Jordan [*q.v.*] from making a unilateral deal with Israel. In early 1985, when King Hussein and Yasser Arafat [*q.v.*], chairman of the Palestine Liberation Organization (PLO) [*q.v.*], devised a plan for a confederation of Jordan and a future state of Palestine, Banna allied with Abu Musa, another Syria-backed Fatah dissident, to destroy the accord and prevent any prospect of an agreement being reached between Hussein, Arafat, and Israel. In late 1985 Banna's gunmen attacked counters of the Israeli El Al airline in Vienna and Rome, and hijacked a Pan-American aircraft on the ground in Karachi.

In mid-1986 Syria expelled Banna and his group from Damascus [*q.v.*]. They reportedly took refuge in Libya, which became their main haven for almost 11 years.

Once the Iran-Iraq War [*q.v.*] was over in 1988, freeing Iraq from the need to placate the United States, Banna turned successfully to Baghdad for assistance. In 1990 he tried to wrest control of the Fatah-dominated Palestinian refugee camps in southern Lebanon, but failed. During the Kuwait crisis (August 1990 to March 1991), caused by Iraq's invasion and occupation of Kuwait, Banna was allegedly bribed by the Saudi government to refrain from carrying out assassinations and sabotage in Saudi Arabia on behalf of Iraq. In January 1991 an agent of Banna, working as a bodyguard of Salah Khalaf [q.v.], the PLO's second-in-command, assassinated him in Tunis.

When, by 1996–97, the Libyan leader Muammar Gaddafi had found him to be a political liability, Banna and his dwindled number of followers reportedly moved to Cairo [q.v.] to offer their mercenary services to Egypt in its drive against Islamist insurgents. This lasted a few years. In 1999, Banna, an isolated figure, returned to Baghdad. There he became a liability to Saddam Hussein after 9/11 when the Iraqi leader realized that U.S. President George W. Bush could use Banna's presence in Baghdad as an excuse to attack Iraq.

Iraq's internal security intelligence agency suspected that Banna was spying for Saudi Arabia and Kuwait to find out any links between Saddam Hussein [q.v.] and al-Qaida [q.v.] in order to provide a basis to America to invade Iraq. When its team arrived at the safe house where Banna was staying to arrest him, he said that he needed a change of clothes. He went into his bedroom and shot himself in the mouth. Efforts to revive him failed. He was buried in a cemetery in Baghdad with his grave identified as "M7."

Barak, Ehud (1942–) *Israeli military and political leader; prime minister 1999–2001*; born Ehud Brog in Kibbutz Mishmar HaSharon. On joining the Israel Defense Forces (IDF) [q.v.] in 1959 he altered his family name to

Barak (Hebrew: *lightning*). During the 1967 Six-Day War [q.v.], he served as a reconnaissance group commander. In 1972, as the head of the *Seyeret* (Hebrew: derivative of *reconnaissance*) *Makal* (Hebrew: acronym for *General Staff*), he led a successful assault on the Palestinians who had hijacked Belgian airliner at Ben-Gurion Airport in Israel. In April 1973, Barak, dressed as a woman, led a commando unit into Beirut [q.v.] to assassinate three Palestinian leaders. During the Arab-Israeli War that erupted six months later, he was a tank battalion commander on the southern front in Sinai [q.v.]. He then enrolled at Hebrew University, Jerusalem [q.v.], where he graduated in physics and mathematics, followed by a master's degree in engineering-economic systems from Stanford University, California, in 1978.

During the Israeli invasion of Lebanon in June 1982 [q.v.] Barak, now a major-general, was the Deputy Commander of the IDF in Lebanon. In April 1983, he was appointed head of the IDF's Intelligence Branch. In January 1986, he was promoted to Commander of the IDF Central Command, and then to Deputy Chief of Staff in May 1987. By the time he was promoted to Lt. General, the highest in the Israeli military, and appointed the 14th Chief of the General Staff, in April 1991, he had become the most decorated soldier in IDF history

Following Israel's agreement with the Palestine Liberation Organization [q.v.] in May 1994, Barak supervised the IDF's redeployment in the Gaza Strip [q.v.] and Jericho [q.v.]. He played a vital role in finalizing the peace treaty with Jordan signed in 1994, and met with his Syrian counterpart as part of the Syrian-Israeli negotiations. By the time he retired from the IDF in mid-1995, he had won the "Distinguished Service Medal" and four other citations for courage and operational excellence, the highest ever by an Israeli soldier.

Prime Minister Yitzhak Rabin [q.v.] then appointed him interior minister. In that capacity he did not vote for the Oslo II Accord [q.v.] that Rabin concluded with the Palestinian leader Yasser Arafat [q.v.]. After Rabin's assassination in November, Prime Minister Shimon Peres [q.v.] appointed Barak foreign minister. In the 1996 general election he was elected to the Knesset, and later that year he was elected chairman of the Labor Party [q.v.]. In 1999 he formed the One Israel Party, an alliance of Labor, Gesher, and Meimad.

In May 1999 he defeated his Likud [q.v.] rival, Benjamin Netanyahu [q.v.], in a prime ministerial contest by a large margin. In the new cabinet Barak also took charge of the defense ministry. He kept his election promise by withdrawing unconditionally from south Lebanon in May 2000. He became the first Israeli leader to state the terms for a final settlement with the PLO on the Palestinian refugees, Jewish settlements, Jerusalem, and final borders. But his talks with Arafat, chaired by U.S. President Bill Clinton at Camp David in July 2000, failed—chiefly on the status of the Noble Sanctuary [q.v.] in the Old City when Barak insisted on giving Israeli sovereignty over the revered Islamic site.

The subsequent eruption of the Second Intifada [q.v.] in September by the Palestinians undermined his standing, and he called a special prime ministerial election on 6 February 2001. At the same time he allowed foreign minister, Shlomo Ben-Ami, to attend the summit with the leadership of the Palestinian Authority at the Egyptian border town of Taba during the run-up to the election. On 27 January, after six days of negotiations, the two sides declared that they had "never been closer to reaching an agreement" on the permanent settlement, and that they believed that "the remaining gaps could be bridged with the resumption of negotiations following the Israeli elections."

This was not to be, because Barak lost to his Likud [q.v.] rival, Ariel Sharon [q.v.]. He resigned as leader of the Labor Party and as a Knesset member. He turned to business and thrived by joining private equity companies in Israel and America.

In 2007 he entered the race for the leader of the Labor Party and won. He replaced the outgoing party chief, Amir Peretz, as defense minister. Under his leadership, Labor did poorly in the 2009 general election, ending up fourth. He decided to join the coalition led by Likud's Netanyahu as defense minister.

In November 2011, when in a TV interview in the United States he was asked whether he would strive for nuclear weapons if he was in Iran's position, he replied: "Probably. I don't delude myself that they are doing it just because of Israel." When his statement was widely criticized in Israel, he became a vociferous advocate of air strikes against Iran's nuclear facilities.

Barghouti, Marwan (1958–): *Palestinian politician* Born in Kobar, a village near Ramallah [*q.v.*], in the household of a day laborer, Barghouti joined Fatah in 1973. Three years later he was arrested for his political activities. He finished his secondary school diploma in prison. His subsequent higher education at Bir Zeit University was interrupted by the First Intifada [*q.v.*] in 1987 when he was expelled to Jordan. As the cofounder of the Fatah Youth Movement he directed the intifada from Amman [*q.v.*]. After the Oslo I Accords [*q.v.*] in 1993, he was allowed to return to the West Bank [*q.v.*]. The next year he became secretary-general of Fatah [*q.v.*] in the West Bank as well as a postgraduate student in international affairs at Bir Zeit. In 1995 he was elected to the Palestine Legislative Council (PLC). He founded *al-Tanzim* (Arabic: *Organization*) militia. In 2000, he cofounded the al-Aqsa Martyrs' Brigades (AAMB). By then he had begun criticizing the corruption and mismanagement of the Palestinian Authority [*q.v.*] under Yasser Arafat [*q.v.*].

With the outbreak of the Second Intifada [*q.v.*] in 2001, he gained popularity as leader of al-Tanzim and the AAMB. He was arrested in 2002 and convicted in May 2004 on five counts of murder and sentenced to five life imprisonments.

He was reelected to the PLC in 2006. While in prison he tried to bring about reconciliation between Fatah and Hamas [*q.v.*]. He was one of the architects of the compromise that led to the formation of the national unity government in February 2007. At the Fatah Conference in Bethlehem [*q.v.*], he was elected to the Central Committee.

In October 2011, the efforts of Hamas to include him in the list of Palestinians to be released in exchange for the captured Israeli soldier Gilad Shalit failed.

Barzani, Masoud (1947–): *Iraqi Kurdish leader; president of Iraqi Kurdistan, 2005–* Born during the tumultuous times that followed the collapse of the Kurdish Republic of Mahabad [*q.v.*], led militarily by his father, Mustafa [*q.v.*], Barzani grew up in Moscow. After a two-year stay in Baghdad [*q.v.*] following the republican coup of 1958, the family returned to Barzan in northern Iraq. With the defection in the early 1970s of one of his elder brothers, Ubaidullah, to the Baghdad government, the burden of assisting their father in his political and military endeavors fell on Barzani and his remaining brother, Idris. After Mustafa Barzani's departure for the United States in 1976, the leadership of the Kurdistan Democratic Party (KDP) [*q.v.*] was exercised by Barzani and Idris. When they moved to Iran after the Islamic revolution in early 1979, the new regime started to lend them its support.

The outbreak of the Iran-Iraq War [*q.v.*] in September 1980 compelled Baghdad to reduce its troops in the Kurdish areas. This enabled the KDP to increase the area under its control in Iraqi Kurdistan. In late 1986 Barzani attended a conference organized in Tehran [*q.v.*] by the Supreme Council of the Islamic Revolution in Iraq (SCIRI) [*q.v.*]. However, SCIRI's attempt to coordinate the military activities of all anti-Saddam parties failed because the secular leadership of the KDP felt uneasy about coalescing with the predominantly Islamic Iraqis. With the death of Idris in 1987, Barzani became the sole leader of the KDP.

During the long Iran-Iraq war the KDP had managed to set up liberated zones along the Iraqi border with Iran. But, when the conflict ended in 1988, Iraqi President Saddam Hussein [q.v.] launched a campaign of vengeance against the KDP stronghold.

Later, when the Iraqi forces were defeated in the Second Gulf War [q.v.] in early 1991, Barzani led a Kurdish rebellion against the central government. Its suppression caused a massive exodus of Kurds into Turkey and intervention by the anti-Iraq Western coalition. Barzani's subsequent talks with the Baghdad government failed to lead to a successful conclusion.

Protected by the air forces of the United States, Britain, and France, the KDP, along with other Kurdish parties, held assembly elections in May 1992. Barzani shared power equally with Jalal Talabani [q.v.], the leader of the Patriotic Union of Kurdistan (PUK) [q.v.]. Yet the traditional rivalry between the two parties continued. In May 1994 intra-Kurdish clashes left over 1,000 people dead. It was not until six months later that, assisted by mediators, Barzani worked out a *modus vivendi* with Talabani.

But Barzani's relations with his rival soured again when their two factions took opposite positions in the anti-Saddam coup plans in March 1995. With this, Kurdistan divided into two hostile zones. By September, Barzani's jurisdiction was reduced to a third of the region. But with the illicit

Iraqi oil supplies passing through his territory, providing hefty customs duties, Barzani had much cash, part of which he used to buy arms and ammunition, some of them from Saddam Hussein.

Talabani's subsequent rapprochement with Iran upset both Barzani and Saddam. When Talabani, freshly armed with Iranian-supplied weapons, attacked KDP's positions in August 1996, Barzani appealed to Saddam for military assistance to retake Irbil [q.v.] from Talabani. Saddam obliged. Barzani captured not only Irbil but all of Talabani's territory, only to lose all except Irbil when Talabani, armed by Iran, counterattacked.

The unprecedented intra-Kurdish violence undermined Washington's strategy of developing Kurdistan as the base for overthrowing Saddam. The United States withdrew its agents and funds from the area. Its efforts to conciliate the two rivals were successful, only partially because Barzani refused to share the large customs duties he collected on the illicit export of Iraqi oil to Turkey. After the passage of the Iraq Liberation Act by U.S. Congress in 1998, Barzani found the KDP certified as a faction that was entitled to Washington's military aid.

When, after defeating the Taliban regime in Afghanistan in December 2001, the administration of U.S. President George W. Bush turned its attention to ousting Saddam's government by force, the importance of Barzani as well as Talabani rose sharply.

After the Anglo-American invasion of Iraq [q.v.] in March 2003, Barzani was appointed to the Interim Iraqi Governing Council. In the January

2005 general election, the KDP and the PUK led the Democratic Patriotic Alliance of Kurdistan, which won 104 of the 111 seats in the parliament of Iraqi Kurdistan, the new name of the region. It elected Barzani as president of the region.

In the July 2009 election, held under the new constitution, Barzani became the first directly elected president of the Kurdistan region, securing nearly 70 percent of the vote. His critics accused him of corruption and nepotism, with one opposition newspaper, *Rozhnama* (Kurdish: *Daily Journal*), mentioning in July 2010 the KDP's siphoning of large amounts of money from illegal oil-smuggling. The central government had agreed to give 17 percent of the national oil income to Kurdistan's government on the condition that it would export oil from its region only through the legal channel sanctioned by Baghdad. But Barzani's critics alleged that his KDP was exporting petroleum through illegal means and pocketing the profits.

Barzani, Mustafa (1904–79): *Iraqi Kurdish leader* Born into the family of a notable in Barzan, northern Iraq, Barzani grew up to be a leader of the Barzani tribe, which was traditionally opposed to the authority of the government whether based in Baghdad [*q.v.*] or in Mosul [*q.v.*]. Along with his elder brother, Ahmad, Barzani led the Kurdish struggle for independence in 1931–32. Following its suppression in 1935, the two brothers were exiled to Suleimaniyah. Escaping in 1942, Barzani led another unsuccessful rebellion.

Along with 1,000 armed followers, he crossed into the Kurdish region of Iran, which, along with the rest of country north of the latitude of Tehran [*q.v.*], had been under Soviet occupation since August 1941. When the State of Kurdistan Republic [*q.v.*] was founded there in December 1945, Barzani was appointed its commander-in-chief. Following the Soviet departure in May 1946, the republic, run by the Kurdish Democratic Party (KDP) [*q.v.*], was crushed by the Tehran government in December 1946. Along with his followers, Barzani crossed the Iranian border into Soviet Trans-Caucasia in June 1947 on his way to Moscow. There he enrolled at the Institute of Languages.

After the 1958 coup against the Iraqi monarchy, Barzani returned to Iraq and backed the new regime under Abdul Karim Qasim [*q.v.*], who legalized the KDP. However, when Barzani advanced a plan for autonomy, Qasim rejected it. The KDP revolted. In September 1961 Qasim mounted an offensive against the Kurdish insurgents. During the subsequent years, despite changes in the regime in Baghdad, relations between the central government and Barzani did not improve. It was not until March 1970 that the two sides reached a settlement, to be implemented over the next four years. This agreement conceded several of the Kurdish demands, including recognition of Kurdish ethnicity on a par with Arab, and the official use of the Kurdish language [*q.v.*] in Kurdish-majority areas. But there was mistrust on both sides, and the pact failed to hold.

In March 1974 Barzani once again led his followers to fight the Iraqi government. This time he had the active backing of Muhammad Reza Shah Pahlavi [*q.v.*] of Iran, who wanted to weaken the pro-Moscow regime in Baghdad. By early 1975 the conflict was threatening to escalate into a full-scale war between Iraq and Iran. In an effort to avert this, Baghdad and Tehran reached an accord in March 1975, which resulted in Iran cutting off military and logistical aid to Barzani's fighters. His rebellion failed. After escaping to Iran, Barzani fled to the United States and settled in northern Virginia, where he died in 1979.

Basra: *Iraqi city* Population: 3.5 million (2011 est.). The second-largest city of Iraq, it is the country's main port. Located beside the Shatt al-Arab [*q.v.*], it is the site of an ancient settlement. Because of its strategic position, Caliph Omar (r. 634–44 A.D.) set up a military camp there in 636 A.D. It was from Basra that Muslim Arabs conducted their campaigns against the Sassanian rulers of Persia. It evolved as a center of literary and scientific knowledge, commerce, and finance. In the early eighth century it fostered rebellions against the Umayyad caliphate based in Damascus [*q.v.*]. When the Abbasids succeeded the Umayyads in 750 A.D. they favored Baghdad [*q.v.*] over Basra. An attack by militant Qarmatian Muslims in 923 A.D. severely damaged the city. It suffered heavily under the Mongol invasions of the 13th century, which finally led to its destruction. In the early 1500s a new settlement, bearing the name of Basra, was founded a few kilometers further up the Shatt al-Arab. The settlement prospered and grew.

In more recent times, a rail link with Baghdad and the discovery of oil in southern Iraq boosted its fortunes. However, the outbreak of the Iran-Iraq War [*q.v.*] in 1980 turned it into a frontline. In 1987, during the Iranian advance, the city center came within the range of artillery fire and suffered heavily, with two-thirds of its population fleeing. At the time of the Second Gulf War [*q.v.*] in 1991, it was near the front line with Kuwait, but the damage this time was a result of air and missile attacks. The city was reconstructed.

During the first phase of the Anglo-American invasion of Iraq in 2003 [*q.v.*], Basra was the scene of fierce fighting. After the war it came under British occupation, which continued until July 2009. It emerged as a stronghold of Shia [*q.v.*] religious parties. With new oilfields being found in the surrounding areas, the city is set to prosper in the coming decades.

bat: (Hebrew: *daughter*) The traditional Jewish custom of identifying a woman as a *bat* of her father is seldom manifested nowadays in secular Western societies. Nonetheless, every female Jew has a Hebrew name given to her at birth, and used in synagogue [*q.v.*] services and at marriage and burial.

al-Baz, Abdul Aziz ibn Abdullah (1911–99): *Saudi Arabian religious leader* Born into a religious family in Riyadh [*q.v.*], Baz studied the Quran [*q.v.*] and Sharia [*q.v.*] at an early age. After going blind at 16 he became a student of Shaikh Muhammad ibn Abdul Wahhab, the grand mufti, to train as an Islamic judge. He was appointed a judge in the Kharj region, where he served from 1938 to 1952. For the next seven years he taught the Sharia and *fiqh* [*q.v.*] at the University of Riyadh. An orthodox cleric, he was made vice president of the Islamic University of Medina [*q.v.*] at its inception in 1961. In an article published in two Saudi newspapers in September 1965 he stated that the sun was moving in its orbit, as God has ordained, and that the earth was stationary and spread out by God for His creation. When this proved controversial he denied saying that the earth was flat, but maintained that it was static.

In 1969 he was promoted to president of Medina Islamic University while continuing to head the Sharia faculty. Rejecting *ijtihad* [*q.v.*] of any kind, he urged a return to the letter of the scriptures. In 1972, Juheiman ibn Saif al-Utaiba [*q.v.*] was one of his students in the Sharia faculty. In 1975 Baz was appointed chairman of the 21-member Council of Senior Ulema, established four years earlier, by the king. In that capacity he concluded in the summer of 1978 that the ideas propagated by al-Utaiba were not treasonable. However, when al-Utaiba led an armed uprising at the Grand Mosque in Mecca [*q.v.*] in late 1979 he ruled that King Khalid ibn Abdul Aziz [*q.v.*] was entitled to use force to regain control of the holy mosque.

When Iraq invaded Kuwait in August 1990, he initially argued against the Council's sanctioning of non-Muslim troops on Saudi soil. Later he changed his stance. In November 1990 his religious verdict barred women from driving. On the eve of the U.S.-led Gulf War [*q.v.*] in January 1991, he issued a call for jihad [*q.v.*] by the forces under King Fahd ibn Abdul Aziz [*q.v.*] against the troops of Iraqi President Saddam Hussein [*q.v.*], whom he described as a blasphemer for claiming to be a descendent of the Prophet Muhammad, something he had done several years earlier.

In May 1991, Baz passed on to King Fahd a petition signed by more than 400 leading religious scholars, judges, and academics, demanding a consultative assembly; full Islamization of all social, economic, administrative, military, and educational institutions; and disassociation from non-Islamic pacts and treaties. King Fahd ignored the demands. The next year he was appointed grand mufti of Saudi Arabia, a job that had been left vacant since 1969, and president of the Supreme Religious Council.

He supported the 1993 Oslo Accord I [*q.v.*] between Israel and the Palestine Liberation Organization [*q.v.*], arguing that the Prophet Muhammad had signed the Treaty of Hudaibiya with non-Muslims in 628 A.D. to avoid loss of life.

His several books include *Inquiry and Clarification of Many Hajj and Umra Issues.*

bazaar, bazaaris: (Persian: *market place, traders*) Originating in Iran, the word *bazaar* spread to Arabia, Turkey, North Africa, and South Asia. The vendors in a bazaar are called *bazaaris*. As the Prophet Muhammad was a trader, bazzaris have been close to the mosque since the founding of Islam [*q.v.*]. In modern times they played a particularly important role in bringing about the 1979 Islamic revolution in Iran [*q.v.*].

Bazargan, Mahdi (1905–95): *Iranian politician; prime minister, 1979* Born into a wealthy trading family in Tabriz [*q.v.*], Bazargan obtained an engineering degree from Paris University. After spending some years in Paris he returned to Iran, where he began to teach engineering at Tehran University in 1941. He joined the Iran Party, which merged with two other groups in 1949 to form the National Front [*q.v.*], headed by Muhammad Mussadiq [*q.v.*]. During Mussadiq's premiership (1951–53), he became the managing director of the newly nationalized petroleum industry, managed by the National Iranian Oil Company.

In May 1955 he was arrested on the charge of treason and detained until 1960. He teamed up with Ayatollah Mahmoud Taleqani [*q.v.*] to form the Liberation Movement of Iran (LMI) [*q.v.*] in 1961. When he called for a boycott of a referendum on the government-inspired "white revolution" [*q.v.*] in 1963, he was given a 10-year sentence. After his release he stayed out of politics until the first stirrings of the anti-regime agitation in the autumn of 1977, when he became a co-founder of the Human Rights Association.

On 1 February 1979 he was nominated by Ayatollah Ruhollah Khomeini [*q.v.*] to head the provisional Islamic government. His appointment reassured the large, modern middle class. He served for nine months, resigning in protest at the militant students' seizure of the U.S. Embassy and diplomats. He had found that most of his authority was being usurped by such bodies as the Islamic Revolutionary Council (of which he was a member) and the Islamic Revolutionary Guards Corps. The following year he was elected leader of the 20 LMI members of parliament.

By the spring of 1983 his party, the LMI, was the only pre-revolutionary political group that was not banned, despite the fact that he opposed the official policy of continuing the war with Iraq after Iran had gained the upper hand in mid-1982. However, in protest against the lack of campaigning facilities, the LMI boycotted the 1984 parliamentary elections. In 1985 his candidacy for president was rejected by the Guardians Council [*q.v.*]. Ignoring calls for action against Bazargan, Khomeini allowed him freedom of movement, including foreign travel, while denying him facilities for propagating his consistently critical views. This policy continued after Khomeini's death in 1989.

B.C.: *Before Christ* The era before the birth of Jesus Christ (derivative of the Greek word *Christos*, Anointed). The date originally assigned to Christ's birth is now believed to be about four to eight years too late—that is, he is believed to have been born between 4 and 8 B.C., and not 0 A.D. [*q.v.*]

B.C.E.: *Before Common Era* Some non-Christians prefer this term to B.C. [*q.v.*] with its religious connotation.

Begin, Menachem Wolfovitch (1913–92): *Israeli politician; prime minister, 1977–83* Born in Brest-Litovsk (then in Poland, later in Russia), Begin obtained a law degree at the University of Warsaw. At 16 he joined the youth organization of the Revisionist Zionists [*q.v.*], *Betar* (Hebrew: an acronym for *Brit Trumpeldor*, Covenant of [Joseph] Trumpeldor [*q.v.*]). More extremist than Vladimir Zeev Jabotinsky [*q.v.*], the founder of the Revisionist movement, Begin challenged him in 1938 after being appointed commander of Betar in Poland. On the eve of the Nazi invasion of Poland in 1939, he fled to Vilnius, Lithuania, then under Soviet occupation. In 1940 he was sentenced to eight years' hard labor in a Siberian camp. But after the Soviet Union had joined World War II in mid-1941, he was released and drafted into the Free Polish army. He arrived in Palestine in 1942 [*q.v.*] as a soldier of that force.

After his demobilization in 1943, he was appointed commander of the underground *Irgun Zvai Leumi* [*q.v.*] (Hebrew: *National Military Organization*). He declared an armed struggle against the British Mandate in January 1944, a call he repeated in October 1945 after the end of the war. The Irgun's terrorist activities led the British authorities to offer a £10,000 reward for his arrest. In July 1946 the Irgun bombed the British Mandate government offices in King David Hotel, Jerusalem [*q.v.*], killing 91 British, Arab, and Jewish officials and staff. After this, the *Haganah* [*q.v.*], the main military forces of the Jewish community in Palestine, stopped cooperating with the Irgun.

Begin was one of the chief planners of the attack on the Arab village of Deir Yassin near Jerusalem on 10 April 1948, resulting in the massacre of 254 men, women, and children—an event that caused the intended massive exodus of Arabs [*q.v.*] from Palestine. At his behest, Irgun ranks refused to be absorbed into the Israel

Defense Forces (IDF) formed by the provisional government of David Ben-Gurion [*q.v.*] on 26 May 1948. They participated in the war against the Arab states as a separate entity. This continued until late June when Ben-Gurion, clashing with Begin on the question of delivery of arms and volunteers to the Irgun aboard a freighter anchored off Tel Aviv [*q.v.*], ordered his forces to destroy the ship. In September Begin disbanded the Irgun, but soon former Irgun ranks and Revisionist Zionist reemerged as the Herut [*q.v.*] Party under his leadership.

In 1949 he was elected to the Knesset [*q.v.*], and remained a member until 1984, his membership interrupted by a 15-month suspension in January 1952 for inciting a mob to attack the Knesset in protest against reparations to Israel by West Germany. In the first five general elections, his Herut Party won about 12 percent of the votes, emerging as the largest opposition faction in the parliament. He led his group in an authoritarian way and brooked no challenge. In 1965, at his behest, the Herut joined with the Liberal Party [*q.v.*] to form the Gahal bloc [*q.v.*], which won 21 percent of the seats in that year's general election.

On the eve of the June 1967 Arab-Israeli War [*q.v.*], Begin joined the national unity government headed by Levi Eshkol [*q.v.*]. He stayed in the cabinet until July 1970 when—protesting against the majority decision to accept the American peace plan that envisaged Israel's withdrawal from Sinai [*q.v.*]—he resigned. He resumed his opposition role. In 1973 when the Likud bloc [*q.v.*], containing all the right-wing parties, was formed, he was elected its leader.

Following Likud's electoral success in May 1977, Begin became the prime minister, a position he held for more than six years. He signed the Camp David Accords [*q.v.*] with Egyptian President Anwar Sadat [*q.v.*] in September 1978, which in turn led to the conclusion of a peace treaty between Israel and Egypt. That year he and Sadat won the Nobel Peace Prize.

He twice ordered the invasion and occupation of Lebanon— in March 1978 and June 1982. The first occupation, limited to southern Lebanon, ended shortly. But the second invasion, when the Israelis advanced as far as Beirut [*q.v.*] and began to dictate the politics of Lebanon, proved controversial. Growing public criticism and the increasing Israeli death toll in Lebanon, combined with an annual inflation rate of 400 percent, led to his resignation in August 1983. On a personal level, he had become depressed in the wake of the death of his wife, Aliza, nine months earlier.

al-Beidh, Ali Salim (1938–): *South Yemeni and Yemeni politician* Born into a religious family in the Hadramaut region, Beidh participated in the armed nationalist struggle of South Yemen, conducted by the National Liberation Front (NLF) [*q.v.*] against Britain. Soon after independence in 1967, the radical Beidh fell foul of the moderate faction then dominant in the NLF. The situation changed when radicals finally gained the upper hand in 1971. Beidh's star rose steadily. In 1973 he became the planning minister, moving three years later to the ministry of municipal affairs. In April

1980—after Premier Ali Nasser Muhammad [*q.v.*] had ousted his rival, President Abdul Fattah Ismail [*q.v.*]—Beidh was promoted to deputy prime minister.

He then allied himself with Vice President Ali Antar to oppose President Muhammad's increasingly moderate policies. The return of Ismail from self-exile in Moscow in 1985 intensified the factional struggle. In the armed confrontation that ensued between the Muhammad and Ismail camps in January 1986, Beidh sided with the latter. When the internecine violence led to the deaths of Ismail, Antar, and other radicals, and the exile of Muhammad, Beidh emerged as the only top party leader to survive the conflict. He was elected secretary-general of the ruling Yemeni Socialist Party [*q.v.*].

With the presidency and premiership going to technocrats Haidar al-Attas and Yassin Numan, Beidh held the reins of real power. He began to moderate his radical stance and introduce economic and political reform— a tendency accelerated by the rapid decline of the Soviet bloc from 1989 onwards. He expedited the plans for the unification of South and North Yemen that had been agreed to in principle earlier. He became vice president of united Yemen—a state with two separate armies—in May 1990.

The unification process proved more problematic than had been anticipated. In August 1993, blaming President Ali Abdullah Saleh [*q.v.*] for lack of progress, Beigh left Sanaa [*q.v.*] for Aden [*q.v.*]. Despite his re-election as vice president two months later by the newly elected parliament, he did not return to Sanaa. The subsequent signing by the two leaders of a Document of Agreement and Bond in Amman [*q.v.*] in February 1994 failed to dissipate the crisis.

After the eruption of a civil war [*q.v.*] between the two former states in April, Beidh declared South Yemen independent in May. This was not formally recognized by any country. Just before the defeat of the South Yemeni military in early July, he fled to neighboring Oman, and then to Saudi Arabia. In 1996, as the leader of the National Opposition Front, Beidh demanded a referendum in the south to secure better terms for the region. Two years later he was sentenced to death in absentia for his role in the 1994 Civil War.

In 2009, against the backdrop of violent clashes between protesting South Yemenis and the central Yemeni security forces, Beidh declared himself leader of the Southern separatists in a televised speech from Germany. As a result, he lost his right to stay in Oman, which was conditional on his abstaining from political activity. He then resumed his exile in Germany. In February 2011, he backed the pro-democracy demonstrations against the regime of President Saleh.

Beirut: *capital of Lebanon* Population: 1.9 million (2011 est.) The principal port of the country at the foot of Mount Lebanon, Beirut has a history stretching back to the Phoenician era (ca 1250 B.C.), when it was known as Berytus. An important commercial center, it thrived under the rule of the Selucuids, Romans, and Byzantines. It fell to Muslim Arabs in 636 A.D. During the Crusades it was seized by the Crusaders in 1110. They retained it until 1291 as part of the Latin Kingdom of Jerusalem. During the Ottoman period it became capital of the Vilayat of Lebanon, an autonomous province of the empire from 1861 onward. In 1920 the French Mandate authorities made it capital of Greater Lebanon, created by adding areas to the east, north, and south of the (Ottoman) Vilayat of Lebanon. It expanded greatly after Lebanon's independence in 1946 and became the leading financial center of the Middle East [*q.v.*], but lost that position after the Lebanese Civil War of 1975–90 [*q.v.*].

During that long conflict the city split between the exclusively Christian East Beirut, situated on al-Ashrafiya hill, and the predominantly Muslim West Beirut on al-Musaitiba hill. From 1972 to 1982 Beirut was the headquarters of the Palestine Liberation Organization [*q.v.*]. The civil war and the Israeli invasion of Lebanon in June–August 1982 [*q.v.*] played havoc with the city. Despite the violence, its two leading educational institutions, the American University in Beirut [*q.v.*] and Beirut Arab University, continued to function. By the mid-1990s reconstruction plans were finalized, and their implementation got started.

With its redesigned city center, marina, and hotels, it once again became a tourist destination. In the Israel-Hizbollah War [*q.v.*] in 2006, the Israeli air raids damaged south Beirut, inhabited predominantly by Shias [*q.v.*]. But by 2009, Beirut had once again become a vibrant city.

ben (Hebrew: *son*): Nowadays the traditional Jewish custom of identifying a man as a *ben* (son) of his father is seldom followed in secular Western societies. Nonetheless every male Jew has a Hebrew name given to him at circumcision (on the eighth day after birth), confirmed at *bar mitzah* (Hebrew: lit., *son of commandments*; fig. *coming of age*), and used in synagogue [*q.v.*] services and at marriage and burial.

Ben-Gurion, David (1886–1973): *Israeli politician; prime minister, 1948–53, 1955–63* Born David Green in Plonsk, Poland, Ben-Gurion, the son of a lawyer, went to Warsaw University in 1904. There he joined the *Poale Zion* [*q.v.*] and two years later left for Palestine [*q.v.*] where he became a farm hand. He was a cofounder of the Poale Zion journal, *HaAhdut* (Hebrew: *The Unity*). In 1912 he enrolled at the University of Istanbul to study Turkish law and government. The outbreak of World War I took him back to Palestine. In 1915 he was deported as a troublemaker and placed on a ship sailing for New York. There he joined an American battalion of the Jewish Legion, which was being formed as part of the British army. Trained in Canada, he arrived in Egypt as a member of the 40th Royal Fusiliers.

In the postwar Palestine the Poale Zion split, its leftist section leaving in 1919 and forming Mopsi (acronym of *Mifleget Poalim Sozialistim*, Socialist Workers Party). Its right-wing nationalist section—led among others by Ben-Gurion—combined with the followers of Berle Katznelson to form Ahdut HaAvodah [*q.v.*]. Soon Ahdut HaAvodah and HaPoale HaTzair [*q.v.*] took the lead in constituting an umbrella organization to encompass all Labor-pioneer parties of Zionist persuasion: Histadrut [*q.v.*]. With successive elections to Histadrut conferences showing Ahdut HaAvodah and HaPoale HaTzair to be the main parties, pressure grew on their leaders to seek a merger. This led to the founding of Mapai [*q.v.*] in January 1930 under the stewardship of Chaim Arlosoroff [*q.v.*]. After the murder of Arlosoroff in 1933, Ben-Gurion was elected head of Mapai. Two years later he became leader of the executive committee of the Jewish Agency for Palestine [*q.v.*], soon to be recognized by the British Mandate as the official representative of the Jews in Palestine.

Differing with his colleagues in the Mapai leadership, Ben-Gurion favored the 1937 Peel Commission's partition proposal. He opposed the British White Paper of 1939, which limited Jewish immigration into Palestine to an annual average of 15,000 for the next five years. But he could not remain anti-British once World War II had erupted in September 1939. He encouraged fellow Jews to join the British Africa Corps.

In 1942 he was the main instigator behind the resolution of the American Zionist Organization that the founding of a Jewish state in Palestine should be the prime objective of Zionism [*q.v.*]. After the war, backed by Jewish Agency funds, Ben-Gurion, in his role of Histadrut chief, began to purchase arms in Europe. His appointment as head of the Zionist Organization's [*q.v.*] Defense department in December 1946 enabled him to bring the various Jewish armed organizations in Palestine under a single command. Early in 1947, noticing the convergence of the

American and Soviet positions on the partitioning of Palestine, the National Council (Hebrew: *Vaad Leumi*) of the Yishuv [*q.v.*], led by Ben-Gurion, started to formulate plans to consolidate the Jewish sector in Palestine, militarily and otherwise. By the time the United Nations adopted the partition plan in November 1947, the Yishuv had a large professional army, supported by 79,000 reserves, armed police, and home guards.

By spring 1948, at the behest of Ben-Gurion, the Jewish Agency had transferred all its executive powers to the people's administrative committee of the Yishuv assembly's National Council. It was this committee of 13, headed by Ben-Gurion, and functioning as the provisional government, that declared the founding of the State of Israel on 14 May 1948 in Tel Aviv [*q.v.*]. Twelve days later it established the Israel Defense Forces (IDF) consisting of 60,000 troops, with Ben-Gurion as defense minister. It performed well in the First Arab-Israeli War I [*q.v.*], also known as the War of Independence (of Israel) [*q.v.*], which lasted from mid-May 1948 to early January 1949, when armistice agreements were signed between Israel and its four neighboring Arab adversaries on the Greek island of Rhodes.

Mapai emerged as the largest party in the January 1949 election, winning 46 of the 120 seats in the Knesset [*q.v.*], and Ben-Gurion became the prime minister. He welcomed the Tripartite (Anglo-American-French) Declaration of May 1950 [*q.v.*], which opposed any attempt to change the armistice boundaries of Israel set in January 1949, and promised to supply arms to Arabs and Israelis only to the

extent that they did not create an "imbalance." The United Religious Front's [*q.v.*] disagreement with Ben-Gurion on the degree of governmental control over religious education in schools caused the downfall of his government in mid-1951. In the Second Knesset, Mapai won 45 seats. Having played a leading role in shaping the basic outline of Israel's internal and external policies, Ben-Gurion resigned as prime minister in December 1953 and retired to his kibbutz in the Negev.

Moshe Sharett [*q.v.*] became the premier. His defense minister, Pinchas Lavon [*q.v.*], authorized a sabotage campaign in Egypt. It backfired, and Lavon resigned. Ben-Gurion was brought into the cabinet in early 1955 as the defense minister. In response to the execution of two ringleaders of the Jewish espionage-sabotage cell in Egypt, Ben-Gurion ordered a massive attack on an Egyptian military camp in Gaza [*q.v.*], which resulted in 39 Egyptian deaths. The escalating tension led to Ben-Gurion's becoming the prime minister in late 1955. Within a year he was involved in invading and occupying the Sinai Peninsula [*q.v.*] in collusion with Britain and France in the Suez War [*q.v.*]. Under pressure from the United States and the Soviet Union, he withdrew the Israeli troops from the Sinai in March 1957.

His next coalition government, formed after elections in November 1959, proved unstable, with the old controversy about Lavon's "security mishap" resurfacing in 1960. When a cabinet committee exonerated Lavon in early 1961, Ben-Gurion threatened to resign as the prime minister and the defense minister, insisting on a judicial enquiry. In exchange for the shelving of further investigation into the affair, Lavon stepped down as secretary-general of Histadrut [*q.v.*]. Ben-Gurion headed the coalition government formed after the August 1961 election, but found that he lacked the kind of authority he had exercised before. He resigned from the government in 1963 and then started campaigning against his successor, Levi Eskhol [*q.v.*].

The declining popularity of Mapai prompted its leaders to recommend an alignment (*maarach*) between their party and Ahdut HaAvodah-Poale Zion [*q.v.*]. This was ratified by the Mapai convention in February 1965. Disagreeing with this, Ben-Gurion and his followers left Mapai and offered their own list, Rafi, in the November 1965 election. Rafi won 10 seats and the Mapai-Ahdut HaAvodah-Poale Zion Maarch [*q.v.*] won 45. Ben-Gurion's personal popularity proved unequal to the institutional strength of his former party.

After the June 1967 Arab-Israeli War [*q.v.*], he opposed the annexation of the Occupied Arab Territories [*q.v.*]. In 1968 the *maarach* was widened to include Rafi, leading to the merger of the three constituents into the Israeli Labor Party [*q.v.*]. Ben-Gurion then founded a new group, *LaAam* (Hebrew: *To the People*), which won four seats in the 1969 election. The following year he quit politics. He died in December 1973, leaving behind many diaries that have been published.

Ben-Zvi, Yitzhak (1884–1963): *Israeli politician; president, 1952–63* Born

Yitzhak Shimshilevitch in Poltava, Ukraine, he became a Zionist [*q.v.*] in his youth. In 1906, Ben-Zvi cofounded Poale Zion [*q.v.*] in Russia, and then migrated to Palestine [*q.v.*] the following year. He was one of the founders of the HaShomer self-defense association, and editor of *HaAhdut* (Hebrew: *The Unity*), the organ of the Poale Zion in Palestine. In 1912 he enrolled at the University of Istanbul to study Turkish law and government. The outbreak of World War I brought him back to Palestine. After his deportation as a trouble-maker in 1915, he traveled to New York City. There he joined an American battalion of the Jewish Legion that was being formed as part of the British army. Trained in Canada, he arrived in Egypt as a member of the 40th Royal Fusiliers.

After the war he returned to Palestine where he cofounded Ahdut HaAvodah [*q.v.*] in 1919, Histadrut [*q.v.*] in 1920, and Mapai [*q.v.*] in 1930. From 1931 to 1948 he was president of the National Council of the representative assembly of the Yishuv [*q.v.*]. He was a Mapai member of the Knesset [*q.v.*] from 1949 until his election as president in December 1952 following the death of President Chaim Weizmann. He was reelected president in 1957 and 1962. Like his predecessor, he died in office.

Berri, Nabih (1938–): *Lebanese politician* Born into a Lebanese Shia [*q.v.*] merchant family that settled in Freetown, Sierra Leone, Berri returned to Tibnin in southern Lebanon, the town of his ancestors. During his days as a law student at the Lebanese University of Beirut [*q.v.*], he joined the semi-clandestine Baath Party [*q.v.*]. After a brief enrollment at Sorbonne University, Paris, and a short stay in Freetown, he went to the United States. There he married a Lebanese-American and raised a family before returning to Lebanon in early 1975. He allied with Imam Musa Sadr [*q.v.*], a radical Shia leader, and helped to establish a militia, Amal [*q.v.*]. Starting as a member of Amal's leadership council, he became its secretary-general in 1978 after the "disappearance" of Sadr in Libya. Under his stewardship Amal became one of the most effective militias in the Lebanese Civil War [*q.v.*]. In October 1981 he led an Amal delegation to Tehran [*q.v.*]. At the Amal conference in April 1982 he shared the leadership with Shaikh Muhammad Mahdi Shams al-Din, a Shia cleric.

Following Israel's occupation of southern and central Lebanon in June 1982, Berr encouraged Shia resistance to the Israeli occupiers. He became one of the leading opponents of President Amin Gemayel [*q.v.*] when the latter initialed a peace treaty with Israel [*q.v.*] in May 1983. Responding to Gemayel's order to the Lebanese army to raze the Shia suburbs of Beirut [*q.v.*] in February 1984, Berri issued a successful call to fellow Muslims in the Lebanese army to defy the president. Aided by the Druze [*q.v.*] militia, Amal captured West Beirut and weakened the presidency of Gemayel, who then abrogated the draft peace treaty with Israel. In the national unity government that followed, Berri became minister of south Lebanon and reconstruction.

He had close ties with Syria. At its behest his militia attacked the Palestinian camps based in Beirut and southern Lebanon in order to weaken the control of Fatah [*q.v.*] over them. He was one of the three leading militia commanders to sign the "National Agreement to Solve the Lebanese Crisis" in December 1985, but the document proved stillborn. From 1988 onwards he allowed Amal to be used by Syrian President Hafiz Assad [*q.v.*] to contain the growth of Hizbollah [*q.v.*], a radical Shia organization, whenever it suited him. Berri had reservations about the Syrian-brokered National Reconciliation Charter [*q.v.*]—agreed on in Taif, Saudi Arabia, in October 1989—because of its inequity toward Shias, but dropped them under pressure from Assad. The next month, following the election of Elias Hrawi [*q.v.*] as president, Berri was given a seat in the new cabinet under Salim Hoss [*q.v.*]. In June 1990 he was one of the 40 nominees to fill the vacant or newly created seats in parliament.

When Amal and other Muslim militias were disbanded after the victory of the pro-Syrian, predominantly Muslim forces over their right-wing Maronite adversaries in October 1990, a proportion of Amal's members was absorbed into the regular army. After a fresh general election in 1992, Berri was elected speaker of the parliament. He was reelected speaker after the 1996, 2000, and 2005 elections. In 2003 he was elected president of the Arab Parliamentary Union.

After the resignation of five Shia ministers from the government in November 2006, Berri refused to convene the parliament for a year and a half. Despite this, he secured 90 out of 128 votes when the freshly elected parliament met in July 2009. Two years later, his gesture to give up one of the Shia seats in the cabinet to a Sunni [*q.v.*], Faisal Karami, enabled Prime Minister Najib Mikati [*q.v.*] to end a five-month backroom bargaining and announce his new government.

In September 2011 he described the ongoing protests in Syria as "part of involvement in a foreign conspiracy" aiming to partition Syria, which would destabilize Lebanon, Iraq, and Turkey.

Bethlehem: *West Bank town* (In Arabic, *Beit lahm*; in Hebrew, *Beth lehem*: *house of bread/Lahmu, a goddess*) Population: 25,266 (2007 census). Known in Old Testament [*q.v.*] times as Ephrat, Bethlehem was the scene of the Book of Ruth and the home of King David (r. ca 1010–970 B.C.). It was the birthplace of Jesus Christ (ca 6 B.C. to 28 A.D.) and is a holy place for Christians [*q.v.*]. Roman Emperor Constantine I (r. 306–337 A.D.) built a basilica at the site of Jesus's birth. When the settlement fell to Muslim Arabs [*q.v.*] in 637 A.D., it was left untouched. The Church of the Nativity standing there today is shared by the Armenian Orthodox Church [*q.v.*] (which has the Grotto of the Nativity, containing the manger that is believed to have warmed the newborn Jesus), the Roman Catholic Church [*q.v.*] (which owns the site of the birth, marked by a 14-point star on a marble stone), and the Greek Orthodox Church [*q.v.*] (which possesses the High Altar standing above the Grotto).

Due to their steady emigration to North America, West Europe, and Australia, Christians now form only about one-third of the town's population.

Bible: *Christian scripture* "Bible" is the diminutive of *byblos*, the Greek word for papyrus (an ancient writing material), meaning *book*. The Bible is regarded by Christians [*q.v.*] as the word of God delivered through divinely directed authors. It is composed of the Old Testament and the New Testament. The longer Old Testament, also called the Hebrew [*q.v.*] Bible, is a record of the testament (i.e., solemn covenant) made by God with man and revealed to Moses (d. ca 1250 B.C.) on Mount Sinai. It was written mostly in Hebrew [*q.v.*] between 1200 B.C. and 100 B.C. and is accepted as a holy scripture by both Jews [*q.v.*] and Christians [*q.v.*]. The shorter New Testament is a record of the fulfillment of the Old Testament and of the fresh covenant, encapsulated in the life and death of Jesus Christ, between God and Christians. It was written mainly in Greek within a century of Christ's death (ca 30 A.D.) and is accepted as a holy scripture by Christians only.

The modern Old Testament is based on the Hebrew Bible which, originally consisting of 24 books, is divided into: (1) The Law/Pentateuch/Torah [*q.v.*], containing five books; (2) The Prophets, containing eight books; and (3) The Holy Writings/Hagiographia, containing 11 books.

(1) The Pentateuch spans the period between the Creation of the universe (ca 3760 B.C.) and the death of Moses (ca 1250 B.C.). Genesis, the first book, begins with the creation of the universe and ends with Joseph, a great-grandson of Abraham (ca 1800 B.C.), becoming an adviser to the Egyptian king. The four remaining works deal with the activities of

Moses and the covenant between God and the Israelites. *Exodus* describes the deliverance of the Israelites from four centuries of bondage in Egypt, God's present of the Law to Moses on Mount Sinai, and God's covenant with the Israelites. *Leviticus* deals chiefly with the rituals of worship. *Numbers* describes the wanderings of the Israelites in the Sinai [*q.v.*] desert for 40 years. In *Deuteronomy* Moses summarizes the Law, and the book ends with a description of his death on the frontiers of the Promised Land.

(2) The Prophets is a record of the activities of the divinely inspired men (prophets), who lived during the ninth century B.C. through the fifth century B.C. Their books cover the history of the period between the death of Moses and the fall of the Kingdom of Judah in the sixth century B.C.

(3) The Holy Writings consist of books of poetry, songs, aphorisms, prophecy, and history. *Psalms* (ca third century B.C.) contains the hymns and prayers used to worship JHVH (pronounced Yahweh), the sacred name of God. *Job* (ca sixth century B.C.) is a narrative poem about a man named Job who was beset by disasters. *Proverbs* (ca fourth century B.C.) is a collection of aphorisms and epigrams about human existence, offering a positive, pragmatic philosophy of life. *Song of Songs* (ca 10th century B.C.) contains wedding songs. *Ruth* (ca fourth century B.C.) is the story of the marriage of Ruth, a Moabite woman, to Boaz, a Hebrew landowner. *Lamentations* (ca mid-sixth century B.C.) consists of poems lamenting the destruction of Jerusalem [*q.v.*] and the First Temple. *Ecclesiastes* (ca third century B.C.), like *Proverbs*, contains

maxims, but their general tone is skeptical. *Esther* (ca second century B.C.) is the tale of Esther, the Hebrew wife of a Persian king, Ahasuerus, whose courageous actions save the Jewish community from an evil prime minister. The next three books—*Chronicles, Ezra,* and *Nehemiah,* which are attributed to a scribe at the Second Temple (537–350 B.C.) and written around 250 B.C.—are historical works that update the chronicle of the Jews, including the return of the exiled Jews to Jerusalem, the restoration of its walls by Nehemia (445 B.C.), and the legal reforms of Ezra (397 B.C.). *Daniel* (ca 165 B.C.), the last book, begins with the capture of the prophet Daniel in Babylon and the fall of the city to the Persians, and ends with a revelation of the end of history, proclaiming the arrival of the Kingdom of God.

Of the 27 books of the New Testament, 21 are epistles. The New Testament begins with *The Gospels*—a book each by Matthew, Mark, Luke, and John, disciples of Jesus Christ, who describe his life and teachings. The first three works, called *Synoptic Gospels,* are somewhat similar and are nowadays judged to be anti-Semitic [*q.v.*]. *The Gospel according to John,* instead of focusing on Jesus's biography as the other disciples did, concentrates on the theme of Jesus as the word of God made flesh. It too is considered anti-Semitic. The fifth book, *The Acts of the Apostles,* ascribed to Luke, describes the history of early Christianity led by Peter (d. 67 A.D.), as well as the missionary work of Paul (d. 65 A.D.). *The Epistles* follow—attributed to Paul (14 epistles), and to James, Peter, John, and Jude, disciples of Jesus Christ. The epistles are addressed to the young churches and deal chiefly with Christian doctrine and worship. The New Testament ends with *Revelation*, a prophetic book written during the rule of Domitian (r. 81–96 A.D.), most probably by more than one person, including John. In the traditional apocalyptic style of Hebrew literature, the book describes the catastrophes that will presage the Day of Judgment at the end of history.

Because Christians later split into three major churches—Roman Catholic [*q.v.*], Orthodox (Catholic) [*q.v.*], and Protestant [*q.v.*]—different versions of the Bible are in use today. Since the Roman Catholic Old Testament in Latin was translated from the Septuagint (the Greek translation of the Hebrew Bible rendered in third century B.C.), and not from the later Hebrew Bible of Jamnia, it includes seven books not contained in the later version. This, and the division of single books into two or more, explains why there are as many as 46 books in the Roman Catholic Old Testament. As a translation of the Septuagint they are arranged differently from the Hebrew Bible: The Pentateuch, The Historical Books, The Didactic Books, The Prophetical Books, and The Historical Books. The Protestant Old Testament has 39 books, arranged in the same way as those in the Roman Catholic Bible, but without the last collection of Historical Books. The Orthodox (Catholic) Church, consisting largely of Greek or Slavic churches, uses either the Septuagint for the Old Testament and the Greek New Testament (for Greek churches), or their translations into Old Church Slavonic (for the Slavic churches).

bin (Arabic: *son*): It is customary for an Arab male from the Arabian Peninsula [*q.v.*] to identify himself as the bin (son), of his father, followed by his surname, often prefixed with al (the). Those of high social rank tend to include more than one generation in the name.

bin Laden, Osama (b. 1957–2011): *Saudi Islamist, leader of al-Qaida* Son of Muhammad Awad bin Laden—a bricklayer from South Yemen [*q.v.*], who after settling in the Saudi city of Jeddah [*q.v.*], became a leading construction magnate—and Alia Hamida Ghanoum, the youngest of his 11 wives, in Jeddah. After finishing his secondary education in 1974 at an elite high school, he graduated in civil engineering at King Abdul Aziz University in 1978. He regarded those who mounted the armed uprising in Mecca [*q.v.*] in November 1979 as "true Muslims" [*q.v.*].

After visiting the Pakistani city of Peshawar in the spring of 1980, he successfully lobbied his brothers, relatives, and friends to support the anti-Soviet struggle in Afghanistan. He returned to Pakistan with the hefty donations he had collected in Saudi Arabia [*q.v.*], and several Afghan and Pakistani employees of Saudi Binladin Group, owned by his family, to set up an office to support non-Afghan mujahedin in cooperation with Pakistan's Inter-Services Intelligence (ISI) and the U.S. Central Intelligence Agency (CIA), which oversaw the conduct of the anti-Soviet campaign. Bin Laden came under the influence of Abdullah Azzam [*q.v.*], who in 1984 established the *Maktab al-Khidmat* (Persian: *Bureau of Service* [to the non-Afghan mujahedin]) in Peshawar. Besides vetting non-Afghan volunteers, and sending them to one of the constituents of the seven-party Afghan Mujahedin Alliance, bin Laden supervised the construction of roads and the refurbishing of caves for storing weapons in the Mujahedin-controlled areas. He also participated in guerrilla actions and armed encounters.

At the ISI-CIA training camps established on both sides of the Afghan-Pakistan frontier, the volunteers underwent military training—based on the manuals used by the Pentagon and the CIA, and translated into Persian [q.v.], Arabic [q.v.], and Urdu—as well as political education, which emphasized nationalism and Islam [q.v.]. In 1986 bin Laden oversaw the construction of a tunnel complex at Zhwahar Killi in the vicinity of Khost near the Pakistani border, to house a training center, weapons store, and medical facility with electricity and piped water as well as a jail for the prisoners of war. The new base was to be an addition to the already existing nearby cave complex at Tora Bora, which had proved impervious to the Soviet-Afghan assaults.

When the Soviets left Afghanistan in February 1989, bin Laden declared it to be a victory for the jihad [q.v.]. After the assassination of Azzam in November, he resolved to continue running Maktab al-Khidmat under the new title of al-Qaida (Arabic: *The Base*), but with a more ambitious aim of creating an international network of jihadis, those who had participated in the anti-Soviet jihad.

Frustrated by the internecine violence among Afghan Mujahedin, centered on ethnicity, that erupted after

the Soviet withdrawal, bin Laden returned to Jeddah in the spring of 1990. Here he became a much sought-after speaker, and his taped speeches became best sellers. During the crisis caused by Iraq's invasion of Kuwait [q.v.] in August, he offered the Saudi government a plan to defend the kingdom by mobilizing citizens as well as his veteran mujahedin. It was rejected. Along with many fellow Saudis, he disapproved of the stationing of more than half a million Western troops, predominantly American, on Saudi soil. When, after the successful end of the Second Gulf War [q.v.] in February 1991, many thousands of U.S. soldiers stayed on in the kingdom, he protested vehemently.

He left the kingdom for Sudan, ruled by an Islamist [q.v.] military government. In Khartoum he set up several different businesses. During his five years there, he ran al-Qaida along corporate lines, with the policy-making Shura Council of 12 served by four executive committees: military (headed by Muhammad Atef [q.v.]), business, Islamic studies, and media and public relations. He kept up his attacks on the continued presence of infidel soldiers on Arabia's holy soil and the regime that allowed it.

He pursued his political-religious agenda of waging jihad against the U.S. by either directly financing al-Qaida's terrorist actions or sponsoring like-minded groups abroad while offering to train their activists at al-Qaida camps in Sudan, thus turning al-Qaida into an umbrella organization, specializing in conducting jihad violently. It established associate relationships with like-minded groups in Algeria, Chechnya, Egypt, Ethiopia, Lebanon, Libya, the Philippines, Syria, and Yemen, and maintained guest houses in different countries. In 1992–93, he intervened in the civil war in Somalia, with Atef supervising the training of the Somali tribes opposed to the UN intervention in the conflict. Later bin Laden would be accused by Washington of aiding and abetting the attacks on U.S. troops within the UN force, as a result of which 18 American soldiers died while hunting for Somali warlord Muhammad Farah Aideed—as did nearly 500 Somalis.

In early 1994 the Saudi government revoked bin Laden's citizenship and froze his assets—estimated to be $20–25 million. There was an unsuccessful attempt on his life. He responded by establishing the Committee for Advice and Reform (CAR) with the purported aim of promoting peaceful reform in Saudi Arabia, and opened an office in London.

To get its name removed from Washington's list of states that support international terrorism, Sudan's government agreed in early 1996 to put bin Laden under surveillance, thus following the lead of the CIA, which had by then set up a special bin Laden Station, an unprecedented step taken regarding an individual. Sudan's gesture was not enough. But, as neither the United States nor Saudi Arabia wanted bin Laden for itself (the United States lacked evidence to prove his guilt of killing Americans), in May 1996 bin Laden and his entourage left for Jalalabad in Afghanistan, then in the throes of a civil war between a ramshackle government in Kabul and the newly arisen Pakistan-backed Taliban. The area where he took refuge was outside the Taliban's control. It was only after it had captured Kabul and the areas to its east in September that bin Laden sought its protection. He got it but only after the Taliban's spiritual leader, Mullah Muhammad Omar, based in Kandahar, had accepted bin Laden's oath of loyalty to him.

In return, bin Laden ordered several hundred of his experienced militia to fight alongside the Taliban in the civil war. His fighters consisted of those veterans of the anti-Soviet jihad who, on returning home, had been intolerably harassed by their governments, and the post-1989 Mujahedin, dispirited by the decline in the jihads in the Balkans, Chechnya, and Kashmir. Assisted by bin Laden's veterans, Mullah Omar's government extended its control over 85 percent of Afghanistan.

On the eve of the formation of the World Islamic Front for Jihad against Crusaders and Jews [q.v.] in February 1998, bin Laden and four other Islamist leaders deplored the suffering of the Palestinians and Iraqi people and declared it to be the religious duty of Muslims everywhere to kill the Americans and their allies—civilian and military—wherever possible in order to liberate the al-Aqsa Mosque (in Jerusalem [q.v.]) and the Holy Mosque (in Mecca [q.v.]) from their control.

Following the detonation of huge bombs at the U.S. Embassies in Nairobi and Dar es Salaam on 7 August 1998, which killed 227 people, Washington held bin Laden responsible for the deadly blasts, and called on the Taliban to hand him over. Mullah Omar refused. By now bin Laden was listed among the "Ten Most Wanted Fugitives" by the U.S. Federal Bureau of Investigation, with $5 million reward for information leading to his arrest, a sum that would later be raised to $25 million.

America saw the hand of al-Qaida in the bombing of U.S.S. *Cole* in Aden [*q.v.*] in October 2000, which killed 17 servicemen. Two months later, working together with Russia, the administration of U.S. President Bill Clinton (r. 1993–2001) had the UN Security Council demand the extradition of bin Laden from the Taliban-controlled Afghanistan within a month on pain of an imposition of arms embargo on the Taliban regime. Mullah Omar defied the resolution. The subsequent ban brought him and bin Laden closer, with al-Qaida's well-trained non-Afghan fighters now forming the Taliban's 55th Brigade.

The public trial in February 2001 in New York of four al-Qaida operatives, charged with conspiracy for the bombings in Nairobi and Dar as Salam, gave bin Laden a higher profile in the Muslim world than before, and raised his influence over Mullah Omar. When, following the terrorist attacks in New York and Washington on 11 September, the U.S. administration of President George W. Bush (r. 2001–2009) held him responsible, and called on Mullah Omar to hand him over to America, the Taliban leader argued that bin Laden could not have been the culprit.

In the course of his videotaped meeting with a visiting radical cleric from Jeddah, named Khalid Harbi, bin Laden named nine of the 9/11 hijackers, adding that they had been instructed to go to America, but were told of the operation just before boarding the planes. Bin Laden also revealed that he and other plotters had discussed the extent of the damage that would be caused to the Twin Towers of the World Trade Center in New York City by the impact of the flying aircraft. The videotape, obtained by the United States in the third week of November (after the flight of the Taliban from Kabul on 12–13 November), was released to the media in mid-December 2001.

After fleeing Afghanistan, bin Laden found refuge in Pakistan's South Waziristan tribal agency, and then returned to the border area of Afghanistan. He took to sending audio-taped statements to Al-Jazeera satellite television, timing them to coincide with the first anniversary of 9/11 or the high point of the hajj [*q.v.*] in February 2003 during the American military buildup to invade Iraq.

In 2004 he made his way to the Swat region of northern Pakistan. After a few months he moved south to Haripur district in Khyber Pakhtunkhwa province. On the eve of the U.S. presidential election in November 2004, the airing of a videotape by bin Laden highlighted his threatening presence as well as the reality of the "war on terror," particularly to the voters in the U.S. That led most of the undecided Americans to favor the incumbent Bush, who managed to garner 51 percent of the popular vote. Thus he became the second Third World leader to impact directly on an American presidential election, the first being Ayatollah Ruhollah Khomeini [*q.v.*].

In May 2005, bin Laden moved from Haripur to the Bilal Town

suburb of Abbottabad, to occupy a newly built three-story house enclosed by a high compound wall. He lived there with his three wives and their many children until the helicopter raid by the Pentagon's Special Forces in the early hours of 2 May 2011. The raiders killed bin Laden and three others, and took his corpse to the Bagram air base in Afghanistan. From there it was flown to the aircraft carrier the *Carl Vinson* in the North Arabian Sea, and given a sea burial.

bint (*Arabic: daughter*) It is customary for an Arab female to identify herself as the bint (daughter), of her father, followed by his surname, often prefixed with al (the).

Bishara, Azmi (1956–) *Israeli Arab academic and politician* Born into a middle-class Roman Catholic [*q.v.*] family in Nazareth [*q.v.*], Bishara founded the National Committee of Arab High School Students in 1974. Later, while enrolled at Haifa University for a degree in political science, he established the Arab Students Union, which elected him its chairman. After receiving a doctorate in philosophy from Humboldt University in Germany in 1986, he taught cultural studies and philosophy at Bir Zeit University near Ramallah [*q.v.*], West Bank [*q.v.*], and also worked as a senior researcher at the Van Leer Institute in Jerusalem [*q.v.*]. Along with his Jewish [*q.v.*] Israeli colleagues, he founded the Palestinian Institute for Research of Democracy.

In 1996 he was elected to the Knesset [*q.v.*] as a member of the United Arab List. On the eve of the 1999 election he founded the National

Democratic Assembly-Balad and won a Knesset seat on its ticket. In early 2001 he became the first Israeli Arab [*q.v.*] to enter the race for prime minister. However, he withdrew at the last moment without endorsing any other candidate.

In November 2001, the Knesset revoked his immunity accorded to parliamentarians. It did so to let the attorney general initiate criminal proceedings against him under the Prevention of Terrorism Ordinance (1948) regarding the speeches he delivered in Israel in June 2000 and at President Hafiz Assad's [*q.v.*] memorial service in Syria a year later, in which he upheld the Palestinians' right to resist the Israeli occupation of their territories. It was the first time that the Knesset stripped the immunity of one of its members because of the political statements made by the member in the course of performing his/her duty as an elected representative.

On the eve of the 2003 parliamentary election, the Israeli election commission barred him by 22 votes to 19 from running for election, but the High Court upturned the ban. He retained his seat. He was reelected to the Seventeenth Knesset in March 2006. He visited Syria in September after the 34-day Israel-Hizbollah War [*q.v.*] which ended on 14 August 2006. By so doing he violated the law passed after his 2001 visit to Syria which barred Knesset members from visiting any enemy state. He also visited Lebanon, where he reportedly told the Lebanese Prime Minister Saad Hariri [*q.v.*] that Hizbollah's resistance to Israel has "lifted the spirit of the Arab people."

Against the backdrop of police investigation into his foreign contacts and accusations of aiding the enemy during wartime and laundering money received from foreign sources, he resigned from the Knesset while on a visit to Cairo [*q.v.*] in April 2007, saying that he would not receive a fair trial in Israel. He then went into self-exile.

In 2010 he was appointed director general of the Arab Center for Research and Policy Studies (Doha Institute) in Doha [*q.v.*]. He is the author of several books in Arabic and English, including *The Arabs in Israel*.

Bitar, Salah al-Din (1912–80): *Syrian politician* Born into a prominent Sunni [*q.v.*] family in Damascus [*q.v.*], Bitar received his higher education at Damascus University followed by Sorbonne University, Paris. Back in the Syrian capital in 1934, he taught mathematics and physics at a prestigious secondary school. In 1940, together with Michel Aflaq [*q.v.*], a fellow teacher, he established a study circle called the Movement of Arab Renaissance (*Baath*, in Arabic). They published pamphlets in which they expounded revolutionary socialist Arab nationalism, committed to achieving Arab unity as the first step. Once the Mandate power, France, had left Syria in April 1946, Bitar and Aflaq secured a license for their group, now called the Party of Arab Renaissance. They decided to merge their faction with the one led by Zaki Arsuzi [*q.v.*]. Out of this in April 1947 emerged the Arab Baath Party [*q.v.*] in Damascus. Bitar was elected to its four-member executive committee.

In 1954 he became a member of parliament. As the foreign minister from 1954 to 1957, he actively backed the idea of a union between Syria and Egypt. The next year, following the formation of the United Arab Republic (UAR) [*q.v.*], Bitar was appointed its minister of national guidance. But when UAR President Abdul Gamal Nasser [*q.v.*] dissolved the Arab Baath Socialist Party [*q.v.*] in 1959, he resigned. After the Baathist coup of March 1963 he became prime minister but lost his seat in the Baath Party's national command.

As the Baathist Military Committee tightened its grip over the party and the government, Bitar, identified with the rival civilian wing of the party, found himself out of favor. After intermittently ceding the premiership to General Hafiz Amin, he lost his office in February 1966, when the civilian faction was purged from the government. He escaped to Lebanon. In 1969 he was sentenced to death in absentia in Damascus. Soon after Hafiz Assad [*q.v.*] seized power in November 1970, he pardoned Bitar.

During his exile in Beirut [*q.v.*] he stayed away from the Baathist national command led by Aflaq, which forged links with the Baathist regime of Iraq. From Beirut he moved to Paris. In January 1978 he was invited to Damascus for talks with President Assad, but the two leaders failed to reconcile their views. After his return to Paris, Bitar started publishing a journal, *Al-Ihya al-Arabi* (Arabic: *The Arab Revival*), which became a mobilizing forum for various Syrian opposition groups in exile. He was assassinated in Paris in July 1980. Syria's complicity in the killing, though not proven, was widely suspected.

Black September Organization: *A Palestinian group* This Palestinian group, led by Wadi Haddad, was formed by militant members of Fatah [*q.v.*] soon after the defeat of the Palestinian commandos by the Jordanian army in September 1970, and was named after that month. Following the assassination in November 1971 of Jordanian Premier Wasfi Tal in Cairo [*q.v.*], the four Palestinians claiming responsibility for it declared that they belonged to the Black September Organization (BSO).

Eight BSO members took hostage nine of the 11 Israeli athletes at the Olympic village near Munich, Germany, on 5 September 1972, the remaining two Israelis having died earlier in the struggle. Their demand that they and their hostages be put aboard an aircraft was met. But at the airport there was a shoot-out between them and the German security forces. All nine Israeli athletes were killed—eight of them by the German security personnel—as were five Palestinians. The remaining three hostage takers were captured.

The macabre drama was reported live by some 6,000 newspersons and the largest gathering of television equipment ever assembled, thus inadvertently highlighting the fate of Palestinians as a people nursing deeply felt grievances. In retribution, Israel's three-day long air raids on Palestinian refugee camps in Syria and Lebanon killed 200 to 500 people, mostly civilians. Over the next few years Mossad [*q.v.*] assassinated 12 Palestinians believed to have been involved in the Munich attack.

Borochov, Dov Ber (1881–1917): *Zionist thinker* Born in Kiev, Ukraine, Borochov became the leading ideologue of Zionist socialism. He started out as a member of the Russian Social Democratic Labor Party, but in 1900 left to become a cofounder of Poale Zion [*q.v.*] in Minsk, Belarus. He offered a program of socialism, Zionism and migration to Palestine [*q.v.*]. He argued that before the Jews could launch a class struggle they first had to achieve nationhood, and for that they had to have a country of their own.

He chose Palestine partly because it was regarded as the historic homeland of the Jews [*q.v.*], and partly because, being a "derelict country," it held interest only for minor and medium-sized Jewish capitalists—not the big ones—and thus offered revolutionary promise for the Jewish proletariat, which was to be fostered there. He regarded local Arabs [*q.v.*] as Turkish subjects, lacking national consciousness, and visualized their assimilation, economic and cultural, into the Jewish nation as it developed economically under Jewish initiative and leadership. He left Russia in 1907 and returned 10 years later to attend the Congress of Minorities called by the Alexander Kerensky regime. He died in Kiev.

Boutros-Ghali, Boutros (1922–): *Egyptian politician; UN secretary-general, 1992–96* Born into a prominent Coptic [*q.v.*] family that was active in nationalist politics in Cairo [*q.v.*], Boutros received higher education at Cairo University and then Paris University, where he obtained diplomas in political science and economics and a doctorate in international law in 1949. He then taught international law and international affairs at Cairo University. In 1960 he founded the *Al-Ahram al-Iqtisadi* (Arabic: *Economic Al-Ahram*) as the weekly magazine of the *Al-Ahram* (Arabic: *The Pyramids*) newspaper, and edited it for the next 15 years. He also authored several studies of international problems.

In 1977 President Anwar Sadat [*q.v.*] appointed him minister of state for foreign affairs. He played a role in the negotiations that led to the Camp David Accords [*q.v.*] between Egypt and Israel in September 1978. He retained his position under the presidency of Hosni Mubarak [*q.v.*]. He was elected to parliament in 1987 as a member of the ruling National Democratic Party [*q.v.*], and was promoted to deputy minister for foreign affairs four years later. On 1 January 1992 he assumed the office of the UN secretary-general. Five years later 14 of the 15 UN Security Council members backed his bid for a second term, but the United States vetoed it.

In 1999, he published his experiences at the United Nations in *Unvanquished: A U.S.-UN Saga.*

Bu (Arabic: *father*): Derivative of abu [*q.v.*]

Byblos: *Lebanese town* Population: 40,000 (2011 est.) Known in Arabic as Jbail, a derivative of biblical Gebal, Byblos is one of the oldest settlements in the world. Some historians describe it as the oldest continuously inhabited town on the planet. Since papyrus, the ancient writing material later used for making paper, was exported from Lebanon to the Aegean region through Byblos, the place-name became the source

word in Greek for *book* and in English for *bible* and *bibliography*.

Archaeological work conducted during the 1920s established that Byblos has been inhabited since the eighth millennium B.C. In ancient times it was part of the Egyptian Empire, and an important trading place for cedar and other wood. After the end of Egyptian suzerainty in the 11th century B.C., Byblos emerged as the leading city of Phoenicia. Later, during the Roman era, it lost its supremacy to Tyre [*q.v.*]. In the course of the Crusades it was captured in 1103 by the Crusaders, who retained it until 1291 as part of the Latin Kingdom of Jerusalem. It then came under the successive rule of the Mamlukes and the Ottomans.

Today its tourist offerings include a necropolis, an Obelisk Temple, Phoenician ramparts, a Roman theatre, and Crusader ramparts. It is a world heritage site of the UN Educational, Scientific, and Cultural Organization.

Cairo: *capital of Egypt* Population: 7.783 million (2011 est.) Cairo's Arabic name, al-Qairah, means "the Victorious." Located at the head of the River Nile [*q.v.*] delta, Cairo is the commercial, financial, industrial, educational, and cultural center of Egypt, and the most populous city of the Middle East [*q.v.*]. The ancient Roman settlement of Babylon was situated nearby; and Memphis, the capital of ancient Egypt, was across the Nile. Near Memphis are the Pyramids of Giza, a suburb of Cairo. The oldest pyramid, the tomb of Pharaoh Khufu (Cheops), dates back to 2640 B.C.

After Muslim [*q.v.*] Arabs [*q.v.*] had conquered Egypt in 641 A.D., they established the new capital, al-Fustat (Arabic: *The Encampment*), near the fortress of Babylon. In 969 A.D., following their conquest of Egypt, the Fatimids, a Shia [*q.v.*] dynasty from Tunis, founded Cairo, located 2 mi./3 km north of al-Fustat, as their capital. Since then Cairo has thrived. In the early 12th century the Crusaders' plan to capture it failed. It became the capital of the Islamic Empire under the Mamlukes (1260–1517). It then came under the suzerainty of the Ottomans. They lost it briefly to Napoleon Bonaparte in 1798, and then to the British in 1882. After Egypt's independence in 1922, the monarchical regime confirmed Cairo as the country's capital.

As a city rich in history since ancient times, it provides numerous tourist attractions. The most important of these, besides the Pyramids, are the Muallaqa Coptic Church [*q.v.*]; the Citadel (1179) built by Saladin (also known as Salah al-Din Ayubi); the mosques of Ibn Tulun (878 A.D.), al-Hakim (1010), and Muhammad Ali (1857); the Antiques Museum, spanning the pre-Islamic era from 3000 B.C. to 641 A.D.; the Coptic Museum; the Museum of Islamic Art; and the medieval Khan-e-Khalili bazaar. The city is the site of 16 universities, including al-Azhar University [*q.v.*] and the American University in Cairo [*q.v.*]. It is the headquarters of the Arab League [*q.v.*].

In late January 2011, the city's Tahrir (Arabic: *Liberation*) Square became the epicenter of the popular protest against President Hosni Mubarak [*q.v.*], with the initial gathering of 50,000 people occupying the square ballooning to two million in 18 days, and succeeding in forcing Mubarak to resign on 11 February.

Cairo Agreement (Lebanese-PLO, 1969): Relations between Lebanon and the Palestine Liberation Organization [*q.v.*] soured when their forces clashed on Lebanese soil in late October 1969. Responding to a mediation offer by Egyptian President Gamal Abdul Nasser [*q.v.*], the two sides signed an accord, popularly known as the Cairo Agreement. According to the unofficial leaks, it allowed the PLO to administer the Palestinian refugee camps and establish armed units and posts inside them, and also to hold transit routes and certain positions in southern Lebanon (which had emerged as a major Palestinian-Israeli battleground), in return for the PLO's promise to respect Lebanese sovereignty. Both sides broke the terms of the accord as and when expedient. After the Israeli invasion of Lebanon in June 1982 [*q.v.*]—resulting in the PLO's expulsion from Beirut [*q.v.*] and the creation of an Israeli-enforced security zone in southern Lebanon—the Cairo Agreement became virtually moribund.

Camp David Accords (Egypt-Israel, 1978): These accords were hammered out at the U.S. presidential retreat of Camp David, Maryland, in September 1978 between Egyptian President Anwar Sadat [*q.v.*] and Israeli Premier Menachem Begin [*q.v.*], with the assistance of U.S. President Jimmy Carter. They were signed in Washington on 18 September 1978. They laid out the framework for a peace treaty between Egypt and Israel, and a resolution of the Palestinian problem.

The highlights of the accord concerning Egypt and Israel were as follows: Egypt would regain Sinai [*q.v.*] in exchange for an agreement to conclude a peace treaty and establish normal relations with Israel. The negotiations would establish security zones in Sinai and limit the forces of both sides stationed there. Once the peace treaty was signed, within three months (in practice it took six months), a phased pull-back by Israeli troops would start, the first such withdrawal to be within three to six months after the treaty, and the last two to three years later.

The highlights of the regional peace, especially concerning the Palestinians, were as follows: Over a five-year transition period the West Bank [*q.v.*] and Gaza Strip [*q.v.*] would gain autonomy and see the end of Israeli military rule, while Israel would maintain military camps on the West Bank. Jordan was to be invited into the negotiations, and could have a security role if it wanted. During the transition period there would be talks on the final status of the West Bank and Gaza Strip between Israel, Egypt, Jordan (if it wished), and the elected representatives of resident Palestinians. During these negotiations there would be a freeze on new Israeli settlements on the West Bank and the Gaza Strip.

The Egypt-Israel peace treaty was signed on 26 March 1979 in Washington, and endorsed by the parliaments of the two countries. In the first

phase of the Israeli withdrawal from the Sinai Peninsula, Israel vacated two-thirds of the peninsula from El Arish on the Mediterranean coast to Ras Muhammad on the Red Sea on 23 January 1980. The two sides exchanged ambassadors on 26 February. The final Israeli withdrawal occurred on 26 April 1982.

The total cost to the United States of military and economic aid to Israel and Egypt, promised in order to secure the Camp David Accords, was put at $10 billion, with two-thirds going to Israel.

Carter Doctrine (1980): *U.S. policy on the Gulf region* Responding to Soviet military intervention in Afghanistan in late December 1979, U.S. President James Carter, in his State of the Union address to the U.S. Congress on 24 January 1980, stated: "An attempt by any outside force to gain control of the Persian Gulf region will be regarded as an assault on the vital interests of the United States. It will be repelled by use of any means necessary, including military force." Conceptually, the Carter Doctrine was a virtual repetition of what President Franklin Roosevelt had said in 1943—"The defense of Saudi Arabia is vital to the defense of the United States"—and a reiteration of the Eisenhower Doctrine [*q.v.*] proclaimed in 1957.

In its application, it advanced the steps taken by the Carter administration soon after the downfall of Muhammad Reza Shah Pahlavi of Iran [*q.v.*] in February 1979: to establish a joint task force of 50,000, to be called the Rapid Deployment Force (RDF), for safeguarding Gulf oil supplies; to build up the U.S.

Fifth Fleet operating from Diego Garcia near Mauritius in the Indian Ocean; and to seek long-term access to air and naval bases in the Gulf. But of the six pro-Western Gulf States approached by Washington, only Oman agreed to let the U.S. use its military bases. The RDF was headquartered in the United States at MacDill Air Force Base near Tampa, Florida, in March 1980. The next U.S. president, Ronald Reagan, declared in October 1982: "An attack on Saudi Arabia would be considered an attack on the United States."

Catholics, Armenian: *see* Armenian Catholic Church.

Catholics, Assyrian: *see* Nestorian Christians.

Catholics, Chaldean: *see* Chaldean Catholic Church.

Catholics, Greek: *see* Greek Catholic Church.

Catholics, Maronite: *see* Maronite Catholic Church.

Catholics, Orthodox: *see* Orthodox Christians Church.

Catholics, Roman: *see* Roman Catholic Christians Church.

Catholics, Syrian: *see* Syrian Catholic Church.

C.E.: *Abbreviation of Common Era* This term is used by some non-Christian writers to denote A.D. [*q.v.*].

Cedar Revolution (Lebanon): *an anti-Syrian movement in Lebanon* Cedar Revolution was the term used for a series of demonstrations sparked by the assassination of the former Lebanese Prime Minister Rafiq Hariri [*q.v.*] on 14 February 2005. It was coined by the U.S. State Department which tried to link it to other color revolutions—Rose and Orange respectively in Georgia (November 2003) and Ukraine (November 2004 to January 2005)—that occurred in the former Soviet republics. The protestors wanted the withdrawal of the 14,000 Syrian troops and intelligence agents from Lebanon and an international investigation into Hariri's assassination. The crowning mass demonstration took place on 14 March 2005, and the subsequent anti-Syrian alliance acquired the moniker of 14 March Alliance [*q.v.*]. Syria withdrew all its forces on 27 April, and a general election, monitored by the United Nations, was held in May and June 2005.

Central Treaty Organization: *multilateral defense pact involving Middle Eastern countries* A Western-sponsored regional alliance, briefly known as the Baghdad Pact [*q.v.*], it started as the Middle East Treaty Organization (METO) in 1954. As part of its global strategy to create a worldwide chain of anti-Soviet alliances, in February 1954 the United States encouraged Turkey, a member of North Atlantic Treaty Organization, to sign a Pact of Mutual Cooperation with Pakistan. In April Washington concluded a military assistance agreement with Iraq, followed by a Pact of Mutual Assistance with Pakistan in May.

This set the scene for the signing of a military agreement in February 1955 between Turkey and Iraq, the nucleus of the Baghdad Pact. Later that year Iran, Pakistan, and Britain joined the Baghdad Pact, which pledged military aid in the event of Communist aggression against a fellow member.

Western pressure on Jordan, Lebanon, and Syria to join failed due to widespread nationalist, pan-Arab [q.v.] feelings expressed in huge demonstrations. After the republican coup in July 1958, Iraq pulled out of the Baghdad Pact in March 1959, which was then officially and popularly called Central Treaty Organization (CENTO), with its headquarters in Ankara. Because it was meant to provide defense against Communist aggression, Pakistan's attempts to invoke it in its wars with India in 1965 and 1971 failed. After its Islamic revolution [q.v.] in February 1979, Iran quit CENTO, destroying its geographical continuity and military effectiveness, and hastening its demise later that year.

Chalabi, Ahmad Abdul Hadi (1945–):
Iraqi politician Born into a rich banking family in Baghdad, Ahmad Chalabi and his parents fled Baghdad [q.v.] in the wake of the anti-royalist coup in 1958. After university education in Beirut [q.v.], Chalabi enrolled at the Massachusetts Institute of Technology, and then obtained a doctorate in mathematics at the University of Chicago. He became a mathematics professor at the American University in Beirut [q.v.]. He stayed there until 1977 when, due to the escalating Lebanese Civil War [q.v.], he moved to Amman [q.v.].

He established Petra Bank there. Within a decade, it became the third-largest bank in Jordan [q.v.], only to be seized by the Central Bank of Jordan in mid-1989 due to shady foreign exchange transactions. His reported flight in the boot of a friend's car to Damascus [q.v.] damaged his reputation. He moved to London where he later became a British citizen. In 1992 the State Security Court in Amman convicted him in absentia in two cases, and sentenced him to a 20-year jail term. In the wake of Iraq's invasion of Kuwait [q.v.] in 1990, he carved out a niche for himself in the Iraqi opposition circles in London.

The U.S. Central Intelligence Agency (CIA) recruited him as an asset partly because he lacked any constituency inside Iraq, so he was the least threatening to other opposition groups, each of which had some sort of contacts at home. In June 1992, at the convention of 300 opposition delegates in Vienna, bankrolled by the CIA, Chalabi was elected leader of the Iraqi National Congress (INC) [q.v.], an umbrella body that gained the affiliation of nearly 20 groups.

He moved to Salahuddin in Iraqi Kurdistan [q.v.], the headquarters of the INC, with a plan to develop the region as the launching pad to overthrow the regime of President Saddam Hussein [q.v.]. But his plan in March 1995 to combine a military coup against Saddam with a popular uprising in the area adjacent to Kurdistan failed when the U.S. withdrew its support for it, preferring to back an alternative plan by the Iraqi National Accord (INA) [q.v.].

In September 1996, following the intra-Kurdish fighting in which the

Kurdistan Democratic Party [*q.v.*] successfully secured Saddam Hussein's military assistance to defeat its rival, the Patriotic Union of Kurdistan [*q.v.*], the CIA decided to pull out all its 5,500 Arab and Kurdish agents, including Chalabi from Kurdistan.

After the passage of Iraq Liberation Act in October 1998, the INC was recognized as one of the six factions that qualified for official U.S. assistance. But, in April 1999, protesting against Chalabi's high-handedness, the INC's executive committee members demoted him from chairman to an ordinary member of the committee.

The hawkish officials of the administration of President George W. Bush (2001-2009) warmly adopted Chalabi, who had by then developed close relations with influential pro-Israeli lawmakers. By contrast, he was now shunned by the state department and the CIA. At the Iraqi Open Opposition Conference in London in December 2002, his proposal for a transitional government in post-Saddam Iraq was rejected.

After the Anglo-American invasion of Iraq [*q.v.*] in March 2003, Chalabi was appointed to the Interim Iraqi Governing Council by the occupying Coalition Provisional Authority. His INC remained on the payroll of the U.S. state department until September 2003 and of the Pentagon until May 2004. In August an arrest warrant was issued for Chalabi for alleged counterfeiting while he lived abroad. But, on his return to Baghdad [*q.v.*], he was not apprehended. The charge was dropped when the investigating judge cited lack of evidence.

On the eve of the January 2005 election to the Interim National Assembly, Chalabi, a secular Shia [*q.v.*], led the INC to join the United Iraqi Alliance (UIA) [*q.v.*], the brainchild of Grand Ayatollah Ali Sistani [*q.v.*]. When the UIA emerged as the majority group in parliament, he made a bid for prime minister. He failed because the UIA was primarily an alliance of the religious Shia parties. However, under the subsequent premiership of Ibrahim al-Jaafari [*q.v.*], he briefly served as the acting oil minister.

He ran in the December 2005 elections for the National Assembly under the new constitution as the leader of the secular National Congress Coalition (NCC), composed of the INC and some small groups. Gaining less than 1 percent of the popular vote, the NCC failed to win a single seat in the parliament.

In 2007, Prime Minister Nouri al-Maliki [*q.v.*] appointed him head of the Iraqi Services Committee—a consortium of eight service ministries and two Baghdad municipal departments—charged with restoring electricity, education and health services, and security services to Baghdad's numerous districts.

On the eve of the March 2010 parliamentary election, he revived the Supreme National De-Baathification Commission, originally set up under his chairmanship after the overthrow of the Baathist regime, to disqualify 500 mainly Sunni [*q.v.*] candidates from running in the election. This controversial move raised inter-sectarian tensions that had been lessening over the past few years.

During the early days of the Shia-led protest in Bahrain in 2011, it became known that Chalabi had helped leaders of Bahrain's al-Wafeq [*q.v.*] to establish contacts in Washington in order to lobby their case in the U.S.

Chaldean Catholic Church: Originally, it was composed of the members of the Nestorian Church [*q.v.*], who split from it to follow John Sulaka, appointed Patriarch of Catholic Nestorians by Roman Catholic [*q.v.*] Pope Julius III in 1551. The term Chaldean was used partly to differentiate it from the Nestorian Church of Cyprus, which had reconciled with Rome earlier, and partly because the followers were originally from Chaldea and Mesopotamia [*q.v.*]. The Chaldean Catholic Church is a Uniate church [*q.v.*], and follows East Syriac liturgy. Its Patriarch Catholicos of Babylon of the Chaldeans is based in Mosul [*q.v.*]. Its adherents in the Middle East [*q.v.*] live mainly in Iraq and Lebanon—as well as Iran.

The roots of Christianity [*q.v.*] in Iraq and Iran go back to the second century. Following its adoption of Nestorianism [*q.v.'*] by the Church of the East in the fifth century, it expanded into Central Asia and China. The rise of Timur Beg in the 14th century led to the decimation of this church in Central Asia and China.

In Iraq, the Chaldean community was 500,000 strong before the Anglo-American invasion of Iraq [*q.v.*] in 2003 when its best-known member was Tariq Aziz [*q.v.*]. Due to the widespread violence in the post-2003 Iraq, in which Christians were frequently targeted by al-Qaida in Mesopotamia [*q.v.*], the size of this group shrank. In Iran, the church is governed by the Chaldean Catholic Metropolitan Archdiocese of Tehran.

Chamoun, Camille Nimr (1900–87): *Lebanese politician; president, 1952– 58* Born into a Maronite [*q.v.*] family in Deiral Qamar, Chamoun acquired a degree from the French Law College of Beirut [*q.v.*] in 1925. He entered parliament nine years later and became finance minister (1938) and interior minister (1943). In 1944 he was Lebanon's envoy to Britain, and two years later he was the chief Lebanese representative at the United Nations. On his return to Beirut in 1947 he served as a minister for a year. He parted company with President Bishara Khouri [*q.v.*] when the latter had the constitution amended to pave the way for his reelection to the presidency. He joined the opposition, and became its choice to succeed Khouri when, facing charges of corruption, he resigned in September 1952.

Disregarding the program of his supporters to concentrate on domestic reform, Chamoun focused on foreign affairs. Despite pressure from Muslim politicians, he did not break his links with Britain and France during the latter's aggression against Egypt in October 1956 in the Suez War [*q.v.*]. His open alignment with the West, coupled with his rigging of the 1957 general election and repression of the opposition, angered the pan-Arab camp. A civil war [*q.v.*] erupted in May 1958. When the pro-Western monarchy in Iraq was overthrown by pan-Arabist military officers in mid-July, he called for the dispatch of U.S. troops to Lebanon under the Eisenhower Doctrine [*q.v.*]. The arrival of these troops intensified the civil conflict. To expedite the departure of foreign troops after the end of the civil war on 31 July, opposition lawmakers agreed to vote for General Fuad Chehab [*q.v.*]—the army commander who had remained neutral in the war—as president in September.

Chamoun then founded the National Liberal Party [*q.v.*]. In the 1968 election it joined the Triple Alliance to oppose those Christian candidates who, as Chehabists, wanted to marry Christian identity with Arab nationalism [*q.v.*]. He took an increasingly anti-Palestinian stance because he feared that, encouraged by the support of armed Palestinians, the Lebanese Muslims would strive to strip the Christians of their traditional power. At the beginning of the 1975–90 Lebanese Civil War [*q.v.*] between the pan-Arab, leftist, predominantly Muslim camp, and the right-wing Christian camp, he emerged as the leader of the Lebanese Front [*q.v.*], a confederation of largely Maronite organizations, committed to maintaining the status quo.

His party set up its own militia, the Tigers, commanded by his son, Danny. But the Tigers were defeated in a series of clashes with the militia of the Phalange Party [*q.v.*], a Maronite faction. After the ascendancy of the Phalange and its leaders, the Gemayels [*q.v.*], in the wake of the Israeli invasion of Lebanon in June 1982 [*q.v.*], the importance of Chamoun waned. The successful Second National Reconciliation Conference in March 1984 in Lausanne paved the way for Chamoun to join the subsequent national unity government, which he served until his death three years later.

Chehab, Fuad (1902–73): *Lebanese military leader and politician; president, 1958–64* Born into a Maronite [*q.v.*]

family, Chehab joined the army during the French Mandate and rose to the rank of colonel. After the independence of Lebanon in 1946 he was promoted to general and appointed commander of the army. He modernized the force and maintained its neutrality during political crises. When the opposition mounted street demonstrations against the corrupt government of President Bishara Khouri [*q.v.*] in September 1952, he kept the army in the barracks. Unable to withstand rising popular pressure, Khouri resigned. Under the new president, Camille Chamoun [*q.v.*], Chehab served briefly as the prime minister as well as the defense and interior minister. In the May 1958 Civil War [*q.v.*] between pro-Western forces, led by President Chamoun, and nationalist-leftist forces, headed by Kamal Jumblat [*q.v.*], Chehab, commanding a force of 8,000, remained neutral. His impartiality paved the way for his election to the presidency and an end to the civil strife.

Reflecting the bipartisan backing he had received, he maintained stability by aligning his external policies with those of the Arab hinterland, and by coopting the leaders of urban Muslims in ruling the country. At home, supported by military officers and technocrats, he tried to modernize the Lebanese political-administrative machine, which was steeped in feudal values and sectarian cleavages. His public works program, including road building in rural north and south, led to increased migration from villages to cities. That in turn resulted in the radicalization of Lebanese politics. After stepping down in 1964 he continued to wield influence through the many lawmakers as well as military and intelligence officers who remained loyal to him.

Christian calendars: *Gregorian and Julian* The Christian [*q.v.*] calendar is solar. The one introduced by Roman Emperor Julius Ceasar (102–44 B.C.) in 46 B.C. was called the Julian calendar, in which the year consisted of 365 days, each fourth year having 366 days, and the months bearing the same names, order, and length as now. But when it was discovered that a solar year consisted of 365.242189, not 365.25, days—a difference of about ll minutes annually—corrections had to be made for the past inconsistency and an appropriate step taken for the future. This was done by Pope Gregory XIII (1502–85) in 1582, and the new calendar was called Gregorian.

By re-dating 5 October 1582 as 15 October 1582, 10 days were lost. For the future it was specified that for the centesimal years—1600, 1700, and so on—only those exactly divisible by 400 should be leap years. In 1582 the difference between the two calendars was 10 days. It extended to 11 days from 1700 to 1800, then 12 from 1800 to 1900, and 13 from 1900 to 2000. It will increase to 14 in 2100.

It was not until September 1752 that Britain and British colonies in the Americas adopted the Gregorian calendar. Russia did so after the Bolshevik Revolution in October 1917.

In 1681 the Pope moved the New Year from the Spring Equinox (on 21 March) to 1 January, being the circumcision day of Jesus. Born a Jew [*q.v.*], Jesus was circumcised on the eighth day of his birth which, according to Christian [*q.v.*] tradition, is 25 December—or 24 December after sunset, according to Jews, for whom a day starts with sunset. The Christian era is computed to start with Jesus Christ's circumcision. It is now recognized that this date has been put four to eight years too late.

Christian fundamentalism: Christian fundamentalism rests primarily on the belief that both the Old Testament [*q.v.*] and the New Testament [*q.v.*] are literal expressions of the Divine Truth, particularly in their moral-ethical commandments and sociopolitical injunctions, and that they are absolutely infallible. It rests secondarily on the belief in the divinity of Christ and in the salvation of the believer's soul by the effective action of Christ's life, death, and resurrection.

The term fundamentalism came into vogue in the United States in the 1920s following the publication of the 12-volume *Fundamentals: The Testimony to Truth*. It was presented as antithetical to modernity and liberalism, which generally informed the Protestant church [*q.v.*] in the United States.

Christian fundamentalism has been particularly strong among Pentecostal Protestants in the southern states of the United States. Growing support for Christian fundamentalism in America, organized through such bodies as the Moral Majority, led to the Republican Party gaining a majority in both Houses of Congress in 1994. Since then the Christian right has carved out a powerful niche within the Republican Party, whose candidate George W. Bush won the presidency in 2000. Its pro-Israeli stance was an important influence on the Bush administration's policies in the Middle East.

Christianity and Christians: Christianity arose out of the birth, crucifixion, and teachings of Jesus of Nazareth [*q.v.*], a settlement in the Roman province of Galilee. Born a Jew [*q.v.*], Jesus (ca. 6 B.C.–28 A.D.) was acclaimed as the Christ (Greek: *Anointed*) by his principal followers, called apostles, most of whom were also Jewish. They regarded Jesus as the Christ who had been sent to earth as part of God's earlier covenants with the prophets Abraham, Isaac, and Jacob.

Initially, Christianity was a sect within Judaism [*q.v.*], a monotheistic religion. But following the unsuccessful Jewish uprising in 66–70 A.D. the Jewish element within the Christian community withered. Those believing in the one eternal truth and salvation, as laid down by Christ, followed the rites prescribed by him—especially baptism and the Eucharist (Greek: *thanksgiving*), which includes the liturgy of the sacrament, consisting of the consecration and distribution of bread and wine, symbolizing the body and blood of Christ offered in sacrifice.

After the death of Christ, his teachings were compiled into four books, called *The Gospels*, which form the early part of the New Testament [*q.v.*]. While the apostle Peter exercised religious authority, the apostle Paul spread Christ's teachings among non-Jews.

The well-organized nature of Christianity made the state hostile to it, and its monotheistic doctrine clashed with pagan practices. As a re-

sult early Christians were persecuted. The situation changed in 313 A.D. when Roman Emperor Constantine I (r. 306–337 A.D.) adopted Christianity and made it the state religion.

The breakup of the Roman Empire in 395 A.D. into the Western and Eastern sections began to undermine the unity of the Christian church. The church council, established in 325 A.D. to adjudicate controversies, produced the dogma of the Trinity—the Father (God), the Son (Christ), and the Holy Spirit—in the sixth century A.D. Increasingly, though, the church was racked with differences on such issues as the number of natures Christ possessed (divine only, or divine and human) and the relationship of the Holy Spirit to the Father and the Son. Also, following the barbarian attacks on the Western Roman Empire in the fifth century A.D., there was a political vacuum that was filled largely by the church, led by the Pope based in Rome, with Latin as the official language. In contrast, in the Eastern Roman Empire the Byzantine rulers exercised control over the church, led by the Patriarch based in Constantinople (now Istanbul), where Greek was the official language.

Guided by Rome and Constantinople, Christian monks spread the faith among pagans all over Europe. (In the Middle East, Asia Minor, and North Africa, Christianity gave way to Islam [*q.v.*] in the seventh century A.D.) The drift between Western (Roman Catholic [*q.v.*]) and Eastern (Orthodox [*q.v.*]) churches became a formal breach in 1054 after mutual excommunications of the Patriarch of Constantinople, Michael Cerularius, and the Rome-based Pope Leo IX. However, both churches experienced increasing conflict between secular and church authorities. When Reformation came in the early 16th century, it produced fresh diversity in the Christian faith, leading to the emergence of reformed churches—commonly called Protestant [*q.v.*], signifying their exclusion from both the Roman Catholic and the Eastern (Orthodox) sects.

While the long-established sects still maintain an elaborate version of early doctrines and rites, the more recent Protestant churches have restored pristine doctrines and forms, removing later additions and developments. Modern Christianity is marked by continued conflict between various sects, periodic attempts at unification, and an ongoing attempt to find a stable, well-defined relationship between religion and state. With 2.184 billion followers among the planet's 6.89 billion inhabitants in 2010, Christianity is the world's most popular religion.

Christians, Catholic: *see* individual Catholic categories.

Christians, Eastern (Orthodox): *see* Orthodox Christians Church and individual Orthodox Christian categories.

Christians, Protestant: *see* Protestant Christians Church.

Christmas: *Christian festival* A derivative of the Old English term *Cristes maesse*, Christ's mass, Christmas is an annual Christian festival celebrated by special gifts, greetings, and food on 25 December, commemorating the birth of Jesus Christ in ca. 6 B.C. *See also*

Christian calendars.

church: The term "church" is used for a community of Christians as well as a building for Christian worship. Early churches, built like Roman basilicas (halls of justice), were later given a cruciform shape by the addition of wings laid perpendicular to the nave. In the Eastern Roman Empire under the Byzantines, churches acquired the form of the Greek cross.

Circassians: Circassians, also known as Cherkess or Adighe, based in North Caucasia and speaking Circassian, abandoned Christianity [*q.v.*] for Islam [*q.v.*] in the 17th century under the influence of the Ottoman Turks. In 1829 the Ottomans ceded the region to Tsarist Russia. But Circassians resisted Russian domination until 1864. After that many Circassian clans fled to Turkey and Greater Syria [*q.v.*]. Because the Ottoman sultan encouraged them to settle around Amman [*q.v.*], they now form a minority group in Jordan, where they are often to be found in the army and the king's bodyguard.

Civil War in Jordan (1970–71): *see* Jordanian Civil War (1970–71).

Civil War in Lebanon (1958): *see* Lebanese Civil War (1958).

Civil War in Lebanon (1975–90): *see* Lebanese Civil War (1975–90).

Civil War in North Yemen (1962–70): *see* North Yemeni Civil War (1962–70).

Civil War in Oman (1963–76): *see* Omani Civil War (1963–76).

Civil War in Yemen (1994): *see* Yemeni Civil War (1994).

Committee for Advice and Reform

(Saudi Arabia): In July 1994 Osama bin Laden [*q.v.*] signed a document describing the Committee for Advice and Reform (CAR) as "an all-encompassing organization that aims at applying the teachings of God to all aspects of life" in general and promoting "peaceful and constructive reform" in the governance of "Arabia"—deliberately omitting the qualifying "Saudi"—and establishing its office in London, with Khalid al-Fawwaz (b. 1962) its director. CAR's specific objectives were to eliminate all forms of *jahiliya* (pre-Islamic) rule and all aspects of injustice; to reform the political system of (Saudi) Arabia by ridding it of corruption and injustice; and to revive the Islamic legal tradition of *hezba*, which entitles a Muslim to initiate a legal case against others to defend the "rights of Allah."

Fawwaz was a civil engineering graduate of King Fahd University in Dhahran who joined the anti-Soviet jihad in the early 1980s in Afghanistan, where he met bin Laden. In early 1994 he came to Britain and took up an English-language course at a local college. He collected all the relevant media publications, video tapes, and newspaper cuttings available in Britain. He employed staff for the task and supplied information to bin Laden. After the bombings of the American Embassies in Nairobi and Dar as Salam in August 1998, and Washington's allegation of his involvement in those attacks, he was detained by the British government. Since then he had been in the custody of Britain while challenging his extradition to the United States.

Committee for the Defense of Legitimate Rights (Saudi

Arabia): Encouraged by the holding of the first multiparty general election in Yemen in April 1993, six Saudi human rights activists—professors, lawyers, and civil servants—established the Committee for the Defense of Legitimate Rights (CDLR). Aiming to strive to eliminate injustice and defend the legitimate rights of citizens, the CDLR called on Saudi citizens to report official acts of injustice to it, and demanded political reform, including elections based on universal suffrage. The government arrested the CDLR's head, Professor Muhammad al-Masaari, and sacked the remaining founders from their jobs.

The CDLR then moved its base to London, from where, led by al-Masaari, it continued its activities, making extensive use of faxes to receive information from Saudi Arabia and communicate with its supporters there. In September 1994 it revealed that, following demonstrations against the detention of two militant clergymen, there had been large-scale arrests. Unprecedentedly, this was later confirmed by the Saudi government, which was believed to be holding up to 300 protestors in jail by early 1995.

The Saudi efforts to get Masaari deported from Britain failed. Later, there was a split in the CDLR, with al-Masaari's erstwhile colleague Saad al-Faqih forming the rival Islamic Reform Movement. This and lack of funds left the CDLR weak and ineffective.

Communist Movement in Egypt: In 1921 a breakaway faction of the Socialist Party of Egypt founded the Communist Party of Egypt (CPE). On the eve of the group's admission to the Moscow-based Communist International (also known as Comintern) in 1923, its program included demands for Egypt's independence from Britain, land reform, and the recognition of existing trade unions. Its policy of calling strikes brought it into conflict with the government, leading to a ban in 1924 on the Confederation of Trade Unions dominated by it.

In the face of persecution, the CPE failed to make much headway among peasants. The situation changed in 1936 when a tide of anti-imperialism swept the country following the unpopular Anglo-Egyptian Treaty [q.v.]. After the Soviet Union's entry into World War II in mid-1941 on the Allied side, the official policy toward Communists turned benign. In 1942 trade unions were legalized. The dramatic increase in the size of the working class, caused by the war, enabled Communists, now represented largely by the Mouvement Egyptien de Liberation Nationale (French: *Movement for National Liberation of Egypt*), and the smaller faction Iskra (meaning *Spark*), to enlarge their influence among workers.

The two Communist groups brought their respective unions under the umbrella of the Congress of Workers' Unions (CWU), with a membership of 115,000 members. In May 1947 they merged to form the Mouvement Democratique de Liberation Nationale (French: *Movement for Democracy and Liberation*; MDLN).

Since a large section of the MDLN's 1,500 members were either Copts [q.v.] or Jews [q.v.], the party's strength was not overly damaged by the Soviet support for the partition of Palestine [q.v.] at the United Nations in November. But the government used the Soviet action to dub Communists pro-Zionist and jail their leaders.

After a poor showing by the Egyptian troops in the Palestine War (1948–49) [q.v.], the much-weakened government released all political prisoners, including Communists. Once the freshly elected Wafd [q.v.] administration had abrogated the 1936 Anglo-Egyptian Treaty in October 1951, the Communists forged a united front with other anti-imperialist groups and participated in the anti-British guerrilla campaign in the Suez Canal [q.v.] zone. On the eve of the July 1952 coup the CPE had 5,000 active members.

Two of the 18-strong ruling Revolutionary Command Council (RCC) were Communist: Major Khalid Mohieddin [q.v.] and Colonel Yusuf Sadiq. But this had no impact on the actions of the RCC, which claimed to be non-ideological. Once Gamal Abdul Nasser [q.v.] had consolidated his hold over the RCC, he removed Mohieddin and Sadiq from it. But facing an Anglo-French-Israeli attack on Egypt in October 1956, Nasser released hundreds of Communist and leftist Wafd prisoners to let them organize popular resistance against the invaders.

Following reconciliation between the MDLN and the CPE, a party congress was held in early 1958. But a split occurred when the leadership was unable to forge an agreed policy toward the Iraqi Communists [*q.v.*] after the antiroyalist coup of July 1958 in Iraq. When Arab socialism [*q.v.*] was enshrined into the Charter of National Action in June 1962, which expressed belief in scientific socialism and commitment to the struggle against exploitation, the two factions reacted differently. The moderates saw it as heralding the beginning of a socialist revolution, while the radicals regarded it as signifying nothing more than the introduction of state capitalism since it rejected the concepts of class conflict and abolition of private property.

Hundreds of radical Communist continued to suffer imprisonment. However, in August 1963 Nasser followed up his nationalization of private companies with a decision to release political prisoners (of both left and right) in order to enlarge the base of the fledgling Arab Socialist Union (ASU) [*q.v.*]. This resulted in the freeing of some 600 Communist prisoners by the spring of 1964. A year later the Communist leadership, declaring that Nasser's regime had been following the road of non-capitalist development toward socialism, dissolved the party and advised individual members to join the ASU.

While using the organizational skills of former Communists, the Egyptian regime treated them with circumspection. Loyal to the Egyptian president, they played a prominent role in organizing pro-Nasser demonstrations after the June 1967 Arab-Israeli War [*q.v.*]. However, Nasser rejected their advice to strengthen the revolutionary cadres of the ASU and changed the ASU structure to placate traditional elements. After Nasser's death in September 1970, former Communists demanded greater representation in the ASU secretariat and trade unions, but to no avail. Because the National Unity Law of September 1972 specified a heavy penalty for political activity outside the ASU, they found themselves in a dilemma. When parliament decided to allow three forums within the ASU, the Communists allied with leftist Nasserites [*q.v.*] to form the National Progressive Unionist Alliance [*q.v.*] in May 1976.

Communist Movement in Israel: *see* Maki and Rakah.

Communist Party of Iran: *see* Tudeh Party of Iran.

Communist Party of Iraq: The Communist Party of Iraq (CPI) was established in March 1934. Two years later it went underground when the government banned the propagation of Bolshevik socialism. It was only after the Soviets had joined the Allies in World War II in mid-1941 that the authorities allowed the Communist front organizations to function openly.

They held their first congress in 1945. Active among workers, the party, with a membership of 3,000, also built up a following among teachers, students, and ethnic minorities in towns as well as peasants in villages. When it organized a strike of oil workers in July 1946 it faced government crackdown. It suffered a setback in late 1947 when the Soviet Union backed the partition plan for Palestine [*q.v.*]. Yet in January 1948 it succeeded in organizing demonstrations against the renegotiated 1930 Anglo-Iraqi Treaty [*q.v.*], called the Portsmouth Agreement. After rescinding the agreement, the government jailed hundreds of Communist activists. Undeterred, they turned prisons into recruiting centers while their comrades outside dominated the largest student body.

In 1956 the CPI joined the United National Front (UNF), which advocated political reform at home and an anti-imperialist and anti-Zionist struggle abroad. The UNF was in touch with the Free Officers Organization, which overthrew the monarchy in mid-1958. The 8,000-member-strong CPI expanded its base among peasants by forming Peasant Leagues to help implement the agrarian reform decreed by the regime of Abdul Karim Qasim [*q.v.*]. It backed Qasim in his conflict with Nasserists [*q.v.*], who wanted to unite Iraq with the United Arab Republic [*q.v.*]. Though Qasim curtailed Communist influence during the latter part of his rule, the CPI was the only party to fight alongside his forces against the Baathists [*q.v.*] in February 1963.

Following their seizure of power, the Baathists, working in coordination with the U.S. Central Intelligence Agency, carried out an anti-Communist pogrom which claimed the lives of 3,000 to 5,000 Communists, the worst fate suffered by any political party in the Arab East [*q.v.*].

With the fall of the Baathist government in November 1963, the CPI returned to a semi-clandestine existence. Its leadership scaled down the party's objective of establishing a socialist regime, led by workers and peasants, to participating in a popular front government based on the alliance of all patriotic forces. This led to splits in the party in 1965 and 1967, but allowed its main body, led by moderate Aziz Muhammad, to reach a rapprochement with the Baathists, who had been driven underground by then.

After the successful Baathist coup of July 1968, the regime permitted the CPI to function. It held its second congress in September 1970. In May 1972 its seven-year old clandestine journal *Tareeq al-Shaab* (Arabic: *The People's Path*), was allowed to appear daily. On the fifth anniversary of the July 1968 revolution the CPI and the Baath Party signed the National Action Charter, heralding the formation of the National Progressive and Patriotic Front (NPPF) [*q.v.*]. This required the CPI to be loyal to the Baathist revolution, and refrain from labor agitation as well as dissemination of its ideology among students and soldiers. In return it was given two cabinet seats out of 28.

The third CPI congress, held in May 1976, concluded that Iraq had entered the stage of non-capitalist development and recommended a series of anti-capitalist measures. But the regime, enriched by booming oil revenues, increased its trade links with the West and relaxed controls over private capital at home. With the Kurdish problem settled for the time being through an accord with Iran in March 1975, the government decided to curb the Communist influence. On their part, in March 1978 CPI leaders coupled their criticism of the regime with calls for a general election and parity with the Baathists in the government until the election.

In April the Marxist military coup in Afghanistan made the Baathist regime in Baghdad [q.v.] wary of the CPI. The result was large-scale arrests of Communist activists and the execution of 36 leaders for trying to form party cells in the army. The CPI left the NPPF, but without publicizing the fact. The official anti-Communist drive intensified to the point where reports circulating in early 1979 mentioned some 1,900 Communists "disappearing." In April the party daily, with a circulation of 50,000, was shut down. In early 1980 President Saddam Hussein [q.v.] barred the CPI from entering the parliamentary elections to be held in June. CPI leaders condemned Saddam Hussein's invasion of Iran in September, arguing that it diverted Arab energy away from confronting the main Arab enemy in the region: Israel. After the 1991 Gulf War [q.v.], the remnants of the party set up a base in the Kurdistan Autonomous Region [q.v.] which was controlled by the anti-Saddam Kurdish parties.

The CPI opposed the UN sanctions against Iraq after the 1991 war. It condemned the Anglo-American invasion of Iraq [q.v.] in 2003. But its leader, Hamid Majid Mousa, accepted a seat on the Interim Iraqi Governing Council appointed by the occupying Coalition Provisional Authority. It entered the January 2005 election to the Interim National Assembly as part of the People's Union, which received about 3 percent of the vote. For the December 2005 general election, it joined the Iraqi National List [q.v.], an alliance of secular parties. Of the 25 seats gained by this bloc, only one went to the Iraqi Communist Party. It failed to win any seat in the 2010 general election.

Communist Party of Israel: *see* Hadash

Communist Party of Jordan: The Communist Party of Jordan (CPJ) evolved under the leadership of Fuad Nassar in June 1951 out of the eight-year-old League of National Liberation (LNL). Two months later it allied with the Baathists [q.v.] and the Arab Nationalist Movement [q.v.] to form the National Bloc to run in a general election. It scored 11 percent of the vote, enough to upset the government, which arrested the Communist leadership and stiffened its anti-Communist law of 1948.

After the promulgation of a new constitution in 1952, which allowed licensed political parties, the CPJ cooperated with the Baathists and the National Socialist Party to form the National Front in the spring of 1954. Despite vote-rigging in the election in the autumn, two Communists won. In 1955 the CPJ participated in the National Front campaign to keep Jordan out of the recently formed Baghdad Pact [q.v.] and get the election results annulled. The struggle was successful. In the election of October 1956 the alliance of the CPJ, Baathists, and National Socialists won 40 percent of the vote, with the CPJ securing 13 percent. The inclusion of a Communist in the government, led by Suleiman Nabulsi [q.v.], was unprecedented in the Arab East [q.v.]. In April 1957 the monarch dismissed the Nabulsi government, dissolved parliament, declared martial law, and jailed 200 of the 2,000 CPJ members. They were incarcerated until late 1964. The chastened party leadership adopted a moderate program of socioeconomic reform at home.

The loss of the West Bank [*q.v.*] to Israel in the June 1967 Arab-Israeli War [*q.v.*] deprived the party of nearly half of its members. But the subsequent increase in the Palestinian refugee population in Jordan, and the emergence of armed Palestinian commandos, radicalized the CPJ's ranks. The party formed its own militia, the Ansars (Arabic: *Helpers*). However, once the government had expelled all Palestinian commandos by mid-1971 after bloody fighting, CPJ leaders dissolved the militia and reverted to the moderate aim of forming a national unity government of all national and progressive forces.

In May 1974 the CPJ resolved to establish a national front of anti-royalist forces in order to set up a "national liberated authority" on the East Bank [*q.v.*]. But the outbreak of civil war in Lebanon a year later diverted the CPJ's attention and energies. It participated in the conference of 10 Arab Communist parties in June 1978 in Beirut [*q.v.*], which decided to sharpen the anti-Zionist struggle. Its semi-clandestine existence ended in 1992 when, following the legalization of political parties, the CPJ became one of the nine parties to secure a license. It participated in the general election of 1993 but failed to win a seat.

In 2005, the CPJ was one of the three regional parties (the others being the Palestinian People's Party [*q.v.*] and the Communist Party of Israel [*q.v.*]) to coordinate their opposition to the implementation of the strategy of U.S. President George W. Bush's "war on terror" repackaged as the Greater Middle East Project. It held a unity conference in 2006 to welcome those who had left the party earlier.

In the wake of the Arab Spring [*q.v.*] it formed an alliance with five other leftist, nationalist, and pan-Arabist groups to demand political reform in February 2012. While standing apart form the main opposition Islamic Action Front [*q.v.*], this coalition had a similar platform: an elections law based on proportional representation, constitutional reform leading to an elected governments, and a reversal of the decade-old privatization program.

Led by Munir Hamarna, the JCP publishes *al-Jamahir* (*The Masses*).

Communist Party of Lebanon: The Communist movement in Lebanon started with the People's Party of Lebanon in 1924, composed of intellectuals and trade unionists. After it had absorbed the Spartacus Party, a leftist group, in 1925, it renamed itself the Communist Party of Syria and Lebanon (CPSL). Because of its support for the Druze [*q.v.*] rebellion (1925–27), its leaders were arrested by the French Mandate. It was not until 1928 that the CPSL, dominated by Armenian Christians [*q.v.*], was admitted to the Moscow-based Communist International (also called Comintern). Accepting Comintern's advice to "Arabise" itself, in 1936 the party hierarchy replaced Fuad Shemali, a Christian [*q.v.*], with Khalid Bakdash [*q.v.*], a Syrian Kurd [*q.v.*].

The CPSL's adoption of a radical program of combining the anti-imperialist struggle with revolutionizing workers and peasants in Lebanon alarmed the French Mandate, which refused to recognize its trade union wing. The situation changed in 1936 when the leftist Popular Front, backed by Communists, assumed power in France. Between then and the outbreak of the Second World War, the party membership rose from 200 to 2000. It participated in Lebanon's parliamentary election in 1943. After the Lebanese independence in 1946, the strength of the CPL soared to 16,000. It suffered a setback when the Soviets endorsed the Palestine partition plan in late 1947. When CPL leaders backed the Soviet decision, the government banned the party and dissolved its trade union wing.

President Camille Chamoun's [q.v.] refusal to condemn the Anglo-French-Israeli invasion of Egypt in 1956 created a climate where the CPL succeeded in reestablishing its Arab nationalist credentials by siding with local Nasserists [q.v.]. In the 1958 Lebanese Civil War [q.v.] it sided with the leftist-nationalist camp against Chamoun. In March 1965 it joined the Front of National and Progressive Parties and Forces, led by Kamal Jumblat [q.v.], a Marxist. The decision of the party congress in 1968 to enlarge its membership was aided by the formal lifting of the ban on it (along with other parties with extra-territorial links) two years later. In 1974 it formed the National Union of Workers and Employees under its aegis.

On the eve of the 1975 Lebanese Civil War [q.v.] the CPL, along with the Organization of the Communist Action in Lebanon (OCAL), formed the hard core of the Lebanese Na-

tional Movement (LNM) [q.v.], which fought the rightist camp. Unlike other Lebanese parties, the CPL combined military action with political education and propaganda. By the end of 1975 the party had 15,000 members, half of whom were Shia [q.v.]. In June 1978 it hosted a conference of 10 Arab Communist parties in Beirut [q.v.], which decided to intensify the anti-Zionist struggle. By the end of the civil war in October 1990, the CPL had lost most of its Shia supporters to Amal [q.v.] and Hizbollah [q.v.]. It was denied any role in the postwar national unity government.

The CPL participated in the general elections of 1992, 1996, and 2000, but without any success. Led by Maurice Nohra, its weekly journal *Al-Akhbar* (Arabic: *The News*), with a circulation of about 20,000, many of them intellectuals.

At its 9th congress in 2003, the CPL delegates elected Khalid Hadadi as the party's general secretary. It failed to win a seat in the 2005 and 2009 general elections. It reiterated its opposition to the sectarian division of parliamentary seats.

Soon after the start of a civil uprising in Syria in March 1939 the party stated that Syrians had the right to use peaceful and democratic means to demand political and economic reforms and wished that their government would implement the ones put forward by President Bashar Assad [q.v.].

Communist Party of Palestine: The Communist Party of Palestine (PCP), founded in 1922, won the recognition of the Moscow-based Communist International (also known as

Comintern) two years later. With the dissolution of the Comintern in May 1943—and thus the loss of an external overseeing organization—the simmering differences between the Jewish and Arab members surfaced. Most of the Arab members left to form the League of National Liberation (LNL). Soon the LNL enlarged its influence by absorbing the existing Arab leftist groups and establishing the Federation of Arab Trade Unions and Labor Societies.

After the Palestine War (1948–49) [q.v.] and the absorption of the West Bank [q.v.] into Jordan, the LNL transformed itself into the Communist Party of Jordan [q.v.] in June 1951. It functioned among the Palestinians of the West Bank. Sixteen years later, following the loss of the West Bank to Israel in the Six-Day Arab-Israeli War [q.v.], the PCP was revived clandestinely in this territory. It also began to function in the Palestinian refugee camps, and was close to the Democratic Front for the Liberation of Palestine [q.v.], which backed the idea of establishing a "national" authority in any part of "liberated" Palestine. It affiliated to the Palestine Liberation Organization (PLO) [q.v.], and participated in the conference of 10 Arab Communist parties in Beirut [q.v.] in June 1978, which decided to intensify the anti-Zionist struggle. In 1987 the party, then led by Suleiman Najab, was given seats on the Palestine National Council.

In 1992 it changed its name to the Palestinian People's Party [q.v.], but retained Najab as its head. Hassan Asfour, one of the party's leaders, participated in the PLO's secret negotiations with Israel which led to the Oslo Accord [q.v.]. It backed the Accord and the resulting Palestinian Authority [q.v.].

Following the death of Najab in 2001, the leadership passed to Bassam al-Salihi. He entered the presidential election in 2005 and received less than 3 percent of the vote. It participated in the parliamentary election of 2006 on a joint list with the Democratic Front for the Liberation of Palestine [q.v.] and secured two seats.

Communist Party of Saudi Arabia: The Communist Party of Saudi Arabia (CPSA), officially established in Baghdad in 1975 Bank [q.v.] evolved out of the National Liberation Front (NLF), a Marxist group formed in 1958, whose roots went back to the Workers' Committees formed in the wake of strikes at oilfields in 1953. These committees continued to function secretly until the next wave of strikes in 1956 when, following government persecution, they disintegrated. Some of their members allied with local Communists to form the National Reform Front, a clandestine organization that subsequently renamed itself the National Liberation Front. The NLF demanded a democratic constitution with rights to establish political parties and trade unions, and to demonstrate or strike, and called on the state to take total control of oil resources, from prospecting to marketing. It supported the coup attempt led by the Saudi section of the Arab Nationalist Movement [q.v.] in June 1969.

In June 1978 the CPSA attended the conference of 10 Arab Communist parties in Beirut [q.v.], which decided to intensify the anti-Zionist struggle.

With opposition in Saudi Arabia turning more toward militant Islam from the late 1970s onwards, the appeal of the CPSA, operating from outside the country, waned. In the early 1990s it renamed itself Democratic Unification in Saudi Arabia. When, a few years later, its leaders agreed to stop political activity, the Saudi government released its jailed members.

Communist Party of Syria: The Communist movement in Syria started in 1924 with the formation of the Communist Party of Syria and Lebanon (CPSL). Because of its support for the Druze [q.v.] rebellion (1925–27), its leaders were arrested by the French Mandate. It was not until 1928 that the CPSL, dominated by Christian Armenians [q.v.], was admitted to the Moscow-based Communist International (also known as Comintern). Accepting Comintern's advice to "Arabise" itself, in 1936 the party hierarchy replaced Fuad Shemali, a Christian [q.v.], with Khalid Bakdash [q.v.], a Syrian Kurd [q.v.].

The CPSL's adoption of a radical program of combining the anti-imperialist struggle with revolutionizing workers and peasants made it unpopular with the French Mandate, which refused to recognize its trade union wing. The situation changed in 1936 when the leftist Popular Front, backed by the Communists, assumed power in France. It continued to function until it was banned, along with other political parties, on the eve of World War II.

Its clandestine existence ended in July 1941, when the British and Free French forces, having defeated the troops loyal to the pro-Nazi French government based in Vichy, legalized all political groups. It participated in the parliamentary elections in the summer of 1943. During the first four years of its legal existence (1941–45), the Communist Party of Syria (CPS) raised its membership from 1000 to 10,000. Later it played a prominent role in frustrating France's plans to reestablish its authority in Syria. But the Soviet decision to back the partition of Palestine in late 1947 severely damaged the CPS's standing. It was not until early 1954, when President Adib Shishkali [q.v.] dissolved parliament and disbanded all political parties, did the CPS lose its pariah status due to the radically changed political environment.

In the 1954 general election the party won as many votes as the Baathists [q.v.]. Following the discovery in late 1956 and mid-1957 of Western-inspired plots against the Syrian government, the CPS was allowed to join the Popular Resistance Force, a paramilitary organization. Its membership rose to 18,000, a record. This unnerved the Baathists, who began to advocate union with Egypt. Anticipating a ban on political parties after the Syrian-Egyptian union in early 1958 under President Gamal Abdul Nasser [q.v.], CPS leaders went into self-exile in Prague, Czechoslovakia. Nasser responded to Bakdash's criticism by repressing the CPS.

After the breakup of the UAR in 1961, the new rulers of Syria did not permit CPS leaders to return home. When the Baathist regime, established in March 1963, moved leftward, the CPS backed it, especially after it had allowed the party's leadership to return to Damascus [*q.v.*] in 1966.

Initially the CPS opposed General Hafiz Assad's [*q.v.*] "correctionist" coup in November 1970. But when two years later, listening to Bakdash's advice, he decided to form the National Progressive Front [*q.v.*], the CPS backed him. Of those elected on a common NPF list in the 1973 election, eight belonged to the CPS, believed to have a membership of 3,000 to 6,000.

Assad's dispatch of Syrian troops in June 1976 to aid the rightist camp in the Lebanese Civil War [*q.v.*] strained relations between him and the CPS. The reduced CPS representation in the parliament of 1977 reflected Assad's lukewarm attitude toward the party. But when, in the face of a serious challenge to Assad from the Muslim Brotherhood [*q.v.*] in 1980–82, the CPS backed the regime, relations between the two sides improved.

In 1986, Bakdash disagreed with the deputy general secretary Yusuf Faisal when the latter backed the reformist policies of Mikhail Gorbachev, the first secretary of the Communist Party of the Soviet Union. Faisal left to lead a breakaway Communist Party. It was allowed to join the NPF.

The parent party held its sixth congress in January 1987. In the 1990 general election the two factions of the CPS together secured eight seats. In the 1994 and 1998 parliamentary elections, they retained their seats. After the death of Bakdash in 1995, his widow, Wisal Farha, was elected the parent party's general secretary. In 2001 it was allowed to publish the *Sawt al-Shaab* (Arabic: *The People's Voice*) fortnightly. In 2004, the party celebrated the 80th anniversary of the founding of the Communist Party of Syria and Lebanon.

In the 2002 and subsequent general election, the quota of eight parliamentary seats for the two factions of the Communist Party remained unchanged.

The CPS described the civil resistance in 2011 as part of a "counter-revolutionary movement" and largely supported the regime of President Bashar Assad [*q.v.*]. It participated in the parliamentary election in 2012 held under the amended constitution in May 2012.

Conference of Islamic Organization: *see* Islamic Conference Organization

confessionalism (in Lebanon): Confessionalism is the term used for a social system that recognizes the principle of religious communities being vested with political authority. It has been operational in Lebanon since March 1943, when the British representative in Beirut, General Edward Spears, mediating between the feuding Muslims [*q.v.*] and Christians [*q.v.*], recommended a ratio of six Christian parliamentary seats to five Muslim, based on the 1932 census, which had classified the population under 16 religions or sects: Armenian Catholic [*q.v.*], Chaldean Catholic [*q.v.*], Greek Catholic [*q.v.*], Maronite Catholic [*q.v.*], Roman Catholic [*q.v.*], Syrian Catholic [*q.v.*], Armenian Orthodox [*q.v.*], Greek Orthodox [*q.v.*], Syrian Orthodox [*q.v.*], Protestant [*q.v.*], Bahai [*q.v.*], Jew [*q.v.*], Alawi [*q.v.*], Druze [*q.v.*], Shia [*q.v.*], and Sunni [*q.v.*]. This was accepted as part of the National Pact [*q.v.*], an unwritten supplement to the Lebanese constitution of 1926, which was given the status of an official decree by the French delegate-general in July 1943.

Conservative Judaism: Conservative Judaism, founded in 1845 in Germany, lies somewhere between Orthodox Judaism [*q.v.*] and Reform Judaism [*q.v.*]. While remaining faithful to the basic features of traditional Judaism, it accepts a certain adjustment of religious practices to suit the modern age. It considers the Jewish religion, culture, and national identity as an integral whole. It regards the Sabbath [*q.v.*] as sacred, respects the dietary injunctions, encourages the learning of Hebrew [*q.v.*], and backs the secular Zionist movement [*q.v.*]. Its chief ideologue, Zacharias Frankel (1801–75), urged examination of the Jewish Written and Oral Law in order to separate its essence from the elements reflective of contemporary times, and then reinterpreting the essence to suit the current era. An estimated 48 percent of the world's Jews [*q.v.*] are followers of Conservative Judaism or Reform Judaism [*q.v.*].

Constitutional Revolution (Iran) (1907–11): Yielding to demonstrations in Tehran [*q.v.*] and Qom [*q.v.*] for an elected parliament, the Shah of Iran, Muzzafar al-Din Qajar (r. 1896–1907), issued a decree in August 1906 stating that an "Assembly of Delegates" be elected by the ulama [*q.v.*], the Qajar family and nobles, landowners, merchants, and guilds. The 106-strong assembly, called the Majlis [*q.v.*], met in October. During the next two months it unanimously passed a set of Fundamental Laws. The document, modeled along the Belgian constitution, was framed within an Islamic context. The mortally ill shah signed it on 30 December, died five days later, and was succeeded by his son, Muhammad Ali (r. 1907–8). Some months later the Majlis produced the longer Supplementary Fundamental Laws, outlining a parliamentary form of government, with power concentrated in the legislature at the expense of the executive. When the shah refused to ratify the new document there were demonstrations, as well as the assassination of his prime minister. He signed it on 7 October 1907. The two sets of laws together formed the Iranian constitution, and ushered in the Constitutional Revolution.

However, the shah was reluctant to become a figurehead monarch. He used an attempt to assassinate him in mid-June 1908 as a pretext to mount a coup against the elected government. On 23 June he ordered his palace guard to bomb the Majlis building, which was being defended by 7,000 lightly armed constitutionalists. In the ensuing fight, over 250 people were killed. He dissolved the First Majlis, declared martial law, and waged a campaign of terror against his opponents. A civil war ensued, which he lost by mid-July. After securing refuge in the Russian embassy, he abdicated in favor of his 12-year-old son, Ahmad.

In November 1909, the Second Majlis approved the appointment of William Shushter, an American economist, as the treasurer-general to increase the state's falling revenue. He organized a special tax-collecting force and deployed it everywhere, including the northern region, regarded as a Russian zone of influence. In November 1911, having ordered his troops to occupy Iran's Caspian Sea ports of Enzali and Rasht, Tsar Nicholas II gave an ultimatum that failure to remove Shuster within two days would lead to the Russian occupation of Tehran. Only after the deadline, when Russian troops had begun to march toward Tehran, did the Majlis vote to dismiss Shuster. To placate the Tsar the Iranian regent dismissed the Majlis for having defied the Russian ultimatum. Though the regent did not formally abrogate the 1906–7 constitution, his dismissal of the Majlis marked the end of the Constitutional Revolution.

Coptic Church and Copts: *main Christian [q.v.] church in Egypt* The term *Copt*—a derivative of the Greek word *Aigyptios*, meaning Egyptian, and derived from the hieroglyphic "Het-Ka Ptah," Temple of Ptah's spirit—was applied to all Egyptians before the Muslim [q.v.] Arab [q.v.] conquest in 641 A.D. After the Muslim rule, Copts meant those Egyptians who did not embrace Islam [q.v.] and continued to practice Christianity [q.v.]. In 451 A.D. the Roman church declared the Coptic church, one of the oldest in the Christian world, heretic because of the latter's adoption of the monophysite doctrine, which states that Christ had only one nature—either divine or a synthesis of divine and human—not two, divine and human. The service books of the Coptic Church continue to be in Coptic [q.v.].

The church's head, the Patriarch of Alexandria and all Egypt, is based in

Cairo [q.v.]. Its best known member is Boutros Boutros-Ghali [q.v.].

The official 1986 census put Copts at 5.6 percent of the national population of 48.2 million, a proportion that remained about the same in the 1996 census, with Egypt's inhabitants numbering 59.3 million. Since Copts and Muslims share the same name and many Copts prefer to be listed as Muslim in official documents to avoid discrimination, the census figures are widely believed to be about half the real ones. The figure of 9 percent in the national population of 77.4 million in 2008 seems more reliable. That made Copts the largest Christian community in the Middle East [q.v.].

Before the 1952 revolution Copts owned almost half of the nation's wealth and were active in the Wafd [q.v.]. They were adversely affected by the nationalization policies of President Gamal Abdul Nasser [q.v.], and began migrating in large numbers to Europe and North America. Nasser reserved certain parliamentary constituencies for Copts, and nominated 10 Copts to parliament.

In the absence of proper political leadership, Copts turned to the religious hierarchy to advance political demands. The draft law on apostasy, making it a capital offense, was withdrawn by President Anwar Sadat [q.v.] in 1977 when Coptic religious leaders fasted for five days.

After the Egyptian-Israeli peace treaty [q.v.] in March 1979, anti-Sadat sentiment turned anti-Copt, since the government had blocked all legitimate channels of expressing opposition to the treaty. In March 1980 several Copts were killed in clashes in southern Egyptian towns. When Pope

Shenudah III canceled official Easter celebrations and retired to a monastery in the Sinai [q.v.], Sadat banished him to internal exile and nominated a committee of five bishops to administer the church. In 1985, President Hosni Mubarak [q.v.] reversed Sadat's order and let Pope Shenudah III resume his office.

The rise of militant Islamic movement in the early- and mid-1990s strained relations between Muslims and Copts, which improved with the decline of Islamic militancy in the late 1990s. In 1995, President Hosni Mubarak [q.v.] nominated six Copts as members of the People's Assembly, followed by four in 2000 and then five in 2005 and 2010.

On the Coptic Christmas [q.v.] eve in 2010, nine Copts were killed when Islamist militants opened fire on the worshipers leaving a church in Naj Hammadi in southern Egypt. In 2011, on the New Year's Eve, celebrated on 6 January, the bombing of a church in Alexandria [q.v.] during a midnight prayer service left 23 Copts dead.

Copts participated in the pro-democracy movement centered on Tahrir Square in Cairo in late January 2011. On Sunday, 6 February, Muslim protestors joined hands with Copts to form a protective cordon around the Copts celebrating Mass in the square. Later they chanted "We are one," and held up a Quran and a cross. Elsewhere joint Muslim-Copt patrols guarded churches in Cairo and Alexandria against attacks by Islamist militants.

The situation changed after the overthrow of Mubarak. When Copts in Cairo protested against the authorities'

failure to act against those who burned down a church in Merinab village in southern Egypt in October, the army fired on the demonstrators, killing 25. Fearing the rise of Islamist parties through the ballot box, about 100,000 Copts emigrated before the end of 2011.

In January 2012, Field Marshal Muhammad Hussein Tantawi [q.v.], head of the ruling military council, appointed five Copts as members of the People's Assembly.

Coptic language: A Hamito-Semitic language, derived from ancient Egyptian, Coptic was a living language in Egypt between the second and the seventh centuries A.D. Written in the Greek alphabet, Coptic supplanted the religious expressions of the earlier Egyptian language with words borrowed from the Greek. Nowadays it is used only in the liturgy of the Coptic Church [q.v.].

Council of Guardians (Iran): *see* Guardian Council (Iran).

D

al-Daawa (Iraq): (Arabic: *The Call*) *Iraqi political party* Official title: *Hizb al-Daawa al-Islamiya*, The Islamic Call Party. After the secular Baathists [q.v.] seized power in Iraq in July 1968, their government censored religious publications, closed several Islamic institutions, and started harassing Shia [q.v.] clerics. When they urged their followers to protest, further repression followed. Against this backdrop al-Daawa al-Islamiya was formed in 1969, clandestinely, with the blessing of the Najaf [q.v.]-based Ayatollah Muhsin Hakim, the senior-most Shia cleric.

When the government, dominated by Sunni [q.v.] leaders, tried to interfere with some Shia rituals and weaken the authority of the religious hierarchy, al-Daawa gained ground. In December 1974 Shia religious processions turned into anti-government demonstrations. The authorities executed five al-Daawa leaders. At the same time they tried to placate the Shia masses by increasing the flow of public development funds to the Shia-dominated south.

Following the Islamic revolution [q.v.] in Shia-majority Iran in early 1979, the leadership in Tehran [q.v.] decided to encourage an Islamic movement in Iraq. It aided al-Daawa. Iraq responded by making al-Daawa membership a capital offense. In March 1980 it executed 94 al-Daawa activists for killing a score of Iraqi officials in 1979. The next month al-Daawa militants tried but failed to assassinate the Christian [q.v.] deputy premier Tariq Aziz [q.v.].

After the outbreak of the Iran-Iraq War [q.v.] in September, which necessitated blackouts, al-Daawa, now backed by Iranian arms and training, intensified its sabotage and assassination campaign. Iraq's task of suppressing al-Daawa became easier once the Iranians had marched into Iraq in June 1982. It was convincingly able to label the allies of Iran as traitors to Iraq. This caused a sharp drop in al-Daawa's support.

Five months later, al-Daawa members in Iran cooperated with other Islamic organizations to form the Supreme Council of Islamic Revolution in Iraq (SCIRI) [q.v.] in Tehran. In December 1983 they set off five bombs in Kuwait, which had been aiding Iraq in its conflict with Iran. In 1985 al-Daawa allied with secular Iraqi opposition, especially the Kurdistan Democratic Party [q.v.], which provided it with refuge in the Kurdish region to carry out its attacks on economic and military targets of the Baathist regime. On 9 April 1987 al-Daawa militants made an unsuccessful attempt to assassinate President Saddam Hussein [q.v.] on the outskirts of Mosul [q.v.].

With the end of the Iran-Iraq War in August 1988, al-Daawa's activities subsided. They revived when, in the wake of the 1991 Gulf War [q.v.], there was a Shia rebellion in the south. With its failure, al-Daawa once again became marginalized within Iraq.

In 2002, it formally split from SCIRI when the latter decided to cooperate with U.S.-sponsored Iraqi opposition groups. It opposed the Anglo-American invasion of Iraq [q.v.]. But after the war, its leader, Ibrahim al-Jaafari [q.v.], accepted a seat on the Interim Iraqi Governing Council appointed by the occupying Coalition Provisional Authority. On the eve of the January 2005 election to the Interim National Assembly, al-Daawa joined the United Iraqi Alliance [q.v.], the brainchild of Grand Ayatollah Ali Sistani [q.v.]. When the Alliance emerged as the majority group in parliament, Ibrahim al-Jaafari [q.v.] became the prime minister.

Following the elections to the National Assembly under a new constitution in December 2005, another al-Daawa leader, Nouri al-Maliki [*q.v.*] succeeded Jaafari as its secretary-general in 2007. Maliki made al-Daawa less religious than before. In 2009 it became part of the State of Law Coalition [*q.v.*] led by Maliki.

al-Daawa al-Islamiya (Iraq): *See* al-Daawa.

Damascus: *capital of Syria* Population: 4.71 million (2011 est.) History of Damascus stretches back to the third millennium B.C., and the city's present name is at least 3,500 years old. In ancient times it was ruled by the Assyrians and the Persians. It fell to Alexander of Macedonia (r. 336–323 B.C.), and then to other rulers. After it was conquered by the Romans in 65 B.C., it became an important city of the Decapolis province east of the Jordan River [*q.v.*]. It was on his way to Damascus that Paul was converted to Christianity [*q.v.*].

After its capture by Muslim [*q.v.*] Arabs [*q.v.*] in 635 A.D., Damascus became the capital of the Islamic Empire of the Umayyads in 661 A.D. Its prosperity continued even after the Abbasids, who succeeded the Umayyads, moved the imperial capital to Baghdad [*q.v.*] in 763 A.D. It was sacked twice by the Mongols, first in 1258 and then about a century later. Conquered by the Ottoman Turks in 1517, it remained part of their empire for the next four centuries. It came under the French Mandate after World War I, and became the capital of semi-independent Syria in 1943. It has expanded since then, and become the commercial, financial, industrial, educational, and cultural center of Syria, and the leading city of the Levant [*q.v.*].

Its prime tourist attraction is the Great Mosque, also called the Umayyad Mosque, one of the finest Islamic monuments. The original site was home to a temple to Jupiter, built by the Greeks. In fourth century A.D. it was replaced by the renowned church of St. John the Baptist, constructed by Roman Emperor Theodosius I (r. 379–395 A.D.). The Umayyads transformed this church, containing the shrine of St. John the Baptist, into a mosque in 715 A.D.

Damascus witnessed its first protest demonstration as part of the Arab Spring [*q.v.*] on 15 March 2011. From May onward such protests built up in the city's eastern suburbs until their violent suppression by the security forces in January 2012. The capital was also the venue of large pro-government demonstrations in October 2011 and again in March 2012.

The situation changed in mid-July after the killing of the defense minister and his deputy during a meeting by a bomb triggered by remote control. The rebels seized some of the capital's suburbs, and it took the government forces considerable time to regain control.

Darwish, Mahmoud (1941–2008): *Palestinian writer and poet* Born into a landowning Sunni [*q.v.*] family in Barwa village near Acre [*q.v.*], Darwish and his family escaped to Lebanon during the 1948–49 Palestine War [*q.v.*]. They later returned and settled in Deir al-Assad village in Galilee. After finishing high school at Kafr Yasid, Darwish found work with an Arabic printer in Acre [*q.v.*]. He began publishing his poems in the Arabic-language press, including the literary monthly *Al-Jadid* (Arabic: *The New*) and the fortnightly *Al-Ittihad* (Arabic: *The Unity*), both being the publications of Maki [*q.v.*], the Israeli Communist Party. After being appointed to the editorial boards of these journals, he became a journalist.

With the publication of three volumes of poetry—*Birds without Wings* (1961), *Lover from Palestine* (1964), and *Olive Leaves* (1964)—he established himself as an outstandingly talented poet who was fluent in both Arabic [*q.v.*] and Hebrew [*q.v.*]. Profoundly original, rich in imagery, and imbued with intense feelings, his lyrical verses conveyed the suffering of Palestinians who had been expelled from their homeland and compelled to live in refugee camps. Though deeply disappointed by the humiliating defeat suffered by the Arabs [*q.v.*] in the June 1967 Arab-Israeli War (*q.v.*), in which Israel occupied the rest of Palestine [*q.v.*], in his poetry he kept up the image of the resistant hero who, inspired by the ideas of valor and self-sacrifice, struggles to achieve freedom.

After spending a year at the University of Moscow (1970), he decided not to return to Israel. He based himself in Cairo [*q.v.*], where he published articles and poems in the leading daily, *Al-Ahram* (Arabic: *The Pyramids*). When the Palestine Liberation Organization (PLO) [*q.v.*] moved to Beirut [*q.v.*] in 1972, he became editor of its monthly publication, *Shuaun Falastiniyya* (Arabic: *Palestinian Affairs*). In 1975 he was appointed director of the PLO Research Center. The involvement of the PLO in the Lebanese Civil War [*q.v.*], in which some 3,000 Palestinian refugees were massacred in Tal Zaatar camp in East Beirut by the Phalangist militia [*q.v.*] in 1976, darkened the tone of Darwish's poetry. The low point came during the long siege of West Beirut during the Israel invasion of Lebanon [*q.v.*] in 1982, when he was with the PLO chairman Yasser Arafat [*q.v.*].

Following the PLO's expulsion from Beirut, he penned poems to recapture the debilitating experience in *Ode to Beirut* (1982) and *A Eulogy for the Tall Shadow* (1983), both narrative works of considerable length. His voice was now tinged with a realism which recognized that bravery, just cause, and readiness to die would not suffice to redeem the hero in the present-day world of global power politics and high technology. His protagonist was now a man stretching himself to his limits, striving in the face of continued exile and defeat. His earlier triumphant tone has given way to the concept of a heroic victim, someone caught in a heroic deadlock, like a man dying while climbing. Such maturity added to the power of his poetry. He often called on the Old Testament [*q.v.*] prophets, notably Isaiah and Jeremiah, to condemn the Israeli acts of injustice against the Palestinians. Equally, he remained unrivalled in his use of the language, style, and motifs of the Quran and the prophetic tradition in his poetry.

During his stay in Cyprus he was elected chairman of the Palestinian Writers and Journalists Association and edited its magazine. He received the Ibn Sina Prize, sponsored by the

Soviet Union, in 1981, followed by the Lenin Peace Prize a year later. When a selection of his poems was translated into English (*The Music of Human Flesh*, 1980), he became known in Britain and the United States, where he took up residence in the late 1980s before moving to Paris.

He was elected to the PLO Executive Committee in 1987 as an independent, and was reelected four years later. Opposed to the Oslo Accord [*q.v.*] of September 1993, he resigned in protest.

In Paris he continued to edit *Al-Karmel* (Arabic: *The Garden of God*), a Palestinian literary review established in 1981. His volumes of poetry in English included *Psalms* (1994) and *The Adam of Two Edens* (2001). Many of his poems were set to music and included in popular albums.

In 2007 he returned to the West Bank [*q.v.*] city of Ramallah [*q.v.*]. He presented himself at the festival organized in his honor in Haifa [*q.v.*] by Hadash [*q.v.*] and the Masharaf (Arabic: *Honored*) magazine. He died the following year while undergoing heart surgery at a hospital in Houston, Texas. The Palestinian Authority [*q.v.*] declared three days of mourning and accorded him a state funeral.

Dashnak Party (Lebanon): *see* Tashnak Party (Lebanon).

Day of Atonement (Jewish): *see* Yom Kippur.

Dayan, Moshe (1915–81): *Israel military and political leader* Born in Degania kibbutz [*q.v.*] near the Sea of Galilee, Dayan joined the Haganah [*q.v.*] when in his teens. Due to his lack of fluency in English he discontinued his studies at the London School of Economics in 1935–36 and returned to Palestine [*q.v.*], where he participated in the Haganah's operations to counter the Arab Revolt (1936–39). Following a change in the British Mandate policy at the start of World War II, the authorities suppressed the Haganah and sentenced Dayan to five years' imprisonment. After his release in early 1941 he led a British reconnaissance unit into Syria, then under a pro-Nazi French regime. He was wounded and lost his left eye.

During the Arab-Israeli War I (1948–49) [*q.v.*], his battalion captured Ramle and Lod, and this led to his appointment as the commander of the Jerusalem [*q.v.*] area. He became a protégé of Prime Minister David Ben-Gurion [*q.v.*], who was also defense minister. After serving as head of the southern command (1950) and the northern command (1952), he was promoted to chief of army operations. In 1953 he was promoted to chief of staff. His military leadership reached its apogee during the Suez War (October–November 1956) [*q.v.*], when Israel mounted its lightning Sinai campaign.

After retiring from the military in 1958, he became a Mapai [*q.v.*] politician. Elected to the Knesset [*q.v.*] in 1959, he served as agriculture minister. He resigned in 1964 because of his differences with Prime Minister Levi Eshkol [*q.v.*]. The next year he joined Rafi and was elected to the Knesset on its list, becoming part of the opposition. On the eve of the 1967 Six-Day War [*q.v.*], however, Premier Eshkol formed a national unity government, which included Dayan as defense minister.

With most Rafi leaders joining the enlarged Mapai-Ahdut HaAvodah-Poale Zion Aligment [*q.v.*] to form the Labor Party [*q.v.*] in 1968, Dayan returned to the political mainstream. He took a hawkish line on the Occupied Arab Territories [*q.v.*] and used threats to establish a breakaway group of his own to impose his views on his Labor colleagues. In April 1973 he mounted a campaign to annex the West Bank [*q.v.*], the Golan Heights [*q.v.*], and parts of the Sinai [*q.v.*]. He used his office to establish Jewish colonies in the Occupied Territories [*q.v.*].

The surprise Egyptian-Syrian attack on the Israeli-occupied Arab territories in October 1973 shattered the invincible image of Israel and Dayan. Though he recovered from the initial shock, and the Israeli military performed well later, the label of failure stuck to him. In March 1974 the official inquiry on the October 1973 Arab-Israeli War [*q.v.*] cleared him and blamed the chief of staff, General David Elazer. When Elazer resigned, the pressure on Dayan to do the same mounted. He refused, forcing Premier Golda Meir [*q.v.*] to submit the resignation of the full cabinet. When Labor lost the May 1977 election to Likud [*q.v.*], Dayan crossed the party lines and became foreign minister under Premier Menachem Begin [*q.v.*].

He played an important part in the peace talks with Egypt, which culminated in the Israeli-Egyptian peace treaty [*q.v.*] in March 1979. Later that year he left the government and established his own group. In the 1981 election it won only two parliamentary seats.

Democratic Alliance (Egypt): *an alliance of Islamist political parties* After the ouster of Egyptian President Hosni Mubarak [*q.v.*] in February 2011, several small groups allied with the Freedom and Justice Party (FJP) [*q.v.*] of the Muslim Brotherhood [*q.v.*] to form the Democratic Alliance in June to fight the parliamentary elections held between November 2011 and January 2012. In the 508-seat People's Assembly all but 10 seats were open to competition, with two-thirds to be won on the basis of a party and one-third on the basis of an individual. The Alliance secured 235 seats with the FJP in the lead at 213. In the elections for the Consultative Council conducted in January-February 2012, of the 180 elected seats the Democratic Alliance garnered 105.

Democratic Front for the Liberation of Palestine: *Palestinian political organization* A breakaway group of the Popular Front for the Liberation of Palestine (PFLP) [*q.v.*], the Democratic Front for the Liberation of Palestine (DFLP) was formed in 1969 by Nayif Hawatmeh [*q.v.*] and Bilal Hassan. By launching guerrilla actions against Israel, it secured an invitation to join the Palestine Armed Struggle Command (PASC) run by the Palestine Liberation Organization (PLO) [*q.v.*]. Within a year the DFLP's guerrilla force of 1,200 became the fourth largest.

The DFLP stressed that the Palestinian and Jordanian struggles were complementary. Its first open congress in August 1970 in Amman [*q.v.*] advocated the overthrow of the Hashemite dynasty and the founding of a democratic regime. But the bitter experience of September 1970—when Palestinian civilians and commandos suffered heavy losses at the hands of the Jordanian army—had a salutary effect on the DFLP.

Following its expulsion from Jordan to Beirut [*q.v.*], it moderated its criticism of other parties and regional Arab regimes. At the Palestine National Council (PNC) session in June 1974 the DFLP was the prime mover behind the PNC's acceptance of resolution calling for the establish-ment of a "national authority" in the West Bank [*q.v.*] and Gaza Strip [*q.v.*] as the first step toward the liberation of the "whole of Palestine." In Lebanon the DFLP allied with the leftist Lebanese National Movement (LNM) [*q.v.*] during the Lebanese Civil War [*q.v.*]. In line with its policy of talking to those Israelis who were either anti-Zionist or simply ready to recognize the Palestinians' right to "an independent national authority" in the West Bank and Gaza Strip, it held talks with the radical left wing Israeli Socialist Organization.

After it expulsion from Beirut in 1982, the DFLP moved its base to Damascus [*q.v.*]. In the mid-1980s it cooperated with other radical Pales-tinian groups to frustrate the plan of the PLO chairman, Yasser Arafat [*q.v.*], and King Hussein [*q.v.*] of Jordan to enter into secret peace talks with Israel. It strongly opposed the PLO-Israeli Accord [*q.v.*] signed in September 1993, refusing to moderate its stance. As a result, a year later the Palestinian Authority (PA) [*q.v.*], arrested 40 DFLP activists in 1994.

It was not until October 1999 that the DFLP made its peace with the PA. This resulted in its name being removed from Washington's list of terrorist organizations. It participated in the al-Aqsa intifada [*q.v.*] launched by the Palestinians in September 2000. About a year later two DFLP members became the first Palestinians to infiltrate an Israeli military outpost in the Gaza Strip and killed three soldiers.

The DFLP opposed attacks inside Israel or on Israeli civilians. In the Palestinian parliamentary elections of 2006, it formed an alliance with the Palestinian People's Party [*q.v.*] called al-Badeel (Arabic: *The Alternative*). It won two seats. With its headquarters in Damascus [*q.v.*], the DFLP en-joyed better support among the Pales-tinian refugees in Syria and Lebanon than the inhabitants of the West Bank or Gaza Strip.

Democratic Front for Peace and Equality (Israel): *see* Hadash.

dhimmis: *non-Muslims in an Islamic state* Dhimmis are members of *ahl al-dhimma* (Arabic: *people of dhimma*, meaning *contract*). Thus dhimma is a contract between Muslims and mem-bers of other religions—Judaism [*q.v.*] and Christianity [*q.v.*]—provided the latter accept Islamic rule. Dhimma is based on a verse in the Quran [*q.v.*] (IX, 29): "Fight those who believe not in God and the Last Day ... until they pay the *jizya* (Arabic: *tribute*) out of their hand, and have been humbled." The Prophet Muhammad concluded pacts of submission and protection with the Jews of Khaibar and the Christians of Najran. Initially, only Jews and Christians were involved. But when it became necessary to consider Zoroastrians [*q.v.*], it was decided that, by writing down their previously orally transmitted scripture, *Avesta*, they had attained the status of *ahl al-kitab* (Arabic: *people of the Book*). The payment of the *jizya*, which developed into a precise poll tax, gave a definite fiscal status to *dhimmis*. Muslim rulers were prohibited to accept *jizya* from apostates or from idolaters in Arabia. However, they could accept it from idolaters in other regions of the world.

diaspora: (Greek: *a scattering)* The term diaspora, meaning *dispersion*, was originally applied to the scattered colonies of Jews [*q.v.*] following their exile from Palestine to Babylon in 586 B.C. Later it was applied collectively to all Jews living outside Palestine [*q.v.*] in the rest of the Old World. With the migration of Europeans to the Western Hemisphere, the Jewish diaspora extended to that region as well. At 5.3 million, the Jews in the United States formed the largest diaspora in the Western Hemisphere in 2011.

Nowadays, however, the term has acquired a secular meaning, and applies to all communities that have been dispersed in recent times: the Armenians [*q.v.*] after their persecution during World War I, the Palestinians after the Palestine War (1948–49) [*q.v.*], and so on.

Doha: *capital of Qatar* Population: 1 million (2011 est.). A hotbed of piracy, the village of Doha (Arabic: *Bay*) was razed in 1867. It was revived by Shaikh Muhammad bin Thani the next year under British patronage. After Qatar [*q.v.*] formally became a British protectorate in 1916, London maintained its political agent in Doha.

Its inhabitants made their living by fishing, pearling, and trading. After oil was found in the nearby Dukhan area in 1939, and exploited on a commercial scale after World War II, Doha prospered and underwent dramatic change. Further expansion came in the wake of Qatar's independence in 1971. By the mid-1980s Doha accounted for three-fifths of the national population. A gleaming modern city with a deep-water harbor, its rising prosperity is underwritten by the enormous natural gas reserves of Qatar. As a cosmopolitan city, Doha has acquired a string of Christian churches but no Hindu or Buddhist temple.

During the first decade of the of the 21st century it became a leading center for regional diplomacy. By the end of that decade it was the base of Al-Jazeera Arabic and English satellite television channels and the site of several outstanding museums. Its Education City housed not only Qatar University but also branch campuses of six leading American universities.

Dome of the Rock: *see* Noble Sanctuary.

donum: area measurement used in the Arab Middle East [q.v.] 1 donum = 0.26 acre = 0.11 hectare.

Dowlatabadi, Mahmoud (1940–): *Iranian writer* Born in Dowlatabad, a village in the eastern province of Khorasan, into a poor peasant family, Dowlatabadi moved to Tehran [*q.v.*] in his mid-teens. After completing a course in acting in 1960, he became a stage actor. He published his first short story in 1962 in the *Anahita* magazine, named after the Zoroastrian [*q.v.*] divinity of the waters, symbolizing fertility, and graduated to writing novels, the first of which, *The Tale of Baba Sobhan*, was published in 1968, and made into a movie titled *Khak* (Persian, *Dust*) in 1972. In 1974 he was hired by the Association for Intellectual Development of Children and Young People. The next year he was arrested for his anti-regime activities and jailed for a year.

After the Islamic revolution [*q.v.*] in 1979, he started publishing a series of novels under the title *Kelidar*, a Kurdish town, about the day-to-day struggle for survival of the people there. He chronicled facts but in such an emotionally charged language that he gripped the reader. This 10-volume saga, published over a decade, established him as a literary giant of modern Persian literature. His other works include *Jay-e Khali-e Solooch* (Persian: *The Unoccupied Place of Solooch*), the story of the survival of a village woman and her three children after her abandonment by her husband, published as *Missing Solooch* in English in 2007, and *Yusuf's Day and Night*, an equally riveting work of social realism.

His latest novel, *Colonel*, written in 2009 and published in its English translation in 2011, was long-listed for the Man Asian Literary Prize. Because it shows how the revolution devoured its children, it has not been cleared by the censors in Iran for publication in the original Persian [*q.v.*].

Druze: *Islamic sect* Druzes are members of a movement called Daraziyya, derived from Muhammad al-Darazi (d. 1019), an Ismaili [*q.v.*] missionary from Bukhara, Uzbekistan, who be-

came an adviser to Fatimid Caliph al-Hakim (r. 996 A.D.–1021) in Cairo in 1017. Accepting the Ismail doctrine, Darazi regarded the *taawil* (Arabic: *inner truth*) and its representative, the imam [*q.v.*], as superior to the *tanzil* (Arabic: *outer truth*) and its representative, the Prophet Muhammad, and attributed the living imam (al-Hakim) with supernatural powers, embodying al-aql al-kulli (Arabic: *the highest cosmic intellect*). This proved controversial.

After al-Darazi's death, this mission was taken over by Hamza bin Ali, an Iranian. He gave the al-Hakim cult a definitive Druze form. He described al-Hakim as the embodiment of the Ultimate One, the present locus of the Creator. He thus went beyond the Ismaili taawil and the Sunni [*q.v.*] tanzil.

Druzes do not feel bound by two of the five pillars of Islam [*q.v.*]: fasting during Ramadan [*q.v.*] and pilgrimage to Mecca [*q.v.*]. They accept the seven commandments prescribed by Hamza and his successors, Baha al-Din al-Muktana: speaking the truth among the faithful; helping and defending one another; renouncing all former faiths; dissociating themselves from unbelievers; recognizing the unity of the Lord in all ages; being content with whatever the Lord does; and submitting to his orders as conveyed by his cosmic ranks. They believe that, when al-Hakim and Hamza bin Ali—both of whom disappeared—reappear to establish universal justice, the especially pious among them will rule the human race.

As a heterodox sect, Druzes suffered persecution by the majority Sunni Muslims. This drove them to the mountainous region of Syria-

Lebanon-Palestine. They are now to be found in southern Syria's Druze Mountain area, Lebanon's Shouf region, and Israel.

Dual Containment policy (United States): In May 1993 the U.S. administration of President Bill Clinton (r. 1993–2001) declared that in the Gulf [*q.v.*] it would contain both Iran [*q.v.*] and Iraq [*q.v.*], thus reversing the policies of the earlier administrations of Presidents George H. W. Bush (r. 1989–93) and Ronald Reagan (r. 1981-1989), based on the doctrine of "zero sum" regarding these two Gulf neighbors—that is, weakening Iraq was tantamount to strengthening Iran, and vice versa. Clinton's successor, President George W. Bush (r. 2001-2009), would adopt a modified version of the Dual Containment policy under the title of the "Axis of Evil" by adding North Korea to the list.

Dubai: *city and emirate in the United Arab Emirates*

Dubai city: *capital of the Dubai Emirate of the United Arab Emirates* Population, 1.9 million (2010 est.) Established in 1799, Dubai became an important pearling center in the early 20th century. With traders from India and Iran settling there, it developed as a trading port. Its commercial and political significance grew to the extent that London transferred its political agent for the Trucial States [*q.v.*] from Sharjah [*q.v.*] to Dubai in 1954 when it was home to 20,000 people.

With discovery of offshore oil in 1966, the city's fortunes improved sharply. Its reputation as a center for free trade in gold, much in demand in the Indian subcontinent, also helped its prosperity. Following the independence of Dubai Emirate in 1971, the city became its capital. It acquired a modern port and dry docks in the 1970s. During the Iran-Iraq War (1980–88) [*q.v.*], the importance of Dubai as a center for re-exporting Western goods to Iran rose dramatically. A cosmopolitan metropolis, with foreigners making up 95 percent of its population, it has excellent financial and telecommunications facilities. It is the largest city of the United Arab Emirates [*q.v.*].

It has been developed as a tourist destination as well as a financial services and media hub. Its International Finance Center, built in 2004, is expected to be the largest between Hong Kong and London.

During the first decade of the 21st century its Jebel Ali port, inaugurated in 1979, became one of the busiest in the world. The Jebel Ali free trade zone was duplicated in Dubai Maritime City, Dubai Internet City, and Dubai Media City. The Burj al-Arab (Arabic: *Tower of the Arabs*), the second-tallest freestanding hotel (shaped like a sail of a boat), which opened for business in 2000, has become the symbol of Dubai just as the Eiffel Tower is for Paris.

An unprecedented boom in construction during the first decade of the 21st century created a host of super-tall skyscrapers, with the Burj Khalifa (Arabic: *Tower of Dubai*) at 2,684 ft./818 m, opened in January 2010, being the tallest on the planet. Dubai has become one of the favorite holiday resorts for Europeans.

The Palm Jumeirah, an artificial archipelago, is the first of the three palm shaped islands to be created in the Gulf, increasing its shoreline by 320 mi./520 km. The first Palm Island was built by pouring seven million tons of rock and 94 million tons of sand into the Gulf. Along with hundreds of privately owned villas and several mega-shopping-malls, it accommodates 30 five-star hotels.

Due to the crash in property values, caused partly by the Great Recession of 2008–09 in the West, the frantic construction activity ended in November 2009 when Dubai World, the heavily indebted conglomerate, told its creditors that it could not repay about $25 billion of debts as planned. With the financial aid of the ruler of the Abu Dhabi Emirates [q.v.], it reached a compromise with its creditors.

Dubai Emirate Area 1,510 sq. mi./3,900 sq. km, population, 2.262 million (2010 est.); *see* United Arab Emirates.

In 2009, its GDP was $47 billion and its total foreign debt was $110 billion, according to the International Monetary Fund.

East Bank: The terms "East Bank" and "West Bank" [q.v.] apply to the Jordan River [q.v.]. The territory on the East Bank belongs to Jordan [q.v.].

East Jerusalem: Area: 2.5 sq. mi./6.5 sq. km in 1948, 27.5 sq. mi./71.2 sq. km in 1967; population 264,100 Arabs (2011 est.); 192,800 Jewish settlers (2011 est.); total 456,900. East

Jerusalem, captured by the Arab forces in the 1948–49 Arab-Israeli War [q.v.] and retained by Jordan, measured 2.5 sq. mi./6.5 sq. km. It included the Old City, measuring about 0.4 sq. mi./1 sq. km and containing the Noble Sanctuary [q.v.], the Wailing Wall [q.v.], and the Church of the Holy Sepulcher, the burial place of Jesus Christ.

It was captured by Israel on 7 June 1967 during the Six-Day War [q.v.]. On 28 June 1967 Israel added 25 sq. mi./65 sq. km of the West Bank [q.v.] territory to (Jordanian) East Jerusalem, and extended its laws to the vastly enlarged area, a step repudiated by UN Security Council Resolution 252 (1968). The census carried out by Israel then showed 44,000 Arabs [q.v.] living in the Jerusalem of the pre-Six-Day War period and another 22,000 in the territory of the West Bank annexed by Israel.

In 1980 the Israeli parliament passed a "basic law," which declared unified Jerusalem to be the indivisible capital of Israel, without stipulating its boundaries. This was repudiated by UN Security Council Revolutions 476 (March 1980) and 478 (June 1980) by 14 votes to none. Though the Arab residents of East Jerusalem were given the right to vote in local elections, no more than 5 percent exercised this right, thus emphasizing their commitment to having East Jerusalem as the capital of a future State of Palestine [q.v.].

By 1997 Israel had established 12 Jewish settlements in East Jerusalem. That number rose to 17 almost a decade later. In 2009, the walled Old City had 35,000 Arab and 4,500 Jewish residents.

It is a cardinal demand of the Palestinian Authority [*q.v.*] and the Palestine Liberation Organization [*q.v.*] that East Jerusalem must be the capital of a future independent Palestine. *See also* Jerusalem and West Jerusalem.

East Syriac rite: *see* Chaldean Catholic Church.

Easter: *Derivative of Eastre, an ancient Teutonic goddess* An annual church celebration commemorating Christ's resurrection on the third day after his crucifixion, for Roman Catholics [*q.v.*] and Protestants [*q.v.*]. Western Easter is the first Sunday after the full moon that falls on, or follows, the spring equinox (21 March in the Gregorian Christian calendar [*q.v.*]). If the full moon happens on a Sunday, Easter is celebrated a week later. Thus Easter Sunday falls between 22 March and 25 April. Due to the somewhat different calculations of the Orthodox Church [*q.v.*], the Orthodox Easter often comes one, four, or five weeks later, but sometimes it coincides with the Western Easter. In both cases, Easter determines the dates of all other movable church festivals, such as Lent and Pentecost [*q.v.*].

Eastern (Orthodox) Church: *see* Orthodox Christian Church.

Ebadi, Shirin (1947–): *Iranian lawyer, human rights campaigner, and winner of Nobel Peace Prize 2003* Born into a family of academics in Hamadan, Ebadi grew up in Tehran [*q.v.*]. She secured her law degree from Tehran University at 21, and became a junior judge after a six-month apprenticeship in adjudication. Two years later she obtained a doctorate with honors in private law from the same university. After serving in various jobs in the Justice Department, she was appointed President of Bench 24 of the Tehran City Court in 1975, the first woman in Iran to hold such a position.

Since the Islamic regime did not allow women to become judges, Ebadi and other female judges were demoted to clerks in 1979. When they protested, the authorities promoted them to "experts" in the Justice Department. She resigned. Her application for an attorney's license to the Justice Ministry was rejected.

Along with being a homemaker and mother, she published books on different aspects of the law, from medical practice to architecture to workers' rights. It was not until 1992 that she was able to secure an attorney's license.

She became involved in human rights violation cases. In 1995 she cofounded the Association for Support of Children's Rights. The next year she was appointed an observer for the New York-based Human Rights Watch. In 2000 she published *History and Documentation of Human Rights in Iran* in the United States. Along with four defense lawyers she founded the Human Rights Defense Center in 2001.

She was awarded the Nobel Peace Prize in 2003 for her pioneering work for the rights of women, children, and refugees. She became the first Iranian and the first Muslim woman to receive this prize.

In her book (written along with Azadeh Moaveni) *Iran Awakening: A Memoir of Revolution and Hope* (2006), she explained her views on Islam, democracy, and gender equality.

Firmly rooted in Iranian soil and history, she treats Islam as her primary premise, and argues for new interpretations to align the Sharia [*q.v.*] with human rights, democracy, and freedom of speech and association.

In her speeches abroad, she was critical of the double standards of the West, particularly America. In 2007 she supported the Iranian government's nuclear program, arguing that aside from its economic justification, the program had become a cause of national pride for an old nation with a glorious history.

In August 2008 when she announced that she would defend seven Bahai [*q.v.*] leaders arrested earlier, threats against her life and those of her family intensified. In December the official raiding and closure of the Human Rights Defense Center was followed by a raid on her private office and the seizure of her computers and files.

She was in Spain at the time of the disputed presidential election in June 2009. She demanded a fresh poll. Later she called on the Western powers to withdraw their ambassadors from Tehran and freeze the assets of Iran's leaders. From her base in London, she continued to speak out about the repression of dissidents, women, and Bahais in Iran in her lectures and seminars around North America and Europe.

In April 2012 she criticized the harsh economic sanctions imposed against Iran for its nuclear program, arguing that they were doing more harm than good and failing to weaken the Iranian regime.

8 March Alliance (Lebanon): A coalition of several pro-Syria groups in Lebanon, it was named after the 8 March 2005 mass demonstration in Beirut [*q.v.*] as a counterforce to a series of anti-Syria marches. It praised Syria for its efforts to end the Lebanese Civil War [*q.v.*] in 1990 and for backing the Lebanese resistance to Israel's occupations of southern Lebanon following its invasions in 1978 and 1982. The leading members of the coalition were Amal [*q.v.*], the Free Patriotic Movement [*q.v.*], the Lebanese Democratic Party, and the Syrian Socialist Nationalist Party [*q.v.*].

In the 2005 parliamentary election, the 8 March Alliance won 56 of the 128 seats, and in the 2009 election it garnered 57 seats on a popular vote of 55.5 percent of the 1.486 million ballots cast, gaining 152,000 votes more than the 14 March Alliance [*q.v.*]. It secured 16 of the 30 cabinet posts in the government of Prime Minister Najib Mikati [*q.v.*] in 2012. When the pro-reform protest spread in Syria during 2011-2012, the Alliance's constituents attributed it to foreign intervention and Salafi [*q.v.*] militants.

Egypt:

OFFICIAL NAME: Arab Republic of Egypt

CAPITAL: Cairo [*q.v.*]

AREA: 385,230 sq. mi./997,740 sq. km

POPULATION: 81.1 million (2011 est.)

GROSS DOMESTIC PRODUCT (nominal) $231 billion; per capita $2,892 (2011 est.)

GROSS DOMESTIC PRODUCT (Purchasing Power Parity) $508 billion; per capita $6,360 (2011 est.)

NATIONAL CURRENCY: Egyptian Pound (EGP); EGP 1 = U.S.$0.166 = £0.105 = € 0.126 (2011)

FORM OF GOVERNMENT: republic, president elected by popular vote

OFFICIAL LANGUAGE: Arabic [*q.v.*]

OFFICIAL RELIGION: Islam [*q.v.*]

ADMINISTRATIVE REGIONS: Egypt is divided into 29 governorates (provinces).

CONSTITUTION: The 1971 constitution, approved by a referendum, was amended in 1990. It described Egypt as an Arab republic with a democratic, socialist system. It prescribed Islam as the state religion and the Sharia [*q.v.*] as the "principal source" of legislation. It labeled the political system as multiparty. The state ensured equality of men and women in accordance with the Sharia. It also safeguarded the public sector, and protected the assets of cooperative societies and trade unions. The constitution banned the propagation of atheism and any attack on "divine religion." It guaranteed the right to peaceful assembly, freedom of the press, and freedom to travel.

The sole presidential candidate who must be endorsed by at least two-thirds of parliamentary deputies was to be offered to voters for approval. He had six-year tenure and could be elected for further terms. He exercised executive authority and appointed or dismissed vice presidents and ministers, including the premier. He also nominated 10 members to the parliament, called the People's Assembly, with at least 350 elected members, to be elected for five years. It had the power to force a minister to resign. In the case of the prime minister, the Assembly had the right to submit an adversarial report to the president. If the president rejected the report, the matter was then put to referendum. If the

voters accepted the report, the full cabinet had to resign. If the voters rejected it, then the president had to dissolve the Assembly.

Wide-ranging changes to the constitution in 2007 banned the use of religion as a political ideology by a party, ended the judicial supervision of elections, and authorized the president to dissolve the People's Assembly. These amendments were endorsed in a referendum in which a little over a quarter of the voters participated.

Following the forced resignation of President Hosni Mubarak [*q.v.*] in February 2011 in the face of escalating popular uprising, which came to be called the Arab Spring [*q.v.*], the ruling Supreme Council of the Armed Forces (SCAF) amended the constitution. These changes limited the presidency to two six-year terms, required the president to appoint at least one vice president, mandated judicial supervision of elections, specified a 100-member panel elected by a post-Mubarak parliament to draft a new constitution, and modest requirements for the presidential candidacy. In a referendum held in March 77 percent approved the amended document on a turnout of 41 percent of the 45 million voters. It came into effect at the end of the month.

In October the Islamist-dominated, 100-strong constituent assembly released a partial draft of the constitution, which excluded military-civilian relations, for public discussion. Among other things it accorded gender equality subject to the rulings of the Sharia [*q.v.*].

CONSULTATIVE COUNCIL: Following amendments to the 1971 constitution in May 1980, a 210-member

Consultative Council, called Shura Council, with three-year term was established to preserve the principles of the 1952 republican revolution and the 1971 "correctionist" revolution by President Anwar Sadat [*q.v.*]. One-third of its members were appointed by the president. Because the first three elections were boycotted by the opposition, the ruling National Democratic Party (NDP) [*q.v.*] filled all the elected seats. The opposition participated in the 1989 election, but failed to win a single seat. In the 1995 election, the NDP won 88 of the 90 seats, and in the mid-term 1998 election, 87 seats out of 90, followed by 74 of the 88 seats in 2001, with most opposition factions continuing their boycott.

The 2007 amended constitution designated the 270-member Consultative Council with six-year tenure as the upper house of a bicameral parliament. Only 180 of its members were elected, with the rest appointed by the president. Half of the Council members were renewed every three years. Its lawmaking powers were limited with the People's Assembly being the dominant chamber. It was dissolved by the SCAF on 11 February 2011 after Mubarak was forced to resign. It was replaced by a fully-elected 180-member Consultative (Shura) Council, and given the status of the upper house of parliament with the same four-year tenure as the lower house, called the People's Assembly. *See further*, Legislature.

The elections in January-February 2012 led to the following result: Democratic Alliance [*q.v.*], 105 seats; Islamist Bloc [*q.v.*], 45 seats; New Wafd [*q.v.*], 14 seats; Egyptian Bloc, 8; others, 8.

ETHNIC COMPOSITION: (2011) Arabs 99 percent, other 1 percent.

EXECUTIVE AUTHORITY: Executive authority rests with the president, who is elected directly by voters.

High officials:

President: Muhammad Morsi, 2012–

Prime minister: Hisham Qandil, 2012–

Speaker of the People's Assembly (before dissolution in June 2012): Saad El Katatny, 2012

Speaker of the Consultative (Shura) Council (before dissolution in June 2012): Ahmad Fahmy, 2012

HISTORY: On the eve of World War I Britain declared Egypt (which had been under its occupation since 1882) a protectorate. In 1922, while recognizing Egypt as a sovereign state under King Ahmad Fuad (r. 1922–36), Britain continued to maintain its military occupation. The anti-imperialist movement, spearheaded by the Wafd [*q.v.*], gained momentum and resulted in the Anglo-Egyptian Treaty of 1936 [*q.v.*]. The treaty preserved many British privileges, including its military presence in the Suez Canal [*q.v.*] zone.

The poor performance of the Egyptian troops in the Palestine War (1948–49) [*q.v.*] encouraged nationalist officers to plan a coup. In 1952, organized as Free Officers, they seized power after overthrowing King Farouq [*q.v.*]. The new Revolutionary Command Council (RCC) was dominated by Gamal Abdul Nasser [*q.v.*]. It started a program of land reform and industrialization at home and advancement of pan-Arabism [*q.v.*] in the region. Egypt combined with Syria in early 1958 to form the United

Arab Republic [*q.v.*], but the UAR split in September 1961 in bitterness. Egypt helped the republican officers in North Yemen to consolidate their regime after an anti-royalist coup there in 1962. But its humiliating defeat by Israel in the 1967 Six-Day War [*q.v.*], resulting in the loss of Sinai [*q.v.*], undermined the leadership of Nasser.

After his death in 1970 the presidency passed to Anwar Sadat. In conjunction with Syria, he launched a surprise attack on the Israeli-occupied Sinai in October 1973. The Egyptians gave their best military performance yet. Sadat cut the 20-year-old ties with the Soviet Union, and turned to the United States for a compromise with Israel. His efforts culminated in an Egyptian-Israeli peace treaty [*q.v.*] in March 1979. To curb domestic opposition to the treaty, Sadat took increasingly repressive measures, thus losing popularity. He was assassinated in October 1981.

His successor, Hosni Mubarak, tried to heal the wounds, and succeeded. During his presidency Egypt was readmitted to the Arab League in 1989, after a decade of suspension. He continued the economic liberalization of Sadat. Equally, there was no change from his predecessor's practice of periodic, rigged elections. Mubarak was reelected to the presidency for the second time in October 1993. He faced increasing opposition from militant Muslim [*q.v.*] groups, especially al-Gammat al-Islamiya [*q.v.*]. By the time he was renominated by the People's Assembly for the presidency in 1999, his government had crushed Islamic militancy by using repulsive methods which caused concern in the

U.S. administration of President Bill Clinton (r. 1993–2001). Following the Islamist terrorist attacks on New York and Washington in September 2001, however, American perceptions at the official level changed. While offering full cooperation to the U.S. in its war against Islamist terrorism, Mubarak advised President George W. Bush (r. 2001-2009) to address the Israeli-Palestinian conflict impartially and help forge an international convention on terrorism—but to no avail.

Under pressure from the Bush administration to democratize his regime, Mubarak allowed a limited number of semi-clandestine Muslim Brotherhood [*q.v.*] members to enter parliamentary elections in 2005. When three-fifths of them won, Washington's ardor for democracy cooled. With that, Mubarak reverted to the old policy of repressing the Brotherhood. In the first popular election for the presidency in 2005, he secured 88.6 percent of the vote, with his nearest rival, Ayman Nour [*q.v.*] garnering 7.3 percent, on a voter turnout of 25 percent. The election was marred by suppression of opposition candidates' campaigns and blatant electoral fraud and vote-rigging.

In the most fraudulent parliamentary election yet, boycotted by the Muslim Brotherhood, in December 2010, the NDP raised its strength by 90 to 420. Soon thereafter the Arab Spring [*q.v.*] arrived in Egypt.

With the overthrow of the Tunisian President Zine el Abidine Ben Ali on 14 January, the recently launched "We are all Khaled Saeed" Facebook page, referring to an innocent citizen in Alexandria [*q.v.*] murdered by the police, became a rallying point for the protest on 25 January. Yet it was only on the following Friday, 28 January, that peaceful demonstrations in the Tahrir Square of Cairo gathered momentum after the weekly Muslim congregational prayers.

Violent clashes between protestors and the security forces broke out as Mubarak coupled his promise on 2 February not to contest the next presidential election in 2013. Demonstrators were not satisfied. On 4 February, Friday, labeled "Day of Departure," an ever-larger gathering of protestors demanded Mubarak's immediate resignation as the economic life of the nation started ebbing.

Behind the scenes Egyptian defense minister Field Marshall Muhammad Hussein Tantawi was in daily contact with his counterpart in Washington, Robert Gates, who stressed U.S. President Barack Obama's advice not to use military force to disband the over one million demonstrators who had camped in the Tahrir Square. The escalating popular protest, coupled with Obama's withdrawal of support for Mubarak, led the fence-sitting generals on the SCAF to join the anti-Mubarak faction.

On 10 February, claiming that a national dialogue on political reform was in progress, Mubarak transferred power to Vice President Omar Suleiman, but refused to step down. But the next day he bowed to the popular will backed by the SCAF. By the time he resigned after 18 days of civil uprising, handing over his powers to the SCAF and retiring to the presidential palace in the sea resort of Sharm al-Shaikh, 846 protestors were dead and 12,000 had been arrested.

After assuming power, the SCF accepted the amendments to the constitution proposed by its appointed committee. These were designed to prepare Egypt for free and fair parliamentary and presidential elections. Once the amended constitution was approved in a referendum on 25 March, the country's revolution entered a new phase.

At his trial in August, a bed-ridden Mubarak denied charges of killing protestors and abuse of power.

Following massive protest at the slow progress toward democracy, Tantawi promised a presidential poll in June 2012. The SCAF appointed Kamal Ganzouri, a former prime minister, as head of a national salvation cabinet.

Staggered elections to the People's Assembly started in late November and continued until early January 2012. The Democratic Alliance led by the Freedom and Justice Party [q.v.] won 235 of the 508-member People's Assembly, with the Islamist Bloc [q.v.] headed by the al-Nour Party [q.v.] gaining 127 seats. In the 180-member Consultative Council elections that followed, the FJP-led Democratic Alliance garnered 105 seats and the al-Nour-led Islamist Bloc gained 45.

In the first round for the presidential poll on 23–24 May there were 12 candidates. Since none of them received 50 percent plus one vote, there was a second round on 16–17 June between the Freedom and Justice Party's Muhammad Morsi [q.v.] and Ahmed Shafiq [q.v.], the last prime minister of Hosni Mubarak, who was given a life sentence on 2 June for his part in the killing of protestors during the 2011 upheaval. Shafiq lost to Morsi by 48.3 percent of the vote to 51.7 percent.

Two days before the presidential election the Supreme Constitutional Court ruled that some of the articles on which the bicameral parliament was formed were unconstitutional. The SCAF dissolved the parliament and reassumed legislative powers.

In August President Morsi forced the 75-year-old Tantawi, head of the armed forces, and 64-year-old Sami Anan, the Army chief of staff, to resign, thereby ending the dual power structure. In October, Morsi granted pardon to all the protestors detained and tried in the civil protest movement between 25 January 2011 and 30 June 2012, the day he assumed the presidency.

LEGISLATURE: The parliament, called the People's Assembly, deals with legislation, general policy matters, and the budget. Of its 454 members, 444 are elected, the rest are appointed by the president. The main opposition parties boycotted the election in November–December 1990, demanding the lifting of the state of emergency and supervision of the election by an independent body, not the interior ministry. Five years later, the NDP won 316 seats, independents 115 (of whom 72 joined the NDP), and four opposition groups 13. In the 2000 elections—when polling stations were supervised by judges and not interior ministry officials—the NDP secured 170 seats, independents 234 (of whom 194 joined the NDP, raising its total to 364) and six opposition parties together 39. In the 2005 election, the NDP's score fell to 311, and the Muslim Brotherhood's total rose to 88.

In the blatantly rigged election of 2010, the NDP secured 420 out of the 444 contested) seats. The Muslim Brotherhood boycotted the election, and the New Wafd did not participate in the second round. This Assembly was dissolved by SCAF in February 2011 after Mubarak's ouster.

The first post-Mubarak era election for the 508-member People's Assembly during November 2011 and January 2012 produced the following results: the Freedom and Justice Party [q.v.]-led Democratic Alliance 235 seats (on 37.5 percent popular vote); the Salafist [q.v.] al-Nour [q.v.]-led Islamist Bloc 123 seats (on 28 percent vote); the New Wafd [q.v.] 38 seats (9 percent); and the secular Egyptian Bloc 35 seats (9 percent). As before, the governing authority was entitled to nominate 10 members. Two-thirds of the contested seats were decided on the basis of a party and one-third on the basis of an individual, with the first past the post being the winner. The voter turnout during the three phases of the election for the People's Assembly varied between 59 and 65 percent.

The result of the Consultative (Shura) Council elections in January–February 2012 was as follows: Democratic Alliance [qv], 105 seats; Islamist Bloc [qv], 45 seats; New Wafd [qv], 14 seats; Egyptian Bloc, 8; others, 8.

On 14 June the Supreme Constitutional Court ruled that some of the articles on which the bicameral parliament was formed were unconstitutional. The SCAF dissolved the parliament and reassumed legislative powers. These powers then passed to Morsi when he assumed the presidency on 30 June.

Fresh elections to the People's Assembly and the Consultative (Shura) Council were to follow after a newly drafted constitution had been passed.

RELIGIOUS COMPOSITION: (2010) Muslim, 90 percent, almost all Sunni [*q.v.*]; Christian [*q.v.*], 9 percent; four out of five Christians are Copts [*q.v.*]; other, 1 percent.

Egyptian-Israeli Peace Treaty

(1979): The Egyptian-Israeli Peace Treaty, signed in March 1979, ended the state of war that had existed between the two countries since the founding of Israel in May 1948. It was based on the principles and procedures outlined in the Camp David Accords [*q.v.*] of September 1978. Within a year of the treaty the signatories had exchanged ambassadors, and Israel had returned two-thirds of the occupied Sinai [*q.v.*] to Egypt. By April 1982 Israel had withdrawn from the rest of the peninsula. Arab League [*q.v.*] members denounced Egypt's deviation from the common Arab policy of working toward a comprehensive peace settlement with Israel, suspended it from the League, and broke all relations with Cairo. Egypt's suspension from the Arab league lasted until 1989. Despite periodic tension between Israel and Egypt—such as during the Israeli invasion and occupation of Lebanon in June 1982 [*q.v.*], the al-Aqsa Intifda [*q.v.*] of 2000, and the Israeli-Hizbollah War [*q.v.*] of 2006—the treaty has held.

Egyptian-Soviet Friendship Treaty

(1971): The Egyptian-Soviet Friendship Treaty, valid for 15 years, was negotiated in Cairo [*q.v.*] by Egyptian President Anwar Sadat [*q.v.*] and signed on 27 May 1971. According to the operative Articles 7 and 8, the signatories agreed to enter into immediate consultation in the event of any threat to peace, and to continue cooperation in developing Egypt's military potential. However, the existence of the treaty did not inhibit Sadat from expelling Soviet military personnel in July 1972. Whatever tensions this act of Sadat created, these subsided quickly. Before, during, and after the October 1973 Arab-Israeli War [*q.v.*] the Soviets supplied Egypt with massive cargoes of arms and ammunition. In 1975 Sadat, burdened with heavy foreign debt and rising budget deficit, approached Soviet leaders for a 10-year moratorium on debt repayments. They rejected his request. In return Sadat refused to renew the annual trade pact. On 14 March 1976 he unilaterally abrogated the friendship treaty 10 years before its expiry date.

Eid al-Adha (Arabic: *Festival of Sacrifice*): *Islamic festival*

One of the two canonical festivals, Eid al-Adha is also known as Eid al-Qurban (Persian: *Sacrifice*) or Eid al-Kabir (Arabic: *Major Festival*). It falls on 10 Dhul Hijja, the last month of the Islamic calendar [*q.v.*], when the hajj [*q.v.*] is undertaken by the faithful from the eighth to the 12th of Dhul Hijja. After the Stoning of the Devil in the form of three walls, the hajj is celebrated by sacrificing a sheep, camel, or bovine animal. Even those Muslims who are not on hajj are required to sacrifice an animal. They are also required to participate in communal prayers. By tradition, wearing their best clothes, they visit friends and relatives and exchange presents.

Eid al-Fitr (Arabic: *the festival of breaking the fast*): *Islamic festival*

One of the

two canonical festivals, Eid al-Fitr is also called Eid al-Saghir, the Minor Festival. It falls on 1 Shawaal, which follows Ramadan [*q.v.*], the month of fasting. Muslims are required to participate in communal prayers, and pay their *zakat* [*q.v.*] before the prayers. The faithful wear their best clothes, visit friends and relatives, and exchange presents. Since Eid al-Fitr comes at the end of a month of fasting, it is a joyous occasion.

Eisenhower Doctrine (1957): Following the strengthening of ties between Egypt and the Soviet Union in late 1956, U.S. President Dwight Eisenhower sent a message on 5 January 1957 to U.S. Congress outlining a countervailing strategy for the Middle East, later to be called the Eisenhower Doctrine. It proposed joint measures by U.S. Congress and the president to accelerate economic development of the region to help it maintain political independence; to provide military aid and cooperation on request; and, most importantly, to safeguard the territorial integrity and political independence of individual countries requesting such aid against overt aggression from any nation "controlled by international Communism," a phrase that included Egypt under President Abdul Gamal Nasser [*q.v.*], who was seen by Washington as being under Soviet control.

In March 1957 U.S. Congress adopted the Eisenhower Doctrine. In the region, Israel and Lebanon, then ruled by President Camille Chamoun [*q.v.*], subscribed to the Doctrine immediately. King Hussein of Jordan [*q.v.*] and Iraqi Prime Minister Nuri al-Said [*q.v.*] followed.

This doctrine enabled the United States to project its power in a region dominated until then by Britain and France.

el (Arabic: *the*): *see* al.

Epiphany (Greek: *from epiphania, manifestation*): *Christian festival* Also called the Twelfth Day, Little Christmas, and the Manifestation of Jesus Christ to the Gentiles, Epiphany is celebrated on 6 January, 12 days after Christmas, to commemorate the baptism of Jesus in the River Jordan [*q.v.*], the showing of Jesus to the Three Wise Men, and the Miracle of Cana. It ranks after Easter [*q.v.*] and Pentecost [*q.v.*].

Erbil: *see* Irbil.

Eretz Yisrael (Hebrew: *Land of Israel*): The term Eretz Yisrael is used to denote the Hebrew kingdom under David (r. 1010–970 B.C.) and Solomon (r. 970–930 B.C.). It measured about 17,500 sq. mi/45,320 sq. km, with half its area lying to the east of River Jordan [*q.v.*]. To the west it was bounded by the Mediterranean, to the east by the Syrian Desert, and to the south by the line connecting the Valley of Arish with Kadesh Barnea and the Valley of Zor south of the Dead Sea, and then running from River Arnon to Mount Hermon to the Valley of Iyon. In ca 930 B.C. the Hebrew kingdom was split into the northern territory called Israel, and the southern called Judah.

Esfahan: *see* Isfahan.

Eshkol, Levi (1895–1969): *Israeli politician; prime minister 1963–69* Born

Levi Shkolnik in Ukraine, Eshkol migrated to Palestine [*q.v.*] in 1914 and worked as a farm hand. Active with HaPoale HaTzair [*q.v.*], he co-founded Degania Beth kibbutz in 1920. Later he participated in establishing the housing company of the Histadrut [*q.v.*]. From 1934 to 1937 he worked in the Palestine Office in Berlin to supervise the transfer of goods bought with money donated by German-Jewish immigrants in Palestine. On his return home he directed the Histadrut's Mekorot Water Company. In 1940 he took charge of the finances of the Haganah [*q.v.*], including arms procurement. During the First Arab-Israeli War (1948–49) [*q.v.*], he became director-general of the defense ministry under David Ben-Gurion [*q.v.*], focusing on the war's economic and financial aspects.

Elected to the Jewish Agency [*q.v.*] executive committee in 1948, he supervised the settlement of immigrants. He encouraged the founding of cooperative villages, *moshavim*. In 1951 he was elected to parliament on the Mapai [*q.v.*] list and kept his seat until his demise. After a year as minister of agriculture and development he served as finance minister, a position he retained until he succeeded Ben-Gurion as the prime minister and defense minister in 1963. He liberalized the economy and detached the broadcasting department from the prime minister's secretariat, transforming it into an independent authority. He removed the travel limitations that had been imposed on Israel's Arab [*q.v.*] citizens since 1948.

By sponsoring a cabinet decision to bring the remains of Vladimir Jabotinsky [*q.v.*] from New York to Israel for reburial in Jerusalem [*q.v.*], Eshkol lowered tensions between the government and right-wing opposition. He reinforced arms purchase agreements with the United States, involving advanced attack aircraft, thus strengthening the Israeli military. He withstood the challenge posed by the defection of Ben-Gurion, who founded his own group, Rafi, in 1965, and led the government formed after the general election later that year.

Eshkol continued the development of nuclear weapons, initiated by Ben-Gurion, at Dimona. In 1968, he clinched a clandestine agreement with West Germany: in exchange for Israel's providing West Germans with laser technology to enrich uranium, the latter shipped 200 tons of uranium to Israel.

On the eve of the 1967 Six-Day War [*q.v.*], he came under increased public pressure to broaden his administration. He set up a government of national unity and gave up the defense ministry to Moshe Dayan [*q.v.*]. By co-opting the right-wing Gahal [*q.v.*] and its leader, Menachem Begin [*q.v.*], into the government, he gave that party the respectability denied to it by Ben-Gurion. Ignoring his critics' charge of vacillation, he governed by consensus until his death.

Euphrates River: Known in biblical times as Perath, the Euphrates River rises in eastern Turkey and flows roughly 1,680 mi./2,700 km to Iraq, there joining the Tigris River [*q.v.*], about 120 mi./260 km from the Persian Gulf [*q.v.*], to form the Shatt al-Arab [*q.v.*]. It provides irrigation for the fertile plain of Mesopotamia [*q.v.*], a cradle of ancient civilization.

F

Fahd bin Abdul Aziz al-Saud (1921–2005): *King of Saudi Arabia, 1982–2005* Born in Riyadh [*q.v.*] to Abdul Aziz bin Abdul Rahman al-Saud [*q.v.*] and Hassa bint Ahmad al Sudairi, Fahd was the 11th son of Ibn Saud. He received a traditional education. During the rule of Saud bin Abdul Aziz [*q.v.*], he served first as education minister (1953–60) and then, from 1962, as interior minister. He continued in that position when Faisal bin Abdul Aziz [*q.v.*] ascended the throne in 1964. Fahd was promoted to second deputy prime minister in 1967 and to first deputy prime minister two years later. When Khalid bin Abdul Aziz [*q.v.*] became king in 1975, he was named crown prince. On Khalid's death in June 1982 Fahd succeeded him. Eldest of the seven sons of Hassa al-Sudairi, his accession implied the dominance of the Sudairi Seven in the kingdom.

Of the two trends that had emerged among senior Saudi princes during Khalid's reign, Fahd belonged to the pro-American school, favoring rapid economic progress funded by Saudi Arabia's vast oil revenues, and opposed the nationalist trend, which was committed to a greater respect for tradition and slower economic development. In August 1981 he presented to the Arab League [*q.v.*] a Middle East peace plan which, in exchange for peaceful coexistence of all the states in the region, required Israeli to evacuate all the Arab territories occupied in 1967, the dismantling of the Jewish settlements in these areas, and the founding of a Palestinian state. It was adopted at the next summit in Fez, Morocco, in September 1982, and remained the common Arab position on a Middle East settlement until the Middle East conference in Madrid, Spain, nine years later. In 1986 he changed his title from "His Majesty" to the "Custodian of the Holy Mosques (of Mecca [*q.v.*] and Medina [*q.v.*])."

In keeping with his vacillating nature, Fahd waited a whole week before making public his position on Iraq's invasion of Kuwait on 2 August 1990. He called on the United States and Arab countries to send troops to help protect Saudi Arabia and end the Iraqi occupation of Kuwait. The huge expenses incurred by Riyadh in the conduct of the 1991 Gulf War [*q.v.*], the rearming of the kingdom that followed the conflict, and the sharply reduced prices of oil led his government to raise foreign loans to balance the budget.

Rising corruption and repression led to the growth of the Islamic fundamentalist movement, which drew its inspiration from the early days of the Ikhwan movement [*q.v.*], which had laid the foundation of the kingdom in the mid-1920s.

In August 1993 he appointed a fully nominated 60-member Consultative Council. Having made some concessions in the political and religious spheres, Fahd moved to repress further the dissident Islamic ulema [*q.v.*] at home and block financial assistance to Islamist militants abroad. He tightened ties with the United States still further while the latter's dependence on Saudi petroleum grew. A quarter of America's oil imports now originated in Saudi Arabia, which had purchased $25 billion worth of U.S. arms between August 1990 and December 1992—by which date a semi-formal defense agreement between Riyadh and Washington was reportedly in place.

To silence the opposition, his government detained 200 political dissidents in 1994. It was distressed when a bomb at the National Guard training center in Riyadh in November 1995 killed seven people, including five American officers. That month, following a stroke, Fahd transferred his powers to Crown Prince Abdullah [q.v.]. Though, on recovery, Faisal nominally retrieved these powers three months later, there was less of his imprint on the administration during the subsequent years as Abdullah became the de facto ruler. After a series of bombings in the kingdom in 2003, a statement attributed to him advocated striking the terrorists with "an iron hand."

One of the richest men in the world, Fahd's personal wealth was estimated to be around $21 billion at the time of his death.

Faisal bin Abdul Aziz al-Saud (1904–75): *King of Saudi Arabia, 1964–75*
Born in Riyadh [q.v.] to Abdul Aziz bin Abdul Rahman al-Saud [q.v.] and Tarfa bint Abdullah al-Shaikh, Faisal was the fourth son of Ibn Saud and the second among those who survived. After receiving a traditional education and military training, Faisal served his father as governor of Hijaz [q.v.] from 1926. He undertook several foreign missions, including an official visit to

the Soviet Union in 1934. During that year he led a successful campaign against North Yemen. Over time he emerged as foreign minister—inter alia leading Saudi delegations to the United Nations—without bearing such a title: autocratic Ibn Saud did not rule with the assistance of a formally appointed cabinet.

When Saud bin Abdul Aziz [q.v.] became king in 1953, he nominated a cabinet as an advisory body, with Faisal as deputy prime minister and foreign minister. He was also named crown prince. When, hit by an economic crisis and the absence of a budget, the kingdom's administration came to a halt in 1958, the king put Faisal in charge of all state affairs, promoting him to prime minister, a position Saud had held so far. Two years later King Saud reappointed himself prime minister but did not interfere with the fiscal policies of Faisal, who cut expenditure, introduced a budget, and paid off state debts.

Following the republican coup in North Yemen in September 1962, King Saud once again promoted Faisal to prime minister. To offset the threat to the future of the Saudi monarchy, Faisal promised constitutional, religious, judicial, social, and economic reforms—including the promulgation of a written constitution, specifying a consultative council. But he was unable to deliver because King Saud refused to give up any of his powers. The resulting crisis was resolved in November 1964 when, pressured by senior princes and clergy, King Saud abdicated.

Faisal ascended the throne. A pious Muslim, and son of a mother who came from the religious House of

Shaikh, he had the respect of the Islamic establishment. He suppressed the opposition harshly. He increased support to the royalist camp in the North Yemeni Civil War [*q.v.*], in which the republicans were being aided by Egyptian President Gamal Abdul Nasser [*q.v.*].

But after the Arab defeat in the 1967 Six-Day War [*q.v.*], Faisal buried his differences with Nasser. His efforts to establish a transnational organization of Muslim states succeeded in 1969, in the aftermath of an arson attempt on the al-Aqsa mosque, Jerusalem [*q.v.*], resulting in the formation of the Islamic Conference Organization [*q.v.*], based in Jeddah [*q.v.*]. On 25 March 1975 he was assassinated by a young nephew, Prince Faisal bin Musaid.

Faisal I bin Hussein al-Hashem

(1885–1933): *King of Iraq, 1921–33*
Third son of Hussein bin Ali al-Hashem [*q.v.*], Faisal was born in Taif, Hijaz [*q.v.*], but was raised in Istanbul, where his father was kept under surveillance by the Ottoman sultan. In 1908 he returned to Hijaz along with his father, who was appointed governor of Mecca [*q.v.*] by the Young Turks after they had succeeded Sultan Abdul Hamid II in 1908. Faisal worked closely with his father, traveling to Damascus [*q.v.*] in 1915 (during World War I) to secure support for him from secret Arab nationalist groups there. The next year Hussein led an Arab revolt in Hijaz against the Ottomans. As commander of the northern force, Faisal focused on harassing the Turkish troops, and marched into Transjordan [*q.v.*] in 1917 along with the victorious British.

Entering Damascus [*q.v.*] in October 1918, he established an Arab government under the aegis of the Allied military administration.

At the Paris Peace Conference he staked the claim of his al-Hashem family as the ruler of either an independent Arab kingdom or a federation of several emirates (principalities). France, which in 1916 had entered into a secret agreement with Britain called the Sykes-Picot Pact [*q.v.*], opposed Faisal's demands and insisted on keeping Syria under its control. An Arab national congress in Damascus in March 1920 declared Faisal king of (Greater) Syria [*q.v.*], composed of present-day Syria, Lebanon, Israel, Palestine [*q.v.*], and Jordan. The next month, at the behest of the Allies, the League of Nations' Supreme Council handed France a mandate to administer Syria. In July there was a fight between the forces of Faisal and France in which Faisal was the loser.

Forced into exile, he accepted Britain's invitation to go to London. To overcome nationalist opposition to its mandate in Iraq, Britain offered to make Faisal king of Iraq in March 1921. He accepted and was crowned in August. Caught between rising Iraqi nationalism and British suzerainty, he pursued a middle course. By ratifying a constitution drafted by an assembly and holding parliamentary elections, he legitimized his regime. In 1930 he signed a treaty with Britain: it required him to coordinate his foreign policy with London and allow the stationing of British troops in Iraq in exchange for a British guarantee to protect Iraq against foreign attack. Britain ended its mandate in October 1932 and sponsored Iraq's membership in the League of Nations.

Faisal II bin Ghazi al-Hashem (1935–58): *King of Iraq, 1939–58*

The only son of King Ghazi bin Faisal I al-Hashem [q.v.], Faisal succeeded his father as an infant, under the regency of his uncle, Abdul Ilah bin Ali. After the 1941 coup by the nationalist Rashid Ali Gailani [q.v.], Faisal and his mother fled, along with Abdul Ilah and other members of the royal family. Gailani was defeated by the British, and that ensured the future of Faisal as king. Following World War II, he was sent to Britain to be educated. On achieving his majority in 1953 he started to exercise royal authority, but found himself hamstrung by the powerful presence of Abdul Ilah. After the formation of the Arab Federation of Iraq and Jordan in February 1958, he became its head. Five months later he was gunned down in the royal courtyard during a coup mounted by republican officers.

faqih: *Islamic jurisprudent*

One who practices *fiqh* [q.v.] (Arabic: *knowledge*), the term for jurisprudence, the science of religious law in Islam [q.v.].

Farouq (1920–65): *King of Egypt, 1936–52*

The only son of King Ahmad Fuad, Farouk received his education in Egypt and Britain. He succeeded his father in April 1936 but did not exercise royal authority until the age of 18 in February 1938. He pursued his father's policy of undermining the nationalist Wafd [q.v.].

Following the outbreak of World War II, he attempted to remain neutral, even though British troops were stationed in Egypt under the Anglo-Egyptian Treaty of 1936 [q.v.]. Italy's entry into the conflict on the German side in May 1940 complicated matters, since Farouq had many close Italian friends and advisers. In February 1942, while German troops were advancing on Egypt from Libya and Farouq was considering appointing a prime minister known to share widely prevalent anti-British views, Britain's ambassador in Cairo [q.v.] ordered British tanks to surround his palace and gave him the choice of abdicating or appointing Mustafa Nahas (Pasha) [q.v.], a pro-British Wafd leader, prime minister. Farouq chose the latter option.

While this secured the Allied position in Egypt for the rest of the war, it destroyed Farouq's prestige among his subjects. He tried to retrieve it by dismissing Nahas Pasha in October 1944. His standing suffered a further setback when the Egyptian army did badly in the Palestine War (1948–49) [q.v.] due to the incompetence and corruption of its senior officers, the obsolescence of its British-supplied arms, and erratic supplies of food and medicine.

To restore the nation's wounded pride Farouq made peace with Wafd leaders and held a general election in 1950. It returned the Wafd to power. The next year, after abrogating the Anglo-Egyptian Treaty of 1936, the Wafd government declared Farouq king of Egypt and Sudan. He was deposed in July 1952 by the Free Officers, led by General Muhammad Neguib and Col. Gamal Abdul Nasser [q.v.]. He and his family were allowed to leave for Italy, where he continued to maintain a luxurious lifestyle until his death 13 years later.

Farsi language: *See* Persian language.

Fatah (Arabic: *Victory;* reverse acronym of *Harkat al-Tahrir al-Falastini,* Movement for the Liberation of Palestine): Fatah was founded in 1958 by Yasser Arafat [*q.v.*], Salah Khalaf [*q.v.*], and Khalil Wazir [*q.v.*] in Kuwait. They set up secret party cells in Kuwait and the Palestinian refugee camps in Jordan, Syria, and Lebanon: a process accelerated by the publication of a monthly magazine, *Falastin-una* (Arabic: *Our Palestine* [*q.v.*]), in Beirut [*q.v.*] in 1959. By then the basic theory of Fatah ideology and tactics was that revolutionary violence, practiced by the masses, was the only way to liberate Palestine and liquidate all forms of Zionism [*q.v.*].

Fatah remained underground until 1964, when the Arab League [*q.v.*] established the Palestine Liberation Organization [*q.v.*] under the leadership of Ahmad Shuqairi. Of the radical Arab states then, only Algeria volunteered in 1963 to provide military training facilities to Fatah. In 1964, in Baathist-run Damascus [*q.v.*], Fatah leaders decided on guerrilla actions against Israel from Syria. The first such act, on 1 January 1965, was aimed at blowing up the pipes of Israel's National Water Carrier at Ain Bone on the west bank of Jordan River [*q.v.*]. Fatah then had about 200 members.

The loss of the West Bank [*q.v.*] and Gaza Strip [*q.v.*] to Israel in the June 1967 Arab-Israeli War [*q.v.*] weakened Shuqairi's position in the PLO, whose Palestine National Council (PNC) [*q.v.*] had been boycotted by Fatah and other armed groups. Egyptian President Gamal

Abdul Nasser [*q.v.*] met Fatah's chairman, Arafat, and promised to aid the organization. In March 1968 Fatah members engaged in a much-publicized battle with Israel near the Jordanian border town of Karameh. This raised Fatah's membership to 15,000.

By now Fatah's overall objective had emerged as the establishment of a democratic, secular state in all of British Mandate Palestine with equal rights to Jews [*q.v.*], Muslims [*q.v.*], and Christians [*q.v.*]. In July 1968 Fatah and other armed groups attended the PNC session in Cairo [*q.v.*], which rejected UN Security Council Resolution 242 [*q.v.*], mainly because it made no mention of Palestinians. Fatah emerged as the PLO's largest constituent.

In early 1969 the PNC elected Arafat chairman of the PLO's executive committee, which included three more Fatah leaders. In 1970 Fatah, based in Amman [*q.v.*], claimed membership of some 40,000, with half of them active in its militia, *al-Assifa* (Arabic: *The Storm*). The party leadership was evenly divided between right and left, with Arafat often acting as a mediator between Salah Khalaf and Farouq Qaddumi on the left, and Khalid Hassan and Khalil Wazir on the right. But Fatah's involvement, along with other mainly leftist forces, in the Palestinian conflict with the Jordanian army in September 1970 moved it leftward. This changed after Fatah's expulsion from Jordan, and its new base in Beirut in 1972.

Prodded by the Democratic Front for the Liberation of Palestine [*q.v.*], in June 1974 Fatah accepted the idea of a transition stage for achieving the liberation of the Mandate Palestine with an independent entity in the West Bank and Gaza Strip [*q.v.*]. In the Lebanese Civil War [*q.v.*], which started in 1975, Fatah, along with other Palestinian commando groups, sided with the leftist Lebanese National Movement [*q.v.*] to fight the right-wing Lebanese Forces [*q.v.*]. Its opposition to the Camp David Accords [*q.v.*] in 1978 led Fatah to adopt a radical stance, with its fourth congress in Damascus [*q.v.*] in May 1980 resolving to "liberate Palestine completely."

Following the Israeli invasion of Lebanon [*q.v.*] in June 1982, Fatah was expelled from Beirut. From its new headquarters in Tunis, Arafat tried to reestablish a base in Lebanon, but failed. In the mid-1980s Fatah's policy of coordinating with King Hussein of Jordan [*q.v.*] with regard to peace talks with Israel failed to take off. In 1988 the Fatah leadership decided to disavow violence against Israel and backed moves for the declaration of the State of Palestine, with Arafat as its president. After failing to build on this moderated policy, the party leaders backed Iraqi President Saddam Hussein [*q.v.*] when, having occupied Kuwait in August 1990, he tried to link Israel's evacuation of the West Bank and Gaza Strip to his evacuation of Kuwait, but in vain.

They were divided on the Oslo Accord [*q.v.*] of September 1993, with Qaddumi opposing it. In the end, Fatah accepted the Accord. It became the political backbone of the Palestinian Authority (PA) [*q.v.*]. In the elections to the Palestinian Legislative Council in 1996, Fatah won 55 of the 86 contested seats, with seven other members describing themselves as Fatah Independents. Following the

eruption of the al-Aqsa intifada [*q.v.*] in September 2000, it set up an armed wing in the West Bank and Gaza Strip, called al-Tanzim (Arabic: *Organization*), which resorted to suicide bombings against Israelis. Led by Marwan Barghouti [*q.v.*], it later morphed into al-Aqsa Martyrs Brigade.

After Arafat's death in 2004, Fatah nominated Mahmoud Abbas [*q.v.*] as its candidate for PA's presidency of the PA in the January 2005 election. He won. But overall, due to the incompetence and corruption of its government, Fatah started losing popular support. It was also weakened by the internal divisions over policy issues, use of funds, and control of intelligence agencies in Gaza and West Bank between the aging exiled leaders and their younger challengers who had lived under the Israeli occupation since 1967. The latter were headed by Marwan Barghouti [*q.v.*]. Due to these reasons, Fatah secured only 45 seats in the Palestine Legislative Council (PLC) election of 2006.

In the subsequent fighting that erupted between it and Hamas [*q.v.*] in the Gaza Strip, Fatah lost control of that territory.

The Sixth General Assembly of Fatah was held in Bethlehem [*q.v.*] in August 2009—20 years after the previous General Assembly. Many Fatah leaders, including Kaddoumi, were denied entry into Bethlehem by Israel. Its 2,000 delegates cast their ballots for 18 of the 23 contested seats on the Central Committee and 81 of the 128 seats on the Revolutionary Council. They specified a dozen preconditions for the resumption of Israeli-Palestinian peace talks. These included the release of all Palestinian prisoners by Israel, freezing of all Israeli settlements in the Occupied Territories [*q.v.*], and the ending of Israel's siege of Gaza. Abbas ignored these pre-conditions when he entered into direct talks with Israeli Prime Minister Benjamin Netanyahu [*q.v.*] in September 2010.

After alleging massive fraud in the election for the Central Committee, Fatah's Higher Committee in the Gaza Strip resigned. In November 2010 the Revolutionary Council rejected Netanyahu's demand that the PLO must accept Israel as the nation-state of the Jewish people.

In April 2011, mediation by Nabil al-Araby, the foreign minister of the first post-Hosni Mubarak [*q.v.*] government in Egypt, led to reconciliation between Fatah and Hamas [*q.v.*] on the basis of sharing power until fresh elections. In February 2012 Abbas signed an agreement with Hamas leader Khaled Mashaal [*q.v.*], spelling out the implementation of the earlier accord.

Fatah: The Revolutionary Council: *See* Abu Nidal.

Fayyad, Salam (1952–): *Palestinian economist and politician; Prime Minister of Palestinian Authority, 2007–* Born in the village of Dir al-Rasoun, West Bank [*q.v.*], in the household of the director of the agriculture department of the Jordanian government, Fayyad graduated in science from the American University in Beirut [*q.v.*] in 1975 and then entered business. He obtained his Ph.D. in economics from the University of Texas in 1986. He then served as an economist with the

World Bank in Washington. In 1995 he returned to the Palestinian Territories [*q.v.*] as a representative of the International Monetary Fund.

In 2001, soon after becoming the West Bank's manager of the Arab Bank, the largest bank in the Middle East, he was appointed finance minister by the Palestinian Authority's [*q.v.*] president, Yasser Arafat [*q.v.*]. He served until 2005 when he co-founded a political party, the Third Way. In the 2006 parliamentary election it won two seats, one of them occupied by Fayyad. When the national unity government split in June 2007, President Mahmoud Abbas [*q.v.*] appointed him prime minister as a measure of national emergency. He was not confirmed by the Palestine Legislative Council as required by the constitution. He resigned in March 2009 but was reappointed prime minister two months later. In August he inaugurated a two-year plan to build the infrastructures and institutions of a future Palestinian State.

Following reconciliation between Fatah [*q.v.*] and Hamas [*q.v.*] in April 2011, Abbas's insistence that Fayyad should remain the prime minister until fresh elections to the Palestinian institutions were held became the main hurdle in sealing the deal. A compromise was reached with the agreement that Abbas should hold both posts. But the implementation plan signed by Abbas and Hamas leader Khaled Mashaal [*q.v.*] in February 2012 met resistance from the Hamas leadership in Gaza [*q.v.*].

Fedai Khalq (Persian: *Popular Self-sacrificers*): *Iranian political party* Official name, Sazman-e Cherakha-ye Fedai

Khalq-e Iran (Persian: *Organization of Iranian People's Self-Sacrificing Guerrillas*) Fedai Khaliq was formed in 1970 by the amalgamation of two leftist groups, established in 1963 by university students inspired by the victorious revolutionary movements led by Fidel Castro in Cuba and Vo Nguyen Giap in Vietnam. Believing in the "Propaganda by the Deed" doctrine of Ernesto "Che" Guevara, a Latin American revolutionary, the party hoped that repression by the pro-Western monarchical regime in the wake of guerrilla attacks on selected targets would lead to increased resistance by the masses, which would culminate in a people's revolution.

Its first attack on a gendarmerie post in the littoral fringes of the Caspian forest in early 1971 received much publicity. This won the party hundreds of young recruits, mostly from middle-class families. The party cadres, often trained by the Popular Front for the Liberation of Palestine [*q.v.*] in the Palestinian camps of Lebanon, attacked police stations and banks as well as police and Savak (secret police) informers. During the next five years some 10,000 Fedai Khaliq members, actual or suspected, were jailed, and about 180 activists were killed. But the anticipated people's revolution failed to materialize. The party split into two factions, with the moderates focusing on political activity among industrial workers. When Savak became overstretched in the autumn of 1977, the Fedai Khalq revived its guerrilla activity, and its supporters participated in the antiregime demonstrations.

After the revolution in early 1979, the party's demand for a share of

power was rejected by Ayatollah Ruhollah Khomeini [*q.v.*]. It went into opposition. As government pressure mounted, hundreds of party activists left for the Kurdish region to join the Kurdish guerrilla movement there.

The party split in June 1980 into "majority" and "minority" factions. Fedai Khalq (majority) advocated cooperation with the Islamic regime and allied with the Tudeh Party [*q.v.*], which followed a similar policy. It was allowed to function openly while the government battled with the Mujahedin-e Khalq [*q.v.*]. But in May 1983, after the Mujahedin-e Khalq had been crushed, the authorities turned against Fedai Khalq (majority). The party, which continued to exist secretly, suffered a setback when one of its safe houses in Tehran [*q.v.*] was discovered by police in 1989. Following the collapse of the Soviet bloc in 1989–91, party members, many of them living abroad, began to drift toward the adoption of secular social democracy as their objective.

Fedai Khalq (minority) opposed the Islamic regime and sided with Abol Hassan Bani-Sadr [*q.v.*] in his confrontation with Khomeini in June 1981, and was repressed severely. It was formally dissolved in 1987.

Fedaiyan-e Islam (Persian: *Self-sacrificers of Islam*): *Iranian religious-political group* Formed in 1945 by a young theological student, Nawab Safavi (alias Mujtaba Mirlohi), Fedaiyan-e Islam went beyond the customary Islamic call for the application of the Sharia [*q.v.*], as provided by the Iranian constitution of 1906–07, and demanded a ban on tobacco, alcohol, cinema, opium, gambling, and the wearing of foreign attire. It advocated the veil for women. It also demanded comprehensive land reform, the nationalization of industry, and various social welfare measures. It drew its following chiefly from the lower sections of the trading community—porters, shop assistants, hawkers, and peddlers.

The group used assassination as a political weapon. In 1948 it assassinated Ahmad Kasravi, a leading secularist lawyer and historian, and Abdul Hussein Hazhir, a court minister who was considered pro-British and pro-Bahai [*q.v.*]. This was followed in March 1951 by the assassination of General Ali Razmara, a pro-British prime minister. When two months later Muhammad Mussadiq [*q.v.*] refused to share power with the party, it turned against him. Its activists tried to assassinate one of his aides, Hussein Fatimi. Even after the August 1953 coup against Mussadiq the party did not moderate its anti-government stance. It condemned the oil agreement that Muhammad Reza Shah Pahlavi [*q.v.*] signed with the Western consortium in August 1954.

In November 1955 a Fedaiyan member tried unsuccessfully to kill Premier Hussein Ala. The authorities mounted an all-out assault on the party. Four top leaders, including Safavi, were executed. Following the release of party members during the shah's last days in 1978, Fedaiyan-e Islam was revived by Sadiq Khalkhali, a prominent cleric in Qom [*q.v.*], as a shadowy organization. The assassination of Mustafa Shafiq, a nephew of the shah, in Paris in December 1979 was widely attributed to Fedaiyan-e Islam.

feddan: *area measurement used in the Arab Middle East* 1 feddan = 4 donums [*q.v.*] = 1.038 acres.

Fertile Crescent: *Crescent-shaped area between the Anatolian Mountains and the Arabian Desert* The Fertile Crescent covers ancient Elam (southwestern Iran), Mesopotamia [*q.v.*] (Iraq), Assyria (Syria), Phoenicia (Lebanon), and Palestine [*q.v.*] (Israel and the Palestinian Territories [*q.v.*]). Sometimes the Nile valley of Egypt is included to emphasize the crescent shape. The cradle of ancient civilization, with irrigated agriculture going back to ca 8000 B.C., it is the region that provided the base for the Greek and Roman civilizations.

fiqh: *Islamic jurisprudence Fiqh* includes all aspects of religious, social, and political life—covering not only ritual and religious observances, the law of inheritance, property and contracts, and criminal law, but also constitutional law, laws concerning state administration, and the conduct of war. Islamic jurisprudence became established within a century of the emergence of Islam [*q.v.*] in 622 A.D.

First Gulf War: *See* Gulf War I (1980–88).

Fiver Shias: *See* Zaidis.

Fotouh, Abdel Moneim Aboul (1951–): *moderate Egyptian Islamist leader* Born into a middle-class family in Cairo [*q.v.*], Fotouh pursued higher education at Cairo University, where he obtained degrees in medicine and law. He joined the Muslim Brotherhood [*q.v.*] after President Anwar Sadat [*q.v.*] had reversed his predecessor's policy in 1971 and released Brotherhood prisoners. He was elected president of the student union of Cairo University in 1975. He protested the arrests of student demonstrators on the campus by Sadat's government. After acquiring a postgraduate degree in hospital management, he practiced as a physician. He was an active member of the Doctors Association which was affiliated to the Brotherhood.

To curb the rising disaffection against his government, Sadat ordered the arrest of hundreds of Brotherhood members, including Fotouh, in September 1981. The next month Sadat was assassinated by Islamist extremists. As his successor, Hosni Mubarak [*q.v.*], considered Brotherhood a moderate organization he released its members. Fotouh's status in the Brotherhood rose steadily, and he was elected to its Guidance Council in 1987. With the rise of Islamist violence in the mid-1990s, Mubarak reversed his policy. In his drive to divest the Brotherhood of its control of important professional syndicates, his government imprisoned Fotouh from 1996 to 2001.

Within the Brotherhood's Guidance Council he belonged to the moderate wing. In the conservative-driven purge of the moderates in 2010, he lost his place on the Guidance Council. After the ouster of Mubarak in February 2011, he defied the Guidance Council's decision not to enter the presidential race. He was expelled from the organization. In his election he wooed moderate Muslims and Egyptians by advocating civilian control of the military, protection of civil liberties, and enhanced public spending on health care and education. Yet he won the backing of the hard-line al-Nour Party [*q.v.*] in April 2012 after its candidate Hazem Salah Abu Ismail was disqualified by the Election Commission. Gaining 17.2 percent of the vote, he ended up in fourth place.

14 March Alliance (Lebanon): A coalition of several anti-Syria groups and individual politicians, it was named after the 14 March 2005 massive demonstration and rally in Beirut [*q.v.*] as the culmination of a series of demonstrations sparked by the assassination of the former Lebanese Prime Minister Rafiq Hariri [*q.v.*] on 14 February. The speakers demanded the withdrawal of the 14,000 Syrian troops and intelligence agents from Lebanon and an international investigation into Hariri's assassination. The leading constituents of the Alliance were the Future Movement [*q.v.*], the Progressive Socialist Party [*q.v.*], the Lebanese Forces [*q.v.*], and the Phalange Party [*q.v.*].

Syria withdrew all its forces on 27 April; a general election, monitored by the United Nations, took place in May and June. In that election, the 14 March Alliance secured 72 seats, and in the 2009 parliamentary election it won 71 seats on a popular vote of 44.5 percent, including 11 by the Progressive Socialist Party, which left the Alliance and functioned as an independent entity in parliament. Its members formed a majority in the national unity government that Prime Minister Saad Haririr [*q.v.*] assembled in November 2009. It collapsed in January 2012. As the pro-democracy movement gathered pace in Syria, its leaders publicly praised the anti-regime demonstrators.

Franco-Lebanese Treaty (1936): This treaty—signed between France (then ruled by the leftist Popular Front government) and Lebanon in November 1936—gave Lebanon considerable autonomy. It was designed to pave the way for the end of the French Mandate.

Franco-Syrian Treaty (1936): Following negotiations between the leftist Popular Front government in France and the nationalists in Syria, the Franco-Syrian Treaty was initialed in September 1936. Paris agreed to end its mandate in three years and sponsor Syria's membership of the League of Nations in exchange for long-term military, political, and economic privileges of France. But the French parliament refused to ratify it in 1939.

Franjieh, Suleiman (1910–93): *Lebanese politician; president, 1970–76* Born into the Maronite [*q.v.*] Franjieh clan [*q.v.*] at the Ihden palace, 12 mi./20 km miles from Zghorta, Franjieh grew up in the shadow of his elder brother, Hamid. While Hamid provided overall leadership to the clan, he supervised its organization and armed guards. After Hamid's retirement from public life in 1957, he became head of the clan and entered politics.

In the 1958 Civil War [*q.v.*] he sided with the pro-Nasser [*q.v.*] camp against the Maronite president, Camille Chamoun [*q.v.*]. Two years later he was elected to parliament. He served as a minister in 1960–61 and again in 1968–70. In his bid for presidency in August 1970, Franjieh re-ceived the support of Chamoun and Pierre Gemayel [*q.v.*]. He defeated Elias Sarkis [*q.v.*], though by only one vote. His adoption of an anti-Palestinian stand, advocated by right-wing Maronites, made him unpopular with the pro-Palestinian, Arab nationalist Muslims [*q.v.*].

When the Lebanese Civil War [*q.v.*] erupted in April 1975, he turned to Syria, aware that only it had the power to end the conflict and introduce political reform. In early 1976, at the behest of Syrian President Hafiz Assad [*q.v.*], he issued a Constitutional Reform Document, which specified changing the current agreement of six Christian seats to five Muslim seats in parliament to parity between the two communities. But the reform failed to materialize.

As the civil conflict intensified, he grew closer to the right-wing Maronites. In September 1976, at the end of his presidential tenure, he joined the Lebanese Front [*q.v.*], led politically by Chamoun and militarily by Bashir Gemayel [*q.v.*]. But when, in Gemayel's bid to eliminate any serious rival to his presidential ambitions, his henchmen assassinated Franjieh's son and heir, Tony, and his family in June 1978, he turned vehemently against the Gemayel clan and allied with the leftist, pro-Syrian camp, led by Walid Jumblat [*q.v.*] and Rashid Karami [*q.v.*].

Along with other anti-Lebanese Front leaders, he denounced the draft peace treaty between Lebanon and Israel [*q.v.*], initialed in May 1983. While remaining close to Assad, he rejected the "National Agreement to Solve the Lebanese Crisis," signed in December 1985 by the three pro-Syrian militia leaders, Walid Jumblat,

Nabih Berri [*q.v.*], and Elie Hobeika. However, still hostile toward the Gemayels, he backed these commanders when their militias attacked the forces loyal to President Amin Gemayel [*q.v.*].

When the end of Gemayel's presidency in September 1988 resulted in the emergence of two governments, he opposed the anti-Syrian administration led by General Michel Aoun [*q.v.*]. A year later he backed the Taif Accord [*q.v.*], which followed the general line of his own Constitutional Reform Document of 1976. He supported the military moves by the pro-Syrian Lebanese forces and Syria against Aoun in October 1990, which ended the civil war. The following spring, in line with other irregulars, his militia surrendered its weapons to the Syrian army. Unlike right-wing Maronites, his party participated in the 1992 parliamentary elections and won half of the 34 seats reserved for the Maronites in a house of 128.

Freedom and Justice Party (Egypt): Soon after the ouster of Egyptian President Hosni Mubarak [*q.v.*] on 11 February 2011, the Guidance Council of the Muslim Brotherhood [*q.v.*] announced its intention to form the Freedom and Justice Party (FJP), open to all Egyptians irrespective of their religion. The list of its founder members included 93 Copts [*q.v.*]. When the party was established on 30 April, Rqfiq Habbi, a Coptic writer-academic, was nominated as one of its two vice presidents. Its chairman was Muhammad Morsi [*q.v.*] and its secretary-general Saad el Katatny. They were both former members of the Brotherhood's Guidance Council; and

so was Essam el Erian, the other vice president.

While commentators often described the FJP as the political wing of the Muslim Brotherhood, the website of the Brotherhood maintained that the FJP was distinct from the Brotherhood. Nonetheless, the two entities assisted each other actively during the parliamentary elections from November 2011 to January 2012. The FPJ's manifesto stated that the party was based on the Sharia [*q.v.*], and argued that the concepts of freedom, social justice, and equality were embedded in the Sharia. It favored market economy while ensuring that it did not lead to monopoly. It accepted the fact that tourism was an important contributor to the GDP. It promised to respect international treaties as long as they achieved their objective of benefiting both sides while noting that the parliament had the right to revise any treaty that failed to do so.

In the election for the 508-member People's Assembly in November 2011 to January 2012, the FJP-led Democratic Alliance won 235 seats on a popular vote of 37.5 percent popular, with the FJP, led by el Katatny, gaining 213 seats. In the elections for the Consultative Council conducted in January-February 2012, of the 180 elected seats the FJP-led Democratic Alliance garnered 105.

Freedom Movement of Iran: *See* Liberation Movement of Iran.

Front for Steadfastness and Resistance: *See* Steadfastness Front.

G

Gahal (Hebrew: acronym of *Gush Herut Liberalim*, Herut-Liberals bloc): *Israeli political party* Gahal was formed in 1965 by the merger of Herut [*q.v.*] and Liberalim (Liberals) [*q.v.*], under the leadership of Menachem Begin [*q.v.*]. The prospect of winning power in the November 1965 general election, following the defection of David Ben-Gurion [*q.v.*] from Mapai [*q.v.*], encouraged Herut and Liberal leaders to paper over their differences on equal rights for women and relations between state and religion. By winning 26 seats, Gahal became the second-largest bloc in the new Knesset [*q.v.*]. An invitation to join the national unity government on the eve of the June 1967 Arab-Israeli War [*q.v.*] made it and Begin politically respectable. In the October 1969 election it retained its 26 seats and joined the national unity cabinet that followed. Rejecting the Rogers cease-fire plan [*q.v.*], prepared by Washington and accepted by all other parties in the cabinet, Gahal left the government in July 1970. On the eve of the December 1973 election, Gahal allied with three small right-wing groups to form Likud [*q.v.*].

Gailani, Rashid Ali (1892–1965): *Iraqi politician; prime minister, 1933, 1940–41* Born into an eminent Sunni [*q.v.*] family in Baghdad [*q.v.*], Gailani obtained a degree from the Baghdad Law School and set up legal practice. After a brief stint as a judge, he entered politics. He served as minister of justice in 1924, then as minister of the interior from 1925 to 1928. A nationalist, he opposed the Anglo-Iraqi Treaty of 1930 [*q.v.*]. He became prime minister briefly in 1933. Two years later he was appointed interior minister, and in late 1938 he became chief of the cabinet secretariat.

During World War II, when politicians and military officers split into pro- and anti-British factions, he headed the anti-British, nationalist camp. He became prime minister in March 1940. Three months later, when Italy declared war against Britain and its allies, he refused to cut links with Italy. He also refused to abide by Article 4 of the Anglo-Iraqi Treaty, which gave landing and transit rights to Britain in the event of war. He withstood British pressure until January 1941, when he stepped down. But his pro-British successor, Taha Hashemi, faced counterpressure from military officers and public opinion. Hashemi's resignation from office in early April 1941 led to Gailani's reassuming the premiership—and to the flight of the pro-British regent Abdul Ilah, Nuri al-Said [*q.v.*], and the child-king Faisal II [*q.v.*]. Britain landed troops in Basra [*q.v.*]. In his combat with the British military in May, he lost, and fled to Germany.

After the war he spent many years in Saudi Arabia, Egypt, and Syria. He returned to Baghdad after the July 1958 coup against King Faisal II. A pan-Arab nationalist, he did not find favor with Abdul Karim Qasim [*q.v.*], who was averse to a merger with another Arab country. After Gailani's failed coup attempt in conjunction with the United Arab Republic [*q.v.*] in December 1958, he was sentenced to death. But Qasim commuted his sentence and freed him in October 1961. He then stayed away from politics.

al-Gamaat al-Islamiya (Egypt) (Arabic: *The Islamic Groups*): *Egyptian Islamist movement* After carrying out a coup against the leftist Ali Sabri [*q.v.*] and his followers in the ruling Arab Socialist Union [*q.v.*] in May 1971, President Anwar Sadat [*q.v.*] instructed General Abdul Moneim Amin, sympathetic to the Muslim Brotherhood [*q.v.*], to establish, train, and arm 1,000 Islamic Groups—al-Gamaat al-Islamiya—in universities and factories to fight "atheist Marxism." The program was so successful that the al-Gamaat acquired an independent existence. al-Gamaat activities accentuated the historical animosity between Muslims [*q.v.*] and Copts [*q.v.*], and led to attacks on Copts and their churches. When the government tried to discourage this, al-Gamaat members demonstrated, calling on Sadat to intensify the struggle against Israel.

The October 1973 Arab-Israeli War [*q.v.*], hailed as a victory for Egypt by the authorities, produced a lull in al-Gamaat's activities. But the postwar economic crisis and Egypt's step-by-step rapprochement with Israel helped Islamic fundamentalists [*q.v.*] to widen their base. In the spring 1978 election of university student union officials, al-Gamaat won 60 percent of the posts. The impending signing of an Egyptian-Israel peace treaty [*q.v.*] in March 1979 so angered al-Gamaat students that they mounted protest demonstrations at Alexandria and Asyut universities—a daring step, since it made them liable

to life imprisonment. Their slogans were: "No peace with Israel," "No privilege for the rich," and "No separation between Islam and state." They cheered the victory of the Islamic revolution [*q.v.*] in Iran and condemned the hospitality that Sadat accorded to the deposed Muhammad Reza Shah Pahlavi [*q.v.*] in Egypt. Sadat set up new disciplinary councils for university students and arrested hundreds of Islamists in September 1981. His assassination the next month was applauded by al-Gamaat.

There was lull in its activities during the early phase of the presidency of Hosni Mubarak [*q.v.*]. But as he upheld the substance of Sadat's policy of maintaining a secular state, the gap between al-Gamaat and the regime widened. The group's first manifesto, *The Program for Islamic Action*, issued in 1984, had a much wider focus than the one specified in that of *Al-Jihad al-Islami* [*q.v.*] with its almost exclusive stress on violent action. al-Gamaat activists, operating at the grass-roots level, continued their social welfare work—religious education and health clinics—through local mosques under the general guidance of Shaikh Muhammad Abu Nasr, an 80-year-old cleric. In the early 1990s, as the authorities began to repress Islamists, al-Gamaat, bolstered by the return of its militants from Afghanistan where they had operated as guerrillas, escalated its anti-regime campaign.

It adopted the strategy of waging an armed struggle against the secular regime, aiming to raise the religious consciousness of the masses as a prelude to a popular insurrection.

To hurt the economy, starting in

October 1992, its activists began attacking foreign tourists. Over the next two years they killed some 450 policemen and tourists. By then there were an estimated 29,000 Islamist political detainees, two-thirds of them al-Gamaat members. In June 1995 their attempt to assassinate President Hosni Mubarak [*q.v.*] during his visit to Addis Ababa, Ethiopia, failed. Five months later, their truck bombing of the Egyptian embassy in Islamabad, Pakistan, led to 16 deaths. In April 1996, their operatives killed 17 Greek tourists in Cairo [*q.v.*], mistaking them for Israelis. This led to an intensified government crackdown. Yet al-Gamaat extremists managed to massacre 72 foreign tourists and Egyptians at an ancient site in Luxor.

Among those who guided al-Gamaat from abroad were Muhammad Shawki Islamboulii, brother of Khalid, one of the assassins of President Sadat, and Talat Fuad Qasim, both based in Afghanistan.

In early 1999, al-Gamaat leaders declared a unilateral cease-fire, which was endorsed by Shaikh Abdul Rahman Omar [*q.v.*], serving a life sentence in an American jail. The government released over 5,000 al-Gamaat members out of an estimated total of 20,000. By tightening its control of mosques and preachers, it reduced the potential for recruits for al-Gamaat. It also frustrated the organization's attempt to transform itself into a recognized political party.

Following the renunciation of violence by its jailed leaders in 2003, the government released more than 1,000 al-Gamaat members. In 2006, a further 1,200 members were freed. The authorities allowed al-Gamaat to function as a semi-clandestine organization engaged in charitable activities centered on mosques in poor areas.

The statement by Ayman al-Zawahiri [*q.v.*], deputy leader of al-Qaida [*q.v.*], in August 2006 that a faction of al-Gamaat had allied with al-Qaida applied to a tiny fraction of the organization.

After the ouster of Mubarak in February 2011, the organization's leaders in Egypt decided to form a political wing called the Construction and Development Party (Arabic*: Hizb al-Benaa wa al-Tanmia*), led by Nasr Abdul Salam. It stood for representative democracy with institutions guided by the principles of the Sharia [*q.v.*], and a free market economy. Once it was accepted as a legal entity by the Supreme Administrative Court in October, it joined the Islamist Bloc [*q.v.*] headed by al-Nour [*q.v.*] party to run in the general election to the People's Assembly. It won 13 seats.

al-Gamaat al-Muslimin (Egypt): *See* al-Takfir wal Hijra (Egypt).

gas: *See* natural gas.

Gas Exporting Countries Forum: Qatar helped establish the Gas Exporting Countries Forum (GECF) whose founding meeting took place in Tehran [*q.v.*] in 2001. By the end of the decade its membership had stabilized at 11: Algeria, Bolivia, Egypt, Equatorial Guinea, Iran, Libya, Nigeria, Qatar, Russia, Trinidad and Tobago, and Venezuela. Kazakhstan and Norway were observers. At different times the following countries attended its annual ministerial meetings: Angola, Azerbaijan, Brunei,

Indonesia, Iraq, Malaysia, the Netherlands, Oman, Saudi Arabia, Turkmenistan, the United Arab Emirates, and Yemen.

Altogether, GECF members possess 70 percent of the world's gas reserves—with Russia, Iran, and Qatar jointly owning 56 percent—and produce more than 40 percent of the global output.

Initially the GECF's main function was to exchange information among its members. It was only in 2008 that it adopted a charter at its meeting in Moscow. It aimed to establish ongoing dialogue among its members, between producers and consumers, and between governments and energy-related industries, while promoting a stable energy market. It decided to establish its secretariat in the Qatari capital of Doha [q.v.].

The next year it elected Qatar's energy minister and deputy Prime Minister Abdullah bin Hamad al-Attiyah its chairman and Leonid Bokhanovsky its secretary general.

Since gas facilities are far more expensive that those for oil, gas supply contracts involve many billions of dollars, and tie up governments and large corporations for decades. The cheapest way to transport gas is by an overland pipeline. But when the distance between the source and the destination is very long, it is best transported as liquefied natural gas (LNG), which occupies a small fraction of its volume in the vaporous form. But handling super-cool LNG is expensive, due to the heavy initial outlay. LNG, pumped into super-heavy, sealed containers on specially designed ships, is discharged into specially constructed storage tanks at the destination terminal, to be pumped through special pipes to re-gasification units to be warmed gradually to its natural vaporous form. So the LNG trade requires special containers, ships, terminals, and pipelines.

GECF members account for nearly 40 percent of the natural gas pipeline trade and 85 percent of LNG output, which is less than 10 percent of the overall global gas demand.

The GECF ministerial meeting in December 2010 in Doha stated that there had to be a balance between spot prices of gas and long-term contract prices linked to oil prices, and that the only adequate price-setting formula for gas was one that took into account prices for diesel and fuel oil.

Gaza City: *capital of the Gaza Strip*
Population: 538,000 (2011 est.) The recorded history of Gaza stretches back to the 15th century B.C. A thriving trading post, it is the reputed site of the temple to Dagon, which was razed by Samson. To punish its residents for their spirited resistance, Alexander of Macedonia (r. 336–23 B.C.) condemned them to slavery. Gaza fell to Muslim [q.v.] Arabs [q.v.] in 635 A.D., and because it is the burial site of Prophet Muhammad's great grandfather, Hashem bin Abdul Manaf, it has acquired religious significance. It changed hands during the Crusades, and in 1517 passed into the control of the Ottoman Turks, who held it until 1917. It was part of the Palestine that came under British Mandate five years later. After the Palestine War (1948–49) [q.v.] it became the capital of the Gaza Strip [q.v.].

In 1994 the Palestinian Authority [q.v.] made Gaza its base. This continued until 2001 when Yasser Arafat [*q.v.*], president of the Palestinian Authority [*q.v.*], moved his headquarters to the West Bank [*q.v.*] town of Ramallah [*q.v.*], north of Jerusalem [*q.v.*].

During the first decade of the 21st century the city became a bastion of Hamas [*q.v.*], an Islamist organization. When Hamas expelled its rival Fatah [*q.v.*] from the Gaza Strip [*q.v.*] in June 2007, the city along with the rest of the territory was put under siege by Israel as well as Egypt.

In the course of the Gaza War [*q.v.*] in December 2008–January 2009, the city became the principal target of Israel's artillery shelling and air strikes, which caused widespread destruction of property and infrastructure as well as loss of life and limb.

A majority of its present population consists of refugees. At nearly 10,000 persons per square kilometer/26,500 per square mile, it is one of densest settlements on the planet. As a result of the economic blockade by Israel and Egypt, almost 70 percent of the city's residents lived below poverty line. The situation improved somewhat when Egypt lifted the blockade after the ouster of President Hosni Mubarak [*q.v.*] in 2011.

Gaza Strip: *Palestinian territory* Also known as Gaza. Area 146 sq. mi./378 sq. km; population 1.59 million (2011 est.), with most inhabitants being refugees from the 1948–49 Palestine War [*q.v.*] or their descendants.

In the Palestine War, the Arab armies managed to retain only a semi-desert strip along the Mediterranean coast, later called the Gaza Strip, and an enclave on the west bank of the Jordan River [*q.v.*], later named the West Bank [*q.v.*]. From January 1949 onward the Gaza Strip was administered by Egypt. It passed into the hands of the invading Israelis during the Suez War (October–November 1956) [*q.v.*]. Israel vacated it in March 1957.

In the June 1967 Arab-Israel War [*q.v.*] the Gaza Strip was once again captured by Israel. An official census put its population at 380,800. On 1 December 1981 it was put under civilian administrators, albeit working under a military command. On the eve of the signing of the Oslo Accord [*q.v.*] in September 1993, one-third of the Strip was taken up by 16 Jewish settlements (4,500 settlers) and the out-of-bounds military zones. As a result of the Israel-Palestine Liberation Organization agreement of May 1994 this area was further expanded due to the creation of buffer zones. Hence only about 60 percent of the Strip came under the administration of the Palestinian Authority [*q.v.*]. This continued until September 2005, when the Jewish settlers and Israeli troops and settlers withdrew from the Strip, while maintaining control over its airspace and shoreline.

Following its electoral victory in the January 2006 parliamentary election, Hamas [*q.v.*] formed the Palestinian government. It was not recognized by Israel or by the United States or the European Union, which considered Hamas a terrorist organization. Tensions between the ruling Hamas and opposition Fatah [*q.v.*] escalated. But Saudi Arabia's mediation led to the formation of a national unity government in March 2007. It proved short-lived. In the renewed violence that erupted, Hamas expelled Fatah from Gaza in June. President Mahmoud Abbas [*q.v.*] declared a state of emergency, appointed a new cabinet excluding Hamas, and ordered the arrest of many Hamas leaders in the West Bank.

The boycott of the Hamas government by Israel and the West continued. And so too did the firing of locally produced short-range Qassam rockets by Hamas and other Islamist organizations at Israel. Between September 2005 and January 2008, nearly 700 rockets and more than 820 mortar bombs were fired at Israeli towns. Following the takeover of Gaza by Hamas, Egypt closed its border with the Strip. During a brief breach in the border barrier between Gaza and Egypt in January 2008, hundreds of thousands of Gaza residents crossed into Egypt in search of food and fuel. This continued only for a fortnight.

On the political front, Abbas insisted on Hamas returning the control of Gaza to the Palestinian Authority based in Ramallah [*q.v.*] as a precondition for resuming talks on forming a coalition government.

The need for survival led many Gaza residents to start smuggling goods from Egypt through hundreds of tunnels. In 2010 there were 800 to 1,000 tunnels with an average depth of 1,800ft./550 m. The Hamas government imposed law and order in the Strip by disarming militias and criminal gangs, and establishing control over supply tunnels. It suppressed even peaceful activities by Fatah supporters.

In March 2008, Israel's air strikes and ground incursions caused more than 100 deaths and wide scale damage to the Jabalia refugee camp.

During the Gaza War [*q.v.*] in December 2008–January 2009 the Strip suffered heavy damage to its infrastructure, factories, and housing. Nearly 21,000 houses, 280 schools, and 16 hospitals were partly or completely destroyed. Of the 1,420 Palestinians killed, 446 were children. More than half of Gazans left home for a safer place.

Due to the economic stranglehold on the Strip, backed by the U.S. and the European Union, 70 percent of Gazans lived on less than $1 a day. The situation improved somewhat when Egypt opened its Rafah border crossing to pedestrians after the overthrow of President Hosni Mubarak [*q.v.*] in February 2011. The unemployment rate declined to 31 percent.

Gaza War (2008–09): *War between Israel and Hamas-controlled Gaza.*

BACKGROUND: Following the electoral victory of Hamas [*q.v.*] in the Palestinian Territories [*q.v.*] in January, there was escalation in the long-running strife between Hamas and other Islamist organizations, who fired homemade rockets and mortars at Israel, and the Israel Defense Forces (IDF), who responded with artillery fire, air strikes, and ground incursions. A massive IDF reprisal in March led to the deaths of over 100 Palestinians and two Israeli soldiers. In the early hours of 25 June 2006, Palestinian militants infiltrated into Israel through an underground tunnel and attacked an Israeli army post, killing two soldiers and capturing one, Corporal Gilad Shalit. His captors demanded the freeing of more than 1,000 Palestinian prisoners in exchange for his release. This was refused.

Relations between Israel and Hamas deteriorated after the armed seizure of the Gaza Strip by Hamas [*q.v.*] in June 2007. Israel controlled the inflow and outflow of goods and services, including water and power, into and from Gaza. Some of the supply tunnels were used for smuggling small arms. On 11 November 2007, Israeli Prime Minister Ehud Olmert [*q.v.*] warned of an impending confrontation between Israel and Hamas. During 2005–07, Hamas and others fired 2,700 homemade rockets and mortars into Israel, and killed four Israelis. In return Israel fired over 14,600 artillery shells into Gaza, killing 59 Palestinians. A cease-fire went into effect on 18 June 2008.

Between 18 June and 4 November rockets fired at Israel decreased by 98 percent compared to the four-and-a-half-month period before the cease-fire. On 18 December Hamas declared an end to the six-month-long cease-fire. On 23 December 2008 the IDF killed three Palestinians, claiming that they were planting explosives along the Gaza-Israeli border. The next day the military wing of Hamas resumed rocket and mortar shell firings. On 25 December Olmert warned of a broad offensive.

OPPOSING FORCES: Israeli Defense Forces; the military wing of Hamas called Izz al-Din Qassam Brigade

EVENTS: On 27 December 2008 the IDF mounted its Operation Cast Lead. Its air force bombed military and police facilities and public buildings, in the process also damaging or destroying civilian structures. Hamas and other Islamist organizations kept up their rocket and mortar attacks throughout the hostilities, targeting among others Beersheba in the Negev and the port of Ashdod with Grad rockets with 40-km/25-mile range.

On 3 January 2009, the IDF mounted a land invasion of the Gaza Strip. This continued for 15 days. The air and ground attacks by warplanes, tanks, and bulldozers combined with phosphorus shelling covered 22.3 sq. kilometers/8.57 sq. mi.. Unsure of the reaction of the incoming U.S. President Barack Obama—to be inaugurated on 21 January—to its ongoing onslaught on the Gaza Strip, the Israeli government announced a unilateral cease-fire on 18 January. Hamas declared a truce for a week. The IDF withdrew from Gaza on 21 January.

HUMAN LOSSES: Palestinians, 1,166 to 1,420; Israelis, 13.

PROPERTY LOSSES: According to the UN Development Program, 68 public buildings, 38 offices of non-governmental organizations, and 14,000 homes were destroyed or damaged. Other losses included 600 to 700 manufacturing plants, small factories, workshops, and businesses, as well as two dozen mosques. In addition, 50 UN facilities were hit. Nearly half of the 122 public health facilities were damaged or destroyed. The damage to 10 water or sewage lines left over 400,000 Palestinians without running water; 187 greenhouses covering 28 hectares were destroyed or badly damaged. Gaza's total loss of assets was put at $2 billion.

UNITED NATIONS INVESTIGATION: The report by a UN committee chaired by South African judge Richard Goldstone, published in September 2009, accused the IDF and the Islamist organizations of committing war crimes and possible crimes against humanity. The next month the UN Human Rights Council endorsed the Goldstone report by 25 votes to six, with 16 abstentions, and reprimanded Israel.

As a result, Israel's experts on international law advised cabinet ministers with security background and senior IDF officers not to visit Britain, Spain, Belgium, or Norway because they risked arrest in these countries on charges of alleged war crimes on the basis of universal jurisdiction, which entitles a state to claim jurisdiction against a person who committed alleged crimes outside its boundaries.

Gemara (Aramaic: *completion*): Gemara is a commentary on and a supplement to Mishna [*q.v.*], the text of the Jewish Oral Law. *See also* Talmud.

Gemayel, Amin (1942–): *Lebanese politician; president, 1982–88* Born in Beirut [*q.v.*] of a notable Maronite [*q.v.*] family, Gemayel obtained a degree in law from St. Joseph University. He started his professional life as a lawyer but soon branched out into business. He entered parliament in 1970 in a by-election, and retained his seat two years later in a general election. Unlike his younger brother, Bashir [*q.v.*], Gemaye was not active in the Phalange Party's [*q.v.*] militia and was not directly involved in the Lebanese Civil War [*q.v.*], which broke out in 1975. Once the Syrians had intervened in the conflict in 1976 on the side of the Maronites [*q.v.*], he established contact with them. He was catapulted into the presidency when Bashir was assassinated soon after being elected president in September 1982. Backed by Syria, he received the votes of all but one of the 78 parliamentarians in attendance.

He initially won much support abroad and at home. In May 1983, under Washington's pressure, he initialed a peace treaty with Israel, then occupying much of Lebanon. But in order to get Israel to vacate Lebanese soil he refused to sign the document, even after parliament had passed it by 64 votes to two. In retaliation Israel withdrew its protection of his regime.

When Israel carried out only partial withdrawal in September 1983, fighting between different communities erupted and engulfed Muslim West Beirut, further reducing the power of Gemayel's government. In February 1984 his attempt to cow the Shia [*q.v.*] residents of West Beirut by deploying the army against them backfired, resulting in the breakup of the Lebanese army along religious lines. Finding himself with no outside protection—Israeli or Western—he decided to bury the Lebanese-Israeli Treaty [*q.v.*] and seek aid from Syria.

Following the Second National Reconciliation Conference in Lausanne, Switzerland, in March 1984, he appointed a national reconciliation government under Rashid Karami [*q.v.*] to implement political and constitutional reform. But after the death of his influential father, Pierre [*q.v.*], in August, his position in the Phalange Party weakened. The internecine fighting within the party damaged the standing of Gemayel, who was also attacked by pro-Syrian militia leaders such as Nabih Berri [*q.v.*] and Walid Jumblat [*q.v.*]. In return he opposed the "National Agreement to Solve the Lebanese Crisis," brokered by Syria and signed by Berri,

Jumblat, and Eli Hobeika of the Lebanese Forces [*q.v.*].

Among other things this pact specified parliamentary parity between Muslims [*q.v.*] and Christians [*q.v.*] instead of the current 6:5 division in favor of Christians. This alienated Gemayel from Syrian President Hafiz Assad [*q.v.*]. The latter tried to undermine his authority by aiding the militias of Berri and Jumblat as well as Suleiman Franjieh [*q.v.*], a Maronite rival of Gemayel. By staying away from the parliamentary session to elect a new president, rightist Maronite deputies deprived it of a quorum, thus defeating Assad's plan to have his nominee elected as president. In September 1988, on his last day of office, Gemayel appointed his chief of staff, General Michel Aoun [*q.v.*], as his successor. A month later he went into exile in France, where he reverted to being a businessman. He returned to Lebanon in 2000.

On the eve of the Anglo-American invasion of Iraq [*q.v.*] in March 2003, he tried to forestall the war by carrying a message from the George W. Bush administration to Iraqi president Saddam Hussein [*q.v.*] to go into exile, but failed. In the August 2007 by-election in Lebanon, he failed to win a parliamentary seat.

Gemayel, Bashir (1947–82): *Lebanese politician; president-elect, 1982* Born into a notable Maronite [*q.v.*] family in Beirut [*q.v.*], Gemayel started his law and political science studies at St. Joseph University but did not finish them. Active in the Phalange Party [*q.v.*], he opposed the presence of Palestinian guerrillas in Lebanon. In the early 1970s he worked for a law

firm in Washington, D.C., where he was recruited by the United States Central Intelligence Agency (CIA).

At the start of the Lebanese Civil War [*q.v.*], beginning in April 1975, he became commander of the Lebanese Forces [*q.v.*], the military wing of the Lebanese Front [*q.v.*], a coalition of right-wing Maronite parties. He formalized his long-existing secret ties with Israel. Intent on becoming the next Lebanese president, he started to eliminate serious rivals, culminating in the assassination by his henchmen of Tony Franjieh, the eldest son of Suleiman Franjieh [*q.v.*], in June 1978. He then overpowered the militia of Camille Chamoun's [*q.v.*] party.

In December 1980, at his initiative, Lebanese Front leaders issued a manifesto that favored a federal or confederal system within a unified Lebanon. Gemayel tightened his links with Israel, which provided arms and training to his militia. During the Israeli invasion of Lebanon in June 1982 [*q.v.*], his forces linked up with the Israelis on the outskirts of Beirut. The expulsion of the PLO and the Syrians from Beirut by the Israelis strengthened the Phalange and improved Gemayel's chances of achieving the highest office. On 23 August 1982 he was elected president, with 57 of the 65 parliamentarians voting for him. In his secret meeting with the Israeli Prime Minister, Menachem Begin, [*q.v.*], on 1 September he agreed to exchange representatives with Israel. On 14 September 1982, eight days before he was to be installed in office, a bomb explosion at the Phalange headquarters in Beirut killed him and 26 others.

Gemayel, Pierre (1905–84): *Lebanese politician* Born into a notable Maronite [*q.v.*] clan in Bikfaya, Gemayel received his university education in Beirut [*q.v.*] and Paris, and trained as a pharmacist. Interested in sports clubs, he was deeply impressed by the Nazi Youth Movement in Germany and by the Berlin Olympics in the summer of 1936. Later that year he founded the Phalange Party [*q.v.*]. He played little or no role in the anti-French nationalist movement and the crisis of 1943. It was only after Camille Chamoun [*q.v.*] had become president nearly a decade later that Gemayel came to the fore. In the Lebanese Civil War of May–July 1958 [*q.v.*] he sided with Chamoun against the pan-Arabist [*q.v.*] forces.

Following the election of Fuad Chehab [*q.v.*] in September 1958, he was appointed to the four-member interim cabinet. After his election to parliament in 1960 he became an almost constant fixture in the governments formed during the presidency of Chehab and Charles Helou (1964–70) [*q.v.*], serving variously as minister of finance, public works, and health. In the 1968 general election he allied with Chamoun and Raymond Edde to form the Triple Alliance, which described the activities of the Palestinian commandos in Lebanon as a serious threat to national security. In the 1970 presidential election he backed Suleiman Franjieh [*q.v.*].

With the onset of civil war in 1975 [*q.v.*], the importance of the Phalange militia increased, and with it the weight carried by his youngest son, Bashir [*q.v.*], the militia commander. After the Maronite camp had overcome the immediate threat from its enemy, the Lebanese National Movement [*q.v.*], with Syrian assistance in 1976–77, it turned to its long-standing though clandestine ally, Israel. In May 1978 Gemayel visited Israel and signed an arms and training agreement.

Two years later, when Bashir Gemayal used his fighters to overpower the militia of Chamoun, the two patriarchs decided to resolve the crisis by merging their political parties. In December they endorsed the Lebanese Front [*q.v.*] manifesto, which favored a federal or confederal system within a unified Lebanon. At the March 1984 National Reconciliation Conference in Lausanne, Gemayel allied with Chamoun in proposing to create a federal system composed of several cantons, but failed to win the backing of the assembly. The next month he joined the National Reconciliation government headed by Rashid Karami [*q.v.*]. In July he stepped down as chairman of the Phalange Party, and the following month he died.

General People's Congress (Yemen): *Yemeni political party* After surviving a few coup attempts by military officers since assuming power in October 1977, President Ali Abdullah Saleh [*q.v.*], a lieutenant general, decided to consolidate his authority through political means. In October 1981 he set up a 1,000-member General People's Congress (GPC), partly by appointment and partly by indirect elections. Its program included the unification of North Yemen and South Yemen. The GPC backed Saleh's reelection as president in 1983 and 1988. It also endorsed his decision to take North

Yemen into the Arab Cooperation Council [*q.v.*] in early 1989.

On the eve of the unification of North and South Yemen in May 1990 the GPC was transformed into a licensed political party. Its program included multiparty democracy at home and friendly relations with neighbors and Islamic countries. It backed Yemen's official stance of neutrality in the 1990–91 Kuwait crisis and the subsequent Gulf War [*q.v.*]. In the multiparty general election in Yemen in April 1993, the GPC won 123 seats in a house of 301 members, and led the coalition government formed with the Yemeni Socialist Party [*q.v.*] and the Yemeni Islah Group [*q.v.*]. It backed President Saleh during the Yemeni Civil War [*q.v.*], which erupted in the spring of 1994. In the 1997 general election, it secured 187 seats, and 25 of the 29 cabinet posts. In the 2003 parliamentary election, its share rose to 238 seats on a popular vote of 58 percent.

During the pro-democracy protest in 2011, GPC leaders organized pro-Saleh demonstrations. Once Saleh had agreed to step down in an orderly fashion, they backed the candidacy of Vice President Abd Rabbu Mansour al-Hadi as president [*q.v.*]. He was elected to that office in February 2012.

General Zionists: *Zionist political party in Palestine* The term General Zionists (Hebrew: *Zionim Klaliyim*) was first used at the Zionist Congress of 1907 to describe delegates attached to neither Labor Zionism [*q.v.*] nor religious Zionism. In Palestine [*q.v.*] the General Zionist party came into being in 1930. Since it had by then come to represent the capitalist strand within Zionism, it drew the support of businessmen, industrialists, planters, and traders.

Four years later the party split into a liberal "A" faction (sympathetic to Labor) and a conservative "B" faction (sympathetic to capital). These factions came together in 1944, but their unity proved short-lived. Soon after the founding of Israel in 1948, the liberal "A" faction left to combine with the German-dominated *Aliya Hadasha* (Hebrew: *New Immigrants*) to form the Progressive Party [*q.v.*]. During the 1950s the General Zionists saw their parliamentary strength fall from 20 to eight. Fear of further decline persuaded its leaders to seek a merger with the Progressives on the eve of the 1961 election and form the Liberal Party [*q.v.*].

Geneva Conventions on War (1949): *International treaties signed in Geneva* The last of the four Conventions—developed by an International Red Cross conference in Stockholm in August 1948 and ratified by UN members in Geneva on 12 August 1949—entitled "Relative to the Protection of Civilian Persons in Time of War"—applies to Israel and the Occupied Arab Territories [*q.v.*], including Jerusalem [*q.v.*], according to several UN Security Council resolutions, including 465 (March 1980). It forbids the Occupying Power doing the following to the Protected Civilians: collective punishment and reprisals; deportation of individuals or groups; hostage-taking; torture; unjustified destruction of property; and discrimination in treatment on the grounds of race, religion, national origin, or political affiliation. Article 47 states: "Protected persons … shall not be deprived of … the benefits of this Convention by any changes introduced, as the result of the occupation of a territory, into the institutions or government of the said territory, nor by any agreement concluded between the authorities of the occupied territories and the Occupying Power, nor by the annexation of the whole or part of the occupied territory." Article 49 (6) states: "The Occupying Power shall not deport or transfer parts of its own civilian population into the territory it occupies."

Ghashmi, Ahmad Hussein (1938–78): *North Yemeni military officer and politician; president 1977–78* Born in Hamada into a clan of the Hashid tribal confederation, Ghashmi was trained as an officer at the Baghdad Military Academy. During North Yemen's Civil War (1962–70) [*q.v.*] he liaised between the republican regime in Sanaa [*q.v.*] and the northern tribal confederations of Hashid and Bakil. His relations with the Hashid chief, Abdullah al-Ahmar [*q.v.*], were tense. After a coup by Colonel Ibrahim Hamdi [*q.v.*] in June 1974, Lieutenant Colonel Ghashmi was appointed deputy chief of staff and a member of the ruling Military Command Council (MCC).

A conservative, Ghashmi was considered pro-Saudi Arabia. After the assassination of Hamdi in October 1977 he became commander-in-chief and chairman of the three-man MCC. He revived the Constituent People's Assembly (CPA), disbanded earlier by Hamdi, and tried to mend fences with al-Ahmar. His government repressed the nationalist-leftist

forces. Guided by Saudi Arabia, he purged the military and civil services of pro-Hamdi personnel. In March 1978 he dissolved the MCC, thus neutralizing the power of the paratroop commander, Major Abdullah Abdul Alim, an erstwhile MCC member and a Hamdi loyalist. In April the CPA replaced the MCC with a presidential council, and elected Ghashmi president. He was assassinated in June by the blast of a bomb hidden in a briefcase carried by an emissary of South Yemeni President Salim Rubai Ali [q.v.] during their meeting to discuss unifying North and South Yemen.

Ghazi bin Faisal I al-Hashem (1912–39): *King of Iraq, 1932–39* The only son of Faisal I bin Hussein al-Hashem [*q.v.*], Ghazi was born in Hijaz [*q.v.*] under the Ottoman rule. Following the installation of his father as king of Iraq in 1921, he became heir apparent. Educated partly in Baghdad [*q.v.*] and partly in Britain, Ghazi succeeded his father in 1933. During his rule factions emerged among military officers. In October 1936 Ghazi encouraged Commander-in-chief Bakr Sidqi to overthrow the unpopular civilian government of Yasin al-Hashemi. His nationalist, anti-British views won him popularity. He died as a result of an alleged car crash.

Ghom: *See* Qom.

Gibran, Kahlil (1883–1931): *Lebanese writer* Born into a Maronite [*q.v.*] family in the village of Bishari, Gibran received his schooling in Beirut [*q.v.*] until the age of 12, when he left with his parents for Boston, Massachusetts.

Three years later he traveled to Beirut [*q.v.*] to study Arabic [*q.v.*] and French at the Maronite al-Hikma Institute. After his return to Boston, he took to writing and painting. He published his literary essays in 1903 in *al-Muhajir* (Arabic: *The Migrant*), a newspaper of expatriate Arabs. The next year, at an exhibition of his drawings, he met Mary Haskel, who became his lifelong benefactor. She sent him to Paris in 1908 to study art.

Soon after his return to Boston in 1910, Gibran formed the Golden Chain, a political group committed to bringing about sociopolitical reform in Lebanon. In 1912 he settled in New York City, where he continued to produce essays, poems, short stories, and paintings.

His collections of short stories— *Nymphs of the Valley* (1906) and *Rebellious Spirits* (1908)—all set in Lebanon, showed his romantic bent, belief in the inherent goodness of humans, admiration for pastoral surroundings, and distrust of the institutions and bonds of civilized society. He expressed these ideas forcefully in his collection of essays, *A Tear and a Smile* (1914). He was influenced by the Bible [*q.v.*], Jean Rousseau, William Blake, and Friedrich Nietzsche. Though religious, he was anticlerical and opposed to the Maronite church hierarchy. He continued writing in Arabic until 1918, when he began to use English as well.

His lyrical style, supported by analogies and biblical metaphors, suited his romantic thoughts, the end result being musically poetic Arabic prose that was unique. His first book in English was *The Madman* (1918), which expressed optimistic pantheism,

followed by *Twenty Drawings* (1919) and *The Forerunner* (1920). In his novel *Broken Wings* (1922), he attacked feudal lords and clerics in Lebanon who stood between the young hero and his rich beloved, a reflection of his personal experience.

In 1920 he became a cofounder of the Pen Association, a literary club, and provided its members, many of them talented poets, with encouragement, inspiration, and intellectual leadership. He published his volume of Arabic poems, *The Processions,* in 1923. But far more important was his volume in English, *The Prophet* (1923), in which he discussed relations between man and man in a mystical fashion, an approach that won him critical acclaim and riches. The book became a classic and kept selling long after he was dead. His next two volumes in English, *Sand and Foam* (1926) and *Jesus, the Son of Man* (1928), were also well received. He published *The Earth Gods* just before he died, and *The Wanderer* and *The Garden of the Prophet* appeared posthumously.

Glubb (Pasha), Sir John Bagot

(1897–1986): *British military officer in the Middle East* Born in Preston, Britain, Glubb was educated at Cheltenham College and the Royal Military Academy in Woolwich, London. During World War I he was wounded in combat and was awarded the Military Cross. After the war he was sent to Iraq.

He left the British army in 1926 to serve the Iraqi government as an administrative inspector. In 1930 he joined Transjordan's Arab Legion, an internal security force. He became the

Legion's second-in-command, rising to commander in 1938 and attaining the rank of lieutenant general.

Led by Glubb, the Arab Legion assisted Britain and its allies in 1941 in their attacks on the government of Rashid Ali Gailani [q.v.] in Iraq and on the troops of the pro-Nazi, French Vichy regime in Syria-Lebanon.

After the Palestine War (1948–49) [q.v.]—when the Arab Legion failed to capture West Jerusalem [q.v.]—Glubb, a symbol of British hegemony in the region, became a hate figure among Arab nationalists. When Britain pressured King Hussein bin Talal al-Hashem [q.v.] to join the Baghdad Pact [q.v.] (in order to regain the privilege of securing military bases in times of war), the tide of nationalism rose and Glubb became the target.

To offset the rising popular charge that he was a puppet of London, King Hussein dismissed Glubb in March 1956. He retired to Britain, where he lectured and wrote books mainly about Arab countries and peoples.

Golan Heights: *Syrian region* Also known as the Golan Plateau. Area 454 sq. mi./1176 sq. km; population in the Syrian sector: 79,000 (2010 est.), population in the Israeli-occupied zone: approximately 19,100 Jews (2010 est.), and 23,500 Syrians, mostly Druze [q.v.] (2010 est.). Part of Syria since World War I, the western border of the Golan Heights, overlooking the Hula Valley and Lake Tiberias/Sea of Galilee, was fortified after the founding of Israel in 1948.

It became a source of sniper and artillery attacks on Israelis in the region. After defeating Jordan in the 1967 Arab-Israeli War [q.v.], Israel attacked the Golan Heights on 9 June and captured its capital, Qunaitra, the next day. A cease-fire went into effect later that day. The fighting and subsequent Israeli actions reduced the Syrian population of 250,000 to about 8,000, mainly Druze. Israel declared that it would keep the Golan Heights.

In 1969 Syria gave Palestinian commandos greater freedom of action in the area. Because the U.S. peace plan presented to the warring parties by secretary of state William Rogers in June 1970 made no mention of Israel evacuating the Heights, Syria rejected it. In the October 1973 Arab-Israeli War [q.v.], the Syrian offensive, launched on 6 October, limited itself to recovering the Golan Heights. Its initial gain was reversed when Israel mounted a successful counteroffensive.

After Syria had signed the Syrian-Soviet Friendship Treaty [q.v.] in October 1980, its spokesman said that any attempt by Israel to annex the occupied Golan Heights would lead Syria to take "any step or measure to secure our rights." But when, on 14 December 1981, the Israeli government extended its laws to the Golan Heights and received parliamentary backing in the form of the Golan Heights Law, Syria merely denounced the Israeli action and put its case before the UN Security Council, which declared the law "null and void."

Israel continued its policy of establishing Jewish settlements, which numbered 34 in 2009 and housed about 18,000 Jews. As for Syria, before joining the Middle East peace process initiated by the United States after the 1991 Gulf War [q.v.], it ensured that Israeli evacuation of the Golan Heights would be the principal subject of discussion in the subsequent bilateral talks.

In mid-1994 the two sides entered into substantive negotiations linking Israel's evacuation of the Golan Heights with normalization of mutual relations. Israel unilaterally broke off these talks in the spring of 1996. These resumed in 1999 after the election of Ehud Barak [q.v.] as Israel's prime minister. But they failed in March 2000 when Barak insisted on keeping a strip of the Golan along Lake Tiberias, which Syrian President Hafiz Assad [q.v.] refused.

Later, indirect negotiations between Israel and Syria resumed in May 2008 through Turkish intermediaries, once Israeli Prime Minister Ehud Olmert [q.v.] had informed Turkish Prime Minister Recep Tayyip Erdogan that he was prepared to hand back all of the Golan Heights. These talks were suspended when Olmert resigned in March 2009 over a corruption inquiry. His successor, Benjamin Netanyahu [q.v.], decided to take a tougher line over the issue, and in June Syrian President Bashar Assad [q.v.] said that there was no negotiating partner on the Israeli side.

Golpaygani, Muhammad Reza Musavi (1899–1993): *Iranian leader* Born in Golpaygan of a religious Shia [q.v.] family, Golpaygani lost his parents when young and was raised by his sisters. When he was 16 he went to Arak to be a pupil of Ayatollah Abdul Karim Hairi-Yazdi, and moved with him to Qom [q.v.] in 1922. Having finished his studies in Arabic and theology, he started teaching Islamic jurisprudence.

After Hairi-Yazdi's death in 1937, Golpaygani rose in stature in the religious hierarchy, now led by Ayatollah Muhammad Hussein Borujerdi. Like Borujerdi, he was a conservative. After the death of Borujerdi in 1961, the leadership of conservative clerics fell on the triumvirate of Ayatollahs Golpaygani, Shehab al-Din Marashi-Najafi, and Muhammad Kazem Shariatmadari [q.v.]. They opposed the idea of state takeover of land above a certain ceiling, an important part of the agrarian reform law of the government of Muhammad Reza Shah Pahlavi [q.v.]. This brought Golpaygani close to Ayatollah Ruhollah Khomeini [q.v.], an opponent of the regime.

When Khomeini was exiled in 1964, Golpaygani took over the administration of the prestigious Faiyziyya seminary in Qom. He offered the concept of *Vilayat-e-Faqih* (Persian: *Rule of the Religious Jurisprudent*) [q.v.], which assigned spiritual and temporal leadership of an Islamic community to jurisprudents. This was to be incorporated into the constitution of the Islamic Republic of Iran, founded in 1979. As a senior *marja-e taqlid* (Persian: *source of emulation*) [q.v.], Golpaygani received *khums* [q.v.] (one-fifth of the income of his followers) as religious dues. With this money he founded and sustained charitable projects in Iran and abroad—building and maintaining clinics, hospitals, orphanages, and religious and educational centers.

After the Islamic revolution in Iran [q.v.] he backed the new regime at crucial moments. In the mid-1980s, when there was growing division between conservative and radical clerics, especially on the issue of Khomeini's succession, the conservatives backed

Golpaygani. When Khomeini died in 1989 without having publicly named a successor, the Assembly of Experts [*q.v.*] reportedly offered the position of the (supreme) Leader to 90-year-old Golpaygani. Due to his advanced age and poor health, he turned it down. As a cleric who had been in close contact with all the leading Shia religious personalities of the 20th century, he was unique.

Greater Syria: Area: 119,690 sq. mi./310,000 sq. km. Greater (or Natural) Syria occupies the piece of territory enclosed by the Taurus Mountains to the north, the Mediterranean Sea to the west, the Arabian Desert to the south, and the Euphrates River [*q.v.*] to the east. It was known historically as *Bilad al-Sham*, or Land on the Left/North (of Mecca [*q.v.*]).

From 1831 to 1840, during an interregnum in the Ottoman rule that started in 1517, Greater Syria was governed as a single entity under the Egyptian viceroy Ibrahim Pasha. When direct Ottoman rule resumed, Greater Syria was divided into several provinces. Following the Ottoman defeat in World War I, the victors—Britain and France—split Greater Syria according to the Sykes-Picot Pact [*q.v.*], with the northern region (later forming the republics of Syria and Lebanon) going to France and the southern section (constituting Palestine and Transjordan) to Britain. This was denounced at the Syrian National Congress meeting in Damascus in July 1919, which demanded sovereignty for a united Syria-Palestine, but in vain.

The League of Nations Supreme Council confirmed the British and French claims in 1920 by giving them mandates over the new entities created out of the old Ottoman provinces. The League of Nations visualized a mandate as guardianship of a young nation to be prepared for full independence. But France toppled the government of Faisal I bin Hussein al-Hashemi [*q.v.*] in Damascus [*q.v.*], established a colonial regime, and rearranged the borders by allocating parts of Syria to the Vilayat of Mount Lebanon to create Greater Lebanon. By surrendering sections of the Syrian province of Aleppo to Turkey in October 1921, France further reduced the size of Syria. As a result the independent Syria that emerged in 1946 occupied only 71,500 sq. mi./185,180 sq. km.

Greater Tumb/Tunb Island: *See* Tumb/Tunb Islands.

Greek Catholic Church: Also known as Greek-Melkite Catholic Church, the Greek Catholic Church is a Uniate Church [*q.v.*]. Those early Christians [*q.v.*] of Egypt and Syria who accepted the church council's ruling in 451 A.D. that Jesus Christ possessed two natures, human and divine, were labeled "malka" (Syriac: *royalist*) by their opponents. Since they followed the Byzantine rite, they stayed with the Eastern Orthodox Church [*q.v.*] after the major church schism in 1054. Due to the predominance of Greek colonizers (in Egypt and Syria) in its congregation, the church came to be known as Greek Orthodox [*q.v.*].

Periodic attempts at unification with the Roman Catholic Church [*q.v.*] did not succeed until 1724, when a Roman Catholic, Cyril VI, was elected Patriarch of Antioch. But only a third of Greek Orthodox members followed his lead, and they came to be called Greek/Greek-Melkite Catholics. They conduct their Byzantine liturgy in Arabic [*q.v.*]. Their head, the Patriarch of Antioch and All the East, resides alternatively in Damascus [*q.v.*], Beirut [*q.v.*], and Cairo [*q.v.*]. Of the 1.3 million Greek Catholics in the Middle East [*q.v.*] and the Western Hemisphere, 160,000 live in Lebanon. They are also to be found in Egypt, Jordan, Syria, and the Palestinian Territories [*q.v.*].

Greek Orthodox Church: Those early Christians [*q.v.*] of Egypt and Syria who accepted the church council's ruling in 451 A.D. that Jesus Christ possessed two natures, human and divine, were labeled "malka" (*Syriac: royalist*) by their opponents. Since they followed the Byzantine rite, they stayed with the Eastern Orthodox Church [*q.v.*] after the major church schism in 1054. Due to the predominance of Greek colonizers (in Egypt and Syria) in its congregation, the church came to be known as Greek Orthodox [*q.v.*]. The Patriarch of Alexandria and all Africa, based in Alexandria [*q.v.*], is the head of a community of 350,000 in Egypt. The Patriarch of Antioch and All the East, based in Damascus [*q.v.*], is the head of a 320,000-strong (in 2010) community in Lebanon, the second-largest Christian sect after the Maronite Catholics [*q.v.*].

Green Path of Hope (Iran): The Green Path of Hope (GPH) is a coalition of social networks, non-governmental organizations, and political groups. It was founded by Mir Hussein Musavi [*q.v.*] on 15 August 2009 to consolidate the wide-scale protest against the rigging of the presidential election in June 2009, demanding its annulment. The title avoids the term "party" or "movement," which require a license from the interior ministry. The symbol of an open knot used by Musavi's election campaign for the presidency was colored green, and it offered a government of hope.

The GPH aimed to keep challenging the legitimacy of the government of Mahmoud Ahmadinejad [*q.v.*] peacefully, and to insist on implementing the Iranian constitution fully rather than partially. The six members of its Central Council include Musavi, former president Muhammad Khatami [*q.v.*], former speaker of parliament Mahdi Karroubi, and Zahra Rahnavard, former chancellor of al-Zahra University.

Because of the heavy-handed methods of the government, protest calls by the GPH became less and less effective. Its efforts to mount a large demonstration on the first anniversary of the rigged election in June 2010 failed. It called for a boycott of the parliamentary election in 2012.

Gregorian calendar: Named after Pope Gregory III in 1582. *See* Christian calendars.

Gregorian Orthodox Church: Since Armenians [*q.v.*] were converted to Christianity [*q.v.*] by Gregory the Illuminator, the Armenian Orthodox Church is also known as the Gregorian Orthodox Church. *See* Armenian

Orthodox Church.

Guardian Council (Iran): Official title, Council of Guardians of the Constitution (Persian: *Shora-ye Negahban-e Qanun-e Assassi*). Established by the 1979 constitution of the Islamic Republic of Iran, the task of the 12-member Council of Guardians is to ensure that all laws and regulations passed by parliament are compatible with the Iranian constitution and Islamic percepts. It consists of (1) six "*faqihs* [Arabic: *Islamic jurisprudents*] conscious of current needs and the issues of the day," to be appointed by the Leader (of the Revolution); and six jurists, specializing in different branches of Islamic law, to be elected by parliament from a list of qualified candidates submitted by the head of the judiciary, who is appointed by the Leader. The tenure of the Council is six years. The parliament is required to submit its regulations and bills to it. All guardians vote on their compatibility with the constitution, but only the six faqihs do so on their compatibility with Islamic precepts. A regulation or law becomes effective only if it is judged to be compatible with both the constitution and Islamic precepts. The Council also vets all candidates for public office at the national level for their loyalty to the constitution and Islam as well as the results of these elections.

Starting with the parliamentary election in 2000, its decisions have proved controversial. This was particularly true of its endorsement of the landslide victory of Mahmoud Ahmadinejad [*q.v.*] in the presidential election of 2009, which was, by most accounts, rigged.

Guardians of the Cedars: *Lebanese political group* Named after the cedar, the national symbol of Lebanon, the Guardians of the Cedars emerged soon after the outbreak of the Lebanese Civil War in April 1975 [*q.v.*]. Led by Eteinne Saqr, the Guardians were ultra-nationalist Maronites [*q.v.*]. They were inspired by the writings of Said Aql [*q.v.*], who believed that Lebanese identity was rooted in its distant Phoenician past and had little to do with pan-Arabism [*q.v.*] or Islam [*q.v.*]. In January 1976 they combined with other Maronite militias to create a unified military command. Open about their links with Israel, many of them joined the Israeli-sponsored South Lebanon Army [*q.v.*], which was formed after the Israeli invasion of southern Lebanon [*q.v.*] in March 1978.

In the fractured Maronite community of the late 1980s they were one of the eight political or military factions. When the civil war ended in favor of their adversaries in October 1990, their influence declined. Their backing of the electoral boycott by the Maronites of the parliamentary election of 1992 further marginalized them politically. With the dissolution of the South Lebanon Army in May 2000 following Israel's unconditional withdrawal from South Lebanon, their military activity ended. They continued to have a minor political presence under the newly acquired title of the Movement of Lebanese Nationalism.

Gulf, the: Surface area, 92,500 sq. mi./240,000 sq. km; length 610 mi./990 km; width, 35–210 mi./56–340 km; depth, 120–300 ft/40–100 m. An extension of the Arabian Sea between Iran [*q.v.*] and the Arabian Peninsula [*q.v.*], the Gulf is connected to the Gulf of Oman by the Strait of Hormuz [*q.v.*]. As the flow of fresh water into it from the Shatt al-Arab [*q.v.*] and the Karun River is limited, and water temperatures are generally high, its salinity of 40 pounds per 1,000 pounds of sea water is above average. Because the eight countries around the Gulf possess 54 percent of global petroleum reserves [*q.v.*] and produce between a quarter and a third of the world's oil, the Gulf is an area of prime importance to the rest of the world.

Gulf Cooperation Council: *Regional body consisting of Bahrain, Kuwait, Oman, Qatar, Saudi Arabia, and the United Arab Emirates* Official title, Cooperation Council for the States of the Arab Gulf (Arabic: *Majlis al-Taawun li Dual al-Khaleej al-Arabiyah*). The idea of a regional body in the Gulf grew out of Saudi Arabia's proposal for an internal security pact with fellow monarchies on the Arabian Peninsula [q.v.] following an armed uprising in Mecca [q.v.] in late 1979. The matter became urgent when the Iran-Iraq War [q.v.] erupted in September 1980. Meeting in Abu Dhabi [q.v.], rulers of the six Gulf monarchies founded the Gulf Cooperation Council (GCC) on 26 May 1981. Its objectives were to coordinate internal security, procurement of arms, national economy of member states, and to settle border disputes under the leadership of the Supreme Council, consisting of the heads of the member states.

Abdullah Bishara, a Kuwaiti diplomat, was appointed secretary general of the GCC, whose secretariat was in Riyadh [*q.v.*]. In June 1982 the GCC foreign ministers' attempt to end the Iran-Iraq War [*q.v.*] failed. A GCC communiqué in November condemned Iran [*q.v.*] for occupying Iraqi territory. However, continuation of the war helped the GCC to become a cohesive body, particularly in defense, where collectively GCC states had 190,000 troops and 300 warplanes. In October 1984 the GCC conducted a three-week joint military exercise in the desert of the United Arab Emirates (UAE).

At the next month's GCC summit it was decided to set up a Peninsula Shield Force (PSF) of two brigades under a Saudi officer based in Riyadh. A year later the GCC summit pledged to continue its efforts to end the Iran-Iraq War in a manner that safeguarded the legitimate rights and interests of "the two sides." The next summit in late 1987 urged the UN Security Council to implement its cease-fire Resolution 598, passed in July.

Following Iraq's [*q.v.*] invasion and occupation of Kuwait in August 1990, the GCC condemned Baghdad's action. It dispatched its PSF to the Saudi-Kuwait border to deter Iraqi intrusion. The GCC summit in December 1990 demanded the unconditional withdrawal of Iraq from Kuwait. The troops and air forces of GCC members participated in the U.S.-led Gulf War [*q.v.*] against Iraq. In March 1991 GCC ministers agreed to give grants to Egypt and Syria for the deployment of the 35,000 Egyptian and 20,000 Syrian troops as part of the backbone of an expanded Gulf defense force. But these plans were later abandoned. The GCC's own Peninsula Shield Force, based near King Khalid Military City at Hafar al-Batin consisted of only one infantry brigade of 5,000 troops drawn from all its members.

The GCC states decided to suspend their subsidies to the Palestine Liberation Organization [*q.v.*] so long as it was headed by Yasser Arafat [*q.v.*], who had sided with Iraq during the Kuwait crisis and the subsequent war. Following the PLO-Israeli accord in Washington in September 1993 [*q.v.*], GCC members ended their ostracizing of the PLO and the Palestinians. Saudi Arabia promised to contribute up to $100 million over a five-year period to a development fund for the West Bank [*q.v.*] and Gaza Strip [*q.v.*]. A year later the GCC ended the secondary and tertiary embargo on trade with Israel.

In 1997 the Supreme Council decided to appoint a 30-member Consultative Council as an advisory body. In March 1999 the GCC condemned Iran for conducting military exercises around the waters of the Abu Musa [*q.v.*] and Tunb Islands [*q.v.*], over which the UAE claimed jurisdiction. Later that year it set up a committee to facilitate direct talks between Iran and the UAE to settle the dispute, but nothing came of it.

In 2002, Abdul Rahman bin Hamad al-Attiyah of Qatar succeeded Saudi Arabia's Jamil Ibrahim Hejailan as the GCC's fourth secretary-general.

On the economic front, the GCC summit in 2005 decided to have a common currency by 2010. But the next year Oman said that it would be unable to meet the target date. And in 2009, soon after it was announced that the central bank for the new currency

would be situated in Riyadh, and not in Abu Dhabi [*q.v.*] or Dubai [*q.v.*], the UAE quit the project. The plan failed.

Breaking with protocol, GCC leaders invited Iran's President Mahmoud Ahmadinejad [*q.v.*] to attend their 2007 summit in Doha [*q.v.*]. He did so. But Tehran's dispute with the UAE on the Abu Musa [*q.v.*] and Tunb Islands [*q.v.*] remained unresolved. The 2010 summit held in Abu Dhabi called on Iran to refrain from using or threatening to use force against the UAE.

In March 2011, the GCC deviated from its core purpose of defense against foreign attack by agreeing to deploy its PSF units in Bahrain to quell its domestic pro-democracy protest. Most of the 1,500 PSF soldiers were Saudis, with small contributions from Kuwait and the UAE. Abdul Latif bin Rashid al-Zayani of Bahrain, who became the GCC's fifth secretary-general on 1 April 2011, argued that a threat to the stability of one GCC member state was a threat to all.

In late April the GCC formulated a three-phase proposal to resolve the political crisis caused by the pro-democracy uprising in Yemen inspired by the Arab Spring [*q.v.*]. It required the reconstitution of the parliament reducing the share of the ruling General People's Congress [*q.v.*] to 50 percent, with the oppositionist Joint Meeting Parties (JMP) getting 40 percent, and the remaining 10 percent to other political entities. Within 30 days of the new parliament's inauguration, President Ali Abdullah Saleh [*q.v.*] would resign after securing immunity from prosecution for himself, his relatives, and senior members of his government. Then within the next 60 days a presidential election would follow. Having agreed to sign the deal three times, Saleh backed out at the last moment. After receiving severe injuries in an attack on the mosque in his presidential palace during Friday congregation on 3 June, he flew to Riyadh for medical treatment. On his sudden return to Sanaa [*q.v.*] in September, clashes between the opposing sides resumed. The GCC revived its peace efforts, this time gaining the support of the UN Security Council for its new plan. On 23 November, Saleh signed the deal, agreeing to relinquish power within 30 days in favor of a transitional government headed by Vice President Abd Rabbu Mansour al-Hadi [*q.v.*], while remaining president until a fresh election in February 2012.

In October the GCC called for an Arab League [*q.v.*] meeting to debate the repression of the pro-democracy protest in Syria. Two months later it urged the Syrian government to end its "killing machine" immediately in accordance with the Arab League's plan, requiring President Bashar Assad [*q.v.*] to step down. Assad rejected the demand.

Gulf States: Though eight countries border the Gulf [*q.v.*], only the six monarchies of Bahrain, Kuwait, Oman, Qatar, Saudi Arabia, and the United Arab Emirates are collectively known as the Gulf States. The remaining states with shorelines along the Gulf are Iran and Iraq.

Gulf War I (1980–88): *war between Iran and Iraq* After a week-long clash be-

tween Iraq and Iran in the disputed border territory in the central sector, Baghdad claimed on 10 September 1980 to have captured the area. A week later Iraqi President Saddam Hussein [*q.v.*] abrogated the 1975 Iran-Iraq Treaty of International Boundaries and Neighborliness [*q.v.*], and claimed full sovereignty over the Shatt al-Arab [*q.v.*]. On 22 September Iraq invaded Iran at eight points along their international border, and bombed Iranian military installations and economic targets.

The armed conflict, the longest conventional war of the 20th century, went through the following phases.

PHASE ONE: September 1980 to March 1981. Iraqi troops advanced into Iran. On 28 September UN Security Council Resolution 479 urged a truce. Iraq announced its readiness to cease fire if Iran accepted its complete rights over the Shatt al-Arab. Tehran rejected the resolution. By mid-November Iraq had captured Khorramshahr and besieged Abadan [*q.v.*]. It occupied 10,000 sq. mi./25,900 sq. km of Iranian territory in the southern and central sectors. The wet winter led to a military standoff.

PHASE TWO: April 1981 to March 1982. While the Iranian military, much enlarged by a surge of patriotism among Iranians, blocked further Iraqi advance, it failed to lift the siege of Abadan. Efforts by the UN and the Islamic Conference Organization [*q.v.*] to end the conflict foundered: Iran refused to negotiate so long as Iraq occupied its land.

PHASE THREE: March 1982 to June 1982. Iran recovered the lost territory. On 24 May 1982 Iran retook Khorramshahr and drove the Iraqis back to the international frontier. Iraq announced its readiness for a truce on 9 June. Tehran refused to cease fire until Saddam Hussein had been removed from office. On 20 June he declared that Iraq's voluntary withdrawal from Iran would be completed within 10 days. But on 30 June Iraq still held some pockets of Iranian territory.

PHASE FOUR: July 1982 to March 1984. Iran's troops marched into Iraq. Having rejected the UN Security Council's call for a truce and the withdrawal of the opposing armies to the international border, Iran tried to conquer Basra [q.v.] in mid-July. With nine divisions locked in the largest infantry combat since World War II, fierce battles raged for a fortnight. Finally Iran managed to hold only 32 sq. mi./83 sq. km of the Iraqi land. In October Iran reclaimed some territory in the northern sector. Iraq's air strikes on Iran's Nowruz offshore oilfield in March 1983 caused the largest oil spill in the history of the Gulf. In April Iran's offensive in the southern sector to reach the strategic Basra-Baghdad highway failed. But its offensive in the north in July yielded it the Iraqi garrison town of Hajj Umran. In mid-February 1984 Iran launched a second attempt to breach the Baghdad-Basra highway, but again failed. After an offensive in the Haur al-Hawizeh marshes in late February, Iran seized Iraq's oil-rich Majnoon Islands.

PHASE FIVE: April 1984 to January 1986. Iraq escalated its attacks on Iranian oil tankers, using French-made Exocet air-to-ship (surface-skimmer) missiles, and intensified its air raids on the Kharg oil terminal, which handled most of Iran's petroleum exports. Iran retaliated by hitting ships serving the ports of Kuwait and Saudi Arabia, which were aiding Iraq, in the Lower Gulf [q.v.]. In October 1983, Iraq started using chemical weapons—at first mustard gas and then nerve gases. In March 1985 an Iranian brigade reached the Baghdad-Basra highway, but was unable to withstand the Iraqi counterattacks. In May Iraq intensified its tanker war and strikes on Kharg, reaching a peak in mid-August. Altogether, Iraq hit 33 ships in the Gulf in 1985, and Iran 14.

PHASE SIX: February 1986 to January 1988. The war of attrition escalated, and the United States began to intervene on the Iraqi side. The Iranian assault in February 1986 in the south, which resulted in the capture of 310 sq. mi./800 sq. km in the Fao Peninsula, broke the stalemate. A relentless effort by Iraq, which mounted 18,648 air missions between 9 February and 25 March 1986 (compared with 20,011 missions in the whole of 1985), to regain Fao failed. In March, following a report by UN experts on Iraq's use of poison gas, the UN Security Council combined its condemnation of Iraq for deploying (universally banned) chemical weapons with its disapproval of the prolongation of the conflict by Iran. The next month, flooding of the oil market by Kuwait and Saudi Arabia caused the price of petroleum to fall below $10 a barrel, down from $27 in the previous December. This sharply reduced the oil income of Iran and Iraq, but the latter was cushioned by the approximately $10 billion a year it received in aid from its Gulf allies, the West, and the Soviet Union.

From July, using covert official U.S. expertise, Iraq began to use its air force more aggressively than before, hitting Iran's economic and infrastructural targets and extending its air strikes to the Iranian oil terminals in the Lower Gulf. During 1986 Iraq struck 86 ships in the Gulf, and Iran 41. In January 1987 Iran's offensives in the south brought its forces within seven miles of Basra, but failed to capture it. During the spring the Iranians and their Iraqi Kurdish allies captured territory in Iraqi Kurdistan [*q.v.*]. On 20 July the UN Security Council unanimously passed Resolution 598, calling for a cease-fire and the withdrawal of warring forces to the international border. The 10-article text included a clause for an impartial commission to determine war responsibility, one of the major demands of Iran. Iraq said it would accept the resolution on condition that Iran did the same. Four days later a Kuwaiti supertanker on the first Gulf convoy escorted by U.S. warships hit a mine, believed to have been planted by Iran. The subsequent naval buildup by the United States, Britain, and France brought 60 Western warships in the region.

On the seventh anniversary of the war on 22 September 1987, Iraq had nearly 400 combat aircraft, six times the number of Iran's airworthy warplanes. Baghdad possessed 4,500 tanks, 3,200 armored fighting vehicles, and 2,800 artillery pieces versus Tehran's respective totals of 1,570; 1,800; and 1,750. Iraq had 955,000 regular troops versus Iran's 655,000; and Iraq's Popular Army, at 650,000, was slightly larger than Iran's Revolutionary Guards Corps, at 625,000.

In October the U.S. Navy sank three Iranian patrol boats near Farsi Island,

claiming that Iran had fired on a U.S. patrol helicopter; and U.S. warships destroyed two Iranian offshore oil platforms in the Lower Gulf in retaliation for an Iranian missile attack on a U.S.-flagged supertanker docked in Kuwaiti waters. Tehran's capacity to mount major offensives was much reduced due to its shortage of manpower and money, and the damage done to its bridges, factories, and power plants by ceaseless Iraqi bombing.

PHASE SEVEN: February to June 1988. Iraq retook its lost territories. By introducing long-range surface-to-surface missiles in February 1988, Iraq was able to hit Tehran [*q.v.*] and demoralize the population. Iran retaliated by hitting Baghdad [*q.v.*], which was much nearer the international border. Between 16 and 18 April Iraq recaptured the Fao Peninsula, using chemical weapons, while U.S. warships blew up two Iranian oil rigs, destroyed one Iranian frigate and immobilized another, and sank an Iranian missile boat. From 23 to 25 May Iraq, using chemical arms, staged offensives in the northern and central sectors, and then in the south, regaining Shalamche. Between 19 and 25 June, Iraq recaptured Mehran in the central zone, using poison gases, and then the Majnoon Islands in the south.

PHASE EIGHT: July to 20 August 1988. Iraq failed to seize Iranian land. On 3 July a U.S. cruiser U.S.S *Vincennes* shot down an Iran Air airbus carrying 290 people over the Lower Gulf, mistaking it for a combat aircraft. On 18 July Iran unconditionally accepted UN Security Council Resolution 598. Two days later Iran's leader, Ayatollah Ruhollah Khomeini [*q.v.*], stated that acceptance of a truce was "in the interest of the revolution and the system at this juncture." From 22 to 29 July, Iraq mounted offensives in the northern, central, and southern sectors to capture Iranian land. It failed in the north but succeeded elsewhere. However, within a week Iran regained its lost territory. On 20 August a truce came into effect under UN supervision. By then, Iraq had used 110,000 chemical munitions against Iran.

HUMAN LOSSES: Iran (official), 194,931 dead, consisting of 183,931 combatants, including those missing in action, and 11,000 civilians; Iran (unofficial est.), 300,000 dead; Iraq (unofficial est.), 160,000–240,000 dead.

COST: Iran (estimated by the Stockholm International Peace Research Institute), $74–91 billion, plus military imports of $11.26 billion; Iraq (est. by the Stockholm International Peace Research Institute), $94–112 billion, plus military imports of $41.94 billion. In July 1990 Iraq's deputy premier, Tariq Aziz [*q.v.*], put the military imports at $102 billion.

OUTCOME: Neither country lost much territory, nor was there a change of regime in Iraq or Iran. The war enabled Khomeini to consolidate the Islamic revolution [*q.v.*]. With a million men in its military, Iraq emerged as the most powerful country in the region, outstripping Turkey and Egypt.

AFTER THE TRUCE: On 12 August 1990 Iraq unilaterally agreed to abide by the 1975 Iran-Iraq Treaty of International Boundaries and Neighborliness, withdraw its forces from the occupied Iranian territory, and exchange prisoners of war. By the spring of 2000, the two countries had repatriated 100,000 prisoners of war. Each side rejected the other's figures on the remainder, with Baghdad claiming that Iran was still holding 13,000 Iraqi prisoners of war, and Tehran alleging that Iraq was holding 2,800 Iranian prisoners. By the time of the Anglo-American invasion of Iraq [*q.v.*] in March 2003, this dispute was almost settled.

Gulf War II (1991): *war between Iraq and the U.S.-led coalition*

BACKGROUND: (mid-July to 1 August 1990) In mid-July Iraq complained to the Arab League [*q.v.*] that the oil glut caused by Kuwait and the United Arab Emirates (UAE) had caused the price to fall to $11–13 a barrel—far below the reference price of $18 set by the Organization of Petroleum Exporting Countries [*q.v.*]—and that a drop of $1 a barrel reduced Iraq's annual revenue by $1 billion. On 31 July Iraqi and Kuwaiti officials met in Jeddah [*q.v.*] against the background of some 100,000 Iraqi troops massed along the Kuwaiti border. The next day the talks failed. According to the Kuwaitis, they had refused to comply with Iraq's demands to write off the $12–14 billion Iraq had received from Kuwait during the Iran-Iraq War [*q.v.*], relinquish some of the Kuwaiti territory along the Iraqi border, and lease its Bubiyan and Warba Islands to Baghdad. According to the Iraqis, they had been unable to see any sign of willingness on the part of Kuwait to repair the economic damage it had inflicted on Iraq by depressing oil prices.

Iraqi invasion of Kuwait and its aftermath:

2 August 1990: At 2 a.m. local time

Iraqi forces invaded Kuwait and occupied it. The ruler, Shaikh Jaber III al-Sabah [*q.v.*], and other members of the royal family fled to Saudi Arabia. The UN Security Council passed Resolution 660 by 14 votes to none, condemning Iraqi aggression against Kuwait and demanding immediate withdrawal. The United States, Britain, and France froze Iraqi and Kuwaiti assets. The Soviet Union halted arms deliveries to Iraq.

3 August: The Arab League [*q.v.*] foreign ministers condemned Iraq's action by 14 votes to one, with five abstentions and one walk-out.

6 August: The UN Security Council passed Resolution 661 by 13 votes to none, imposed mandatory sanctions and an embargo on Iraq and occupied Kuwait. Following a request by Saudi King Fahd bin Abdul Aziz [*q.v.*] for the United States to bolster his country's defenses, U.S. President George Bush ordered fighter aircraft and troops to leave for Saudi Arabia.

8 August: Baghdad annexed Kuwait.

9 August: King Fahd condemned Iraq's invasion of Kuwait.

12 August: Iraqi President Saddam Hussein [*q.v.*] offered a peace initiative that involved the withdrawal of Israel from the Occupied Arab Territories [*q.v.*] in "Palestine, Syria and Lebanon," and the formulation of arrangements for the "situation in Kuwait" in line with the UN resolutions.

2 October: Amnesty International, a London-based human rights organization, published a report portraying widespread arrests, torture, and summary executions in Kuwait by the occupying Iraqi forces.

8 November: Bush ordered a doubling of U.S. troops in the Gulf to 400,000.

15 November: Saddam Hussein proposed talks between Iraq and Saudi Arabia on regional problems as well as between Iraq and the United States on wider issues. There was no response from Riyadh or Washington.

19 November: Iraq mobilized an additional 250,000 troops, with 100,000 to be sent to Kuwait immediately.

27 November: Testimonies of experts before the U.S. Senate Armed Services Committee showed a large majority favoring the economic option over the military option in forcing Iraq out of Kuwait.

29 November: The UN Security Council adopted Resolution 678 by 12 votes to two (Cuba and Yemen), with one abstention (China), authorizing "all necessary means" to implement the earlier resolutions in order "to restore international peace and security in the area," unless Iraq fully implemented these resolutions before 15 January 1991.

9 January 1991: Talks in Geneva between Tariq Aziz [*q.v.*], Iraq's foreign minister, and James Baker, U.S. Secretary of State, to resolve the crisis failed.

12 January: The U.S. Senate authorized President Bush by 53 votes to 47 to use the armed forces pursuant to UN Security Council Resolution 678; the House of Representatives did likewise by 250 votes to 183.

14 January: Iraqi parliament unanimously decided to go to war rather than withdraw from Kuwait, and empowered Saddam Hussein to conduct it.

OPPOSING FORCES (at the start):
Iraq: Baghdad had 545,000 troops in Kuwait and southern Iraq, equipped with 4,200 tanks and 150 combat hel-

icopters, supported by 550 combat-ready warplanes.

U.S.-led coalition: Coalition of the United States and 28 other UN members: Argentina (naval); Australia (naval); Bahrain (ground, air); Bangladesh (ground); Belgium (air—in Turkey, naval); Canada (air, naval); Czechoslovakia (ground); Denmark (naval); Kuwait; Egypt (ground); France (ground, air, naval); Germany (air—in Turkey); Greece (naval); Italy (air, naval); Morocco (ground); the Netherlands (naval); New Zealand (air); Niger (ground); Norway (naval); Oman (ground, air); Pakistan (ground, naval); Qatar (ground, air); Saudi Arabia (ground, air, naval); Senegal (ground); Spain (naval); Syria (ground); United Arab Emirates (ground, air); United Kingdom (ground, air, naval). Of the 425,000 U.S. troops, 250,000 were army troops; 75,000 marines; 60,000 naval soldiers; and 45,000 air force personnel. They were equipped with 2,200 tanks, 500 combat helicopters, and 1500 warplanes. By the end of the war the number of troops from the U.S., the United Kingdom, and France rose to 697,000, 52,000, and 25,000 respectively. The 12 North Atlantic Treaty Organization members involved had deployed 107 warships in the Gulf, the northern Arabian Sea, the Gulf of Oman, the Red Sea, and the eastern Mediterranean, with most of them enforcing the UN embargo. The Pentagon's naval personnel were armed with 700-plus nuclear weapons on warships and submarines. The Arab and Muslim troops totaled 220,000. They were under the command of Prince Khalid bin Sultan of Saudi Arabia, and were equipped with 1,200 tanks, 150 combat helicopters, and 350 warplanes. The overall commander of the coalition was General Norman Schwarzkopf of the U.S. Army. (The combined figures at the end of the war were: 700,000 troops equipped with 4,000 tanks and 2,900 warplanes and helicopters.)

EVENTS:

Air campaign (Operation Desert Storm) 16 January to 24 February:

16–23 January: The air campaign of the U.S.-led coalition started at 23:30 GMT on 16 January (02:30 local time on 17 January) with aerial bombing and the firing of cruise missiles from U.S. warships. On 18 January Iraq fired 12 Scud ground-to ground missiles at Tel Aviv [*q.v.*] and Haifa [*q.v.*] in Israel, and four days later three more Iraqi Scuds landed in Tel Aviv. Coalition air sorties in the first week totaled 12,000 (half of which were combat sorties), and cruise missile firings numbered 216.

24–30 January: The coalition increased the number of daily air sorties to 3,000.

31 January–6 February: On 3 February the number of coalition air missions reached a total of 41,000, with the U.S. share at 87 percent. Iraq broke diplomatic ties with the United States, Britain, France, Canada, Italy, Egypt, and Saudi Arabia.

7–13 February: During the fourth week the coalition concentrated on destroying Iraq's transport infrastructure of bridges and roads.

14–20 February: On 15 February Iraq agreed to deal with UN Security Council Resolution 660 if the coalition forces left the region, if Israel withdrew from the Occupied Arab Territories, and if the nationalist and

Islamic forces of Kuwait were allowed to settle the country's future. Moscow saw this as opening up a new stage in the ongoing conflict, but Kuwait, Saudi Arabia, and Egypt rejected it. Bush called on the Iraqi people and military to remove Saddam Hussein from office, and then comply with the UN resolutions. The five-week total of coalition air sorties reached 86,000.

21–24 February: On 21 February Iraq welcomed the Soviet Union's eight-point peace plan, including Iraq's statement of intent to withdraw from Kuwait; a cease-fire; the actual evacuation; the abrogation of the UN sanctions once two-thirds of the Iraqi force had left Kuwait, and then the rest of the UN resolutions once all Iraqi troops had departed; and the monitoring of the cease-fire by a UN force. Bush rejected the plan, and offered a list of 12 conditions, including total Iraqi withdrawal within a week, to be accepted by 17:30 GMT on 23 February. At 12:00 GMT on 23 February Iraq said that, following its acceptance of the Soviet peace plan, it had decided to withdraw from Kuwait immediately and unconditionally. At 16:30 GMT the UN Security Council began a closed-door session, with the Western powers declaring that they were not interested in bridging the gap between the Soviet plan and the U.S. terms. At 18:00 GMT Bush ordered General Schwarzkopf to expel the Iraqis from Kuwait. By then retreating Iraqis had begun to set Kuwaiti oil wells ablaze.

Ground campaign (Operation Desert Saber) 24–28 February:

At 01:00 on 24 February the coalition launched its ground offensive, with ground troops advancing on two axes. The next day at 21:30 GMT the Soviet Union presented a new peace plan, and an hour later Iraq accepted it. Baghdad ordered a withdrawal from Kuwait as part of its compliance with Security Council Resolution 660. On 26 February at 11:50 the Iraqi forces were out of Kuwait City. U.S. troops blocked all exits for the Iraqi forces in the Kuwaiti theatre of war. The killing of the retreating Iraqi soldiers continued until a cease-fire 40 hours later. On 27 February at 05:30 GMT Iraq said that it had completed its evacuation of Kuwait. By then some 640 Kuwaiti oil wells were ablaze. The next day at 02:00 GMT Bush ordered a truce if Iraq put down its arms. At 04:40 GMT Iraq complied, and a temporary cease-fire went into effect at 05:00 GMT, thus ending 167 days of prewar crisis and 42 days of warfare.

The final total of the coalition's air sorties reached 106,000. They dropped 141,000 tonnes of explosives, equivalent to seven nuclear bombs dropped on the Japanese city of Hiroshima in 1945, and hit 700 targets, many of them repeatedly. The number of cruise missiles fired was 325.

HUMAN LOSSES: The U.S. Defense Intelligence Agency issued an estimate of 100,000 Iraqi deaths with an error factor of 50 percent. According to Iraq's deputy premier, Sadoun Hamadi, in the first 26 days of the war the coalition bombing (in 65,000 air sorties) had killed 20,000 Iraqis. Therefore, the remaining 41,000 sorties probably killed another 12,600 people. During the ground campaign, involving attacks on 12 retreating Iraqi divisions (180,000 troops), the fatalities were estimated at 25,000 to

30,000. The total estimated dead were therefore 57,600 to 62,600. Other estimates put this figure higher—at 100,000. Iraq did not release its official statistics.

Of the 376 Coalition deaths, the United States sustained 266 (including 125 due to the accidents during the seven-month field training prior to the war), and Britain 29. An estimated 2,000 to 5,000 Kuwaitis, mostly civilians, died.

WEAPONS LOSSES: Iraq, 30 warplanes; Coalition, 21 warplanes

Cost: Coalition total, $82 billion—Japan, $13 billion; Kuwait $22 billion; Saudi Arabia, $29 billion; and the United States, $18 billion. Saudi Arabia put its indirect costs at $22 billion. No official figures were released by Iraq. According to Sadoun Hamadi, the damage to Iraq's infrastructure during the first 26 days of war was $200 billion. Other estimates also put the total damage to Iraq at $200 billion.

AFTER THE TRUCE: UN Security Council Resolution 687 required Iraq to implement a U.N.-monitored program of disarming itself of weapons of mass destruction and intermediate and long-range ground-to-ground missiles before UN sanctions against it could be lifted. *See also* Operation Desert Fox.

Gulf War III (2003): *war between Iraq and the U.S.-led alliance*

BACKGROUND: (May 1991–December 1998) During this period the UN Special Commission (UNSCOM) [*q.v.*], charged with disarming Iraq of weapons of mass destruction, disarmed it of 90 to 95 percent of its proscribed arms. By mid-June 1998 Iraq claimed to have disarmed fully, and demanded that the UN economic

sanctions be lifted as specified in Paragraphs 20 and 21 of the UN Security Council Resolution 687. Richard Butler, head of UNSCOM, disagreed. Tension mounted between the U.S. administration of President Bill Clinton and Iraq. To enable Washington to mount its Operation Desert Fox [*q.v.*] in coordination with the United Kingdom against the regime of Iraqi President Saddam Hussein [*q.v.*] as a penalty for its failure to provide unhindered, unconditional access to UN inspectors to visit any sites they wished, Butler withdrew his inspectors from Iraq. At the Security Council, China, France, and Russia condemned the U.S.-U.K. action.

December 1998–November 2003: The breach among the permanent five members of the Security Council was so profound that it took a year before the Council adopted a new resolution on the subject—1284—with China, France, and Russia abstaining. Iraq did not accept this resolution. Starting in August 2000, when several regional countries resumed air flights to Baghdad [*q.v.*], the UN sanctions began to crumble, with Syria reopening its oil pipeline with Iraq. George W. Bush, who became U.S. president in January 2001, continued the hardline policy of his predecessor. Following the terrorist attacks on America in September 2001, commonly denoted as 9/11, he stiffened further his stance toward Iraq even though no evidence turned up to support his administration's early speculation that Saddam Hussein was in cahoots with al-Qaida [*q.v.*] and Osama bin Laden [*q.v.*] in perpetrating 9/11.

But when, having overthrown the Taliban regime in Afghanistan and put bin Laden on the run, Bush looked for the next target in his global war on terror, Iraq reappeared as a prime candidate in the spring of 2002. Washington ratcheted up its anti-Saddam rhetoric after the Labor Day holiday in September, claiming that the Iraqi president had restarted his program of making nuclear weapons, and asserting that the Iraqis had made an unsuccessful attempt to buy 500 tons of uranium oxide from Niger in 2000 and had obtained aluminum tubing for centrifuges to enrich uranium. (Later both these claims would be proved false, with the International Atomic Energy Agency [IAEA] declaring the Niger documents to be forgeries.) These statements proved highly effective in persuading the U.S. Congress to give Bush war powers by a comfortable majority in October, even though on 16 September Iraq had agreed to the return of the inspectors of the UN Monitoring, Verification and Inspection Commission (UNMOVIC) [q.v.] headed by Hans Blix, a former Swedish foreign minister and director-general of the LAEA, and Muhammad El Baradei, the Egyptian head of the IAEA. Both Bush and British Prime Minister Tony Blair began building up a military presence in the Gulf [q.v.], with Kuwait providing its territory for the posting of American and British troops, and Qatar allowing the U.S. Central Command (Centcom) to set up its regional headquarters at al-Sayliya near Doha [q.v.]. Against this background the UN Security Council adopted Resolution 1441 unanimously on 8 November, with France and Russia asserting, rightly, that the resolution did not authorize automatic

military action against Iraq if the Baghdad government failed to meet its requirements. It specified the most intrusive inspection regime ever devised. After some equivocation, Saddam Hussein accepted the resolution.

UN inspections started on 27 November. As specified in Resolution 1441, Iraq submitted a 12,000-page document detailing its programs of weapons of mass destruction and missiles. In their reports to the Security Council on 19 December, Blix and Baradei said that Iraq had provided prompt access to the 150 sites their teams had visited. The aluminum tubing that America and Britain had alluded to was for permissible Iraqi rockets and not for the proscribed nuclear weapons. By 18 January 2003, the UN teams had visited all 11 sites mentioned by Bush and Blair as the premises used by Iraq in its revived program of weapons of mass destruction, and found no evidence to that effect. On 19–20 January Iraq signed a 10-point agreement with Blix and Baradei promising further cooperation. Yet Bush kept saying that Saddam must disarm, and, in the event of his refusal, the U.S.-led coalition would force him to do so and free the Iraqi people. He was aware that 52 percent of Americans would believe the White House if it asserted that it had evidence of proscribed weapons program by Baghdad, even if UN inspectors found nothing. At the same time, the Special Forces of America and Britain began infiltrating Iraq to facilitate the invasion of the country by the Anglo-American troops.

In their 27 January report, covering two months and 300 inspections (of which about a third concerned the nuclear program) of 230 sites (out of a total of 700) by a staff of 260 drawn from 60 countries, Blix and Baradei reported to the Security Council that on the whole Iraq had cooperated well, giving their teams prompt access to all sites. Baradei said that his inspectors had visited presidential compounds and private residences but had discovered no evidence that Iraq has revived its nuclear weapons program since its elimination in the 1990s.

By contrast, in his presentation to the Security Council on 5 February U.S. Secretary of State Colin Powell claimed that (1) there were up to two dozen al-Qaida operatives in Iraq, the most important being Abu Mussab Zarqawi [q.v.]; (2) the Ansar-e Islam operated a chemical poison factory in an enclave of Iraqi Kurdistan [q.v.]; (3) a missile brigade operating from outside Baghdad was dispersing proscribed rockets in the country; (4) Iraq possessed about 18 mobile biological weapons laboratories; (5) Baghdad had a model of an unmanned drone capable of spraying chemical or germ weapons within a radius of 550 miles; and (6) Iraq moved contraband, with soldiers relocating munitions just before inspectors arrived. Finally, Powell referred to Tony Blair's 19-page dossier, "Iraq: Its Infrastructure of Concealment, Deception, and Intimidation," posted on his official website on 3 February, as a fine piece of evidence.

Critics argued that the presence of al-Qaida operatives in Iraq did not prove the government's involvement. Such operatives lived not only in other Arab [q.v.] and Muslim [q.v.] countries but also in many Western states. The visiting Western journalists found

that the Ansar-e Islam's poison factory was nothing but a derelict dump. Following the overthrow of Saddam Hussein's regime, the Anglo-American troops failed to find the alleged Iraqi missile brigade or the proscribed missiles. Four days before the start of the Anglo-American invasion of Iraq on 20 March 2003, Iraq handed over to UNMOVIC videos of mobile biological laboratories, arguing that the videos showed that Iraq did not violate UN resolutions. When checked out by the UN inspectors, Iraq's single unmanned drone turned out to be a machine rusting on an airfield north of Baghdad. Likewise, when verified on the ground, Powell's interpretation of the satellite images of trucks moving banned parts turned out to be false. Equally damaging was the discovery made by a British researcher at Cambridge University that large chunks of what Blair had tried to pass of as official U.K. intelligence were lifted verbatim from old academic journals and magazines posted on the Internet. Yet 70 percent in America agreed with Powell that Iraq was being deceptive.

Powell's presentation marked the end of the Bush administration's support of continued UN inspections. It prepared the ground for military action, despite Blix's report on 14 February that the 300 biological and chemical samples examined by UN-MOVIC were consistent with Iraq's declarations, and that the inspections were bridging the gap in the United Nations's knowledge that arose between December 1998 and November 2002. It ignored rising public opposition to war both in America and Europe.

On 15 February, 15 to 20 million people in 60 countries marched in antiwar protest in 600 towns and cities, a quarter of them in America. The marches in London (1.5 million strong), Rome (over 2 million), and Barcelona (over 1 million) were the largest ever. Overall, more than 70 percent in Britain, Italy, and Spain opposed the war. Yet their governments continued to back Bush in his belligerent stance.

Indeed, Spain was one of the three sponsors of the draft resolution—the others being America and Britain—presented to the Security Council on 24 February. It stated that Iraq had failed to comply with and cooperate fully in the implementation of Resolution 1441, and must therefore face "serious consequences." Disagreeing with this document, France, Russia, and Germany (as a non-permanent member of the Security Council) issued a memorandum saying that a verifiable disarmament could be reached through the implementation of a clear program of action by the inspection agencies, with each task clearly defined; reinforced inspections; and a timeline for inspections and assessment, with the chief inspectors reporting every three weeks. This was rejected by the U.S.-U.K.-Spain trio.

In America, opposition to war rose from 18 percent at the end of January to 37 percent a month later, almost equal to the support for it.

On 6 March Blix declared that Iraq was involved in "real and very fine disarmament" and that its cooperation had been "pro-active." It had begun taking inspectors to the sites where it said it unilaterally destroyed biological weapons.

At the Security Council the U.S.-U.K.-Spanish draft attracted one more vote, while five members— China, France, Germany, Russia, and Syria—opposed it. Of the remaining six, Pakistan and Guinea indicated they would abstain while a top official of Cameroon said that his country and France were "old friends." Given this, there was no prospect of the Anglo-American alliance getting its draft resolution adopted by the Council. Yet so strongly opposed were France and Russia to a war on Iraq that they individually threatened to veto the resolution if passed. When Angola, Cameroon, Chile, Guinea, Mexico, and Pakistan proposed giving Iraq 45 days to disarm (versus France's 120 days), the U.S. rejected the proposal summarily.

In the United States, the anti-Saddam rhetoric reached a point where 42 percent believed that he was "personally" responsible for 9/11, and 55 percent believed that he gave direct support to al-Qaida.

On 14 March, when Bush, Blair, and Spanish Prime Minister Jose Maria Aznar decided to meet on the Portuguese Island of St. Azores, Iraq gave UNMOVIC a 20-page document detailing the destruction of 3.9 tons of VX nerve agent. The next day UN Secretary-General Kofi Annan said he believed war without the second resolution by the Security Council would break international law, meaning a violation of the UN Charter. Following the Bush-Blair-Aznar meeting on 16 March, when they decided to abandon their draft resolution at the Security Council, Bush gave Saddam Hussein and his sons— Uday and Qusay [q.v.]—48 hours to leave

Iraq, failing which Washington would mount military operations. Saddam rejected the ultimatum. On 18 March the House of Commons in London passed a motion by 412 to 149 votes—with the opposition Conservatives voting with most of the governing Labor Party members—stating that "the U.K. must uphold the UN's authority as set out in [Resolution] 1441 and many resolutions preceding it, and therefore supports the decision that the U.K. should use all means to disarm Iraq."

OPPOSING FORCES:

Iraq: Baghdad had 389,000 troops, including 82,000 in the Republican Guard and 20,000 in the Special Republican Guard, equipped with 2,200–2,600 tanks and 100 combat helicopters, backed by 300 combat aircraft, only half of which were serviceable. Its active paramilitary force included 5,000 armed personnel of the Special Security Organization, 18,000 members of the *Fedayeen* (Arabic: *Self-sacrificers*) Saddam, and 6,000 non-Iraqi Arab volunteers.

U.S.-led coalition: A nominal coalition of 48 countries, with only five contributing combat troops—America (255,000), Australia (2000), Britain (45,000), Czech Republic (200), Poland (200), and Slovakia (200)—the rest either merely expressing support for Washington's position or allowing U.S. military aircraft passage through their air spaces. The Anglo-American forces were equipped with 920 tanks, 600 warplanes, 300 combat helicopters, and 50 unmanned aerial vehicles. The U.S. navy deployed five aircraft-carrier battle groups, and the U.K. navy one.

EVENTS:

20–26 March (Week 1): The Pentagon started its Operation Iraqi Freedom [*q.v.*] on 20 March at 02:33 GMT (05:33 Iraqi time) with four guided bunker-busting bombs, released by Stealth bombers, to strike the Republican Presidential Palace Complex in Baghdad where Saddam Hussein and his two sons were suspected of holding a meeting. Cruise missiles hit surrounding targets while Tomahawk missiles struck targets around Baghdad. At 05:30 GMT the Iraqi president appeared on television to declare that "Iraq will carry out jihad [*q.v.*] against the invaders with the heroic army in the vanguard of Iraq of civilization, history, and belief…Iraq will be victorious." Four hours later, Group Captain Al Lockwood, spokesman for the British forces in the Gulf said, "If I was a betting man, hopefully, we'll be in Baghdad in the next three or four days." At the Rumeila oil field west of Basra [*q.v.*], Iraqis set oil wells ablaze. At night, when U.S. Navy Seals and Royal Marine commandos under British command tried to capture oil and gas platforms in the Fao Peninsula, they encountered resistance.

Next morning, the Centcom mounted a four-pronged ground attack on Iraq from Kuwait, with the U.S. Third Infantry Division heading north toward Baghdad. American and British Special Forces, infiltrating Iraq from Jordan *[q.v.]*, claimed the capture of Iraq's H2 and H3 airfields in the western desert. The Centcom's claim of the capture of Umm Qasr (pop. 45,000) port was disputed, rightly, by Al-Jazeera TV. The Centcom's swift and surgical strikes on public buildings and presidential compounds in Baghdad, combined with emails and mobile phone calls to Iraqi generals to defect, failed to bring about the predicted collapse of the regime.

At 17:20 GMT (20:20 Iraqi Time) the Centcom unleashed its "shock and awe" strategy, with a series of staggering explosions, most of them in Baghdad's Republican Presidential Palace Complex, in an unprecedentedly murderous fireworks display.

Later the Centcom hit targets in Mosul [*q.v.*] and Kirkuk [*q.v.*]. In Kurdistan, the Kurdistan Democratic Party [*q.v.*] and the Patriotic Union of Kurdistan [*q.v.*] agreed to put their 35,000 militia, called *peshmargas* (Kurdish: *those prepared to die*) under the Centcom command.

On 20-21 March, the Centcom undertook 1,000 combat missions and discharged 600 cruise missiles.

On 22 March, the Iraqi TV showed Saddam Hussein meeting senior advisers. The Iraqi military set fire to oil-filled trenches around Baghdad to create smoke to obscure targets from the U.S. pilots dropping dumb bombs. The Centcom claim of the capture of Nasiriya (pop. 750,000), was disputed, rightly, by Al-Jazeera TV. The Anglo-American forces approached Basra. The Pentagon sources said that the Special Activities Division of Central Intelligence Agency's (CIA) might be involved in talks between the U.S. and the Republican Guard generals. The total of the cruise missiles to hit Iraq reached 1,000.

In America, Bush's approval rating rose from 51 percent 10 days previously to 70 percent, while disapproval points fell from 42 to 27. A poll in Britain showed 56 percent saying that America and Britain were "right" to go to war, against 36 percent saying

"wrong."

On 23 March the Centcom's claim of the capture of Zubair naval base remained unverified. Iraq claimed that 77 civilians had died in the fighting in Basra. As U.S. troops approached Najaf [*q.v.*] and Karbala [*q.v.*] they met stiff resistance. Nightly bombing of Baghdad continued.

On 24 March there were reports of resistance to the invading forces in Zubair. The next day the Centcom claimed control of all of the Rumeila oil field. But its claim of a civilian uprising in Basra was contradicted by the images shown by Al-Jazeera's reporter inside the city, which was now besieged. The Iraqi resistance in Nasiriya continued. A fierce sandstorm hit Baghdad.

There were large antiwar protest marches in Amman [*q.v.*], Beirut [*q.v.*], and Damascus [*q.v.*].

On 26 March a sandstorm and Iraqi resistance slowed down the American advance. The Centcom's final capture of Umm Qasr was confirmed by Al-Jazeera TV. On the outskirts of Baghdad, the Anglo-American Special Forces pointed targets with lasers to guide bombs. U.S. paratroopers arrived at Bashur air strip in Kurdistan to open a front in the north.

In the first week of its invasion, the Centcom mounted 5,700 air sorties, dropped 2,000 guided bombs, and fired 500 Tomahawks missiles.

27 March–2 April (Week 2): On 27 March U.S. troops began consolidating their positions outside Karbala. Across the Karbala Gap, however, they faced 6,000 Iraqi regular army and Republican Guard soldiers. Small bands of Iraqi irregulars harassed U.S. supply lines. There were big explosions in central Baghdad. Two bunker-busting bombs destroyed the communications tower.

On 29 March, there were world-wide protest demonstrations against the war, including one in Port Said, Egypt, organized by the ruling National Democratic Party [*q.v.*].

On 30 March, there was fierce fighting between the two warring sides in Najaf. In Nasiriya the Americans started building an extra bridge over the Euphrates [*q.v.*] to help unclog the supply lines to the forces northwards. U.S. troops captured the airfield near Karbala after an intense combat. The Centcom's round-the-clock bombardment of Baghdad continued.

On 31 March, the British Marines captured the Abu Qassib suburb of Basra after a 15-hour battle. In Nasiriya U.S. Marines engaged in street fighting in Nasiriya. The next day, on reaching Kut, they fought the units of the Iraqi Republican Guard, regular army, and Fedayeen Saddam. U.S. soldiers besieged Najaf. Fighting broke out in Hillah. There was heavy bombing of Baghdad with low-flying aircraft swooping over.

On 2 April, American troops encircled Karbala.

At the end of two weeks, the Centcom had flown 18,000 air sorties, launched 725 Tomahawk missiles, discharged 12,000 precision-guided munitions, and dropped 50 cluster bombs as well as several phosphorous bombs in Nasiriya. It had seized 600 of the 1,000 oil wells in southern and central Iraq.

3–9 April (Week 3): On 3 April the Kurdish peshmargas attacked the Iraqi front lines in a big way. The Centcom's black-out bombs, which showered power cables with graphite filament

and short-circuited electric grids, plunged Baghdad into darkness. U.S. troops seized Furat near Saddam International Airport, located six miles from Baghdad's city boundary. The capital was (in theory) safeguarded by 20,000 soldiers of the Special Republican Guard, whose commanders were unable to communicate with their Central Command, and an unknown number of the Fedayeen Saddam and foreign volunteers.

The following day, a British Special Forces unit staged a lightning raid on an official site inside Basra and killed Gen. Ali Hassan al-Majid, commander of the southern Iraqi forces, and his bodyguards. After a day's combat, the U.S. troops captured Saddam International Airport. Central Baghdad was quiet, with little evidence of troops, road blocks, or other defenses. Most of the capital was without power or water after another night of bombing.

On 5 April, an armored column of 30 U.S. tanks went around in an arc in the southwest of Baghdad, adjacent to the Saddam Airport. Iraqi TV showed Saddam Hussein attending a meeting with his sons, top aides, and military commanders. The black-uniformed Fedayeen Saddam appeared on the streets for the first time.

On 6 April, in a three-pronged attack, the British troops, who had so far fired inter alia 2,000-plus cluster munitions around Basra, entered the city center while the Americans seized Karbala's central district. The 7,000 American soldiers stationed at the Saddam Airport repulsed an Iraqi counterattack.

The next day there was looting in Basra, and a large statue of Saddam

Hussein was pulled down in Karbala. In Baghdad, with an advance of special mine-clearing tanks forging a path through 400 yards/366 meters of minefields, a column of 70 U.S. tanks and 60 fighting vehicles, with air cover, captured the district housing government offices and the Parade Ground and Victory Arches. American soldiers raided the New Presidential Palace, which contained Saddam Hussein's official residence.

On 8 April at 12:00 GMT (15:00 Iraqi Time), the Centcom directed two satellite guided bombs and two bunker-busting bombs at a restaurant in Mansour district following an intelligence tip-off that Saddam Hussein and his two sons and senior aides were there. The bombs left a 60-ft./20-meter crater and 14 ordinary citizens dead. Separately, U.S. attacks killed Tariq Ayub, a producer of Al-Jazeera TV in his office in Baghdad, and two news agency photographers based at Palestine Hotel. Iraqi TV went off the air. That day all Republican Guard and Special Republican Guard soldiers melted away, reportedly as a result of a secret deal negotiated by top CIA officials between the Centcom and the Republican Guard General Command, which had lost contact with the Central Command due to the disruption of the Iraqi communications system caused by the Pentagon. It had also realized the impossibility of defending Baghdad without air cover. Its deal with the CIA required the generals to order their ranks to throw away their uniforms and go home in return for the Centcom's assurance that the deserters would not be chased and that the Republican Guard commanders would

be flown out of Iraq. This left Special Republican Guard commanders no option but to follow suit. As a result, the number of Iraqi prisoners of war remained unchanged—at 8,302. When the regular army troops and Fedayeen Saddam sniped at the American troops from building tops, they were targeted by the Centcom's attack aircraft.

On 9 April celebrating crowds in Baghdad danced, looted, and defaced the ubiquitous images of Saddam Hussein. The 20-ft./6-meter bronze statue of Saddam at the Fardaus Square in downtown Baghdad was pulled down with the help of a U.S. Marine tank. The Centcom declared the end of the regime of Saddam Hussein, who was to be sighted later that day in the streets of the northern neighborhood of Adhimiya.

During the past three weeks the Centcom staged 30,000 air sorties, dropped 30,000 bombs, and discharged 750 cruise missiles.

10–16 April (Week 4): On 10 April Baghdad descended into anarchy, as underprivileged Shia [q.v.] mobs resorted to arson and looting. With the exception of the ministries of oil and the interior, heavily guarded by U.S. troops, all ministries were ransacked and burnt. In the north, Kurdish peshmargas entered Kirkuk—after the Iraqi troops abandoned the city following heavy U.S. air raids. Tikrit, the home town of Saddam Hussein, was bombed heavily, with the U.S. Special Forces guiding the bombing. At Diwaniva there was an eight-hour firefight as the Iraqis attacked U.S. supply lines, and there was intense combat in Hillah between the American troops and the Fedayeen Saddam. Umm

Qasr was named as the base of the U.S. Office for Reconstruction and Humanitarian Assistance (ORHA) to be headed by retired U.S. general Jay Rayner. In Paris, President Chirac said, "France, like all democracies, rejoices [in the fall of Saddam]."

On 11 April, the Kurdish peshmargas and U.S. Special Forces entered Mosul after signs of Iraqi withdrawal. There was celebration as well as looting. The next day there was fighting between Kurds [q.v.] and Arabs in Mosul, which was two-thirds Arab. In central Baghdad, Iraq's largest Museum of Antiquities, with its unique collection of relics from the Mesopotamian civilization, was looted, and many ancient artifacts were destroyed or stolen.

On 13 April U.S. soldiers entered Tikrit, which looked deserted. But once inside they faced a fierce attack by Iraqi tanks. The Pentagon claimed that, of the 60 zones in which the Centcom had divided Baghdad, only 15 were not under its control, and whatever resistance persisted was mainly from the non-Iraqi foreign volunteers.

On 14 April the Bush administration put a $200,000 bounty on Saddam's head. The next day Centcom conceded that it controlled only the western part of Tikrit, with its eastern part on the other side of the Tigris still under pro-Saddam forces. A meeting of 80 Iraqi delegates held at Talil air base near Nasiriya, opened by Jay Garner, head of the ORHA, and chaired by Zalmay Khalilzad, a personal envoy of President Bush, was attended by the two main Kurdish parties but boycotted by the Supreme Assembly of Islamic Revolution in Iraq [q.v.]. In nearby Nasiriya, 20,000

Shias demonstrated against the U.S. and for an Islamic Iraq, shouting "No to America, No to Saddam."

On 16 April 40 U.S. Marines raided the home of British-trained Dr. Rihad Taha, the biologist wife of General Amr Muhammad Rashid, former oil minister, but failed to find evidence of Iraq's alleged weapons of mass destruction.

In the past four weeks, the Centcom mounted 37,000 air sorties, launched 23,000 precision-guided missiles, fired 750 cruise missiles, and dropped 1,566 cluster bombs (1,500 by the U.S. and the rest by Britain).

For all practical purposes the Gulf War III ended on 16 April although it was not until 1 May that President Bush announced a formal end to the hostilities against Iraq.

HUMAN LOSSES UP TO 3 APRIL 2003: Iraq: civilians 1,254, soldiers 3,650; U.K.: soldiers 31; U.S.: soldiers 119.

HUMAN LOSSES UP TO 15 DECEMBER 2011: 4,487 U.S. soldiers. A conservative estimate of the dead Iraqis was put at 105,000. In 2006, the London-based general medical journal Lancet published an estimate of 654,965 excess Iraqi deaths related to the war, with 601,027 caused by violence.

COST: $30 billion for the first 28 days, with Britain bearing about 8 percent of the total. The total cost of the eight years and nine months' long war to the U.S. treasury was $802 billion.

AFTERMATH: A poll of Iraqis in 2009 by the British Broadcasting Corporation, ABC News (America), and NHK (Japan) showed that 56 percent thought that the invasion was wrong. On 31 August 2010, U.S. President Barack Obama announced the end of the Pentagon's combat missions in Iraq. Almost 1.5 million Americans served in the war. Of those military personnel who served in Iraq, 4,487 were killed, and about 32,000 were injured. The number of Iraqis killed varied from 106,147 to several hundreds of thousands. In 2009, the Pentagon had 3.4 million pieces of equipment at 357 bases in Iraq. In August 2010 the respective figures were down to 1.2 million and 94.

Gush Emunim (Hebrew: *Bloc of the Faithful*): *Israeli political-religious movement* Founded in early 1974, the Gush Emunim grew out of a ginger group within the National Religious Party (NRP) [*q.v.*], formed after the 1967 Six-Day War [*q.v.*] to advocate the Jewish settlement of the Occupied Arab Territories [*q.v.*]. In 1970 it captured popular attention by establishing an unauthorized settlement at Kiryat Arba near Hebron [*q.v.*]. The presence of the NRP inside the cabinet, and the fact that the Labor-dominated [*q.v.*] government itself had initiated a program of colonization within six months of the 1967 War, meant that no action was taken against the settlers. The assumption of power by the Likud [*q.v.*]-led coalition in May 1977 boosted the morale of the Gush, whose views on historical Jewish claims on Judea [*q.v.*] and Samaria [*q.v.*] had been endorsed by the powerful Ashkenazim [*q.v.*] Rabbinical Council.

Within three years of the start of the Likud administration, the Gush had established 20 illegal colonies on the West Bank [*q.v.*]. The plans of Gush extremists—known as "the Jewish Underground"—to blow up the Dome of the Rock [*q.v.*] and al-Aqsa Mosque in order to trigger a fresh war between Israel and the Arabs [*q.v.*] were diverted by their involvement in the attacks on two Palestinian mayors in June 1980 in retaliation for the death of six Jewish militants in Hebron in May. When the final phase of the Israeli evacuation of Sinai [*q.v.*], including Yamit settlement, in April 1982 aroused little public protest, Gush militants postponed their plan to demolish the Dome of the Rock and al-Aqsa Mosque.

In July 1983 the stabbing of a Jewish settler in Hebron led to retribution by the Jewish settlers of Kiryat Arba. This in turn led to attacks on Israeli buses in early 1984. Gush extremists responded by planting bombs on five Arab buses, which were defused. The arrest in April 1984 of Gush militants revealed their plans against Muslim [*q.v.*] shrines, which were condemned by secular and religious authorities.

It was only after the Palestinian intifada [*q.v.*] had gathered momentum in the late 1980s that the Gush's influence began to wane, after reaching a peak of 50,000 members. It opposed the Oslo Accord [*q.v.*] of September 1993. Its militants applauded the murder of 29 Palestinians who were praying at Hebron's Ibrahimi Mosque (called Tomb of the Patriarchs by the Jews [*q.v.*]) in February 1994 by a Kiryat Arba resident, Baruch Goldstein—an acolyte of Kiryat Arba-based Moshe Levinger, the best known leader of the Gush Emunim. *See also* Jewish fundamentalism.

ha: (Hebrew: *the*) Used as a prefix, the definite article in Hebrew is often joined in European languages to the noun by a hyphen, or is written with no intervening space, for instance Ha-Poale or HaPoale.

Habash, George (1925–2008): *Palestinian leader* Born into a Greek Orthodox [*q.v.*] family in Lydda (later Lod), Habash moved to Amman [*q.v.*] with his parents after the Palestine War (1948–49) [*q.v.*]. He graduated in medicine from the American University in Beirut (AUB) [*q.v.*]. While at the AUB, he cofounded the Arab Nationalist Movement (ANM) [*q.v.*] in 1952 soon after the anti-royalist coup by Arab nationalist officers in Egypt. Under his leadership the ANM's Palestinian members formed a "Preparatory Committee for Unified Palestinian Action" in early 1966. Overall, though, Habash put his faith in Egyptian President Gamal Abdul Nasser [*q.v.*] as the leader who would liberate Palestine [*q.v.*] through a conventional war with Israel. But the Arab defeat in the 1967 Six-Day War [*q.v.*] destroyed this scenario.

He founded the Popular Front for the Liberation of Palestine (PFLP) [*q.v.*], which affiliated with the Palestine Liberation Organization (PLO) [*q.v.*]. Believing that hijacking an airliner was more effective in drawing world attention to the plight of Palestinians than killing Israelis, he started organizing hijacks—the first target being an Israeli aircraft at Athens airport in December 1968. His conversion to Marxism-Leninism led him to add international Zionism [*q.v.*], world imperialism, and Arab reaction to Israel as the enemies. He used the hijacking of three Western airliners on 9 September 1970 to trigger a clash between Palestinian commandos and King Hussein of Jordan [*q.v.*], which escalated into large-scale fighting in which the Palestinians suffered a defeat. The expulsion of all the Palestinian parties from Amman followed.

He relocated the PFLP in Beirut [*q.v.*]. When in 1974 the Palestine National Council (PNC) accepted the idea of a Palestinian state on the West Bank [*q.v.*] and the Gaza Strip [*q.v.*] as an "intermediate step" toward the liberation of Palestine, he rejected it. He boycotted the PLO executive committee, of which he was a member. He maintained this stance until 1981.

After the expulsion of the PLO from Beirut in September 1982, he refrained from joining the Syrian-instigated attack against Yasser Arafat [*q.v.*] and Fatah [*q.v.*]. But following Arafat's agreement with King Hussein in early 1985 to initiate talks with Israel, he joined the Syrian-inspired Palestine National Salvation front of radical Palestinian groups. Two years later, after the Arafat-Hussein agreement had been reversed, he rejoined the PLO executive committee. In November 1988, while opposing the resolution before the PNC to accept a Palestinian state in part of Palestine and peaceful coexistence with Israel, he declared that he would abide by the decision of the majority (which adopted the resolution).

During the crisis created by Iraq's invasion of Kuwait in August 1990,

Habash backed President Saddam Hussein [*q.v.*], especially after the latter tried to link the Kuwaiti issue to Israel's occupation of the Arab territories. He opposed the Oslo Accord [*q.v.*] of September 1993. Afflicted with cancer, he gave up his leadership of the PFLP to his deputy, Mustafa Zifri, also known as Abu Ali Mustafa, in 2000.

Habibi, Emile Shukri (1921–96): *Palestinian writer and politician* Born into an Anglican Christian [*q.v.*] family in Haifa [*q.v.*], Habibi received his secondary school education in Haifa and Acre [*q.v.*]. After working in sundry jobs he became an announcer with the Palestinian Broadcasting Service in 1940, the year he joined the Palestine Communist Party [*q.v.*]. Following the party line, he backed the 1947 UN partition plan for Palestine [*q.v.*]. After the founding of Israel in 1948, he stayed in the newly established state.

As a leading member of Maki [*q.v.*] (the Israeli Communist Party), he opposed military administration of Arab-inhabited areas and fought discrimination against Arab [*q.v.*] citizens. He was elected to the Knesset [*q.v.*] in 1951, 1955, and 1961. Four years later, together with Emile Touma [*q.v.*] and Meir Vilner, he left Maki and established Rakah [*q.v.*] (New Communist List). He failed to get reelected to the Knesset in 1965 and 1969, but was successful in 1973.

A prolific journalist dealing with literary, cultural, and political subjects, Habibi served on the editorial boards of important Communist publications, becoming chief editor of the party organ, *Al-Ittihad* (Arabic: *The Unity*) from 1985 to 1989. His collec-

tion of short stories, *The Sextet of the Six-Day War* (1969), relates meetings between Israeli Arabs [*q.v.*] and their relatives living elsewhere. His best-known volume, *The Secret Life of Saeed, the Ill-fated Pessoptimist* (1974), is a sardonic novel about an Arab anti-hero who wants to cooperate with the Israelis. Then followed *Lukaa bin Lukaa* (Arabic: *Lukaa, son of Lukaa*) (1980), *Ikhtiyaa* (1985), and *Suraya bint al-Ghoul* (Arabic: *Saraya, daughter of the Ghoul*) (1991). He won the Israel prize for literature in 1992, the first Israeli Arab to do so.

Hadash (Hebrew: acronym of *Hazit Demokratit le Shalom ve Leshivyon,* Democratic Front for Peace and Equality): *Israeli political party* Formed in Haifa [*q.v.*] in 1977 by the merger of Rakah [*q.v.*] and the Black Panther Party, Hadash adopted the following program: Israeli withdrawal from all Occupied Arab Territories [*q.v.*], the establishment of a Palestinian state in the West Bank [*q.v.*] and Gaza [*q.v.*], and an end to discrimination against Israeli Arabs [*q.v.*] and Oriental Jews [*q.v.*]. The number of Knesset [*q.v.*] seats won by Hadash has varied between two (in 2003) and five (in 1977, 1981, and 1988). Its secretary-general is Muhammad Barake, who has been a Knesset member since 1999. In 2003, the party entered the parliamentary elections on a joint list with Ta'al, an Israeli Arab group led by Ahmad Tibi, but returned to an independent participation in the subsequent elections. In the 2006 Knesset election it secured three seats. Its 2009 election manifesto called for the eradication of all weapons of mass destruction in Israel, meaning nuclear bombs and chemical and biological weapons. It won four seats, divided equally between Jews [*q.v.*] and Israeli Arabs.

al-Hadi, Abd Rabbu Mansour (1945–): *Yemeni politician, president 2012–* Born in the village of Thakin in the Abyan province of South Yemen [*q.v.*], then a British colony, he graduated from Aden Protectorate Military School. He won a scholarship to study briefly in Britain, where he became flunet in English. Soon after his return to Aden [*q.v.*], he was sent to Cairo [*q.v.*] for a four-year-long military training, which ended in 1970. He rose in the hierarchy from a commander of an armored battalion to an administrative assistant to the chief of general staff. In 1976, the Marxist government of South Yemen arranged an advanced four-year training for him at a Soviet military academy. After his return home, he was promoted to deputy chief of staff for logistics and administration in 1983. In the civil war that erupted between President Ali Nasser Muhammad [*q.v.*] and his rivals in January 1986, al-Hadi sided with Muhammad, who lost. He fled to North Yemen along with the troops loyal to him. He reorganized them as the Brigades of Yemen Unity.

After the unification of North and South Yemen in May 1990, he cooperated with the newly appointed Yemeni Vice President, Ali Salim al-Beidh [*q.v.*], a native of South Yemen. But when civil war erupted in April 1994 he sided with the North Yemeni forces. Yemeni President Ali Abdullah Saleh [*q.v.*] appointed him defense minister in May, and then promoted him to vice president in October. In

1997 Saleh raised his military rank to lieutenant general.

Following his reelection as president in 1999 and 2006, Saleh reappointed al-Hadi vice president. When pro-democracy protests, inspired by the Arab Spring [*q.v.*], escalated in 2011, he stood by Saleh. During Saleh"s absence between 4 June and 23 September to undergo medical treatment in Saudi Arabia, he became the acting president. Once Saleh had accepted the transitional plan of the Gulf Cooperation Council [*q.v.*] on 23 November, he became the acting president again. In the presidential election that followed in February 2012, he was the sole candidate. He then succeeded Saleh as president. He faced a challenge to reform the political-administrative system, including the military.

Hadith (Arabic*: Narrative*): *sayings and doings of the Prophet Muhammad* The original term al-Hadith, meaning *The Tradition*—an account of the words and deeds of the Prophet Muhammad—is now used without "Al." With the spread of Islam [*q.v.*] after the Prophet Muhammad's death in 632 A.D., many of his companions settled in the conquered territories, which were administered first by the Umayyads (661–750 A.D.) and then by the Abbasids (751–1258). Of the 6,616 verses in the Quran [*q.v.*], only 80 concerned legal issues, mainly about women, marriage, family, and inheritance. But since the Prophet Muhammad had governed a realm there was an oral record of what he had said and done as a judge and administrator. As most of his companions had made note of what he did or said for their own guidance, their diligence later paved the way for codification of the Prophet's *sunna* (Arabic: *practice*) when the eminent jurist Muhammad bin Idris al-Shafii (767–820 A.D.) ruled that all legal decisions not stemming directly from the Quran [*q.v.*] must be based on a tradition going back to the Prophet Muhammad himself.

The result was the Hadith—books of traditions, each tradition described by text and the chain of authority, going back to the original source. Some 2,700 acts and sayings of the Prophet were collected and published in six canonical works, called *Al-Hadith*, the first collection being by Muhammad al-Bukhari (d. 870 A.D.). These were accepted by Sunnis [*q.v.*] and became a secondary source of guidance, the primary source being the Quran. Shias [*q.v.*], who accepted only those traditions that were traced through Imam Ali bin Abu Talib, came up with their collections, compiled by Abu Jaafar Muhammad al-Kulini (d. 939 A.D.), Abu Jaafar Muhammad al-Kummi (d. 991 A.D.), and Abu Jaafar Muhammad al-Tusi (d. 1068). In the event of dispute, a tradition can only be abrogated by another tradition.

Hafiz, Amin (1921–2009): *Syrian politician; president, 1963–66* The son of a Sunni [*q.v.*] policeman in Aleppo [*q.v.*], Hafiz became a non-commissioned officer in the French-Syrian Special Forces during World War II. He graduated from the Homs Military Academy in 1947. Following his participation in the coup by Hashem al-Attasi against Adib Shishakli [*q.v.*] in 1954, he was appointed commandant of the Homs Military Academy. After the merger of Syria and Egypt

into the United Arab Republic [*q.v.*] in 1958, he was sent to the Cairo military staff college as an instructor. When Syria seceded from the UAR in September 1961, he was recalled to Damascus [*q.v.*], then dispatched to Argentina as military attaché.

After the Baath Party [*q.v.*] seized power in March 1963, the powerful Military Committee promoted Hafiz to lieutenant general and appointed him interior minister and deputy premier. He joined the Baath Party. Having foiled the Syrian Nasserists' [*q.v.*] attempt to capture power, he became defense minister and acting chief of staff as well as chairman of the Presidential Council. When Salah al-Din Bitar [*q.v.*] resigned as prime minister in October 1963, Hafiz succeeded him. But his order in April 1964 to shell the al-Sultan Mosque in Damascus to counter the Islamist challenge to the regime backfired. He gave up his premiership.

Despite his high governmental and party positions, he lacked real power, which belonged to the Military Committee from which he was excluded. In protest he went over to the civilian faction of the Baath Party, led by Michel Aflaq [*q.v.*] and Bitar, which lacked a military figure. In August 1965 he ousted Salah Jadid [*q.v.*], head of the Military Committee, as chief of staff. But in the final showdown between the Military Committee and its rival faction in February 1966, his side lost.

On his release from jail in June 1967, he went into exile in Lebanon. When the Aflaq-led faction of the Baath party seized power in Iraq about a year later, he moved to Baghdad [*q.v.*]. Following the seizure of power by Hafiz Assad [q.v.] in November 1970, more than 100 Syrians, including Hafiz and Aflaq, were tried for conspiring with Iraq to overthrow the Syrian regime in 1970 (before Assad's takeover). Hafiz, Aflaq, and three others were sentenced to capital punishment, which was commuted by Assad. Hafiz continued his anti-Assad activities, later heading the National Alliance of the Liberation of Syria, an umbrella body of 18 anti-Assad factions.

He was allowed to return to Syria in 2005 by President Bashar Assad [q.v.].

Haganah (Hebrew*: defense*): *Zionist military Organization* Aware of the deep Arab resentment against Jewish immigration into Palestine [q.v.], young Zionists [q.v.] secretly transformed a voluntary body, HaShomer (Hebrew: *The Watchmen*), into Haganah, a militia, in 1920. After the Arab-Jewish clashes of 1929, they accelerated the process of training and equipping Haganah volunteers with smuggled weapons. It was the discovery of such arms in the autumn of 1935 that triggered the Arab revolt of 1936–39. Haganah then had more than 10,000 relatively well-equipped recruits. During the latter, post-1938 phase of the Arab revolt, when the Arabs [q.v.] attacked not only British targets but also Jewish settlements, Haganah was fostered and armed by the British Mandate. It carried out operations against the Arabs and manufactured arms at a clandestine factory.

Following the outbreak of World War II, the British legalized Haganah. It instructed its members to join the Jewish units within the British army. More than 27,000 Palestinian Jews

[q.v.] did so. However, when the war was over Haganah turned against the British and engaged in the smuggling of Jewish immigrants into Palestine. The British mounted a major campaign against it in June 1947, but met with only partial success.

By the time the United Nations adopted the partition plan in November 1947, Haganah had emerged as a professional army, supported by 79,000 reserves, armed police, and home guards. As 15 May 1948—the British withdrawal date—approached, interethnic violence intensified. Conscious of the fact that the area about to constitute the Jewish state, according to the UN plan, had almost as many Arabs as Jews [q.v.], Haganah, along with Irgun Zvai Leumi [q.v.] and Lehi [q.v.], focused on expelling as many Arabs from these areas as possible. With the founding of Israel in 1948, Haganah members were transferred to the *Zvai Haganah Le Israel* (Hebrew: *Military Defense of Israel*), known as Zahal [q.v.].

Haifa: *Israeli city* Population: 858,000 (2011 est.) An important port whose recorded history goes back two millennia. Haifa was captured by Muslim Arabs [q.v.] in 638 A.D. and changed hands during the Crusades. It formed part of the Ottoman Empire in the 16th century. At the turn of the 20th century, Haifa began to overtake Acre [q.v.], situated at the northern end of the same bay, as a port. After the defeat of the Ottomans in 1918 it became part of the Palestine [q.v.] that was placed under British Mandate. It was the site of bitter battles between the Arabs [q.v.] and the Zionists [q.v.] on the eve of the founding of Israel in 1948, which resulted in all but 3,000 of its 50,000 Arab residents fleeing. At present Israeli Arabs form 9 percent of its population.

The city, located on Mount Carmel, is picturesque and has a large deep-water harbor. It is an important commercial, industrial, and communications center. The burial place of Abdul Baha, son of the founder of the Bahai faith [q.v.], Haifa is the international headquarters of this religion.

hajj (Arabic: *setting out*): The fifth pillar of Islam [q.v.], hajj is decreed by the Quran [q.v.] (3:97): "And pilgrimage to the House [of Allah] is incumbent upon people for the sake of Allah, [upon] everyone who is able to undertake the journey to it." The pilgrimage takes place from 8 to 12 Dhul Hijja, the last month of the Islamic calendar [q.v.].

The House of Allah, containing the sacred Black Stone, the Kaaba [q.v.], in the Saudi city of Mecca [q.v.], is believed to have been rebuilt several times since its original construction by Adam. Before entering Mecca—during 8–10 Dhul Hijja—the pilgrim performs a ritual ablution and puts on two seamless pieces of white cloth (men only—women wear ordinary dress).

After entering the city the pilgrim circumambulates the Kaaba anti-clockwise seven times. Then he strides between the Safa and Marwa hillocks, respectively symbols of caution and hope, pertaining to the search for water by Hagar for her son Ishmael/Ismail by the Prophet Abraham. Along with fellow pilgrims he must then stand on Arafat Hill, situated 12 mi/19 km to the east of the

Kaaba, from midday to sunset, seeking enlightenment and salvation.

Then the pilgrim must reach Mina, a site located 3 mi/5 km east of Mecca on the way to the Arafat Hill, the site of the Prophet Muhammad's last sermon, to throw seven pebbles at each of the three pillars, the first of which is called the Great Devil. This is a reenactment of Abraham's stoning of the devil, when an inner voice whispered to him not to sacrifice his son, Ishmael, as he had been commanded to do. In 2004 these pillars were replaced by three walls, each 85 ft/27 m long.

Next, in a further reenactment of Abraham (when, having resolved to sacrifice his son, Ishmael, in the way of God, the ram of his renunciation appeared) the pilgrim sacrifices an animal: a sheep, goat, camel, or cow. In the past, the pilgrim either slaughtered the animal himself/herself or witnessed the killing. Nowadays most pilgrims purchase a sacrifice voucher in Mecca whereby an animal is sacrificed in their names without their presence. The pilgrim then has his face and head shaved, a preamble to his acquiring the title of *hajji* or *haaji*.

On each of the subsequent two days the haaji must hit each of the three walls with seven pebbles.

Hajj is the most dramatic manifestation of the Muslim [q.v.] *umma* [q.v.]. In 1988 the Saudi government fixed a quota of one pilgrim per thousand foreign Muslims. Yet, due to the flawed crowd control, there were a series of fatal accidents. In 1990 a stampede in the pedestrian tunnel leading to Mina caused 1,426 deaths. Four years later a stampede at the Stoning of the Devil ritual led to the deaths of 270 pilgrims, and in 1998 a similar event left 118 people dead. Similar accidents in 2001, 2003, and 2004 caused a total of 400 fatalities.

Between 1996 and 2011, the number of foreign Muslims doing the hajj rose from 1 million to 1.828 million. The size of the Saudi-based pilgrims with or without the hajj permit varies around 900,000.

The Saudi government deploys 100,000 policemen and soldiers in and near Jeddah [*q.v.*], Mecca, and Medina [*q.v.*] during the hajj season, and 1,850 closed-circuit TV cameras to monitor the pilgrims at the Grand Mosque of Mecca, which has a capacity to hold 1.5 million people.

al-Hakim, Tawfiq (1898–1987): *Egyptian writer* Born of a Turkish father and an Egyptian mother in Alexandria [*q.v.*], Hakim secured a law degree from Cairo University. In 1925 he went to Paris to obtain a doctorate in law. Instead of concentrating on his studies he soaked himself in the cultural, artistic, and theatrical life of the city. Having written two plays before arriving in Paris, he took a keen interest in the works of George Bernard Shaw, Henrik Ibsen, Maurice Maeterlinck, and Luigi Pirandello. After his return to Egypt in 1928, albeit without a doctorate in law, he was appointed deputy prosecutor in Alexandria and then transferred to several towns as the county district attorney. In 1934 he became director of the education ministry's research department, moving five years later to information department of the ministry of social affairs.

By then his literary career was well established. Having attempted light entertainment in *Ali Baba* (1926),

Hakim opted for intellectual plays full of ideas and philosophic reflections. He retained his outstanding ability to write lucid dialogue in colloquial Arabic [*q.v.*], and single-handedly raised prose drama, until then considered low art, to the exalted level of Arabic poetry. He dealt with the conflict between pragmatic and idealist behavior in *A Bullet in the Heart* (1931), a comedy, and with the search for knowledge in *Shahrazad* (1934). *The Men of the Cave* (1935) is another play of ideas, offering a Quranic version of the Christian legend of the Seven Sleepers of Ephesus. Inspired by Aristophanes' *Lysistrata*, he wrote *Praxa or: How to Govern* (1939), in which the entertaining element was stronger than the intellectual. It was the same in *Pygmalion* (1942). During the next decade he penned *Solomon the Wise* (1943); *King Oedipus* (1949); *Mr Kanduz's Property* (1950), a contemporary social comedy; and *If Youth Only Knew* (1950), in which an old man regains his youth by taking an elixir.

At the time of the 1952 revolution, Hafiz was director of the National Library in Cairo [*q.v.*]. He supported the new regime. In 1956 he was made a member of the National Arts Council, and four years later received the state prize for literature. His *Soft Hands* (1954) is about the dignity of labor, and *The Deal* (1956) centers on a small village's attempt to purchase land from a foreign company.

The Sultan's Dilemma (1960) is an entertaining fantasy with a political message: a ruler who uses force to uphold freedom is hardly free himself. This indicated Hakim's disappointment with the rule of President

Gamal Abdul Nasser [*q.v.*]. He expressed this feeling more strongly after the publication of *The Tree Climber* (1962) (a variation of the story of Adam, Eve, and the tree) and *Shams al-Nahr* (1965) (about a princess in the *Arabian Nights* who refuses to marry a rich prince), and in such political plays as *Fate of a Cockroach* (1966), *Not a Thing out of Place* (1966), and *The Bank of Worry* (1967). After Nasser's death in 1970, Hafiz criticized him in his booklet *The Return of Consciousness* (1975). By then his plays had been translated into foreign languages and performed abroad. His novels *Return of the Soul* (1933) and *Diary of a County District Attorney* (1937) also had been translated abroad.

Hakimiya: *Islamic sect* Hakimiya is the term used for those who followed the Fatimid Caliph Abu Ali Tariq al-Hakim. *See* Druzes.

Halabja: *Kurdish Iraqi town, site of poison gas attacks by Iraq* Population: 80,000 (2010 est.). During the Iran-Iraq War [*q.v.*], Iran and its Iraqi Kurdish allies captured Halabja, 15 miles from the international border, on 13 March 1988. Three days later the Iraqi air force attacked it with poison gas bombs, killing between 3,200 and 6,800 people, mainly civilians, and injuring another 10,000. The pictures of men, women, and children frozen in instant death, relayed by the Iranian media, shocked the world. In killing its own unarmed citizens with chemical weapons, Iraq did something unprecedented in history. The U.S. defense department put it about that Iran was partly responsible for the

event. It was seven weeks before the UN Security Council condemned the use of chemical weapons by "both sides (Iraq and Iran)" and called on them to refrain from using them in the future. In March 2010, Iraq's High Criminal Court ruled that the Halabja massacre was an act of genocide.

Halacha (Hebrew: *The Way*): *Jewish religious law* Also spelled Halakha, a derivative of halach, meaning "to go."

Halacha is a set of laws and ordinances that governs religious observances as well as daily life and conduct of Jews [*q.v.*]. It preserves the Oral Law, originating with the revelation on Mount Sinai to Moses. The project of compiling the oral traditions of the law and their interpretations, begun at the turn of the second century A.D., was completed in the early third century A.D. by Judah HaNasi and was called Mishna [*q.v.*]. Then the commentaries on Mishna, known as Gemara [*q.v.*], followed. The two together formed the Talmud [*q.v.*].

Halacha is the legal section of the Talmud and excludes the non-legal text—poetical digressions, fables, etc.—known as Hagadda. To take into account the changes caused by the passage of time, the original version of Halacha was revised by Moses Ben Maimon/Maimonides (d. 1204), Joseph Karo (d. 1575), and Abraham Danzig (d. 1820). In more recent times, Halacha has come to include Midrash Halacha [*q.v.*], which pertains to the Written Law as revealed in the written scripture, the Torah [*q.v.*].

Hama: *Syrian city* Population: 700,000 (2011 est.) An important ancient settlement, the recorded history of Hama goes back more than three millenniums when it was called Hamath. It underwent changes of names as well as rulers until it fell to Muslim [*q.v.*] Arabs [*q.v.*] in 638 A.D. It changed hands again during the Crusades. It came under Ottoman suzerainty in the early 16th century. After the defeat of the Ottomans in 1918, it became part of the Syria placed under the French Mandate.

As the leading center of the Sunni [*q.v.*] religious establishment, Hama witnessed major skirmishes between Islamists and the security forces of the secular Baath Party [*q.v.*] regime in 1964 and 1980. In February 1982 there was an Islamist-inspired insurrection there. Before it was crushed, between 5,000 and 10,000 people died, including about 1,000 soldiers, and nearly a quarter of the old city was razed.

During the Arab Spring [*q.v.*] of 2011, Hama emerged as a strong center of opposition to the regime of President Bashar Assad [*q.v.*]. Following a vast pro-democracy demonstration on 1 July, the authorities imposed an armed blockade of the city. In late July-early August, in a concerted rive to crush the protest the security forces, using tanks, artillery, and snipers killed 200 people, and regained control of the city.

Its tourist attractions include the seventh-century al-Sultan mosque, originally a church; the citadel; and the gardens along the Orontes River, irrigated by giant, six-century-old waterwheels.

Hamas (Arabic*: zeal*; acronym of *Harakat al-Muqawama al-Islami,*

Movement of Islamic Resistance): *Islamic organization in the West Bank, Gaza, and East Jerusalem* Hamas was established on 27 December 1987 by Shaikh Ahmad Yasin [*q.v.*] and six other leaders of the Muslim Brotherhood [*q.v.*] in the Occupied Territories [*q.v.*] soon after the outbreak of the intifada [*q.v.*]. Its 1988 Charter described its short-term aim as reversing Israel's occupation of the West Bank [*q.v.*], Gaza Strip [*q.v.*], and East Jerusalem [*q.v.*], and founding an Islamic state approved by a referendum; and its long-term objective as establishing an Islamic state in all of (Mandate) Palestine. Strongly opposed to drugs and alcohol, it called for a struggle against corruption and bribery.

It was financed mainly by its supporters worldwide, who made contributions to it as part of *zakat* [*q.v.*], an Islamic tax. Most of its funds were spent on charity and the construction and running of clinics and mosques. It participated in both trade unions and chambers of commerce.

Active in the intifada, it set up its armed wing, and named it after Izz al-Din Qassam [*q.v.*], leader of the Arab intifada of 1936–39. Due to its decentralized structure it was unaffected by Yasin's imprisonment in 1989 when the leadership of Hamas passed to Abdul Aziz Rantisi. It became a recipient of grants from the Gulf States [*q.v.*] after their decision to stop funding the Palestine Liberation Organization (PLO) [*q.v.*] for siding with Iraq during the 1990–91 Kuwait Crisis. It opposed the PLO's decision to participate in the Middle East peace process initiated in October 1991 in Madrid, and rejected the Oslo Accord I [*q.v.*], signed in Washington nearly two years later. By then it had emerged as the foremost opponent of Israel, which in December 1992 deported 413 leaders of Hamas and Islamic Jihad [q.v.] to south Lebanon.

When the PLO established the Palestinian Authority (PA) [q.v.] in the Gaza Strip in May 1994, with several Jewish settlements in the Strip still intact, Hamas reiterated its earlier position that it considered Jewish settlers and Israeli troops in the Palestinian Territories [q.v.] as an occupying force to be resisted. Following the arrest of 350 Hamas supporters in the Gaza Strip by the PA police in October 1994, in the wake of the kidnapping of an Israeli soldier near Tel Aviv [q.v.] by Izz al-Din Qassam Brigade members, Hamas intensified its opposition to the PA.

By the mid-1990s, Hamas ran a network of mosques, clinics, schools, youth clubs, and day care centers. Its funds, amounting to $50 to $70 million a year, came mostly from charitable organizations based in the Gulf States which in turn received the bulk of their contributions from expatriate Palestinians working in the region. The annual contribution of Iran was put at $3 million.

Hamas did not participate in the elections for the presidency of the Palestinian Authority and the Palestinian Legislative Council in January 1996 as these stemmed from the Oslo Accord I.

In retaliation for the killing of 29 Palestinian worshippers in the Mosque of Abraham in Hebron [q.v.] on 25 February 1994 by a Jewish zealot, the Qassam Brigade embarked on a program of suicide attacks inside Israel. In turn Israel assassinated

Yahya Ayash, the chief bomb-maker of the Qassam Brigade, in Gaza City [q.v.] in January 1996. To avenge his death, the Qassam Brigade mounted a series of suicide bombings in Jerusalem [q.v.] and elsewhere during the run-up to the elections for the Israeli prime minister and parliament in May. These damaged the prospects of the incumbent Prime Minister Shimon Peres [q.v.] who lost to Benjamin Netanyahu. [q.v.].

Following Netanyahu's decision to authorize a controversial Jewish settlement at Har Homa/Jabal Abu Ghneim on the southern outskirts of Jerusalem in early 1997, the Qassam Brigade resumed suicide bombings. Pressured by Israel, the PA suppressed Hamas. But in October Israel freed Shaikh Yasin in order to secure the release of its two intelligence agents caught trying to assassinate Khaled Mashaal [q.v.], a Hamas leader, in Amman [q.v.].

A year later the PA arrested Hamas leaders for criticizing it for its latest agreement with Israel, called the Wye River Memorandum [q.v.]. Its leaders criticized the PA for attending the final settlement talks with Israel chaired by the U.S. President Bill Clinton (r. 1993–2001) at the presidential retreat of Camp David in July 2000. These negotiations failed.

However, once the Al Aqsa intifada [q.v.] erupted two months later, and PA President Yasser Arafat [q.v.] resisted Israeli pressure to arrest Hamas leaders, the differences between the two rivals disappeared. Indeed, Hamas became an important member of the newly formed local Popular Resistance Committees, its other constituents being the Islamic Jihad [q.v.] and radical members of Fatah [*q.v.*]. The Qassam Brigade stepped up its suicide bomb attacks on Israelis. While the reoccupation of the West Bank towns and cities by the Israeli government of Ariel Sharon from the spring of 2002 onward curtailed the terrorist activities of the Qassam Brigade it failed to stop them.

Because of the clandestine structure of its local cells and a scattered leadership that functions by consensus, Hamas has proved to be resilient to attacks by its adversaries. To rebut the charges of anti-Semitism [*q.v.*], the Hamas Politburo described its conflict with Israel as "political, not religious."

In 2003, the European Union (EU) listed Hamas as a terrorist organization—nine years after the United States had done so. In January 2004, Hamas leader in Gaza, Abdul Aziz Rantisi, proposed a 10-year truce between Israel and his organization in exchange for the founding of an independent Palestine on the territories occupied by Israel since the June 1967 Arab-Israel War. [*q.v.*]. This was rejected by Israel whose intelligence services assassinated Rantisi in an air strike in April 2004—two months after a similar strike had killed Yasin.

Reversing its earlier policy, Hamas entered the parliamentary elections in January 2006. It won 74 of the 132 seats—with a half of the total elected on the basis of popular vote for a party and the other half by ballots for individual candidates. Its total consisted of 29 seats in the parties' category and 45 in the other category. The voter turnout was 77 percent; and the election, overseen by 900 foreign observers, was certified as "free and fair." Hamas formed the government under

Ismail Haniyeh [*q.v.*]. But it was not recognized by the U.S. and the EU. They insisted that Hamas must renounce violence, recognize Israel, and accept all the previous agreements between the Palestinian Authority and Israel. The Hainyeh government refused. The U.S. and the EU cut off their financial aid. Iran stepped in and raised its annual contribution to Hamas to $23 million.

Tensions rose between Hamas and Fatah. But Saudi mediators succeeded in reconciling the two, and that led to the formation of a national unity government under Haniyeh in March 2007.

This was unacceptable to the U.S. and Israel. They backed a clandestine plan to fund and arm a militia commanded by Fatah's Gaza-based strongman, Muhammad Dahlan, to overthrow the Haniyeh-led government. To abort this plot, Hamas mounted an armed offensive against Fatah in June, seized full control of the Gaza Strip, and expelled Fatah activists from it. In response, PA President Mahmoud Abbas [*q.v.*] dismissed all Hamas officials in the West Bank. Israel jailed 27 Hamas parliamentarians and other leaders in the West Bank areas under its control. It imposed an economic blockade on Gaza. The Qassam Brigade fired missiles at Israel from the Gaza Strip.

The classified U.S. cables, leaked by the anti-secrecy group WikiLeaks in December 2010, showed Yuvan Diskin, head of Israel's Shin Beth [*q.v.*], saying that Fatah [*q.v.*] forces asked Israel to attack Hamas in Gaza. Israel declined to get involved. Also Diskin opposed the idea of General Keith Dayton, then U.S. Security Coordinator for Israel-Palestinian Authority to arm Fatah's forces, arguing that these weapons and equipment would ultimately fall into the hands of Hamas. Diskin told U.S. ambassador Richard Jones that the PA shared intelligence on Hamas fully with Israel.

The conflict between Hamas-controlled Gaza and Israel continued with the Israeli Defense Forces [*q.v.*] retaliating with artillery firings, air strikes, and occasional incursions into Gaza to the missile and mortar attacks by the Qassam Brigade. In 2008, following mediation by Egypt, Hamas and Israel agreed to a six-month cease-fire from 19 June. But on 4 November, an Israeli incursion into Gaza led to the deaths of seven Hamas activists. The cease-fire broke down, and rocket and mortar attacks on Israel resumed. An armed conflict between Hamas and Israel, called the Gaza War [*q.v.*], ensued on 27 December.

At the end of this conflict in January 2009, rocket and mortar firings ceased. But Israel's blockade of land and sea borders and airspace continued. Later that year Hamas Politburo chief Khaled Mashaal repeated the earlier offer of his predecessor for a 10-year truce with Israel on the following basis: Hamas will accept the founding of an independent Palestinian state based on the 1967 frontiers—provided the Palestinian refugees were given the right to return to Israel, and East Jerusalem was recognized as the capital of the State of Palestine. In May 2010, he moderated the party's stance by saying that if the Palestinian state were established along the lines mentioned before, that would end the Palestinian resistance, and that the subsequent relationship

with Israel would be decided by all the Palestinians around the world democratically. In December Ismail Haniyeh confirmed that Hamas would accept the result of such a referendum even if "it contradicted our policies and convictions."

The overthrow of Egyptian President Hosni Mubarak [*q.v.*] and his pro-Israeli intelligence minister Omar Suleiman in February 2011 benefited Hamas. The post-Mubarak foreign minister Nabil al-Araby was even-handed in his efforts to reconcile Hamas with Fatah. The erstwhile rivals' decision to share power in April was followed by an agreement between Mashaal and Abbas in February 2012 in Doha [*q.v.*].

Against the background of popular protests in Syria, President Bashar Assad [*q.v.*] expected Mashaal, based in Damascus [*q.v.*], to support him publicly. As beneficiaries of free and fair vote in the Palestinian Territories [*q.v.*], Mashaal and other Hamas leaders failed to do so. The headquarters of Hamas was shifted temporarily to Doha so that Hamas could maintain and cultivate its contacts with diplomats and other foreign officials. While Mashaal moved to Doha, other Politburo members stayed on in Damascus.

Hamdi, Ibrahim (1943–77): *North Yemeni politician; president, 1974–77* Born to a religious Zaidi Shia [*q.v.*] father and a Shafii Sunni [*q.v.*] mother in Dhamar, he trained as an Islamic judge. After the 1962 anti-royalist coup he joined the army on the republican side. Rising through the ranks, he became a close aide of General Hassan al-Amri, who served as chief of staff and premier from 1967 to 1969. In 1971 Prime Minister Muhsin al-Aini appointed Hamdi deputy premier and interior minister. A year later he was promoted to lieutenant colonel and made deputy chief of staff.

On 13 June 1974 he carried out a bloodless coup by forcing the ruling Republican Council members and Abdullah Hussein al-Ahmar [q.v.], speaker of the Constituent People's Assembly (CPA), to resign. He assumed power as head of the newly created Military Command Council. He replaced many of the 3,000 army officers, who were often illiterate tribal chiefs, with young officers freshly trained at the military academies of the Soviet bloc countries. He dissolved the CPA, which was dominated by tribal nominees, in October 1975.

Distancing himself from Saudi Arabia, he started pursuing independent domestic and foreign policies. While maintaining a ban on political parties, he tolerated the clandestine formation of the National Democratic Front [q.v.] in 1976. As a result, he fell foul of the tribal leaders at home and the Saudi royal family abroad. The disgruntled tribal chiefs attempted two coups, but in vain. Negotiations between them and Hamdi, initiated in early 1977, collapsed when Shaikh al-Ahmar and his supporters occupied Saada and Khamir in the north, which led Hamdi to use force in July to quell the rebellion.

He improved relations with South Yemen as well as the Soviet Union. During his visit to Sanaa [q.v.] in August 1977, South Yemeni President Salim Rubai Ali [q.v.] and Hamdi agreed to unify their countries in four

years. But two days before Hamdi's departure for Aden [q.v.] in October 1977 to sign a mutual defense pact, he was assassinated along with his brother Lieutenant Colonel Abdullah Hamdi, commander of an elite brigade. These killings were widely believed to have been inspired by Saudi Arabia.

Hanafi Code: *Sunni Islamic legal school*
The Hanafi Code is the school of the Sharia [q.v.] founded by Abu Hanifa al-Numan (699–767 A.D.), an Iranian merchant-scholar based in Kufa [q.v.], Iraq. Instead of codifying established practices, Abu Hanifa applied logic and consistency in legal doctrines, thus establishing a method for tackling future problems and expanding the jurisdiction of law in a Muslim [q.v.] society.

On the whole the Hanafi Code is liberal and oriented toward urban communities. Adopted by the Abbasid caliphs (751A.D.–1258), it spread east to Afghanistan and then the Indian subcontinent, Central Asia, and Western China. It became the favored school of the Ottoman Turks. Once they had usurped the caliphate from the Mamlukes and established an Islamic empire (1517–1918) of their own, the Hanafi doctrine became their official code. It has continued to enjoy official status even in those former Ottoman territories where a majority of local Muslims follows a different doctrine.

Hanbali Code: *Sunni Islamic legal school*
The Hanbali Code is the school of the Sharia [q.v.] founded by Ahmad bin Hanbal (780–855 A.D.). Opposed to the legal superstructure built upon the

Quran [*q.v.*] and the *sunna* [*q.v.*], Hanbal argued that a legal decision must be reached by referring directly to the Quran and the *sunna*. He maintained that they constituted the law itself, and were not merely its source, thus standing apart from those schools—Hanafi [*q.v.*], Maliki [*q.v.*], and Shafii [*q.v.*]—that had codified the Quran and the *sunna* into a comprehensive jurisprudential system.

Over time Hanbal's fundamentalist approach lost support in the sophisticated societies of the Fertile Crescent [*q.v.*] but retained its hold among the nomadic tribes of the Najd [*q.v.*]. In the early 14th century Ahmad bin Taimiya (d. 1328) emerged as an eminent Hanbali reformist. He condemned the practices of saint worship and tomb cult common among Sufis [*q.v.*] and opposed the contemporary ulema's [*q.v.*] assertion that there was no further need of *ijtihad* [*q.v.*], interpretative reasoning. Thus Hanbali jurists continued to practice *ijtihad* in those areas where the Quran and the *sunna* are vague. Timaya's views were well received by the Mamluke caliphs (1250–1517) in Cairo [*q.v.*]. During the subsequent Ottoman Empire, Muhammad bin Abdul Wahhab (1703–1787), a Najdi cleric, was inspired by Hanbal and Taimiya. In 1745 he formed an alliance with the ruler of Najd, Muhammad bin Saud, who adopted the Wahhabi doctrine [*q.v.*].

Haniyeh, Ismail (1963–): *prime minister of the Palestinian Authority, 2006–;* (also spelled Hainya or Haniyah) Born to refugee parents in Gaza [*q.v.*], Haniyeh acquired an undergraduate degree in Arabic literature from the Islamic University in Gaza city [*q.v.*] in 1987. Two years later he was jailed for participating in the Palestinian Intifada [*q.v.*] as a member of Hamas [*q.v.*]. He was one of the 413 leaders of Hamas and Islamic Jihad [*q.v.*] to be banished to south Lebanon in December 1992, then under the control of Israel. After his return to Gaza in 1993, he served as the dean of the Islamic University. Four years later he became the chief of staff of the spiritual leader of Hamas, Shaikh Ahmad Yasin [*q.v.*].

During the Al Aqsa Intifada [*q.v.*], launched in 2000, several senior leaders of Hamas, including Yasin and Rantisi, were assassinated by Israel. As a result the status of such surviving figures as Haniyeh rose. When the Hamas Politburo decided to run in the parliamentary elections in January 2006, he topped the party list. After the electoral victory of Hamas, he was appointed prime minister in March.

Despite pressures from America, the European Union, and President Mahmoud Abbas [*q.v.*] of the Palestinian Authority (PA) [*q.v.*] on Hamas to renounce violence, recognize Israel, and accept all the previous agreements between the PA and Israel, the Haniyeh government refused to change its policies. However, in his interview with the German magazine *Der Spiegel* (The Star) in December 2006, he said that, if Israel agreed to a Palestinian state along the 1967 borders, then Hamas would offer Israel a 50-year-long truce.

Due to the economic blockade and the severing of all foreign aid, except from the Islamic Republic of Iran, the living standards of Gazans declined. To reverse the trend, Haniyeh resigned in February 2007 as a prelude to forming a national unity government, which came into being in March. But it proved short-lived. Following the seizure of the Gaza Strip in June 2007 by Hamas forces, Haniyeh was dismissed by Abbas as prime minister.

But since Abbas's appointment of Salam Fayyad [q.v.] as the prime minister was not endorsed by the parliament, as required by the constitution, Haniyeh continued to operate as the premier from Gaza. In line with the constitution, his government regarded Professor Aziz Duwaik, a native of the West Bank town of Tulkarm—speaker of the parliament, then serving a three-year jail sentence for his membership in Hamas in an Israeli prison—as the acting president of the PA [q.v.].

Reflecting the moderated views expressed by Khaled Mashaal [q.v.] in May 2010, Haniyeh said in December that he accepted the establishment of the Palestinian state on the borders of 1967 along with "a resolution of the issue of the Palestinian refugees," and added that if Palestinian voters worldwide endorsed such an accord with Israel his government would abide by it.

After remaining silent for many months, Haniyeh came out in support of the pro-reform protestors in Syria and elsewhere. In February 2012, addressing Friday worshippers at al-Azhar Mosque [q.v.] in Cairo [q.v.], he said: "I salute all the nations of the Arab Spring [q.v.], and I salute the heroic people of Syria who are striving for freedom, democracy, and reform." Two weeks earlier, disregarding the contrary advice by the rulers of the Gulf States [q.v.], he had paid a state visit to Tehran [q.v.].

Hanukkah (Hebrew: *dedication*): *Jewish festival* Hanukkah is an eight-day celebration, from 25 Kislev to 3 Tevet, to mark the rededication of the Holy Temple and altar in Jerusalem [q.v.] following the successful revolt in 165 B.C. by Judah the Maccabee against Antiochus IV, the Greek ruler of Syria. After the razing of the Second Holy Temple in 70 A.D., the festival was associated with the miracle of the cup of oil that burned for eight days on one day's supply of oil, and thus with the concept of an eternal flame. The celebration consists of lighting candles placed in a special eight-branched *menorah*—a candelabrum—with a candle added on each of the eight days, and playing games of chance with a dreidel, a four-sided top inscribed with Hebrew [q.v.] letters on its sides.

Haram al-Sharif: *See* Noble Sanctuary.

Hariri, Rafiq (1944–2005): *Lebanese politician; prime minister, 1992–98; 2000–2004* (also spelled Rafic Harirri) Born into a Sunni [q.v.] family in Sidon [q.v.], Hariri enrolled as a student of business administration at Beirut Arab University in 1965. The next year he left to become a teacher in Jeddah [q.v.]. Soon he joined a construction company, and worked there until 1970. He then established his own construction company. It thrived, and he took over a French firm in 1978. He set up a branch of the company in Lebanon in 1980 in the midst of the Lebanese Civil War [q.v.]. By 1983 his business empire included banking, insurance, construction, light engineering, computer, and advertising companies.

Following the Israeli invasion of Lebanon in 1982 [*q.v.*], he offered the services of his firms to counter the effects of the long Israeli siege of Beirut [*q.v.*]. He participated in the National Reconciliation Conferences respectively in Geneva and Lausanne, Switzerland, in 1983 and 1984. Once the civil war was over in 1990, his multinational companies, possessing assets worth billions of dollars, became involved in reconstruction.

After the general election in August–October 1992, followed by a government led by Prime Minister Omar Karami, public attention focused on reconstruction and rehabilitation. Aware of his business acumen and high standing in international financial centers, President Elias Hrawi [*q.v.*] named Hariri prime minister in October 1992. His appointment began to attract foreign investment. In late 1994, stung by charges of corruption, he resigned, but was persuaded to withdraw his resignation.

Frustrated by the parliament's resistance to his reconstruction plans, he resigned again in May 1995, but was recalled. He formed a new government. He backed the extension of President Elias Hrawi's [*q.v.*] term of office. In October 1996 he was invited to become the prime minister for the third time. Two years later President Emile Lahoud [*q.v.*] did not repeat the invitation. But, in the parliamentary election of 2000, Hariri's supporters scored such an overwhelming victory that Lahoud had no option but to call on him to form the next cabinet. He served as the prime minister until October 2004 when he resigned due to differences with Lahoud. Overall, he presided over a reconstruction boom in Beirut. But during his administrations, corruption increased, as did public debt, which shot up 16-fold to $40 billion.

He and 22 others were killed in February 2005 when a powerful bomb hit his motorcade in Beirut. Following an agreement between the United Nations and the Lebanese government in February 2007, the UN Security Council passed a resolution in May to set up a Special Tribunal on Lebanon (STL) to investigate the killing of Hariri and bring the guilty to justice. The STL started functioning in March 2009. The next month it called on the Lebanese government to free the four top security and intelligence officers it had arrested in September 2005, due to the absence of credible evidence against them. In January 2011, the STL's prosecutor submitted a sealed indictment for the pre-trial judge, Daniel Fransen, to confirm. Once this was done, the STL submitted four confidential arrest warrants to the Lebanese government on 30 June. These warrants were believed to name four senior members of Hizbollah [*q.v.*]. Its leader, Hassan Nasrallah [*q.v.*], questioned the legitimacy of the STL. The warrants could not be served since the named persons went missing.

Hariri, Saad (1970–): *Lebanese politician; prime minister, 2009–2011 (*also known as Saadeddine Hariri) Born to Rafiq Hariri [*q.v.*] and Nidal al-Bustani in Riyadh [*q.v.*], Saad acquired a business administration degree from Georgetown University in Washington, D.C. He then supervised his father's extensive business interests in Saudi Arabia.

Following his father's assassination in 2005, he inherited assets worth an estimated $1.4 billion. He entered the Lebanese politics as a leader of the Sunnis [*q.v.*]. On the founding of the 14 March Alliance [*q.v.*], he was elected its chairman. After the success of the 14 March Alliance in the May–June 2009 parliamentary election, he was invited to form the government. He succeeded in putting together a national unity cabinet in November only after he had agreed to give the opposition 8 March Alliance [*q.v.*] 11 of the 30 cabinet seats. A year later, following his meetings with President Bashar Assad [*q.v.*] in Damascus [*q.v.*], Hariri announced the beginning of a new phase in Lebanese-Syrian relations.

During his state visit to Washington in January 2011, all opposition ministers resigned from the cabinet in anticipation of the indictment of some senior members of Hizbollah [*q.v.*] by the U.N.-appointed Special Tribunal on Lebanon to investigate the assassination of Rafiq Hariri. With more than a third of the ministers quitting, Hariri's government fell. But he stayed on as caretaker premier until June when his successor, Najib Mikati [*q.v.*], succeeded in forming a new cabinet.

al-Hashem clan: *Jordan's ruling dynasty* Named after Hashem bin Abdul Manaf, the great-grandfather of the Prophet Muhammad, the Banu Hashem clan was part of the Qureish tribe of Arabia [*q.v.*]. In the 10th century, al-Hashems became the ruling family of Mecca [*q.v.*] and the surrounding province of Hijaz [*q.v.*]. This continued until 1517 when—following the Ottoman Sultan Salim I's victory over the Mamlukes in Egypt—the head of al-Hashem ruling family, known as the Sharif (Arabic: *Noble*), sent an envoy to present the keys of Mecca to the Ottoman sultan and offer him the title of the Protector of the Holy Places. The sultan accepted both.

In 1893 Sultan Abdul Hamid II exiled Sharif Hussein bin Ali al-Hashem—the 37th in line of descent from the Prophet Muhammad, through his daughter Fatima and her husband, Imam Ali, and their son Hassan—by forcing him to live in Constantinople (now Istanbul). His exile ended when the sultan was deposed in 1908 by the Young Turks.

In 1916, during World War I, Sharif Hussein, allying with Britain against the Ottoman Turks, led the Arab revolt with the help of his sons: Ali, Abdullah [*q.v.*], Faisal [*q.v.*], and Zaid.

Hassidic Jews (Hebrew: *from hasedim, pious*): *leading ultra-Orthodox sect* The Hassidic sect was established in Poland by Israel Baal Shem Tov (1698–1740), a pious Jew [*q.v.*] who, rebelling against the literalism of the Talmud [*q.v.*], attempted to help religious but illiterate Jews relate to the Jewish law and doctrine through emotional means. He devised a method of total surrender by the believer to God through mystical elevation, involving singing and dancing. As the leader of his group of disciples, a Hassidic rabbi acts as an intercessor between them and God, offering inspired advice.

Despite being branded heretics by the Talmudists in 1781, the size of the Hassidic community grew, especially in Poland and Russia. Beginning in the early 20th century, a small minority migrated to Palestine [*q.v.*], preferring to live either in Jerusalem's [*q.v.*] Mea Shearim district or in self-enclosed communities such as the Bnei Brak agricultural settlement near Tel Aviv [*q.v.*]. Politically, they supported Agudat Israel [*q.v.*].

Hawatmeh, Nayef (1934–): *Palestinian leader* Born into a Greek Catholic [*q.v.*] family in Salt, Jordan, Hawatmeh was a cofounder of the Arab Nationalist Movement [*q.v.*] in 1952 in Beirut [*q.v.*]. With the Arab defeat in the 1967 Six-Day War [*q.v.*], he became disillusioned with Egyptian President Gamal Abdul Nasser [*q.v.*], whom he had seen as the leader to liberate Palestine [*q.v.*] through a conventional war with Israel.

When the Popular Front for the Liberation of Palestine (PFLP) [*q.v.*] was formed in 1968, Hawatmeh was one of its founders. But the PFLP's failure to form a broad national front of Palestinian organizations led him and Bilal Hassan to quit and establish the Democratic Front for the Liberation of Palestine (DFLP) [*q.v.*] in 1969 and affiliate it with the Palestine Liberation Organization (PLO) [*q.v.*]. Within a year he had expanded the DFLP's commando force to make it the fourth-largest among Palestinian militias.

Stressing the complementary nature of the Palestinian and Jordanian struggles, he advocated the overthrow of the Hashemite dynasty. But the bitter experience of September 1970—when the Palestinians suffered heavy losses at the hands of Jordanian troops—chastened him.

He maintained good relations with the Communist Party of the Soviet Union, and was instrumental in persuading the Kremlin to recognize the PLO as the sole legitimate, representative body of the Palestinian people in the wake of the October 1973 Arab-Israeli War [*q.v.*]. He was also the prime mover in persuading the Palestine National Council (PNC) [*q.v.*], in mid-1974, to accept the idea of establishing a "national authority" in the West Bank [*q.v.*] and Gaza [*q.v.*] as the first step toward the liberation of all of Palestine.

After his expulsion from Beirut [*q.v.*], Hawatmeh relocated the DFLP in Damascus [*q.v.*]. He began to cooperate with the PFLP leader, George Habash [*q.v.*], in their policies toward Yasser Arafat [*q.v.*] and the peace process. He accepted the PNC decision in late 1988 to reject terrorism and limit the use of violence to military targets inside Israel and the Occupied Territories. He opposed the Israeli-PLO Accord [*q.v.*] of September 1993.

Six years later he met Yasser Arafat [*q.v.*] in Cairo [*q.v.*], when they agreed to coordinate their positions on the PLO's final status talks with Israel. His later request to be allowed to return to the Palestinian Territories [*q.v.*] was rejected by Israel even though the DFLP was removed from the list of the terrorist organizations by the United States in 1999.

In 2002, he opposed suicide bombings inside Israel. Two years later he called for an end to the Second Intifada [*q.v.*]. In 2007, he was allowed by Israel to attend the meeting of the PLO's Central Council [*q.v.*] in Ramallah [*q.v.*].

Hebrew Bible: *See* Old Testament.

Hebrew language: A member of the Canaanite group of Semitic languages [*q.v.*], Hebrew was the language of the ancient Hebrews [*q.v.*]. The biblical Hebrew of the period before the Jewish Exile in 586 B.C. evolved into a more precise language (as used in the Mishna [*q.v.*]) in the first century A.D. The subsequent forms have been mixtures of these two variants. Literary Hebrew had come into its own by the early sixth century. From then until the late 15th century, it was the only written medium of communication for the Jews [*q.v.*] of northwest Europe. By contrast, the Jews in the Arab [*q.v.*] world and Spain used it only for artistic expression.

The emergence of Modern Hebrew—an amalgam of the language at different stages—coincided with the rise of Jewish nationalism [*q.v.*] around 1880. Once again Hebrew became a spoken language among Jews. The Jewish community in Palestine [*q.v.*] made it the medium of instruction in Jewish schools in 1913. Later the British Mandate recognized it as one of the three languages in Palestine, on a par with Arabic [*q.v.*] and English. It became one of the two official languages of Israel upon its founding in May 1948, the other being Arabic [*q.v.*].

Hebrews: This term stands for the Jews [*q.v.*], as used in the Old Testament [*q.v.*].

Hebron: *West Bank city* Population: 166,000 (2011 est.) Called Hevron by the Jews [*q.v.*] and Al Khalil al-Rahman (the Friend of the Merciful, a reference to Abraham) by the Arabs [*q.v.*], Hebron is sacred to both Jews and Muslims [*q.v.*], the latter revering Abraham as a founder of monotheism and an antecedent of the Prophet Muhammad.

Hebron was established in the 18th century B.C. by the Hittites. Tradition has it that Abraham, the founder of Judaism [*q.v.*], lived there and bought the Machpelah cave, which became the burial place for him and his wife, Sarah; their son Isaac and his wife, Rebecca and their son Jacob and his wife, Leah. In ca 1010 B.C. King David was anointed in Hebron, his capital for eight years, and King Herod the Great (r. 37–4 B.C.) tried to protect the Machpelah cave—the site of Abraham's tomb—by enclosing it within a wall. In the Bible Hebron also appears as Kiryat Arba (Hebrew: *Four Towns*) and Marme.

Hebron fell to Arab [*q.v.*] Muslims [*q.v.*] in 635 A.D. It changed hands during the Crusades, with the Crusaders administering it from 1100 to 1260. In 1267 Mamluke Sultan Baybar banned worship by non-Muslims at the Machpelah cave. Hebron came under Ottoman suzerainty in 1516. After the fall of the Ottomans in 1918, it became part of the Palestine [*q.v.*] under the British Mandate. Modern Hebron is situated east of the old settlement.

Following the Arab-Jewish riots in 1929, in which 67 of the town's 700 Jews were killed, the rest of the community fled. Two years later some 30 Jewish families returned, but they left after the Arab uprising of 1936–39. After the Palestine War (1948–49) [*q.v.*] Hebron came under Jordanian authority. This lasted until the 1967 Six-Day War [*q.v.*], when the town, with a population of 38,310, fell to the

Israelis. They opened the Cave of Machpelah, now enclosed within the Mosque of Ibrahim/ Abraham, called by Arabs the Haram al-Khalil (Arabic: *Sanctuary of the Friend*), to worship by Jews.

An attempt by militant Jews in 1968 to establish a Jewish settlement in a rented Palestinian hotel in Hebron failed, and they were moved to an Israeli military base near the city. In 1971 they were allowed to build a settlement, called Kiryat Arba, east of Hebron. Eight years later Jewish families returned to the old Jewish neighborhood in the city center. By the early 1990s Kiryat Arba, with a population of nearly 5,000, had become the second-largest Jewish colony on the West Bank [*q.v.*] and a hotbed of Jewish extremists. One of them, Baruch Goldstein, shot dead 29 Palestinians at prayer in the Mosque of Abraham (called Ibrahimi Mosque by Arabs, and Tomb of Patriarchs by Jews) on 25 February 1994.

Though included in the list of the Palestinian cities to be evacuated according to the Oslo II Accord [*q.v.*] of September 1995, Israel did not withdraw from it. A later agreement between Israel and the Palestinian Authority (PA) [*q.v.*] left the city divided into two parts, with the one containing the Ibrahimi Mosque/Tomb of the Patriarchs and the Jewish settlers under exclusive Israeli control.

In 2009, there were 800 Jewish settlers in central Hebron. The Kriyat Arba settlement adjacent to the city had a population of 7,300.

Heikal, Muhammad Hassanein

(1923–): *Egyptian journalist, historian,* *and politician* Born into a middle-class family in Cairo [*q.v.*], Heikal secured a degree in law and economics from Cairo University. After a year at the *Egyptian Gazette* in 1943 as a reporter, he joined the weekly *Rose al-Yusuf*, named after a famous Lebanese actress who had turned to journalism in 1925, and then the *Akhbar al-Yom* (Arabic: *The Daily News*), covering World War II, the Greek Civil War, and the Palestine War (1948–49) [*q.v.*]. In 1953 he became editor of *Akhar Saa* (Arabic: *Last Hour*), an illustrated weekly, and in 1956 of the daily *Al-Akhbar* (Arabic: *The News*).

After the July 1952 revolution he had become a friend of President Gamal Abdul Nasser and his aides. This led to his appointment in 1957 as the chief editor of *Al-Ahram* (Arabic: *The Pyramids*), the semi-official newspaper of Egypt. Under his stewardship *Al-Ahram* shed its sensational style and became a sober, objective newspaper of quality in the Arab world. He became the country's most influential journalist and a confidant of Nasser. The circulation of *Al-Ahram* rose to 500,000 daily and 750,000 on Fridays in the mid-1960s.

In 1968 he was appointed to the central committee of the Arab Socialist Union [*q.v.*], where he advocated less reliance on the Soviet Union and political liberalization at home. He became minister of information and national guidance in April 1970. After Nasser's death five months later, he lost his ministerial position but remained editor of *Al-Ahram*.

While maintaining his personal friendship with the new president, Anwar Sadat [*q.v.*], Heikal started criticizing his deviation from the

Nasserist principles. Following *Al-Ahram*'s criticism of the U.S.-brokered Sinai I Agreement [*q.v.*] between Egypt and Israel in January 1974, Sadat removed Heikal from his job and prohibited him from publishing articles in the Egyptian press. He took to writing for the foreign press in the Arab world and elsewhere. After Heikal's opposition to Sadat's dramatic peace moves with Israel in late 1978, he was harassed by the police and deprived of his passport. He was one of the important opponents that Sadat imprisoned in September 1981, a month before his assassination. Released by President Hosni Mubarak [*q.v.*], Heikal resumed his journalistic career in Egypt, but failed to develop a rapport with the new leader.

He continued to publish books in English. The titles included *Nasser: the Cairo Documents* (1972), *The Road to Ramadan* (1975), *The Sphinx and the Commissar* (1978), *Return of the Ayatollah* (1981), *Autumn of Fury: the Assassination of Sadat* (1983), *Illusions of Triumph: An Arab View of the Gulf War* (1992), and *Secret Channels: The Inside Story of Arab-Israeli Peace Negotiations* (1997).

In 2003, at the age of 80, Heikal decided to stop writing and limit himself to commenting on the electronic media. He soon acquired a weekly slot on the Al-Jazeera satellite TV channel to dwell at length on such subjects as the decline of the Ottoman Empire, the rise of Arab nationalism [*q.v.*], the Arab wars, and the rise and fall of superpowers in history. He criticized the reelection of Hosni Mubarak in 2006, and, in an interview with a British newspaper in 2007, he said that Mubarak lived in a "world of fantasy."

In 2009 he covered the U.S. presidential contest for Al-Jazeera. The exposure on that TV channel gave him a wide audience throughout the Arabic [*q.v.*]-speaking world.

In 2011, he supported the Arab Spring [*q.v.*] which, in his view, had repositioned Egypt as a leading regional power. At the same time he lamented Egyptians' immersion in reforming their domestic political system to the exclusion of enabling their country to become an important actor in shaping the future of the Middle East [*q.v.*].

Helou, Charles (1912–2001): *Lebanese politician; president, 1964–70* (also spelled Hilou) Born into a middle-class Maronite [*q.v.*] family in Beirut [*q.v.*], Helou studied law and practiced as a lawyer and journalist. From 1935 to 1946 he was the managing editor of the daily *L'Orient le Jour* (French: *The Oriental Morning*).

One of the founders of the Phalange Party [*q.v.*], he left it to joint the Constitutional Bloc of Bishara Khouri [*q.v.*]. He was elected to parliament in 1951 and held his seat for a decade, becoming minister of justice from 1954 to 1955. Though he opposed the attempt by Camille Chamoun [*q.v.*] to win the presidency for a second term, he stayed out of the 1958 Lebanese Civil War [*q.v.*]. This helped him to win the presidency in 1964 as a nonpartisan candidate who also had the backing of the incumbent, Fuad Chehab [*q.v.*].

A weak leader, he lacked a political or military base of his own. The reforming drive initiated by Chehab slowed under him. But he maintained stability in the country by aligning his foreign policy with that of the Arab hinterland and co-opting the urban Muslim [*q.v.*] leadership in the running of the state, thus blending Lebanon's Christian identity with Arab nationalism [*q.v.*]. He kept Lebanon out of the June 1967 Arab-Israeli War [*q.v.*].

Realizing that the unity of the Lebanese army would be threatened if the clashes between the army and the Palestinian commandos became more bloody and frequent, he approved the Cairo Agreement of 1969 [*q.v.*], by which Lebanon allowed the Palestine Liberation Organization [*q.v.*] control of the Palestinian refugee camps. During the 1975–90 Lebanese Civil War [*q.v.*] he was often consulted as someone whose mediation might help to end the conflict.

Herut (Hebrew: *Freedom*): *Israeli political party* (official title: *Gush Herut* [Hebrew: *Freedom Bloc*]) After the disbandment of Irgun [*q.v.*] in July 1948, its former ranks and Revisionist Zionists [*q.v.*] reemerged jointly as Gush Herut, headed by Menachem Begin [*q.v.*]. The party advocated establishing biblical Eretz Yisrael [*q.v.*] and separating trade unions from the various social services and business activities of the Labor [*q.v.*]-dominated Histadrut [*q.v.*]. It attracted those Jewish immigrants, especially from the Arab states, who had experienced difficulty in getting assimilated into the new social order. Herut secured 14 seats in the first Knesset [*q.v.*], eight in the second, 15 in the third, 17 in the fourth, and 17 in the fifth (1961). In 1963, the rift in Labor's ranks encouraged Herut to merge with the Liberal Party [*q.v.*] to form Gahal [*q.v.*].

Herzog, Chaim (1918–97): *Israeli politician; president, 1983–93* Son of Isaac Herzog, the chief rabbi of Ireland, Herzog was born in Belfast, United Kingdom. When his father was appointed the Ashkenazi [*q.v.*] chief rabbi of Palestine [*q.v.*] in 1936, the family migrated to Palestine. After attending Jewish schools, Herzog studied law at the Palestine Law School, Jerusalem [*q.v.*], and then in London and Cambridge.

During World War II he worked as an intelligence officer in the British army. After the founding of Israel in 1948 he was appointed director of military intelligence. He then served as military attaché in Washington (1950–54), commander of the Jerusalem district and head of the southern command (1954–59), and chief of military intelligence (1959–62).

After his retirement from the military he took up law practice. He joined Rafi, led by David Ben-Gurion [*q.v.*] in 1965. During the June 1967 Arab-Israeli War [*q.v.*], he was a commentator on Israeli radio. After serving briefly as the military governor of the West Bank [*q.v.*], he returned to his law practice. During the October 1973 Arab-Israeli War [*q.v.*] he once again became a commentator on Israeli radio.

He served as Israel's ambassador to the United Nations from 1975 to 1978. On his return home he resumed his political career with the Labor [*q.v.*] movement. In 1983 he was elected to the Knesset [*q.v.*], and two years later he narrowly won the contest for the presidency. He was reelected in 1988. His seven books include *Israel's Finest Hour* (1967), *The War of Atonement* (1975), and *Heroes of Israel* (1990).

hijab (Arabic: *cover or screen*): *See* Islamic dress.

Hijaz: *western region of Saudi Arabia* Area 150,000 sq. mi./388,500 sq. km. As the birthplace and spiritual center of Islam [*q.v.*], Hijaz is the Holy Land of Muslims [*q.v.*]. It contains Islam's holiest shrines—in Mecca [*q.v.*], the site of the Kaaba [*q.v.*], and the birthplace of the Prophet Muhammad; and in Medina [*q.v.*], the burial place of the Prophet Muhammad. It was the nucleus of the early Islamic Empire.

In more recent times, having been a province of the Ottoman Empire since 1517, it became after World War I an independent kingdom under Sharif Hussein bin Ali al-Hashem, who had been appointed the Protector of the Holy Places (of Mecca and Medina) by the Ottoman regime in 1908.

Following the abolition of the caliphate by the secular republic of Turkey in 1924, Sharif Hussein declared himself caliph. This angered Abdul Aziz bin Abdul Rahman bin Saud [*q.v.*], then king of Najd [*q.v.*], who conquered Hijaz in 1926 and declared himself king of Hijaz as well as of Najd. In 1932 he combined his two realms into the Kingdom of Saudi Arabia. The Hijaz region now covers four of Saudi Arabia's 13 provinces.

Histadrut (Hebrew: *Federation*) (abbreviation of *HaHistadrut HaKelalit shel HaOvedim HaIvirim be Eretz Yisrael*, The General Federation of Workers in the Land of Israel): *Israeli trade union federation and social welfare agency* In 1920 Ahdut HaAvodah [q.v.] and HaPoale HaTzair [q.v.] agreed to form an umbrella organization to encompass all Labor-pioneer parties of the Zionist [q.v.] persuasion. The result was the General Federation of Hebrew Workers in the Land of Israel. Its membership was limited to Jewish workers, artisans, and tradesmen. About three-fifths of the 7,000 Jewish workers in Palestine [q.v.] participated in electing delegates to the founding convention of the Histadrut in December 1920. The next year the Histadrut established Solel Boneh (Hebrew: *Paving and Building*), a large construction and public works company, and, in association with the World Zionist Organization [q.v.], the Workers' Bank. It thus emerged as a general-purpose body rather than an exclusively trade union organization.

Though claiming to be a non-political trade union federation, the Histadrut encouraged Jewish immigration, settled newcomers, and organized defense through Haganah [*q.v.*]. Under the leadership of David Ben-Gurion [*q.v.*], its general secretary from 1920 to 1935, it emerged as a central pillar of the Zionist enterprise in Palestine: it ran a social security system, an educational network, and its own production and service cooperatives.

In 1943 it set up an Arab [*q.v.*] Department in Haifa [*q.v.*]. But it barely functioned outside the city. It was only when the increasing alienation of Israeli Arabs [*q.v.*] from agricultural land purchased by Jewish immigrants led to their large-scale migration to urban areas, resulting in a dramatic rise in wage-earning Arab labor force, that the Histadrut opened its membership to Arabs in stages from 1959. Their enrollment changed the ethnic composition. As a consequence, the leadership of the Federation, elected every four years, dropped the term

"Hebrew" from the organization's name in 1966.

Following a growing challenge to the Histadrut from non-Histadrut "action committees" in 1971, the Labor Party [*q.v.*]-led government passed a law that formalized its monopoly as the "legal representative of workers." The Histadrut opened its membership to all workers, including the self-employed and professionals, as well as students, housewives, pensioners, and the jobless. Nearly 85 percent of all those eligible belonged to the Histadrut. The Histadrut engaged in trade union organization, involving unions, labor councils, and professional federations; social services, including health insurance (until 1995), pensions, and welfare; educational and cultural activities; and economic development undertaken by Hevrat HaOvedim (Hebrew: *The Workers' Company*).

In trade unions the Histadrut's primary unit is the workers' committee at the workplace; its secondary unit the trade union; and its tertiary unit the Labor Council, which is elected by all local trade unions, and oversees union as well as economic and cultural affairs. Then there are nationwide professional bodies and other national organizations. The Labor Councils and nationwide federations report to the Histadrut Executive Committee. Its educational and cultural activities include workers' colleges, vocational schools, sports clubs, and theater and dance groups. The activities undertaken by the Workers' Company include the running of factories, construction companies, agricultural and transport cooperatives, a bank, an insurance company, and a publishing house.

In the 1994 Histadrut elections, the Labor Party lost control of the executive committee. The subsequent leadership renamed the organization as New Histadrut. At that time it had 1,573,000 members, including dependents of the workers. Of these, 170,000 were Israeli Arabs. The Histadrut employed about a third of the working labor force in Israel.

The following year the Labor-led government of Yitzhak Rabin [*q.v.*] passed the National Health Insurance Law, which separated the Histadrut from health care, whose social services had included the General Sick Fund (Hebrew: *Kupat Holim Kelalit*), covering half of the adult population, and pension funds. With this the Histadrut's membership fell to 627,000 in 1998.

In 2009, when it was 650,000 strong, its executive committee opened its membership to 250,000 foreign workers employed in Israel. Its support of Israel's Gaza War [*q.v.*] was criticized both at home and abroad.

In 2010, Ofer Eini, elected chairman three years earlier, appointed a non-member, Daniel Avi Nissan Korn, as chairman of the trade union division, the second most important post in the Histadrut. But that did not lead to any softening on the trade union front. In February 2011 its leaders called a general strike to demand better wages for 250,000 contract workers who received about a third less than directly hired employees. The strike by more than half a million workers closed banks, the stock exchange, ports, airports, and most public offices. It ended after thee days when the government agreed to improve the wages of contract employees.

Hizbollah (Arabic: *Party of Allah*): *Lebanese political-religious movement.* (also spelled Hezbollah and Hizbullah) More a movement than a party, its origins lay in the expulsion of the Lebanese Shia [*q.v.*] students from Najaf [*q.v.*] by the Baathist [*q.v.*] government in Iraq. Among them were Abbas Mousavi and Hassan Nasrallah [*q.v.*], who established a Shia seminary in Baalbek [*q.v.*]. Many of the seminary students joined Nasrallah in offering armed resistance to the Israeli invasion of Lebanon in June 1982 [*q.v.*]. Such fighting groups evolved into Hizbollah under the leadership of Shaikh Muhammad Hussein Fadlallah, a Shia cleric. The chief catalyst was Ali Akbar Mohtashemi, the Iranian ambassador to Syria from 1982 to 1983. Yet it was not until 1985 that Hizbollah published its charter, decrying the West and Israel for its mistreatment of the Muslim [*q.v.*] world.

In its domestic politics, it allied with the Islamic Jihad [*q.v.*] and the Islamic Amal [*q.v.*] to oppose the government of President Amin Gemayel [*q.v.*]. The three organizations together confronted the Lebanese army in early 1984. Hizbollah was close to the contingent of 2,000 Iranian revolutionary guards, based in Baalbek, who had been sent to Lebanon in mid-1982 to fight the Israeli invaders. As it escalated its guerilla attacks on Israeli targets in southern Lebanon, its military aid from Iran increased. By the spring of 1987, when Hizbollah had established its military wing, called *al-Muqawama al-Islamiya*, the Islamic

Resistance, its armory included cannons as well as anti-tank and anti-aircraft missiles. It had emerged as the leading Lebanese recipient of financial assistance from Iran, which funded its health, education, and other public services through its (domestic) Martyrs' Foundation.

In return Hizbollah tried to assist Iran by taking Western, especially American, hostages in Lebanon (under such labels as the Revolutionary Justice Organization and the Organization of the Oppressed of the Earth, which seized Terry Waite, the envoy of the Archbishop of Canterbury, in early 1987), on the ground that their captivity would inhibit the Pentagon's intervention in the Iran-Iraq War (1980–88) [*q.v.*] on the Iraqi side. It also used the hostages as bargaining chips to secure supplies of U.S.-made weapons to Iran, which were needed to replenish the military hardware bought by the regime of Muhammad Reza Shah Pahlavi [*q.v.*]. This led to the Iran-Contra Affair [*q.v.*].

Though unsympathetic to its religious militancy, Syrian President Hafiz Assad [*q.v.*] found the party a suitable instrument to pressure Israeli and South Lebanon Army (SLA) [*q.v.*] troops in Israel's self-declared security zone in southern Lebanon. In January–February 1988 the skirmishes between Hizbollah and the SLA claimed 40 Hizbollah lives. Later, to ensure that Hizbollah did not acquire political monopoly among Shias, Assad encouraged members of Amal [*q.v.*], a Shia party, to attack Hizbollah fighters in the southern suburbs of Beirut [*q.v.*]. But Hizbollah performed well. Its activities also brought it into direct conflict with Israel, whose commandos abducted Shaikh Abdul Karim Obeid, the party leader in the south, in July 1989.

The next month Hizbollah joined the front formed to confront the government of Gen. Michel Aoun [*q.v.*], the Maronite army commander. It criticized the Taif Accord [*q.v.*] as perpetuating the old system, with its downgrading of Shias, now the largest single sect in Lebanon, and hindering the creation of an Islamic state in Muslim-majority Lebanon, its ultimate goal. But it desisted from pressing its objections too far. Syria allowed Hizbollah to play an important, though subsidiary, role in the final, successful, attack on Aoun's forces in October 1990. But, protesting at the lack of any official plan to reverse Israel's occupation of the south, Hizbollah refused to join the national unity government formed in December. Opposed to confessionalism [*q.v.*]—a system which allocates parliamentary seats by religious sects—it demanded a revised electoral law to make parliament truly representative of voters.

After the disarming of all militias in Greater Beirut, Hizbollah moved its men and weapons to the southern part of the Beqaa governorate and the mountain caves near the Israeli-occupied region, and increased its attacks on Israeli and SLA patrols in the area. As before, Israel responded with air raids and artillery fire. In May 1991 the party's newly elected secretary-general, Shaikh Abbas Mousavi, stated that so long as Israel remained inside Lebanon his irregulars would not surrender their weapons to the Lebanese government. Unwilling to cause a split within its ranks by attack-ing Hizbollah—demanding an unconditional Israeli withdrawal from southern Lebanon as required by UN Security Council Resolution 425 of March 1978—the government settled for merely receiving a list of 3,500 Hizbollah militiamen active in the south.

In late 1991 a three-way swap—involving 450 Lebanese and Palestinian detainees under the Israelis, seven dead or captured Israeli servicemen, and the remaining Western hostages—ended Hizbollah's involvement in hostage taking. It won eight of the 27 seats reserved for Shias in the 1992 parliamentary elections. Its killing of two Israeli soldiers in July 1993 brought about a week-long artillery bombardment by Israel under the codename Operation Accountability, which left 139 dead and 250,000 homeless. During 1994–95 Hizbollah mounted sporadic attacks on Israeli targets in south Lebanon. In April 1996, to stop Hizbollah's rocket attacks on northern Israel, the Israeli government mounted Operation Grapes of Wrath, which targeted a power station north of Beirut, and which killed 170 to 200 Lebanese, mostly civilians, including 100 refugees sheltering at the UN base at Qana, and displaced 400,000.

Hizbollah started its own TV channel in Arabic [*q.v.*], called Al Manar (The Tower), in 1991. During the next quarter-century, it acquired an estimated worldwide audience of 12 to 13 million.

In the 1996 parliamentary election Hizbollah retained its four seats in the South and Nabatiya governorates and, allying with Amal, won 22 of the 23 seats in the Beqaa governorate.

Limiting itself to Israeli and SLA targets in the occupied southern Lebanon, Hizbollah mounted 715 attacks in 1997 and 1,200 in 1998. It intensified its activities in the run-up to the Israeli elections in May 1999, when Ehud Barak [*q.v.*], Labor's candidate for the prime minister, promised to disengage Israel from southern Lebanon. In May 2000, Israel withdrew unconditionally from southern Lebanon as required by the 22-year-old UN Security Council resolution. But, because Israel did not withdraw from the Shaaba Farm adjacent to the Syrian border, Hizbollah did not regard its evacuation as complete and attacked its targets periodically.

Hizbollah was placed on Washington's list of terrorist organizations in 1995. It was removed from the list after it condemned the 9/11 attacks. This was reversed in 2005.

In the 2005 parliamentary election, as part of the Amal-Hizbollah alliance, it secured 14 seats.

In the five-week-long Israel-Hizbollah War [*q.v.*] in 2006, Hizbollah was the principal enemy of Israel, with the Amal militia playing a minor role. The ruler of Qatar stepped forward to help financially all those who lost their homes and businesses in the conflict.

The nonviolent impasse in central Beirut between Hizbollah and its allies and the pro-Western government of Fouad Siniora [*q.v.*] over the election of the successor to Emile Lahoud [*q.v.*], which started in October 2007, turned violent on 6 May 2008 when Siniora ordered an investigation of Hizbollah's private telecommunications network and dismissed the airport security chief. Hizbollah and its allies attacked the airport and stormed Sunni streets and properties in central and west Beirut as well as the Government Palace housing the prime minister's office. Counterattacks followed. Fighting spread to other parts of Lebanon as well and altogether claimed 200 lives. To avert Lebanon's descent into fully fledged civil war, Qatar's ruler, Shaikh Hamad ibn Khlaifa al-Thani [*q.v.*], invited the rivals to Doha [*q.v.*]. The concord reached in Doha on 21 May favored Hizbollah, which was allowed to continue bearing arms as a means of protecting Lebanon from Israel's military moves and maintain its own telecommunications system. In the subsequent national unity government the opposition 8 March Alliance [*q.v.*] got 11 of the 30 cabinet places, thus acquiring veto power.

As part of the 8 March Alliance, Hizbollah gained 13 seats in the 2009 general election. Saad Hariri [*q.v.*], leader of the 14 March Alliance [*q.v.*], was able to form his cabinet only after signing a power-sharing agreement which required giving two posts to Hizbollah in the 30-member national unity government. This arrangement broke down when the indictment of four senior Hizbollah members by the Special Tribunal on Lebanon was anticipated in January 2011. At the urging of Hizbollah, 11 of the ministers resigned, bringing down the Saad Hariri administration. The succeeding government of Najib Mikati [*q.v.*] was dependent on the good will of Hizbollah.

Hizbollah maintained close ties with Iran, its leading arms supplier, using Syria as the conduit. It refuses to surrender its weapons.

As the Arab Spring [*q.v.*] started in early 2012, Hizbollah expressed solidarity with the protesting Egyptian and Tunisian peoples. Later it praised the pro-democracy movements in Bahrain, Yemen, and Libya. It applauded this development because the demonstrators in these countries shared its resistance ideology. But when it came to the uprising in Syria, Hizbollah stood by the regime of President Bashar Assad [*q.v.*], and accused the opposition of committing treason.

Holy City: *See* Jerusalem.

Holy Land: The term was first used in the Old Testament [*q.v.*] in Zechariah 2.12. *See* Palestine.

Homs: *Syrian city* Population: 1.276 million (2011 est.) Known in ancient times as Emesa, it was the site of a renowned temple to the sun god. It was the capital of Roman Emperor Aurelian (r. 270–275 A.D.). With Christianity [*q.v.*] becoming the state religion under Emperor Constantine I (r. 306–337 A.D.), most of the local residents embraced the new faith. The city fell to Muslim [*q.v.*] Arabs [*q.v.*] in 636 A.D. and was renamed Hims. A failed Christian uprising in 855 A.D. resulted in the eradication of Christianity. Since then its Muslim character has remained strong. It became part of the Ottoman Empire in 1517, and remained so until the dissolution of the empire four centuries later. It was then included in the Syria placed under the French Mandate. The French established a military academy there, the only one of its kind in the country.

It is an important commercial, industrial, and transport center. A stronghold of Sunni Islam [*q.v.*], in 1973 it witnessed violent skirmishes between the security forces and demonstrators protesting against the secular nature of the new constitution.

Unsurprisingly, when the wave of Arab unrest reached Syria in March 2011, Homs emerged as one of the four major centers of resistance to the secular Baathist [*q.v.*] regime, with protestors demanding the removal of Syrian President Bashar Assad [*q.v.*] from office. The government's strategy of besieging restive areas with tanks, then letting security forces and snipers open fire on demonstrators, failed to quash the uprising. The emergence of the Free Army of Syria (FSA) escalated the conflict in the city and elsewhere in the country. Most of Homs city fell to the FSA.

Angered by the FSA's killing of 10 soldiers on 3 February 2012, the Syrian government besieged the districts under the FSA's control. After three weeks of firing artillery shells and mortars at the rebellious stronghold of Bab Amr, the military launched a ground attack and recaptured the neighborhood. It then retook several other districts, bringing three-quarters of the city under its control by the end of March. Sporadic violence continued until the cease-fire in mid-April. The total death toll consisted of 700 civilians and FSA fighters and 50 soldiers.

In early September, an officer of the FSA announced the formation of the Revolutionary Military Council in Homs to unify all FSA units in Homs province. A month later the government mounted a major offensive, using intense aerial and artillery bombing to regain control of all of Homs and the surrounding towns, and claimed near-success by early November.

The tourist offerings of Homs include Roman ruins, the Citadel of Salah al-Din (aka Saladin) built in the Middle Ages, and the Grand Mosque of al-Nouri, which originated as a temple dedicated to the sun god and was later turned into the Church of St John.

Hormuz, Strait of: Situated between Iran and the northern tip of Trucial Oman, the Strait of Hormuz is only 21 mi./34 km wide at its narrowest point. But the width of the shipping lane in either direction is only two mi./3.2 km, separated by a two-mi./3.2-km buffer zone. The territorial waters of Iran and Oman, each 12 mi./19 km wide, overlap in the Strait. In late 1979, when 40 percent of the world's exported oil carried by tankers passed through the Strait, rising tension between the United States and the newly emergent Islamic Republic of Iran made the Strait the focus of attention for both Washington and Moscow. Scores of warships from both sides assembled in the international waters of the north Arabian Sea at the mouth of the strait.

During the 1980–88 Iran-Iraq War [*q.v.*] the importance of the strait increased. In September 1983 the Iranian leader, Ayatollah Ruhollah Khomeini [*q.v.*], threatened to close it if Iran's Kharg oil terminal in the Gulf was destroyed by Iraq. U.S. President Ronald Reagan reiterated the earlier official position that Washington would intervene militarily to keep the Strait open to international shipping. He increased the U.S. naval presence in the area to 30 warships. Britain and France followed suit. The Soviets increased their presence in the Arabian Sea to 26 war vessels. The crisis subsided, and the strait remained open.

In the course of the periodic crises between Iran and the U.S., the Iranian regime threatened to block the Strait. In 2011, of the 45 million barrels per day (bpd) of oil that were transported by tankers, 17 million bpd passed through the Strait of Hormuz.

Hoss, Salim (1929–): *Lebanese politician; prime minister, 1976–78, 1979–80, 1987–90, 1998–2000* Born into a Sunni [*q.v.*] family in Beirut [*q.v.*], Hoss received his postgraduate degree in economics and business administration from the American University in Beirut (AUB) [*q.v.*], and capped it with a doctorate in economics from Indiana University in the United States in 1961.

After teaching economics at the AUB he joined the Kuwait Development Fund as a financial adviser in 1964. Two years later he was appointed chairman of the Lebanese Banking Control Commission, and in 1973 he was named chairman of the Industrial Development Bank. He worked in conjunction with Elias Sarkis [*q.v.*], the Central Bank governor who was elected president in September 1976 in the midst of a civil war. Three months later he was invited to lead the Lebanese government. He selected an eight-member cabinet consisting wholly of technocrats.

In the civil conflict he generally took a pro-Muslim and pro-Damascus line. His second government of 12 ministers, formed in July 1979, inclined toward Syria. Whereas Sarkis viewed national reconciliation as a prelude to reducing Syria's influence in Lebanon, Hoss considered it as a prelude to implementing a security plan in cooperation with Syria and the institutionalization of Lebanon's relationship with Syria. He served as the premier until October 1980.

He accepted a ministerial post when a national unity government was formed in April 1984 under Rashid Karami [*q.v.*]. After Karami's assassination in June 1987, he was named acting prime minister. With General Michel Aoun [*q.v.*] appointing a military cabinet in September 1988, Hoss became head of a parallel government. His relations with the Aoun administration soured, with Aoun dissolving parliament in early November 1989 and Hoss condemning his action as illegal.

Following the election of Elias Hrawi [*q.v.*] as president in November 1989, he was called to form the next government. He announced a cabinet of 14, divided equally between Christians [*q.v.*] and Muslims [*q.v.*]. In December 1990, after all heavy weapons had been removed from Greater Beirut and the 15-year-long division of the city ended, he resigned. After the election of Emile Lahoud [*q.v.*] as president in November 1998, he was invited to head the next cabinet. He did so. He resigned two years later when the supporters of his predecessor, Rafiq Hariri [*q.v.*], won overwhelmingly in the parliamentary election.

Hostage-taking and hostages: *During Roman times; American hostages in Iran; Western hostages in Lebanon*
Hostage-taking for political reasons in the West and elsewhere has a long history, dating back at least to Roman Emperor Julius Caesar (102–44 B.C.) who, referring to his crossing of the Rhine River in 55 B.C., mentioned the conquered Ubii tribe establishing ties of friendship and giving hostages as a guarantee of good behavior in the future. In more recent times in the Middle East [*q.v.*], the ruler of North Yemen, Imam Yahya Hamid al-Din (1869–1948), held the sons of the tribal leaders from the north hostage while maintaining that they were being given religious instruction at his court. Following the repression of the Iraqi Communist Party [*q.v.*] in 1978, the Baathist regime [*q.v.*] in Baghdad adopted an official policy of holding hostage a member of the family of an absconding Communist to force him to surrender.

AMERICAN HOSTAGES IN IRAN: On 4 November 1979 militant Islamist students in Tehran [*q.v.*] occupied the Embassy and took hostage 67 American diplomats. This was done to secure the extradition of Muhammad Reza Shah Pahlavi [*q.v.*], then receiving medical treatment in New York, to face charges of corruption and violation of Iran's 1906–07 constitution, and stop the United States from courting dissident elements in Iran, especially military officers.

The U.S. administration, under President Jimmy Carter (r. 1977–81), immediately froze Iran's large reserves in America, severed diplomatic relations, and, together with the European Community, imposed economic sanctions against Iran. Its clandestine attempt to rescue the hostages in April 1980 failed, and its agents in Iran, including the commander of the Iranian air force, Amir Bahman

Bagheri, were exposed. The hostages were then dispersed to different locations.

Various secret attempts to resolve the crisis proved futile. Carter made the release of the American hostages a central issue in his campaign for reelection. This made the Iranian leader, Ayatollah Ruhollah Khomeini [q.v.], intransigent. Along with the sluggish U.S. economy the hostage issue was instrumental in the defeat of Carter by Ronald Reagan in the November 1980 presidential election. It was the first time that a stance taken by a Third World leader had impacted directly on an American presidential election. In line with a secret deal between Iran and the U.S., brokered by Algeria, the American hostages (now reduced to 52 due to earlier, individual releases) were freed in Algiers, after 444 days in captivity, within minutes of President Carter's handing over the office to Reagan on 21 January 1981.

WESTERN HOSTAGES IN LEBANON: During the first 12 years of the 1975–90 Lebanese Civil War [q.v.], some 14,000 people were kidnapped, of whom about 10,000 were killed. The practice of kidnapping foreigners for political purposes was initiated by the Phalange Party [q.v.] in mid-March 1982 with the abduction in Beirut [q.v.] of four Iranian diplomats: Kazem Allaf, Ahmad Motevaselian, Muhsin Musavi, and Muhammad Muqadam (they were later killed). In retaliation, three months later the Islamic Jihad [q.v.] kidnapped David Dodge, acting president of the American University in Beirut [q.v.].

Two months after the United States had put Iran on the list of nations that support international terrorism in January 1984 and decided to harden its policy of blocking arms sales to Iran— then engaged in the Iran-Iraq War [q.v.]—came the abduction of William Buckley, the U.S. Central Intelligence Agency (CIA) station chief in Beirut [q.v.]. Securing his release became the chief motive for the U.S. to enter into clandestine talks with Iran on the basis of arms-for-hostages, which surfaced as the Iran Contra Affair (Irangate) [q.v.] in November 1986. By then the pro-Iranian groups in Lebanon held more than a dozen Western, mainly American and British, hostages. Buckley was believed to have died in captivity.

A further addition to the list came in January 1987: Terry Waite, an envoy of the British Archbishop of Canterbury, who had been engaged in an effort to secure the release of earlier captives. The reasons for taking Western hostages were threefold: to undermine the Western policy of a ban on arms supplies to Iran in its war with Iraq; to prevent Western military involvement on the Christian side in the Lebanese Civil War, as had happened in early 1984; and to secure the release of hundreds of Lebanese and Palestinian prisoners held without charge by Israel in the wake of the 1982 Israeli invasion of Lebanon [q.v.].

Once the Iran-Iraq War had ended in August 1988, the motives behind holding Western hostages narrowed to preventing the West's intervention in the long-running Lebanese Civil War, and gaining the freedom of Lebanese and Palestinian prisoners held by Israel. The Western powers endorsed the Taif Accord [q.v.] of October 1989, and the Lebanese Civil War ended a year later. The intervention of the UN secretary-general brought about the release of John McCarthy, a British journalist, in early August 1991. Four months later the exchange of the last three American captives and 450 Lebanese and Palestinian prisoners ended the decade-long saga.

House of Saud: *The ruling dynasty of Saudi Arabia* The House of Saud is named after Saud, a member of the Musalikh clan of the Ruwalla tribe of the Anaiza tribal federation [*q.v.*] at the turn of the 18th century in the Diraiya-Riyadh region. His son, Muhammad, who ruled the Diraiya Emirate during 1726–1765, embraced Wahhabism [*q.v.*] in 1745. Armed with this doctrine he expanded his domain, an enterprise continued by his successors, Abdul Aziz bin Muhammad (r. 1766–1803) and Saud bin Abdul Aziz (r. 1803–1814), who reached the Syrian and Iraqi frontiers. But under Abdullah bin Saud (r. 1814–1818) the House of Saud's fortunes waned, with Abdullah suffering defeat and eventual execution by the Ottoman sultan.

Over the next three-quarters of a century the House of Saud rose again, only to be suppressed when the rival House of Rashid of the Shammar tribe, backed by the Ottomans, overpowered Abdul Rahman bin Faisal al-Saud in his bastion of Diraiya in 1891. The surviving members of the House of Saud, including Abdul Aziz bin Abdul Rahman al-Saud (1879–1953) [*q.v.*], took refuge in Kuwait.

He regained Riyadh in 1902, and began to expand his realm, which he named Saudi Arabia in 1932. With this, the House of Saud, Aal [*q.v.*]

Saud (consisting of Abdul Aziz and his five brothers), became the ruling dynasty of Saudi Arabia. Of Abdul Aziz al-Saud's nearly 70 children 16 were known to be alive in 2010. They and their almost 200 children and grandchildren exercise most of the state authority. It is estimated that there are 7,000-plus male progeny entitled to call themselves princes and receive generous government stipends.

Houthis: *Zaidi insurgents in Yemen, 2004–* Since the overthrow of the Zaidi [*q.v.*] Imamate in North Yemen in 1962, Zaidis, concentrated in the northern provinces of the country, have felt neglected by the central government in Sanaa [*q.v.*], and have expressed their discontent by staging periodic uprisings. The central authority used force and concessions to meet the challenge.

In theological terms, Zaidis and Wahhabis [*q.v.*] are poles apart. So when Zaidis found the Wahhabi minority in Yemen being rewarded unduly for its active participation in the Yemeni Civil War of 1994 [*q.v.*], they disapproved. Their protest was led by Shaikh Hussein Badr al-Din al-Houthi, a religious and tribal leader of Zaidis.

Relations with the government of President Ali Abdullah Saleh [*q.v.*] frayed when the Yemeni leader joined the "war on terror" by U.S. President George W. Bush (r. 2001–2009) and aligned Yemen closely with Washington. Al Houthi and his followers led a campaign against the pro-American policies of the central government in the mosques of the three Zaidi-dominated northern provinces. His popularity grew to the extent that in June 2004 he called himself Emir al-Mumineen (Arabic: *Commander of the Believers*) and declared the Zaidi region independent. A military reprisal by the central government followed. In September al-Houthi was killed. With that the traditional Zadi rebellion acquired the title of the Houthi Movement.

In the following years there were several rounds of fighting between the Zaidi insurgents and the central military forces. During the longest combat from August 2009 to February 2010, Saudi Arabia's troops joined to curb the Houthi rebels.

When the pro-democracy protest started in February 2011 as part of the Arab Spring [*q.v.*], Houthis participated. In the nation-wide turmoil that followed, the size of the armed and unarmed Houthis rose to 120,000. They gained control of the Sadaa province. By the spring of 2012 they had extended their control to the two neighboring predominantly Zaidi provinces. The eight-year conflict had led to 25,000 fatalities.

Hoveida, Amir Abbas (1919–79): *Iranian politician; prime minister, 1968–77* Son of aristocratic Bahai [*q.v.*] parents, Hoveida was born in Tehran [*q.v.*]. He received his graduate degree in political science from Universite Libre de Bruxelles in Brussels. After serving briefly in the army he joined the foreign ministry. As a diplomat, he served the Iranian missions in France, Germany, and Turkey. From 1952 to 1956 he worked at the Geneva headquarters of the UN Relief and Work Agency [*q.v.*].

Back home, in 1958 he was appointed to the board of directors of the National Iranian Oil Company, and in 1964 he was promoted to treasury secretary. When the New Iran Party was formed in 1963 at the behest of Muhammad Reza Shah Pahlavi [*q.v.*], he was nominated its assistant secretary. By then, he had firmly established his loyalty to the monarch. The shah rewarded him with the premiership in 1968. Willing to accept a subservient role, he learned to interpret adroitly what the monarch wanted. As a consequence he retained his high office until August 1977, the longest uninterrupted tenure for a prime minister since the promulgation of the 1906–07 constitution. When the shah decided to do away with the formula of ruling and opposition parties in 1975 and establish a single party—Rastakhiz (Persian: *Renaissance*) [*q.v.*]—he chose Hoveida as its secretary-general. In October 1976 Hoveida relinquished this post to Jamshid Amuzgar.

Despite his long, loyal service, the shah dismissed Hoveida when he needed a scapegoat to stem the rising revolutionary tide in mid-1977, and named him court minister. But as popular pressure rose, the shah arrested Hoveida along with 11 other leading personalities. He was tried and executed by the Islamic regime in April 1979.

Hrawi, Elias (1930–2006): *Lebanese politician; president, 1989–98* Born into a landowning Maronite [*q.v.*] family in a village near Zahle, the capital of the Beqaa governorate, Hrawi obtained a degree in business administration from Saint Joseph University in Beirut [*q.v.*]. He then managed the family lands. He became a parliamentary deputy in 1972, representing Zahle. Appointed minister of public works in 1980, Hrawi served for two years. During most of the 1975–90 Lebanese Civil War [*q.v.*], Zahle was under Syrian control, and Hrawi maintained amiable relations with Damascus. Following the assassination of President Rene Muawad two and a half weeks after his election in November 1989, Hrawi emerged as the favorite. He was elected president by 47 of the 52 lawmakers meeting in Shtuara (also spelled Chtuara), a town in the Beqaa Valley. He called for special bonds between Lebanon and Syria.

His attempt to overthrow the rival government of Gen. Michel Aoun [*q.v.*] through economic and diplomatic pressure failed. But he succeeded in securing support for the Taif Accord [*q.v.*] from a section of the Maronite community, and reducing the area under Aoun's control to about a third of the Christian sector. In August 1990 he navigated the constitutional reform outlined in the Taif Accord through the parliament. Two months later he allied with Syria in a joint military plan to topple Aoun, which succeeded.

He then created Greater Beirut, free of armed militias, and appointed a government of national unity. He cooperated with Syria on security matters. In May 1991 he signed the Lebanese-Syrian Treaty of Brotherhood, Cooperation, and Coordination [*q.v.*], thus formalizing links with Syria in all important matters, including security and foreign affairs. His government participated in the Middle East peace process, inaugurated by the Middle East Peace Conference in Madrid in October 1991, coordinating Lebanon's stance with Syria's. His supporters' success in the general election of 1992, which was boycotted by right-wing Maronites, strengthened his hand. In 1995 the parliament extended his presidency by three years.

hudud (Arabic: *limit*; plural of *hadd*): *It defines the limits of acceptable behavior in Islam* [*q.v.*]. In the Sharia [*q.v.*], *hudud* covers a set of punishments for such transgressions against religiously acceptable behavior as stealing or robbing, fornication and adultery, making a false accusation, and consumption of alcohol or other intoxicants. In the case of major theft or robbery without murder, the penalty is cutting off a hand or a foot. For robbery coupled with murder, the death sentence is mandatory. In the case of adultery by married adults, the punishment is death by stoning, or 100 lashes. Drinking of alcohol or any other intoxicant usually results in the guilty person's subjection to a certain number of lashes. In every instance hard evidence by eye-witnesses is required. Someone making a false accusation is punished with lashes.

Hardline ulema [*q.v.*] stress that *hudud* punishments are applicable to all times and cannot be amended. But moderate ulema argue that these punishments were appropriate within the historical and social contexts in which they originated and that in today's modernizing societies the underpinning Islamic principles and values should be expressed differently.

Hudud is one of the four systems of crime punishment, others being *qisas* [*q.v.*], based on the concept of equal retaliation for the harm inflicted on a victim; *diyya* (Arabic: *balanced*), compensation paid to the heirs of a victim; and *tazir* (Arabic: *corporal punishment*), penalties for misdemeanors at the discretion of a religious judge.

Hussein, Qusay Saddam (1966–2006): *Iraqi politician* Born to Saddam Hussein [*q.v.*] and Sajida Talfa in Baghdad [*q.v.*], Hussein attended Exemplary Kharkh School, run by his mother, until 1979, when his father became president. To mobilize the population during the Iran-Iraq War [*q.v.*] he resorted to going to official meetings in a tank. He married Sahour, daughter of Gen. Mahir Abdul Rashid, commander of Seventh Army Corps and one of the heroes of the war.

After the 1991 Gulf War [*q.v.*], Saddam Hussein put him in charge of the Concealment Operations Committee (COC) to oversee and safeguard crucial information and material about the military programs prohibited by the UN Security Council Resolution 687 [*q.v.*] passed in April 1991.

The next year he became head of the National Security Bureau, consisting of five intelligence agencies: General Security (GS, *Amn al-Aam*), General Intelligence Department (GID, *Dairat al-Mukhabarat al-Ammaa*), Military Intelligence (MI, *Istikhabarat al-Askariya*), Special Security Directorate (*Muderiye al-Amn al-Khas*), and Military Security (MS, *Amn al-Askariya*). He also supervised the elite Republican Guard.

During the mid-1990s, in the internal debates that raged in Saddam Hussein's extended family on how to

deal with the UN Special Commission (UNSCOM) [*q.v.*] and the International Atomic Energy Agency (IAEA), he and his elder brother, Uday, opposed concessions to the UN Against the background of intensified suffering that the Iraqi people experienced due to the punishing UN sanctions, security around the president tightened to the extent that only Hussein and the president's private secretary, Abid Hamid Mahmoud, knew his whereabouts.

In 2001, when Hussein was elected to the Baath Party [*q.v.*] Regional Command, he held the rank of a major-general. Unlike Uday—notorious for his violence, short temper, and public tantrums—Hussein was intelligent, calculating, and quietly ruthless

On the eve of the Anglo-American invasion of Iraq [*q.v.*] in March 2003, he was assigned the task of defending the Baghdad-Tikrit region. After the fall of the Baathist regime, he and Uday became fugitives. Betrayed by their host in Mosul [*q.v.*] in July, Hussein and his brother—each carrying a U.S. bounty of $15 million for information leading to his arrest—were surrounded by 200 American troops, backed by helicopter gun ships, and killed.

Hussein, Saddam (1937–2006): *Iraqi politician; president, 1979–2003* Born into the Begat clan of the al-Bu Nasir tribe in Auja, a village near Tikrit, the son of Hussein Abd al-Majid, a landless peasant, and Subha Talfa al-Massallat, Hussein was raised by his maternal uncle, Khairallah Talfa due to the death of his father before his birth. After his arrival in Baghdad [*q.v.*] in 1955 for further education, he joined

the Arab Baath Socialist Party [*q.v.*].
After the 1958 anti-royalist coup he engaged in fights between the Baathists
and the followers of Premier Abdul
Karim Qasim [*q.v.*]. A member of the
team that tried, unsuccessfully, to assassinate Qasim in October 1959, Hussein
was injured in the leg. He escaped to
Syria and then to Egypt, where he
studied law at Cairo University.

Following the Baathist seizure of
power in 1963, he returned to Iraq.
When Abdul Salam Arif [*q.v.*] usurped
power from the Baathists, he was involved in an abortive attempt to overthrow Arif. He was imprisoned but
managed to escape in July 1966.
Elected assistant general secretary of
the Baath Party, he spent the next two
years reorganizing the party. He was 31
when the Baath recaptured power in
1968.

Though not a member of the ruling
Revolutionary Command Council
(RCC), Hussein was quite influential
due to his blood ties with RCC
Chairman Ahmad Hassan Bakr [*q.v.*],
a cousin of Khairallah Talfa. In late
1969 he secured a place on the RCC.
Thereafter the Bakr-Hussein duo
came to dominate the Baath Party,
mainly because of their cunning decimation of their RCC colleagues.
Hussen busied himself with strengthening the party as well as resolving the
long-running dispute with ethnic
Kurds [*q.v.*]. His foreign travels in
1972 in the wake of Iraq's nationalization of Western-owned Iraq Petroleum Company, took him to Moscow
and Paris.

By the mid-1970s, he had outstripped Bakr in leadership, cunning,
ruthlessness, and organizational ability. It was he who signed the Algiers

Accord [*q.v.*] with Muhammad Reza
Shah Pahlavi [*q.v.*] of Iran in 1975,
thus ending a bitter feud with Tehran.
By the late 1970s he felt powerful
enough to overrule Bakr's strategy of
conciliating Shia [*q.v.*] dissidents, inspired by the Islamic revolution in the
Shia-majority Iran. When Hussein
found out in mid-June 1979 that Bakr
had sent a secret message to Syrian
President Hafiz Assad [*q.v.*] to expedite negotiations on unity between
Syria and Iraq, he compelled Bakr to
resign. On the 11th anniversary of the
Baathist revolution in mid-July, Hussein assumed supreme power.

In late July he discovered a major
"anti-state conspiracy" involving 68 top
Baathist civilian and military leaders.
All were tried summarily, and 21 were
executed. He purged trade unions, the
party militia, student unions, and local
and provincial governments of the
elements he considered half-hearted in
their support of him. While generous
in funding the improvement of Shia
shrines and conciliatory toward senior
Shia clergy, he severely repressed such
militant Shia bodies as al-Daawa [*q.v.*].

In September 1980 he invaded Iran
to recover the eastern half of the Shatt
al-Arab [*q.v.*], which he had conceded
to Tehran in the 1975 Algiers Accord.
But as his troops made inroads into
Iran, he expanded his war aims to include the annexation of the captured
areas on the basis that the majority of
its inhabitants were ethnic Arabs
[*q.v.*]. By mid-1982, when the Iranians had expelled the Iraqis from their
territory, two outcomes were possible:
a draw or an Iranian triumph. Afraid
that Tehran's victory would destabilize
the region, including the oil-rich Gulf
States [*q.v.*], the United States, the

Soviet Union, and France enhanced their military, economic, and intelligence aid to Hussein's regime.

By extending the fight to include the Gulf [*q.v.*] and its shipping from 1984 onwards, he succeeded in involving the U.S. in the conflict in the name of protecting oil shipping lanes—against Iran. By mid-1987 Tehran found itself with a second front, in the Gulf, facing the U.S. Navy.

Against this background, in the spring of 1988 Iraq, making extensive use of chemical weapons, staged a series of successful offensives to regain territory it had lost to Iran from 1984 to 1986. This compelled Tehran to accept unconditionally UN Security Council Resolution 598 [*q.v.*] of July 1987. The truce came into effect on 20 August 1988.

In the course of the eight-year Iran-Iraq War [*q.v.*], Hussein enlarged his military from 250,000 to 1,250,000; vastly expanded the industrial-military complex; and made considerable progress in developing or producing chemical, biological, and nuclear arms. After the war he applied his vastly increased intelligence and military machines—including chemical weapons—to root out insurgent nationalist Kurds in the north, who had largely allied with Iran during the 1980–1988 Gulf War [*q.v.*].

In August 1990 Hussein invaded Kuwait, a neighbor that had aided Iraq materially and logistically during its war with Iran. U.S. President George H. W. Bush (r. 1989–93) took the lead in rallying the support of the international community to reverse the Iraqi aggression, and cobbled together an alliance of 29 Western and Arab nations. The UN imposed a military and economic embargo on Iraq. When Hussein refused to withdraw Iraqi troops from Kuwait by the UN deadline of 15 January 1991, the U.S.-led coalition began an air campaign against Iraq and Iraqi-occupied Kuwait, thus initiating the 1991 Gulf War [*q.v.*].

The coalition's unparalleled intense bombing continued for 39 days and was followed by a ground offensive that lasted four days. Defeated, Hussein withdrew his forces from Kuwait, and a temporary truce came into effect on 28 February. In April he accepted a humiliating UN Security Council Resolution 687 [*q.v.*], which outlined the cease-fire and war reparations as well as the main conditions for the lifting of sanctions against Iraq: destruction of its medium-range missiles and all non-conventional arms and manufacturing facilities.

Despite intense efforts by the leading Western powers, Israel, and Saudi Arabia to have Hussein assassinated, or his regime overthrown by a coup, he survived. His military and intelligence apparatus remained effective. However, the Western imposition of a "no fly" restriction in the area above the 36th parallel in October 1991 virtually ended his control over the Kurdish. His power was cut further in August 1992 when the allies declared the predominantly Shia area of Iraq below the 32nd parallel as a "no fly" zone for the central government.

While economic sanctions caused high inflation and a dramatic drop in living standards, there were no signs that popular discontent against Hussein's regime had reached such proportions as to destabilize it. But his elation at Bush's defeat in the U.S. presidential election in November 1992 proved premature when President Bill Clinton continued his predecessor's hard-line policy toward Hussein. A denouement came in late June 1993, when the U.S. navy hit the Iraqi intelligence complex in Baghdad with missiles on the basis that Hussein had planned Bush's assassination during his trip to Kuwait two months earlier.

By October 1994, having complied with all the conditions of UN Security Resolution 687 (after the Gulf War cease-fire) and Resolution 715 (mandating long-term monitoring of Iraq's military industry), Hussein felt that it was time for the UN to lift the economic sanctions. To force the issue to the top of the agenda, he moved Iraqi troops southward. Washington construed this as a plan by Hussein to re-invade Kuwait, and dispatched its forces to the region. Hussein withdrew Iraqi troops to their pre-crisis positions. At the U.N. Security Council Russia called for the lifting of the sanctions by the spring of 1995. The defection to Jordan in August 1995 of Gen. Hussein Kamil Hassan, a son-in-law of Hussein and minister of industry, created a crisis for Hussein. He overcame it by winning 99.96 percent backing in a referendum on another seven-year presidential term in October.

In February 1996, after the return of Hussein Kamil Hassan and his family to Baghdad, the erstwhile defector was killed in a gun battle by his uncle, Gen. Ali al-Majid. The next month, Hussein called parliamentary elections after seven years. In September, he was invited by Masoud Barzani

[q.v.] of the Kurdistan Democratic Party [q.v.] to assist him in expelling his rival, Jalal Talabani [q.v.], from the regional capital of Irbil [q.v.]. He did. In the process the Iraqi troops and intelligence agents destroyed the base that the U.S. had established in the region to overthrow Hussein before withdrawing from the area.

Hussein's relations with the UN Special Commission (UNSCOM) [q.v.] on disarming Iraq of weapons of mass destruction deteriorated when Richard Butler, an Australian disarmament specialist, replaced Rolf Ekeus, a Swedish diplomat, as head of UNSCOM in mid-1997. A crisis with the UN in February 1998 was defused by the last-minute intervention by UN Secretary General Kofi Annan, who met Hussein in Baghdad. But the agreement lasted only until December, when the U.S., assisted by Britain, mounted its Operation Desert Fox [q.v.]. The Pentagon fired 415 Cruise and Tomahawk missiles and dropped 600 laser-guided bombs on 100 Iraqi targets. Hussein's efforts to have an Arab League [q.v.] summit condemn the Anglo-American action and demand the lifting of sanctions on Iraq failed. Equally, the American attempt to get the Gulf monarchies involved in overthrowing Hussein got nowhere.

He rejected the new, comprehensive UN Security Council Resolution 1284 [q.v.] passed in December 1999, which required Iraq to re-admit UN inspectors who had been withdrawn by Butler to enable the Pentagon to mount its Operation Desert Fox. Confident of his improved standing at home, he called a parliamentary election in March 2000. Five months later he received President Hugo

Chavez of Venezuela, the current chairman of the Organization of Oil Exporting Countries [q.v.], in Baghdad. Soon the air travel ban on Iraq collapsed. In October, Hussein was invited to an Arab League summit after 10 years, but he did not attend. He backed the Palestinian Al Aqsa intifada [q.v.] by sending food and medical aid to the Palestinian Territories [q.v.] and paying generous compensation to the families of the Palestinians killed in the uprising. This made him all the more unpopular with the newly elected U.S. president, George W. Bush (r. 2001-2009), whose father, President George H.W. Bush, had inflicted a humiliating defeat on Hussein in 1991. Within weeks of taking office in January 2001, Bush Jr. ordered air strikes against Iraqi targets on the grounds that Iraq was improving its air defenses.

After the terrorist attacks on the U.S. in September, known as 9/11, the Bush administration tried to show that Hussein had links with Al Qaida [q.v.], but failed to provide convincing evidence. After the administration's failure to capture or kill Osama bin Laden [q.v.] during its Afghanistan War, it attempted to divert popular opinion in the U.S. against Hussein on the premise that he had failed to disarm Iraq of its weapons of mass destruction. The propaganda war against Hussein built up after the first anniversary of 9/11. When Hussein agreed to the return of UN inspectors unconditionally on 16 September 2002, the U.S., backed by Britain, successfully lobbied the UN Security Council to adopt a much more rigorous regime of inspections, which was spelled out in Resolution 1441 in November.

Hussein accepted the new resolution. Within weeks, UN inspectors started working in Iraq. They found no evidence of weapons of mass destruction by mid-March 2003. But that did not alter the earlier agenda of President Bush to bring about regime change in Iraq. He gave Hussein two days to leave Iraq. When, as expected, he did not, Bush, backed by British Prime Minister Tony Blair, ordered an invasion of Iraq, thus starting Gulf War III [q.v.]

During the armed conflict, Hussein appeared on television or in person on the streets of Baghdad until and including 9 April, when the capital fell to the invading forces. He then disappeared, reportedly carrying part of the large amount of cash collected from the Central Bank by his son Qusay [q.v.].

While on the run, he issued audio-taped statements calling on Iraqis to resist "the foreigners." Washington offered a $25 million award for information leading to his arrest. Betrayed by an accomplice, Hussein was arrested in December 2003 by American troops at a farm house 15 mi./24 km from his hometown of Tikrit, where he was hiding in an underground cellar. During his subsequent incarceration, he penned poetry and romantic novels.

Following his trial under the Interim Iraqi government in the U.S.-occupied Iraq, related to the killing of 148 Shia residents of Dujail, the site of a failed assassination attempt on him in 1982, Hussein was sentenced to capital punishment in November 2006. He was hanged the next month.

Hussein bin Talal al-Hashem (1935–99): *King of Jordan, 1952–99* Born in

Amman [*q.v.*], Hussein was educated at Victoria College, Alexandria [*q.v.*], and then at Harrow, a private school, and Sandhurst Military Academy in Britain. After the deposition of his father, Talal bin Abdullah al-Hashem [*q.v.*], in August 1952 due to mental illness, Hussein was named king. But power was exercised by a regency council until the following May, when he turned 18.

The new constitution promulgated in 1952 nominally provided a multiparty, two-chamber parliament, with the king as the constitutional head of state. Following Hussein's rigging of the general election in the autumn of 1954, the opposition demonstrated against the electoral malpractices and the Baghdad Pact [*q.v.*], which he was poised to join in December 1955. Bowing to popular pressure, he dismissed Gen. John Glubb [*q.v.*], and ordered fresh elections. The nationalist-leftist alliance won the largest bloc of seats in the autumn 1956 election.

When the government, headed by Premier Suleiman Nabulsi [*q.v.*], abrogated the 1948 Anglo-Jordanian Treaty [*q.v.*], which entitled Britain to maintain military bases in Jordan, Hussein acquiesced. In April 1957 he crushed an incipient coup by the Free Officers, led by his recently appointed chief of staff, General Ali Abu Nawar, and received U.S. aid under the Eisenhower Doctrine [*q.v.*]. He dismissed the Nabulsi government, dissolved parliament and political parties, and imposed martial law.

He countered the emergence of the United Arab Republic [*q.v.*] in early 1958 by sponsoring a federation of Jordan and Iraq, becoming its deputy head. But the federation disintegrated as a result of the Free Officers' anti-royalist coup in Iraq in July.

Despite several attempts, inspired by Egypt or Syria, to overthrow him, Hussein survived, partly because, in exchange for a financial subsidy, he allowed Washington's Central Intelligence Agency (CIA) to operate freely in his kingdom, which kept him fully apprised of local or regional plots against his regime. To forestall competition upon his succession, he named his youngest brother, Hassan, crown prince in 1965.

In the supercharged atmosphere in the buildup to the June 1967 Arab-Israeli War [*q.v.*], he joined the Egyptian-Syrian defense pact. The subsequent loss of the West Bank [*q.v.*] and East Jerusalem [*q.v.*] had a traumatic effect on him and his subjects. A rise in the number of refugees from these territories, and growing militancy among the Palestinians in Jordan, led to fighting between Palestinian commandos and the Jordanian army in September 1970, which the latter won. A major offensive by the Jordanian army in July 1971 pushed the last of the Palestinian commandos out of the kingdom. The Palestine National Council (PNC) [*q.v.*], meeting in April 1972, rejected Hussein's plan for a United Arab Kingdom, consisting of the federated provinces of Jordan and Palestine, with East Jerusalem [*q.v.*] as its capital after Israel's withdrawal from the West Bank and East Jerusalem.

During the October 1973 Arab-Israeli War [*q.v.*] Hussein rejected calls by Egypt, Syria, and Saudi Arabia to open a third front against Israel, and accepted Washington's advice to stay out of the conflict.

With enhanced U.S. military and diplomatic backing, he felt confident enough to resume face-to-face talks with Israeli leaders which he had initiated clandestinely before the 1967 war and included Yigal Allon, a former Israeli brigadier general, and Golda Meir [q.v.].

He continued to press for Israel's evacuation of the West Bank. This ceased only when a summit conference of the Arab League in October–November 1974 recognized the Palestine Liberation Organization (PLO) [q.v.] as the sole and legitimate representative of the Palestinian people, and supported the right of the Palestinian people to establish an independent national authority on any liberated territory of Palestine. He reluctantly accepted the Arab League resolution. Dismissing West Bank members of the parliament, elected in April 1967, he suspended the chamber. He advocated a comprehensive peace settlement through a U.N.-sponsored conference.

By receiving a PLO delegation to Amman in February 1977, he enhanced his standing in the Arab world. At the same time, during the presidency of Jimmy Carter (r. 1977–81) in the U.S., it became public knowledge that he had been on the payroll of the CIA as an "asset" since 1957. To repair the subsequent damage to his reputation, he refused to join the peace process initiated by the Camp David Accords [q.v.] between Egypt and Israel in September 1978. He strengthened Jordan's ties with the Soviet Union, which he had first visited in 1967. He concluded an arms deal with Moscow in 1981 and backed the Soviet leader Leonid Brezhnev's call for an international conference on the Middle East crisis.

In the Iran-Iraq War (1980–88) [q.v.], Hussein sided with Baghdad. This accelerated Jordan's economic integration with Iraq. Emulating Iraqi President Saddam Hussein's [q.v.] example of giving his regime a parliamentary veneer, he revived the suspended Jordanian parliament in January 1984. Ignoring the Arab League's suspension of Egypt from its membership since 1979, he started improving relations with Cairo from 1984 onward. In early 1985 he concluded an agreement with the PLO chairman, Yasser Arafat [q.v.], on a future confederation of the Palestinian state and Jordan, and a joint approach to a Middle East peace settlement. But this deal was rejected by the Palestine National Council (PNC) [q.v.] in April 1987. He responded by severing all legal and administrative links of Jordan with the West Bank in July 1988.

He actively backed a move to establish the Arab Cooperation Council (ACC) [q.v.], an alliance of Jordan, Egypt, Iraq, and North Yemen. Following Iraq's invasion of Kuwait in August 1990, he worked hard to provide an Arab solution to the crisis, but failed. He blamed the U.S., Egypt, and Saudi Arabia for his failure and the subsequent escalation of the crisis into a full-scale war. Reflecting public opinion at home—well captured by the 80-strong parliament elected in a free and fair election in November 1989, returning 32 Islamist deputies—Hussein combined his critical stance toward Washington with a pro-Baghdad tilt. This cost him dearly in Western capitals.

After the end of the 1991 Gulf War [*q.v.*], he tried to repair the damage by distancing himself from Saddam Hussein. He participated in the negotiations that preceded the holding of the Middle East peace conference in Madrid in October 1991, and agreed to a joint Jordanian-Palestinian delegation, as proposed by Israel. In August 1993, when the secret Israeli-PLO Accord [*q.v.*] became public, he denounced it because it contradicted the agreed-on policy of the four Arab parties—Syria, Lebanon, Jordan, and th PLO—to pursue a joint strategy in their bilateral talks with Israel. But after a meeting with Arafat, he moderated his stance.

He continued to coordinate Jordan's position with Syria and Lebanon in his peace talks with Israel. He allowed a fresh parliamentary election in November 1993 (as scheduled), and was satisfied to see the Islamist forces doing less well than before. With the implementation of the Israeli-PLO Accord progressing, Hussein felt the need to join the process by resuming bilateral talks with Israel. He did so without consulting Syria and Lebanon. He signed the resulting agreement with Israeli Premier Yitzhak Rabin [*q.v.*], ending the state of belligerency between Jordan and Israel, on 25 July 1994 in Washington. Three months later the two leaders signed a peace treaty at a site in the Araba Valley along the Jordanian-Israeli border about 30 mi./48 km north of the Gulf of Aqaba.

In October 1998, invited by U.S. President Bill Clinton (r.1993–2001), Hussein intervened, successfully, in the Israeli-Palestinian talks at the Wye River Plantation near Washington, D.C. Just before his death due to lymph cancer, to the dismay and shock of Crown Prince Hassan, who had been deputing as the monarch during Hussein's extended medical treatment in the U.S., Hussein named his eldest son, Abdullah [*q.v.*], as his heir.

al-Husseini, Faisal (1940-2001): Born in Baghdad [*q.v.*] to Abdul Qadir, the field commander during the 1936–39 Arab Revolt in Palestine [*q.v.*], and Khair Fatima during the time his family took refuge there, Husseini grew up in Cairo [*q.v.*], where he obtained a university degree. He returned to East Jerusalem [*q.v.*]. After the establishment of the Palestine Liberation Organization [*q.v.*] in 1964, Husseini worked briefly in the PLO's Jerusalem office. He then graduated from the Homs [*q.v.*] Military Academy as an officer of the Palestine Liberation Army [*q.v.*]. After the June 1967 Arab-Israeli war [*q.v.*], he worked with Yasser Arafat [*q.v.*] to set up a guerrilla infrastructure in the West Bank [*q.v.*]. He was arrested by the Israeli government and sentenced to a year in jail.

In 1979 he opened the Arab Studies Center in East Jerusalem, which the Israeli authorities regarded as a front for coordinating PLO activities in the Occupied Territories [*q.v.*]. They closed down the Center, and imprisoned him without leveling any charges against him under the system known as "administrative detention." After his release he was placed under city arrest for the next five years. Yet he emerged as the chief spokesman of the PLO on the West Bank [*q.v.*] in the late 1980s. He supported the Intifada [*q.v.*] that erupted in 1987.

During the preliminary talks that led to the Middle East peace conference in Madrid in October 1991, he acted as a bridge between Arafat and U.S. Secretary of State James Baker. He led the Palestinian delegation that negotiated with the Israelis after the Madrid conference.

In the cabinet of the Palestinian Authority [*q.v.*] appointed in 1994, he was given the portfolio of Jerusalem [*q.v.*]. He reopened the Arab Studies Center. Under Israeli Prime Minister Benjamin Netanyahu (r. 1996–99) [*q.v.*], the government closed it down. During his trip to Kuwait to repair the damaged relations between the Emirate and the PLO, dating back to 1991, he died of a heart attack.

al-Husseini, Haajj Muhammad Amin

(1897–1974): *Palestinian religious and political leader* Born into a prominent religious family in Jerusalem [*q.v.*], Husseini received his secondary education in the city, studied for a year at al-Azhar University [*q.v.*] in Cairo [*q.v.*], and then enrolled at the Ottoman school of administration in Istanbul. He served briefly as an officer in the Ottoman army during World War I. After the war he became a recruiting officer for the army of Faisal bin Hussein [*q.v.*] in Syria.

As leader of an Arab nationalist group in Jerusalem, the Arab Club, he considered Palestine [*q.v.*] to be part of Greater Syria [*q.v.*] and opposed Jewish immigration into Palestine. Holding him responsible for anti-Jewish violence in April 1920, a British military court sentenced him in absentia to 15 years in jail. He escaped to Damascus [*q.v.*]. The British high commissioner, Sir Herbert

Samuel, pardoned him in August. The following March, to conciliate Arab opinion, Sir Herbert recommended that Husseini should be made the grand mufti (religious judge) of Jerusalem when the job fell vacant on the death of his step-brother, Kamel al-Husseini. This happened in May.

In December Sir Herbert ordered the establishment of a five-member Supreme Muslim Council—charged with running religious endowments, courts, and mosques—to be elected indirectly. It chose 25-year-old Husseini as its chairman. Having achieved supreme office among Palestinian Muslims, he opted for persuasion rather than violence. But that did not deflect him from pursuing his aim of making Palestine an independent Arab state. He started restoring the Dome of the Rock [*q.v.*] and al-Aqsa mosque, a step that enhanced his popularity among Arabs [*q.v.*]. His attempt to restrict Jewish rights at the Wailing Wall [*q.v.*] triggered a severe riot in August 1929.

His insistent demand that restrictions on Jewish immigration should be coupled with the establishment of an Arab national government made him the most significant political leader of Arab Palestinians. In April 1936, at his behest, various Arab groups united to form the Arab Higher Committee (AHC) [*q.v.*] under his leadership. When the AHC discovered that the Zionists [*q.v.*] were smuggling arms, it called a general strike, which escalated into a general Arab revolt. It won the backing of the Syrian and Iraqi volunteers.

Following the recommendation in July 1937 of the British-appointed Peel Commission to partition Palestine, Arab violence escalated. Three months later the British government dismissed Husseini as chairman of the Supreme Muslim Council, which was disbanded, and banned the AHC, banishing its members to Seychelles in the Indian Ocean. Husseini took refuge in the Muslim shrines of Jerusalem, and then managed to flee first to Lebanon and then Syria. From there he continued to direct the Arab revolt, which ended in March 1939 with a death toll of 3,232 Arabs, 329 Jews, and 135 Britons.

Soon after the outbreak of World War II in September 1939, Husseini arrived in Baghdad [*q.v.*] as a political refugee and began rallying anti-Zionist and anti-British sentiments in Iraq. He aided Rashid Ali Gailani [*q.v.*] in his revolt against the royal family and the British in 1941. After the failure of Gailani's venture, he fled to Iran, then to (neutral) Turkey and the Balkans under the Axis Powers, and finally Germany, where he met Adolf Hitler, who received him as a leader of anti-British Arab nationalism [*q.v.*]. He attended Nazi rallies in Berlin, and blessed those Bosnian Muslims who had joined the German military.

At the end of the war Husseini was arrested by the French forces, but soon managed to escape (aboard a U.S. military aircraft) to Cairo [*q.v.*]. The Arab League [*q.v.*] appointed him chairman of the revived Arab Higher Committee to represent Arab Palestinians. Through his cousin Abdul Qadir al-Husseini, who led the Palestinian fighters in the civil conflict that preceded the Palestine War (1948–49) [*q.v.*], Husseini exercised influence inside Palestine. He lobbied successfully

to get Egypt to join the Arab struggle against Israel.

After the Palestine War his attempts to form a government of all Palestine in the Egyptian-occupied Gaza Strip [*q.v.*] were cold-shouldered by Cairo. He moved to Beirut [*q.v.*] in 1959. With the establishment of the Palestine Liberation Organization [*q.v.*] in 1964, Husseini's influence declined sharply, and he led an uneventful existence until his death a decade later.

Ibadhis: *Islamic sect* Ibadhis are named after Abdullah bin Ibadh, a member of the Azd tribe of Oman, who started his life as a Khariji [*q.v.*]. In 685 A.D. he split with Khariji extremists, who considered that non-Khariji Muslims [*q.v.*] were polytheists, whereas he regarded them as mere infidels. Thus Ibadhism emerged as a pragmatic school within the Khariji movement. It sought to restore the concept of Islam [*q.v.*] and the Islamic state before it was allegedly corrupted by Caliph Othman bin Affan (r. 644–56 A.D.). Ibadhis were then to be found in Iraq, Hijaz [*q.v.*], Central Arabia, Oman, and Iran. In 850 A.D. the Omani tribes, professing Ibadhism, split from the Abbasid Caliphate, based in Baghdad [*q.v.*], and set up an independent domain in the plateau of Jebel Akhdar, Green Mountain. Today two-thirds of Omani Muslims are Ibadhi.

ibn: *See* bin [*q.v.*].

Ibn Baz, Abdul Aziz bin Abdullah: *See* al-Baz, Abdul Aziz bin Abdullah.

Ibn Saud: *See* Abdul Aziz bin Abdul Rahman al-Saud.

ijma: (Arabic: *consensus*) One of the four pillars of Islamic jurisprudence, *ijma* means consensus of the community, *umma* [*q.v.*], the other remaining pillars being the Quran [*q.v.*]; Prophet Muhammad's *sunna* [*q.v.*], later codified as the Hadith [*q.v.*]; and *ijtihad* [*q.v.*], interpretative reasoning. The function of *ijma* is to settle the theory or practice concerning the believer's behavior in matters specified by Allah (through the Quran) and the Prophet Muhammad (through the Hadith). Until Muhammad bin Idris al-Shafii (d. 820 A.D.) founded the discipline of religious jurisprudence (*fiqh* [*q.v.*]), based on these pillars, *ijma* had been construed as consensus of "*ahl al-hall wal aqd*" (Arabic: *people of loosening and binding*), a term that embraces various types of representatives of the community, including religious intellectuals. But Shafii enlarged it to include the whole community. In the modern era Muhammad Abdu (d. 1905), an Egyptian Islamic thinker, interpreted *ijma* as public opinion.

ijtihad (Arabic: *applying effort* [*to form an opinion*]): *interpretative reasoning* With time it became necessary for Muslims [*q.v.*] and their rulers to interpret the Quran [*q.v.*] and the Prophet Muhammad's *sunna* [*q.v.*] (together forming the Islamic law) to address unprecedented situations. During the early Islamic era, *ijtihad* was freely practiced by the learned to interpret the Quran and the *sunna*, the interpretation being either arbitrary or based on analogy, *qiyas* [*q.v.*]. Its practitioners were called *mujtahids* [*q.v.*]. Muhammad bin Idris al-Shafii (d. 820 A.D.) restricted *ijtihad* to analogy from the Quran and the *sunna*.

By the mid-9th century A.D., four major schools of Islamic law—ranging between the rigid Hanbali school [*q.v.*] and the liberal Hanafi school [*q.v.*]—had emerged within Sunni Islam [*q.v.*]. In order not to upset the consensus thus gained with some new radical innovation, the clergy from the 10th century onward declared that the gates of *ijtihad* had been shut. As late as the early 19th century the Mufti of Cairo's al-Azhar University [*q.v.*] declared: "He who believes himself to be a *mujtahid* must be under the influence of his hallucinations and of the devil." This view was challenged by Jamal al-Din Afghani (d. 1897), a leading Islamic reformer, who stated that each believer had the right and responsibility to interpret the Quran and the Hadith himself. His stance was adopted later by Muhammad Abdu (d. 1905), an Egyptian Islamic scholar, and his acolyte Muhammad Rashid Rida (d. 1935). Rida inspired Hassan al-Banna [*q.v.*], the founder of the Muslim Brotherhood [*q.v.*] in Egypt, who favored *ijtihad* so that Islam could face the problems of the modern world.

Unlike in Sunnism, in Shia Islam [*q.v.*] *ijtihad* did not remain dormant for long. The destruction in 1258 of the (Sunni) Abbasid caliphate by the Mongol ruler Hulagu Khan (1217–1265) created a political-ideological vacuum in which the Shia doctrine thrived. Jamal al-Din bin Yusuf al-Hilli (1250–1325), a Shia thinker, rehabilitated the concept and practice of *ijtihad*.

Ikhwan (Arabic: *Brethren or brotherhood*): *Islamic military movement in Arabia* Abdul Aziz bin Abdul Rahman al-Saud [*q.v.*], the ruler of Najd [*q.v.*], conceived the idea of settling the nomadic tribes in colonies in order to teach them the tenets of Islam [*q.v.*] as a step toward replacing their customary law with the Islamic Law [*q.v.*] and their traditional tribal bonds with religious ones. Implementing this idea after 1913, he called the settlements *hijra* (Arabic: *migration*—i.e., from a life of ignorance to one of enlightenment) and the settlers *al-Ikhwan*. They were fired with zeal to spread the Wahhabi [*q.v.*] version of Islam to the farthest corners of the Arabian Peninsula [*q.v.*] and beyond.

By 1920 their colonies had become the primary source of soldiery to Abdul Aziz al-Saud. During the next several years the Ikhwan helped him to expand his realm to nearly four-fifths of the Arabian Peninsula. In 1927 Britain, the most powerful foreign power in the Persian Gulf [*q.v.*] region, recognized Abdul Aziz al-Saud as King of Hijaz and Sultan of Najd and its Dependencies on one condition: he had to accept Britain as the protector of Oman and the Gulf principalities as well as the territorial integrity of Iraq and Transjordan [*q.v.*], then under British Mandate.

Ignoring al-Saud's agreement with Britain, some of the Ikhwan commanders continued to raid territories outside his domain. This led to conflict between the Ikhwan and al-Saud in March 1929, with 8,000 Ikhwan facing 30,000 well-armed soldiers of al-Saud. The rebels were defeated. Further battles followed, and it was not until January 1930 that the last of the defiant Ikhwan chiefs surrendered. Those Ikhwan commanders who had stayed loyal to al-Saud received regular stipends. Soon their units were transformed into the National Guard [*q.v.*].

Ikhwan al-Muslimin: *See* Muslim Brotherhood.

imam (Arabic: *model, one whose leadership or example is to be followed*): *religious leader* "Imam" is used as a noun and as a title. Shias [*q.v.*] use it for the religious leader at the highest level instead of the honorific caliph, a derivative of *khalifa* (Arabic: *vice regent*), used by Sunnis [*q.v.*]. Thus Shias refer to Ali bin Abu Talib as Imam Ali, whereas Sunnis call him Caliph Ali. Sunnis refer to the founders of their four legal schools as imams—for example, Imam Muhammad bin Idris al-Shafii. As the religious leader of Zaidi [*q.v.*] Shias in his country, the ruler of North Yemen carried the honorific of Imam. In modern times Ayatollah Ruhollah Khomeini [*q.v.*] was given this title by Iranian Shias to place him above the highest Shia religious rank of Grand Ayatollah. Finally, the leader of prayers at any mosque is called an imam.

imamat: *supreme leadership of Muslims after the Prophet Muhammad* Sunnis [*q.v.*] distinguish between the early caliphate of the (four) Rightly Guided Caliphs—Abu Bakr bin Abu Quhafa, Omar bin Khattab, Othman bin Affan, and Ali bin Abu Talib—and the latter *imamat*, which was characterized by worldly monarchy. Only the caliphs met the conditions of the true *imamat*. The required qualifications were membership in the Quraish tribe, to which the Prophet Muhammad belonged; thorough knowledge of Islamic law and probity in upholding it; physical fitness; and an ability to discharge the political-military duties of the high office. The Imam could be appointed by his predecessor or elected. The size of the electorate—or *"ahl al-hall wal aqd"* (Arabic: *people of loosening and binding)*—necessary to make their choice binding on the Muslim community varied between one and the "generality" of the electors, the election amounting to a selection of the "most exemplary" Muslim [*q.v.*]. His duties were to protect Islam [*q.v.*] from heterodoxy; dispense Islamic punishment and justice between disputants; maintain peace within the Muslim domain and defend it against foreign enemies; collect Islamic alms and taxes and spend the revenue according to the law; and appoint sincere Muslims to assist him in the discharge of his duties.

Shias [*q.v.*] do not accept the *imamat* of Abu Bakr, Omar, and Othman, arguing that the Prophet Muhammad had designated Ali as his successor. The Twelver Shia [*q.v.*] doctrine, formulated by Imam Jaafar al-Sadiq (d. 765 A.D.), maintains that the Imam must be designated by Allah through the Prophet Muhammad or another Imam, he must be free from sin and error, and he must be the "most exemplary" of all Muslims. In short, Imams, being divinely inspired, are infallible, a view not shared by Sunnis.

Imamis: *See* Twelver Shias.

intifada (Arabic: *shivering or shaking off*): *Palestinian uprising against the Israeli occupation, 1987–93* Intifada erupted spontaneously in the Palestinian refugee camp of Jabaliya in the Gaza Strip [*q.v.*] on 9 December 1987, when thousands marched in protest against the killing of four Palestinians by an Israeli truck near the settlement. During the next several days rioting spread throughout the Gaza Strip and the West Bank [*q.v.*], including East Jerusalem [*q.v.*], with predominantly young protestors hurling stones and gasoline bombs at the Israeli forces, and the latter responding with tear gas and live ammunition, killing 24 Palestinians by the end of December. By then, the Palestine Liberation Organization (PLO) [*q.v.*], headquartered in Tunis, and the Islamic Center, the front organization of the Muslim Brotherhood [*q.v.*], based in the Occupied Territories [*q.v.*], had given the spontaneous movement their support.

The intifada stemmed from 20 years of collective and individual frustration and humiliation that the Palestinians had endured in their dealings with the Jews [*q.v.*] and the Israeli authorities, both military and civilian. By early January 1988 the secular PLO had set up the United National Leadership of the Uprising (UNLU) [*q.v.*] to direct the movement, while the Islamic Center formed Hamas [*q.v.*] for the same purpose. Many of those involved were young, educated Palestinians, fluent in Hebrew [*q.v.*] and familiar with Israeli norms, who took over the communal leadership from the older generation of Arab notables who professed peaceful coexistence with the Israelis.

UNLU and Hamas urged the Palestinians to resign from all government posts, stop using public services, withdraw money from Israeli banks, boycott all Israeli products, cease paying taxes, and join the strikes it called. UNLU committees issued circulars containing instructions in these matters, and urged all Palestinians to share the sacrifices required by the intifada. The Palestinians used charity funds to support the large number of families whose husbands or brothers were jailed. Actions by the Israeli security forces—involving firings, curfews, harassment, arrests, and house searches and demolitions—severely disrupted Palestinian life.

During the first four years of the intifada, 1,413 Palestinians were killed—most of them by the Israeli security forces and a minority by fellow Palestinians for being Israeli agents—and 90,000 (about one-sixth of all Palestinian males above 15) were arrested.

The campaign against the Israeli agents intensified in the early 1990s and destroyed Shin Beth's [*q.v.*] 20,000-strong intelligence network among the Palestinians, making it extremely hard for the occupying Israeli authorities to re-impose full control and restore law and order.

This, and the refusal of Palestinians to call off the intifada, convinced the Israeli government of the futility of continued suppression of them, and denial of their national identity and the right to self-rule, and paved the way for the Israeli-Palestine Liberation Organization Accord [*q.v.*] in September 1993. By the end of the intifada, 1,636 Palestinians, including 316 mi-

nors, had been killed—1,346 by the Israeli security forces and 290 by Jewish civilians. This figure excluded those who were murdered by fellow Palestinians for collaborating with Israel. By contrast, the total death toll of the Israelis, 70, amounted to one a month.

Iran:

OFFICIAL NAME: Islamic Republic of Iran

CAPITAL: Tehran [*q.v.*]

AREA: 636,296 sq. mi./1,648,000 sq. km

POPULATION: 74.7 million (2011 census)

GROSS DOMESTIC PRODUCT (nominal): $420.9 billion (2011 est.); per capita, $6,260 (2011 est.)

GROSS DOMESTIC PRODUCT (Purchasing Power Parity): $827.3 billion (2011 est.); per capita, U.S.$10,800 (2011 est.)

NATIONAL CURRENCY: Iranian Rial (IRR); 12,260 IRRs= U.S.$1; 20,000 IRRs= £1; 15,460 IRRS= €1

FORM OF GOVERNMENT: republic, under Leader (of the Revolution), also known as Supreme Leader

OFFICIAL LANGUAGE: Persian [*q.v.*]

OFFICIAL RELIGION: Islam [*q.v.*]

ADMINISTRATIVE REGIONS: Iran is divided into 31 provinces.

ASSEMBLY OF EXPERTS: The 1979 constitution provided for the Assembly of Experts [*q.v.*] to select the Leader or Leadership Council of three to five members. The First Assembly, elected in 1982, was followed by the Second in 1990 after the constitution was amended in 1989 and the provision of the Leadership Council removed. The Third Assembly was elected in 1990, and the subsequent ones every eight years.

CONSTITUTION: A draft constitution, submitted to the Assembly of Experts (1979) by the government in August 1979, was modified and then approved by a referendum in December. Another referendum in July 1989 approved 50 amendments to the constitution, including abolishing the premiership and creating the Expediency Consultation Council System (ECCS) to resolve differences between parliament, the presidency, and the Guardian Council [*q.v.*].

Iran is an Islamic republic, where social, political, and economic affairs are conducted according to the tenets of Islam [*q.v.*]. The constitution provides for an outstanding Islamic jurisprudent to be the Leader (of the Revolution). Standing above the executive, legislative, and judicial branches of the state, he has extensive powers, including exercising the supreme command of the armed forces and declaring war or peace in consultation with the Supreme National Security Council and outlining general policies after consultation with the ECCS. He has the authority to appoint half the members of the Council of Guardians, the head of the judiciary, and the chief of the joint staff. He can dismiss the (elected) president if the Supreme Court finds him derelict in his duties or the parliament declares him politically incompetent. Ayatollah Ruhollah Khomeini [*q.v.*], named as the first Leader, was assigned these powers for life. His successor is required to be chosen by a popularly elected Assembly of Experts (on Islam), consisting of clerics, for the eight-year tenure of the Assembly.

The president is the chief executive, and is elected directly for a four-year term. Legislative authority rests with the Majlis, with four-year tenure. Bills passed by the Majlis are vetted by the Guardian Council to ensure that they are in line with the constitution and Islamic precepts. The articles dealing with the basic rights of the individual provide for equal human, political, economic, social, and cultural rights for men and women.

The press and other publications are given a free rein except in matters deemed detrimental to Islamic principles and public morality. The formation of political and professional parties and associations, as well as religious societies, is allowed provided they do not violate the principles of independence, national unity, or Islamic criteria.

The constitution specifies Islam of the Twelver Jaafari doctrine [*q.v.*] as the official religion, with other Islamic schools, including the Hanafi [*q.v.*], Maliki [*q.v.*], Shafii [*q.v.*], and Zaidi [*q.v.*], being accorded full respect. It recognizes Christians [*q.v.*], Jews [*q.v.*], and Zoroastrians [*q.v.*] as religious minorities, and allocates them a certain number of parliamentary seats.

ETHNIC COMPOSITION: (2010) Persians [*q.v.*] 65 percent, Azeris [*q.v.*] 16 percent, Kurds [*q.v.*] 7 percent, Luris 6 percent, Baluchis [*q.v.*] 2.5 percent, Arabs [*q.v.*] 2 percent, Turkmen [*q.v.*] 2 percent, Armenians [*q.v.*] 0.5 percent

EXECUTIVE AUTHORITY: Executive authority rests with the president, who is elected directly by voters.

High officials:

Leader: Ayatollah Ali Hussein Khamanei [*q.v.*], 2006–

President: Mahmoud Ahmadinejad [*q.v.*], 2009–

First vice president: Muhammad Reza Rahimi, 2009–

Speaker of Parliament: Ali Larijani, 2008–

Speaker of the Assembly of Experts: Ayatollah Muhammad Reza Mahdavi-Kani, 2011–

Chairman of the Council of Guardians: Ayatollah Ahmad Jannati, 1989–

Expediency Consultation Council System: Ali Akbar Hashemi Rafsanjani [*q.v.*] 2012–

HISTORY The Constitutional Revolution [*q.v.*] in 1907, during the reign of Muzzafar al-Din Qajar (r. 1896–1907), which introduced a written constitution and an elected Majlis, collapsed in 1911 with the dissolution of the Second Majlis. By the end of World War I the financial position of Iran (then Persia) was so dire that only British subsidies could keep it afloat. London and Tehran concluded the secret Anglo-Persian Agreement [*q.v.*] in 1919, which turned Iran into a virtual protectorate of Britain. The Majlis refused to ratify it. Britain decided to supplant the weak Qajar power with a strong authority represented by Col. Reza Khan, commander of the elite Cossak Brigade. Reza Khan carried out a coup against the government of Fathullah Gilani in February 1921. He persuaded the Majlis to depose the Qajar monarch, Ahmad Shah, and appoint him king in December 1925.

As Reza Shah Pahlavi [*q.v.*], the new ruler established a strong, centralized state in Iran, implemented social reform, and renegotiated the oil concessions given to the British-owned Anglo-Persian (later Anglo-Iranian) Oil Company. In foreign affairs, he cultivated Germany in the 1930s in order to offset the traditional influence of Britain and Russia (then the Soviet Union). In 1933 he changed the name of the country from Persia to Iran. Opposed to Reza Shah's neutrality during World War II, Britain and the Soviet Union occupied Iran in August 1941 and forced Reza Shah to abdicate in favor of his son Muhammad [*q.v.*].

Following the departure of the British and the Soviets after the war, Muhammad Reza Shah Pahlavi faced leftist autonomous governments in Azerbaijan [*q.v.*] and Kurdistan [*q.v.*]. After overpowering them with Washington's assistance, he consolidated his authority.

In May 1951 nationalist Premier Muhammad Mussadiq [*q.v.*] nationalized the Anglo-Iranian Oil Company. Britain protested, and oil exports stopped. In August 1952 the Majlis gave Mussadiq emergency powers for six months, and renewed them for a year in January 1953. Mussadiq came into conflict with the shah over the control of the defense ministry. On 16 August the shah left the country.

However, the jubilation of the pro-Mussadiq forces was short-lived. Royalist officers, working in conjunction with the U.S. Central Intelligence Agency, mounted a counter-coup that resulted in the arrest of Mussadiq and the return of the shah on 19 August. A year later the shah offered oil concessions to a Western consortium. He strengthened links with the West by joining the Baghdad Pact [*q.v.*]. He repressed domestic opposition, secular and Islamic, and set up a police state. By implementing the "white revolution" [*q.v.*], he broke the hold of the landed aristocracy and prepared the ground for the rise of capitalism. The enormous jump in oil revenues in the mid-1970s fueled his ambition to make Iran the fifth most powerful nation in the world.

The discontent of the burgeoning modern middle class—which had emerged during a quarter-century of repression that had destroyed all avenues of opposition, except the mosque, whose extensive network remained intact—combined with the alienation experienced by a large underclass of recent rural migrants fostered by an overheated economy, created a protest movement that began to stir in the autumn of 1977. Within a year the movement—guided by Ayatollah Ruhollah Khomeini [*q.v.*], exiled in Najaf [*q.v.*], Iraq—acquired revolutionary proportions. It succeeded in overthrowing the shah, heralding an Islamic order under Khomeini in early 1979.

Several attempts were made by the displaced Iranian leaders to overthrow the new regime through a military coup. When the last of these failed in July 1980, the scene was set for a frontal attack on Islamic Iran, which had alienated not only the U.S. but also the neighboring royalist Gulf States [*q.v.*]. Iraq invaded Iran in September 1980. Despite the chaotic state of its military, Iran was able to stop the Iraqi advance. Overall, the eight-year conflict enabled Khomeini to consolidate the revolution. When in the early summer of 1988 he realized that further military reverses at Iraqi hands would threaten the future of his regime, he agreed to a cease-fire. He died within a year.

The succession to Khomeini's office by Ayatollah Ali Khamanei, the erstwhile president, was smooth. So too was the elevation of Ali Akbar Hashemi Rafsanjani, the Majlis speaker, to the presidency by popular vote. His liberalization of the economy achieved mixed results. That is why his vote declined to 63 percent at the next election in 1993. Continued low prices for oil, the predominant export of Iran, was another factor in the country's economic ills.

In the 1997 general election, the Majlis speaker, Hojatalislam Ali Akbar Nateq Nouri, the favored candidate of the religious establishment, was defeated by Hojatalislam Muhammad Khatami by a landslide. He initiated much-needed political reform, which was resisted by the conservative-dominated Majlis and orthodox clerics. Under his leadership the regime held the first local elections in February 1999, an exercise that created tens of thousands of elected representatives. Facing the crisis caused by the student protest in July, Khatami and Khamanei worked together to defuse it. That Khatami's reformist agenda had popular backing became apparent when, in the 2000 general election, voters gave a thumping majority to reformers in the Majlis. In the presidential election in 2001, Khatami improved his vote by nine percent, to 78. He continued the economic liberalization initiated by his predecessor.

After the terrorist attacks on the U.S. in September 2001, both Khatami and Khamanei condemned the killing of innocent civilians. In the Afghanistan campaign of the Pentagon that followed, Iran—hostile to the

Taliban administration in Kabul since its inception in 1996—stayed neutral, while welcoming the overthrow of the Taliban, which it had regarded as the brainchild of Pakistan and Saudi Arabia. But that did not stop U.S. President George W. Bush (r. 2001–2009) from including Iran in his "Axis of Evil" along with Iraq and North Korea, thus continuing the Dual Containment policy [q.v.] of the previous administration. That did not deter Iran from letting the Tehran-based Supreme Council of Islamic Revolution in Iraq [q.v.] join the Washington-backed Iraqi opposition groups.

While covertly ignoring the violations of its airspace by the Pentagon in the run-up to the Anglo-American invasion of Iraq [q.v.] in March 2003, Iran criticized America's attack on a fellow Muslim country.

In the 2005 presidential election, Mahmoud Ahmadinejad, mayor of Tehran, emerged with the second-largest number of ballots, slightly ahead of Mahdi Karrubi, former Majlis speaker—allegedly due to the vote-rigging in the Isfahan [q.v.] region—in the first run. He went on to defeat Hashemi Rafsanjani in the second round by a large margin. In foreign affairs a standoff developed between Iran and the United Nation Security Council when—lacking confidence in Iran's declarations that its uranium enrichment program was for generating electricity—a majority of the 35 governors of the International Atomic Energy Agency (IAEA) voted to refer Iran's case to the UN Security Council in 2006. The council imposed three sets of fairly modest economic sanctions on Iran when it refused to cease enriching uranium, which it was entitled to do

under the nuclear Non-Proliferation Treaty (NPT) to which it was a signatory. At home, due to the rising oil prices [q.v.] which peaked at $147 a barrel in July 2008, the government was able to raise salaries and pensions and give generous loans to small farmers and businessmen. In the 2008 parliamentary election, conservatives won 170 seats and reformists only 46, with the rest going to independents.

Yet Ahmadinejad faced stiff competition when he sought reelection in 2009. His main rival, Mir Hussein Musavi/Mousavi [q.v.], proved popular with women and young voters. The race looked so close that most observers expected a second round, with neither of the leading candidates gaining 50 percent plus one vote. The result announced post-haste that Ahmadinejad had secured 62.5 percent of the ballots versus Mousavi's 33.9 percent set off a protest involving millions of people nationwide. It was brutally suppressed, leaving 69 people dead, and caused fissures at the top leadership with Khamanei, Jannati, and Ahmadinejad on one side and Mousavi, Khatami, and Hashemi Rafsanjani on the other. Abroad, while the United States and the 27-member European Union (EU) doubted the veracity of the election result, Russia, China, India, Brazil, and most Muslim states, including Turkey, congratulated Ahmadinejad on his reelection.

Resorting to communication by Internet, the opposition kept up its protest, using the celebration of important secular or religious events as a cover for demonstrations. This lasted about a year.

Islamic Iran's generally hostile policy toward the United States, dating back to the time of the revolution, continued. Responding to Washington's success in getting the UN Security Council to impose a series of sanctions against it on the nuclear issue from 2008 onwards, it hardened its stance. The official line on the nuclear program in Iran had the backing of the reformist opposition.

Iran continued to support Hizbollah [q.v.] and Hamas [q.v.] politically and financially. It strengthened ties with China, Russia, Brazil, and Venezuela.

The government decided in December 2010 to remove subsidies on petroleum products and agricultural produce. This spiked inflation. As a compensatory measure the government distributed part of the expected annual savings of $60 billion by making monthly payments of $43 to each citizen who applied for it. These measures won the praise of the International Monetary Fund because they reduced the government's burden and lowered domestic energy consumption.

Tensions arose between Ahmadinejad and Khamanei when the president attempted to strengthen his office at the expense of the clerical establishment. The result of the parliamentary election in March 2012 showed overwhelming support for the Khamanei camp. But both sides were united in withstanding the increasingly stringent economic sanctions against Iran by the U.S. and the EU as well as the frequent threats by Israel to bomb Iran's nuclear facilities to deprive Tehran of its capability to produce an atom bomb in the future.

The Iranian regime considered the events of the Arab Spring [q.v.] as a reprise of the Islamic Revolution [q.v.]

in Iran that toppled the pro-Washington shah, Muhammad Reza Pahlavi [q.v.], and described it as the Islamic Awakening [q.v.].

LEGISLATURE: The parliament, officially called Majlis, deals with legislation, general policy matters, and the budget. Its 290 members, elected for a four-year term, include three Christians, one Zoroastrian, and one Jew. It has the right to impeach the president, who is then dismissed by the Leader.

RELIGIOUS COMPOSITION: (2011) Muslims [q.v.], 99 percent, of which Shia [q.v.] 90 percent, Sunni [q.v.] 9 percent; Bahai [q.v.], 0.4 percent; Christian [q.v.], 0.5 percent, affiliated mainly to the Armenian Orthodox [q.v.] and the Assyrian Churches [q.v.]; Jewish, 0.05 percent; Zoroastrian, 0.05 percent. Bahais are considered heretics; and their institutions and worship in public were banned in 1983.

Iran-Contra Affair: : *Secret U.S. arms-for-hostages deal with Iran* On 3 November 1986, *Al-Shira* (Arabic, *The Sail*), a Beirut-based magazine, disclosed that the United States had secretly sold weapons to Iran. Aware of Iran's geo-strategic importance, Washington wanted to end the hostility that Tehran had shown toward the U.S. since the 1979 Islamic revolution [q.v.]. It also wanted to gain the freedom of the American captives taken by pro-Iranian groups in Lebanon, then in the midst of the long Lebanese Civil War [q.v.]. This sale of arms was contrary to the declared policies of U.S. President Ronald Reagan (r. 1981-89), which were to maintain an arms embargo on Tehran and not to deal with terrorists and hostage takers.

The Islamic Jihad [*q.v.*] had captured William Buckley, the U.S. Central Intelligence Agency station chief in Beirut [*q.v.*], in March 1984. It coupled its demand for the freeing of 17 Shias convicted in Kuwait on charges of bombing the U.S. and French embassies with a call on Washington and Paris to end their arms embargo against Iran, then engaged in war with Iraq. By the end of May the number of American captives taken by the pro-Iranian groups in Lebanon had risen to five.

In early July 1985 Reagan allowed his National Security Adviser, Robert McFarlane, to propose that Tehran might influence the pro-Iranian Lebanese groups to free their American hostages in exchange for the sale of U.S.-made weapons to Iran. The money thus obtained was to be channeled to the Contra guerrillas fighting the leftist regime in Nicaragua, thus subverting the ban that the U.S. Congress had imposed on aiding the Contras.

Two months later, in exchange for the sale of 508 U.S.-made anti-tank missiles, one American hostage was released. But the second swap of 120 anti-aircraft missiles and 4,000 anti-tank missiles for the remaining captives (excluding Buckley, who had died) became entangled. A U.S. delegation, led by McFarlane, arrived in Tehran on 25 May 1986 but made no progress in repairing U.S. relations with Iran. After further shipment of seven metric tons of U.S.-made arms and ammunition in early July, one American hostage was freed. The release of a further captive came after

500 anti-tank missiles had been delivered to Iran in late October. With three Americans still in captivity, the Iranians had managed to make the American negotiators appear poor bargainers.

The disclosure of secret U.S. arms sales to Iran had a devastating impact on American and world public opinion. Reagan's approval rating fell from 67 percent to 46 percent and paralyzed his administration for several months. Washington's Arab allies were shocked and incensed. This was particularly true of Iraq, which had been assured clandestinely since November 1983 that the United States would ensure that it was not defeated in its war with Iran.

Irangate Affair (1986). *See* Irangate Affair

Iran-Iraq Frontier Treaty (1937): Signed on 4 July 1937, the Iran-Iraq Frontier Treaty declared the Shatt al-Arab [*q.v.*] open for navigation to all countries of the world. It confirmed the land boundaries as set out in the 1913 Protocol of Constantinople [*q.v.*], and the *procès-verbaux* of the Delimitation of the Frontier Commission of 1914; and amended the Shatt al-Arab frontiers, with Iraq conceding the thalweg (that is, the median line of the main navigable channel) principle for four miles facing Abadan [*q.v.*], the site of the Anglo-Persian Oil Company's refinery. Later Iraq said it had signed the treaty under duress.

Iran-Iraq Treaty of International Boundaries and Good Neighborliness (1975): The Treaty of International Boundaries and Good

Neighborliness between Iran and Iraq evolved out of the accord concluded on 6 March 1975 in Algiers between Muhammad Reza Shah Pahlavi [*q.v.*] and Saddam Hussein [*q.v.*], then vice president of Iraq. The signatories agreed to delimit the land boundaries of their countries according to the 1913 Protocol of Constantinople [*q.v.*] and the *procès-verbaux* of the Delimitation of the Frontier Commission of 1914, to demarcate the fluvial frontiers of their countries according to the thalweg line (that is, along the median line of the main navigable channel), and to end all infiltrations of a subversive nature.

Once the demarcation of the land and river boundaries had been accomplished according to the Accord, Iran and Iraq signed the Treaty of International Boundaries and Good Neighborliness in Baghdad on 13 June 1975. Article 4 of the treaty stated that the provisions about the land and river frontiers and stopping subversive infiltration "shall be final and permanent." After the respective constitutional requirements about international treaties had been met in both states, the treaty went into effect on 17 September 1975.

Since the treaty incorporated Iran's demand, first made 60 years earlier, that the thalweg principle be applied to the frontier along the Shatt al-Arab [*q.v.*], it signified a victory for Iran.

Later Iraq said that it had signed the treaty under duress. It unilaterally abrogated it on 17 September 1980 before invading Iran. Iran protested. The subsequent war lasted nearly eight years. In mid-August 1990, following its invasion of Kuwait, Iraq agreed to abide by the treaty to ensure that its eastern frontier remained quiet.

Iran-Iraq War (1980–88): *See* Gulf War I.

Iranian calendar: In 1925 the Iranian parliament adopted the solar calendar beginning with the *hijra*, the migration of the Prophet Muhammad from Mecca [*q.v.*] to Medina [*q.v.*] in 622 A.D. which is also the starting point of the Islamic (lunar) era. The Iranian (solar) year begins on the spring equinox, 21 or 22 March, and is divided into six consecutive months of 31 days, and the rest of 30 days, except the last, which is normally 29 days long. The months—named after Zoroastarian [*q.v.*] angels—are Farvardin (31 days), Urdibehesht (31), Khurdad (31), Tir (31), Murdad (31), Shahrivar (31), Mihr (30), Aban (30), Azar (30), Dey (30), Bahman (30), and Isfand (29 days normally, 30 days in a leap year). To change an Iranian calendar date to a Christian [*q.v.*] date, add 621 or 622 depending on the month of the year. The Islamic Republic of Iran, founded in 1979, uses the Iranian calendar along with the Islamic one.

Iranian-Russian Treaty (1921): A 25-article treaty was signed between Iran (then Persia) and Soviet Russia on 26 February 1921. Article 5 required the two parties to prohibit the formation or presence of "any organization or groups of persons ... whose object is to engage in acts of hostility against Persia or Russia." This applied equally to troops. Both signatories agreed to prevent the presence of forces of a third party in cases where the presence of such forces would be regarded as "menace to the frontiers, interests or safety" of the other party. "If a third party should carry out a policy of usurpation by means of armed intervention in Persia, or if such power should desire to use Persian territory as a base of operations against Russia, or if a foreign power should threaten the frontiers of Federal Russia or those of its allies, and if the Persian government should not be able to put a stop to such menace after having been once called upon to do so by Russia, Russia shall have the right to advance her troops into the Persian interior for the purpose of carrying out the military options necessary for its defense," stated Article 6. "Russia undertakes, however, to withdraw her troops from Persian territory as soon as possible when the danger has been removed." In August 1941 these articles formed the basis for the Soviet march into northern Iran (which took place in coordination with Britain, its ally in World War II, after June 1941, whose troops advanced from the south).

When the revolutionary movement in Iran against the pro-Washington Muhammad Reza Shah Pahlavi [*q.v.*] started to escalate sharply during the autumn of 1978, raising the possibility of intervention by the United States, the Soviet leader, Leonid Brezhnev, warned the United States against interfering in Iran's domestic affairs. Aware that Articles 5 and 6 of the 1921 Treaty entitled Moscow to move its troops into Iran if it felt threatened by an armed intervention by a third party in Iran, U.S. Secretary of State Cyrus Vance stated publicly that Washington had no intention of becoming involved in Iran's internal affairs: a statement that boosted the morale of the anti-shah forces.

Iranian-Soviet Treaty of Guarantee and Neutrality (1927): On 1 October 1927 the Soviet Union signed a Treaty of Guarantee and Neutrality with Iran. The signatories agreed to refrain from aggression against each other and to remain neutral in the event of aggression by a third country. "Each of the contracting parties agrees to take no part … in political alliances or agreements directed against the safety of the territory or territorial waters of the contracting party or against the integrity, independence or sovereignty," stated Article 3. The same applied to economic boycotts or blockades organized by third parties. One of the two protocols accompanying the document reiterated that Article 6 of the 1921 Iranian-Russian Treaty [*q.v.*] should remain in force. Following the 1979 Islamic revolution in Iran, when the United States and the European Economic Community imposed economic sanctions against Iran after militant Iranian students had taken U.S. diplomats hostage, the Soviet Union refused to join the embargo.

Iraq: *derivative of eraq* (Middle Persian, *lowland*)

OFFICIAL NAME: Republic of Iraq

CAPITAL: Baghdad [*q.v.*]

AREA: 169,235 sq. mi./438,317 sq. km, excluding the Iraqi share of the Saudi Arabia-Iraq Neutral Zone [*q.v.*] at 1,360 sq. mi./3,522 sq. km

POPULATION: 33.33 million (2010 est.)

GROSS DOMESTIC PRODUCT (nominal): $108 billion (2011 est.); per capita, $3,300 (2011 est.)

Gross domestic product (Purchasing Power Parity): $126 billion (2011 est.); $3,830

National currency: Iraqi Dinar (IQD); IQD 10,000 = $8.63 = £5.46 = € 6.52 (2011)

Form of government: republic, with president as head of state and prime minister as chief executive

Official language(s): Arabic [*q.v.*] in all of Iraq and Kurdish [*q.v.*] only in the Kurdistan Autonomous Region [*q.v.*]

Official religion: Islam [*q.v.*]

Administrative regions: Iraq is divided into 18 governorates (provinces), including the three—Irbil, Dohak, and Suleimaniya—forming the Kurdistan Autonomous Region which has its own regional assembly and president.

Constitution: After a coup by the Baath Socialist Party [*q.v.*] in July 1968, an interim constitution was promulgated in September. Amended in November 1969, it was replaced by another provisional version in July 1970. The latest document was amended in 1973 and 1974. A draft of the permanent constitution was submitted in March 1989 to the National Assembly [*q.v.*], an institution established in 1980. Though the Assembly approved it in July 1990, it remained to be put to a referendum for approval before its implementation.

The September 1968 constitution described Iraq as "democratic and sovereign," and Islam as the state religion. The state undertakes to safeguard freedom of religion, speech, and opinion. It also guarantees freedom of the press and the right to establish associations and trade unions within the law.

The highest authority in Iraq was the Revolutionary Command Council (RCC), which ruled by two-thirds majority, and which was authorized to issue laws until the establishment of a parliament. The 1969 amendments made Iraq's president the supreme commander of the armed forces and chairman of the RCC.

The 15-article peace agreement that the Iraqi government signed with the Kurdish insurgents in March 1970 included a promise by it to amend the existing constitution to declare that the people of Iraq consisted of two principal nationalities—the Arab [*q.v.*] and the Kurdish—and to confirm the national rights of Kurds [*q.v.*] and all other minorities within the framework of Iraqi unity, and to appoint a Kurd as a vice president of Iraq.

The 1970 interim constitution required that the president and vice president(s) should be elected by a two-thirds majority of the RCC, and that cabinet ministers should be responsible to the president. The National Charter promulgated by the president in July 1973 mentioned the creation of a National Assembly. The law for autonomy in Kurdistan, issued in March 1974, provided for a Legislative Council there. Following an RCC decree in March 1980, elections to the National Assembly and the Legislative Council were held respectively in June and September.

Following an amendment to the interim constitution by the RCC in September 1995, the elected chairman of the RCC became the Republic's president for seven years after approval by the National Assembly followed by an endorsement in a referendum.

After the Anglo-American invasion

of Iraq [*q.v.*] in March 2003, a multinational coalition, led by the United States and the United Kingdom, occupied Iraq. A new constitution followed. Drafted by the Interim National Assembly (the elections to which were boycotted by the Sunnis [*q.v.*] in January 2005) in October 2005, it was ratified in a referendum in December by 78 percent of the voters. It described Iraq as an Islamic, democratic, federal parliamentary republic. It specified Islam as a main source of legislation and stated that no Iraqi law would violate the basic tenets of Islam. It stipulated a parliamentary system with an executive prime minister to be elected by the 275-member Council of Representatives. But it also required that all bills passed by the National Assembly must be approved unanimously by a three-member Presidential Council, consisting of a Shia [*q.v.*], a Sunni, and a Kurd before it could become law.

ETHNIC COMPOSITION: (2011) Arab 78 percent, Kurd 18 percent, Turkmen [*q.v.*] 1.5 percent, other 2.5 percent.

EXECUTIVE AUTHORITY: Executive power rests with the republic's prime minister, who is elected by the Council of Representatives. It also elects the Presidential Council consisting of President and two vice presidents.

High officials:
President: Jalal Talabani, 2010–
First Vice President: Tariq al-Hashemi, 2011–
Second Vice President: Khudayar Khuzai, 2011–
Speaker of the Council of Representatives: Osama Najafi, 2010–

HISTORY (ca 1900): At the turn of the 20th century the provinces of Basra [*q.v.*] and Baghdad in the Mesopotamian plain [*q.v.*] had been part of the Ottoman Empire since 1638. After the dissolution of the Ottoman Empire in 1918 the mandate over these provinces was given to the British. They constituted them as Iraq and put them under the authority of King Faisal I bin Hussein al-Hashem [*q.v.*] in 1921. Four years later, a League of Nations arbitration committee awarded Mosul [*q.v.*] province to Iraq, thus enlarging the country.

In 1932 the British Mandate ended, but most Iraqis considered their independence incomplete so long as British troops were stationed on their soil. In April 1941 Premier Rashid Ali Gailani [*q.v.*] led a successful coup against the British. However, he was unable to withstand a British counteroffensive in May.

After World War II the national sentiment turned strongly anti-Western and anti-Zionist [*q.v.*] in the aftermath of the Arab defeat in the Palestine War (1948–49) [*q.v.*]. But the Iraqi strongman Premier Nuri al-Said [*q.v.*] overrode popular feelings, took Iraq into the Western-led Baghdad Pact [*q.v.*], and refused to condemn the Anglo-French-Israeli aggression in the Suez War (1956) [*q.v.*]. The result was an anti-royalist military coup by Free Officers led by Brigadier Abdul Karim Qasim [*q.v.*] in July 1958. He carried out socioeconomic reform, but was overthrown in 1963 by a group of Baathist [*q.v.*] officers, working in conjunction with the U.S. Central Intelligence Agency.

Due to a division among the Baathists, power passed to the non-Baathist, pro-Egyptian Abdul Salam Arif [*q.v.*], and then to his brother

Abdul Rahman Arif [*q.v.*], who was overthrown by a Baathist coup in July 1968. Better organized than before, the Baathists consolidated their hold over power, and started an ambitious program of economic development. They were helped by a dramatic jump in oil prices in the mid-1970s.

The rebellion by nationalist Kurds that flared up in 1974 was pacified by striking a deal with Iran, which had been arming the Iraqi Kurds, in March 1975, known as the Algiers Accord [*q.v.*]. But with the rise of an Islamic republic in Iran, a Shia [*q.v.*] majority country, in 1979, the Iraqi government found Islamic militancy gaining ground among its Shias. Iraq's President Saddam Hussein tried to tackle the problem by suppressing militant Shias at home and invading the oil-rich Iranian province of Khuzistan in September 1980. He had expected the conflict to last a month, with Iraq emerging triumphant. But it continued for 95 months, ending in August 1988. Nonetheless, thanks to the aid Iraq received from the Gulf States [*q.v.*] and the West, Iraq became the most powerful Arab country.

Determined to make his weight felt in the region, in August 1990 Saddam Hussein invaded and occupied Kuwait, an emirate to which Iraq had in the past laid claim. In response the United States, under President George H. W. Bush (r. 1989–93), led a coalition of 28 nations in a successful war in early 1991, which ended the Iraqi occupation of Kuwait. Due to the UN embargo imposed in August 1990 the living standards of Iraqis declined sharply.

Though by late 1994 Iraq claimed to have met almost all the conditions required for the lifting of the UN embargo, such a prospect was not in sight. It receded altogether when, after his defection in August 1995, Gen. Hussein Kamil Hassan, a former minister of military industrialization, revealed the true extent to which the Iraqi government had withheld information on its program of weapons of mass destruction, to Rolf Ekeus, head of the UN Special Commission (UN-SCOM) [*q.v.*].

Following the succession of Ekeus, a career diplomat, by Richard Butler, a disarmament specialist, two years later, there was further pressure on Iraq to submit full information on its program of unconventional weapons, particularly biological warfare agents. The heightened tension between the two sides led to a four-day bombing of Iraq by America, backed by Britain, in December 1998, called Operation Desert Fox [*q.v.*], after Butler had withdrawn UN inspectors from Iraq.

The efforts of the UN Security Council to get weapons inspectors back into Iraq under a new resolution a year later were spurned by Baghdad. The UN's agreement to let Iraq export oil to purchase food and medicine for its citizens that came into operation from December 1996 reduced the suffering of ordinary Iraqis. However, the fact that Iraq could sell oil only under UN supervision, and deposit its earnings in a UN escrow account, meant that the UN's economic mandate over the country's most prized resource remained in place.

For the first time since the Iran-Iraq War, Iraq held its parliamentary election on time—in March 2000. Five months later, the arrival in Baghdad of President Hugo Chavez of

Venezuela, then chairman of the Organization of Petroleum Exporting Countries (OPEC) [*q.v.*], in August by air in the course of his visits to the capitals of the OPEC member-states, started an erosion of the strict UN sanctions. In the wake of the outbreak of the Second Intifada [*q.v.*] by Palestinians in September, Iraq was invited to an Arab League summit after 10 years. But Saddam Hussein dispatched his deputy to the summit. Iraq sent food and medical aid to the Palestinian Territories [*q.v.*] via Jordan. And, following the lead of the Palestinian Authority [*q.v.*], Iraq paid compensation to the families of the Palestinians killed in the Intifada.

The succession to Democrat U.S. President Bill Clinton by Republican George W. Bush (r. 2001-2009) made no difference to Washington-Baghdad relations. The newly installed American president ordered air strikes against Iraqi targets on the ground that Iraq was improving its air defenses. And, in the aftermath of the attacks on the U.S. in September, Washington tried hard to link Iraq with Al Qaida [*q.v.*], but failed. However, after overthrowing the Taliban regime in Afghanistan, Bush targeted Iraq, arguing that it had failed to disarm itself of weapons of mass destruction as required by the UN. His administration succeeded in getting the UN Security Council to adopt Resolution 1441 in November 2002, stipulating a rigorous inspection and monitoring regime in Iraq. Baghdad accepted the resolution, which authorized the formation of the UN Monitoring, Verification, and Inspection Commission (UNMOVIC) [*q.v.*].

UN inspections started on 27 No-

vember under the leadership of Hans Blix. As required by Resolution 1441, Iraq submitted a 12,000-page document detailing its programs of weapons of mass destruction and missiles. In their reports to the Security Council on 19 December, Blix and Muhammad el Baradei, director general of the International Atomic Energy Agency, said that Iraq had provided prompt access to the 150 sites their teams had visited. The aluminum tubing that America and Britain had alluded to was for permissible Iraqi rockets and not for the proscribed nuclear weapons. By 18 January 2003 the UN teams had visited all 11 sites mentioned by Bush and Blair as the premises used by Iraq in its revived program of weapons of mass destruction, and found no evidence to that effect. On 19–20 January Iraq signed a 10-point agreement with Blix and Baradei promising further cooperation. Yet Bush kept saying that Saddam must disarm, and, in the case of his refusal, the U.S.-led coalition would force him to do so and free the Iraqi people. At the same time the Special Forces of America and Britain began infiltrating Iraq to facilitate the invasion of the country by the Anglo-American troops.

In their 27 January report, covering two months of inspections and 300 inspections (of which about 100 concerned the nuclear program) of 230 sites (out of a total of 700) by a staff of 260 drawn from 60 countries, Blix and Baradei reported to the Security Council that on the whole Iraq had cooperated well, giving their teams prompt access to all sites. Baradei said that his inspectors had visited presidential compounds and private residences but had discovered no evidence that Iraq has revived its nuclear weapons program since its elimination in the 1990s.

By contrast, in his presentation to the Security Council on 5 February, U.S. Secretary of State Colin Powell made the following claims: there were up to two dozen Al Qaida operatives in Iraq, the most important being Abu Mussab Zarqawi; the terrorist Ansar-e Islam operated a chemical poison factory in an enclave of Iraqi Kurdistan [q.v.]; a missile brigade operating from outside Baghdad was dispersing proscribed rockets in the country; Iraq possessed about 18 mobile biological weapons laboratories; Baghdad had a model of an unmanned drone capable of spraying chemical or germ weapons within a radius of 550 miles; and Iraq moved contraband, with soldiers relocating munitions just before inspectors arrived. Lastly, Powell referred to Tony Blair's 19-page dossier, "Iraq: Its Infrastructure of Concealment, Deception and Intimidation," posted on his official website on 3 February, as a fine piece of evidence.

Critics argued that the presence of Al Qaida operatives in Iraq did not prove the government's involvement: such operatives lived not only in other Arab and Muslim countries but also in many western states. The visiting western journalists found the Ansar-e Islam's poison factory nothing but a derelict dump. Following the overthrow of Saddam Hussein's regime, the Anglo-American troops failed to find the alleged Iraqi missile brigade or the proscribed missiles. Four days before the start of the Gulf War III [q.v.] on 20 March 2003, Iraq handed over to UNMOVIC videos of mobile

biological laboratories, arguing that the videos showed that Iraq did not violate UN resolutions. When checked out by UN inspectors, Iraq's single unmanned drone turned out to be a machine rusting on an airfield north of Baghdad. Likewise, when verified on the ground, Powell's interpretation of the satellite images of trucks moving banned parts turned out to be false. Equally damaging was the discovery made by a British researcher at Cambridge University that large chunks of what Blair had tried to pass off as official U.K. intelligence were lifted verbatim from old academic journals and magazines posted on the Internet. Yet 70 percent in America agreed with Powell that Iraq was deceptive.

Powell's presentation marked the end of the Bush administration's support of continued UN inspections and prepared the ground for military action, despite Blix's report on 14 February that the 300 biological and chemical samples examined by UNMOVIC were consistent with Iraq's declarations, and that the inspections were bridging the gap in the United Nations' knowledge that arose due to its absence during December 1998–November 2002.

On 15 February, 15 to 20 million people in 60 countries marched in antiwar protests in 600 towns and cities, a quarter of them in America. The marches in London (1. 5 million strong), Rome (over 2 million), and Barcelona (over I million) were the largest ever. Overall, more than 70 percent in Britain, Italy, and Spain opposed the war. Yet their governments continued to back Bush in his belligerency.

Indeed, Spain was one of the three sponsors of the draft resolution—the others being America and Britain—presented to the Security Council on 24 February. It stated that Iraq had failed to comply with, and cooperate fully in the implementation of Resolution 1441 and must therefore face "serious consequences. " Disagreeing with this document, France, Russia, and Germany (as a non-permanent member of the Security Council) issued a memorandum saying that a verifiable disarmament could be reached through the implementation of a clear program of action by the inspection agencies, with each task clearly defined; reinforced inspections; and a timeline for inspections and assessment, with the chief inspectors reporting every three weeks. This was rejected by the U.S.-U.K.-Spain trio.

In the United States, opposition to war rose from 18 percent at the end of January to 37 percent a month later, almost equal to the support for it.

On 6 March Blix declared that Iraq was involved in "real and very fine disarmament" and that its cooperation had been "proactive." It had begun taking inspectors to the sites where it said it unilaterally destroyed biological weapons. At the Security Council the U.S.-U.K.-Spanish draft attracted one more vote, while five members—China, France, Germany, Russia, and Syria—opposed it. Of the remaining six, Pakistan and Guinea indicated they would abstain, while a top official of Cameroon said that his country and France were "old friends." Given this, there was no prospect of the Anglo-American alliance getting its draft resolution adopted by the Council. Yet so strongly opposed were

France and Russia to a war on Iraq that they individually threatened to veto the resolution if passed. When Angola, Cameroon, Chile, Guinea, Mexico, and Pakistan proposed giving Iraq 45 days to disarm (versus France's 120 days), the U.S. rejected the proposal summarily.

In the U.S., the anti-Saddam rhetoric reached a point where 42 percent believed that he was "personally" responsible for 9/11, and 55 percent believed that he gave direct support to Al Qaida.

On 14 March, when Bush, Blair, and Spanish Prime Minister Jose Maria Aznar decided to meet on the Portuguese Island of St. Azores, Iraq gave UNMOVIC a 20-page document detailing the destruction of 3.9 tons of VX nerve agent. The next day UN Secretary-General Kofi Annan said he believed war without the second resolution by the Security Council would break international law, meaning a violation of the UN Charter. Following the Bush-Blair-Aznar meeting on 16 March, when they decided to abandon their draft resolution at the Security Council, Bush gave Saddam Hussein and his sons—Uday and Qusay [q.v.]—48 hours to leave Iraq, failing which Washington would mount military operations. Saddam rejected the ultimatum. On 18 March the House of Commons in London passed a motion by 412 to 149 votes—with the opposition Conservatives voting with most of the governing Labor Party members—which stated that "the U.K. must uphold the U.N.'s authority as set out in [Resolution] 1441 and many resolutions preceding it, and therefore supports the decision that the U.K.

should use all means to disarm Iraq."

The Anglo-American invasion of Iraq started on 20 March 2003. For all practical purposes the Gulf War III [q.v.] ended on 16 April, although it was not until 1 May that President Bush announced a formal end to the hostilities against Iraq.

The Anglo-American occupation of Iraq followed. In June 2004 Iraq became nominally sovereign. The Interim National Assembly elected in January 2005 drafted a new constitution, which was ratified in a referendum in October. The election to the Council of Representatives under the new constitution was held in December 2005 and a new government formed under Ibrahim al-Jaafari [q.v.] in May. A year later Jaafari ceded his position to Nouri al-Maliki [q.v.].

In 2006–07 the inter-sectarian violence between Sunnis [q.v.] and Shias [q.v.] threatened to escalate into a fully-fledged civil war. But the Sunni tribal leaders' severance of links with Al Qaida in Mesopotamia [q.v.] and the infusion of additional American soldiers led to the lowering of Sunni-Shia tensions. In 2008, therefore, the Pentagon began planning to reduce its troops, then numbering 140,000, starting with their withdrawal from cities and towns to their rural bases. When Barack Obama succeeded Bush as president in January 2009, he accelerated the evacuation plans. On the last day of June the withdrawal of all U.S. troops from the urban areas was completed. The Maliki government declared 30 June 2009 as National Sovereignty Day. Yet the airspace of Iraq remained under U.S. control. By August 2010, the Pentagon's phased troop withdrawal brought the total down from the peak of 170,000 to 50,000. It was on 18 December 2011 that U.S. military presence in Iraq finally ended.

LEGISLATURE: Nationally, legislative power rests with the Council of Representatives and, regionally, with the Regional Council of Representatives of Kurdistan. In the February 2010 national election, 10.81 million ballots were cast. The popular vote and the number of seats won by the major alliances were as follows: al-Iraqiya List [q.v.] (Iraqi National Movement), 24.7 percent, 91 seats; (Shia) State of the Law coalition, 24.2 percent, 89 seats; (Shia) National Iraqi Alliance, 18.2 percent, 70 seats; Kurdistan List, 15.5 percent, 43 seats; others, 17.4 percent, 32 seats.

RELIGIOUS COMPOSITION: (2011) Muslim, 97.5 percent, of which Shia 63.5 percent, Sunni 34 percent; Christian [q.v.], 1.5 percent, of which Chaldean Catholic [q.v.] 0.8 percent, Nestorian [q.v.] 0.5 percent, Orthodox [q.v.] 0.2 percent; and Yazidi [q.v.], 1 percent.

Iraqi Kurdistan: *See* Kurdistan Autonomous Region [q.v.].

Iraq-Najd Neutral Zone: *See* Saudi Arabia- Iraq Neutral Zone.

Iraq-Saudi Arabia Neutral Zone: *See* Saudi Arabia-Iraq Neutral Zone.

Iraqi National Accord: Funded by Saudi Arabia's intelligence agency, *Riasat al-Istikhabart al-Aama* (Arabic: *General Intelligence Leadership*), the Iraqi National Accord (INA) was established in 1990 by Adnan Nouri; Iyad Muhammad Allawi [q.v.], a physician; and Omar Ali al-Tikriti, a diplomat—all of them defectors. As a former general in Iraq's Republican Guard, London-based Nouri maintained contacts with U.S. Central Intelligence Agency (CIA). Their sole objective was the overthrow of Iraqi President Saddam Hussein [*q.v.*] through a military coup, and they focused on recruiting defectors from the Iraqi military and Baath Party [*q.v.*].

Though the INA formally affiliated to the newly formed Iraqi National Congress [*q.v.*] in June 1992, it opened its own office in Iraqi Kurdistan [*q.v.*] and maintained direct contacts with the CIA. When, in March 1995, Nouri learned of the INC's plan to mount a frontal attack on the Iraqi troops, he successfully convinced U.S. National Security Adviser Tony Lake to withdraw Washington's support for the plan. Nonetheless, the INC went ahead. Its resulting failure soured relations between it and the INA. In October the INA was accused of blowing up the INC office in Salahuddin.

The INA's own plan for a coup—conceived by its specially formed Jordan-based military council—backed not only by the CIA but also by the intelligence agencies of Britain, Saudi Arabia, Jordan, and Kuwait—was scheduled for 26 June 1996. In it, U.S. intelligence and communications operatives, working as inspectors and support staff for the United Nations Special Commission (UNSCOM) [*q.v.*] on disarming Iraq, were assigned the job of conveying coded messages to some of the leading Iraqi military conspirators. But, starting in mid-June, the Iraqi government began arresting the plotters.

Following the bitter intra-Kurdish violence in September, when the CIA withdrew its agents and informers from Iraqi Kurdistan, the INA left the region. Nouri split with Allawi and moved to Turkey. After the passage of the Iraq Liberation Act in October 1998, Washington recognized the INA as a group eligible for U.S. assistance. During the administration of U.S. President George W. Bush (r. 2001-2009), the INA became the favorite of the CIA and the state department. It participated in the Iraqi Open Opposition conference in London in late 2002.

The INA was the conduit for the dubious intelligence—originating with a former Iraqi officer exiled in Germany in contacts with the German foreign intelligence agency—that Iraq was capable of deploying its weapons of mass destruction within 45 minutes, which was supplied to the British Secret Intelligence Service, known as MI6. This was used as a leading piece of evidence in the dossier presented to the British parliament in September 2002 to gain legislative and popular support for invading Iraq.

After the Anglo-American invasion of Iraq [*q.v.*] in March 2003, Allawi was appointed a member of the Interim Iraqi Governing Council, and then in June 2004 prime minister of the Iraqi Interim government. On the eve of the December 2005 parliamentary election, the Iraqi National Accord formed an alliance with other secular groups to form the Iraqi National List. It won 25 seats in a house of 275. It participated in Nouri al-Maliki's coalition government until 2007. Two years later, with Allawi coalescing with Sunni leaders to form the Iraqi National Movement, popularly called al-Iraqiya List [*q.v.*], the original INA ceased to exist.

Iraqi National Congress: The Iraqi National Congress was formed as an umbrella organization in Vienna at the meeting of 300 Iraqi delegates, funded by the U.S. Central Intelligence Agency (CIA), which used Ahmad Chalabi [*q.v.*] as the front man. Among the 20 factions that affiliated to it were the Iraqi National Accord [*q.v.*], Kurdistan Democratic Party (KDP) [*q.v.*], and Patriotic Union of Kurdistan (PUK) [*q.v.*].

Led by Ahmad Chalabi [*q.v.*], it committed itself to waging a war of liberation against the regime of Iraqi President Saddam Hussein [*q.v.*] with the objective of establishing a democratic Iraq. Working with the KDP and the PUK, it set up its headquarters in Salahuddin to develop Iraqi Kurdistan [*q.v.*] as the staging area for the overthrow of Saddam. Encouraged by the defection in late 1994 of Gen. Wafiq Samarrai, who headed Iraq's military intelligence in 1991–92, Chalabi and Samarrai devised a plan that was in theory an amalgam of a popular revolt and a military coup to oust Saddam. But since it involved mounting frontal assaults on Iraqi troops, necessitating U.S. intervention with its air force and even ground forces, the National Security Adviser, Tony Lake, withdrew all American support. Nonetheless, the INC along with the PUK mounted assaults on 5 March 1995 which the KDP and the INA refused to join. Nothing came of the INC-PUK offensives. Relations between the INC and the INA deteriorated to the extent that the INC headquarters was blown up in October, allegedly by the INA.

Following the bitter intra-Kurdish violence in September 1996, when the CIA withdrew its agents and informers from Iraqi Kurdistan, the INC left the region and moved its head office to London. After the passing of the Iraq Liberation Act in October 1998, the U.S. recognized the INC as a group eligible for its assistance. During the administration of President George W. Bush (r. 2001–2009), the INC became the favorite of the defense department and Vice President Dick Cheney's office. At the Iraqi Open Opposition conference in London in December 2002, the INC failed to get its proposal for a transitional government for the post-Saddam Iraq [*q.v.*] accepted.

After the Anglo-American invasion of Iraq [*q.v.*] in March 2003, Chalabi was appointed to the Interim Iraqi Governing Council by the occupying Coalition Provisional Authority. His INC remained on the payroll of the state department until September 2003 and of the Pentagon until May 2004. In August, when Chalabi was abroad, an arrest warrant was issued for him for alleged counterfeiting. But on his return to Baghdad [*q.v.*], he was not arrested. The charge was dropped when the investigating judge cited lack of evidence.

On the eve of the January 2005 election to the Interim National Assembly, the INC joined the United Iraqi Alliance [*q.v.*], the brainchild of Grand Ayatollah Ali Sistani [*q.v.*]. Under the premiership of Ibrahim al-Jaafari [*q.v.*], Chalabi briefly served as the acting oil minister. Later the INC allied with small secular groups to form the secular National Congress Coalition (NCC). It failed to gain a single seat in the parliament. With that the INC became a paper organization.

Iraqi Kurdistan: *See* Kurdistan Autonomous Region (Iraq).

Iraqi-Saudi Non-Aggression Pact
(1989): The Iraqi-Saudi Non-Aggression Pact was signed in Baghdad [*q.v.*] on 27 March 1979 during a visit by Saudi King Fahd bin Abdul Aziz [*q.v.*]. It spelled out the principles of "non-interference in the internal affairs of the two sisterly countries" and "non-use of force and armies between the two states." Following the Iraqi invasion of Kuwait in August 1990 and Saudi Arabia's participation in the U.S.-led anti-Iraq coalition, the pact lost its purpose.

Iraqi-Soviet Friendship Treaty (1972): In 1972 Iraq and the Soviet Union cemented their friendship, based on their common opposition to Western imperialism and Zionism [*q.v.*], with a 20-year Iraqi-Soviet Friendship Treaty. It was signed in Baghdad [*q.v.*] on 9 April 1972. The signatories agreed to contact each other in case of "danger to the peace of either party or … danger to peace," and to refrain from joining any alliance with another country or group of countries against the other. They also resolved to "develop cooperation in the strengthening of their defense capacity." Following its invasion of Kuwait in August 1990, Iraq fell foul of the UN Security Council, and the Soviet Union, a permanent Council member, condemned the Iraqi action. With the disintegration of the Soviet Union in December 1991, the treaty expired.

al-Iraqiya List: After quitting the government of Nouri al-Maliki [*q.v.*] in 2009, Iyad Allawi [*q.v.*], a secular Shia [*q.v.*] leader, cobbled together a coalition of his Iraqi National List [*q.v.*] with two Sunni factions—the Renewal List of Tariq al-Hashmi and the Iraqi National Dialogue Front—to form the Iraqi National Movement (Arabic: *al-Harka al-Wataniya al-Iraqiya*), popularly called the al-Iraqiya List. It emphasized its nonsectarian, secular character, and won political and financial support from Saudi Arabia. In the March 2010 general election, it won 91 seats, two more than its rival the State of Law Coalition. However, it was denied the first chance to form the government because in May its rival State of the Law Party and the Iraqi National Alliance united to form the National Alliance, with the combined strength of 159 seats.

Irbil: *Iraqi city* (Also spelled Arbil, Erbil) Population: 1 million (2011 est.). One of the oldest settlements in the world, Irbil has a history dating back to antiquity. In more modern times it was part of Mosul province under the Ottomans (1517–1918). With the transfer in 1925 of Mosul to Iraq, it came under the jurisdiction of Baghdad. Discovery of oil [*q.v.*] in the region helped to improve the economy of Irbil, already an important trading center.

When, following an agreement between Kurdish nationalists and the central government, the Kurdistan Autonomous Region [*q.v.*] was created in 1974, Irbil was chosen as its capital. After the 1991 Gulf War [*q.v.*], the victorious Washington-led Coalition declared the Iraqi territory above the 36th parallel as a "no fly zone" for the Baghdad government.

This forced the Irbil-based Fifth Army to leave. With that, the city became the capital of a semi-independent Iraqi Kurdistan. During the next five years, it changed hands between the competing Kurdistan Democratic Party [*q.v.*] and the Patriotic Union of Kurdistan [*q.v.*]. But its status as Iraqi Kurdistan's capital remained intact.

In the post-Saddam Hussein [*q.v.*] years, the city has prospered. Its several tourist attractions include a medieval citadel.

Irgun Zvai Leumi (Hebrew: *National Military Organization*): Irgun was formed by the Revisionist Zionists [*q.v.*] in Palestine [*q.v.*] in 1937, during the Arab revolt (1936–39), as a result of their disagreement with Haganah [*q.v.*], which limited itself to responding to Arab guerrilla activity. Irgun organized "preventive strikes" against Arab targets.

Following the publication of the British White Paper of 1939, which limited Jewish migration to Palestine, it turned against the British Mandate—except briefly during World War II, when it respected the official Zionist policy of cooperation with the Allies. After the war Irgun, with 3,000 to 5,000 members and led by Menachem Begin [*q.v.*], began sabotaging military installations, attacking barracks and executing British soldiers. It cooperated with the Stern Group [*q.v.*] in raiding armories, blowing up bridges and warplanes, mining roads, derailing trains, and sinking patrol boats. On 22 July 1946 in Jerusalem [*q.v.*] it blew up the King David Hotel, the site of the British Mandate's civilian and military offices, killing 91 people, including 15 Jews

[*q.v.*], the first massive terrorist act in the post-World War II era.

During the months preceding the founding of Israel in mid-May 1948, it cooperated with the Stern Group in carrying out concerted attacks on Arabs [*q.v.*]. On 9–10 April 1948, in an eight-hour attack on Deir Yassin village near Jerusalem, their joint forces killed 254 men, women, and children—two-thirds of all inhabitants. They dynamited houses, looted, and raped. The tactic was effective. In the five weeks leading up to the establishment of Israel, some 300,000 Arabs fled from the areas included in the UN plan for a Jewish state, and another 80,000 from the territory marked for the Arab state.

Though Irgun, while retaining its own military structure, agreed on 13 April 1948 to accept overarching Haganah command, Begin refused to let Irgun members be transferred along with Haganah personnel to the Israel Defense Forces [*q.v.*], formed by the provisional government of David Ben-Gurion [*q.v.*] on 26 May 1948. Irgun continued its fight against the Arab armies as a separate entity. In late June Ben-Gurion forbade Irgun leaders to deliver arms to their troops, scattered along the beaches, from the ship *Altalena*. When the latter defied him, Ben-Gurion ordered his forces to attack the ship. They did. This led to the death of 40 Irgun soldiers and the organization's disbandment.

al-Iryani, Abdul Rahman (1908–98): *Yemeni politician; president of North Yemen, 1967–74* Born into a notable Zaidi [*q.v.*] family in Saada, Iryani received religious education and trained as an Islamic judge. An opponent of the ruler, Imam Ahmad bin Yahya [*q.v.*], he participated in an abortive coup in 1948. After serving a six-year prison sentence, he left first for Aden [*q.v.*] and then Cairo [*q.v.*], where he cofounded the Free Yemen movement. Following the successful republican coup in September 1962, he returned home and participated in the Yemeni Civil War [*q.v.*] on the republican side. He served as minister of justice (1962–63) and then minister of local government (1964).

He belonged to the conservative faction that had links with the Zaidi tribes in the north. When, in a move to placate the royalists, the pro-republican Egyptian President Gamal Abdul Nasser [*q.v.*] compelled North Yemeni President Abdullah Sallal [*q.v.*] in April 1965 to move to Cairo [*q.v.*], Iryani was made a member of the powerful Republican Council of Yemen. He helped organize a pro-republican tribal conference to bolster the influence of the conservative faction within the government.

Having failed to strike a deal with the royalists, Nasser freed Sallal in September 1966. On his return home Sallal purged his rivals, including Iryani. Following Nasser's decision to withdraw the Egyptian troops from North Yemen by December 1967, Sallal's position became untenable. He was overthrown in November by a group of leaders, who later formed the five-member Republican Council, with Iryani as chairman and therefore president of North Yemen.

He helped to reconcile the warring sides and end the civil strife in March 1970. After the promulgation of a new constitution in December he was confirmed as president in March 1971 by a Consultative Council. In 1972, following clashes between North Yemen and South Yemen, Iryani and his South Yemeni counterpart agreed to work toward uniting their two countries. He was overthrown in a bloodless coup by Col. Ibrahim Hamdi [*q.v.*] in June 1974. He went into exile to Lebanon, and then to Syria. He was allowed to return home in 1981.

Isfahan: *Iranian city* (Also spelled Esfahan) Population: 1.70 million (2011 est.) It is known as *Nasf-e Jahan* (Persian: *Half of the World*). Its recorded history goes back to the Sassanian period (226–640 A.D.), when it was called Aspadana. Captured by Muslim [*q.v.*] Arabs [*q.v.*] in 642 A.D., it became the capital of the Seljuk dynasty in the mid-11th century. After the fall of the Seljuks in 1200 it lost its prominence. It survived a sacking by Tamerlane in 1387 to become the capital of Persia in 1598 under Shah Abbas I (r. 1588–1629). Abbas built the royal palace as well as the magnificent Shah Mosque (also known as the Blue Mosque), one of the finest examples of Iranian architecture, on the south side of the *Naqsh-e Jahan* (Persian: *Map of the world*) Square, which is one of the largest city squares on the planet. When Isfahan fell to the invading Ghalzai Afghans in 1723, it lost its capital status.

Some two centuries later an effort was made by the ruler, Reza Shah Pahlavi [*q.v.*], to rebuild and enlarge the city. Its traditional textile and metalwork industries expanded, and it became the site of an oil refinery and a steel plant. Its tourist attractions include the Royal Mosque and the Julfa quarters of the Armenians [*q.v.*], dating back to 1605.

Islam and Muslims (Arabic: *submission [to God's will]*): The last of the three important monotheistic religions, and drawing upon Judaism [*q.v.*] and Christianity [*q.v.*], Islam was founded by the Prophet Muhammad (570–632 A.D.), who was born in Mecca [*q.v.*]. Those who followed this religion were initially called Believers. Muslim, the term for those who followed Islam, came into vogue only in the 8th century. Their scripture is the Quran [*q.v.*], the Word of Allah, which was revealed to Muhammad (Arabic: *praiseworthy*) bin Abdullah al-Hashem, the last of a series of messengers of Allah to humans, beginning with Adam and including Abraham, Moses, and Jesus. Next in importance to Muslims is the *sunna* [*q.v.*] (Arabic: *custom*)—the words and deeds of the Prophet Muhammad. The Quran and the *sunna*, later codified as the Hadith [*q.v.*], together form the Sharia [*q.v.*] (Arabic: *Path*), which covers all aspects of religious, social, and political life, including state administration and conduct of war.

The Islamic credo rests on belief in Allah, the revealed books, the prophets, and the Day of Judgment. Five duties (called Pillars of Islam) are prescribed for Muslims. Believers must say at least once in their life: "There is no god but God, and Muhammad is the prophet of God." They must pray five times daily while facing Mecca, and must take part in collective noon prayers on Fridays. They must pay *zakat* [*q.v.*] (Arabic: *purification*), a religious tax, to support the poor and needy. They must fast from dawn to dusk during Ramadan [*q.v.*]. They must undertake a hajj [*q.v.*] to Mecca once in their lives, if they can afford it.

After the death of the Prophet Muhammad who, during the last decade of his life governed a domain (capital: Medina [*q.v.*]), fought wars and acted as a judge and administrator, his duties were taken over by his vice regent, Caliph (Arabic: *khalif*) Abu Bakr bin Abu Quhafa (r. 632–634 A.D.). He was followed by Omar bin Khattab (r. 634–644 A.D.) and Othman bin Affan (r. 644–656 A.D.), who was assassinated by Muhammad bin Abu Bakr and other conspirators for his maladministration.

During the reign of Omar and Othman, the Islamic state expanded far beyond the Arabian Peninsula [*q.v.*], with local governors administering its distant parts. The rule of Caliph Ali bin Abu Talib (r. 656–661 A.D.), a cousin and son-in-law of the Prophet Muhammad, was challenged by Muwaiya bin Abu Sufian, governor of Syria. A civil war ensued, creating Shiat Ali, or Shias [*q.v.*], and Kharijis [*q.v.*], thus fracturing the unity of the Islamic world. Over the next two centuries four different codes of the Sharia developed among Sunnis [*q.v.*], the orthodox sect. Sufism [*q.v.*], a mystical streak within Islam, was developed by, among others, Abu Hamid Muhammad al-Ghazali (1058–1111).

The spread of Islam was rapid during the two centuries after the Prophet Muhammad's death, reaching central France in 732 A.D. From the 12th century onward, Sufis were at the forefront of the religious expansion that took Islam into Turkey, Central Asia, the

Indian subcontinent, and sub-Saharan Africa. Pious Muslims, trading over land and sea, became the harbingers of Islam in East Africa, West Africa, and Indonesia. At 1.62 billion, Muslims were 23.5 percent of the global population of 6.89 billion in 2010. Only about one-fifth of them lived in the Middle East [*q.v.*] and North Africa; three-fifths lived in Asia-Pacific.

Islamicism and Islamicists: *See* Islamism and Islamists.

Islamic Action Front (Jordan): *See* Muslim Brotherhood (Jordan).

Islamic Amal (Lebanon): *Lebanese religious–political organization* The Islamic Amal was established in July 1982 by Hussein Mousavi, a member of the command council of Amal [*q.v.*], after he had left Amal in protest at its leaders' passivity toward Israel's occupation of two-fifths of Lebanon. He allied with the Iranian revolutionary guards based in Baalbek [*q.v.*], and attacked and occupied the nearby Lebanese army's barracks. Islamic Amal activists conducted guerrilla actions against the Israeli troops in southern Lebanon. At the behest of Ali Akbar Mohtashemi, Iran's ambassador to Syria, the Islamic Amal allied with the Islamic Jihad [*q.v.*] and the Hizbollah [*q.v.*] to conduct anti-Israeli and anti-U.S. activities. In early 1984 the three organizations together confronted the Lebanese army. When General Michel Aoun [*q.v.*] escalated his struggle against Syria and its Lebanese allies in 1989, the Islamic Amal joined an anti-Aoun front of 18 groups. Following the end of the

Lebanese Civil War [*q.v.*] in October 1990, the influence of the Islamic Amal declined as the Hizbollah emerged as the main party of radical Shias.

Islamic Awakening (2011): This is the term used by the Iranian regime and media to describe the events of the Arab Spring [*q.v.*], which they regarded as a reprise of the Islamic Revolution [*q.v.*] in Iran that toppled the pro-American shah, Muhammad Reza Pahlavi [*q.v.*], on 11 February 1979. As it happened, pro-Washington Egyptian President Hosni Mubarak was ousted on 11 February 2011.

Islamic banking: The Quran [*q.v.*] forbids usury: "Oh believers, fear you God; and give up the usury that is outstanding, if you are believers" (2:279), and "Oh believers, devour not usury, doubled and redoubled, and fear you God" (3:25). Money must be used only as a means of exchange. But since money is also used as commodity, this injunction has proved problematic. From the early days of Islam, legalistic innovations have been employed to get around this prohibition. The extreme example is the Islamic doctrine that states, "Necessity makes prohibited things permissible." In the Ottoman Empire (1517–1918) banks charged and paid interest, sometimes disguised as commission.

The circumventing devices are *muraabaha* (Arabic: derivative of *ribh, profit*), *mudaaraba* (Arabic: derivative of *zarab, to struggle*), and *mushaaraka* (Arabic: *partnership*). *Muraabaha* involves selling a commodity with a contract that it would be bought back later at a premium equaling the agreed interest. *Mudaaraba*, meaning sleeping partnership, involves a sleeping partner providing cash for an activity undertaken by an active partner, any profits being shared. *Mushaaraka* entails a depositor being treated as a partner who shares in the profits or losses. Over the past few decades many banks that use one or more of these methods have been established in Muslim countries, especially where laws are derived exclusively from the Quran and the Hadith [*q.v.*].

Islamic banking was virtually unscathed by the credit crunch that swept through the Western world in 2008–09.

Islamic calendar: In Islam, as in Judaism [*q.v.*], a day starts with sunset. The Islamic calendar is dated from the sunset on 15 July 622 A.D., the start of the *hijra* (Arabic: *migration*) of the Prophet Muhammad from Mecca [*q.v.*] to Medina [*q.v.*]. The Islamic year is lunar and contains 354 days, 8 hours, and 4.8 minutes. The Islamic months, and their duration, are Muharram (30 days), Safar (29), Rabia Awal (30), Rabia Thani (29), Jumada Awal (30), Jumada Thani (29), Rajab (30), Shaaban (29), Ramadan (29), Shawal (30), Dhul Qaada (29), and Dhul Hijja (30).

Since a lunar year is shorter than a solar one by about 11 days, it takes roughly 34 lunar years to equal 33 solar years. There is thus an approximate difference of three years between a lunar century and a solar one. A person aged 100 years by a solar calendar is 103 according to a lunar calendar. To convert an Islamic date to a Christian [*q.v.*] date, divide it by 1.031 and then add 621 or 622, depending on the month of the year.

Islamic Conference Organization: An arson attack on al-Aqsa mosque in Jerusalem [*q.v.*], the third-holiest shrine of Islam [*q.v.*], by Michael Rohan, an Australian fundamentalist Christian [*q.v.*], in August 1969 shocked the Muslim world. At the initiative of Saudi King Faisal bin Abdul Aziz [*q.v.*], an Islamic summit conference attended by 24 Muslim countries met in Rabat, Morocco, in September. Out of this emerged the Islamic Conference Organization (ICO), the first official pan-Islamic institution of intergovernmental cooperation. Open to all Muslim-majority states, the ICO based itself in Jeddah [*q.v.*] in May 1971. Its charter, adopted in 1972, aimed to promote Islamic solidarity; to coordinate efforts to safeguard Islamic holy places and support the Palestinian struggle for national rights; and to increase social, cultural, and economic cooperation among members.

Funded primarily by Saudi Arabia, it provided the kingdom with an opportunity to project itself as the leader of the Islamic world. In 1975 it set up the al-Quds [*q.v.*] committee to implement ICO resolutions on the status of Jerusalem. The ICO's attempt to emerge as a mediator in the Islamic world suffered a setback when its efforts to bring about a cease-fire in the war between two Muslim countries, Iran and Iraq, in 1981 failed. Tehran boycotted the fourth summit in Casablanca, Morocco, in January 1984 because the ICO failed to send a team to Iran to inspect the damage done by Iraqi bombing of Iran's civilian areas.

When the ICO secretariat refused to change the venue of the fifth summit in January 1987 in Kuwait, which was closely allied to Iraq in its conflict against Iran, Tehran again boycotted the meeting. The summit urged a cease-fire in the Iran-Iraq War [*q.v.*].

The sixth summit in Dakar, Senegal, in December 1991 was boycotted by 12 Arab heads of state in protest at the invitation extended to the Palestine Liberation Organization (PLO) [*q.v.*] and Jordan [*q.v.*], the ICO members that had sided with Iraq in the 1991 Gulf War [*q.v.*]. At the next summit in Morocco in 1994, the ICO adopted a code of conduct on terrorism which required member states not to aid terrorism and to ensure that extremist organizations did not use their territory for attacks on other states. At the extraordinary summit held in Islamabad, Pakistan, the ICO resolved to apply international pressure on Israel to honor its agreements with the PLO. The seventh summit in Tehran in December 1997 called on ICO members to consider Washington's Iran-Libya Sanctions Act of 1996 as invalid. It condemned terrorism but upheld the right of those under military occupation to resist the occupiers by all means. The next summit was held in Doha [*q.v.*] in 2000 after Qatar [*q.v.*] had closed down the Israeli trade mission in its capital.

In April 2002, the ICO foreign ministers, meeting in Kuala Lumpur, Malaysia, failed to agree on the definition of terror or terrorism [*q.v.*]. While calling for an internationally agreed definition of terrorism, their final communiqué specifically differentiated it from the resistance of a people under colonial or foreign occu-

pation. The tenth summit of the ICO was held in the Malaysian capital of Putrajaya in October 2003. And following the publication of a cartoon by a Danish newspaper in September 2005, showing the Prophet Muhammad with a turban containing a bomb, an extraordinary summit was held in Mecca [*q.v.*], where it was decided to boycott Danish goods.

At its eleventh summit in Dakar in March 2008, the leaders adopted a renewed charter and decided to rename the organization the Conference of Islamic Cooperation from 2011.

In 2011 it had 57 members, including the PLO, which was only an organization, not a fully fledged state. The five countries that enjoyed observer status included Russia. Since 2005 its secretary-general has been Ekmeleddin Ihsanoglu, an Arabic-speaking Turk.

Islamic Consultative Assembly (Iran): *See* Majlis.

Islamic Cooperation Organization (2011): *See* Islamic Conference Organization.

Islamic dress: Islamic dress applies to women, who are required to behave as stated in the Quranic verse (24:30–31): "And say to the believing women that they cast their eyes and guard their private parts … and let them cast their veils over their bosoms, and not reveal their adornment save to their husbands, or their fathers, or their husbands' fathers, or their sons, or their husbands' sons, or their brothers, or their brothers' sons, or their sisters' sons, or their women … or children who have not yet attained knowledge of women's private parts." The intention is to avoid arousing sexual passion between men and women who are not spouses or are not intending to be. The *hijab* (Arabic: *veil*), traditionally worn by Muslim women in public, always covers the head but not necessarily the face.

Islamic dress has been compulsory for women in Saudi Arabia since its founding in 1932. Following the Islamic revolution in Iran in 1979, it was made compulsory by law. Iran's urban working-class and rural women wear a *chador*, an all-encompassing shroud.

Islamic Front of Syria: *Syrian political alliance* In 1980 the moderate faction of the Muslim Brotherhood [*q.v.*] combined with the Islamic Liberation Party (ILP), the Society of Abu Dharr (SAD), and the Northern Circle (NC) to form the Islamic Front of Syria (IFS). It was led by Shaikh Muhammad Bayununi of SAD, Adnan Saad al-Din of the Muslim Brotherhood, and Said Hawa of the NC. To reassure the leftist and secular opposition, the IFS offered a program that was an amalgam of Islamic concepts and liberal democracy.

Once IFS leaders had reorganized their cadres they resumed their armed struggle against the regime of President Hafiz Assad [*q.v.*]. In February 1981 they initiated an insurrection in Hama [*q.v.*] and, operating from Iraq, they appealed to Syrians to declare a "civil mutiny" against the regime. Assad repressed the uprising in Hama brutally. Israel invaded Lebanon [*q.v.*], an event in which the Syrian troops stationed in Lebanon became partially involved. This turned public attention away from Islamic resistance toward the government's anti-Israel fight, and weakened the Islamic movement.

The Muslim Brotherhood, the IFS's leading constituent, wanted the IFS to adopt its pro-Iraq policy. This split the IFS into "compromisers," led by Saad al-Din, and "purists," headed by Adnan Uqla. The latter held that, since Iraqi President Saddam Hussein [*q.v.*] had invaded the Islamic Republic of Iran, he was anti-Islamic, and therefore cooperation with him could not be contemplated. The compromisers were prepared to work with anybody who was willing to help them overthrow the Assad regime.

In March 1982 Saad al-Din led the IFS into an alliance with 17 other opposition groups to form the National Alliance for the Liberation of Syria under Amin Hafiz [*q.v.*] in Baghdad [*q.v.*]. It demanded a constitutional parliamentary regime, Islam as the state religion, and the Sharia [*q.v.*] as the main source of legislation. When the purists condemned Saad al-Din's move their leader, Uqla, was expelled from the IFS. The infighting caused a dramatic drop in the fundamentalists' activities and popular support.

Islamic fundamentalism: Fundamentalism is the term used for the effort to define the fundamentals of a religion and adhere to them. One of the cardinal tenets of Islamic fundamentalism is to protect the purity of Islamic precepts from the adulteration of speculative exercises. Related to fundamentalism is Islamic revival or resurgence, a renewed interest in Islam. Behind all this is a drive to purify Islam in order to release all its vital force. In medieval times the drive for purification meant ridding Islam of superstition and/or scholastic legalism. That is, the fundamentalist response was purely internal. Today the response is both internal and external: to release Islam from its scholastic cobwebs as well as to rid it of ideas imbibed from the West.

Whether a Muslim-majority state today is fundamentalist or not can be judged by a single criterion: is its legislation derived *solely* from the Sharia [*q.v.*] (Islamic Law)? By this standard Saudi Arabia is the oldest Islamic fundamentalist state in the world: since its inception in 1932 it has known nothing but the Sharia. However, what the Islamic revolution did in Iran in 1979 was to transform a secular state and society into a religious one, thus pioneering a model for Muslim countries with a secular background, the majority in the 57-member Islamic Conference Organization (ICO) [*q.v.*]. In the mid-1990s about a dozen of the ICO member-states were being run solely according to the Sharia.

See also Omar Abdul Rahman; Muhammad Atef; Hassan al-Banna; Osama bin Laden; al-Gamaat al-Islamiya (Egypt); Hamas; Hizbollah; Islamic Action Front (Jordan); Islamic Amal (Lebanon); Islamic Front of Syria; Islamic Jihad (Lebanon); Islamic Jihad (Palestine); Islamic Revolution (Iran); al-Jihad al-Islami (Egypt); Ali Mohamad; Muslim Brotherhood (Egypt); Muslim Brotherhood (Jordan); Muslim Brotherhood (Palestine); Muslim Brotherhood (Saudi Arabia); Muslim Brotherhood (Syria); Al Qaida; Al Qaida in Arabian Peninsula; Al Qaida in Mesopotamia; al-Takfir wal Hijra;

Abu Mussab Zarqawi; and Ayman Zawahiri.

Islamic Iranian Participation Front

(Iran): Popularly known as *Moshakerat* (Persian: *participation*) Formed on the eve of the first local elections in Iran in early 1999, the left-of-center Islamic Iranian Participation Front was led by Muhammad Reza Khatami, a younger brother of President Muhammad Khatami (r. 1997–2005) [*q.v.*]. It was the leader of the alliance of 22 factions constituting the 2nd Khrdad/23rd May Front, named after the date on which Khatami had scored his landslide victory in 1997, formed to run in the 2000 Majlis [*q.v.*] elections. Its program included greater social, cultural, and media freedom, including private radio and television channels, and reform of government bureaucracy. While favoring attractive conditions for private capital in industry, it opposed privatizing state-owned oil, power, telecommunications, and tobacco industries. The IIPF won 95 Majlis seats. Muhammad Reza Khatami was elected deputy speaker of the Majlis. It remained the main bulwark of political reform in the country that was resisted by the conservative lawmakers and judiciary.

On the eve of the 2004 parliamentary election, when the Guardian Council [*q.v.*] rejected many of its candidates, the second Khordad Front split, with 14 factions boycotting the election. The voter turnout of 51 percent was well below the 63 percent in 2000, signifying that a substantial proportion of women, university students, and middle-class professionals abstained. The number of reformist deputies fell to 50. Mostafa Mon, the IIPF's candidate for president in 2005, did poorly. In the 2008 general election for parliament, reformists held on to 46 seats.

Following the widespread protest at the controversial presidential election in 2009, and the repression that followed, many IIPF leaders were among those who were imprisoned and later given jail sentences.

Islamic Jihad (Egypt): *See* al-Jihad al-Islami (Egypt).

Islamic Jihad (Lebanon): The Islamic Jihad (IJ), a pro-Iranian Shia [*q.v.*] group, was formed in Lebanon in the spring of 1982. In retaliation for the kidnapping of four Iranian diplomats in Beirut [*q.v.*] in mid-March 1982 by Maronite [*q.v.*] militiamen, it abducted David Dodge, the acting president of the American University of Beirut (AUB) [*q.v.*], in July. It was close to Ali Akbar Mohtashemi, Iran's ambassador to Syria (1982–83).

In April 1983 its rigged truck bombed the American Embassy in West Beirut. Seventeen of the 63 people killed were American, most of them senior Central Intelligence Agency (CIA) operators. On 23 October 1983, IJ militants truck-bombed the U.S. Marines headquarters at Beirut International Airport, killing 241 troops, and the French paratroops in Bir Hassan district, killing 59 soldiers. A similar explosion, caused by another IJ activist, destroyed the Israeli military headquarters in Tyre [*q.v.*], leaving 60 people dead, half of them Israelis. It allied with the Islamic Amal [*q.v.*] and Hizbollah [*q.v.*] in early 1984 to confront the Lebanese army.

The IJ kidnapped William Buckley, the CIA station chief in Beirut in March 1984. It promised to free him in exchange for the release of 17 Shias [*q.v.*], who had been convicted in Kuwait on charges of bombing the U.S. and French embassies. In September the IJ exploded a car-bomb inside the U.S. Embassy compound in East Beirut, killing eight people. The next month it released David Jacobsen, an American, as part of the hostages-for-arms deal between the United States and Iran, known as the Irangate Affair [*q.v.*].

In 1985, a grand jury in the United States meeting in secret indicted IJ leader, Imad Mougneih, as the mastermind of the 1983 explosion in Beirut.

Following the IJ's freeing of John McCarthy, a British journalist, in August 1991 United Nations Secretary-General Javier Perez de Cuellar became involved in securing the release of the remaining Western hostages and 450 Lebanese and Palestinians held without charge by Israel. In late 1991 a three-way swap—involving 450 Lebanese and Palestinian detainees under the Israelis, seven dead or captured Israeli servicemen, and the remaining Western hostages—ended the IJ's involvement in hostage taking.

With Hizbollah dominating radical Shia politics, the IJ, led by shadowy Mougneih, faded away. He was assassinated in 2008 by a car bomb detonated by Israeli agents in Damascus [*q.v.*].

Islamic Jihad Movement in Palestine: (Also known as Palestinian Islamic Jihad) A split in the Muslim Brotherhood in the Occupied Territories [*q.v.*] in 1981 led to the formation of the Islamic Jihad (Palestine) as a radical organization. It captured media headlines when its activists threw hand grenades at a military graduation ceremony at the Western Wall [*q.v.*] in Jerusalem [*q.v.*] in October 1986. It claimed to be the main force behind the eruption of the Palestinian intifada [*q.v.*] a little over a year later. It cooperated with other groups in continuing the intifada.

Opposed to the Israeli-Palestine Liberation Organization Accord of September 1993 [*q.v.*], it maintained its policy of violent attacks on Israeli targets in the West Bank [*q.v.*] and Gaza Strip [*q.v.*], and came into open conflict with the Palestinian Authority [*q.v.*] in late 1994. Its collective leadership kept a low profile, except for Shaikh Abdullah Shammi in Gaza [*q.v.*], where the group published a weekly paper, *Al-Istiqlal* (Arabic: *The Independence*). Its leader, Fathi Abdul Aziz Shikaki, was assassinated by Mossad [*q.v.*] agents in Malta in October 1995. He was succeeded by Abdullah Ramadan Shallah.

It participated actively in the Al Aqsa intifada [*q.v.*] that erupted in September 2000. Between 2001 and 2003 it carried out suicide bombings inside Israel—targeting a night club in Tel Aviv [*q.v.*], a bus in Jerusalem [*q.v.*], the Meggido railway station, and a restaurant in Haifa [*q.v.*]. A suicide attack in April 2006 in Tel Aviv proved to be its last terrorist act inside Israel. In that year it started firing its own fabricated rockets at Israeli targets. Some of its leaders became victims of Israel's policy of "targeted killings." Following the assassination of one of its senior commanders in Gaza by Israel in March 2009 its

spokesman unveiled an advanced rocket, called Al Quds-4, to be fired at Israeli targets. Under the guise of non-governmental organizations, it also runs free schools and health clinics.

Islamic Law: *See* Sharia.

Islamic Majlis (Iran): *See* Majlis.

Islamic Republican Party (Iran): The Islamic Republican Party (IRP) was established within a month of the February 1979 revolution by Iran's leading clerics, including Ali Akbar Hashemi Rafsanjani [*q.v.*] and Ali Hussein Khamanei [*q.v.*]. Its main aim was to guard the revolution and infuse Islamic principles into political, economic, cultural, and military spheres of society. As well as encouraging individuals to join it, the founders of the IRP urged the local Islamic Associations to affiliate to it.

In the elections to the Assembly of Experts [*q.v.*], which was charged with drafting the constitution, 47 of the 73 members either belonged to the IRP or were sympathetic to it. IRP leaders were at the forefront of the opposition to President Abol Hassan Bani-Sadr [*q.v.*] and his policies. Due to their endeavors, Bani-Sadr was impeached by 177 deputies, with one vote opposing, on 20 June 1981. Eight days later a bomb explosion triggered by Mujahedin-e Khalq [*q.v.*] activists killed 74 IRP leaders.

After President Muhammad Ali Rajai's [*q.v.*] assassination in August, the IRP's secretary-general, Ali Khamanei, successfully ran for the office in October 1981. Within two years the IRP and its allied groups occupied all political space. Yet by late

1984 its importance within the regime had declined: the factions of the party had become so deeply divided on socioeconomic issues, between conservatives and radicals, that their infighting was impeding the workings of the executive and the legislature. The differences between the two party wings became acute by mid-1986, and Ayatollah Ruhollah Khomeini [*q.v.*], the Supreme Leader, appointed a mediation council to conciliate them. It failed. So he had the party dissolved in July 1987.

Islamic Revolution (Iran): What started in early 1977 as a demand by Iranian intellectuals to abolish censorship ended up as a revolutionary overthrow of the most powerful pro-Western monarchy in the Middle East [*q.v.*], the Pahlavi shahs, two years later. The protest movement went through several stages, beginning with the revival of opposition parties at home and leading to the assuming of its stewardship by Ayatollah Ruhollah Khomeini [*q.v.*], then in exile in Najaf [*q.v.*], Iraq.

Khomeini made adroit use of Shia [*q.v.*] history and Iranian nationalism to attract ever-increasing support, and he united disparate anti-shah forces, both secular and religious, by his most radical demand: the deposition of Muhammad Reza Shah Pahlavi [*q.v.*]. Khomeini also devised an original set of strategies and tactics to neutralize the shah's 413,000-strong military. He advised his followers to confront the soldiers through martyrdom [*q.v.*], to let them kill as many as they wanted until they felt disgusted at their brutal behavior. At the same time he warned troops that firing at their brothers and

sisters amounted to firing at the Quran [*q.v.*]. These words, coming as they did from an eminent religious authority, had a strong impact on the soldiers, who were often conscripts and overwhelmingly Shia.

Though the revolutionary movement included secular elements, only the religious segment could provide a national network down to the village level in the form of the mosque. Both as an institution and as a place of congregation, the mosque proved crucial. Since the state could not stop mosques functioning normally, they became the only places where revolutionaries could meet in safety. This led Khomeini to instruct the clergy to base the Revolutionary Komitehs [*q.v.*] in mosques.

What finally sealed the fate of the Pahlavi state was an indefinite strike by oil workers, ordered by Khomeini on 31 October 1978. This was a body blow to the state treasury, already reeling from the effects of strikes by bazaar merchants, bank employees, customs officers, postal workers, and miners. Forced by the military government, appointed by the shah in early November, to return to work, the oil workers did so, but only to produce enough to satisfy domestic demand.

The 10-day Shia ritual of Ashura [*q.v.*] in December enhanced religious feeling in the nation, now paralyzed by a strike of civil servants. The first signs of cracks in the army appeared, with soldiers deserting with their weapons. In desperation the shah appointed Shahpur Bakhtiar [*q.v.*], a secular opposition leader, as prime minister, and agreed to go abroad on holiday immediately. He did so on 16 January 1979. But it was only after

Khomeini had returned home and appointed Mahdi Bazargan [*q.v.*] prime minister, and after the pro-Khomeini forces had crushed an attempted coup by the Imperial Guard, that the Pahlavi rule finally ended on 11 February.

The human cost in terms of anti-royalist deaths was 10,000 to 40,000. The Iranian military was down to 110,000 armed personnel. The soldiers of the monarchical elite forces either fled or ended up behind bars.

Though secular opposition had contributed substantially to the success of the revolution, it was denied its share of power. Because Khomeini, the movement's unrivaled leader, was a religious authority, and the mosque provided the base for the popular uprising, the end result was an Islamic revolution. Though other Middle Eastern countries had experienced dramatic change, often accompanied by the overthrow of the monarchy, the prime mover had been the military, and the means an overnight coup. This was the first time that millions of ordinary, unarmed citizens actively participated in a political process lasting many months, and ended up not only toppling the ruler but also decimating such state institutions as the military, the police, and intelligence agencies.

Since then no other Muslim-majority country in the Middle East [*q.v.*] or elsewhere has undergone such a thoroughgoing revolutionary transformation as a result of a single continuous political process. The Arab Spring [*q.v.*] in Tunisia and Egypt left the security forces and intelligence agencies intact. In Libya it turned into a civil war in which the North Atlantic Treaty Organization intervened actively against the regime of Colonel Muammar Gaddafi. In Yemen, the end result of the protest movement was the handing over of power from President Ali Abdullah Saleh [*q.v.*], in office since 1978, to his vice president, Abd Rabbu Mansour al-Hadi [*q.v.*].

Islamic Revolutionary Komitehs (Iran): *See* Revolutionary Komitehs (Iran).

Islamism and Islamists: When Islam [*q.v.*] is used as a political ideology, it is described as Islamism, and its adherents are called Islamists. *See* Islamic fundamentalism.

Islamist Bloc (Egypt): On the eve of the first post-Hosni Mubarak [*q.v.*] election to the 508-member People's Assembly in November 2011, the Al Nour [*q.v.*] Party coalesced with such other Salafi [*q.v.*] groups as Hizb *Al-Asala* (Arabic: *Originality Party*) and the Construction and Development Party set up by the Gamaat al-Islamiya [*q.v.*] to form the Islamist Bloc. The breakdown of the 127 seats it won on a popular vote of 28 percent was Al Nour, 114; Construction and Development Party, 10; and Al Asla Party, three. In the subsequent 180-member Consultative (Shura) Council election, the Islamist Bloc gained 45 seats on a popular vote of 29 percent.

Ismail, Abdul Fattah (1936–86): *South Yemeni politician, president 1978–80* Born into a peasant family in the Hujairiah region of North Yemen, Ismail traveled to Aden [*q.v.*] for further education. Employed by the British Petroleum Company, he took a keen interest in trade unionism. Active in the National Liberation Front (NLF) [*q.v.*], he became one of its leaders in 1964 and specialized in political and military affairs. After South Yemen's independence in 1967 he was named minister of national guidance. In June 1969 his leftist faction overthrew President Qahtan al-Shaabi [*q.v.*], and he became secretary-general of the NLF and a member of the Presidential Council under Salim Rubai Ali [*q.v.*].

Together with Ali Nasser Muhammad [*q.v.*], he continued to lead the leftist wing, and built up the party militia and the intelligence network. After a coup in August 1971 he and Muhammad consolidated their positions. In June 1978 they clashed with President Ali, who lost his life. Muhammad became chairman of the Presidential Council, but six months later ceded that position to Ismail. The radical policies of Ismail alienated Muhammad, who espoused a more pragmatic approach. In April 1980 Ismail was forced to resign his position and go into exile in Moscow for "medical reasons." He spent five years there. Following the Soviet Communist Party's successful mediation between the South Yemeni factions, he returned home. He was made secretary-general of the ruling Yemeni Socialist Party's [*q.v.*] central committee, a position that lacked power. The rapprochement between the factions broke down in January 1986. In the subsequent violence, which lasted a month and caused nearly 10,000 deaths, Muhammad was defeated, but Ismail was killed.

Ismailis: *Islamic group* Part of Shia [*q.v.*] Islam, Ismailis are distinguished from the other sub-sects—Zaidis [*q.v.*] and Imamis or Twelvers [*q.v.*]—by the number of revered figures they regard as Imams [*q.v.*]. They share the first six Imams with Twelvers (Ali, Hassan, Hussein, Zain al-Abidin, Muhammad al-Baqir, and Jaafar al-Sadiq). The seventh is Ismail, the older, militant son of al-Sadiq, who died in 765 A.D., five years before his father. This created a rift among Shias, since not all of them accepted Ismail's younger brother, Abdullah bin Jaafar, as their Imam. He died without a son.

They interpret the Quran [*q.v.*] symbolically and allegorically, seeing the inner meaning in the holy book as superior to the literal meaning. Because they value esoteric exegeses, which are revealed only to the elite, they believe in a religious hierarchy.

Ismailis are also known as Seveners since they subscribe to the concept that the number seven, being the total of spatial directions—forward, backward, above, below, right, left, and center—is symbolic, and that in the case of Imams signifies the end of a cycle.

An Ismaili group set up the Fatimid (named after a daughter of the Prophet Muhammad and the wife of Imam Ali) caliphate in Tunis which, after conquering Egypt in 969 A.D., rivaled the Abbasids, based in Baghdad [*q.v.*]. Their rule lasted until 1171. Today in the Middle East Ismailis are to be found in Iran, Syria, and Yemen.

Israel:

OFFICIAL NAME: State of Israel

CAPITAL: Tel Aviv [*q.v.*] (internationally recognized); Jerusalem [*q.v.*] (self-declared)

AREA (pre-1967 borders): 7820 sq. mi./20,255 sq. km

POPULATION: 7.8 million (2011, official est.), including ca. 508,600 Jewish settlers in Occupied Arab Territories [*q.v.*] (2011 est.): East Jerusalem [*q.v.*] 192,800; Golan Heights [*q.v.*] 20,100; West Bank [*q.v.*]) 340,000 in 121 recognized settlements and 102 unrecognized outposts

GROSS DOMESTIC PRODUCT (nominal): $245.3 billion (2011 est.); per capita, $32,300 (2011 est.)

GROSS DOMESTIC PRODUCT (Purchasing Power Parity): $235.4 billion (2011 est.); per capita, $31,000 (2011 est.)

NATIONAL CURRENCY: New Israeli Shekel (NIS); NIS 1 = U.S. $0.27 = £0.17 = €0.20 (2011)

FORM OF GOVERNMENT: republic, parliamentary

OFFICIAL LANGUAGES: Hebrew and Arabic

Official religion: None

ADMINISTRATIVE REGIONS: Israel is divided into six districts.

CONSTITUTION: The Constituent Assembly, elected in January 1949, adopted the Transition Law [*q.v.*] in February. It declared Israel a republic, to be headed by a president who would be elected for a five-year term by the Knesset [*q.v.*] (parliament; a single chamber of 120 members) by a simple majority. The Knesset was to be elected by adult franchise under a system of proportional representation, with the election threshold at 1 percent. The leader of the largest group would be invited by the president to become the prime minister and form the government, which would exercise executive authority. The Constituent Assembly then transformed itself into the First Knesset.

Following a debate on a report on the question of a written constitution by the Knesset's Committee on Constitution, Law, and Justice, the house decided in June 1950 to assign the task of preparing a draft constitution to the Committee "chapter by chapter … [with] each chapter submitted to the Knesset" and "all the chapters [after the Committee had finished its work] shall be incorporated into the Constitution." Between then and 1968, four such "chapters" were adopted by the Knesset: Basic Law: the Knesset (1958), fixing its term to four years; Basic Law: Lands in Israel (1959) creating the National Land Authority; Basic Law: the State President (1964), requiring him/her to be an Israeli citizen, resident in the country; and Basic Law: the Government (1968).

ETHNIC COMPOSITION (2011): Jews 75.3 percent, Arabs 24.7 percent

EXECUTIVE AUTHORITY: Executive authority rests with the cabinet, headed by the prime minister, who is the leader of the largest group in parliament.

High officials:

President: Shimon Peres, 2007–

Prime minister: Benjamin Netanyahu, 2009–

Speaker of the Knesset: Reuven Revlin, 2009–

HISTORY: Israel was established on 14 May 1948 at the end of the British Mandate over Palestine [*q.v.*], which dated back to 1922. An immediate war with its Arab neighbors ended in January 1949, with Israel acquiring 21 percent more land than the 54 percent allocated to it by the UN General Assembly Resolution 181 adopted in

November 1947. Israel was admitted to the United Nations on 11 May 1949 after it agreed to implement the General Assembly's resolution on partition as well as Resolution 194, passed in December 1948, which inter alia called for the return of the Palestinian refugees.

Following Egypt's nationalization of the Suez Canal [q.v.] in July 1956, Israel colluded with Britain and France to invade Egypt. It did so in October and occupied Sinai [q.v.] and Gaza [q.v.]. Under UN and U.S. pressure it vacated these territories in March 1957.

During the heightened tension in early June 1967 Israel staged preemptive strikes on the air forces of Egypt, Syria, and Jordan, and occupied the West Bank [q.v.], Gaza [q.v.], and the Golan Heights [q.v.]. This firmly established Israel's military superiority over its Arab neighbors, and made it somewhat complacent. The attacks in October 1973 by Egypt and Syria on Israel to regain their lost territories of Sinai and the Golan respectively came as a surprise to the Israelis. They rallied quickly but failed to reestablish the status quo. Mediation by the United States led to a peace treaty between Israel and Egypt in March 1979 on the principle of "land for peace."

Within six weeks of returning the last segment of Sinai and Egypt on 25 April 1982, Israel invaded Lebanon, occupying two-fifths of the country, including its capital, Beirut [q.v.]—a far more serious venture than the one in March 1978, when Israel had restricted itself to occupying about half of southern Lebanon, which was being used by the Palestinian guerril-

las to attack Israel. After phased withdrawals from Lebanon ending in June 1985, Israel maintained a military presence in its self-declared security zone in southern Lebanon.

The situation in the occupied West Bank and Gaza deteriorated to the extent that in 1987 the Palestinian population mounted an uprising, or intifada [q.v.]. The intifada continued year after year, compelling Israel first to recognize and then to negotiate with the Palestine Liberation Organization (PLO) [q.v.]. The resulting Israeli-PLO Accord [q.v.] of September 1993 led to the formation of the Palestinian Authority [q.v.] in Gaza and the West Bank town of Jericho [q.v.] as a first step toward autonomy for the areas of the Palestine under British Mandate that had been occupied by Israel since 1967.

The dominance of the Ashkenazi Jews [q.v.], a feature of Israel at its inception, lessened as large numbers of Jews arrived from the Arab states. This affected the political balance in the country, with the left-of-center Labor Party [q.v.], which had dominated governments since 1948, being relegated to opposition in 1977 by the right-wing Likud [q.v.]. But Likud's dominance did not last long. After the 1984 election the two leading parties formed a national unity government, with premiership divided into a two-year term for each of the leaders: Labor's Shimon Peres [q.v.] and Likud's Yitzhak Shamir [q.v.].

This arrangement was repeated after the 1988 general election. But in 1990, disagreeing with Shamir's policy on pursuing peace, Labor withdrew from the national unity administration, hoping Likud would lose power. It did not. It co-opted ultranationalist groups into the government and finished its term in 1992. At the next election Labor emerged as the leading party and became the dominant partner in the new coalition. Having achieved positive results in the peace process—an accord with the PLO and a peace treaty with Jordan—Labor planned to keep on this path with a view to gaining the directly elected premiership, to be introduced in 1996. It failed because its popular leader, Yitzhak Rabin [*q.v.*], was assassinated by a Jewish extremist in November 1995, and his successor Shimon Peres [*q.v.*] lost to his Likud rival, Benjamin Netanyahu [*q.v.*], in the May 1996 election.

Without formally renouncing the Oslo Accord, Netanyahu tried to wriggle out of it, in the process weakening it. But when, under American pressure, he signed a fresh deal under it, his ultra-right-wing supporters abandoned him, depriving him of a majority in the Knesset. He lost to the Labor rival, Ehud Barak [*q.v.*], in the elections—for the prime minister and the parliament—in May 1999. Barak withdrew Israeli troops from southern Lebanon a year later. But his final status talks with PLO leader Yasser Arafat [*q.v.*], chaired by U.S. President Bill Clinton (r. 1993–2001) at Camp David in July 2000 failed when Arafat found Barak's terms unacceptable. A visit by Ariel Sharon [*q.v.*], the Likud leader, to the Noble Sanctuary/Temple Mount [*q.v.*] in September triggered the Palestinian Al Aqsa intifada [*q.v.*]. With his coalition government disintegrating, Barak resigned in December. He lost to Sharon in the prime ministerial contest in February 2001.

Sharon demanded total cessation of violence by the Palestinians before peace talks could resume. Following that, he held out the prospect of freezing the present arrangement—whereby the Palestinian Authority (PA) [*q.v.*] controlled about 20 percent of the Palestinian Territories [*q.v.*]—and signing an extended truce with the Palestinians. Soon the Palestinian intifada escalated from stones thrown at the Israeli troops to armed assaults on Israeli soldiers and settlers. The Sharon government escalated its response from army firings to besieging Palestinian enclaves to making military incursions into the areas under PA jurisdiction and assassinating suspected terrorists.

After the terrorist attacks on the U.S. in September 2001, Sharon tried, unsuccessfully, to bracket Arafat with Osama bin Laden [*q.v.*]. By ordering tanks and helicopter gun-ships into refugee camps in the West Bank in February 2002 to arrest wanted terrorists, Israel crossed a red line. Responding to the killing of seven Israeli soldiers in early March, Israel sent 20,000 troops and scores of tanks in the West Bank. For the first time the PA publicly called on the Palestinians to confront the invaders. A more severe reprisal followed the murder of 27 Israeli Jews on Passover [*q.v.*], on 27 March, by a Palestinian suicide bomber, when Israel mounted its Operation Defensive wall, reoccupying all Palestinian towns and cities except Hebron [*q.v.*] and Jericho [*q.v.*], destroying Arafat's headquarters in Ramallah, and placing him under house arrest. By the time the Israeli offensive had ended a month later, 250 Palestinians were dead. In April the European Union parliament called on member states to impose political and trade sanctions against Israel for violating international and humanitarian law in its offensive against the Palestinians. With no end to periodic suicide bombings by the Palestinians, Israel reoccupied the West Bank towns and cities.

In 2002, Sharon ordered building a barrier to separate Israel from the West Bank which would annex nearly 10 percent of the Palestinian territory into Israel. After announcing his decision to end the military occupation of the Gaza Strip [*q.v.*] in 2004, he implemented it in September 2005, while retaining Israeli control over the airspace and the shoreline of the Palestinian territory. When he was incapacitated in April 2006, he was succeeded by Ehud Olmert [*q.v.*]. In July, under his leadership, Israel went to war with Hizbollah [*q.v.*] in Lebanon, which lasted a month. His numerous meetings with President Mahmoud Abbas [*q.v.*] of the Palestinian Authority failed to move the peace process forward.

Following Olmert's resignation in the wake of corruption charges and the Knesset elections in 2009, Benjamin Netanyahu became prime minister. His hardline stance on the peace process ended meetings with Abbas. After the war between Israel and Hamas [*q.v.*] in December 2008–January 2009, the cease-fire between the parties held. The brief resumption of talks between Netanyahu and Abbas in 2010 ended when Netanyahu refused to freeze the expansion of the Jewish settlements in the West Bank.

In October 2011, after five-year-long secret negotiations with Hamas through Egyptian and German intelligence officials, Israel agreed to free 1,027 Palestinian prisoners to secure the release of its soldier Gilad Shalit, captured by Hamas inside Israel in June 2006. On the strategic issue of peace with the Palestinians, Netanyahu asserted repeatedly that "by embracing Hamas, Abbas is walking away from peace."

LEGISLATURE: The Knesset deals with legislation, general policy matters, the budget, and international treaties. It has the right to elect the state president by a simple majority, or dismiss him/her for misdemeanor. But a two-thirds majority is needed to declare the president too ill to perform his or her duties. In order to reduce the number of political parties, the Knesset passed a law in 1992 to raise the qualifying threshold for a political party to secure a place in the legislature from 1 percent to 1.5 percent, and introduced direct election for the prime minister charged with forming a government. The new rules applied to the elections in 1996 and 1999 for both the Knesset and the prime minister. But in 2001, there was only the prime ministerial contest, the last such exercise. In 2003 the electoral system reverted to the old arrangement, since the new system had failed to reduce the number of political factions. However, the 2003 Knesset raised the qualifying threshold for a political group from 1.5 percent to 2 percent.

RELIGIOUS COMPOSITION (2011): Jews, 75.3 percent, of which 20 percent secular, 55 percent traditional, 17 percent Orthodox [*q.v.*], and 8.3 percent ultra-Orthodox; Muslims [*q.v.*], 20.5 percent, of which 18 percent are Sunni [*q.v.*] and 2.5 percent Druze [*q.v.*]; Christian [*q.v.*], 2.2 percent;

unclassified, 2 percent.

Israel Defense Forces: *See* Military in Israel.

Israel BeAliya (Hebrew: *Ascent into Israel*): *Israeli political party* (Official title *Yisrael BeAliya BeRashut*) Israel BeAliya was formed by Natan Sharansky in 1995. Born in Moscow in 1948, he migrated to Israel [*q.v.*] in 1986. As the number of Jews [*q.v.*] from the Soviet Union arriving in Israel rose sharply from the late 1980s, he saw a potential for a political party that catered to the needs of such migrants. In the 1996 Knesset [*q.v.*] election, Israel BeAliya won seven seats. In the coalition government headed by Benjamin Netanyahu [*q.v.*], Sharansky served as minister of industry and trade. He took a hard-line position on the peace process with the Palestinians [*q.v.*]. In the 1999 parliamentary election, his faction secured six seats. It joined the coalition government led by Ehud Barak [*q.v.*], with Sharanksy becoming minister of internal affairs. When Ariel Sharon [*q.v.*] succeeded Barak as the prime minister, Sharansky retained his ministry. In the 2003 general election, Israel BeAliya secured only two seats. Sharanksy then merged the party with Likud [*q.v.*]

Israel Beitainu (Hebrew: *Israel our home*): *Israeli political party* Israel Beitainu was formed on the eve of the 1999 Knesset [*q.v.*] election by Avigdor Lieberman [*q.v.*], until then a close aide to Prime Minister Benjamin Netanyahu [*q.v.*], leader of Likud [*q.v.*]. Born in the Soviet Republic of Moldavia, Lieberman was active in Likud politics, where he backed ultra-right-wing policies. He founded the party as a rival to the older Israel BeAliyah [*q.v.*] which was popular with the Jewish immigrants from the former Soviet Union, who numbered almost one million by 1999. It won four seats on a secular, ultra-nationalist platform, opposing statehood for the Palestinians [*q.v.*] and proposing exile for their leader, Yasser Arafat [*q.v.*]. It did not join the national unity government formed by Ariel Sharon [*q.v.*] in March 2001.

Following the assassination of the Moledet leader and tourism minister Rechavam Ze'evi in October, it formed an alliance with Moledet, called the National Union [*q.v.*]. When Sharon's government faced defeat in the Knesset after the exit of the Labor Party [*q.v.*] from the coalition in November 2002, the National Union backed Sharon, and Lieberman became a minister.

In the 2003 general election it retained its share of four seats within the National Union's score of seven. It joined the coalition government of Ariel Sharon [*q.v.*] but quit when Sharon decided to vacate the Gaza Strip [*q.v.*]. The 2006 parliamentary election saw the party's strength rise to 11. It participated in the coalition government of Ehud Olmert [*q.v.*], but left in 2008 when Olmert resumed talks with the Palestinian Authority's [*q.v.*] president, Mahmoud Abbas [*q.v.*]. In the 2009 Knesset election, the party demanded that every Israeli Arab [*q.v.*] should take a loyalty oath—"No loyalty, no citizenship." Winning 15 seats, Israel Beitainu emerged as the third-largest group in the Knesset. It joined the coalition government led by

Benjamin Netanyahu [*q.v.*], with Lieberman becoming foreign minister. In December 2011 he said that he did not believe that a peace deal between Israel and the Palestinians would be agreed within the next decade, and, therefore, Israel must work to manage the conflict and not solve it.

Israel-Hamas War (2008–09): *See* Gaza War (2008–09).

Israel-Hizbollah War (2006): *From 12 July to 14 August 2006* In this conflict, Hizbollah [*q.v.*] was the principal enemy of Israel, with the Amal [*q.v.*] militia playing a minor role.

The war started when, in the midst of rising tension along the Israeli-Lebanese border, Hizbollah ambushed an Israeli patrol, killing three soldiers and capturing two more. In its rescue operation, Israel lost five more troops. It then mounted a ground offensive on 12 July.

During the first fortnight Hizbollah fired rockets at targets in north Israel, including Haifa [*q.v.*], while Israeli military hit Lebanese civilian infrastructure, including the Beirut [*q.v.*] airport and the Beirut-Damascus [*q.v.*] highway, and imposed an aerial and naval blockade on Lebanon. On an average, Hizbollah directed about 100 rockets a day at Israel, and the Israeli army fired 300 artillery shells, with its air force carrying out 330 combat missions and its Navy firing 75 shells.

On 18 July an Israeli general said that Israel's offensive would last several more weeks in order to rout Hezbollah. At the UN Security Council, the United States stalled a cease-fire resolution to let the Israeli

Defense Forces (IDF) decimate Hizbollah. On 23 July the IDF expanded its offensive by penetrating Lebanon in the Maroun al-Ras area. Two days later, U.S. Secretary of State Condoleezza Rice described the plight of the heavily bombed Lebanon as part of "the birth pangs of a new Middle East," and added that Israel should ignore calls for a cease-fire.

But the IDF's attempt on 25 July to capture Bint Jbeil, two miles/3 km from the Israeli-Lebanese border, failed. Its infantry withdrew from the outskirts of the town on 29 July. Hizbollah had divided a three mile-wide strip along the Israeli-Lebanese border into numerous fortified bunkers, with booby-traps, land mines, and even closed circuit TV cameras to closely watch the enemy forces. It was from these bunkers that Hizbollah fired their anti-tank missiles, damaging 52 Israeli tanks. Their missiles also hit buildings sheltering Israeli troops. International opinion began to change after Israel's night air-raid on 30 July on a three-story building with 63 civilian occupants near the Lebanese village of Qana, which killed 41 civilians.

Between then and 14 August, when the UN Security Council cease-fire resolution 1701 of 11 August went into effect, Israel bombed a Shia [*q.v.*] suburb of Beirut, and launched an offensive by crossing the Litani River. Toward the end of the fighting, the IDF had three times more soldiers in Lebanon than at the beginning.

During the conflict the armed members of the Popular Front for the Liberation of Palestine-General Command assisted Hizbollah. While Lebanon did not declare war against

Israel, its president, Emile Lahoud [*q.v.*], condemned Israel's attacks and canceled a scheduled meeting with Rice in Beirut.

LOSSES IN LEBANON: An estimated 1,200 Lebanese militants and civilians were killed and 4,400 injured; one million people were displaced, with 150,000 fleeing to Syria and 40,000 to Cyprus; about 100,000 were trapped in the south, with declining food, water, medicine, and fuel reserves. The total economic losses were put at $12 billion, including $3.5 billion to the country's infrastructure, covering 400 mi./640 km of roads, 73 bridges, and 31 other targets, such as Beirut's international airport, ports, water and sewage treatment plants, electrical facilities, 25 fuel stations, 900 commercial structures, up to 350 schools and two hospitals, and 15,000 destroyed homes. The government of Qatar volunteered to help financially all those who had lost their homes and businesses. And backed by Iran, Hizbollah also provided financial aid to those who had suffered losses.

LOSSES IN ISRAEL: 19 soldiers and 43 civilians were killed, and 894 civilians were injured; 400,000 people were displaced; 12,000 buildings, including schools and hospitals, and 6,000 homes were damaged. The war cost the government $5.3 billion. The economy suffered a loss of $1.6 billion, and private businesses lost $1.4 billion.

AFTERMATH: In July 2008, the remains of the two Israeli soldiers captured by Hizbollah were returned to Israel as part of a prisoner exchange.

Israeli Arabs: The term Israeli Arabs applies to those Arabs [*q.v.*] who did not leave Palestine before or during the 1948–49 Arab-Israeli War [*q.v.*] and acquired Israeli nationality. According to the Israeli census taken in November 1948, the 156,000 Israeli Arabs represented 18 percent of the total population. Due to natural growth this figure had increased to 1.9 million by 2011, including 264,100 living in East Jerusalem [*q.v.*], forming 24 percent of the Israeli population, including East Jerusalem.

Three-quarters of Israeli Arabs were Sunni Muslim [*q.v.*], about one-tenth Druze Muslim [*q.v.*], and the rest Christian [*q.v.*] and unclassified. More than 70 percent lived in the Northern District of Israel. Until 1966 they were severely restricted: for instance, they could not travel without the permission of the local military governor. They are barred from joining the military, the exception being Druze males, who have their own units within the armed forces.

The education system for Israeli Arabs is separate from the Jewish, except at university level, where the medium of instruction is Hebrew [*q.v.*]. They suffer discrimination. The average hourly wage for an Israeli Arab worker is 30 percent lower than for Israeli Jewish workers. The 5 percent of the public funds they receive for development projects nationally is a fraction of their proportion in the population.

Politically, until 1958 Israeli Arabs were allowed to join only auxiliary bodies attached to the mainstream secular political parties. The lead of Mapam [*q.v.*] to open direct membership to Israeli Arabs in 1958 was not followed by Labor [*q.v.*] until 1971. When that happened, the practice of

Labor and Mapam offering separate Arab lists lost its raison d'être. The 1973 election was the last one in which Labor won a parliamentary seat for its Arab list. For the next two decades, the overall strength of Israeli Arab members of the 120-member Knesset [q.v.] varied between five and six, with the left-wing Maki [q.v.]/Rakah [q.v.]/Hadash [q.v.] gaining the majority of these seats.

In the 1992 election eight Israeli Arabs were elected to parliament, and two were appointed deputy ministers. Angered by Operation Grapes of Wrath [q.v.] in Lebanon, ordered by Prime Minister Shimon Peres [q.v.], which killed 160 civilians, including 102 refugees sheltering at a hilltop in Qana, in April 1996, enough Israeli Arabs abstained to cause his defeat in the prime ministerial context. In the 1999 Knesset election, the number of Israeli Arab members rose to 12. Of these, nine belonged to the groups that were either exclusively or predominantly Arab, and rejected Zionism [q.v.]. The 2003 general election saw the number of Israeli Arab Knesset [q.v.] members decline to 10.

Israeli Arabs largely back the idea of a Palestinian state on the West Bank [q.v.] and Gaza [q.v.], and have been keen supporters of the Oslo Accords [q.v.] of 1993 and 1995. Soon after the eruption of the Second Intifada [q.v.] in September 2000, Israeli Arabs mounted a demonstration in support of the Palestinians. Firing by the Israeli security forces left 13 protestors dead. This alienated Israeli Arabs from Prime Minister Ehud Barak [q.v.]. By abstaining in the prime ministerial contest in February 2001, they contributed to his defeat by an unprecedented 25 percent to Ariel Sharon [q.v.].

In the national unity government of Sharon, formed in March 2001, Salah Tarif, a Druze [q.v.] member of the Labor Party, became the first Israeli Arab to serve as a cabinet minister, albeit without portfolio. In 2007 Raleb Majadele, a Sunni [q.v.] member of the Labor Party, became the first Muslim [q.v.] Arab member of the Israeli government when he was appointed minister without portfolio. He failed to get reelected in 2009, when the Labor Party's strength in the Knesset sank to a record low of 13, and he was 15th on its list. However, he returned to the Knesset in April 2010 to succeed Yuli Tamir when she resigned her seat. That raised the number of Israeli Arab Knesset members to 10.

Israeli Invasion of Lebanon (1978): Eleven Lebanon-based Palestinians reached northern Israel [q.v.] near Haifa [q.v.] secretly by boat on 11 March 1978. In their attacks on the beach and on a bus on the Haifa-Tel Aviv [q.v.] road they killed 35 Israelis. Nine of them died when they were overpowered by the Israeli forces.

Given the severity of the Palestinian action on the highway in central Israel, the government decided to solve the south Lebanese problem by removing about 5,000 Palestinian guerrillas and their infrastructure from the area. On 14 March, under the code of Operation Peace in Galilee, Israel invaded Lebanon with the aim of creating a 6-mi./10-km-wide buffer zone along the 62 mi./100 km border. It dispatched 20,000 to 25,000 troops and used U.S.-made F-1 fighter planes and cluster bombs. Finding the

Palestinians on the run, the Israelis captured half of southern Lebanon, about 10 percent of the country. By the time the Israelis had accepted UN Security Council Resolution 425 [*q.v.*] (calling for a cease-fire and an unconditional withdrawal) adopted on 19 March, they had destroyed 82 villages, killed 2,000 people, mostly civilian, and displaced 160,000.

The Israeli withdrawal, which started on 11 April, took two months to complete and resulted in the Lebanese border zone (2–6-mi./4–12-km-wide and 50 mi./80 km long) being put under the jurisdiction of an Israeli-funded and armed Christian [*q.v.*] militia, called the South Lebanon Army (SLA) [*q.v.*], commanded by Saad Haddad, a former Lebanese army major, as well as 1,000 Israeli soldiers. In the rest of the territory evacuated by the Israelis, the UN Interim Force in Lebanon (UNIFIL) [*q.v.*] took over from the departing troops.

The SLA acted as part of the Israel Defense Forces (IDF) when the latter invaded Lebanon in June 1982. When Haddad died in January 1984, Israel appointed Antoine Lahad, a retired (Christian) Lebanese army major, to succeed him. The final and unconditional withdrawal of the Israeli forces from the Lebanese border zone, as demanded by the UN Security Council in March 1978, did not take place until May 2000.

Israeli Invasion of Lebanon (1982):

The second Israeli invasion of Lebanon, launched under the code of Operation Big Pines, lasting from 6 June to 3 September 1982, went through the following phases.

PHASE 1: On the morning of 6 June 1982, Israel mounted Operation Peace in Galilee with the dual aim of securing the evacuation of all foreign forces from Lebanon and installing a regime in Beirut [*q.v.*] that would conclude a peace treaty with it. About 40,000 Israel Defense Forces (IDF) [*q.v.*] soldiers marched under heavy air cover into Lebanon across the land frontier, divided into eastern, central, and western sectors. This was supplemented by amphibious landings near Sidon [*q.v.*] and Tyre [*q.v.*].

Ignoring the UN Security Council Resolution 509 of 6 June, which called on Israel to withdraw immediately to its border with Lebanon, the IDF advanced along the coastal highway to Tyre and captured it the next day. Backed by more amphibious landings near Sidon, the IDF seized the city on 8 June. That night Israel's amphibious landings near Damour prepared the ground for the fall of the town the following day.

In the central sector the IDF column captured Litani River bridges and encircled Nabatiye, then pushed northwest to Sidon to link up with the other columns to besiege Sidon. By nightfall on 8 June the central IDF column had outflanked the Syrian forces in the southern Beqaa Valley, while its western column pressed eastwards from Sidon into the Shouf Mountains to envelop Syria's forward positions at Jezzine before heading north. The IDF's eastern column concentrated on getting a foothold in southern Beqaa in order to advance to the strategic Beirut-Damascus [*q.v.*] highway.

PHASE 2: On the afternoon of 9 June, after Israeli electronic counter-measures had crippled Syria's radar, the IDF destroyed 17 of the 19 Syrian anti-aircraft batteries. The ensuing air battle, involving 70 Syrian and 100 IDF supersonic jets, resulted in the loss of 29 Syrian planes. Despite these losses, Syrian President Hafiz Assad [*q.v.*] deployed his air force on a large scale to slow down the Israeli advance. Syria lost 35 more warplanes but gained valuable time.

On 10 June a Syrian armored division engaged an IDF armored brigade in the Rashaya area near the Lebanese-Syrian border, forcing the Israelis back several kilometers. The western IDF column reached the outskirts of Khalde, 3 mi./5 km from Beirut's international airport. Assad dashed to Moscow, which led to the activation of the hotline between the Soviet leader, Leonid Brezhnev, and U.S. President Ronald Reagan. Washington pressed its special envoy, Philip Habib, to intensify his peacemaking efforts.

PHASE 3: On 11 June a cease-fire between Israel and Syria went into effect, ending the fight in the eastern and central sectors. The next day Habib brokered a truce between Israel and the Palestine Liberation Organization (PLO) [*q.v.*].

PHASE 4: Ignoring the cease-fire with the PLO, on 13 June the IDF expelled Lebanese President Elias Sarkis [*q.v.*] from his palace in Baabda, an easterly suburb of Beirut, and linked up with the militia of the Phalange Party [*q.v.*], thus besieging half a million Lebanese and Palestinians in the 3 sq. mi./8 sq. km of West Beirut. From 13 June to 12 July the Israeli defense minister, Gen. Ariel Sharon [*q.v.*], who was directing the

invasion, tried to secure unconditional PLO surrender, first by heavy artillery salvos and then by staging air raids. This was coupled with the severing of water and electricity supplies as well as fuel and food.

Breaking the truce with the Syrians, the IDF attacked them on 22 June along the Beirut-Damascus highway east of Baabda, and removed them from the road for 9 mi./15 km, up to Sofar. By the time the next cease-fire came into effect on 26 June, the Israelis had seized the Dahr al-Baidar pass, east of Sofar, along the Beirut-Damascus road.

PHASE 5: A truce between the PLO and the IDF lasted from 12 July to 21 July, when the Palestinians attacked the IDF behind its lines. From 22 July to 29 July the IDF staged a more intense bombing of West Beirut, combining it with a bombardment of the entire Syrian front in the Beqaa Valley. After a brief cease-fire, lasting until 31 July, from 1 August to 12 August the IDF subjected West Beirut to a more intense bombardment from the air, land, and sea, with Sharon resorting to saturation bombing for 11½ hours, using phosphorus shells and concussion bombs. Water supplies were cut off to let the city burn. Sharon's action angered Washington, which pressured Israeli Prime Minister Menachem Begin [*q.v.*] to intervene. As a result, the 63-day siege of West Beirut ended, and peace returned on 13 August.

PHASE 6: On 19 August Israel accepted the evacuation plans of the PLO and Syria that had been brokered by Habib. Two days later contingents of about 1,000 men each from the United States, Britain,

France, and Italy—constituting the Multi-National Force (MNF) [*q.v.*] for peacekeeping—were deployed to ensure the safe withdrawal of PLO and Syrian troops. The last of the 8,144 PLO commandos, 3,500 Syrian-controlled Palestine Liberation Army (PLA) [*q.v.*] troops, and 2,700 Syrian soldiers left West Beirut on 1 September 1982.

At their peak the IDF deployed 76,000 troops; PLO fighters and their Lebanese allies amounted to 18,000, and the Syrian units to 25,000.

HUMAN LOSSES: Lebanese and Palestinians: 15,700 dead, including 1,110 PLO fighters and 1,350 Syrian troops; Israel: 350 dead. By the time of the final Israeli withdrawal from southern Lebanon in May 2000, the number had risen to over 1,000.

WEAPON LOSSES: Syria, 92 aircraft, 42 tanks; PLO, 20 tanks; Israel, 2 aircraft, 2 tanks.

Israeli Labor Party: *See* Labor Party, Israeli.

Israeli-Palestine Liberation Organization Accord (1993): (Popularly known as the Oslo Accord I) Following secret talks in Norway between Israeli and Palestine Liberation Organization (PLO) officials (called at the behest of Terje Larsen, a Norwegian sociologist, and his wife, Mona Juul, a diplomat, and lasting nearly a year) the two sides initialed a deal in Oslo in late August 1993. On 10 September Israel formally recognized the PLO after its chairman, Yasser Arafat [*q.v.*], had addressed a letter to Israeli Premier Yitzhak Rabin [*q.v.*] recognizing Israel's right to exist in peace and security. He also renounced violence and

promised to ensure compliance of this by all PLO elements. The accord, called the Declaration of Principles (DOP), was signed on 13 September in Washington at the White House by Mahmoud Abbas [*q.v.*], the second-in-command of the PLO, and Shimon Peres [*q.v.*], the Israeli foreign minister, in the presence of Rabin, Arafat, and U.S. President Bill Clinton.

The accord provided for Palestinian self-rule for the Gaza Strip [*q.v.*] and the West Bank town of Jericho [*q.v.*]—with Israeli sovereignty over Jewish settlements in the Occupied Territories [*q.v.*]—as an interim stage, with talks on permanent agreement to begin after two years. The timetable was as follows:

13 October: The accord to come into force. Joint Israel-PLO Liaison Committee formed to implement it.

By 13 December: The two sides to agree on a protocol for the withdrawal of Israeli forces from the Gaza Strip and Jericho.

By 13 April 1994: Israel to complete military withdrawal from the Gaza Strip and Jericho. Israel to transfer powers to the Palestinian Authority [*q.v.*] nominated by the PLO.

By 13 July 1994: Elections to the Palestinian Council to be held, followed by the dissolution of Israel's military-run civil administration in the Occupied Territories, with its powers transferred to the Palestinian Authority.

By 13 December 1995: Israel and the Palestinians to start talks on permanent settlement, including the status of East Jerusalem [*q.v.*].

By 13 December 1999: Permanent settlement to take effect.

In practice, the implementation

agreement was signed on 4 May 1994; and, as head of the Palestinian Authority, Arafat set up his headquarters in Gaza City on 1 July. The implementation agreement on extending the jurisdiction of the Palestinian Authority to the West Bank [*q.v.*] and the holding of elections to the Palestinian Council was signed in September 1995, with the implementation to be completed by early 1996, a few months before the extended deadline (May 1996) for negotiation on the final status of the Occupied Territories and the Jewish settlements built there.

These plans went awry when Rabin was assassinated in November 1995, and his successor, Peres, was defeated by Likud leader Benjamin Netanyahu [*q.v.*] six months later in the prime-ministerial electoral contest. Short of unilaterally abrogating the Oslo Accord I, he crippled it severely. His defeat by his Labor rival Ehud Barak [*q.v.*] in May 1999 raised hopes. But the terms for the final settlement that Barak offered at the summit with Arafat and Clinton at Camp David in July 2000 did not satisfy Arafat. The talks were inconclusive. Nonetheless, the two sides found enough common ground to resume negotiations in Sharm El Shaikh, Egypt, in January 2001. These proved fruitful but were suspended because of the prime ministerial election on 6 February. Barak lost to Netanyahu at a time when the Palestinian Al Aqsa intifada [*q.v.*] was gathering momentum. With that the foundation on which the Oslo Accord I was built collapsed.

J

Jaafari, Ibrahim (1947–): Born Ibrahim Abdul Karim al-Eshaiker in a religious Shia [*q.v.*] family in the holy city of Karbala [*q.v.*], he joined the clandestine al-Daawa party [*q.v.*] as a medical student at Mosul University in 1968. When President Saddam Hussein [*q.v.*] cracked down on al-Daawa, he fled to Iran in 1980. In Tehran [*q.v.*], he collaborated with the Supreme Council of Islamic Revolution in Iraq [*q.v.*] after its formation in 1982.

In 1989 he moved to London where he became the spokesman of al-Daawa. He opposed the Anglo-American invasion of Iraq [*q.v.*] in March 2003, but returned to Iraq after the overthrow of the Saddam Hussein regime. As leader of al-Daawa, he secured a seat on the U.S.-sponsored Iraqi Governing Council in July 2003. A year later he was nominated a vice president of Iraq's Interim government. In an opinion poll he ranked the third-most-popular leader—after Grand Ayatollah Ali Sistani [*q.v.*] and Muqtada al-Sadr [*q.v.*].

Under his stewardship, al-Daawa joined the United Iraqi Alliance (UIA) of major Shia parties in the January 2005 election. With the UIA emerging as the majority bloc in parliament, he became the prime minister in April. After the December 2005 general election held under the new constitution, the UIA again won a majority of seats. In his contest for the premiership, he beat his rival, Adel Abdul Mahdi, by one vote with the support of the Sadrist members, who decried the U.S. military presence in Iraq. U.S. President George W. Bush publicly opposed Jaafari's reelection as prime minister. To end the subsequent stalemate, Sistani persuaded him to step down. Nouri al-Maliki [*q.v.*] succeeded him first as the prime minister and then as the general secretary of al-Daawa.

In 2008, he left al-Daawa to establish his own party, National Reform Trend. It joined the Iraqi National Alliance, the predominantly Shia bloc, on the eve of the March 2010 general election. The Alliance secured 70 seats, with Jaafari as its nominal leader.

Jaafari Code: *Shia Islamic legal school* This Islamic legal code is named after Imam Jaafar al-Sadiq (699–765 A.D.), the sixth Imam of Twelver Shias [*q.v.*]. It is the predominant code in the Islamic Republic of Iran. *See also* Hadith [*q.v.*].

Jabotinsky, Vladimir Zeev (1880–1940): *Revisionist Zionist leader* Born into a middle-class family in Odessa, Russia, Jabotinsky studied law in Berne, Switzerland, and Rome. On his return home he worked as a journalist with an Odessa newspaper. During the 1903 pogroms he helped to organize local Jewish self-defense. Shocked by the pogroms, he joined the Zionist movement and attended the Sixth Zionist Congress [*q.v.*] in 1904. Two years later, as a delegate to the Congress of Russian Zionists [*q.v.*], he helped to draft its program.

The outbreak World War I found him working in Cairo [*q.v.*] as the correspondent of a Moscow-based newspaper. He met Joseph Trumpeldor [*q.v.*] in Alexandria [*q.v.*], and together they formed the Zion Mule Corps of young Jews [*q.v.*] who had been deported from Palestine [*q.v.*] by the Ottomans. They promoted the idea of establishing Jewish battalions to fight alongside the British to conquer Palestine. In 1917 London authorized the formation of the First Judean Regiment, popularly known as the Jewish Legion, and attached it to the British forces of General Edmund Allenby. As a lieutenant in the Legion, Jabotinsky engaged in combat in the Middle East, and was decorated.

After the war he settled in Jerusalem [*q.v.*]. For his role in the Arab-Jewish riots in 1920 he was sentenced to 15 years' imprisonment, but was freed the next year as part of a general amnesty. He moved to London, and was elected to the executive committee of the World Zionist Organization (WZO) [*q.v.*]. He resigned this post in 1923, when the committee refused to endorse his proposal to pressure the British Mandate to build a Jewish homeland in Palestine with its resources.

He formed the World Union of Revisionist Zionists in 1925, which affiliated to the WZO. He also founded *Betar* (acronym of *Berit Trumpeldor:* Covenant with Trumpeldor), a youth organization. At the 1931 Zionist Congress the 52 Revisionist Zionist [*q.v.*] delegates were the third-largest group. Efforts to conciliate them with Labor Zionists failed.

In Palestine, the Revisionists' attempt to seize the leadership of the Zionist movement was frustrated by Labor Zionists, headed by David Ben-Gurion [*q.v.*]. Seceding from the

WZO in 1935, the Revisionists established the New Zionist Organization (NZO), led by Jabotinsky. He advocated giving primacy to private capital to develop Palestine, and was opposed to the Marxist concept of class struggle. He moved Palestine to edit the NZO's newspaper there. Fluent in several languages, he was an essayist, poet, novelist, playwright, and translator.

When he went abroad in 1936, the British refused to let him return to Palestine. By then the Irgun Zvai Leumi [q.v.], which had splintered from Haganah [q.v.] five years earlier, had volunteered to take orders from him. Later he became Iran's formal supreme commander, even though, barred from Palestine, he spent his time in Eastern Europe, Paris, London, and New York.

When World War II erupted in 1939 he declared that the NZO would support the war effort. Determined to form a Jewish army, he visited the United States for this purpose in mid-1940. He died there and was buried in New York City. His remains were exhumed and reburied in Israel in 1964.

Jacobite Christians: *See* Orthodox Christians, Syrian.

Jadid, Salah (1926–93): *Syrian military leader and politician* Born into a notable Alawi [q.v.] family in Duwair Baabda, a village near Jablah port, Jadid trained as an officer at the Homs Military Academy. He began his army career as a lieutenant. Politically active, he was at first a member of the Syrian Social Nationalist Party [q.v.], then the Arab Socialist Party [q.v.], and finally the Baath Socialist Party [q.v.]. Following the merger of

Syria and Egypt into the United Arab Republic (UAR) [q.v.] in early 1958, he was transferred to Egypt.

Angered at President Gamal Abdul Nasser's [q.v.] decision to dissolve the Baath Party in Syria, he joined Hafiz Assad [q.v.] and two other Baathist officers to form, secretly, the Military Committee in 1959. It succeeded in taking Syria out of the UAR in September 1961. It also carried out a Baathist coup in Damascus [q.v.] on 8 March 1963. As a Military Committee leader, he started purging non-Baathist officers from the armed forces.

In October, promoted to major-general, he was named chief of staff. But a year later he lost his high office as a result of party infighting and was relegated to deputy secretary-general of the Baath regional command. But he fought back. The climax came in February 1966 when the military faction, led among others by Jadid, won an armed confrontation with its rival. Having gained a monopoly of authority, he packed the government and the party regional command with his supporters, while remaining simply deputy secretary-general of the party. He promoted Nur al-Din Attasi [q.v.] to secretary-general of the party and Assad to defense minister. He continued to lead a spartan existence and espouse leftist policies. Following an abortive military coup in September, he and Assad purged the officer corps.

The Syrian defeat in the June 1967 Arab-Israeli War [q.v.], involving the loss of the Golan Heights [q.v.], was a strong blow to Jadid's regime. Among other things it created a rift between him and Assad, who advocated pragmatic policies. With Jadid maintaining a tight grip over the party machine, Assad increased his control over the armed forces. In February 1969 Assad tried to usurp his power, but compromised in order to avoid bloodshed. But matters came to a head in September 1970, when, contrary to Jadid's promise, Assad failed to provide military aid to the Palestinian commandos battling the Jordanian army.

When he convened an emergency National (i.e., pan-Arab) Congress of the Baath Party on 30 October 1970 in Damascus, the meeting place was surrounded by pro-Assad soldiers. Once the congress had ended in acrimony on 12 November, the opponents of Assad, including Jadid, were arrested. He was held in the Mezze fortress prison until his death.

Jaffa: Incorporated into Tel Aviv [*q.v.*] in 1949. *See* Tel Aviv-Jaffa.

Jbail: *See* Byblos.

Jeddah: *Administrative capital of Saudi Arabia* (Also spelled Jiddah) Population: 3.856 million (2010 est.). The reputed site of the tomb of Eve, Jeddah means female ancestor. Situated on a narrow coastal plain, it has been an important port on the Red Sea since the pre-Islamic era. After the rise of Islam [*q.v.*], Caliph Othman (r. 644–656 A.D.) designated it as the port for Muslims undertaking a hajj [*q.v.*] to Mecca [*q.v.*] by sea. This contributed to its prosperity. It also developed as a transit point for maritime trade between India and the Mediterranean region via Egypt. However, this settlement was to the south of present-day Jeddah.

When the Ottoman Turks conquered Egypt in 1517, Jeddah came under their authority. Sultan Muhammad IV (r. 1648–1687) made it the official port of Mecca, a position until then held by the older port to the south. The opening of the Suez Canal [*q.v.*] in 1869 ended the trans-shipping role of Jeddah, but boosted the hajj travel, which became the lifeline of the city.

During World War I, when the provincial governor Sharif Hussein bin Ali al-Hashem led the Arab revolt against the Ottomans in 1916, Jeddah's Ottoman garrison surrendered to the British. Sharif Hussein's rule ended with his defeat by Abdul Aziz al-Saud [*q.v.*] in 1924, and Jeddah passed to the victor. It was here in 1927 that Britain signed a treaty with Abdul Aziz al-Saud, recognizing him as King of Hijaz and Najd [*q.v.*] and its Dependencies. As a Wahhabi [*q.v.*], King Abdul Aziz regarded the tomb of Eve as an idolatrous shrine and destroyed it in 1928.

For the next two decades Jeddah remained a walled settlement. Then, rid of its walls and funded by the fast-rising oil revenue of Saudi Arabia, it expanded rapidly. It acquired new apartment blocks, hotels, banks, private and public offices, a university, and such industries as cement, food processing, oil refining, and pottery. A new dock complex, named after King Faisal [*q.v.*], opened in 1973 to serve the growing commercial and pilgrimage traffic. In 1980 came the King Abdul Aziz international airport, occupying an area of 40 sq. mi./104 sq. km. Both these facilities are needed to serve the more than one million foreign Muslims who undertake the hajj annually. Until 1982, Jeddah was the kingdom's diplomatic capital.

It is the most cosmopolitan Saudi city, its residents coming not only from other parts of the Arab world but also Asia, Africa, and Europe. It is the headquarters of the Islamic Conference Organization [*q.v.*], renamed Islamic Cooperation Organization [*q.v.*] in 2011, and the World Muslim League [*q.v.*].

Jericho: *West Bank town* Population: 20,700 (2011 est.). Jericho is one of the oldest settlements in the world; its history dates back to ca 9000 B.C. A millennium or so later its few thousand inhabitants built a stone wall around the village. There were intermittent breaks in Jericho's history until 2300 B.C., when it was settled by Amorites, who were followed by Canaanites in ca 1900 B.C. Its capture by Joshua, successor to Moses, around 1220 B.C. heralded the entry of Hebrews into Canaan, the Promised Land, and its fall to Babylon in 586 B.C. marked the end of the Kingdom of Judah.

During the reign of King Herod the Great (37–4 B.C.), the settlement was moved about a mile southward. The king built a palace there. In 68 A.D. the Romans destroyed the town. The Crusaders rebuilt it on a site about a mile east of the Old Testament [*q.v.*] settlement. A center of balsam groves, it became known as the City of Palms.

Jericho was part of the Palestine [*q.v.*] under the British Mandate. After the Palestine War (1948–49) [*q.v.*] it was incorporated into Jordan. When two camps for the Arab

refugees from Palestine were opened nearby, it became a vibrant town. In the June 1967 Arab-Israeli War [*q.v.*] it fell to the Israelis and became depopulated. It was the only West Bank [*q.v.*] town to be included in the Oslo Accord I [*q.v.*] of September 1993 for transfer to the Palestinian Authority [*q.v.*], along with the Gaza Strip [*q.v.*] in the first round. In 1998 it became the site of a casino, which proved popular with Israelis, who are not allowed to gamble inside Israel. The casino closed down during the Al Aqsa Second Intifada [*q.v.*].

Jerusalem: *Israeli/Palestinian city; self-declared capital of Israel* Area: East Jerusalem [*q.v.*] 2.5 sq. mi./6.5 sq. km in 1948, 28.5 sq. mi./73.7 sq. km in 1967; West Jerusalem [*q.v.*] 13 sq. mi./34 sq. km in 1948, 20 sq. mi./54 sq. km in 1993; East Jerusalem population: 456,900 (2011 est.); West Jerusalem population: 403,800 (2011 est.); total population: 860,700 (2011 est.). Jerusalem is derivative of Yerushalayim (Hebrew: *Founded by [god] Shalem*).

Mentioned as Salem in the Old Testament [*q.v.*] (Genesis 14:18), Jerusalem is a settlement with a recorded history dating back to ca 1900 B.C., when it was the capital of a Canaanite city state and the site where Abraham was greeted by King Melchizedek. Though its ruler was defeated by the Hebrews under Joshua, the successor to Moses, around ca 1220 B.C., it maintained its independence until its capture by David (r. 1010–970 B.C.) in ca 1010 B.C. He made it the capital of united Israel and also—by transferring the Ark of the Covenant from Hebron [q.v.]—the religious center of his kingdom. He built the fortress of Zion, and his successor, King Solomon (970–930 B.C.), the First Temple in 952 B.C.

After the division of Israel, which followed Solomon, Jerusalem became the capital of the southern Kingdom of Judah until it was overrun by the Babylonian ruler Nebuchadnezzar (r. 605–562 B.C.) in 586 B.C., when most of the population was expelled and the First Temple razed. Under the succeeding Persian rule, Jewish sectarianism hardened. Allowed to return to Jerusalem in 538 B.C., the Jews [q.v.] started to construct the Second Temple, finishing it in 515 B.C. The Persians in Palestine [q.v.] were overpowered by Alexander of Macedonia (r. 336–323 B.C.) in 333 B.C., and the succeeding Greek rulers tried to found a parallel city on Jerusalem's western edge.

The banning of Judaism [q.v.] in 168 B.C. by Antiochus IV (r. 175–163 B.C.) led to a Jewish revolt, headed by Judas Maccabeus. It was successful and resulted in the restoration of the Second Temple in 163 B.C. and the revival of the Jewish rule in Jerusalem under Jonathan in 152 B.C. The city became the capital of Judaea.

In 63 B.C. the Roman general Pompey captured Jerusalem, which fell in 40 B.C. to the Parthians, who were in turn overpowered by Roman King Herod the Great (r. 37–4 B.C.) three years later. In 20 B.C. Herod started reconstructing the Second Temple on a large scale, building a surrounding esplanade, part of whose outer wall, built partly with stones from Solomon's First Temple, came to be known as the Western Wall [q.v.].

After Herod the city was governed by Roman procurators, called Pontius. Under one of them, Pilate, Jesus of Nazareth [q.v.], born a Jew, was crucified at nearby Calvary in ca 29 A.D.

The repressive Roman administration led to another revolt by the Jews in 66 A.D. and its siege by Roman Emperor Titus (r. 40–81 A.D.). When it fell to Titus in 70 A.D., he razed the Second Temple. Roman Emperor Hadrian (r. 117–138 A.D.) seized and destroyed Jerusalem in 132 A.D. He then reconstructed it as a Roman colony, named Aelia Capitalina (Latin: *Capital of Memory*), and banned Jews.

With the conversion of Roman Emperor Constantine I (r. 306–337 A.D.) to Christianity [q.v.] in 313 A.D., Jerusalem underwent a revival. The Church of the Holy Sepulchre, begun in 325 A.D., on the site of Jesus Christ's crucifixion at Calvary, was completed 10 years later, and Jerusalem became a holy Christian city. In 614 A.D. it was seized by the Persians, who were overpowered by Byzantine Emperor Heraclius (r. 610–641 A.D.) in 628 A.D. The Byzantines were defeated by Muslim [q.v.] Arabs [q.v.] led by Caliph Omar (r. 634–644 A.D.) in 637 A.D.

Jerusalem had been mentioned in the Quran [q.v.] (17:1): "Celebrated be the praises of Him who by night took His servant from the Masjid al-Haram [the Sacred Mosque in Mecca, q.v.] to the Masjid al-Aqsa [the Remote Mosque in Jerusalem] the precinct of which we have blessed." At the site of the Sacred Rock, where the Prophet Muhammad had purportedly been carried on a winged animal on the night of his ascent to heaven, a mosque was built by Abdul Malik bin

Marwan (r. 684–705 A.D.), an Umayyad ruler, in 691 A.D. and called the Dome of the Rock [q.v.]. Under the Muslim rulers Jews were allowed to return, and Christians were given freedom of worship.

In 969 A.D. the city fell into the hands of the Fatimid ruler al-Muizz (r. 955–978 A.D.), and the church of the Holy Sepulchre was burnt down. The persecution of Christians continued and resulted in the First Crusade (1095–1099). The Crusaders, led by Godfrey of Bouillon, captured Jerusalem and carried out a massacre of Muslims and Jews. The city became the capital of the Latin Kingdom until its fall to the Muslim general Salah al-Din (Saladin) Ayubi in 1187.

With brief interruptions, Jerusalem remained under Muslim control until 1917. Sacked by the Mongols in 1244, it came under Ottoman rule in 1517. Sultan Suleiman the Magnificent (r. 1520–1566) rebuilt the city walls in 1541. By the late 18th–early 19th century, Jerusalem, confined to the Old City and measuring 0.4 sq. mi./1 sq. km, had fewer than 10,000 residents, a quarter of them Jewish. The Old City contained the Western Wall (sacred to Jews), the Church of the Holy Sepulchre (sacred to Christians), and the Dome of the Rock and al-Aqsa Mosque (sacred to Muslims). Once new buildings had been constructed outside the walled Old City, from 1855 onward, Jerusalem's population increased, reaching 68,000 in 1910. It was captured by British forces in December 1917.

During the British Mandate (1922–48), Jerusalem was the capital of Palestine. Tension between local Arabs and new Jewish immigrants led to riots in 1920, 1929, and 1936. After World War II the city's population was 165,000, three-fifths of whom were Jewish. The UN partition plan of November 1947 specified an independent Jerusalem under UN administration.

After the Palestine War (1948–49) [q.v.] the city was divided into two parts: the Israeli sector included the west and south of the New City and was known as West Jerusalem [q.v.]; the Jordanian sector comprised the east and north of the New City and all of the Old City, and was known as East Jerusalem [q.v.]. In January 1950 Israel declared (West) Jerusalem its capital, but this was not recognized by foreign governments, which continued to maintain their embassies in Tel Aviv [q.v.].

During the June 1967 Arab-Israeli War [q.v.] the Israelis seized East Jerusalem from Jordan. They then attached 25 sq. mi./65 sq. km of the West Bank territory to it, and extended Israeli laws to Greater East Jerusalem. The Jerusalem Law of 1980 extended Israeli sovereignty over the entire city. UN Security Council Resolution 476 of 30 June 1980 reaffirmed its earlier resolutions on the Holy City of Jerusalem—252 (1968), 267 (1969), 271 (1969), 298 (1971), and 465 (1980)—and reconfirmed that all measures taken by Israel (as the occupying power) that altered the character and status of the Holy City were legally invalid and violated the last of the four Geneva Conventions on War [q.v.]. With the exception of Costa Rica and El Salvador, all the countries with diplomatic relations with Israel maintain their embassies in Tel Aviv.

Since 1972 the number of the Jewish settlers in East Jerusalem has shot up from 10,600 to 192,800 in 2011.

Jewish Agency: *a Jewish organization for the ingathering of Jews in Israel* Full title: The Jewish Agency for Palestine [*q.v.*]/Land of Israel. The 1922 British Mandate for Palestine provided for the recognition of "an appropriate Jewish agency" for "advising and co-operating with the administration of Palestine in such economic, social and other matters as may affect the establishment of the Jewish national home and the interests of the Jewish population in Palestine," and that "the Zionist Organization [*q.v.*] … shall be recognized as such agency."

The Zionist Organization appointed a Zionist executive committee in Palestine, with its own chairman and based in Jerusalem [*q.v.*]. Its functions were to act as the political representative of the Jews [*q.v.*] in Palestine, and to encourage and finance the ingathering of diaspora [*q.v.*] Jews in Palestine. The Sixteenth Zionist Congress [*q.v.*] in 1929 formally created the Jewish Agency in Palestine "for discharging the functions of the Jewish agency as set forth in the Mandate" on the basis of parity between Zionists [*q.v.*] and non-Zionists (i.e., those who backed the idea of a Jewish national home without subscribing to political Zionism). Both the Zionist and the Jewish Agency executive committees shared the same chairman. The Jewish Agency negotiated with Britain and represented Jewish interests at the League of Nations.

In May 1942 David Ben-Gurion [*q.v.*]—chairman of both the Jewish Agency Executive Committee and the Zionist Organization Executive Committee in Palestine—convened an American Zionist Congress at the Biltmore Hotel, New York City. It coupled its call for unrestricted Jewish immigration to Palestine with a demand that "Palestine be established as a Jewish Commonwealth integrated into the structure of the new democratic world." This led to the steady departure of non-Zionists from the Agency Executive, accelerated in December 1946 by the endorsing of the Biltmore Hotel resolution by the 22nd Zionist Congress in Basle, Switzerland. This turned the agency into a purely Zionist organization by early 1947. It lobbied strongly at the newly formed United Nations, which finally offered a partition plan for Palestine in November 1947.

By May 1948, when Israel was established, the Agency had transferred all its executive powers to the people's administrative committee of the National Council of the Yishuv [*q.v.*] assembly while retaining the functions of Jewish immigration and settlement in Israel. Its functions as an international non-governmental body, coordinating all Jewish overseas endeavors in Israel, were formalized by Israel's Law of Status (1951), which codified statutory and conventional links between the Jewish Agency and Israel. The law states: "The [World] Zionist Organization, which is also the Jewish Agency for Palestine, deals as hitherto with immigration and directs the projects of absorption and settlement in the state."

A major reorganization in 1971 put the Jewish Agency in Israel in charge of practical work in Israel, leaving the

World Zionist Organization [*q.v.*] to concentrate on the diaspora [*q.v.*]. Its Assembly decides the basic policy, with the board of governors doing so between the Assembly sessions, and the executive committee conducting day-to-day affairs.

The Jewish Agency is the overall collector of contributions to the Zionist cause throughout the world, with the *Keren Hayesod* (Hebrew: *Foundation Fund*) being one its three constituent bodies, the others being the World Zionist Organization and the United Israel Appeal in America. The Keren Hayesod operates in 46 countries, often using local names. In 2007 its budget was $177 million.

Jewish Bible: *See* Old Testament.

Jewish calendar: The Jewish dating system is a compendium of lunar and solar cycles. The Jewish calendar consists of a lunar cycle of 19 years. There is also a solar cycle of 28 years, at the beginning of which the *tekufah* of Nisan (month)—the spring equinox—returns to the same day and the same hour. In the Jewish calendar, a day is counted from sunset to sunrise; a week consists of seven days; a month contains 29 days, 12 hours, and 793 portions (1080 portions equaling one hour); and a year has 12 lunar months (totaling 353 to 355 days) and about 11 days. In order to bring the calendar into line with the annual solar cycle, a 13th month of 30 days is intercalated in the 3rd, 6th, 8th, 11th, 14th, 17th, and 19th years of a 19-year cycle. A leap year may therefore have 383, 384, or 385 days, and is called defective, regular, or abundant. The same terms apply to a regular year with 353, 354,

and 355 days.

The names of the months, arranged according to religious usage, are: Nisan (30 days, March–April of the Christian Gregorian calendar [*q.v.*]), Iyar (29, April–May), Sivan (30, May–June), Tammuz (29, June–July), Av (30, July–August), Elul (29, August–September), Tishri (30, September–October), Heshvan/Marheshvan (29/30, October–November), Kislev (29/30, November–December), Tevet (29, December–January), Shevat (30, January–February), and Adar (29/30, February–March). The 13th month of the leap year, Adar Sheni/Ve-Adar (29), is intercalated before Adar and so contains the religious observances normally occurring in Adar. The calendar begins with Tishri, its first day heralding Rosh HaShana (Hebrew: *The New Year*) [*q.v.*], which falls between 6 September and 4 October.

Formalized by Hillel II in 358 A.D., it originates in 3761 B.C., the date traditionally given for the Creation in the Old Testament [*q.v.*]. The Jewish year is denoted by A.M. [*q.v.*]. The 301st lunar cycle started in 5701 A.M.(1940–41 A.D.).

To convert a Jewish year into Christian [*q.v.*], deduct 3760 from it.

Jewish festivals: Jewish festivals are divided into major and minor. The four major festivals—when work is prohibited and all males are required to attend religious observances at a synagogue [*q.v.*]—are: Pesah/Passover [*q.v.*] (15–22 Nisan), commemorating the Israelites' servitude in Egypt and the subsequent exodus; Shabout (Feast of Weeks, or Pentecost [*q.v.*]), the anniversary of the revelation of the Torah [*q.v.*] at Mount Sinai, celebrated on 6–7 Sivan; the Days of Penitence/Judgement, beginning with Rosh Hashana [*q.v.*] on 1–2 Tishri and ending with Yom Kippur [*q.v.*] on 10 Tishri; and Sukkot/Tabernacles/Booths, 15–21 Tishri, commemorating the Israelites' wanderings after the exodus. Minor holidays, when work is not prohibited, are: Simhath Torah (Rejoicing over the Law) on 23 Tishri; Hannukah [*q.v.*] from 25 Kislev to 2/3 Tebet; and Purim (Feast of Lots) on 14 Adar.

Jewish/Judaistic fundamentalism: Fundamentalism is the term used for the effort to define the fundamentals of a religion and adhere to them. In the case of Judaism, these fundamentals are contained in the Halacha [*q.v.*] (Jewish Law). The expunging of current Jewish precepts and practices of secular influences is a primary goal of Jewish fundamentalists. Related to fundamentalism is Judaistic revival or resurgence, renewed interest in Judaism [*q.v.*], or the *teshuva* (return) movement—a return to full observance of the Halacha, i.e., all 613 religious prohibitions and obligations that regulate Jewish life, from trivial daily bodily functions to the organization of life in society—and the separation of Jews [*q.v.*] and gentiles. Whether the Jewish state of Israel is fundamentalist or not can be judged by a single criterion: is its legislation derived solely from the Halacha? The answer is no.

There is also the belief held by ultra-Orthodox Jews that Israel as a "peoplehood" would be redeemed only by a messiah, from which stems their opposition to Zionism [*q.v.*], which is seen as a Jewish version of secular nationalism. Later a synthesis of "the divine concept" and "national sentiment"—offered by Abraham Yitzhak Kook (d. 1935), the first Ashkenazi [*q.v.*] chief rabbi of Palestine [*q.v.*]—gave rise to religious Zionism. After the founding of Israel in 1948, his son, Zvi Yehuda Kook (d. 1982), argued that the Zionists, despite their lack of religiosity, were the inadvertent bearers of a messianic redemption, and that the State of Israel was an unconscious instrument of the divine will. He attributed Israel's spectacular victory in June 1967 to divine intervention, and his followers called 1967 the Year One of the Era of Redemption.

In early 1974 they established the Gush Emunim [*q.v.*]. It was one of the several manifestations of a rising *teshuva* movement in Israel in the mid-1970s, the others being the opening of the great Talmudic colleges in Jerusalem [*q.v.*] for penitents, and the coming to power of a religious-conservative coalition led by Likud [*q.v.*] in 1977. With Prime Minister Menachem Begin [*q.v.*] officially backing Jewish settlements in the West Bank [*q.v.*], the Gush made an advance in its program of re-Judaization from above. However, it opposed Begin's peace talks with Egypt and looked for ways of sabotaging the peace process. The foiling of a conspiracy involving Gush extremists in a plan to blow up the Muslim holy shrines on the Temple Mount [*q.v.*] in 1984 was a setback to the fundamentalist cause. Its proponents then returned to fundamentalism from below, which has been the program of several religious parties.

In the 11 general elections between 1949 and 1984 the fundamentalists won 12–15 percent of the votes—with two-thirds going to religious Zionists organized as the National Religious Party (NRP) [*q.v.*], and only one-third to the non-Zionists of Agudat Israel [*q.v.*]. But in the 1988 election, out of the total of 15 percent religious votes, the NRP secured only a quarter, with the ultra-Orthodox votes—consisting of Shas [*q.v.*] and United Torah Judaism [*q.v.*]—rising to three-quarters. In 1999, with Shas gaining 13 percent of the vote, the total for the religious parties rose to 21 percent.

Without specifically recognizing the legitimacy of the Zionist state of Israel, the non-Zionist religious parties have often delivered their supporters' votes in exchange for substantial government handouts, including enlarged subsidies for religious educational institutions. They have pursued a strategy of forcing the secular Israeli government to institute creeping Judaization, affecting all Jews in Israel. For instance, they made it accept their definition of Jewish identity "in accordance with the Halacha" when determining the credentials of Jewish converts coming from abroad.

Jewish National Fund: *fund for the purchase and development of land in Palestine/Israel* Official title: *Keren Kayemet LeIsrael* (Hebrew: *Perpetual Fund for Israel*). The Fifth Zionist Congress in 1901 set up a land and development section, which established the *Keren Kayemet LeIsrael*, popularly known as the Jewish National Fund (JNF), to buy land in Palestine [*q.v.*] for the settlement of Jews there. The JNF, an organ of the World Zionist Organization [*q.v.*], adopted the following principles: the purchase of land with communal contributions for communal ownership;

plots to be available only for lease to Jews; land use to be supervised; and speculation to be prevented.

Starting modestly in 1905, the JNF resorted to large-scale land purchases from local Arabs [*q.v.*] from 1921 onwards. It leased land for 49 years on the condition that lessees would forfeit their right to the land if they failed to work it or did so with the help of hired labor. By the time Israel was established in May 1948 the JNF, now operating from Jerusalem [*q.v.*], had acquired nearly a quarter of a million acres. In 1949–50 the Israeli government handed over to it a further 600,000 acres belonging to the Arabs who had fled.

The JNF was turned into an Israeli-registered company in 1953. It collects funds in about 70 countries. In 1960 the JNF, owning 13 percent of all land, signed a treaty with the Israeli government to place all its land holdings under the authority of the Israel Lands Administration, which operates through the Israel Lands Council. JNF lands can only be leased, never sold. It is estimated that nearly four-fifths of the Israeli population lives on the land owned by the JNF.

Jewish nationalism: Jewish nationalism is the concept that Jews [*q.v.*] form a nation that is entitled to develop its own distinctive identity. The Jewish commonwealth, established in ancient Israel under King David (r. 1010–970 B.C.), underwent divisions, decimation, and revival before its final destruction by the Romans in 70 A.D. Spread throughout the rest of the Roman Empire, Jews continued to believe in their nationhood.

Over the centuries anti-Jewish persecution pushed European Jews toward the less hospitable northeastern and central-northern parts of the continent. Here the idea of nationhood acquired a spiritual dimension at the expense of the political, and gave rise to a belief that a messiah would restore sovereignty to Jews in their historical land.

Barred from agriculture, most Jews took to commerce and finance. The feeling of being stifled in ghettoes became stronger as Jews became increasingly familiar with liberal ideas following the 1789 French Revolution. Gradually they began to abandon the religious traditions of their antecedents. But their assimilative tendency, encouraged by their emancipation in the late 19th century, was checked by the emergence and popularity of pseudoscientific theories proving the racial inferiority of Jews. The result was the rise of Jewish nationalism which, on the eve of World War I, fell into three categories: diaspora [*q.v.*] nationalism, Zionism [*q.v.*], and Territorialism.

Arguing that Jews could develop their own special identity and culture as a minority regardless of where they lived, diaspora nationalists advocated that they should strive for cultural autonomy within their countries of domicile. Zionists emphasized the need for a Jewish homeland for Jews who were unwilling or unable to live elsewhere, which would also be a cultural-spiritual center for international Jewry. For historical reasons they focused on Palestine [*q.v.*] as the Jewish homeland. The Territorialists, while subscribing to the concept of the Jewish homeland, were prepared to explore such alternatives to Palestine as Argentina, Angola, Australia, and Iraq. They were overtaken by the Zionists because of the Balfour Declaration of 1917 [*q.v.*].

Jews: *See* Judaism and Jews.

Jews in Arab Middle East: In 1945 there were 870,000 Jews [*q.v.*] in the Arab Middle East [*q.v.*]. After the establishment of Israel in 1948 and the 1948–49 Palestine War [*q.v.*], their number fell to 70,000, with 600,000 migrating to Israel and the rest to other countries.

BAHRAIN: In the 1880s some Iraqi Jews began settling in Bahrain. At the time of the founding of Israel in 1948, they numbered nearly 600. As a result of rioting against the Jews during the 1948–49 Palestine War, the community shrank. Further depletion came in the wake of the June 1967 Arab-Israeli War [*q.v.*]. Forty years later, there were only 36 Jews left, but they maintained their synagogue and cemetery. In 2008, a Jewish woman, Huda Ezra Ebrahim Noona, then a member of the nominated Consultative (Shura) Council, was appointed Bahrain's ambassador to the United States.

EGYPT: The recorded history of the Jewish community in Egypt dates back to 494 B.C. and the reign of Darius I (r. 521–486 B.C.). At the turn of the 20th century there were about 40,000 Jews, mostly Sephardic [*q.v.*], and concentrated in Cairo [*q.v.*]. After World War II their number rose to 70,000, with Cairo and Alexandria [*q.v.*] their main centers of settlement.

Jewish intellectuals were active in the leftist Mouvement Egyptien de

Liberation National and the Iskra group, led respectively by Henri Curiel and Hillel Schwartz, both Jews.

After the Palestine War (1948–49) most of the Jews left, with only 5,000 remaining. Still more departed after the arrest in 1954 of a group of 13 Jews who were found to be working for Israeli defense minister Pinchas Lavon to destabilize the Egyptian regime and ruin its relations with the West by planting bombs in cinemas, post offices, and railway stations, as well as U.S. consulates and information centers. The 1956 census showed just 450 Jews. The total rose to 1,631 in the 1976 census.

With the establishment of an Israeli Embassy in Cairo in 1979, the local Jews were free to travel to Israel. The synagogues [q.v.] in Cairo and Alexandria functioned normally. The government actively discouraged anti-Semitism [q.v.]. In 2007, the Shaar HaShamayim synagogue in Cairo celebrated its century-old existence.

In March 2010, the Egyptian Antiquities Authority completed the restoration of the Rav Moshe Synagogue and its attached yeshiva, which was once the private study of Rabbi Moses Ben Maimon, known as Maimonides, (aka Mousa bin Maimon bin Abdullah al-Qurtubi al-Israeli), the 12th-century physician and philosopher regarded as one of the most important rabbinic scholars in Jewish history. The culture ministry reaffirmed its commitment to restore all 10 synagogues in Cairo and one in Alexandria.

During the January–February 2011 civil uprising in Cairo, though the synagogues were left unguarded by security forces, they were untouched by protestors or others.

IRAQ: Iraq under the British Mandate had a substantial community of Jews, many of whom could trace their ancestry to ancient times. After the passage of a law in 1931 that gave the community autonomy in its internal affairs, a network of Jewish schools, hospitals, and charitable institutions grew, mostly in Baghdad [q.v.]. On the eve of the Palestine War in 1948, there were an estimated 150,000 Jews in Iraq. After this conflict, most of them departed, mainly for Israel. A second exodus occurred after the Suez War [q.v.] of 1956. Unofficial estimates on the eve of the 1991 Gulf War [q.v.] put the number of Jews in Iraq at 2,500, chiefly in Baghdad. By the time of the Anglo-American invasion of Iraq [q.v.] in 2003, the figure had fallen to 60. Due to the violence and chaos that followed, encouraging kidnappings and murders, the remaining Jews often confined themselves to their homes. Their number in Baghdad fell below 10.

JORDAN: Article 25 of the League of Nations Mandate for Britain, which went into force in September 1922, exempted Jordan (then Transjordan) from the application of the Balfour Declaration [q.v.]. Jews were barred from acquiring land or settling in the country. During the 1948–49 Arab-Israeli war, some 2,000 Jews living in the Old City of East Jerusalem [q.v.] surrendered to the Jordanian army and were later transferred to Israel. After the Jordanian-Israeli Peace Treaty [q.v.] in 1994, the Jews from Israel started visiting Jordan as tourists.

LEBANON: A region under the Ottomans that proved popular with minority Islamic sects, Lebanon also attracted Jews. In the late 19th century they formed a small, thriving community in Beirut [*q.v.*]. The 1932 census showed Jews to be about 15,000 strong. The National Pact [*q.v.*] of 1943 included Jews in a grouping of non-Muslim minorities along with Bahais [*q.v.*] and Protestant Christians [*q.v.*], and allotted the community one parliamentary seat.

After the Palestine War (1948–49) many Jews left, and more did so after the Suez War. In 1968 there were some 7,000 Jews in the country. The community was down to 3,000 on the eve of the civil war in 1975. The long conflict and the prevailing chaotic conditions, involving abductions and hostage-taking, made life for Jews difficult. During Israel's invasion of Lebanon in 1982 [*q.v.*], its shelling of Beirut damaged the largest Maghen Abraham synagogue, built in 1926, leading to its abandonment for almost three decades.

By the early 1990s unofficial estimates put the Jewish population at 500 to 700. It dwindled to about 150 in 2010. Yet the tradition of having a Jewish Community president continues. Issac Arazi has been the president since 2005. Under his leadership, the Maghen Abraham synagogue was renovated in 2011 with the funds supplied by Lebanese Jews living abroad.

SYRIA: The small, long-established Jewish communities in Damascus [*q.v.*], Aleppo [*q.v.*], and Latakia [*q.v.*] together totaled 25,000 on the eve of the Palestine War (1948–49). A majority of them departed after this conflict, and more did so after the Suez War. In the mid-1960s the Jewish total declined to some 5,000. By 1994 it fell to 1,250. In 2009 there

were approximately 200 Jews left, most of them in Damascus, which had two synagogues.

Following his meeting with Malcolm Hoenlein, executive vice chairman of the Conference of Presidents of Major American Jewish Organizations, in December 2010, Syrian President Bashar Assad [*q.v.*] reiterated his commitment to renovate all the 11 synagogues in the country. Early the next year the restoration of the Al Raqi Synagogue in the old Jewish quarter of the capital was completed.

YEMEN: North Yemen had a substantial community of Jews, mostly settled in Sanaa [*q.v.*] and the northern town of Saada. Many of them could trace their ancestry to ancient times. A unique feature of Yemenite Jews is that they read the Torah [*q.v.*] in Hebrew [*q.v.*] as well as in Aramaic [*q.v.*]. Following the 1948–49 Palestine War, 42,000 Jews migrated to Israel. Less than 6,000 remained, and many of them left after the Suez War [*q.v.*]. In the early 1990s unofficial estimates put their number at 2,000 to 2,500. In South Yemen some 7,000 Jews departed from the Aden Protectorate during and after the 1948–49 Palestine War. In 2000, there were about 400 Jews in united Yemen, most of them in Sanaa [*q.v.*].

After the killing of a Jew and the firebombing of a Jewish home in the capital in December 2008, President Ali Abdullah Saleh [*q.v.*] ordered extra security for the Jews and offered free housing to some. Despite this, 60 Jews migrated to the United States. During the initial period of the pro-democracy demonstrations in 2011, Saleh provided protection to most of the remaining 250 Jews at an official compound in Sanaa. They in turn joined pro-Saleh demonstrations.

Jews in Iran: Jews in Iran have a history dating back to antiquity. That was also the case with the Jews who traced their Iranian heritage to the exile from Babylon in the late 6th century B.C. In the Book of Ezra, the Persian emperors—Cyrus, Darius, and Artaxerxes—are mentioned as the ones who allowed the Jews to return to Jerusalem and reconstruct their Temple (Ezra 6:14). Among the prominent Jewish monuments in Iran are the shrines of Esther and her cousin Mordecai, and Habakkuk in Hamadan, as well as the mausoleum of Daniel in Susa. Regarded as one of the prophets of monotheism—starting with Adam and ending with Muhammad—Daniel is revered by Muslims, thousands of whom make the pilgrimage to his tomb.

In latter-day Iran, Jews settled in Shiraz [*q.v.*], Isfahan [*q.v.*], and Tehran [*q.v.*], the capitals of the country at different times. In the mid-20th century there were 150,000 Jews in the country. Due to the emigration to Israel and North America, their size declined to about 80,000 in the late 1970s. Within a few months of the Islamic Revolution [*q.v.*] in 1979, that number shrank to about 20,000 even though, on his return to Tehran from a long exile, Ayatollah Ruhollah Khomeini [*q.v.*] issued a fatwa (religious decree) saying that the Jews must be protected.

During the reign of Muhammad Reza Shah Pahlavi (r. 1941–79) [*q.v.*], Jews—along with other non-Muslim recognized minorities—voted as a distinct group in parliamentary elections.

This practice continued after the 1979 revolution.

The community elected one member to the Assembly of Experts (1979) [*q.v.*]—convened to draft an Islamic constitution, which recognized Jews as the People of the [Holy] Book—and entitled them to elect one deputy to the Majlis [*q.v.*]. In 1999, there were an estimated 35,000 Jews with 56 synagogues. The trial of 13 Jews and nine Muslims [*q.v.*] in Shiraz on spying charges drew international attention. All but three Jews and two Muslims were found guilty, with the Jews sentenced to 4 to 13 years in jail. On appeal, their sentence was reduced by two to four years. However, those still in prison in 2002 were released.

In 2003 President Muhammad Khatami [*q.v.*] became the first Iranian president to meet Chief Rabbi Yousef Hamadan Cohen and the Jewish parliamentarian Morris Motamed at a synagogue in Tehran. In an open letter to Mahmoud Ahmadinejad [*q.v.*] in 2007, the Jewish community's official leader, Haroun Yashayaei, protested the Iranian president's denial of the Holocaust.

In 2011, there were 25,000 Jews and 25 synagogues, with 18 in Tehran, many of them teaching Hebrew [*q.v.*] The Jewish community has its own newspaper, *Ofogh-e Bina*, (Hebrew: *Horizon of Knowledge*) and its own charity hospital. The Central Library of Jewish Association has 20,000 volumes.

Jibril, Ahmad (1937–): *Palestinian leader* Born of a Palestinian father and a Syrian mother in Yazour, a village near Jaffa [*q.v.*], Jibril and his family fled to Syria during the Palestine War (1948–

49) [*q.v.*]. After finishing his education he joined the Syrian army and rose to be captain.

In the early 1960s he quit the army to participate in Palestinian politics, founding the Palestine Liberation Front. It was one of the constituents of the Popular Front for the Liberation of Palestine (PFLP) [*q.v.*], formed some months after the Arab defeat in the June 1967 Arab-Israeli War [*q.v.*]. Soon after the first clandestine PFLP congress in August 1968, Jibril and his supporters split to form the PFLP-General Command (PFLP-GC) [*q.v.*], which joined the Palestine Liberation Organization (PLO) [*q.v.*].

His small, tightly controlled faction carried out several operations against Israel and Israeli targets, including planting a bomb aboard a Swissair flight from Zurich to Tel Aviv [*q.v.*] in February 1970, which exploded and killed 47 passengers and crew. Four years later, in a failed attempt to exchange their Israeli hostages, taken in northern Israel, for 100 Palestinian prisoners, three members of Jibril's party and 18 Israelis were killed.

Following the expulsion of the PLO from Beirut in 1982, he made Damascus [*q.v.*] the base of his group. He joined an anti-Yasser Arafat [*q.v.*] rebellion masterminded by Syrian President Hafiz Assad [*q.v.*]. In May 1985 Israel released 1,150 Palestinian prisoners in exchange for three Israeli soldiers that the PFLP-GC had captured during the 1982 Israeli invasion of Lebanon [*q.v.*]. In late November 1987 a hang glider raid from southern Lebanon by three PFLP-GC activists on an Israeli military outpost, which resulted in six Israeli deaths, proved pivotal in sparking the Palestinian intifada [*q.v.*] on 9 December.

Though Jibril's faction was secular, socialist, and nationalist, in the late 1980s he started to form links with Iran and traveled to Tehran [*q.v.*]. His party propaganda began referring to the "Arab and Islamic people" and the "Arab and Islamic region." Despite threatening statements before and during the 1990–91 Kuwait crisis following Iraq's invasion of Kuwait, his faction did not carry out any terrorist acts. He rejected the Israeli-PLO Accord [*q.v.*] of September 1993, primarily because the PLO failed to obtain Israeli agreement on the Palestinians' right to self-determination and the Palestinian refugees' right to return home. His continued opposition to the peace process led to a split in his party in 1999, with its radical elements opting for either Hamas [*q.v.*] or the better established secular PFLP. The support for Jibril declined sharply.

During the Israel-Hizbollah War in 2006 [*q.v.*], PFLP-GC activists assisted the Hizbollah [*q.v.*] in the fight.

jihad: (Arabic: *effort*) Full title: *jihad fi sabil Allah* (Arabic: *striving in the way of God*) Literally, jihad means effort or struggle, which is waged in various forms—such as internal and external—and degrees, war being the most extreme. In its internal form, jihad is the inner struggle of moral discipline and commitment to Islam [*q.v.*] by a Muslim [*q.v.*]. However, it is jihad's external form that has engaged the attention of most chroniclers.

Historically the term "jihad" has been used to describe an armed struggle against unbelievers by Muslims in their mission to advance Islam or counter danger to it. Among the several verses in the Quran [q.v.] that enjoin religious war to be waged by believers is (9:5): "Then, when the sacred months are away,/slay the idolaters wherever you find them,/and take them, and confine them, and lie in wait/for them at every place of ambush. But if they/repent, and perform the prayer, and pay the alms, then/let them go their way."

According to the *sunna* [q.v.], jihad is to be launched only after unbelievers have turned down the offer to embrace Islam [q.v.] or become *dhimmis* [q.v.]. When a Muslim community is ruled by non-Muslims, a jihad can be justified only if Islam is suppressed. Kharijis [q.v.] and Ibadhis [q.v.] regard jihad as the sixth pillar of Islam [q.v.]. Later, Sufi [q.v.] thinkers distinguished between the "greater jihad," a struggle against one's base instincts, and the "lesser jihad," a struggle against unbelievers.

Nowadays those who wage jihad's external form are called jihadis or jihadists.

al-Jihad al-Islami (Egypt): *Egyptian Islamic organization* The Egyptian authorities discovered the existence of al-Jihad al-Islami, often called Al Jihad (AJ), in 1978 during Muslim-Copt [q.v.] riots. Its leadership council included Ismail Tantawi; Shaikh Omar Abdul Rahman [q.v.]; Muhammad Abdul Salam Faraj, an Islamist ideologue; Abbud Abdul Latif Zumur, a colonel in military intelligence who ran the group's operational wing; and Ayman Zawahiri [q.v.], a young surgeon. In his books, *Al-Jihad: the Forgotten Pillar* and *The Absent*

Obligation, Faraj argued that a true Muslim is obliged to struggle for the revival of the Islamic *umma* [q.v.] and those Muslim groups or leaders who have turned away from the Sharia [q.v.] are apostates. Those who want to revive the Islamic *umma* [q.v.] are obliged to wage a jihad [q.v.] against the infidel state, the only acceptable form of jihad being the armed struggle. A true Muslim must first confront the internal infidel (i.e., the Egyptian state) and then the external infidel (i.e., the non-Muslim world at large).

In early 1979 over 100 AJ members were charged with forming an anti-government party. The next year Abdul Rahman issued a religious verdict that declared Egyptian President Anwar Sadat [q.v.] an infidel, thus making him a legitimate target for assassination. In early 1981 Faraj and Zumur devised a plan to assassinate Sadat and set up an Islamic state. On 6 October Lt. Khalid Ahmad Islambouli and three of his colleagues, armed with automatic weapons and hand grenades, attacked the review stand at the military parade in a Cairo [q.v.] suburb, killing Sadat and seven others.

Al Jihad leaders had visualized Sadat's assassination as a catalyst for a nationwide insurrection for the founding of an Islamic state. But there was an uprising only in Asyut, southern Egypt [q.v.], which left 188 dead. Most of the 3,000 Islamists jailed belonged to Al Jihad. It continued to have cells in the armed forces. Following his release after three years in jail for his participation in the plot to assassinate Sadat, in 1984, Zawahiri became the group's ideologue. He issued its first manifesto, *The Philosophy of Confrontation*. Its very title emphasized violence as a means of turning

Egypt into an Islamic fundamentalist state. Thirty of its military members, including two majors, were tried in December 1986 for running training centers for subversives. After a series of Muslim-Copt clashes in the spring of 1987, the government arrested hundreds of Al Jihad members.

With Abdul Rahman emigrating in 1989, its activities declined. But, with the return home of many veteran Islamist commandos after a successful jihad in Afghanistan against the leftist regime there in April 1992, Al Jihad, now calling itself the New Al Jihad, revived. It concentrated on assassinating high officials, such as ministers, but two such attempts in 1993 failed. Government repression followed, including trials by military courts. In 1995, the AJ cooperated with Al Gamaat al-Islamiya [*q.v.*] to assassinate Egyptian President Hosni Mubarak during his visit to Addis Ababa, Ethiopia, but failed.

Severe repression followed. By early 1997 these courts handed down 87 death penalties to Islamist extremists. In 1999 Al Jihad's military leader, Adim Sigam, was killed, and 107 AJ members were tried for attempting to overthrow the government. Nine were given capital punishment. In early 2000 the leadership called on its followers to cease military activities and focus their attention on liberating Jerusalem [*q.v.*] from the Zionists [*q.v.*]. The government released a few hundred AJ detainees.

In 2001, the exiled Zawahiri merged the AJ with Al Qaida [*q.v.*], with the new organization acquiring the official title of Jamaat Qaidat al-Jihad.

Joint Defense and Economic Cooperation Treaty (Arab League, 1950): After the failure of their military action against the newly founded Israel in the Palestine War (1948–49) [*q.v.*], the seven members of the Arab League [*q.v.*] signed a Joint Defense and Economic Cooperation Treaty (JDECT), aimed primarily at Israel, and ratified it in 1950. An early decision taken under this treaty was the League's resolution in November 1950 to continue the wartime blockade of Israel on the premise that the truce of January 1949 did not amount to a state of peace. When a new member was admitted to the League, it was required to join the JDECT.

In the Arab-Israeli wars of 1967 [*q.v.*] (when the League had 13 members) and 1973 [*q.v.*] (when the League had 19 members), the combatant Arab states called for and received military aid from fellow members under the JDECT. But when in May 1982, during the Iran-Iraq War [*q.v.*], Iraq invoked the pact to secure military aid from members, it failed. This happened partly because the enemy was not Israel [*q.v.*], partly because Iraq [*q.v.*] had started the war, and partly because such leading Arab League members as Syria and Libya had sided with Iran.

Jordan:

OFFICIAL NAME: Hashemite Kingdom of Jordan

CAPITAL: Amman [*q.v.*]

AREA: 34,442 sq. mi./89,206 sq. km

POPULATION: 6.5 million (2011 est.)

GROSS DOMESTIC PRODUCT (nominal): $29.96 billion (2011 est.); per capita $4,790 (2011 est.)

GROSS DOMESTIC PRODUCT (Purchasing Power Parity): $36 billion (2011 est.); per capita $5,760

NATIONAL CURRENCY: Jordanian Dinar (JOD); JOD 1 = U.S. $1.41 = £0.90 = €1.08 (2011)

FORM OF GOVERNMENT: monarchy

OFFICIAL LANGUAGE: Arabic [q.v.]

OFFICIAL RELIGION: Islam [q.v.]

ADMINISTRATIVE REGIONS: Jordan is divided into eight governorates (provinces).

CONSTITUTION: The Hashemite Kingdom of Jordan is an independent sovereign state. Its governmental form is monarchical, with a parliament. The present constitution, approved by King Talal bin Abdullah al-Hashemi [q.v.], has been in force since 1952. Executive power rests with the king, who exercises it through ministers. He appoints, dismisses, or accepts the resignation of the prime minister; and on his recommendation other ministers are appointed or dismissed, or their resignation accepted. He also appoints the members and president of the Senate, also called House of Notables, the upper house of parliament. The cabinet manages all state affairs. If the parliament's lower chamber, the House of Representatives (HoR), also called the Chamber of Deputies, withdraws its confidence from the cabinet or any minister, the latter must resign. The king is the supreme commander of the armed forces.

ETHNIC COMPOSITION: (2010) Arab 98 percent, of which almost half are of Palestinian origin; Armenian [q.v.] 1 percent; Circassian [q.v.] 1 percent.

EXECUTIVE AUTHORITY: Executive authority rests with the king, who exercises it through ministers appointed by him.

High officials:

Head of state: King Abdullah II bin Hussein al-Hashem [q.v.], 1999–

Crown Prince: Prince Hussein bin Abdullah II al-Hashem, 2009–

Prime minister: Fayez al-Tarawneh, 2012–

Speaker of the Senate: Taher al-Masri: 2010–

Speaker of the House of Representatives: Faisal Al Fayez, 2011–

HISTORY: Following the disintegration of the Ottoman Empire in 1918, Abdullah bin Hussein al-Hashem [q.v.] and his army entered the British-Mandated area east of the Jordan River [q.v.] called Transjordan [q.v.], and set up a government in Amman in 1921. Britain agreed to recognize Abdullah's rule if he accepted Britain's Mandate over it and Palestine [q.v.]. He did. In 1923 Transjordan became an autonomous emirate, which agreed to formulate a common foreign policy with London and allowed Britain to station troops on its soil.

When Transjordan acquired independence in May 1946, Abdullah assumed the title of king and renamed the Emirate of Transjordan the Hashemite Kingdom of Jordan. The 1923 treaty was replaced by a new document in 1948. As a result of the Palestine War (1948–49) [q.v.], Jordan occupied 22 percent of Palestine, called the West Bank [q.v.]. West Bankers were given full Jordanian citizenship, and equal parliamentary representation with East Bankers. After a general election in 1950 the new parliament declared the East Bank [q.v.] and West Bank united in the Hashemite Kingdom of Jordan.

After the assassination of King Abdullah in 1951, his son Talal [q.v.] ascended the throne. Due to mental illness he abdicated the next year in favor of his son, Hussein bin Talal. His poll-rigging in the 1954 general election led to massive protest. Following a fair and free election in 1956, a national-leftist government under Suleiman Nabulsi [*q.v.*] came to power. It abrogated the 1948 treaty with Britain, and King Hussein acquiesced. But after he had crushed an incipient coup by his newly appointed chief of staff in 1957, he dismissed the Nabulsi government and dissolved parliament and all political parties. Though parliament was revived in 1963, political parties remained banned.

In the charged atmosphere during the buildup to the June 1967 Arab-Israeli War [*q.v.*], Jordan joined the Egyptian-Syrian defense treaty. In addition to losing the West Bank to Israel, Jordan ended up with 250,000 refugees from the territory. Growing militancy among them and the Palestinians who had settled earlier in Jordan led to fighting between the Palestinian commandos and the Jordanian army in September 1970, which the latter won. Jordan stayed out of the October 1973 Arab-Israeli War [*q.v.*].

When the Arab League summit in October–November 1974 recognized the Palestine Liberation Organization (PLO) [*q.v.*] as the sole and legitimate representative of the Palestinian people, Jordan reluctantly accepted the resolution. Dismissing the West Bank half of the HoR, King Hussein suspended it. Jordan refused to join the peace process begun by the Camp David Accords [*q.v.*] in 1978. It sided with Iraq [*q.v.*] in the Iran-Iraq War

(1980–88) [*q.v.*], thus accelerating its economic integration with Iraq. In 1984 King Hussein revived the HoR. His agreement with PLO Chairman Yasser Arafat [*q.v.*] in 1985 on a joint approach to a Middle East peace settlement was rejected by the Palestine National Council [*q.v.*] two years later. A free and fair election in 1989 resulted in an HoR with 40 percent Islamist membership.

During the Kuwait crisis following Iraq's invasion of Kuwait in August 1990, Jordan tried to find an Arab solution, but failed. Its stance during the subsequent Gulf War [*q.v.*] was pro-Iraq. Later it tried to repair the damage done to its standing in the West by distancing itself from Iraq. Before the Middle East peace conference in Madrid in October 1991, Jordan agreed to a joint Jordanian-Palestinian delegation. Three years later it became the second Arab country to sign a peace treaty with Israel. At the same time, Jordan's economic links with Iraq remained strong, with Baghdad supplying 75,000 barrels of oil per day, half of it free and the rest at a discount. These ties became stronger when Iraq was allowed to purchase food and medicine by selling its oil. It gave large contracts to Jordanian businessmen to supply food and medicine.

Whenever the Israeli-Palestinian talks ran into trouble, King Hussein intervened, successfully. The last time he did so was in October 1998 at the Wye River Plantation near Washington, D.C. His successor, King Abdullah II, lacked the seniority and experience of his father to play a mediating role in the Israeli-Palestinian peace process. Indeed the outbreak of the Al Aqsa Intifada [*q.v.*] of the

Palestinians in September 2000 created a crisis in Jordan. As the host of the Arab summit in March 2001, Abdullah II tried to conciliate Iraq and Kuwait, but failed. At home, he dissolved the HoR in June 2001, and then postponed the general election due in November.

Two months earlier, following the terrorist attacks on the United States, the George W. Bush administration increased Washington's economic assistance to Jordan by giving it free access to the American market, in order to secure the monarch's active cooperation in its war on terrorism and to wean him away from Iraq. But that proved insufficient to counter the economic downturn that came toward the end of the decade.

In the wake of the chaos and violence that followed the Anglo-American invasion of Iraq [q.v.] in 2003, up to 700,000 Iraqis sought refuge in Jordan. They included such prominent politicians as Iyad Allawi [q.v.]. Almost simultaneous explosions in three upscale hotels in Amman in November 2005, attributed to Al Qaida in Mesopotamia [q.v.], showed the Iraqi violence spreading to neighboring states.

During the war between Israel and Hamas in Gaza in December 2008–January 2009, Abdullah II had no choice but to reflect the anti-Israel sentiment that swept the country. Even Jordan's wealthy elite publicly urged him to harden his stance toward Israel. He allowed large pro-Gaza demonstrations calling for an immediate cease-fire and humanitarian assistance to Palestinians. He also eased up on the Islamic Action Front [q.v.], which had been deprived of many

HoR seats through electoral fraud.

The onset of the Arab Spring [q.v.] in 2011 led the monarch to replace his prime minister three times in 15 months, with his second choice, Awm Shawkat al-Khasawneh, a former judge of the International Court of Justice, lasting only six months. Following the recommendations of the Royal Commission on Constitutional Review, the parliament amended the constitution to set up an independent commission to supervise and conduct general elections, and outlawed the issuing of "temporary laws" by the king except during a natural disaster, war, or other emergency, or when the parliament was dissolved. These changes did not meet the opposition's demands, but the incipient protest movement remained stillborn because of the fear of the bloodshed then ravaging neighboring Syria.

LEGISLATURE: The parliament, called the National Assembly, consists of a fully nominated Senate of 30, and a popularly elected House of Representatives of 80, which has tenure of four years. In case either chamber turns down a bill acceptable to the other, or the monarch withholds his consent, then only a joint session of the two houses can pass it. Following the dissolution of the HoR and political parties in 1957, fresh elections were held in July 1963, and then in April 1967. After dismissing all 30 West Bank deputies, the king suspended the 60-member house in February 1975. He revived it in January 1984. In July 1988 he dissolved it and formally cut Jordan's legal and administrative links with the West Bank. In November 1989 a fresh election was held for the HoR, confined to the

East Bank. After the legalization of political parties in September 1992, nine parties were licensed. In November 1993, in the first multiparty election since October 1956, the majority of the seats went to independents, with the Islamic Action Front (IAF) [*q.v.*] securing 16 seats, being the only party to win more than one seat. In the 1997 election, its share dropped to eight seats, with the pro-government independents winning 60.

King Abdullah II dissolved the HoR in June 2001 and ruled by decree for two years. In the 2003 general election to 110 seats (including six seats reserved for women if less numbers got elected), despite electoral fraud, the Islamic Action Front won 17 seats, with 84 going to the candidates representing tribes and other conservative social forces. Flagrant electoral fraud in the 2007 parliamentary election reduced the number of IAF representatives to 6, with the conservative and tribal members totaling 98.

The monarch dissolved the HoR in 2009 and imposed direct rule for a year. The election in November 2010 was boycotted by seven opposition groups, including the Islamic Action Front, in protest at the new electoral law, which reduced representation of urban area and increased the rural share. Of the 86 candidates of political groups, only 17 won. The vast majority of the 120 seats went to loyalists and tribal-linked rural candidates.

RELIGIOUS COMPOSITION: (2011) Muslim [*q.v.*], 94 percent, of whom Sunni [*q.v.*] 91 percent, Shia [*q.v.*] 2 percent, Druze 1 percent [*q.v.*]; Christian [*q.v.*], 6 percent.

Jordan River: Rising primarily at the foot of Mount Herman in Syria and secondarily in Mount Anti-Lebanon, the Jordan River is fed by the Hasbani, Banias, and Dan rivers, and flows 220 mi./355 km into the Dead Sea. Its northern half delineates parts of the Jordanian-Israeli border and the Syrian-Israeli border. Its southern half lies in Jordan. Often mentioned in the Bible [*q.v.*], it was the scene of the baptism of Jesus Christ.

Jordanian Civil War (1970–71): Involving the Jordanian military and an alliance of Palestinian guerrillas and radical Jordanians, the civil conflict lasted from 15 to 25 September 1970. It resulted in a Jordanian victory and came to be known among Palestinians as Black September.

With the increased presence of armed Palestinians in Jordan, there were periodic clashes between them and the 55,000-strong Jordanian military in the spring of 1970.

The truce between them, brokered by the Arab League [*q.v.*] in June, became tenuous when King Hussein bin Talal [*q.v.*] accepted Washington's Rogers Peace Plan [*q.v.*] in early August. Since his action contradicted the stance on peace with Israel adopted by the Fourth Arab League summit [*q.v.*] in Khartoum, relations between him and the Palestine Liberation Organization (PLO) [*q.v.*] soured. Tension heightened following the blowing-up of three Western airliners at an airfield near Amman [*q.v.*] by the Popular Front for the Liberation of Palestine (PFLP) [*q.v.*] on 12 September, after Israel had refused to release its Palestinian prisoners.

As the United States moved its warships and warplanes to the region, Hussein formed a military cabinet on 15 September. Fighting erupted between the two sides in Amman and northern Jordan. On 19 September the tank units of the Syrian-based Palestine Liberation Army (PLA) [*q.v.*] crossed into the north of Jordan and captured Irbid. Hussein requested U.S. intervention, but Washington opted for a joint U.S.-Israel operation. However, the Jordanian army managed to check the Palestinian tank advance.

Assured of U.S. and Israeli backing, Hussein deployed his air force against the Palestinians in the Irbid area. With the Syrian air force under Gen. Hafiz Assad [*q.v.*] refusing to intervene on their behalf, the Palestinian armored units withdrew to Syria. A truce, mediated by the Arab League, went into force on 25 September.

Since Palestinian militia units were often posted inside refugee camps and used them as their bases, there was much fighting in the camps, and high casualties. About 4,000 Palestinians died. The U.S. airlifted arms to Jordan and increased its financial aid. Thus fortified, Hussein kept up pressure on the Palestinian commandos and finally expelled them in July 1971 after destroying the last centers of resistance in the hills near Ajloun.

Jordanian-Israeli Peace Treaty

(1994): King Hussein bin Talal [*q.v.*] of Jordan and Israeli Premier Yitzhak Rabin [*q.v.*] signed a peace treaty between the two countries on 26 October 1994 at a site in the Araba Valley along the Jordanian-Israeli border about 30 mi./48 km north of the Gulf of Aqaba. It was witnessed by U.S. President Bill Clinton. The treaty fixed the Israeli-Jordanian border along the lines demarcated at the time of the British Mandate in 1922. Israel conceded Jordanian sovereignty over the 147 sq. mi./381 sq. km occupied by it, while Jordan leased 116 sq. mi./300 sq. km of it to Israel.

Jordan agreed that the Palestinian refugees would be settled where they were in Jordan in return for aid from the United States, thus forfeiting their right to return home. The treaty recognized Jordan's custodianship of the Muslim [*q.v.*] holy places in East Jerusalem [*q.v.*], thereby undermining the Palestinian position. The treaty was condemned by Syria, Lebanon, the Palestine Liberation Organization (PLO) [*q.v.*], and Hamas [*q.v.*]—and ordinary Palestinians in Gaza [*q.v.*], the West Bank [*q.v.*], and East Jerusalem, who staged a protest strike.

Judaism and Jews:

The oldest of major monotheistic creeds, Judaism is a compendium of law, tradition, and doctrine dating back to the Prophet Abraham in ca 1900/1800 B.C. According to tradition, he was directed by God to leave his native Harran in northern Mesopotamia for Canaan (present-day Israel, Palestine, and southern Lebanon) with a solemn promise, the Covenant, that he would become the father of great nations there. His grandson, Jacob, received the name Israel and had 12 sons, the source of the Twelve Tribes of Israel. They migrated to Egypt, where they were enslaved in 1700 B.C., a condition they endured until God renewed his Covenant to Abraham by calling on Moses in the mid-13th century

B.C. to lead the descendants of Israel (the Israelites) out of Egypt, and giving them the Law through Moses on Mount Sinai during their 40 years of wandering in the Sinai Peninsula [q.v.]. This provided a strong ethical foundation to the creed, with its stress on virtuous action.

The Israelites began to conquer and settle Canaan, but they were not yet a nation, only a confederation of tribes led by personages called Judges, such as Gideon and Samson. They set up altars and sanctuaries in Canaan, with the Ark of the Covenant deposited at Shiloh. These tribes were brought together under Saul (r. ca 1030–1010 B.C.), who established the Kingdom of Israel. His successor David, son of Jesse (r. ca 1010–970 B.C.), led the Israelite nation in obedience to God, and brought the Ark of the Covenant to Jerusalem [q.v.] as a shrine for the God of Israel. His son Solomon (r. ca 970–930 B.C.) built the First Temple.

The opposition to the evolution of a dynastic rule led the northern tribes—who called their domain Israel—to break with the southern part, ruled by David's descendants and called Judah, with Jerusalem as its capital.

During the 8th century B.C., Prophet Amos declared that violations of the moral-ethical code of the Covenant would bring the wrath of God upon the Israelites.

In 722 B.C. Israel fell to Assyria, and many Israelites were expelled. Judah continued to exist, but from 605 B.C. the people of Judah, called Jews [q.v.], were taken into exile by the Babylonians. In 586 B.C. Jerusalem was destroyed and the First Temple razed, and the Israelites/Jews were ex-

iled. They were allowed to return to Jerusalem in 538 B.C. by Persian King Cyrus the Great (600–529 B.C.). The Second Temple was completed by 515 B.C.

Though the new Covenant of God, promising a kingdom under a descendant of King David, was not fulfilled, Persian King Artaxerxes (r. 464–424 B.C.) declared the Torah [q.v.] (Written Law) to be the law for the Jews. This in turn led to the Oral Law. The region fell to Alexander of Macedonia (r. 336–323 B.C.) in 333 B.C., resulting in the emergence of Hellenstic Judaism. The banning of Judaism by the Greek ruler Antiochus IV (r. 175–163 B.C.) in 168 B.C. led to a Jewish revolt in 166 B.C., headed by Judas Maccabaeus of the Hasmonaean family. He succeeded in gaining religious freedom for the Jews three years later, but not political freedom. In his attempt to secure the latter, he was killed in 160 B.C. That gave rise to the concept of martyrdom [q.v.] in monotheistic religions.

The Jewish commonwealth was revived under Jonathan in 152 B.C. However, the Hellenization of Judaism continued, and the Torah, written originally in Hebrew [q.v.], was translated into Greek. Later the Jewish community split into Sadducees—often rich, conservative, and ecclesiastical—who believed in the divinity of the Written Law, and Pharisees—often poor, progressive, and lay—who espoused the Oral Law.

In 63 B.C. the Roman general Pompey captured the region, named it Judea (derivative of Judah), and incorporated it into the Roman Empire. Various attempts by the Jews to set up an independent Jewish state failed.

Christianity [*q.v.*] emerged initially as a sect within Judaism. Restrictive decrees from Rome led to a Jewish revolt in 66–70 A.D., during which the Second Temple was destroyed.

With the Jews now turning inward, their leadership increasingly came under eminent rabbis (Hebrew: *my teachers*), beginning with Judah HaNasi (175–220 A.D.), who concentrated on developing the Talmud [*q.v.*]. During the Middle Ages (476 A.D.–1492), two branches of Jewish culture evolved: Sephardim [*q.v.*] and Ashkenazim [*q.v.*]. Attempts to conciliate them, initiated in France, were thwarted when the Jews were expelled from that country in 1306.

German Jews underwent enlightenment, *haskala*, in the 18th century. From this emerged a religious reform of doctrine and worship, especially among the Jews of Germany and France. The reform among German Jews became institutionalized as Reform Judaism [*q.v.*] in the 1840s. This in turn spawned Conservative Judaism [*q.v.*], also in Germany. Most Jews, unaffected by either movement, remained Orthodox [*q.v.*] in their religious beliefs and practices. Modern secular Jewish thinkers tend to reinterpret Judaism as an historical process, centered on ethics and morals, or as religious nationalism.

In 2010, a little over two-fifths of the world's 14.3 million Jews lived in Israel and the Jewish settlements it had established in occupied East Jerusalem [*q.v.*] and the West Bank [*q.v.*]. Of the 8.44 million Jews in the Diaspora [*q.v.*], 5.275 million lived in the United States. Elsewhere, with 483,000 Jews, France had the largest number—followed by Canada with 375,000, Britain 292,000, and Russia 205,000.

Judaism, Conservative: *See* Conservative Judaism.

Judaism, Orthodox: *See* Orthodox Judaism.

Judaism, Reform: *See* Reform Judaism.

Judea: Judea was the name given by the Romans to the vassal kingdom in Palestine [*q.v.*], which came under their rule in 63 B.C. This lasted until 135 A.D., when it was renamed Palestina (Prima and Secunda). The term Judea was revived by Israel's right-wing government in 1977.

Judeo-Spanish language: *See* Ladino language.

Julian calendar: Introduced by Roman Emperor Julius Caesar (r. 59–44 B.C.) in 46 B.C.; *see* Christian Calendars.

Jumblat, Kamal (1917–77): *Lebanese politician, leader of the Lebanese National Movement, 1975–77* Born into a notable Druze [*q.v.*] family in Mukhtara village, Jumblat obtained a diploma in philosophy in Lebanon, and then spent two years at Sorbonne University in Paris where he earned a degree in sociology and psychology. He was elected to parliament in 1947. The next year he became head of his clan. In 1949 he established the Progressive Socialist Party [*q.v.*]. Though predominantly Druze, the party had Sunni [*q.v.*], Shia [*q.v.*], and Christian [*q.v.*] members; and it advocated abolition of the country's political system based on confessionalism [*q.v.*]. Earlier, by marrying May Arsalan, he had softened the traditional rivalry between the Jumblat and the Arsalan clans. She bore him one child, Walid [*q.v.*].

Starting out as a supporter of Bishara Khouri [*q.v.*], Jumblat turned against him when he was accused of corruption in the summer of 1952. In alliance with Camille Chamoun [*q.v.*], Jumblat established the Socialist National Front [*q.v.*]. Chamoun succeeded Khouri after his resignation in September. When Chamoun abandoned the Arab nationalist program on which he had been elected president, Jumblat led an opposition alliance against him in May 1958. The resulting Lebanese Civil War [*q.v.*] lasted until the end of July. He served as education minister (1960–61) and interior minister (1961–64).

His feudal background accorded him an influential role among fellow Druzes, and his leftist, Arab nationalist [*q.v.*] views made him popular with urban, mainstream Sunnis. A consistent opponent of confessionalism, he provided a common framework to the leftist Lebanese groups and the Palestinian factions in the form of the National and Progressive Front (NPF) in 1969. As interior minister in 1970, he legalized such transnational parties as Communists [*q.v.*] and Baathists [*q.v.*]. That enabled the NPF to enlarge in 1972 and 1975, and emerge as the Lebanese National Movement (LNM) [*q.v.*], with Jumblat as its leader.

In the Lebanese Civil War [*q.v.*], which erupted in April 1975, he led the LNM against its opponent—the rightist Maronite coalition called the Lebanese Front [*q.v.*]. He formed an alliance with the Palestine Liberation Organization (PLO) [*q.v.*], which was friendly with Syria. But when it captured two-thirds of Lebanon by April 1976, Syrian President Hafiz Assad [*q.v.*] reversed his policy, fearing that total victory by the radical LNM-PLO alliance would result in Israeli military intervention and destabilization of the whole region, including Syria. In June, Syria attacked LNM-PLO positions and thus rescued the Lebanese Front from a humiliating defeat.

Following the election of Elias Sarkis [*q.v.*], a Syrian nominee, as president in September, and a ceasefire in the civil war two months later, Jumblat accepted Sarkis as president. But as a Lebanese patriot committed to maintaining a multiparty system in Lebanon, he resented the role of authoritarian Assad as the sole power broker in Beirut [*q.v.*]. In early 1977, when he attacked Assad's rule in Syria itself, Assad was furious. He was assassinated in March 1977 by the agents of the Syrian government.

An intellectual of high caliber, Jumblat taught history of economic thought at Beirut University for several years, and authored a few books on Lebanese politics. He was awarded the Lenin Peace Prize by the Soviet government in 1971.

Jumblat, Walid (1949–): *Lebanese politician* Born into a notable Druze [*q.v.*] family in Mukhtara village, Jumblat obtained a political science degree from the American University in Beirut [*q.v.*]. At the age of 20, he broke with tradition by his marriage, outside the Druze clans, to an Iranian actress, which alienated him from his father, Kamal [q.v.]. Later he became active with the militia of the Progressive Socialist Party (PSP) [q.v.] formed after the start of the civil war in 1975.

After the assassination of his father in March 1977, Walid succeeded him as head of his clan, of the PSP, and of the Lebanese National Movement (LNM) [q.v.]. Yet, after divorcing his Iranian wife, he remarried outside the Druze community, to Gervette, an ethnic Circassian [q.v.] from Jordan. Politically, he moderated the LNM's stress on ending confessionalism, and tried to work in cooperation with Syria. He condemned the election of Bashir Gemayel [q.v.] as president in August 1982.

After the initialing of a peace treaty between Israel and Lebanon [q.v.] in May 1983, he joined the alliance that was formed to overturn it. Once the Israelis had withdrawn from the Druze-dominated Shouf region in September 1983, his militia expelled the Maronite [q.v.] forces that had arrived earlier on the coattails of the Israeli occupiers. In March the Lebanese-Israeli draft treaty was annulled.

Jumblat joined the national government formed under Rashid Karami [q.v.] as minister of public works. In October 1983 he helped form an alliance of six parties opposed to President Amin Gemayel [q.v.]. He extended Druze control to the Mediterranean coast and the hills overlooking Beirut [q.v.] and its southeastern suburbs.

He had reservations about the Taif Accord [q.v.], signed in September 1989, which he saw as giving too many concessions to the Maronites,

but he suppressed his misgivings at Syria's behest. Two months later he was named minister of public works in the government of Salim Hoss [q.v.].

Following the end of the Lebanese Civil War [q.v.] in October 1990, when a national reconciliation government was formed under Omar Karami, Jumblat was made a minister without portfolio. In June 1991 he was nominated to the expanded parliament. His party ran in the general election in September 1992. Elected to parliament, he was appointed minister of displaced persons. In the 1996 election his party won all the eight Druze seats. In 1998, he and his party deputies abstained from voting for Syria's choice for president, Emile Lahoud [q.v.].

Once Israel had withdrawn its troops unconditionally from south Lebanon in May 2000, he saw no rationale for Syria to deploy its troops in Lebanon. In the run-up to the general election three months later, he joined the Maronite [q.v.] leaders in demanding the withdrawal of the Syrian troops from Lebanon.

After the assassination of Rafiq Hariri [q.v.] in February 2005, Jumblat led his party to join the anti-Syrian 14 March Alliance [q.v.]. In the general election that followed, the PSP won 16 seats. With the departure of the last Syrian soldiers from Lebanon, his anti-Syrian sentiment cooled. In the 2009 parliamentary election he decided not to join the pro-Syrian 8 March Alliance [q.v.] or the 14 March Alliance. As an independent entity, the PSP garnered 10 seats. Later that year he visited Damascus [q.v.] to reconcile with President Bashar Assad [q.v.]. In the presidential contest in January 2011 his party voted for the 8 March Alliance candidate, Najib Mikati.

He condemned Assad for his violent suppression of the pro-democracy demonstrations that started in March 2011. A year later he ruled out the prospect of any Syrian party reaching a peaceful settlement with Assad, and called on Russia to help Syrians to remove Assad from power.

K

Kaaba (Arabic: *cube*): *Islamic shrine* The holiest shrine of Islam, the Kaaba, containing the sacred Black Stone, stands at the center of the Grand Mosque of Mecca [*q.v.*]. Built of grey stone, it is a 50-foot/15-meter-high boxlike structure, 40 ft./12 m by 35 ft./10.5 m resting on a marble base, 1 ft./30 cm thick. Apart from its entrance door and a gilt water spout, it is covered with a black silk cloth displaying verses from the Quran [*q.v.*] embroidered with gold and silver threads, which is changed after each hajj [*q.v.*].

Entry to the marble-floored interior is by a door in the northeastern wall. In the eastern corner near the door the holy Black Stone is built into the wall 5 ft./1.5 m above the ground. It consists of three large pieces of stone and several small ones, which are surrounded by a ring of stones held together by a silver band. Either solidified basaltic lava or basalt, the Black Stone has been worn smooth by touching and kissing over the centuries.

Opposite the northwest wall of the Kaaba is a semi-circular white marble wall 3 ft./1 m high, about 6 ft./2 m from the north and west corners of the Kaaba. The space between the Kaaba and this wall is believed to contain the graves of Ismail/Ishmael and his mother, Hagar, the slave wife of Ibrahim/Abraham. Nearby is a trough where legend has it that Ibrahim/Abraham and Ismail/Ishamael mixed the mortar to build the Kaaba.

Within two years of his migration from Mecca to Medina [*q.v.*] in 622 A.D., after failing to conciliate the local Jewish tribes, the Prophet Muhammad instructed that during prayer, instead of turning to Jerusalem [*q.v.*], believers should turn to the Kaaba in Mecca.

kabbala (Hebrew: *receiving or accepting [tradition]*): *See* mysticism in Judaism.

Kach (Hebrew: *Thus*): *Israeli political party* Kach was established in 1976 by Rabbi Meir Kahane [*q.v.*], an American Jew [*q.v.*] who settled in Israel in 1971. The group, known widely by its symbol of a clenched fist, was a Jewish fundamentalist [*q.v.*] party. That is, it regarded Jews to be an exclusivist community, opposed to social or sexual intercourse with non-Jews, and insisted that only Jews had the right to live in the biblical Eretz Israel [*q.v.*]. It therefore advocated expulsion of Arabs [*q.v.*] from the West Bank [*q.v.*] and the Gaza Strip [*q.v.*] as well as Israel. Its members harassed Arabs, assaulted them in their homes, and smashed cars and shop windows in Arab districts.

In the 1984 Knesset [*q.v.*] elections, Kach won 25,000 votes and Kahane became a deputy. The Knesset then passed a law barring parties with a racist policy from entering elections. When the high court upheld the legislation and declared Kach racist in 1988, it was prevented from participating in the general election later that year. With opinion polls showing its support at 5 percent, it would have won six seats if it had been allowed to enter the electoral arena. After Kahane's assassination in 1990, his son, Baruch, set up the Kahane Hai (Hebrew: *Kahane Lives*) group. Following Yitzhak Rabin's [*q.v.*] assassination in 1995, both Kach and Kahane Hai were banned in Israel.

Kadima (Hebrew: *Forward*): The decision of Likud [*q.v.*] prime minister Ariel Sharon [*q.v.*] to withdraw the Israeli military from the Gaza Strip [*q.v.*] in September 2005 was opposed by hard-liners in his party. So he quit Likud to form Kadima in November. The new party attracted moderates from Likud as well as the veteran Labor leader Shimon Peres [*q.v.*] and former Histadrut [*q.v.*] chairman Haim Ramon.

Kadima aimed to end the Israeli-Palestinian conflict and achieve separate states for the two nations by dismantling terrorist organizations, collecting firearms, and instilling security reforms in the Palestinian Authority [*q.v.*] as a prelude to accepting a demilitarized Palestinian state.

When Sharon suffered a debilitating hemorrhagic stroke in January 2006, Ehud Olmet [*q.v.*] became the acting prime minister and acting chairman of Kadima. In the March 2006 Knesset election, Kadima won 29 seats, and led the coalition cabinet with Olmert as the premier.

Facing corruption charges, Olmert stepped down from the high office in 2008. In the election of the party chairperson in September by 74,000 party members, Tzipi Livni [*q.v.*] beat Shaul Mofaz [*q.v.*] by a wafer-thin majority of 431 votes. Her failure to form a coalition government led to a general election in February 2009. Kadima won 28 seats, one more than Likud, but once again Livni failed to cobble together a cabinet. As the leading opposition leader Livni emphasized security of Israel security as well as pursuit of the peace process.

In March 2012 she lost her party leadership to Mofaz, who secured 62 percent of the members' votes. Two months later she resigned from the Knesset.

Kahane, Meir (1932–90): *Israeli politician* Born Martin David Kahane, the son of a rabbi in Brooklyn, New York, he joined the Betar, the youth movement of the Revisionist Zionists [*q.v.*] as a teenager. He obtained a law degree from New York University and was ordained as an Orthodox [*q.v.*] rabbi. He combined his religious work with editing the Brooklyn-based *Jewish Press*.

His increasingly militant views led him to establish in the mid-1960s the Jewish Defense League, which resorted to such violent acts as bombing as a means of defending the Jews [*q.v.*]. He coupled this with harassing the Soviet missions in New York to highlight Moscow's ill treatment of Jews. During this period he operated as the Federal Bureau of Investigation's undercover agent, named Michael King, the pseudonym he used to coauthor the book

The Jewish Stake in Vietnam, Kahane would later reveal.

Declaring that the only way a Jew could escape from imbibing Gentile values was to live in Israel [*q.v.*], he migrated there in 1971. After the October 1973 Arab-Israeli War [*q.v.*] he became vehemently anti-Arab. In 1976 he set up Kach [*q.v.*]. He advocated the creation of a Jewish state exclusively for Jews so that they would be free from non-Jewish influences.

He became a Knesset [*q.v.*] deputy when his party, Kach, won 25,000 votes in the 1984 general election. His often controversial behavior in the Knesset led to a number of suspensions. But his popular standing rose, so that on the eve of the 1988 election his party was poised to win six parliamentary seats. However, his party was considered racist, and therefore unlawful, by the High Court, and was barred from running in the general election. He was assassinated by El Sayyid Nosair, an Egyptian-American, in New York in 1990.

Karami, Omar (1934–): *Lebanese politician; prime minister, 1990-92 and 2004–05* Born into the religious Sunni [*q.v.*] family of Abdul Hamid Karami near Tripoli [*q.v.*], Omar obtained a law degree from the Lebanese University and became an attorney. After the assassination of his elder brother Prime Minister Rashid Karam [*qv]* in 1987, he entered public life. At the end of the Lebanese Civil War of 1975–90 [*q.v.*], Prime Minister Salim Hoss [*q.v.*] resigned in his favor. In the 1991 general election Karami was elected to the National Assembly. He maintained close relations with Syria. He resigned in May 1992 against the

backdrop of the falling value of the Lebanese pound. He was reelected in the subsequent parliamentary elections. Following the resignation of Prime Minister Rafiq Hariri [*q.v.*] in October 2004, Karami led the next cabinet. He resigned in the wake of Hariri's assassination in February 2005 but stayed on as a caretaker premier until April.

Karami, Rashid (1921–87): *Lebanese politician; prime minister, 1955–60, 1961–64, 1965–66, 1966–68, 1969–70, 1975–76, and 1984–87* Born into a religious Sunni [*q.v.*] family near Tripoli [*q.v.*], Karami secured a law degree from Cairo University. He set up legal practice in Tripoli.

After the death in 1950 of his father, Abdul Hamid, the chief Islamic judge of the city, he became the leader of local Muslims and their representative in parliament. He was named justice minister in 1951, then economy and social affairs minister (1953), and finally prime minister (1955).

Unlike traditional, conservative Sunni leaders such as Saeb Salam [*q.v.*], he was a radical who supported the pan-Arabism [*q.v.*] of Egyptian President Gamal Abdul Nasser [*q.v.*]. In the 1958 Lebanese Civil War [*q.v.*] he sided with the pan-Arabists who fought the pro-Western President Camille Chamoun [*q.v.*]. After the conflict he led a national unity government from September 1958 to May 1960. For most of the 1960s he was the premier. During the June 1967 Arab-Israeli War [*q.v.*] he wanted Lebanon to enter the conflict but was opposed by the Maronite [*q.v.*] commander of the military, Gen. Emile Boustani.

In the May 1968 election he led the Democratic Parliamentary Forum, which emerged slightly behind its rival, the Triple Alliance of Camille Chamoun, Pierre Gemayel [*q.v.*], and Raymond Edde. However, the subsequent government, led by Abdullah Yafi, fell in December. The new cabinet, headed by Karami, excluded Triple Alliance leaders. In April he resigned when clashes between the Palestinian commandos and the Lebanese army got out of hand. But since no other premier was appointed by President Charles Helou [*q.v.*], he resumed his office after a satisfactory accord had been signed between the Palestine Liberation Organization (PLO) [*q.v.*] and the Lebanese government in November in Cairo [*q.v.*].

Following the election of Suleiman Franjieh [*q.v.*] as president in 1970, Karami failed to win a further mandate for his premiership. But after the start of the Lebanese civil war in April 1975 [*q.v.*], Franjieh appointed him prime minister in the hope that his stature would enable him to end the war. He failed, but continued as premier until December 1976, when the newly elected president, Elias Sarkis [*q.v.*], turned to Salim Hoss to lead the cabinet. To his dismay, Tripoli, his bastion, became the battleground between Islamists [*q.v.*] and secular Baathists [*q.v.*].

After the Israeli invasion of Lebanon [*q.v.*] in June 1982, he joined the anti-Israeli camp and called for deferment of the presidential election until after Israel's evacuation. This did not happen. When Amin Gemayel [*q.v.*] became president in September 1982, he lined up with anti-Gemayel politicians. He opposed the draft Lebanese-Israeli Peace Treaty [*q.v.*], which was trashed in early March 1984.

As a result of the successful national reconciliation conference in Lausanne, Switzerland, he headed a national reconciliation government in April. He fell out with President Gemayel in 1986 after the latter refused to endorse the "National Agreement to Solve the Lebanese Crisis," signed by three leading militia leaders. Their relations became very tense in the following spring. But when Karami submitted his resignation in May 1987, Gemayel refused to accept it, as he saw no alternative to Karami. He was assassinated on 1 June.

Karbala: *Iraqi city* Also called Mashhad al-Hussein (Arabic: *Witness to Hussein*). Population: 675,000 (2011 est.) It is the site of the martyrdom [*q.v.*] of Imam Hussein bin Ali at the hands of Yazid bin Muwaiya in 681 A.D., which forms the climax of the Shia [*q.v.*] festival of Ashura [*q.v.*]. Over the centuries Karbala emerged as a center of Shia learning, and after the construction of the shrine of Imam Hussein, called the Great Martyr, became one of the holiest cities of Shias. It was attacked by Wahhabis [*q.v.*] in 1802, and Imam Hussein's shrine was stripped of all its embellishments. Before long, it was restored to its earlier splendor and capped with a golden dome. It became a major tourist attraction.

After the seizure of power in Iraq by secular Baathists [*q.v.*] in 1968, Karbala and its religious establishment came under a shadow. Unsurprisingly, in the aftermath of the 1991 Gulf War [*q.v.*], the city became an important center of Shia uprising against President Saddam Hussein [*q.v.*]. But the government forces quickly crushed the rebellion.

Twelve years later, following the overthrow of the Saddam Hussein's regime on 9 April 2003, nearly 1.5 million Shias assembled in Karbala on 25 April to commemorate the 40th day of mourning of the death of Imam Hussein, a ritual banned by the Baathist government.

From then onward, Shias gathering in Karbala for the Ashura ritual were often targeted by militant Sunni [*q.v.*] suicide bombers attached to Al Qaida in Mesopotamia [*q.v.*]. In 2004 this led to the deaths of 170 people. Yet the number of Shia pilgrims to Karbala to commemorate Ashura kept rising, reaching 3 million in December 2011, including 650,000 from abroad.

Karman, Tawakul (1979–): *Yemeni journalist, co-recipient of 2011 Nobel Peace Prize* Born in the village of Mekhlaf in Taizz province in the household of Abdul Salam Karman, a lawyer-politician, Karman obtained a post-degree in political science from the University of Sanaa [*q.v.*] in 2003. She became a journalist and went on to cofound the Women Journalists without Chains (WJWC), which advocated press freedom. When the WJWC was denied a license for a mobile phone news service in 2007, she mounted a protest campaign of weekly demonstrations outside the interior ministry from 2007, demanding investigations into corruption and other forms of social and legal injustice and the lifting of limitations on press freedoms.

Being married to Muhammad al-Nahmi and raising two children did not blunt her fight for social-political reform. When the opposition alliance, called the Joint Meeting Parties (JMP), faced pressure from the government of President Ali Abdullah Saleh [*q.v.*], the WJWC came to its aid, and called for the release of political prisoners.

She joined the Yemen Islah Group [*q.v.*], a conservative religious party which called for reform in accordance with the Sharia [*q.v.*]. In 2007 she was one of the 13 women elected to the 130-member Shura (Consultative) Council of the party.

Because of her activities she was harassed and occasionally arrested by the government. When she organized a demonstration in favor of the pro-democracy uprisings in Tunisia and Egypt in January 2011, she was thrown into jail. Widespread protest followed. As a leader of the anti-Saleh movement she focused on women and youths, always stressing nonviolence. Inspired by her, tens of thousands of women took part in anti-Saleh demonstrations.

Like almost all Yemeni women, she grew up wearing the *niqab* (Arabic: *mask*), a garb that covers the face and head except the eyes. But in 2010, just before delivering a speech at a human rights conference in Washington, she realized that wearing a niqab was unsuitable for a woman wishing to work in the public domain. So she switched to a *hijab*, a scarf that covers the head and neck and leaves the face open. She took to wearing a headscarf and a long black *abaya* (Arabic: *cloak*), a loose robe covering the body from head to toe.

In October 2011, the Norwegian Nobel Committee named her and

Liberian President Ellen Johnson Sirleaf and Liberian human rights activist Leymah Gbowee as the joint winners of the Nobel Peace Prize for their "nonviolent struggle for the safety of women and for women's rights to full participation in peace-building work." She became the youngest person to receive this 110-year-old prize and the second Muslim woman to do so, the first being Shirian Ebadi [q.v.].

She supported the deal between Saleh and the opposition centered on the transitional plan offered by the Gulf Cooperation Council [q.v.] and backed by the UN Security Council, and voted in the presidential election in February 2012 for the sole candidate, Abd Rabbu Mansour al-Hadi [q.v.].

Kashani, Abol Qasim (1884–1962):
Iranian religious-political leader Born into a religious Shia [q.v.] family in Tehran [q.v.], Kashani grew up in Najaf [q.v.], Iraq, where he pursued religious studies. He returned to Iran in 1921 after Iraq had been placed under British Mandate. During the interwar years he emerged as a radical who opposed senior clerics' advice to juniors to stay away from politics. He became popular with second-rank clerics and itinerant mullahs. He was arrested for his anti-British activities after the British had occupied Iran in August 1941 during World War II.

On his release after the war, he founded a political party, Mujahedin-e Islam [q.v.]. It demanded abrogation of all secular laws passed by the regime, the application of the Sharia [q.v.], as stated in the 1906–07 constitution, and the reintroduction of the veil for women.

He was sent into internal exile in the northern city of Qazvin until late 1947. His third arrest, followed by his banishment to Lebanon, came in the wake of a failed attempt on the life of Muhammad Reza Shah Pahlavi (r. 1941–79) [q.v.] on 4 February 1949. He was permitted to return home after a year.

The issue of the nationalization of the Anglo-Iranian Oil Company dominated the general election held from July 1949 to February 1950, in which Kashani participated as a candidate. Elected to parliament, he advocated oil nationalization. In March parliament voted for it and then for the appointment of Muhammad Mussadiq [q.v.] as premier. Kashani was moved as much by anti-imperialism as by a symbiotic relationship between religion and politics in Islam [q.v.]—the two major themes that were later to inspire Ayatollah Ruhollah Khomeini [q.v.] and fuel the forces of Islamic revolution [q.v.]. In August he was elected speaker of parliament for a year.

At his intercession, Mussadiq released 28 members of the Fedaiyan-e Islam [q.v.], including the assassin of a prime minister. But the Kashani-Mussadiq alliance broke down when, in order to survive politically, Mussadiq began to rely increasingly on secular leftists. In January 1953 Kashani opposed Mussadiq's request for an extension of his emergency powers by a year. Following his failure to be reelected speaker of parliament in July, Kashani joined the anti-Mussadiq camp and, whether by design or chance, contributed to his overthrow in August 1953.

He opposed the oil agreement that the shah made with a Western oil consortium a year later. Following a failed attempt by a Fedaiyan-e Islam [*q.v.*] activist to assassinate Prime Minister Hussein Ala, the government arrested Kashani, releasing him only after he had dissociated himself from the group. After his death his mantle of radical religious opposition to the shah was taken over by Khomeini.

Kataeb Party: *See* Phalange Party.

Katsav, Moshe (1945–): *Israeli president, 2000–07* Born in Yazd to parents who migrated to Israel in 1951, Katsav grew up in Kiryat Malachi. At 24, while still a student at Hebrew University in Jerusalem [*q.v.*], he was elected mayor of his town. In 1977 he won a seat in the Knesset [*q.v.*] as a member of Likud [*q.v.*], and retained it until 2000. He served as minister of labor and welfare in the national unity government of 1984–88, then as transportation minister under Yitzhak Shamir [*q.v.*] for the next four years. In the administration of Benjamin Netanyahu's [*q.v.*] he was appointed deputy prime minister and minister of tourism.

Following Netanyahu's defeat in 1999 in the prime ministerial contest, he became chairman of the opposition Likud in the Knesset. When President Ezer Weizman [*q.v.*] resigned in 2000, Katsav faced Shimon Peres [*q.v.*] as his rival in his bid for the presidency. He won by a majority of six in a chamber of 120 and became Israel's eighth president.

He resigned in July 2007, a fortnight prior to the end of his term, after pleading guilty to charges of sexual harassment and indecent acts toward his female subordinates—but not of rape—in his plea bargain with state prosecutors. Later he abandoned the deal to prove his innocence. The new trial went on for a year mostly behind closed doors. In December 2010 the court found him guilty of two counts of rape and several instances of sexual harassment, and sentenced him to seven years in jail.

Katzir, Ephraim (1916–2009): *Israeli scientist; president, 1973–78* Born Katchalsky in Kiev, Russia, Katzir arrived in Palestine [*q.v.*] as a child in 1925. He pursued his undergraduate and postgraduate studies in biochemistry at the Hebrew University in Jerusalem [*q.v.*], and then taught there. In 1951 he became head of the biophysics department at the Weizmann Institute of Science. He was awarded the Israel Prize for Life Sciences in 1959 and the Rothschild Prize in Life Sciences the following year. He served as the chief scientist to the ministry of defense from 1966 to 1968.

Interested in public affairs, he was a member of Mapai [*q.v.*]. As the candidate of the Labor Party [*q.v.*] for the presidency in 1973, he defeated his rival, Yitzhak Navon [*q.v.*], by 66 votes to 41. During his term of office Israel witnessed the October 1973 Arab-Israeli War [*q.v.*], the Likud [*q.v.*] victory in the 1977 election, and President Anwar Sadat's [*q.v.*] trip to Jerusalem [*q.v.*].

In 1980 he established the Center for Biotechnology at Tel Aviv University and resumed his career as a scientist.

Khaddam, Abdul Halim (1932–): *Syrian politician, first vice president 1984–2005* Born into a poor Sunni [*q.v.*]

family in Banias, Khaddam obtained a law degree from Damascus University, where he joined the Baath party [*q.v.*]. He worked as a lawyer and school teacher in the capital before entering civil service as a provincial governor under the Baathist regime from 1963—first in Hama [*q.v.*], then Qunaitra, and finally Damascus [*q.v.*].

Khaddam was a friend of Hafiz Assad [*q.v.*] from their senior school days (1949–51), and his career advanced in line with Assad's. In May 1969, after Assad had made his first, partly successful move to acquire supreme power, Khaddam was appointed minister of economics and foreign trade. Once Assad had assumed full authority in late 1970, he became foreign minister and deputy premier.

Over time he established himself as a brilliant executor of Assad's foreign policies. Assad put him in charge of implementing Syria's policy in Lebanon, especially after the outbreak of the Lebanese Civil War [*q.v.*] there in April 1975. He helped to assemble a Committee for National Dialogue in September, which secured a month-long truce. Later he was the moving spirit behind the First and Second Lebanese National Reconciliation Conferences in Switzerland (November 1983 and March 1984). In May 1984 Assad appointed him as one of the three vice presidents, with special responsibility for Lebanese and foreign affairs.

Two months later he narrowly escaped death from a car bomb. He was the main force behind the forging of the Taif Accord [*q.v.*] in October 1989. His moment of glory came a year later when the Lebanese Civil War ended, on Syria's terms.

He was confirmed in his vice presidency in 2000 by President Bashar Assad [*q.v.*]. Five years later he resigned his post and moved to Paris to write his memoirs. There he criticized Assad's policies in Lebanon. Forecasting the fall of the Assad regime by the end of 2006, he formed the National Salvation Front in Syria in Brussels. It aimed to change the Syrian regime through peaceful means. Its first conference in Berlin in 2007 was attended by more than 40 opposition leaders, including those of the Syrian Muslim Brotherhood [*q.v.*].

In his interview on Channel 2 TV of Israel in May 2011, he acknowledged receiving funds from the United States and the European Union to bring about the downfall of Assad's regime. In March 2012 he called for the formation of a military coalition of the Arab and Western nations to overthrow Assad.

Khalaf, Salah (1932–91): *Palestinian leader* Khalaf was born into a middle-class household in Jaffa [*q.v.*]. He and his family became refugees in al-Bureij camp in the Gaza Strip [*q.v.*] in 1948. After graduating from a teacher training college in Cairo [*q.v.*] he worked as a teacher in the Gaza Strip, then under Egyptian administration. Spotted in 1954 by the Egyptian army as someone with leadership potential, he was given advanced military training. During a visit to Cairo he met Yasser Arafat [*q.v.*], then leader of the local Palestinian Student Federation. During the 1956 Suez War [*q.v.*], when Gaza fell to the Israelis, Khalaf left the territory. Later he enrolled as a student in Stuttgart, Germany.

In March 1959 Arafat, then working in Kuwait, secured him an entry permit for Kuwait. That summer, together with Arafat and Khalil Wazir [*q.v.*], he cofounded Fatah [*q.v.*]. After his involvement in an attack on the Israeli National Water Carrier at Beit Netopha on 1 January 1965, launched from the Ein Hilwa Palestinian camp in southern Lebanon, he was arrested along with Arafat and jailed for two months. In prison they decided to adopt *noms de guerre*, Khalaf choosing Abu Iyad.

Helped by the Baathist [*q.v.*] government in Syria, Khalaf began to recruit members for Fatah in Gaza and Jordan. In 1969 he and other Fatah leaders assumed control of the Palestine Liberation Organization (PLO). In the 1970s he emerged as a member of a triumvirate that dominated both Fatah and the PLO, his colleagues being Arafat and Wazir. With Arafat somewhere in the middle, Khalaf balanced the rightist tendencies of Wazir. During the June 1982 Israeli invasion of Lebanon [*q.v.*], when he was head of Fatah's security apparatus, the defense of West Beirut fell mainly upon him.

After the banishment of the PLO from Beirut [*q.v.*] to Tunis and other setbacks that followed in the mid-1980s, he mellowed. In November 1988 he endorsed the resolution of the Palestine National Council (PNC) [*q.v.*] to abandon violence and accept peaceful coexistence with Israel, along with a Palestinian state to be established on the West Bank and Gaza. This, and the victory of the Fatah forces over the Abu Nidal [*q.v.*] group in the southern Lebanese Palestinian camps in mid-1990, turned him into a hated figure among militant Palestinian circles. He was assassinated in January 1991 at the PLO headquarters in Tunis by his bodyguard, described by PLO sources as an agent of Abu Nidal.

Khalid bin Abdul Aziz al-Saud (1912–82): *King of Saudi Arabia, 1975–82*
Born in Riyadh to Ibn Saud [*q.v.*] and Jawhara bint Musaid al-Jiluwi, Khalid learned the Quran [*q.v.*] as a boy—as well as riding, tracking, and marksmanship. He then had his apprenticeship in politics, attending the daily assembly of his father. Khalid helped his father to suppress the Ikhwan [*q.v.*] rebellion in 1929. After the establishment of Saudi Arabia three years later, he carried out royal missions in Germany and Britain. In 1943 he and his elder brother Faisal bin Abdul Aziz [*q.v.*] traveled to the United States on an official assignment.

When Faisal was promoted to prime minister in September 1962, he appointed Khalid deputy prime minister. In 1963 he was named commander of the newly formed National Guard [*q.v.*]. Once King Saud bin Abdul Aziz [*q.v.*] had abdicated in late 1964, and his elder brother Muhammad bin Abdul Aziz, being ill, had given up his claim to the throne a few months later, Khalid was named crown prince in March 1965. A decade later he ascended the throne after the assassination of Faisal. He freed 150 political prisoners held by his predecessor.

His cabinet of 25 contained 15 commoners, but retained the crucial foreign, defense, interior, and National Guard ministries with the House of

Saud [*q.v.*]. He delegated authority to Crown Prince Fahd bin Abdul Aziz [*q.v.*], partly because he himself was susceptible to heart attacks. He supported the plans to end the civil war in Lebanon [*q.v.*], and funded the Arab Deterrent Force, which was stationed there.

He gave grants to the Palestine Liberation Organization (PLO) and opposed the Camp David Accords [*q.v.*] of September 1978. He cut off all links with Egypt after it had signed a peace treaty with Israel in March 1979. Convinced that the United States, which failed to rescue the Pahlavi dynasty [*q.v.*] in Iran in early 1979, would be unable to save the House of Saud, Khalid rebuffed U.S. President Jimmy Carter's efforts to persuade him to join the Middle East peace process inaugurated by the Camp David Accords.

In domestic affairs, along with Muhammad bin Abdul Aziz and Abdullah bin Abdul Aziz [*q.v.*], Khalid represented the nationalist trend (committed to greater respect for tradition and slower economic development), which was in conflict with the pro-U.S. trend (stressing rapid economic development funded by vast oil revenues) espoused by three Sudairi brothers: Fahd, Sultan bin Abdul Aziz (defense minister), and Nayif bin Abdul Aziz (interior minister) [*q.v.*].

When faced with an armed uprising at the Grand Mosque of Mecca [*q.v.*] in November 1979, Khalid prevaricated while Sultan urged rapid, massive action. It was a fortnight before the uprising was crushed, leaving 117 insurgents dead, followed by the execution of 67 more. Facing the challenge posed by the revolutionary Islamic regime in Iran, Khalid, a pious Muslim, moved toward stricter enforcement of orthodox Islam and Islamic practices in the kingdom.

Despite open heart surgery in 1978, he suffered a minor coronary attack in February 1980. He succumbed to a major heart attack in June 1982.

al-Khalifa, Hamad bin Isa (1950–): *ruler of Bahrain, 1999–* Born in Riffa, he was educated in Nanama [*q.v.*]. On completing his junior secondary schooling in 1964, he was named crown prince. He finished his secondary education in Godalming and Cambridge, U.K., and then joined Mons Officer Cadet School in Aldershot. After graduating as a cadet in 1968, he returned home to command the newly established Bahrain Defense Force. In 1970, as head of the Defense Directorate, he became a member of the 12-member advisory Council of State. On the eve of Bahraini independence in 1971, he became the country's defense minister, a position he held until his elevation to ruler. In 1972 he enrolled at the U.S. Army Command and Staff College at Fort Leavenworth, Kansas, and graduated the following year.

As deputy head of the al-Khalifa Family Council, he had much say in the running of the emirate. Yet it was only after he ascended the throne in 1999 that he could implement the long overdue political reform. He immediately reshuffled the cabinet and freed more than 300 political detainees. When the State Security Court sentenced the leading opposition figure, Shaikh Abdul Amir al-Jamri, to 10 years in jail, Khalifa pardoned him.

The stationing of the revived U.S. Fifth Fleet in Bahrain, dating back to 1995, continued. In 2001, Khalifa renewed the defense agreement with the United States for 10 years. A year later, Washington secretly extended the agreement by another five years, a fact that became known only in September 2011.

In 2000 when the Supreme National Committee, appointed by Khalifa, drafted a National Action Charter, which recommended a constitutional monarchy and a bicameral parliament, he put it to vote in early 2001. Once the electorate voted for the Charter, he declared Bahrain to be a constitutional monarchy. He held an election, based on universal suffrage, to the 40-member National Assembly in 2002. It was boycotted by popular political parties because Khalifa had compromised the assembly's legislative authority by creating a nominated upper house. Even though in the subsequent general election a Shia [q.v.] religious party emerged as the leading group in the National Assembly, the government continued its traditional policy of repressing Shia leaders. He refused to consult any political group on political reform.

According to the classified U.S. cables leaked by the anti-secrecy group WikiLeaks in December 2010, during a private conversation between U.S. ambassador William Monroe and Khalifa on 15 February 2005, the ruler revealed that Bahrain already had contacts with Israel at the intelligence/security level—that is, with Mossad [q.v.]—and indicated that Bahrain would be willing to move forward in other areas to cooperate with Israel.

The participation of the religious parties in the 2006 general election altered the political environment. Due to its close links with the Ulema Council of the Shia sect, Al Wefaq won 17 of the 18 seats it vied for. On the Sunni side their two parties together garnered 13 seats. So three-quarters of the 40 elected members of parliament (MPs) belonged to religious parties. With that the influence of clerics in politics rose. The most prominent among them was Shaikh Isa Qasim, a Shia, who had returned from exile in Iran in 1990. He became the spiritual guide of Al Wefaq and the leading authority on such issues as codification of personal law and participating in or boycotting elections.

Starting late 2009, Shias in rural areas staged regular protests, demanding the release of dozens of political prisoners. Inspired by the overthrow of the autocratic presidents in Tunisia and Egypt as part of the Arab Spring [q.v.], members of the Shia majority began demonstrating against discrimination in housing, education, and employment and their exclusion from command positions in the military and security forces from mid-February 2011 onward. Khalifa responded with a crackdown in which 30 demonstrators were killed. After bloody clashes, protestors occupied the Pearl Square, where they stayed in tents. In mid-March Khalifa declared a state of emergency, which empowered the security forces to dissolve any organization they considered a danger to the state. With the support of 1,100 Saudi soldiers, the government crushed the protest, with the security forces demolishing the 300-ft. sculpture, topped by a giant pearl, at the center of the Pearl Square. Over 1,400 people were arrested and more than 4,000 were sacked from their jobs. The National Security Courts handed out stiff jail sentences to protestors. Washington issued tempered criticisms of the crackdown but did not press for political reform. On 1 June Khalifa lifted the state of emergency.

He appointed a five-member Bahrain Independent Commission of Inquiry (BICI) of jurists and legal experts of international repute. In its report in November it concluded that the government had used excessive force and that there were many instances of torture of the detainees. It recommended reorganization of the National Security Agency (NSA). A subsequent royal decree termed the NSA an intelligence gathering agency without powers of law enforcement and arrest.

In January 2012 Khalifa announced amendments to the constitution to give the parliament the right to approve cabinets proposed by the ruler and question and remove cabinet ministers. The opposition leaders noted that the parliament would not have the power to question or dismiss the hard-line Prime Minister Shaikh Khalifa bin Salman al-Khalifa in office since 1971. Therefore, street demonstrations for democratic transformation continued, albeit with reduced frequency.

al-Khalifa, Isa II bin Salman II (1933–99): *ruler of Bahrain, 1961–99* Born in Manama [*q.v.*], Khalifa was named heir apparent at the age of 24. He succeeded his father three years later. He faced growing agitation by his subjects—including a strike by oil workers

in 1965—for political reform. But it was not until January 1970 that he appointed an advisory 12-member Council of State. As the British prepared to leave in 1971 he transformed it into a cabinet and charged it with framing a constitution. Severe rioting and strikes in March and September 1972 led Khalifa to concede a 42-member constituent assembly, half-elected and half-appointed, to draft a constitution. It did so in mid-1973, and Khalifa approved the document, which provided for a National Assembly with a four-year tenure. The elections to the Assembly were held on a limited franchise in December 1973. He dissolved the parliament and suspended the constitution in August 1975.

Bahrain, with a Shia [*q.v.*] majority, was inspired by the Islamic revolution [*q.v.*] in Shia-majority Iran. When the Islamic opposition demanded that Bahrain be declared an Islamic republic, Khalifa, a Sunni [*q.v.*], reacted with a heavy hand. In May 1981 he became one of the cofounders of the Gulf Cooperation Council [*q.v.*], which was established with the primary aim of coordinating internal security arrangements of the Gulf States [*q.v.*]. In January 1982 his government arrested 73 members of the Islamic Front for the Liberation of Bahrain, accusing them of plotting an Iranian-instigated coup. Most of them were given a life sentence. Khalifa sided with Iraq during the Iran-Iraq War (1980–88) [*q.v.*]. During the Kuwait crisis (1990–91) he took a firm pro-Kuwaiti line and contributed troops and warplanes to the war against Iraq.

To meet the rising demand for reform, he appointed a 30-member Advisory Council in 1993, but kept the 1973 constitution in suspension as advised by his hard-line Prime Minister Shaikh Khalifa bin Salman al-Khalifa, in office since 1971.

al-Khalifa, Salman II bin Hamad

(1895–61): *ruler of Bahrain, 1942–61* Born in Manama [*q.v.*], Khalifa started to acquire administrative experience in his early 20s. He became head of the department dealing with the properties of minors, and then graduated to the departments overseeing courts. During World War II he sided with the Allies. After the war, he allowed the British navy to use Bahrain's docks and other facilities, later extending this privilege to the U.S. Middle East Force [*q.v.*]. His close ties with Britain became a point of contention during the 1956 Suez War [*q.v.*], when the Anglo-French-Israeli alliance invaded Egypt, and his subjects mounted massive pro-Egyptian demonstrations.

al-Khalifa dynasty: *Bahraini ruling dynasty*

Following the migration of the al-Khalifa clan of the Utaiba tribe of the Anaiza tribal federation [*q.v.*] from the Arabian Peninsula [*q.v.*] to the offshore islands of Bahrain, in 1783, the clan succeeded in wresting control of the islands from Iran (then Persia). The al-Khalifas consolidated their hold by signing treaties with Britain in 1861, 1880, and 1892, turning Bahrain into a British protectorate.

After Shaikh Isa I bin Ali was deposed by the British in 1923, his son Hamad (1873–1942) became the ruler. Under his rule oil was discovered in 1932, with output reaching 19,000 barrels a day in 1940. Oil revenue funded expanding public services while the ruler maintained tight control over his subjects, refusing trade union rights to workers despite a strike in the oil industry in 1938.

Khamanei, Ali Husseini

(1939–): *Iranian religious-political leader; Supreme Leader, 1989–* (Also spelled Khamenei) Born into a religious family in Mashhad [*q.v.*], Khamanei pursued his theological studies in Najaf [*q.v.*], Iraq, and then Qom [*q.v.*], where he became a student of Ayatollah Ruhollah Khomeini [*q.v.*]. He participated in the June 1963 protest against Muhammad Reza Shah Pahlavi [*q.v.*]. After Khomeini's deportation to Turkey in late 1964, he returned to Mashhad, where he taught at the local theological college. During the next decade he was arrested six times for his anti-government activities. His release from jail in 1975 was followed by an internal exile in Iranshahr in the border province of Baluchistan-Sistan. This ended during the revolutionary upsurge of 1977–78, and enabled him to return to Mashhad and participate in the movement.

He was one of Khomeini's first appointees to the Islamic Revolutionary Council (IRC), which assumed supreme power after the Islamic revolution [*q.v.*]. He was a cofounder of the Islamic Republican Party [*q.v.*], which became the ruling party. Later the IRC appointed him its representative at the defense ministry, where he headed the political-ideological bureau, which was charged with inculcating the troops with Islamic ideology and keeping a watchful eye on the officer corps. Later he was elected to the Assembly of Experts [*q.v.*], which drafted the constitution. Following the death in September of Ayatollah Mahmoud Taleqani [*q.v.*], Khomeini appointed Khamanei, then a *hojatalislam* (a grade lower than ayatollah), as the Friday prayer leader of Tehran [*q.v.*], a highly prestigious position.

Elected to the Majlis [*q.v.*] in early 1980, he was active in the IRP's parliamentary wing. In May he became Khomeini's personal representative on the Supreme Defense Council. During his sermon at a Tehran mosque on 27 June 1981 a bomb, hidden in a tape recorder placed near him, exploded, injuring his arm, lungs, and vocal cords. After the assassination of the IRP's secretary-general, Muhammad Beheshti, the next day, he was elected to this office. And following the assassination of President Muhammad Ali Rajai [*q.v.*] on 30 August, he was chosen as the IRP's candidate for the presidency. He gained 95 percent of votes. He was elected to the Assembly of Experts [*q.v.*] in 1982. In the summer of 1984 he toured Syria, Libya, and Algeria, the Arab countries that were backing Iran in its war with Iraq.

He won 88.5 percent of the vote in the August 1985 presidential election. But when he tried to replace radical Prime Minister Hussein Musavi [*q.v.*], he found his hands tied. He and Musavi belonged to the opposing factions within the IRP and could not reconcile their differences. As a result, Khomeini ordered the dissolution of the IRP in July 1987. A year later, instructed by Khomeini, Khamanei accepted the UN Security Council Resolution 598 for a cease-fire in the Iran-Iraq War [*q.v.*].

Promoted to ayatollah by Khomeini on his deathbed, Khamanei became a *mujtahid* [*q.v.*], a constitutional requirement for the Leader. After Khomeini's death on 3 June 1989, the hastily assembled Assembly of Experts implemented his deathbed wish by electing Khamanei the Leader by 60 votes to 12.

While maintaining Khomeini's pattern of periodically issuing radical statements, he encouraged pragmatic President Ali Akbar Hashemi Rafsanjani [*q.v.*] to liberalize the economy, which had become highly centralized due to the eight-year-long Iran-Iraq War. The newly elected Second Assembly of Experts in 1990 confirmed Khamanei as the Leader for the duration of its tenure of eight years. He maintained a hard-line stance toward America which, in his view, became the sole "arrogant power" in the world after the collapse of the Soviet Union in 1991. At home he worked closely with Rafsanjani after his reelection in 1993 to advance economic reform.

Khamanei endorsed the result of the 1997 presidential election unhesitatingly, even though it resulted in the defeat of Ali Akbar Nateq Nouri, the favorite of the religious establishment. The crisis caused by student rioting in Tehran in July 1999 brought him and the reformist President Muhammad Khatami [*q.v.*] together. They diffused the crisis by a mixture of firm action, mobilization of popular support for the regime, and placating of student leaders.

Alarmed by the euphoria displayed by reformers following their overwhelming success in the first run of the parliamentary election in March 2000, Khamanei ordered a clampdown of the reformist press through the judiciary on the ground that, if unchecked, the forces unleashed by reformers would replace the Islamic order with a secular one. His nomination of conservatives to the Guardian Council [q.v.] ensured an effective control of the reformist-dominated parliament.

He endorsed the repeat landslide victory of Khatami in the presidential election in 2001. With the United States extending its 1996 Iran-Libya Sanctions Act for another five years in 2001, the chances of Washington-Tehran rapprochement receded, and this suited Khamanei.

On the other hand, his strong condemnation of the terrorist attacks on the U.S. in September 2001 thawed relations between the two countries, which continued as the Pentagon attacked the Taliban regime in Afghanistan, much detested by his government. But when U.S. President George W. Bush included Iran in his so-called "Axis of Evil" in early 2002, Khamanei and his aides lambasted Washington. He maintained silence as America ratcheted up pressure on Iraqi President Saddam Hussein [q.v.], whose aggression against Iran in 1980 had not been forgotten.

But on the eve of the Anglo-American invasion of Iraq in March 2003 [q.v.], he warned Washington against attacking Iraq. After the war, he described the U.S. occupation of Iraq as "worse than Saddam's dictatorship."

The massive victory of the conservatives in the 2004 parliamentary election removed the friction between Khamanei and the Majlis that had developed during the previous four years. The election of hard-liner Mah-moud Ahmadinejad [q.v.] as president in 2005 aligned the presidency with the Majlis.

As the supreme Leader, Khamanei had the final say on national security and foreign relations. In November 2004, he declared that developing, producing, or stockpiling nuclear weapons was forbidden under Islam and in "our Islamic nation." Two years later he reiterated Iran's right to pursue its nuclear program for peaceful purposes despite the United Nation Security Council's demand for Iran to stop enriching uranium. At home he called on the Ahmadinejad government to expedite privatization.

The initial expectation of a change in Washington's policy toward Iran under President Barack Obama (r. 2009–), raised by Obama's promise of a "new beginning," failed to materialize. Following the widespread protest at the disputed reelection of Ahmadinejad in June, he described the public disapproval as "the greatest domestic challenge in 30 years" to the Islamic regime, and authorized singularly severe measures to crush it.

Responding to Washington's success in getting the UN Security Council to impose a series of sanctions against it on the nuclear issue from 2008 onwards, Khamanei hardened his stance. The official policy of continuing with the enrichment of uranium had the backing of the reformist opposition. Under Khamanei's watch, Iran continued to support Hizbullah [q.v.] and Hamas [q.v.] politically and financially. It strengthened ties with China, Russia, Brazil, and Venezuela.

Tensions arose between him and Ahmadinejad when the president attempted to strengthen his office at the expense of the clerical establishment. The result of the parliamentary election in March 2012 showed overwhelming support for the Khamanei camp.

In his Eid al-Fitr [*q.v.*] message in August 2011, Khamanei praised the protest movements in Bahrain, Egypt, Libya, Tunisia, and Yemen, describing the phenomenon as an "Islamic Awakening" [*q.v.*], not an Arab Spring [*q.v.*]. He called on the people of these countries to be vigilant and "not to allow enemies to confiscate the victories they have achieved." Pointedly, he did not include Syria in his list, since the regime of Syrian President Bashar Assad [*q.v.*] continued to maintain the strategic alliance his father, Hafiz Assad [*q.v.*], had forged with Islamic Iran in 1980.

Khamanei is the author of several books on Islam and history.

Khan, Reza: *See* Pahlavi, Reza Shah.

Kharijis: (Arabic: *Khawarij*, singular *Khariji*, meaning *Seceder*): *Islamic sect* During the battle of Siffin on the banks of the Euphrates [*q.v.*] in July 657 A.D. between Ali bin Abu Talib and Muawiya bin Suffian about the succession to the caliphate, Muawiya proposed that he and Ali should settle their differences by referring them to two arbitrators, who would judge the matter according to the Quran [*q.v.*]. While a majority of Ali's forces accepted the proposal, several hundred protested against establishing a human tribunal above the divine word. They withdrew to a nearby village. Over the months their ranks swelled as more of Ali's soldiers deserted, especially after the arbitrators had ruled against Ali in

March 658 A.D. They came to be called *Khawarij*.

They denounced Ali's claim to the caliphate, declaring that that any pious Muslim was worthy of becoming caliph, and did not have to belong either to the household of the Prophet Muhammad or his Quarish tribe. They branded anyone disagreeing with them as an infidel. In July 658 A.D. Ali attacked the Khawarij in their camp at Nahrawan and defeated them. But enough of them survived to continue the Kharaji movement and avenge the deaths of their comrades by Ali's forces. One of them, Abdul Rahman bin Mujlam al-Muradi, fatally stabbed Ali in January 661 A.D. A moderate school of Khawarij, known as Ibadhis [*q.v.*], is predominant in Oman today.

Khatami, Muhammad (1943–): *Iranian politician and scholar; president of Iran, 1997–2005* He was born to Ruhollah and Sakineh Ziayi in Yazd. As his father was a sayyid, a descendant of the Prophet Muhammad, he pursued religious education in Qom [*q.v.*] where he obtained a degree in advanced theology. He then secured degrees in philosophy from Isfahan University and in educational sciences from Tehran University. In Tehran [*q.v.*] he became an active member of the Association of Militant Clergy [*q.v.*]. In 1978 he was sent to Hamburg, Germany, to head the Islamic Center and the associated Shia [*q.v.*] mosque. There he learned English and German.

After the revolution, he was elected to the First Majlis [*q.v.*]. Ayatollah Khomeini appointed him head of the state-owned Kayhan Newspapers. In

1982 he became minister of culture and Islamic guidance in the cabinet of Prime Minister Mir Hussein Musavi [*q.v.*], a position that was confirmed by the two subsequent parliaments. When the conservative-dominated 1992 Majlis objected to his liberal views, he resigned. President Rafsanjani then appointed him an adviser to the presidential office. He also became head of the National Library.

On 23 May (2 Khordad in Iranian calendar [*q.v.*]) 1997, an unprecedented 88 percent of the 33 million electors participated in the presidential election. Of these, 69 percent favored Khatami, and only 25 percent Ali Akbar Nateq Nouri. In general, voters wanted the government to tone down its ideological rhetoric and focus more on tackling such problems as inflation, joblessness, drug addiction, and pollution in cities. In Khatami they saw a potential for a more down-to-earth approach by the authorities. Women and youth voted overwhelmingly for him. The nation's youth perceived in him a mild, tolerant personality, ready to pay attention to their grievances, both social (such as strict segregation of sexes) and economic (such as the dearth of jobs). He advocated freedom and equality for women within an Islamic context. His emphasis on the rule of law appealed especially to the modern middle class. Finally, by having the courage to discuss publicly the role of ethnic and religious minorities—Christians [*q.v.*], Jews l*q.v.*], Zoroastrians l*q.v.*], Azeris l*q.v.*], and Baluchis [*q.v.*]—he won their vote.

At home, his government accorded greater freedoms to citizens. The crisis caused by the student rioting in Tehran in July 1999 brought Khatami and supreme Leader Ali Khamanei [*q.v.*] together. They defused it by a combination of firm action, mobilization of popular support for their regime, and placating of student leaders. Hopes rose when the reformist camp, headed by the left-of-center Islamic Iranian Participation Front [*q.v.*], led by Khatami's younger brother, Muhammad Reza, achieved overwhelming success in the first run of the parliamentary election in February 2000. When Khamanei clamped down on the exuberant reformist press through the judiciary, Khatami did not protest, knowing well that the final authority lay with Khamanei.

Abroad, Khatarni's government mended its fences with the Gulf monarchies as well as Iraq. His hosting of the Islamic Conference Organization [*q.v.*] in December 1997 added to Iran's prestige abroad. His government also normalized relations with the leading European nations.

In the June 2001 presidential election, Khatami won 78 percent of the vote on a lower turnout of 67 percent, with his nearest rival getting a mere 16 percent of the ballots. Khatami was quick to condemn the terrorist attacks on the United States, and his government was glad to see the downfall of the Taliban regime in Afghanistan, with which it nearly went to war in September 1998. Since his administration cooperated with Washington to stabilize post-Taliban Afghanistan after the overthrow of the Taliban in November 2001, Khatami was surprised and disappointed when President George W. Bush included Iran in his "Axis of Evil" in January 2002.

Given the continued resistance by

the conservative judiciary, the pace of political reform at home slowed. At the same time firm oil prices helped Iran's economy. As the United States began its military buildup in the Gulf region, Khatami warned against attacking Iraq. And once the Anglo-American forces had occupied Iraq in April 2003, Khatami demanded that they leave the country.

After stepping down as president in 2005, he founded the International Institute for Dialogue among Cultures and Civilizations with a branch in Geneva. In his worldwide lectures he advocated religious and cultural tolerance. He announced his candidacy in the 2009 presidential election, but withdrew in favor of Mir Hussein Mousavi [*q.v.*] After the disputed re-election of Mahmoud Ahmadinejad [*q.v.*], he called for a referendum on the legitimacy of the government. But he voted in the 2012 parliamentary election, ignoring the call of the Green Movement [*q.v.*] to boycott it.

Fluent in Arabic, English, and German, he is the author of several books, including *Fear of the Wave, From the World of the City to the City of the World, and Faith* and *Thought Trapped by Despotism*.

Khoei, Abol Qasim (1899–1992): *Iraqi Islamic leader* Born into a religious Shia [*q.v.*] family in Khoy, Iranian Azerbaijan [*q.v.*], Khoei migrated along with his parents to Najaf [*q.v.*], Iraq, in 1912. There he pursued his Islamic studies and became an outstanding theological teacher. Settled in Najaf, he rose steadily in the Shia hierarchy, reaching the rank of ayatollah in the mid-1930s. Because of his Iranian origins, Khoei acquired a sub-

stantial following in Iran, where he was represented by his nominees in Qom [*q.v.*] and Mashhad [*q.v.*]. Following the death in 1961 of Ayatollah Muhammad Hussein Borujerdi, the most senior Shia cleric in Iran, Khoei's status rose.

He kept up his teaching and a steady output of books on the Sharia [*q.v.*], religious biography, and Quranic commentary. He belonged to the quietist school among Shia clergy, who wanted to concentrate on providing succor to the community in its spiritual life and social welfare. He thus stood apart from Ayatollah Ruhollah Khomeini [*q.v.*], an Iranian Shia leader who went to live in Najaf in 1965 and urged clerics to get involved in politics.

On the death in 1970 of Ayatollah Muhsin Hakim, the status of *marja-e taqlid* (Arabic/Persian: *source of emulation*) [*q.v.*] passed to Khoei, who also acquired the title of grand ayatollah. His followers now spanned the Shia world, as did the activities of the al-Khoei Foundation.

In the late 1970s he stayed out of the revolutionary movement in Iran. Equally, when Shahbanu Farah, wife of Muhammad Reza Shah Pahlavi [*q.v.*], during her visit to Najaf in November 1978, called on him to make a conciliatory statement, he refused.

Following Iraq's invasion of Iran, President Saddam Hussein [*q.v.*] sought Khoei's approval for his action, but he maintained a studied silence. He did not break it when the Iraqi media claimed in May 1981 that Khoei had prayed for Saddam Hussein's health. The government sharply curtailed the size of his seminary in Najaf and imprisoned many of his students. When in April 1983 it organized the First Popular Islamic Conference in Baghdad [*q.v.*], Khoei and his family spurned the invitation to attend.

After the collapse of the Shia uprising in southern Iraq in the wake of the 1991 Gulf War [*q.v.*], Khoei, then seriously ill, was put under house arrest and coerced into appearing on television with Saddam Hussein. He was then moved to Kufa [*q.v.*], where he died in August 1992. He left behind some 90 books and pamphlets.

Khomeini, Ruhollah Musavi (1902–89): *Iranian religious-political leader: Supreme Leader, 1979–89* Born into a religious Shia [*q.v.*] family in Khomein, Khomeini was educated in theology at a religious school run by Ayatollah Abdul Karim Hairi-Yazdi in Arak. When Hairi-Yazdi moved to Qom [*q.v.*] in 1922, Khomeini went with him. Three years later he graduated in the Sharia [*q.v.*], ethics, and spiritual philosophy. Over the years he related ethical and spiritual problems to contemporary issues and taught his students to regard the addressing of current social problems as part of their religious duty.

In 1941 he published a book in which he attacked secularism. Four years later he graduated to the clerical rank of *hojatalislam* (Arabic: *proof of Islam*), which allowed him to collect his own circle of disciples, who would accept his interpretations of the Sharia. After the death of Ayatollah Muhammad Hussein Borujerdi in 1961, urged by his students, he published a book entitled *Clarification of Points of the Sharia*. It secured him promotion to ayatollah (Arabic: *sign of Allah*). This enabled Khomeini to assume the leadership of radical clergy.

In 1963 he combined his criticism of the White Revolution [*q.v.*] with a personal attack on Muhammad Reza Shah Pahlavi [*q.v.*]. His arrest on 5 June 1963 in Qom triggered a countrywide uprising. The shah used the army to crush it, reportedly causing the death of thousands. Pressured by clerics, the shah released Khomeini two months later and placed him under house arrest in a Tehran [*q.v.*] suburb.

After his release in April 1964, Khomeini resumed his oppositional activities. In November he was expelled to Turkey. After living in the Turkish city of Bursa for a year, he moved to Najaf [*q.v.*], Iraq. From there he kept up his campaign against the shah—an enterprise that the leftist Baathists [*q.v.*], who seized power in Iraq in 1968, found convenient since they too were opposed to the pro-Western shah. In 1971 Khomeini condemned the celebrations of 2500 years of unbroken monarchy in Iran, a claim that lacked historical evidence.

That year his book, *Islamic Government: Rule of the Faqih*, based on a series of lectures, was published. In it he argued that instead of prescribing dos and don'ts for believers and waiting passively for the return of the Hidden Imam, the (Shia) clergy must attempt to oust corrupt officials and repressive regimes and replace them with the ones led by just Islamic jurists. Unhappy at the mistreatment of Shia clerics by the Baathist regime, he sought permission in 1972 to leave for Lebanon, but was denied it.

In 1975 he attacked the inauguration of a single party, the Rastakhiz [*q.v.*], in Iran. His call was taken up by many clergy and theological students. As a result of a rapprochement between Iraq and Iran in the wake of the Algiers Accord [*q.v.*], the number of Iranian pilgrims to Najaf and Karbala [*q.v.*] rose sharply; and this made it easier for Khomeini to guide his followers in their anti-shah campaign through smuggled tape recordings. These audio tapes became all the more important as the revolutionary process, consisting of massive and repeated demonstrations and strikes, gathered momentum through successive stages, from February 1977 to October 1978, when he was exiled to France.

The turning point in the movement had come in January 1978, when a scurrilous attack on him in a Tehran-based pro-government newspaper inflamed popular feelings and placed the initiative in the ongoing struggle firmly with Khomeini. He made astute use of Shia history and Iranian nationalism to engender and intensify anti-royalist militancy among a rapidly growing circle of Iranians. He showed considerable shrewdness in uniting various disparate forces along the most radical demand—the deposition of the shah—and in causing the disintegration of the 413,000-strong military of the regime.

By November 1978, operating from Neuphle-le-Chateau, a Paris suburb, he had put the shah on the defensive, and the economy, crippled by the stoppage of vital oil exports, was in a tailspin. On 13 January 1979, three days before the shah's final departure from Iran, he appointed the Islamic Revolutionary Council (IRC) to facilitate the formation of a provisional government to produce a constitution for an Islamic republic in Iran.

On his return to Tehran on 1 February 1979, Khomeini appointed Mahdi Bazargan [*q.v.*], a member of the IRC, as prime minister. Following a referendum, based on universal suffrage, he announced the establishment of the Islamic Republic of Iran on 1 April. In August an elected Assembly of Experts (1979) [*q.v.*] debated the draft constitution, which incorporated the principle that Islamic jurisprudents would provide the leadership of the republic. Khomeini was named *marja-e taqlid* (Arabic: *source of emulation*) [*q.v.*], leading mujtahid [*q.v.*], and the (Supreme) Leader.

He first isolated and then repressed all non-Islamic forces that had backed the revolutionary movement. He was equally hostile to the Mujahedin-e Khalq [*q.v.*], which combined Islam [*q.v.*] with Marxism. He turned against President Abol Hassan Bani-Sadr [*q.v.*] when the latter tried to foster a constituency outside the Khomenist circles. Having brought about Bani-Sadr's dismissal, constitutionally, Khomeini endorsed only those candidates for the presidency— Muhammad Ali Rajai [*q.v.*] and Ali Husseini Khamanei [*q.v.*]—who were his proven acolytes.

In the early crisis-ridden years of the Islamic Republic, he provided strong leadership and showed ruthlessness in crushing opposition, bent on either staging a military coup against the regime (the monarchist strategy) or triggering a civil war (the Mujahedin-e Khalq strategy).

Convinced that Iran could never be truly independent until it had excised American influence from all walks of

Iranian life, he kept up his campaign against the United States, the prime source to him of moral corruption and imperialist domination, describing it routinely as the "Great Satan." He was pleased when, following the storming of the U.S. Embassy in Tehran in November 1979 and the taking of diplomats as hostages, Washington cut off its diplomatic links with Iran. By refusing to sanction the release of the American diplomats before the U.S. presidential election in November 1980, Khomeini highlighted the weakness of President Jimmy Carter, thereby drastically reducing his chance of reelection.

Khomeini was incensed when neither the United Nations nor the Islamic Conference Organization (ICO) [*q.v.*] condemned Iraq's invasion of Iran in September 1980. However, Iraq's aggression helped him to rally Iranians on a patriotic platform, and make his fractious supporters sink their differences on how to run the country, especially the economy. Conscious of the cementing effect of the Iran-Iraq War [*q.v.*], he repeatedly rejected offers of mediation and a cease-fire.

His attempts to export Islamic revolution to the neighboring countries failed. The Gulf monarchs, all Sunni [*q.v.*], managed to sideline Khomini by successfully portraying him as a Shia leader of a non-Arab country. The only success he had in this regard was among the Shias of Lebanon. At home he managed to keep together the moderates and radicals within the ruling establishment by intermittently favoring one side and then the other. When he realized that the governing Islamic Republican Party (IRP) [*q.v.*]

had become incurably faction-ridden, he ordered its disbandment in 1987.

His radicalism did not blind him to reality. The military setbacks suffered by Iran in its war with Iraq in the spring of 1988 made him realize that, if he did not stop fighting, the Islamic Republic would disintegrate. That led him to accept the U.N.-brokered cease-fire in July 1988. Nonetheless this was a bitter blow, described by him as "taking poison." He died within a year of taking that decision—on 3 June 1989. He left behind an Iran with its territorial integrity intact, its Islamic regime well-entrenched, but its economy shattered.

Khouri, Bishara (1890–1964): *Lebanese politician, president 1943–52* Born into a Maronite [*q.v.*] family in Beirut [*q.v.*], Khouri went to Paris to pursue his law studies. Returning home in 1911, he set up a legal practice. It was interrupted by World War I, when he left for Egypt. After returning to Beirut in 1919, he briefly practiced as a lawyer, and then joined the judicial system, becoming a judge in 1923.

When the republican constitution went into effect under the French Mandate in 1927, Khouri was named interior minister, and then promoted to prime minister (1927–29). In 1932, when he was about to succeed Charles Debbas as president, the French suspended the constitution. This turned him into a nationalist. He demanded a return to the constitution. When this happened in 1936, he ran for the presidency but lost to Emile Edde by a thin margin. The constitution was suspended again by the pro-German government of France, based in Vichy, which assumed power in 1940. It was only after the Vichy forces were defeated by the Allies in Lebanon that the Free French reinstated the constitution.

He led the Christian [*q.v.*] camp in its dispute with the Muslim [*q.v.*] camp about sharing parliamentary seats. After the matter had been settled with the National Pact [*q.v.*] in March 1943, and approved by the Free French government, Khouri was elected president, unopposed, in September for a six-year term. Before the end of his office he instigated an amendment to the constitution to allow a second presidential term. This proved controversial, especially when it followed widespread charges of poll-rigging in the 1947 parliamentary election. It inspired a concerted campaign by the opposition, which accused him of corruption. Unable to withstand rising popular pressure, he resigned in September 1952, midway through his second term.

At home he co-opted urban Muslim leaders in administering the state; he aligned his foreign policies with those of the Arab hinterland, and participated in the Palestine War (1948–49) [*q.v.*].

khums (Arabic: *one-fifth*): *religious tithe applicable to Shia Muslims* One of the several duties incumbent upon Shias [*q.v.*], *khums*, amounting to one-fifth of a believer's trading profits, should be used for charitable purposes. Often a Shia hands over this amount to his *marja-e taqlid* (Arabic: *source of emulation*) [*q.v.*], a leading *mujtahid* [*q.v.*] whose interpretations of the Sharia [*q.v.*] he has agreed to accept, and who uses these sums for social welfare.

kibbutzim (Hebrew: *communes*; singular, *kibbutz*): *rural communes in Palestine/Israel* Kibbutz is the term used for a settlement centered on a village and based on communal ownership of the means of production, with each member supplied with his/her personal needs. Sometimes the term *kvutzah* (plural, *kvutzot*) is used. Early Zionists [*q.v.*] thought collective or cooperative settlements to be the best way to reclaim Palestine [*q.v.*], and they established the first kibbutz in 1909 during the second *aliya* (1904–14), a wave of migration into Palestine. In the course of the third *aliya* (1919–23) collectivism became popular within the labor movement. During the subsequent *aliya* (1924–31) there was a split in the kibbutz movement, with the moderates being prepared to coexist with an expanding private sector and the radicals resolving to establish a countrywide commune.

Initially most of these settlements were affiliated to a federation called the *Kibbutz Muhad* (Hebrew: *United Kibbutz*), which was controlled by Mapai [*q.v.*]. But in 1927, with the formation of *HaShomer Hatzair* (Hebrew: *The Young Guard*), a revolutionary socialist group, nearly half of the kibbutzim affiliated to the left-wing federation called *Kibbutz Artzi* (Hebrew: *Countrywide Kibbutz*). At the end of the fifth *aliya* (1932–40), some 25,000 Jews, forming about 5 percent of the Jewish population, lived in kibbutizm or kvutzot.

During World War II many of their members joined the Jewish units of the British army. When Haganah [*q.v.*] decided to form the elite

Palmah [*q.v.*] units, the Kibbutz Muhad helped with the project.

After the founding of Israel in May 1948 the importance of kibbutzim in absorbing new arrivals declined sharply. In 1949 the concept of combining collectivism with military defense was realized in *Nahal* (acronym of *Noar Halutzi Lohem*; Hebrew: *Fighting Pioneer Youth*) settlements. The first Nahal settlement in Upper Galilee in 1951 was followed by many others in the border areas. In 1967 the Kibbutz Artzi, with 28,800 members on 76 settlements, became the largest kibbutz federation, followed by *Ihud HaKvutzot HaKibbutzim* (Hebrew: *The Union of Kvutzot and Kibbutzim*), with 25,300 members in 76 settlements, and the *Kibbutz Muhad*, with 22,800 members in 58 settlements.

After the economic boom of 1968, labor shortages in Israel led many kibbutzim to break with the past and employ Arab [*q.v.*] labor. The number of kibbutzim fell from 300 in 1976 to about 250 in 1993, when, housing only 2.5 percent of Israel's population, they produced 40 percent of its agricultural and 8 percent of its industrial output. These figures declined further during the 1990s.

In 2010, nearly 127,000 Israelis, forming 1.6 percent of the population, lived on 270 kibbutzim, producing nearly 40 percent of the nation's agricultural output and 9 percent of its industrial output.

King-Crane Commission (1919): *U.S. commission on the Middle East* Pursuing the self-determination doctrine he had been advocating, U.S. President Woodrow Wilson, at the Paris Peace Conference of the Council of Four in March 1919, proposed that an Allied Commission on Mandates in (Ottoman) Turkey—consisting of American, British, French, and Italian members—be sent to the Middle East [*q.v.*] to consult the inhabitants on their political future. The Peace Conference endorsed the idea. But since the French were really against it, and the British were at best lukewarm, three of the four Allied members soon withdrew from the Commission. As a result only the U.S. appointees (Dr Henri King, president of Oberlin College, Ohio, and Charles Crane, a businessman interested in Christian missions in the Middle East) left for the region in May.

King and Crane received numerous petitions from varied quarters, and interviewed all political leaders in Syria and Palestine [*q.v.*]. In their report, submitted in August, they concluded that an overwhelming majority, while opposed to the concept of Mandate, agreed that there was a need for foreign assistance, provided it came from the United States or, as a second alternative, Britain. They recommended a single Mandate for a United Syria consisting of Syria and Palestine, provided the Mandate was for a limited period and its holder did not act as a colonial power. They further recommended that Faisal bin Hussein [*q.v.*] should become king of United Syria and that Iraq should have an Arab monarch.

While sympathizing with Zionist aspirations and plans, they concluded that the "extreme Zionist program must be greatly modified if the civil and religious rights of the non-Jewish inhabitants of Palestine are to be protected in accordance with the terms of the Balfour Declaration [*q.v.*]." After discussions with Zionist leaders in Jerusalem [*q.v.*] they had concluded that "the Zionists [*q.v.*] looked forward to a practically complete dispossession of the present non-Jewish inhabitants of Palestine, by various forms of purchase." They therefore recommended that "Jewish immigration should be definitely limited and the project of making Palestine a distinctly Jewish commonwealth should be given up. There would then be no reason why Palestine could not be included in a united Syrian state." Britain and France ignored the report.

Since the U.S. withdrew from the Peace Conference in December 1919—a preamble to its refusal to join the League of Nations, which was formed the following month—the report lost its importance. It was not until December 1922 that it was published unofficially.

Knesset (Hebrew: *Assembly*): *Parliament of Israel* The Knesset and government of Israel evolved out of the People's Council, which was formed according to a joint decision by the National Council of the Jewish Community in Palestine and the Executive Committee of the Jewish Agency [*q.v.*] on 1 March 1948. The People's Council's 37 members, appointed on 15 April 1948, came from the National Council of the Jewish Community, the Jewish Agency Executive Committee, and other groups not represented in either of these bodies. Of these 13 were chosen to form the People's Administration.

On 15 May 1948, the end of the British Mandate in Palestine, the People's Council became the Provisional State Council, and the People's Administration the provisional government of the State of Israel. The Provisional State Council passed a law for the election of 120 members to the Constituent Assembly. Following this election in January 1949, the Constituent Assembly adopted a Transition Law, which specified a unicameral parliament, to be called the Knesset, of 120 deputies, elected by universal suffrage using a proportional representation system, with the whole country forming a single constituency and the election threshold at 1 percent. The Constituent Assembly then transformed itself into the First Knesset.

It was not until 1958 that the "Basic Law: the Knesset" was passed. It gave the Knesset the same powers as exercised by the British parliament, i.e., the Knesset is sovereign, and its authority in legislative and other affairs is unlimited. Its tenure is four years, but it can dissolve itself before that. No quorum is needed. It elects the state president (a constitutional head) for a five-year term by a simple majority of those present and voting. The president invites the leader of the largest group in the Knesset to form a government. Once he or she has succeeded in doing so, with himself/herself as the prime minister, and secured a vote of confidence in the Knesset, the cabinet is sworn in within a week. Starting with the 1992 Knesset election, the election threshold was raised to 1.5 percent with a view to reducing political parties. When this did not happen, the Knesset passed a law mandating direct election for the prime minister, who then cobbled together a coalition government. The first such election took place in 1996 along with the one for the Knesset, with the second such set of elections held in 1999. There was no decrease in the number of groups winning parliamentary seats. In 2001, however, there was only the prime ministerial contest, the last such exercise. In 2003 the electoral system reverted to the old arrangement with the election threshold raised from 1.5 percent to 2 percent.

Komala-e Jaan-e Kordestan (Kurdish: *Association of Revival of Kurdistan*): *Kurdish Organization in Iran*
During the Soviet occupation of northern Iran (1941–46), nationalist Kurds secretly established the Komala-e Jaan-e Kordestan, often called Komala, in 1943 in Mahabad. It had the support of the Soviet forces. Following the founding of the Kurdish Democratic Party (KDP) [*q.v.*] in 1945, Komala members joined it after dissolving their group. It was revived as the Kurdish wing of the Communist Party of Iran (Marxist-Leninist) in 1969.

Under the leadership of Jaafar Shafii it participated in the 1977–78 revolutionary movement. In its strongholds in the northern Kurdish area it seized power through Revolutionary Komitehs [*q.v.*]. After the 1979 revolution it allied with the KDP and the followers of Shaikh Izz al-Din Husseini, a Mahabad-based Sunni [*q.v.*] religious leader, and demanded autonomy for the Kurds. When this was rejected by the Islamic regime in Tehran [*q.v.*], it took up arms against it. Government persecution followed.

In the confrontation between Ayatollah Ruhollah Khomeini [*q.v.*] and President Abol Hassan Bani-Sadr [*q.v.*] in 1981, it sided with the latter. It then joined the National Resistance Council [*q.v.*]. As the Iran-Iraq War (1980–88) [*q.v.*] dragged on, Komala started to cooperate with Iraq. Therefore, Iran often combined its offensives against Iraq in the northern sector with attacks on Komala strongholds. After the war Komala merged into the Communist Party of Iran, and became the Kordestan Organization of the Communist Party of Iran (KOCPI). Following the 1991 Gulf War [*q.v.*], it moved its base to Iraqi Kurdistan near Suleimaniyah, then administered by the Patriotic Union of Kurdistan (PUK) [*q.v.*]. But, once the PUK had decided on repairing its strained relations with Iran in September 1996 after suffering a humiliating defeat by the rival Kurdistan Democratic Party [*q.v.*], the KOPCI lost its base in Iraq—and with it any importance it had.

Koran: *See* Quran.

Kordestan (Iran): *See* Kurdistan (Iran).

Kordestan Democratic Party of Iran: *See* Kurdistan Democratic Party of Iran.

Kufa: *Iraqi town* Population: 110,000 (2011 est.) Situated north of Najaf [*q.v.*], Kufa lies along the banks of the Euphrates [*q.v.*] and has a history dating back to antiquity. A military base of Muslim [*q.v.*] Arabs [*q.v.*] in Mesopotamia [*q.v.*], Kufa grew in importance during early Islam [*q.v.*]. It was a center of rebellion against Caliph Othman (r. 644–656 A.D.), and a bastion of support for Ali bin

Abu Talib in his struggle for the caliphate against Muwaiya bin Abu Sufian, which led to the battle of Siffin. It was in the main mosque of Kufa that Ali bin Abu Talib was assassinated in 661 A.D.

It remained a leading political-military center until 750 A.D. when it turned into a cultural center. This lasted for a century, during which it nurtured such scholars as Abu Hanifa al-Numan (d. 767 A.D.), the founder of the Hanafi Code [*q.v.*]. It then became the cradle of Shia Islam [*q.v.*] for the next century. With the emergence of Najaf and Karbala [*q.v.*] as leading Shia holy shrines, the religious significance of Kufa declined. But the importance of its Great Mosque remained undiminished.

During the Baathist rule of Iraq (1968–2003), Grand Ayatollah Muhammad Baqir al-Sadr often delivered his Friday prayer sermon at the town's Great Mosque, demanding the release of Shia political prisoners and religious freedom. After the Anglo-American invasion of Iraq in 2003 [*q.v.*], this mosque became the bastion of the followers of Muqtada al-Sadr [*q.v.*].

Kurdish Democratic Party (Iraq): *See* Kurdistan Democratic Party (Iraq).

Kurdish language: The language of Kurds [*q.v.*], Kurdish is part of the Iranian branch of the Indo-Iranian subfamily of the Eastern/Satem division of the Indo-European languages. Spoken in Kurdistan [*q.v.*], its northern dialect is called Kermanji and the southern Surani, the latter being the literary form of the language. It is written in Arabic script using the Per-

sian alphabet. In the Soviet Republic of Armenia, a modified version of the Cyrillic script was used for Kurdish.

Kurdish Republic of Mahabad (1945–46): *See* Kurdistan Republic (1945–46).

Kurdish Revolutionary Party (Iraq): *a breakaway group of the Kurdistan Democratic Party* The Kurdish Revolutionary Party (KRP) was formed in 1964 in protest against the authoritarian leadership of Mustafa Barzani [*q.v.*]. After the agreement of the Kurdistan Democratic Party (KDP) with Baghdad in 1970, many KRP members returned to the parent body. But when the KDP failed to join the institutions inaugurated by the 1970 accord, there was a reverse flow led by Obeidallah Barzani, a son of Mustafa. The KRP had by then joined the National Progressive and Patriotic Front [*q.v.*], which collapsed after the Anglo-American invasion of Iraq in 2003 [*q.v.*].

Kurdistan (Kurdish/Persian: *Place of Kurds*): Geographically, Kurdistan means the Kurdish-majority region in southwest Asia. It covers about 193,000 sq. mi./500,000 sq. km spread over northwestern Iran, northern Iraq, the northeastern corner of Syria, southeastern Turkey, the Nakhichevan enclave of Azerbaijan, and southern Armenia. The estimated number of Kurds living in these countries in 2011 was 28 million: Turkey, 15 million; Iraq, 6 million; Iran, 5.3 million; Syria 1.4 million; and Azerbaijan and Armenia, 0.3 million.

Kurdistan (Iran): *Iranian province* (Also spelled Kordestan) Area 9652 sq. mi./24,998 sq. km; population, 1.574

million (2006 census). Established in 1961, Kurdistan is bordered by West Azerbaijan to its north, Gilan and Hamdan to its east, Kerman to its south, and Iraq to its west. Its population is predominantly Kurdish.

Kurdistan Autonomous Region

(Iraq): Area 14,923 sq. mi./38,650 sq. km; population, 4.9 million (2011 est.). An agreement between the Kurdistan Democratic Party (KDP) [q.v.] and the Iraqi government in March 1970 led to a Kurdistan Autonomous Region (KAR) being inaugurated four years later. Consisting of three Kurdish-majority governorates of Dohak, Irbil, and Suleimaniyah in the north-northwest, it had an 80-member Legislative Council and an Executive Council. The legislative deputies are elected, but the Executive Council members and chairman were appointed by the central government in Baghdad [q.v.]. Elections to the Legislative Council were held in September 1980, August 1986, and September 1989.

Kurdish [q.v.] was the official language for administration and education, and Arabic [q.v.] was the compulsory language in schools.

After the 1991 Gulf War [q.v.] the Baghdad government was deprived by the actions of the United States, Britain, and France (including the imposition of "no fly" restrictions) of its control of the KAR, which began to function as a semi-independent entity. Fresh elections in May 1992 led to the sharing of power by the Kurdistan Democratic Party [q.v.] and the Patriotic Union of Kurdistan [q.v.], with the new government adopting its own flag. The power-sharing arrangement

broke down after two years, and the American plan to develop the region as the springboard for overthrowing the Baathist regime was scuttled in 1996. Following the general election in 1996, the region split into two, with one part ruled by the KDP and the other by the PUK.

In the post-Saddam Hussein [q.v.] era, the KDP and the PUK formed a coalition, along with smaller parties, called the Democratic Patriotic Alliance of Kurdistan. In the January 2005 elections the Alliance won 104 of the 111 seats in the parliament. These deputies elected Masoud Barzani [q.v.] as president of the autonomous region now renamed Iraqi Kurdistan. It maintained its own armed forces. After the December 2005 elections held under the new national constitution, Nechirvan Idris Barzani of the KDP became the prime minister. His cabinet's unilateral decision to sign oil prospecting and extracting contracts with foreign companies was questioned by the central government in Baghdad, and created tensions. In 2007 the Kurdistan Regional Government established its lobbying office in Washington.

In the July 2009 election for the regional Assembly, the KDP-PUK alliance, now called the Kurdistan List, won only 59 seats because of the widespread perception of corruption in the coalition government, with the opposition Change party gaining 25, and Service and Reform alliance 13, followed by the Islamic movement's two—with 11 seats reserved for ethnic minorities parties: Turkmen [q.v.], 5; Assyrian Christians [q.v.], 5; and Armenian [q.v.], 1. In the presidential contest on the basis of popular vote,

Masoud Barzani won 70 percent of the ballots. *See also* Kurds (Iraq), Kurdistan Democratic Party, and Patriotic Union of Kurdistan.

Kurdistan Democratic Party (Iraq):

(Official Kurdish title, *Partiya Demokrata Kurdistan*) In the interregnum between the demise of the Kurdish Republic of Mahabad [*q.v.*] in December 1946 and his crossing into the Soviet Union from Iran in June 1947, Mustafa Barzani [*q.v.*] set the guidelines for an Iraq-based Kurdish Democratic Party (KDP) [*q.v.*]. Inspired by Marxism-Leninism, it would dedicate itself to liberating Iraq from foreign imperialism and domestic reaction, and would fight for Kurdish autonomy within Iraq.

After the July 1958 revolution, Barzani was allowed to return home. He backed the new regime under Abdul Karim Qasim [*q.v.*], who legalized the KDP. The KDP renamed itself the Kurdistan Democratic Party (KDP) in 1959. But when Barzani advanced a plan for Kurdish autonomy, Qasim rejected it. In September 1961 he mounted an offensive against the strongholds of the KDP. During the subsequent years, despite changes in the regimes in Baghdad [*q.v.*], relations between the central government and the KDP remained poor.

In March 1969 the KDP resumed its armed struggle against the central government, now run by the Baath Party [*q.v.*]. The fighting ended a year later with an accord that was to be implemented over a four-year period. It conceded to several of the KDP's demands, including recognition of Kurdish ethnicity on a par with Arab [*q.v.*], and the official use of Kurdish

[*q.v.*] in Kurdish-majority areas. But due to mistrust on both sides, the pact failed to hold.

After March 1974, when the government created the promised Kurdistan Autonomous Region (KAR) [*q.v.*], the KDP went on a warpath. Fighting ensued anew. This time the KDP had the backing of Iran's Muhammad Reza Shah Pahlavi [*q.v.*], who wanted to weaken the pro-Moscow regime in Iraq. By early 1975 four-fifths of Iraq's 100,000 troops and nearly half of its 1,390 tanks were pinned down by 45,000 Kurdish guerrillas. The conflict threatened to escalate into a full-scale war between Iran and Iraq. To avert this, the two countries signed the Algiers Accord [*q.v.*], which resulted in Iran's stopping military and logistical aid to the KDP. Barzani escaped to Iran.

The KDP leadership passed on to Barzani's sons, Idris and Masoud [*q.v.*]. When they moved into Iran after the 1979 Islamic revolution [*q.v.*], Teheran began to provide them with aid. The outbreak of the Iran-Iraq War [*q.v.*] in 1980 compelled Baghdad to reduce its troops in the Kurdish areas. This led to an expansion in the Iraqi border area under KDP control. The KDP began to increase its cooperation with Iran. With the death of Idris Barzani in 1987, Masoud became the KDP's sole leader. During the Iran-Iraq War it set up liberated zones, totaling 4,000 square mi./10,360 sq. km, along the Iraqi border with Iran. In retaliation, in February 1988 Iraqi President Saddam Hussein [*q.v.*] unleashed a seven-month-long campaign of vengeance against KDP strongholds that affected 3,800 villages, and reclaimed the lost area.

KDP leaders escaped to Iran or

Syria, but during the crisis created by Iraq's occupation of Kuwait in August 1990, which drew most of the Iraqi troops away from the KAR, they returned to the region. When Iraq was defeated in the 1991 Gulf War [*q.v.*], Masoud Barzani led a Kurdish rebellion against Baghdad. Its suppression caused a massive exodus of Kurds into Turkey and Iran, and the intervention of the Unites States-led anti-Iraq coalition.

Barzani's subsequent talks with Baghdad failed. Protected by the air forces of the U.S., Britain, and France, the KDP along with other Kurdish parties, held Legislative Council elections in May 1992. The KDP, commanding 25,000 troops and backed by 30,000 militiamen, shared power equally with the Patriotic Union of Kurdistan (PUK) [*q.v.*]. Two years later the arrangement broke down, with KDP and PUK partisans clashing violently. To reduce the PUK's area of control, the KDP began to ally itself with the Islamic Movement of Kurdistan.

Yet the traditional rivalry between the two parties continued. In May 1994 intra-Kurdish clashes left over 1,000 people dead. It was not until six months later that, assisted by mediators, Barzani worked out a modus vivendi with Talabani. But Barzani's relations with his rival soured again when their two factions took opposite positions in the anti-Saddam coup plans in March 1995. With this, Kurdistan divided into two hostile zones. By September, Barzani's jurisdiction was reduced to a third of the region. But with the illicit Iraqi oil supplies passing through his territory, providing hefty customs duties, Barzani had much cash, part of which he used to

buy arms and ammunition, some of them from Saddam Hussein.

Talabani's rapprochement with Iran upset both Barzani and Saddam Hussein. When Talabani, freshly armed with Iranian-supplied weapons, attacked KDP's positions in August 1996, Barzani appealed to Saddam for military assistance to retake Irbil [*q.v.*] from Talabani. Saddam obliged. Barzani captured not only Irbil but all of Talabani's territory, only to lose all except Irbil when Talabani, armed by Iran, counterattacked.

The unprecedented intra-Kurdish violence undermined the American strategy of developing Kurdistan as the base for overthrowing Saddam. The U.S. withdrew its agents and funds from the area. Washington's efforts to conciliate the two rivals were successful only partially because Barzani refused to share the large customs duties he collected on the illicit export of Iraqi oil to Turkey. After the passage of the Iraq Liberation Act by U.S. Congress in 1998, he found the KDP certified as a faction that was entitled to Washington's military aid.

When, after defeating the Taliban regime in Afghanistan in December 2001, the U.S. administration of President George W. Bush turned its attention to ousting Saddam's government by force, the importance of Barzani as well as Talabani rose. The KDP cooperated actively with the invading Anglo-American invasion of Iraq in March 2003.

In the post-Saddam Hussein period, it became an integral part of the successive government that followed, with one its leaders, Hoshyar Zebari, becoming foreign minister in 2003 in the Iraqi Governing Council and then all the subsequent governments. Barzani was elected president of the Kurdistan Autonomous Region in 2005, and reelected four years later. *See also* Masoud Barzani and Kurdistan Autonomous Region (Iraq)

Kurdistan Democratic Party of Iran: *Iranian political party* In September 1945, when Iran's Kurdish region was under Soviet occupation, the Kurdish Democratic Party (KDP) (Kurdish: *Hizbi Demokirati Kurdistani Iran*) was established in Mahabad by Qazi Muhammad, who had led an autonomous local council since 1941. The KDP demanded autonomy for the Kurds within Iran. Three months later it founded the State of Republic of Kurdistan/Kordestan (Kurdish: *Dawlat-e Jumhouri-ye Kurdistan*), popularly known as the the National Government of Kordestan (Kurdish: *Hukumat-e Milli Kurdistan*) and often labeled by outsiders as the Kurdish Republic of Mahabad. Qazi Muhammad was appointed president. The republic lasted a year before being overthrown by the forces of Muhammad Reza Shah Pahlavi [*q.v.*] after the Soviet withdrawal in May 1946. The KDP went underground.

With a mild revival of armed resistance against the shah in the early 1970s, the party, now renamed the Kordestan Democratic Party of Iran (KDPI), began to flex its muscles. A complicating factor entered the equation when the shah began to arm Kurdish autonomists in Iraq in 1973–74, a policy that ended with the Algiers Accord [*q.v.*] of 1975.

The KDPI participated in the revolutionary movement of 1977–78, when local power was seized in north-

ern Kurdish areas by the Revolutionary Komitehs [*q.v.*], composed of the followers of Shaikh Izz al-Din Husseini, a Mahabad-based Sunni [*q.v.*] religious leader, and KDPI members.

After the revolution, when the central government, led by Ayatollah Ruhollah Khomeini [*q.v.*], tried to establish control in the Kurdish areas, the KDPI resisted. At its congress in April 1980 the KDPI demanded the use of the Kurdish language [*q.v.*] in schools, offices, and courts, and the redrawing of provincial borders to include all Kurds in one province. Efforts to reach a compromise with Tehran failed, and fighting broke out between the two sides.

The Iraqi invasion of Iran in September 1980 helped Khomeini in that it created a surge of nationalism in which ethnic differences were forgotten, for the time being. The KDPI backed President Abol Hassan Bani-Sadr [*q.v.*] in his confrontation with Khomeini in June 1981, and lost. Later both the KDPI and Komala [*q.v.*] joined the National Resistance Council [*q.v.*], headed by Bani-Sadr and Masoud Rajavi [*q.v.*].

As the Iran-Iraq War (1980–88) [*q.v.*] dragged on, the KDPI began to side with Iraq. Its leader, Abdul Rahman Qasimlou, tried to reconcile Baghdad with its Kurdish nationalists, and managed to get the central government and Jalal Talabani [*q.v.*] of the Patriotic Union of Kurdistan [*q.v.*] to negotiate in 1984–85. The talks failed. After the war, Talabani brokered a meeting between Qasimlou and Iranian officials in Vienna, Austria, in the autumn of 1989. Qasimlou was assassinated in Vienna, allegedly by Iranian agents. But the KDPI, having a 10,000-strong militia, withstood the shock.

Following the establishment of the no-fly zones in northern Iraq by America and Britain in late 1991, the Iraqi PUK began providing refuge to the KDPI forces, with their headquarters in the Iraqi border town of Qala Diza. They made a point of killing the personnel of Iran's Revolutionary Guard Corps, which in turn hit back. It was against this background that KDPI chief Sadiq Sharaf-Kindi and his three colleagues were murdered at a restaurant in Berlin in September 1992 by Kazem Darabi, an Iranian intelligence agent and his four Lebanese cohorts.

Tension between the KDPI and Iran rose sharply after Washington's adoption of the Dual Containment policy [q.v.] in May 1993. This continued until the summer of 1996 when Talabani reached a rapprochement with Tehran in order to get even with the rival Kurdistan Democratic Party [q.v.] of Masoud Barzani [q.v.]. The Iranian forces then captured the KDPI stronghold inside Iraqi Kurdistan at Koy Sanjak, delivering an almost fatal blow to the group by reducing its fighting force to about 1,500.

It remained a member of the National Resistance Council. After the disputed presidential election in June 2009, its supporters joined a one-day protest strike in the Kurdish areas of Iran.

Kurdistan Republic (1945–46): Official title: State of Republic of Kurdistan (Kurdish: *Dawlat-e Jumhouri-ye Kurdistan*), popularly known as the National Government of Kurdistan (Kurdish: *Hukumat-e Milli Kurdistan*). It was formed in December 1945 by the Kurdish Democratic Party [q.v.], with Qazi Muhammad as its president and Mustafa Barzani [q.v.] as its commander-in-chief. Its capital was Mahabad. Kurdish [q.v.] became the official language in the government and schools, and the Iranian imperial army was replaced by a national army. The republic was overthrown by the forces of Tehran in December 1946, seven months after the Soviet troops, stationed in the area since August 1941, had withdrawn.

Kurds: Kurds are members of an ethnic group that inhabit the Zagros and Taurus Mountains of southeastern Turkey, northwestern Iran, northern Iraq, and the adjacent areas in Syria and Nakhichevan. Descendants of Indo-European tribes, they appear in the history of the early empires of Mesopotamia [q.v.], where they are described as "Kardouchoi." They trace their distinct history as mountain people to the seventh century B.C., and this has been substantiated by recent excavations at Saaqez in Iran. These show Saaqez as the capital of a Kurdish region that was part of the Scythian Empire, from the ninth to the third century B.C. It was not until the seventh century A.D. that they embraced Islam [q.v.]. Like Persians, who also embraced Islam, they retained their language, but unlike them they remained predominantly Sunni [q.v.].

The Kurdish general, Salah al-Din (Saladin) Ayubi, overpowered the Shia [q.v.] Fatimid dynasty in Egypt and established the Ayubid dynasty (1169–1250). During the Ottoman and Persian Empires there were periodic uprisings by Kurds against the central power. Kurdish nationalism manifested itself in the late 19th century inter alia in the publication of the first periodical in Kurdish (1897). Because the Treaty of Sèvres (1920) [q.v.], which specified an autonomous Kurdistan, was not ratified, and because the subsequent Treaty of Lausanne (1923) [q.v.] made no mention of it, the aspirations of Kurdish nationalists remained unfulfilled. *See also* Kurds in Iran, Kurds in Iraq, and Kurds in Syria.

Kurds in Iran: Nationally, Kurds make up about 7 percent of the Iranian population of 75 million. They are predominant in Kurdistan [q.v.] and are a substantial community in the provinces of East Azerbaijan (population, 3.62 million), West Azerbaijan (population, 2.95 million), Kerman (population, 2.66 million), and Ilam (population, 0.55 million). During the rule of the Pahlavi dynasty [q.v.], the teaching of Kurdish in schools was banned. *See also* Komala and Kurdistan Democratic Party (Iran).

Kurds in Iraq: Nationally, Kurds [q.v.] account for 18 percent of the Iraqi population. Of the 6 million Kurds in the country in 2011, nearly two-thirds were in the Kurdistan Autonomous Region [q.v.]. By amalgamating (in December 1925) the predominantly Kurdish province of Mosul, which was part of Turkey before World War I, with Baghdad and Basra (former provinces of Mesopotamia [q.v.]) to create modern Iraq, the British unwittingly engendered a Kurdish problem for the enlarged country. In 1927 the importance of Mosul province rose

sharply when a British-dominated company struck oil near Kirkuk.

During World War II, Mustafa Barzani [q.v.] led a failed rebellion. He fled to Iran, and later to the Soviet Union. Following the 1958 coup in Iraq, he returned home and backed the new republican regime. In exchange Baghdad legalized the Kurdistan Democratic Party (KDP) [q.v.] and promulgated a constitution that stated: "Arabs and Kurds are associated in this nation." But when Barzani advanced an autonomy plan, Baghdad rejected it. Fighting broke out between the two sides in September 1961 and continued until June 1966, when an agreement granted official recognition of the Kurdish language [q.v.] and proportional representation of Kurds in the civil service.

However, the accord failed to dissipate mutual mistrust. In March 1969 the KDP resumed its armed struggle against the central government, now run by the Baath Party [q.v.]. The fighting ended a year later with an accord that was to be implemented over the next four years. The constitution of July 1970 recognized Kurds as one of the two nationalities of Iraq, and Kurdish as one of the two languages in the Kurdish region. But once again the agreement failed to hold.

Ignoring the non-cooperation of the KDP, the Baghdad government enforced the Kurdish autonomy law in March 1974, including the appointment of a Kurd, Taha Muhyi al-Din Maruf, a diplomat, as a vice president of the republic; the formation of the Kurdistan Autonomous Region (KAR) [q.v.], comprising the provinces of Dohak, Irbil, and Suleimaniyah; and establishment of the (largely nominated) Kurdistan Legislative Council.

Fighting erupted again. This time the KDP had the active backing of Iran's Muhammad Reza Shah Pahlavi [q.v.], who wanted to weaken the pro-Moscow regime in Baghdad. At one point the KDP controlled a third of the KAR, and its 45,000 guerrillas pinned down four-fifths of Iraq's 100,000 troops and nearly half of its 1,390 tanks. The conflict resulted in 60,000 civilian and military casualties, the destruction of 40,000 homes in 700 villages, and 300,000 refugees. To avert the danger of the conflict escalating into a full-scale war between Iran and Iraq, the two countries signed the Algiers Accord [q.v.] in March 1975, which resulted in Iran's cutting off military and logistical aid to the KDP. Barzani escaped to Iran.

During the 1980–88 Iran-Iraq War [q.v.] the activities of the Kurdish insurgents, allied with Tehran, compelled Iraq to deploy divisions in the north to the detriment of its war effort elsewhere. Taking advantage of the pressure of war on Baghdad, the KDP (now led by Masoud Barzani [q.v.]) and the Patriotic Union of Kurdistan (PUK) [q.v.], headed by Jalal Talabani [q.v.], set up liberated zones along the borders with Iran and Turkey. Starting in February 1988, Iraqi President Saddam Hussein [q.v.] unleashed a seven-month campaign of vengeance against KDP strongholds, involving the use of chemical weapons and affecting 3,800 villages. He reclaimed the area that had been lost to the insurgents, and the Kurdish leaders escaped to Iran or Syria.

During the crisis created by Iraq's occupation of Kuwait in August 1990,

which drew most of the troops away from the KAR, the KDP leaders returned to Kurdistan. After Iraq's defeat in the 1991 Gulf War [q.v.], the Kurdish nationalists persuaded the 100,000-strong local Iraqi army auxiliary force, made up of Kurds, to change sides. Within a week the rebels controlled the KAR and large parts of the oil-rich province of Tamim, including its capital, Kirkuk. In late March a government counterattack reversed the situation, causing an exodus of 1.5 million Kurds into Iran and Turkey.

Having fully regained the region, Baghdad signed a truce with the insurgents in mid-April. In the subsequent talks with the central government, Barzani, acting as leader of the Iraqi Kurdistan Front (IKF), reached a draft agreement in June whereby the Kurds would have predominant military and political authority over the KAR, with joint control of the army and police by the Kurdish authorities and Baghdad. In return the Kurds had to surrender their heavy weapons and cut all links with outside powers. But, despite further clarification of the agreement from Baghdad, Barzani failed to win the approval of the majority of IKF leaders.

With 16,000 Western troops deployed in the 3,600 sq. mi./9,325 sq. km security zone created by the Washington-led anti-Iraq coalition in the Iraqi-Turkish border region, Baghdad was forced to withdraw its forces from the KAR by late October. Even after America, Britain, and France, the three permanent Western members of the UN Security Council, had pulled out their troops from the area by the end of 1991, they continued their air surveillance of Iraq north of latitude 36 degree from the Turkish air base of Incirlik. Thus protected, the Kurds conducted their own elections for parliament in May 1992, and chose their own government, which among other things had its own army, and adopted its own flag. Kurds thus acquired a semi-independent administrative-political entity. *See also* Kurdistan Democratic Party and Patriotic Union of Kurdistan.

Kurds in Syria: Nationally, Kurds [*q.v.*] make up nearly 6 percent of the Syrian population of 22.5 million. Apart from a small community in Damascus [*q.v.*] dating back to the times of Salah al-Din (Saladin) Ayubi (r. 1169–93), himself a Kurd, they are concentrated in the Jazira region in the northeast corner of the country, and in the mountainous area north of Aleppo [*q.v.*] among the border with Turkey. Most of them arrived from Turkey during the interwar years, when a Kurdish revolt against the regime of Mustafa Kemal Ataturk failed in 1925.

Mirroring the situation in adjoining Iraq, the Kurds in Syria established the Kurdish Democratic Party (KDP) in 1957, demanding that Kurds be recognized as an ethnic group entitled to develop its own culture.

Following the merger of Syria with Egypt to form the United Arab Republic (UAR) [*q.v.*] in 1958, the new pan-Arabist regime repressed the KDP. This policy continued after Syria seceded from the UAR in 1961. A special census conducted in Jazira in late 1962 deprived 120,000 Kurds of Syrian nationality. After the pan-Ara-

bist [*q.v.*] Baath Party [*q.v.*] seized power in 1963, the government expelled many of the Kurds along the Turkish frontier and stripped many thousands of others of their Syrian nationality. It joined the Iraqi Baath [*q.v.*] government's war against the Kurds, and adopted a policy of settling Arabs in the Jazira region while scattering the local Kurds into the interior, especially after oil had been found in the area. Applied haphazardly, this policy resulted in some 30,000 Jezira Kurds leaving the area by early 1971.

Later that year the government adopted a conciliatory position similar to the one taken by the Iraqi regime in its March 1970 declaration. The Baath congress recognized that the Kurdish and Arab peoples had equal rights and that the Kurds had a right to their own nationality, though not to separation. In late 1971 the government for the first time distributed land-reform land to Kurdish peasants in Jazira. In 1976 President Hafiz Assad [*q.v.*] officially renounced the population transfer plans for Jazira.

Since then, because of the discovery of oil in Jazira, it has become strategically important to the government. The region has been virtually free from anti-regime protest which started in March 2011. Many Kurdish leaders fear that collapse of a strong central authority would jeopardize the security of such minorities as Kurds and Christians [*q.v.*], as happened in Iraq after 2003.

Kuwait:

OFFICIAL NAME: State of Kuwait
CAPITAL: Kuwait city
AREA: 6,880 sq. mi./17,820 sq.

km—including the Kuwaiti share of the Kuwait-Saudi Arabia Neutral Zone [*q.v.*], and the Bubiyan and Warba offshore islands with a combined area of 348 sq. mi./900 sq. km

Population: 3.632 million, of which 1.16 million were Kuwaiti nationals (2011 est.)

Gross domestic product (nominal): $172.78 billion; per capita, $39,500 (2011 est.)

Gross domestic product (Purchasing Power Parity): $136.50 billion; per capita, $37,580 (2011 est.)

National currency: Kuwaiti Dinar (KD); KD1= U.S. $3.60 = £2.31 = €2.70 (2011)

Form of government: monarchy

Official language: Arabic [*q.v.*]

Official religion: Islam [*q.v.*]

Administrative regions: Kuwait is divided into five governorates (provinces).

Constitution: After Kuwait's independence on 19 June 1961, the ruler appointed a constituent assembly in December. The constitution drafted by it was promulgated in November 1962. Kuwait is a hereditary emirate (principality) under the ruler of the descendants of Shaikh Mubarak I al-Sabah (d. 1915). The constitution guarantees freedom of opinion, freedom of the press, and the freedom to perform religious rites, and allows the formation of trade unions and peaceful societies that stay within the law. A unicameral National Assembly of 50 members is elected for a four-year term by literate male Kuwaiti citizens who can prove that their family has been domiciled in Kuwait since 1921. The ruler can dissolve the Assembly, provided fresh elections are held within two months.

Ethnic composition (2011): Kuwait Arab, 31 percent; other Arab, 28 percent; South Asian, 37 percent; other, 4 percent.

Executive authority: Executive authority rests with the emir, who exercises it through a council of ministers. He appoints or dismisses the prime minister, or accepts his resignation. After consultation with the prime minister, the emir appoints or dismisses ministers, or accepts their resignation. Non-parliamentary ministers become ex-officio members of the National Assembly. A minister is responsible to the National Assembly, and, following a vote of no confidence, must resign. The emir is the supreme commander of the military and is authorized to declare defensive war, conclude peace agreements, and sign treaties.

High officials:

Head of state: Shaikh Sabah IV al-Ahmad al-Jaber al-Sabah, 2006–

Crown prince: Shaikh Nawaf al-Ahmad al-Jaber al-Sabah, 2006–

Prime minister: Shaikh Jaber al-Mubarak al-Hamad al-Sabah, 2011–

Speaker of the National Assembly: Ahmad Abdul Aziz al-Sadoun, 2012–

History (ca 1900): At the turn of the 20th century Kuwait was a British protectorate following a secret treaty between Shaikh Mubarak I al-Sabah (r. 1896–1915) and London in 1899. The Anglo-Ottoman Convention of 1913 [*q.v.*], which recognized Kuwait as an autonomous *caza* (Arabic: *administrative unit*) of the Ottoman Empire under Shaikh Mubarak I, became invalid when the Ottomans joined the Germans in World War I. London now publicly declared Kuwait to be "an independent shaikhdom under British protectorate." After the war the 1922 Protocol of Uqair [*q.v.*] defined Kuwait's borders and created the Kuwait-Najd [*q.v.*] (later Saudi Arabia) Neutral Zone. In 1937 the 14-member (elected) Kuwait Legislative Council voted by 10 to 4 for a union with Iraq [*q.v.*] then ruled by King Ghazi bin Faisal [*q.v.*]. But nothing changed.

Following the development of the oil industry in Iraq and Iran [*q.v.*], the trading economy of Kuwait improved. Kuwait's oil exploration bore fruit in 1938 at Burgan, but the wells were plugged during World War II. In the postwar years oil extraction and exports reached commercial proportions. The stoppage of Iran's oil exports from 1951 to 1953 led to a rapid increase in the Kuwaiti output and a rise in local living standards.

Popular demand for political reform, including parliament, was not conceded by the ruler, Shaikh Abdullah III al-Sabah [*q.v.*], until after political independence in June 1961. He appointed a constituent assembly in December and promulgated the constitution drafted by it in November 1962. Elections to the National Assembly on a limited franchise were held in 1963, 1967, 1971, and 1975.

Over the years the Assembly evolved into an institutional means of expression and access to the main sociopolitical elements—nomadic and sedentary tribes, urban merchants and businessmen, and political intellectuals and professionals. In August 1976 the ruler suspended four articles concerning the National Assembly as well as the Assembly, accusing it of "malicious behavior" and wasting time on legislation, and dissolved the Assembly a year later.

Kuwait prospered from the steep rise in the price of oil in the mid-1970s, and the state set up a national fund for future generations.

Yielding to popular pressure, Shaikh Jaber III al-Sabah [*q.v.*] reinstated the National Assembly with depleted powers in early 1981. The new parliament proved to be a handmaiden of the ruler. However, in the Sixth National Assembly, elected in early 1985, there were five nationalist-leftists and 11 Islamists [*q.v.*] in a house of 50. By offering a combined opposition and demanding an official inquiry into the disastrous collapse of the unofficial stock exchange in 1982, involving $97 billion in paper debts, they caused the al-Sabah dynasty [*q.v.*] some unease. In July 1986 Shaikh Jaber III dissolved the Assembly again.

Once the Iran-Iraq War (1980–88) [*q.v.*], in which Kuwait had sided with Iraq, ended in August 1988, there was agitation for the restoration of the Assembly. When the ruler conceded a 75-member National Council (one-third of whom were nominated), but with the power only to make recommendations, protest continued. The June 1990 election was boycotted by the opposition. This crisis and Kuwait's attempt to weaken Iraq's economy by depressing oil prices by flooding the market were major factors behind Iraqi President Saddam Hussein's [*q.v.*] decision to invade Kuwait in August 1990.

During the seven months of Iraqi occupation Kuwait suffered wanton damage, and Kuwaitis suffered exile and unprecedented brutality, including rape, summary execution, and arbitrary confiscation of property. The Second Gulf War [*q.v.*] ended with the U.S.-

led coalition expelling Iraq from Kuwait in February 1991. The country's funding of the 1991 Gulf War and its aftermath reduced the Kuwait Investment Authority's assets from $88.5 billion to $31.5 billion. Kuwait was restored to Shaikh Jaber III. He declared 25 February as the National Day of the "liberated" Kuwait which until then was celebrated on 19 June. He held elections to the Seventh National Assembly in October 1992. Of the 50 members, 31 belonged to the opposition, despite the government's success in quickly rebuilding the country's shattered oil economy.

Following Kuwait's signing of a 10-year defense pact with Washington, 5,000 U.S. troops were based in the country. In the recurring crises between Iraq and the United Nations during the 1990s, Kuwait stood out as the only Gulf monarchy that publicly backed Washington's plans to bomb Iraq. At home, due to the recurring conflict between the National Assembly and the cabinet, the ruler dissolved the parliament a year earlier. In the subsequent general election the size of the government supporters fell from 18 to 12. In regional affairs, Kuwait's growing rapprochement with Iran and Iraq was halted by the terrorist attacks on the U.S. in September 2001, followed by President George W. Bush's description of Iran and Iraq as members of the "Axis of Evil."

Kuwait became the forward base for the American and British troops before and during the 2003 Anglo-American invasion of Iraq [q.v.]. During this period nearly a third of Kuwait was out of bounds to the local population. Kuwait's close links with America grew tighter. After the over-throw of President Saddam Hussein [q.v.], relations between Kuwait and Iraq improved. Yet, despite Washington's pressure, Kuwait refused to cancel the reparations that Iraq's fallen regime was required to pay it. And it was only in 2008 that Kuwait agreed to exchange ambassadors with Iraq.

The Arab Spring [q.v.] arrived in January 2011 at a time when there was a rising tension between the National Assembly and the cabinet dominated by al-Sabah ruling family amidst allegation of corruption at the highest level of government. Major demonstrations, attracting tens of thousands of protestors, occurred with increasing frequency. At these gatherings, the ruling family was criticized publicly. In November the demonstrators broke into the National Assembly building. The cabinet led by the ruler's nephew, Nasser Muhammad al-Ahmad al-Sabah, since 2006, resigned. Shaikh Sabah IV al-Sabah dissolved the parliament and ordered a fresh election. The opposition won more than two-thirds of the seats.

LEGISLATURE: A single-chamber National Assembly of 50 members with four-year tenure is elected by literate male Kuwaiti citizens belonging to families domiciled in Kuwait since 1921. The emir can dissolve the Assembly provided fresh elections are held within two months. But in August 1976 he suspended the four constitutional articles concerning the Assembly and dissolved it in 1977. After its restoration in early 1981, it was suspended again by the emir in July 1986.

Ministers are responsible, individually and collectively, to the Assembly, which must approve bills before the emir promulgates them as laws. If dissatisfied with the prime minister, the National Assembly can convey its lack of confidence in him to the emir, who must then dismiss him or dissolve the Assembly. Though political groups are not permitted, several semi-political organizations are known to exist. In the October 1992 general election, among the factions that secured Assembly seats were the Islamic Constitutional Movement, a moderate Sunni [*q.v.*] group; the Kuwait Democratic Forum, a secular body; and Salafin [*q.v.*], a Sunni fundamentalist group.

In the 1999 general election, when only 113,000 Kuwait males (out of 793,000 Kuwait adult nationals) were entitled to vote, 20 seats were secured by Islamists—both Sunni [*q.v.*] and Shia [*q.v.*] (represented by the National Islamic Coalition)—14 by secular liberals, represented by the National Democratic Rally, founded in 1997, and the older Kuwait Democratic Front; 12 by government supporters; and the rest by independents.

In the 2003 parliamentary election, Islamists won 21 seats, liberals 3, and independents 12, reducing the pro-government members to 14. When the majority of legislators demanded to reduce the electoral districts from 25 to 5 in order to enlarge the size of the electorate and thus minimize the chance of vote-buying, which was commonly practiced in the electoral districts of a smaller size, the emir objected. In the spring of 2006 he dissolved the National Assembly, which had earlier enfranchised women.

In the subsequent election held in June, the Sunni Islamic bloc won 17 seats, the populist Popular Bloc 9, and the Liberals 7, reducing the pro-government group to 13. None of the new

members were women. Relations between the parliament and the government remained tense. So the Emir dissolved the chamber in 2008. In the next election, which followed within two months of the dissolution of the Assembly, the Sunni Islamic bloc improved its strength to 21, and the Popular Bloc remained steady at 9, with the pro-government members rising to 16. The royalists' failure to gain a majority of the seats kept alive the tension between the legislature and the palace. Once again the emir dissolved the Assembly in March 2009. By now women had won the right to vote. Of the 340,000 voters, 187,000 were women. Sixteen of them stood as candidates. This time the size of the pro-government bloc rose by 5 to 21 at the cost of the Sunni Islamic bloc, with the newly established Shia Islamist bloc gaining six seats. The new National Assembly had four women members. Once again the Assembly was not allowed to complete its four-year term.

The next general election, held in early February 2012 against the background of Islamist parties in Egypt sweeping the polls, resulted in the opposition Islamic groups making headway and the previous women parliamentarians failing to get reelected. Three Sunni Islamist factions, including the Islamic Salafi Alliance and the Islamic Constitutional Movement gained 20 seats, the Popular Action Bloc 9, and Shia Islamists 7, with the pro-government Sunnis, Liberals, and independents reduced collectively to 14 seats. Ahmad Abdul Aziz al-Sadoun, leader of the Popular Action Bloc, was elected speaker.

RELIGIOUS COMPOSITION (2011): Muslims [*q.v.*], 85 percent, among whom Sunni [*q.v.*] 70 percent, Shia [*q.v.*] 30 percent; other (including Christian, Hindu, Buddhist, and Zoroastrian), 15 percent.

Kuwait City: *capital of Kuwait* Population: 509,700 (2010 est.). Kuwait (Arabic: *Little Fort*) was founded in 1710 by members of the Anaiza tribal confederation [*q.v.*] who migrated from the interior of the Arabian Peninsula [*q.v.*]. In 1776 the (British) East India Company established a base there, and it became an important link in the communication system between India and Britain.

Until 1921 the settlement was surrounded by a mud wall, and its residents lived by fishing, pearling, and trading with India and East Africa. Following the development of the emirate's petroleum industry after World War II, Kuwait city and its environs grew dramatically, a process accelerated by the razing of the mud wall in 1957. It emerged as a prosperous administrative, commercial, and financial center with tree-lined roads, and dotted with parks and gardens.

The damage done to the city during its seven-month occupation by the Iraqis was repaired after the defeat of Iraq in the 1991 Gulf War [*q.v.*]. The subsequent reconstruction turned the city into an important regional business center, full of high-quality hotels and shopping malls. Its historical museum contains prehistoric artifacts from Failakah Island.

Kuwaiti-Saudi Neutral Zone: *See* Saudi Arabia-Kuwait Neutral Zone.

L

Labor Alignment, Israel: *Israeli political bloc See* Labor-Mapam Alignment.

Labor Islamic Alliance (Egypt): *Egyptian political party* (Also called Islamic Alliance) On the eve of the April 1987 parliamentary election, the semi-clandestine Muslim Brotherhood [*q.v.*] allied with the opposition Socialist Labor Party [*q.v.*] and the Liberal Socialist Party [*q.v.*] to form the Labor Islamic Alliance (LSA). The secular groups joined the alliance in order to meet the electoral threshold of 8 percent of the total vote. Adopting the slogan "Islam is the solution," the LSA demanded that the Sharia [*q.v.*] should be the sole source of legislation.

Despite political harassment and the stuffing of ballot boxes with the votes of the dead, absent, and under-aged for the ruling National Democratic Party [*q.v.*], the LSA won 17 percent of the vote and 60 seats, displacing the Neo-Wafd Party [*q.v.*] as the main opposition group. LSA constituents boycotted the next general election in 1990 when their demands that the emergency should be lifted and that the election should be supervised by an independent, non-governmental body, instead of the interior ministry, were rejected. The LSA extended its boycott to the 1995 general election. In the 2000 election, when judges supervised polling stations, the LSA participated, winning 17 seats. In the 2005 election, the Muslim Brotherhood candidates ran as independents.

After the ouster of President Hosni Mubarak [*q.v.*] in February 2011, the LSA joined the Democratic Alliance led by the Freedom and Justice Party [*q.v.*] and secured one seat in the People's Assembly.

Labor Party (Israeli): The alignment formed in 1965 between Mapai [*q.v.*] and *Ahdut HaAvodah-Poale Zion* [*q.v.*] was widened in January 1968 to include Rafi, leading finally to the merger of the three into *Mifleget HaAvodah HaYisraelit* (Hebrew: *The Israeli Labor Party*). Entering the 1969 and 1973 elections in alliance with Mapam [*q.v.*] as the Labor-Mapam Alignment [*q.v.*], its total score in the 1969 and 1973 elections was 56 and 51 seats respectively. The Alignment became the leader of the coalition government. In the 1977 and 1981 elections, Labor continued the same arrangement, but won only 32 and 47 seats respectively. It lost power to Likud [*q.v.*]. In the 1984 election the Alignment won 44 seats, three more than Likud, but the Labor leadership decided to form a national unity government with Likud. Disagreeing with this, Mapam (six seats) left the Alignment. In January 1987 the three-member Yahad group merged with the Labor Party.

In the 1988 and 1992 elections Labor ran independently, and won 39 and 44 seats respectively. The national unity government that Labor formed with Likud in 1988 fell in March 1990 when its differences with Likud Premier Yitzhak Shamir [*q.v.*] on the Middle East peace process became irreconcilable. It acted as opposition until the June 1992 election when, led by Yitzhak Rabin [*q.v.*], it secured 44 seats, 12 more than Likud. It formed a coalition government with Meretz [*q.v.*] and Shas [*q.v.*].

The Rabin government signed a limited self-rule accord for the Palestinians with the Palestine Liberation Organization [*q.v.*] in September 1993, followed by the Jordanian-Israel Peace Treaty [*q.v.*] in October 1994. In the 1996 general election, Labor won 34 seats. The One Israel alliance, led by Labor in the May 1999 election, secured 26 seats. Following the defeat of its leader, Ehud Barak [*q.v.*], in the 2001 prime ministerial contest, Labor, led by Binyamin Ben Eliezer, joined the national unity government formed by Ariel Sharon [*q.v.*].

There was a quick turnover of leaders of the party, from Amiran Mitzna (2002–03), Shimon Perez [*q.v.*] (2003–05), and Amir Peretz (2005–07), back to Barak. During the chairmanship of Peretz, the party fought the 2006 Knesset election on a mildly social-democratic platform. That enabled it to regain the two seats it had lost in the 2003 election to return to the total of 21. Under Barak, the party's strength in the Knesset election of 2009 fell to a record low of 13, behind Likud, the centrist Kadima [*q.v.*], and the ultra right-wing Israel Beitainu [*q.v.*].

Labor Zionism and Zionists: *political movement among Jews* The term Labor Zionist applies to those Zionists who wanted to blend Zionism [*q.v.*] with socialism. A month after the first Zionist Congress met in Basle, Switzerland, in August 1897, the Bund (German: *League*) was established in Vilna, Lithuania, as the general union for Jewish workers in

Lithuania, Poland, and Russia. Three years later Poale Zion [*q.v.*] was established in Minsk, Russia, with a program of socialism, Zionism, and migration to Palestine [*q.v.*]. From Russia it spread to Austria and then to the United States. A survey of European Jews [*q.v.*] showed that less than a third of them worked in manufacturing or the construction industry, while nearly a half were engaged in distributive trades, with none in agriculture.

A leading Poale Zion ideologue, Don Ber Borochov [*q.v.*], argued that Jews in the diaspora [*q.v.*] were excluded from the larger class struggle because of being rootless. The solution lay in concentrating Jews in a country of their own, where they could develop the base of their own socioeconomic pyramid. What was needed, he concluded, was a land with a small population but a large potential for agricultural development. Borochov chose Palestine, partly because it was regarded as the historic homeland of Jews, and partly because, being a "derelict country," it was of interest only to small and medium Jewish capitalists—not the big ones—and thus offered revolutionary promise for the Jewish proletariat that was to be fostered there. He considered local Arabs [*q.v.*] as Turkish subjects, lacking national consciousness, and visualized their assimilation, economic and cultural, into the Jewish nation as it developed economically under Jewish initiative and leadership.

This emphasis on creating a Jewish working class in Palestine dovetailed with the views and actions of Aaron David Gordon (a Ukrainian Jew who arrived in Palestine in 1904) and his followers, who formed the HaPoale HaTzair [*q.v.*]. Gordon believed that the Jewish nation would recapture its lost spiritual values through manual Labor, and that the crux of the Jewish problem was not capital against Labor but production versus parasitism. By draining marshes and setting up agricultural outposts, HaPoale HaTzair members helped to create Jewish wage labor in agriculture.

In 1919 the leftists within Poale Zion left to form Mopsi (the Socialist Workers Party). The Poale Zion's rightist, nationalist members merged with another group to form Ahdut HaAvodah [*q.v.*]. In January 1930 Ahdut HaAvodah and HaPoale HaTzair merged to form Mapai [*q.v.*]. Fifteen years later, having failed to persuade Mapai to adopt the ideas of class struggle and bi-national (Arab-Jewish) socialist revolution, Hashomer HaTzair members left Mapai, merged with the leftist Tanua LeAhdut HaAvodah [*q.v.*] a year later, and emerged as Mapam [*q.v.*] in early 1948.

In Israel, Borochov's influence was most marked in Mapam and Ahdut HaAvodah-Poale Zion [*q.v.*]—in Mapai, Gordon's. As the dominant element in the coalition governments for the next three decades, the Labor Zionist parties were at the forefront of building the nation and the state. In January 1968 a merger of Mapai [*q.v.*] with Ahdut HaAvodah-Poale Zion and Rafi created the Israeli Labor Party [*q.v.*]. The Labor Zionist groups in the diaspora supported their counterparts in Israel, and each of them had its own world confederation.

Labor-Mapam Alignment: *Israeli political bloc* The Israeli Labor Party, which arose in January 1968 out of the merger of Mapai [*q.v.*], Ahdut HaAvodah-Poale Zion [*q.v.*], and Rafi, forged an alliance with Mapam [*q.v.*]. Popularly called *Maarach* (Hebrew: *Alignment*), it won 46.2 percent of the vote and 56 parliamentary seats. The Alignment arrangement continued in the elections in 1973 (42.5 percent, 51 seats), 1977 (26.7 percent, 32 seats), 1981 (39.2 percent, 47 seats), and 1984 (36.7 percent, 44 seats). When Labor decided to form a national unity government with Likud [*q.v.*] in 1984, Mapam left the Alignment and became an opposition group with its six deputies.

Ladino language: Ladino, also known as Judeo-Spanish, the mother tongue of Sephardic Jews [*q.v.*], is a language of medieval Spanish origin. Written in Hebrew script, its vocabulary consists of Hebrew [*q.v.*] words as well as Portuguese, Greek, and Turkish. The first book in Ladino appeared in 1510, published in Istanbul.

Lahoud, Emile (1936–): *Lebanese military and political leader, president, 1998–2007* Son of General Jamil Lahoud and Adrenee Bajakian in Baabdate, Lahoud was educated locally. After joining the Beirut Military Academy as a cadet in 1956, he graduated with the rank of lieutenant four years later after passing a naval engineering course in Britain.

He became commander of the Second Fleet in 1966. By the time he acquired the rank of rear admiral in 1985, he had been through naval staff courses at the Naval Command College in Rhode Island, U.S., twice. Two years earlier he had been ap-

pointed president of the military office in the defense ministry where Gen. Michel Aoun [*q.v.*] was chief of staff. In September 1989, toward the end of the 1975–90 Lebanese Civil War [*q.v.*], he fell out with Aoun. Two months later, President Elias Hrawi [*q.v.*] promoted him to general and appointed him military chief of staff after dismissing Aoun. Lahoud led the campaign against Aoun in October 1990 that ended the civil war.

He rebuilt the shattered Lebanese armed forces and introduced conscription for male adults. He managed to maintain friendly relations with both Syria and America. In October 1998 he was elected president by 118 out of 128 parliamentarians. He invited Salim Hoss [*q.v.*] to form the next government, and exercised greater presidential powers than his predecessor.

When the pro-Rafiq Hariri [*q.v.*] groups did well in the 2000 parliamentary election, he called on Hariri to head the next cabinet. While Hariri agreed to focus on the economy, Lahoud took charge of defense and security. In that role he tried to curb the rising protest against the continued presence of Syrian troops in Lebanon [*q.v.*], which showed little sign of abating even after Syria had withdrawn 6,000 to 10,000 soldiers from Beirut [*q.v.*] and suburbs in the summer of 2001. He chaired the Twenty-second Arab League summit [*q.v.*] in March 2002, the first to be held in Beirut, where there was public reconciliation between Iraq and Kuwait, and Iraq and Saudi Arabia.

In September 2004, encouraged by Syria, lawmakers extended Lahoud's term by three years. In April 2005 he oversaw the total withdrawal of the Syrian troops from Lebanon.

Land of Israel: *See* Eretz Yisrael.

Latakia: *Syrian city* Population. 667,000 (2011 est.) Latakia's Arabic name, Ladhikiya, is derived from Laodicea, mother of Selecus II (d. 226 B.C.), a Greek ruler. A leading port during the Seleucid period in the third and second centuries B.C., it was destroyed by earthquakes twice before falling into the hands of invading Muslim [*q.v.*] Arabs [*q.v.*] in 638 A.D. From then until the French Mandate in 1920, it came under the intermittent authority of Crusaders, Arabs, and Ottoman Turks.

Endowed with an excellent harbor, today it is the main port of Syria. Its local industry includes fishing, vegetable-oil extraction, tanning, and cotton ginning. Among its surviving monuments are Corinthian columns, called the Colonnade of Bacchus, and a Roman victory arch.

During the 2011 uprising, there were anti-regime demonstrations in the Ramel neighborhood, where a Palestinian refugee camp was located. In August the security forces besieged the area and then entered it with tanks and armored vehicles to regain control. The ensuing violent skirmishes left 25 people dead.

Lavon, Pinchas (1904–76): *Israeli politician* Born Lubianker in Lwow, Poland, Lavon was a cofounder of the Jewish youth movement built around the ideas of Aaron David Gordon. He migrated to Palestine [*q.v.*] in 1929. He became a joint secretary of Mapai [*q.v.*](1938–39). After serving as a member of the Histadrut [*q.v.*] executive for several years, he was elected its secretary-general (1949–50). Elected to the First Knesset [*q.v.*] in 1949, he retained a seat until 1961. He was minister of agriculture (1950–51) and then minister of defense (1954–55).

As defense minister, he became the focus of the longest and most controversial political dispute in Israeli history. In 1954 an attempt by an Israeli spy network in Egypt, made up of local Jews [*q.v.*], to destabilize the Egyptian regime and ruin its relations with the West—by planting bombs in cinemas, post offices, and railway stations as well as U.S. consulates and information centers—backfired. All 13 Israeli agents were arrested. In February 1955, despite Lavon's protestations that the operation had been undertaken by a senior army officer without his knowledge, he was forced to resign as defense minister. The next year he was elected secretary-general of the Histadrut, and stayed on until 1961.

In the summer of 1960, when new evidence backing Lavon's version of the "security mishap" surfaced, he demanded that his name be cleared. Prime Minister David Ben-Gurion [*q.v.*] refused to accept a ministerial inquiry into the affair, as proposed by a majority in the cabinet, and insisted on a judicial inquiry. Ben-Gurion resigned as premier in January 1961, but that was not the end of the Lavon Affair. Indeed it continued until the mid-1960s, dragging the ruling party, Mapai, into a whirlpool, and weakening both it and its leader, Ben-Gurion. The Levi Eshkol [*q.v.*] government, formed in June 1963, fell in December 1964 amidst continuing controversy about the Lavon affair.

He led a political group named *Min HaYesod* (Hebrew: *From the Foundation*), consisting chiefly of intellectuals and members of the kibbutzim [*q.v.*] who had split from Mapai in November 1964. Following the June 1967 Arab-Israeli War [*q.v.*], Lavon favored Israel's withdrawal from the Occupied Territories [*q.v.*].

Law of Return 1950 (Israel): Adopted in July 1950, the Law of Return confirmed a provision in the 1948 Declaration of Independence of Israel [*q.v.*] by guaranteeing that "every Jew has the right to this country as an immigrant." Any Jew [*q.v.*] in the diaspora [*q.v.*] wishing to settle in Israel is guaranteed an immigration visa, except those engaged in an activity "against the Jewish people" or likely to "endanger public health or security of the state." In August 1954 another exception was added: Jews "with a criminal past, likely to endanger public welfare." During the first 20 years of Israel, 1,290,771 Jews entered the country under the Law of Return. Of the nearly one million people from the former Soviet Union who migrated to Israel between 1989 and 1998 under this law, about a third of them were not Jews; they were allowed to settle in Israel because they were married to Jews.

Lawrence, Thomas Edward (1888–1935): (Also known as Lawrence of Arabia) Son of an Anglo-Irish baronet, Sir Thomas Chapman, Lawrence grew up in Oxford, Britain, and graduated from the city's Jesus College, specializing in medieval military architecture. Between 1911 and 1913 he worked under D. G.

Hogarth, an Oxford archaeologist, in Mesopotamia [*q.v.*]. The next year he joined an exploratory project that took him from Gaza [*q.v.*] to Aqaba.

After the outbreak of the World War I, he was sent to Cairo [*q.v.*], where he was assigned to military intelligence. In January 1916 he became part of the Arab Bureau of Intelligence and diplomatic officers, which was established to define and implement Britain's role in the Arab revolt against Ottoman Turkey. In October he joined the British mission in Jeddah [*q.v.*]. Leading a small force behind the Ottoman lines, he carried out sabotage and guerilla operations. After mid-1917 he coordinated the Arab revolt with the British campaign, led by General Edmund Allenby. In December he was captured by the Ottoman army, but managed to escape. In September 1918 Lawrence, now promoted to lieutenant colonel, entered Damascus [*q.v.*] with the Arab [*q.v.*] forces.

As a member of the British delegation to the Paris Peace Conference of the Council of Four in March 1919, he liaised with the Arabs and acted as adviser to Faisal bin Hussein [*q.v.*]. His lobbying for Arab independence failed. This meant the end of the agreement that he had managed to broker between Faisal bin Hussein and Chaim Weizmann, the Zionist [*q.v.*] leader, in London in January 1919, involving acceptance of Jewish immigration into Palestine [*q.v.*], since it was conditional on the Arabs obtaining their independence "as demanded."

When Colonial Secretary Winston Churchill set up the Middle East department in March 1921, he appointed

Lawrence as his Arab affairs adviser. He was involved in Churchill's negotiations with Abdullah bin Hussein [*q.v.*], as a result of which Transjordan [*q.v.*] was handed over to Abdullah under British protection.

Having finished his long memoirs recounting his wartime experiences (*Seven Pillars of Wisdom*, 1922), he spent a few years pruning it and finding a publisher. It was published privately in 1926, and was followed by a summary, *Revolt in the Desert*, a year later. He was then posted at a Royal Air Force (RAF) base in India. He retired from the RAF in 1935, and died in a motorcycle accident soon after.

Lawrence of Arabia: *See* Lawrence, Thomas Edward.

League of Arab States: *See* Arab League.

Lebanese Civil War (1958): The 1958 Lebanese civil war lasted from May to July. The gap between President Camille Chamoun [*q.v.*] and the mainly Muslim [*q.v.*] Socialist National Front (SNF) [*q.v.*], led by Kamal Jumblat [*q.v.*], widened after the formation of the United Arab Republic [*q.v.*] in February 1958, with Chamoun becoming increasingly intolerant of opposition. On 8 May Nasib Metni, a Christian [*q.v.*] newspaper publisher, who had just served a jail sentence for criticizing the president, was killed. This led to anti-government rioting in Tripoli [*q.v.*] that left 35 dead. The SNF organized countrywide strikes and Chamoun declared a state of emergency.

On 12 May civil war started between Chamoun's partisans—the gendarmerie

and the Maronite [*q.v.*] militia—and Jumblat's supporters, with the army staying neutral. But when the fighting between the two sides intensified, the army intervened to end it. In mid-July, when the Jumblat camp controlled about a third of Lebanon, the pro-Western Iraqi monarch, Faisal II bin Ghazi [*q.v.*], was overthrown by republican army officers.

Deprived of his only strong ally in the region, Chamoun requested military aid from the United States under the Eisenhower Doctrine [*q.v.*]. Soon 14,300 U.S. marines and airborne ground troops arrived with a backup of the 76-ship U.S. Sixth Fleet. The civil strife intensified briefly before coming to an end on 31 July, with both sides accepting the army commander, General Fuad Chehab [*q.v.*], as the sole presidential candidate. The war took a toll of 1,400 to 4,000 Lebanese. All American troops withdrew by 25 October.

Lebanese Civil War (1975–90): Traditional rivalry between left-leaning Muslim [*q.v.*] and right-wing, mainly Maronite, Christians [*q.v.*] was accentuated with the arrival in Lebanon in the early 1970s of the Palestinian commandos and the Palestine Liberation Organization (PLO) [*q.v.*]. Also by March 1975 the shuttle diplomacy of U.S. Secretary of State Henry Kissinger to further the Middle East peace process had run out of steam. It suited Washington to see the Arabs [*q.v.*] mired in a civil conflict that would distract their attention from the failure of U.S. diplomacy. An attack on the Palestinians by the Phalange [*q.v.*] militia in East Beirut [*q.v.*] on 13 April 1975 heralded the start of a civil war, that lasted until 13 October 1990 and went through the following phases:

PHASE 1: April 1975 to May 1976—ascendancy of the reformist alliance. Violence spread throughout the country. The main opposing camps were the Lebanese National Movement (LNM) [*q.v.*], led by Kamal Jumblat [*q.v.*], and the Lebanese Front [*q.v.*], headed by Camille Chamoun [*q.v.*], with its militia, the Lebanese Forces [*q.v.*], commanded by Bashir Gemayel [*q.v.*]. The PLO allied with the LNM, and set up a joint command. The LNM demanded an end to confessionalism [*q.v.*], and reform of the political system to make it equitable to Muslims, who were now known to constitute a majority.

The Lebanese Front insisted on the expulsion of the armed Palestinians from Lebanon before discussing political and constitutional reform. During this period both sides decided to eliminate hostile pockets within their enclaves. Intense countrywide fighting in January 1976 destroyed vital state institutions and public buildings, and caused the breakup of the Lebanese army. By early April the LNM-PLO alliance controlled two-thirds of the country. In desperation the Lebanese Front turned to Syria through President Suleiman Franjieh [*q.v.*]. Realizing that radicalized Lebanon would give the PLO wide latitude in its struggle against Israel, which would lead to Israel's lashing out in blind fury and would destabilize the whole region, Syrian President Hafiz Assad [*q.v.*] decided to aid the Maronite-dominated Lebanese Front.

PHASE 2: June 1976 to February 1978—Syrian intervention and hege-mony. The Syrian military intervention saved the Lebanese Front from total defeat. A subsequent cease-fire, brokered by Libya, prepared the ground for the presidential election. Elias Sarkis [*q.v.*], a Syrian nominee, won and took office in September 1976. Within two months a truce had taken hold in the country, except in southern Lebanon where the PLO's activities against Israel were being hampered by an Israeli-backed Christian militia.

PHASE 3: March to October 1978—the first Israeli invasion [*q.v.*]. Following a Palestinian guerrilla attack inside Israel on 11 March 1978, Israel invaded southern Lebanon [*q.v.*]. In May Maronite leaders Pierre Gemayel [*q.v.*] and Camille Chamoun visited Israel for arms supplies. On 13 June a Phalange squad assassinated Tony Franjieh, son of Suleiman Franjieh, to eliminate any serious rival to Bashir Gemayel in his bid for the presidency.

PHASE 4: November 1978 to May 1982—consolidation of the Christian mini-state. In May–June 1979 the Phalange began to clash with the National Liberal Party (NLP) [*q.v.*] militia. The conflict reached a climax in July 1980, with the Phalange defeating the NLP fighters. In the fighting between the Phalange and its Syrian opponents for the control of Mount Sanin, northwest of Zahle, in late April 1981, Israel intervened and shot down two Syrian helicopters. Three months later, following a three-way understanding between Israel, Syria, and the PLO brokered by the United States, a cease-fire went into effect in southern Lebanon. After the Israeli defense minister, Ariel Sharon [*q.v.*], had conferred with Lebanese Forces

(LF) commanders in January 1982 to plan an invasion of Lebanon, Israel resumed arms shipments to the Maronite militias.

PHASE 5: June 1982 to February 1984—the second Israeli invasion and its aftermath. Following a failed assassination attempt on the Israeli ambassador to Britain, Shlomo Argov, on 3 June, Israel invaded Lebanon three days later. This conflict lasted until 1 September (*See* Israeli Invasion of Lebanon [1982]). On 13 September president-elect Bashir Gemayel [*q.v.*] was killed in an explosion that destroyed the headquarters of his Phalange Party [*q.v.*]. Israeli units occupied Beirut with the aim of maintaining order and preventing retaliatory violence. Between 16 and 18 September some 2,000 Palestinian refugees were massacred by the Phalange militia in Beirut's Sabra and Shatila camps. On 20 September deployment of the Western Multi-National Force (MNF) [*q.v.*]—consisting of U.S., British, French, and Italian units—began. The next day Amin Gemayel [*q.v.*] was elected president by the parliament. On 29 September the Israelis left Beirut.

On 17 May 1983 Israel signed the Lebanese-Israeli Peace Treaty [*q.v.*] after the Lebanese parliament had adopted it by an overwhelming majority, but President Amin Gemayel withheld his signature. After the Israelis withdrew from the Shouf region on 3 September, their positions were taken up by the Phalange militia and the Lebanese army. This led to fighting between them and the Druze-PLO alliance. The U.S. and France intervened with warplanes and warships on the side of the Lebanese

army. A cease-fire was mediated by Saudi Arabia on 25 September. But the Pentagon continued its reconnaissance missions over west-central Lebanon from its aircraft carriers. On 23 October truck-bombing of U.S. and French military headquarters killed 241 American and 59 French troops. The First National Reconciliation Conference was held in Geneva in early November.

After an attack on West Beirut's Shia [*q.v.*] suburbs by the Lebanese army and the LF on 3 February 1984, fighting erupted between the army and the LF on the one side and the Amal-Druze [*q.v.*] alliance on the other. U.S. warships intervened against the Muslims forces. Following the defection of Muslims from the Lebanese army, the Amal-Druze alliance expelled the (Christian) army from West Beirut. On 7 February 1984 the U.S. withdrew its troops from Beirut. The other members of the Western MNF followed suit.

PHASE 6: March 1984 to January 1986—return of the Syrian hegemony. Encouraged by Assad, President Gemayel decided to abrogate the draft Lebanese-Israeli peace treaty: the Lebanese parliament did so on 5 March. After the Second National Reconciliation Conference in Lausanne, Switzerland, in mid-March, a national reconciliation government was formed. On 6 June 1985 Israel completed the last phase of its withdrawal from Lebanon by handing over its positions in southern Lebanon to the Christian militia run by it, but leaving behind 1,000 Israeli troops. In late December the commanders of Amal, the Druze militia, and the LF signed the National Agreement to

Solve the Lebanese Crisis, outlining political reform and Lebanese-Syrian relations; but the agreement was still-born, as the LF commander was unable to secure the endorsement of his executive committee.

PHASE 7: February 1986 to September 1988—limits of Syrian power. When Amal and the Druze militia in West Beirut started fighting in February 1987, Syria sent its troops, withdrawn in September 1982, to restore order. In early April 1988 there were clashes between Amal and Hizbollah [*q.v.*] in southern Lebanon. These continued until late May. Meanwhile, in mid-April Assad and U.S. Secretary of State George Shultz agreed to coordinate policy on political reform in Lebanon. When the Lebanese parliament failed to elect a new president, on 22 September 1988 the outgoing President Gemayel instructed his chief of staff, General Michel Aoun [*q.v.*], to form a temporary military government. Of the five other officers he appointed to his cabinet, three Muslim officers refused to serve.

PHASE 8: October 1988 to September 1989—war of liberation, Aoun style. Following his attack and suppression of the LF in the Christian enclave in February 1989, Aoun declared a war of liberation against Syria in mid-March. Syria imposed land and sea blockades on the Christian enclave. On 25 May the Sixteenth Arab League [*q.v.*] summit appointed a committee of the heads of Algeria, Morocco, and Saudi Arabia to settle the Lebanese crisis within six months. In mid-August, 14 Lebanese groups formed an anti-Aoun front.

PHASE 9: October 1989 to October 1990—the Taif Accord [*q.v.*]. Be-tween 30 September and 22 October, 58 of the 62 (surviving) Lebanese parliamentarians debated the National Reconciliation Charter [*q.v.*] in Taif, Saudi Arabia, and adopted it. Aoun rejected it but the Maronite Lebanese Front accepted it. After endorsing the Taif Accord on Lebanese soil at Qulayaat in northern Lebanon on 5 November, the Lebanese parliament elected Rene Muawad as president. He was assassinated on 22 November. Two days later parliament elected Elias Hrawi [*q.v.*] president.

From January to March 1990 there was intense fighting between Aoun loyalists and the LF. As a result Aoun ended up with only a third of the Christian enclave. The LF declared allegiance to Hrawi. On 21 August the parliament decided to overhaul the constitution as outlined in the Taif Accord. A month later Hrawi's decision to impose a land blockade on Aoun's enclave was backed by the LF. By now, in the midst of the crisis created by Iraq's invasion and occupation of Kuwait, Syria had joined the U.S.-led coalition against Iraq. On 13 October, in a joint air and ground campaign, the Lebanese and Syrian troops defeated Aoun's soldiers and brought the civil war to an end.

HUMAN LOSSES: The number of fatalities during the 15½ years of war, including the 15,700 killed in the Israeli invasion of 1982, mainly civilians, was put at 150,000.

ECONOMIC DAMAGE: During the first seven years of conflict (before the Second Israeli invasion), the direct annual cost of the war was put at $900 million.

AFTER THE WAR: On 9 May 1991 parliament passed a law giving Muslims and Christians parity in the chamber, thus changing the 6:5 Christian-Muslim ratio of the 1943 National Pact [*q.v.*] and raising the size of the chamber from 99 to 108 members. On 22 May Presidents Hrawi and Assad signed the Lebanese-Syrian Treaty of Brotherhood, Cooperation, and Coordination [*q.v.*] which required the two neighbors to coordinate their policies in foreign affairs, defense, and economy.

Lebanese Forces: *Lebanese militia and political party* Formed in January 1976, the Lebanese Forces (LF) consisted of the Maronite [*q.v.*] militias of the Phalange [*q.v.*], the National Liberal Party [*q.v.*], the Guardians of the Cedars [*q.v.*], and al-Tanzim. Its unified military command was headed by Bashir Gemayel [*q.v.*]. After his assassination in 1982 the new commander, Fadi Afram, adopted an openly pro-Israeli line, calling for talks between Lebanon and Israel. He fell from grace when the draft Lebanese-Israeli Peace Treaty [*q.v.*] was abrogated in March 1984. The LF's leadership passed to Fuad Abu Nadr. After a bloodless coup in March 1985, Samir Geagea assumed command of the LF.

In December 1989 Geagea's backing for the Taif Accord [*q.v.*] led to fighting between the LF and Gen. Michel Aoun [*q.v.*] commanding the (Christian) Lebanese army based in the Christian enclave. It intensified after Geagea declared his allegiance in April 1990 to President Elias Hrawi [*q.v.*], who rivaled Aoun as the head of state. Five months later the LF backed Hrawi's blockading of Aoun's enclave, now reduced to about a third of the Christian sector. At the time of

Aoun's fall in October 1990, marking the end of the civil war, the LF was 10,000 strong, down from its peak of 20,000 under Bashir Gemayel, with 25,000 reserves.

Geagea was included in the national unity cabinet formed in December. The next year, in line with the official policy of integrating all militiamen under the age of 25 into the regular armed forces, the government absorbed 6,500 LF men into the military. The LF then transformed itself into a political party. It boycotted the 1992 general election. Following the bombing of a Maronite church in Jonieh in February 1994, which killed nine worshippers, the LF was banned and Geagea was arrested on charges of complicity in the explosion and the assassinations of Rashid Karami [*q.v.*] in 1987 and Danny Chamoun, a son of Camille Chamoun [*q.v.*], in October 1990. Geagea was sentenced to life imprisonment. The LF entered the 2005 general election as part of the 14 March Alliance [*q.v.*] and gained six seats. Its deputies included Geagea. So the parliament passed a law to release him. In the 2009 election, the LF's share rose to eight.

Lebanese Front: *Lebanese political alliance* The Lebanese Front was formed in September 1976 as a confederation of the following Maronite [*q.v.*] Christian political parties: the Phalange Party [*q.v.*], the National Liberal Party [*q.v.*], the Guardians of the Cedars [*q.v.*], and the Maronite League. It was headed by Camille Chamoun [*q.v.*]. The Front's constituents stressed their distinctness from the Arab world by emphasizing that Maronite history, centering on the church and Mount Lebanon, stood apart from mainstream Muslim [*q.v.*] Arabs [*q.v.*] and even non-Maronite Christians. In December 1980 the Front issued a manifesto calling for the replacement of the 1943 National Pact [*q.v.*] by a federation or confederation within a unified Lebanon.

Whereas Chamoun was the nominal leader, Bashir Gemayel [*q.v.*] and his father, Pierre [*q.v.*], mattered more. Since Christians [*q.v.*] played a special role in Lebanon, they argued, they were entitled to a special position, irrespective of their minority status. The Front tightened its links with Israel, which found it more convenient to deal with a single Maronite political entity than with several. However, with Bashir Gemayel's murder in September 1982 and Israel's withdrawal from Lebanon in June 1985, the Front moderated its stance.

With the rise of Gen. Michel Aoun [*q.v.*] as a pretender to the presidency in September 1988, the Front became one of the three power centers in the Christian enclave, the remaining one being the Lebanese Forces [*q.v.*]. A year later the Front's parliamentary leader, Georges Saade, successfully opposed a proposal by the Lebanese parliament, meeting in Taif, Saudi Arabia, to discard confessionalism [*q.v.*] by a certain deadline. The internecine Christian fighting in early 1990 weakened the Front. With the end of the civil war [*q.v.*] in October, the Front, a creature of the conflict, lost its relevance.

Lebanese National Movement:
Lebanese-Palestinian political alliance
Formed on the eve of the April 1975–October 1990 Lebanese Civil War [*q.v.*], the Lebanese National Movement (LNM) was a confederation of various nationalist and progressive Muslim-dominated parties—including the Arab Baath Socialist Party [*q.v.*], the Progressive Socialist Party (PSP) [*q.v.*], the Syrian Social Nationalist Party [*q.v.*], the Communist Party [*q.v.*], the Communist Action Organization, the Popular Nasserist Organization, and the Independent Nasserites. Led by Kamal Jumblat [*q.v.*], it demanded the abolition of the confessional system, amendment of the constitution to redefine the prerogatives of the various branches of the executive, and reorganization of the army.

It formed an alliance with the Palestine Liberation Organization (PLO) [*q.v.*] in its fight with the Maronite [*q.v.*] Lebanese Front [*q.v.*] and the Lebanese Forces [*q.v.*]. When the LNM-PLO alliance gained the upper hand in the fighting, Syria intervened in June 1976 on the side of the Christians [*q.v.*]. Its troops expelled LNM-PLO forces from the Christian areas they had captured. This, and the subsequent Syrian plan to legitimize its occupation of eastern and northern Lebanon, turned Jumblat into a vocal adversary of Syrian President Hafiz Assad [*q.v.*].

Jumblat's assassination in March 1977 deprived the LNM of a charismatic figure. The mantle passed to his son, Walid [*q.v.*], who lacked experience and leadership qualities. He made his peace with Syria. Indeed, as the leader of both the PSP and the LNM, he coordinated his policies and actions with Damascus. Whereas the Lebanese Front insisted on resolving the problem of the Syrian and Palestinian military presence before tackling the issue of political reform, the LNM wanted immediate reform while its Syrian and Palestinian allies were able to lend it their support.

Israel's siege of Beirut [*q.v.*] in August 1982 resulted in the departure of both PLO and LNM fighters from West Beirut. This enfeebled the LNM. A year later, in July 1983, the constituents of the LNM gathered again (in Tripoli [*q.v.*]) to consult all other groups opposing the draft Lebanese-Israeli peace treaty [*q.v.*] that had been initialed two months earlier. After it succeeded in getting the treaty abrogated, the LNM ceased to function as a coherent body. Its erstwhile constituents participated in the civil strife through their respective militias. They came together again briefly as the Lebanese National Front in August 1989 to overthrow Gen. Michel Aoun [*q.v.*]. Having achieved its aim, the Front disintegrated.

Lebanese-Israeli (Putative) Peace Treaty (1983–84): Soon after assuming office in September 1982, President Amin Gemayel [*q.v.*] yielded to Washington's pressure to enter into talks with Israel provided the United States acted as the mediator. This led to an agreed draft of a peace treaty between Lebanon and Israel in early May 1983. It formally ended the state of war between the two countries, and banned Lebanon from allowing the use of its territory or airspace for the passage of troops or military equipment from any state that did not have diplomatic relations with Israel. It also required Lebanon to abrogate any regulations, laws, or treaties that were in conflict with the Lebanese-Israeli accord, including all the commitments

that Lebanon had made as a founder member of the Arab League [*q.v.*] since 1945. It curtailed the Lebanese government's power to station troops between the Zahrani and Awali rivers, and required it to recognize the Israeli-backed Christian militia, commanded by Saad Haddad, called the South Lebanon Army [*q.v.*], as the sole force authorized to patrol the area up to Zahrani, and allow the stationing of Lebanese-Israeli supervisory teams charged with detecting and destroying any armed guerrillas in the area.

The document was denounced by left-of-center forces in Lebanon and by Syrian President Hafiz Assad [*q.v.*]. Its adoption by 64 Lebanese members of parliament (with only two opposing), followed by the signing of it by Israel, made little difference to their stance. They continued to express their opposition publicly. Protesting at Israel's continued occupation of a large part of Lebanon in the aftermath of the June 1982 Israeli invasion [*q.v.*], President Gemayel withheld his signature on the treaty. Following the truck-bombing of their military barracks that resulted in 300 American and French deaths in October 1983, the United States, France, Britain, and Italy withdrew their peace-keeping contingents from Beirut [*q.v.*] in February 1984. With that, Gemayel lost his Western guardians. He therefore decided to abrogate the treaty. At his behest, the parliament did so almost unanimously on 5 March 1984.

Lebanese-Palestine Liberation Organization Agreement (1969): *See* Cairo Agreement (Lebanese-PLO, 1969).

Lebanese-Syrian Treaty of Brotherhood, Cooperation, and Coordination (1991): The six-article Lebanese-Syrian Treaty of Brotherhood, Cooperation, and Coordination was signed by the presidents of the two countries in Damascus [*q.v.*] in May 1991. Article 1 enjoins the parties to "realize the highest degree of cooperation and coordination between them in all political, security, cultural, scientific, and other concerns… within the framework of the sovereignty and independence of each of them." Article 2 requires the signatories to achieve cooperation and coordination in economics, agriculture, industry, commerce, transportation, communications, customs, and development. "The interrelationship of the two countries' security requires that Lebanon not be made the source of a threat to Syria's security or Syria to Lebanon's in any circumstances whatsoever," states Article 3. "Lebanon shall therefore not allow itself to become a passage or a base for any power or state or organization the purpose of which is the violation of Lebanon's security or Syria's security." Equally, Syria "shall not allow any action that threatens Lebanon's security, independence, or sovereignty."

The next article specifies the formation of a Lebanese-Syrian military committee to determine the size and duration of the Syrian troops' presence in Lebanon. Article 5 focuses on the contracting parties' foreign policy, and requires them to coordinate their Arab and international policies. The last article specifies the formation of joint agencies at different levels to implement the treaty—from the Higher Council, cochaired by their presidents, and consisting of the prime ministers, deputy prime ministers, and parliamentary speakers, to the level of joint committees on defense and security, foreign affairs, and economic and social affairs.

In September 1991 a defense and security pact between the two neighbors went into effect. And in 2001, Lebanon and Syria created a customs union. After the unconditional withdrawal of Israel from south Lebanon in May 2000, and the death of Hafiz Assad [*q.v.*] in June, the presence of Syrian troops in Lebanon faced increasing criticism. But the total withdrawal of the Syrian troops from Lebanon in April 2005 left intact the Syrian Lebanese Higher Council with its secretariat in Damascus [*q.v.*].

Lebanon:

OFFICIAL NAME: Republic of Lebanon

CAPITAL: Beirut [*q.v.*]

AREA: 4,036 sq. mi./10,452 sq. km

POPULATION: 4.22 million (2011 est.), including 375,000 Palestinian refugees in camps and Iraqi asylum seekers

GROSS DOMESTIC PRODUCT (nominal): $42.54 billion; per capita, $10,100 (2011 est.)

GROSS DOMESTIC PRODUCT (Purchasing Power Parity): $61.58 billion; per capita, $14,590 (2011 est.)

NATIONAL CURRENCY: Lebanese Pound (LBP); LBP 1000 = U.S. $0.66 = £0.42 = €0.50 (2001)

FORM OF GOVERNMENT: republic, president elected by parliament

OFFICIAL LANGUAGE: Arabic [*q.v.*]

OFFICIAL RELIGION: None

ADMINISTRATIVE REGIONS: Lebanon is divided into six governorates (provinces).

CONSTITUTION: Promulgated by the French Mandate in May 1926, the constitution was amended in 1927, 1929, and 1943 by France—and in 1947 and 1990 by the Lebanese parliament, the last exercise resulting in changes to 31 articles. Lebanon is a multiparty, multi-religious republic, where since 1943 confessionalism [*q.v.*] has been built into the political-administrative system. It specifies that the president of the republic is to be a Maronite Christian [*q.v.*], the prime minister a Sunni Muslim [*q.v.*], and the parliamentary speaker a Shia Muslim [*q.v.*].

ETHNIC COMPOSITION: (2011) Arab 95 percent, Armenian [*q.v.*] 4 percent, other 1 percent.

EXECUTIVE: The 1990 amendments to the constitution curtailed the power of the president, elected for a six-year term by parliament, and increased the authority of the cabinet, making it more autonomous. The president has the power to approve and implement laws passed by the National Assembly. However, his decisions must be cosigned by the prime minister, except when it is a question of appointing a prime minister—something he must do in consultation with the speaker of the Assembly and senior deputies. Cabinet ministers need not be Assembly members, but are responsible to it.

High officials:

President: Michel Suleiman [*q.v.*], 2008–

Prime minister: Najib Mikati [*q.v.*], 2011–

Speaker of the parliament: Nabih Berri [*q.v.*], 2009–

HISTORY: After receiving a Mandate for (Greater) Syria from the League of Nations in 1920, France enlarged the ex-Ottoman Vilayat of Lebanon by adding areas to its north, west, and south hitherto belonging to Syria, and calling the new entity Greater Lebanon. In 1926 it promulgated a republican constitution, with a parliament and an executive president elected by parliament, and the country was renamed the Republic of Lebanon. France suspended the constitution in 1932, and a census held in that year produced figures for 16 recognized religious sects. In 1936 Paris reinstated the constitution, and the Franco-Lebanese Treaty [*q.v.*], signed in November, gave considerable autonomy to Lebanon.

During World War II the pro-German government—formed in Vichy, central France—took over overseas French territories, including Lebanon, in 1940. The Vichy government's occupation of Lebanon was overturned by British and Free French forces in June 1941, and Lebanon was given (nominal) independence. The National Pact [*q.v.*] of March 1943 provided a formula of six Christian to five Muslim parliamentarians. In September Bishara Khouri [*q.v.*] was elected president. In 1945 Lebanon was one of the founder members of the Arab League [*q.v.*].

With the departure of the French in December 1946, Lebanon became fully independent. It participated in the Palestine War (1948–49) [*q.v.*] and signed a truce with Israel in March 1949. Khouri was reelected later that year, but was forced to resign in 1952 and was followed by Camille Chamoun [*q.v.*]. Chamoun subscribed to the Eisenhower Doctrine [*q.v.*] and solicited the help of U.S. troops in the midst of the May–July 1958 Lebanese

Civil War [*q.v.*] between his forces and those of Kamal Jumblat [*q.v.*]. The succeeding president, Fuad Chehab [*q.v.*], tried to modernize Lebanon's political-administrative machinery, which was steeped in feudal values and sectarian cleavage. The reforming pace slowed down during the presidency of Charles Helou [*q.v.*].

Lebanon did not participate in the June 1967 Arab-Israeli War [*q.v.*]. The increasing presence of armed Palestinians led to clashes between them and the Lebanese army, but a modus vivendi was worked out through the 1969 Cairo Agreement [*q.v.*]. During the presidency of Suleiman Franjieh [*q.v.*], the Palestine Liberation Organization (PLO) [*q.v.*] set up its headquarters in Beirut [*q.v.*] in 1972. Lebanon stayed out of the 1973 Arab-Israeli War [*q.v.*].

In April 1975 the long Lebanese Civil War [*q.v.*] erupted. By the spring of 1976 the Lebanese National Movement (LNM)-PLO alliance controlled two-thirds of the country, and Syria intervened on the side of the Christian Lebanese Front [*q.v.*]. In September Elias Sarkis [*q.v.*], a Syrian nominee, was elected president. After the assassination of the LNM leader, Kamal Jumblat [*q.v.*], in March 1977, his son Walid [*q.v.*] succeeded him.

Israel invaded southern Lebanon in March 1978 to destroy the PLO bases there. In June Israel withdrew, but handed over its posts in southern Lebanon to a Christian militia sponsored by it. The Maronite militias forged strong ties with Israel, but their joint attempts to extend their sway to Zahle in the Beqaa Valley in mid-1981 were frustrated by Syria, now

maintaining 30,000 peacekeeping troops under the aegis of the Arab League, and backing the Muslim camp.

In early June 1982, six weeks after completing its withdrawal from the Sinai Peninsula [*q.v.*] in late April 1982, under the terms of the Egyptian-Israeli Peace Treaty [*q.v.*], Israel again invaded Lebanon. It occupied two-fifths of the country, including Beirut [*q.v.*], and was instrumental in getting Bashir Gemayel [*q.v.*] elected president. But before he could take office Gemayel was assassinated. The Israeli invasion ended on 1 September, after 11,644 PLO fighters and 2,700 Syrian troops had left West Beirut.

Amin Gemayel [*q.v.*] was elected president. Under U.S. pressure he initialed a draft peace treaty with Israel in May 1983. But strong domestic hostility to it, combined with Syrian opposition, resulted in the treaty's being annulled in March 1984. Following a reconciliation conference in Lausanne, Switzerland, a national unity government was formed. In June 1985 Israel completed the last phase of its withdrawal, handing over its positions in southern Lebanon to its surrogate force, the South Lebanon Army (SLA) [*q.v.*], backed by its 1,000 soldiers. In early 1987 Syria dispatched its troops into West Beirut to restore order following fighting between Amal [*q.v.*], a Shia [*q.v.*] militia, and an alliance of left-of-center non-Shia Muslim forces.

Following parliament's failure to elect a new president to succeed Gemayel, on 22 September 1988 he called on his chief of staff, Gen. Michel Aoun [*q.v.*], to form a temporary military government. Of the five officers appointed to the cabinet, all three Muslim officers refused to serve. In May 1989 Aoun launched a "war of liberation" from Syria. Five months later Lebanon's parliamentarians, meeting in Taif, Saudi Arabia, adopted the National Reconciliation Charter [*q.v.*], containing political reform. It was later approved at a meeting held inside Lebanon. They also elected Elias Hrawi [*q.v.*], a Syrian nominee, as president.

Aoun rejected the Taif Accord [*q.v.*], whereas the Maronite Lebanese Forces [*q.v.*] accepted it. This led to intra-Christian violence in which Aoun did badly. After parliament had translated the Taif Accord into law, giving parity to Muslims and Christians in the legislature and curtailing the powers of the Maronite president in August, the Lebanese and Syrian forces defeated Aoun's troops on 13 October 1990, thus ending the civil war. A national unity government disarmed the various militias, ended the division of the capital into East and West Beirut, and signed a Treaty of Brotherhood, Cooperation, and Coordination with Syria [*q.v.*] in May 1991.

Elections to an enlarged parliament were held between August and October 1992. Due to the boycott by the Maronite-dominated parties, the new chamber and the consequent government were strongly pro-Syrian. Lebanon participated in the Middle East peace process that had been inaugurated by the Middle East Peace Conference in Madrid in October 1991 [*q.v.*]. But, mirroring the impasse between Syria and Israel, its bilateral talks with Israel made little progress.

The government called on Israel to vacate southern Lebanon unconditionally, as demanded by the 1978 UN Security Council Resolution 425 [*q.v.*], and allowed Hizbollah [*q.v.*] to function in the region as a counterforce to the SLA. Bound by the 1991 Lebanese-Syrian Treaty of Brotherhood, Cooperation, and Coordination [*q.v.*], it consulted Syria in its peace talks with Israel. Since Syria's negotiations with Israel made little progress, the Lebanese-Isreali talks proved inconclusive. Pressured by Hizbollah's relentless attacks, Israel unconditionally quit southern Lebanon in May 2000.

After the terrorist attacks on the United States in September 2001, Washington pressured Lebanon to ban Hizbollah. But the Lebanese government refused, arguing that it was a legitimate political group with a substantial presence in the parliament as well as a social welfare organization. President Emile Lahoud [*q.v.*] chaired the Twenty-second Arab League summit [*q.v.*] in March 2002 in Beirut, which called for devising a universally accepted definition of terrorism [*q.v.*]. Reconstruction of Beirut advanced steadily.

The assassination of Rafiq Hariri [*q.v.*] in 2005 caused a political earthquake and resulted in a popular anti-Syria movement, called the Cedar Revolution [*q.v.*]. It led to the withdrawal of the remaining 15,000 Syrian soldiers from Lebanon. In the general election that followed, the anti-Syrian 14 March Alliance [*q.v.*] won a majority and formed the government under Fouad Siniora [*q.v.*].

The war between Israel and the Hizbollah from 12 July to 14 August

2006 caused significant civilian fatalities and much damage to Lebanon's infrastructure and private property. Qatar was preeminent in providing financial assistance to those Lebanese who suffered losses.

Following the end of President Lahoud's term of office in October 2007, the opposition 8 March Alliance [q.v.] demanded a national unity government as its price for participating in the election for the next president. When this was rejected, Speaker Nabih Berri refused to convene parliament. The government was paralyzed. In the ensuing civil unrest, which turned violent, nearly 200 people lost their lives. A deal brokered by Qatar in May 2008 ended the crisis with an agreement to form a national unity government and elected Michel Suleiman [q.v.], the current chief of staff, as president.

As agreed in principle before, Syria opened its embassy in Beirut in December 2008, followed by Lebanon doing the same in Damascus three months later, thus creating diplomatic parity between them for the first time.

Though the 14 March Alliance won a majority in the 2009 parliamentary election while polling fewer votes than its rival, it agreed to form a national unity government with the opposition 8 March Alliance. This was the most intensely contested election as well as the most expensive. More than 120,000 Lebanese expatiates were flown in and accommodated in hotels at the estimated expense of $30 million, most of them being Maronite or Sunni.

The coalition government formed by Saad Hariri [q.v.] in November 2009 collapsed in January 2011 when, following his refusal to withhold funds for the United Nations's Special Tribunal for Lebanon (STL), 11 of the 30 ministers resigned. In the succeeding government of Najib Mikati [q.v.], deputies of the pro-Syria 8 March Alliance [q.v.] formed a majority.

Because multiparty electoral politics have been the traditional mode of public life, except during the 1975–90 Civil War [q.v.], there were almost no pro-democracy demonstrations in Lebanon during 2011–2012. Nonetheless, political factions were divided on how they viewed the uprising in Syria, with the 8 March Alliance constituents attributing the protest to foreign intervention and Salafi [q.v.] militants, and their rivals in the 14 March Alliance openly identifying with the Syrian opposition.

LEGISLATURE: The National Assembly is a unicameral house with 128 members, divided equally among Christians and Muslims, who are elected on universal suffrage for a four-year term. It has legislative and constitutional powers. It is also an electoral college for the election of president. If it fails to choose a president by a two-thirds majority in the first secret ballot, it then makes its choice by a simple majority. On constitutional matters, such as electing the president, a quorum of two-thirds is required. That is not the case with the routine business of law-making.

After the outbreak of the Lebanese Civil War in April 1975, the Assembly, elected in 1972, periodically, extended its life until September 1992, when a fresh election was held under the amended constitution. The new share of Islamic sects, with the old share in parenthesis, was: Sunni 27

(20), Shia 27 (19), Druze [*q.v.*] 8 (6), and Alawi [*q.v.*] 2 (none). The new share of Christian sects was: Maronites 34 (30), Greek Orthodox 14 [*q.v.*] (11), Greek Catholics 6 [*q.v.*] (6), Armenian Catholic and Armenian Orthodox [*q.v.*] 6 (5), Protestants [*q.v.*] and non-Muslim minorities 4 (2).

RELIGIOUS COMPOSITION (2011, unofficial estimate): Muslim, ca. 61 percent, of which Shia 28 percent, Sunni 27 percent, Druze 5 percent, Alawi 1 percent; Christian, ca. 39 percent, of which Maronites 21 percent, Greek Orthodox 8 percent, Greek Catholic, 4 percent, Armenian Catholic and Orthodox 4 percent; other, 2 percent. As many as 18 religious sects are now recognized officially.

Lehi/Lehy (Hebrew: acronym of *Lohemei Herut Israel/Yisrael*, Fighters for Free Israel): *Zionist militia* In June 1940 Avraham Stern [*q.v.*] and his followers, disagreeing with Irgun's [*q.v.*] decision to suspend its armed campaign against the British Mandate, left Irgun and established Lehi in September. Commonly known as the Stern Gang or Stern Group, Lehi argued that since the British were the number-one enemy of Jews [*q.v.*], and since fighting them was the top Jewish priority, there was no harm in negotiating with the German Nazis to achieve this aim. As a result, it contacted the German Embassy in Ankara. This, and the terrorist attacks against the British Mandate, marginalized Lehi and Stern, who went underground.

Stern's death in February 1942 left Lehi almost intact. In November, the leadership formally passed to the triumvirate of Yitzhak Shamir [*q.v.*], Nathan Yellin-Mor, and Israel Schieb. Its assassinations policy resulted in the murder of Lord Moyne, British minister of state in Cairo [*q.v.*], in November 1944. After the war, in order to coordinate underground activities, it joined with Irgun and Histadrut [*q.v.*] to form the Hebrew Resistance Movement (HRM) in November 1945.

Among the joint operations it carried out with Irgun were the blowing up of the British embassy in Rome and the posting of letter-bombs to British ministers, as well as killing British soldiers in Palestine [*q.v.*] and hanging their officers. Lehi attacked a military airfield as well as several railway depots and workshops. After the disbanding of the HRM in October 1946, Lehi felt free to intensify its guerrilla activities: it attacked oil installations, military trains and vehicles, and British troops and policemen.

Between November 1947 (when the United Nations adopted a partition plan for Palestine) and May 1948 (when Israel was founded), the 1,000-strong Lehi allied with the larger Irgun in concerted attacks on Arabs [*q.v.*], including a fully fledged offensive against the Arabs of Jaffa [*q.v.*] and an attack on Deir Yassin village near Jerusalem [*q.v.*] on 9–10 April 1948, killing 254 men, women, and children.

After the establishment of Israel, the decision to dissolve Lehi and absorb its members into the Israel Defense Forces (IDF) did not apply to Jerusalem, which was given a separate status. Therefore, Lehi units continued to function in the city. In September the assassination of Count Folke Bernadotte, a Swedish diplomat acting as the UN mediator between Arabs and Jews, in Jerusalem was claimed by *Hazit HaMoledet* (Hebrew: *The Homeland Front*), a sub-group of Lehi. Two Lehi leaders, Nathan Yellin-Mor and Matitiahu Schmulevitz, were found guilty and given eight and five years' imprisonment, respectively, by a military court. But they were soon released as part of the general amnesty. Yellin-Mor was elected to the Knesset [*q.v.*] in January 1949 on a Lehi ticket. The group was disbanded later that year.

The Israeli government treated Lehi members on a par with Haganah [*q.v.*] and Irgun when calculating pensions or redundancy payments for its civil servants.

Lesser Tumb Island: (also spelled Lesser Tunb Island) *See* Tumb/Tunb Islands.

Levant: (French: *derivative of lever, to rise, e.g. sunrise*) Early historians applied this term to the lands along the eastern shores of the Mediterranean. Subsequent to the French Mandate of Syria and Lebanon in 1920, these countries were called the Levant States. Today the term Levant applies to the independent states of Syria and Lebanon.

Liberal Party (Israel): *Israeli political party* (Official title: *Liberalim* [Hebrew: *Liberals*]) The fear of a further fall in their electoral popularity drove the General Zionists [*q.v.*] to merge with the Progressive Party [*q.v.*] to form the Liberal Party on the eve of the 1961 general election. While en-

dorsing the concept of a welfare state, it demanded encouragement for private enterprise. It won 17 seats in the Knesset [*q.v.*]. In the 1965 election it allied with Herut [*q.v.*] to form a bloc called Gahal [*q.v.*], under the leadership of Menachem Begin [*q.v.*].

Liberal Socialist Party (Egypt): *Egyptian political party* (Also called Socialist Liberal Party) The Liberal Socialist Party (LSP) was formed in May 1976 by Mustafa Kamel Murad to represent the rightist forum within the Arab Socialist Union [*q.v.*]. It advocated liberal economic policies and greater freedom for private enterprise. It was allowed to publish a weekly magazine, *Al-Ahrar* (Arabic: *The Free*). In the general election in November it won 12 seats. This declined to three in the 1979 election when Murad failed to be reelected.

The LSP's poor performance in the next two elections led its leadership to form an alliance with the Socialist Labor Party [*q.v.*] and the Muslim Brotherhood [*q.v.*] on the eve of the 1987 election, especially as it had no chance of crossing the newly specified threshold of 8 percent of the total vote to qualify for seats in parliament. The resulting Labor Islamic Alliance (LSA) [*q.v.*] won 60 seats, with the LSP's share at 10. Like its allies in the LSA, it boycotted the 1990 election when the government rejected their call to lift the state of emergency and conduct the election under the supervision of a non-governmental organization. In the 1995 election it secured one seat, retaining it in the 2000 election.

It failed to win a seat in 2005 and went into oblivion.

Liberation Movement of Iran: *Iranian political party* (Official title: *Nahzat-e Azadi-e Iran*) After his release from jail in 1961, Mahdi Bazargan [*q.v.*], a leader of the National Front [*q.v.*], teamed up with Ayatollah Mahmoud Taleqani [*q.v.*] to form the Liberation Movement of Iran (LMI). They saw it as a link between Shia Islam [*q.v.*] and modern political ideas and movements. It was open to both lay and clerical Iranians. Bazargan urged the clergy to participate in politics.

After Bazargan's call for a boycott of the referendum on the White Revolution [*q.v.*] in January 1963, he was given a 10-year prison sentence. But that did not slow down the spread of the LMI among Iranian students in Europe and North America. In late 1977, with the revolutionary movement gathering pace in Iran, the LMI revived at home.

Its status rose when, after the 1979 Islamic revolution [*q.v.*], Ayatollah Ruhollah Khomeini [*q.v.*] appointed Bazargan as prime minister. In the first parliamentary election it won 20 seats in a house of 270. Since it functioned as opposition it came under official pressure. The government shut down its paper, *Mizan* (Persian: *Scales*), on the ground that it had divulged military secrets. However, by the spring of 1983, when the political scene was occupied by the governing Islamic Republican Party [*q.v.*] and its smaller allies, the LMI was the only opposition group allowed to function.

In a parliamentary speech in August, Bazargan, who had opposed Iran's advance into Iraq two months earlier, criticized the government for labeling dissidents as heretics. In April 1985 Khomeini criticized his appeals

for a truce with Iraq, arguing that they demoralized the military. Undaunted, Bazargan and the LMI continued to describe war as harmful to Islam [*q.v.*] and revolution. In August 1985 Bazargan was disqualified as a candidate for the presidency.

Once the Iran-Iraq War [*q.v.*] ended in 1988, the party lost its strongest card against the government. While a sharp decline in the majority for President Ali Akbar Hashemi Rafsanjani [*q.v.*] in 1993 showed that opposition to the government was rising, there was little evidence to show that the LMI was the main beneficiary.

The death of Bazargan in 1995 caused a decline in the LMI's following. Though the party lacked an official license, the authorities allowed it to function. During the student protest in mid-1999, it emerged that some students favored the LMI. In 2001 the conservative-dominated judiciary arrested many party leaders, and next year the group was formally banned.

Lieberman, Avigdor (1958–): *Israeli politician* Born Evet Lvovich Lieberman in Kishinev (now Chisinau) in Soviet Moldova, he migrated to Israel in 1978, where he changed his name to Avigdor. After serving his military draft, he graduated in political science from Hebrew University in Jerusalem [*q.v.*]. During his studies he took a part-time job as a bouncer at the university student club called Shablul (Hebrew: *Snail*). He was an active member of the Zionist Forum for the Soviet Jewry.

In 1988, he started working with Benjamin Netanyahu [*q.v.*]. On becoming leader of Likud [*q.v.*] in 1993,

Netanyahu appointed him director general of the party. When Netanyahu was elected prime minister in 1996 he named Lieberman director general of the prime minister's office.

On the eve of the 1999 Knesset [*q.v.*] election, Lieberman formed Israel Beiteinu [*q.v.*] with the aim of attracting the votes of the Jews [*q.v.*] from the former Soviet Union. It secured four seats in the Knesset [*q.v.*], including one for him. In March 2001, Prime Minister Ariel Sharon [*q.v.*] appointed him national infrastructure minister. He resigned the post a year later. After getting reelected to the Knesset in January 2003, he became transportation minister under Sharon. But, when he opposed Sharon's plan to disengage from the Gaza Strip [*q.v.*], he lost his post in May 2004.

With his party winning 11 seats in the 2006 general election, Lieberman's importance rose. He joined the coalition government of Ehud Olmert [*q.v.*] as minister of strategic affairs only after Olmert reneged on Kadima's election pledge to withdraw from a number of Jewish settlements in the West Bank [*q.v.*]. He quit the cabinet in January 2008 when Olmert agreed to peace talks with the Palestinians on core issues after the U.S.-sponsored Middle East Conference in Annapolis [*q.v.*] in November 2007.

Following his party's increased Knesset membership to 15 in the 2009 election, he became foreign minister as well as deputy prime minister in the government led by Netanyahu. At a joint press conference with U.S. Secretary of State Hillary Clinton, he clashed with her on the issue of the Jewish settlement in the West Bank,

which Washington wanted frozen.

As a resident of the Jewish settlement of Nokdim in the West Bank since 1988, he is a staunch supporter of Jewish settlers. He advocates an exchange of territories whereby Israel would keep major Jewish settlement blocs in the West Bank, and a future Palestinian state would acquire large Israeli Arab [*q.v.*] population centers. Under the slogan "No loyalty, no citizenship," he demanded a law specifying Israeli Arabs' allegiance to Israel as a Jewish state.

After a three-year-long investigation, Israeli police recommended in 2009 that he should be indicted for bribe-taking, fraud, violation of public confidence, obstruction of justice, and money laundering, involving transfer of millions of Israeli shekels to shell companies and accounts belonging to people close to him over the past nine years.

In December 2011 he said that he did not believe that a peace deal between Israel and the Palestinians would be agreed within the next decade, and therefore Israel must work to manage the conflict and not solve it.

Likud (Hebrew: *Unity): Israeli political bloc* In the wake of the October 1973 Arab-Israeli War [*q.v.*], Gahal [*q.v.*] combined with the Free Center, the State Party (a remnant of Rafi), and the Eretz Yisrael movement to form Likud. What brought them together was their commitment to incorporating into Israel the Palestinian Arab territories occupied since the June 1967 Arab-Israeli War [*q.v.*].

Ideologically, Likud was an alliance of the conservative, capitalist, and ultranationalist trends within secular

Zionism [*q.v.*]. It won 30.2 percent of the votes (39 seats) in the December 1973 election and secured 33.4 percent of the votes (43 seats) in the May 1977 election, becoming the senior partner in the coalition government, including religious parties, headed by its leader, Menachem Begin [*q.v.*]. It repeated its winning performance in the July 1981 election and secured 47 seats.

Due to Israel's invasion of Lebanon [*q.v.*] in 1982 and its aftermath, resulting in the death of more than 500 soldiers, Likud's popularity declined. Begin resigned in August 1983 and was succeeded by Yitzhak Shamir [*q.v.*]. Likud's share of 41 seats in the 1984 general election was a little more than Labor's [*q.v.*] at 38. It formed a national unity government with Labor, with its leader becoming prime minister for a two-year term. The same happened after the 1988 election when, faced with the loss of a further two seats (to 39), Likud agreed to share power with Labor in a national unity administration.

When this arrangement broke down in March 1990 on the issue of the terms of a Middle East peace process, Likud managed to put together a coalition cabinet with the help of religious and ultra-right-wing parties. In the June 1992 election, with its share of seats down to 32, it lost power. Its leadership passed to Benjamin Netanyahu [*q.v.*]. In the May 1996 general election, it won 22 seats. After Netanyahu had stepped down as the party leader in the wake of his defeat in the prime ministerial contest in May 1999, and Likud's Knesset [*q.v.*] strength had fallen to 19, its leadership went to Ariel Sharon [*q.v.*].

Sharon won the prime ministerial election in 2001. In the Knesset election that followed in 2003, Likud's share of seats rose to 38. Sharon formed a national unity government with Labor as the main partner. After his government's withdrawal from Gaza in September 2005, disaffection among Likud ranks rose. Sharon quit the party to found the centrist Kadima [*q.v.*] in November. Kadima gained 11 Knesset members because of the defections from Likud, whose leadership passed to Netanyahu. In the 2006 general election, Likud's strength fell to 12, a record. But its fortunes rose in the 2009 Knesset election: its 27 seats were just one short of the leading Kadima. But when Kadima's leader Tzipi Livni [*q.v.*] failed to cobble together a coalition government, Netanyahu formed one consisting of right-wing and ultra-right-wing groups. In May 2012 he co-opted Kadima, led by Shaul Mofaz, and expanded his coalition.

Little Tumb Island: also spelled Little Tunb Island; *See* Tumb Tunb Islands.

Livni, Tzipi (1958–): *Israeli politician*
Born to Tzipora Malka to Eitan Livni and Sara Rosenberg—both leading members of Irgun [*q.v.*], her father being its chief operations officer—in Tel Aviv [*q.v.*]; she was educated in that city.

After serving in the military, she joined Mossad [*q.v.*]. She was part of the intelligence unit involved in Israel's invasion of Lebanon in 1982 [*q.v.*]. She left Mossad in 1983 to marry and finish her law studies at Bar Ilan University in Tel Aviv. She practiced law for a decade before joining

Likud [*q.v.*] in 1996. Prime Minister Benjamin Netanyahu [*q.v.*] named her chairperson of the state-owned companies, and she supervised the privatization process.

She was elected to the Knesset [*q.v.*] in 1999. Two years later Prime Minister Ariel Sharon [*q.v.*] appointed her minister for regional development. After her reelection in 2003, she was named minister for housing and construction, and then moved to justice ministry. Livni quit Likud in November 2005 to join Kadima [*q.v.*], founded by Sharon. With the resignation of many Likud members from the cabinet, she was given the additional post of foreign minister in 2006.

Following the March 2006 Knesset election, she was named deputy prime minister by Prime Minister Ehud Olmert [*q.v.*]. During the Israeli-Hizbollah War [*q.v.*] in July-August, she was kept out of the conduct of the armed conflict. Her strained relations with Olmert continued until, facing corruption allegations, Olmert announced his intention to resign in July 2008.

In the subsequent contest for Kadima's leadership with Shaul Mofaz [*q.v.*], a former defense minister, she won by a margin of 1 percent of the vote. This marked a break in the traditional ascendancy of former generals in Israeli politics. However, she failed to form a coalition government headed by her. This led President Shimon Peres [*q.v.*] to let Olmert continue as the caretaker prime minister until the next general election.

Livni was part of the three-member team, with Olmert and defense minis-

ter Ehud Barak [*q.v.*], that launched and supervised the Gaza War of 2008–09 [*q.v.*]. In the February 2009 election Kadima won 28 seats, one more than Likud. But once again she failed to form a coalition government. As the opposition leader she stressed equally security of Israel and furthering the peace process. In March 2012 she lost the party's leadership to Mofaz by a wide margin. Two months later she gave up her Knesset seat.

M

Maarach (Hebrew: *Alignment*): *Israeli political alliance* Maarach is the popular term that was applied to the alliance between Mapai [*q.v.*] and Ahdut HaAvodah-Poale Zion [*q.v.*] in 1965—and then from 1969 to 1984 to the alliance between the Labor Party [*q.v.*] and Mapam [*q.v.*].

Mafdal (Hebrew: acronym of *Mifleget Datit Leumit,* National Religious Party*): See* National Religious Party (Israel).

mahdi (Arabic: *the guided one, leader*) (Also spelled Mehdi) The concept of mahdi, the Rightly Guided One, who will end injustice and restore faith while claiming divine sanction, is well defined in Judaism [*q.v.*], Christianity [*q.v.*], and Twelver Shiism [*q.v.*]. Twelver Shias believe that the Twelfth Imam, Muhammad al-Qasim, the infant son of the Eleventh Imam, Hassan al-Askari, is their mahdi, who has been in spiritual occultation since 874 A.D. but will reappear to institute the rule of justice on earth before the Day of Judgment. Among Sunnis [*q.v.*] the prevalent concept is that of a *mujaddid* (Arabic: *one who renews*), who appears at the turn of every Islamic century to defend the *sunna* [*q.v.*] from innovation.

Mahfouz, Naguib (1911–2006): *Egyptian writer, winner of the Nobel Prize for Literature, 1988* Born into a merchant family in Cairo [*q.v.*], Mahfouz graduated in philosophy from Cairo University in 1934. After a brief period of teaching philosophy, he joined the civil service in 1939 and stayed on for 33 years. After serving in the ministry of religious endowments (1939–54), he moved to the ministry of culture and national guidance as director of technical supervision, and later as director of the State Cinema Organization.

He discovered European fiction at university, and avidly read in French such writers as Honoré de Balzac, Albert Camus, Fyodor Dostoevsky, Gustave Flaubert, Walter Scott, Leo Tolstoy, and Emile Zola. *A Game of Fates* (1939), his first novel, was influenced by Walter Scott. Set in the era of the pharaohs, it dealt with an oppressive regime and the overthrow of foreign rule. As monarchical Egypt was then under British tutelage, the subject was contemporary.

After two more historical novels, Mahfouz turned to social realism with *A New Cairo* (1946). The book centered on three university students— one a socialist, the second a pious Muslim, and the third an opportunist. The next three novels—*Khan al-Khalili* (1945), *Midaqq Alley* (1947), and *The Beginning and the End*

(1949)—revolved around the lower middle classes in Cairo. The novels had a large cast and examined the prevailing social tensions. Balzac was his inspiration. Mahfouz stretched the bounds of literary Arabic [*q.v.*]— which is understood from the Persian Gulf [*q.v.*] to the Atlantic—to compose realistic dialogue, a unique achievement, thus fashioning a device that allowed him and other Arabic writers to infuse social realism into their creative works and broaden their readership.

Next followed his most mature work, *The Trilogy* (1956–57): *Bayn al-Qasryn (The Palace Walk)*, *Qasr al-Shawq (The Palace of Desire)*, and *al-Sukkariyya (The Sugar Street)*, named after Cairo streets. In it he offered an eye-witness account of Egypt between the World Wars I and II through a 30-year history of one Cairene family, using a vernacular that had not been penned before, with religious and political themes entertainingly intertwined. It made him a literary star in Egypt and elsewhere in the Arab world. In its length and scale *The Trilogy* remains unrivalled in Arabic literature.

After seven years of silence came a serialization in *al-Ahram* (Arabic: *The Pyramids*), the country's leading daily newspaper, of his *Children of Gebelaawi* (1964), an iconoclastic allegory of human life from Genesis to the present day, which concluded with a vision of man searching in a rubbish dump for clues about his salvation. So unsettling was this work that the authorities did not allow it to be issued as a book in Egypt.

At the film broadcasting division of the ministry of culture and national guidance, he adapted several of his novels as movies. He became a full-time writer in 1973 and continued his steady output of novels and short stories. By the time he won the Nobel Prize for Literature at the age of 77 he had authored 32 novels, 13 volumes of short stories, and 30 screenplays. He had also emerged as the most widely translated Egyptian writer. After the Nobel Prize his novels were immediately translated into several languages.

Adrift in the Nile was published in 1993, followed by *The Harafish* in 1994, a story of a Egyptian family living in an alley over several centuries. While his works are not partisan they are certainly political. A modest man of regular habits, he had always been a writer with a highly developed social conscience, committed to social justice.

He was also robustly independent-minded, and was stabbed in the neck outside his home in 1994 by a Muslim [*q.v.*] fanatic after he had been denounced as an "infidel" by Islamist extremists. Due to permanently damaged nerves, he lost the full use of his right (writing) hand, and his output declined drastically. His post-attack works of nonfiction were *The Rehabilitation Period* (2004) and *The Seventh Heaven* (2005).

His fiction and nonfiction works translated into English included *Arabian Nights and Days* (1995); *The Honeymoon* (1995); *The Beggar, the Thief and the Dogs* (2000); *The Day the Leader Was Killed* (2001); *Naguib Mahfouz at Sidi Gaber: Reflections of a Nobel Laureate, 1994–2001* (2001); and *Voices from the Arab World: Ancient Egyptian Tales* (2003)—capped by *The Complete Mahfouz Library* (2002).

Majlis (Arabic/Persian: *Assembly*): *parliament in Iran* Majlis is the popular term that has been used for the Iranian parliament since its inception during the 1906–07 Constitutional Revolution [*q.v.*]. It is the oldest elected legislative body in the Middle East [*q.v.*]. *See also* Iran: Constitution and Legislature.

Maki (Hebrew: acronym of *Miflaga Kommunistit Israelit*, Israeli Communist Party): *Israeli political party* Maki emerged in October 1948 out of the merger of the Communist Party of Palestine (CPP) [*q.v.*] and the remnants of the League of National Liberation (LNL). It recognized the State of Israel without accepting the Zionist doctrine of a link between the Jews [*q.v.*] in Israel and the diaspora [*q.v.*]. It backed the right of Arab refugees to return to their homes, as well as the founding of a Palestinian state in the territory allotted to the Arabs [*q.v.*] in the UN partition plan of November 1947.

In the First Knesset (1949–51) [*q.v.*] it won four seats. It had 8,000 members in 1951. Benefiting from a split in Mapam [*q.v.*] in 1953, it increased its Knesset seats to six in the 1955 election. Opposed to the military administration of the Arab-inhabited areas, it fought discrimination against Arab citizens, then 4 percent of the population. It was the only party to oppose the Israeli aggression in the 1956 Suez War [*q.v.*].

In the early 1960s, when the Soviet Union began to pursue pro-Arab policies, a cleavage developed in Maki. The pro-Arab faction proposed cooperation with the Arab Communist parties whereas the pro-Jewish faction advocated alliance with certain Zionist workers' groups to form a popular front. Moscow's sympathy for the Palestine Liberation Organization [*q.v.*], and its continued refusal to allow Soviet Jews to emigrate, accentuated the division within Maki. In mid-1965, the pro-Arab wing led by Meir Vilner and Tawfiq Toubi left Maki to form Rakah [*q.v.*]. In the general election later that year, Maki, led by Moshe Sneh [*q.v.*] and Shamuel Mikunis, gained only one seat.

Maki supported the June 1967 Arab-Israeli War [*q.v.*] and opposed unconditional Israeli withdrawal from the Occupied Arab Territories [*q.v.*]. In the 1969 election it retained its single seat, but failed to do so in the election four years later. The party disintegrated in 1975.

al-Maktoum, Muhammad bin Rashid

Muhammad al-Maktoun (1949–): *ruler of Dubai emirate in the United Arab Emirates, 2006–; prime minister and vice president of the United Arab Emirates, 2006–* Born in Dubai [q.v.], he was educated privately there and at Bell Language School in Cambridge, U.K. He received his military training at Mons Officer Cadet School in Aldershot, U.K.

After his nomination as the Crown Prince in 1995 by the ruler, Shaikh Maktoum bin Rashid al-Maktoum [*q.v.*] in 1995, he supervised the development of many construction projects, including the creation of the artificial Palm Islands, the seven-star Bur al-Arab Hotel, and Burj Khalifa, which became the tallest free-standing building on the planet in 2010.

On his elder brother's death, he became the ruler of Dubai, and was appointed Prime Minister and Vice

President of the United Arab Emirates by UAE President Khalifa bin Zayed al-Nahyan [*q.v.*]

He possesses 99.7 percent of Dubai Holdings, owning diversified businesses and investments, which ran into financial straits in the wake of the international credit crunch of 2008–09. His horses have won numerous Group One races in Britain, France, Ireland, and the United States.

al-Maktoum, Maktoum bin Rashid

(1943–2006): *ruler of Dubai Emirate in the United Arab Emirates, 1990–2006 ; vice president of the UAE, 1990–2006 ; prime minister of the UAE, 1971–79, 1990–2006* Born in Dubai [q.v.], Maktoum was educated there and in Britain. He then began to acquire administrative experience in the Emirate of Dubai [q.v.]. After the formation of the United Arab Emirates (UAE) in December 1971 he was elected prime minister by the Supreme Council of Emirs. As a Western-educated royal, he got on well with the substantial community of Western oil and financial experts. He continued as the UAE premier until July 1979 when he stepped down in favor of his father, Shaikh Rashid bin Said al-Maktoum [q.v.], becoming his deputy. After Shaikh Rashid's death, Maktoum inherited his father's positions as the vice president and prime minister of the UAE and the ruler of the Dubai emirate. Under his leadership, Dubai was developed successfully as a tourist destination for Europeans. He died during his tour of Australia.

al-Maktoum, Rashid bin Said (1910–

90): ruler of the Dubai emirate in the United Arab Emirates, 1958–90; vice president of the UAE, 1971–90; prime minister of the UAE, 1979–90 Born in Dubai [q.v.], Maktoum belonged to the Aal bu Falasa section of the Bani Yas tribe. Despite his lack of formal schooling, he proved to be a good administrator and economist when he became ruler of the Dubai Emirate in 1958. He turned Dubai into a leading entrepôt of eastern Arabia, basing its commercial prosperity initially on the import and export of gold bars, the source of supply being banks in Switzerland and the destination India and Pakistan. Commercial oil production, which started in 1969, boosted the local economy.

Following the founding of the United Arab Emirates in July 1971 a Supreme Council of seven rulers was established, with Shaikh Zaid al-Nahyan [q.v.] of Abu Dhabi [q.v.] as its president and Maktoum its vice president. Though both leaders realized the importance of cooperation to make a success of the fledgling UAE federation, personal rivalry between them persisted: Maktoum was a sophisticated entrepreneur whereas Shaikh Zaid was a bedouin chief.

But when the UAE faced the stormy winds of republicanism from Islamic Iran, both leaders realized the danger of internal discord and banded together. At the behest of Shaikh Zaid, the Supreme Council called on Maktoum to become the UAE's prime minister in July 1979. He agreed, and took over from his eldest son Maktoum bin Rashid al-Maktoum [q.v.]. He applied his considerable administrative and financial skills to the running of all of the UAE for the next decade.

Malaika, Nazik (1923–2007): *Iraqi poet* Born in Baghdad [q.v.] into a literary family— both her parents were poets—Malakia composed her first poem in classical Arabic [q.v.] at the age of 10. While a student at the Higher Teachers' Training College, she published her poetry—characterized by extraordinary terseness, eloquence, original use of imagery, and a sensitive ear for music—in newspapers and magazines.

Her first collection of poems, *Aashiqat Al-Layl* (Arabic: *Lover of Night*), was published in 1947. Two years later, her next collection, *Shazaya wa ramad* (Arabic: *Ashes and Shrapnel*), helped launch free verse in Arabic as a new form for avant-garde poets—as part of the literary movement also pioneered by Badr Shakir Sayyab [q.v.]. At the same time she became a strong advocate of women's rights. Her lectures on women's status in patriarchal societies appeared as books: *Woman between Passivity and Positive Morality* (1953) and *Fragmentation in Arab Society* (1954). She obtained a postgraduate degree in comparative literature from the University of Wisconsin, Madison, in 1959.

On her return home, she became a lecturer at the Arabic department of the Education College in Baghdad. In 1961 she married Abdul Hadi Mahbooba. The next year she published a collection of essays on the merits and demerits of free verse and metrical poetry, *Qadaya 'l-shiar al-muaasir* (Arabic: *The Contemporary Poetry Issues*). At the end of the decade, however, she began to distance herself from experimentalism while advocating socially conservative views, and reverted to traditional metrical poetry. These collections of her poems appeared between 1970 and 1978. She moved to Kuwait [*q.v.*] to teach at University of Kuwait. A festschrift, containing many essays on her work, was published in 1985.

Following the invasion of Kuwait by Iraq [*q.v.*] in August 1990, she returned to Baghdad because of the turmoil in the emirate. On the eve of the 1991 Gulf War [*q.v.*] she moved to Cairo [*q.v.*]. There, a collection of her poems, *Youghiyar Alouanah Al-Bahr* (Arabic: *Leaving the Sea of Sorrow*), most of them written a quarter-century ago, appeared in 1999.

Maliki Code: *Sunni Islamic school* The Maliki Code is the canonical school of Sunni Islam [*q.v.*], founded by Malik bin Anas (714–96 A.D.), a jurist based in Medina [*q.v.*]. Like other schools, it is based on the Quran [*q.v.*], the *sunna* [*q.v.*], and *ijma* [*q.v.*]. But in the tradition of the Prophet Muhammad and his Companions, Malik bin Anas excludes Caliph Ali bin Abu Talib, a cousin and son-in-law of Muhammad, who is regarded by Sunnis as the last of the four Rightly Guided Caliphs. Regarding ijma, consensus of the community, Malik bin Anas stated that if the community fails to produce a solution to a problem, then *qiyas* [*q.v.*], reasoning by analogy, should be practiced by a jurist to find one.

The Maliki Code's initial dominance of the Arab heartland of Islam gave way to the Shafii Code [*q.v.*]. An essentially conservative doctrine, it has persisted more in pastoral communities than in the urbanizing ones, and is today the leading code in North Africa, West Africa, and Sudan.

al-Maliki, Nouri (1950–): *Iraqi politician, prime minister 2006–* Nouri Muhammad Hassan Maliki was born into an influential Shia [*q.v.*] family in Hindiya, near Hillah. He acquired a master's degree in Arabic literature at Baghdad University, where he joined al-Daawa party [*q.v.*] in the late 1960s. He worked in the education department in Hillah. When President Saddam Hussein [*q.v.*] started repressing al-Daawa in 1979, he fled to Syria. To protect his relatives in Iraq from official persecution, he changed his family name to Jawad. In 1982 he moved to Tehran [*q.v.*] and stayed there until 1990. He then returned to Damascus [*q.v.*], where, as an al-Daawa leader, he forged links with Hizbollah [*q.v.*] and Iran.

After his return to post-Saddam Hussein Iraq in 2003, he was appointed deputy chairman of the Supreme National De-Baathification Commission by the Iraqi Interim Government to purge Baathist [*q.v.*] officials from the government. He was a member of the committee that drafted the new constitution which was passed in October 2005. He served as a spokesman for al-Daawa, as well as for the broader coalition of Shia parties, the United Iraqi Alliance (UIA), which won most seats in the parliamentary election in December 2005 under the new constitution.

When U.S. President George W. Bush ruled out the continuation of Ibrahmi Jaafari [*q.v.*] as the prime minister after the latest election, Maliki was one of the four prospective candidates that the U.S. embassy in Baghdad [*q.v.*] considered. The American ambassador, James Jeffrey, regarded Maliki as someone who was independent of Iran and was easy to maneuver. He was sworn in as prime minister on 22 April 2006.

Once in power, he acted as independently as he could to project himself as an Iraqi nationalist. The first foreign capital he visited was Tehran [*q.v.*], where he was warmly welcomed by Iranian President Mahmoud Ahmadinejad [*q.v.*] and Supreme Leader Ayatollah Ali Khamenei [*q.v.*].

In May 2007 he succeeded Jaafari as the general secretary of al-Daawa. To curb the violence of the Sunni [*q.v.*] militants affiliated to Al Qaida [*q.v.*], he authorized the increase of 21,500 U.S. troops in Iraq. The next year he led a successful campaign against Shia militias loyal to radical cleric Muqtada Sadr [*q.v.*].

He pressed the Bush administration to agree to a withdrawal of American forces in stages, arguing in June 2008 that 16 months would be the right time-frame to complete the process. His joint press conference with Bush in Baghdad in December became memorable when an irate Iraqi journalist Muntadhar al-Zaidi threw his shoes at Bush to express his anger at his policies on Iraq, but missed.

In February 2009 U.S. President Barack Obama announced that all American troops would leave Iraq by the end of 2011. When on 30 June 2009 U.S. soldiers withdrew from the urban areas, Maliki's government declared it National Sovereignty Day.

Criticized by his Shia allies, and pressured by Washington to reconcile with the disaffected Sunnis, Maliki split from the UIA in early 2009, and formed the broader-based State of Law coalition. In the March 2010 general elections it gained two seats

less than the 91 won by the mostly Sunni-backed alliance of Iyad Allawi [*q.v.*]. To enable Maliki to exceed the strength of Allawi's alliance, Sadr, then pursuing advanced theological studies at the Iranian city of Qom [*q.v.*], facilitated the merger of the State of the Law coalition with Jaafari-led National Iraqi Alliance. But the only way Maliki could conciliate the Sunnis was by forming a national unity government. It wasn't until November that he was able to co-opt Allawi's al-Iraqia List [*q.v.*].

Feeling the wind of the Arab Spring [*q.v.*], Maliki announced that he would not run for a third term. In August 2011, he said that there would be no American military bases in Iraq after December, and that any U.S. military presence in Iraq after that date would be limited to trainers for the 18 F-16 warplanes that Iraq had purchased from the American manufacturers.

Manama: *capital of Bahrain* Population: 157,850 (2011 est.). Situated on the Bahrain Island, Manama's recorded history dates back to 1345. It fell to the Portuguese in 1521, and then to the Iranians in 1602. Iran's authority was overthrown by the local al-Khalifa family [*q.v.*] in 1783. The treaties that al-Khalifas signed with Britain between 1861 and 1892 turned Bahrain into a British protectorate. Manama became the seat of a British political agent under the regional political resident based in Bushehr, Iran. In 1946 Britain's regional political resident set up his office in Manama. In that year the ruler allowed the British navy to use Manama's docks and other facilities. This continued until Bahrain's independence in 1971, when Manama became the emirate's capital. The ruler then extended the use of the city's docks to the Pentagon, an arrangement that has been renewed under different contracts and titles since then.

Before the discovery of oil in 1932 the local economy depended on fishing, pearling, and trade. After World War II the city rapidly developed as a commercial and financial center. It became a free port in 1958 and acquired deep-water shipping facilities four years later. With its modern harbor and ship-repair facilities, it has emerged as one of the leading ports in the Gulf [q.v.]. It has also acquired a worldwide reputation as an offshore banking center.

When, after a gap of 48 years, the Pentagon relaunched its Fifth Fleet it chose the Naval Support Activity Bahrain in Manama as its home, with its responsibilities extending over the Persian Gulf, Red Sea, Arabian Sea, and the coast off East Africa up to Kenya. Thus Manama became the combined headquarters of the U.S. Fifth Fleet and the U.S. Naval Forces Central Command.

Mapai (Hebrew: acronym of *Mifleget Poalei Israel,* Israel Workers Party): *Israeli political party* Mapai resulted from the merger of Ahdut HaAvodah-Poale Zion [q.v.] and HaPoale HaTzair [q.v.] in Palestine [q.v.] in 1930. Of its 5,650 members, three-fifths were agriculturists. After the murder of its head, Chaim Arlosoroff [q.v.], in 1933, its leadership passed to David Ben-Gurion [q.v.]. Mapai dominated most of the institutions of the Yishuv [q.v.]: kibbutzim [q.v.], trade unions, militia, schools, and par-

liament. In the 23-member National Council (i.e., cabinet) of the Yishuv Assembly, it often held 11 seats.

As its leaders began to focus on building a nation, they diluted their socialist commitment. Despite strong opposition from leftists, the Mapai conference of 1941, representing some 20,000 members, adopted a program that focused on the founding of a Jewish state in Palestine [q.v.]. The party split on this issue in February 1944, with the leftists leaving. After World War II, Mapai started an anti-British campaign, which won the backing of Haganah [q.v.], Irgun [q.v.], and Lehi [q.v.]. It favored partitioning Palestine into Jewish and Arab states, and participated in the Arab-Israeli War (1948–49) [q.v.].

In the 1949 general election it emerged as the leading party, gaining 46 seats out of 120, a performance it repeated in the 1951 election. It became the dominant partner in the coalition governments that followed. The crucial decisions taken between 1948 and 1952, which set the foundations of the State of Israel, reflected its leaders' views. They chose a secular, not a theocratic, system; a capitalist economy managed by social democratic bureaucracy, not socialism; and pro-Western foreign policy. After a dip in the 1955 election to 40 seats, Mapai's share rose to 47 in the 1959 election, but fell to 42 in 1961.

During Israel's first quarter-century, when the population increased dramatically, the state and society changed considerably. Mapai's decision to open its membership to all socioeconomic groups further diluted its pioneering socialist ideals. The sharp growth in its size, reaching 200,000 members in 1964, created an unwieldy party bureaucracy.

The rivalry between Ben-Gurion and Pinchas Lavon [*q.v.*], centered on the latter's "security mishap" in 1954, which dragged on for a decade and damaged the party, reducing its vote in the 1960 Histadrut [*q.v.*] election to 55 percent, down from the 80 percent it used to win in the 1930s. Having rid Lavon of his office in Histadrut and the government, Ben-Gurion did not rest content. He left the government in 1963 and started campaigning against Prime Minister Levi Eshkol [*q.v.*]. To meet the challenge, party leaders recommended an alliance with Ahdut HaAvodah-Poale Zion [*q.v.*]. The Mapai conference in 1964 accepted the recommendation. On the eve of the 1965 election Mapai signed an agreement for a *maarach* (Hebrew: *alignment*) with Ahdut HaAvodah-Poale Zion, the resulting block winning 45 seats. The Maarach, widened in 1968 to include Rafi, finally resulted in the merger of the three constituent parties into the Israeli Labor Party [*q.v.*].

Mapam (Hebrew: acronym of *Mifleget Poalei Meuhedet*, United Workers Party): *Israeli political party* Once the November 1947 UN partition plan for Palestine [*q.v.*] had extinguished the idea of a bi-national (Arab-Jewish) state in Palestine, the barrier between the two major leftist organizations—Ahdut HaAvodah-Poale Zion [*q.v.*] and HaShomer HaTzair (Hebrew: *The Young Guards*)—was lifted, paving the way for their merger. This happened in January 1948, and the result was Mapam under the leadership of Moshe Sneh [*q.v.*].

It became the leading leftist force inside and outside parliament in Israel. Its 19-member bloc in the First Knesset [*q.v.*] (1949–51) attacked the Mapai [*q.v.*]-led government for accepting a large amount of financial aid from the United States. Mapam advocated organizing new immigrants into collective agrarian and industrial units, and nationalizing natural resources and large capitalist enterprises. In the elections to the Second Knesset in 1951 it won 15 seats. But during the term of this parliament it lost two deputies to Mapai; two, including Sneh, to Maki [*q.v.*]; and four to the revived Ahdut HaAvodah-Poale Zion. The smaller contingent of nine in the Third Knesset (1955–59) was less leftist and less pro-Soviet. Indeed it became a partner in the coalition government led by Mapai [*q.v.*].

After the Suez War [*q.v.*] Mapam held demonstrations against Israel's withdrawal from the Sinai Peninsula [*q.v.*]. In the elections of 1959, 1961, and 1965, it won eight or nine seats, and coalesced with Mapai to form the government. When it supported the June 1967 Arab-Israeli War [*q.v.*] it lost some leftist members.

In January 1969 Mapam allied with the newly formed Labor Party [*q.v.*] to form the Labor-Mapam Alignment [*q.v.*], which performed erratically—down from 56 seats in 1969 to 32 in 1977, then rising to 47 in 1981. The Alignment held until September 1984 when, protesting against Labor's decision to form a national unity government with Likud [*q.v.*], Mapam ended the arrangement, taking its six deputies into opposition. In the 1988 election Mapam won three seats on its own. As part of the Meretz [*q.v.*]

alliance in the 1992 election it secured four seats. Its share fell to two seats in the 1996 general election and rose to three in 1999. With the steady decline of the Meretz alliance in the succeeding elections, Mapam lost its identity.

marja-e taqlid (Arabic/Persian: *source of emulation*): Among Twelver Shias [*q.v.*] the idea of a living *mujtahid* [*q.v.*] interpreting the Sharia [*q.v.*] took hold in the late 18th century. Muhammad Baqir Behbehani (d. 1793), a mujtahid based in Karbala [*q.v.*], ruled that every believer must choose a mujtahid to emulate, who was given the honorific of marja-e taqlid. In the religious establishment his standing was above that of ayatollah *ozma*, grand ayatollah, a title that came into vogue in Iran during the 1907–11 Constitutional Revolution [*q.v.*]. He exercised far greater power than an outstanding Sunni [*q.v.*] cleric. He issued judgments on political matters impinging on Islamic principles independently of the temporal ruler, a development that had a profound impact on the subsequent history of Iran, a predominantly Shia [*q.v.*] country. Among the best-known Shia marja-e taqlids of recent times have been Abol Qasim Khoei [*q.v.*], Ruhollah Khomeini [*q.v.*], Musa al-Sadr [*q.v.*], and Muhammad Kazem Shariatmadari [*q.v.*]. They carried the title of Grand Ayatollah. *See also* mujtahid and Titles, Religious (Shia Islam).

Maronite Catholic Church: *Christian sect* Member of the Uniate churches [*q.v.*]—i.e., affiliated to the Roman Catholic Church [*q.v.*] but allowed to practice its own Eastern rites and customs—its adherents are called Maronites. They are followers of Saint Maron/Maro, a Christian hermit who lived in northeast Syria in the late fourth–early fifth centuries. Their migration to Mount Lebanon occurred in the late seventh century, and was led by St. John Maron, patriarch of Antioch. As the persecuted Christians [*q.v.*] from the plains took refuge in these mountains over the next few centuries, the Maronite ranks grew steadily. During the Crusades (1095–1272), they sided with the Crusaders.

In 1182 their church acquired semi-autonomous affiliation with the Vatican, which allowed them to retain their own West Syriac liturgy [*q.v.*] and have their own resident patriarch in Lebanon. Pope Gregory XIII established the Maronite College in Rome in 1585. In 1648 France proclaimed itself protector of Catholics in the Ottoman Empire (1517–1918), and was so accepted. This was the beginning of a special relationship between France and the Maronites, which bloomed when Syria-Lebanon was placed under the French Mandate after World War I. Maronite and other Christian leaders cooperated actively with Paris in the creation of a Christian-dominated Greater Lebanon, later to be called the Republic of Lebanon.

Centuries of isolation in the mountains, combined with successful resistance to direct control by Muslim [*q.v.*] overlords, turned Maronites into a community where religion and politics were inextricably mixed. Its immediate spiritual head is the Patriarch of Antioch and All the East, who resides in Bkirki near Jounieh port. Today Maronites are the largest Christian community in Lebanon whose constitution requires the republic's president to belong to this sect.

martyrdom (Greek: *derivative of martus, witness*): *the concept of dying in the cause of religion* In the course of securing political independence for the Jews [*q.v.*] from their Greek rulers, their leader, Judas Maccabaeus of the Hasmonaean family, lost his life in 160 B.C., thus giving rise to the concept of martyrdom in monotheistic religions. A martyr is one who dies for his or her faith. The concept of martyrdom was formalized and elevated by the Prophet Muhammad (570–632 A.D.). The appropriate verse in the Quran [*q.v.*] (3:163) reads: "Count not those who are slain in God's way as dead,/but rather living with their Lord, by Him provided,/rejoicing in the bounty that God has given them,/and joyful in those who remain behind and have not joined them."

The popular belief in the West that a martyr would enjoy the favors of 72 virgins in Paradise has no Quranic origins. The two Quranic verses describing Paradise read: "Surely the God-fearing shall be in gardens and bliss/Rejoicing in what the Lord has given them;/… Reclining upon couches ranged in rows;/and We shall espouse them to wide-eyed houris." [52:20]; and "In the Gardens of delight… upon close-wrought couches, reclining upon them, set face to face, and such fruits as they shall choose, and such flesh of fowl as they desire, and wide-eyed houris as the likeness of hidden pearls, a recompense for what they labored." [56:22].

In modern times martyrdom motivated the Ikhwan [*q.v.*], operating under Abdul Aziz al-Saud [*q.v.*] from 1913 to 1928, to expand the realm of Wahhabi Islam [*q.v.*]. During the 1977–78 revolutionary movement in Iran, the deeply rooted martyr complex of Shias [*q.v.*]—which led thousands of Iranians, wearing white shrouds, used to cover corpses, to face the bullets of the army—was an important factor in demoralizing soldiers, who started to desert. In December 1978 the onset of the Ashura festival [*q.v.*] focused on the martyrdom of Imam Hussein, called the Great Martyr, irrevocably turned the tide against the secular regime of Muhammad Reza Shah Pahlavi [*q.v.*].

The newly formed Islamic Republic of Iran established the Martyrs Foundation to look after the families of those who had died as martyrs before, during, and after the Islamic Revolution [*q.v.*]—a category that also included those who were killed in the 1980–88 Iran-Iraq War [*q.v.*], since they had perished while defending an Islamic republic. The concept of martyrdom was also instrumental in actions such as truck-bombing, involving the instant death of the driver, carried out by such Shia organizations in Lebanon as the Islamic Jihad [*q.v.*] and Hizbollah [*q.v.*]. Later it inspired similar actions by Hamas [*q.v.*] and Islamic Jihad [*q.v.*], both Sunni [*q.v.*] groups, in the Occupied Territories [*q.v.*]—as well as secular Fatah [*q.v.*]. *See also* suicide bombing.

Mashhad (Arabic: *a place of witness/ sepulchral shrine*): *Iranian city* Population: 3.173 million (2011 est.). The settlement of Nukan, where Caliph Haroon al-Rashid (r. 786–809 A.D.)

and Imam Ali al-Rida/Reza (d. 818 A.D.), the eighth imam of the Twelver Shias [*q.v.*], were buried, acquired the name Mashhad or Mashhad-e Rida. It is the birthplace of the author of Persian epic poem *Shahnama*—Abul Qasim Mansour, popularly known as Firdausi (c. 940 A.D.–1020)—who left a mark on the Persian language [*q.v.*] and culture that survives to this day.

In 1220 the Mongol invaders damaged it considerably. When the founder of the Safavid dynasty, Shah Ismail (r. 1501–1524), adopted Shia Islam [*q.v.*] as the state religion, the importance of Mashhad rose.

It fell into the hands of Uzbek invaders and was not recovered until 1598 by Shah Abbas I (r. 1587–1629). He made the city attractive and a leading place of pilgrimage for Shias. Nadir Shah Afshar (r. 1736–47) made it into the capital of Iran and built several monuments, including a mausoleum for himself. After his assassination and a civil war, Mashhad became the capital of Khurasan province, a buffer zone between Iran and Afghanistan. It was finally brought under Iranian control in the early 19th century by Fath Ali Shah of the Qajar dynasty. The palace started by Crown Prince Mirza in 1833 was completed in 1876.

The leading city of eastern Iran, Mashhad serves the prosperous agricultural region of the country. It is the center of the wool trade and of carpet making. In recent times the quadrupling of the oil price in 1973–74, which boosted the income of Iran, had a beneficial effect on Mashhad. In 1974 the city received 3,200,000 pilgrims who came to visit the shrine

of Imam Ali al-Rida/Reza, a 15-fold increase over the previous decade.

Following the establishment of the Islamic Republic of Iran in 1979, religious fervor rose sharply. In 2011, the city received nearly 20 million Iranian and foreign pilgrims to the revered shrine.

Mashaal, Khaled (1956–): *Palestinian leader* Born in the village of Silwad near Ramallah [*q.v.*], then under Jordanian control, he was educated there until the 1967 Arab-Israeli War [*q.v.*], when the family moved to Kuwait. While at a secondary school he joined the Muslim Brotherhood [*q.v.*] at the age of 15. As an undergraduate at Kuwait University he formed a student body called Islamic Justice List in the General Union of Palestinian Students. After graduation in 1978 he taught physics at local schools and then at Kuwait University.

In the mid-1980s he was involved in forming an Islamic movement among Palestinians. This culminated in the founding of Hamas [*q.v.*] in 1987 and his inclusion in its Politburo. He was the leader of the Kuwait contingent of Hamas.

Following Iraq's invasion of Kuwait in 1990, he moved to Amman [*q.v.*] and ran the Hamas bureau there, focusing on raising funds for the welfare activities of Hamas in the West Bank [*q.v.*] and Gaza [*q.v.*], and forging ties with the governments of Syria and Iran. In 1996, he was elected chairman of the Politburo.

The next year, two agents of Israel's Mossad [*q.v.*], posing as Canadian tourists, injected a lethal chemical agent into his ear. He was rushed to hospital before it took hold. Pressured

407

by King Hussein [*q.v.*], Israel provided an antidote. After Hussein's death in February 1999, his son King Abdullah II [*q.v.*] shut down the Hamas bureau and expelled Mashaal.

He stayed in Qatar, and in 2001 moved to Damascus [*q.v.*], which became the base of the Politburo. Unimpeded by Israel's travel restrictions on Hamas leaders in Gaza and the West Bank, he has represented the organization at meetings with foreign governments and other interested parties. After Israel's assassination of Hamas leader Abdul Aziz Rantisi in Gaza in 2004, Mashaal's importance rose.

He was instrumental in raising $100 million from Iran and Qatar in 2006 to support the freshly formed Hamas government in the West Bank and Gaza. In that year, he declared that Hamas would end the armed struggle against Israel if it withdrew to its pre-1967 borders and recognized the Palestinian right of return.

In his meeting with former U.S. President Jimmy Carter in 2008, he said that Hamas would respect the creation of a Palestinian state in pre-1967 areas provided it was ratified by the Palestinian people in a referendum. Until then Hamas would continue its resistance to Israeli occupation. After his meeting with him in Damascus in 2010, Russian President Dmitry Medvedev said that peace between Israelis and Palestinians would not be achieved unless Hamas joined the negotiations.

As the anti-regime protest in Syria escalated in 2011, Syrian President Bashar Assad [*q.v.*] expected Mashaal to support him publicly. As beneficiaries of a free and fair vote in the Palestinian Territories [*q.v.*], Mashaal and other Hamas leaders failed to do so. Mashaal shifted the Hamas headquarters temporarily to Doha so that it could maintain and cultivate its contacts with diplomats and other foreign officials.

Mecca: *Saudi Arabian city* Population 1.73 million (2011 est.) Known as Macoraba during the (Greco-Egyptian) Ptolemaic period (323–330 B.C.), Mecca was an ancient center of commerce. It was situated on the incense route from India to the Mediterranean region, and had developed around the well of Zamzam and the sanctuary of Kaaba [*q.v.*], which were holy to Arab [*q.v.*] tribes before the rise of Islam [*q.v.*].

The birthplace of the Prophet Muhammad bin Abdullah al-Quraish (570–632 A.D.), Mecca was where he conveyed his first revelations to early believers. The Prophet Muhammad's migration from Mecca in 622 A.D. marked the beginning of the Islamic era. Eight years later he conquered Mecca. As the site of the annual hajj [*q.v.*], Mecca became the most sacred city of Islam.

It was looted in 930 A.D. by Karmathians, a crypto-Muslim sect, which removed the Black Stone from the Kaaba and held on to it for 20 years. By the late 11th century Mecca was administered by the al-Hashem [*q.v.*] family, the governor bearing the title of *sharif* (Arabic: *noble*). Together with the surrounding region of Hijaz [*q.v.*], it was dependent for its food on Egypt, being under the suzerainty of whoever controlled Cairo [*q.v.*].

When the Ottomans conquered Egypt in 1517, the control of Mecca fell to them. It came under Wahhabi [*q.v.*] rule from 1804 to 1813. After the opening of the Suez Canal [*q.v.*] in 1869 there was improved communication between Istanbul and Mecca, now the capital of Hijaz. Hussein bin Ali al-Hashem became the sharif in 1908. In June 1916 he declared himself king of Hijaz, with Mecca as its capital. He was overthrown by Abdul Aziz al-Saud [*q.v.*] in 1924. Mecca became part of Saudi Arabia, and was closed to non-Muslims.

The economic and religious life of the city revolves around the hajj, which lasts five days. The heart of Mecca is the *Haram* (Arabic: *Sanctuary*), the Grand Mosque. Situated at the center of the Old City and containing the Kaaba, it was extensively renovated after a two-week siege by security forces to quell an armed uprising by over 300 Islamic militants, led by Juheiman al-Utaiba [*q.v.*] on 1 Muharram 1400 A.H./20 November 1979.

Served by the seaport and airport facilities of Jeddah [*q.v.*], and transformed into a modern metropolis, Mecca is well equipped to serve some two million pilgrims who arrive during the hajj. In the course of the hajj in 1987 it became the site of rioting, in which 402 people were killed, including 275 Iranians, 85 Saudis, and 45 other pilgrims as a result of police gunfire and stampedes.

Besides the 2.5 to 3 million Muslims who visit the city during the hajj [*q.v.*], another 12 million visit it annually as religious tourists. The ban on the entry of non-Muslims into Mecca continues.

By 2011, as part of the city's massive makeover, the area around the Grand Mosque was turned into a complex of luxury hotels, malls, and apartments. Its 1,600-ft./485-m-high clock tower—resembling Big Ben in London but capped with gold crescent and adorned with Arabic calligraphy—is a landmark that is visible from 25 miles.

Medina (*Arabic: town*): *Saudi Arabian city* Population 1.32 million (2011 est.) Also known in Arabic as *Madinat al-Rasul Allah* (Town of the Messenger of Allah), Medina is the second-holiest city of Islam [*q.v.*]. Called Yathrib in pre-Islamic times, this oasis town was possibly settled by some of the Jews [*q.v.*] expelled from Palestine [*q.v.*] in 135 A.D. After his migration from Mecca [*q.v.*] in 622 A.D., the Prophet Muhammad established a base here. It became the capital of the Islamic caliphate after his death a decade later. This continued until 661 A.D., when the capital was moved to Damascus [*q.v.*].

It remained a center of Islamic learning, especially with regard to the Quran [*q.v.*] and the *sunna* [*q.v.*], and was the base, among others, of the founder of the Maliki Code [*q.v.*] in the eighth century. Later it came under the intermittent control of the *sharifs* of Mecca and of Egypt.

The Prophet's Mosque, built on the site of his modest mosque, was the main attraction. After lightning destroyed much of the earlier stricture, the mosque was expanded during the rule of the Ottoman Turks, who gained control of Medina as a result of their seizure of Egypt in 1517. The Ottoman suzerainty ended during World War I. The subsequent rule by Sharif Hussein bin Ali al-Hashem gave way in 1924 to that of Abdul

Aziz al-Saud [*q.v.*]. It became part of Saudi Arabia, and was closed to non-Muslims.

The economic and religious life of the city revolves around the hajj [*q.v.*], when most pilgrims combine their visit to Mecca with one to Medina. Its Great Mosque, the renamed Prophet's Mosque, contains the tombs of the Prophet Muhammad; his daughter Fatima, wife of Caliph/Imam Ali; and Caliphs Abu Bakr and Omar.

After the hajj [*q.v.*], most of the 2.5 to 3 million Muslims pilgrims visit Medina to pray at the Great Mosque. In addition, the city attracts another 12 million Muslims as religious tourists.

Meir (Meyerson), Golda (1898–1978):
Israeli politician; prime minister, 1969–74 The daughter of Moshe Mabovitch, a carpenter in Kiev, Ukraine, Meir migrated with her family to Milwaukee in the United States when she was eight. She trained as a teacher, and married Morris Meyerson, a bookkeeper, in 1917. Four years later they migrated to Palestine [*q.v.*] and joined a kibbutz [*q.v.*]. From 1926 she became active in the Histadrut [*q.v.*] and later Mapai [*q.v.*]. After separating from her husband in 1932 she spent two years in the United States with the Pioneer Women's Organization.

In 1936 she became head of the Histadrut's political department. She opposed the partition plan proposed by Britain's Peel Commission in 1937. After the arrest in 1946 of Moshe Sharett [*q.v.*], head of the Jewish Agency's [*q.v.*] political department, dealing with foreign affairs, she replaced him. In that capacity she had secret meetings with Transjordan's ruler, Abdullah bin Hussein [*q.v.*], in late November 1947 and again on 10 May 1948 to dissuade him from joining other members of the Arab League [*q.v.*] in attacking the imminent State of Israel [*q.v.*]. She failed.

She served briefly as head of the Israeli legation in Moscow until her election in early 1949 to the Knesset [*q.v.*], where she was to retain a seat for the next quarter of a century. She served as labor minister (1949–56) and then as foreign minister (1956–66). After she resigned from the cabinet in 1966, she was drafted as secretary-general of Mapai to heal internecine wounds. When Mapai transformed itself into the Labor Party [*q.v.*] in 1968, she retired from public life. But following the sudden death of Prime Minister Levi Eshkol [*q.v.*] in February 1969, she was elected to head the national unity government in order to stave off a power struggle within Labor.

In September 1969, she signed a secret agreement with U.S. President Richard Nixon (r. 1969–74) that, so long as Israel did not advertise its possession of nuclear arms by testing them or publicly admitting ownership, Washington would tolerate and protect its nuclear program.

Her acceptance of Washington's Rogers Peace Plan [*q.v.*] in July 1970 led to the exit of Gahal [*q.v.*] from the cabinet.

The attention of all political parties was focused on the impending general election in late October 1973, when Israel was attacked by Egypt and Syria on 6 October. During the conflict she provided strong leadership, including ordering the mounting of Israel's entire stock of 25 atomic bombs on specially adapted bombers. Though praised for her leadership during the October 1973 Arab-Israeli War [*q.v.*] by the official inquiry commission in March 1974, she decided to resign as the prime minister, thus causing the entire cabinet to fall, partly to bring about the resignation of defense minister Moshe Dayan [*q.v.*]. In 1975 she received the Israel Prize for her contribution to Israeli society.

Melkite Christians: *See* Greek Catholic Church.

Meretz (Hebrew: *Energy*): *Israeli political alliance* (Official title: *Meretz—Israel HaDemokratit* [Hebrew: *Energy—The Democratic Israel*]): Having ended its alignment with the Labor Party [*q.v.*] in the aftermath of Labor's decision to form a national unity government with Likud [*q.v.*] in September 1984, Mapam [*q.v.*] formed the Meretz alliance with Shinui [*q.v.*] and Ratz [*q.v.*] after the 1988 general election, giving it a total strength of 10 deputies. Its program included separation of religion and state, electoral reform, discontinuation of the construction of Jewish settlements in the Arab Occupied Territories [*q.v.*], and self-determination for Palestinians. It functioned as an opposition group. In the 1992 election it secured 12 seats and joined the Labor-led coalition government. In 1996 it won nine seats, and went into opposition. It secured 10 seats in 1999, and joined the Labor-led coalition government headed by Ehud Barak [*q.v.*]. It stayed out of the national unity cabinet headed by Ariel Sharon [*q.v.*] in 2001.

In the 2003 Knesset election, the party won six seats, with its strength declining to five in the 2006 general election. On the eve of the 2009 parliamentary election, it combined with a smaller group called the New Movement (Hebrew: *Hatnua HaHadasha*). Yet its score fell to three. This was symptomatic of the overall right-wing drift of Israeli politics that started in the first decade of the 21st century, partly as a result of the Al Aqsa Intifada [*q.v.*] of the Palestinians [*q.v.*].

Mesopotamia (Greek: *Land between the Rivers [Tigris and Euphrates]*): Covering the territory between the Tigris [*q.v.*] and Euphrates [*q.v.*] rivers and extending from the mountains of southern Turkey to the Persian Gulf [*q.v.*], Mesopotamia constitutes the greater part of modern Iraq [*q.v.*]. Archeological excavations, conducted over the past one and a half centuries, have provided evidence of civilization dating back to ca. 10 millennia B.C. Mesopotamia is the region where the earliest settled agrarian society evolved, with its irrigation systems, crafts, and buildings made of clay bricks. It was there that one of the first cities was built, around 4000 B.C., and writing was invented in ca. 300 B.C. Incorporated into the Parthian Empire (250 B.C.–226 A.D.) in the second century B.C., it declined steadily. After 38 B.C. it became a buffer zone—first between the Parthian, and later Sassanian (226–640 A.D.) Empires followed by the Roman (27 B.C.–395 A.D.) and Byzantine (395 A.D.–1453) Empires. It was conquered by Muslim [*q.v.*] Arabs [*q.v.*] in 637 A.D. Since then its history has been that of Iraq.

messiah (Hebrew: *derivative of mashiach, meaning anointed*): Judaism [*q.v.*] and Christianity [*q.v.*] share the concept of messiah but their respective followers view it differently. Following their exile in 586 B.C., Jews [*q.v.*] aspired for restoration by a leader who, like David (r. 1010–970 B.C.), would be a monarch as well as an epitome of piety. After their final dispersion in 135 A.D., Jews began to think of the messiah as someone who would end injustice, lead them to a restored Israel, and initiate the resurrection of the dead. Christians [*q.v.*] regard Jesus Christ as the messiah promised in the Old Testament [*q.v.*]. The fact that, far from ending injustice, he became its victim makes no difference to his messianic status, according to Christians. *See also* mahdi.

Middle East: Early Western geographers divided the East into the Near East [*q.v.*] (the area extending from the Mediterranean Sea to the Persian Gulf [*q.v.*]), the Middle East (the region extending from the Persian Gulf to Southeast Asia), and the Far East (covering the regions facing the Pacific Ocean). But during World War II, when the term Middle East was applied to the British military command in Egypt, the traditional definitions underwent a change, and the Middle East encompassed the region previously called the Near East. Later, when the independent states of Libya, Tunisia, Algeria, and Morocco joined the Arab League [*q.v.*], the term Middle East was considered to include these countries as well. The Middle East can be seen as consisting of a core and peripheries. The core includes Iran, the Fertile Crescent [*q.v.*], the Arabian Peninsula [*q.v.*], and Egypt. To its south lies Sudan; to its west Arab North Africa; and to its north Turkey and Cyprus. The narrowest definition of the Middle East includes only the core, and the widest includes the core and its three peripheries.

Middle East Defense Organization: In an effort to link various Middle Eastern countries in a military alliance against the Soviet Union, Britain, backed by the United States, conceived the Middle East Defense Organization (MEDO) as a multilateral defense pact. Since it was centered on Britain's Middle East Defense Command, based in the Suez Canal [*q.v.*] zone, the nationalist government of Egypt rejected it in late October 1951. This led to efforts by Britain and the United States to encourage bilateral agreements with a view to creating a multilateral defense pact, which materialized in 1955 as the Baghdad Pact [*q.v.*].

Middle East Peace Conference (Geneva, 1973): After the October 1973 Arab-Israeli War [*q.v.*], a Middle East Peace Conference was convened in Geneva on 21 December under the cochairmanship of the United States and the Soviet Union. It was attended by Egypt, Israel, and Jordan, but boycotted by Syria. Having instructed Israel and Egypt to negotiate the disengagement of their forces, the conference adjourned the next day because of the imminent general election in Israel. But, having won the election on 31 December, Israel's Labor [*q.v.*]-dominated government did not return to Geneva on 7 January as agreed. Instead it approached U.S. Secretary of State Henry Kissinger to use his personal diplomacy to bring about an agreement with Egypt. Egyptian president Anwar Sadat [*q.v.*] went along with this. Efforts by Washington and Moscow to reconvene the conference during the tenure of U.S. President Jimmy Carter (r. 1977–1981) failed.

Middle East Peace Conference

(Madrid, 1991): After the Second Gulf War [*q.v.*] the United States began to lobby actively for a Middle East Peace Conference. On 18 July 1991, following Syrian President Hafiz Assad's [*q.v.*] dramatic concessions on his terms for attending a peace conference, U.S. Secretary of State James Baker met him in Damascus [*q.v.*]. On 30 September the Palestine National Council [*q.v.*] agreed to attend such a gathering. It was held in Madrid, Spain, on 30 October 1991 under the cochairmanship of the United States and the Soviet Union (later Russia), and was attended by Israel, Syria, Lebanon, and Jordan (whose delegation included Palestinians from the Occupied Territories [*q.v.*]). All parties agreed to honor UN Security Council Resolution 242 of November 1967, which called for the withdrawal of Israel from the Occupied Arab Territories [*q.v.*] in exchange for the peaceful coexistence of all the states in the region, and Resolution 338 of October 1973, which called on the concerned parties to implement the UN Security Council Resolution 242.

The Madrid conference was followed by bilateral talks between Israel and the three Arab parties, held outside the Middle East. The bilateral negotiations between Israel and Jordan evolved into separate talks between the Israeli delegation and the Jordanian, and the Israeli delegation and the Palestinian, with the latter taking its orders from the Palestine Liberation Organization (PLO) [*q.v.*]. Secret negotiations between the PLO and Israel led to the Israeli-PLO Accord [*q.v.*] in September 1993. Thirteen months later a Jordanian-Israeli Peace Treaty [*q.v.*] was signed. Starting in 1994, talks between Israel and Syria were mediated by the United States, but those between Israel and Lebanon were put on hold, waiting for tangible progress on the Israeli-Syrian front in line with the 1991 Lebanese-Syrian Treaty of Brotherhood, Cooperation, and Coordination [*q.v.*].

Middle East Peace Conference

(Annapolis, Maryland, 2007): This was the first time that Israelis and Palestinians entered a conference with a common understanding that a two-state solution would be the end-result of the Israeli-Palestinian peace process. The conference ended with the issuing of a joint statement signed by all parties. Summarizing the event, U.S. President George W. Bush referred to the commitment by the negotiating parties to implement their respective obligations under the performance-based road map to a permanent two-state solution to the Israel-Palestinian conflict, issued by the Quartet (the United Nations, the United States, the European Union, and Russia) on 30 April 2003—called the road map—and agree to form an American-Palestinian-Israeli mechanism, led by the United States, to follow up on the implementation of the road map. The subsequent talks between the Israelis and the Palestinians involved American participation. The Palestinian team made far-reaching concessions in the negotiations during 2008–09, as revealed by the Palestine Papers [*q.v.*] in January 2011, but the Israeli and American officials found them inadequate.

Middle East Peace Process: *See* Peace Process, Middle East.

Midrash (Hebrew: *investigation or study*) Homiletic interpretations and embellishments of the Hebrew Bible [*q.v.*] by rabbis since ca. 200 A.D., Midrash is incorporated in the Mishna [*q.v.*]. Like the Gemara [*q.v.*], it contains material that pertains to Jewish Law, called Midrash Halacha [*q.v.*], and digressions in the form of rabbinic folklore, called Midrash Hagaada.

Mikati, Najib (1955–): Born into a middle-class Sunni [*q.v.*] family in Tripoli [*q.v.*], Mikati gained a Master's degree in Business Administration from the American University of Beirut [*q.v.*], and pursued further studies at the INSEAD (acronym for *INStitut Européen d'ADministration des Affaires*, European Institute of Business Administration) in Fountainebleau, France, and Harvard Business School in Cambridge, U.S.

During his postgraduate studies, he and his elder brother, Taha, established the company M1 Group. Starting with construction, the founder brothers entered the emerging telecom business in 1982; their company Investcom steadily became a major mobile phone operator around the globe.

In 1998 Najib Mikati was appointed minister of public works and transport by Prime Minister Salim Hoss [*q.v.*]. In that capacity he condemned Israel's extensive bombing of bridges and power plants, including the one near the presidential palace, in June 1999, purportedly as retribution for the rocket attacks on northern Israel by Hizbollah [*q.v.*]. That gave him a high political profile. He was elected to the National Assembly in 2000. He established normal working relations with the newly installed Syrian President Bashar Assad [*q.v.*].

He served as the caretaker prime minister from April to July 2005 to oversee the first general election in Lebanon without the presence of Syrian troops since 1976.

In June 2006 he and his brother Taha sold Investcom to MTN Group of South Africa for $5.5 billion. He was reelected to the National Assembly in 2009 but did not join the national unity cabinet of Saad Hariri [*q.v.*]. When Hariri's government fell in January 2011, Mikati was called to form the new administration. He succeeded in June with the active cooperation of the 14 March Alliance [*q.v.*] at a time when the protest movement in Syria was gathering momentum.

He has followed a consistent policy of distancing Lebanon from the turmoil in Syria by stressing that his priority was to maintain stability and unity in Lebanon. In January 2012, when the Arab League [*q.v.*] asked him to send Lebanese observers to Syria to monitor the implementation of the League's peace plan, he declined, arguing that he did not want to take on additional problems that his government could not solve.

Military in Bahrain (2011): Total armed forces 8,200: active, 8,200. Military expenditure as percent of GDP: 2.8 (2011).

GROUND FORCES: regular army, active, 6,000.

In-service equipment: tanks, 180; armored personnel carriers, 375; major artillery, 151.

AIR FORCES: regular air force, 1,500.

In-service equipment: combat aircraft, 39; combat helicopters, 28.

NAVAL FORCES: regular navy, 700.

In-service equipment: surface combatants, 1 (frigate 1); patrol and coastal combatants, 12.

Military in Egypt (2011): Total armed forces: active, 438,500; reserves, 479,000. Military expenditure as percent of GDP: 2.0 (2011).

GROUND FORCES: regular army, active 310,000; reserves 375,000.

In-service equipment: tanks, 2,410; armored personnel carriers, 3,560; major artillery, 4,470.

AIR FORCES:

(a) regular air force, active, 30,000; reserves, 20,000.

(b) Regular air defense, active, 80,000; reserves, 70,000.

In-service equipment: combat aircraft, 589; combat helicopters, 124.

NAVAL FORCES: regular navy, active, 15,500; reserves, 14,000.

In-service equipment: submarines, 4; surface combatants, 8 (frigates 8); patrol and coastal combatants, 51; mine warfare vessels, 14.

PARAMILITARY: active, 397,000: Central Security Forces, 325,000; National Guard, 60,000; Border Guard, 12,000.

Military in Iran (2011): Total armed forces: active, 523,000; reserves, 350,000. Military expenditure as percent of GDP: 2.4 (2011).

GROUND FORCES:

(a) regular army, active, 350,000; reserves, 350,000.

(b) Revolutionary Guard Corps, active, 125,000.

In-service equipment: tanks, 1,665; armored personnel carriers, 640; major artillery, 8,800; combat helicopters, 50; aircraft, 17.

AIR FORCES: regular air force, 37,000; air defense, 15,000.

In-service equipment: combat aircraft, 336; combat helicopters, 32.

NAVAL FORCES:

(a) regular navy, 18,000.

(b) Revolutionary Guard Corps, 20,000.

In-service equipment: submarines, 23; patrol and coastal combatants, 68; mine warfare vessels, 5.

PARAMILITARY: active, Law Enforcement Forces, 40,000 to 60,000; on mobilization, 450,000; reserves, Resistance Mobilization Force (Persian: *Niruyeh Moqawemat Basij*), 100,000.

NON-CONVENTIONAL WEAPONS:

Chemical: There were unconfirmed reports of Iran deploying chemical weapons during its offensive against Basra in early 1987 during the Iran-Iraq War [*q.v.*]. Further use of such arms was discontinued when it was judged un-Islamic by Ayatollah Ruhollah Khomeini [*q.v.*]. In 1993 Iran signed the Chemical Weapons Convention and its parliament ratified it in 1997.

Nuclear: After examining the nuclear power project in Bushehr in January 1995, the inspectors of the International Atomic Energy Agency (IAEA) said that they saw no evidence of military use of the power plant. Similar statements were issued by the IAEA after their six monthly visits to the site. When in early 2003 the Iranian government announced that it had discovered uranium mines and that it proposed to process the mineral for peaceful purposes, the IAEA said that it had known about these plans before.

As it turned out, it had started enriching uranium at Natanz, northeast of Isfahan [q.v.], which had had a research reactor for many years. Under the nuclear Non-Proliferation Treaty (NPT) of 1970 that Iran had signed, it was entitled to enrich uranium. It claimed to be doing so up to 5 percent purity to be used in the civilian nuclear power plant. The key question was whether Iran would then take the process further, to the point of 90 percent purity, to be used as fuel for an atom bomb. The driving force for militarization of Iran's nuclear program was the plan of Iraqi President Saddam Hussein [q.v.] to produce an atom bomb. By the autumn of 2003, when it became abundantly clear after a thorough search of Iraq by the occupying Anglo-American troops that the Iraqi leader had destroyed all facilities for producing weapons of mass destruction (WMD), the Iranian government discontinued their tentative moves toward militarization of their nuclear activities. According to the National Intelligence Estimate on Iran, prepared by the 16 U.S. intelligence agencies, published in December 2007, Tehran halted a covert nuclear weapons program in 2003.

At the same time, fearful of the prospect of U.S. President George W. Bush overthrowing their regime as he had done Saddam Hussein's, the Iranian leaders signed an agreement with the European Union (EU) Troika of Britain, France, and Germany in October 2003 to resolve with "full transparency" all the remaining questions of the International Atomic Energy Agency (IAEA). As a confidence-building measure Iran suspended its uranium enrichment activities. In September 2004, Iran's Supreme Leader Ayatollah Ali Khamanei issued a fatwa that it was "un-Islamic" to use an atom bomb. Two months later, Iran suspended its uranium enrichment program until there was a "grand bargain" between it and the EU Troika, with the EU guaranteeing nuclear, political, and trade concessions to Iran for Tehran's indefinite suspension of its enrichment program.

Though the United States was not involved in direct talks with Iran, its hard-line stance, expressed in its opposition to the building of a civilian nuclear power plant by Russia, impacted on the EU Troika. In August 2005, the EU Troika's "grand bargain" boiled down to Iran's giving up its right to enrich uranium permanently in return for the improving commerce with Tehran and guaranteeing supplies of nuclear fuel from Europe for Iran's civilian nuclear power plants. Crucially, there was no mention of Iran's right to enrich uranium as accorded by the NPT. Tehran rejected the offer. It removed the IAEA seals on its uranium enrichment facility at Natanz.

In February 2006 the 35-strong

Board of Governors of the IAEA decided by 27 votes to 3 to refer Iran's case to the UN Security Council. Two months later Iranian President Mahmoud Ahmadinejad [*q.v.*] announced that Iran had succeeded in enriching uranium to 3.5 percent purity. When his government ignored the UN Security Council's demand in July that Iran should cease enriching uranium, the Council imposed the first of its three sets of economic sanctions against individuals,and organizations involved in Iran's nuclear program in December 2006. By then Bush had authorized a clandestine cyber-program to access Natanz's industrial computer controls to obtain a blueprint of how it worked.

Once that was achieved, a joint U.S.-Israeli team started building a worm to attack the Natanz plant and make its centrifuges, which enrich uranium, run out of control. The resulting Stuxnet worm was then introduced into the Natanz facility with contaminated computer drives around June 2009, five months after Barack Obama succeeded Bush. But it was about a year before the existence of Stuxnet became known. By then it had damaged up to 1,000 high-speed centrifuges.

But the Iranians' plans to enrich uranium above 3.5 to 5.0 percent remained on track. On the eve of the 31st anniversary of the Islamic Revolution [*q.v.*] in February 2010, Ahmadinejad announced that Iran had enriched uranium to 20 percent, which was required for the nuclear reactor built in Tehran in 1967 to produce medical isotopes. Four months later the UN Security Council Resolution 1929 imposed a complete arms embargo on Iran, banned Iran from

any activities related to ballistic missiles, authorized the inspection and seizure of shipments violating these restrictions, and extended the asset freeze to the Islamic Revolutionary Guard Corps. The resolution was adopted by 12 votes to 2 (Turkey and Brazil), with Lebanon abstaining. Russia and China cooperated with the three Western members with veto power on the understanding that they would not act beyond this resolution. This was not to be.

Washington decided to penalize any financial institution that did business with Iran's Central Bank after 1 June 2012, and the EU banned imports of Iranian oil from July 2012. There was an agreement among U.S. and other leading Western intelligence agencies that Iran's supreme leader had not decided to build an atom bomb. So the overall Western objective, dictated by Israel, boiled down to depriving Iran of the capability of producing a nuclear weapon in the future.

Military in Iraq (2011): Total armed forces: active 271,000; reserves 69,400. Military expenditure as percent of GDP: 4.5 (2011).

GROUND FORCES: regular army, active, 193,400; reserves, 69,350.

In-service equipment: tanks, 335; armored personnel carriers, 2,800; major artillery, 1,400; combat helicopters, 30.

AIR FORCES: regular air force, 5,050.

In-service equipment: 3 combat planes. 7 squadrons of training and transport aircraft.

NAVAL FORCES: regular navy, active, 3,600.

In-service equipment: patrol and coastal combatants, 28.

NON-CONVENTIONAL WEAPONS:

Biological: Research in biological weapons began in 1985. Production of the biological warfare agents anthrax (*bacillus anthracis*) and botulinum (*clostridium botulinum*) started in 1989 and continued for a year. Implementing the UN Security Council Resolution 687 [*q.v.*] of April 1991, the inspectors of UN Special Commission (UNSCOM) [*q.v.*] for disarming Iraq demolished research facilities. By 1995 Iraq's claim to have destroyed all its stored agents was yet to be fully verified by UNSCOM. Later Iraq declared that it had 8,400 liters (1,850 gallons) of anthrax; 19,000 liters (4,180 gallons) of botulinum; 3,400 liters (750 gallons) of clostridium (gangrene gas); 2,200 liters (485 gallons) of aflatoxin; 10 liters (2 gallons) of ricin. These were destroyed by UNSCOM. That left 15,300 kilograms (34,000 pounds) of bio-weapons growth media unaccounted for.

Chemical: Iraq began to use chemical weapons (mustard and nerve gases) in the 1980–88 Iran-Iraq War [*q.v.*] from 1983 onwards, culminating in large-scale deployment during the last months of the war, which ended in August 1988. During that year the government also used chemical weapons against Kurdish insurgents and civilians in the Kurdistan Autonomous Region [*q.v.*], resulting in an estimated 100,000 deaths. After the implementation of UN Security Council Cease-fire Resolution 687 [*q.v.*] of April 1991, the four facilities for developing, producing, and storing were destroyed by UNSOCM.

The chemical warfare agents and quantities destroyed were 500–600 tons of mustard gas; 100–150 tons of nerve gases—sarin and tabun; and 50–100 tons of VX nerve gas. Also destroyed were 480,000 liters (105,600 gallons) of chemical weapons agents; over 450,000 gallons of precursor chemicals; and 30 chemical warheads, as well as 38,537 filled and empty chemical weapons munitions.

Nuclear: Research and development in the nuclear weapons program was well advanced at the time of the 1991 Gulf War. In the course of implementing UN Security Council Resolution 687, the UNSCOM and the International Atomic Energy Agency examined 25,000 pages of documents, 700 rolls of film, and 19 hours of videotape to assess the Iraqi Atomic Energy Commission's personnel and procurement of materials. They concluded that Iraq had not produced a detonator for an atom bomb, and had not accumulated sufficient enriched uranium to produce a nuclear weapon. If Iraq had been able to overcome these barriers it would have acquired the ability to produce two or three atom bombs annually by 1995 or 1996 at the earliest. All military nuclear research and development facilities had been destroyed by UN inspectors by 1993. In its April 1998 report, the IAEA said, "Based on all credible information to date, the IAEA has found no indication of Iraq having achieved its program goal of producing nuclear weapons or of Iraq having retained a physical capability for the production of weapon-usable nuclear material or having clandestinely obtained such material." In February 2003, after carrying out 177 inspections at 125 sites since the previous November, IAEA chief Muhammad El Baradei basically repeated the earlier summary. *See also* Gulf War III, Saddam Hussein, and Iraq: History.

Military in Jordan (2011): Total armed forces: active, 100,500; reserves, 65,000. Military expenditure as percent of GDP: 8.5 (2011).

GROUND FORCES: regular army, active, 88,000; reserves, 60,000.

In-service equipment: tanks, 750; armored personnel carriers, 450; major artillery, 1,340.

AIR FORCES: regular air force, active, 12,000; reserves, 5,000.

In-service equipment: combat aircraft, 115; combat helicopters, 25.

NAVAL FORCES: regular navy, active, 540; reserves, 500.

In-service equipment: patrol and coastal combatants, 7.

PARAMILITARY: active, 10,000 (of which, public security police 10,000); reserves (civil militia), 35,000.

Military in Kuwait (2011): Total armed forces: active, 15,500; reserves, 23,700. Military expenditure as percent of GDP: 2.6 (2011).

GROUND FORCES: regular army, active, 11,000; reserves, 19,000.

In-service equipment: tanks, 290; armored personnel carriers, 260; major artillery, 220.

AIR FORCES: regular air force, active, 2,500; reserves, 3,000.

In-service equipment: combat aircraft, 66; combat helicopters, 16.

NAVAL FORCES: regular navy, active, 2,000; reserves, 1,700.

In-service equipment: patrol and coastal combatants, 11.

PARAMILITARY: active (National Guard), 6,600.

Military in Lebanon (2011): Total armed forces: active, 59,100. Military expenditure as percent of GDP: 2.7 (2011).

GROUND FORCES: regular army, 57,000.

In-service equipment: tanks, 327; armored personnel carriers, 1,240; major artillery, 520.

AIR FORCES: regular air force, 1,000.

In-service equipment: combat aircraft, 7; combat helicopters, 14.

NAVAL FORCES: regular navy, 1,000.

In-service equipment: patrol and coastal combatants, 11.

PARAMILITARY: active, 20,000 (of which, internal security force 20,000).

Military in Oman (2011): Total armed forces: active, 42,600. Military expenditure as percent of GDP: 6.3 (2011).

GROUND FORCES: regular army, 25,000.

In-service equipment: tanks, 117; armored personnel carriers, 206; major artillery, 233.

AIR FORCES: regular air force, 5,000.

In-service equipment: combat aircraft, 54; combat helicopters, 15.

NAVAL FORCES: regular navy, 4,200.

In-service equipment: submarines, 2; primary surface combatants, 1; patrol and coastal combatants, 13.

Royal household: ground force, 6,000; air force, 250; naval force, 150.

PARAMILITARY: active, 4,400: tribal home guard, 4,000; coast guard, 400.

Military in Qatar (2011): Total armed forces: active 11,800. Military expenditure as percent of GDP: 2.0 (2011).

GROUND FORCES: regular army, 8,500.

In-service equipment: tanks, 30; armored personnel carriers, 225; major artillery, 90.

AIR FORCES: regular air force, 1,500.

In-service equipment: combat aircraft, 18; combat helicopters, 19.

NAVAL FORCES: regular navy, 1,800.

In-service equipment: patrol and coastal combatants, 10.

Military in Saudi Arabia (2011): Total armed forces: active, 233,500; reserves, 25,000. Military expenditure as percent of GDP: 8.1 (2011).

GROUND FORCES:

(a) regular army, active, 75,000.

(b) National Guard [q.v.], active, 75,000; tribal levies as reserves, 25,000.

In-service equipment: tanks, 565; armored personnel carriers, 1,800; major artillery, 860; combat helicopters, 33.

AIR FORCES:

(a) regular air force, 20,000.

(b) air defense forces, 16,000.

In-service equipment: combat aircraft, 295; combat helicopters, 15.

NAVAL FORCES: regular navy, 13,500; regular marines, 3,000.

In-service equipment: surface combatants, 7 (destroyers, 3; frigates, 4); patrol and coastal combatants, 30; mine warfare, 7.

PARAMILITARY: active, 15,500: frontier force, 10,500; coast guard, 5,000.

Military in Syria (2011): Total armed forces: active, 285,000; reserves, 314,000. Military expenditure as percent of GDP: 3.7 (2011).

GROUND FORCES: regular army, active, 220,000; reserves, 280,000.

In-service equipment: tanks, 4,950;

armored personnel carriers, 1,500; major artillery, 3,440.

AIR FORCES:

(a) regular air force, active, 30,000; reserves, 10,000.

(b) regular air defense, active, 40,000; reserves, 20,000.

In-service equipment: combat aircraft, 365; combat helicopters, 103.

NAVAL FORCES: regular navy, active, 5,000; reserves, 4,000.

In-service equipment: patrol and coastal combatants, 32; mine warfare, 7.

PARAMILITARY: active 108,000: gendarmerie, 8,000; people's militia, 100,000.

NON-CONVENTIONAL WEAPONS:

Biological: Although, in its July 2012 foreign ministry statement, Syria mentioned the option of using biological and chemical weapons if it was exposed to external aggression, there was no evidence that it possessed biological weapons.

Chemical: Syria embarked on a chemical weapons program in the late 1970s, initially with the assistance of the Soviet Union and North Korea, and later the Islamic Republic of Iran. It set up four production facilities near Aleppo [q.v.], Hama [q.v.], Homs [q.v.], and Latakia [q.v.], producing nerve agents and mustard gas. During the 2011–2012 upheaval, it shifted its stocks of chemical weapons from the northern zone, which was caught up in intense violence, to more secure locations.

Nuclear: After Israel's clandestine bombing of the Al Kibar nuclear reactor in northeastern Syria, built with North Korean assistance, in September 2007, the International Atomic Energy Agency carried out an investigation. It concluded in 2011 that the design of this reactor was similar to that of North Korea's Yongbyon reactor used to produce weapons-grade plutonium from nuclear power plant waste. But the Syria government lacked such material domestically.

Military in United Arab Emirates
(2011): Total armed forces: active, 51,000. Military expenditure as percent of GDP: 9.6 (2011).

GROUND FORCES: regular army, 34,000.

In-service equipment: tanks, 381; armored personnel carriers, 650; major artillery, 271.

AIR FORCES: regular air force, 4,500.

In-service equipment: combat aircraft, 178; combat helicopters, 31.

NAVAL FORCES: regular navy, 2,500.

In-service equipment: submarines, 10; patrol and coastal combatants, 17; mine warfare, 2.

Military in Yemen (2011): Total armed
forces: active, 66,700. Military expenditure as percent of GDP: 4.9 (2011).

GROUND FORCES: regular army, active, 60,000; reserves 40,000.

In-service equipment: tanks, 850; armored personnel carriers, 260; major artillery, 1,300.

AIR FORCES:
(a) regular air force, 3,000.
(b) air defense force, 2,000.

In-service equipment: combat aircraft, 79; combat helicopters, 31.

NAVAL FORCES: regular navy, 1,700.

In-service equipment: patrol and coastal combatants, 22; mine warfare, 1.

PARAMILITARY: active, 71,200 (interior ministry force, 50,000); reserves 20,000 (tribal levies, 20,000); coast guard, 1,200.

Mishna: Text of the Jewish Oral Law. *See* Talmud.

Mizrachi (Hebrew: *Oriental*): *the term commonly used for Edot Mizrachi* (Hebrew: *Oriental Peoples*). *See* Oriental Jews.

Mizrahi (Hebrew: acronym of *Merkaz Rouhani,* Spiritual Center): *political party in Palestine/Israel* Mizrahi was formed in 1902 by a group of rabbis in Vilnius, Lithuania, to counter growing secularization in the education of the Jews [*q.v.*] in Europe. It marked the rise of religious Zionism [*q.v.*] as a distinct faction within the Zionist movement [*q.v.*], represented by the World Zionist Organization [*q.v.*]. The party advocated establishing a Jewish national home in Palestine [*q.v.*], based on the written Jewish law, the Torah [*q.v.*]. In Palestine, Mizrahi ensured that the chief rabbinate was organized within the framework of the elected assembly.

In 1922 its younger members formed Poale HaMizrahi [*q.v.*]. Mizrahi had one minister in the provisional government of Israel in 1948. It and the Poale HaMizrahi allied with other religious groups to form the United Religious Front (URF) to run in the first general election in 1949. The URF won 16 seats and joined the government to run inter alia the ministry of religious affairs. The ministry decided how to finance religious councils and religious courts, and influenced the composition and working of the powerful Rabbinical Council.

In mid-1951 it brought down the government led by David Ben-Gurion [*q.v.*] on the issue of educating immigrant families and the URF's degree of control over religious education in schools. In the following election, Mizrahi and the Poale HaMizrahi together won 10 seats and joined the coalition government. In 1956 the two groups combined to form the National Religious Party [*q.v.*].

Mohieddin, Khaled (1922–): *Egyptian politician* (Also spelled Khalid Mohieddin)Born into a land-owning family in the Nile [*q.v.*] delta, Mohieddin graduated from the Royal Military Academy in Cairo [*q.v.*] and became a cavalry officer, reaching the rank of major. He also obtained an economics degree from the University of Cairo.

Active with the Free Officers Organization, which staged a coup in July 1952, Mohieddin was one of the two leftist members of the ruling 18-member Revolutionary Command Council (RCC). In the power struggle between President Muhammad Neguib [*q.v.*] and his deputy, Gamal Abdul Nasser [*q.v.*], the Communists, including Mohieddin, backed Neguib because he favored returning to a parliamentary system. When Nasser won, he dismissed Mohieddin from the RCC and put him under house arrest. But during the 1956 Suez War [*q.v.*] Nasser released hundreds of leftists, including Mohieddin, so that they could organize resistance against the invaders of the Suez Canal zone.

He was named editor of a new pro-government daily, *Al-Massaa* (Arabic: *The Evening*), but he lost this job in 1959 when, reacting to the Iraqi Communists' [*q.v.*] opposition to the unification of Iraq with the United Arab Republic [*q.v.*], Nasser turned against local Communists. It was not until 1964 that Nasser, responding to the changed situation in the region, began to co-opt Communists. He was appointed chairman of the board of *Al-Akhbar* (Arabic: *The News*). He also became a member of the secretariat of the Arab Socialist Union (ASU) [*q.v.*], the new ruling party, and headed the ASU section responsible for the press.

After Egypt's debacle in the June 1967 Arab-Israeli War [*q.v.*], Nasser began to cold-shoulder leftists and rejected Mohieddin's proposal that the armed services be controlled by the ASU, with its cadre penetrating their institution, thus ending their isolation from society.

He received the Lenin Peace Prize from the Soviet Union in 1970. After Nasser's death that year, his ties with the new government became tenuous. He criticized President Anwar Sadat's [*q.v.*] growing alliance with the United States, especially after the October 1973 Arab-Israeli War [*q.v.*], and economic liberalization, which hurt the poor. After the forums within the ASU were allowed to graduate to parties in 1977, he was elected leader of the National Progressive Unionist Party (NPUP) [*q.v.*]. The next year he became editor of its weekly paper, *Al-Ahali* (Arabic: *The People*). He opposed the Egyptian-Israeli Peace Treaty [*q.v.*].

Mohieddin was one of the 240 secular dissidents arrested in September 1981, a month before Sadat's assassination. He was released soon after. Having failed to win a parliamentary seat in 1984 and 1987, he succeeded in 1990. The number of seats for his party rose to five and six respectively in the elections of 1995 and 2000. In the 2005 election the total fell to two, with one seat going to Mohieddin, and the other to Muhammad Rafaat El Saeed who succeeded him as party chairman.

His book *For this We Oppose Mubarak* (1987) was a powerful indictment of the government of Hosni Mubarak [*q.v.*]. He backed the civil uprising against Mubarak in January-February 2011, which led to his ouster.

Mohamad, Ali (1952–): *Egyptian military officer, Al-Qaida leader* Born Ali Abdul Sauond into a well-to-do family in Alexandria [*q.v.*], Mohamed enrolled at the military academy in Heliopolis, a suburb of Cairo [*q.v.*]. A tall, powerfully built man, he underwent paratrooper training and rose to the rank of major before leaving the army in 1984. During his military service he secretly joined the al-Jihad al-Islami [*q.v.*]. In 1980 he tried to ingratiate himself with the U.S. Central Intelligence Agency (CIA) in Egypt. Though rebuffed, he did not give up; nor did the CIA.

In early 1986 he arrived in the United States with a visa waiver, a privilege that could be conferred on a visitor only with the blessing of the CIA or the state department. He found a job as a security officer in Sunnyvale, California, and married Linda Sanchez, an American medical technician. In November he enlisted in the U.S. army on a three-year contract and served as an army sergeant at the Special Forces headquarters at Fort Bragg, North Carolina. As an assistant instructor at the John F. Kennedy Special Warfare Center, he helped the seminar director prepare classes on the history, politics, culture, and armed forces of the Middle East [*q.v.*]. A multilinguist, he was fluent in Hebrew [*q.v.*]. He was a frequent visitor at Al Khifa Refugee Center in Brooklyn, a recruiting center for American Muslim [*q.v.*] volunteers to join the anti-Soviet jihad [*q.v.*] in Afghanistan. During his annual army leave he traveled to Afghanistan to fight the Soviets there. He returned with a belt of a *Spetsnaz* (Russian: *Special Forces*) soldier whom he claimed to have killed.

After an honorable discharge from the Pentagon, he started a leather import-export business. During his visits to New York, he imparted weapons training to the American Muslim militants attending Al Khifa Refugee Center. He found time and inclination to pursue a doctorate in Islamic studies.

In 1993 he applied unsuccessfully for a translator's job at the Federal Bureau of Investigation (FBI). He traveled to Sudan where, following a failed assassination attempt on Osama bin Laden [*q.v.*] in Khartoum, Mohamad retrained his bodyguards. He reportedly conceded this action of his in an FBI interview in 1997, when he and his wife moved from Santa Clara to Sacramento, where he was employed as a computer specialist at a music and video wholesaler. A search of their home revealed documents on surveillance of government targets, assassination techniques, planning of terrorist acts, and use of explosives.

Following his arrest in 1998, he chose a plea bargain and turned a state witness in the U.S. case against bin Laden. His own trial was so sensitive that it was held in camera when it opened in late October 1998 in Manhattan—two and a half months after the bombing of the two American embassies in East Africa. Mohamad told the court that he had "scouted out" the U.S. Embassy in Nairobi at bin Laden's request.

According to CBS television news report in February 2002, he had pleaded guilty to five counts of conspiracy to kill American nationals and damage U.S. property, and was awaiting sentencing. Another report said that his sentencing had been postponed indefinitely. Speaking in 2006, his wife, Linda Sanchez, said that he had not been sentenced and that nobody could get to him as everything about him was top secret.

Moledet (Hebrew: *Homeland*): *Israeli political party* The Moledet was established in 1988 by Ze'evi Rechavam Ze'evi, a retired general, with a program of bringing about "voluntary transfer" of Palestinians from the West Bank [*q.v.*] and Gaza [*q.v.*]. It won two seats in the 1988 election and backed the national unity government that followed. Protesting against Israel's participation in the Middle East Peace Conference in Madrid [*q.v.*] in October 1991, it withdrew its backing from the administration three months later. In the June 1992 election it won three parliamentary seats. In 1994 it combined with the Tehiya [*q.v.*] to form the Moledet-Eretz Israel Faithful and the Tehiya. Four years later it joined the coalition government led by Benjamin Netanyahu [*q.v.*]. On the eve of the 1999 general election, it was absorbed into the National Union, which won three seats. It joined the

national unity government under Ariel Sharon [*q.v.*] in March 2001, and its leader Ze'evi became minister of tourism. He was assassinated in October by the militants of the Popular Front for Liberation of Palestine [*q.v.*] at an East Jerusalem [*q.v.*] hotel where he had taken up residence. It then combined with Israel Beitainu [*q.v.*] to form the National Union [*q.v.*]. Binyamin Elon, who succeeded Ze'evi, left the government in 2004 when Sharon decided to end the occupation of Gaza the following year. In the 2006 Knesset Moledet's size was reduced to two. On the eve of the 2009 election it revived its alliance with the National Union, but managed to gain only one seat.

Montazeri, Hussein Ali (1921–2009): *Iranian religious-political leader* Born into a poor peasant family in Najafabad, Montazeri had his early theological education in Isfahan [*q.v.*]. He then went to Qom [*q.v.*], where he became a student of Ayatollah Ruhollah Khomeini [*q.v.*]. In the early 1960s he taught at the Faiziyya seminary in Qom, and participated in the anti-government protest in June 1963.

An active member of the anti-shah clerical circles, he was close to Ayatollah Mahmoud Taleqani [*q.v.*]. During the latter part of his exile, from 1964 to 1978, Khomeini appointed him his personal representative in Iran. He was arrested during the anti-Rastakhiz Party [*q.v.*] protest in March 1975. Tortured in jail, he was released in November 1978 in the midst of a rising revolutionary movement.

On his return to Iran in February 1979, Khomeini appointed him the Friday prayer leader of Qom, a highly prestigious position, and gave him a seat on the governing Islamic Revolutionary Council. He was elected leader of the Association of Combatant Clergy [*q.v.*] and chairman of the Assembly of Experts (1979) [*q.v.*], which was convened to draft a constitution. In 1980 Khomeini put him in charge of the secretariat of the Friday prayer leaders, based in Qom.

Montazeri took a radical stance on many issues. The official campaign to bolster his standing gathered pace in the spring of 1983, when in all government offices Khomeini's portraits were accompanied by smaller pictures of Montazeri. But the radicals' attempt to have him named as successor to Khomeini by the Assembly of Experts (1982) [*q.v.*] failed. However, after a brief session of the Assembly in November 1985, one of its members, Ahmad Barkbin, revealed that the Assembly had in fact chosen Montazeri as Khomeini's successor. He retained this position until March 1989, when Khomeini changed his mind.

Instead of following Khomeini's example of intermittently backing one or other faction within the ruling establishment, Montazeri consistently advocated moderate policies, such as allowing a fair degree of opposition and liberalizing the economy, thus alienating centrists and radicals. He also repeatedly stressed the failure of the Islamic revolution to deliver on its promises, while ignoring its achievements. When he was offered the choice of sharing power with two others to constitute a Leadership Council of three, he rejected it, preferring to resign. He then immersed himself in delivering lectures on Islamic jurisprudence. When Khomeini died in June

1989, he was not on the list of candidates considered by the Assembly of Experts.

In 1997, when he publicly questioned the religious learning and standing of Khomeini's successor, Ayatollah Ali Khamanei [*q.v.*], he was put under house arrest. That ended in 2003. He then set up his own website to express his views and communicate with others.

After the controversial presidential election in June 2009, he lambasted the exercise as fraudulent, strongly condemned the authorities for their heavy-handed repression of the peaceful protest, and argued that the regime was neither Islamic nor a republic. He died of natural causes in December.

His funeral rites in Qom, attended by, among others, Mir Hussein Mousavi [*q.v.*] and Mahdi Karroubi [*q.v.*], provided a rallying platform for the opposition supporters who gathered in their hundreds of thousands. Even Khamanei was moved to send his condolences, describing Montazeri one of the great jurists of Islam.

Morsi, Muhammad (1951–): *Egyptian Islamist leader; president 2012–* Also spelled Mohamed Morsi) Born in a village in the northern Egyptian province of Sharqiya province, Morsi obtained an engineering degree in 1975 followed by a postgraduate degree in metallurgy in 1978 from Cairo University. Four years later, he received a doctorate in engineering from University of Southern California. After teaching at California State University, Northridge, until 1985, he returned home to join Zagazig University in northern Egypt as a professor of engineering.

He became an active member of the quasi-legal Muslim Brotherhood [*q.v.*], and cofounded The Egyptians Resist the Zionist Project Committee. He was elected to the Brotherhood's Guidance Council. In 2000 he won a seat at the People's assembly, and became the leader of the 17-strong Muslim Brotherhood group. He protested against the rigging of the 2005 parliamentary election, and was arrested along with 500 other demonstrating Brotherhood members in 2006 and jailed for seven months. He was a coauthor of the Brotherhood's revised political platform in 2007.

During the civil uprising against Egyptian President Hosni Mubarak [*q.v.*], he was arrested on 28 January 2011 in Cairo [*q.v.*]. When, in the midst of the subsequent turmoil there was a jail break, he refused to flee. Instead he contacted the media to visit his prison and check the conditions under which he and other Brotherhood members had been detained.

In April, when the Brotherhood's Guidance Council decided to form the Justice and Freedom Party (JFP) [*q.v.*], it named him its chairman. He entered the presidential race as the JFP's candidate. But after Khairat el Shater, the Brotherhood's nominee, was disqualified from running because of his failure to meet all the conditions required for the candidacy, the Guidance Council adopted Morsi as the Brotherhood's official candidate.

In the course of electioneering, he promised that the Sharia [*q.v.*] would be the foundation of a future constitution, while the Guidance Council appealed to conservative clerics to urge their followers to vote for him. In the second round of the presidential poll on 16–17 June 2012 he secured 51.7 percent of the vote. He resigned as leader of the Freedom and Justice Party, and the SCAF transferred power to him on 30 June.

On 10 July, the Supreme Constitutional Court (SCC) suspended his order to reinstate the Islamist-dominated bicameral parliament. In early August he appointed Hisham Qandil, a technocrat with no ties to any political party, as prime minister. On 12 August he forced the 75-year-old Muhammad Hussein Tantawi, head of the armed forces, and 64-year-old Sami Anan, the Army chief of staff, to resign. He then replaced the commander of the presidential guard and the intelligence chief. His team of 21 advisers and aides was dominated by pro-Islamist personalities but included two Copts [*q.v.*] and three women. In October he granted pardon to all the protestors detained and tried in the incidents relating to the Arab Spring [q.v.], from 25 January 2011 to 30 June 2012.

Starting with Riyadh [*q.v.*] in July, he visited Addis Ababa, Beijing, and Tehran [*q.v.*] to attend the summit of the Non-Aligned Movement at the end of August. In his speech at this conference he said it was an "ethical duty" to support the Syrian people against their "oppressive regime."

mosque: *a place of public worship for Muslims,* called *masjid* (Arabic: *place of prostration*). The first mosque, built by the Prophet Muhammad (570–632 A.D.) at Quba near Medina [*q.v.*], was a simple courtyard. During the rule of Caliph al-Walid (705–715 A.D.) the following elements were added to mosques: the *mihrab*, a semi-circular niche in the center of the wall pointing to the *qibla* (the direction of Mecca [*q.v.*]); and the *minbar*, a seat at the top of steps to the right of the niche used as a pulpit by the preacher (Arabic: *khatib*) to deliver a sermon (Arabic: *khutba*). Since then mosques have often been fully or partially covered, and provided with one or more minarets. Large mosques sometimes have cloisters for students of religion.

The head of a mosque is called the imam [*q.v.*] and acts as the prayer leader. Sometimes he also acts as a religious instructor. There is also a muezzin (derivative of *muadhdhin*, Arabic: *announcer*), who uses the minaret to call believers to worship five times a day. Ritual prayers, called *salat* (in Arabic) or *namaz* (in Persian), are offered by barefoot men, gathered in rows on the floor, who bow and prostrate themselves under the guidance of the imam.

Ritual objects, pictures, and statues are not allowed inside mosques. Since believers are required to cleanse themselves before praying, a place for ablution, containing running water, is often either attached to the mosque or enclosed by it.

Muslims are required to pray collectively on Fridays, the Islamic holy day, and the Friday prayer sermon is especially important. This led to the evolution of collective mosques (*jami masjid*) in cities with a large Muslim population. Over time such mosques became multipurpose public buildings, serving military, political, judicial, social, and educational purposes. A prime example of this was the al-Azhar mosque in Cairo, which evolved into the al-Azhar University [*q.v.*] in 969 A.D. In modern times

the non-religious functions of mosques have been taken over by secular institutions, but they continue to impart elementary Islamic education to Muslim children in many countries.

After the establishment of an Islamic republic in Iran, mosques were put to traditional use, with neighborhood Revolutionary Komitehs [*q.v.*] basing itself in mosques and conducting such state administration as issuing ration cards and recruiting volunteers to the Basij militia.

Mossad (Hebrew: *Institute*): *Israeli foreign intelligence service* (Official title: HaMossad LeModein Ve Tafkidim Meyuhadim [Hebrew: *Institute for Intelligence and Special Tasks*]). In April 1951 the Israeli government replaced the foreign ministry's political department (charged with gathering intelligence outside Israel) with Mossad and transferred it to the prime minister's office. Within two months of taking office its first director, Reuven Shiloah, signed a clandestine cooperation agreement with the U.S. Central Intelligence Agency (CIA).

After Shiloah's resignation in September 1952, Isser Harel became director (1952–63). His successors were Gen. Meir Amit (1963–68); Major-Gen. Zvi Zamir (1968–74); Major-Gen. Yitzhak Hofi (1974–82); Nahum Admoni (1982–89); Danny Yatom (1989–97); Efraim Halevy (1998–2002); Meir Dagam (2002–11); Tamir Pardo, 2011–present. The number of full-time Mossad employees, known to be 1,700 in 1997, has increased. Together with Shin Beth [*q.v.*], it spent $1.31 billion in 2011, about 10 percent of Israel's defense budget.

A list of some of the better known

operations of Mossad since the early 1970s follows. Within a year of the killing of 11 Israeli athletes by Black September Organization [*q.v.*] commandos at the Munich Olympics in September 1972, Mossad operatives assassinated 12 Palestinians involved directly or indirectly with the murders. Mossad arranged secret meetings between Prime Minister Yitzhak Rabin [*q.v.*] and King Hussein of Jordan [*q.v.*] between 1975 and 1977, one of which took place in Tel Aviv [*q.v.*]. In July 1976 it organized the storming of the airport in Entebbe, Uganda, where 100 passengers on an Air France flight from Tel Aviv were being held hostage by two Palestinian guerillas and two members of the German Baader-Meinhoff group to secure the release of 40 Palestinian prisoners. In April 1979 Mossad operatives blew up two cores for the Tammuz nuclear reactor that were awaiting shipment to Iraq from the French port of La Seyne-sur-Mer. Fourteen months later in Paris, Mossad agents assassinated Yahya al-Meshad, an Egyptian nuclear physicist overseeing an Iraq-Egyptian cooperation on nuclear development. On 4 June 1981 Mossad and Aman (Hebrew: acronym of *Agaf* [*Branch*] *Modein* [*Intelligence*]), the military intelligence arm, organized an Israeli air raid on Iraq and destroyed the nuclear facility being constructed near Baghdad [*q.v.*].

Based since 1975–76 in Jounieh, capital of the Christian enclave during the Lebanese Civil War [*q.v.*], and working in tandem with Bashir Gemayel [*q.v.*], the Mossad participated in the plan of defense minister Ariel Sharon [*q.v.*] for an Israeli invasion of Lebanon [*q.v.*], which was im-plemented in June 1982. Mossad and Amn organized an air raid on the headquarters of the Palestine Liberation Organization (PLO) [*q.v.*] in Tunis on 1 October 1985, killing 56 Palestinians. Mossad was deeply involved in the Irangate Affair [*q.v.*], which came to light in November 1986. Earlier, in late September 1986, a Mossad agent, "Cindy," had lured Mordechai Vanunu—a shift manager at Israeli's Dimona nuclear plant from August 1977 to November 1985—to Rome from London, where he had passed on details of Israel's nuclear weapons production to the *Sunday Times*, which published them on 5 October. In Rome, Vanunu was drugged by Mossad agents and taken to Israel, where he was sentenced to a long prison term. On 16 April 1988 a Mossad hit team assassinated a top Palestinian leader, Khalil Wazir [*q.v.*], in Tunis. But Mossad's repeated efforts to kill President Saddam Hussein [*q.v.*] before, during, and after the 1991 Gulf War [*q.v.*] failed.

Mossad is widely believed to have assassinated Gerald Bull, a Canadian ballistic expert working on a super-gun for Iraq, in Brussels in 1990. And two years later, it assassinated Abbas Mousavi, the leader of Hizbollah [*q.v.*], in Beirut [*q.v.*].

In 1990 Mossad recruited Adnan Yassin, deputy to Abdul Hakam Balawi, head of the PLO's internal security in Tunis, as an agent. During the ultra-secret talks among the top PLO leaders in 1992–93, Mossad had Yassin plant bugs in the offices of Mahmoud Abbas [*q.v.*] and Ahmad Qurei, and convey the information by a radio transmitter to the Israeli embassies in Paris and Rome, from where it was passed on to top Israeli leadership engaged in sensitive negotiations with the PLO, which culminated in the Oslo Accord I [*q.v.*] in 1993. Thus Mossad enabled its political superiors to strike the most important accord with the PLO in the full knowledge of the strategy and tactics of Yasser Arafat [*q.v.*] and his second-in-command, Abbas.

In October 1995 its agents assassinated Fathi Abdul Aziz Shikaki, leader of the Islamic Jihad of Palestine [*q.v.*] in Sliema, Malta. But its attempt to kill Khaled Mashaal [*q.v.*], a Hamas [*q.v.*] leader, by pumping a chemical agent into his ear, in Amman [*q.v.*] in September 1997 failed. It resulted in the arrest of two of its agents, carrying Canadian passports, and led to Israel's freeing of Shaikh Ahmad Yassin [*q.v.*] and 72 other Palestinian prisoners in return for the agents' release.

Mossad was believed to be the intelligence agency that facilitated the defection of Ali Reza Askari, a former general of Iran's Revolutionary Guard Corps and a member of the government of President Muhammad Khatami [*q.v.*] in 2007. The CIA was also credited with Askari's disappearance after arriving in Turkey. In 2008 Mossad assassinated Imad Mughniyeh, a former military commander of Hizbollah, in Damascus [*q.v.*].

In January 2010, Mossad agents killed Mahmoud Mabhouh, a co-founder of Hamas's military wing and the organization's leading contact with Iran in a hotel in Dubai [*q.v.*]. During the next two years, operating from Iraqi Kurdistan [*q.v.*], Mossad agents organized the assassinations of four Iranian nuclear experts—Masoud Ali

Mohammadi, Majid Shahriari, Darioush Rezaei, and Mostafa Ahmadi Roshan—as part of Israel's campaign to sabotage Iran's nuclear program.

In Lebanon, Hizbollah leaders uncovered more than 10 Mossad agents within the party's ranks and officials in March 2011.

The best-known former Mossad operator is Tzipi Livni [*q.v.*], who served as the leader of Kadima [*q.v.*] from 2008 to 2012.

Mosul: *Iraqi city* Population: 1.8 million (2009 est.). A settlement with a long history and situated by the Tigris River [*q.v.*] opposite the ancient ruins of Nineveh, Mosul was the leading city of northern Mesopotamia [*q.v.*] by the time of the Abbasid caliphate (751 A.D.–1258). It was sacked by the Mongol invader Hulagu in 1258 and subsequently lacked proper administration until its capture by Iran's Shah Ismail (r. 1501–1524) in 1508. It fell to the Ottoman Turks in 1538. As an important commercial center, it thrived during the Turkish rule. Following the Ottoman defeat in World War I it lost its preeminence. But the discovery of oil in the region in 1927 changed its fortunes. It is the site of several mosques, including the one originally built in 640 A.D. with its minaret leaning like the Tower of Pisa, and churches, one of them dating back to the 10th century and another to the 13th century.

The capital of Nineveh province, Mosul is Iraq's third-largest city. After the Anglo-American invasion of Iraq [*q.v.*] in 2003, when the U.S. Army's 101st Airborne Division was headquartered in Mosul, it became a bastion of resistance to the occupation, with the Sunni [q.v.] Arab [q.v.] majority on the western side of the Tigris backing it, and the Kurds [q.v.] on the eastern side opposing it. The subsequent violence and mayhem led to the exodus of thousands of professionals as well as Christians [q.v.]. It was not until 2009 that a semblance of normality returned.

Moussa, Amr, (1936 –) *Egyptian diplomat and politician; secretary-general of the Arab League, 2001–2011* Born into a middle-class family in Cairo [q.v.], Moussa graduated in law from Cairo University in 1957. He then joined the foreign service of Egypt. He served as director of the International Organizations Department of the foreign ministry from 1977 to 1981. For the next four years he was Egypt's alternative representative at the United Nations. After his posting as his country's ambassador to India (1987–1990), he served as the permanent representative of Egypt to the UN for a year. He was then promoted to foreign minister, a job he held for 10 years.

He and President Hosni Mubarak [q.v.] actively advised the Palestinian leadership during its secret talks with Israel [q.v.], which led to the Oslo Accords [q.v.] in September 1993. They were equally involved in getting the two sides to sign an agreement involving the Gaza Strip [q.v.] and Jericho [q.v.], which led inter alia to the establishment of the Palestinian Authority [q.v.] in 1994. But their efforts to put the Middle East peace process back on track during the rule of Israeli Prime Minister Benjamin Netanyahu (1996–99) were largely unsuccessful.

Against the background of worsen-

ing Israeli-Palestinian relations in the wake of the Al Aqsa Intifada [q.v.], Moussa and Mubarak came under pressure by radical Arab states to sever diplomatic relations with Israel, especially after the election of Ariel Sharon [q.v.] as Israel's prime minister. They managed to fend off the pressure at the Twenty-second Arab League summit [q.v.], which appointed Moussa as its new secretary-general to succeed Ahmad Esmat Abdul Maguid [q.v.].

In 2007 he failed to reconcile the opposing camps in Lebanon about power sharing and the election of the new president. The credit for defusing that crisis went to Qatar in 2008. After Moussa's failure to convene an Arab League summit during the Israeli-Hamas War [q.v.], Qatar took the initiative. Because pro-Washington Egypt and Saudi Arabia refused to attend this conference on January 15, 2009, Moussa stayed away. After his meeting with Hamas [q.v.] leader, Khaled Mashaal [q.v.], in Cairo in September, he ruled out Arab normalization of relations with Israel before a total freeze on Jewish settlements in the occupied West Bank [q.v.] and East Jerusalem [q.v.].

In mid-March 2011, by a majority vote, the Arab League asked the UN Security Council to impose a no-flight zone over Libya to halt the killing of civilians. Following the Security Council's resolution to that effect, leading members of the North Atlantic Treaty Organization (NATO) unleashed a bombing campaign against the regime of Colonel Muammar Gaddafi. Moussa condemned the broad scope of NATO bombing but to no avail.

In July he was succeeded by Nabil al-Araby [q.v.] as the Arab League's secretary-general. In the race for Egypt's presidency in May 2012, he ended up with a mere 10 percent of the vote.

Mubarak, (Muhammad) Hosni (1928–): *Egyptian military leader and politician; president, 1981–2011* Son of a court functionary and born in the Nile [q.v.] delta village of Kafr al-Musaliha, Mubarak graduated from the Air Force Academy with a pilot's license in 1950. After serving as a fighter pilot from 1950 to 1954, he taught at the Air Force Academy, where he later became director general. Appointed commander of the West Cairo [q.v.] airbase in 1961, he underwent advanced aviation and command courses in the Soviet Union near Moscow and at the Kant Air Base in Soviet Kyrgyzstan, ending with a year-long enrollment at the Frunze Military Academy in Moscow.

After Egypt's debacle in the June 1967 Arab-Israeli War [q.v.], he was returned to his earlier job of director general of the Air Force Academy. Two years later he was appointed chief of staff of the air force and promoted to air vice-marshal. In the October 1973 Arab-Israeli War [q.v.], under his command the air force performed well during the crucial initial hours, and he was promoted next year to air marshal. In April 1975 President Anwar Sadat [q.v.] appointed him vice president, since he lacked the potential of developing into a competing center of power. He became vice-chairman of the ruling National Democratic Party (NDP) [q.v.] in 1976.

He succeeded Sadat as president after his assassination in October 1981. He also became leader of the NDP. After briefly moderating his stance toward Islamic fundamentalists [q.v.], he reverted to Sadat's iron-fist policy. While continuing a close alliance with the United States he thawed Egypt's relations with the Soviet Union. He withdrew the Egyptian ambassador from Tel Aviv [q.v.] in protest against Israel's invasion of Lebanon in 1982, but rejected Arab demands to break diplomatic ties with Israel. He continued his predecessor's policy of aiding Iraq militarily in the Iran-Iraq War [q.v.], hoping thus to erode the Arab League's [q.v.] policy of boycotting Egypt since the signing of the Egyptian-Israeli Peace Treaty [q.v.]. His success came in September 1984 when Jordan, Iraq's ally, resumed diplomatic ties with Cairo. After the final expulsion of Yasser Arafat [q.v.] from Lebanon in 1983, Mubarak helped him to reassemble his scattered forces.

In February 1986 a riotous mutiny by 17,000 conscripts of the Central Security Forces in Cairo threatened his regime. Its suppression by defense minister Field Marshal Abdul Halim Abu Ghazala so enhanced his prestige that Mubarak sacked him in April to get rid of a serious potential rival to his own authority. As the sole candidate for the presidency, he was re-elected to the high office in 1987.

Mubarak led Egypt into the Arab Cooperation Council (ACC) [q.v.] in February 1989, and three months later Egypt was allowed to return to the Arab League. When Iraqi President Saddam Hussein [q.v.] occupied Kuwait in August 1990, Mubarak condemned his action. In the Arab

League he led the majority that demanded Iraq's immediate and unconditional withdrawal. That ended the ACC. He sent Egyptian troops to Saudi Arabia to bolster Saudi defenses. As part of the U.S.-led coalition, the Egyptians participated in the 1991 Gulf War [*q.v.*], taking care not to enter Iraq.

His policies proved unpopular with a growing segment of Egyptian society. Almost all opposition groups boycotted the general election of 1990. Militant Islamist groups such as Gamaat al-Islamiya [*q.v.*] and Jihad al-Islami [*q.v.*] intensified their campaign against his regime in 1992. Nonetheless he was reelected president in 1993. He played an important role in bringing about an accord between Israel and the Palestine Liberation Organization [*q.v.*] in September 1993, and in its subsequent implementation.

An attempt by al-Gamaat al-Islamiya to assassinate him during his visit to Addis Ababa to attend the Organization of African Union summit in June 1995 failed. By the late 1990s his campaign against Islamic militants had succeeded, and the economy had improved. In the referendum that followed his nomination for president by the parliament in 1999, he secured 94 percent of the vote on an official turnout of 79 percent. In July 2000 he advised Arafat not to compromise on the future status of Jerusalem [*q.v.*] by conceding the sovereignty of the Dome of the Rock to Israel in his talks with Israeli prime minister Ehud Barak [*q.v.*] at Camp David, and called for a united Arab stance in support of the Palestinians according to the UN Security Council Resolution 242. Later, at his behest, Saddam Hussein was invited to the Arab League summit in Cairo after a decade.

Following the terrorist attacks on the United States in September 2001, his calls for an international convention to define terrorism as a preamble to a worldwide campaign against it went unheeded by the administration of President George W. Bush. Nor were his repeated warning against invading Iraq heeded by Washington, which carried out its invasion and occupation in 2003.

In 2005, Mubarak won a multi-candidate contest for presidency, securing 89 percent of the ballots with his nearest rival, Ayman Nour, who scored 7 percent. The turnout of 23 percent reflected accurately the popular feeling of disenchantment with the system.

Mubarak allowed the semi-clandestine Muslim Brotherhood [*q.v.*] to run for about a third of the 444 parliamentary seats in 2005. Despite the state's well practiced strong-arm tactics deployed against the Brotherhood, its candidates won 60 percent of the races they entered. Mubarak thus succeeded in conveying strongly his earlier assertions to the Bush administration: If you want to see democracy installed to the full in Egypt you will have the Brotherhood in power. Washington got the message. Its fervor for democracy cooled.

Israel's wars with Hizbollah [*q.v.*] in 2006 and Hamas [*q.v.*] in January 2009 put Mubarak on the defensive as public opinion was strongly with Hizbollah and Hamas. He could not afford to reflect popular sentiment as that would have displeased the U.S., the leading benefactor of Egypt under his leadership.

He tried to broker reconciliation between Hamas and Fatah [*q.v.*], but failed, partly because Washington wished to see the division in the Palestinian ranks continue. His effort to bring about a cease-fire between Israel and Hamas in Gaza [*q.v.*] succeeded in June 2008. But the uneasy truce broke down in late December. And when Israel mounted a disproportionate attack on the Gaza Strip in January, Mubarak authorized his foreign minister, Ahmad Abu Gheit, to say that Hamas had brought the catastrophic response upon itself. Mubarak went on to ban the holding of an antiwar conference in Cairo because it was expected to condemn Israel.

The blatant rigging of the parliamentary election in 2010 by his government was widely seen as a preamble to his getting his son, Gamal, elected to the presidency in the following year.

The popular uprising against Mubarak's rule that started at the Tahrir Square in Cairo on 25 January 2011 built up to the extent that the U.S. administration of President Barack Obama called on him to step down. Once the 20-strong Supreme Council of the Armed Forces (SCAF) withdrew its support to him, he resigned on 11 February in favor of SCAF. He and his sons Ala and Gamal were confined to a mansion in the sea resort of Sharm el Shaikh, and then arrested on charges of corruption.

Responding to further anti-Mubarak demonstrations, SCAF put the bedridden Mubarak on trial in August, charged with ordering the killing of unarmed demonstrators in Tahrir Square. In June 2012 he was sentenced to life imprisonment as "an accomplice to murder" in the killing of more than 240 protestors during the last six days of January 2011. Because of his failing health, he was moved from prison to an army hospital in Cairo.

Muhammad, Ali Nasser (1939–): *South Yemeni politician; president, 1978, 1980–86* Born in the Dathina tribal region of South Yemen, Muhammad trained as a teacher in Aden [*q.v.*]. While working as the headmaster of a school in his native area, he played an active role in the founding of the National Liberation Front (NLF) [*q.v.*] in 1963. During the armed campaign he led NLF guerrillas in the Beihan region. When South Yemen became independent in November 1967, he was appointed governor of Lahej province.

After the ousting of President Qahtan al-Shaabi [*q.v.*] in June 1969, he was named defense minister. In August 1971, along with Salim Rubai Ali [*q.v.*] and Abdul Fattah Ismail [*q.v.*], he became a member of the Presidential Council and the prime minister. The next year, when Saudi Arabia was poised to intervene in the conflict between South Yemen and North Yemen on the latter's side, his warning that the Soviet Union would not stand idly by if South Yemen were invaded by its neighbors proved effective.

Once the NLF had devised a three-year plan for transition from national democracy to socialism differences arose between moderate President Ali and radical Muhammad and Ismail. The NLF central committee decided in September 1977, and again in January 1978, to divest Ali of some of his many functions. In June he agreed to resign but then reneged, leading to a one-day fight in which he lost his life.

Muhammad took over the presidency, but ceded it to Ismail in December while retaining the premiership and membership of the Presidential Council. Gradually he came into conflict with Ismail as the latter insisted on maintaining a hard line at home and abroad while Muhammad advocated a pragmatic approach. Ismail lost in April 1980 and went into exile to Moscow.

As head of the state, the government and the ruling Yemeni Socialist Party [*q.v.*], Muhammad monopolized power and used it to moderate official policies. This earned him the disapproval of the deputy premier, Ali Salim al-Beidh [*q.v.*], and the defense minister, Ali Antar, among others. The return of Ismail from Moscow in 1985 intensified factionalism. Muhammad's attempted coup to eliminate his radical rivals in January 1986 set off bitter fighting. Though Ismail and Antar were killed, Muhammad lost the battle, and he fled to Ethiopia. He was sentenced to death for treason.

The partial amnesty and introduction of a multiparty system on the eve of the unification of North and South Yemen in May 1990 did not apply to Muhammad. However, he was appointed to the five-member Presidential Council nominated by al-Beidh after the latter's declaration of independence for South Yemen in 1994. The Council did not last long.

He settled in Damascus [*q.v.*], where he founded the Arab Center for Strategic Studies in 1995. He was allowed to return to Yemen 1997 but, finding himself under virtual house arrest in Sanaa [*q.v.*], left. He divided his time between Damascus, where he lived with his Syrian architect, and Cairo [*q.v.*]. He maintained contacts with the Southern Movement in Yemen and al-Beidh. He backed the Yemen uprising in 2011 and was named to the 17-member Transition Council by some opposition groups, which was not backed by the Joint Meeting Parties, the chief opposition coalition.

Muhammad, Khalid Shaikh (1965–):

Al-Qaida leader Born to Pakistani Baluchi [q.v.] parents, settled in Kuwait since 1961, Muhammad grew up in a suburb of Kuwait City [q.v.]. After finishing his secondary education in Kuwait, he went to the United States on a government grant. There he obtained a diploma in mechanical engineering from North Carolina Agricultural and Technical University, Greensboro, a largely African American college, in 1986. Instead of returning home, he went to Peshawar, Pakistan, to join his elder brother, Zahid, and his Kuwait-born nephew, Ramzi Ahmad Yousef, an electrical engineering graduate from a British university. Zahid and Ramzi Yousef had earlier joined the anti-Soviet jihad [q.v.] orchestrated and funded by America, Pakistan, and Saudi Arabia.

When Yousef was arrested in Pakistan in February 1995 in connection with the bombing of the World Trade Center in New York two years earlier, which killed six people and injured 1,200, his chief coconspirator turned out to be Muhammad. It was Yousef who originally came up with the idea of deploying a hijacked passenger plane as a missile to hit a target. In January 1995, when Yousef and Muhammad were living in the Filipino capital of Manila, their apartment caught fire and the police ended up discovering a laptop computer with a plan to blow up 10 U.S.-bound passenger jets over the Pacific. They fled, with Muhammad moving to Qatar [q.v.], where he worked as a civil servant. But by the time the Qatari government, tipped off by the U.S. Federal Bureau of Investigation (FBI), got around to issuing an arrest warrant in 1996, Muhammad had absconded.

He then formally joined Al Qaida [q.v.]. After the formation of the World Islamic Front for Jihad against Crusaders and Jews [q.v.] in February 1998, he was appointed to the military committee headed by Muhammad Atef [q.v.]. Impressed by his record, Atef reportedly made him his deputy. In that capacity, Muhammad is believed to have coordinated the bombings of the American embassies in Nairobi and Dar as Salam in August 1998, the bombing of the USS Cole in Aden [q.v.] in October 2000, and the attacks in New York and Washington on 11 September 2001. With the death of Atef during the Afghan campaign by the United States in November, Muhammad became the head of the military committee. The FBI put a reward of $25 million on his head. He was believed to be the mastermind behind the bombing of a synagogue in the Dierba Island of Tunisia in 2002, which killed 21 people, mainly German tourists. He was arrested in the Pakistani city of Rawalpindi in February 2003 and handed over to U.S. authorities.

mujahid (pl. mujahedin): One who engages in jihad [q.v.].

Mujahedin-e Islam (Iran) (Persian: *Combatants of Islam*): *Iranian political party* The Mujahedin-e Islam was formed in 1945 by Ayatollah Abol Qasim Kashani [q.v.], a nationalist cleric. It drew its strength from small traders, theological students, and older leaders of merchant families. It demanded cancellation of all the secular laws passed by Reza Shah Pahlavi [q.v.], the application of the Sharia [q.v.] as stated in the constitution of 1906–07, the veil for women, and protection for Iranian industries. It suffered a near-fatal blow in early 1949 when the banishment of Kashani to Lebanon was combined with official repression. His return home in mid-1950 failed to revive the party, especially as another semi-clandestine group, Fedaiyan-e Islam [q.v.], had by then struck roots and won Kashani's patronage.

Mujahedin-e Khalq (Persian: *The People's Combatants*): *Iranian political party* (Also known as People's Mujahedin Organization of Iran) (Official title: *Sazman-e Mujahedin-e Khalq-e Iran* ([Persian: *Iranian People's Combatants' Organization]*) The Mujahedin-e Khalq (MEK) was founded secretly in 1965 by young former members of the Liberation Movement of Iran [q.v.] who felt that their leaders were too moderate. It stressed the importance of religion, believing that Shia Islam [q.v.] would play a major role in inspiring the masses to joint the revolution. Its chief ideologue, Ahmad Rezai, argued that the rebellions led by Shia Imams [*q.v.*], especially Hussein bin Ali, were as much against the usurping Caliphs, who had abandoned the objective of establishing the Order of the Divine Unity (worship of One God and the founding of a classless society for universal good) as they were against feudalists and rich merchants. In modern times true Muslims must strive to create a classless society by struggling against imperialism, capitalism, dictatorship, and conservative clericalism.

The party activists started their guerilla actions in August 1971 with a view to disrupting the celebration of 2,500 years of monarchy in October. The resulting government repression led to the killing or detention of virtually all founder members. But the party's action-oriented program attracted a steady stream of young recruits. Severe repression and an inflow of pro-Marxist recruits led to an attempt by party leaders to combine Islam [*q.v.*] and Marxism. While continuing to be inspired by Islam as an ideology and culture, they increasingly used Marxism as an analytical tool. This alienated many anti-Marxists, who, finding themselves in a minority, left, thus strengthening the position of the Marxists at the expense of others.

In mid-1975 the central committee, dominated by Tehran-based leftists, adopted a manifesto that described Islam as "the ideology of the middle classes" and Marxism as "the ideology of the working class," concluding that Marxism was the truly revolutionary creed. The centrists, opposed to the philosophy of Marxism, split the party. Both wings carried out guerrilla actions and lost many cadres. In 1976 they decided to focus on propaganda, with the centrists targeting students,

and the Marxist workers.

Yielding to popular pressure in 1977–78, the government freed most Mujahedin prisoners. This strengthened both factions, who participated in many demonstrations. The release in December 1978 of Masoud Rajavi [*q.v.*], the only surviving member of the original central committee, boosted the Mujahedin's morale. Both factions were active during the events that culminated in the victory of the revolution in February 1979. The Marxist Mujahedin-e Khalq changed its name to the *Sazman-e Paykar dar Rah-e Azadi-e Tabaqah-e Kargar* (Combat Organization on the Road to Liberation of the Working Class), popularly called Paykar, with the centrist group retaining the original name under Rajavi's leadership.

When Mujahedin-e Khalq members refused to surrender their arms to the Islamic government, as ordered by Ayatollah Ruhollah Khomeini [*q.v.*], they came into conflict with the new regime. This culminated in open warfare on the eve of the impeachment of President Abol Hassan Bani-Sadr [*q.v.*] on 21 June 1981. Both Rajavi and Bani-Sadr went underground. On 28 June a bomb planted by Mujahedin-e Khalq members killed 74 leaders of the Islamic republic. A month later Rajavi and Bani-Sadr flew clandestinely from Tehran [*q.v.*] to France. In Paris, Rajavi and Bani-Sadr formed the National Council of Resistance in Iran (NCRI) [*q.v.*] to violently oppose the regime in Tehran.

The party's armed struggle against the Khomeini regime continued, with its guerrillas, led by Musa Khiyabani, targeting revolutionary guards and parliamentarians. On 30 August the

NCRI claimed that its activists detonated an incendiary device that killed President Muhammad Ali Rajai [q.v.] and Premier Muhammad Javad Bahonar. The government responded by imposing summary justice on those found guilty of violence. In February 1982, in a single attack, the security forces shot dead 10 Mujahedin-e Khalq central committee members, including Khiyabani. By then the party claimed to have killed over 1,200 religious and political leaders of the regime. The government put the number of executed Mujahedin at 4,000, with the party claiming twice that number.

With war against Iraq [q.v.] raging along the international border, the Tehran government successfully labeled those creating disorder at home as unpatriotic agents of Baghdad. Its efforts received a boost when the Mujahedin leader, Rajavi, publicly met the Iraqi deputy premier, Tariq Aziz [q.v.], in Paris in January 1983, a move that also caused a split between Rajavi and Bani-Sadr, who quit the NCRI.

After the replacement of a socialist administration in France sympathetic to the Mujahedin-e Khalq, with a center-right government, the authorities expelled Rajavi in June 1986 at the behest of Iran. He set up the party's headquarters in Baghdad [q.v.] and continued his activities from there. A year later, assisted by Iraq, Rajavi formed an armed wing of the party: the National Liberation Army (NLA). Toward the end of the Iran-Iraq War, in late July 1988, the 7,000-strong NLA, operating under heavy Iraqi air cover, seized towns 60 mi./100 km into Iran along the Baghdad-Tehran highway. The Iranians cut off their supply lines and counterattacked. Up to 4,500 NLA and Iraqi troops were killed. As further punishment to the MEK, the Iranian government also executed hundreds of jailed party members.

After Khomeini's death in June 1989, Iraqi President Saddam Hussein [q.v.] halted all anti-Iranian activities, including hostile broadcasts of the Mujahedin-e Khalq radio, in order to improve relations with post-Khomeini Iran. But the thaw did not last long.

The Mujahedin-e Khalq continued to maintain its headquarters in Baghdad in the same way that the Iranian-backed Supreme Council of the Islamic Revolution in Iraq [q.v.] did in Tehran—as an embarrassing irritant to the other side. Of the seven sites allocated to the MEK by Saddam Hussein, Camp Ashraf, 40 miles/60 km north of Baghdad, was maintained as its military headquarters and the main training center, equipped with artillery, armored personnel carriers, and tanks.

In 1991 the MEK's forces aided Iraqi troops in massacring the Kurdish [q.v.] and Shia rebels in Iraq in the aftermath of the January–February 1991 Gulf War [q.v.].

Inside Iran, the government blamed the MEK for the periodic bomb explosions—such as the one in Mashhad [q.v.] on 21 June 1994. In retribution it fired missiles at the MEK bases near the Iran-Iraq border. The MEK continued its periodic pinprick attacks on Iran.

In October 1997 the United States declared the Mujahedin-e Khalq a terrorist organization, thus barring it from collecting funds in America, its chief source of income. The decision was based on the MEK's role in the seizure of the American Embassy in Tehran in 1979 and the earlier assassinations of American military officers and civilians. A decade later, the U.S. state department would add to its list the MEK's assistance to the Iraqi forces in their massacres of the Kurdish and Shia rebels in Iraq in 1991.

Due to the student rioting in mid-1999 in Tehran, and the reformist victory in Iran's parliamentary election in the following year, the MEK leadership visualized an intensified struggle between reformists and conservatives, providing an opportunity for its organization to seize power. In March 2000 its activists fired 13 mortars at a residential area near the headquarters of the Islamic Revolutionary Guard Corps, their obvious target. Iran hit the group's military camps in Iraq, and the members of the Tehran-based Supreme Council of Islamic Revolution in Iraq [q.v.] fired mortars at a neighborhood in Baghdad.

During the Anglo-American invasion of Iraq [q.v.] in March 2003, the U.S. air force bombarded the MEK camps in Iraq. Its commanders signed a cease-fire with the Americans occupiers on 23 April 2003, which permitted them to keep their weaponry. In June the Pentagon took control of Camp Ashraf while MEK commanders consolidated all their weapons from other sites. The Americans confiscated the MEK's arms and destroyed its arsenal. They screened almost 4,000 MEK fighters for past terrorist activities. Once the camp's inmates had surrendered all their small arms and renounced violence in writing, the Pentagon recognized

them as "protected persons" under the Fourth Geneva Convention to safeguard them from attacks by the Iraqi groups or Iran. Its forces escorted supplies from Baghdad to the 28-square-mile, self-regulated Ashraf camp.

This continued until January 2009, when the Pentagon passed on the control of Camp Ashraf to the Baghdad government, which agreed to an American military presence at the camp, and the Iraqi authorities promised to treat the inmates humanely and to refrain from forced relocation to a country where they feared persecution.

In July 2009, when the Iraqi security forces tried to set up a police station inside Camp Ashraf, now housing 3,400 people, including about 1,000 women, violent clashes ensued. Eleven inmates lost their lives due to the use of live ammunition by the Iraqis. In December, when the Iraqi government decided to shift the inmates of the camp to a former detention center at Neqrat al-Salman in the south by March 2010, the inmates refused to leave, claiming that under the Geneva Convention, they had protected status. They successfully resisted the second attempt by the Iraqi forces in April 2011.

In December the United Nations mediated an agreement between the Iraqi authorities and the MRK under which the prisoners would move from Camp Ashraf to the recently vacated Camp Liberty near Baghdad airport, where they would be screened by the UN for asylum eligibility in a third country. All but 400 diehard members were transferred to Camp Liberty by March 2012.

While the MEK functions from its

headquarters in the Paris suburb of Auvers-sur-Oise under the leadership of Mariam Rajavi, the whereabouts of her husband, Masoud Rajavi, are not known.

mujtahid (Arabic: *one who strives*): A mujtahid is one who practices *ijtihad* [*q.v.*], and the term applies to both Sunni [*q.v.*] and Shia [*q.v.*] clerics. Among Twelver Shias [*q.v.*] the idea of a living mujtahid interpreting the Sharia [*q.v.*] took hold in the late 18th century. This gave the mujtahid a far greater degree of power than that of a leading Sunni [*q.v.*] cleric. Shia mujtahids announced their judgments on political matters impinging on Islamic principles independently of the temporal ruler, a development that had a profound impact on the subsequent history of Iran [*q.v.*], a predominantly Shia country. In the Shia world the honorific "mujtahid" was replaced by ayatollah around the time of the 1907–11 Constitutional Revolution [*q.v.*] in Iran. In 2000 there were 27 ayatollahs in that country. The number rose to about 40 a decade later.

Mukhabarat (Arabic: lit., *intelligence*; fig., *organization collecting information*): Mukhabarat is the popular term used in Arab countries for the intelligence apparatus used at home and abroad. More specifically, *Amn al-Aam* (Arabic: *General Security*) focuses on the general public and governmental property, with some of its employees monitoring the daily life of the populace, looking for any sign of dissent, and others, operating at major police stations, specializing in interrogating and, if necessary, torturing suspects. It maintains a large network of inform-ers. By contrast, *Amn al-Khas* (Arabic: *Special Security*) concentrates on protecting the head of state and his palaces and guesthouses. The largest intelligence organ, *Dairat al-Mukhabarat al-Ammaa* (Arabic: *General Intelligence Department*), the official title of Mukhabarat, operates both internally and externally, with its agents attached to the country's embassies abroad. Its functions include keeping tabs on the governing and other political parties (if they are allowed); curbing local opposition; monitoring subversive activities and engaging in counter-espionage; maintaining surveillance of all embassies and other foreign missions in the country and monitoring the state's embassies abroad; collecting intelligence overseas; and conducting sabotage and subversion against hostile countries and aiding the groups opposed to their regimes. Its armed forces counterpart is *Istikhabarat al-Askariya* (Arabic: *Military Intelligence*). Its mandate includes assessing chief military threats to the country, overseeing security and counterintelligence in the armed forces, ensuring the officers' loyalty to the regime, maintaining a network of informers in the countries of the region, and cooperating with foreign intelligence agencies. In addition, there is *Amn al-Askariya* (Arabic: *Military Security*). It is charged with maintaining internal security within the armed forces, a task it often performs by posting at least one unquestionably loyal officer in every military unit. So the generic term Mukhabart normally covers up to five intelligence agencies.

In Iraq ruled by President Saddam Hussein [*q.v.*], for instance, the five intelligence agencies under the National Security Bureau consisted of the General Security (GS, *Amn al-Aam*), General Intelligence Department (GID, *Dairat al-Mukhabarat al-Ammaa*), Military Intelligence (MI, *Istikhabarat al-Askariya*), Special Security Directorate (*Muderiye al-Amn al-Khas*), and Military Security (MS, *Amn al-Askariya*). Syria came to acquire an Air Force Intelligence because its leader Hafiz Assad [*q.v.*] was air force commander before he seized the presidency. Fiercely loyal to him, it reported to him.

Multi-National Force (in Lebanon, 1982–84): Following a 70-day siege of Beirut [*q.v.*] during the 1982 Israeli invasion of Lebanon [*q.v.*], an agreement was brokered in August by the United States between Israel, Syria, and Lebanon that a Multi-National Force (MNF) composed of about 1,200 troops each from the United States, France, and Italy would be deployed to ensure the safe withdrawal of Palestine Liberation Organization (PLO) [*q.v.*] and Syrian forces from West Beirut [*q.v.*]. The evacuation was completed by 3 September and the MNF left within a week.

On 13 September president-elect Bashir Gemayel [*q.v.*] was assassinated. Between 16 and 18 September, Christian Phalangist [*q.v.*] militiamen killed some 2,000 men, women, and children in the Palestinian camps of Sabra and Shatila in Beirut. The MNF was recalled and took up positions between the airport and the outskirts of the city. A British contingent of 150 men was added to the MNF.

About a year later the United States and France intervened with warplanes and warships in the Lebanese Civil War [*q.v.*] on the side of the Maronite-dominated [*q.v.*] Lebanese army. This angered the opposing, predominantly Muslim camp. On 23 October 1983 the truck-bombing of the U.S. and French military headquarters in West Beirut left 241 U.S. and 59 French troops dead. This shook the resolve of the United States and France to back the Lebanese army. In February 1984, despite the intervention of the American warplanes against them, the Muslim forces succeeded in expelling the Lebanese army from West Beirut. Washington ordered the withdrawal of its troops from Beirut, and London, Rome, and Paris followed suit. The MNF withdrawal was completed by 31 March 1984.

Multinational Force and Observers (1979): To ensure compliance with the provisions of the 1979 Egyptian-Israeli Peace Treaty [*q.v.*] concerning the level of forces of the two neighbors in and near the Sinai Peninsula [*q.v.*], a Multinational Force and Observers (MFO) of 2,600 troops from 11 countries was posted in the peninsula in August 1981. The contributing countries included Australia, New Zealand, and Fiji in Asia-Pacific; France and Italy in Europe; the United States and Canada in North America; and Colombia in South America. The MFO is also required to ensure freedom of navigation through the Strait of Tiran. In 2009 the Czech Republic became the 12th member of the MFO.

Mousavi, Mir Hussein (1941–): *Iranian politician, prime minister 1981-89*

Born in Khamane near Tabriz [*q.v.*], Mousavi obtained a maser's degree in architecture from the National University of Tehran in 1969. An activist in Islamic circles, he was jailed briefly in 1973 for anti-government activities. On his release he went to London to study interior design. After the Islamic revolution [*q.v.*] in February 1979, he became a cofounder of the Islamic Republican Party [*q.v.*]. He was appointed chief editor of the party's daily paper, *Jumhouri-ye Islami* (Persian: *Islamic Republic*).

An economic radical, he favored nationalization of foreign and domestic trading. After a brief tenure as foreign minister, he was named prime minister in October 1981. His government accelerated the pace of Islamization and the purging of official institutions of those with insufficient Islamic convictions. But its effort to implement radical land reform, involving the purchase of excess land by the state, was thwarted by the Guardian Council [*q.v.*] on the ground of inviolability of private property. His policies favoring the public sector were unpopular with traders and businessmen.

When, after his reelection as president in 1985, Ali Hussein Khamanei [*q.v.*] considered dropping Musavi as premier, Ayatollah Ruhollah Khomeini [*q.v.*], intent on maintaining a balance between radicals and moderates, publicly praised Mousavi. An amendment to the constitution in 1989 abolished the office of premier.

Upon his election as president in July 1989, Ali Akbar Hashemi Rafsanjani [*q.v.*] appointed Mousavi as his adviser on political matters, and Supreme Leader Ayatollah Ali

Khamanei [*q.v.*] nominated him to the Expediency Consultation Council System. Neither of these posts carried the power that Mousavi had exercised before. He continued as an adviser to the president when Muhammad Khatami [*q.v.*] was elected to that office in 1997.

For the next two decades, he shunned politics and devoted his energies to painting, architecture, and teaching. He was elected president of the Iranian Academy of Arts in 2000.

Critical of the government of President Mahmoud Ahmadinejad [*q.v.*] for its mismanagement of the economy and its unnecessarily provocative stance toward the West, he entered the presidential race in 2009. He called for transparent governance, transferring of the control of the security forces from the Supreme Leader to the popularly elected president, equal rights for women, disbanding of the morality police, and privatization of the electronic media. He supported the official policy that Iran's nuclear program was for peaceful purposes. He condemned both the Holocaust-denial by Ahmadinejad and the mass murder of the Jews [*q.v.*]. His election campaign, in which his academic wife, Professor Zahra Rahnavard, participated actively caught the imagination of women and young people. The support for him rose sharply in the last two weeks before the election.

After the election on 12 June he challenged the official figures of 62.5 percent vote for Ahmadinejad and 33.9 percent for himself. He claimed the figures had been reversed. He provided calm leadership to the massive protest that ensued, always stressing nonviolence. That did not stop the government from using brutal tactics to quash it. He set up the Green Path of Hope as a movement, popularly known as the Green Movement [*q.v.*], to continue the protest through lawful means and demand full implementation of the constitution. But its attempts to stage peaceful demonstrations were foiled by the government.

After the downfall of the president of Tunisia in January 2011 followed by Egyptian President Hosni Mubarak [*q.v.*] on 11 February, Mousavi and Mahdi Karrubi, a former speaker of parliament, applied for an official permission to hold a solidarity rally. Though their application was rejected, thousands of protestors across Iran demonstrated their support for the Arab uprisings. He, Zahra Rahnavard, and Karroubi were placed under house arrest on the direct orders of Khamanei.

Muscat: *Capital of Oman* Population: 775,900 (2010 census). A port with a long history, Muscat was an important center for trading with the Gulf [*q.v.*] and East Africa by the 13th century. The Hormuzis, who then administered it, held supreme for three centuries before being overthrown by the Portuguese in 1508. After a century and a half the Portuguese gave way to the forces of the local Imam [*q.v.*]. After Sultan Hamad had captured the port in the late 18th century the country was called Muscat and Oman, a name it retained until 1970.

Encircled by mountains, Muscat is a striking city with two 16th-century forts. It is an architectural museum, showing influences of the regions it has traded with over the centuries:

India, Portugal, East Africa and Zanzibar, Iran and the Persian Gulf. Its population is equally cosmopolitan.

In February-March 2011, the city witnessed small demonstrations calling for higher salaries and political reform.

Muslim Brotherhood (Egypt): *Egyptian political-religious party* (Official title: *al-Ikhwan al-Muslimin*, [Arabic, *The Brotherhood of Muslims*]) In 1928 Hassan al-Banna [*q.v.*] established the Muslim Brotherhood as a youth club committed to effecting moral and social reform through information and propaganda. But in 1939, responding to the popular movement against the Anglo-Egyptian Treaty [*q.v.*] and the 1936 Palestinian Arab [*q.v.*] uprising against the British Mandate and Zionist colonization, it transformed itself into a political entity. It declared that Islam [*q.v.*], based on the Quran [*q.v.*] and the Hadith [*q.v.*], is a comprehensive, self-evolving system, applicable to all times and places. According to al-Banna, the Brotherhood was "a salafiya [*q.v.*] message, a Sunni [*q.v.*] way, a Sufi [*q.v.*] truth, a political organization, an athletic group, a scientific and cultural union, an economic enterprise, and a social idea." By 1940 it had established 500 branches, each with its own center, mosque, school, and club.

During World War II the Brotherhood's ranks swelled with students, civil servants, artisans, petty traders, and middle-income peasants. After the war it helped escalate anti-British struggle. In 1946 it claimed 500,000 members with as many sympathizers, organized among 5,000 branches. Its volunteers fought in the 1948–49

Palestine War [*q.v.*]. Many Egyptian officers subscribed to the Brotherhood's ideology, and the Brethren acquired military training from them.

Blaming Egypt's political establishment for the debacle in the Palestine War, the Brotherhood resorted to terrorist and subversive activities. The government declared martial law and banned the party in December 1948. Three weeks later Premier Mahmoud Fahmi Nokrashi (Pasha) was assassinated by a Brotherhood activist. This led to further repression of the party. Hassan al-Banna argued that since the Brotherhood had been disbanded after the ban, the assassin could not be described as its member. In February 1949 al-Banna was assassinated by secret service agents in Cairo [*q.v.*].

When martial law was lifted in 1950 the ban on the Brotherhood was removed, and it was allowed to function as a religious body. However, the next year, following the election of moderate Hassan Islam al-Hudaibi as leader, it was permitted to participate in politics. Supporting the government's abrogation of the Anglo-Egyptian Treaty, it declared a campaign against the British occupiers, and participated in the January 1952 riots in Cairo.

The ban on political parties by the ruling Revolutionary Command Council (RCC) after the July 1952 coup did not apply to the Brotherhood, which was described as a religious body. Of the 18 RCC members, four, including Anwar Sadat [*q.v.*], had close contacts with the Brotherhood. When the Brotherhood's leaders realized that the RCC was more interested in spreading secular education, giving equal rights to women,

and implementing land reform than in applying the Sharia [*q.v.*] to all spheres of life, they started opposing the new regime. The RCC banned the Brotherhood in February 1954.

On 23 October a Brotherhood activist, Abdul Munim Abdul Rauf, tried unsuccessfully to assassinate President Gamal Abdul Nasser [*q.v.*]. He and five other Brethren were executed and more than 4,000 party activists were arrested. Several thousand Brethren fled to Syria, Saudi Arabia, Jordan, and Lebanon. In 1964, as part of a general amnesty, Nasser released the Brethren in order to co-opt them into the newly formed Arab Socialist Union [*q.v.*] as a counterforce to the Communists [*q.v.*], who were also freed. But reconciliation between the two sides proved temporary. During the next two years there were three attempts by the Brethren to assassinate Nasser. This resulted in a trial of 365 Brethren followed by the execution of their top leaders, including Sayid Muhammad Quttb [*q.v.*], in August 1966.

The humiliating defeat the Israelis inflicted on Egypt in June 1967 created a popular feeling that God had punished Arabs for turning away from their faith and tinkering with alien concepts such as Arab socialism [*q.v.*]. Sensing a change in the popular mood, Nasser released 1,000 Brethren in April 1968.

Reversing Nasser's policies, President Anwar Sadat promised that the Sharia would be the chief source of legislation, and released all Brotherhood prisoners. The exiled Brethren started returning from Saudi Arabia and elsewhere, and this strengthened the Islamists [*q.v.*] at home. The changed conditions enabled the Brethren to reintegrate themselves into al-Azhar University [*q.v.*], the official center of Islam, which had been purged of them by Nasser.

Fearful of the popular appeal of the Brotherhood, Sadat denied it a license to enter the 1976 general election as a distinct forum. Therefore, the Brethren ran either as independents or as members of the ruling Arab Socialist Party (ASP) [*q.v.*]. Nine were elected as independents, and another six as ASP members. When independent Brethren offered to cooperate with the government on certain conditions, the radicals within the party left to form militant groups. But, because Sadat's economic policies increased disparity between rich and poor, and because he agreed to make peace with Israel without addressing the crucial Palestinian problem, Brotherhood leaders turned against him. Most of the nearly 2,000 dissidents arrested in September 1981 were Brethren or other Islamic fundamentalists [*q.v.*]. On 6 October Sadat was assassinated by four Islamist soldiers.

After an intense drive to crush Islamic militants, President Hosni Mubarak [*q.v.*] engaged al-Azhar clerics to reeducate the imprisoned Brethren and other Islamists, two-fifths of whom were college or university students. Because the 1983 Election Law, like its predecessor, banned parties based on religion or atheism, the Brotherhood was barred from running in the 1984 elections. It therefore allied with the Neo-Wafd Party [*q.v.*] and won eight seats, despite the fact that the election was flagrantly rigged. Outside parliament,

the Brotherhood, working in alliance with the Neo-Wafd [*q.v.*], succeeded in dominating the ruling bodies of influential syndicates of journalists, lawyers, doctors, and engineers.

In the 1987 elections the Brotherhood allied with the opposition Socialist Labor Party [*q.v.*] and the Liberal Socialist Party [*q.v.*] to form the Islamic Alliance. Despite the customary vote-rigging and harassment of the opposition, the Brotherhood-led Alliance won 17 percent of the vote and 60 seats, of which 37 were secured by the Brethren. They demanded the immediate application of the Sharia, the ending of Egypt's strategic and economic links with the United States, and the abrogation of the Egyptian-Israeli Peace Treaty [*q.v.*]. Like its allies in the Islamic Alliance, the Brotherhood boycotted the 1990 election when the government rejected their joint call to lift the state of emergency and conduct the election under the supervision of a non-governmental body.

During the Kuwait crisis and the 1991 Gulf War [*q.v.*], the Brotherhood, a traditional ally of Saudi Arabia, largely supported Iraqi President Saddam Hussein [*q.v.*]. It fueled pan-Islamic [*q.v.*] feelings at the expense of the West. Due to its absence from parliament it could no longer act as an intermediary between the government and the militant Islamic groups as they escalated their anti-regime campaign.

Allowed to run in the general election in 1995, the Brotherhood fielded 150 candidates, all of whom lost. In 1996 it was divested of its domination of the Bar Association, leaving only the Doctors Association under its control. Three years later 20 Brotherhood leaders were arrested on charges of plotting to overthrow the government and infiltrating professional syndicates. However, the Brotherhood was allowed to enter the 2000 general election, and won 17 seats.

When, in the aftermath of the terrorist attacks on the United States in September, the administration of President George W. Bush pressured Mubarak to democratize his regime, Mubarak temporized. He allowed the Brotherhood to run for about a third of the 444 parliamentary seats in 2005. Despite the state's standard strong-arm tactics deployed against the Brotherhood, now led by Muhammad Mahdi Akef, who succeeded the deceased Mamoun al-Hudaybi, its candidates won 60 percent of the races they entered, with the 88 successful Brotherhood members electing Muhammad Morsi [q.v.] as their leader. The result provided Mubarak with the evidence that installing democracy in Egypt would catapult the Brotherhood into power. He presented it to the Bush administration, which got the message. From then on, its fervor for democracy in the Middle East [q.v.] cooled.

After the 2005 election, the Mubarak government mounted a relentless repressive campaign against the Brotherhood, involving thousands of arrests of its ordinary members and military trials for its leaders. By sentencing its treasurer, Khairat al-Shater, a successful businessman, to seven years' imprisonment in 2007 for funding an illegal organization, the authorities disrupted the Brotherhood's funding of its social network. The state-run media slandered the Brotherhood as an agent of Iran.

In its moderated manifesto of 2007 it called for the establishment of a council of Islamic jurists—as a consultative body—to review laws and official policies to judge whether or not they were in line with the basic Islamic precepts.

In 2010, Muhammad Badie, an academic, succeeded Akef as the supreme guide of the Brotherhood. It joined the National Association for Change (NAC), an umbrella organization of all opposition groups, formed by Muhammad El Baradei, a former director general of the International Atomic Energy Agency. When the NAC launched a campaign to secure one million signatures for a petition to lift emergency rule and change election laws, the Brotherhood secured seven times more signatures than all the secular factions combined. Its strong support in urban areas and the villages of the heavily populated Nile Delta remained intact. It boycotted the parliamentary election in November 2010, which was marred by flagrant electoral fraud.

After the ouster of Mubarak [q.v.] in February 2011, the Brotherhood's Guidance Council established the Freedom and Justice Party (FJP) [q.v.] open to all Egyptians irrespective of their religion in April. In the parliamentary elections held between November 2011 and January 2012, the FJP-led Democratic Alliance [q.v.] gained 235 seats on 37.5 percent popular vote and in the Consultative Council elections in January–February 2012 the Alliance won 105 of the 180 elected seats. In the presidential election in June 2012, Muhammad Morsi [q.v.], the candidate of the Muslim Brotherhood's Freedom and Justice

Party [*q.v.*], secured 51.7 percent of the vote.

The Brotherhood's leadership was dominated by urban-based successful businessmen and professionals with advanced degrees in law, medicine, or science. Its economic policy was an amalgam of business-friendly free market capitalism with plans to build up strong manufacturing base and train a labor force with enhanced skills.

Muslim Brotherhood (Jordan): *Jordanian religious body with a political wing, called the Islamic Action Front* During his visits to Jordan (then Transjordan [*q.v.*]) between 1942 and 1945, Hassan al-Banna [*q.v.*] set up Muslim Brotherhood branches in many towns. When the Brotherhood was first banned in Egypt in 1948, hundreds of its activists went into exile in other Arab states, including Jordan. The same happened in 1954, when the Brotherhood in Egypt was dissolved by President Abdul Gamal Nasser [*q.v.*].

Since King Hussein of Jordan [*q.v.*] was one of the Arab leaders Nasser tried to overthrow, the Jordanian Brotherhood turned increasingly pro-Hussein. When his throne was threatened by opposition demonstrations in 1956, it actively sided with him. In return, Hussein's ban on political parties in 1957 exempted the Brotherhood on the ground that it had been registered as a religious charity. His growing stress on the religious eminence of his antecedents as governors of Hijaz [*q.v.*], and thus guardians of Mecca [*q.v.*], endeared him to the Brotherhood.

During the decade after the June 1967 Arab-Israeli War [*q.v.*], with the star of Saudi Arabia rising in the Arab East [*q.v.*], King Hussein grew closer to Riyadh for financial and ideological reasons, and started co-opting Brotherhood leaders into his regime. In the 1970s he allowed them to impart military training to members of Syria's Muslim Brotherhood [*q.v.*]. This enabled him to overcome their disapproval of his opposition to the 1979 Islamic revolution [*q.v.*] in Iran.

The Brotherhood participated in the November 1989 election to the House of Representatives (HoR) through its political wing, the Islamic Action Front (IAF) [*q.v.*]. The IAF emerged as the single largest group, with 23 deputies in a chamber of 80; another nine, while describing themselves as independent Islamists [*q.v.*], worked in tow with it. In October 1990 the IAF joined the government and ran five ministries. During the Kuwait crisis and the 1991 Gulf War [*q.v.*], the Brotherhood, deviating from its traditional pro-Saudi stance, supported Iraqi President Saddam Hussein [*q.v.*]. It was partly in deference to the IAF policy that King Hussein refused to join the Washington-led alliance against Iraq. On the eve of the Middle East Peace Conference in Madrid [*q.v.*], IAF ministers resigned in protest at Jordan's participation in the conference.

To thwart the possibility of the IAF's emerging as a majority party in the November 1993 elections, conducted officially on a multiparty basis, the monarch modified the election law by decree, and introduced single-member-district system which favored tribal and family links over political or ideological affiliation. Unwilling to confront the king, the IAF decided to run for only 36 seats. It won 16 and again emerged as the largest group in the HoR. It opposed the Jordanian-Israeli Peace Treaty [q.v.] signed in October 1994. In the 1997 general election its score fell to eight seats.

After dissolving the HoR in June 2001, King Abdullah II [q.v.] ruled by decree for two years. In the 2003 general election to 110 seats (including six seats reserved for women, if a lesser number got elected), despite electoral fraud, the Islamic Action Front won 17 seats, with 84 going to the candidates representing tribes and other conservative social forces. Flagrant electoral fraud in the 2007 parliamentary election reduced the number of IAF representatives to 6, with the conservative and tribal members totaling 98.

The IAF was one of the seven opposition parties that boycotted the general election in 2010 in protest at the new electoral law. It divided the country into 45 constituencies, with each of them subdivided into as many subdistricts as the number of seats, with eligible citizens casting one non-transferable vote. The system was designed to reduce the representation of urban areas and increase the pro-government rural share.

In early 2011 the IAF participated actively in demonstrations, demanding economic and political reform, with focus on the iniquitous electoral law. It found the constitutional and other concessions by King Abdullah II insufficient. But, led by Hamza Mansour, it refrained from criticizing him, aware that such a stance would open the fault lines between the royalist East Bankers and citizens of Palestinian origin. Unhappy about the repres-

sion of the largely Sunni [q.v.] protestors in Syria, the IAF pressured the monarch to abandon his neutrality on the Syrian crisis. In August King Abdullah II became the first Arab leader to openly call on President Bashar Assad [q.v.] to step down.

Muslim Brotherhood (Palestine): *religious–political organization in Palestine/the West Bank and Gaza* During his visits to Palestine [q.v.] between 1942 and 1945, Hassan al-Banna [q.v.] set up Muslim Brotherhood branches in many towns. After the 1948–49 Palestine War [q.v.], the Gaza Strip [q.v.] came under Egyptian authority and the West Bank [q.v.] was annexed by Jordan. With this, the fate of the Brotherhood in Gaza became intertwined with its Egyptian counterpart and that of the Brotherhood in the West Bank with its Jordanian counterpart.

Following the June 1967 Arab-Israeli War [q.v.], Israel occupied the West Bank and Gaza. In order to weaken the Palestine Liberation Organization [q.v.] in the Occupied Territories [q.v.], in 1973 Israel issued a license to Shaikh Ahmad Yasin [q.v.], the Brotherhood leader in the Occupied Territories, to set up the Islamic Center as a charity to run social, religious, and welfare institutions. It encouraged the growth of Islamic Center/Muslim Brotherhood—funded chiefly by contributions from private and official sources in the Gulf States [q.v.]—as a counterpoint to the secular PLO. It resorted to providing funds covertly to the mosques in the Occupied Territories, especially the Gaza Strip, considered sympathetic to it. But following the dramatic rise of Hizbollah [*q.v.*] in Lebanon, the Israeli government had second thoughts. It arrested Yasin in 1983 for illegal possession of arms, and sentenced him to a long prison term. However, he was released two years later as part of a prison exchange deal between Israel and the Popular Front for the Liberation of Palestine-General Command [*q.v.*].

Yasin built on the popularity he had gained as a political prisoner of Israel, and rapidly increased the membership of the Islamic Center/Muslim Brotherhood. With the eruption of the Intifada [*q.v.*] in December 1987, Yasin and six other leaders of the Brotherhood decided to join the mass movement against the Israeli occupiers. The result was the founding of Hamas [*q.v.*] as the activist arm of the Brotherhood. *See also* Hamas.

Muslim Brotherhood (Saudi Arabia): Following the dissolution of the Muslim Brotherhood in Egypt in 1954, hundreds of Brethren took refuge in Saudi Arabia. After their leaders had convinced the Saudi monarch that Egyptian President Abdul Gamal Nasser [*q.v.*] was misusing al-Azhar University [*q.v.*], they were given funds to set up the Islamic University of Medina in 1961. The university emerged as a bastion of the Brotherhood, which is allowed to function as a religious charity under the leadership of eminent theologians such as Shaikh Muhammad al-Khattar. In their struggle against Nasser and Nasserism [*q.v.*], the Saudi monarchs started funding the Brotherhood in different Arab countries, a practice that continued after Nasser's death in 1970 until the 1991 Gulf War [*q.v.*].

Thousands of Brethren found jobs in the Saudi kingdom as teachers, lawyers, engineers, and accountants in government department and helped establish Islamic banks and revise curricula at schools and universities. Funded by the royal treasury, they founded the World Muslim League [*q.v.*] in 1963 and the World Assembly of Muslim Youth a decade later. They played a major role in rallying active support for the anti-Soviet jihad in Afghanistan in the 1980s.

With the Brotherhood in most Arab states criticizing the pro-Washington policies of the Saudi kingdom, and publicly opposing the alignment of King Fahd [*q.v.*] with the non-Muslim United States in the 1991 Gulf War [*q.v.*] to expel the Iraqis from Kuwait, relations between the Brotherhood in Saudi Arabia and the authorities soured. The Saudi government responded by reducing its funding to the Brotherhood.

Following the terrorist attacks on the United States in September 2001, the Saudi royal family started criticizing the Brotherhood and downgrading the role of the clerics associated with it. In 2004 Saudi interior minister Prince Nayif bin Abdul Aziz [q.v.] accused the Brotherhood of ingratitude but refrained from banning it. In early 2011, in its drive to weed out books that incited violence and extremism, the Saudi government ordered their removal from school and college libraries. The list included works by such Muslim Brotherhood stalwarts as Hassan al-Banna [q.v.] and Sayid Muhammad Quttb [q.v.] that had been popular over the past four decades.

Muslim Brotherhood (Syria): The Muslim Brotherhood in Syria emerged in the mid-1930s when Syrian students of theology returning from Egypt started forming branches in different cities under the title Shabab Muhammad (Arabic: *Youths of Muhammad*). The most important of these, established in 1935 in Aleppo [*q.v.*], became the organization's headquarters. It stood for an end to the French Mandate and for sociopolitical reform along Islamic lines. In 1944 the headquarters was moved to Damascus [*q.v.*]. Once the French had departed in 1946, it focused on socioeconomic issues. Most of its support came from urban craftsmen and small traders. The founding of Israel and the Arab defeat in the Palestine War [*q.v.*] gave a boost to the Brotherhood, and politicized it.

After the dissolution of Egypt's Muslim Brotherhood in 1954, many Egyptian activists took refuge in Syria, and strengthened and radicalized the local variant. Its program now demanded the founding of "a virtuous polity" which would implement the rules and teachings of Islam.

When Syria joined Egypt in 1958 to form the United Arab Republic (UAR) [*q.v.*], and the ban on political parties in Egypt was extended to Syria, the Brotherhood was formally dissolved. However, it continued to function underground. Growing disaffection with Gamal Abdul Nasser's [*q.v.*] presidency helped it to expand its base. In the election held in December 1961, a few months after Syria's secession from the UAR, it won 10 seats, nearly half as many as the mainstream National Bloc. Following the Baathist [*q.v.*] coup in March 1963, the Brotherhood and other political parties were banned, and the parliament was dissolved. It fared badly in its confrontation with the government in 1964.

The Arabs' defeat in the June 1967 Arab-Israeli War [*q.v.*] led to a split in the party, with the moderates advising caution and radicals advocating a jihad [*q.v.*] against the Baathists. With young Brethren receiving commando training from the Muslim Brotherhood [*q.v.*] in Jordan in the 1970s, the party's militarization gathered pace.

When Hafiz Assad [*q.v.*] became president in late 1971 the Brotherhood attacked the regime strongly because Assad was an Alawi [*q.v.*]. The party, composed of Sunnis [*q.v.*], who formed two-thirds of the population, argued that since Alawis were neither Muslim nor People of the Book (Christian [*q.v.*] or Jew [*q.v.*]), they were infidels and idolaters, who worshipped Imam Ali. Assad countered this by participating in prayers in various Sunni mosques throughout Syria. The Brotherhood condemned the 1973 constitution, which sanctified the leading position of the Baath Party in Syria, described as a "democratic, popular, socialist state."

Pro-Brotherhood clerics demanded that Islam [*q.v.*] be declared the state religion. Anti-government rioting followed. Assad compromised by directing the parliament to specify that the head of state must be Muslim, and it complied. Unsatisfied, the clergy called for demonstrations, which turned violent. Heeding their call, many Sunnis boycotted the referendum on the constitution. Assad combined repression with co-option and offered state honors and higher salaries to the clergy. He described the October 1973 Arab-Israeli War [q.v.] as a jihad against the enemies of Islam, and referred to the Syrian troops as soldiers of Allah. In early 1974 he undertook an *umra* [q.v.] to Mecca [q.v.]. Later Imam Musa al-Sadr [q.v.], an eminent Shia [q.v.] theologian, issued a religious verdict that Alawis were part of Shia Islam [q.v.].

These developments reduced tension between the two sides, but not for long. In mid-1976 Assad intervened militarily in the year-old Lebanese Civil War [q.v.] on the side of Maronite Christians [q.v.] against the alliance of Lebanese Muslims and Palestinians. This angered the Brotherhood, now led by Adnan Saad al-Din. The jihad it launched against the regime in July 1976 lasted four years. Its activists assassinated Baathist officials, Alawi leaders, and security personnel and informers in order to goad the government into increasing its repressive activities, thereby alienating large sections of society.

The increased activity swelled the party ranks. Between 1975 and 1978 the number of Brethren in Aleppo [q.v.] rose from 800 to 7,000. The national total of 30,000 members compared favorably with the ruling Baath Party's 200,000. A study of 1,384 fundamentalist prisoners (in 1982) showed 27.7 percent to be college or university students and 13.3 percent professionals.

In a calculated escalation in mid-1979 the party combined attacks on police stations, Baath Party offices, and army units with large-scale demonstrations and strikes. In a daring assault on the Aleppo artillery

school it killed 83 Alawi cadets. Assad convened a special Baathist congress in January 1980 to debate the composition of the party and its policies. Two-thirds of the national command of the party was replaced, often by Sunnis. Assad raised the proportion of Sunnis in his cabinet.

Unimpressed, the Brotherhood called indefinite strikes in Aleppo and Hama [q.v.] that paralyzed these cities. Soon the national syndicates of lawyers, engineers, doctors, and academics joined in, demanding free elections and the freeing of political prisoners. Assad released 200 political prisoners, sacked several unpopular provincial governors, and increased imports of consumer goods. But the Aleppo and Hama merchants continued their shutdown. Assad dispatched elite troops to the defiant cities. They arrested some 5,000 people and summarily executed several hundred. The protest petered out.

Another wave of official retribution followed an unsuccessful assassination attempt on Assad on 25 June 1980. The next month parliament passed Emergency Law 49 making membership in or even association with the Muslim Brotherhood a capital offense. Armed with this, the security forces went on a rampage, meting out summary justice, especially in Aleppo. The Islamist rebellion virtually collapsed. The Brotherhood split, with the moderate faction led by Issam Attar allying with smaller Islamic Organizations to form the Islamic Front of Syria [q.v.] in October 1980.

The radical faction, led by the erstwhile deputy leader, Ali Sadreddine Bayanouni, then in exile in Jordan, retained the original title of the organization. In 1996 he entered into secret talks with Assad, and two years later the president freed some Brotherhood leaders.

Soon after succeeding his father in 2000, Bashar Assad [*q.v.*] ordered more releases. By then Bayanouni had secured political asylum in Britain. After a meeting of Syrian opposition groups in London in 2002, the Brotherhood issued a document in which it committed itself to democracy, pluralism, and nonviolence. In December 2004 it reaffirmed its commitment to creating a civil state with a provision for peaceful transfer of power from one party to another. But, by joining the National Salvation Front (NSF) [*q.v.*] in 2006, it subscribed to the Front's program of regime change, albeit through peaceful means. After the Western governments reengaged with the Assad regime by late 2008, Bayanouni quit the NSF (in April 2009) and suspended the Brotherhood's opposition to the Syrian government.

In July 2010, the Brotherhood's General Council, meeting in Istanbul, elected Muhammad Riad Shaqfa as the secretary-general. The efforts of Turkey's moderately Islamic government tried but failed to reconcile the Brotherhood, demanding the immediate repeal of the Emergency Law 49 and the Assad regime.

With the inception of civil resistance to the Assad regime in March 2011, the Brotherhood revived inside Syria, albeit clandestinely. It demanded political reform. Assad's refusal to make concessions led its officials to call for his overthrow. In October it joined six other opposition groups in Istanbul to form the Syrian National Council (SNC) [*q.v.*] under the stewardship of Burhan Ghalioun, an academic at Sorbonne University in Paris. To reassure the Western audience and governments, Ghalioun downplayed the strength of the Muslim Brotherhood within the SNC, whereas Riad Shaqfa, president of the Brotherhood, baldly highlighted the long roots and strong network it had inside Syria. Within the SNC the Brotherhood dominated the relief committee in charge of distributing humanitarian aid and cash to the Syrian rebels. Using the donations received from individuals and more importantly the Gulf States, it purchased and distributed arms inside Syria. It forged strong ties with Qatar, which provided it with the bulk of its financial support as well as wide exposure in the Arab world through its Al-Jazeera satellite channel. *See also* Islamic Front of Syria and Syrian National Council.

Muslims: *See* Islam and Muslims.

Mussadiq, Muhammad (1881–1967): *Iranian politician; prime minister, 1951–53* (Also spelled Mohammad Mossadegh) Son of a wealthy public official in the village of Ahmadabad, Mussadiq pursued his university education in Paris and then obtained his doctorate in law at Lausanne University, Switzerland. On his return to Iran in 1914 he was named governor general of Fars province. After the coup by Reza Khan [*q.v.*] in 1921, he joined the cabinet as minister of finance. He was elected to the Majlis [*q.v.*] in 1923, but when he opposed the coronation of Reza Khan as the shah of Iran in 1925, he was forced to retire from public life.

With the deposition of Reza Shah in 1941, his fortunes rose. He was elected to the Majlis in 1944. A nationalist, he led a successful campaign to deny granting of an oil concession to the Soviet Union in 1945. Three years later he challenged Muhammad Reza Shah Pahlavi's [*q.v.*] nominee for the prime minister, Ibrahim Hakimi, and lost by a single vote. In 1949 he cofounded the National Front [*q.v.*]. His call to nationalize the oil concession given to the British-owned Anglo-Iranian Oil Company proved popular. In late April 1951 the Majlis decided by a large majority to go ahead with the nationalization and to appoint him as the prime minister. This happened on 1 May 1951. Britain and other Western powers boycotted Iran's nationalized oil industry, and the economy suffered as a result.

With the middle classes forsaking him, Mussadiq depended increasingly on the support that the Tudeh Party [*q.v.*] could muster on the street and among oil workers and civil servants. This alienated him from clerical circles. In mid-January 1953 he won a year-long extension of his emergency powers from the Majlis. He clashed with the shah over the command of the armed forces. In July 1953, by asking his supporters in the Majlis to resign, he caused its de facto dissolution because of the lack of a quorum. Having won the endorsement of his decision in a referendum, he declared on 12 August 1953 that he would order fresh parliamentary elections.

When the shah's attempt to dismiss Mussadiq failed, the shah fled. After three days of demonstrations and counterdemonstrations, his civilian and military opponents, actively aided by Washington's Central Intelligence Agency, mounted a successful coup against him. By 19 August the shah was back in power. Tried for treason, he was jailed for three years and barred from public life. After his release he was kept under house arrest in Ahmadabad.

Muwahhidun (Arabic*: Unitarianism*): *See* Wahhabism and Wahhabis.

mysticism (Greek: derivative of *mystikos,* belonging to secret rites): Mysticism is the doctrine that direct knowledge of God, or some ultimate reality or spiritual truth, can be attained through intuition or insight, and in a way that is distinct from ordinary sense perception or the application of logical reasoning. The experience of the presence of God, or some ultimate reality or spiritual truth, often results in heightened consciousness and a sense of transcending the mundane world. During this experience new knowledge and awareness are often believed to be passed on to the mystic in unfamiliar ways. Forms of mysticism are to be found in all major religions as well as in secular experience.

mysticism in Christianity: An early example of Christian mysticism is Gnosticism, a religious philosophical movement of the pre-Christian era, with the central doctrine that spiritual emancipation is attained through gnosis (knowledge), which saves the initiate from the intrinsic evil of matter. According to St. John of the Cross, union with God is the highest mystical experience and is attained by pursuing the path of purgatory, intended to excise sin, and then the path of illumination, which illuminates whatever is spiritual. Later the Desert Fathers developed the hermetic method of attaining mystical enlightenment. St. Augustine elaborated the concept of the Divine Light of Being, drawing heavily on neo-platonic ideas, which continued to interest later Christian mystics, including Meister Eckhart (d. 1329).

Mysticism has continued to thrive in the church and outside, and the long list of great Christian mystics includes St. Gregory I, St. Hildegard of Bingen, Hugh of St. Victor, St. Thomas Aquinas, St. Theresa of Avila, and St. Catherine of Siena. Its influence in Eastern Orthodox [*q.v.*] and Catholic [*q.v.*] Churches continues.

mysticism in Islam: *See* Sufism.

mysticism in Judaism: The desire for immediate awareness of and communion with God is basic to Judaism. The visions of the Old Testament [*q.v.*] prophets and the apocalyptic images of later Judaism provided the foundations for Jewish mysticism. In the 12th century Jewish mystics adopted the term *kabbala* (Hebrew: *received [tradition]*)—originally used to denote the (received) oral tradition, along with the Written Law—to stress the continuity of their mystical tradition since antiquity.

Kabbala reached its apogee at the beginning of the 14th century in the *Sepher HaZohar* (The Book of Splendor), attributed to Moses de Leon (d. 1305). It narrated the power and inner life of God and laid out the principles and commandments by which the true

believer could regain the adherence to God that had been lost by the fall of humans from their original purity. Subsequent Jewish mysticism continued to be built upon this base. Rabbi Isaac Luria (d. 1572) and his followers, and the Hassidic [*q.v.*] masters of the 18th and 19th centuries represent important developments of kabbala.

N

Nablus: *West Bank city* (Also spelled Nabulus) Population: 150,000 (2009 est.). The site of an ancient settlement with the Greek name of Neapolis (New City), Nablus sits between two mountains: Jerizim, a place where, according to legend, God issued his commandments to Moses, and Ebal, from where curses were hurled at those who defied Moses's Law. It is a twin of Shechem, a biblical settlement associated with Abraham (Genesis: 12:6) and Jacob (Genesis: 34:2).

Established by Roman Emperor Vespasian (r. 69–79 A.D.) in 72 A.D., it thrived as an east-west gate between Mount Jerizim and Mount Ebal because it was endowed with an abundant water supply from springs. Captured by Muslim [*q.v.*] Arabs [*q.v.*] in 636 A.D., it remained under Muslim rule until 1917, except between 1099 and 1187 when it was ruled by the Crusaders. A severe earthquake destroyed much of it in 1927.

In the 1930s it was a leading center of Arab resistance to the Jewish immigration into Palestine, and the birthplace of the Arab Higher Committee in 1936. After the 1948–49 Palestine War [*q.v.*] it became part of Jordan, and later a base for Palestinian guerrilla activities directed against Israeli targets. Following its occupation by Israeli in 1967, it once again became a forefront of resistance. In 1976 Jewish militants set up a colony at Elon Moreh near the city. In 2002, its *kasbah* (Arabic: *older section of a town*), the historic old city center, was destroyed by the reoccupying Israeli forces. Their bulldozers partially destroyed the historic al-Kabir (Arabic: *The Great*) Mosque as well as the leading Greek Orthodox Church [*q.v.*]. The estimated damage to public and private property caused by Israel's military action, involving attacks by helicopter gunships and warplanes, was put at $80 million.

The four Palestinian refugee camps surrounding the town have an aggregate population of 50,000. Its industry continues to be dominated by olive oil and soap production, furniture, and stone quarries. It is home to Al Najah National University, the largest in the West Bank, with nearly 22,000 students.

Its tourist attractions include Jacob's Well and Joseph's grave as well as the al-Kabir and al-Nour mosques, both constructed on the ruins of Byzantine churches.

Nabulsi, Suleiman (1908–76): *Jordanian politician; prime minister, 1956–57* Born into a notable family in Salt, Jordan, Nabulsi graduated in law and social studies from the American University in Beirut [*q.v.*]. He joined the civil service and rose to be director of the state-owned Agricultural Bank, a post he held until 1946. He served

as minister of finance and economy (1947–49 and 1950–51).

He was Jordan's ambassador to Britain from 1953 to 1954. This experience turned him into a staunch Arab nationalist and anti-Zionist, and alienated him from the regime of King Hussein bin Talal [*q.v.*]. He was exiled from the capital, Amman [*q.v.*], to a provincial town. Undaunted, he co-founded the National Socialist Party (NSP) and was elected its leader. He entered into an electoral alliance with the Baathists [*q.v.*] and the Communist Front [*q.v.*], and formed the National Front (NF). Its attempt to win a majority in the 40-member parliament in the autumn of 1954 was frustrated by official poll-rigging. It won 12 seats. Nonetheless, as leader of the NF, the largest bloc in parliament, he succeeded in preventing King Hussein from joining the Baghdad Pact [*q.v.*] in December 1955. He also succeeded in getting the monarch to dissolve parliament, which lacked legitimacy.

In the free election of October 1956 the NF won 16 seats, and Nabulsi was asked to form a government. He did. His cabinet merged the Arab Legion with the (Palestinian-dominated) National Guard to create a 35,000-strong army. When the parliament abrogated the 1948 Anglo-Jordanian Treaty [*q.v.*] the monarch did not overrule it. But when the government decided to establish diplomatic relations with the Soviet Union, and allow the Communist Front to publish a weekly newspaper, King Hussein warned it of the dangers of Communist infiltration. Heeding this, Nabulsi banned the Communist publication.

In April 1957 the monarch resisted a challenge from the Free Officers led by Ali Abu Nawar, who had succeeded Sir John Bagot Glubb [*q.v.*] as the chief of staff. He then dismissed Nabulsi's government, declared martial law, dissolved parliament as well as political parties and trade unions, and placed Nabulsi under house arrest. Once freed, he resumed his leadership of the NSP. But with martial law in force, his area of operation was limited. When the Jordanian army and the Palestine Liberation Organization (PLO) [*q.v.*] clashed in 1970, he backed the PLO. But by the mid-1970s he had changed sufficiently to merit royal appointment to the fully nominated Senate in 1976.

Nahas (Pasha), Mustafa (1879–1965): *Egyptian politician; prime minister, 1928, 1930, 1935–37, 1942–44, 1950–52* Born into a wealthy Cairene family, Nahas obtained a law degree from the University of Cairo. After practicing as a lawyer he joined the judicial system and served as a judge from 1904 to 1919. He then participated in the nationalist movement and was exiled along with its leader, Saad Zaghlul, to the British-controlled Seychelles Islands. After their release they won parliamentary seats as Wafd Party [*q.v.*] candidates in the first general election under the 1923 constitution.

Nahas served in the Wafd government under Zaghlul. When Zaghlul died in 1927, Nahas succeeded him as leader of the party. In 1928 and 1930 he served as the prime minister, but was forced by the monarch to resign. His efforts to see the parliamentary constitution reinstated succeeded in 1935, and his stewardship of the party's election campaign in May 1936 resulted in a Wafd victory. He

formed the next government, and three months later signed the new Anglo-Egyptian Treaty [*q.v.*], which granted Egypt independence but fell short of total sovereignty.

He was dismissed from office in December 1937 by King Farouq [*q.v.*]. In February 1942, when German troops were advancing on Egypt from Libya, the British intervened militarily by surrounding the royal palace with tanks and gave Farouq the choice of abdicating or appointing the pro-British Nahas as the prime minister. Farouq invited Nahas to form a government. He played a key role in the establishment of the Arab League [*q.v.*], a British-inspired enterprise. Soon after he had inaugurated the League's preparatory conference in Alexandria [*q.v.*] in October 1944, he lost his top post. His party boycotted the election of January 1945.

But it entered the election in January 1950 on an Arab nationalist platform. It won. Nahas led the next government. When his talks on the future of the 1936 Treaty and the British military presence in the Suez Canal [*q.v.*] zone failed, he unilaterally abrogated the treaty in 1951. He initiated a popular struggle to eject the British troops. This led to mounting violence, culminating in battles between the Egyptian and British troops, the eruption of mob fury in January 1952, and the fall of his government.

Following the July 1952 coup all political parties, including the Wafd, were outlawed. Unlike many other politicians, who were tried for corruption, Nahas was left alone. He retired from public life.

al-Nahyan, Khalifa bin Zayid (1948–):
President, United Arab Emirates, 2004–;
ruler, Abu Dhabi Emirate, 1966– Born
to Shaikh Zayid bin Sultan al-Nahyan
[*q.v.*] and Hassa bint Muhammad bin
Khalifa al-Nahyan of the Aal [*q.v.*]
Bu Falah branch of the ruling Bani
Yas tribe, he grew up in the oasis settlement of al-Ain. He received traditional education in Arabic [*q.v.*],
memorizing and reciting of the Quran
[*q.v.*] and the study of the Hadith
[*q.v.*]. After the introduction of formal school system in the principality,
he learned English. Later he spent
time at the Royal Military College in
Sandhurst, Britain.

In 1969, his father named him
Crown Prince of Abu Dhabi [*q.v.*].
He became the head of the defense
department, which later formed the
core of the United Arab Emirates
[*q.v.*] military. At the independence of
the UAE, he was appointed the prime
minister of Abu Dhabi. Two years
later he assumed the office of the
deputy prime minister in the UAE's
federal cabinet. In 1976 he became the
deputy supreme commander of the
UAE armed forces. In 1989 he was
appointed head of the Supreme Petroleum Council.

Due to his father's ill health in the
1990s, he served as the acting ruler of
Abu Dhabi. A year after assuming the
supreme office in the UAE in 2004,
he decreed that half of the members of
the 40-strong Federal National Council should be elected indirectly.

In January 2010, the world's tallest
building, originally known as Burj
Dubai, in Dubai was renamed Burj
Khalifa after he had provided emer-
gency funds to the debit-ridden Dubai
Holdings, the owner of the tower. His

net worth of $15 billion is second only
to that of Saudi Arabia's King Abdullah [*q.v.*] in the region.

al-Nahyan, Zayid bin Sultan (1915–
2004): *President, United Arab Emirates,*
1971–2004; ruler, Abu Dhabi Emirate,
1966– Born in al-Ain to the ruling
Aal [*q.v.*] Nahyan family of the Aal
Bu Falah branch of the ruling Bani
Yas tribe, Nahyan learned the Quran
[*q.v.*] as a boy, as well as falconry,
riding, and marksmanship. He was
appointed governor of the eastern
province of the Abu Dhabi Emirate
(capital, al-Ain) in 1946. He ruled it
as a bedouin chief, consulting tribal
notables and being accessible to ordinary people. When his elder brother
Shakbut bin Sultan, ruler of the emirate since 1928, refused to use the revenue accruing from oil production,
which started in 1960, to promote
economic development, he was overthrown with the aid of Britain, the
imperial power, in 1966 and replaced
by Nahyan. He appointed highly
trained advisers and administrators to
handle the emirate's burgeoning government revenues and activities.

It was primarily Abu Dhabi's rapidly growing oil revenues that encouraged the small neighboring emirates
to agree to form the United Arab
Emirates (UAE) in July 1971, five
months before the scheduled British
departure in December. Nahyan was
elected president of the UAE for a
five-year term, and reelected four
times.

As ruler of the Abu Dhabi Emirate
he appointed a cabinet led by a premier, responsible to him, in July 1971.
When a single federal council of ministers came into being in December

1973, he abolished the Abu Dhabi cabinet and appointed a 50-member consultative council.

To the detriment of the UAE, personal rivalry between Nahyan and Shaikh Rashid bin Said al-Maktum [*q.v.*], vice president of the UAE, persisted for many years. In the aftermath of the Islamic republican revolution in Iran [*q.v.*] in early 1979, the nominated Federal National Council and the federal cabinet demanded parliamentary democracy and a unitary state. This alarmed Nahyan and Shaikh Rashid, who buried their differences. Rashid became the prime minister of the UAE.

During the early phase of the 1980–88 Iran-Iraq War [*q.v.*] Nahyan sided with Baghdad. But as the conflict dragged on and Iran's position grew stronger, he took an increasingly neutral stance. Later, during the spring of 1990, he allied with Kuwait in its strategy to hurt the Iraqi economy by flooding the oil market and thus lowering prices. Later, troubled by the impoverishment and suffering of the Iraqi people caused by the UN sanctions, he called for their lifting, but to no avail.

During his rule the UAE evolved from a collective of medieval emirates to an efficiently run modern state with one of the highest per capita incomes in the world.

With personal assets of $24 billion, Nahyan died as one of the richest men in the world, and yet he maintained a simple, traditional lifestyle throughout his existence.

Najaf: *Iraqi city* Population: 1.286 million (2011 est.). Also called *Mashhad Ali* (Arabic: *Witness to Ali*), Najaf is the burial place of Imam Ali bin Abi Talib, a caliph (r. 656–661 A.D.) and a cousin and son-in-law of the Prophet Muhammad (d. 632 A.D.). Since Shias [*q.v.*] consider Ali to be the only legitimate caliph after the Prophet Muhammad, they regard his tomb in Najaf as the most sacred shrine after the Kaaba [*q.v.*] in Mecca [*q.v.*] and the Prophet Muhammad's grave in Medina [*q.v.*].

The town is believed to have been established by Caliph Haroon al-Rashid (r. 786–809 A.D.). It has undergone dramatic vicissitudes since then. It was burned down by zealot Sunnis [*q.v.*] from Baghdad [*q.v.*] in 1051, but was soon rebuilt. When under Ottoman rule (1638–1918), the city was sacked twice by Wahhabi [*q.v.*] raiders (in 1806 and 1810), and Ali's mausoleum was stripped of all its furnishings. Led by resident *mujtahids* [*q.v.*], its Shia population rebelled against the Sunni [*q.v.*] Ottomans in 1842, 1852, and 1854, but was repressed. In 1920, the locals offered stiff resistance to the British Mandate and opposed King Faisal I bin Hussein [*q.v.*], considering him a British stooge.

During the republican era, beginning in 1958, Najaf emerged as a seat of opposition to the secular regime of the Baath Party [*q.v.*], which seized power in 1968. From 1965 to 1978 it was the base of exiled Ayatollah Ruhollah Khomeini [*q.v.*]. After the 1991 Gulf War [*q.v.*] it participated in the Shia uprising in southern Iraq against the regime of President Saddam Hussein [*q.v.*], which was quickly quelled.

After the Anglo-American invasion of Iraq [*q.v.*] in 2003, Najaf became a bastion of resistance against the occupation, led by the radical Shia cleric Muqtada al-Sadr [*q.v.*].

Najaf remains a leading center of Shia pilgrimage and burial. The Place of Learning (Arabic: *Al-Hawza al-Ilmiyya*), supervised by four grand ayatollahs, is the leading seminary for the training of Shia clergy. With its encircling wall mostly intact, it has retained the aura of a medieval settlement. Unlike Mecca and Medina, the city is open to non-Muslims, but they are not allowed to enter the shrine of Imam Ali.

Najd: *central region of Saudi Arabia* (Also spelled Nejd) Population: 8.59 million (2011 est.). A chiefly rocky plateau with mountains to the west and desert to the east, north, and south, Najd has a string of oases. It was politically fragmented until 1745, when it became the center of the Wahhabi movement [*q.v.*]. More recently, Abdul Aziz bin Abdul Rahman bin Saud [*q.v.*] conquered the region from the Ottoman Turks in 1902. Since then it has been the geographical and ideological nucleus of the Saudi realm that Abdul Aziz created, which was finally named the Kingdom of Saudi Arabia in 1932, with the Najdi capital of Riyadh [*q.v.*] as its national capital. Now officially called the Najd (central) Region, it is divided into the provinces of Riyadh, Qassim, and Hail, and covers 224,265 sq. mi./581,000 sq. km.

Nasrallah, Hassan (1960–): *Lebanese political and military leader* Born in the household of Abdul Karim, a poor Shia [*q.v.*] grocer, in East Beirut's [*q.v.*] neighborhood of Bourj Hammoud, he went to a government school in the Christian [*q.v.*] area of Sinal Fil. At the start of the 1975 civil war the family moved to the ancestral village of Bazouriyah near Tyre [*q.v.*] in the south. While at school in Tyre, he joined the Amal Movement [*q.v.*] led by Musa al-Sadr [*q.v.*]. He went to Najaf [*q.v.*] to study Shia theology but returned home in 1978 when Iraq's Baathist government pressured foreign theological students to leave.

He became Amal's representative for the Beqaa region and taught religion at a school founded by Shaikh Abbas Mousavi who later became the secretary-general of Hizbollah [*q.v.*]. After the 1982 Israeli invasion of Lebanon [*q.v.*], he joined Hizbollah and became one of its organizers. In 1987, he went to Qom [*q.v.*] for further studies, and later represented Hizbollah in Iran.

He returned to Lebanon in 1991. After Mousavi's assassination in an Israeli helicopter attack on his motorcade in 1992, Nasrallah was elected the secretary-general of Hizbollah. While continuing Hizbollah's social welfare activities, he strengthened its military wing and accentuated the low-intensity war with Israel's occupation forces in southern Lebanon. In 1997, his eldest son, Muhammad Hadi, was killed in a battle with an Israeli Navy commando unit operating in southern Lebanon in which 13 Israeli soldiers lost their lives. In May 2000, when Israel withdrew from southern Lebanon unconditionally, Nasrallah's prestige surged in Lebanon and the rest of the Arab [*q.v.*] world.

In 2004, in return for the release of one Israeli civilian and the corpses of three Israeli soldiers, Nasrallah secured the freedom of over 400 Palestinian and Lebanese prisoners, and also secured the corpse of his son Muhammad Hadi.

After the assassination of Rafik Hariri [q.v.] in February 2005, Nasrallah emerged as an influential arbitrator between Lebanon's many political factions because of his widely recognized erudition and politically savvy. The following year, he signed a 10-point pact with Michel Aoun [q.v.], leader of the Free Patriotic Movement.

Under his leadership Hizbollah brought the Israeli military to a standstill in the five-week war in July–August 2006 [q.v.]. After the cease-fire, he declared a "divine, historic and strategic victory" over Israel, and refused to disarm Hizbollah's military wing. By providing material help for the reconstruction of the homes of the displaced Lebanese, he enhanced his standing further. In several public opinion surveys in the region, he emerged as a very popular leader.

Following the 2009 general election, he readily conceded the defeat of the pro-Syrian 8 March Alliance [q.v.]. Yet he managed to obtain more than a third of the cabinet seats for the defeated camp in the national unity government of Saad Hariri [q.v.]. A month later the Hariri administration adopted a bill that permitted Hizbollah to retain its weapons. But when Hariri refused to discontinue part-funding for the United Nations Special Tribunal for Lebanon (STL), Nasrallah brought about the downfall of his government in January 2011. The efforts of Najib Miktai [q.v.] to form his cabinet suc-

ceeded in June only after he had agreed to allocate 18 of the ministerial posts to the Hizbollah-dominated 8 March Alliance.

The next month Nasrallah rejected indictments against four Hizbollah members (whose names were leaked) by the STL for the murder of Rafiq Hariri and 21 others in 2005, and denounced the STL. In February 2012 the STL's trial chamber said it would try the accused in absentia after all reasonable steps to arrest them had failed.

During the uprisings in Syria in 2011–2012, Nasrallah emerged as the strongest supporter of President Bashar Assad [q.v.]. Once the option of foreign military intervention in Syria had been ruled out by March 2012, he urged peaceful resolution of the crisis through dialogue and simultaneous reform under the leadership of Assad.

Nasser, Gamal Abdul (1918–70): *Egyptian military leader and politician; president, 1956–70; prime minister, 1954–56* Born in Bani Mor village, Asyut province, Nasser, son of a postal clerk, was a graduate of the Royal Military Academy in Cairo [q.v.]. After serving in Sudan for two years, he returned to the military academy as an instructor in 1941. He underwent further training at the staff college, and participated in the Palestine War (1948–49) [q.v.] as a major in the Egyptian army. Promoted to colonel in 1950, he was appointed lecturer at the Royal Military Academy.

Nasser was a charismatic leader of the clandestine Free Officers Organization, which ousted King Farouq [q.v.] on 22 July 1952, and set up the ruling Revolutionary Command Council (RCC) [*q.v.*], with Brigadier-General Muhammad Neguib [*q.v.*] as its head. Neguib favored reinstating the parliamentary system but Nasser disagreed. He won. Having banned political groups in January 1953, the regime sponsored a single party, the Liberation Rally. The power struggle between Nasser and Neguib intensified after the RCC declared a republic in June 1953 and appointed Prime Minister Neguib as the republic's president.

The differences between Nasser and Neguib came to the fore in February 1954 when the RCC banned the Muslim Brotherhood [*q.v.*] without consulting Neguib. His resignation as president and premier created a crisis, involving the mobilization of different military units by the two rivals. A compromise in April allowed Neguib to retain the presidency but give up the premiership. This lasted until November when the RCC dismissed Neguib as president and put him under house arrest. It chose Nasser as its chairman. After a new constitution was proclaimed in 1956, Nasser was elected president for a six-year term, and reelected twice.

Starting out as a non-ideological officer, committed only to ridding public life of corruption, Nasser became increasingly ideological and radical as conservatives at home and the Western powers abroad tried to smother his Arab nationalist regime. At the first conference of 29 nations—28 Afro-Asian and one European—in Bandung, Indonesia, in April 1955, he came under the influence of Prime Minister Jawaharlal Nehru of India and President Josip Tito of Yugoslavia,

both committed to non-alignment in international affairs. Nasser succeeded in stopping the expansion of the Western-sponsored Baghdad Pact [*q.v.*].

After America had refused to sell him weapons, he accepted an arms sales offer from Czechoslovakia. When the United States reacted by withdrawing its offer of aid for the Aswan High Dam [*q.v.*] project, and getting the World Bank to do the same, Nasser nationalized the Suez Canal [*q.v.*], and accepted aid from the Soviet Union. The resulting, aggressive anti-Egyptian alliance of Britain, France, and Israel, which culminated in the Suez War [*q.v.*] in October–November 1956, further radicalized Nasser. He became the top political demon of the West and Israel. America, Britain, France, and Israel fielded teams to assassinate him. They failed. The withdrawal of the aggressors from Egypt by March 1957 raised his prestige at home and in the region.

Following the merger of Egypt and Syria into the United Arab Republic (UAR) [*q.v.*] in early 1958, Nasser was elected president of the UAR. He visited the Soviet Union for the first time as a leader of the Non-Aligned Movement. At home he suffered a major setback when Syria seceded from the UAR in September 1961, ending his hopes of gradually uniting the Arab East [*q.v.*] under his leadership. As Syria turned increasingly radical in its policies, he quickened the pace of socioeconomic reform in Egypt so as not to be seen less militant than the Syrians. The land reform, launched a decade earlier, was consolidated along with further nationalization of industries and services.

In 1962, at a convention of the delegates of peasants, workers, and intellectuals, he inaugurated the Arab Socialist Union (ASU) [*q.v.*]. Later that year he sided with the republicans in the civil war that erupted in the wake of a coup in North Yemen. In 1964 he hosted a summit of the Organization of African Unity in Cairo.

With the ascendancy in Damascus [*q.v.*] in early 1966 of radical Baathists, who escalated the Palestinian guerrilla attacks against Israel, Nasser once again found himself upstaged by the Syrians. To meet the problem, in November 1966 he signed a defense pact with Syria, which specified a joint command for the Egyptian and Syrian forces in the event of war. As tension rose in the spring of 1967, Israel warned Syria against allowing Palestinian guerrilla operations from its soil. In mid-May, stung by taunts that he was hiding behind the protection of the UN Emergency Force (UNEF) [*q.v.*], stationed in Sinai [*q.v.*] on the Egyptian side, Nasser called on UN Secretary-General U Thant to withdraw it. When this was done, Nasser closed the Strait of Tiran to Israeli shipping, thus raising the stakes. King Hussein of Jordan [*q.v.*], who hitherto had been hostile to Nasser, rushed to sign a mutual defense pact with Egypt on 30 May. This was the zenith of Nasser's power and prestige.

Once Israel had realized that the international community would not force Nasser to reopen the Strait of Tiran to Israeli ships, on 5 June it mounted devastating preemptive attacks on the air forces of Egypt, Syria and Jordan. The resulting debacle of the June 1967 Arab-Israeli War [*q.v.*]

virtually destroyed Nasser and Nasserism [*q.v.*]. For the time being, though, he contrived to turn defeat into victory. Taking responsibility for the defeat, he resigned. Popular demonstrations, combined with the Soviet Union's pledge to replace all the heavy weaponry lost in the war free of charge only if he were to remain president, made him retract.

But his retraction went beyond resignation. It covered the whole gamut of his domestic and foreign policies. He moderated the stance of the ASU at home. In November 1967, he accepted UN Security Council Resolution 242 [*q.v.*], which called for the peaceful coexistence of Israel and the Arab states in return for Israel's evacuation of the Occupied Arab Territories [*q.v.*]. However, to prevent Israel from consolidating its occupation of Egyptian territory, Nasser initiated the War of Attrition [*q.v.*] in 1968 after reequipping his military with Soviet weaponry.

In the Arab world he reached a compromise with his archenemy, the conservative Saudi King Faisal bin Abdul Aziz [*q.v.*]. He withdrew Egyptian troops from the North Yemeni Civil War [*q.v.*] in December 1967. Yet he remained the elder statesman of the progressive Arab world. When conflict between the Palestine Liberation Organization (PLO) [*q.v.*] and Lebanon became explosive, both parties turned to him for mediation. The result was the November 1969 Cairo Agreement [*q.v.*]. Equally, after the fight between the PLO and the Jordanian army in mid-September 1970, the two sides approached Nasser for a rapprochement. It was the strain of these negotiations that caused him to suffer a fatal heart attack.

A charismatic figure, Nasser was the first Egyptian to rule Egypt for a very long time, since King Farouq's family was originally from Albania.

Nasserism and Nasserites: Nasserism is a sociopolitical doctrine based on the thoughts and actions of Gamal Abdul Nasser, president of Egypt [*q.v.*] (1954–70). Beginning as pan-Arab nationalism [*q.v.*], it evolved into Arab socialism [*q.v.*]. Unlike Baathism [*q.v.*], Nasserism was not a well-conceived thesis by one or more ideologues, but emerged as an ideology out of a series of practical responses to the problems, domestic and foreign, that Egypt, ruled by military officers from 1952 onward, faced as it tried to consolidate its newly won political and economic independence. Egyptian military officers led by Nasser developed an ideology and created, as a state fiat, a political organization to implement it after they had seized power, whereas the Baathists were a party with an ideology and a cadre long before they acquired power.

Nasser's drift toward socialism reflected an emerging trend among Egyptian intellectuals and workers. But instead of implementing egalitarian socioeconomic reform with the assistance of a political party committed to the doctrine, he relied basically on state bureaucracy, with the Arab Socialist Union (ASU) [*q.v.*] acting more as an organizational façade than a real cadre-based party.

During Nasser's rule, Nasserite parties sprouted in several Arab countries, including Syria, Iraq, Jordan, Lebanon, Saudi Arabia, North Yemen, and South Yemen. But within a few years of his death these disappeared or became insignificant, except in Lebanon—where the Independent Nasserite Movement and its militia Murabitun continued to draw their support from Sunni Muslims [*q.v.*]—and in Yemen [*q.v.*]. In Egypt, denied a license to constitute a party of their own, most of the Nasserites joined the National Progressive Unionist Alliance (NPUA)[*q.v.*]. In the early 1990s, they were allowed to form a party. The NPUA's score in the parliamentary elections until and including the one in 2010 varied between two and six seats.

In the first round of the post-Mubarak presidential race in May 2012, the independent Nasserite Hamdeen Sabbahi came third, with 20.4 percent of the vote.

National and Progressive Front (Lebanon): In 1969 Kamal Jumblat [*q.v.*] established the National and Progressive Front (NPF), consisting of leftist Lebanese parties and major Palestinian groups based in Lebanon. As interior minister he legalized such transnational parties as the Communist Party [*q.v.*] and the Baathist Party [*q.v.*] in the summer of 1970, and they joined the NPF. In 1972 it was renamed the Front of National and Progressive Parties and Forces. *See also* the Lebanese National Movement.

National Consultative Assembly (Iran): *See* Majlis.

National Coordination Committee for Democratic Change (Syria): An umbrella organization of a dozen opposition factions, it was formed after the start of civil uprisings in March 2011 at a conference in Damascus [*q.v.*]. A largely home-based organization, the National Coordination Committee for Democratic Change (NCCDC) consisted mainly of secular groups of leftist, or Arab or Kurdish nationalist, orientation. Its leadership included Hassan Abdul Azim, chairman of the Nasserite [q.v.] Democratic Arab Socialist Union, called the General Coordinator, and Michel Kilo, a veteran dissident who had spent six years in jail. The NCCDC committed itself to dismantling the present dictatorial system and the removal of President Bashar Assad [q.v.] from power, but strictly through non-violent means. It staged periodic anti-Assad demonstrations. Strongly opposed to foreign military intervention, it called on the UN Security Council to adopt a resolution allowing observers to monitor and protect civilians. Unlike the Syrian National Council [q.v.], it was prepared to negotiate with Assad's regime.

In April 2012, its delegation was received by Russian foreign minister Sergey Lavrov in Moscow when both sides backed the recent UN-brokered ceasefire. Invited by the Chinese People's Institute of Foreign Affairs, its delegation, led by Abdul Azim, met the Chinese foreign minister Yang Jiechi in Beijing in mid-September. It reaffirmed its four-point plan: an end to violence, release of prisoners, ensuring humanitarian access, and initiating a political transition process.

Later that month it sponsored the National Conference for Syria Salvation in Damascus. The conference adopted an eight-point program, including the overthrow of the regime

through non-violent resistance, and "extracting" the Syrian military from "the clutches of the regime."

National Council of Resistance in Iran: *See* National Resistance Council (Iran).

National Democratic Assembly—Balad: *Israeli Arab political party* Its official title, Balad, is the Hebrew [*q.v.*] acronym of *Brit Leumit Demokratit*, meaning National Democratic Assembly; its title in Arabic [*q.v.*] is *Tajama al-Watan al-Dimuqrati*. Formed by Palestinian professionals led by Azmi Bishara [*q.v.*], Balad in 1995 allied with Taal, another Israeli Arab group, to fight the 1999 parliamentary election; it secured two seats. It aimed to transform Israel from a Jewish state into a democratic state according equal treatment to all its citizens, Jews [*q.v.*] and Arabs [*q.v.*] alike, and demanded autonomy over the Arab educational system and affirmative action for the Arab minority. It advocates Israel's withdrawal from all the Occupied Arab Territories [*q.v.*], the establishment of an independent Palestinian state in the Occupied Territories [*q.v.*] with East Jerusalem [*q.v.*] as its capital, and the implementation of the UN General Assembly Resolution 194, passed in December 1948, which inter alia called for the return of the Palestinian refugees.

Before the 2003 Knesset election, the party was banned by the Central Election Committee, whose decision was overturned by the Supreme Court. It won three seats. It repeated the performance in the 2006 election. In April 2007 Bishara resigned his set by contacting the Israeli Embassy in Cairo [*q.v.*] after a police investigation into his alleged assistance to Hizbollah [*q.v.*] during its war with Israel in July–August, and money laundering.

On the eve of the 2009 Knesset election, the Central Election Commission's ban on Balad was once again overturned by the Supreme Court, and the party, now led by Jamal Zahalka, maintained its strength of three.

National Democratic Front (North Yemen): *North Yemeni political party*
In 1976 the Revolutionary Democratic party, the (Marxist) Democratic Party of Popular Unity, and the Baathists [*q.v.*] secretly merged to form the National Democratic Front under the leadership of Sultan Ahmad Omar. Its aims were to consolidate national independence, which was threatened by reactionary Saudi Arabia, and to end feudalism.

Ignoring the ban on political parties, President Ibrahim Hamdi [*q.v.*] allowed the NDF to exist semi-clandestinely. It held its first secret congress in July 1978, when it called for unity between North and South Yemen. Its ranks were swelled by the defection in late 1978 of the paratroop commander, Major Abdullah Abdul Alim, and his troops from the government of President Ali Abdullah Saleh [*q.v.*]. Aided by South Yemen, the NDF captured the southern town of Harib in February 1979 and tried to extend its area of control. The fighting continued until early March, when South Yemen yielded to regional pressures and accepted a cease-fire.

The agreement of the presidents of the two Yemens to unite within a year was welcomed by the NDF. But when

nothing came of it the NDF reached a compromise with Saleh. He would allow the NDF to publish a newspaper in North Yemen if it stopped its radio broadcasts from South Yemen. As Saleh consolidated his power in the 1980s he squeezed out the NDF from North Yemen, leaving it with a base in Aden [*q.v.*], the South Yemeni capital. The NDF welcomed the unity of the two Yemens in 1990. On the eve of the general election of 1993 it merged with the Arab Baath Socialist Party, which won seven seats.

National Democratic Party (Egypt):
The National Democratic Party (NDP) was founded by President Anwar Sadat [*q.v.*] in August 1978 after the parliament, at his behest, had outlawed wide-ranging political activities such as preaching Marxism and class struggle, advocating laissez-faire capitalism, demanding a religion-based state, and so on. He called on Mustafa Khalil, then heading the much weakened Arab Socialist Union [*q.v.*], to be its (nominal) president. Even before it had published its program, 275 of the 300 Arab Socialist Party [*q.v.*] parliamentarians joined it, thus assuring it of power.

Describing itself as "national, democratic, socialist, scientific, faithful, popular, revolutionary, humanist, and nationalist," the NDP listed its enemies: the "followers of foreign ideologies" (i.e., Marxists), "those trying to take Egypt back to the pre-1952 era" (i.e., New Wafdists [*q.v.*]), and "the remnants of the totalitarian regime" (i.e., Nasserites [*q.v.*]). It stated that the effort to rebuild Egyptian society after the 1952 revolution had failed because the regime had tried to imitate "the system and culture of foreign occupation," the word *foreign* implying the Soviet Union. Describing its socioeconomic philosophy as "socialist democracy, Arab Islamic and Christian values, and the principles of the 1952 revolution after being corrected [in 1971 by Sadat]," its program stated that the public sector must be limited to projects that "the people" felt necessary, and that the economic policy of providing an open door to foreign capital must remain.

After the Camp David Accords [*q.v.*] in September 1978, Sadat appointed Khalil as the prime minister to lead "the peace government," and took over the presidency of the NDP. In the 1979 parliamentary election the NDP won 302 of the 362 elected seats. After Sadat's assassination in 1981, Hosni Mubarak [*q.v.*] became the NDP's president.

In the general elections of 1984, 1987, and 1990—which, as in Sadat's period, were blatantly rigged—the NDP won 379, 380, and 354 seats respectively in a house of 438 to 444 seats, the last election having been boycotted by all the major opposition parties. In the 1995 general election it secured 316 seats and then gained the loyalty of another 99 independents. In the 2000 election it won 176 places, with a further 212 deputies, having been elected as independents, joining the party later, raising its total to 388. Its strength fell to 317 in the 2005 parliamentary election, when it yielded its losses to the semi-clandestine Muslim Brotherhood [*q.v.*], whose members were allowed, begrudgingly, to run as independents.

In the grossly rigged election of 2010, boycotted by the opposition

parties, the NDP won 420 of the 444 contested seats.

During the anti-regime demonstrations in Cairo [*q.v.*] in January–February 2011, NDP militants attacked the protestors, who retaliated by burning down the party headquarters. In April, accepting the charges of corruption against the NDP, the Higher Administrative Court ordered its dissolution and the transfer of its funds to the state. Its former members entered the parliamentary elections between November 2011 and January 2012, using seven different party names, ranging from National Party to Freedom Party. Altogether they won 7 percent of the popular vote and 17 seats in the 508-member chamber.

National Front (Iran): *Iranian political party* The Iran Party and the Democrat Party combined in 1949 to form the National Front (NF) [*q.v.*] under the leadership of Muhammad Mussadiq [*q.v.*]. A secular nationalist group, the NF demanded nationalization of the oil industry, which at the time was controlled by the British-owned Anglo-Iranian Oil Company (AIOC). This proved a popular move. In May 1951, its leaders succeeded in getting a majority backing for Mussadiq in the Majlis [*q.v.*], thus compelling Muhammad Reza Shah Pahlavi [*q.v.*] to name Mussadiq as the prime minister. The NF supported Mussadiq during the 1951–53 crisis caused by the nationalization of the AIOC.

When the shah fled in mid-August 1953 the party split, with one section calling for a republic and the other for a constitutional monarchy. After the return of the shah, the NF was repressed. It made a comeback in the early 1960s, and urged a boycott of the referendum on the state-sponsored White Revolution [*q.v.*] in 1963. Once again official repression and the jailing of its leaders followed.

The NF continued to attract support among Iranian students studying in the West. It revived at home in the early stages of the 1977–78 revolutionary movement, participating actively as one of the three major strands of the movement, the others being Islamic fundamentalism [*q.v.*] and Marxism. After the revolution the liberal, secular forces represented by the NF aspired to create social democracy in Iran.

In February 1979 Prime Minister Mahdi Bazargan [*q.v.*] appointed Karim Sanjabi, the NF leader, as foreign minister. Sanjabi resigned after the occupation of the American Embassy in Tehran [*q.v.*] by militant students in November. The NF failed to win any seats in the 1980 general election. Later it was wooed by President Abol Hassan Bani-Sadr [*q.v.*], even though it was considered an opposition group. But with most of the moderate democrats siding with the Liberation Movement of Iran [*q.v.*], the NF lost support steeply.

National Front for the Liberation of South Yemen: *See* National Liberation Front (South Yemen).

National Guard (Saudi Arabia): An armed force drawn from the most loyal of the tribes in Saudi Arabia, the National Guard was the new name given to the White Guard (formed in 1932) after the dissolution of the Ikhwan [*q.v.*]. The need to rename, rearm, and retrain this force arose in

the aftermath of the overthrow of the monarchy in North Yemen [*q.v.*] in September 1962. The National Guard was put under the command of Prince Khalid bin Abdul Aziz [*q.v.*]. Its personnel were billeted outside the main urban centers, and its officers were the most pampered outside the royal family. King Faisal bin Abdul Aziz [*q.v.*] rejected a proposal to merge the military and the National Guard, mainly because having two separate armed services enabled him to maintain a balance between the competing clans inside the kingdom. Also the National Guard's role covered both foreign and domestic threats to the royal Saudi regime.

As the kingdom's most reliable armed force, the National Guard deals with anything that remotely threatens the regime—be it a strike, a demonstration, a tribal revolt, or disaffection in the military. It was at the forefront of quelling the uprising by Islamic militants in Mecca [*q.v.*] and the demonstrations by Shias [*q.v.*] in the eastern province of Hasa in late 1979. With the ascendancy of Fahd bin Abdul Aziz [*q.v.*] to the throne in 1982, Crown Prince Abdullah bin Abdul Aziz [*q.v.*] became its commander.

Since the early 1980s the Guard has been thoroughly reorganized and retrained by the Pentagon as well as private defense contractors. In 1995 a car bomb in the parking lot of the U.S. Office of the Program Manager in charge of the National Guard Modernization Program killed six, including five Americans. The National Guard's modernization continues under the supervision of the Pentagon.

In 2010 King Abdullah appointed his son Prince Mutaib commander of the 100,000-strong National Guard, including its 25,000 tribal levies as reserves. Its recruits are drawn invariably from the Sunni [*q.v.*] tribes in the Najd [*q.v.*]. Their equipment includes armored personnel carriers and armored fighting vehicles as well as artillery, armed helicopters, and light aircraft.

National Liberal Party (Lebanon): Camille Chamoun [*q.v.*] established the National Liberal Party (NLP) soon after stepping down as president in September 1958. It stressed Lebanese (as opposed to Arab) nationalism and economic liberalism based on private enterprise. It succeeded in attracting Lebanese outside the Maronite [*q.v.*] community. In the 1972 general election, campaigning in alliance with the Phalange [*q.v.*], it secured 13 seats, the largest number won by any party.

During the initial phase of the 1975–90 Lebanese Civil War [*q.v.*], the NLP cooperated with the Phalange in building up state infrastructure in the Christian region, with its capital in Jounieh, working for a "decentralized unity" of Lebanon, and strengthening links with Israel. But, once they had jointly thwarted the plans of the Lebanese government and the Syrian peacekeeping force to patrol Christian areas, the simmering tension between them over such matters as control over the illegal ports in the Christian enclave, often used for drug trafficking, boiled over. The NLP militia suffered heavily in the bloody clashes with the Phalangists in July 1980 and again in October. But after the assassination of Bashir Gemayel [*q.v.*] in September 1982, the party's

chances of survival improved. When the Phalange militia split in early 1986, the NLP's relative standing in the Christian enclave rose considerably.

After Chamoun's death in August 1987, the mantle of the NLP's leadership passed to his son, Danny. In August 1990 he backed Gen. Michel Aoun [*q.v.*] when the latter challenged the parliament's power to alter the constitution and pass reform laws. Danny Chamoun and his family were murdered in the aftermath of Aoun's defeat in mid-October 1990.

His younger brother, Dory Chamoun, became party president. He joined other Maronite parties in boycotting the 1992 general election. He kept out of the 1996 parliamentary election, but not the 1998 municipal elections when the NLP captured several local councils. He boycotted the parliamentary election in 2000 in protest at the continued presence of Syrian troops in Lebanon.

As part of the 8 March Alliance [*q.v.*] in the 2005 general election, the NLP won a single seat. It retained it in the 2009 election.

National Liberation Front (South Yemen): *South Yemeni political party* (Official title: National Front for the Liberation of South Yemen) The National Liberation Front (NLF) was set up in Sanaa [*q.v.*], North Yemen, in early 1963 to achieve independence from Britain through an armed struggle. It launched its first armed attack in the Rafdan Mountains in October. During the course of two years it opened four fronts against the British and took the fight to Aden [*q.v.*].

The NLF also came into conflict with the moderate Front for the

Liberation for the Occupied South Yemen (FLOSY). London's declaration in early 1966 that it would leave by December 1968 intensified the fight between the NLF and FLOSY. By August 1967 the NLF emerged as the stronger party. After the departure of the British three months later, it founded the People's Republic of South Yemen. The republic's constitution described the NLF as an alliance of the people's democratic forces, and its central committee, elected by the party congress, as the leading political organ.

Following a split in the regime in June 1969, the victorious leftists replaced the republic's presidency with a presidential council of five NLF leaders, later reduced to three. In March 1975 the party's sixth congress laid down a three-year political-economic plan for transition from national democracy to socialism. In October a unification congress decided to weld the NLF, the (Baathist [*q.v.*]) Vanguard Party, and the (Marxist) Popular Democratic Union into the United Political Organization-National Front, to be reconstituted as the Yemeni Socialist Party [*q.v.*] in 1978.

National Pact, 1943 (Lebanon): *constitutional agreement* In March 1943, prodded by the British, the Free French, led by Charles de Gaulle—who had retaken Lebanon from the pro-German French government in June 1941 with British assistance—restored Lebanon's 1926 constitution. Gen. Edward Spears, the British representative in Beirut [*q.v.*], mediated between feuding Muslims [*q.v.*] and Christians [*q.v.*] about the division of parliamentary seats. Using the 1932

census showing Christians as 54 percent of the population, Spears recommended a ratio of six Christian seats to five Muslim. (Later this ratio was also applied to posts in the civil service, judiciary, and military.) This was agreed by Riad Solh [*q.v.*], the Muslim leader, and Bishara Khouri [*q.v.*], the Christian leader, as part of the National Pact, an unwritten supplement to the constitution. It stipulated that the republic's president should be a Maronite Christian [*q.v.*], its prime minister a Sunni Muslim [*q.v.*], its parliamentary speaker a Shia Muslim [*q.v.*], and his deputy a Greek Orthodox [*q.v.*].

The National Pact sealed a wider compromise. While Muslim leaders accepted the existing frontiers of Lebanon, abandoning their demand for union with Syria to recreate Greater Syria [*q.v.*], their Christian counterparts agreed that Arabic should be the only official language of the republic, and that Lebanon should be free of any foreign (i.e., European) ties and should present an "Arab face" to the world. Some months later the National Pact was given the status of an official decree by the Free French government's General Georges Catroux.

In 1960 the number of parliamentary seats was increased from 77 to 99, with 54 going to Christians and 45 to Muslims. This lasted for 30 years and then, as a result of the National Reconciliation Charter of 1989 [*q.v.*], popularly called the Taif Accord [*q.v.*], the number of seats was raised to 128 and the proportion altered to parity between Christians and Muslims. *See also* Lebanon: Legislature.

National Progressive and Patriotic

Front (Iraq): *Iraqi political alliance* In July 1973, on the fifth anniversary of the Baathist coup, the parties that had earlier signed the National Action Charter formed the National Progressive and Patriotic Front (NPPF). It included the Baath Party [*q.v.*], the Communist Party [*q.v.*], and the smaller Nasserist [*q.v.*] and Kurdish groups. Its secretary-general was Naim Haddad, a Baathist leader.

The non-Baathist signatories to the charter agreed to be loyal to the Baathist revolution and refrain from spreading their ideologies among students and soldiers, as well as abstain from labor agitation and help to avert strikes. In return, some of the non-Baathist constituents of the NPPF were given seats in the cabinet, the Communists receiving two, and the others one or none. But cabinet ministers were more heads of departments than makers of policy, which was formulated by the ruling (Baathist) Revolutionary Command Council. Due to growing differences with the Baathist leadership, the Communist Party quit the NPPF in 1978 but did not publicize its decision.

When parliamentary elections were introduced in 1980, only NPPF constituents were allowed to run. The Baathist candidates won 183 of the 250 seats, the rest going to the non-Baathist groups or independents. In the 1984 election the Baathist share rose marginally to 188, but in the general election of 1989 it fell to 138, with non-Baathist NPPF groups and independents making gains. During the crisis leading to the 1991 Gulf War [*q.v.*] the NPPF was prominent in organizing pro-regime demonstrations. Its importance declined sharply after the war.

National Progressive Front (Syria):

Syrian political alliance The National Progressive Front (NPF), formed in March 1972 on the ninth anniversary of the Baathist revolution, comprised the Baath Party [*q.v.*], the Communist Party [*q.v.*], the Arab Socialist Union (ASU), the Arab Socialist Movement (ASM), and the Organization of Socialist Unionists (OSU). Its 18-member leadership, headed by President Hafiz Assad [*q.v.*], included nine other Baathists and two members each from the four non-Baathist groups. The latter were given seats in the cabinet, but they were barred from enrolling members among students or military personnel. PNF policies were to be modeled along Baath congress resolutions. On such weighty matters as going to war with Israel in October 1973, Assad consulted leaders of the PNF as well as the Baath Regional Command.

PNF constituents were allowed to enter elections. In the 1986 general election the Baath Party won 129 of the 250 seats, the Communist Party 9, the three remaining parties of the NPF 57, the rest going to independents. The figures for the 1990 election were Baathists 134 seats, Communists 8, the ASU 8, the ASM 5, the OSU 7, and independents 84. In 1994 the Organization of Socialist Unionists split, with the breakaway faction calling itself Organization of Democratic Socialist Unionists (ODSU). It was allowed to join the PNF. In the 1994 election the Baath Party won less than half of the seats, with the

PNF gaining a total of 167. In the 1998 parliamentary election, the result was Baath 135, Communists 8, the ASU 7, the ASM 6, OSU 7, and ODSU 4. Of the 169 seats garnered by the PNF in 2007, Baath won 134, Communists (both factions) 8, the ASU 8, the ASM 3, ODSU 4.

By the time the parliamentary election was conducted under an amended constitution in May 2012, the PNF's membership had increased to 10. Altogether it won 168 seats, with the rest going to the newly formed Popular Front for Change and Liberation (5 seats) and independents. Among the PNF's constituents, the Baath Party led with 134 seats followed by Socialist Unionists (18 seats).

National Progressive Unionist Party

(Egypt): *Egyptian political party* (Official title: *Hizb al-Tagammu al-Watani al-Taqadomi al-Wahdawi*, commonly known as *Tagammu* [Arabic: *rally*]) When, in May 1976, the government allowed the political role of the Arab Socialist Union [*q.v.*] to be taken over by three tribunes, the leftist forum was represented by the National Progressive Unionist Party (NPUP). Consisting largely of Marxists and leftist Nasserists [*q.v.*], the NPUP was led by Khaled Mohieddin [*q.v.*]. In the parliamentary election of 1976 the NPUP won only two seats. This was in contrast to the large circulation of the party's weekly journal, *Al-Ahali* (Arabic: *The Masses*).

To silence the journal, which vehemently opposed the Egyptian-Israeli Peace Treaty of March 1979 [*q.v.*], the government of President Anwar Sadat [*q.v.*] amended the law so that only a party with 10 parliamentary seats could publish a newspaper. In the subsequent elections the party failed to win a single seat because of the high threshold of 8 percent specified by the successive electoral laws. In the 1990 general election, held under changed electoral rules and boycotted by all the major opposition parties, the NPUP won 1.4 percent of the vote and two seats. At the next election in 1995 its strength rose to five, and then to six in 2000, when the party leadership claimed 160,000 members. After a dip to two seats in the 2005 election, the party's share of seats in the People's Assembly rose to five in the 2010 election.

Led by Muhammad Rifaat el Saeed, the party participated in the civil uprising against President Hosni Mubarak [*q.v.*] in 2011.

National Reconciliation Charter, 1989

(Lebanon): The National Reconciliation Charter is the document adopted by the Lebanese lawmakers at their session in Taif, Saudi Arabia, in October 1989 to resolve the issues at the core of the Lebanese Civil War [*q.v.*]. The draft, prepared by the Arab League's [*q.v.*] troika (Algeria, Morocco, and Saudi Arabia) proposed parity in parliament between Christians [*q.v.*] and Muslims [*q.v.*]. It was debated by 62 deputies, accounting for all but nine of the surviving members, with their election dating back to 1972.

Despite the widely acknowledged fact that the demographic changes, caused by higher birth rates among Muslims and the increased emigration of Christians, had turned Muslims into a majority community, accounting for more than 60 percent of the population, Muslim lawmakers agreed to equal sharing of the 128 parliamentary seats between Christians and Muslims. They also consented to allow Christians to keep the presidency, albeit with reduced powers. All but four (Muslim) deputies voted for the final version of the charter.

By accepting the continued Syrian military presence in Lebanon for at least two years after the national unity government had agreed on constitutional reform, Christian deputies provided Syria with legitimacy—something it had lost with the expiry of the 1976 Arab League mandate in mid-1982—and conceded Syria's strategic concerns in Lebanon.

On 4 November, 58 deputies, forming four-fifths of the surviving members, and the speaker, met at the Qulayaat airstrip in northern Lebanon to ratify the charter, popularly called the Taif Accord. A national unity government was then formed to implement it. By the end of 1989 most of the important foreign powers had declared their backing for it. Within the Christian camp, Gen. Michel Aoun [*q.v.*] rejected it, whereas most other Maronite [*q.v.*] leaders accepted it.

Its implementation started in August 1990. Of the 49 deputies participating in the voting, all but one opted to overhaul the 1926 constitution by altering three articles, specifically Articles 17, 52, and 53. Article 17, which stated that executive power should be vested in the president of the republic, was amended to read: "Executive power is assigned to the Council of Ministers." This council was to consist of an equal number of Muslim and Christian ministers. Article 53 formerly empowered the president to

designate a prime minister for approval by parliament, and appoint or dismiss ministers. Now the president was required to consult the speaker and senior deputies before designating the prime minister, and the right to dismiss ministers became the prerogative of the cabinet. Likewise, Article 52, which authorized the president to negotiate and ratify international treaties, was amended to require the president to secure the consent of the prime minister and the approval of the cabinet before an international treaty could become operative. Overall, the agreed reform favored the cabinet, which emerged with greater power than the president, but, crucially, a two-thirds majority was required for cabinet decisions.

The civil war ended in October 1990. To implement the next stage of the charter, a second national unity government was formed in late December 1990. Its main task was to effect the administrative decentralization stipulated by the charter.

National Religious Party (Israel):

Israeli political party Known by its Hebrew acronym, Mafdal [*q.v.*], Miflaga Datid Leumit, the National Religious Party (NRP) was formed in 1956 by the merger of Mizrahi [*q.v.*] and Poale HaMizrahi [*q.v.*]. In the general elections of 1959, 1961, 1965, and 1969, the NRP won 11 to 12 seats and joined Mapai [*q.v.*] or Labor [*q.v.*] to form a coalition government, and to run the education, religious affairs, and interior ministries.

Following the June 1967 Arab-Israeli War [*q.v.*], the NRP's commitment to creating the Eretz Yisrael [*q.v.*] of biblical times strengthened the hand of Labor hard-liners and stiffened official policies toward the Occupied Arab Territories [*q.v.*]. The NRP spawned Gush Emunim [*q.v.*] with a program to colonize the Occupied Arab Territories, and ensured that no action was taken against Gush settlers.

After the December 1973 election, when it obtained 10 seats, as a precondition for joining a Labor-led coalition government of Golda Meir [*q.v.*], the NRP demanded that the Law of Return [*q.v.*] be amended to exclude non-Orthodox [*q.v.*] converts to Judaism [*q.v.*]. When Meir rejected its demand, it stayed out of the government. However, it joined the next administration led by Yitzhak Rabin [*q.v.*] in October 1974.

Winning 12 seats in the 1977 election, NRP became part of the Likud-led [*q.v.*] coalition government. A split in the party halved its Knesset [*q.v.*] strength to six in the 1981 election. In the three subsequent general elections its presence in the Knesset fluctuated between four and six. It opposed the 1993 Oslo Accords [*q.v.*].

In the 1996 election it secured nine seats, and joined the coalition government led by Benjamin Netanyahu [*q.v.*]. The party's strength declined to five in the 1999 election. It joined the administration of Ehud Barak [*q.v.*]. And it was also part of the national unity government formed by Ariel Sharon [*q.v.*] in 2001. In the post-1977 cabinets, it continued to hold the education ministry.

The next election in 2003 saw the party raise its total to six. Weakened by a split caused in the party by Sharon's decision to withdraw the Israeli military from the Gaza Strip

[*q.v.*], it formed an alliance with the National Union [*q.v.*] to participate in the 2006 parliamentary election. Its share of the Knesset seats won fell to two. The joint list of the NRP-National Union secured six seats in the 2009 election, divided equally between the two constituents. The NRP continues to publish a daily newspaper, *Hazofeh*.

National Resistance Council of Iran: *Iranian political alliance* After their escape from Iran by air to Paris in July 1981 Abol Hassan Bani-Sadr [*q.v.*] and Masoud Rajavi [*q.v.*], head of the Mujahedin-e Khalq (MEK) [*q.v.*], formed the National Resistance Council of Iran (NRCI) to violently oppose the Islamic regime of Iran. The NRCI claimed responsibility for the bomb explosion in Tehran [*q.v.*] on 30 August that killed President Muhammad Ali Rajai [*q.v.*] and Premier Muhammad Javad Bahonar. Three months later it won the affiliation of the Kurdistan Democratic Party of Iran [*q.v.*] and the Komala-e Jian-e Kordestan [*q.v.*].

Among its constituents, the MEK was the most active in the Persian-speaking heartland of Iran. In August 1983 it claimed that during its two years of existence it had killed 2,800 Islamic officials and revolutionary guards in hundreds of offensive and defensive operations.

With the Iran-Iraq War [*q.v.*] dragging on, the NRCI concentrated on this issue, advocating an immediate cease-fire and blaming Ayatollah Ruhollah Khomeini [*q.v.*] for continuing the conflict in order to divert public attention away from the worsening domestic problems. Rajavi's public meeting with the Iraqi vice premier, Tariq Aziz [*q.v.*], in Paris in January 1983 angered Bani-Sadr, who considered Iraq an enemy country. When efforts to patch up their differences failed, Bani-Sadr quit the NRCI in early 1984.

When Rajavi moved the MEK's headquarters moved to Baghdad [*q.v.*] in 1986, the Iraqi capital became the center of NRCI activities as well. Washington's ban on the MEK in 1997 did not extend to the NRCI. And even when the ban was imposed in the wake of the terrorists attacks on the United States in September 2001, it was not applied in practice. Indeed, the NCRI, maintaining an office in Washington, periodically called for the lifting of the ban on the MEK with advertisements in American newspapers, endorsed by many members of the House of Representatives.

By informing the U.S. administration of Iran's clandestine uranium enrichment facilities in Natanz in 2002, it won some goodwill. But U.S. Secretary of State Colin Powell called the organization's American affiliate a terrorist front of the MEK. In August 2003 the Federal Bureau of Investigation closed the Washington office of NRCI.

During that month Masoud Rajavi's wife, Mariam, based in a suburb of Paris, was elected president of the NCRI. It has remained active in Europe, holding rallies and collecting funds.

National Union: *Israeli political bloc* (Official title: Hebrew, *Halchund HaLeumi*). Israel Beitainu [*q.v.*] and Moledet [*q.v.*] combined in 2001 to form the National Union on the common platform of their opposition to the establishment of a Palestinian state, and their advocacy of "transfer" of the Palestinians [*q.v.*] from the Occupied Palestinian Territories [*q.v.*] and total Israeli jurisdiction over all of Jerusalem [*q.v.*]. In the 2003 Knesset [*q.v.*] election, it won seven seats, with four for Israel Beitainu [*q.v.*] and the rest for Moledet. By allying with the National Religious Party [*q.v.*] in the 2006 general election, it managed to gain four seats. In the 2009 Knesset election, that number declined to three while the alliance with the NRP remained intact.

National Unity Front (Qatar): *Qatari political party* The National Unity Front (NUF) was formed in 1963 to channel the discontent Qatari citizens felt at the squandering of oil wealth by the ruling al-Thani clan [*q.v.*], coupled with its tight grip over political and economic power. The NUF organized a series of anti-government demonstrations to demand a proper state budget, a representative council, and curbs on the unlimited prerogatives of the al-Thanis. The ruler, Shaikh Ahmad bin Ali al-Thani [*q.v.*], combined his repression of the NUF with the appointment in 1964 of an advisory council with authority to issue laws and decrees concerning basic state policy. The Front fizzled out.

natural gas: Natural gas is a mixture of several hydrocarbons and such inert gases as nitrogen and carbon dioxide. Among the hydrocarbons, methane (CH_4), a colorless, odorless gas, accounts for at least three-quarters of natural gas by volume, the other hydrocarbons being ethane, butane, and propane. Natural gas is found in two forms: on its own, called unassociated, or along with petroleum [q.v.], called associated. The associated gas exists partly as a cap above an oil reservoir and partly dissolved into it. In the newly exploited oilfields the presence of gas under pressure pushes the oil to the surface. The associated gas produced with petroleum is either used as fuel, or re-injected into a well to bring oil to surface, or burnt. The natural gas that is piped to domestic or industrial outlets is pure methane.

Navon, Yitzhak (1921–): *Israeli politician; president, 1978–83* Born into a long-settled Sephardic Jewish [q.v.] family in Jerusalem [q.v.], Navon was fluent in Arabic [q.v.]. He became active in the Zionist movement [q.v.] in his youth. He enrolled with Haganah [q.v.] in the early 1940s and worked for its intelligence section. On the founding of Israel he joined its foreign service. After serving briefly as a diplomat in Argentina, he served as political secretary to foreign minister Moshe Sharett [q.v.]. From 1952 to 1963 he worked as secretary to Prime Minister David Ben-Gurion [q.v.] and became quite influential.

He joined the breakaway Rafi group formed by Ben-Gurion in 1965 and was elected to the Knesset [q.v.] in that year. During his 13 years in parliament he became deputy speaker (1966–73) and chairman of the foreign affairs and defense committee (1974–77). In 1978 he was elected president by a parliament in which the right wing had the majority. He returned to the Knesset on the Labor [q.v.] list in 1984, and became deputy

premier and minister of culture and education. Reelected in 1988, he resumed his earlier posts and held them until 1990. He retained his seat in Knesset until 1992, when he retired from politics.

Among politicians he stood out as the only one who wrote two successful musicals, which were performed by the national theater in Tel Aviv [q.v.].

Nawruz (Kurdish/Persian: *New Day*): It is the first day of the Iranian solar calendar [q.v.] and falls on the spring equinox. It is celebrated by Iranians, Kurds [q.v.], and Zoroastrians [q.v.].

Nazareth: *Israeli town* Population: 82,200, of which Christians [q.v.] 25,500, and Muslims [q.v.] 56,700 (2009 est.). The New Testament [q.v.] makes several mentions of Nazareth, a Jewish settlement, as the home town of Joseph and a place associated with the childhood of Jesus. It became a center of Christian pilgrimage after Roman Emperor Constantine (306–37 A.D.) had adopted Christianity [q.v.] as the state religion in 313 A.D. and built a church there.

Nazareth was one of the most prized towns during the Crusades. Having captured it in 1099, the Crusaders turned it into a leading ecclesiastical center. But once Salah al-Din (Saladin) Ayubi (r. 1169–1193) had defeated the Crusaders in 1187, Christian influence declined rapidly.

Following their conquest of Palestine [q.v.] in 1517, the Ottomans expelled the Christians from the town. This policy was reversed when Emir Fakhr al-Din Maan (r. 1591–1633) extended his Vilayat of Lebanon to Lower Galilee. Following his permission to Christians to return to Nazareth, Franciscan monks resettled the old Crusader foundation in 1620 and constructed a church in 1730, which in 1909 was replaced by a basilica, the Roman Catholic Church [*q.v.*] of the Annunciation. It contains the Grotto of the Annunciation where, according to the New Testament [*q.v.*], Archangel Gabriel appeared to the Virgin Mary to announce that she was to be the mother of Jesus.

Among the two dozen religious premises and monasteries are St. Mary's Well, the Church of Joseph on the site of Joseph's carpentry shop, the Synagogue-Church on the site of the synagogue [*q.v.*] where Jesus preached, and the Mensa Christi (Latin: *Table of Christ*) Church where Jesus reputedly dined with the Apostles after his resurrection.

Included in the Arab [*q.v.*] sector by the UN partition plan of 1947, Nazareth fell to Zionist [*q.v.*] forces in 1948. It is now the largest Arab town in Israel, and an important market and trading center. In the first popular election for mayor in 1973, Tawfiq Zayyad, belonging to the Rakah [*q.v.*] Communist party, was elected with a large majority, and administered the town with the Communist-dominated local council. He was reelected four years later as a leader of Hadash [*q.v.*] repeatedly until his death in 1994. After that his deputy Ramiz Jaraisy, a Greek Orthodox [*q.v.*] Christian and a Hadash member, has been the mayor.

Near East: The term Near East was coined by Western geographers to distinguish it from the Middle East (running from the Persian Gulf [*q.v.*] to Southeast Asia) and the Far East (the region facing the Pacific Ocean). Extending from the Mediterranean Sea to the Persian Gulf, the Near East virtually coincided with the Ottoman Empire. But when the British government prefaced its military command in Egypt with the Middle East during World War II (1939–45), the nomenclature became confused. Since then the term Near East has disappeared in common parlance, although the foreign ministries of a few Western governments, chiefly the United States, continue to use it in the pre-World War II context.

Neguib, Muhammad (1901–84): *Egyptian military leader and politician; prime minister 1952–53, president 1953–54* Born to an Egyptian military officer and his wife in Khartoum, Sudan, Neigub graduated from the Royal Military Academy in Cairo [*q.v.*]. As an army officer he rose steadily in rank, and was a brigadier in 1948 when Egypt participated in the Palestine War [*q.v.*]. Promoted to brigadier-general in 1950, he became commander of the ground forces the following year.

Through his operations officer, Abdul Hakim Amer, he was in touch with the Free Officers Organization. He accepted its offer to head the Revolutionary Command Council (RCC) after the July 1952 coup. He also became commander in chief of the armed forces. When the civilian government resigned in September, the RCC appointed him the prime minister and defense minister. Following the declaration of the republic in June 1953, the RCC confirmed him as the prime minister and appointed him president, but relieved him of his top military office.

His differences with Gamal Abdul Nasser [*q.v.*], the real leader of the RCC and the republic, came to the fore in February 1954 when the RCC banned the Muslim Brotherhood [*q.v.*] without consulting him. His resignation as president and premier created a crisis when the two rivals mobilized different military units. A compromise in April allowed Neguib to retain the presidency, albeit with diminished powers, but give up the premiership. This lasted until November when the RCC dismissed him as president and put him under house arrest. He was freed in 1971 after the death of Nasser. He backed Anwar Sadat [*q.v.*], but did not reenter public life.

Neo-Wafd Party: *Egyptian political party* The Neo-Wafd Party was established by Fuad Serag al-Din, a veteran of the Wafd Party [*q.v.*], in early 1978 when he won the loyalty of 22 parliamentarians, thus meeting the legal requirement for new political groups. The party, which was committed to secularism, private enterprise, and close ties with the United States, proved particularly attractive to Copts [*q.v.*]. But when parliament, guided by President Anwar Sadat [*q.v.*], passed a law specifying various penalties for those who inter alia had a record of belonging to "the corrupt elements before or after the 1952 revolution," the Neo-Wafd leadership disbanded the party in September 1978.

Serag al-Din was one of the opposition leaders to be rounded up by Sadat three years later. President Hosni Mubarak [*q.v.*] reversed Sadat's policy,

and the Neo-Wafd reemerged in August 1983. In the 1984 general election it allied with the (unlicensed) Muslim Brotherhood [*q.v.*], arguing that both parties had been suppressed by President Gamal Abdul Nasser [*q.v.*]. However, it adopted only 18 of the candidates the Brotherhood offered. Of the 58 Neo-Wafd deputies, only eight belonged to the Brotherhood.

In the 1987 election the Neo-Wafd, running on its own, managed to cross the 8 percent threshold fixed by the electoral law and won 36 seats. Along with other major opposition groups, it boycotted the 1990 election, protesting against the continuing state of emergency and demanding supervision of the election by a non-governmental body. In the 1995 election, it won six seats, followed by seven in 2000. After the death of Serag al-Din during that year, Numan Jumaah became the party leader. In the 2005 general election it secured six seats on a popular vote of 1.3 percent.

Following the fall of Mubarak in February 2011, the New Wafd entered the parliamentary elections held between November 2011 and January under the leadership of El Sayyid el-Badawi Shehata, and won 42 seats on a popular vote of 9 percent. In the subsequent elections to the 180-member Consultative (Shura) Council, it gained 14 seats.

Nestorian Christians: *Christian sect* The Nestorian Church is based on the theology of Nestorius (d. ca 451 A.D.), patriarch of Constantinople, who asserted that there were two separate persons in Christ—human and divine—morally united through the cooperation of their two wills. This contradicted the orthodox doctrine that the human and divine natures of Christ were inseparably joined in one person and partook of one divine substance—a doctrine reaffirmed by the Councils of Ephesus in 431 A.D., Chalcedon in 451 A.D., and Constantinople in 553 A.D. Only the Persian Church remained faithful to Nestorianism and emerged as the Nestorian Church. The invasion of the region by Tamerlane (d. 1405) virtually destroyed the church, leaving a few pockets of followers in Iran and Iraq. When a section of Nestorians reunited with the Roman Catholic Church [*q.v.*] in 1551, their church was called Chaldean/Chaldean Catholic [*q.v.*]/East Syriac [*q.v.*]. The rest of the community then became known as Assyrian Christians [*q.v.*].

Netanyahu, Benjamin (1950–): *Israeli politician, prime minister 1996–99*
Born into the household of Bentzion Netanyahu, a right-wing academic, Netanyahu left for the United States when his father got a teaching job there in 1964. He returned to Israel three years later to do his military service and became a commander in an elite commando force, then returned to America to resume his university education at the Massachusetts Institute of Technology in Cambridge. He obtained a master's degree in business administration in 1976. He worked in the United States for three years, and then became a furniture sales executive in Israel (1980–82).

In 1982 Moshe Arens, Israel's ambassador to the U.S., hired him as political counselor. Later he served as Israel's ambassador to the United Nations until 1984. On his return to Is-

rael, he became a full-time director of the Jonathan Institute, which specialized in study of terrorism.

Elected to the Knesset [*q.v.*] on the Likud [*q.v.*] list in 1988, he became deputy foreign minister (1988–91). He then served as deputy minister in Prime Minster Yitzhak Shamir's [*q.v.*] office (1991–92). He was reelected to parliament in 1992. Generously assisted by the expertise and funds of his American Jewish friends, he won the contest for the Likud's leadership in 1993. He opposed the Oslo Accords [*q.v.*].

In the 1996 prime ministerial contest, he defeated his rival Shimon Peres by one percent of the vote. His coalition government had the backing of 62 of the 120 members of the Knesset. By refusing to implement the previous government's agreement on troops withdrawal from the Occupied Territories [*q.v.*], and by pursuing such hard-line policies as authorizing the construction of a highly controversial Jewish settlement at Har Homa/Jabal abu Ghnaim on the outskirts of Jerusalem [*q.v.*], Netanyahu severely impaired the Oslo Accords, much to the disapproval and frustration of the administration of U.S. President Bill Clinton (r. 1993–2001).

Following his signing of the Wye River Memorandum [*q.v.*], which required Israel to withdraw from 13 percent of the West Bank [*q.v.*], Netanyahu lost the support of the ultra-right-wing factions in the Knesset. This resulted in the downfall of his government. In the May 1999 prime ministerial contest he lost to Ehud Barak [*q.v.*] by a plurality of 56–44 percent. He resigned as the Likud leader and a member of the Knesset, and did a lecture tour of the Unites States.

He served in the Ariel Sharon [*q.v.*] cabinet, first as foreign minister and then as finance minister. He quit the government on the eve of Israel's military withdrawal from Gaza [*q.v.*] in September 2005. Later that year, following Sharon's defection from the Likud, he was elected its head. Under his leadership Likud's score in the Knesset election of 2006 fell to 12, a record low. Yet the next year he managed to retain its leadership in the party's elections. In the 2009 general election, the Likud emerged as the second-largest, one member short of Kadima [*q.v.*]. Whereas Kadima leader failed to form a viable coalition to govern Israel, he succeeded in cobbling together right- and ultra-right-wing factions to win a majority in the Knesset, and became the prime minister in March.

Netanyahu said that he would accept a Palestinian state only if the Palestinians recognized Israel as the Jewish national state with undivided Jerusalem as its capital; agreed to have a state that would be demilitarized, possessing neither an army nor rockets and missiles nor the control of its airspace; and gave up the right of return for the Palestinian refugees to the areas within Israel.

He defied the demand of the newly elected U.S. President Barrack Obama (r. 2009–) for a complete freeze of settlements in the Occupied Palestinian Territories [*q.v.*], as required in the 2003 Road Map peace proposal of the Quartet on the Middle East [*q.v.*], consisting of the United Nations, the United States, the European Union, and Russia. His government went on to sanction enough new housing units in the occupied territories to cover the next 10 months and then declared a temporary moratorium on further building for that period.

Given this, Palestinian Authority [*q.v.*] President Mahmoud Abbas refused to engage in any peace talks with Netanyahu, insisting that a complete freeze on Jewish settlements was a precondition to resuming peace negotiations. His stance was backed by the Arab League [*q.v.*]. Defying Washington's pressure, Netanyahu refused to extend the moratorium on Jewish settlement building in the West Bank and East Jerusalem [*q.v.*]. Peace talks with the Palestinians ceased.

By urging Obama during the January–February 2011 pro-democracy demonstrations in Egypt not to press Egyptian President Hosni Mubarak [*q.v.*] to step down, Netanyahu came out on the same side as King Abdullah [*q.v.*] of Saudi Arabia. In November he described Obama and other Western leaders as "naive" for backing the Arab Spring [*q.v.*], which, in his view, was "Islamic, anti-Western, anti-liberal, anti-Israeli and anti-democratic." Describing the transition to democracy in Tunisia and Egypt as "period of instability and uncertainty in the region," he ruled out any concessions to the Palestinians. By then he had succeeded in diverting Obama's attention away from the resolution of the Israeli-Palestinian conflict and making the issue of Iran's nuclear program Washington's top priority in the region.

Neturei Karta (Aramaic: *Guardians of the [Holy] City*): *an ultra-Orthodox Jewish sect in Israel* The name Neturei Karta is derived from an allusion in the Talmud [*q.v.*] to students of the Torah [*q.v.*] as "guardians of the [holy] city." The group emerged in Palestine [*q.v.*] in 1935 following a split in Agudat Israel [*q.v.*] when it compromised its Poland-based parent body's policy of non-cooperation with the (World) Zionist Organization [*q.v.*]. Ten years later Neturei Karta and its sympathizers won a majority on the committee representing the Ashkenazi [*q.v.*] community of Jerusalem [*q.v.*].

During the run-up to the founding of Israel in 1948, Neturei Karta opposed the creation of a Jewish state in Palestine on the ground that such a state would not be founded exclusively on Jewish law and tradition, and that the return to Zion [*q.v.*] of the diaspora [*q.v.*] Jews could not be taken in isolation from their redemption by the awaited messiah [*q.v.*], who was charged with establishing a Jewish state and whose time had not yet come. During the 1948–49 Arab-Israeli War [*q.v.*] it called for the internationalization of Jerusalem. Later it became the most-known Jewish organization in Israel to refuse to recognize the Zionist [*q.v.*] state.

In 1980 the sect had about 6,000 members, living mainly in the Mea Shearim district of Jerusalem and the Bene Brak suburb of Tel Aviv [*q.v.*]. Periodically its adherents resort to stoning cars that pass near their neighborhoods on the Sabbath [*q.v.*].

After the split in the sect, the larger faction was headed by Rabbi Reuven Katznellenbogen, and the smaller one by his son-in-law Rabbi Moshe Hirsch in Jerusalem. The Hirsch-led group holds that the Orthodox Jews can and should live as a minority in an independent Palestinian-dominated state. Hirsch was appointed to the Palestinian Authority [*q.v.*] in 1994 to deal with the Jewish affairs of the Occupied Territories [*q.v.*]. He and other members of his faction attended Arafat's funeral in Ramallah [*q.v.*] in 2004. After his death in 2010, his son Israel-Meir Hirsch became the leader of the faction.

New Testament: *See* Bible.

Nile River: Length 4,150 mi./6,680 km from its remotest headstream to the Mediterranean, including 1,875 mi./3,020 km of the Nile proper, formed by the junction of the Blue Nile and the White Nile at Khartoum, Sudan. The world's longest river, the Nile rises in the highlands south of the equator, flows through northeast Africa into the Mediterranean Sea and drains 1,294,000 sq. mi./3,351,000 sq. km. Between Khartoum and Aswan the Nile falls 935 ft./285 m in a series of six rapids. Flooding is caused by the Blue Nile being fed by heavy monsoon rains in Ethiopia. Efforts to tame the Nile go back six millennia. The building of several barrages and waterworks by the late 19th century made perennial irrigation possible. The Aswan Dam was completed in 1902, and the Aswan High Dam [*q.v.*] in 1971. After Cairo [*q.v.*], the Nile waters enter the delta, dividing chiefly between the Damietta and Rosetta channels. The river is an important means of transportation.

Noble Sanctuary: *Islamic site in Jerusalem* (called *Haram al-Sharif* by Arabs [*q.v.*], *Har HaBayit* [Hebrew:

The Mountain Home] by Jews [*q.v.*], and Temple Mount in the English-speaking world) Built on Mount Moriah in the Old City of Jerusalem [*q.v.*], the Noble Sanctuary—which houses the Dome of the Rock and al-Aqsa Mosque (The Distant Mosque) and measures 35 acres/0.14 sq. km—takes up about a third of the Muslim Quarter, which occupies nearly two-fifths of the historic Old City. It was from this spot that, having arrived there in the course of his night journey by a winged animal, and having prayed at the Rock of Foundation, the Prophet Muhammad, guided by Archangel Gabriel, ascended into the heavens by a ladder of light, where (it is believed) he received Allah's injunction on the prayers his followers were to perform.

The rock that the Dome of the Rock protects is the Rock of Foundation (of the world) of the Jewish legend, the Jewish temple's inner sanctum. The octagonal shape of the building surmounted by a dome—that is, a circle within an octagon—modeled on the then-existing Church of Resurrection (later renamed the Church of the Holy Sepulcher), was symbolic in ancient times of the center of the world. Thus the Dome of the Rock is a synthesis in form and content of Judaism [*q.v.*], Christianity [*q.v.*], and Islam [*q.v.*]. It was built in 691 A.D. by Abdul Malik bin Marwan (r. 684–705 A.D.), an Umayyad ruler based in Damascus [*q.v.*]. During the Crusaders' rule (1099–1187), it was reconverted into a church and renamed the Temple of the Lord.

Al Aqsa is a plainer, traditionally built mosque. It has prayer niches dedicated to Moses and Jesus. An arson attack on it by Michael Rohan, an Australian fundamentalist Christian [*q.v.*], in August 1969, shocked the Muslim world and led inter alia to the founding of the Islamic Conference Organization [*q.v.*].

Following the annexation of East Jerusalem [*q.v.*] by Jordan, the Jordanian monarch acquired the custody of the Noble Sanctuary in 1950. When Israel occupied East Jerusalem in June 1967 it accepted the Jordanian custodianship. This was confirmed by the Jordanian-Israeli Peace Treaty [*q.v.*], which was signed in October 1994 and hotly disputed by the Palestine Liberation Organization [*q.v.*]. The future of the Noble Sanctuary proved to be main stumbling block in the Israeli-PLO final settlement talks in July 2000 at Camp David in Maryland. And it was the controversial tour of the Nobel Sanctuary by Ariel Sharon [*q.v.*], guarded by hundreds of Israeli policemen, that set off the Al Aqsa intifada [*q.v.*] in September.

Non-Conventional weapons (Arab Middle East, Iran and Israel): *See* each individual country's military: non-conventional weapons.

North Yemen: (Official title: Yemen Arab Republic) *See* Yemen: history.

North Yemeni Civil War (1962–70): Following the overthrow of Imam Muhammad al-Badr [*q.v.*] by pan-Arabist [*q.v.*] military officers in September 1962, Egyptian President Gamal Abdul Nasser [*q.v.*] agreed to help the republican side, which had only 6,000 troops. In January 1963 the Saudi White Guard, later renamed the National Guard [*q.v.*], moved to the North Yemen border at Jizan and Najran to help al-Badr. This led to fighting between Saudi and Egyptian forces.

Initially the Zayidi [*q.v.*] tribesmen, inhabiting the northern region bordering Saudi Arabia, supported al-Badr. But in the absence of a strong central authority, tribal leaders such as Shaikh Naji al-Ghadr of the Bakil tribal confederation, commanding a private army of 12,000, and Shaikh Abdullah al-Ahmar [*q.v.*], head of the Hashid tribal confederation, found it more profitable to distance themselves from the conflict or offer their services to the highest bidder. By August 1965 the royalists had regained about half of North Yemen.

After inviting the republican president, Abdullah Sallal [*q.v.*], to Cairo [*q.v.*], and placing him under house arrest, Nasser met King Faisal in Jeddah [*q.v.*]. Talks between them went on for about a year, but ended in failure. Meanwhile Abdul Rahman al-Iryani [*q.v.*], a conservative member of the Republican Council, had managed to neutralize the tribal leaders. Though Sallal returned to Sanaa [*q.v.*] and resumed his office, his position was weakened when, following the Egyptian debacle in the June 1967 Arab-Israeli War [*q.v.*], Nasser agreed with the Saudi king to pull out his troops from North Yemen by December.

When al-Iryani replaced Sallal in November 1967, the political hue of the republican regime changed. The royalists made a bid to capture Sanaa [*q.v.*], but the republicans, assisted by the tribes and the leftists, ended the siege in February 1968. The tribal forces then attacked the leftists. The subsequent ascendancy of conserva-

tives in the republican regime made it acceptable to more and more tribal fighters.

By early 1969 Riyadh had ceased to back al-Badr militarily. In March 1970 President al-Iryani reached an agreement with Riyadh whereby Saudi subsidies to the royalists were stopped. Once the Saudis were reassured that a republican regime in Sanaa, dependent for its financial survival on them, would be no threat, they formally recognized it. A coalition government, including royalist ministers, was formed, and the Consultative Council of 45 was expanded by 18 nominees, all of them royalists.

The eight-year conflict caused an estimated 200,000 deaths.

North Yemeni-Soviet Friendship Treaty (1984) It was signed by President Ali Abdullah Saleh [*q.v.*] and Konstantin Chernenko, general secretary of the Communist Party of the Soviet Union in Moscow.

Al Nour Party (Egypt): *Political party* (Official title: *Hizb al-Nour* [Arabic: *The Party of Light*]) It is the political wing of the Call of the Salafiya (Arabic: *al-Daawa al-Salafiya*) movement that originated in Alexandria [*q.v.*] in 1977 when many Islamist students at Alexandria University came under the influence of the Salafi [*q.v.*] ideology blended with the core elements of the Wahhabi doctrine [*q.v.*]. Their leader was Muhammad Abdul Fattah.

By shunning politics, and focusing on providing social welfare to the needy through orphanages and health clinics, funded by the group's *zakat* [*q.v.*] committees, the adherents of the Salafiya Call grew roots in the community by the mid-1980s, aided by their magazine, *Sawt al-Daawa* (Arabic: *Voice of the Call*). The group achieved this despite the periodic arrests of its leaders and the banning of its publication by the government of President Hosni Mubarak [*q.v.*].

During the pro-democracy protest in January–February 2011, Salafiya Call leaders actively discouraged their followers from joining the pro-democracy demonstrations in order not to raise alarm in Washington. Nonetheless, Salafiya Call activists joined the popular committees formed to maintain security in neighborhoods throughout Egypt following the nationwide withdrawal of police forces on 28 January.

After the fall of Mubarak on 11 February 2011, the Salafiya Call leadership established Al Nour Party in May with Emad Abdel Ghaffour as its chairman. It was recognized as a legal entity a month later. It aimed to reform Muslim lives according to the Quran [*q.v.*] and the Sunna [*q.v.*], and run a modern state based on Islamic ethics. It wanted strict application of the Sharia [*q.v.*], such as implementing Islamic punishments known as Hudud [*q.v.*]. It believed in private property and free market economy so long as it did not harm public interest. It was committed to granting freedoms and rights to citizens according to the Sharia. Within that framework it was willing to abandon its earlier demand for an Islamic state in favor of a civil state, and allow Copts [*q.v.*] to have their separate personal status laws and their freedom of religion.

The party sought amendments to the 1979 peace treaty with Israel to secure full Egyptian rights in the Sinai Peninsula [*q.v.*] as well as self-determination for the Palestinians. This would be the preamble to normalization of relations with Israel which was to be ruled out as long as Israel occupied Arab lands and imposed a siege on the Palestinians.

Al Nour joined the Democratic Alliance [*q.v.*] headed by the Freedom and Justice Party [*q.v.*], but withdrew in November to coalesce with Hizb *Al-Asala* (Arabic: *Originality Party*) and the Construction and Development Party set up by the Gamaat al-Islamiya [*q.v.*]. In the parliamentary elections of 2011–2012 it won 113 seats out of the total of 127 for the Islamist Bloc [*q.v.*] on a popular vote or 28 percent, with 10 seats going to the Construction and Development Party and three to the Al Asla Party. In the Consultative (Shura) Council, the Al Nour Party-led Islamist Bloc gained 45 seats on a popular vote of 29 percent. As local preachers, many Al Nour politicians were close to their rural constituents, nursing populist resentments of poor villagers toward the urban elite.

Hazem Salah Abu Ismail, the party's candidate for president, was disqualified by the Election Commission because he did not meet the legal requirement that both parents of a candidate had to be Egyptian citizens, since his dead mother had acquired American citizenship. Al Nour leaders then backed Abdel Moneim Aboul Fotouh, who lost.

Nuclear weapons (Arab Middle East, Iran, and Israel): *See* each individual country's military: non-conventional weapons.

Nusairis: *See* Alawis.

Occupied Arab Territories (1967): During the June 1967 Arab-Israeli War [*q.v.*], Israel occupied the following Arab territories: Egypt's Sinai Peninsula [*q.v.*]; the Gaza Strip [*q.v.*], which had been administered by Egypt since 1949; the West Bank [*q.v.*], including East Jerusalem [*q.v.*], which had been annexed by Jordan in 1950; and Syria's Golan Heights [*q.v.*]. The annexation by Israel of East Jerusalem in late June 1967 and of the Golan Heights in December 1981 was not formally recognized by any foreign government or the United Nations. The UN Security Council Resolution 242 [*q.v.*], adopted in November 1967, demanded "withdrawal of Israel's armed forces from territories occupied in the recent conflict."

After its peace treaty with Egypt in March 1979, Israel returned the Sinai Peninsula to Egypt in three stages, ending in April 1982. Having accepted the Palestine Liberation Organization (PLO) [*q.v.*] as the sole representatives of the Palestinians in November 1974, King Hussein [*q.v.*] of Jordan severed all legal and administrative ties with the West Bank, including East Jerusalem, in July 1988. The Israeli-PLO Accord of September 1993 [*q.v.*] involved interim Palestinian self-rule in Gaza and the West Bank town of Jericho [*q.v.*], followed by an extension of autonomy to other parts of the West Bank, and negotiations on the future of East Jerusalem and the final settlement. In 1994 the Israeli-Syrian talks centered around Syria's insistence on Israel's acceptance of full withdrawal from the Golan Heights on the model of the 1979 Egyptian-Israeli Peace Treaty [*q.v.*]. In 2005, Israel withdrew its forces from the Gaza Strip but maintained control over its airspace and shoreline. In May 2008 indirect negotiations between Israel and Syria started in Istanbul with the Turkish Prime Minister Recep Tayyip Erdogan acting as the mediator. The two sides came very close to a peace agreement but with the resignation of Israeli Prime Minister Ehud Olmert [*q.v.*] in March 2009 over corruption charges, the deal was not finalized. The issue remained unresolved.

Occupied Territories (1967): The term Occupied Territories refers to those areas of Palestine [*q.v.*] under British Mandate that were occupied by Israel in the June 1967 Arab-Israeli War [*q.v.*]—that is, the West Bank [*q.v.*], including East Jerusalem [*q.v.*] and the Gaza Strip [*q.v.*]. With Israel's withdrawal from the Gaza Strip in September 2005, the term applied to the West Bank, including East Jerusalem. In 2008, it was estimated that about one-fifth of all Palestinian male adults had at one time been jailed for offering resistance against the Israeli occupation since 1967.

October 1973 Arab-Israeli War: *See* Arab-Israeli War IV (1973).

oil: In its geological context "oil" is a shortened version of crude oil, or more appropriately petroleum [*q.v.*]. A mixture of hydrocarbons found underground in a gaseous or liquid state, the term *oil* is applied to the liquid form.

It is often greenish or dark brown, and sometimes black. Archaeological excavations in Iraq and Iran indicate that oil in the form of bitumen was used for building roads and for coating the hulls of ships and walls. In more modern times petroleum replaced whale oil in lamps as an illuminating fuel. Its mining involves prospecting, drilling, and extraction. The first commercial drilling for petroleum occurred in 1848 near Baku, the capital of Azerbaijan. It was not until 1859 that oil was struck first in the United States, the site being Titusville, Pennsylvania. In the Middle East [q.v.] the first commercial drilling for petroleum took place in 1908 at Masjid-e Suleiman, Iran [q.v.].

After extraction, often called recovery, oil is refined by distillation, which separates it into fractions of varying volatility. These are put through chemical conversion processes, known as cracking and reforming, to produce a variety of end products: asphalt, cleaning agents, explosives, fertilizers, fibers, gasoline/petrol, jellies, jet fuel, paraffin/kerosene, medicines, naptha, paints, plastics, synthetic rubber, and waxes. Carbon accounts for 82–87 percent of the weight of crude oil, and hydrogen 12–15 percent. Of the three series of compounds contained in oil, the paraffin series is the most extensive, ranging from methane gas to petrol/gasoline to waxes; followed by the naphthene series, yielding volatile liquids to tarry bitumen; and the aromatic series, yielding mainly benzene.

The arrival of the motor car, run on gasoline, at the turn of the 20th century provided the single most important incentive to develop the oil industry. The introduction of a tank powered by an internal combustion engine in 1916 during World War I elevated petroleum to an essential element in modern warfare.

Oil and gas embargoes (1956, 1967, and 1973–74): Oil embargoes were imposed by the Arab petroleum-exporting countries in 1956, 1967, and 1973–74 against Western states that directly aided Israel in its war with Arab adversaries.

During the Suez War [q.v.] of 1956, when Britain, France, and Israel attacked Egypt, the oil workers in Syria blew up the pumping stations along the pipeline carrying petroleum from Iraq to the Mediterranean ports of Banias, Syria, and Tripoli, Lebanon. Popular pressure led the Saudi king, Saud bin Abdul Aziz [q.v.], to embargo oil supplies to Britain and France.

The scale and speed of Israeli attacks on the Egyptian, Syrian, and Jordanian air bases in early June 1967 led Cairo and Amman to accuse Washington and London of direct participation in the Arab-Israeli conflict. An emergency meeting of the Arab petroleum-exporting countries in Baghdad [q.v.] decided to cut off oil supplies to the United States, Britain, and West Germany, but not France, which had condemned the Israeli action. The boycott lasted until the end of August 1967. It led to the formation in January 1968 of the Organization of Arab Petroleum Exporting Countries (OAPEC) [q.v.].

During the October 1973 Arab-Israeli War [q.v.], OAPEC oil ministers met in Kuwait [q.v.] on 16 October. The next day, reacting to U.S. President Richard Nixon's decision to airlift weapons to Israel on a massive scale, OAPEC members decided that "all Arab oil exporting countries shall forthwith cut production by no less than 5 percent of the September production, and maintain the same rate of reduction each month until the Israeli forces are fully withdrawn from all Arab territories occupied during the [June] 1967 [Arab-Israeli] War [q.v.], and the legitimate rights of the Palestinian people are restored." They categorized the consumer countries as friendly, neutral, or hostile to the Arab cause, with the friendly nations to be supplied at the September level, the neutrals at a reduced level, and the hostile ones not at all. They also confirmed the steep price rise decided earlier by the Organization of Petroleum Exporting Countries (OPEC) [q.v.]. Saudi Arabia ordered a 25 percent cut in its output, then running at 8 million barrels a day, but Iraq ignored the OAPEC decision.

Unlike the June 1967 embargo, this one hurt the United States—partly because it was applied during autumn and winter when demand for heating oil was high, and partly because the U.S. had become more dependent on Arab oil than before. The OAPEC move reduced the annual U.S. gross domestic product by $10–20 billion.

The resolve of OAPEC members, especially of Saudi Arabia, began to falter. Aware of the staunchly anti-Communist views of the Saudi monarch, Faisal bin Abdul Aziz [q.v.], Edward Heath, prime minister of Britain (which was not on the Arab oil boycott list), argued publicly in late December that any prolonged oil squeeze would, by weakening the West, strengthen Communism. It did not take long for President Anwar

Sadat [q.v.], working in conjunction with U.S. Secretary of State Henry Kissinger, to convince Faisal to end the boycott. Faisal and Sadat then prevailed upon other members of OAPEC to end the five-month embargo on 18 March 1974 "as a token of Arab goodwill" to the West—even though the Israelis had not withdrawn from anywhere in the Occupied Arab Territories [q.v.] and the legitimate rights of the Palestinian people had not been restored.

Oil and gas industry in Bahrain: Oil reserves: 125 million barrels (2010), 0.1 percent of the world total; gas reserves: 200 billion cu m (2010), 0.1 percent of the world total.

In 1929 the Standard Oil Company of California combined with the Texas Company to form the Bahrain Petroleum Company (BAPCO) and registered it in Canada, a British dominion. BAPCO commenced commercial production in 1932. Output rose from 19,000 barrels per day (bpd) in 1940 to 77,000 in 1970. It then declined, stabilizing around 42,000 bpd in the early 1990s. It then fell to 40,000 bpd in 2011, yet provided the island state with two-fifths of its annual revenue. At this rate the petroleum reserves were expected to last for about 10 years.

In 2002, the upstream Bahrain National Oil Company merged with BAPCO to form the Bahrain Petroleum Company. Three years later, the government replaced the Ministry of Oil with the National Oil and Gas Authority.

Its gas output of 13.1 billion cu m in 2010 was expected to last about 16 years.

Bahrain is a founder member of the Organization of Arab Petroleum Exporting Countries [*q.v.*].

Oil and gas industry in Egypt: Oil reserves: 4.50 billion barrels (2010), 0.3 percent of the world total; gas reserves: 2.20 trillion cu m (2010), 1.2 percent of the world total

Though oil was first struck in 1886 it was not extracted commercially until 1913. It was only after the 1952 revolution that the government tried seriously to develop the industry. The loss of oilfields in the Sinai [*q.v.*] to Israel in 1967 was compensated by fresh discoveries in the Gulf of Suez and the Western Desert.

Following the establishment of the oil ministry in 1973, exploration and extraction gained pace, with output reaching 420,000 barrels per day in 1977 and then stabilizing around 730,000 million barrels per day in 2009. At this production rate, Egypt's reserves will last another 17 years. Egypt, a founder member of the Organization of Arab Petroleum Exporting Countries (OAPEC) [*q.v.*], was suspended from OAPEC in 1979 as a result of the Egyptian-Israeli Peace Treaty [*q.v.*] but was readmitted a decade later.

Gas production, which began in 1974, reached 61.3 billon cu m a year in 2010. At this rate, Egypt's reserves will last 36 years.

Oil and gas industry in Iran: Oil reserves: 137.0 billion barrels (2010), 9.9 percent of the world total; gas reserves: 29.6 trillion cu m (2010), 15.8 percent of the world total.

Oil was found at Masjid-e Suleiman, southwest Iran, in 1908 by a British prospector, William Knox d'Arcy, and commercially mined four years later. His firm expanded to become the Anglo-Persian Oil Company (APOC). With the British admiralty's decision in 1913 to switch from coal to oil, the importance of petroleum increased. To ensure supplies Britain acquired a controlling share in APOC, whose name was changed to the Anglo-Iranian Oil Company (AIOC) following the renaming of Persia as Iran in 1933, and then British Petroleum.

After the nationalization of the AIOC in 1951 and the founding of the National Iranian Oil Company (NIOC) in that year, the West boycotted Iran's oil, thus creating a crisis that culminated in a clash between nationalist Premier Muhammad Mussadiq [*q.v.*] and pro-Western Muhammad Reza Shah Pahlavi [*q.v.*] in August 1953, in which Mussadiq lost. On the advice of the United States, the shah kept the oil nationalization law on the statute books, but downgraded the role of the NIOC. It leased the rights to, and management of, Iranian oil in 1954 for the next 25 years to a Western consortium, with the following share-out: AIOC 40 percent; Royal Dutch Shell 14 percent; five major U.S. oil companies (Exxon, Gulf, Mobil, Socal, and Texaco) 8 percent each; and Compagnie Française des Petroles 6 percent. It was only in 1967 that NIOC was able to market 100,000 barrels per day (bpd) on its own.

Encouraged by the self-reliant policies advocated by the Organization of Petroleum Exporting Countries (OPEC) [*q.v.*], of which Iran was a founder member, the shah pressed the consortium to renegotiate the leasing agreement. In July 1973 the NIOC took over all the operations and ownership of the Western oil consortium. Buoyed by the rise in production at 6 million bpd in 1974, and the quadrupling of oil prices in 1973–74, the shah visualized Iran becoming the fifth most powerful nation in the world. In 1977 the oil revenue of $19.5 billion provided three-quarters of the government's annual income. The strike of oil workers in October 1978 (when oil production was at 5.3 million bpd and domestic consumption at about 800,000 bpd), played a crucial role in the overthrow of the Pahlavi dynasty [q.v.]. The loss of Iran's supplies to the international oil market pushed the price from $13 to $20 a barrel. Therefore, with the resumption of exports at 3.2 million bpd in the spring of 1979, Iran earned more than it did with larger exports before the revolution of February 1979.

Article 81 of the 1979 constitution of the Islamic Republic of Iran forbade "the granting of concessions to foreigners for the formation of companies or institutions dealing with commerce, industry, industry, agriculture, services, or mineral extraction."

With the Western economic boycott of Iran following the takeover of the U.S. Embassy in Tehran in November 1979, there was disruption of the Iranian oil supplies into the market, resulting in another price rise. The outbreak of the Iran-Iraq War [q.v.] in September 1980, primarily in the Iranian oil province of Khuzistan, destabilized the market further, pushing the dollar price into the upper 30s in the spring of 1981. In the mid-

1980s Iran's output fell to 1.4 million bpd, and then stagnated at 2.5 million bpd during the war.

Iran's chief oil terminal at Kharg Island became vulnerable to Iraqi air attacks. Iran survived by pumping oil at Kharg into its own tankers, which delivered the commodity to its customers at its offshore islands in the Lower Gulf [q.v.] outside the range of the Iraqi bombers.

The steep decline in the oil price from $28 to below $10 a barrel, caused by the flooding of the market by Saudi Arabia and Kuwait during the spring of 1986, reduced Tehran's oil income from $13.1 billion in 1985 to $7.2 billion, earned by exporting 1.6 million bpd. This severely damaged its ability to conduct the war, which ended in August 1988.

The exigencies of the long running Iran-Iraq War [q.v.] compelled the government to seek foreign assistance to reverse the continuing degrading of its oil industry. The Petroleum Law of 1987 allowed agreements between the Ministry of Petroleum, state-owned companies, and local and foreign persons or legal entities. This opened the door for a variant of a production-sharing agreement (PSA). According to a PSA contract, a hydrocarbon corporation bears the cost of exploring and developing a field and is then allowed to extract enough oil and/or gas to recover the capital and operational costs it has incurred—after which it shares the production with the government. The share varies from 80 to 85 percent for the government and the rest for the company.

The variant that Iran used was called the Buy-Back Agreement (BBA), valid for 5 to 10 years; it is also known as a short-term service contract. The chief difference between the PSA and the BBA is that in the former case the foreign hydrocarbon corporation shares proprietary rights with the government, whereas in the latter case it merely receives an agreed fee in cash or kind from the state, nothing more. In return for the costs incurred by the foreign firm, it receives an agreed share of extracted oil—enough to give it a return of 10 to 15 percent on its investment—with the stipulation of handing over the operation of the oil field to the ministry of petroleum at the end of the contract. Initially, Tehran used BBAs only for offshore fields.

After the eight year war Iran increased its output steadily from 2.87 million bpd in 1989 to 3.62 million bpd in 1993, with exports around 2.5 million bpd and oil revenue at $14.5 billion. The government decided to give contracts to foreign petroleum corporations to develop off shore fields on the basis of production sharing agreements (PSAs).

In 1998, during the presidency of the reformist Muhammad Khatami [*q.v.*], the parliament approved the government's plan to open up much of the hydrocarbon sector, including onshore fields, to foreign companies on the basis of production sharing agreements. The increased foreign participation involved energy corporations from Brazil, Britain, Canada, France, Italy, Malaysia, the Netherlands, Norway, Russia, and Spain. By 2009, the contracts signed by the state-owned Chinese oil companies amounted to $120 billion.

At the 2010 oil output rate of 4.25 million bpd, Iran's reserves will last 88 years.

At 9,700 sq. km the North Dome-South Pars gas field is the largest in the world, with South Pars, measuring 3,700 sq. km, lying in the Iranian waters. The aggregate recoverable gas reserves of the North Dome-South Pars are the equivalent of 230 billion barrels of oil, second only to Saudi Arabia's reserves of the conventional oil.

Discovered in 1990, South Pars gas field came on stream in 2002. Its numerous phases have been developed by Iran's Petropars and such foreign corporations as Petronas of Malaysia, ENI of Italy, Repsol of Spain, Gazprom of Russia, and Royal Dutch Shell.

With the world's second-largest gas reserves after Russia's being consumed at the rate of 138.5 billion cu m a year in 2010, it will take Iran 214 years to exhaust them.

Oil and gas industry in Iraq: Oil reserves: 115.0 billion barrels (2010), 8.3 percent of the world total; gas reserves: 3.2 trillion cu m (2010), 1.7 percent of the world total.

The efforts of the Turkish Petroleum Company (TPC), owned largely by the Anglo-Persian Oil Company (APOC) after World War I, bore fruit in 1927 when it struck oil in commercial quantities in the Kirkuk area. This increased the strategic and economic value of Palestine [*q.v.*], since it provided a gateway to the Iraqi oilfields through the British protectorate of Transjordan (now Jordan). Under Washington's pressure the TPC was reconstituted in 1931 as the Iraq Petroleum Company (IPC)—a 23.5 percent share each was held by government-owned British, French, and Dutch companies and two U.S. corporations, the remaining 6 percent by Partex, owned by C.S. Gulbenkian, a Portuguese businessman.

The oil output had reached such proportions by World War II that Britain intervened militarily to overthrow the nationalist government of Rashid Ali Gailani [q.v.] in 1941. In the late 1940s the Iraqi government required IPC to pay half of its profit as tax. After the 1958 revolution, Abdul Karim Qasim [q.v.] issued a decree in 1961 that deprived IPC of 99.5 percent of the 160,000 sq. mi./414,400 sq. km originally allocated to it for prospecting, covering almost the whole country, including oil-rich Rumeila [q.v.] in the south. The government set up its own Iraq National Oil Company (INOC). IPC challenged the law, and a partial compromise was reached in 1969.

Meanwhile, government decrees of August and October 1967 gave the INOC wider powers and the exclusive right to develop the Rumeila oilfield. To pressure Baghdad to reverse its hard-line policy, IPC halved the output of the Kirkuk oilfields in March 1972. In mid-May 1972 Iraq warned IPC that it would end negotiations if its demands were not met within a fortnight. They were not, and IPC was nationalized in June. This marked the end of an era that had begun in 1912 under the rule of an Ottoman sultan.

The Soviet Union played an important role in giving confidence to Iraq to go ahead with nationalizing IPC. It also helped to develop Iraq's petroleum industry in exploration and extraction—as in the Rumeila oilfields—and in refining. The general message of the Soviets was that Iraq need not be totally dependent on Western capital and/or expertise in this industry.

Once it had consolidated its position, Iraq nationalized American and Dutch interests in the Basrah Petroleum Company, operating in the south. It did so during the October 1973 Arab-Israeli War [q.v.], when feelings in the Arab world were running high against the United States and the Netherlands, which openly and materially sided with Israel. On the other hand, Baghdad did not join the Organization of Arab Petroleum Exporting Countries (OAPEC) [q.v.] oil embargo against the states that aided Israel in the war.

The fivefold increase in revenue from petroleum exports in the mid-1970s provided an unprecedented boost to the morale of the ruling Baath Socialist Party [q.v.], which had seized power in 1968. The government raised the salaries of its civil servants and military personnel substantially. Its ambitious Five-Year Plan, 1976–80, promised a prosperous future for all. In 1979 and 1980, when the national population was less than 13 million, the oil output exceeded 3.5 million barrels per day (bpd), with exports at 3.3 million bpd, and oil income at $21.3 billion and $26.3 billion respectively. The amended constitution of 1974 outlawed giving proprietary rights over natural resources to local or foreign private companies.

The war with Iran started in September 1980, and oil output fell to 800,000 bpd in 1982. It rose to 1.75 million bpd in 1986. But with petroleum selling below $10 a barrel, Iraq's oil income plummeted to $7 billion a year. Baghdad was able to withstand the price crash because of the large grants it received from Saudi Arabia and Kuwait. Later, Iraq built a pipeline that connected with a Saudi pipeline leading to the Red Sea port of Yanbu, thus supplementing its earlier pipeline running to the Turkish port of Dortyol.

Demanding parity with Iran in its export quota, from October 1986 to May 1988 Iraq ignored the output quotas agreed by the Organization of Petroleum Exporting Countries (OPEC) [*q.v.*]. Following the end of the Iran-Iraq War [*q.v.*] in August 1988, Iraq returned to the OPEC system when OPEC agreed to parity between Iraq and Iran, at 2.64 million bpd. The following year Iraqi production reached 2.83 million bpd, with exports at 2.4 million bpd and export earnings at $12 billion. In the first half of 1990 production was 3.1 million bpd, but flooding of the market by Kuwait and the United Arab Emirates depressed the price from $18 to $12 a barrel, causing Iraq to lose nearly $20 million a day.

With Iraq's invasion of Kuwait in early August 1990, followed by immediate economic sanctions by the United Nations, Baghdad's oil exports ceased. From then on, Iraqi oil output fell to 400,000 bpd, enough for domestic needs, lowering the annual average for 1990 to two million bpd. Three years later the figure was 455,000 bpd, including the 65,000 bpd that Jordan was allowed to import from Iraq as a special case.

Starting in December 1996, when Iraq was allowed by the UN Security Council to export enough petroleum to earn $2 billion in six months, the output rose. With the Security Council raising the six-monthly limit to $5.2 billion in the spring of 1998, the

production for that year reached 2.2 million bpd. Further improvement occurred when the Security Council sanctioned sufficient funds for Iraq to repair its dilapidated oil industry. When the Council removed the ceiling on Iraq's oil output in December 1999, the figure for 2000 topped 2.63 million bpd, with Baghdad's oil exports earnings reaching $7.1 billion in the first half of the year.

Following the Anglo-American invasion of Iraq [*q.v.*] in 2003, the petroleum production went into free fall, reduced to almost half of the pre-war total, just enough for domestic consumption. It took four years for Iraq to manage to maintain a steady rate of oil exports through official channels.

Only in 2007 was the Iraqi government able to present its national oil and gas legislation to the parliament. It contained a provision for 20-year Exploration and Development Production Risk Service Contracts, also called Technical Support Agreements. But the passage of the draft legislation got stalled, due to the resistance of the Kurdish [*q.v.*] deputies. Instead of waiting for a law applicable to all of Iraq, the Kurdistan Regional Government (KRG) [*q.v.*] got its regional assembly to pass a law with a provision for 25-year Exploration and Production Sharing Agreements (EPSAs). It went on to sign 29 such contracts with foreign oil corporations.

The basic difference between a production sharing contract and a service contract is that, whereas the former allows a foreign oil corporation to share proprietary rights with the government, the latter entitles it to receive only an agreed fee in cash or kind from the state. Therefore, some experts in Iraq and outside argued that by signing the EPSAs, the KRG had violated the article on natural resources in the 1974 constitution which, in the absence of a fresh law on hydrocarbons, remained in force. Disregarding this argument, the KRG stood by the contracts it had signed.

Meanwhile, the Baghdad government awarded contracts to foreign corporations during the second half of 2009 and early 2010, thus reversing the expulsion of the last non-Iraqi oil company from Iraq in 1972. But these were service contracts, and the total share of foreign companies in a joint venture was limited to 75 percent of the equity. In a service contract an energy firm is paid a fixed fee for each oil barrel it extracts. The bulk of these contracts in 2009, covering reserves of nearly 40 billion barrels, went to such non-Western energy corporations as China National Petroleum Corporation (CNPC), Petronas of Malaysia, and Sonangol of Angola. Among the contracts signed in January 2010, covering 62 billion barrels in reserves, Exxon was the only American oil company to win a contract for West Qurna Phase One oilfield, with reserves of 8.7 billion barrels, in a consortium where it held 60 percent interest. All other winners were non-American, ranging from CNPC to Sonangol, Petronas, and Gazprom Neft of Russia.

Despite their best efforts, by mid-2012, the Baghdad government and the KRG had not succeeded in resolving their differences on a national oil and gas law.

Iraq's oil output in 2009 was 2.46 million bpd. At that rate its oil reserves will last 128 years.

Gas production, starting in 1966, rose to 55.2 million cu m per day in 1979, but then declined sharply due to the conflict with Iran in the 1980s. With its output running at 1.3 billion cu m a year in 2009, it will be several centuries before the reserves are exhausted.

Oil and gas industry in Israel: Oil was first found in southern Israel in 1955 near Ashkelon. The output peaked at 6,000 barrels per day (bpd). By 2008, more than 17 million barrels of oil had been extracted from a field with the recoverable reserves of 19 million barrels. In 2011 the output was down to a few dozen bpd.

The production of natural gas, found in the Dead Sea region, remained steady around 700 million cu m a year. And by 2009, the reserves of an offshore gas field near Ashkelon were down to 10 billion cu m from the initial 32 billion cu m. In that year, a new find 50 mi./80 km off Haifa [q.v.] added 240 billion cu m of gas to the national total. At the present rate of consumption, gas deposits would be exhausted in 21 years.

Oil and gas industry in Jordan: There is no oil extraction industry in Jordan. The production of natural gas, found first in the northeast in 1987, was less than 350 million cu m a year in 2000, with the country's total deposits estimated at 6.44 billion cu m, or 0.3 percent of the global total. In 2009 it produced 250 million cu m of gas.

Oil and gas industry in Kuwait: Oil reserves: 101.5 billion barrels (2010), 7.3 percent of the world total; gas reserves: 1.8 trillion cu m (2010), 1.0 percent of the global total.

The Kuwait Oil Company (KOC), owned equally by the Anglo-Iranian Oil Company (now British Petroleum) and the (U.S.) Gulf Oil Company, obtained petroleum concessions in Kuwait in 1934 for 74 years. Commercial extraction began in 1938, the Burgan field proving to be a gigantic reserve of oil. But the extraction of oil had to wait until after the end of World War II in 1945. Due to the Western boycott of the nationalized oil company in Iran in 1951, the output of Kuwaiti petroleum rose sharply. In 1956 Kuwait became the leading oil exporter in the region, with a total output of 1.1 million barrels per day (bpd), a position it maintained for a decade.

Pursuing the self-reliance policy of the Organization of Petroleum Exporting Countries (OPEC) [q.v.], Kuwait, one of OPEC's founder members, acquired 25 percent of the shares of KOC in October 1972, with provision for a further 2.5 percent annual increase in shareholding over the next decade. But after the October 1973 Arab-Israeli War [q.v.] and a dramatic jump in oil prices, the government acquired a majority holding in KOC immediately, buying the rest of the shares in March 1975. It also responded positively to parliament's demand that oil output be limited to a maximum of 2 million bpd.

Following the disruption of Iraqi oil supplies due to the outbreak of the Iran-Iraq War [q.v.] in September 1980, Kuwait volunteered to meet Iraq's obligations. Later it used oil as a weapon when, in alliance with Saudi Arabia, it flooded the market in early 1986, depressing the price from $28 to $10 a barrel, thus severely damaging Iran's ability to finance its war. The negative impact on Iraq was compensated by subventions to it from Kuwait and Saudi Arabia. After the war's end in August 1988, Kuwait insisted that Iraq should repay the $10–12 billion loaned to it by way of the oil supplied to Iraq's customers during the conflict. When Baghdad refused, Kuwait began to flood the petroleum market by exceeding its OPEC quota of 1.5 million bpd by 40 percent, thus depressing the price and hurting Iraq. This was the background to the Iraqi invasion and occupation of Kuwait in early August 1990.

Just before retreating at the end of the 1991 Gulf War [q.v.], Iraqi troops set ablaze 640 of Kuwait's 790 oil wells. After the cease-fire the Kuwaiti government successfully concentrated on extinguishing the fires and repairing the damage to the industry.

In 1992 OPEC gave a special dispensation to Kuwait to produce without a fixed quota. In early 1993 OPEC fixed Kuwait's share at 1.6 million bpd, one-fifth less than its current output. Though its quota was increased to 1.7 million bpd later in the year, Kuwait insisted on 2 million bpd and produced nearly that much. In 2010 its output was 2.50 million bpd. At this rate Kuwait's reserves will last another 110 years.

Kuwait's gas reserves, being consumed at the rate of 11.6 billion cu m a year in 2009, will last until 2163.

Oil and gas industry in Oman: Oil reserves: 5.5 billion barrels (2010), 0.4 percent of the global total; gas reserves: 0.7 trillion cu m (2010), 0.4

percent of the world total.

Exploration by the Anglo-Iranian Oil Company (AIOC), which obtained concessions in 1925, yielded nothing. In 1937 a subsidiary of the Iraq Petroleum Company (IPC), Petroleum Concessions (Oman), received a 75-year concession for the whole country except Dhofar province, where a separate concession was granted to Dhofar Cities Service Petroleum Corporation in 1953. In that year Petroleum Development Oman (PDO), the successor to Petroleum Concessions (Oman), started serious exploration. Due to the continued failure to strike oil, all corporations except Royal Dutch Shell and Partex, owned by C.S. Gulbenkian, withdrew, leaving them respectively with 85 percent and 15 percent of the shares. The reconstituted company found oil in commercial quantities in 1962 in the central region. In 1967, when exports started, Partex sold part of its shares to Compagnie Française des Petroles.

Oil revenue rose from $21 million in 1964 to $117 million in 1970, when Sultan Said bin Taimur [*q.v.*] was succeeded by his son Qaboos [*q.v.*]. Rising income from oil, though modest by Gulf standards, enabled Qaboos to build up Oman's infrastructure and provide public services to his subjects. In 1975 his government acquired a 60 percent share of the PDO, leaving the rest with Royal Dutch Shell (34 percent) and Compagnie Française des Petroles. During the 1970s oil output averaged 300,000 bpd. Production in Dhofar, which started in 1980, boosted the total. After reaching a nationwide peak of 961,000 barrels per day in 2001, output started declining.

At its production of 865,000 bpd in 2010, Oman's reserves will last 17 years.

Oman's gas reserves, being consumed at the rate of 27.4 billion cu m a year in 2010, will last until 2049.

Oil and gas industry in Qatar: Oil reserves: 25.9 billion barrels (2010), 1.9 percent of the world total; gas reserves: 25.3 trillion cu m (2010), 13.5 percent of the global total.

The concession given in 1925 to the Anglo-Persian Oil Company, which yielded nothing, was transferred in 1935 to an Iraq Petroleum Company subsidiary, Petroleum Development (Qatar)—later renamed Qatar National Petroleum Company (QNPC). It struck oil in 1939, but work was interrupted by World War II and did not resume until 1948. Output rose from 32,000 barrels per day (bpd) in 1950 to 600,000 bpd in 1973.

After its independence in 1971, Qatar, a member of the Organization of Petroleum Exporting Countries (OPEC) [*q.v.*] since 1961, pursued self-reliant policies. A dramatic increase in its oil revenue due to a sharp price rise in 1973–74 enabled the Qatari government to buy the QNPC in two stages, in 1974 and 1976. In 1977 the state-owned Qatar General Petroleum Company (QGPC) became solely responsible for oil and gas production. After a peak of 510,000 bpd in 1979, output averaged 350,000 bpd during the 1980s. Rising steadily from 420,000 bpd in 1991, it reached 757,000 bpd in 2000, when the name of the owning company was changed to Qatar Petroleum. At the output of 1.57 million bpd in 2010, the Qatari oil reserves will last until 2055.

At 9,700 sq. km the North Dome-South Pars gas field is the largest in the world, with North Dome's 6,000 sq. km lying in Qatari territorial waters and the rest in Iranian waters. The aggregate recoverable gas reserves of the North Dome-South Pars are the equivalent of 230 billion barrels of conventional oil.

Discovered in 1971, the production at the North Dome Qatari side started in 1989. In a decade the output grew to 22.1 billion cu m a year. Qatar began exporting the commodity as Liquefied Natural Gas (LNG) in specially made tankers. Its first shipment was to Japan in 1997. At the 2010 production rate of 116.7 billion cu m a year, the Qatari reserves will last 217 years.

Oil and gas industry in Saudi Arabia:

Oil reserves: 264.5 billion barrels (2010), 19.1 percent of the world total; gas reserves: 8.0 trillion cu m (2010), 4.3 percent of the global total.

In 1933 the Standard Oil Company of California (SOCAL) secured exploration rights in the eastern Hasa province with preferential rights elsewhere in the kingdom. In 1936 SOCAL invited Texaco to form a joint company called Caltex. It struck oil in 1938. World War II intervened. Exports resumed in 1946. Two years later Caltex expanded into a consortium of four U.S. companies—SOCAL (later Chevron) 30 percent, Texaco 30 percent, Standard Oil Company of New Jersey (later Esso, then Exxon) 30 percent, and Mobil Oil 10 percent—called Arabian American Oil Company (Aramco). Output rose so sharply that Aramco's earnings jumped from $2.8 million in

1944 to $115 million five years later. The Saudi monarch decreed that Aramco should pay half of its profits as tax.

In 1962, as part of its administrative and fiscal reform, the government set up the General Petroleum and Mineral Organization, known as Petromin, to increase state participation in the oil and gas industry. Petroleum output shot up from 1.3 million barrels per day (bpd) in 1940 to 8 million bpd in 1973 before the Arab-Israeli War [q.v.] in October. Saudi Arabia joined the oil embargo imposed by the Organization of Arab Petroleum Exporting Countries (OAPEC) [q.v.] during the fighting, and ensured its continuation. Equally, when it decided to see it end in March 1974, its will prevailed at the OAPEC.

Due to increased output and a sharp rise in price in 1973–74, Saudi oil income reached $22.57 billion in 1974, a 36-fold increase in a decade. Among other things this allowed Riyadh to pursue the self-reliance policy advocated by the Organization of Petroleum Exporting Countries (OPEC) [q.v.], of which it was a founder member. Saudi Arabia acquired a 25 percent share of Aramco, with provision for a further 2.5 percent annual increase in shareholding until the total reached 51 percent.

To fill the gap created in late 1978 by the stoppage of oil exports from Iran, which was in the midst of revolutionary turmoil, Saudi Arabia increased its output to 9.5 million bpd in 1979 and 10 million bpd a year later. Political turbulence in Iran after the Islamic revolution [q.v.] raised the price from $13 a barrel in early 1979 to $28 in May 1980, increasing Saudi

Arabia's oil income to $106 billion in 1980. This enabled it to buy up the remaining Aramco shares, thus completing the nationalization of Aramco announced in 1978. It renamed the company Saudi Aramco.

The outbreak of the Iran-Iraq War [*q.v.*] in September, resulting in extensive damage to both countries' oil industries and a drop in their exports, led to higher prices during 1981, reaching a spot price peak of $41 a barrel. With Saudi production steady at 10 million bpd, oil income reached a record $110 billion in 1981. To aid Iraq in its war against Iran, Saudi Arabia volunteered to honor Iraq's oil contracts.

When, due to high prices, worldwide demand for oil began to decline, Saudi Arabia cut its output sharply, first to 6.6 million bpd (1982) and then 4.8 million bpd (1984), to stabilize the price at $29 a barrel. It thus underlined its role as the swing producer within OPEC, with the leverage to adjust its production to stabilize the price and maintain the overall OPEC output within the agreed limits. However, as a result, its oil income fell to $27 billion in 1985 when its output was 3.6 million bpd.

Partly to increase OPEC's overall share of the world market in the face of price cutting by non-OPEC producers, and partly to depress the oil income of Iran, thus weakening its capacity to prolong its war with Iraq, Saudi Arabia, in alliance with Kuwait, started to flood the market by raising their production by an average of 50 percent. This depressed the price from $28 a barrel in December 1985 to below $10 a barrel in July, and began to hurt the kingdom's economy. King Fahd bin Abdul Aziz [*q.v.*] intervened

in October, and sacked Ahmad Zaki Yamani [*q.v.*], the oil minister since 1962, and reversed his policy to raise prices. Fahd's stance prevailed at OPEC, which cut its total production by 7.5 percent to 15.8 million bpd for the first half of 1987, the Saudi share being 4.1 million bpd. The price stabilized at little over the OPEC reference level of $18 a barrel.

It held until the spring of 1990 when flooding of the market by Kuwait and the United Arab Emirates depressed the price to $12 a barrel. However, the Iraqi invasion and occupation of Kuwait in early August caused the spot price of oil to shoot up to $28 a barrel. An emergency meeting of OPEC allowed members to increase their output beyond the allocated quota due to the loss of 4 million bpd of oil previously exported by Iraq and Kuwait. With an average output of 6.84 million bpd, Saudi Arabia ended 1990 with oil income of $40.7 billion, more than twice the average figure for the past four years.

With output running at 8.6–8.9 million bpd during the early 1990s, and the price fluctuating between $12 and $22 a barrel, Saudi Arabia's oil income in 1993 was nearly $43 billion. Oil prices fell sharply in 1998 due to the reduced demand in the Asian market caused by an economic downturn. Saudi Arabia played a leading role in securing output cuts by OPEC and leading non-OPEC producers in 1999, and succeeded in getting the prices stabilized in the $22–28 per barrel range. By and large this range held for the next few years.

Those who expected that following the overthrow of the Saddam Hussein [*q.v.*] regime in Iraq in 2003, the Iraqi oil industry would come under American management, resulting in an upsurge in output and leading to the fall in price to $20 a barrel, were disappointed.

In 2010, Saudi Arabia yielded its place as the holder of the world's largest oil reserves to Venezuela. At 10 million bpd output in 2010, its reserves will be exhausted by 2082.

Saudi Arabia has the globe's fourth-largest gas reserves. Its gas industry got started in the early 1980s. By the turn of the century it reached 50 billion cu m a year. At its 2010 rate of 84 billion cu m a year, the Saudi reserves will last 95 years.

Oil and gas industry in Syria: Oil reserves: 2.5 billion barrels (2010), 0.2 percent of the world total; gas reserves: 0.3 trillion cu m (2010), 0.15 percent of the world total.

The Iraq Petroleum Company (IPC), which acquired oil concessions in Syria [q.v.] during the French Mandate (1920–41), surrendered these to the government in 1951 after having failed to find petroleum. The concessions given in the mid-1950s to a West German-led consortium and an American company, which led to the discovery of petroleum, were cancelled when the Baathist [q.v.] regime nationalized the oil industry in 1964 and set up the Syrian Petroleum Company (SPC) under the aegis of the General Petroleum Authority. Modest production started in 1968. In the mid-1970s Syria granted concessions to foreign companies. Their discoveries a decade later, especially in the country's northeast corner, nearly doubled the national output to 400,000 bpd in 1990. Continued

steady increase took the figure to 600,000 bpd in 1995, when a decline set in, reducing the total to 385,000 bpd in 2010. At this rate, the Syrian reserves will last until 2028.

Natural gas production started in 1994, and peaked at 6.4 billion cu m a year in 2004, and then began declining. It increased to 7.8 billion cu m its 2010. At this rate Syria's gas reserves will last 39 years.

Oil and gas industry in United Arab Emirates (UAE): Oil reserves: 97.8 billion barrels (2009), 7.1 percent of the world total; gas reserves: 6.0 trillion cu m (2010), 3.2 percent of the global total.

In 1939 the Trucial Coast Development Oil Company, later Abu Dhabi Petroleum company (ADPC), subsidiary of the Iraq Petroleum Company (IPC), acquired exploration rights in Abu Dhabi Emirate [q.v.]. Another company to secure concessions was Abu Dhabi Marines Area (ADMA), formed in 1954 by British Petroleum and Compagnie Française des Petroles. Oil production started in 1962 on a modest scale. By 1978 the ADPC and ADMA had been restructured into the Abu Dhabi Company for Onshore Oil (ADCO) and ADMA-OPCO for offshore work. These companies accounted for 93 percent of Abu Dhabi's oil output, which amounted to 1.8 million barrels per day (bpd) on the eve of Iraq's invasion of Kuwait in August 1990.

Oil was discovered in Dubai Emirate [q.v.] in 1966 by the Dubai Petroleum Company (DPC), which in 1961 had taken over IPC's concession, held since 1937. Commercial production, which started in 1969, rose to

420,000 bpd at the time of Iraq's attack on Kuwait in August 1990. Petroleum was struck in Sharjah Emirate [*q.v.*] in 1974, and production reached 60,000 bpd in mid-1990. Oil was found in Ras al-Khaima Emirate [*q.v.*] in 1984, but by the late 1980s output had not exceeded 12,000 bpd.

The two sharp rises in the price of oil in the mid and late 1970s made the UAE, with less than a million people, one of the top five richest countries in the world. In July 1990 the UAE was producing 2.3 million bpd, more than twice the quota fixed by the Organization of Petroleum Exporting Countries (OPEC) [*q.v.*], of which it had been a member since 1974, thus causing the price to fall to $12 a barrel, a third below the $18 OPEC reference price.

With the temporary loss of Iraqi and Kuwaiti oil to the world market, the UAE raised its output, which reached 2.6 million bpd in 1991, stabilized around 2.4 million bpd (marginally above the OPEC limit of 2.24 million bpd) and earned the country an annual income of some $14 billion.

Another bump in production came with the Anglo-American invasion of Iraq [*q.v.*] in 2003 and its aftermath, when Iraq's oil exports nose-dived. At the 2010 output of 2.85 million bpd, the UAE's reserves will last until 2104.

With the sixth-largest gas reserves in the world being consumed at a rate of 51.0 billion cu m a year in 2010, it will take 117 years to exhaust them.

Oil and gas industry in Yemen: Oil reserves: 2.7 billion barrels (2010), 0.2 percent of the world total; gas reserves: 0.5 trillion cu m (2010), 0.25 percent of the world total.

The efforts of the state-owned oil company in North Yemen to find petroleum from the 1970s onward failed. However, in 1984 the Yemeni subsidiary of the United States-based Hunt Oil Company discovered oil in commercial quantities. Production increased rapidly and reached 200,000 barrels per day (bpd) on the eve of the unification of North and South Yemen in May 1990. In South Yemen oil was struck in commercial quantities in 1987, and output remained at 10,000 bpd until the unification of the two Yemens in 1990. The aggregate Yemeni output rose steadily, reaching the peak of 457,000 bpd in 2002, and then began declining. At its 2010 production rate of 264,000 bpd, Yemen's reserves will last until 2038.

With its gas deposits being consumed at the rate of 6.2 billion cu m a year in 2001, Yemen's reserves will last until 2074.

Oil industry, Middle East: Of the world's proven oil reserves of 1,383 billion barrels in 2010, the Middle East [*q.v.*] had 753 billion barrels, or 54.7 percent of the total, with 54 percent in the Gulf States [*q.v.*], Iran and Iraq, and the rest in Egypt, Syria, and Yemen.

Oil was first extracted commercially in 1908 by a British prospector, William Knox D'Arcy, at Masjid-e Suleiman in southwest Iran. His firm expanded to become the Anglo-Persian Oil Company (APOC). With the British admiralty's decision in 1913 to switch from coal to oil, the importance of petroleum increased. To ensure supplies Britain acquired a controlling share in APOC. It also imposed a series of agreements on the rulers of Kuwait (1913), Bahrain (1914), Qatar (1916), the Lower Gulf emirates (mid-1920s), and Oman (mid-1920s), whereby they were barred from giving oil concessions to non-British companies without London's prior permission. The terms of oil concessions to British interests included long duration (60–95 years), vast areas (160,000 sq. mi./414,000 sq. km in Iraq, more than 500,000 sq. mi./1,295,000 sq. km in Saudi Arabia), exemption from local taxes, and paltry royalties to the host country, with the royalty treated as a rental proportional to the size of the yield, irrespective of the price of the extracted commodity. It varied between 3–8 British pennies/8–20 American cents per barrel of 35 imperial gallons.

After World War I, APOC acquired three-quarters of the shares of the Turkish Petroleum Company (TPC), which had originally consisted of British, French, and German interests. The TPC had started to operate in Iraq in 1912 after winning an oil concession from the Ottoman sultan. APOC found oil in commercial quantities in the northern region of Kirkuk in 1927. Petroleum on a commercial scale was next discovered in Bahrain in 1932, followed by Kuwait and Saudi Arabia in 1938.

By then the Anglo-Persian Oil Company had changed its name to the Anglo-Iranian Oil Company (now British Petroleum) following the renaming of Persia as Iran in 1933; and the Iraq Petroleum Company (IPC) had been created in 1931. Government-owned British, French, and Dutch companies and two privately owned American companies each held 23.5 percent of the shares of the IPC; the remaining 6 percent held by Partex, owned by C.S. Gulbenkian, a Portuguese businessman who had acted as a middleman during the Ottoman times.

After a halt in production during World War II, output rose sharply as more oil fields were discovered and tapped. By the late 1960s production in the Gulf [*q.v.*] amounted to 30 percent of the global total. In 2001 the Gulf region's output was 28.5 percent of the world aggregate and 70 percent of the Organization of Petroleum Exporting Countries' (OPEC) [*q.v.*] total.

The recent histories of the following countries have been shaped largely or exclusively by oil: all six Gulf States [*q.v.*], Iran, Iraq, and Palestine [*q.v.*] under the British Mandate.

Oil measurements (Based on world average crude oil gravity):

1 barrel = 35 Imperial gallons/42 U.S. gallons

1 short ton (2,000 lbs.) = 7.00 barrels (used in North America)

1 metric ton (2,205 lbs.) = 7.30 barrels (also called tonne)

1 long ton (2,240 lbs.) = 7.42 barrels (used in Britain)

1 tonne (2,205 lbs.) = 7.30 barrels

CONVERSION TABLE:

Long tons per year to barrels per day, divide by 49.2

Metric tons per year to barrels per day, divide by 50.0

Short tons per year to barrels per day, divide by 52.14

Tonnes per year to barrels per day, divide by 50.0

Oil prices: In the early days of the petroleum industry, when Standard Oil Company had a virtual monopoly in the United States, it fixed the price. Between 1861 and 1880, the average worldwide price of a barrel of oil fluctuated between U.S. $1 and $9 in money of the day, equivalent to U.S. $10 to $90 in 2001. Following the breakup of Standard Oil Company in 1911 in the wake of the anti-trust law, a free market of sorts emerged. After settling down to $1 a barrel the price rose to $3.50 during World War I ($28 in today's money), and did not return to its $1 level until the early 1930s. During World War II the price rose modestly, but picked up during postwar reconstruction.

After World War II seven oil majors set up a cartel. It exercised a stranglehold on the oil industry, from exploration to retailing, and fixed prices to suit the interests of its members. The price moved up to $2 a barrel in the wake of the loss of Iranian supplies from 1951 to 1953 and the Suez War [q.v.] of 1956, which closed the Suez Canal [q.v.]. On the eve of the October 1973 Arab-Israeli War [q.v.] the average price of a barrel of oil from the Gulf [q.v.] region was $2.55. Between mid-October 1973 and 1 January 1974 the price of oil was raised from $2.55 to $11.65 a barrel ($43 in today's cash) by the Organization of Petroleum Exporting Countries (OPEC) [q.v.], with the host government's average earnings rising fivefold, from $1.38 to $7 a barrel. For the next four years price increases kept pace with inflation, with oil in late 1978 selling for $14 a barrel.

The overthrow of Muhammad Reza Shah Pahlavi [q.v.] of Iran in early 1979, partly caused by a strike in the Iranian oil industry, raised the price from $14 to $28 a barrel within a few months. The outbreak of the Iran-Iraq War [q.v.] in September 1980, resulting in extensive damage to both countries' oil industries and a drop in their oil exports, led to higher prices during 1981, reaching a spot-price peak of $47 a barrel (equivalent to today's $78) but stabilizing around $34 a barrel in the early 1980s.

On 30 March 1983, OPEC received a blow when New York Mercantile Exchange (Nymex) introduced crude oil futures. This development, introduced against the background of falling oil demand in the West, weakened OPEC's price-setting clout further. Prices started sliding. Saudi Arabia, the largest OPEC producer, curtailed its output sharply to stabilize the price at $29 a barrel in 1984.

To meet the price-cutting challenge by non-OPEC Western producers such as Britain and Norway, and to enlarge OPEC's share of the market and damage Iran's war effort, Saudi Arabia and Kuwait started to flood the oil market from December 1985, depressing the price from $28 to less than $10 in July 1986. Hurt by the steep fall in its oil revenue, Saudi Arabia reversed the strategy, and in alliance with Iran, encouraged OPEC to aim for $18 a barrel by cutting overall production. By and large this aim was achieved, the dollar price rising to the low 20s in the spring of 1989.

However, in early 1990, once again for political reasons (this time to put pressure on Iraq), Kuwait and the United Arab Emirates [q.v.] overproduced and reduced the price to $11 a barrel. The Iraqi invasion and occupation of Kuwait in early August caused the spot price of oil to reach $28 a barrel within a few weeks, the dollar price briefly rising to the high 30s. An emergency meeting of OPEC allowed members to increase their output beyond their allocated quotas because of the loss of the 4 million barrels per day (bpd) that had previously been exported by Iraq and Kuwait.

After the 1991 Gulf War [*q.v.*], the price fluctuated around $20 until mid-1992, when Kuwait returned to its prewar production levels and resumed its exports. During the next two years the price hovered around $16 a barrel (equivalent to today's $20), only $2 above the prevalent figure in 1978. The reentry of Iraq, albeit on a limited scale, into the oil export market in December 1996 had a depressing effect on prices. They fell sharply in 1998 due to the reduced demand in the Asian market caused by an economic downturn combined with OPEC's decision to increase output. Saudi Arabia played a leading role in securing output cuts by OPEC and such leading non-OPEC producers as Mexico, Norway, Oman, and Russia in 1999, and succeeded in pushing up the prices to the $22–28 per barrel range. By and large this range held for the next few years, with the price shooting the $30 mark in 2000.

At the turn of the century, oil prices since 1861 as computed in terms of the 2001 U.S. dollar, could be summarized as follows. Between 1861 and 1880, the price of a barrel of crude oil fluctuated between $10 and $90. A century later, in 1960, it was still $11 a barrel. The 1973 Arab-Israeli War and the 1979 Iranian Islamic revolution [*q.v.*] pushed the price to a peak of

$78 in 1980. It then declined to $13 in 1998 (registering a decline of 70 percent in real terms since 1981)—reaching its mid-1950s level—before rising above $30 in 2000, and then falling to $27.

It was in the aftermath of the Anglo-American invasion of Iraq [*q.v.*] in 2003 that the price of a barrel of crude oil crossed the $30 mark. It kept rising until it hit the peak of $147 in July 2008. Against the background of the deepening recession worldwide—except in China and India—that started in September 2008, the price collapsed to $33 in December. With OPEC cutting overall output by 4.2 million bpd, and the GDPs improving during the second half of 2009, the price stabilized around $75 a barrel. Another reason for the price recovery was that fresh petroleum reserves were being found in inaccessible areas like deep ocean waters and were far more expensive to exploit than the earlier finds. The average cost of extracting one barrel of oil from these fields was put at $70. With North America and the European Union (EU) recovering from the Great Recession of 2008–09, and the economies of China and India growing by 8 to 10 percent a year, oil prices rose to $90 a barrel at the end of 2010.

Even though the 17-nation Eurozone in the EU struggled to shore up the sinking GDP of Greece, and the economy of the United States failed to show consistent improvement, oil prices in 2011 remained above $100 a barrel, and rose to an average of $120 a barrel in the spring of 2012 before softening a little in the summer.

Breaking with the long-established tradition of oil being priced in U.S.

dollars, Iran and Venezuela started pricing their oil in euros in 2009.

Oil and gas reserves (2010):

OIL RESERVES (2010):

World: 1,383 billion barrels

Middle East: 730 billion barrels, 54.8 percent of global total

The Gulf region: 54. 0 percent of world total.

Bahrain	0.1 percent
Iran	9.9 percent
Iraq	8.3 percent
Kuwait	7.3 percent
Oman	0.4 percent
Qatar	1.9 percent
Saudi Arabia	19.1 percent
United Arab Emirates	7.0 percent

Outside the Gulf region: 0.7 percent of world total

Egypt	0.3 percent
Syria	0.2 percent
Yemen	0.2 percent

North America: 5.4 percent of world total. At the 2010 output of 13.8 million barrels per day (bpd) for the United States, Canada, and Mexico, the North American reserves will last until 2025.

South and Central America: 17.3 percent of world total. At the 2010 output of 6.99 million bpd for the region, including Venezuela, with the largest reserves in the world, the regional reserves will last until 2104.

Europe and Eurasia: 10.1 percent. At the 2010 production of 17.66 million bpd, their reserves will last until 2031. In 2010, of the global conventional oil reserves of 1,383 billion barrels, 88 percent were owned by the governments of the petroleum-bearing states, with only 12 percent possessed by the mainly Western oil corporations in North America and the 27-nation European Union.

GAS RESERVES (2009):

World: 187.1 trillion cu m

Middle East: 78.0 trillion cu m, 41.0 percent of global total

The Gulf region: 39.0 percent

Bahrain	0.1 percent
Iran	15.8 percent
Iraq	1.7 percent
Kuwait	1.0 percent
Oman	0.4 percent
Qatar	13.5 percent
Saudi Arabia	4.3 percent
United Arab Emirates	3.2 percent

Outside the Gulf region: 2.0 percent of world total

Egypt	1.2 percent
Jordan	0.3 percent
Syria	0.2 percent
Yemen	0.3 percent

North America: 5.3 percent of the world total. At the 2010 output of 826 billion cu m a year, the reserves of North America (Canada, Mexico, and the United States) will last 12 years.

South and Central America: 4.0 percent of the world total. At the 2010 production rate of 161.2 billion cu m a year, these reserves will last 46 years.

Europe and Eurasia: 33.7 percent of world total. At the 2010 production rate of 1,043.1 billion cu m a year, these reserves will last 61 years.

Old Testament: *See* Bible.

Olmert, Ehud (1945–): *Israeli politician; prime minister 2006–09* Born to Mordechai and Bella Olmert, members of Irgun [*q.v.*], in Binyamina, Palestine [*q.v.*], Ehud grew up as a member of the *Betar* (Hebrew: acronym of *Berit Trumpledor*, Covenant with Trumpledor) youth organization, affiliated to the Revisionist Zionists [*q.v.*]. He obtained a law degree from the Hebrew

University in Jerusalem [*q.v.*]. During his military service, he trained as a journalist with the armed forces' magazine *BaMahane* (Hebrew: *In the Base Camp*). Following his father's politics, he joined Herut [*q.v.*], which later merged with Liberalim [*q.v.*] to form Gahal [*q.v.*].

During the October 1973 Arab-Israeli War [*q.v.*], he served as a military correspondent at the headquarters of General Ariel Sharon [*q.v.*]. In the general election that followed in December he was elected to the Knesset [*q.v.*] as a member of the newly formed Likud [*q.v.*]. At the same time he practiced law in Jerusalem.

In 1988 Prime Minister Yitzhak Shamir [*q.v.*] appointed him minister for minorities and then moved him to the health ministry. After Likud's loss of power in the 1992 Knesset election, he ran as the party's candidate for Jerusalem's mayor in 1993. He won. During his two five-year terms as mayor, he improved the city's infrastructure. He also encouraged the expansion of the Jewish settlements in the West Bank [*q.v.*] surrounding Jerusalem.

He reentered the Knesset after the general election in January 2003 and became deputy prime minister in the cabinet led by Sharon. In his interview with the mass circulation newspaper *Yediot Aharonot* (Hebrew: *Latest News*) in December, he argued that Israel should withdraw from the West Bank and Gaza Strip [*q.v.*] in order to remain democratic and Jewish. If Israel retained these territories, then, because of the high birthrate among Palestinian Arabs [*q.v.*], the Jews would become a minority, he argued.

When Benjamin Netanyahu [*q.v.*] resigned as finance minister in protest at Sharon's plan to withdraw from Gaza, Olmert took over the ministry. He followed Sharon to join Kadima [*q.v.*] in November 2005.

He succeeded Sharon when the latter suffered a severe hemorrhage attack in January 2006. When Kadmia won most seats in the April 2006 election, Olmert became the prime minister. His conduct of the war with Hizbollah [*q.v.*] in July–August 2006 [*q.v.*] was criticized widely. The Winograd Commission's inquiry into the conflict concluded that Olmert had failed gravely to exercise "judgment, responsibility, and prudence." In May 2007 his approval rating fell to 3 percent.

Olmert attended the Middle East Conference in Annapolis [*q.v.*] in November and backed the two-state solution to resolve the 60-year-old Israel-Palestinian conflict. But his subsequent talks with President Mahmoud Abbas [*q.v.*] of the Palestinian Authority [*q.v.*] did not lead to any agreement.

Facing multiple corruption investigations, he decided in July 2008 to resign as Kadima leader. He was succeeded by Tzipi Livni [*q.v.*]. But because she failed to cobble together a coalition government, he continued as acting prime minister. After the February 2009 Knesset election, he gave way to Netanyahu as prime minister. His trial on corruption charges opened in September.

In November 2010 Olmert claimed that in his talks with Abbas he offered the following deal: A two-stage solution based on the 1967 border with agreed land swaps in exchange for

Israel keeping large settlement blocks in the West Ban; a division of Jerusalem; the holy sites of Jerusalem to be governed jointly by Israel, Palestine, America, Saudi Arabia, and Jordan; a symbolic number of Palestinian refugees to be permitted to return to Israel; compensation for the Palestinians and Jews displaced as a result of wars between Israel and the Arab countries; and a demilitarized Palestinian state. He claimed that the Palestinians did not formally respond to his comprehensive proposal. His statement contradicted the evidence provided by the Palestine Papers [*q.v.*], which were leaked the next month.

In January 2012 he was indicted for allegedly taking bribes totaling $400,000 in a massive property scandal in Jerusalem during his tenure as the city's mayor.

Oman:

OFFICIAL NAME: Sultanate of Oman

CAPITAL: Muscat [*q.v.*]

AREA: 119,500 sq. mi./309,500 sq. km

POPULATION: 3.03 million, including 577,300 non-nationals (2011 est.)

GROSS DOMESTIC PRODUCT (nominal): $66 billion; per capita $21,420 (2011 est.)

GROSS DOMESTIC PRODUCT (Purchasing Power Parity): $80 billion; per capita; $25,950 (2011 est.)

NATIONAL CURRENCY: Omani Rial (OMR); OR 1 = $2.60 = £1.67 = €2.00 (2011)

FORM OF GOVERNMENT: monarchy

OFFICIAL LANGUAGE: Arabic [*q.v.*]

OFFICIAL RELIGION: Islam [*q.v.*]

ADMINISTRATIVE SYSTEM: Oman consists of 11 governorates.

CONSTITUTION: In 1996 Sultan Qaboos issued the Basic Statute of State, the first such document. It describes Oman as Arab, Islamic, and independent, with its system of government being Sultani (i.e., royal), hereditary in the male descendants of Sayyid Turki bin Said bin Sultan. It describes the Sultan as head of state as well as prime minister and supreme commander of the military. He heads a nominated council of ministers. While the constitution provides for a bicameral parliament, called the Council of Oman, consisting of the Consultative Council and the State Council, it has no provision for political parties or trade unions.

COUNCIL OF OMAN: Bicameral Majlis Oman (i.e., Council of Oman) consists of the upper chamber, called Majlis al-Dawla; the State Council; and the lower chamber, called Majlis al-Shura (i.e., Consultative Council). In 1981 the Sultan established a 45-member Consultative Council as an advisory body. Ten years later he added 15 members and restructured it. This council was incorporated into the 1996 Basic Statute of the State. Initially, the local caucus in each of the 59 districts forwarded three names which, after vetting by a ministerial committee, were submitted to the Sultan who made the final choice. In 2000, this system was replaced by direct election based on limited franchise. In 2003 came the universal franchise for adults aged 21 or more. Women were also allowed to stand as candidates in elections. In the first such election, nearly three-fourths of the registered voters cast their ballots to elect 83 members of the Consultative Council, with four-year tenure. Its speaker is appointed by the Sultan. This council meets at the Sultan's discretion. It deals with the legislation only on social and economic affairs. After the cabinet has presented a drafted law to the Sultan, he passes it on the council for debate and adoption. In the 2007 election, 46 new candidates won seats. The Sultan then appointed a new speaker of the Consultative Council as well as a new cabinet that included three women.

The State Council was established in 1997 to serve as a liaison between the government and its citizens. It is nominated fully by the Sultan and has four-year tenure. Its annual session lasts at least eight months. It reviews matters referred to it by the Sultan, and drafts laws. Its membership has risen from 41 to 71.

In October 2011 the Sultan enhanced the powers of the Council of Oman at the expense of the appointed cabinet. The authority to present draft laws to the Sultan was transferred from the cabinet to the Council of Oman after the council had debated and amended the bills submitted to it by the cabinet. The changed procedure also applied to the annual budget and draft development plans.

ETHNIC COMPOSITION (2011): Arab 83 percent; South Asian 15 percent; other 2 percent.

High officials:

Head of state: Sultan Qaboos bin Said [q.v.], 1970–

Prime minister: Sultan Qaboos bin Said, 1972–

Speaker of the Consultative Council: Khalid bin Hilal al-Mawaly, 2011–

Speaker of the Council of State: Yahya bin Mahfoudh al-Manthri, 2011–

HISTORY SINCE CA 1850: The ruling Aal Bu Said dynasty reached its peak in the 1850s, when its empire extended to the eastern shores of Africa. The empire collapsed in the following decade. This so weakened the ruling family that it was overpowered by tribal leaders from the interior. In 1871 the British attacked Muscat and restored the Aal Bu Saids to power. Oman thus became a de facto colony of Britain.

In 1915 the traditional rivalry between the coast and the hinterland resurfaced, and the tribes of the interior, led by the Imam [q.v.], attacked Muscat. Britain intervened on behalf of the sultan. The subsequent uneasy peace was formalized in 1920 in the Treaty of Sib [q.v.] between Sultan Taimur bin Faisal [q.v.] and the tribal leaders, who recognized the sultan's authority in external affairs. The treaty guaranteed freedom of movement to the tribes and urban dwellers, with the sultan agreeing not to raise taxes above 5 percent of the value of trade in coastal towns. The signing of a treaty with the Imam implied autonomy for the interior. But its extent became contentious, with the sultan maintaining that the treaty recognized the imamate as autonomous only in local and socio-religious affairs.

The reasonable modus vivendi between the sultan and the tribal chiefs of the interior broke down again in the mid-1950s. Encouraged by Saudi Arabia, which was feuding with Oman over the Buraimi oasis straddling their borders, Imam Ghalib bin Ali proclaimed the independent Imamate of Oman in 1954. The forces of Sultan Said bin Taimur [q.v.], armed and led by the British, quelled the uprising. Acting in collusion with the forces of Abu Dhabi, they also recovered the area of Buraimi oasis occupied by the Saudis.

In 1957 the imam's brother Talib bin Ali, urged on by Saudi Arabia and Egypt, mounted a rebellion in the interior. With the assistance of the British, the sultan reduced the uprising to sporadic guerrilla actions. Claiming that Britain had committed an act of aggression against the Imamate of Oman, Egypt and other Arab states placed the matter before the United Nations. While the UN Commission of Inquiry failed to uphold the claim of popular opposition to the sultan, several Arab countries succeeded in persuading the UN General Assembly to adopt a resolution demanding the end of British colonial presence in Oman.

Though oil revenues started to rise in the 1960s, Sultan Said showed no sign of spending these funds on building the infrastructure of a modern state. He also faced armed rebellion in the southwestern region of Dhofar, which received an impetus from the victory of the leftist forces in the adjoining South Yemen in 1967. The British engineered a coup in July 1970 to replace Said with his only son, Qaboos [q.v.].

Under Qaboos, Oman joined the Arab League and the United Nations. With the funds provided by oil revenues and subventions by Kuwait and the United Arab Emirates, the new ruler expanded the economic infrastructure and public services. In 1975, assisted militarily by Britain and the Shah of Iran, the government succeeded in ending the insurgency in Dhofar.

Alone among the Arab Gulf States [q.v.], Oman showed a willingness for U.S. troops to use its military facilities, especially the ones on its offshore Masirah Island after Britain had withdrawn its forces from it in 1977. Again, as a sole dissident among Arab League members, it refused to cut relations with Egypt after the latter's peace treaty with Israel in 1979 [q.v.]. In June 1980 it signed a military cooperation agreement with Washington whereby, in exchange for U.S. military and economic aid, the Pentagon could use Oman's air and naval facilities and conduct military exercises.

Oman joined the Gulf Cooperation Council [q.v.] in May 1981. Later that year Sultan Qaboos nominated a 45-member consultative council as an advisory body. Having sided with Iraq in the early phases of the 1980–88 Iran-Iraq War [q.v.], Oman later adopted a neutral stance. Along with other GCC members it backed Kuwait after the latter's occupation by Iraq in August 1990. It joined the U.S.-led coalition against Iraq in the 1991 Gulf War [q.v.].

Later that year Sultan Qaboos expanded and restructured the consultative council. The arrest of 200 Omanis in 1994 was attributed to the authorities' efforts to curb Islamist militancy. There were increasing signs of popular disaffection at the absence of a written constitution and the Sultan's refusal to share his absolute power. In response, he promulgated a constitution in late 1996. But it failed to give legislative powers to the Consultative Council. There were riots in Hajar, which were curbed by the military. In the first directly elected Consultative Council in 2003, two women won seats.

Earlier, Oman renewed its 10-year military access agreement with America in 2001. In Washington's war against the Taliban-administered Afghanistan in October 2001, Oman allowed the Pentagon use of its military facilities. Though Oman opposed the Anglo-American invasion of Iraq [q.v.], it allowed the stationing of 3,600 American military personnel, 100 elite British Special Forces, and 40 U.S. warplanes on the eve of the invasion in March 2003.

In the region Oman has maintained consistently good relations with Iran, partly because the territorial waters of the two countries overlap in the narrow, strategic Strait of Hormuz [q.v.].

In 2005, the government arrested 31 citizens suspected of being members of the secret Bashaer military group aiming to subvert the government. After the court had found them guilty and sentenced them to one to 20 years in jail, Sultan Qaboos pardoned them.

The next year Oman signed a Free Trade Agreement with the United States. And in 2007 it became a member of the World Trade Organization.

Inspired by the peaceful demonstrations in Bahrain in mid-February 2011, the protestors in Muscat demanded higher salaries, an end to corruption, less official control of the media, and an equitable distribution of oil wealth. Those participating in a sit-in outside the Consultative Council building from 1 March onward demanded that the council be given real powers of legislation. The 27 February protest in the industrial port of Sohar, with an oil terminal for exports, had turned violent, with a shopping mall set ablaze, and the police firings of

rubber bullets had killed two demonstrators. With this, the unrest had spread to a few oilfields.

Sultan Qaboos appointed a committee to draft proposals for boosting the power of the elected Consultative Council. He reshuffled the cabinet, firing unpopular ministers, and abolished ministry of national economy, known to be corrupt. After raising the salaries in the public sector, he mandated increase in the minimum wages in the private sector from $364 a month to $520. He doubled social security benefits.

RELIGIOUS COMPOSITION (2011 est.): Among Muslim [q.v.] nationals, Ibadhi [q.v.] 75 percent, Sunnis [q.v.] 18 percent, Shia [q.v.] 9 percent. The non-nationals were affiliated to Islam, Christianity [q.v.], and Hinduism.

Omani Civil War (1963–76): In 1963 the Dhofar region, annexed by the Sultan of Oman in 1876 and covering two-fifths of the sultanate, erupted into a secessionist rebellion. Within two years the uprising had turned into a sustained armed struggle led by the Dhofari Liberation Front (DLF). The leftists' capture of power in adjoining South Yemen in November 1967 gave a boost to the DLF. In September 1968 it decided to extend its revolutionary activities to the rest of Oman and other Gulf states, and changed its name to the Popular Front for the Liberation of the Occupied Arab Gulf (PFLOAG) [q.v.]. Having secured large parts of Dhofar, the PFLOAG launched campaigns against slavery, illiteracy, tribalism, and the oppression of women.

With two-thirds of Dhofar under its control, the PFLOAG extended its guerrilla activity to the core region of the sultanate in June 1970. This alarmed the British government, the dominant political and commercial power in the country, which engineered a coup in July and replaced the old, inflexible Sultan Said bin Taimur [*q.v.*] with his young son, Qaboos [*q.v.*]. Qaboos initiated socio-political reform and modernization, and rapid expansion of the military under the British aegis. In response, the PFLOAG decided in July 1971 to lower the party's objective of achieving a socialist revolution to that of a national democratic revolution, and opened its membership to non-Marxist nationalists. The party was renamed the Popular Front for the Liberation of Oman and the Arab Gulf [*q.v.*], but the acronym remained the same (PFLOAG).

The resulting increase in the strength of the PFLOAG enabled it to withstand the repeated offensives that the British-led Omani troops, in conjunction with Britain's counterinsurgency force, the Special Air Service (SAS), mounted between October 1971 and December 1972. By recruiting a large number of Pakistani mercenaries, Sultan Qaboos expanded his military—fivefold, to 12,500. He also received generous funding from Saudi Arabia to purchase arms, and Iran lent him helicopters. When these measures failed to defeat PFLOAG insurgents, Tehran dispatched troops to Dhofar in 1973, and the guerrillas suffered setbacks as a result of the increased size of their enemy.

In July 1974, PFLOAG leaders decided to concentrate on Oman, and therefore renamed their Organization the Popular Front for the Liberation of Oman (PFLO) [*q.v.*]. In 1975,

whereas foreign assistance to Oman increased sharply, with Iran introducing more combat troops, Jordan and Egypt sending military advisers, and Saudi Arabia donating money, the external aid for the PFLO dried up. Following the Algiers Accord in March 1975 [*q.v.*], Iraq withdrew its backing for the PFLO. With Saudi Arabia offering a rapprochement to South Yemen, the latter ceased to assist the PFLO.

In October 1975 the Omani military, working in conjunction with some 25,000 Iranian troops and Britain's SAS units, launched a major offensive against PFLO guerrillas, estimated to be 5,000 to 10,000 strong. By December, the Omani government claimed to have crushed the revolutionary movement at the cost of some 400 Omani, British, Iranian, and Jordanian troops. Saudi Arabia helped to negotiate a truce in 1976, whereby an amnesty was offered to those who had fought on the PFLO side.

Operation Cast Lead: *See* Gaza War (2008–09)/Israel-Hamas War (2008–09).

Operation Desert Fox: Relations between Iraqi President Saddam Hussein [*q.v.*] and the UN Special Commission (UNSCOM) [*q.v.*] on disarming Iraq of weapons of mass destruction deteriorated when Richard Butler, an Australian disarmament specialist, replaced Rolf Ekeus, a Swedish diplomat, as head of UNSCOM in mid-1997. A crisis with the UN in February 1998 was defused by the last-minute intervention of UN Secretary-General, Kofi Annan, who met Saddam Hussein in Baghdad [*q.v.*]. But the agreement lasted only until mid-December when the United States, assisted by the United Kingdom, mounted its four-day Operation Desert Fox after Butler had withdrawn UN inspectors from Iraq on the private advice of Peter Burleigh, the U.S. ambassador to the UN, without even informing other Security Council members. The U.S. fired 415 Cruise and Tomahawk missiles (90 more than during the 1991 Gulf War [*q.v.*]) and dropped 600 laser-guided bombs on 100 Iraqi targets.

China, France, and Russia condemned the U.S.-U.K. action. The breach among the Permanent Five members of the Security Council was so severe that it took a whole year before the Council adopted a new resolution on the subject—1284—with China, France, and Russia abstaining. Saddam Hussein's efforts to have the Arab League [*q.v.*] foreign ministers' meeting in January 1999 condemn the Anglo-American action and demand the lifting of sanctions on Iraq failed. Equally, Washington's attempt to get the Gulf monarchies involved in overthrowing Saddam Hussein got nowhere.

Operation Big Pines: *See* Israeli Invasion of Lebanon (1982).

Operation Desert Saber: *See* Gulf War II (1991).

Operation Desert Storm: *See* Gulf War II (1991).

Operation Grapes of Wrath: *See* Israel-Hizbollah War (2006).

Operation Litani: *See* Israeli Invasion of Lebanon (1978).

Organization of Arab Petroleum Exporting Countries: The Organization of Arab Petroleum Exporting Countries (OAPEC) was formed in Kuwait [*q.v.*] in January 1968 in the aftermath of the Arab defeat in the June 1967 Arab-Israeli War [*q.v.*], and consisted of Algeria, Iraq, Kuwait, Libya, and Saudi Arabia. Membership in OAPEC required oil to be the main source of national income, and its objective was to safeguard the interests of its members. In 1970 Qatar joined the organization. In 1971 the condition that oil be the chief source of income was dropped. With the subsequent addition of Bahrain, Egypt, Syria, and the United Arab Emirates, its membership rose to 10 by 1973.

During the October 1973 Arab-Israeli War [*q.v.*], OAPEC members, reacting to U.S. President Richard Nixon's order to airlift weapons to Israel on a massive scale, decided on 17 October to cut output by 5 percent of the September figure, and to maintain the same rate of reduction each month until the Israeli forces had withdrawn from all Arab territories occupied during the 1967 War and the Palestinians' legitimate rights had been restored. Consumer countries were categorized as friendly, neutral, or hostile to the Arab cause. Friendly nations were to be supplied at the September level, neutral nations at a reduced level, and hostile ones not at all. OAPEC also confirmed the steep price rise decided earlier by the Organization of Petroleum Exporting Countries (OPEC) [*q.v.*]. Saudi Arabia ordered a 25 percent cut in its output, then running at 8 million barrels a day, but Iraq ignored the OAPEC decision.

The embargo hurt the U.S., reducing its annual gross domestic product by $10–20 billion. Aware of the anti-communist views of the Saudi monarch, Faisal bin Abdul Aziz [*q.v.*], Edward Heath, prime minister of Britain (which was not on the Arab oil boycott list), warned him that any prolonged oil squeeze would, by weakening the West, strengthen Communism. Egyptian President Anwar Sadat [*q.v.*], working in conjunction with U.S. Secretary of State Henry Kissinger, convinced Faisal to end the boycott. Faisal and Sadat then prevailed upon the other members of OAPEC to end the five-month embargo on 18 March 1974 as a token of Arab goodwill to the West—even though the Israelis had not withdrawn from anywhere in the Occupied Arab Territories [*q.v.*] and the legitimate rights of the Palestinian people had not been restored.

Following the Egyptian-Israeli Peace Treaty [*q.v.*] in 1979, Egypt was suspended from OAPEC's membership. It was readmitted a decade later. During the Kuwait crisis of 1990–91 caused by the emirate's occupation by Iraq, OAPEC headquarters was moved to Cairo [*q.v.*].

Even though its output was more than 700,000 barrels a day in the early 1990s, Oman did not apply to join OAPEC. In 2009 its membership rose to 11 with the addition of Tunisia.

In 2010, OAPEC's total output of 21.38 million barrels per day was 26 percent of the global aggregate.

Organization of Islamic Conference: *See* Islamic Conference Organization.

Organization of Islamic Cooperation: *See* Islamic Cooperation Organization.

Organization of Petroleum Exporting Countries: The Organization of Petroleum Exporting Countries (OPEC) [*q.v.*] is an international body to coordinate the hydrocarbon policies of its constituents. Following a meeting in Baghdad [*q.v.*] in September 1960 of the representatives of Iran, Iraq, Kuwait, Saudi Arabia, and Venezuela, it was formally inaugurated in January 1961 in Geneva (the headquarters was moved to Vienna in 1965). Its subsequent members included Qatar (1961), Indonesia, and Libya (1962); Abu Dhabi (1967), which transferred to the United Arab Emirates (UAE) in 1974; Algeria (1969); Nigeria (1971); Ecuador (1973); and Gabon (1975).

The major oil companies were opposed to OPEC's aims and policies, outlined in June 1962. The OPEC document stated that, until the final goal of nationalization of hydrocarbon resources had been achieved, the government of a member state should ensure that the contracted arrangements with the concessionaires specify maximum governmental participation and control over all aspects of their operations. It called on the member states to set a tax reference price and gradually reduce the area of existing concessions. The oil majors were particularly opposed to OPEC's demand that they must maintain accounts as stipulated by the local government and make them available at all times for official inspection.

Between 1948 and 1960 the average rate of return on the capital of oil corporations operating in the Gulf [*q.v.*], producing nearly a third of the global output in 1960, was 111 percent. In 1968 British Petroleum, Royal Dutch-Shell, and five American oil majors—Exxon, Gulf, Mobil, SOCAL, and Texaco—together controlled 77.9 percent of world oil production, 60.9 percent of refining, and 55.6 percent of the marketing facilities. But with many independent American petroleum corporations, as well as Japanese and Italian companies, offering favorable terms to the producing countries and acquiring an increasingly important role in the industry, the situation changed.

In 1970 Libya's year-old radical republican regime imposed production cuts on oil companies as a pressure tactic to secure higher taxes and royalties. To offset the ripple effect, the oil majors negotiated with Iran, Iraq, and Saudi Arabia as the representatives of all Gulf [*q.v.*] producer territories, reaching a satisfactory arrangement in February 1971. In October 1972 the national oil companies of Abu Dhabi, Kuwait, Qatar, and Saudi Arabia acquired 25 percent of the shares of the foreign concessionaires, with an agreement for a further 2.5 percent annual increase in shareholding for the next decade.

In September 1973, aware of the energy crisis facing their main Western consumer countries and intent on securing compensation for the latest devaluation of the U.S. dollar (the currency used in oil trade), OPEC members decided to double the price, from $2.55 to $5.09 a barrel. The talks with the oil majors on the subject scheduled for October were postponed due to the outbreak of the Arab-Israeli War [*q.v.*]. The hawkish stand taken by the Organization of Arab Petroleum Exporting Countries (OAPEC) [*q.v.*] during the conflict led to the earlier OPEC price rise remaining in force without the consent of the oil majors. In late November Algeria raised the price of its crude from $4.80 to $9.25 a barrel, and three weeks later the oil ministers of the eight Gulf States [*q.v.*] pushed the figure to $11.65, effective from 1 January 1974. This became the price of OPEC, then producing 55 percent of the world's oil. Thus within three months the price jumped from $2.55 to $11.65, with the host government's average earnings per barrel rising from $1.38 to $7.

In 1976 OPEC produced more than half of the global output and provided seven-eighths of the exports. Within OPEC Saudi Arabia became the swing producer to quickly raise or reduce output to balance the market and to help maintain the price fixed by OPEC.

To offset inflation in the West and the concomitant diminution in the value of the U.S. dollar, OPEC raised the oil price thrice in five years, taking it to about $14 a barrel in mid-1977. The comparative stability of price and supplies was shaken in late 1978 by the political turmoil in Iran. Responding to a call by Ayatollah Ruhollah Khomeini [*q.v.*], the oil workers of Iran went on strike, halting Iranian oil exports, then running at 4.5 million barrels a day. The disruption of supplies in the winter of 1978–79 pushed up the price to $28 a barrel. After the price rise in 1980, when OPEC produced 45 percent of the global total, its unity became frayed mainly because of the outbreak of war between its two important members, Iran and Iraq.

On 30 March 1983, OPEC received a blow when the New York Mercantile Exchange (Nymex) introduced crude oil futures. This development, introduced against the background of falling oil demand in the West, weakened OPEC's price-setting clout further. Prices started sliding.

The flooding of the market by Kuwait and Saudi Arabia in 1986, aimed at weakening Iran in its war with Iraq, lowered the price to below $10 a barrel in April and severely damaged OPEC's clout. With the departure in 1992 of Ecuador, following its failure to obtain a higher quota, OPEC's membership stood at 12. Ecuador's example was followed by Gabon in 1996, and this reduced OPEC's size to 11 members—with all, except Venezuela, being Muslim majority states.

In December 1996, when Iraq reentered the world oil market after an absence of over eight years, OPEC made it exempt from its quota system to enable it to repair and rebuild its shattered infrastructure. Its decision in late 1997 to increase its overall output by 10 percent at the behest of Saudi Arabia caused a dramatic drop in price which fell below $10 a barrel in early 1999. Subsequent cuts in production lifted the price to above $34 in March 2000. Six months later at the OPEC summit hosted by the current chairman, President Hugo Chavez of Venezuela, in Caracas, to celebrate OPEC's 40th anniversary, the leaders resolved to promote market stability

by developing "remunerative, stable, and competitive" pricing policies. The result was an agreement to maintain the price of an oil barrel in the $22–28 range.

A spike in oil prices came in the wake of the Anglo-American invasion of Iraq [q.v.] in 2003, a decision in which none of the OPEC members was involved. Equally, the price explosion, which pushed the figure to a record $147 a barrel, had more to do with the falling exchange value of the U.S. dollar, leading investors and speculators to direct their funds into such commodities as oil and gold, than any decisions taken by OPEC members. Nonetheless, with the deepest recession in the West since the Great Depression of the 1930s ravaging the economies of the Western nations in 2008–09, OPEC curtailed its aggregate output by a record 4.2 million barrels per day. And yet the price plummeted to $33 a barrel in December 2008 before stabilizing at around $75 a barrel for most of 2009.

When Indonesia became a net importer of oil in 2008, it withdrew from OPEC. A year earlier OPEC had acquired Angola as its latest member. So its total membership stood at 12. In 2009 Iran and Venezuela became the first OPEC members to price their petroleum in euros instead of U.S. dollars.

The main weakness of OPEC is that it lacks the authority to enforce the quotas it decides for its members every quarter. There is also an inbuilt conflict between OPEC members with (a) large populations—Algeria, Iran, Iraq, and Nigeria, and (b) small populations and large reserves—Kuwait, Qatar, Saudi Arabia, and the

UAE. Those in category (b) are more interested in extracting as much oil as soon as possible—even if that lowers price—whereas those in category (a) want to restrict output and achieve higher prices in order to improve the living standards of their people. Over the years, buffeted by wild price swings, the two groups have managed to devise a compromise. And, to offset low prices of oil, OPEC has made successful deals with such leading non-OPEC producers as Mexico, Norway, Oman, and Russia to cut output in order to improve prices.

In 2010, at 34.32 million barrels per day, OPEC's output was 41.2 percent of the global total. *See also* Oil Prices.

Oriental Jews: The term applied to non-Ladino–speaking Jews [*q.v.*] from the Arab countries, Iran, India, or Central Asia. In biblical times their ancestors left Palestine [*q.v.*] for North Africa or the Middle East [*q.v.*]—from where they migrated to Central Asia or the Indian subcontinent. While their religion set them apart from their hosts, they underwent cultural assimilation and adopted the local language as their own. In the late 1960s the 1.5 million Oriental Jews formed about one-ninth of the world's Jewry. They were the dominant group among the Jews in Palestine under the Ottomans. But since the Jewish migrations into Palestine between 1882 and 1939 did not include Oriental Jews (except 45,000 from North Yemen), their proportion in the Jewish community in Palestine declined to about one-fifth of the total on the eve of World War II. However, following the 1948–49 Arab-Israeli War [*q.v.*], Oriental Jews started to arrive in Israel in large numbers.

Given their higher birth rate, within a generation they formed half of the Jewish population and became a majority during the next decade. But due to the influx of 540,000 Jews from the former Soviet Union between 1990 and 1994, they lost their majority status to Ashkenazim [*q.v.*], a trend that continued with further immigration of the ex-Soviet Jews. Even though only the Jews who originated in the countries surrounding the Mediterranean followed Sephardic [*q.v.*] rituals and practices, others coming from such countries as Yemen, Iraq, and India, following different rituals and practices, affiliated to the Sephardic chief rabbinate in order to receive public funds for their newly established synagogues [*q.v.*].

As for the government, it classifies those Jews born abroad in its annual *Statistical Abstract of Israel* according to the continent(s) of origin: Europe-America-Oceania (meaning, for all practical purposes, Ashkenazim), Asia, and Africa (taken together, meaning Sephardim). Strictly speaking, the term "Oriental Jew" is geographical, whereas the label "Sephardim" is sectarian. However, to describe someone originating in Morocco, Algeria, or Tunisia—part of the Arab West [*q.v.*]—as "Oriental" is inexact. The most logical, and ethnically correct, term is "Arab/Arabic Jew" [*q.v.*], which parallels "European Jew" or "American Jew." *See also* Arab Jews and Sephardim.

Orthodox Christians/Church (Greek: *derivative of orthodoxos, right opinion*): (Official title: Orthodox Catholic Church; also known as the Orthodox Eastern Church or the Eastern

Church) The term applies, literally, to those who follow the right doctrine and not a heretical or heterodox one. As for church denominations, the term applies to the historic churches of Eastern Europe and Southwest Asia, which split from the Western Church based in Rome. They accepted the decrees of the first seven ecumenical councils, held between 325 A.D. and 787 A.D. But the drift between the Western Church led by the Pope in Rome, with Latin as the official language, and the (Orthodox) Eastern Church, led by the Patriarch and based in Constantinople (now Istanbul), with Greek as the official language, became unbridgeable with the challenge to papal authority by Patriarch Photius in the ninth century A.D., and irreversible with the mutual excommunication of the Patriarch of Constantinople, Michael Cerularius, and Pope Leo IX in 1054. The Crusades (1095–1272) further embittered feelings between the two sides, and numerous attempts at reconciliation failed.

The Orthodox churches are noted for their rich liturgical practices and devotional use of icons, but the relationship of various churches with one another is complex. The term Greek Church is applied to the Church of Greece, churches whose liturgy is in Greek, and those affiliated to the Patriarchate of Constantinople. There are six other national churches in the (Orthodox) Eastern community: the Churches of Bulgaria, Cyprus, Poland, Rumania, Russia, and Yugoslavia, the most important being the Russian [*q.v.*].

Orthodox Christians, Armenian: *See* Armenian Orthodox Church.

Orthodox Christians, Greek: *See* Greek Orthodox Church.

Orthodox Christians, Gregorian: *See* Armenian Orthodox Church.

Orthodox Christians, Russian: *See* Russian Orthodox Church.

Orthodox Christians, Syrian: (Also known as the Jacobite Church) Unlike other Orthodox churches, the Syrian Orthodox Church rejects the doctrine of the fourth ecumenical council at Chalcedon (451 A.D.), which defined Christ as one person with two natures (human and divine), and accepts that Christ had one nature, as in the monophystic doctrine. The Church was founded in the sixth century by Jacob Baradaeus, assisted by Empress Theodara. Its head is the Patriarch of Antioch and All the East, based in Damascus [*q.v.*]; its rite is the Antiochene [*q.v.*]; and its liturgical language is Syriac. The church has a following in Syria, Iraq, and India.

Orthodox Eastern Church: *See* Orthodox Christians/Church.

Orthodox Judaism: Orthodox Jews are those who follow strictly traditional beliefs and practices. They believe, among other things, that Halacha [*q.v.*] does not change with time, and that only exceptionally well-qualified authorities can interpret it. They engage in daily worship as well as participate in traditional prayers and ceremonies, study Torah [*q.v.*], and observe dietary laws and the Sabbath [*q.v.*]. They separate men and women in the synagogue, where music during the communal service is banned. Orthodox rabbis have successfully challenged the legitimacy of certain non-Orthodox marriages, divorces, and conversions in Israel [*q.v.*].

In 2010, of the 14.3 million Jews [*q.v.*] worldwide, nearly two million were Orthodox. Of these about a half lived in Israel, and another 750,000 in the United States.

Oslo Accord I: *See* Israeli-Palestine Organization Accord.

Oslo Accord II: *See* Washington Accord (1995).

Oslo Accords: The term includes Oslo Accord I [*q.v.*] and Oslo Accord II [*q.v.*].

Oz, Amos (1939–): *Israeli writer* Born Amos Klausner of a scholarly family in Jerusalem [*q.v.*], Oz left the city to live in a kibbutz (Hulda), and pursued his further education from there. His first collection of short stories, *Lands of the Jackals* (1965), and his first novel, *Another Place* (1966), were set in kibbutz surroundings. His novella *Unto Death* (1971) was an allegory about a group of crusaders intent on exorcising the Jew among them. In *My Michael* (1972) he used the central character, Hannah Gonen, as a metaphor for Jerusalem between 1948 and 1967. In *Touch the Water, Touch the Wind* (1973) he returned to the kibbutz with the story of two Jews [*q.v.*] who had survived the Holocaust. In his novels *Perfect Peace* (1982) and *Black Box* (1987), he argued that ideological conviction was a crutch an individual leaned on when his inner world collapsed. *To Know a Woman* (1991) was about a former Mossad

[*q.v.*] agent who scoured the world deciphering codes and unraveling plots but failed to understand his wife. *Fima* (1993) centered on a Jewish Walter Mitty, a man with big dreams but a shaky grip on reality.

A political activist, Oz was close to Pinchas Lavon [*q.v.*] and joined his Min HaYesod group. He was injured in the 1956 Suez War [*q.v.*] and the June 1967 Arab-Israeli War [*q.v.*]. Following the latter conflict he opposed those who wanted to annex the Occupied Arab Territories [*q.v.*]. One of the cofounders of the dovish Moked (1973) and Shelli (1977) groups, he was prominent in the Peace Now [*q.v.*] movement, which emerged in late 1977 after Egyptian president Anwar Sadat's [*q.v.*] visit to Jerusalem. On the eve of the 1981 general election, he returned to the Labor [*q.v.*] fold and campaigned for it.

His essays and articles on politics, ideology, and literature have been published in several volumes: *In the Powerful Blue Light* (1979); *In the Land of Israel* (1983); *Perfect Peace* (1993); *Israel, Palestine and Peace* (1994); *Under This Blazing Light* (1996); *The Story Begins: Essays on Literature* (1999); *The Story Begins: Essays on Literature* (2003); and *The Story Begins: Essays on Literature* (2006). *A Tale of Love and Darkness* (2003), his memoir of coming of age during the birth pangs of Israel, was translated into 25 languages, won prizes in nine countries, and sold more than one million copies.

His fiction includes *Panther in the Basement* (1998), a story of a 12-year old Jewish boy in Palestine [*q.v.*] during the last year of the British Mandate; *The Same Sea* (1999), a prose poem centered on accountant

Albert, a tale of family love and erotic longing; *The Silence of Heaven* (2000); *Suddenly in the Depth of the Forest* (2005); *Rhyming Life and Death* (2007); *Scenes from Village Life* (2009); and *Between Friends* (2012).

He was awarded the Israel Prize for literature in 1998. Ten years later he received the German President's High Honor Award.

P

Pahlavi, Muhammad Reza Shah

(1919–80): *Shah-en-shah (King of Kings) of Iran, 1941–79* Born in Tehran [*q.v.*], Pahlavi was educated at a private school in Switzerland and the Tehran Military Academy. He succeeded his father, Reza Shah Pahlavi [*q.v.*], in September 1941, who abdicated in his favor when, angered at his neutrality in World War II, British and Soviet troops started marching toward Tehran.

Pahlavi allowed Iranian territory to be used by the Allies for supplies to the Soviet Union to bolster its capacity to fight Nazi Germany. At home he placated the clerical establishment, which had been alienated by his father. It was only after the Soviet troops had withdrawn in May 1946 and the Iranian forces had quelled autonomous governments in Kurdistan [*q.v.*] and Azerbaijan [*q.v.*] in December that he was able to exercise authority over all of Iran.

Following a failed assassination attempt on him in February 1949, he imposed martial law and banned the Tudeh Party [*q.v.*]. However, in his

tussle with the nationalist Premier Muhammad Mussadiq [*q.v.*], Pahlavi reluctantly yielded to the parliament's decision to nationalize the British-owned Anglo-Iranian Oil Company (AIOC) in 1951. The subsequent power struggle led to the flight of Pahlavi to Rome on 16 August 1953. But three days later, aided by the U.S. Central Intelligence Agency (CIA) and royalist military officers, he staged a comeback.

This inaugurated a period in Iran's history when the U.S. replaced Britain as the dominant Western power. American companies were preeminent in the Western oil consortium, which was given a contract to run Iran's petroleum industry on behalf of the National Iranian Oil Company (NIOC). After joining the Western-sponsored Baghdad Pact [*q.v.*] in 1955, Pahlavi subscribed to the Eisenhower Doctrine [*q.v.*] two years later. At home he established a political police force under military officers, later called *Savak* (Persian: *Sazman-e Amniyat Va Ittilaat-e Keshvar*, Organization of National Security and Intelligence), with strong ties with the CIA, Israel's Mossad [*q.v.*], and Turkey's National Intelligence Service.

Under pressure from U.S. President John F. Kennedy, Pahlavi initiated a land reform program in 1961. To overcome resistance by the parliament, he dissolved it and ruled by decree. This led to increased opposition, including from Ayatollah Ruhollah Khomeini [*q.v.*]. In January 1963 he launched a six-point White Revolution [*q.v.*] and called a referendum on it. By repressing the groups that called for a boycott of the referendum, he won 91 percent approval.

His conflict with Khomeini reached a climax in June, and led to a nation-wide uprising. He crushed it by deploying the army, reportedly causing thousands of deaths. Following a general election in September 1963, he eased his grip over the nation slightly. But when, after his release from prison in April 1964, Khomeini resumed his opposition, Pahlavi expelled him from Iran in November.

He further strengthened Iran's economic, military, and cultural ties with the West. To persuade the Western oil consortium to increase its output his government gave it additional concessions. The two ambitious Five-Year Plans between 1963 and 1972 accelerated economic development in agriculture and industry, and raised literacy. In October 1971, Pahlavi celebrated 2,500 years of "unbroken" monarchy in Iran (a claim disputed by most historians) at the ancient capital of Persepolis, near Shiraz [*q.v.*].

On the 10th anniversary of the White Revolution in January 1973, Pahlavi announced nationalization of the Western oil consortium. The petroleum price jump in 1973–74 boosted Iran's export revenue and fired the grandiose ambitions of Pahlavi. The inflated Five-Year Plan of 1973–77, involving inter alia high expenditure on Western arms purchases, overheated the economy, causing rapid migration of rural workers to cities, high inflation, and rampant corruption.

With all avenues of secular opposition blocked by Pahlavi's regime, more and more Iranians turned to the mosque and clergy to express their growing discontent. Under pressure from the newly elected U.S. President Jimmy Carter, Pahlavi started to mod-erate his repression of the opposition. This emboldened the dissenters, both secular and religious. Guided by Khomeini, based since 1965 in the Iraqi city of Najaf [*q.v.*], religious and secular opposition forces banded together to mount a popular revolutionary movement aiming to depose Pahlavi. It surged to the extent that it immobilized the vital oil industry and caused the disintegration of Pahlavi's 413,000-strong military. His last-minute ploy to appoint a dissenter, Shahpur Bakhtiar [*q.v.*], as prime minister failed.

On 16 January 1979 he left Iran, ostensibly for a holiday in Aswan, Egypt. He was allowed to enter the U.S. clandestinely in October for medical treatment. The post-Pahlavi government of Iran demanded his extradition to face charges of violating the country's 1906–07 constitution, which was refused. In March 1980, Egyptian President Anwar Sadat [*q.v.*] invited him to Cairo [*q.v.*]. He died there four months later, leaving behind his widow, Farah, and their only son, Reza Cyrus.

Pahlavi, Reza Shah (1878–1944): *Shah-en-shah (King of Kings) of Iran, 1925–41* Son of a military officer in a village in northern Mazandaran province, Pahlavi joined the army as a youth. He rose through the ranks, becoming commander of the elite Cossack Brigade with the rank of colonel. At Britain's behest, he overthrew the government in February 1921 and forced the monarch, Ahmad Shah Qajar, to appoint his nominee as premier. Pahlavi became war minister in the first cabinet. Later he took over the premiership as well.

By crushing tribal and other revolts he raised his popular standing. In October 1925, at his instigation, parliament deposed Ahmad Shah Qajar and appointed Pahlavi as regent. Two months later, a freshly elected constituent assembly proclaimed Pahlavi (who had chosen Pahlavi [*q.v.*] as his surname) shah-en-shah (king of kings) of Iran.

Pahlavi centralized and modernized the state, creating a national civil service and police force. He quickened the pace of economic development, fueled by oil revenues. He unilaterally cancelled the economic privileges given to leading European nations over the past century, and increased tariffs on imports. He pressured the Anglo-Persian Oil Company in 1932 to increase its oil royalties and reduced its concessionaire area by 80 percent.

To create a national Iranian identity out of many ethnic ones, he required all males, by law, to wear Western-style dress and a round peaked cap. He ordered all public places and educational institutions to admit women. He reduced the powers and scope of the Sharia [*q.v.*] courts and strengthened the secular, state courts. By manipulating elections he reduced the share of clerics in parliament from 40 percent in the Sixth Majlis [*q.v.*] (1926–28) to none in the Eleventh Majlis (1936–38). The building of 14,000 miles of roads and the Trans-Iranian Railway by August 1938 boosted industrialization.

After the rise of Adolf Hitler in Germany in 1933, Pahlavi tried to use Berlin as a counterpoint to the commercial and political dominance of London and Moscow. By the time World War II started in September 1939, Germany accounted for nearly half of Iran's foreign trade. Pahlavi declared Iran's neutrality in the conflict. The Allies saw the German invasion of the Soviet Union in June 1941 as part of a pincer movement, its other arm being Germany's thrust into North Africa. In late August, Soviet and British troops invaded Iran at five points. Fearing an imminent march of Soviet troops into Tehran, Pahlavi abdicated on 16 September in favor of his eldest son, Muhammad Reza [*q.v.*]. He left for the British-ruled island of Mauritius, and then for South Africa.

Pahlavi dynasty: Following a law passed in the spring of 1925, which required all Iranian citizens to acquire a birth certificate and a surname, Reza Khan (later Reza Shah) [*q.v.*], then Iran's prime minister and commander in chief, chose his family name, Pahlavi [*q.v.*]. It was the language of Persians [*q.v.*] from the third to the tenth century A.D. The dynastic rule of the Pahlavis lasted from 1925 to January 1979, when Muhammad Reza Shah Pahlavi [*q.v.*] left the country.

Pahlavi language: Pahlavi evolved in the second century B.C. under the rule of the kings of Parthia, modern northeast Iran [*q.v.*]. Its alphabet, developed from Aramaic, was written from right to left. It was the principal language of Persians from the third to the tenth century A.D., and the official language of the Sassanians (r. 226–640 A.D.). Zoroastrian [*q.v.*] literature was written in Pahlavi.

Palestine: (Greek: *Palaistina*, derivative of *Pleshet, Land of Philistines* in Hebrew) Also known as the Holy Land because it is sacred to Jews [*q.v.*], Christians [*q.v.*], and Muslims [*q.v.*].

INHABITANTS AND CONQUERORS:
Canaanites and Philistines, before 1250 B.C. and from 1250–1030 B.C.
Israelites, 1030–586 B.C.
Babylonians, 586–538 B.C.
Persians, 538–332 B.C.
Greeks, 332–166 B.C.
Maccabeans (Jews), 166–63 B.C.
(Pagan) Romans, 63 B.C.–323 A.D.
(Christian) Romans, 323–614 A.D.
Persians, 614–628 A.D.
(Christian) Byzantine Romans, 628–637 A.D.
(Muslim) Arabs, 637–1072 A.D.
(Muslim) Turks, 1072–1092.
(Muslim) Arabs, 1092–1099.
(Christian) Kingdom of Jerusalem, 1100–1187.
(Muslim) Arabs, 1187–1517.
(Muslim) Turks/Ottomans, 1517–1917.
(Christian) British, 1918–48.

HISTORY: In the second century A.D. the Roman emperors called the southern third of their province of Syria, including former Judea [*q.v.*], Syria Palestina. There has been much variation in the boundaries of Palestine, which has been ruled by Egyptians, Assyrians, Israelites, Babylonians, Persians, Greeks under Alexander of Macedonia and his successors, the Ptolemies and Seleucids, Maccabeans (Jews), Byzantine Romans, Umayyads, Abbasids, Fatimids, Crusaders, Ayubids, Malmukes, Ottomans, and British.

Under the Ottomans (r. 1517–1917) there was no single administrative unit called Palestine. What was to emerge as Palestine under the British Mandate (area 10,435 sq. mi./27,027 sq. km) had existed as three territories under the Ottomans: the southern zone, called the *sanjak* (Turkish: *district*) of Jerusalem [*q.v.*]; the northern area as part of the *vilayat* (Turkish: *province*) of Beirut; and Jerusalem and its suburbs, administered directly by Constantinople (now Istanbul). Yet Britain's Balfour Declaration [*q.v.*] of November 1917 referred to the "establishment in Palestine of a National Home for the Jewish people."

The Ottoman offensive against the Allies in Palestine in 1915 had made Britain realize the strategic importance of Palestine as a buffer to safeguard Egypt and the Suez Canal [*q.v.*], Britain's lifeline to its empire in India. Therefore, Britain insisted on, and acquired, a mandate—a variant of trusteeship—over Palestine at the meeting of the Supreme Council of the League of Nations in San Remo, Italy, in April 1920. Approved by the League in July 1922, the Mandate went into effect in September 1923.

Instead of preparing Palestine for independence—which London had visualized for Iraq—Britain contrived to hold on to it, making full use of the Balfour Declaration, which had been incorporated into the Mandate. The discovery of oil in Iraq in 1927 gave further impetus to the British government to consolidate its grip over Palestine, which was a gateway to the Iraqi oilfields through the British protectorate of Transjordan [*q.v.*] (now Jordan).

As a result the percentage of Jews [*q.v.*] in the Palestinian population rose from 8 percent in 1918 to 18 in 1931. The fifth Jewish wave of immigration, from 1932 to May 1939, brought a further 225,000 Jewish migrants into Palestine. Among other things this led to an Arab uprising that lasted from 1936 to 1939 and resulted in the death of 3,232 Arabs [*q.v.*], 329 Jews, and 135 Britons. Responding to the persistent uprising, and anxious to retain Arab goodwill in the region and access to the crucial oilfields in Iran in the increasingly likely event of war with Germany, Britain's White Paper of May 1939 limited Jewish immigration to 75,000 over the next five years and offered an outline of an independent, bi-national state in Palestinian by 1949. Earlier, in 1937, the Arabs had rejected the Peel Commission's recommendation to partition Palestine, creating a Jewish state on the coastal plain and Galilee, and an Arab state to be attached to Transjordan.

Tensions were eased by World War II, in which both Arabs and Jews cooperated with Britain. Nearly 43,000 Jews of both sexes joined the Allied military, and 10,000 of them became part of the British Nile Army. After the war the Anglo-American Commission on Palestine recommended in April 1946 that the British should continue the Mandate. The decision of the Zionist Organization [*q.v.*] in December to demand an independent Jewish state in Palestine ended whatever hopes London had of solving the problem on its own. It therefore placed the issue before the General Assembly of the United Nations. Its Special Committee on Palestine recommended in August 1947 that Palestine be partitioned—with 45.4 percent of the area going to the Arabs, who made up 70 percent of the population, and 53.5 percent to the Jews, who constituted 30 percent of the population and owned 6 percent of

the land. The remaining 1.1 percent, covering Jerusalem and its suburbs, was to be placed under international control.

On 29 November the UN General Assembly adopted Resolution 181, specifying partition, by 33 votes (including the eight-strong Soviet bloc) to 13, with 12 abstentions (including Britain). The Arab states challenged the right of the UN General Assembly to partition a country against the wishes of the majority of its inhabitants, proposing that the International Court of Justice should rule on the subject. But their proposal was defeated by 21 votes to 20 in the General Assembly. The Jews accepted the partition plan warmly, the Arabs rejected it angrily. Interethnic violence erupted immediately, and intensified as Britain's withdrawal date of 15 May 1948 approached. By that date some 300,000 Arabs had fled from the areas allocated to the Jews by the UN partition plan. The establishment of the State of Israel led to war between the Zionist forces and the Arab armies. *See* Arab-Israeli War I.

Palestine Liberation Army: The Palestine Liberation Army (PLA), the military wing of the Palestine Liberation Organization (PLO) [*q.v.*], was established in 1964. It was posted in different Arab countries, including Egypt and Syria. Its tank units, stationed in Syria, advanced into northern Jordan during the fighting between the PLO and the Jordanian army in September 1970. Lacking air cover from Syria, they retreated when attacked by the Jordanian air force.

After the PLO moved to Beirut [*q.v.*] in 1972, the PLA consisted of

8,000 to 10,000 troops organized into three brigades, two of which were integrated into the Syrian army. During the Lebanese Civil War [*q.v.*], between October 1975 and January 1976, Syrian President Hafiz Assad [*q.v.*] dispatched two brigades of the Syrian-officered PLA from Damascus [*q.v.*] to Lebanon to help the PLO-Lebanese National Movement [*q.v.*] alliance. But in June, under orders from Assad, these brigades changed sides and backed the right-wing Maronite [*q.v.*] forces. When Syria redeployed its peacekeeping forces in Lebanon in early 1980, it ceded many of their positions to the PLA. After the June 1982 Israeli invasion [*q.v.*], the Palestinian forces that left Beirut in early September included 3,500 PLA troops.

Following the break between PLO Chairman Yasser Arafat [*q.v.*] and Assad in 1983, the PLA in Syria became estranged from the mainstream PLO. In late 1983 the PLA units, backed by the Syrians, encircled Arafat's 5,000 commandos in Tripoli [*q.v.*], Lebanon, and defeated them.

The 8,144 PLO commandos who had been dispersed from Beirut in 1982 to Tunisia, Libya, North Yemen, Jordan, and Iraq were reconstituted as the Palestine National Liberation Army (PNLA), with the host country supervising them. A decade later the strength of the PNLA was put at 11,000. They were stationed in Algeria, Egypt, Iraq, Jordan, Lebanon, Libya, Sudan, and Yemen. Another 4,500 troops, still bearing the old name of Palestine Liberation Army and based in Syria, had nothing to do with the PNLA.

Following the Israeli-PLO Accord [*q.v.*] in September 1993, a minority

of the PNLA ranks, having retrained as policemen in Egypt, were recruited into the 10,500-strong police force of the Palestinian Authority (PA) [*q.v.*]. The estimated strength of Palestinian troops stationed in other Arab countries was 8,000. Later most of them returned to the Palestinian areas controlled by the PA as civilians.

Palestine Liberation Organization: An umbrella body, the Palestine Liberation Organization (PLO) was set up in early 1964 to enable Palestinians to play their part in liberating Palestine [*q.v.*] and determining their own future. The decision to form the PLO was taken at a summit of the Arab League [*q.v.*] which, by virtue of an annex to its charter, had assumed the right to select an Arab [*q.v.*] Palestinian to take part in its activities.

The PLO held its first congress in May–June 1964 in East Jerusalem [*q.v.*], then under Jordanian control, where it adopted the Palestine National Charter [*q.v.*], which called for the establishment of a democratic and secular state in the Palestine constituted by the British Mandate. Each of the affiliated bodies was represented on the Palestine National Council (PNC) [*q.v.*], which elected a central council and an executive committee.

The PLO's importance increased in the aftermath of the defeat suffered by the Arab states in the June 1967 Arab-Israeli War [*q.v.*]. A change in the charter in 1968, which declared armed struggle to be the only way to liberate Palestine, paved the way for the affiliation of radical groups. In 1969 Yasser Arafat [*q.v.*], leader of Fatah [*q.v.*], the largest of the parties affiliated to the PLO, became its chairman, replacing

Yahya Hamuda, who had taken over from Ahmad Shuqairi [*q.v.*] after the June 1967 War.

After the Arab-Israeli War of October 1973 [*q.v.*], the PNC adopted the idea of a Palestinian state in the Occupied Territories [*q.v.*] as a transient stage for the liberation of all Mandate Palestine in June 1974. Later that year the Arab League recognized the PLO as the sole representative of the Palestinian people and granted it membership of the League.

Arafat participated in a debate on the Palestine question at the UN General Assembly in mid-November 1974. On 22 November, UN General Assembly Resolution 3236, describing the PLO as "the representative of the Palestinian people," reaffirmed the Palestinians' right to self-determination and national independence and the right of Palestinian refugees to return to their homes and property. The motion was carried by 89 votes to 8, with 37 abstentions. The PLO was given observer status at the UN by 95 votes to 17, with 19 abstentions. Dr. Zehdi Terzi became the PLO's first representative to the UN, and he was invited to a UN Security Council session on the Palestinian issue in December to participate in the debate. On 22 January 1975 the UN Security Council endorsed the General Assembly's stand by adopting a resolution affirming the Palestinians right to establish an independent state. But the resolution was vetoed by the U.S. administration of President Gerald Ford.

By the late 1970s the PLO had won the formal recognition of over 100 countries, far more than Israel. Its annual budget of $500 million consisted of $350 million in grants by oil-rich Arab states and $150 million in indirect Palestine taxes collected by the Arab states, mainly in the Gulf [*q.v.*], all of which were paid into the Palestine National Fund [*q.v.*]. It commanded about 23,000 armed guerrillas and 8,000 to 10,000 troops of the Palestine Liberation Army (PLA).

The groups affiliated to the PLO were the Arab Liberation Front, the Democratic Front for the Liberation of Palestine [*q.v.*], Fatah [*q.v.*], the Palestine Communist Party [*q.v.*], the Popular Front for the Liberation of Palestine [*q.v.*], the Popular Front for the Liberation of Palestine-General Command [*q.v.*], the Popular Struggle Front, and Saiqa [*q.v.*]. The PLO's affiliates also included 14 organizations for students, workers, women, journalists, lawyers, doctors, and others.

Following the Israeli invasion of Lebanon [*q.v.*] in June 1982, the PLO, including its commandos and PLA troops, was evacuated from Beirut [*q.v.*] and dispersed to several Arab countries. The PLO headquarters was moved to Tunis. Here its policies became progressively moderate. Yet the Israelis bombed the PLO headquarters on 1 October 1985, killing 71 people but missing their main target, Arafat. After the outbreak of Intifada [*q.v.*] in the Gaza Strip [*q.v.*] in December 1987, the PLO backed it, and its adherents in the Occupied Territories became part of the United National Leadership of the Uprising [*q.v.*].

After the declaration on 15 November 1988 by the PNC of the independence and establishment of the State of Palestine "on our Palestinian land," on the basis of the UN General Assembly's Resolution 181 of November 1947, 70 of the 103 countries that had recognized the PLO accorded it full diplomatic status. On the same day, Arafat, named president of the State of Palestine by the PNC, renounced the use of violence to achieve the PLO's aims, and accepted the idea of the Palestinian self-determination coexisting with Israel. At the UN, the PLO's representation was renamed "Palestine."

In December Arafat addressed the UN General Assembly, specially convened in Geneva, to reiterate the new PLO position. There was no positive response from Israel, which was on the verge of receiving a rising tide of Jewish immigration from the Soviet Union, resulting in the number of immigrants shooting up from 13,300 in 1988 to 199,500 in 1990.

As a result, the PLO's policy became hard-line, with Arafat tilting toward the radical views of Iraqi President Saddam Hussein [q.v.]. He sided with the Iraqi leader in the latter's conflict with the UN following his invasion of Kuwait in August 1990. Saddam linked Iraqi's future withdrawal from Kuwait with Israel's evacuation of the Occupied Arab Territories [q.v.]. This stance gained the backing of the Palestinians in the West Bank [q.v.] and Gaza [q.v.]. Arafat's support of Saddam led to the severance of grants for the PLO by the oil-rich Gulf States [q.v.], a near-fatal blow to its finances.

Chastened by Iraq's defeat in the Gulf War II [q.v.] in early 1991, the PLO backed the idea of a Middle East peace conference, where Palestinians were to be included in a joint Jordanian-Palestinian delegation. Though this delegation was to exclude any PLO members, the organization was active behind the scenes before and after the conference, which was held in Madrid in October 1991. The subsequent bilateral talks between the Israeli and Jordanian-Palestinian (later functioning separately) delegations made little progress.

Once Israel, now led by a Labor [q.v.] government, had lifted its ban on contact with the PLO in January 1993, the scene was set for secret talks between the two sides. These took place in Norway. The resulting accord, based on mutual recognition of Israel and the PLO (as the representative of the Palestinian people), and providing for limited autonomy for the Palestinians in the Gaza Strip and the West Bank town of Jericho [q.v.], was signed in Washington on 13 September 1993. Of the 10 groups then affiliated to the PLO, only four—the Democratic Palestinian Union, Fatah, the Palestine People's Party [q.v.], and the Popular Struggle Front— accepted the deal. Nonetheless this agreement on principles was transformed into a working document in Cairo [q.v.] in early May 1994.

Among other things this gave rise to the Palestinian Authority [q.v.]. Arafat left Tunis in July to administer Gaza and Jericho. The PLO maintained offices in Tunis and Amman [q.v.]. It was the prime mover behind the convening of the joint session of its Central Council, the Palestine National Council, and the Palestinian Authority [q.v.] in Gaza in December 1998 to radically alter the Palestine National Charter. After this, its delegates were permitted to participate in the UN General Assembly proceedings without being able to vote.

In 2002, the PLO had diplomatic relations with 93 countries.

After the death of Arafat in 2004, Mahmoud Abbas [q.v.], then secretary-general of the PLO, was promoted to chairman of the PLO's 18-member executive committee, which includes chairman of the Palestine National Fund [q.v.]. As before, the political department, meaning the foreign affairs department, remained under Farouq Kaddoumi, a radical, based at the PLO headquarters in Tunis. Relations between Kaddoumi and Abbas became fraught when Abbas dismissed the national unity government in June 2007 and appointed Salam Fayyad [q.v.], a technocrat, prime minister. Kaddoumi publicly criticized Abbas. In retaliation, Abbas removed Kaddoumi loyalists as PLO ambassadors worldwide, and required international contacts to pass through his foreign minister.

On 15 November 2008—the 20th anniversary of the PNC's declaration of the independence and establishment of the State of Palestine—the PLO's central committee elected Abbas president of the State of Palestine. Egypt's efforts to conciliate the PLO and Hamas [q.v.] in 2009 failed.

In July 2010, the United States upgraded the status of the 16-year-old Washington-based PLO Mission in the U.S. to "General Delegation of the PLO." After their meeting in Cairo in December 2011, Mahmoud Abbas and Khaled Mashaal [q.v.] of Hamas [q.v.] decided to form a committee to prepare for the inclusion of Hamas and Islamic Jihad [q.v.] in the PLO.

Palestine National Charter: Though originally adopted by the Palestine National Council (PNC) [q.v.] at its inaugural session in East Jerusalem [q.v.] in May–June 1964, the Palestine National Charter became significant only in July 1968, when the Fourth PNC Congress in Cairo [q.v.] inserted the statement: "Armed struggle is the only way to liberate Palestine" (Article 9). Of the 33 articles in the charter the other important ones were: "Palestine, with the boundaries under the British Mandate, is the homeland of Palestinian Arabs [q.v.], and is indivisible" (Articles 1 and 2); "the Jews [q.v.] who lived in Palestine before the Zionist immigration are considered Palestinian" (Article 6); "the partition of Palestine and the founding of Israel are illegal since they violated the will of Palestinians and the principle of self-Mandate for Palestine are null and void" (Article 20); "the Palestinians reject all solutions which are substitutes for total liberation of Palestine" (Article 21); and "Zionism [q.v.], associated with international imperialism, is racist, expansionist, and colonial, and Israel is the instrument of the Zionist movement" (Article 22).

Although in November 1988 the PNC abandoned some of the basic principles of the Charter (such as the use of armed struggle to liberate Palestine, as constituted under the British Mandate) it did not amend the charter. But, on the eve of the signing of an accord between the Palestine Liberation Organization (PLO) [q.v.] and Israel in September 1993, PLO Chairman Yasser Arafat [q.v.] stated in a letter to Israeli Premier Yitzhak Rabin [q.v.] that those articles in the Palestine National Charter that denied Israel's right to exist and contradicted the PLO's commitment to renounce terrorism and other acts of violence would henceforth be "inoperative and no longer valid." and added that the PLO would submit to the PNC for formal approval the necessary changes in the Charter. Article 33 of the Charter requires a vote of two-thirds of all PNC members at a special session to amend it.

At the joint session of the PLO's 124-member Central Council, the 700-strong Palestine National Council, and the Palestinian Authority's [q.v.] 87 parliamentarians and 34 cabinet members in Gaza [q.v.] in December 1998—witnessed by U.S. President Bill Clinton—the Palestinian representatives passed a resolution radically altering the Palestine National Charter, with only a few dozen dissenting. The resolution endorsed the letter that Yasser Arafat had addressed to Clinton in January 1998, revoking those paragraphs of the Charter that clashed with the 1993 Oslo Accords [q.v.].

Palestine National Council: (Official title: National Council of the Palestine Liberation Organization [PLO] [q.v.]) Founded in May 1964 in East Jerusalem [q.v.], with 350 delegates representing the various groups affiliated to the Palestine Liberation Organization (PLO) [q.v.], the Palestine National Council (PNC) was inaugurated by King Hussein [q.v.] of Jordan. It adopted the Palestine National Charter [q.v.] and elected a central council and an executive committee. The 50-member Central Council, meeting once every three months, acted as an intermediary between the PNC (which was considered a Palestinian parliament in exile), and the ex-

ecutive committee handling day-to-day affairs, as well as deciding broad policy between the sessions of the PNC.

Any Palestinian Arab [q.v.] born in Palestine before 1947 or born of a Palestinian father after that, irrespective of his/her birthplace, was entitled to PNC membership. PNC membership was allocated to the affiliated political groups as well as the affiliated mass organizations of workers, students, women, teachers, doctors, and others, and representatives from the Occupied Territories [q.v.], and the Palestinian diaspora in Jordan, Syria, Lebanon, and the Gulf States [q.v.]. Normally the PNC met once a year.

Its acceptance of the resignation of Ahmad Shuqairi [q.v.] in 1967, followed by its stiffening of the charter in July 1968 in Cairo [q.v.], which became its headquarters after the 1967 Arab-Israeli War [q.v.], paved the way for hard-line Palestinian groups to affiliate to the PLO.

With the election of Yasser Arafat [q.v.] as chairman of the PLO, a new chapter opened in the history of PNC. At its seventh session in April 1972 it rejected King Hussein's plan for a united kingdom of two federated parts: Jordan and a Palestine consisting of the West Bank [q.v.] and Gaza [q.v.]. Yet overall it remained a middle-of-the-road body. Of its 292 members at the 13th session in March 1977 in Cairo, 172 were moderate and only 69 radical. After the Egyptian-Israeli Peace Treaty [q.v.] in 1979, the PNC headquarters was moved from Cairo to Damascus [q.v.].

The expulsion of the PLO from Beirut [q.v.] in September 1982, followed by the conflict between Arafat and Syrian President Hafiz Assad [*q.v.*], had divided the PNC. The PNC session in November 1984 in Amman [*q.v.*] was boycotted by the radicals, which made it easier to shift the headquarters from Damascus to Amman.

The radicals returned to the 18th session of the PNC, now 426-strong, in April 1987 in Algiers only after Arafat had abandoned his earlier agreement with King Hussein on a confederation of Jordan and a future Palestinian state. At the subsequent session in Algiers in November 1988, the radicals, though unhappy at the PNC's acceptance of a Palestinian state in the Occupied Territories [*q.v.*] and peaceful coexistence with Israel, accepted the majority decision. Here the PLO formally declared the establishment of the State of Palestine. Among the countries that would recognize this state was the Soviet Union.

The 20th session held in Algiers in September 1991 elected a new 18-member executive committee, with Arafat continuing as chairman. Protesting at the signing of the Israeli-PLO Accord [*q.v.*] in September 1993, seven of them, including Mahmoud Darwish [*q.v.*], resigned. Of the remaining 10, one each belonged to the Democratic People's Union, the Palestine People's Party [*q.v.*], and the Popular Struggle Front, and five were independent, including Archbishop Ilya Khouri.

On the eve of the signing of an accord with Israel, Arafat promised to submit necessary changes to the charter to the PNC. But it was only at the 21st session in April 1996 in Gaza that the PNC abrogated those articles of its Charter that denied Israel's existence. This was deemed insufficient by Benjamin Netanyahu [*q.v.*], elected Israeli prime minister in May. Therefore, at its 22nd session in December 1998—bolstered by the PLO's Central Council (with 88 of the 124 members attending) and the Palestinian Authority's [*q.v.*] parliamentarians and cabinet ministers in Gaza—the PNC (with the nominal membership of 700) overwhelmingly passed a resolution endorsing the letter that Yasser Arafat had addressed to U.S. President Bill Clinton in January, revoking all those paragraphs of the Charter that clashed with the 1993 Oslo Accord.

In 2003, the PNC, chaired by Salim Zanoun, had 669 members. Of these, 483 represented the Palestinian diaspora [*q.v.*], with the rest representing the Palestinians living in the West Bank, Gaza, and East Jerusalem [*q.v.*], including the 88 members of the Palestine Legislative Council.

During the reconciliation talks between Palestinian Authority [*q.v.*] President Mahmoud Abbas [*q.v.*] and Khaled Mashaal [*q.v.*] of Hamas [*q.v.*] in December 2011 in Cairo [*q.v.*], Zanoun acted as an effective mediator.

Palestine National Fund: The Palestine National Fund (PNF) was set up by the Palestine Liberation Organization (PLO) to meet its financial requirements. Contributions were in the form of grants from Arab and other friendly countries, a general Palestine tax collected by certain Arab states, income tax on the Palestinians living in the diaspora [*q.v.*], and returns on the investments made by the PNF's directors. The size of the contributions from these sources varied, with the taxes most likely providing majority of the revenue.

As the recipient of all income, the PNF funded the PLO according to the budget approved by the PLO's executive committee. It supervised the PLO's expenditure and set up channels for collecting funds. The PNF's chapters in many Arab states ensured that the Palestine taxes collected by the government and private companies were remitted to the PNF.

It shared its headquarters with the Palestine National Council [*q.v.*], first in Cairo [*q.v.*] and then in Damascus [*q.v.*] and Amman [*q.v.*]. In 1987 it moved to Abu Dhabi [*q.v.*].

The chairman of the PNF sits as a member of the PLO's executive committee. From 1984 to 1996 its chairman was Jaweed al-Ghussein, a successful businessman in Abu Dhabi. After the establishment of the Palestinian Authority [*q.v.*] in Gaza [*q.v.*] in 1994 with its own finance minsitry, the importance of the PNF declined sharply.

Palestine Papers: The Palestine Papers, published in January 2011, is the title given to a cache of 1,684 confidential documents—emails, maps, memorandums, minutes of private meetings, records of high level exchanges, strategy papers, and Power Point presentations—obtained by Al-Jazeera TV Channel, which shared it with the London-based *Guardian* newspaper. Leaked by Ziyad Clot, a member of the Negotiations Support Unit of Saeb Erekat, head of the Steering and Monitoring Committee of the Palestine Liberation Organization (PLO) [*q.v.*], these papers provided details of the negotiations between Israel and the Palestinians

from September 1999 to September 2010. The Palestine Papers covered the status of Jerusalem [*q.v.*] and the Jewish settlements and borders; Palestinian refugees and their right of return; and security coordination between Israel and the Palestinian Authority [*q.v.*].

Following the Middle East Peace Conference in Annapolis, Maryland, in 2007 [*q.v.*], American officials participated in the Israeli-Palestinian talks. Desperate to reach a peace accord, the Palestinian team led by Erekat made far-reaching concessions in the negotiations during 2008–09.

The Palestinians agreed to let Israel annex all its illegal Jewish settlements in the occupied East Jerusalem [*q.v.*], except Har Homa. On Haram al-Sharif/Temple Mount [*q.v.*] in the Old City of Jerusalem, the Palestinians proposed a joint committee of the Palestinian Authority [*q.v.*], Israel, Egypt, Jordan, Saudi Arabia, and the United States to administer the holy site until a permanent solution was reached. Regarding the right of return to the 4.7 million Palestinian refugees registered with the UN Relief and Work Agency for Palestinian Refugees in the Near East [*q.v.*], the Palestinian team agreed to a nominal figure of 10,000 to be allowed to return to their homes in Israel on "humanitarian" grounds. But the Israeli and American officials found these concessions inadequate.

For their part, the Palestinians rejected the option of a state with provisional borders or any further transitional or interim solution.

The publication of the Palestine Papers led to the resignatoin of Erekat as the chief Palestinian negotiator.

Palestine People's Party: *See* Communist Party of Palestine.

Palestine War (1948–49): *See* Arab-Israeli War I (1948–49).

Palestinian Authority: (Official title in Arabic: *Al-Sulta al-Watanniyya al-Filistiniyya*, the Palestinian National Authority, used by Arab [*q.v.*] countries and organizations) The Palestinian Authority (PA) is the name of the legislative and executive body responsible for exercising all powers and functions devolved by Israel to the autonomous Palestinian areas under the Oslo Accord I [*q.v.*] in September 1993. The maximum strength of its executive body was fixed at 24.

In June 1994 Yasser Arafat [*q.v.*], its president/chairman (Arabic: *raees*) and interior minister, appointed 19 other members, including Ahmed Qurei, who had conducted secret talks with Israel in Norway; Faisal Husseini [*q.v.*], a nephew of Haajj Muhammad Amin al-Husseini [*q.v.*]; Elias Freij, the Christian [*q.v.*] mayor of Bethlehem [*q.v.*]; and Intisar Wazir, widow of the assassinated Khalil Wazir [*q.v.*].

This arrangement continued until elections were held in the West Bank [*q.v.*] and Gaza [*q.v.*] to the 87-member Palestinian Legislative Council (PLC) in January 1996, after Israel had vacated most towns and cities in the West Bank [*q.v.*] following the signing of the Oslo Accord II [*q.v.*]. These were boycotted by Hamas [*q.v.*] and Islamic Jihad [*q.v.*]. Of those elected, 54 belonged to Fatah [*q.v.*], one each belonged to the Popular Front for the Liberation of Palestine [*q.v.*] and the Palestinian Democratic Union, and four were independent Is-

lamists [*q.v.*]. Among the rest, 11 were pro-Fatah independents and the remainder truly independent. Azmi Shuaibi was elected speaker of the PLC. The reconstituted cabinet had 28 ministers, chaired by the newly elected President Arafat. According to the law passed by the PLC, its tenure was scheduled to expire when Israel had implemented all its obligations under the Oslo Accord II, originally by September 1998. Within a year the PLC passed a draft constitution, which Arafat failed to sign.

With the election of Benjamin Netanyahu [*q.v.*] as Israel's prime minister in 1996, the Oslo Accords [*q.v.*] suffered a hemorrhage from which they did not recover fully during the premiership of Ehud Barak [*q.v.*] from 1999 to 2001. By 1999, Israel had finally allowed the establishment of a 20-mi./32-km-long safe corridor for Palestinians between the West Bank and the Gaza Strip, and the PA had gained full civilian control over seven percent of the West Bank and joint control over another 23 percent, and acquired an armed police force of 40,000.

At the same time complaints about the PA's inefficiency and corruption had risen to the extent that both the European Union [*q.v.*] and the International Monetary Fund, the chief financial backers of the PA, publicly demanded reform. In January 2000 the PA set up the Higher Council for Development, chaired by Arafat, to ensure transparency of public finances. By then the headquarters of the PA had moved from Gaza [*q.v.*] to the West Bank town of Ramallah [*q.v.*].

Following the outbreak of the Second Intifada [*q.v.*], supported by all Palestinian parties, in September 2000, Israel hit the PA's offices in Gaza and the West Bank. As violence escalated, the Israeli government under Prime Minister Ariel Sharon systematically destroyed the security, administrative, and economic infrastructure of the PA, leaving only one of the buildings standing in the PA's Ramallah headquarters, where Arafat was placed under house arrest in April 2002. This reduced the PA to a threadbare organization.

Arafat's government acquired notoriety for ineptitude, corruption, and mismanagement. It was only in 2002 that Arafat signed the Basic Law passed by the PLC in 1999, which specified three independent organs of the state: executive, legislative, and judiciary. But, ignoring the new reality, Arafat maintained monopoly of power. It was not until March 2003 when, unable to withstand pressure by Western governments providing most of the funds to the PA, that he agreed to appoint a prime minister to share some of his power.

His first prime minsiter, Mahmoud Abbas [q.v.], resigned after six months when Arafat refused to transfer authority over security forces to him. Ahmad Qurie, his second prime minister, also resigned after six months. After Arafat's death in November 2004, Abbas succeeded him as the acting president of the PA. In the election for president that followed in Jnuary 2005, Abbas secured 62 percent of the vote.

In 2005, once Israel had evacuated the Gaza Strip, the area under the PA's jurisdiction rose from 60 percent to 100 percent, but it did not extend to Gaza's air space or territorial waters.

In the elections to the 132-member PLC in January 2006, Hamas [q.v.] emerged as the victor, and Ismail Haniyah [q.v.] became prime minister in March. When his government refused to recognize Israel, renounce violence, and accept all the previous agreements of the Palestine Liberation Organization (PLO) [q.v.] and the PA with Israel, the United States, the EU, and Israel froze all funds due to the PA.

To resolve the resulting crisis, Hamas agreed with Fatah to form a national unity government. This was done in mid-March 2007. Three months later it fell apart when, in a violent confrontation, Hamas expelled Fatah from the Gaza Strip.

Abbas appointed a new government led by a technocrat, Salam Fayyad [q.v.], and based it in Ramallah. It was recognized by Saudi Arabia, Jordan, and Egypt, which moved its embassy from Gaza City to Ramallah. The division between the Fatah-ruled West Bank and Hamas-governed Gaza continued until April 2011 when mediation by Egypt's post-Mubarak foreign minister Nabil al-Araby [q.v.] reconciled the rivals. But the subsequent agreement on power-sharing between the two organizations until a fresh election, signed in February 2012, remained to be implemented.

While the PA's application to the UN Security Council in September 2011 that Palestine should be admitted as a full member of the United Nations failed, Palestine gained membership of the UN Education, Scientific, and Cultural Organization in October, with 107 voting for it and 14 against.

Palestinian National Authority (Arabic: *Al-Sulta al-Watanniyya al*

Filistiniyya): This is the term used by Arab countries and organizations for the Palestinian Authority [*q.v.*].

Palestinian Territories: They consist of East Jerusalem [*q.v.*], the Gaza Strip [*q.v.*], and the West Bank [*q.v.*]. *See* Occupied Territories.

Palmah (Hebrew: acronym of *Plugot Mahatz,* Shock Units): The Palmah, the elite command force of Haganah [*q.v.*], was formed in May 1941 to implement special assignments. It drew its recruits from left-wing kibbutizm [*q.v.*]. Though illegal, it cooperated with British troops and participated in reconnaissance for their Lebanese campaign in June 1941. At the end of World War II it was 2,000 strong. It cooperated with the right-wing Irgun [*q.v.*] and the Stern Group [*q.v.*] in a violent campaign against the British Mandate, blowing up railroad tracks, bridges, and radar and other installations. In mid-1946, when the British turned against Haganah and the Palmah, the Haganah leadership ordered the Palmah to focus on furthering illegal Jewish immigration. By the time the United Nations adopted a partition plan in November 1947 the Palmah was 5,000 strong.

During the run-up to the Palestine War (1948–49) [*q.v.*], the Palmah often cooperated with Irgun and the Stern Group, providing one of its units for an attack on Deir Yassin village in April 1948, which resulted in the massacre of 254 Arabs—men, women, and children. In the first months of the Palestine War, Palmah and Haganah troops carried out dozens of raids on Arab villages with the primary aim of razing them. Thus

472 of the 755 Arab villages disappeared without a trace.

After the establishment of Israel in May 1948, Prime Minister David Ben-Gurion [*q.v.*] decided to merge all Zionist [*q.v.*] militias into a national military organization. Therefore, the general staff of the Palmah was dissolved in 1949.

pan-Arabism: Pan-Arabism is a doctrine that maintains that no matter where Arabs [*q.v.*] live they are part of a single community. It first manifested itself in the Arab territory of the Ottoman Empire from 1876–1878 when a written constitution, promulgated by Sultan Abdul Hamid II, provided some element of free expression. It reemerged in 1908 after the Young Turks in Istanbul had mounted a successful coup against the sultan, only to go underground soon after the new rulers adopted the traditional stance of Turkish superiority.

The outbreak of World War I provided the Ottoman's Arab subjects and notables an option to further their nationalist cause by siding with the anti-Ottoman forces. By declaring an Arab revolt in 1916, Hussein bin Ali, the Hashemite governor of Hijaz [*q.v.*], became the leader of pan-Arabism, with a plan to see the Arab territories formed into a single independent Arab state after the defeat of the Ottomans. But this scenario contradicted the aims of the clandestine 1916 Sykes-Picot Pact [*q.v.*] signed by Britain and France.

During the interwar period the al-Hashem clan [*q.v.*], which ruled Iraq and Transjordan [*q.v.*], remained the repository of pan-Arabism. This changed in 1948 when, in order to annex parts of Palestine [*q.v.*] to his realm, King Abdullah bin Hussein [*q.v.*] of Jordan tried to make a secret deal with the Zionists [*q.v.*]. Thereafter, pan-Arab nationalists came to regard him as a traitor to their cause.

Following the 1948–49 Palestine War [*q.v.*] and the establishment of Israel, pan-Arabism centered on the Arab struggle for the retrieval of Palestine from the Zionists [*q.v.*]. With the Free Officers' successful coup in Egypt in 1952, the mantle of pan-Arab leadership fell on Abdul Gamal Nasser [*q.v.*], president of the most populous and strategic Arab country, which had so far contributed little to pan-Arabism, except to provide headquarters, since its inception in 1945, to the Arab League [*q.v.*], a pan-Arab institution conceived originally by the British to further their interests in the region.

Nasser's first step toward creating a unified Arab state in 1958—the merger of Egypt and Syria into the United Arab Republic [*q.v.*]—failed three years later. Yet on the eve of the June 1967 Arab-Israeli War [*q.v.*], he was able to lead a joint military command of Egypt, Syria, and Jordan.

After this conflict, which ended with Arab defeat, pan-Arabism revolved around the objective of recovering all Arab territories lost to Israel in Egypt, Syria, and Jordan. The military alliance of Egypt and Syria in October 1973, backed by the military and oil muscle of the rest of the Arab world, was the next manifestation of pan-Arabism. It proved to be the pinnacle of the movement.

By signing a peace treaty with Israel in 1979, Egypt, under President Anwar Sadat [*q.v.*], destroyed the Arab con-

sensus that there should be no unilateral peace treaty with Israel. With this, Egypt lost its leadership of pan-Arabism, leaving Syrian President Hafiz Assad [*q.v.*] to carry the banner. Assad was committed to retrieving all Occupied Arab Territories [*q.v.*] from Israel.

The attempt by President Saddam Hussein [*q.v.*] of Iraq to portray his war with Iran as a struggle for "all of Arab homeland" against Persian expansionism, masquerading as pan-Islamism [*q.v.*], was only partially successful. With such important Arab states as Syria, Algeria, and Libya siding with Iran, Saddam Hussein failed to project himself as a latter-day Nasser. Indeed his invasion and annexation of Kuwait in August 1990 severely split the Arab League and mortally weakened pan-Arabism. This became clear a year later when the Arab neighbors of Israel and the Palestinians agreed to negotiate with Israel, not collectively under UN auspices as they had hitherto unanimously insisted, but bilaterally, as Israel had proposed.

What remains of pan-Arabism is the Arab League, consisting of 22 Arabic-speaking member countries, but even that institution was somewhat undermined by the emergence of the Gulf Cooperation Council [*q.v.*] in 1981, and the Arab Maghreb Union, encompassing five North African Arab states of Algeria, Libya, Mauritania, Morocco, and Tunisia in 1989.

A final blow to pan-Arabism came in the wake of the Arab Spring (2011-2012) when, at the instigation of Saudi Arabia and Qatar, the Arab League paved the way for the violent downfall of Colonel Muammar Gaddafi in Libya in September 2011 followed by its ostracizing of Syria ruled by Arab Baath Party [*q.v.*], wedded to the doctrine of pan-Arabism since its inception in 1947.

pan-Islamism: Pan-Islamism is a traditional doctrine that maintains that, no matter where Muslims live, they belong to a universal Islamic *umma* (Arabic: community) [*q.v.*]. It transcends linguistic, cultural, and other ethnic differences among Muslims.

Pan-Islamism proved useful to the Ottoman rulers in the late 19th century. Sultan Abdul Hamid II (r. 1876–1909) tried to regenerate cohesion in Ottoman society by mobilizing the masses around the Islamic banner and engendering a pan-Islamic movement. By manifesting personal piety, appointing Arabs [*q.v.*] to important posts at the court, and constructing a railway from Damascus [*q.v.*] to Mecca [*q.v.*] to promote the hajj [*q.v.*], he showed his commitment to pan-Islamism. In this he had the active backing of Jamal al-Din Afghani (1838–1897), a religious personality of varied talents, whom he invited to Constantinople (now Istanbul) in 1892. Since Afghani played an active role in the religious-political life of all the important Islamic regions—Ottoman Turkey, Egypt, Iran, India, and Central Asia—he acquired a truly pan-Islamic perspective and realized that the Islamic *umma* as a whole was threatened by European powers.

The dissolution of the Ottoman Empire—the last in the series of Islamic empires—in the wake of World War I, followed by the abolition of the caliphate in 1924 by the Republic of Turkey, was a blow to pan-Islamism. But a few years later the pan-Islamic concept was relaunched on a popular basis in Egypt by the Muslim Brotherhood [*q.v.*] established by Hassan al-Banna [*q.v.*]. The Egyptian Brotherhood set up sister organizations in Syria, Transjordan (now Jordan), and Palestine [*q.v.*]. The pan-Islamic movement in Egypt reached a climax in 1949, the year when al-Banna [*q.v.*] was assassinated.

In the course of popularizing pan-Arabism [*q.v.*] and then Arab socialism [*q.v.*], Egyptian President Abdul Gamal Nasser [*q.v.*] suppressed the Brotherhood. The mantle of pan-Islamism was then taken up by the House of Saud [*q.v.*], specifically King Faisal bin Abdul Aziz [*q.v.*], a devout Muslim, who promoted it in the mid-1960s as a competing ideology to Nasser's Arab socialism [*q.v.*]. He failed, but in 1969 an abortive attempt to set fire to Islam's third-holiest shrine, the al-Aqsa Mosque in Jerusalem [*q.v.*], created an environment in which Faisal was able to sponsor the Islamic Conference Organization (ICO) [*q.v.*], composed of Muslim states throughout the world, and base it in Jeddah [*q.v.*].

As a multinational body representing governments, the ICO paralleled the Arab League [*q.v.*]. However, what caught popular attention in both the Muslim and non-Muslim world was the successful Islamic revolution [*q.v.*] in Iran in early 1979, which overthrew the secular, pro-Western regime of Muhammad Reza Shah Pahlavi [*q.v.*]. Article 10 of Iran's constitution requires the government to formulate its general policies with a view to "the merging and union of all Muslim peoples"; and Article 152 requires Iranian foreign policy to be based on "the defense of the rights of all Muslims." However, as Iran is populated mainly by Shias [*q.v.*], a minority sect within Islam [*q.v.*], its impact has been limited to such pockets in the Muslim world as Bahrain and the Shia communities in Lebanon and Iraq.

In 1991 the military regime in Algeria struck a blow against pan-Islamism by aborting the imminent electoral victory of the Front for Islamic Salvation.

The electoral successes of the Muslim Brotherhood and Al Nour party [*q.v.*] in a democratic Egypt in 2011–2012, have unveiled the possibility of a revival of pan-Islamism in a much changed world.

Pasha, Nahas: *See* Nahas (Pasha), Mustafa.

Passover (Hebrew: *Pesach,* derivative of the root meaning "pass over"): One of the four major Jewish festivals, lasting seven (in Israel) to eight (in the diaspora [*q.v.*]) days, the term *Passover* applies strictly to the first day. It celebrates the "passing over" by destructive forces (on the eve of the exodus when the Lord "smote the Land of Egypt," Exodus 12:13) of the Israelites, who had poured the blood of a lamb on their door posts to show they were children of God. The festival begins on the 15th of Nisan, the first month of the Jewish calendar [*q.v.*]. At the ceremonial evening meals on the first and second day of the festival, there is a recitation of certain passages of Exodus. During the festival only unleavened bread is eaten as a reminder that the Jews [*q.v.*] fleeing Egypt had no time to leaven their bread.

Patriotic Union of Kurdistan: *Iraqi Kurdish party* The Patriotic Union of Kurdistan (PUK) was formed in mid-1976 by the merger of the Kurdish Workers League and the Social Democratic Movement under the leadership of Jalal Talabani [*q.v.*]. Both PUK constituents had emerged from the Kurdistan Democratic Party (KDP) [*q.v.*] after its leader, Mustafa Barzani [*q.v.*], fled to Iran in the wake of the March 1975 Algiers Accord [*q.v.*].

Under Talabani—who, during his tenure as the KDP's envoy to Syria, had been influenced by the leftist Palestinian leaders George Habash [*q.v.*] and Nayif Hawatmeh [*q.v.*]—the PUK described itself as Marxist-Leninist. It conducted its armed struggle against the Baghdad regime as well as the KDP, which had its bastion in the northwest of the Kurdistan Autonomous Region (KAR) [*q.v.*]. Based at Yakhsamar in Suleimaniyah province, the PUK was strong in the southeast.

With the outbreak of the Iran-Iraq War [*q.v.*] in September 1980 the chances of Kurdish guerrilla activity improved sharply, with the PUK concentrating its operations in its stronghold. A PUK agreement with the KDP in 1982 to open all of the KAR to both parties failed to endure. Overall the PUK expanded at the KDP's expense. In 1984, yielding to the pressure of its war with Iran, the Baghdad government started negotiating with the PUK, but nothing came of it. This laid the groundwork for the PUK's subsequent ties with Iran, which began arming PUK activists. Iran tried to reconcile the PUK and the KDP. It succeeded in May 1987, when the two parties combined with six others to form the Iraqi Kurdistan Front (IKF).

Both the PUK and the KDP set up liberated areas along Iraq's borders with Iran and Turkey. But with Iraq prevailing over Iran in 1988 the situation changed. Following the Baghdad regime's onslaught on nationalist Kurds in 1988, the PUK and other IKF constituents fled across the border to Iran or Syria. Baghdad demanded public recantation from PUK leaders before they could be allowed to submit their demands to the government.

The crisis created by the Iraqi invasion of Kuwait [*q.v.*] in August 1990 revived the PUK and other IKF members. In March 1991, soon after the end of the Gulf War II [*q.v.*], the PUK and the KDP revolted against the central government. Within a few weeks they captured three-quarters of the KAR. But they were unable to withstand Baghdad's counteroffensive. The crushing of the rebellion caused an exodus of some 1.5 million Kurdish refugees.

Pressured by the UN Security Council, Iraq declared a cease-fire in the KAR in mid-April. Talabani was deputy leader of the IKF delegation that negotiated with Baghdad on the basis of the 1970 pact between the central government and Kurdish autonomists. These talks ended in mid-June with an agreement on the extent of Kurdish autonomy, which was meant to encourage the return of Kurdish refugees to revive the 3,800 villages that had been razed by the Iraqi government over the past 17 years. However, Talabani recommended to IKF leaders that the deal should be rejected. It was. Pressured by the Western powers, the Iraqi government

withdrew its last troops from the KAR in October.

Following the general election in the KAR in May 1992, held under the protection of Western air forces, the PUK shared power equally with the KDP. This arrangement was applied even to teachers and policemen. In the ministries two different command structures emerged. With each party allowed to open offices in the other's bastion, enabling it to raise its strength at the expense of the other, traditional tensions between them rose sharply. As a party directed by urban-based leaders, the PUK remained antipathetic to the KDP's continuing tribal ways.

In May 1994 clashes between them left more than 1,000 fighters and civilians dead. Despite periodic cease-fires, relations soured further when the PUK participated in the military plan by the Washington-funded Iraqi National Congress (INC) [*q.v.*] to overthrow President Saddam Hussein [*q.v.*] in March 1995, while the KDP did not. The intermittent intra-Kurdish violence raised the total death toll to 3,000 by September 1995. The PUK's capture of the regional capital of Irbil [*q.v.*] in December left the two sides intensely embittered.

It was against this background that the PUK found itself under attack in Irbil in late August 1996 by the KDP bolstered by Saddam Hussein's tanks and artillery. The retreating PUK lost not only Irbil but also all of its territory in the southeast, and its leaders and fighters took shelter in Iran. From their haven they launched a counteroffensive and recaptured all the lost territory except Irbil at the cost of 2,000 fatalities. Initialing a temporary accord in October, mediated by American and British diplomats, the two sides agreed to discuss sharing of the customs revenue currently monopolized by the KDP as well as conducting a new parliamentary election. Nothing came of it.

After the passage of the Iraq Liberation Act in Washington in October 1998, which authorized the White House to designate Iraqi opposition groups eligible for military aid by America, the PUK found itself included in the list of seven such factions. On the ground very little changed, with Kurdistan divided administratively into two sectors, with the PUK's territory ruled from Suleimaniyah.

It was not until September 2002, when Washington's plans to invade Iraq went into a higher gear, that the PUK decided to bury its hatchet with the KDP.

This modus vivendi continued in the post-Saddam Hussein Iraq. To run in the elections to the Interim Iraqi Parliament as well as the Kurdistan National Assembly and three provincial councils, in January 2005, the PUK allied with the KDP and a few small groups to form the Democratic Patriotic Alliance of Kurdistan. In the national parliament the Alliance won 26 percent of the vote and 53 seats out of 275. It played an important role in the drafting of the new constitution which among other things described Iraq as composed of two nations, Arabs and Kurds.

Under the new constitution, Talabani was elected president of Iraq and Masoud Barazani president of the Kurdistan Regional Government. The PUK-KDP Alliance won 78 of the 111 seats in the regional legislative as-

sembly with a four-year tenure. In the 2009 election, when the turnout was 79 percent, the Alliance did less well, securing only 59 seats. Its main challenger, the Reform Movement, claimed 25 seats. Following its lackluster performance amid widespread allegations of corruption, the PUK held a much-postponed plenum in October 2009, which promised unity and reform. There was no noticeable change.

Peace Now: *An extra-parliamentary Israeli group* (Official title, Hebrew *Shalom Achshav.*) It was founded by 348 reserve officers and soldiers of the Israel Defense Forces (IDF) [*q.v.*] to support the Camp David Accords [*q.v.*] between Israel [*q.v.*] and Egypt [*q.v.*] in 1978. Its primary function was to pressure the Israeli government to seek peace with its Arab [*q.v.*] neighbors as well as the Palestinians, whose right to an independent state it recognized. It also accepted the idea that the municipal borders of Jerusalem [*q.v.*], expanded by Israel after the 1967 Six-Day War [*q.v.*], could be readjusted, and that the two states could have their capitals in Jerusalem: the Palestinians in the Arab areas, the Israelis in the Jewish neighborhoods. It advocated a peace treaty with Syria, on the basis of total Israeli withdrawal from the Golan Heights [*q.v.*], for total normalization of relations with Israel by Syria.

A nonpartisan, volunteer movement with branches throughout the country, Peace Now's national secretariat, based in Tel Aviv [*q.v.*], decides policy, with its branches conducting activities on an almost autonomous basis. It has sister Organizations in America, Britain, Belgium, and the Netherlands.

As part of the final settlement with the Palestinians, Peace Now visualized some Jewish settlements being absorbed into Israel, some disbanded, and the rest allowed to exist under Palestinian sovereignty and law. In the late 1980s, its Settlement Watch section started monitoring and documenting the expropriation of Palestinian land and houses, the building of new Jewish settlements, and the expansion of the existing ones in the West Bank [*q.v.*], Gaza Strip [*q.v.*], and East Jerusalem [*q.v.*]. It publishes periodic updates on the subject, and uses this information in appeals to the judiciary and for lobbying politicians.

Before the Oslo Accord of 1993 [*q.v.*], Peace Now leaders held clandestine talks with the Palestinian leaders abroad. After it, they organized many joint activities, vigils, marches, and symposia with the Palestinians. As a result of its persistent lobbying, the Israeli public opinion favoring a Palestinian state rose from 1 percent in 1977 to over 50 percent in 1997.

Its most dramatic achievement was in the case of Lebanon [*q.v.*]. It led the mass movement against Israel's 1982 invasion of Lebanon, mobilizing 400,000 people in a protest rally in the aftermath of the conflict, and finally succeeding in securing Israel's withdrawal from south Lebanon in May 2000.

But the launching of the Al Aqsa intifada [*q.v.*] in September had an adverse effect on the Peace Now movement, as many Israelis interpreted the fresh intifada as signifying the end of the peace process that started with the Oslo Accord I in 1993.

The movement then started focusing on monitoring the expansion of the Jewish settlements in the Occupied Palestinian Territories [*q.v.*] and the setting up of illegal outposts on hilltops by using aerial photography. Its Settlement Watch Committee soon established itself as the most authoritative on the subject.

When ultra-right-wing groups mounted a campaign against the evacuation of Gaza, Peace Now organized a 10,000 strong pro-evacuation rally in Tel Aviv in March 2005.

According to classified U.S. cables leaked by the anti-secrecy group WikiLeaks in April 2011, this committee supplies information to the Israeli defense ministry and the United States. It also continued to approach courts to bring about the removeal of unauthorized Jewish outposts in the West Bank. Following one such move, the Supreme Court ordered the government in March 2011 to dismantle all illegal West Bank outposts built on private Palestinian land within a year. The implementation of this blanket order remained unclear.

Peace Process, Middle East:

(1) AFTER THE ARAB-ISRAELI WAR, 1948–49 [*q.v.*]: Following the truces signed between Israel and its Arab [*q.v.*] enemies in 1949, behind-the-scene efforts were made by the United States to secure Israel's recognition by one or more of its Arab neighbors. Washington was behind the military coup in Syria in March 1949 that put Col. Hosni Zaim [*q.v.*] in power. But when, as promised, he opened secret talks with Israel, he was overthrown in August. When King Abdullah I bin Hussein [*q.v.*] of Jordan established

clandestine contacts with Israeli leaders he was assassinated in 1951. Israel's aggression toward Egypt in collusion with Britain and France in 1956 hardened the stance of the Arab states toward Israel. In the mid-1960s competition between radical Egyptian President Gamal Abdul Nasser [*q.v.*] and conservative Saudi King Faisal bin Abdul Aziz [*q.v.*] for leadership of the Arab world intensified, and neither could afford to be less than militantly anti-Zionist [*q.v.*].

(2) AFTER THE JUNE 1967 ARAB-ISRAELI WAR [*q.v.*]: The Arab summit in Khartoum from 29 August to 1 September 1967 combined its rejection of Israel—no peace, no recognition, and no negotiation—with its insistence on the Palestinians exercising their self-determination right. To ensure that Israel did not consolidate the territorial gains it had made in the 1967 conflict, Egypt initiated a War of Attrition [*q.v.*] in March 1969, which continued until mid-1970. In December 1969 U.S. Secretary of State William Rogers offered a peace plan, later called the Rogers Plan [*q.v.*], which opposed Israeli expansionism and recommended that any boundary modifications to the pre-June 1967 Israel be limited to "insubstantial alternatives required for mutual security." This was rejected by both Egypt and Israel. Egypt wanted unconditional Israeli withdrawal from the Occupied Arab Territories [*q.v.*] before negotiating a peace agreement with it. In contrast, Israel wanted direct unconditional talks with its Arab adversaries.

As the War of Attrition escalated in 1970, Rogers revived his initiative and focused on securing a cease-fire, en-

abling the UN mediator, Gunnar Jarring, to get the peace process going under UN Security Council Resolution 242 (November 1967, requiring return of captured Arab lands for peace for Israel). He presented this proposal to Egypt, Israel, Jordan, and Syria on 19 June 1970. After consulting the Soviet Union, Nasser accepted the Rogers proposal on 22 July. Jordan did so on 25 July, and the Israeli parliament followed suit on 31 July after the government had received certain secret assurances from U.S. President Richard Nixon. The 90-day truce went into effect on 7 August 1970. After Nasser's death in September, his successor, Anwar Sadat [*q.v.*], renewed the cease-fire. But the UN mediator's peace efforts got nowhere. Having failed to secure Israel's withdrawal from Sinai [*q.v.*], Sadat planned a military campaign, in coordination with Syria, to retrieve the Arab territories occupied by Israel in 1967.

(3) AFTER THE OCTOBER 1973 ARAB-ISRAELI WAR [*q.v.*]: The one-day UN peace conference in Geneva on 22 December 1973, under the cochairmanship of the U.S. and the Soviet Union and attended by Israel, Egypt, and Jordan, did not reassemble as planned because Sadat chose to pursue a unilateral path in his talks with Israel through U.S. Secretary of State Henry Kissinger. The result was the Sinai I Agreement [*q.v.*] between Egypt and Israel in January 1974. A truce between Syria and Israel on the Golan Heights [*q.v.*] was signed in June 1974. Next followed the Sinai II Agreement [*q.v.*] between Egypt and Israel, valid for three years, and signed on 4 September 1975. Israel agreed to

this deal only after it had received written guarantees from the U.S. that it would not have talks with the Palestine Liberation Organization (PLO) [*q.v.*] unless it ceased its terrorist activity against Israel and recognized Israel's right to exist in tranquility.

In 1976, an American presidential election year, the peace process came to a halt. It was only in October 1977, when the new U.S. President Jimmy Carter had settled into his job, that a joint U.S.-Soviet Union declaration stated the terms for reconvening the Geneva conference in December. But because of the Israeli disapproval, no such meeting took place. In November the dramatic visit of Sadat to Jerusalem [*q.v.*] to address the Israeli Knesset [*q.v.*] altered the course of the peace process. The accords between Israel and Egypt, signed at Camp David, Maryland, in September 1978, covered relations between the two countries, and between Israel and the Palestinians, even though their sole representative, the PLO, did not participate in the talks. On 26 March 1979 Egypt and Israel signed a peace treaty in Washington. By the time the two countries exchanged ambassadors in February 1980, Israel had returned two-thirds of Sinai to Egypt. But 26 May 1980—the target date for an agreement on Palestinian self-rule—passed unnoticed. On 26 April 1982 Israel returned the last part of Sinai to Egypt.

After the expulsion of the PLO from Beirut [*q.v.*], on 1 September 1982, U.S. President Ronald Reagan presented a peace plan that reaffirmed UN Security Council Resolution 242 [*q.v.*]. While explicitly excluding Israeli annexation, sovereignty, or domination over the Occupied Territories [*q.v.*], it also ruled out an independent Palestinian state. Instead it favored Palestinian self-government "in association with Jordan" and called on Jordan and the Palestinians to widen the 1978 Camp David Accords [*q.v.*] so that a self-governing Palestinian authority could be elected to succeed the Israeli rule. Israeli Prime Minister Menachem Begin [*q.v.*] summarily rejected this proposal because he had not been consulted, and the Reagan Plan was dead on arrival.

On 6 September 1982 the Arab League summit in Fez adopted an eight-point peace plan, which included Israel's withdrawal to its pre-1967 borders, the dismantling of the Jewish settlements in the Occupied Arab Territories [*q.v.*], the exercising of Palestinian self-determination under the PLO to create a State of Palestine with its capital in East Jerusalem [*q.v.*], the right of Palestinian refugees to return home or receive compensation, and a UN Security Council guarantee of peace for all the states of the region, including Palestine. Syria backed this plan. There was no comment by Israel.

After falling out with Syrian President Hafiz Assad [*q.v.*] in 1983, PLO Chairman Yasser Arafat [*q.v.*] initiated talks with King Hussein [*q.v.*] of Jordan early the following year. In February 1985 they announced a peace plan that envisaged Palestinians exercising their right to self-determination within the framework of a confederation of Jordan and Palestine, and a joint Jordanian-Palestinian delegation participating in peace talks organized under UN auspices. When

Israel failed to respond to the proposal, Jordan ended its diplomatic collaboration with the PLO. The Palestine National Council [q.v.] cancelled the 1985plan in April 1987. Meanwhile Syria pursued a policy of achieving strategic parity with Israel.

In February 1988 George Shultz, the U.S. secretary of state, offered a plan, specifying a negotiating period of six months between Israel and a Jordanian-Palestinian delegation to work out details of a transitional autonomy arrangement for the West Bank [q.v.] and Gaza [q.v.]. The arrangement would remain in force for three years, during which a final settlement would be negotiated. The talks would run concurrently with an international peace conference, involving the five permanent members of the UN Security Council and all the interested parties, on the basis of Security Council Resolutions 242 and 338 (on 22 October 1973, calling on warring parties to cease fire and start implementing Resolution 242). Israeli Prime Minister Yitzhak Shamir [q.v.] rejected the plan, calling it impractical. Since the Shultz Plan lacked any provision for a Palestinian state, the PLO turned it down. So did other Palestinian leaders, who saw it as a ploy to defuse the Intifada [q.v.], which had started two months earlier.

With King Hussein finally cutting administrative and legal links with the West Bank in July 1988, Israel's strategy of persuading Jordan to join the enlarged Camp David Accords became redundant. On the other hand it opened the way for the Palestine National Council to issue a declaration of independence for "our Palestinian land" and renounce violence and terrorism, at its session in Algiers in November 1988. This opened the way for the U.S. to establish low-level contact with the PLO headquarters in Tunis.

During 1989, with the tide of Soviet Jewish immigration building up due to Moscow's relaxed policies—raising the total number of immigrants from 13,300 in 1988 to 199,500 two years later—a new factor entered the process. In June 1990 Washington suspended talks with the PLO when the latter failed to condemn attacks on Israel by the radical Palestine Liberation Front, affiliated to the PLO, because its target was military.

During the crisis preceding Gulf War II [q.v.] the PLO backed Iraqi President Saddam Hussein [q.v.] because he tied Iraq's evacuation of Kuwait to Israel's withdrawal from the Occupied Arab Territories, a linkage summarily rejected by Washington. On the other hand, when during his meeting with U.S. President George H. W. Bush in Geneva in November 1990, President Assad pointed out the double standards used by Washington regarding Iraq and Israel, Bush assured him that after the war he would act as a catalyst between Israel and the Arabs in bringing about a peace settlement.

(4) After the 1991 Gulf War [q.v.]: The defeat of Iraq, the only independently radical Arab state, provided an incentive to U.S. Secretary of State James Baker to revive the peace process. The chances of this improved in mid-July 1991 because of Assad's concessions on his terms for attending an international conference on Middle East peace in the belief that his accommodating gesture would shift the blame for the failure to convene

such a gathering on the obdurate Israel. The preconditions by Israel, now ruled by a right-wing coalition government headed by Yitzhak Shamir [*q.v.*], were the exclusion of the PLO from the talks; the inclusion of the Palestinians resident in the Occupied Territories but unconnected with the PLO in a joint Jordanian-Palestinian delegation; any settlement with the Palestinians to include a transitional period of autonomy under the Israelis; and the negotiations to be bilateral, with no third country acting as a mediator or arbiter. In return, Israel conceded the principle of land for peace as contained in UN Security Council Resolution 242.

The Middle East Peace Conference was held in Madrid on 30 October under the cochairmanship of the U.S. and the Soviet Union (later Russia). When in his speech, Shamir described Syria as a "terrorist state," the Syrian foreign minister, Farouq al-Shaara, responded by holding up a picture of a poster showing Shamir as a wanted fugitive concerning the assassination of Lord Moyne, the British resident minister in the Middle East.

After the preliminaries, bilateral talks started between Israel and Syria, and Lebanon and the Jordanians-Palestinians. A second stream of multilateral negotiations concerning regional matters was also initiated. These included issues such as refugees, water, the economy, ecology, and regional security and disarmament. Syria and Lebanon boycotted these talks.

In the course of the bilateral negotiations the Jordanian-Palestinian delegation split into two, and the contact between the Palestinian delegates and the PLO gradually became public.

Moreover, the four Arab delegations coordinated their strategies at joint sessions, often held in Damascus [*q.v.*], before attending new rounds of talks. The bilateral talks made little progress despite the installation of a Labor-led [*q.v.*] government following the defeat in June 1992 of Likud [*q.v.*] led by Shamir—who later revealed that he had planned to keep the negotiations going for 10 years. Nor did the situation alter when Bill Clinton succeeded George H. W. Bush as U.S. president in January 1993. The 10th round, held in Washington in June–July, was as sterile as the preceding nine.

Unknown to the Americans or anybody else, the Israeli government and the PLO had entered into Norwegian-organized secret talks in Norway in January 1993. These resulted in an agreement on principles in late August, which was initialed by the Israeli foreign minister, Shimon Peres [*q.v.*], and the PLO official, Ahmad Qurei, in Oslo. The formal signing of the Israeli-PLO Accord [*q.v.*] took place in Washington on 13 September in the presence of President Clinton.

(5) AFTER THE ISRAELI-PLO ACCORD, SEPTEMBER 1993 [*q.v.*]: Having ended the state of war between Jordan and Israel at a meeting in Washington in July 1994, King Hussein and Israeli Premier Yitzhak Rabin [*q.v.*] signed the Jordanian-Israeli Peace Treaty [*q.v.*] in October 1994.

In May 1994 the PLO and Israel signed an agreement in Cairo [*q.v.*] on interim Palestinian self-rule in the Gaza Strip and the West Bank town of Jericho [*q.v.*] under the Palestinian Authority (PA) [*q.v.*]. The PA started functioning in July in Gaza [*q.v.*]. In

September 1995 the PLO and Israel signed an agreement in Washington on interim Palestinian self-rule in the West Bank under the PA, requiring withdrawal of Israeli troops from seven West Bank cities by December, joint PA-Israeli control of 450 Palestinian villages, and continued Israeli control of 128 Jewish settlements. This became known as the Washington Accord [q.v.] or Oslo II Accord [q.v.]

After the assassination of Rabin in November 1995, his successor, Shimon Peres, carried out the Israeli withdrawal from the West Bank villages as well as six West Bank cities (Hebron [q.v.] being the exception) by late December 1995. In January there were elections to the 88-member Palestinian Council, followed by the election of the executive president of the Palestinian Authority, in which Yasser Araft won seven-eighths of the vote. Peres's defeat by his right wing rival, Benjamin Netanyahu [q.v.], who described the Oslo Accords [q.v.] as "evil," in May 1996 was a heavy blow to the peace process.

(6) NETANYAHU'S PREMIERSHIP, MAY 1996–MAY 1999: After renegotiating the terms for a partial withdrawal from Hebron, Netanyahu authorized the construction of a large Jewish settlement southeast of Jerusalem at Jabal abu Ghunaim, called Har Homa. This brought the peace process to a virtual standstill while Netanyahu stated that any progress was conditional on the PA's curbing the Islamist opposition and ending its political activities in Jerusalem.

The deadline of September 1998 for further Israeli withdrawal specified in the Oslo II Accord passed without any movement in the peace process. In October at the Arafat-Netanyahu summit, chaired by President Clinton at the Wye Plantation, Maryland, Israel agreed to withdraw from a further 13 percent of the West Bank in three phases, each conditional on the PA meeting specific security arrangements to be verified by the U.S. Central Intelligence Agency (CIA). Talks on the final settlement, involving Palestinian refugees, Jewish settlements, and Jerusalem, were set to start in November and continue until the expiry of the Oslo Accords on 4 May 1999. In practice the Israelis carried out only the first of the three redeployments.

To dissuade Arafat from declaring unilaterally the establishment of the sovereign State of Palestine on 4 May 1999, Clinton addressed a letter to him reasserting his backing for the right of Palestinians to determine their future as "a free people on their own land."

(7) EHUD BARAK [q.v.] AS ISRAELI PRIME MINISTER, MAY 1999–FEBRUARY 2001: In September 1999 Israel withdrew from 7 percent of the West Bank, and in October opened a safe passageway between the West Bank and Gaza through the Israeli territory as specified in the Oslo Accords. In May 2000 Israel withdrew unconditionally from southern Lebanon as demanded by the UN Security Council Resolution 425 [q.v.] of March 1978.

In early July Clinton invited Arafat and Barak to an open-ended summit at Camp David to reach a framework agreement on the final settlement. On 26 July the summit ended in failure, chiefly due to unbridgeable differences between the two sides on the fate of the Palestinian refugees and the future of Jerusalem. Clinton announced that the negotiations were being deferred.

On 25 September Arafat visited Barak at the latter's home and they said they would meet again four days later. But on 28 September, Likud leader Ariel Sharon [q.v.], protected by 1,000 armed police, toured the Noble Sanctuary/Temple Mount [q.v.] in Jerusalem's Old City, normally out of bounds to the Jews [q.v.]. Regarding this as a provocative move by Sharon to underscore Israeli sovereignty over Islam's third-holiest site, Palestinians protested by throwing stones. The next day there was a demonstration by the Palestinians after Friday's midday prayers at the al-Aqsa Mosque. It was dispersed by the Israeli security forces firing live ammunition, which killed seven Palestinians. This marked the start of the al-Aqsa Intifada [q.v.], also known as the Second Intifada [q.v.]. Against the background of rising violence and weakening coalition government, Barak called for the prime ministerial election in late November 2000.

A month later the print media in the region published the Clinton Plan which visualized a demilitarized Palestinian state in Gaza and 95 percent of the West Bank, with the Palestinians getting an equivalent land in the Negev desert next to the Gaza Strip. Whereas the Israelis would exercise sovereignty over the Jewish settlements in East Jerusalem, the Palestinians would do so only over the Arab neighborhoods. In the Old City Israel would annex the Jewish Quarter and the Western Wall [q.v.] as well as enjoy "shared functional sovereignty" both "behind" the Western Wall and

"under" the Noble Sanctuary/Temple Mount. The estimated 3.75 million Palestinian refugees would have the right of return to the newly established State of Palestine but not to Israel. Those rejecting this choice would be entitled to compensation and resettlement. In his meeting with Clinton on 3 January 2001, when Arafat sought clarifications, he was told that his plan would expire when Clinton left the White House on 20 January.

However, the Israeli and Palestinian delegations, led respectively by foreign minister Shlomo Ben-Ami and chief negotiator Saeb Erekat, met at the Egyptian sea resort of Taba on 21 January, and began negotiating, with the Clinton Plan as the starting point. Their joint statement issued on 27 January said that they had progressed on the core issues of refuges, security, borders, and Jerusalem much further than ever before and that the remaining gaps could be bridged following the resumption of talks after the Israeli election on 6 February. On that day Barak lost to Ariel Sharon [q.v.].

(8) ARIEL SHARON [q.v.] AS ISRAELI PRIME MINISTER, FEBRUARY 2001–DECEMBER 2005: Sharon got elected on the platform of continued expansion of Jewish settlements, Israeli sovereignty over all of the expanded Jerusalem, and no talks with the Palestinians until there was complete cessation of terrorism.

Reporting in May, former U.S. Senator George Mitchell described Sharon's walkabout at the Noble Sanctuary in September 2000 as "provocative" and Israel's use against the Palestinian demonstrators as excessive. Equally, he criticized the Palestinians for firing on Israeli soldiers and Jewish settlers from the PA-controlled areas, and rejected their demand for an international protection force due to Israel's opposition. Stating that a cessation of violence would be hard to sustain unless Israel stopped its settlement construction activity, he recommended a freeze on all such activity. The PA accepted the Mitchell Report. While disputing any link between Jewish settlement policy and Palestinian terrorism, Sharon accepted the report "in principle." Later that month, for the first time Israel used F16 jet fighters to attack targets in Nablus [*q.v.*], killing 13 Palestinian policemen, thus escalating the conflict.

In his talks with officials of the new U.S. administration of President George W. Bush, Arafat offered a cease-fire if Israel froze settlements, removed the blockades of the Palestinian urban centers, implemented the third redeployment under the Wye River Memorandum [*q.v.*], and resumed talks on final settlement from the point where they were left off at Taba in January. But, after a suicide bomb attack in Tel Aviv [*q.v.*] in June that killed 20 young Israelis, Arafat dropped his conditions and promised a full cease-fire while refusing to arrest Islamist leaders.

Following the terrorist attacks on the United States in September 2001, both Arafat and Sharon condemned them. Arafat ordered total cease-fire which did not hold.

By reoccupying the territories under the PA's jurisdiction, and destroying the security and administrative infrastructure of the PA, Sharon systematically undermined all the elements of the peace process painstakingly built up by Rabin and Peres in the 1990s in cooperation with the Palestinians.

The 14th Arab League summit in March 2002 adopted a peace plan of Saudi Crown Prince Abdullah [*q.v.*]. It offered Israel total peace with all the League members in exchange for its total withdrawal from all of the Occupied Arab Territories [*q.v.*], the establishment of an independent Palestine state, and the granting of the right of return to the Palestinian refugees according to the UN General Assembly Resolution 194. There was no response from Israel.

In April 2003, the quartet of the United States, the European Union, Russia, and the United Nations [*q.v.*] issued a "road map" for peace which among other things called for the establishment of a sovereign Palestinian state. The document required the PA to upgrade its security apparatus and focus on disrupting and arresting groups and individuals conducting or planning attacks on Israelis and on dismantling all terrorist capabilities and infrastructure. Israel was required to dismantle Jewish settlements built in the Palestinian territories after 1 March 2001; freeze all settlement activity; and end curfews and ease movement of people and goods. In defiance, Israel continued to expand Jewish settlements, a process that continued throughout the decade.

While the Israeli military evacuated the Gaza Strip in September 2005, it continued to patrol the West Bank, including the areas nominally controlled by the Palestinian Authority.

(9) Ehud Olmert [*q.v.*] as Israeli Prime Minister, January 2006– March 2009: Though Ehud Olmert [*q.v.*], as the successor to Sharon as the leader of Kadima [*q.v.*], became

the prime minister of Israel in January 2006, he did not start peace talks with PA president Mahmoud Abbas [*q.v.*] until June 2007. However, the process got a boost when a Middle East Peace Conference [*q.v.*] was held under U.S. sponsorship in Annapolis, Maryland, in November 2007.

Abbas and Olmert attended it on the prior understanding that the final Israeli-Palestinian peace treaty would yield an independent State of Palestine. That became the official position of the Annapolis Conference. But Olmert continued Sharon's policy of allowing "natural growth" of the Jewish settlements in the West Bank.

The violent conflict between Fatah [*q.v.*] led by Abbas and Hamas [*q.v.*] in Gaza, which led to the expulsion of Fatah from the Strip in June 2007, impeded progress in the peace process.

The leaking of the confidential Palestine Papers [*q.v.*] in January 2011 revealed that during the negotiatoins in 2008–09 the Israeli and American teams were not satisfied with the far-reaching concesssions the Palestinians made on East Jerusalem, Haram al-Sharif/Temple Mount [*q.v.*], and the right to retrun for Palestinian refugees.

Matters grew worse when Israel mounted a fully-fledged military attack on the Gaza Strip in December 2008–January 2009.

(10) BENJAMIN NETANYAHU AS ISRAELI PRIME MINISTER, MARCH 2009– : Soon after assuming office in January 2009, U.S. President Barack Obama called on Israel to freeze Jewish settlements in the Occupied Palestinian Territories. Israeli Prime Minister Benjamin Netanyahu defied Obama. After a lengthy meeting with

Obama at the White House he succeeded in linking the Israeli-Palestinian peace process with Iran's nuclear program—two unrelated issues. Obama gave Tehran until December 2009 to abide by the UN Security Council resolutions on its nuclear program or face stiff economic sanctions. Netanyahu's government then sanctioned the building of enough new housing units in the Occupied Palestinian Territories to cover the next 10 months, and then announced a moratorium on further construction for 10 months. Once the moratorium ended in September 2010, there was accelerated construction activity.

On the cardinal subject of an independent Palestinian state, Netanyahu said that he would accept it only if the Palestinians recognized Israel as the Jewish national state with undivided Jerusalem as its capital; agreed to have a Palestinian state that would be demilitarized, possessing neither an army nor rockets and missiles nor the control of its airspace; and gave up the right of return for the Palestinian refugees to the areas within Israel. Abbas and other Palestinian leaders found this new set of Israeli demands unacceptable. Bilateral peace talks ceased.

Pentecost: (Greek: derivative of *pentekostos*, fiftieth): *Christian and Jewish Festival* (also known as Whitsunday [*q.v.*]) In the Jewish calendar [*q.v.*] Pentecost comes 50 days after Passover [*q.v.*] and marks the end of the biblical Palestinian grain harvest, a period of 49 days or 7 weeks. In the Bible [*q.v.*], it is called the Feast of Weeks/Harvest/First Fruits (*Shabuot* [*q.v.*] in Hebrew). It is also known as the anniversary of receiving of the Jewish Law, an aspect stressed by Reform Jews [q.v.]. In the Christian calendar [q.v.], Pentecost is celebrated on the seventh Sunday after Easter [q.v.] in memory of the day when the Holy Spirit descended upon the followers of Jesus Christ on the 50th day after his resurrection. The Church celebrates Pentecost as the Feast of the Holy Spirit and as its own birthday. During early Christianity [q.v.] converts were baptized during the festival. Since they wore white garments the festival acquired the title Whit(e)sunday in the English-speaking world.

People's Democratic Republic of Yemen (1970–90): *See* South Yemen.

People's Republic of South Yemen (1967–70): *See* South Yemen.

Peres, Shimon (1923–): *Israeli politician; prime minister, 1984–86, 1995–96; president, 2007–* Born Shimon Persky into a middle-class household in Poland, Peres was 11 when his family migrated to Palestine [q.v.]. After studying at an agricultural school, he joined a kibbutz. From 1941 to 1944 he was secretary of a Zionist youth group. Active within Haganah [q.v.] since 1941, he was promoted to its command six years later and assigned the task of procuring weapons. By the end of the Arab-Israeli War (1948–49) [q.v.] he had become commander of the Israeli Navy. Between 1953 and 1959 he served as the defense ministry's director-general. Among other things he reinforced Israel's military links with the Western nations, especially in the nuclear weapons program, developed with the assistance of France.

He entered the Knesset [q.v.] in 1959 on a Mapai [q.v.] ticket and retained a seat under different party labels for the next 48 years. From 1960 to 1965 he served as deputy defense minister. He left Mapai and became secretary-general of Rafi, a breakaway group led by David Ben-Gurion [q.v.], in 1965. When the Labor Party [q.v.] was formed in 1968 Peres joined it and became its deputy secretary-general. The next year Golda Meir [q.v.] included him in her cabinet as minister without portfolio. He served as transport minister from 1971 to 1974, followed by a short stint as information minister. Prime Minister Yitzhak Rabin [q.v.] appointed him defense minister (1974–77).

Violating his party's policy, Peres compromised with the ultranationalist Gush Emunim [q.v.] when its members set up a settlement in Kadum, thus setting the stage for Jewish colonization in the West Bank [q.v.].

In a determined challenge to Rabin for party leadership in 1976, Peres lost by 1,404 votes to 1,445. But, when Rabin resigned after the disclosure that, when he was Israel's ambassador to the United States his wife Lea Rabin had maintained an active bank account there, an illegal act, Labor Party delegates elected Peres their leader. In the May 1977 election Labor Party lost to Likud [q.v.], led by Menachem Begin [q.v.].

After the indecisive result of the 1984 election, Peres forged a coalition and rotation deal with Likud led by Yitzhak Shamir [q.v.], and became prime minister of a national unity government for two years. He oversaw Israel's withdrawal from Lebanon, except the border security strip, and reduced the runaway inflation to a manageable level. From 1986 to 1988, he served as deputy premier and foreign minister. With the 1988 election mirroring the previous stalemate, Peres renewed his power-sharing agreement with Likud. In the Shamir-led cabinet he became deputy premier and finance minister. His differences with Shamir on how to proceed with the Middle East peace process [q.v.] led to his resignation from the government in March 1990 and Labor's withdrawal from the ruling coalition.

In the 1992 leadership contest he lost to his longtime rival, Rabin. After Labor's victory in the June 1992 election Peres was appointed foreign minister. But Prime Minister Rabin allowed him to deal only with multilateral talks with the Arab countries, initiated by the Middle East peace conference in Madrid in October 1991. But, once Israel had lifted its ban on contact with the Palestine Liberation Organization (PLO) [q.v.] in January 1993, Peres became involved in the secret talks with the PLO in Norway. The resulting Israeli-PLO Accord [q.v.], concluded in September 1993 in Washington and signed by him, was a personal triumph for Peres. A year later he saw his peace efforts elsewhere culminate in a Jordanian-Israeli Peace Treaty [q.v.]. He shared the 1994 Nobel Peace Prize with Rabin and Yasser Arafat [q.v.]. Following the assassination of Rabin in November 1995, he became prime minister.

In the prime ministerial contest of May 1996, he lost to Benjamin Netanyahu [q.v.]. He remained a member of the Knesset. After the May 1999 election, Prime Minister Ehud

Barak [q.v.] included him in his cabinet as minister without portfolio. In the national unity government of Ariel Sharon [q.v.], formed in March 2001, he became foreign minister. As a member of the inner cabinet, which included him and Labor defense minister Binyamin Ben-Eliezer, he claimed to have moderated the more extreme actions proposed by Sharon to quell the Palestinians' Al Aqsa Intifada [q.v.] and Islamist militants. He resigned his post when the Labor Party decided to quit the national unity administration in November 2002.

When the Labor Party under the leadership of Amram Mitzna did badly in the 2003 Knesset election, resulting in Mitzna's resignation, Peres became its interim leader. He joined the Sharon-led coalition government toward the end of 2004. When he lost the party's leadership in November 2005 to Amir Peretz by a margin of 2.4 percent, he defected to the newly formed Kadima [q.v.]

Following Kadima's success in the March 2006 Knesset election, Prime Minister Ehud Olmert [q.v.] appointed Peres vice prime minister and minister for regional economy.

He was elected president of Israel by 86 votes to 23 in June 2007 for a seven-year term. In 2008, British Queen Elizabeth II awarded him an honorary knighthood of the Order of St. Michael and St. George. He is the author of 11 books, the latest being *The Imaginary Voyage: With Theodor Herzl in Israel.*

Persia and Persians: Persia is a derivative of Parsa, modern Fars, the southern region of Iran. The Indo-European nomads who migrated into the area from the Caucasus around 1000 B.C. were known as Parsa. By the seventh century B.C. they were established in southern Iran, then part of the Assyrian Empire. From early on, Persian rulers were associated with the Medes. Cyrus the Great (600–529 B.C.), first of the Achaemenians, declared himself ruler of Media in 559 B.C. and expanded his realm into the great Persian Empire. The Persians borrowed Assyrian political structures and Babylonian and Egyptian arts. Darius I (r. 521–486 B.C.) established a centralized government and extended his empire east into modern Afghanistan and northwest India, and as far north as the Danube River.

The empire began to decline from the mid-fifth century B.C., with regional governors acquiring greater powers and Egypt breaking away. Its death knell came when Alexander of Macedonia (r. 336–323 B.C.) defeated the Achaemenians on the Granicus in 334 B.C. and in the Battle of Guagamela in 331 B.C. After Alexander's death, most of the Persian Empire fell to his successors, the Selecuids, who were unable to maintain control.

Parthia, which seceded in 250 B.C., emerged as a successor to the Persian Empire. Following its decline a new empire of Sassanians emerged in 226 A.D. It reestablished Zoroastrianism [*q.v.*] as the state religion. The Sassanian Empire reached its peak under Anushirvan (r. 531–579) and then declined until its overthrow by the invading Muslim [*q.v.*] Arabs [*q.v.*] in 640 A.D. Islam [*q.v.*] replaced Zoroastrianism as the official religion and the caliphate made Persia part of an Islamic empire, from which modern Iran was to emerge later.

Persian Gulf: *See* The Gulf.

Persian language: (Also known as Farsi) The principal language of the Iranian branch of the Indo-European family, Persian is divided into Old Persian, the language of ancient Persia [*q.v.*], written in cuneiform characters and in use until the third century B.C.; Middle Persian, including Pahlavi [*q.v.*] and Parsi, the chief language of Zoroastrian [*q.v.*] and Manichaean literature, both written in Aramaic script and dominant between the third century B.C. and the ninth century A.D.; and Modern Persian, dating from the ninth century A.D., written in the Arabic script [*q.v.*], the language used in the finest examples of Persian literature.

Pesach (Hebrew: *Passover*): *See* Passover.

petroleum (Latin: from *petra*, a rock + *oleum*, oil): *See* oil.

Phalange and Phalangists (Lebanon): *Lebanese political party and militia* (Official title: Lebanese Kataeb Social Democratic Party) The Phalange is a derivative of phalanx (or battalion), the literal translation of the Arabic word *Kataeb*. It was established in November 1936 by Pierre Gemayel [*q.v.*], who had been inspired by the Nazi Youth Movement rallies he had seen during his visit to the Berlin Olympics in the summer.

The party attracted Christian [*q.v.*] youths from the mountainous Metn region, the heartland of the Maronites [*q.v.*], and Christian students in Beirut [*q.v.*]. It participated in the talks that led to the National Pact of

1943 [*q.v.*], which formalized
Christian domination of the state. Its
popularity was enhanced by the
discovery in 1949 of a plot by the
Syrian Social Nationalist Party [*q.v.*]
to merge Lebanon with Syria and the
nationalist reaction it generated
among Christians.

Its pro-Western stance and opposition to pan-Arabism [*q.v.*] led it to
back President Camille Chamoun [*q.v.*]
in the 1958 Lebanese Civil War [*q.v.*].
Its initial support for President Fuad
Chehab [*q.v.*] waned when he tried to
strengthen state powers at the expense
of the financial and commercial oli-
garchs who led the Phalange. By aligning with the parties of Chamoun and
Raymond Edde in the 1968 election, it
increased its parliamentary share from
four to nine among the 30 Maronite
seats.

Its leaders began to highlight the
presence of Palestinians, whose numbers had increased because of the June
1967 Arab-Israeli War [*q.v.*] and the
1970–71 Jordanian Civil War [*q.v.*].
On the eve of the Lebanese Civil War
of 1975–90 [*q.v.*], the party, now
20,000 strong, had a militia under the
command of Bashir Gemayel [*q.v.*],
who later became commander of a
coalition of Maronite militias, the
Lebanese Forces (LF) [*q.v.*]. Politically it was part of an umbrella organization called the Lebanese Front
[*q.v.*], led by Chamoun. Working in
collaboration with the American and
Israeli intelligence agencies, it confronted its adversaries, the Lebanese
National Movement [*q.v.*], which was
allied with the Palestinians. In mid-
June 1976, facing defeat, its leaders
welcomed Syria's armed intervention
on their side. But since they refused to

sever their ties with Israel, their relations with Syria turned frosty.

Intent on eliminating any serious rivals to his dominance in the Christian
camp, in the summer of 1980 Bashir
Gemayel used the Phalange militia to
wipe out the militia of Chamoun's National Liberal Party [*q.v.*]. He succeeded to a large extent. In early 1982
he started to liaise with Israel in its
plans to attack Lebanon. The invasion
occurred in June, and by September the
Phalange had been catapulted into the
leading position, with Bashir Gemayel
elected to the presidency. But his assassination some days before taking office
changed the situation. Though his
elder brother, Amin [*q.v.*], a Phalange
member, won the subsequent presidential election, the party had lost its most
ambitious leader. The death of Pierre
Gemayel in August 1984 deprived it of
a much-respected patriarch.

In early 1985 Samir Geagea, a leading member of the LF Command
Council, declared the LF independent
of the Phalange in security, policing,
and finance, thus depriving it of much
of its influence. This occurred just at
the point when it had agreed to hand
over to the Lebanese government various public departments it had usurped
and run in the Christian enclave for
several years. In the subsequent fighting, Geagea won full control of the
LF, further reducing the power of
Amin Gemayel.

After Gemayel had stepped down as
president of Lebanon in September
1988 and left the country, the influence
of Phalange declined further. Guided
by Geagea, the party backed the Taif
Accord [*q.v.*]. This caused a rift in the
Lebanese Front, with the anti-Geagea
faction siding with Gen. Michel Aoun

[*q.v.*], who challenged the newly elected President Elias Hrawi [*q.v.*].

In the wake of Aoun's defeat in October 1990, many Phalange offices were taken over by the pro-Syrian forces. Later the party cooperated with the government in its plans to disarm the militias. The national unity government formed in December 1990 included Geagea and another Phalange leader, Georges Saade. But in March 1991 Geagea resigned, and went on to transform the LF into a political party. Due to its decision to boycott the 1992 general election, the Phalange's influence waned. Its headquarters was blown up in December.

Poale Agudat Israel (Hebrew: *Workers of the Union of Israel*): *Israeli political party* Formed in Katowice, Poland, in 1922 as the worker's section of Agudat Israel [*q.v.*] to safeguard the rights of religious Jewish workers, Poale Agudat Israel (PAI) set up a branch in Palestine [*q.v.*] a year later. In 1933 it founded its first kibbutz [*q.v.*]. It began cooperating with the World Zionist Organization (WZO) [*q.v.*] in the colonization of Palestine, including organizing illegal immigration. After the establishment of Israel in 1948 it expanded its educational and settlement activities.

On the eve of the general election in 1949 it allied with Agudat Israel as well as Mizrahi [*q.v.*] and Poale HaMizrahi [*q.v.*] to form the United Religious Front [*q.v.*]. In the 1951 election it joined with Agudat Israel to form the Torah Religious Front [*q.v.*], which won five seats. The Front participated in the next Mapai-led [*q.v.*] government but quit in 1952 in protest against the law mandating conscription

for women. While maintaining a separate existence, the two Agudat groups, winning two to six seats, stayed in opposition throughout the Mapai/Labor-led [*q.v.*] governments until May 1977, when the PAI won one seat and merged with Agudat Israel.

Poale HaMizrahi (Hebrew: *Workers of the Spiritual Center*): *Israeli political party* (Also known as HaPoale HaMizrahi) Since the branch of the Mizrahi [*q.v.*] in Palestine had many workers, its younger members formed Poale HaMizrahi in 1921. In turn Poale HaMizrahi formed a confederation of trade unions, a group of kibbutizim [*q.v.*], and a network of religiously oriented schools. It acquired a separate identity from its parent body. Both organizations participated in the Zionist movement [*q.v.*] and in the quasi-governmental organs of Yishuv [*q.v.*]. After World War II it actively encouraged illegal Jewish immigration.

In the run-up to the Israeli general election in 1949 it allied with three other religious parties to form the United Religious Front [*q.v.*], which won 16 seats and joined the government. In the 1951 election it allied with Mizrahi and secured 10 seats, improving the total by one in the next election in 1955 and rejoining the coalition government. The next year Poale HaMizrahi united with Mizrahi to form Mafdal, the National Religious Party [*q.v.*].

Poale Zion (Hebrew: *Workers of Zion*): *Zionist Organization in Palestine* The first Zionist workers' party, Poale Zion was formed in the Russian city of Minsk (now in Belarus) in 1900 with a program of socialism, Zionism [*q.v.*], and migration to Palestine [*q.v.*]. It set up a branch in Palestine. Growing cooperation between socialist pioneers and the World Zionist Organization (WZO) [*q.v.*] caused a split in Poale Zion, its leftist section leaving in 1919 to form Mopsi (Socialist Workers Party), and its rightist, nationalist faction merging with the followers of Berle Katznelson to found Ahdut HaAvodah [*q.v.*].

poll tax: *an across-the-board tax on every member of a group* To keep the Arab conquerors separate from the conquered people, the early caliphs of the Umayyad period (661–750 A.D.) confined their soldiers to garrison towns. They provided protection to the non-Muslim population on payment of a poll tax, a practice initiated by the Prophet Muhammad after his victory at Khaibar, an oasis populated by Jewish tribes. The practice continued among Muslim [*q.v.*] rulers, who exempted non-Muslim subjects from military service and charged them a poll tax in exchange for providing them security, the last such example being during the Ottoman Empire, which ended in 1918. *See also* dhimmis.

Popular Bloc (Bahrain): *Bahraini political party* After the Bahraini constitution had been promulgated in June 1973, the Bahrain National Liberation Front allied with the Bahrain Nationalist Movement to form the Popular Bloc, with a nationalist-leftist program, under the leadership of Hussein Musa. In the election for the 42-member National Assembly, held on a restricted franchise of 30,000 adult males, it secured 21 of the 30 elected seats. Led by Muhsin Mahrun, Popular Bloc members demanded the introduction of income tax, trade union rights, votes for women, and the nationalization of large Western-owned companies. The ruler, Shaikh Isa al-Khalifa [*q.v.*], responded by issuing a draconian state security law in October 1974. The Popular Bloc protested. Alleging that parliament had debated "foreign" ideas and principles, the ruler dissolved it in August 1975, arresting most Popular Bloc leaders and closing down their party.

Popular Democratic Party (Saudi Arabia): *Saudi political party* In 1970, former members of the Arab Nationalist Movement [*q.v.*], remnants of the local Baath Party, and the Marxists outside the National Liberation Front combined to form the Popular Democratic Party (PDP). Committed to liberating Saudi Arabia from Western imperialism by an armed struggle, it stressed the need to form a broad national front to oppose the royal dictatorship. Unusually for a Saudi group, it set up a special women's section. It drew most of its support from students and petty civil servants. Since belonging to it was a capital offense, its membership inside the country was minuscule. As a largely expatriate body, active among Saudi students studying abroad and long-term exiles, it had no impact on domestic events. With the decline of radical politics by the late 1980s, it lost support even among Saudi expatriates.

Popular Front for the Liberation of the Occupied Arab Gulf (1968–71): At its second congress in September 1968 in South Yemen, a Marxist state, the Dhofari Liberation Front (DLF) decided to extend its revolutionary activities to the rest of Oman and other Gulf states [q.v.] and changed its name to the Popular Front for the Liberation of the Occupied Arab Gulf (PFLOAG). Opposed to imperialism, neocolonialism, and local oligarchies, the PFLOAG committed itself to achieving a socialist revolution and stressed the importance of Dhofar as a link between South Yemen and the Gulf States [q.v.]. Besides South Yemen, the People's Republic of China backed it.

Nearly two years later, having brought two-thirds of Dhofar under its control, the PFLOAG extended its activities to the Omani core of the sultanate. This alarmed the British, the dominant political power in the country, and led to a London-engineered coup that replaced Sultan Said bin Taimur [q.v.] with his son, Qaboos [q.v.]. The latter initiated socio-political reform and modernization, and expanded the military under the British aegis. In response, the third congress of the PFLOAG in 1971 lowered its sights from engineering a socialist revolution to accomplishing a national democratic revolution. It opened party membership to non-Marxist nationalists and renamed itself the Popular Front for the Liberation of Oman and the Arab Gulf [q.v.].

Popular Front for the Liberation of Oman (1974–82):

Faced with a vigorous onslaught by its enemy, the congress of the Popular Front for the Liberation of Oman and the Arab Gulf (PFLOAG) [q.v.], meeting in July 1974, decided to narrow its field of action to Oman and renamed its organization the Popular Front for the Liberation of Oman (PFLO). Within a year the Soviet Union had begun supplying arms to the PFLO and training its cadres.

But this was not enough to enable it to withstand the offensives that the Omani army along with the Iranian troops—ssisted by Britain, Egypt, and Jordan—launched in 1975. With South Yemen stopping its assistance in order to placate Saudi Arabia, the PFLO agreed to a cease-fire in 1976. But once Iran had withdrawn most of its troops in early 1977, PFLO fighters began to regroup. However, their activities from 1978–79 did not go beyond sporadic attacks and assassinations. Once Oman and South Yemen had formally recognized each other and signed a normalization agreement in 1982, the PFLO ceased to exist.

Popular Front for the Liberation of Oman and the Arab Gulf (1971–74):

In 1971 the third congress of the Popular Front for the Liberation of the Occupied Arab Gulf [q.v.] lowered its sights from engineering a socialist revolution to accomplishing a national democratic revolution. It opened party membership to non-Marxist nationalists and renamed itself the Popular Front for the Liberation of Oman and the Arab Gulf (PFLOAG).

The resulting increase in its strength enabled it to withstand three offensives by the British-led Omani forces, backed by British counterinsurgency units, between October 1971 and September 1972. The Omani sultan and his British backers redoubled their efforts, securing aid and assistance from Saudi Arabia and Jordan, and finally from Iran, which entered the fray in 1973. Faced with this opposition, the next PFLOAG congress in July 1974 decided to limit its activities to Oman, and the organization was renamed the Popular Front for the Liberation of Oman (PFLO) [*q.v.*]. However, a PFLOAG branch was set up in Bahrain.

Once the British had departed from Bahrain in mid-1971 and the ruler, Shaikh Isa al-Khalifa [*q.v.*], had made desultory moves to share power with his ministers, the PFLOAG's Bahraini section began to flex its muscles. Along with the Bahrain National Liberation Front, it called a general strike twice. Shaikh Isa agreed to hold elections to a constituent assembly, but because of his refusal to release all political prisoners and grant votes to women, the PFLOAG boycotted the election. It did the same when a general election was held in December 1973. In the crackdown that followed the dissolution of parliament in August 1975, many PFLOAG leaders were jailed.

Popular Front for the Liberation of Palestine: *Palestinian political party*

The Popular Front for the Liberation of Palestine (PFLP) was formed in December 1967 by the merger between the Palestinian section of the Arab Nationalist Movement [*q.v.*] and the Syria-based Palestine Liberation Front, under the leadership of George Habash [*q.v.*]. The next year it affiliated to the Palestine Liberation Organization (PLO) [*q.v.*]. At its first (open) congress in February 1969 the PFLP described Israel, the World Zionist movement [*q.v.*], world imperialism, and Arab reaction in the re-

gion as the enemies of the Palestinian cause. It adopted a program of mobilizing Palestinian workers and peasants in alliance with the petty bourgeoisie, and starting a guerrilla struggle as a step toward a national liberation war.

It emulated the organizational structure of a cadre-based Communist party. The congress, elected by members every four years and meeting every alternate year, was the PFLP's highest body. It elected the central committee, which in turn chose the political bureau (politburo). The congress also had the authority to elect the secretary-general, a position occupied by Habash from the party's inception until his formal retirement due to ill health in April 2000.

The PFLP's campaign inside the Occupied Territories [*q.v.*] involved 220 armed operations in 1970. Abroad, its activists hijacked three airliners between 7 and 9 September 1970, took them to an abandoned airfield near Amman [*q.v.*], emptied them of passengers, and blew them up. This triggered fighting between the Palestinian commandos and the Jordanian army, resulting in the Palestinians' defeat. The PFLP then moved its main operational base to Lebanon. Its militia was the third-largest after Fatah [*q.v.*] and Saiqa [*q.v.*].

Making no distinction between Zionist persons or organizations inside Israel or outside, it attacked Israeli targets abroad—mainly by hijacking airliners and making political demands. Between July 1968 and December 1973, when the party congress suspended its activity against Israeli targets abroad, the PFLP conducted 16 foreign operations.

In 1974, when the Palestine National Council (PNC) [*q.v.*] accepted the idea of a Palestinian state on the West Bank [*q.v.*] and Gaza [*q.v.*] as an intermediate step toward the liberation of all of Mandate Palestine, the PFLP boycotted the PLO Executive Committee and the central council. In the late 1970s, when the Soviet Union started offering military training to PLO activists, the PFLP was included in the program. It ended its boycott of the PLO institutions in 1981.

After the expulsion of the PLO from Beirut [*q.v.*] in September 1982, the PFLP moved its headquarters to Damascus [*q.v.*], but did not join the Syrian-instigated fight against Yasser Arafat [*q.v.*] and Fatah [*q.v.*]. However, after Arafat's agreement with King Hussein [*q.v.*] of Jordan to pursue a joint negotiating strategy in 1985, the PFLP allied with the pro-Syrian Palestinian factions to form the Palestine National Salvation Front. After the PNC had disowned Arafat's deal with King Hussein in April 1987, the PFLP rejoined the PLO Executive Committee and other PLO institutions. In November 1988, while opposing the resolution before the PNC to accept a Palestinian state in part of Palestine and peaceful coexistence with Israel, the PFLP accepted the majority decision in favor of the resolution.

During the crisis created by Iraq's invasion of Kuwait in August 1990, the PFLP backed President Saddam Hussein [*q.v.*], especially when the latter tried to link Iraq's evacuation of Kuwait to Israel's withdrawal from the Occupied Arab Territories [*q.v.*]. The PFLP opposed the Israeli-PLO Accord [*q.v.*] of September 1993 and the Jordanian-Israeli Peace Treaty [*q.v.*] of October 1994.

In 1999, when the PFLP lifted its objections to the PLO leadership's talks with Israel, Abu Ali Mustafa, the moderate deputy of Habash, was allowed to return to the West Bank. He set up an office in Ramallah [*q.v.*]. After the formal retirement of Habash as the party's secretary-general in 2000, Mustafa succeeded Habash.

Following the assassination of Mustafa in August 2001 by the Israeli military, which fired a rocket at the PFLP's Ramallah office, Ahmad Saadat, a hard-liner, was elected secretary-general. To avenge Mustafa's killing, PFLP activists assassinated ultra-right-wing tourism minister Rehavam Zee'vi in an East Jerusalem hotel in October. Pressured by the United States, the Palestinian Authority (PA) [*q.v.*] arrested Saadat in January 2002 and imprisoned him in Jericho [*q.v.*] along with five other PFLP members. During the Al Aqsa Intifada [*q.v.*], the PFLP carried out five suicide bombing attacks inside Israel between 2002 and 2004.

In a military operation in March 2006, the Israelis besieged the Jericho prison, and after a 10-hour battle, which left two people dead, abducted Saadat and five other inmates for a trial in Israel. Saadat was sentenced to 30 years' imprisonment in December 2008.

In the 2006 Palestinian parliamentary election, the PFLP won three seats in a house of 132. Its appeal is limited to Christian pockets in the West Bank and Gaza. Its supporters are often urban university graduates of liberal-leftist disposition.

At the time of massive pro-democracy demonstrations in Cairo [*q.v.*] in January 2011, the PFLP declared its solidarity with "the popular classes" of Egypt.

Popular Front for the Liberation of Palestine-General Command:

Palestinian political party Having merged his Palestine Liberation Front with the Palestinian section of the Arab Nationalist Movement [*q.v.*] to form the Popular Front for the Liberation of Palestine (PFLP) [*q.v.*] in late 1967, Ahmad Jibril [*q.v.*] led his supporters out of the PFLP about a year later to form the Popular Front for the Liberation of Palestine-General Command (PFLP-GC). It then affiliated to the Palestine Liberation Organization (PLO) [*q.v.*].

The PFLP-GC carried out several operations against Israel and Israeli targets, including planting a bomb onboard a Swissair flight from Zurich to Tel Aviv [*q.v.*] in February 1970, which exploded and killed 47 passengers and crew. Four years later, in a failed attempt to exchange their Israeli hostages—taken at Kiryat Shimona—for 100 Palestinian prisoners, three members of the PFLP-GC and 18 Israelis were killed.

After the 1982 Israeli invasion of Lebanon [*q.v.*], when the PLO's constituents were forced to vacate Beirut [*q.v.*], the PFLP-GC moved its headquarters to Damascus [*q.v.*]. In 1983 it joined an anti-Yasser Arafat [*q.v.*] rebellion masterminded by Syrian President Hafiz Assad [*q.v.*]. In May 1985 Israel granted the release of 1,150 Palestinian detainees and convicted prisoners in exchange for three Israeli soldiers captured by the PFLP-GC during the 1982 Israeli invasion of Lebanon. In late November 1987 three PFLP-GC activists mounted a hang-glider raid from southern Lebanon on an Israeli military outpost, resulting in six Israeli deaths. This proved pivotal in sparking the Intifada [*q.v.*] on 9 December.

Although the PFLP-GC was secular, socialist, and nationalist, in the late-1980s it started to form links with Iran, with Jibril visiting Tehran [*q.v.*] periodically and receiving financial aid. PFLP-GC propaganda began referring to the "Arab and Islamic people" and the "Arab and Islamic region."

In the Kuwait crisis and the subsequent Gulf War II [*q.v.*], the PFLP-GC backed Iraqi President Saddam Hussein [*q.v.*]. But, despite brave statements before and during the conflict, it did not carry out any terrorist acts.

It rejected the Israeli-PLO Accord [*q.v.*] of September 1993 because it failed to concede Palestinians' right to self-determination and the right of refugees to return home. It quit the PLO.

With Jibril moving closer to Iran, the PFLP-GC split in 1999. Its breakaway faction acquired the name of the Palestinian Liberation Front.

The PFLP-GC maintains its head office in Damascus [*q.v.*] and, given its cordial relations with the government there, it continues to enjoy support in the Palestinian refugee camps in Syria. Also, so long as the Syrian troops were present in Lebanon, it maintained a substantial presence in the Palestinian refugee camps there. With the departure of the last Syrian soldier from Lebanon in 2005, it lost its protective cover. On the other hand, its links with Hizbollah [*q.v.*], a Lebanese organization, assured its survival in Lebanon. Of all the Palestinian factions, it remained the most hard-line. In the Israel-Hizbollah War in 2006 [*q.v.*], its armed activists assisted Hizbollah.

During the uprisings in Syria in 2011, it sided with the regime of Syrian President Bashar Assad [*q.v.*].

Progressive Party (Israel): *Israel political party* Shortly after the founding of Israel in May 1948 the liberal "A" faction of the General Zionists [*q.v.*] left its parent body to combine with the German-dominated *Aliyah Hadasha* (Hebrew: *New Immigrants*) Party, a moderate faction, and *HaOved HaTzioni* (Hebrew: *The Zionist Worker*) to form the Progressive Party. With four to six deputies in the first four parliaments (1949 to 1959), it participated in most of the Mapai-dominated [*q.v.*] governments. In 1961 it merged with the General Zionists [*q.v.*] to form the Liberal Party [*q.v.*].

Progressive Socialist Party (Lebanon): The Progressive Socialist Party (PSP) was formed in 1949 by Kamal Jumblat [*q.v.*]. Predominantly Druze [*q.v.*], it had some Sunni [*q.v.*], Shia [*q.v.*], and Christian [*q.v.*] members. The party adopted a pan-Arabist [*q.v.*], left-of-center program that opposed the confessionalism [*q.v.*] built into the 1943 National Pact [*q.v.*]. In the 1958 Lebanese Civil War [*q.v.*] Jumblat assumed leadership of the camp opposed to the pro-Western President Camille Chamoun [*q.v.*].

As political consciousness among Muslims increased because of the events in the region and the growing presence of armed Palestinian commandos, the importance of the party and its leader rose. It was an important member of the National Progressive Front, forged by Jumblat in 1969, and enlarged and renamed the Front of National and Progressive Parties and Forces in 1972. With the outbreak of the Lebanese Civil War in April 1975 [*q.v.*] the leadership of the nationalist-leftist camp once again rested with the PSP chief, Kamal Jumblat. After his assassination in March 1977, his son Walid [*q.v.*] became the PSP leader. He moderated the party line and repaired relations with Syria, which had been soured by his father.

Following the Israeli invasion of Lebanon [*q.v.*] in June 1982, the PSP found itself on the defensive against the onslaught of the Israeli-backed Maronite [*q.v.*] militias. In September 1983 the PSP militia played an important role in frustrating the Western attempt to bolster the Lebanese army, which was commanded largely by Maronite officers. In February 1984 the party militia allied with the fighters of Amal [*q.v.*] and expelled the Maronite-controlled Lebanese army from West Beirut [*q.v.*]. The PSP was a leading actor at the reconciliation conference held in Lausanne, Switzerland, in March 1984.

To frustrate the designs of Gen. Michel Aoun [*q.v.*], the PSP joined 13 other parties in August 1989 to form the Lebanese National Front, which was committed to defeating Aoun's political and military program. The PSP had reservations about the

Taif Accord [*q.v.*] because it did not sufficiently curtail presidential powers and did not treat Muslim Lebanese equitably. But, aware of Syria's strong backing for the Accord, it desisted from protesting.

After the end of the civil war in October 1990, some 2,800 fighters from the PSP militia, which at its peak had 15,500 armed men, were taken into the regular Lebanese army. Jumblat was appointed a minister in the national unity government that followed. The PSP participated in the 1992 general election, and, after his election to parliament, Jumblat became minister for displaced persons. Following the 1996 parliamentary election, in which the PSP won 10 seats, including all eight of the seats reserved for Druzes, Jumblat returned to his old ministerial post.

In 1998, the party's deputies abstained from voting for Emile Lahoud [*q.v.*], the choice of Syria for president. Therefore, Walid Jumblat did not find a place in the cabinet of Salim Hoss [*q.v.*]. During the run-up to the 2000 parliamentary election, the PSP demanded the withdrawal of the Syrian troops from Lebanon, thus appearing to make a common cause with Maronite Christian [*q.v.*] politicians. It won 16 seats, including the eight allocated to the Druzes. As a result, Jumblat's deputy, Marwan Hamadeh, became minister of displaced persons in the cabinet led by Prime Minister Rafiq Hariri [*q.v.*].

Emboldened by the UN Security Council Resolution 1559 in 2004 demanding the withdrawal of Syrian forces from Lebanon, the PSP reiterated its earlier stance. It cofounded the anti-Syria 14 March Alliance [*q.v.*]. In the 2005 general election it gained 16 seats. Once the Syrian forces had pulled out completely from Lebanon, the party lost its anti-Syrian thrust. It entered the 2009 parliamentary election as an independent entity and secured 10 seats.

In January 2011, PSP lawmakers were among the 68 members of parliament who elected Najib Mikati [*q.v.*], backed by pro-Syria Hizbollah [*q.v.*], as president.

Protestant Christians/Church: *Christian sect* A Christian not belonging to the Roman Catholic Church [*q.v.*] or the Orthodox Church [*q.v.*] is generally described as Protestant. Protestants consider the Bible [*q.v.*] to be the central source of Christian teaching. Protestant churches emerged as part of a religious revolution in Western Europe in the 16th century, starting as a reform movement in the Catholic Church. The major Protestant schools are Adventist, Anabaptist, Baptist, Calvinist, Congregationalist, Lutheran, Methodist, Modernist, Presbyterian, Puritan, and Unitarian.

Protocol of Constantinople (1913): Under the terms of the Protocol of Tehran (1911) [*q.v.*], representatives of the Ottoman Empire, Persia (now Iran), Russia, and Britain met in Constantinople (now Istanbul) to delineate the boundary from Mount Ararat to the Persian Gulf [*q.v.*] and redefine navigational rights in the Shatt al-Arab [*q.v.*], which formed the fluvial border between Iran and the easternmost province of the Ottoman Empire. Since Britain, keen to develop an oil industry in Iran, needed extensive port facilities along the waterway, the new protocol awarded to Iran five small islands and one largish one in the Shatt al-Arab between Muhammara (later Khorramshahr) and the sea. It was confirmed in 1914 and followed by the appointment of a Delimitation Commission, in which Britain and Russia had powers of arbitration. By the time World War I started in mid-1914, a definitive map of the frontier had been produced and 227 boundary pillars installed.

Protocol of Tehran (1911): The Protocol of Tehran, signed in 1911, outlined a basis for negotiations between Persia (now Iran) and the Ottoman Empire, and set up a Joint Delimitation Commission consisting of representatives of the Ottoman Empire, Persia, Russia, and Britain.

Protocol of Uqair (1922): The Protocol of Uqair was imposed by Sir Percy Cox, the British high commissioner in Baghdad [*q.v.*], on Kuwait and Najd [*q.v.*] (later Saudi Arabia) in December 1922. It carved out a neutral zone between Najd and Kuwait (the Saudi Arabia-Kuwait Neutral Zone [*q.v.*]). It confirmed the inner (red) line of the 1913 Anglo-Ottoman Convention [*q.v.*] regarding Kuwait's southern border with Najd, but did not define Kuwait's northern frontier with Iraq. In April 1923, when Shaikh Ahmad I al-Sabah [*q.v.*] of Kuwait claimed the outer (green) line of the 1913 Anglo-Ottoman Convention as applying to the area north of Kuwait port, Sir Percy replied that his claim to the frontier and offshore islands was recognized as far as Britain was concerned. This limited Iraq's access to the Gulf [*q.v.*] to mere 36 mi./58 km

of coastline infested with swamps and marshland, thus denying it a deep-water harbor and the possibility of becoming an important naval power in the region. King Faisal I of Iraq [*q.v.*] was disappointed, but with his country under the British Mandate he had no choice but to ratify Iraq's boundaries with its neighbors as decided by a British high commissioner.

Qaboos bin Said (1940–): *Sultan of Oman, 1970– ; prime minister, 1970–* Born in Salalah, Qaboos was educated privately at the royal palace and then at a private college in Bury St. Edmunds, Britain. After graduating from the Royal Military Academy at Sandhurst, he served briefly with the British forces stationed in West Germany, and then took courses in social studies at a British university but did not graduate.

He was recalled home in 1965 and put under surveillance at the Salalah royal palace where he spent time studying Islam [*q.v.*]. Among his visitors were British expatriates whom his father Sultan Said bin Taimur [*q.v.*] trusted. Some of them were used by the British government to plot the deposition of Sultan Said, which occurred on 23 July 1970.

After becoming sultan as well as prime minister and defense and foreign minister, Qaboos ended Oman's isolation by securing it membership in the Arab League [*q.v.*] and the United Nations. Aided by rising oil output, which reached a peak of 400,000 barrels per day (bpd) in the mid-1970s, he built or expanded the economic infrastructure and provided social services to Omani nationals. He intensified the campaign against the leftist insurgency in Dhofar that had started in 1963. He expanded the army with a large intake of foreign mercenaries, especially Pakistanis. In 1973 he turned to the shah of Iran for extra troops. With British, Saudi, Egyptian, Jordanian, and Iranian backing, he crushed the Dhofari rebellion by late 1975.

At the age of 36, he married his 14-year-old cousin Kamila (née Nawwal bint Tariq bin Taimur). The marriage ended in divorce five years later. They had no children.

Qaboos was alone in the Arab world in endorsing Egypt's Camp David Accords [q.v.] with Israel, and did not cut ties with it after the signing of a peace treaty between the two countries. He was the only Gulf leader to sign a military accord with Washington in mid-1980, allowing it to use Oman's harbors and airports, and to stockpile arms and ammunition on its soil. He ended his regional isolation after the start of the Iran-Iraq War [q.v.] in September 1980 by taking a pro-Iraqi position along with other Gulf rulers. He was a cofounder of the Gulf Cooperation Council (GCC) [q.v.] in 1981. However, belated awareness of Oman's proximity to Iran at the mouth of the Hormuz Strait [q.v.] made him adopt a neutral stance in the Iran-Iraq War. Along with other GCC rulers he backed Kuwait after it had been occupied by Iraq in August 1990. He joined the U.S.-led coalition against Iraq. After the war he signed a 10-year military access agreement with Washington.

While refusing to provide Oman with a written constitution or abandon any of his arbitrary powers, he expanded and restructured the fully nominated 45-member consultative council acting as an advisory body on socioeconomic affairs. This proved insufficient to counter growing public disaffection. He then promulgated a written constitution in 1996, which incorporated the existing consultative council with scant legislative authority. It was only when rioting broke out in Hajar in 2000 that he turned the council into an elected body.

He renewed Oman's 10-year military access agreement with America in 2001. In its war against the Taliban-administered Afghanistan later that year, he allowed the Pentagon to use Oman's military facilities after it agreed to sell the sultanate advanced weapons worth $1.2 billion.

His opposition to the Anglo-American invasion of Iraq [q.v.] did not stop him from letting 3,600 American military personnel, 100 elite British special forces, and 40 U.S. warplanes be stationed in Oman in early 2003. At the same time he continued to maintain cordial relations with Iran, partly because the territorial waters of the two neighbors overlap in the narrow Strait of Hormuz.

In 2005, his government arrested 31 suspects for being members of the secret al-Bashaer military group aiming to subvert the government. After the court had found them guilty and sentenced them to one to 20 years' imprisonment, Qaboos pardoned them.

He indulged his fondness for super-yachts in 2007 by purchasing a 510-foot/155-meter-long yacht, named

Al-Said, equipped with a helipad and an auditorium large enough for a symphony orchestra.

When the wave of popular demonstrations emanating from Cairo [*q.v.*], demanding political reform, reached the sultanate in February–March 2011, culminating in violent rioting in the industrial port city of Sohar, Qaboos temporized. He combined the dismissal of corrupt ministers, raising the minimum wage, and doubling social benefits with the appointment of a commission to recommend political reform. Following its report in the autumn he enhanced the powers of the two-tier Council of Oman at the expense of the appointed cabinet. He transferred the authority to present draft laws to him from the cabinet to the Council of Oman after it had debated and amended the bills submitted to it by the cabinet. The changed procedure also applied to the annual budget and draft development plans.

Al Qaida (Arabic: *The Base*): *Extremist Islamist organization* Al Qaida evolved out of *the Maktab al-Khidmat* (Arabic: *Bureau of Service* [to the non-Afghan mujahedin]) established by Abdullah Azzam [*q.v.*] in Peshawar, Pakistan, in 1984. At the training camps on both sides of the Afghan-Pakistan frontier set up by Pakistan's Inter-Services Intelligence (ISI) and the U.S. Central Intelligence Agency (CIA), the non-Afghan mujahedin underwent military training. It was based on the manuals used by the U.S. Defense Department and the CIA, and translated into Persian [*q.v.*], Arabic [*q.v.*], and Urdu. Their complementary political education emphasized nationalism and Islam [*q.v.*]. Their leader was

Osama bin Laden [*q.v.*]. He declared the departure of the Soviet troops from Afghanistan in February 1989 a victory for the anti-Soviet jihad.

Following the assassination of Azzam in November, bin Laden decided to run Maktab al-Khidmat under the new title of Al Qaida, but with a more ambitious aim of creating an international network of jihadists, those who had participated in the anti-Soviet jihad.

His scheme took concrete shape during his five-year stay (May 1991–May 1996) in Sudan, where he set up a string of companies. He ran Al Qaida along corporate lines, with the policy-making Shura Council of 12 served by five executive committees: military (headed by Muhammad Atef [*q.v.*]), political, business, Islamic jurisprudence, and media and public relations. The military committee handled training recruits, procuring arms and explosives, and planning attacks. The political committee assessed the political situation in a particular country. The business committee focused on acquiring and spending funds. The Islamic jurisprudence committee evaluated whether a particular action or decision was in line with the Sharia [*q.v.*]) and issued religious decrees. The media committee handled public relations and propaganda, including production of audio- and videotapes.

In 1993 Al Qaida had an estimated 1,000 members, most of them Afghan veterans.

Bin Laden used his financial resources to fund the activities of Al Qaida, which focused on waging jihad against the United States by either directly financing Al Qaida's terrorist actions or sponsoring like-minded groups worldwide, with their activists coming to Sudan for weapons training. Thus he turned Al Qaida into an umbrella organization specializing in conducting jihad through violent means.

By the mid-1990s, besides supporting about 5,000 mainly Arab fighters in the Balkans, where a civil war raged in Bosnia during 1992–95, al-Qaida's members were established in Albania, Britain, Lebanon, Malaysia, the Netherlands, Pakistan, Romania, Russia, Saudi Arabia, Turkey, and the United Arab Emirates. Also, Al Qaida established associate relationship with like-minded groups in Algeria, Chechnya, Egypt, Ethiopia, the Horn of Africa, Lebanon, Libya, Philippines, south Asia, southeast Asia, Syria, Tunisia, and Yemen.

After bin Laden had moved his entourage to Afghanistan in 1996, Al Qaida expanded further, partly because Mullah Muhammad Omar, the ruler of the Taliban-controlled Afghanistan, gave it a free rein; partly because of the return of the veterans of the anti-Soviet jihad after being harassed by their governments; and partly because of the decline in the jihads in the Balkans, Chechnya, and Kashmir. It opened military training camps. Four years later, Al Qaida's 3,000 fighters would become the Taliban's 55th Brigade. Outside Afghanistan, the estimated size of Al Qaida activists and sympathizers was put at 4,500 in 60 countries.

The United States held Al Qaida responsible for the bombing of the American Embassies in Nairobi and Dar es Salaam in August 1998 that killed 227 people. It saw the hand of

Al Qaida in the bombing of USS *Cole* in Aden [q.v.] in October 2000. And, following the terrorist attacks in New York and Washington in September 2001, popularly known as 9/11, U.S. President George W. Bush held al-Qaida and bin Laden responsible. The Al Qaida official responsible for organizing and supervising 9/11 was believed to be Khalid Shaikh Muhammad [q.v.], a Pakistani of Baluchi origins born in Kuwait. During Washington's Afghanistan campaign from October to December 2001, two-thirds of Al Qaida fighters, including Atef, either died or were taken prisoner. The rest, including bin Laden and his ideological mentor, Ayman Zawahiri [q.v.] escaped, mainly to Pakistan.

By the end of 2002, the arrest of some 3,000 Al Qaida activists and sympathizers in 98 countries had cut the size of the organization by two-thirds. Al Qaida now lacked a headquarters and training camps. Faced with enhanced security in the United States and other Western countries, it switched to Western targets in non-Western countries. In 2002 it or its associates hit German tourists in Tunisia, French naval technicians in Pakistan, and Australian and Western tourists in Bali, Indonesia, using vehicles carrying liquid gas (in Tunisia) or chlorate (Bali). Also, with the transfer of terrorist technology and expertise from the center to the periphery, Al Qaida's associate groups became more active. By early 2003, the remnants of al-Qaida inside Afghanistan had established an underground network to carry out guerrilla actions and assassinations and had set up a radio station.

The Anglo-American invasion of

Iraq [*q.v.*] in 2003, and the subsequent chaos provided an unprecedented opportunity to Al Qaida to establish itself in the war-ravaged Iraq, an Arab state with its capital in Baghdad [*q.v.*], which had been the seat of the caliphate from 754 A.D. to 1258. As leader of the *Jamaat al-Tawihid wal Jihad* (Arabic: *Society of Divine Unity and Jihad*), Abu Musssab Zarqawi, trained in Al Qaida camps in Afghanistan, readily affiliated his organization with Al Qaida and renamed it Al Qaida in Mesopotamia [*q.v.*]. It became an important player in the anti-American resistance movement and also in the violent anti-Shia [*q.v.*] campaign.

Al Qaida viewed itself as a vanguard movement dedicated to founding genuinely Islamic states free of such non-Muslim concepts as socialism and nationalism as a step to reviving the caliphate. This was to be done by simultaneous selected terrorist actions against Western powers that continued to dominate and exploit the Muslim world, and by undermining and overthrowing the regimes in most Muslim countries that were under Christian-Jewish influence.

Overall, its modus operandi could be described as centralized decision-making and decentralized implementation, with national or regional organizations using Al Qaida as a brand name. The leading examples of this were Al Qaida in Mesopotamia [*q.v.*] and Al Qaida in the Arabian Peninsula [*q.v.*].

The number of commanders [emirs] in the field had fallen from a few thousand in the mid-2000s to a few hundred by 2010. With the assassination of bin Laden by U.S. Special Forces in the Pakistani city of Abbottabad on 2 May 2011, the leadership of Al Qaida passed to Zawahiri, believed to be hiding in the tribal belt along the Afghan-Pakistani border. The success of largely nonviolent popular movements to bring about regime change in Tunisia and Egypt in 2011 undermined Al Qaida's strategy of violent attacks on the interests of America, perceived as the puppet mater of these Arab regimes. *See also* Al Qaida in Mesopotamia and Al Qaida in the Arabian Peninsula.

Al Qaida in the Arabian Peninsula:

(Official title, *Al-Qaida fi Jazirat al-Arab* [Arabic: *Al-Qaida in the Arabian Peninsula*]) It came into existence in January 2009 following the merger of the Al Qaida branches in Saudi Arabia and Yemen, established seven years earlier. Its aim was to overthrow the regimes in Saudi Arabia and Yemen and establish an Islamic caliphate.

With its suicide attacks on three Western housing compounds in Riyadh [*q.v.*], which claimed 19 lives, in May 2003, Al Qaida's Saudi branch—led by Khalid Ali Hajj, a former bodyguard of Osama bin Laden [*q.v.*]—acquired a high profile. Despite the government's severe response to the terrorist event, the network attacked another residential compound in November, causing 17 fatalities. When Ali Hajj was killed by the Saudi forces in early 2004, he was replaced by Abdul Aziz Muqrin. In the spring the group shot dead five Western employees at a petrochemical complex in Yanbu, killed 22 foreign and Saudi nationals in attacks on three sites in Khobar, and beheaded an American aerospace employee. In retaliation, the kingdom's security forces stormed a hideout in Riyadh [*q.v.*] and shot Muqrin dead.

Under the leadership of Salhi al-Awfi, the network raided the U.S. consulate in Jeddah [*q.v.*] and murdered a dozen people in December 2004. Awfi died in a police raid in Medina [*q.v.*] in 2005. In February 2006, in a meticulously planned operation, Al Qaida activists dressed in the Saudi Aramco Company's uniforms and driving official vehicles went past two of the three guarded perimeters of the Abqaiq oil facility, which processed seven-eighths of the kingdom's petroleum exports, only to be challenged at the last gate. In the ensuing firefight they were killed.

The subsequent crackdown by the Saudi authorities forced many of the group's several hundred members to seek refuge in Yemen.

The suicide attack by Al Qaida's Yemeni operators aboard a speedboat, led by Jamal al-Badawi, on USS *Cole* in Aden in October 2000, resulting in the death of 17 U.S. sailors, gave the group a high profile. In November 2002, the killing of an American citizen along with a group of Al Qaida operatives, by a drone operated by the U.S. Central Intelligence Agency (CIA), grabbed headlines in Yemen. The ongoing cooperation between the Yemeni and American governments kept Al Qaida's activists subdued.

But the escape of 23 Al Qaida extremists from a high-security prison in Sanaa [*q.v.*] in February 2006 changed the situation. Two escapees, Nasser Abdul Karim al-Wuhayshi and Qasim al-Raymi, formally established Al Qaida in Yemen. Its members included the veterans of jihad in

Afghanistan and Iraq as well as new recruits. Wuhayshi's credentials as a participant in the anti-Soviet jihad in Afghanistan, when he became an assistant to bin Laden, impressed his colleagues. After the fall of the Taliban in December 2001, he had fled to Iran where he was imprisoned. In 2003 the Iranian government extradited him to Yemen. As the military commander of the network, Raymi, an expert organizer, proved innovative.

The newly formed group set up bases in the tribal areas under nominal control of the central government, which was held in low esteem because of its ineptitude and rampant corruption. Following small-scale attacks on security forces and foreign tourists, the network assaulted the U.S. Embassy in Sanaa in September 2008, deploying detonated bombs and firing rocket-propelled grenades. The toll of 20 included 14 Yemeni guards and civilians.

The video announcing the formation of Al Qaida in the Arabian Peninsula (AQAP) in January 2009 showed Said Ali al-Shihri, a Saudi national, as the deputy leader. Freed from the U.S. military detention center at Guantánamo Bay, Cuba, in November 2007, Shihri was inducted into Saudi Arabia's de-radicalization program, only to abscond soon after. Anwar Awlaki, a U.S. citizen settled in Yemen, was believed to have played an important role in the founding of the AQAP.

In August the AQAP tried, but failed, to kill Saudi security chief Prince Muhammad bin Nayef, in charge of the kingdom's anti-terrorism campaign. Equally, the attempt by Umar Farouk Abdulmutallab, a Nigerian, to blow up a passenger plane over

Detroit on Christmas Day by igniting plastic explosive PETN (pentaerythritol tetranitrate), sewn to his underwear, failed. He told his U.S. interrogators that AQAP operatives had trained and equipped him in Yemen to carry out the attack. During that year about 20 Islamist British nationals arrived in Yemen for training with the AQAP.

Working in collaboration with Washington, the Yemeni government mounted a major offensive against AQAP in the provinces of Abyan, Marib, and Shabwa, with the CIA making frequent use of its drones for "targeted" killings, and the Pentagon firing cruise missiles. Yet the continued AQAP armed attacks and bombings on military, civilian, and diplomatic targets during 2010 left more than 90 security officers and civilians dead.

In October 2010, two packages originating in Sanaa—each containing a bomb of 300 to 400 grams/11–14 ounces of plastic explosives and a detonating mechanism hidden inside electronic printers—were discovered on separate cargo planes after a tip-off from Prince Muhammad bin Nayef. Bound for the United States, they were found at en route stopovers in British Midlands and in Dubai [*q.v.*]. They were designed to detonate midair, with the debris falling over the destined American cities.

During the lengthy pro-democracy protests in Yemen in 2011, the army split, with the opposing units fighting each other, particularly in the south. This allowed the militia of the *Ansar al-Sharia* (Arabic: *Helpers of the Sharia*), affiliated with the AQAP, to leave their highland hideouts and cap-

ture large swathes of the Abyan, Bayda, and Shabwa provinces in the south, including many urban centers. They established a parallel government, free of corruption and run strictly according to the Sharia [*q.v.*], which provided much needed public services.

The AQAP's gains were unaffected by the killing of Awlaki and Samir Khan—a Pakistani-American editor of the organization's quarterly online magazine *Inspire*—in a U.S. drone attack in September 2011.

Al Qaida in Mesopotamia:

(Official title, Organization of Jihad's Base in the Land of Two Rivers; Arabic: *Tanzim Qaidat al-Jihad fi Bilad al-Rafidain*) Its origins lie in Ansar al-Islam founded by Abu Musab Zarqawi [*q.v.*], which was renamed Society of Divine Unity and Jihad (Arabic: *Jamaat al-Tawhid wal Jihad*), after the overthrow of Iraqi President Saddam Hussein [*q.v.*] in April, and acquired the commonly used title of Al Qaida in Mesopotamia (AQM) in October 2004 when Zarqawi took an oath of loyalty to Osama bin Laden [*q.v.*].

It offered resistance to the U.S.-led occupation authority by attacking it and those Iraqis cooperating with it as well as Iraqi Shias [*q.v.*]. It emerged as the most lethal among the Sunni [*q.v.*] groups resisting the foreign occupation. It claimed responsibility for such dramatic acts as the bombing of the UN mission in Baghdad [*q.v.*] in 2003 and the assassination of the Iraqi Governing Council president Izzeddine Salim 10 months later. It sent suicide bombers into Shia gatherings in Baghdad and Karbala [*q.v.*] to devastating effect. It took westerners as hostages and beheaded some. The Pentagon raised the price on Zarqawi's head from $10 million to $25 million.

Arguing that the authority to legislate rested with Allah's word as revealed in the Quran [*q.v.*], the AQM opposed democracy and elections. It backed the decision of the Sunni tribal leaders to boycott the election for the Interim National Assembly in January 2005. It focused on high-profile and coordinated suicide attacks, and created insecurity among the general public. Because of its addiction to violence for its own sake and intolerance of those who differed from it, the AQM started to lose whatever popular support it had.

To regain the lost ground, in January 2006 Zarqawi created the Islamic World Council (IWC) to gather all Sunni resistance groups under one banner. He had made scant progress when he was killed in June in a joint operation by the American and Iraqi forces.

His successor, Abu Ayub al-Masri, an Egyptian extremist, replaced the Islamic World Council with the Islamic State of Iraq, under the leadership of Abu Omar al-Baghdadi, by co-opting small militant groups. It aimed to seize power in Iraq and transform it into an orthodox Sunni Islamist state.

The AQM's attack on the Al Askirya Mosque—containing the remains of the Shias' Tenth and Eleventh Imams, Ali al-Hadi and Hassan al-Askari—in Samarra [*q.v.*] in February 2006, blew out its golden dome. The event triggered low intensity inter-sectarian warfare between Shias and Sunnis. It continued well into 2007 when the second attack on the same holy place in June 2007 destroyed its two minarets. The retaliation by the Shia militias raised the temperature.

The unpredicted internecine violence turned many Sunni tribal leaders against the AQM. They began cooperating with the U.S. troops to quash the AQM. By mounting a series of joint offensives, the American and Iraqi troops expelled the AQM and its allies from their bastions in Anbar and Diyala provinces by 2008. As a result, in April 2008 the Pentagon reduced its prize for the head of al-Masri from $5 million to $100,000. Nonetheless the AQM continued to target Shia gatherings and neighborhoods.

As the Pentagon started to reduce U.S. troop presence in cities for eventual withdrawal from all urban areas by June 2009, the AQM tried to make a comeback with massive bomb attacks on government ministries in Baghdad. But the killing of al-Masri and al-Baghdadi in a joint operation by American and Iraqi forces in April 2010 weakened the AQM. By June, of the AQM's 42 leaders, only eight remained at large. Of these, the single most important, Nasser al-Din Allah Abu Suleiman, the war minister of the Islamic State of Iraq, was killed in February 2011. The next top figure to fall was Huthaifi al-Batawi, the AQM commander of Baghdad, three months later. The current AQM chief, Abu Dua, carries Washington's bounty of $10 million for information leading to his capture or death.

With the total withdrawal of U.S. troops from Iraq in December 2011, the AQM lost its primary aim. It kept up its occasional suicide attacks on Shia gatherings in a country where Shias were 63.5 percent of the population.

Qasim, Abdul Karim (1914–63): *Iraqi military leader and politician; prime minister, 1958–63* Born to a Sunni [*q.v.*] father and a Shia [*q.v.*] mother in a lower-middle-class home in Baghdad [*q.v.*], Qasim graduated from the local military academy and became a commissioned officer in 1938. He fought in the 1948–49 Palestine War [*q.v.*] as a lieutenant colonel. Along with Col. Abdul Salam Arif [*q.v.*], he led the Free Officers group since its formation in 1956. It overthrew King Faisal II [*q.v.*] on 14 July 1958, assassinated the royal family, and declared a republic.

Instead of forming a military revolutionary command council as the coup leaders in Egypt had done in 1952, Qasim headed a civilian-dominated cabinet of 14 as the prime minister, with additional authority as defense minister and military chief of staff. He became known as the Sole Leader.

In the debate that followed on Iraq's unification with the United Arab Republic (UAR) [*q.v.*], Qasim led the anti-unity camp and ousted the pan-Arabist [*q.v.*] Arif from office in September. A year later he curbed the Communist Party [*q.v.*], which had backed him in his opposition to the union with the UAR, and his implementation of long-overdue agrarian reform, thus alienating it. His strategy of manipulating the pro-union and anti-union camps proved counterproductive. He became isolated, and inadvertently paved the way for his own downfall.

Having made peace with Kurdish nationalists, Qasim invited their leader, Mustafa Barzani [*q.v.*], to return home from the Soviet Union. But, when Barzani demanded autonomy, he mounted a campaign against the Kurds [*q.v.*].

Qasim withdrew Iraq from the Baghdad Pact [*q.v.*]. He hosted a conference of Iran, Iraq, Kuwait, Saudi Arabia, and Venezuela in September 1960 to form the Organization of Petroleum Exporting Countries (OPEC) [*q.v.*] to serve as a collective bargaining agency. His decree in 1961 deprived the Western-owned Iraq Petroleum Company (IPC) of 99.5 percent of the 160,000 sq. mi./414,400 sq. km originally allocated to it for prospecting. In June 1961, when Kuwait became independent, Qasim claimed that it was part of Iraq. In the subsequent crisis that followed, he found himself being opposed by, among others, the Arab League [*q.v.*], which sent a Joint Emergency Force to Kuwait. This defused the crisis, but only after Kuwait had made substantial secret subventions to Iraq.

An alliance of Baathist [*q.v.*] civilians and military officers and Abdul Salam Arif toppled Qasim's regime on 8 February 1963, and executed him and his close aides.

Qassam, Izz al-Din (1881–1935): *Palestinian lender* Born into a religious family in Jabla, northern Syria, Qassam received an Islamic education in Latakia [*q.v.*], and joined al-Azhar University [*q.v.*] in Cairo [*q.v.*]. There he came under the influence of Muhammad Abdu, an Islamic thinker. On his return to Syria he worked as a preacher. When France received the League of Nations' mandate to administer Greater Syria [*q.v.*] in 1920, he opposed the foreign rule. Because of his participation in the resistance to the French Mandate in the mid-

1920s, he was sentenced to death in absentia.

Qassam fled to the Palestinian city of Haifa [*q.v.*] and became a preacher there. Calling for a jihad [*q.v.*] against the British Mandate and the Zionist [*q.v.*] colonizers, he coined the slogan: "Allah's book in one hand and a rifle in the other." He thus became the first Arab [*q.v.*] leader in Palestine [*q.v.*] to advocate an armed struggle against foreign colonizers and rulers.

Because he considered workers and peasants to be the most dedicated classes, ready to sacrifice everything to gain the independence of Palestine, he was seen as a guardian of the poor. This won him popularity among those Palestinians who were not particularly religious. In late 1935 Qassam gathered some 800 armed men in Haifa and started marching toward the hills of the West Bank [*q.v.*] to defeat the British forces and make Palestine independent. After British reconnaissance planes had tracked down his militiamen, the British army engaged them in an uneven battle at Yaabad near Jenin. They lost, and Qassam was killed.

However, this first armed confrontation between the Palestinians and the British, coupled with Qassam's martyrdom [*q.v.*], boosted Arab morale. It paved the way for the Arab Revolt, the first Palestinian intifada, which erupted in 1936 and lasted three years. It is widely recognized that Qassam's philosophy, leadership, and advocacy of an armed struggle left a lasting impression on the Palestinian political culture. This became apparent when, during the Intifada [*q.v.*] in the Occupied Territories [*q.v.*] in 1987, both Hamas [*q.v.*] and Islamic Jihad [*q.v.*] named their respective military wings the Izz al-Din Qassam Brigade.

Qatar:

OFFICIAL NAME: State of Qatar
CAPITAL: Doha [*q.v.*]
AREA: 4,416 sq. mi./11,437 sq. km
POPULATION: 1.7 million (2011 est.), of which 1.4 million were non-nationals.
GROSS DOMESTIC PRODUCT (nominal): $173.8 billion; per capita, $98,330 (2011 est.)
GROSS DOMESTIC PRODUCT (Purchasing Power Parity): $182.0 billion; per capita, $102,940 (2011 est.)
NATIONAL CURRENCY: Qatari Rial (QAR); QAR 1 = U.S.$0.275 = £0.169 = €0.207 (2011)
FORM OF GOVERNMENT: monarchy
OFFICIAL LANGUAGE: Arabic [*q.v.*]
OFFICIAL RELIGION: Islam [*q.v.*]
ADMINISTRATIVE SYSTEM: Qatar consists of 10 municipalities.
CONSTITUTION: An interim constitution, promulgated in April 1970 by Shaikh Ahmad bin Ali al-Thani [*q.v.*], named the al-Thanis [*q.v.*] as hereditary ruling family and invested the emir (head of state) with supreme power. It specified a 10-member cabinet, appointed and led by the emir as the chief executive. The cabinet ministers were to be additional members of the 23-strong Consultative Council, with 20 of its members chosen from among the 40 popularly elected representatives. In 1999 the ruler set up a 29-member Central Municipal Council, elected by universal adult suffrage, as a consultative body to the Ministry of Municipal Affairs and Agriculture. It has a four-year tenure.

A new constitution, endorsed in a referendum in 2003 and ratified by Shaikh Hamad bin Khalifa al-Thani [*q.v.*] a year later, was promulgated in June 2005. It provides for a 45-member Consultative Council, with two-thirds of its members to be elected by universal suffrage. It is to be entitled to debate and vote on proposed legislation, which must win two-thirds majority and the ruler's endorsement before it becomes law; to monitor the performance of ministers; and to approve the budget presented to it. The last of the several promises by the ruler to hold elections to this Council, made in the midst of the Arab Spring [*q.v.*] in 2011, mentioned 2013 as the date for the first general election.

CONSULTATIVE COUNCIL: After ascending the throne in February 1972, Shaikh Khalifa bin Hamad al-Thani [*q.v.*] appointed a fully nominated Consultative Council of 20 members, who were empowered to advise the cabinet only on matters referred to it by the emir. The Council was expanded to 30 members in 1975 and 35 in 1988. Since its formation, its four-year tenure has been extended repeatedly.

ETHNIC COMPOSITION: (2010 est.): Arab 28 percent, South Asian 54 percent, East Asian 11 percent, other 7 percent.

High officials:

Head of state: Shaikh Hamad bin Khalifa al-Thani, 1995–

Crown Prince: Tamim bin Hamad Khalifa al-Thani, 2003–

Prime minister: Shaikh Hamad bin Khalifa al-Thani, 2007–

Speaker of Consultative Council: Abduallah al-Khalifa al-Thani, 2007–

HISTORY: By intervening in the Qatari-Bahraini battles of 1867–68,

Britain became the dominant foreign influence in the politics of Qatar, ruled by the al-Thani family. During the Ottoman suzerainty (1872–1916) the al-Thanis, adherents of Wahhabism [*q.v.*], remained preeminent. The end of the Ottoman rule brought Abdullah bin Qasim al-Thani (1876–1948) closer to the British, a relationship that was formalized in the 1916 Anglo-Qatari Treaty [*q.v.*]. Britain guaranteed Qatar's territorial integrity against external aggression while Qatar promised not to cede any rights, including mineral rights, to a third party without British consent. A subsidiary of the Iraq Petroleum Company, owned largely by Britain, struck oil in 1939, but commercial extraction did not start until 1948. Output rose to 32,000 barrels per day (bpd) toward the end of Shaikh Abdullah's reign.

His successor, Shaikh Ali bin Abdullah al-Thani (r. 1948–60) [*q.v.*], was deposed by the British in 1960 in favor of Shaikh Ahmad bin Ali al-Thani (r. 1960–72). He took Qatar into the Organization of Petroleum Exporting Countries (OPEC) [*q.v.*] in 1961 and into the Organization of Arab Petroleum Exporting Countries (OAPEC) [*q.v.*] nine years later. In 1964, yielding to pressure from the National Unity Front [*q.v.*] and Britain, he appointed an advisory council with the authority to issue laws and decrees for "the fundamental principles and basic rules of overall policy." He promulgated an interim constitution in April 1970, which, by specifying a largely elected consultative council, marked an important step toward a representative government. It was only in that year that the apparatus of a modern state was established in Qatar. But that left untouched the "rule of four quarters"—the first quarter of revenues for administration; the second for the princes; the third to be credited to the reserves controlled by the royal clan, consisting of some 1,000 adult male al-Thanis; and the remainder for economic development.

Shaikh Ali al-Thani negotiated the termination of the 1916 Anglo-Qatari Treaty and declared Qatar independent in September 1971. But in February 1972 he was overthrown in a bloodless coup by Prime Minister Khalifa bin Hamad al-Thani [q.v.]. By then Qatar's petroleum output had reached 600,000 bpd. Its oil revenue soared to $5.4 billion in 1980, when its population was less than 250,000. The next year it became a cofounder of the Gulf Cooperation Council [q.v.]. Qatar supported Iraq in the Iran-Iraq War [q.v.]. It backed Kuwait after it had been occupied by Iraq in August 1990, and joined the Washington-led coalition against Iraq in Gulf War II [q.v.].

In June 1995 Shaikh Khalifa was overthrown by his son Shaikh Hamad al-Thani. Later that year he allowed Israel to open a trade mission in Doha. His decision in 1996 to partly fund the Al-Jazeera satellite television channel, which was licensed to operate without censorship, broke new ground. It gave the tiny emirate a high profile in the region and in the Arab world at large. Defying pressure from Arab and Muslim countries, Qatar presided over the U.S.-sponsored Fourth Middle East and North Africa Economic Conference, aiming to foster economic ties between Israel and the Arab world, in Doha in November 1997.

The emir held the first direct election to the nation-wide Municipal Council on the basis of universal franchise in 1999. The following year Qatar acquired the chairmanship of the Islamic Conference Organization [q.v.], but only after it had closed down the Israeli trade office in Doha.

When popular sentiment in Saudi Arabia turned against the U.S. military presence, dating back to the 1991 Gulf War, Shaikh Hamad al-Thani allowed the Pentagon to shift most of its military hardware and personnel to Qatar's al-Udaid air base in 2002. During the run-up to the Anglo-American invasion of Iraq in March 2003 [q.v.], the Pentagon's Central Command set up a forward base at al-Saliyah Camp near Doha. Both these military bases were key elements in the conduct of Washington's war against Iraq.

With the increased exploitation of the enormous North Dome gas field, the income from gas and oil provided more than three-fifths of the GDP and nearly seven-eights of Qatar's export income.

Buoyed by the ballooning income from hydrocarbons, Shaikh Hamad al-Thani started playing an important role in regional affairs. After the Israeli-Hizbollah War [q.v.] in 2006, he stepped forward to help financially all those who had lost their homes and businesses. He also tried to conciliate Hamas [q.v.] and Fatah [q.v.]. In May 2008 he mediated successfully between the rival camps in Lebanon and thus helped avert the possibility of full-scale civil war. When the Arab League [q.v.] headquarters refused to hold an emergency session of Arab leaders during the Israeli attack on the

Gaza Strip [*q.v.*] in December 2008–January 2009, he hosted a meeting of 13 Arab leaders in Doha. Later in 2009, he succeeded in resolving the long-running political crisis in Lebanon, which had paralyzed the state machinery.

During the 2011 Arab Spring, the Qatari government and the Al-Jazeera TV channel backed the uprisings, except in Bahrain. Qatar was among the most vociferous Arab supporters of the opposition to the regime of President Bashar Assad [*q.v.*] in Syria.

RELIGIOUS COMPOSITION (2010 est.): Muslim, 74 percent, of which Sunnis [*q.v.*] 70 percent (mostly Wahhabi [*q.v.*]), Shias [*q.v.*] 7 percent; Hindu 11 percent; Christian [*q.v.*] 10 percent; other, 6 percent.

qisas (Arabic: *derivative of* qasas, *tracking the enemy's footsteps*): The concept in Islam [*q.v.*] of equal retaliation for harm inflicted, with a provision for forgiveness, is encapsulated in the Quran [*q.v.*] (5:49): "A life for a life, an eye for an eye/a nose for a nose, an ear for an ear/a tooth for a tooth, and for wounds/retaliation; but whosoever foregoes it/as a freewill offering, that shall be for him/an expiation."

It is one of the four systems of crime punishment in Islam, the others being *hudud* [*q.v.*], *diyya* (Arabic: *balanced*), compensation paid to the heirs of a victim, and *tazir* (Arabic: *corporal punishment*), penalties for misdemeanors at the discretion of a religious judge.

qiyas (Arabic: *to compare*): Qiyas is the method by which statements in the Quran [*q.v.*] and the Hadith [*q.v.*] are applied to situations not explicitly

covered by these sources of the Islamic law. *See also* ijtihad.

Qom: *city in Iran* Population. 1.1 million (2011 est.). As the burial place of Fatima *Maasuma* (Arabic: *one who shuns sin*), sister of Imam Ali al-Rida/Reza, the eighth imam of Twelver Shias [*q.v.*], Qom is the holiest place for Shias [*q.v.*] after Mecca [*q.v.*], Medina [*q.v.*], Najaf [*q.v.*], Karbala [*q.v.*], and Mashhad [*q.v.*]. It became an important religious settlement in the early eighth century A.D., with its Shia inhabitants resisting Sunni [*q.v.*] governors and their tax demands. Fatima Maasuma was buried here in 816 A.D., but the first dome over her grave was not built until the 13th century. The founders of the Safavid dynasty (1501–1736), Shah Ismail and Shah Tahmasp, continued the tradition of using Qom as the winter capital. The city became a place of Shia pilgrimage in the 17th century. The Qajar dynasty (1790–1925) continued the tradition of placing royal and noble mausoleums at Fatima's shrine, now adorned by a gilded dome.

The uncertain conditions in Iraq that followed the collapse of the Ottoman Empire in 1918 encouraged the leading Shia clerics of Najaf and Karbala to resurrect Qom as a center of Shia learning. This led to the founding of Iran's largest theological college, Faiziyya, there in 1920. Five years later, in his drive to gain legitimacy for his rule, Reza Khan Pahlavi [*q.v.*] canvassed support among the clerical leaders of Qom.

During the reign of his son, Muhammad Reza Shah Pahlavi [*q.v.*], the importance of Qom continued. Among the clerics it spawned was Ayatollah Ruhollah Khomeini [q.v.], who came to prominence in the early 1960s. Qom was the site of Khomeini's challenge to the shah's rule in June 1963. Matters settled down after his deportation the following year. But when the anti-shah movement began nationally in late 1977, Qom soon became a leading center of protest and resistance. With the success of the Islamic revolution [q.v.] in February 1979, the city's preeminence grew. It was the Khomeini's base after his return from abroad. Later he left it for Tehran [q.v.], mainly to avail himself of better medical facilities after suffering a heart ailment. Qom then became the headquarters of his deputy, Ayatollah Hussein Ali Montazeri [q.v.], who set up the secretariat of the World Organization of the Islamic Liberation Movements there.

Qom is an important junction for the petroleum and gas pipelines which run between the oilfields of Khuzistan and Tehran. The discovery of an oilfield near the city in 1956 boosted its prosperity.

Since the founding of the Islamic Republic of Iran in 1979, it has been the republic's ideological heart. Its theological student body has expanded to nearly 50,000, least a fifth of them foreigners. It is the base of several grand ayatollahs.

Quartet on the Middle East: As the rotating president of the European Council in the first half of 2002, Spanish Prime Minister Jose Maria Aznar urged coordination of efforts to energize the peace process in the Middle East [q.v.]. In June U.S. President George W. Bush outlined a road map for peace. It called for Israel and the Palestinians to take a series of parallel and reciprocal steps leading to the emergence of an independent, peaceful Palestinian state living side by side with a secure State of Israel. This led to the formation of the Quartet on the Middle East consisting of the United Nations, the European Union (EU), the U.S., and Russia. The Quartet adopted this road map in April 2003.

To further its main objective, the Quartet appointed a special envoy whose mission was funded by the UN. In April 2005 the job went to Sir James Wolfensohn, former World Bank president, to smooth the way for Israel's withdrawal from the Gaza Strip [q.v.]. He found it hard to continue in the job when the U.S. and the EU refused to deal with the government formed by Hamas [q.v.] after its victory in the parliamentary elections in January 2006, and Israel stopped transferring funds to the Palestinian Authority (PA) [q.v.] as required by the agreement between them, to bring about the collapse of the PA. He resigned.

In June 2007, after stepping down as British prime minister, Tony Blair succeeded Sir James as the Special Envoy of the Quartet. A year later Blair came up with a plan for economic cooperation between Israel, Jordan, and the Palestinians to initiate joint industrial and economic projects as a means of promoting mutual cooperation. Given the political stalemate, nothing came of it.

In August 2009, in his interview with Terrasanta.net, Blair said that he backed the idea of involving Hamas [q.v.] and Hizbollah [q.v.] in the peace negotiations, but only if they renounced violence and supported a two-state solution. (In January 2004, Abdul Aziz Rantisi, the leader of Hamas in Gaza [*q.v.*], proposed a 10-year truce between Israel and Hamas in exchange for the founding of an independent Palestine on the territories occupied by Israel since the June 1967 Arab-Israel War [*q.v.*]. This was rejected by Israel, and Rantisi was assassinated by its forces.)

Following its meeting in Moscow in March 2010, the Quartet condemned Israel's plan to construct new homes in disputed East Jerusalem [*q.v.*], since this move undermined attempts to revive peace talks. It also called for the establishment of the Palestinian state within 24 months.

On the eve of the Palestinian Authority's application to the UN Security Council in September 2011 that Palestine should be admitted as a full member of the United Nations, the Quartet called on the PA and Israel to start negotiations within a month to reach a final agreement before the end of 2012.

al-Quds (Arabic: *The holy*—short form of Beit al-Muqudus, *The House of Holiness*): See Jerusalem.

Quran (Arabic: *Recitation*): Muslims [*q.v.*] regard the Quran, which is composed of the divine revelations received by the Prophet Muhammad (570–632 A.D.) over the last 20 years of his life from the eternal, heavenly Book, *al-kitab*, accessible only to the immaculate, as the Word of Allah. According to the Prophet Muhammad, the revelations of the earlier (monotheistic) prophets and the scriptures of Jews [*q.v.*] and Christians [*q.v.*] were also based on the same heavenly tablet, so that they coincided in part with what Allah revealed later. The Quran confirmed that the law was given to Moses, the Gospel to Jesus Christ, and the Book of Psalms to David. Jews and Christians were called *ahl al-kitab*, people of the Book.

The revelations, conveyed piecemeal to the Prophet Muhammad and delivered in rhythmic Arabic [*q.v.*] prose, were initially memorized by his followers and used in prayers. These were subsequently taken down on palm leaves, camel bones, or leather patches. The work of compilation, assigned by Caliph Abu Bakr (r. 632–634 A.D.) to the Prophet's secretary, Muhammad Zaid bin Thabit, involved collecting scattered discourses and transcribing memorized revelations. It was completed before Abu Bakr's death in the form of a sheaf of separate inscribed leaves.

The authorized version of the Quran was not issued until 651 A.D. by Caliph Othman (r. 644–656 A.D.), who destroyed all other versions. It consists of 114 *suras* (Arabic: *chapters*) of varying length to form a book of some 6,616 verses. Until his migration in mid-622 A.D. to Medina [*q.v.*] from Mecca [*q.v.*], the Prophet Muhammad was under attack by his opponents. In contrast, in Medina he became a civil and military governor and judge. This is reflected in the suras, the earlier ones often being shorter, more imaginative, and in rhymed prose; the later ones being generally longer and down-to-earth, full of legal and moral guidelines. Except for the short introductory sura, the others are arranged approximately according to their length, starting with the longest. Therefore, the earlier, shorter suras of the Meccan period appear later in the Quran. These advocate obedience to Allah in view of the forthcoming Day of Judgment. The later, longer suras of the Medinese period offer guidelines for the creation of a social environment that is conducive to the moral existence demanded by Allah.

All the suras are emphatic about monotheism, urging the audience to accept no divinity except Allah. He is the one who has created the universe, and maintains it, and is the most powerful and wise. He has given guidelines to human beings as to how they should conduct themselves in His revelations conveyed through the prophets, and He will judge them on that basis on the Day of Judgment. His strictness is balanced by His mercy and compassion. Human beings, who are capable of doing good or evil, have a choice. They are responsible for their deeds as individuals and members of a group. They are enjoined to heed the Quran. It demands total submission to the will of Allah, and to His message as conveyed by His messenger, the Prophet Muhammad. This means living within the moral-ethical guidelines as an individual believer and as a member of the community. On the Day of Reckoning each person's actions will be examined and judgment delivered. He/she will either enjoy the gardens of heaven or suffer the horror of hell.

The Medinese section of the Quran is concerned with commenting on social affairs and providing a corpus of law.

It deals firstly with the external and internal security of the Islamic *umma* [*q.v.*] (Arabic: *community*). The task of protecting it from external threats lies

with all its members. The security of the individual and the property of individuals within the community is ensured through the old tribal custom of retribution, *qisas* [*q.v.*]. Secondly, family life is regulated. Thirdly, certain ethical and legal injunctions must be obeyed. Intoxicants, flesh of swine, games of chance, and hoarding are forbidden. Fraud, slander, perjury, hypocrisy, corruption, extravagance, and arrogance are condemned. Punishments for stealing, murder, and adultery are stated.

As the paramount authority for the Muslim community, the Quran is the ultimate source and continual inspiration of Islam [*q.v.*]. Pious Muslims memorize it. Often social and political gatherings begin with recitations from it. Together with the Hadith [*q.v.*], it constitutes the Sharia [*q.v.*].

Quttb, Sayyid Muhammad (1906–66): *Islamist ideologue* Born into a poor, but notable, family near Asyut, Sayyid Quttb trained as a teacher in Cairo [*q.v.*] and became a school inspector with the ministry of education. He was a prolific writer, as much at home with essays and literary criticism as with fiction.

In 1948 the ministry sent him to Colorado State College of Education (now University of Northern Colorado) in Greeley for further studies. His three-year long experience in the United States convinced him that that American society was racist and sexually depraved, and that Western civilization was in terminal decline. He became interested in his Islamic roots and Islam [*q.v.*]. On his return to Egypt, the education ministry found his anti-American views so objectionable that it asked him to resign. Later, in his book *Islam and the Problem of Civilization*, he wrote, "What should be done about America and the West, given their overwhelming danger to humanity…? Should we not issue a sentence of death? Is it not the verdict most appropriate to the nature of the crime?" Decades later, such views would be expressed by Osama bin Laden [*q.v.*] and his intellectual mentor, Ayman Zawahiri [*q.v.*].

He joined the Muslim Brotherhood [*q.v.*] and became director of its propaganda department in 1952. After the ban on the Brotherhood in 1954, he was arrested and held in a concentration camp. Here he wrote his classic, *Maalim fi al-Tariq* (Arabic: *Signposts on the Road*), which would become the primer for radical Islamists [*q.v.*] worldwide. The manuscript was smuggled out, and published in 1964, when Quttb and other Brotherhood detainees were released.

In his book, Quttb divided social systems into two categories: the Order of Islam and the Order of *Jahiliya* (Arabic: *Ignorance*), which was decadent and ignorant, the sort that existed in Arabia before the Prophet Muhammad had received the Word of God, when men revered not God but other men disguised as deities. Quttb argued that the regime of President Abdul Gamal Nasser [*q.v.*] was a modern version of Jahiliya. This earned him the approval and respect of young Brothers and the opprobrium of the political and religious establishment.

The militant members of the (still clandestine) Muslim Brotherhood drafted Quttb into the leadership. They wanted him to avenge the persecution of the Brotherhood in the mid-1950s. By inclination a thinker, he wished to avoid violence. But when his radical followers pressed for a jihad [*q.v.*] to be waged against the social order he had himself labeled Jahiliya because of its betrayal of Islamic precepts, he could find no way out.

During his trial in 1966 he did not contest the charge of sedition, and instead tried to explain his position ideologically, arguing that the bonds of ideology and belief were sturdier than those of patriotism based upon a region, and that the false distinction made among Muslims on a regional basis was an expression of the Crusading and Zionist [*q.v.*] imperialism which had to be eradicated. In his view, *watan* (Arabic: *homeland*) was not a land but the community of believers, *umma* [*q.v.*]. He argued that, once the Brothers had declared someone to be *jahil* (Arabic: *ignorant* [of Allah]), they had the right to attack his person or property, a right granted in Islam, and that if in the course of performing the religious duty of waging a jihad against unbelievers, a Brother found himself on the path of sedition, so be it. The responsibility for creating such a situation lay with those who through their policies had created such circumstances. His subsequent execution turned him into a martyr in the eyes of his followers, gaining his thesis a wider acceptance in the Arab [*q.v.*] world.

Among his books translated into English are *Signposts on the Road*; *Islam: The Religion of the Future;* and *Social Justice In Islam*.

al-Quwatli, Shukri (1891–1967): *Syrian politician; president 1943–49, 1955–58*
Born into a rich landowning family in

Damascus [*q.v.*], Quwatli was active in Arab nationalist politics as a youth, joining the clandestine *Jamiat al-Arabiya al-Fatat* (Arabic: *Society of Young Arabs*). The Ottoman government imprisoned him during World War I.

Soon after the war ended, Faisal I bin Hussein [*q.v.*] appointed him governor of Damascus [*q.v.*]. When the French defeated Faisal in 1920, he went into exile, operating mainly from Egypt or Europe. The French Mandate in Syria condemned him to death in absentia. The lifting of this sentence enabled him to return home and head the National Bloc, which demanded independence. Following the Franco-Syrian Treaty of 1936 [*q.v.*], he became minister of defense and finance (1936–39).

After a brief exile from 1941–43, when the pro-Nazi French government, based in Vichy, controlled Syria, he returned to Damascus to lead the National Bloc. It won overwhelmingly at the polls, and Quwatli became president. He led the final struggle for total independence. The National Bloc split into the National Party, led by Quwatli, and the People's Party. He was reelected president in 1948, but was overthrown by the army chief of staff, Col. Hosni Zaim [*q.v.*], in March 1949.

He went into exile in Egypt, and returned home after five years, following the downfall of Adib Shishkali [*q.v.*]. In the September 1954 elections his National Party did not do as well as the People's Party, but in the August 1955 presidential election, backed by the People's Party and Saudi funds, he beat his leftist rival, Khalid Azm.

Following an Israeli attack on the Syrian posts near Lake Tiberias in December, Quwatli strengthened Syria's ties with the Soviet Union. Buffeted by the American and Iraqi plots to overthrow him, and pressured by his pan-Arabist military officers, he backed the idea of an Egyptian-Syrian federation. However, he was overruled by the officer corps, who advocated a merger. When this occurred in February 1958, he resigned, proposing Gamal Abdul Nasser [*q.v.*] as president of the United Arab Republic [*q.v.*].

R

Rabin, Yitzhak (1922–95): *Israeli military leader and politician; prime minister, 1974–77, 1992–95* Born into a middle-class Jewish family in Jerusalem [*q.v.*], Rabin grew up in Tel Aviv [*q.v.*]. He graduated from Kadoon Agricultural High School in 1940. As a member of Palmah [*q.v.*], he participated in the Allied campaign in 1941 in Syria, then under a pro-Nazi French government.

In the 1948–49 Arab-Israeli War [*q.v.*] he commanded a brigade that saw combat on the Jerusalem and Negev fronts. He headed the Israeli military's tactical operations branch (1950–52). After his graduation from the Camberly Staff College in Britain, he was promoted to brigadier-general in 1954. He served as chief of the military's training department (1954–56), commander of the Northern Command (1956–59), chief of operations (1959–61), and deputy chief of staff (1961–63) before being promoted to chief of staff on 1 January 1964. Under his command the Israeli armed forces performed brilliantly in the June 1967 Arab-Israeli War [*q.v.*]. Even when posted as ambassador to the United States (1968–73) he advised the prime minister on important military matters.

After returning home, Rabin joined the Labor Party [*q.v.*] and was elected to the Knesset [*q.v.*] in December 1973. He was given the labor portfolio in the cabinet formed by Golda Meir [*q.v.*] in March 1974. Following her resignation, he challenged Shimon Peres [*q.v.*] for the party's leadership. He won by 298 votes to 254, and became prime minister in June 1974. His achievements included the Sinai II Agreement [*q.v.*] with Egypt in September 1975 and the rebuilding of the military and the economy after the October 1973 Arab-Israeli War [*q.v.*].

Division within the Labor Party on the issue of the Occupied Arab Territories [*q.v.*] intensified, and a series of financial scandals involving party leaders came to the surface. In addition, Rabin's inexperience in civil administration, poor communicating skills, and strained relations with defense minister Shimon Peres hurt the government's popular standing. Yet, in a fresh challenge by Peres to his leadership in early 1977, he scraped through by 41 votes in an electoral college of 3,000. In March it was revealed that, during his ambassadorship in the United States, his wife, Leah, had maintained an active bank account in Washington, an illegal act according to the Israeli law. The next month he resigned as party leader.

Labor lost the general election in May, but Rabin remained politically active, becoming defense minister in the national unity government formed in 1984. Noting the unpopularity of Israel's continued military involvement in Lebanon, he withdrew the Israeli troops from there, except for a small force posted in the border security strip. He retained the defense ministry in the next national unity government that assumed office in 1988, and continued his hard-line policy toward the Palestinian Intifada [*q.v.*] until Labor's withdrawal from the cabinet in 1990. He was elected Labor leader in 1992, and became prime minister of a Labor-led coalition after elections in June.

Rabin closely supervised the secret negotiations with the Palestine Liberation Organization (PLO) [*q.v.*] initiated by his foreign minister, Peres, and sanctified the Israeli-PLO Accord [*q.v.*]—signed in Washington in September 1993—by shaking the hand of his long-term enemy, Yasser Arafat [*q.v.*]. In October 1994 he signed the Jordanian-Israeli Peace Treaty [*q.v.*] with King Hussein [*q.v.*] at a common border site. He shared the 1994 Nobel Peace Prize with Peres and Arafat. In September 1995 he signed an agreement on self-rule for the Palestinians in the West Bank, called Oslo Accord II [*q.v.*]. He was assassinated in November in Tel Aviv by Yigal Amir, a fanatic Jewish Israeli.

Rafsanjani, Ali Akbar Hashemi (1933–): *Iranian religious and political leader; president 1989–1997* Born into a religious family in Behraman, Kerman province, Rafsanjani went to Qom [*q.v.*] for his theological studies. During the power struggle between

Premier Muhammad Mussadiq [*q.v.*] and Muhammad Reza Shah Pahlavi [*q.v.*] from 1951 to 1953, he sided with Mussadiq. Later he became a student of Ayatollah Ruhollah Khomeini [*q.v.*]. After Khomeini's deportation in 1964, Rafsanjani stayed in contact with him, handled Islamic charities on his behalf and consulted him on political affairs. He was arrested and tortured in 1975.

One of the cofounders of the Tehran [*q.v.*] branch of the Organization of Militant Clergy (OMC) [*q.v.*], Rafsanjani was actively involved in the 1977–78 revolutionary movement, particularly the formation of the Revolutionary Komitehs [*q.v.*]. He was one of the members of the Islamic Revolutionary Council and a cofounder of the Islamic Republican Party (IRP) [*q.v.*]. He was later appointed deputy minister of the interior.

He was an active member of the 1979 Assembly of Experts [*q.v.*], charged with drafting the constitution. After his election as a Majlis [*q.v.*] deputy from Tehran [*q.v.*], he was voted speaker of the house in July 1980, a post to which he was reelected every year until 1984. As the Majlis speaker, he played a pivotal role in the impeachment of President Bani-Sadr [*q.v.*] in June 1981. In 1982, after the election of a new Assembly of Experts, Rafsanjani was chosen its vice president. He acted as Khomeini's personal representative on the Supreme Defense Council.

During the Iran-Iraq War [*q.v.*], when in mid-1982 Iran recovered the area lost earlier to its foe, he advocated advancing into Iraq if Iraqi President Saddam Hussein [*q.v.*] did not meet

Iran's demands, including a compensation of $100 billion for war damages. Hussein dismissed the demands, and Iran's troops advanced into Iraq.

After his election to the Majlis in 1984, he was reelected speaker, a position confirmed annually for the next four years. On the sixth anniversary of the armed conflict (September 1986), he remarked that the regime had been able to use the war to awaken the people and confront the problems threatening the revolution. Following Iran's military setbacks in the spring of 1988, Khomeini put him in overall charge of the war effort. Having realistically assessed the deteriorating situation, in mid-July 1988 he persuaded the Assembly of Experts to recommend to Khomeini the acceptance of the truce proposed by the UN Security Council in July 1987. Khomeini accepted the recommendation.

After Khomeini's death in June 1989, when President Ali Husseini Khamanei [*q.v.*] was promoted to succeed him, Rafsanjani resigned his post in the Majlis, and ran in the presidential election. He secured 95 percent of the votes on a turnout of 70 percent. According to the amended constitution, he ruled without the premier, becoming the executive president. He excluded radicals from his government and introduced economic liberalization. He pursued a pragmatic path in foreign policy, and improved relations with Germany, France, Japan, and the Soviet Union (later Russia). But, due to a drop in oil prices, the economy suffered and inflation rose. As a result his popular vote in the 1993 presidential election fell to 63 percent on a voter turnout of 56 percent. His performance during the second term was lackluster.

In 1997 Supreme Leader Khamanei appointed him president of the Expediency Consultation Council System. In that capacity he acted as a mediator to resolve differences between the president, parliament, and the Guardian Council [q.v.]—as well as a consultant to the Leader on the formulation of general policies.

His efforts to return to the leadership of the Majlis failed when he trailed embarrassingly poorly in the parliamentary election of 2001, which he entered from Tehran, once his stronghold. The majority of the reform-orientated residents of the capital regarded him as a conservative surrounded by a coterie of corrupt men.

In the 2005 presidential election, he faced the newcomer Mahmoud Ahmadinejad [q.v.] as his rival in the second run, and lost to him by nearly 2:1, despite running a lavishly funded election campaign. Nonetheless he remained influential in the religious hierarchy.

In 2007, after winning a seat in the Assembly of Experts [q.v.], to which he had belonged since its inception, he was elected its chairman. In the 2009 presidential election he backed Mir Hussein Mousavi with funds and strategic planning. After Mousavi's defeat in a controversial election, Rafsanjani limited himself to bemoaning the crisis that had been caused by the Khamanei regime's repression of the peaceful protestors. He reportedly consulted some members of the Assembly of Experts regarding convening an emergency session, but did not find much support for the idea. Aware of his waning influence, in March 2011 he did not offer his candidacy for the Assembly's chairmanship.

Rajai, Muhammad Ali (1933–81): *Iranian politician; prime minister, 1980–81, president, 1981* Born to a poor shopkeeper in Qasvin, Rajai left school at 16 and traveled to Tehran [q.v.], where he became a bricklayer. In 1951 he joined the air force as an orderly and then as a maintenance trainee. He was in contact with the Fedaiyan-e Islam [q.v.]. Five years later he enrolled at a teacher training college, graduating in 1959. He then taught in a provincial town. He was imprisoned briefly during the June 1963 uprising. After his release he became a high school teacher in Tehran.

Rajai joined the Liberation Movement of Iran [q.v.], and in 1967 he cofounded the Islamic Welfare and Mutual Assistance Foundation, a front organization for political activity. He joined the Mujahedin-e Khalq [q.v.] in 1970, but was unhappy with the leftward drift of the organization and left two years later. In November 1974 he was arrested on suspicion of planting a bomb outside the Tehran office of El Al, the Israeli airline. He was tortured, and scars were left on his feet. During his imprisonment he came into contact with Ayatollah Mahmoud Taleqani [q.v.] and Ali Husseini Khamanei [q.v.]. He was released in November 1978.

After the revolution in February 1979, Rajai was appointed education minister. He accelerated the Islamization of the educational system. In August 1980, after he had been elected a deputy of the Majlis, he became its leading choice for prime minister. A reluctant President Abol Hassan Bani-Sadr [q.v.] appointed him to that post.

Following the Iraqi invasion of Iran

in September 1980, Rajai argued at the UN Security Council that the United States was the chief instigator of the aggression against the Islamic Republic.

Poles apart, socially and politically, Rajai and Bani-Sadr clashed often, and this was one of the factors that caused the downfall of the president in June 1981. In the presidential election that followed, Rajai was one of the four candidates. He won 88 percent of the vote. Under his presidency the government set up ad hoc committees in many places to deal with the violence of the guerrillas led by the National Resistance Council in Iran [*q.v.*], and declared a state of emergency in the worst affected areas. An incendiary bomb killed him and Premier Muhammad Javad Bahonar on 30 August during a National Security Council meeting.

Rajavi, Masoud (1947–): *Iranian politician* Born into a middle-class family in Tabas, Khorasan province, Rajavi studied political science at Tehran University. In 1965 he joined the Mujahedin-e Khalq [*q.v.*], and five years later became a member of its central committee. He received guerrilla training at a Palestinian camp in Jordan. In 1971 he was one of the two Mujahedin-e Khalq (MEK) leaders arrested for trying to abduct a top Western diplomat, and was condemned to death. But under international pressure the government commuted his sentence. By the time he was released in December 1978 he was the only surviving central committee member of the MEK, which participated actively in the revolutionary movement. After the victory of the Islamic revolution [*q.v.*], Rajavi supported autonomy for the Kurds [*q.v.*] and opposed secret revolutionary courts.

Since the MEK abstained in the referendum on the constitution, Ayatollah Ruhollah Khomeini [*q.v.*] disqualified Rajavi from entering the presidential election in January 1980. He then backed Abol Hassan Bani-Sadr [*q.v.*], who was elected president. Later he cooperated with Bani-Sadr in the latter's struggle with the clerical leadership, which wanted to undermine his authority. Rajavi and his party were denounced by Khomeini as "hypocrites"—those claiming to be good Muslims while following the secular ideology of Marxism and misguiding the faithful with their Marxist interpretations. He supported Bani-Sadr in June 1981 in the latter's confrontation with Khomeini.

After Bani-Sadr's dismissal from office, both he and Rajavi went underground. In July they flew to Paris together. There they jointly established the National Resistance Council in Iran (NRCI) [*q.v.*], which conducted sabotage and guerrilla attacks on suitable targets in Iran. The Islamic regime surmounted the challenge, which lasted from July 1981 to September 1982, by using unrestrained force and propaganda. With the war against Iraq raging along the border, it convincingly labeled those creating disorder at home as unpatriotic agents of Baghdad. By holding a public meeting with Iraqi deputy premier Tariq Aziz [*q.v.*] in Paris in January 1983, Rajavi provided Iran with a propaganda tool and angered Bani-Sadr, who quit the NRCI. Yielding to Iran's pressure, the French government expelled Rajavi from France. He then moved the MEK headquarters to Baghdad [*q.v.*].

Toward the end of the Iran-Iraq War [*q*] in July 1988, Rajavi's forces, operating as the National Liberation Army, penetrated deep into Iran, only to be surrounded by the Iranian troops and decimated. Despite Iraq's defeat in Gulf War II [*q.v.*] in 1991, followed by growing economic hardship in the country due to the UN economic sanctions, Rajavi continued to receive aid from the Iraqi government. He came to share his leadership of the MEK with his wife, Miryam.

In the 1990s the MEK mounted pinprick attacks along the Iraqi-Iranian border interspersed with rocket assaults on government offices in central Tehran [*q.v.*]. After many years of enjoying substantial support among American lawmakers, the MEK's standing in the United States suffered when the administration of President Bill Clinton listed it as a terrorist organization in 1997. This made it illegal for the MEK to raise funds in the U.S. However, that left its support among the Iranian exiles living in Europe largely intact. With the United States mounting a global war on terrorism in the wake of the attacks on it on 11 September 2001, there was no prospect of its rehabilitation in America. In Iraq, President Saddam Hussein [*q.v.*], facing increasing pressure by Washington, ensured that both Rajavi and the MEK kept a very low profile.

During the Anglo-American invasion of Iraq [*q.v.*], the U.S. air force bombarded MEK camps. The commanders, who signed a cease-fire agreement with the Pentagon on 23 April 2003, did not include Rajavi. He went into hiding, and nothing about him has become public knowledge since then.

Rakah (Hebrew: acronym of *Reshima Kommunistit Hadash,* New Communist List): *Israeli political party* Rakah emerged as a result of a split in Maki [*q.v.*] in August 1965, when 2,000 Arab members and a section of the equally numerous Jewish members left the parent body. In the November 1965 election Rakah won three Knesset [*q.v.*] seats. It blamed Israel for its aggression in the June 1967 Arab-Israeli War [*q.v.*] and opposed annexing any part of the Occupied Arab Territories [*q.v.*]. In the 1969 election the party retained its three seats. In the 1973 election Rakah was the only group to demand Israeli withdrawal from all Occupied Arab Territories, and recognition of Palestinian national rights. Its strength rose to four seats. In early 1977 Rakah delegates to an international conference in Prague, Czechoslovakia, met the delegates of the Palestine Liberation Organization (PLO) [*q.v.*]. On the eve of the May 1977 election Rakah merged with the Black Panther Party to form the Democratic Front for Peace and Equality, with the Hebrew acronym *Hadash* [*q.v.*], and secured five seats. *See also* Hadash.

Ramadan: *Islamic holy month of fasting* The Arabic root, r-m-d, refers to the heat of summer. The ninth month in the Islamic calendar [*q.v.*], Ramadan is regarded as holy in Islam [*q.v.*] because it was on the night of 26–27 Ramadan, *Lailat al-kadr* (Arabic: *Night of Power*), that the first divine revelation was made to the Prophet Muhammad. During this month the faithful are required to undertake fasting, as stated in the Quran [*q.v.*] (2: 179): "O believers, prescribed for you/is the Fast, even as it was prescribed for/those that were before you… the month of Ramadan, wherein the Quran/was sent down to be a guidance/to the people, and as clear signs/of the Guidance and the Salvation." During the month, between sunrise and sunset all adult Muslims are required to abstain from eating, drinking, smoking, and conjugal relations. Among other things this helps them to develop self-control.

Ramadan War (1973): Since Egypt and Syria started the war against Israel during Ramadan 1393 A.H. [*q.v.*], Arabs [*q.v.*] refer to the October 1973 Arab-Israeli War [*q.v.*] as the Ramadan War. *See* Arab-Israeli War IV.

Ras al-Khaimah Emirate: *a constituent of the United Arab Emirates* Area 660 sq. mi./1,700 sq. km; population 300,000 (2010 est.). Ras al-Khaimah joined the United Arab Emirates only in February 1972 during the rule of Shaikh Saqr bin Muhammad al-Qasimi (r. 1948–2010). Commercial extraction of petroleum started on a small scale in 1984. Its oil reserves of 400 million barrels are modest, and so too are its gas deposits—at 34 million cu m.

Rastakhiz Party (Iran) (Persian*; Resurgence*): *Iranian political party* The Rastakhiz Party was established by Muhammad Reza Shah Pahlavi [*q.v.*] in March 1975 as the sole governing party after he had dissolved the ruling

New Iran Party, founded by him in 1963, and the Mardom Party, the official opposition. By setting up a single governing party under Prime Minister Amir Abbas Hoveida [*q.v.*], the shah co-opted the loyal opposition. In the Majlis elections of June 1975, Rastakhiz won 70 percent of the popular vote.

To tackle rising inflation, the Rastakhiz government passed an anti-profiteering law and used Rastakhiz volunteers to monitor prices. They resorted to exacting levies from traders. When protest mounted in the autumn of 1977, the shah replaced Hoveida with Jamshid Amuzgar, leader of the liberal wing within Rastakhiz. To counter the rising protest movement, Rastakhiz officials set up a Resistance Corps, consisting of policemen in civilian clothes, to break up opposition meetings. This led to attacks on Rastakhiz offices by anti-regime demonstrators. With the revolutionary movement gaining strength during the summer of 1978, the shah dissolved the party in September.

However, so hostile was the Islamic Republic of Iran to this party that any Iranian who had ever belonged to it was automatically disqualified from running for any public office, and this ban was applied strictly.

Ratz (Hebrew: acronym of *Reshima Tzibori*, Citizens' List): *Israeli political party* Ratz was formed by Shulamit Aloni in 1973 after her departure from the Labor Party [*q.v.*]. It opposed Jewish settlements in the Occupied Territories [*q.v.*]. Its opposition to discrimination on the basis of religion, gender, or ethnicity made it attractive to secularists and women. It won three Knesset [*q.v.*] seats in the 1973 election, but only one in 1977. Having failed to secure a place in the subsequent parliamentary elections, it eventually won five seats in 1988. It then allied with Mapam [*q.v.*] and Shinui [*q.v.*] to form the Meretz [*q.v.*] alliance. Of the 12 seats won by Meretz in the 1992 election, six belonged to Ratz. It joined the Labor-led coalition. Its three ministers in the cabinet were notable for their strong support for the Oslo Accord I [*q.v.*] of September 1993. On the eve of the 1996 Knesset [*q.v.*] election, Aloni lost the party leadership and retired from politics. After this election, Ratz formally merged into Meretz.

Reform Judaism: The Jewish enlightenment, called *halaska*, during the latter half of the 18th century in eastern and central Europe led Jews [*q.v.*] away from the traditional belief in messianic redemption and toward a search for personal and communal fulfillment. In his book *Jerusalem* (1783), Moses Mendelssohn, a German Jew, argued that there was no contradiction between believing in a secular religion of reason and believing in Judaism [*q.v.*]. The movement gathered pace after the 1789 French Revolution. It manifested itself among West European Jews in religious reform, with French Jews concentrating on reforming doctrine by emphasizing Judaism as a prophetic tradition and repudiating the binding nature of rabbinic law, and German Jews concentrating on worship—the latter institutionalizing reform in the mid-1840s. Thus Reform Jews reject many of the restrictions of the Halacha [*q.v.*], use the

vernacular in religious ceremonies, and dispense with much of the ritual.

Religious endowment/trust: *Islamic institution. See* waqf.

Revisionist Zionists: *Zionist Organization* Founded as the World Union of Revisionist Zionists in 1925 by Vladimir Jabotinsky [*q.v.*], it derived its name from its program of revising the Labor Zionist strategy of establishing a Jewish state in Palestine [*q.v.*] through colonization, and returning to the original concept of Theodor Herzl (1860–1904) of Jewish statehood through international recognition of Jewish sovereignty over Palestine. Advocating a Jewish state on both sides of the Jordan River [*q.v.*], it opposed the 1922 decision of Britain, the Mandate power in Palestine, to apply the idea of a Jewish homeland only to the west of the Jordan. Unlike Labor Zionists [*q.v.*], it gave priority to private capital to develop Palestine. At the Seventeenth Zionist Congress [*q.v.*] in 1931, one-fifth of the delegates supported its stance. Efforts made later to conciliate its members with Labor Zionists in Palestine failed.

After the Zionist Congress in 1933 had resolved that "in all Zionist matters discipline in regard of the Zionist Organization [*q.v.*] must take precedence over the discipline of any other body," the Revisionists left and formed the New Zionist Organization (NZO) in 1935. In Palestine the party's youth movement, Betar, and the Revisionists within Haganah [*q.v.*], established Irgun Zvai Leumi [*q.v.*] in 1937. After David Ben-Gurion [*q.v.*], head of Israel's provisional government, had brought about the disbandment of Irgun in 1948, the Revisionists and former Irgun ranks combined to form the Herut [*q.v.*] Party under the leadership of Menachem Begin [*q.v.*].

Riyadh: *Capital of Saudi Arabia* Population: 5.254 million (2011 est.), with 40 percent being foreigners. Located in the middle of three valleys in the central Najd [*q.v.*] region, the oasis town of Riyadh became the center of the Wahhabi [*q.v.*] movement from the early 19th century. It was the capital of the House of Saud [*q.v.*] from 1824 to 1881, when it fell to the Rashid dynasty of Hail to the north. But the House of Saud returned when Abdul Aziz bin Abdul Rahman al-Saud [*q.v.*] recaptured Najd in 1902. Using Riyadh as his base, he extended his realm from the eastern Hasa region to the western Hijaz [*q.v.*] and Asir. With the founding of the Kingdom of Saudi Arabia in 1932, Riyadh became its capital.

The discovery of oil in the east in 1933, followed by commercial production after World War II, had a dramatic impact on Riyadh, catapulting it from a medieval existence to modern life and turning it into a variant of a modern American city but, due to Islamic strictures, without the leisure activities commonly available in the United States. It is the country's leading educational and communications center, and is served by an airport, a railway, and highways. It is the most populous city in the Arabian Peninsula [*q.v.*], with two-fifths of its residents being non-Saudi, mostly from South Asia.

Rogers Plan (1969): *a U.S. peace plan* In December 1969 U.S. Secretary of State William Rogers made public a peace plan he had earlier submitted to Israel, Egypt, and Jordan—as well as to the Soviet Union, Britain, and France. It envisaged Israel's withdrawal to its 1967 borders, subject to minor modifications for mutual security, except for the Gaza Strip [*q.v.*], which was to be negotiated between Israel, Egypt, and Jordan. Palestinian refugees were to be either repatriated according to an agreed annual quota or given compensation. Other provisions included security arrangements to be hammered out by the concerned parties. The final accords were to be negotiated under the chairmanship of Gunnar Jarring, the UN mediator. Israel rejected the plan, having been assured by U.S. President Richard Nixon that Washington would not "impose" anything on Israel. Egypt followed suit. This virtually killed the plan.

In August 1970, Rogers unveiled a second plan. It no longer aimed at a comprehensive peace agreement but only an "interim" one. It sought to bring about a truce in the War of Attrition [*q.v.*]. This was accepted by Egypt and Israel.

Roman Catholic Christians/Church: *Christian sect* The term Roman Catholic Church came into vogue only in the 19th century. It applies to the Christian Church under the supreme authority of the pope, the historic Bishop of Rome. It took on a distinctive identity as a result of two major splits in the church—with the (Eastern) Orthodox Church [*q.v.*] in 1054, and within the Western church at the time of the Protestant [*q.v.*]

Reformation in the mid-16th century. The members of this church perform the Roman rites, the liturgy being said in Latin until the 1960s, and follow the practices of the church in Rome. They accept the teachings of the Bible [*q.v.*] and the interpretations offered by the Church, and subscribe to the doctrine that God conveys His grace to humans through sacraments. The Eucharist is therefore the center of Roman Catholic worship, and is often performed with pomp and color. Particular emphasis is laid on the oneness and wholeness of the Christian body, which includes the dead as well as the living.

Different orders of priests, monks, and nuns are part of the body of the Roman Catholic Church. It has a hierarchical structure, extending from parish priests to the pope at Vatican City in Rome, where the central administration is conducted by papal officials and commissions. The supremacy of the Bishop of Rome, the title first applied to Apostle Peter, is derived from the New Testament [*q.v.*] (Matthew 16: 18): "Peter: you are a rock and on this rock foundation I will build my church."

After the fall of the Western Roman Empire in 476 A.D., the pope also assumed the title of Pontifex Maximus, used earlier by Roman emperors in their high priestly functions. Rivalry between the pope and monarchs in Europe with regard to lay and religious power was a running theme in the Middle Ages (476 A.D.–1492). During the last two centuries of the medieval era, most churchmen were involved in politics and other worldly affairs. Before a belated attempt at reform within the church during these centuries and the first half of the 16th

century could succeed in holding the Church together, the Protestant Reformation caused its breakup.

The papacy was beset by "Catholic princes" until the late 18th century. In the 19th century, during the papacy of Pius IX (1846–78), came the declaration of papal infallibility in faith and doctrine, which hardened the rift between the Roman Catholic Church and its two major rivals—the Orthodox and Protestant Churches.

Changes in the liturgy introduced since the 1960s have led to greater use of the vernacular and increased participation by the congregation. With its worldwide membership of 1.196 billion in 2011, the Roman Catholic Church accounted for nearly half of all Christians, and a sixth of the global population.

In the Middle East [*q.v.*], Roman Catholics have a patriarch in Jerusalem [*q.v.*] and apostolic delegates, called nuncios, in Baghdad [*q.v.*], Beirut [*q.v.*], and Cairo [*q.v.*].

Those churches that accept the supremacy of the pope but follow their own Eastern rites and customs are called Uniate [*q.v.*].

Rosh HaShana (Hebrew: *Head of the Year*): *Jewish festival* Rosh HaShana is the Jewish New Year festival and is held on the first two days of Tishri (September–October, according to the Christian Gregorian calendar [*q.v.*]; the seventh month of the Jewish calendar [*q.v.*] when arranged according to religious usage), which is believed to mark the creation of the world. It marks the start of the Ten Days of Penitence, which end on the Day of Atonement—Yom Kippur [*q.v.*]. Rosh HaShana should be spent in prayer. The distinctive feature of the religious ritual of the day is the sounding of a ram's horn. Requesting a good year is the central theme of petitionary prayers. Because Rosh HaShana is a major Jewish festival, work is prohibited.

Russian Orthodox Church: *Christian sect* Of the six national churches in the Orthodox [*q.v.*] group, the Russian Orthodox Church, with its liturgy performed in Old Slavonic, is the most important. Its patriarchal see, originally based in Kiev (now capital of Ukraine) under the supervision of the Patriarchate of Constantinople, was moved to Moscow in 1589, where an independent patriarchate was established. This was replaced by a synod by Peter the Great (r. 1682–1725) in 1721. On the eve of the Bolshevik Revolution in 1917, the patriarchate was revived, only to be suppressed by the Bolsheviks, later Communists. It was again revived in 1943 during World War II in an attempt to foster Russian nationalism. Later the church and the state reached a modus vivendi, which survived until the collapse of the Communist system in 1991, when the church became autonomous in post-Soviet Russia. The Russian Cathedral is an important landmark in Jerusalem [*q.v.*] today.

S

Saadeh, Antun (1902–49): *Lebanese politician and intellectual* Born to a Greek Orthodox [*q.v.*] doctor, Khalil, and his wife, who migrated to Brazil,

Saadeh grew up there and worked on a magazine started by his father. In 1929 he traveled to Damascus [*q.v.*], where he became a journalist with *Al-Ayyam* (Arabic: *The Days*). Soon he moved to Beirut [*q.v.*], where he worked his way into the social and intellectual life of the American University of Beirut (AUB) [*q.v.*].

In 1932 he established a secret society, which by 1935 had acquired several thousand members, with branches in Syria as well as Lebanon. Arguing that geography and history had given the inhabitants of Greater Syria [*q.v.*] a distinct identity, he expounded the concepts of a Greater Syrian nation (an ethnic fusion of Canaanites, Akkadians, Chaldeans, Assyrians, Aramaeans, and Hittites) and Syrian nationalism, which was at odds with both pan-Arabism [*q.v.*] and Lebanese nationalism, which was popular among the country's Christians [*q.v.*].

Saadeh demanded an end to the French Mandate and independence for Syria-Lebanon. After he had brought the organization into the open as the Syrian Nationalist Party and held its first plenary conference in December 1935, he was jailed by the French. Following the electoral victory of the leftist Popular Front in France in 1936, he was freed. The next year his party was allowed to function legally after he had assured the authorities that it did not advocate destruction of the Lebanese entity.

In his book *Nushu al-umam* (Arabic: *Rise of Nations*), published in 1938, he outlined the principles of his philosophy, the leading ones being that Syrians were a complete nation, and that Syria's interests overrode all others. He allied his thesis with a call for reform, including the separation of church and state, the removal of barriers between various sects and confessions, and the abolition of feudalism. His secular and anti-sectarian stance appealed to religious and racial minorities—Alawis [*q.v.*], Christians, Druzes [*q.v.*], and Kurds [*q.v.*]—who became a majority in the party leadership.

He visited Italy and Germany in late 1938, and was in the midst of his tour of South America when World War II broke out in September 1939. The French banned his party, charging its leaders with complicity with the Axis Powers, but they failed to prove their allegation. In 1941, after the party's leaders had altered the organization's name to the National Party, they were released.

When Saadeh returned to Lebanon in 1947 the country had gained its full independence. He resumed his control over the organization, renaming it the Syrian Social Nationalist Party (SSNP) [*q.v.*]. Conflict between it and the Lebanese government revived, and he went underground. A compromise was reached, with Saadeh reaffirming his respect for Lebanon as an independent country.

Following the Arab defeat in the 1948–49 Palestine War [*q.v.*], his argument against pan-Arabism and for Greater Syrian nationalism became attractive enough to make traditional political leaders feel insecure. When Hosni Zaim [*q.v.*] seized power in Syria in March 1949, Saadeh hoped for his backing, but this did not happen. In June there were armed clashes between his party members and the Phalangists [*q.v.*] in Beirut during an alleged coup attempt by Saadeh. He

escaped to Syria to a warm welcome by Zaim. But under pressure from Lebanon and the anti-SSNP forces in Syria, Zaim agreed to his extradition to Lebanon. After a secret military trial, he was executed in July.

el Saadawi, Nawal (1931–): *Egyptian writer and feminist campaigner* Born into a middle-class family in the village of Kafr Tahla, Saadawi trained as a doctor in 1955. As a member of the Egyptian civil service, she rose through the ranks to become director-general of health education at the health ministry. After the publication of her first book, *Women and Sex* (1971), which showed linkage between poverty and politics, and disease and politics, she was sacked from her job. The book was banned by the government of President Anwar Sadat [*q.v.*]. While working for the United Nations in Lebanon and Ethiopia as a doctor, she continued to publish novels, including *Two Women in One* (1975), which were banned in Egypt. She campaigned for women's rights and expressed her left-wing views.

Saadawi was among the several hundred dissident Egyptian intellectuals who were arrested in September 1981. Freed three months later by President Hosni Mubarak [*q.v.*], she resumed her writing and campaigning for women's rights in the Arab world. She founded the Arab Women's Solidarity Association to help repair the damage done to women by oppression and poverty. Her novel *The Fall of the Imam* (1987) drew a death threat from Islamic fundamentalists [*q.v.*], and for two years she lived under armed protection ordered by the government.

Due to her opposition to the U.S.-led war against Iraq following Iraq's invasion of Kuwait in 1990, the authorities closed down the Arab Women's Solidarity Association. Though by then the government had stopped banning her books, she was barred from appearing on state-run television or radio. She went into self-exile and took teaching jobs at American universities before returning home in 1996.

In the searing prose of her novels lies a passionate commitment to fighting injustice. At the same time she is conscious as a writer that a well-crafted story is one that can sustain itself without the politics. In 1991 she published an autobiographical work, *My Travels around the World*. Then came *The Well of Life* (1993), containing two novellas focusing on the suffering of Arab women, and *The Innocence of the Devil* (1994), centered on two women in a mental hospital. She covered the subject of women's status in society in *Memoirs from the Women's Prison* (1984, translated into English in 1994) and *Women at Point Zero* (1997). *North/South: The Nawal el Saadawi Reader* appeared in 1997. Since then she has published three works of fiction and nonfiction: *A Daughter of Isis: The Autobiography of Nawal el Saadawi* (1999), *Dissidenza e scrittura* (2008), and *L'amore ai tempi del petrolio*, (2009).

Altogether she is the author of 11 novels, eight short story collections, several plays, and a few works of nonfiction. She is best known for *Woman at Point Zero*, *God Dies by the Nile*, *The Hidden Face of Eve*, *Memoirs of a Woman Doctor*, and *Memoirs from the Women's Prison*. Her novels have been translated from Arabic into English by her husband, Sherif Hetata, a leftist writer who has spent 13 years in jail for his political beliefs.

She participated in the pro-democracy demonstrations in the Tahrir Square of Cairo [*q.v.*] in January-February 2011. She described the experience as "a dream in which we are all equal."

In 2004 the Council of Europe awarded her the North-South Prize. She was the recipient of the Women of the Year Outstanding Achievement Award sponsored by the London-based *Good Housekeeping* in 2011.

al-Sabah, Abdullah III bin Salim I

(1895–1965): *ruler of Kuwait, 1950–65* Son of Shaikh Salim I, Abdullah was 10 years younger than his rival in the Jaber branch, Shaikh Ahmad I bin Jaber II al-Sabah, and at odds with the latter's pro-British leanings. His moment of glory came in July 1938, when he became president of the first elected parliament. But this lasted only until December, when the parliament was dissolved by Shaikh Ahmad I [*q.v.*]. During World War II, suspecting Abdullah of pro-German sympathies, the British excluded him from any position of authority.

Soon after Abdullah's accession to the throne in 1950, the Iranian oil crisis of 1951–53 boosted Kuwait's petroleum output. By 1955 Kuwait was the leading oil exporter in the Gulf, a position it maintained until 1965. In between, Kuwait became a cofounder of the Organization of Petroleum Exporting Countries (OPEC) [*q.v.*] in 1960.

As a result of London's complicity in the Suez War [*q.v.*] in 1956, anti-

British feelings arose. Abdullah demanded greater latitude in home affairs, and Britain met him half way. But following the overthrow of the pro-Western monarchy in Iraq in July 1958, he came under growing popular pressure to abrogate the 1899 Anglo-Kuwaiti Agreement [q.v.].

This happened in June 1961, and Britain officially recognized Kuwait as an independent country. When the Iraqi government claimed that Kuwait was Iraqi territory, Abdullah appealed for help from Britain and Saudi Arabia. London sent 6,000 troops and Riyadh a small contingent. After acquiring membership of the Arab League [q.v.] for Kuwait, Abdullah called for its assistance. The resulting Arab League's Joint Emergency Force replaced the British troops.

In November 1962 Abdullah promulgated a constitution drafted by an assembly nominated by him. It specified a National Assembly elected on a franchise of one-tenth of adult male citizens. With the ruler having the exclusive right to appoint the cabinet, the assembly lacked executive power. Having conceded an elected parliament, Abdullah tried to determine its composition by manipulating the electoral system. Therefore, the parliament that emerged in January 1963 was a virtual rubber-stamp of the government. Under his rule Kuwait was transformed from an obscure principality into a high profile, oil-rich state.

al-Sabah, Ahmad I bin Jaber II (1885–1950): *ruler of Kuwait, 1921–50* Son of Shaikh Jaber II al-Sabah, Ahmad was the first in the Jaber line to administer the principality. His relations with Abdul Aziz bin Saud [q.v.], the ruler of Najd [q.v.], deteriorated because of the attacks by Ikhwan [q.v.], border disputes, and the embargo on Kuwait's transit trade with the Arabian hinterland. The 1922 Protocol of Uqair [q.v.] resolved these problems, except for the embargo, which continued for the rest of the decade. In the early 1930s the domestic economy faltered due to the decline of the pearling industry, which had been damaged by cheap Japanese imports. However, there was an improvement in relations with Najd, which became part of Saudi Arabia in 1932.

Ahmad granted the first oil concession in 1934 to the Western-owned Kuwait Oil Company (KOC). But it was not until 1938 that petroleum was found in commercial quantities. Meanwhile he treated the fees and advance royalties paid by the KOC as his personal property. This angered the Kuwaiti notables, who demanded that these funds should be treated as government income and that he should restore the 12-member advisory council he had disbanded on becoming the emir. Yielding to popular pressure, Ahmad accepted a constitution drafted by a committee elected by the local Merchant Society. It passed on his powers in domestic affairs to an elected parliament of 14. In July 1938 the parliament elected Shaikh Abdullah bin Salim I al-Sabah [q.v.] as its president. The diminution of Ahmad's authority was against the interests of Britain and the KOC. Encouraged by them, Ahmad dissolved parliament in December and suppressed opposition. The sudden death in April 1939 of King Ghazi [q.v.] of Iraq, who had backed the opposition, further helped Ahmad.

During World War II, ignoring the pro-German sentiment prevalent among his subjects, Ahmad sided with Britain as required by the 1899 Anglo-Kuwaiti Agreement. Popular discontent rose further due to the sealing of oil wells and food shortages caused by the war. It was only in mid-1946 that petroleum exports could be resumed, which helped to turn Kuwait into an oil state.

al-Sabah, Jaber III bin Ahmad I

(1928–2006): *ruler of Kuwait, 1977–2006* Son of Shaikh Ahmad I bin Jaber II al-Sabah [*q.v.*], Jaber continued the domestic policies of his predecessor, Shaikh Sabah III bin Salim I al-Sabah [*q.v.*], and showed no sign of reviving the National Assembly, which had been dissolved in 1976. Freed from the Assembly's scrutiny, the ruling family had resorted to lining its pockets at the expense of the state and leading merchants. This created distrust between the emir and his subjects. Following Iran's Islamic revolution [*q.v.*] in early 1979 and the subsequent Shia [*q.v.*] protest in Kuwait, Jaber put further restrictions on the press and public gatherings. That failed to curb the opposition.

Therefore, he reinstated the suspended articles of the constitution in 1980 and called elections for the 50-member National Assembly in February 1981. As no nationalist-leftist won a seat, and the Islamic fundamentalists [*q.v.*] secured only six, he found the results satisfactory. But his regime was tarnished by the disastrous collapse of Kuwait's unofficial stock exchange in September 1982, leaving $180 billion in paper debt. The voters, restricted to only about a 10th of the adult popula-

tion, showed their disapproval in the 1985 election by selecting five nationalist-leftists and 11 fundamentalists.

His policy of aiding Iraq in the Iran-Iraq War [*q.v.*], both financially and logistically, was unpopular with the Shias, who wanted Kuwait to stay neutral. On 25 May 1985 a suicide bomber driving a car packed with explosives made an unsuccessful attempt to assassinate Jaber. Three weeks later a fire at the petroleum complex in Mina Ahmadi raged for two days. The security lapse angered the National Assembly, and the government resigned. On 3 July 1985 he dissolved the chamber and imposed censorship.

Kuwait's close alliance with Iraq in its war with Iran made its oil tankers vulnerable to attacks by Tehran. In the spring of 1987 Jaber secured the assistance of the U.S. Navy, which protected Kuwaiti oil tankers by transferring their ownership to a U.S.-based company.

When the Iran-Iraq War ended in August 1988, popular pressure built up for the restoration of parliament. Instead of reviving it, he introduced a National Council as an advisory body without legislative powers. When he held elections to it in June 1990, the opposition boycotted them.

He tried to use the $12–14 billion Kuwait had lent to Iraq during the Iran-Iraq War as a lever to settle a border dispute with Iraq dating back to 1961. He failed. He then flooded the oil market in order to lower the price and thus hurt Iraq economically. In retaliation Iraqi President Saddam Hussein [*q.v.*] invaded and occupied Kuwait on 3 August 1990. Jaber and most other members of the ruling family escaped first to Bahrain and then to Saudi Arabia.

Operating from his temporary headquarters in Taif, Saudi Arabia, he contributed $5 billion toward the cost of the war against Iraq that was being planned by the United States. On his return home in March 1991, following the expulsion of Iraq from Kuwait by the Washington-led coalition, he resisted the opposition's demand for an immediate revival of the National Assembly. In September he signed a 10-year defense cooperation agreement with the United States, allowing it to stockpile military supplies and conduct training exercises, as well as granting it access to Kuwait ports and airfields and the stationing of American troops.

The election of 31 opposition candidates to the 50-member parliament in the October 1992 election indicated the degree of disaffection with his reign. During the crises between Iraq and the UN over weapons inspection between 1995 and 1998, he was the only regional leader who publicly backed Washington's hawkish line against Baghdad. In 1999, due to the recurring conflict between the National Assembly and the cabinet, he dissolved the legislature a year earlier. In the subsequent election the number of government supporters fell from 18 to 12.

His efforts to repair relations with Iraq and Iran stalled when, in the aftermath of the terrorist attacks on the United States in September 2001, U.S. President George W. Bush described Iran and Iraq as members of the "Axis of Evil." He cooperated with the Bush administration in its preparations for invading Iraq in 2003 to the extent of letting U.S. forces occupy large parts of Kuwait. After the end of the hot war, Kuwait remained a vital transit point for the arrival and departure of American and British troops.

By the time of his death at the age of 78, he had fathered 40 children.

al-Sabah, Sabah III bin Salim I

(1913–77): *ruler of Kuwait, 1965–77* Son of Shaikh Salim I bin Mubarak, Sabah began his career as commander of the police force in 1938, a position he held until 1959. He then headed the public health department. After Kuwait's independence in June 1961, he established the ministry of foreign affairs and became its head as well as deputy premier. In October 1962 Shaikh Abdullah III bin Salim I al-Sabah [*q.v.*] named Sabah, a member of the ruling family's Salim branch, crown prince, even though, by precedence, the position should have gone to someone from the Jaber branch. Three months later Shaikh Abdullah III appointed him as prime minister, an office held until then by the emir.

On ascending the throne in November 1965, Sabah nominated a new cabinet. Several parliamentary deputies found his choices so unacceptable that they resigned in protest. To prevent this from happening again, Sabah decided to rig the next general election. He instructed Shaikh Jaber III bin Ahmad I al-Sabah [*q.v.*], prime minister since May 1966, and Shaikh Saad bin Abdullah (later crown prince), minister of defense and interior, to curb the opposition. They imposed censorship and disbanded journalists' and teachers' syndicates. The opposition demanded a rerun of the rigged 1967 general election, but to no avail.

During the June 1967 and October

1973 Arab-Israeli Wars [*q.v.*], Sabah joined the Arab oil embargo [*q.v.*] against Israel's allies. The steep petroleum price rise in 1973–74 benefited his regime. In 1975 Kuwait's annual oil income soared to $7.2 billion, but the state budget was able to absorb only $2.9 billion. Pressed by radical parliamentarians, his government nationalized the Western-owned Kuwait Oil Company.

The Lebanese Civil War [*q.v.*], which started in April 1975 and involved the Palestinians living in Lebanon, had an impact on Kuwait, as it had nearly 250,0000 Palestinian residents. The disruption of the Lebanese press, considered the freest in the Arab world, encouraged the Kuwaiti papers (staffed largely by Palestinians) to provide uncensored news, which heightened the Assembly's opposition to Sabah's policies. In August 1976 he suspended four articles of the constitution concerning freedom of the press and dissolution of the legislature as well as the National Assembly. He dissolved the chamber in September 1977.

al-Sabah, Sabah IV al-Ahmad I al-Jaber (1929–): *ruler of Kuwait, 2006–* The fourth son of Ahmad I al-Jaber al-Sabah [*q.v.*], he was educated in Kuwait by private tutors. Two years after Kuwait's independence in 1961, Abdullah III Salim al-Sabah [*q.v.*] appointed him foreign minister. He held that position for the next 40 years under different rulers. His main challenge came after Gulf War II [*q.v.*], when Kuwait had to reestablish diplomatic relations with numerous countries following the rupture caused by Iraq's invasion of the emirate in August 1990.

In 2003 Shaikh Jaber III al-Sabah [*q.v.*] appointed him prime minister, thus separating that office from that of Crown Prince Shaikh Saad Abdullah III al-Sabah, who was in poor health.

On the death of Shaikh Jaber III al-Sabah on 15 January 2006, Saad bin Abdullah III was unable to take the oath of office before the National Assembly, as required by the constitution, because of the loss of speech caused by his grave illness. An impasse ensued. On 24 January he abdicated. Two days later, with the approval of the cabinet, Shaikh Sabah was sworn in as the emir before the National Assembly.

He inherited the tense relations between the National Assembly and the government. Disagreeing with the parliament's demand to reduce the electoral districts from 25 to five, thus raising the size of the electorate and minimizing vote-buying, he dissolved the assembly. In the new parliament the pro-ruler faction occupied only a quarter of the seats. Claiming that some members of parliament (MPs) were misusing parliamentary privilege, he called fresh elections in May 2008. This time the size of the pro-ruler faction rose to 16. Within a year, once again there was a standoff between the National Assembly and the cabinet. The election held in May 2009 saw the strength of the pro-ruler faction rise to 21, including four women MPs.

The Arab Spring [*q.v.*] arrived in January 2011 at a time when there was a rising tension between the National Assembly and the cabinet dominated by al-Sabah ruling family amidst allegation of corruption at the highest level of government. Major demonstrations, attracting tens of thousands of protestors, occurred with increasing frequency. In November the demonstrators broke into the National Assembly building. The cabinet, led by the ruler's nephew, Nasser Muhammad al-Ahmad al-Sabah, since 2006, resigned. Sabah dissolved the parliament and ordered a fresh election. Held in February 2012 against the background of Islamist parties in Egypt sweeping the polls, it ended with the opposition Islamic groups garnering 34 seats.

al-Sabah clan: *Kuwaiti ruling clan* The al-Sabah clan is part of the Amarat tribe of the Anaiza tribal federation [*q.v.*]. After settling on the shores of Kuwait in 1710, the Anaiza's members developed trading facilities under the suzerainty of the Ottoman Turks. Of the three leading families who managed communal affairs, the al-Sabahs were charged with administration and defense. Out of this arose, from 1752 onwards, the al-Sabahs' dynastic reign, the first ruler being Shaikh Sabah I al-Sabah and the second Abdullah I al-Sabah (r. 1756–1814).

In 1899 Shaikh Mubarak I al-Sabah (r. 1896–1915) signed a secret treaty with the British whereby, for an annual subsidy of £1500, the Kuwaiti ruler accorded Britain the right of exclusive presence in Kuwait and control over its foreign policy. Shaikh Mubarak I was followed briefly by his older son, Shaikh Jaber II (b. 1865, r. 1915–17), who was deposed by the British for suspected pro-Ottoman sympathies during World War I, and then by his younger son, Shaikh Salim I (b. 1875, r. 1917–21). Both sons es-

tablished succession lines within the dynasty that were to share power, though not necessarily alternately. The Jaber branch ruled from 1921 to 1950 (Shaikh Ahmad I bin Jaber II al-Sabah [*q.v.*]), and again from 1977 (Shaikh Jaber III bin Ahmad I bin al-Sabah [*q.v.*]). The Salim branch reigned from 1950 to 1965 (Shaikh Abdullah III bin Salim I al-Sabah [*q.v.*]), and again from 1965 to 1977 (Shaikh Sabah III bin Salim al-Sabah [*q.v.*]). Shaikh Saad bin Abdullah III (1930-2008), who ruled nominally for 9 days in January 2006 before abdicating due to ill health, belonged to the Salim branch.

In 1965—four years after Kuwaiti independence—the title of the ruler was changed from shaikh to emir (Arabic: *ruler/commander*). In addition, the practice of having the head of the branch not currently occupying the throne act as crown prince and prime minister was introduced. The leading members of the clan hold such vital ministerial portfolios as oil, defense, interior, and finance.

Sabastiya: *See* Samaria city.

Sabbath (Hebrew: derivative of *shabbat, repose*): Sabbath is the weekly day of rest prescribed for Jews [*q.v.*], Christians [*q.v.*], and Muslims [*q.v.*], although the precise day for each group is different. Since, according to Genesis, God rested from the creation of the world on the seventh day (seven being the total number of spatial directions—forward, backward, above, below, right, left, and center), Jews are required to abstain from constructive activity on the Shabbath, and to praise the Creator (Exodus 20:11), or give thanks for their redemption (Deuteronomy 5:14). The Sabbath as a regular weekly fixture probably evolved during the Exile of the Israelites (586–400 B.C.), and replaced the earlier, irregular practice. The Jewish Sabbath, which falls on Saturday, is marked by three special meals and special prayers. An extract from the Torah [q.v.] is read in synagogues [q.v.] during morning service, followed by the chanting of the Haftara—a selection from Prophets. According to Genesis (1:5) "Evening passed and morning came—that was the first day," so a Jewish day begins in the evening. Hence the Jewish Sabbath lasts from Friday sunset to Saturday sunset.

Likewise, the Muslim [q.v.] Sabbath lasts from Thursday nightfall to Friday nightfall. *Jumah*, the Arabic word for Friday, means Assembling, when the believer is required to gather in the *jami masjid* (Arabic: *assembling mosque*) for midday prayers. In the Hadith [q.v.], the Prophet Muhammad (570–632 A.D.) states: "Friday was ordered as a divine day of worship both for the Jew and the Christian, but they have acted contrary to the command. The Jew fixed Saturday and the Christian Sunday."

Since early Christians observed the first day of the week, Monday, in commemoration of the Resurrection of Jesus Christ, Sunday became the Christian Sabbath.

sabra (Arabic: *cactus*): Sabra is the popular term for native-born Israeli Jews [q.v.] who, like the local cactus plant, are thought to be prickly on the outside but soft and sweet on the inside. In 2011, approximately 70 percent of Israeli Jews were sabra, which was twice the figure in 1948.

Sabri, Ali (1920–91): *Egyptian military officer and politician; prime minister, 1962–65* Born in Cairo [q.v.], Sabri graduated from the Cairo Military Academy in 1939. A member of the Free Officers group, he liaised between its leadership and the U.S. Embassy before and during the July 1952 coup. Later he became close to President Gamal Abdul Nasser [q.v.], becoming director of his office. When Egypt and Syria merged to form the United Arab Republic (UAR) [q.v.] in 1958, he was appointed minister for presidential affairs. Although the UAR split three years later, he retained his post in the Egyptian administration. He was promoted to prime minister in September 1962 and stayed in that position for three years, after which he became one of the four vice presidents.

In July 1965 Nasser appointed him secretary-general of the Arab Socialist Union (ASU) [q.v.] with a mandate to transform it into a cadre-based popular organization. He replaced the provincial and district ASU committees with executive bureaus run by salaried functionaries who were drawn from different social groups: factory foremen, teachers, lawyers, business managers, landowners, and government bureaucrats. He set up the Socialist Youth Organization (SYO) as an auxiliary to the ASU, but with its own cadre, and led the leftist faction within the ASU, advocating a larger public sector and closer ties with the Soviet Union. In 1966 the SYO carried out a campaign against feudalism.

ASU and SYO activists played a crucial role in the demonstrations in Cairo on 9–10 June 1967 to persuade Nasser to reverse his decision to resign in the wake of Egypt's defeat in the Six-Day War [*q.v.*]. Nasser stayed, but replaced his vice presidents, including Sabri.

In a further rightward shift in his policies, Nasser returned the ASU's structure back to that of the pre-1965 period. In September 1969 he demoted Sabri and his supporters in the ASU; and in December he appointed rightist Anwar Sadat [*q.v.*] as the only vice president of the republic.

After Nasser's death in September 1970, President Sadat named Sabri as one of his two vice presidents. But the power struggle between the two continued, with Sabri advocating maintaining the ASU as an independent body and Sadat favoring making it subservient to the state executive. Sadat's wishes prevailed, and Sabri and his close aides were arrested in May 1971. He was charged with treason and abuse of power during Nasser's presidency. He was found guilty and condemned to death, but his sentence was commuted to life imprisonment. After his release in May 1981 he kept out of politics.

Sadat, (Muhammad) Anwar (1918–81): *Egyptian military officer and politician; president, 1970–81; prime minister, 1973–74, 1980–81* Son of a petty civil servant in Mit Abul Kom village in the Nile [*q.v.*] delta, Sadat grew up in Cairo [*q.v.*]. He graduated from the Cairo Military Academy in 1938. Found guilty of spying for the Germans, Sadat, a captain in the signals corps, was jailed in the summer of

1942. He escaped in 1944 and went underground until the lifting of the detention order. He spent two years in jail (1946–48) as a suspect in the assassination of Ahmad Osman, a cabinet minister, but was acquitted.

He tried his hand at business, which failed. He rejoined the army in late 1949, regaining his rank of captain. He was posted to Rafah in the Sinai [*q.v.*], where he came into contact with Gamal Abdul Nasser [*q.v.*]. Sadat participated in the 22 July 1952 coup mounted by the Free Officers organization, and secured a seat on the ruling 18-member Revolutionary Command Council (RCC). He liaised with the Muslim Brotherhood [*q.v.*], with which he had friendly relations. He edited *Al-Gumhuriya* (Arabic: *The Republic*), the regime's mouthpiece, until 1959. For the next decade he served as speaker of the parliament. And during 1964–66 he was one of the four vice presidents.

When in 1965 Egypt established the Islamic Congress in Cairo to rally Muslim opinion abroad behind it, Sadat was chosen as its secretary-general. He was Egypt's representative at international Islamic gatherings, including a summit that led to the formation of the Islamic Conference Organization [*q.v.*] in September 1969. Three months later, President Nasser made a sharp rightward turn in his policies at home, and made Sadat his sole vice president. On Nasser's death the following September, Sadat became acting president. In mid-October he was elected president in a referendum, having been the sole candidate.

His power struggle with Ali Sabri [*q.v.*] ended in May 1971 when he imprisoned Sabri and his close aides. In September he promulgated a new constitution, which played down the socialist guidelines of the earlier document. In mid-1973 he purged the leadership of the Arab Socialist Union (ASU) [*q.v.*] of leftists.

Sadat signed a 15-year Egyptian-Soviet Friendship Treaty [*q.v.*] in late May 1971. But in July 1972 he demanded that all Soviet military advisers in Egypt, who had arrived after the June 1967 Arab-Israeli War [*q.v.*], must leave the country within 10 days. Some 15,000 Soviet personnel left, taking with them fighter aircraft, interceptors, and surface-to-air missiles. However, some of them gradually returned after October 1972 and again after February 1973. After his rapprochement with Moscow in March 1973, Soviet arms shipments resumed.

He started planning an invasion of the Israeli-occupied Arab territories [*q.v.*]. During the October 1973 Arab-Israeli War [*q.v.*] the Egyptian troops performed unprecedentedly well, capturing land in the Sinai from the Israelis and retaining it. This enhanced his standing at home and in the region. But, instead of pursuing peace under the auspices of the United Nations, he opted for Washington's mediation in his talks with Israel, thus breaking Arab ranks. After two interim disengagement agreements with Israel (Sinai I and Sinai II [*q.v.*] in 1974 and 1975) the peace process stalled.

His economic liberalization, involving the removal or reduction of subsidies on essentials, triggered countrywide bread riots in January 1977, the most serious upheaval since the anti-British rioting a quarter of a century earlier. It ceased only when he canceled the price increases. He appealed for aid to the United States, which responded positively. After Moscow had refused to reschedule the Egyptian debts of $10–12 billion, he unilaterally abrogated the Egyptian-Soviet Friendship Treaty.

In November 1977, in a dramatic move he addressed the Israeli Knesset [*q.v.*] in Jerusalem [*q.v.*], and this made him something of a hero in the Western world, a factor that paved the way for the commercial success of his autobiography, *In Search of Identity* (1978). Washington started to provide military aid to Egypt. He signed the Camp David Accords [*q.v.*] with Israeli Premier Menachem Begin [*q.v.*] at the White House in Washington on 18 September 1978 in the presence of President Jimmy Carter.

At home, fearing a military coup, he dismissed his chief of staff and defense minister, General Abdul Ghani Gamassy. He appointed Mustafa Khalil, leader of the National Democratic Party (NDP) [*q.v.*], as prime minister to lead a "peace government" of technocrats and academics.

In March 1979 Sadat and Begin signed the bilateral Egyptian-Israeli Peace Treaty [*q.v.*] at the White House. This resulted in the immediate suspension of Egypt from the Arab League [*q.v.*] and the Islamic Conference Organization (ICO) [*q.v.*], which led all League members, except Oman, to cut diplomatic ties with Cairo.

To overcome the increasing isolation of Egypt, Sadat assumed increased powers at home. He dissolved parliament two years short of its normal tenure, and rigged the first multiparty election in June 1979, with his NDP securing 83 percent of the seats. He expelled the last of the remaining 200 Soviet civilian experts. Egypt became more dependent on the U.S. for economic survival. After securing Khalil's resignation in May 1980, Sadat appointed himself prime minister. By immediately holding a stage-managed referendum he abrogated the constitutional provision that limited the presidency to one six-year term.

His peace treaty with Israel, and the rising corruption and ostentatious behavior of the new rich, alienated the Islamic forces in Egypt, whom he had courted in the early years of his regime. The dismantling of the pricing mechanism introduced by the Nasser regime fueled inflation and brought much hardship to the working and lower-middle classes.

Contemptuous of opposition, both secular and religious, Sadat banned strikes and demonstrations and became increasingly autocratic. His sweeping crackdown on dissidents in September 1981 resulted in some 2,000 arrests. The next month he was assassinated by four Islamic militants, led by Khlaid Ahmad Shawki Islambouli, during a military parade on the anniversary of the October 1973 Arab-Israeli war. In contrast to the mass grief demonstrated at the death of Nasser, most Egyptians were unmoved by his demise.

Muqtada al-Sadr (1973–): *Iraqi political and religious leader* Born in Najaf [*q.v.*], he was the fourth son of Ayatollah Muhammad Sadiq al-Sadr. As a member of a prominent Shia religious family, he undertook theological studies. In 1995, he married a daughter of Grand Ayatollah Muhammad Baqir al-Sadr, who had been executed by the government of Iraqi President Saddam Hussein [*q.v.*] in 1980. After the killing of his father and two elder brothers by Iraqi government agents in Najaf in 1999, he went into hiding.

It was only after the downfall of Saddam Hussein's regime in April 2003 that Sadr reappeared in Najaf. The leading Iraqi Shia [*q.v.*] cleric, Grand Ayatollah Kadhim Husseini Hairi, then based in the holy Iranian city of Qom [*q.v.*], named Sadr as his deputy in Iraq. Operating from the *Hawza al-Ilmiya* (Arabic: *Center for Learning*), Sadr started sending out signed letters and cash by couriers to Shia clerics who in turn appointed qualified people to run the civil administration and restore security which had broken down. They were paid by the *Hawza*.

He opposed the Iraqi Governing Council appointed by the U.S.-led Coalition Provisional Authority (CPA) and formed a militia group, called the Mahdi Army, to protect the holy Shia sites in Najaf. The weekly magazine *Al-Hawza* became his mouthpiece. When Paul Bremer of the CPA banned it in March 2004, there were clashes between Mahdi Army and the American forces in Najaf, Basra, and Baghdad's Sadr City, the former Saddam City. Uneasy peace followed. Fighting resumed in August and ended only when Grand Ayatollah Ali Sistani [*q.v.*] intervened and the Americans agreed to withdraw the warrant for Sadr's arrest.

In the December 2005 election for the interim parliament, his Sadrist Trend [*q.v.*] joined the United Iraqi Alliance of Shias, the brainchild of

Sistani. He lobbied successfully for Nouri al-Maliki [*q.v.*] as the prime minister, and in return the Sadrist Trend got six ministries.

When such extremist Sunni factions as Al Qaida in Mesopotamia [*q.v.*] started attacking Shias, the Mahdi Army reciprocated by hitting Sunni targets. After the blowing up of the Shias' Al Askariya shrine in Samarra [*q.v.*] in February 2006, the intersectarian violence intensified.

In April 2007, when Maliki ignored Sadr's call to finalize a timetable for the withdrawal of the U.S.-led foreign troops, the Sadrist Trend ministers left the government. Sadr, then bearing the religious title of *hojatalislam* (Arabic: *proof of Islam*) went to Qom to pursue advanced theological studies to raise his status to *ayatollah* (Arabic: *sign of Allah*).

After the Maliki government had retaken the control of Basra from the Mahdi Army and other Shia militias in March 2008, Sadr launched a nationwide civil disobedience campaign across Iraq in protest. In August, he ordered most of his militiamen to disarm but retained the elite fighting units to resist the Americans if a timetable for their withdrawal was not set. He renamed the rest of the militia into a socio-cultural organization called Mumahidoun.

Politically, his Sadrist Trend did well in the local elections of 2009 and the parliamentary election of 2010. On his return to Najaf from Iran in January 2011 he reiterated his opposition to the United States while appealing to fellow Iraqis to overcome their divisions. With the unconditional withdrawal of the American forces from Iraq by the end of the year, Sadr's popular standing rose.

al-Sadr, Musa (1928–78):
Lebanese/Iranian Islamic leader
Born into a religious family of Lebanese origin in Qom [*q.v.*], Sadr was educated in secular and Islamic traditions before being sent to Tehran University, where he acquired a postgraduate degree in Islamic studies in 1956. Three years later the Shia [*q.v.*] establishment in Qom sent him to Lebanon as its representative to provide religious guidance to Lebanese Shias. Following his condemnation of Muhammad Reza Shah Pahlavi [*q.v.*] for suppressing the countrywide protest in Iran led by Ayatollah Ruhollah Khomeini [*q.v.*] in June 1963, his Iranian nationality was revoked.

He then became a Lebanese citizen. In 1967 he formed the Higher Shia Communal Council (HSCC), the first of its kind in the country, which made him a leading spokesman of Shias. Five years later the HSCC presented social, administrative, and economic demands to the government to ameliorate the living and working conditions of Shias. This charter became the manifesto of the multi-confessional Movement of the Disinherited that Sadr founded in February 1973. It proved popular with Shias who were dissatisfied with their traditional leaders.

Through rallies, demonstrations and strikes Sadr made Shias, the single largest sect in Lebanon, aware of their strength. When the Lebanese Civil War [*q.v.*] erupted in April 1975, he realized that, unlike most other important religious sects, Shias did not have their own militia. He set up a militia adjunct to the Movement of the Disinherited in June 1975, and called it the Lebanese Resistance Detachments, which became popularly known by its Arabic acronym, Amal [*q.v.*]. It fought the Phalange militia [*q.v.*]. While opposed to the traditional Shia leadership, Sadr remained friendly with the Sunni [*q.v.*] establishment, with whom he shared the demand for political parity between Muslims [*q.v.*] and Christians [*q.v.*].

During a trip to Libya in August 1978, Sadr "disappeared." Libya insisted that he had left by plane for Italy, but his followers alleged that he had been detained or assassinated by his Libyan hosts. Most Lebanese Shias regard him as a martyr, worthy of their veneration.

Sadrist Trend (Iraq) (Arabic: *Al-Tayyar al-Sadri*): This is the official title of the party founded by Muqtada al-Sadr [*q.v.*] in 2003 along with its militant wing, called the Mahdi Army. It is a national party open to all Iraqis but has a strong base among poor urban Shias [*q.v.*].

In the December 2005 election for the interim parliament, it joined the United Iraqi Alliance of Shias, the brainchild of Grand Ayatollah Sistani [*q.v.*]. It lobbied successfully for Nouri al-Maliki [*q.v.*] as the prime minister and in return it got six ministries. It did well on its own in the local elections of 2009, but decided to enter the March 2010 general election under the umbrella of the Iraqi National Alliance (INA), which also included the Supreme Islamic Iraq Council [*q.v.*]. It secured 40 seats out of the total of 70 for the INA. But it was not until October that its leader, Sadr, overcame his hostility toward Maliki to back his reelection as the prime minister after

securing eight ministries for the Sadrist Trend.

After achieving one of its major aims, to end the American occupation of Iraq in December 2011, it has focused more on the improvement of the underprivileged Iraqis, irrespective of their religious affiliation. It favors strengthening the central government under a unitary system.

al-Said, Nouri (1888–1958): *Iraqi military officer and politician; prime minister, 1930–32, 1939–40, 1941–44, 1946–47, 1949, 1950–52, 1954–57, 1958* Born in Baghdad [q.v.] to a Sunni [q.v.] family of mixed Arab-Kurdish [q.v.] origin, Said graduated from the Istanbul Military Academy and became a commissioned officer in the Ottoman army. In 1914 he joined the clandestine Arab nationalist group Al Ahd (Arabic: *The Covenant*). During World War I, having defected from the Ottoman military in 1916, he joined the Arab revolt led by Sharif Hussein bin Ali. He became chief of staff in the army of Faisal I bin Hussein [q.v.]. After gaining the throne of Iraq in 1921, Faisal I appointed Said his chief of army staff. He became defense minister during 1922 to 24 and 1926 to 28, and was promoted to prime minister in 1930.

He. founded a political party named after the secret group he had joined earlier, Al Ahd, even though he had abandoned his pan-Arabism [*q.v.*] and reached accommodation with the British Mandate, an arrangement formalized in the Anglo-Iraqi Treaty of 1930 [*q.v.*], which provided the trappings but not the substance of independence. He was reappointed prime minister in 1939.

During World War II the anti-British feeling in Iraq was so strong that, despite his pro-British learning, Said dared not join the Allies against the Axis Powers. In March 1940 he resigned as premier but agreed to join the next cabinet, led by Rashid Ali Gailani [q.v.], which lasted until January 1941. He stayed out of the next Gailani government, which took office in April. After he had been restored to premiership by the British following their overthrow of Gailani in May 1941, he declared war against Germany in 1943. By the time he stepped down in June 1944, the groundwork for the founding of the Arab League [q.v.], inspired by the British, had been laid.

After the war he served as prime minister three times (1946–47, 1949 and 1950–52) before Faisal II [q.v.] came of age in 1953. Following a general election in June 1954, he was appointed prime minister because the 1930 Anglo-Iraqi Treaty needed to be renegotiated before its expiry in 1955. His decision to join the Baghdad Pact [q.v.] in 1955, and his failure to condemn Egypt's aggressors in the Suez War [q.v.] of 1956, isolated Iraq from the rest of the Arab world. In 1957 he endorsed the Eisenhower Doctrine [q.v.], which offered help to Middle Eastern countries threatened by world Communism or its regional allies.

His increasingly dictatorial ways, and his manipulation of the electoral system and banning of political parties, made Iraq's monarchical regime unpopular. When the Free Officers' group launched a successful coup in July 1958, it assassinated Said along with the members of the royal family.

Said bin Taimur bin Faisal (1911–72): *Sultan of Oman, 1932–70* Son of Taimur bin Faisal [q.v.], Said was enthroned by the British in 1932 after they had dethroned Sultan Taimur on the ground of fiscal irresponsibility. Reacting to his father's extravagance, Said took parsimony to extremes. He also monopolized power. Opposed to progress, he prevented his subjects from using, for instance, patent medicines, trousers, radios, books, and even spectacles.

In 1937 he gave an oil concession to Petroleum Concessions (Oman). When, after World War II, it started exploring for oil in the interior, which was controlled by Imam [q.v.] Ghalib bin Ali, problems ensued. Its activities near the Buraimi oasis in 1951 upset Saudi Arabia, which claimed part of the oasis and occupied it. Said was also challenged by Imam Ghalib bin Ali, who proclaimed the independent Imamate of Oman in 1954 and applied for membership in the Arab League [q.v.], which then did not include the Sultanate of Oman. Said's forces, armed and led by the British, crushed the challenge to his authority by the end of 1955. Acting in collusion with the forces of Abu Dhabi, the British also recovered the part of the Buraimi oasis occupied by the Saudis.

In 1957 the Imam's brother, Talib bin Ali, encouraged by Saudi Arabia and Egypt, mounted a rebellion in the interior and declared the establishment of the Imamate of Oman. Said called on the British to render him military assistance according to the Anglo-Omani Agreement of 1925 [q.v.]. The armed uprising dwindled into guerrilla actions. Egypt and the other states charged that Britain had committed armed aggression against the Imamate of Oman and placed the matter before the United Nations. While the UN commission of enquiry failed to uphold the claim against Britain, several Arab countries succeeded in persuading the UN General Assembly to adopt a resolution demanding the end of the British colonial presence in Oman. Nonetheless, after Said had withdrawn to his palace in Salalah, 620 mi./1,000 km southwest of Muscat [*q.v.*], in 1958, control of the country passed almost totally into the hands of British civil servants, with London providing the funds for all development projects.

In 1962 the successor to Petroleum Concessions (Oman), called Petroleum Development Oman, struck oil in commercial quantities. Petroleum income rose from $21 million in 1967 to $117 million three years later, but Said left the money untouched. Now he found his authority challenged by the inhabitants of the Dhofar region. The victory of the leftist forces in the adjoining South Yemen on the eve on the British withdrawal in November 1967 boosted the morale of Dhofari revolutionaries. This, and Said's inflexibility, made the British apprehensive. They engineered a coup in July 1970 and replaced Said with his son, Qaboos [*q.v.*].

Saiqa (Arabic: *Thunderbolt*): *Palestinian commando force* Saiqa was the name given to the military wing of the Vanguards of the Popular War of Liberation, sponsored by the Syrian Baath Party [*q.v.*] after the June 1967 Arab-Israeli War [*q.v.*]. It started commando actions against Israel from Jordan and joined the Palestine Liber-

ation Organization (PLO) [*q.v.*]. It became the first Palestinian group to receive arms, secretly, from the Soviet Union, followed by military training for its members in the Soviet Union. It was second in size only to the guerilla force of Fatah [*q.v.*]. When fighting broke out between Palestinian commandos and Jordanian troops in September 1970, it was Saiqa, then about 5,000-strong, that persuaded Syrian President Salah Jadid [*q.v.*] to give military aid to the Palestinians. Arms supplies to the Palestinians followed. But when Jordan mounted a counteroffensive using tanks and planes, Syria's defense minister, Hafiz Assad [*q.v.*], refused to commit his air force.

After seizing power in November, Assad purged Saiqa of its leftist elements, appointed his protégé Zuhair Mohsin as the secretary-general, and brought it under the control of the Syrian defense ministry. For most of the 1970s Mohsen headed the PLO's military department. At the Palestine National Council (PNC) [*q.v.*] session in June 1974, Saiqa backed the idea of setting up a "national authority" in the West Bank [*q.v.*] and Gaza [*q.v.*] as an intermediate step toward liberating all of Mandate Palestine. Mohsen's assassination in 1979 was a severe blow to Saiqa.

Following its expulsion from Beirut [*q.v.*] in 1982, Saiqa based itself in Damascus [*q.v.*]. It joined the pro-Syrian Palestine National Salvation Front against PLO Chairman Yasser Arafat [*q.v.*]. It opposed his attempts to make the PLO work in tandem with King Hussein [*q.v.*] of Jordan in the mid-1980s. It continued to derive most of its strength from the Palestinian refugee camps in Syria. After the PNC had repudiated Arafat's deal with King Hussein in April 1987, it ended its boycott of the PLO institutions.

During the Kuwait crisis of 1990–91, it took its cue from Syria and opposed Arafat's backing of Iraqi President Saddam Hussein [*q.v.*]. In September 1993 it rejected Oslo Accord I [*q.v.*].

As Saiqa has not carried out any terrorist actions since the early 1990s, it does not appear on Washington's list of terrorist organizations. Its ideology of pan-Arab [*q.v.*] secularism and socialism remains close to that of the Syrian Baath Party.

Since 2007, its leader has been Farhan Abu al-Hayja. It became marginal because of the reduced support from Syrian President Bashar Assad [*q.v.*], more inclined to bolster Hamas [*q.v.*]. The situation changed after the uprisings in Syria in 2011-2012, when it backed Assad.

Salafiya movement and salafin (Arabic: plural of *salafi*, follower of ancestors): *A Sunni Islamic reformist movement* A derivative of *salaf al-Salihin* (Arabic: *the pious ancestors*), the Salafiya movement was influenced by Jamal al-Din Afghani (1838–1897), an Islamic thinker who noted the militancy of the salaf (ancestors) of the early Islam. One of his disciples, Muhammad Abdu (1849–1905), stressed the impact that the salaf had on the shaping of the Sharia [*q.v.*]. Muhammad Rashid Rida (1865–1935), a follower of Abdu, researched what the Prophet Muhammad and the *salaf al-Salehin* had done and said in order to apply it to contemporary conditions. He preferred to follow the concepts of the *salaf al-Salihin* rather than any of the four Sunni [*q.v.*] legal schools.

From the 1920s onwards it became clear that the salafiya could be realized only if it won popular support. The movement's current adherents wanted conformity with the Islam of their salaf at the political level. They argued that, since the Prophet Muhammad was succeeded by a caliph chosen by the community, there could be no place for hereditary power in Islam.

As such they became part of the religious opposition that emerged, largely clandestinely, in the member states of the Gulf Cooperation Council [*q.v.*]. They have been especially active in Kuwait since the mid-1970s, and want to establish a democratic republican regime there. Some Kuwaiti salafin participated in the armed uprising against the Saudi royal family at the Grand Mosque of Mecca [*q.v.*] in November 1979. As a quasi-political organization, the salafin won four seats in the Kuwaiti general election of 1992. They performed better in the subsequent elections, winning seven seats in 1999. As the Islamic Salafi Alliance in the 2012 general election, their score fell to four seats. In Bahrain, functioning as Al Asalah (Arabic: *of noble descent*), they won three seats in the 2010 parliamentary election.

A far greater success for them came in Egypt after the fall of President Hosni Mubarak [*q.v.*] in 2011. In the subsequent free and fair election to the National Assembly, the Islamist Bloc led by the Al Nour Party [*q.v.*], the political wing of the Call of the Salafiya, won 113 seats out of the total of 127 for the Islamist Bloc on a popular vote of 28 percent. In the Consultative (Shura) Council, the Islamist Bloc gained 45 seats on a popular vote of 29 percent.

Salam, Saeb (1905–2000): *Lebanese politician, prime minister, 1952, 1953, 1960–61, 1970–73* Born into a notable Sunni [*q.v.*] family in Beirut [*q.v.*], Salam graduated from the American University of Beirut [*q.v.*] and finished his postgraduate studies at the London School of Economics and Political Science. He then managed the varied family agrarian and industrial interests. Elected to parliament in 1943, he retained a seat in the chamber until the 1972 election, except in 1957, when the general election was rigged by President Camille Chamoun [*q.v.*]. In 1946 he became interior minister and served briefly as prime minister in 1952 and 1953. He was deputy prime minister in 1956, but resigned his post in protest at Chamoun's refusal to condemn the Anglo-French-Israeli aggression against Egypt in the Suez War [*q.v.*].

In the 1958 civil strife he sided with the anti-Chamounist camp led by Kamal Jumblat [*q.v.*]. After serving as prime minister from 1960 to 1961, he headed a group of Beirut-based Sunni parliamentarians that rivaled the one led by the Tripoli-based Rashid Karami [*q.v.*], who was the premier for most of the 1960s. When Suleiman Franjieh [*q.v.*] became president in 1970, he called on Salam to form the next government. He purged the army and civil service of the reformists inspired by ex-president Fuad Chehab [*q.v.*].

With the emergence of the Front of National and Progressive Parties and Forces under Jumblat in 1972, such traditional leaders as Salam lost ground. He resigned as prime minister in April 1973. Two years later, on the eve of the Lebanese Civil War [*q.v.*], he was one of the six former premiers who demanded that the army command council be reconstituted to give parity to Muslims [*q.v.*] and Christians [*q.v.*]. During the Israeli siege of Beirut in June–August 1982, he supervised the evacuation of the Palestinian and Syrian forces from West Beirut.

After the assassination of Bashir Gemayel [*q.v.*] in September, he played a crucial role in the election of Amin Gemayel [*q.v.*] as president. Later, when Gemayel fell out with the nationalist-leftist constituents of the Lebanese National Movement [*q.v.*], Salam failed to mobilize Muslims behind the president, highlighting the virtual collapse of Sunni power, mainly because the sect had failed to form a powerful militia of its own. As the civil conflict continued well into the 1980s, his influence declined sharply.

Saleh, Ali Abdullah (1942–): *Yemeni military officer and politician; president of North Yemen, 1978–90; president of Yemen, 1990–2012* A member of the Sanhan tribe of the Hashid tribal confederation, Saleh was born in the northern region. After receiving rudimentary education he enrolled in the army as a soldier, and rose rapidly through the ranks. After the assassination of President Ibrahim Hamid [*q.v.*] in October 1977, as commander of the Taiz region he assisted Ahmad

Ghashmi [*q.v.*], chairman of the Military Council, to crush a rebellion by rival officers in April 1978. Ghashmi promoted him to deputy commander-in-chief of the army.

Following Ghashmi's assassination in June 1978, he became chief of staff and a member of the Presidential Council. A month later the 96 People's Constituent Assembly members elected him president by a large majority. To rally domestic support he blamed South Yemen for Ghashmi's murder. In October he survived an attempted coup by a section of the army.

In October 1980 Saleh replaced Prime Minister Abdul Aziz Abdul Ghani [*q.v.*] with Abdul Karim Iryani [*q.v.*]. However, having consolidated his power by purging the officer corps and placing his family and tribal kin in key positions, he did not invite the NDF to share power in a national unity government. In October 1981 he set up a 1,000-member General People's Congress (GPC) [*q.v.*], partly by appointment and partly by indirect election.

When the need for arms rose sharply due to the introduction of conscription in 1979, he opted for Soviet weapons because of their cheapness. This upset Saudi Arabia, which suspended its budgetary aid of $300 million a year and all other economic assistance. Following his visit to Riyadh [*q.v.*] in August 1980, the Saudis partially resumed the aid. Two months later, he visited Moscow. In 1984, when the Yemeni subsidiary of an American oil company started to extract petroleum, he signed a Friendship and Cooperation Treaty with the Soviet Union [*q.v.*] during his second visit to Moscow.

At home he maintained a balance between the conservative tribal confederations in the north and the left-wing National Democratic Front (NDF) in the south, and managed to survive several assassination attempts. After being reelected president in 1983 he recalled Abdul Ghani to head the government. He maintained friendly relations with Saudi Arabia, the chief paymaster of North Yemen, while cultivating the leftist South Yemeni regime by periodically renewing the earlier agreement of eventual unity between the two Yemens.

After his reelection as president in 1988 he responded positively to the idea of an alliance of North Yemen with Egypt, Iraq, and Jordan, which materialized as the Arab Cooperation Council [*q.v.*] in early 1989. A steep decline in the economy of South Yemen resulted in the unification of the two Yemens in May 1990, with Saleh becoming president of the united country.

In the Kuwait crisis of 1990–91 he refused to side with the Saudi-U.S. alliance against Iraq. Yemen, the only Arab member of the UN Security Council, voted against the U.S. stance, and abstained on crucial resolutions on the Kuwait crisis and Gulf War II [*q.v.*]. The consequent Saudi retribution, including the expulsion of 850,000 Yemeni workers and petty traders from the kingdom, damaged Yemen's economy.

When the outcome of the April 1993 general election confirmed the existence of a political division along the old North-South divide, his relations with his vice president, Ali Salim al-Beidh [*q.v.*], soured. He won the subsequent Yemeni Civil War [*q.v.*]

between the northern and southern forces in May–June 1994, when Saudi Arabia backed the southern camp. His prestige at home rose sharply.

In 1995 Saleh was elevated to chairman of the GPC, a new post. Two years later his GPC improved its parliamentary strength from 123 to 187 seats.

But his government encountered violent protest during 1997–98 when it tried to implement economic reform by cutting subsidies on basic necessities and fuel. Nonetheless, in the first direct presidential election in 1999, he won 96.3 percent of the vote. In 2001 he replaced Iryani as prime minister with Abdul Qadir Bajammal.

Whereas Yemen's armed forces conducted their first joint military exercise with the U.S. forces in November 1998, Saleh condemned Washington's Operation Desert Fox [q.v.], launched in December. In October 2000 a suicide bomb attack by a fast boat rammed into the USS *Cole* while it was refueling in Aden [q.v.], killing 17 sailors. The Islamic Army of Aden-Abyan claimed responsibility.

After 9/11, Washington started training the Yemeni forces in anti-terrorist tactics and allied skills of intelligence gathering. Saleh cooperated actively with the United States to curb the activities of Al Qaida [q.v.] operatives in Yemen. That helped reduce Al Qaida's presence in the republic.

In the 2006 presidential election, Saleh was reelected with 77 percent of the popular vote, defeating Faisal bin Shalman, the candidate of the Joint Parties Meeting, an alliance of all opposition parties. The escape of 23 Al Qaida extremists from a high-security prison in Sanaa [q.v.] led to the revival of Al Qaida terrorism with renewed intensity. Saleh's links with Washington tightened, with the Central Intelligence Agency making increased use of drones to hit terrorist targets. This in turn led to the Al Qaida network's attack on the U.S. Embassy in Sanaa in September 2008.

Because of the prevalent corruption and ineptitude of his government, the standing of Saleh among the tribes fell. The emergence of Al Qaida in the Arabian Peninsula [q.v.] with its base in southeastern Yemen in 2009 damaged his image further.

Starting in January 2011, the protesting demonstrators escalated their demands from ending unemployment and corruption to Saleh's resignation. Pro-Saleh supporters staged counterdemonstrations. In late April, he accepted the three-point plan offered by the Gulf Cooperation Council [q.v.], which required him to step down in favor of Vice President Abd Rabbu Mansour al-Hadi [q.v.] in exchange for immunity from prosecution for himself, his relatives, and senior members of his government. But when it came to signing the agreement he balked three times. The GCC suspended its mediation on 22 May. The next day when Sadiq al-Ahmar, leader of the powerful Hashid tribal federation declared his support for the opposition, the army split. Armed clashes, involving artillery and mortars, ensued in different parts of the country.

An explosive attack on the presidential palace's mosque during Friday congregation on 3 June left Saleh and several others badly injured. He flew to Riyadh for medical treatment after transferring his power to al-Hadi. By broadcasting an address to the Yemeni people from Riyadh on 7 July, he underlined his presidential power. But on 12 September he instructed al-Hadi to revive the GCC mediation. Then he suddenly returned to Sanaa on 23 September. Clashes between the opposing camps resumed.

The GCC's revived peace efforts gained the support of the UN Security Council. On 23 November, Saleh signed the deal, agreeing to relinquish power within 30 days in favor of a transitional government headed by al-Hadi, while remaining president until fresh new election in February 2012. After the election he stepped down, but did not leave the country.

Sallal, Abdullah (1917–2001): *Yemeni military officer and politician; president, 1962–67; prime minister, 1962–63, 1966–67* Born in a Zaidi [*q.v.*] blacksmith family in the north, Sallal was sent to Baghdad Military Academy, where he graduated in 1938. On his return home he was jailed briefly for suspected anti-regime activities. After his release he was permitted to resume his military career. He participated in the coup against Imam Yahya in early 1948, led by his personal adviser, Abdullah Wazir. But Wazir was overthrown the following month by Yahya's son, Crown Prince Ahmad bin Yahya [*q.v.*], who succeeded his father. Sallal found himself condemned to death, but his sentence was commuted to a seven-year prison term. After his release he was appointed governor of Hodeida province.

Sallal became a protégé of Crown Prince Muhammad al-Badr [*q.v.*],

who made him commander of his guard in 1956 and of the newly established Military Academy three years later. After his accession to the throne, al-Badr promoted Sallal to commander of the royal guard. Supported by a secret Nasserite [*q.v.*] group among military officers, he carried out a successful coup against Imam al-Badr on 26 September, but the ruler escaped unhurt. Sallal became president of the republic, promoting himself to field marshal. He led the republican camp in the Yemeni Civil War [*q.v.*], which continued until 1970. He concurrently served as the prime minister during 1962–63.

The republicans, deriving their main support from the Shafei (Sunni [*q.v.*]) tribes inhabiting the coastal plain and southern hills, were aided by Egypt, while the royalists, with a solid base among the Zaidi tribes in the north, were helped by the Saudis. There was intense fighting for two and a half years. A year of comparative lull followed. To placate the royalists with a view to reaching an accommodation with them, Egyptian President Gamal Abdul Nasser [*q.v.*] invited Sallal to Cairo [*q.v.*] and then put him under house arrest. He let the Presidential Council run North Yemen.

With the failure of Nasser's peace-making efforts, Sallal was allowed to return to Sanaa [*q.v.*] in September 1966. Besides resuming the presidency, he appointed himself prime minister and carried out a purge. He tried to regain the area lost to the monarchists in the war but failed, partly because of the June 1967 Arab-Israeli War [*q.v.*], which diverted Egypt's resources. Cairo decided to withdraw its forces from North

Yemen, and this weakened the position of Sallal, who was seen as an Egyptian protégé. He was overthrown in November 1967 during his visit to Moscow. He went into exile in Baghdad [*q.v.*] in October 1981. During the presidency of Ali Abdullah Saleh [*q.v.*], he was allowed to return home, where he stayed away from public life.

Samaria: *Ancient kingdom* Called Shomron in Hebrew, Samaria covers the central zone of ancient Canaan/Palestine lying between the Jordan River [*q.v.*] and the Mediterranean Sea, and delineated by Galilee, the area to the west of Lake Galilee to the north and Judea/Judah [*q.v.*] to the south. Its political and geographical center was Shechem, near present-day Nablus [*q.v.*].

It took the Israelites more than two centuries, from ca 1250 B.C. to ca 1030 B.C., to conquer and colonize Canaan. During the united Israelite Kingdom under King David (r. 1010–970 B.C.), northern Samaria was given to half of the tribe of Manasseh (the other half were settled to the east of the Jordan) and southern Samaria to the tribe of Ephraim.

After the demise of King Solomon (r. 970–930 B.C.), the northern tribes, including Ephraim and Manasseh, split from their southern kinsmen, but retained the name Israelite Kingdom. Its capital at Tirzah (now Tall al-Fariah) was shifted in 880 B.C. to Samaria City [*q.v.*]—these settlements and Shechem together forming an equilateral triangle, each side being 7 mi./10 km long. The kingdom fell to the Assyrians in 722 B.C. During the time of Jesus Christ (ca 6 B.C.–30 A.D.) Samaria was ruled by the Romans.

Samaria City: *Modern village of Sabastiya, also called Sebaste* Archaeological excavations during the early part of the 20th century established that the history of Samaria City dates back to the late fourth millennium B.C. During Old Testament [*q.v.*] times it became the capital of the (northern) Israelite Kingdom in 880 B.C. It became the site of an acropolis, which contained a royal palace.

It was captured by the Assyrians, who enslaved most of its inhabitants and colonized it with Cutheans. The succeeding Persians retained it as an administrative center. After the capture of the region by Alexander of Macedonia in 332 B.C., it became a Greek colony. It was destroyed by John Hyrcanus in 120 B.C., restored by the Roman general Pompey (106–48 B.C.), and renamed Sebaste (Greek for Augusta) in honor of Roman Emperor Augustus (Sebastos in Greek) by Herod the Great (37–4 B.C.), and endowed with an Augustine temple, a forum, and a basilica. After reaching a zenith in the late Roman Empire, it declined steadily during the Byzantine era (476 A.D.–1453), shrinking to a village called Sabastiya during the Ottoman Empire (1517–1918).

Samaritans: *quasi-Jewish community* A 2,500-year-old sect with a claim that after the death of King Solomon its adherents formed the Kingdom of Israel, and the Jews [*q.v.*] formed the Kingdom of Judah. Samaritans speak ancient Hebrew [*q.v.*], believe that Moses was the only prophet, and accept only the first five books of the Hebrew Bible. According to them, Abraham prepared to sacrifice his son Isaac not in Jerusalem [*q.v.*] but at

Mount Gerizim, the mountain towering above Nablus [*q.v.*]. In 1917 there were only 146 Samaritans. Their number had grown to 583 in 1997. They have retained their own language and culture. They live in their settlement of Kiryat Luza, on Mount Gerizim, and in Holon, south of Tel Aviv [*q.v.*]. Those based in the West Bank [*q.v.*] have one representative in the Palestinian parliament. Those resident in Holon are Israeli nationals and serve in the army. At Passover [*q.v.*], the entire community gathers on Mount Girizim to sacrifice sheep in a ritual similar to that of the ancient Jews.

Samarra: *Iraqi city* Population: 377,000 (2011 est.) According to the archaeological excavations of the 20th century, the history of Samarra, located on the Tigris River [*q.v.*], dates back to the fifth millennium B.C. The present town, established during the third century A.D, reached its apogee when Caliph al-Mutasim (r. 833–841 A.D.) abandoned Baghdad [*q.v.*] as the capital of the Abbasid Empire in 836 A.D. in its favor, endowing it with gardens and a palace. Though he renamed it Surra Manraa, the old name survived. By the time Caliph al Mutamid (r. 870–892 A.D.) had returned the capital to Baghdad in 892 A.D., Samarra had spread many miles along the river. It was here that the last imam [*q.v.*] of the Twelver Shias [*q.v.*], Muhammad al-Qasim, the infant son of the 11th Imam Hassan al-Askari, went into spiritual occultation in 873 A.D.

Over the next four centuries the town declined dramatically. It has since revived. Its tourist offerings today include the minaret al-Malwiya,

the ziggurat, a temple tower of ancient Mesopotamia [*q.v.*] in the form of a stepped pyramid, and the Great Friday Mosque and the Abu Dulaf Mosque, built during the ninth century. As the site of the gold-domed Al Askriya Mosque, containing the shrines of the Twelver Shias' Tenth and Eleventh Imams, Ali bin Muhammad Naqi al-Hadi and Hassan bin Ali al-Askari, it is a place of pilgrimage for them. It was severely damaged by bombings by Al Qaida in Mesopotamia [*q.v.*] operatives in 2006 and 2007. It has since then been repaired.

San Remo Agreement (1920): The San Remo Agreement is the title given to decisions regarding the Middle East [*q.v.*] made by the Supreme Council of the League of Nations (1920–45), consisting of the major Allied powers—Belgium, Britain, France, Greece, Italy, and Japan (the United States did not join the League of Nations)—at its meeting in San Remo, Italy, in April 1920. The main decisions were as follows. Britain and France would decide the nature of the Mandates for the region and submit their proposals to the League for debate and voting. Later, France was awarded the mandates for Syria and Lebanon, and Britain for Palestine [*q.v.*] and Mesopotamia [*q.v.*] (later Iraq). The British Mandate for Palestine included the Balfour Declaration [*q.v.*].

Sanaa: *capital of Yemen* Population: 1.94 million (2011 est.) Called Ghumdan in pre-Islamic times, Sanaa was a center of the Sabaeans, who arrived from the north in the 10th century B.C.

They surrendered to the Arabs [*q.v.*] in the second century A.D. They were converted to Islam [*q.v.*] in 632 A.D. by Ali, a cousin and son-in-law of the Prophet Muhammad.

Because of its central place in the Yemeni highlands its fate has been shaped by the region's history, dominated by the Zaidi (Shia) [*q.v.*] tribes whose rulers, called imams [*q.v.*], were in the habit of changing their capital. After losing its primacy for nearly four centuries, Sanaa found favor with Imam Abdul Wahhab bin Tahir al-Rassi (r. 1478–1488).

The Ottoman suzerainty over North Yemen from 1517 meant little to Sanaa, where the local imams held sway until 1872. Indigenous resistance to the Ottomans continued, culminating in a rebellion by Imam Yahya in 1911, which was suppressed. The treaty of 1913 limited him to the highlands, with Sanaa as his capital. After the Ottomans' collapse he reasserted his control of the coastal plain and the southern Shafii (Sunni) [*q.v.*] areas to the south, upgrading Sanaa into the national capital. But his son, Ahmad (r. 1948–62), moved the capital south to Taiz.

After the 1962 revolution Sanaa once again became the premier city. During the 1962–70 Civil War [*q.v.*] it suffered extensive damage. During the pro-democracy demonstrations and fighting in 2011, the city suffered also considerable damage to its buildings and infrastructure.

It is an important commercial and communications center. Its tourist attractions include the walled Old City, a Jewish quarter with gold and silver metalwork and embroidery workshops, and the Great Mosque.

Sarkis, Elias (1924–85): *Lebanese politician; president, 1976–82* Born into a middle-class Maronite [*q.v.*] family in Beirut [*q.v.*], Sarkis obtained a law degree from Saint Joseph University. From 1953 he worked in the legal section of the government's audit department. While investigating financial irregularities at the defense ministry, he came to the attention of President Fuad Chehab (r. 1958–64) [*q.v.*], who transferred him to his secretariat. Sarkis made the presidential bureau a leading center of power and became its director-general in 1962.

After briefly serving President Charles Helou (r. 1964–70) [*q.v.*], he became governor of the Central Bank in 1966. Four years later he lost to Suleiman Franjieh [*q.v.*] in the presidential race by one vote. He came to represent moderate Maronite opinion, which was rare after the start of the Lebanese Civil War in April 1975 [*q.v.*].

Sarkis became a favorite of Syrian President Hafiz Assad [*q.v.*] following the latter's intervention in the war on the Maronite side in June 1976. As the only candidate in the presidential election three months later, he won. Working in conjunction with Assad, he replaced top officials with pro-Syrian nominees. When the Phalangists [*q.v.*] protested, he tried to limit Syrian power, but in vain.

His differences with Prime Minister Salim Hoss [*q.v.*] deepened. He saw national reconciliation as a prelude to curtailing Syria's influence in Lebanon, whereas Hoss regarded it as a preamble to implementing a security plan in coordination with the Syrian peacekeeping force. Efforts to bridge the gap between the two failed, and

Hoss resigned in June 1980. Later in the year the cabinet, led by Shafiq Wazzan, split in the face of a crisis created by a confrontation between the Phalangists and the Syrians in Zahle, a largely Greek Orthodox [*q.v.*] city.

In June 1982, within a week of invading Lebanon, the Israeli forces expelled Sarkis from his presidential palace in Baabda. By the time his term officially expired in September, Israel was very much in charge of Beirut [*q.v.*]. He retired from public life.

al-Saud clan: *See* House of Saud.

al-Saud, Abdul Aziz bin Abdul Rahman: *See* Abdul Aziz bin Abdul Rahman al-Saud.

al-Saud, Abdullah bin Abdul Aziz: *See* Abdullah bin Abdul Aziz al-Saud.

al-Saud, Fahd bin Abdul Aziz: *See* Fahd bin Abdul Aziz al-Saud.

al-Saud, Faisal bin Abdul Aziz: *See* Faisal bin Abdul Aziz al-Saud.

al-Saud, Khalid bin Abdul Aziz: *See* Khalid bin Abdul Aziz al-Saud.

al-Saud, Nayef bin Abdul Aziz (1933– 2012): *Crown Prince of Saudi Arabia, 2011–12* Born in Taif [*q.v.*] to Abdul Aziz bin Abdul Rahman al-Saud [*q.v.*] and Hassa bint Ahmad al-Sudairi, Fahd was the 23rd son of the founder of the Saudi kingdom. He was educated at the Princes' School and by senior ulema.

At the age of 20, he was appointed governor of Riyadh [*q.v.*]. As one of the "Sudairi Seven" princes, his career was advanced by one or more of his full brothers. In 1970 King Faisal bin Abdul Aziz [*q.v.*] named him deputy interior minister to serve under his full brother Fahd [*q.v.*]. When Fahd was named crown prince in 1975, Nayef was promoted to interior minister, a position he has held since then.

His ministry controls 130,000 security personnel as well as the ubiquitous morality police, which enforce the veil for women and the closing of businesses during prayer times.

Intolerant of any criticism of the House of Saud [*q.v.*], he has dealt harshly with dissenters, filling jails with political prisoners. He moved strongly against Osama bin Laden [*q.v.*] in 1994, depriving him of Saudi citizenship, among other things. And, working with the kingdom's intelligence agencies, he closed down charities that collected donations for Osama bin Laden and his network.

Commenting on 9/11 a year after the event, he said, "It is impossible that 19 youths carried out the operation of September 11, or that bin Laden or Al Qaida [*q.v.*] did that alone.... I think [the Zionists] are behind these events." And yet when Al Qaida in Arabia carried out terrorist attacks on the Western expatriate housing compounds, oil infrastructure, and industrial facilities in the Saudi kingdom from 2003 onward, he mounted a relentless crackdown, smashed the group by 2006, and forced its remaining activists to seek refuge in Yemen.

In March 2009 King Abdullah [*q.v.*] promoted him to second deputy prime minister, the first deputy prime minister being Crown Prince Sultan bin Abdul Aziz al-Saud. He played a key role in Abdullah's decision to host Tunisia's ousted dictator, Zine El Abidine Ben Ali, in January 2011, and to send troops in March to Bahrain to help end pro-democracy protests led by Shias [*q.v.*], whom he detests.

After Sultan's death in October 2011, he was named crown prince.

al-Saud, Salman bin Abdul Aziz

(1935–) *Crown Prince of Saudi Arabia, 2012–* Born to King Abdul Aziz al-Saud [q.v.] and Hassa al-Sudairi, he was educated at the Princes School in Riyadh [q.v.]. He started his political career at 19 when his father appointed him mayor of the capital, and a year later King Saud bin Abdul Aziz al-Saud [*q.v.*] promoted him to governor of Riyadh province. He resigned in 1960, but was reappointed to the same post three years later. He held that position until 2011 when, following the death of his brother Crown Prince Sultan al-Saud, he became the defense minister. Under his rule, Riyadh grew into a bustling metropolis and attracted much foreign investment. After the demise of his brother Crown Prince Nayef al-Saud [*q.v.*] in June 2012, King Abdullah bin Abdul Aziz al-Saud [q.v.] named him crown prince. Unlike Nayef, he is pragmatic and diplomatic.

al-Saud, Saud bin Abdul Aziz (1902–

69): *King of Saudi Arabia, 1953–64* After the death of his elder brother, Turki bin Abdul Aziz, in 1919, Saud became the eldest son of King Abdul Aziz bin Abdul Rahman al-Saud [*q.v.*]. In 1926 the monarch appointed Saud his viceroy in Najd [*q.v.*]. On the founding of the kingdom of Saudi Arabia in 1932, he named Saud crown

prince. Two years later, along with his younger brother, Faisal [*q.v.*], Saud carried out a victorious campaign against North Yemen [*q.v.*]. When, a month before his death in November 1953, King Abdul Aziz appointed a council of ministers, he named Saud its chairman.

On succeeding his father, Saud remained prime minister and named Faisal crown prince. With the sharp rise in oil revenues due to the growing demand for Saudi oil to fill the gap caused by the 1951–53 Iranian oil nationalization crisis, traditional, direct governance by the monarch proved inadequate when it came to handling the increasing fiscal and administrative complexities. The resulting chaos, compounded by Saud's extravagance and mismanagement, created a crisis.

In 1958 he was compelled to appoint a new cabinet and hand over the premiership to Faisal. His deteriorating health led him to go abroad frequently for medical treatment. Yet he tried to regain full executive authority, and in 1960, after he had promised a constitutional monarchy, including a predominantly elected parliament, he succeeded. However, he reneged on his pledge for political reform.

After the republican coup in North Yemen in 1962, which implicitly threatened the future of the Saudi monarchy, Saud ceded his executive powers once again to Faisal, and Saudi Arabia became involved in the North Yemeni civil war [*q.v.*]. During his long absences abroad for medical treatment in 1963 his opponents consolidated their position. As a result, in March 1964, Saud transferred all his powers to Faisal, who was named viceroy. In November the Supreme

Religious Council and a group of most senior princes deposed Saud and named Faisal king.

He went into exile in Europe. In 1966, when rivalry between Egyptian president Gamal Abdul Nasser [*q.v.*] and King Faisal intensified, Nasser allowed Saud to settle in Cairo [*q.v.*] to strengthen his own anti-Faisal position. But when, following Egypt's defeat in the June 1967 Arab-Israeli War [*q.v.*], Nasser sought a rapprochement with Faisal, Saud lost his importance. He died in Athens, Greece, in February 1969, leaving behind 52 sons and 55 daughters.

Saudi Arabia:
   OFFICIAL NAME: Kingdom of Saudi Arabia
   CAPITAL: Riyadh [*q.v.*]
   AREA: 865,000 sq. mi./2,240,000 sq. km, including parts of the Saudi Arabia-Iraq and Saudi Arabia-Kuwait Neutral Zones [*q.v.*]
   POPULATION: 26.173 million (2011 est.), including 5.60 million foreigners
   GROSS DOMESTIC PRODUCT (nominal): $651.65 billion; per capita, $22,630 (2011 est.)
   GROSS DOMESTIC PRODUCT (Purchasing Power Parity): $681.5 billion; per capita, $24,270 (2011 est.)
   NATIONAL CURRENCY: Saudi Rial (SAR); SAR 1 = $0.267 = £0.164 = €0.20 (2011)
   FORM OF GOVERNMENT: monarchy
   OFFICIAL LANGUAGE: Arabic [*q.v.*]
   OFFICIAL RELIGION: Islam [*q.v.*]
   ADMINISTRATIVE REGIONS: Saudi Arabia consists of 13 provinces divided into five regions: East, West (Hijaz [*q.v.*]), North, South, and Center (Najd [*q.v.*]). These are administered by governors appointed by the monarch.

   CONSTITUTION: In March 1992, 60 years after the founding of Saudi Arabia, King Fahd bin Abdul Aziz al-Saud [*q.v.*] issued the Basic Law of Government as a decree. It declared the Quran [*q.v.*] and the *Sunna* [*q.v.*] as the constitution of the Kingdom of Saudi Arabia, to be governed by the male descendants of Abdul Aziz bin Abdul Rahman al-Saud [*q.v.*]. The monarch is the head of state and the council of ministers, and is also the commander-in-chief of the military. He appoints the prime minister and other members of the cabinet. The Basic Law provided for the appointment of a Consultative Council of 60 members and its chairman by the monarch for a four-year term. There was no provision for a legislature, political parties, or trade unions. In 2006 an Allegiance Institution, consisting chiefly of the sons and grandsons of Abdul Aziz al-Saud, was established to vote for one of the three royal princes chosen by the ruling monarch to succeed him. But this protocol will come into force only after the enthronement of the current crown prince.

   CONSULTATIVE COUNCIL: In August 1993 the first fully nominated 60-member Consultative Council, with four-year tenure, was named by the king. It was authorized to question the government and to refer any official action it disputed to the monarch. Its number was raised successively to 150 in 2005. In early 2005 there were elections to the municipalities, with their members having tenure of four years. But the next election, due in 2009, was held in September 2011 during the course of the Arab Spring [*q.v.*], with their tenure extended to six years.

ETHNIC COMPOSITION: (2010) Arab 79 percent, South Asian 12 percent, other 9 percent.

EXECUTIVE AUTHORITY: Executive authority rests with the king, who rules through a council of ministers, containing many royal princes, responsible to him.

High officials:

Head of state: King Abdullah bin Abdul Aziz al-Saud [*q.v.*] 2005–

Prime minister: King Abdullah bin Abdul Aziz al-Saud 2005–

Crown prince and first deputy prime minister: Nayef bin Abdul Aziz al-Saud [*q.v.*], 201–

Chairman of Council of Senior Ulema: Grand Mufti Abdul-Aziz Aal Shaikh, 2009–

Chairman of the Consultative Council: Abdullah al-Shaikh 2009–

HISTORY: (since ca 1900): In 1902 Abdul Aziz bin Abdul Rahman al-Saud [*q.v.*] regained Diraiya and neighboring Riyadh from the rival Rashid clan, which was allied with the Ottoman Empire. After consolidating his domain, he captured the eastern Hasa region in 1913. Following the downfall of the Ottoman Empire in 1918, he conquered the Asir region on the Red Sea in 1920. The next year he defeated his rival, Muhammad bin Rashid, based in Shammar. After he had added more territories to his domain in 1922 and called himself the Sultan of Najd and its Dependencies. He couched his campaigns in Islamic terms, as a struggle to punish either religious dissenters or those who had strayed from true Islam as represented by the Wahhabi doctrine [*q.v.*]. In 1924 he defeated Sharif Hussein bin Ali al-Hashem in Hijaz, and deposed him.

Having declared himself King of Hijaz and Sultan of Najd and its Dependencies in January 1926, Abdul Aziz sought international recognition. The following year Britain recognized him as King of Hijaz and Najd and its Dependencies. In 1929 he fell out with the militant section of the Ikhwan [*q.v.*], the armed wing of the Wahhabis, which so far had been his fighting force. Assisted by the British, then controlling Kuwait and Iraq, he quelled the Ikhwan rebellion. In September 1932 he combined his domains, comprising about three-quarters of 1.12 million sq. mi./3.1 million sq. km of the Arabian Peninsula [*q.v.*], into one—the Kingdom of Saudi Arabia—and called himself King of Saudi Arabia.

Abdul Aziz granted an oil concession to the Standard Oil Company of California in 1933. Modest commercial extraction, which started in 1938, was interrupted by World War II, in which he remained neutral. As a domineering and militarily successful tribal chief, he behaved like an autocrat. Following a dramatic increase in oil output after World War II, the economic boom overstretched the rudimentary institutions of the state, supervised by him and some of his close aides, and undermined the traditional spartan Wahhabi lifestyle of the House of Saud [*q.v.*]. Yet it was not until October 1953—a month before his death—that he appointed a council of ministers, chaired by his eldest son, Saud [*q.v.*], as an advisory body.

When Saud became king he retained the premiership. However, he proved incapable of handling the fiscal

and administrative complexities aris-
ing from the sharp growth in oil revenues caused by increased demand for
Saudi oil due to the oil nationalization
crisis in Iran during 1951-1953. The
resulting chaos, compounded by
Saud's extravagance and mismanagement, created a crisis and led to a
power struggle between him and his
brother, Crown Prince Faisal [q.v.]. It
was finally settled against Saud, who
was forced to abdicate in 1964.

On ascending the throne Faisal reneged on his promise of political reform that he had made as crown
prince in 1962—especially the promulgation of a written constitution
specifying a consultative council. Instead he harshly suppressed the opposition. He increased support to the
royalist camp in the North Yemeni
Civil War [q.v.], in which the republicans were being aided by Egyptian
President Gamal Abdul Nasser [q.v.].
However, following the Arab defeat in
the 1967 Six-Day War [q.v.], he
buried his differences with Nasser.

Faisal's efforts to establish a transnational organization of Muslim states
succeeded in 1969, in the wake of an
arson attempt on the al-Aqsa Mosque
in Jerusalem [q.v.], resulting in the formation of the Islamic Conference Organization [q.v.], based in Jeddah [q.v.].

During the 1973 Arab-Israeli War
[q.v.] Faisal led the Arab oil embargo
[q.v.] against the Western allies of Israel, and backed the quadrupling of oil
prices in 1973–74. As a result of increased output and a sharp rise in
price in 1973–74, Saudi oil income
reached $22.57 billion in 1974, a 36-
fold rise in a decade. Though Faisal
succeeded in having the oil embargo
against Israel's Western allies lifted in

March 1974, he was unwilling to go
along fully with Washington's policy
on the Middle East peace process
[q.v.]. On 25 March 1975 he was assassinated by his young nephew,
Prince Faisal bin Musaid.

On becoming king, Khalid bin
Abdul Aziz [q.v.] freed political prisoners. He appointed a cabinet in
which 15 of the 25 ministers were
commoners, but he ensured that the
crucial foreign, defense, interior, and
National Guard [q.v.] ministries
stayed with the House of Saud. He
tried to end the Lebanese Civil War
[q.v.], gave grants to the Palestine
Liberation Organization (PLO) [q.v.],
and opposed the Camp David Accords [q.v.]. He cut all links with
Egypt after it had signed the Egyptian-Israeli Peace Treaty [q.v.] in
March 1979.

In domestic affairs, Khalid represented the nationalist trend, committed to greater respect for tradition and
slower economic development, which
was in conflict with the pro-U.S.
trend, stressing rapid economic development. When faced with an armed
uprising at the Grand Mosque of
Mecca [q.v.] in November 1979, he
prevaricated and took a fortnight to
quell it. Responding to the rise of a
revolutionary Islamic regime in Iran,
he opted for stricter enforcement of
Islamic injunctions in the kingdom.
During 1981, the last full year of his
reign, the kingdom earned record oil
revenue of $110 billion.

Of the two trends that had emerged
among senior Saudi princes during
Khalid's reign, King Fahd bin Abdul
Aziz belonged to the pro-U.S. school,
favoring rapid economic progress. His
Middle East peace plan (in exchange

for the peaceful coexistence of all the states in the region, Israel would be required to evacuate all the Arab territories occupied in 1967, dismantle the Jewish settlements in these areas, and accept the founding of a Palestinian state) was adopted by the Arab League [q.v.] summit in September 1982. It remained the common Arab position on a comprehensive settlement until the Middle East Peace Conference [q.v.] in Madrid, Spain, nine years later.

In keeping with his vacillating manner, Fahd waited a whole week before making public his position on Iraq's invasion of Kuwait on 2 August 1990. He called on the United States and the Arab countries to send troops to help protect Saudi Arabia and end the Iraqi occupation of Kuwait. The huge expenses incurred by Riyadh in the conduct of Gulf War II [q.v.], the rearming of the kingdom that followed the conflict, and the sharply reduced prices of oil, with annual petroleum income down to $43 billion, led his government to raise foreign loans to balance the budget.

In May 1991 Shaikh Abdul Aziz al-Baz [q.v.] handed Faisal a "Letter of Demands," signed by 400 leading ulema, judges, and academics, demanding a consultative council with powers to decide all domestic and foreign affairs; greater Islamization of state, social, economic, and educational institutions; punishment of those who had enriched themselves illegally; and freedom of expression within the Sharia [q.v.]. Fahd ignored the petition.

Having made some concessions in the political and religious spheres, Fahd repressed further the dissident Islamic ulema at home and blocked financial assistance to Islamist militants abroad. He tightened ties with Washington still further just as the latter's dependence on Saudi petroleum grew. A quarter of America's oil imports now originated in Saudi Arabia, which had purchased $25 billion worth of U.S. arms between August 1990 and December 1992—by which time a formalized defense understanding between Riyadh and Washington was in place.

The establishment of the fully nominated Consultative Council in 1993 did little to diminish disaffection. To silence opposition, the government detained 200 political dissidents in 1994. It was distressed when a bomb at the National Guard training center in Riyadh in November 1995 killed seven people, including five American officers. That month, following a stroke, Faisal passed on his powers to Crown Prince Abdullah. Though, on recovery, Faisal nominally retrieved these powers three months later, there was less of his imprint on the administration during the subsequent years as Abdullah became the de facto ruler.

Abdullah continued the policy of aiding the Taliban (Arabic: *plural of* talib-e-ilm, *student of knowledge*), a faction of hard-line Islamic fundamentalists [q.v.] in Afghanistan, created largely by Pakistan in late 1994, which would later give refuge to Osama bin Laden [q.v.], a Saudi renegade. Saudi Arabia's financial and other assistance to the Taliban helped it to capture Kabul in September 1996. With this, the kingdom became part of the Islamabad-Kabul-Riyadh triumvirate, which solidified when

Saudi Arabia became the second country after Pakistan to recognize the Taliban regime in May 1997.

Relations with the U.S. began to fray in mid-1996. A huge explosion in June outside the Khobar Towers, a multistory residential block for American military personnel near the Dhahran air base, left 19 U.S. servicemen dead and another 400 injured, including 107 Americans. Despite Washington's request to let its Federal Bureau of Investigation agents interrogate the suspects, the Saudi authorities refused to compromise their monopoly over investigations.

In 1998, unemployment among Saudi citizens soared to 27 percent, twice the rate of five years earlier. But the House of Saud showed little sign of sharing its power with its subjects.

As the custodian of Islam's two holiest shrines in Mecca and Medina [q.v.], the Saudi government advised Palestinian leader Yasser Arafat [q.v.] not to compromise on the sovereignty of the Noble Sanctuary [q.v.] in Jerusalem in his talks with Israeli Prime Minister Ehud Barak [q.v.] in July 2000. After the outbreak of the Al Aqsa Intifada [q.v.] in September, Saudi Crown Prince Abdullah backed the plan at the Arab League summit [q.v.] to set up two funds to aid the Palestinians.

In September 2001, following the attacks on three American targets by hijacked aircraft, Saudi-American relations soured further when 15 of the 19 hijackers turned out to be Saudi nationals. During the succeeding years, the Saudi regime itself became the target of Al Qaida in Arabia. To overcome the challenge, the government of King Abdullah carried out a series of crackdowns, involving simultaneous raids by security forces, wide scale detentions, torture, and public beheadings.

To ease the pressure by the administration of U.S. President George W. Bush for its democracy crusade, the government held municipal elections on a franchise, which excluded women, for the first time in 2005. Another first was to receive Russian President Vladimir Putin in Riyadh in 2007. The kingdom strengthened economic ties with China, which became an important buyer of its petroleum.

The renewed backing of the 1982 Middle East peace plan in the form of King Abdullah's plan, adopted by the Arab League summit in 2002, failed to thaw the impasse between Israelis and Palestinians. But Saudi Arabia's proposal to have Islamic scholars hold interfaith dialogue with their Christian [q.v.] and Jewish [q.v.] counterparts in Madrid, Spain, in 2008 was implemented.

In 2009 Abdullah reconstituted the 21-member Council of Senior Ulema (CSU) while retaining as its chairman Grand Mufti Abdul Aziz bin Abdullah Aal Shaikh who had succeeded Abdul Aziz bin Abdullah al-Baz in 1999 after the latter's death. In April 2010 the CSU issued a fatwa against terrorism, which stated that any Muslim committing it was acting "criminally" and so too was any Muslim who provided financial or moral support to terrorist groups.

During the early days of the Arab Spring in 2011, Abdullah urged U.S. President Barack Obama not to withdraw support for Egyptian President Hosni Mubarak [q.v.]. When this failed, he offered refuge to Mubarak who rejected it. In March his government dispatched tanks and 1,000 troops to Bahrain to help quell pro-democracy demonstrations. In August, it reversed its policy of backing Syrian President Bashar Assad [*q.v.*] and became an active supporter of the opposition, providing it with money and weapons. At the first sight of an incipient protest in the kingdom, the government committed $130 billion to raise social benefits to citizens, reduce unemployment, and provide housing for its subjects, whose numbers were rapidly growing.

RELIGIOUS COMPOSITION: (2011 est.): Muslim, 92 percent, of which Sunni [*q.v.*] 85 percent, mostly Shafii [*q.v.*] and Wahhabi; Shia 10-12 percent; Ismailis [*q.v.*] 2–3 percent; Christian, 4 percent; others, 4 percent.

Saudi Arabia-Iraq Neutral Zone: Area 2,720 sq. mi./7,044 sq. km. Among other things, the Protocol of Uqair [*q.v.*] in December 1922 demarcated a neutral zone between Najd [*q.v.*] (later Saudi Arabia) and Iraq, adjacent to the western tip of the Saudi-Kuwaiti frontier. While open to the nomad tribes of both countries for water and cattle grazing, it was a prohibited area for the construction of permanent (civilian or military) buildings. In 1938 Saudi Arabia and Iraq signed an agreement on administering the zone. In July 1975 the two neighbors divided the zone equally, with the new frontier running straight through it, and each side assuming sovereignty over its part.

Saudi Arabia-Kuwait Neutral Zone: Area: 2,230 sq. mi./5,770 sq. km. Among other things, the Protocol of Uqair [*q.v.*] in December 1922 demarcated, to the south of Kuwait, a neutral zone between Najd [*q.v.*] (later Saudi Arabia) and Kuwait. While remaining open to the nomad tribes of both countries for water and cattle grazing, it was a prohibited area for the construction of permanent (civilian or military) buildings. Two years after its independence in 1961, Kuwait concluded a further agreement with Saudi Arabia on the zone. In 1966 the two neighbors divided the area equally, each country integrating its respective territory into its central administration—except for natural resources, such as petroleum, which remain undivided, the offshore oil concessions being shared equally by the concessionaires of Saudi Arabia and Kuwait.

Sazman-e Cherikha-ye Fedai Khalq-e Iran (Persian: *Organization of People's Self-sacrificing Guerrillas*): *See* Fedai Khalq.

Sazman-e Mujahedin-e Khalq (Persian: *Organization of People's Holy Warriors*): *See* Mujahedin-e Khalq.

Sayyab, Badr Shakir (1926–64): *Iraqi poet* Born into a Shia [*q.v.*] family near Basra [*q.v.*], Sayyab secured a diploma from the Teachers' College, Baghdad [*q.v.*], where he specialized in Arabic and English literature. As a poet he came under the influence of T.S. Eliot (1888–1965), especially his poem *The Wasteland* (1922). Sayyab made his debut with a collection of poems, *The Wilted Flowers* (1947). Like Eliot, he discarded the idea of time as a linear progression, and employed it flexibly as a permutation of the past, present, and future, merging and interlocking different eras and experiences. He made use of eternal images, historical archetypes, myths, proverbs, and folklore. Endowed with impressive linguistic power, he was outstandingly original in his imagery and exact in the choice of his words.

Overall, in the Arab world the impetus to discard the old and experiment with the new grew in the wake of the Arab defeat in the 1948–49 Palestine War [*q.v.*]. He and his fellow Iraqi, Nazik al-Malika [*q.v.*], a highly talented poet—known later as part of "the generation of the catastrophe [of the Palestine War]"—became pioneers of the modernist movement in Arabic poetry. Their concepts dominated the poetry of the 1950s and most of the 1960s.

The volumes published by Sayyab in the mid-1950s (*In the Arab Maghreb*, *Song in the Month of August*, *Jaykur and the City*) were especially notable for the elevating rhythmical construction of the poems. Yet each collection had a different aura: *In the Arab Maghreb* had an enthusiastically heroic tone; *Song in the Month of August* was remarkable for its irony, a rare quality in Arabic literature; and *Jaykur and the City* made a tragic plea.

As a member of the underground Iraqi Communist Party [*q.v.*]—an act that cost him his teaching job in Baghdad—Sayyab's view was that society needed a redeemer, but redemption lay not with a heroic figure but with the masses who, taking their destiny in their hands, would struggle and triumph. Since the defeat in Palestine [*q.v.*] was fresh and the feeling of redemption strong, and there was a popular yearning for Arab unity, his

perspectives were attractive. He aptly captured this perspective in the poem *The Song of Rain* (1954). In it he subtly incorporated the myth of Tammuz, the fertility god of Babylonia, to redeem life through rain and the arrival of spring.

He applauded the revolution of July 1958 in Iraq, which saw the end of the pro-British monarchy. He celebrated the victory of the Algerian Front for National Liberation against French imperialism in 1962 by using the symbol of Sisyphus discarding his rock. During the regime of Abdul Karim Qasim [*q.v.*], he left the Communist Party.

After being fired again from his job, he left for Beirut, where he worked for *Shiar* (Arabic: *Poetry*) magazine, coedited by Ali Ahmad Said Asbar [*q.v.*]. During his terminal illness he produced poetry of despair, often portraying himself as Job, an Old Testament [*q.v.*] prophet who suffered afflictions with fortitude and faith.

Second Gulf War: *See* Gulf War II (1991).

Second Intifada (2000–2005): Despite the failure of their talks in July 2000 at Camp David to reach a final settlement between Israel and the Palestinians, Israeli Prime Minister Ehud Barak [*q.v.*] and Palestine Liberation Organization [*q.v.*] Chairman Yasser Arafat [*q.v.*] had a cordial meeting at the former's home near Tel Aviv [*q.v.*] on 25 September, when they agreed to meet again four days later. But on 28 September, Likud leader Ariel Sharon [*q.v.*], surrounded by 1,000 armed police, toured the Noble Sanctuary/ Temple Mount [*q.v.*] in Jerusalem's

Old City, normally out of bounds to the Jews [*q.v.*]—a move designed to underscore Israeli sovereignty over Islam's third-holiest site. Viewing this as a provocative move by Sharon, the Palestinians protested by throwing stones.

Their demonstration after the Friday midday prayers at the al-Aqsa Mosque on 29 September was dispersed by the Israeli security forces with live ammunition, which left seven protestors dead. This marked the start of the Al Aqsa Intifada [*q.v.*], also known as the Second Intifada.

Barak sealed off the West Bank [*q.v.*] and Gaza Strip [*q.v.*] in October, as a result of which the Palestinian economy would lose $2.9 billion in the next six months, while Israel held back $430 million in tax revenue collected on behalf of the Palestinian Authority [*q.v.*].

Against the background of rising violence and weakening coalition government, Barak called for the prime ministerial election in February 2001. He lost to Sharon, who ran on a platform of continued expansion of Jewish settlements, Israeli sovereignty over all of Jerusalem [*q.v.*], and no talks with the Palestinians until there was complete cessation of terrorism.

Consequently, the intifada became more violent, with the Palestinians resorting to using small arms, and Islamist Palestinians groups like Hamas [*q.v.*] and the Islamic Jihad [*q.v.*] increasingly resorting to suicide bombings [*q.v.*] in the Occupied Territories [*q.v.*] and Israel. It also led to the emergence of the Popular Resistance Committees (PRC), made up of all factions, including the secular Fatah

[*q.v.*], which would go on to form its military wing, Tanzim (Arabic: *Organization*), to specialize in suicide bombings.

Following the terrorist attacks on the American targets in September 2001, Sharon made an unsuccessful attempt to get the U.S. administration of George W. Bush to equate the Palestinian resistance to the Israeli military occupation with terrorism. He responded to periodic suicide bombings by the Palestinians with escalating force, pursuing his strategic aim of destroying the security and administrative infrastructure of the Palestinian Authority (PA) [*q.v.*] by deploying armed helicopters, fighter aircraft, and gunboats, and ordering assassinations of suspected terrorists.

Retaliating for a particularly lethal Palestinian suicide bombing in Israel on 27 March 2002, Sharon ordered the reoccupation of all the towns administered by the PA (except Hebron [*q.v.*] and Jericho [*q.v.*]), thus effectively abrogating the Oslo Accords [*q.v.*], and placing Arafat under house arrest in Ramallah [*q.v.*].

The first two years of the Second Intifada left 1,800 Palestinians dead and another 40,000 injured—directly affecting the life or limb of more than one out of a hundred Palestinians—as well as 570 Israelis dead and another 3,000 wounded.

After the death of Arafat in November 2004, the intifada lost its momentum. His successor, Mahmoud Abbas [*q.v.*], publicly disapproved of it. He participated in the summit meeting with Egyptian president Hosni Mubarak [*q.v.*], Jordanian monarch Abdullah II [*q.v.*], and Sharon in the Egyptian resort town of

Sharm el Shaikh on 8 February 2005 which decided to bring about an end to the intifada. He soon succeeded in persuading Hamas leaders to call off the intifada. Its lingering elements disappeared after the electoral victory of Hamas in the January 2006 Palestinian Legislative Council elections.

According to B'Tselem, an Israeli human rights group, between 29 September 2000 and 15 January 2005, 3,223 Palestinians and 945 Israelis lost their lives during the intifada. Overall, the Al Aqsa Intifada led to the hardening of popular opinion against the Palestinians among Jewish Israelis.

Semitic languages: A member of the Hamito-Semitic language family, the Semitic languages are divided into northern peripheral, consisting of Akkadian (extinct); northern central, including Canaanite, Amorite, Ugaritic, Phoenician and Punic, Aramaic, and ancient and modern Syriac and Hebrew [q.v.] (all extinct except modern Hebrew); southern central, including Arabic [q.v.] and Maltese; and southern peripheral, including southern Arabic and the languages of northern Ethiopia, such as Amharic and Tigre.

In the 10th century A.D., Judah ibn Quraish, a Hebrew grammarian and lexicographer, showed connections between Arabic, Aramaic, and Hebrew. But it was not until 1890 that W. Wright, the author of *Arabic Grammar*, came up with a systematic demonstration of this link. In between—referring to Genesis (10:1): "These are the descendants of Noah's sons: Shem, Ham, and Japheth"—A. L. Schlozer coined the title Shemitic/

Semitic for these languages, which has since then stuck. Words in these languages are founded on a root made up of consonants that provides the basic meaning of the word, and a vowel pattern that defines various shades of this meaning.

Semite: The term Semite/Shemite is based on Genesis (10:1): "These are the descendants of Noah's sons: Shem, Ham, and Japheth." Initially, those believed to be the descendants of Shem were called Semite. Nowadays the term applies to Arabs [q.v.], Akkadians of ancient Babylon, Assyrians, Canaanites (including Phoenicians), Aramaean tribes (including Hebrews [q.v.]), and a large segment of northern Ethiopians, because their languages are derived from the common Semitic root.

Sephardim (*Hebrew: plural of* Sephardi, *derivative of Sepharad/Spain*): In the Middle Ages (476 A.D.–1492), *Sepharad* meant Spain, and the term *Sephardi* was applied to the Jews [q.v.] of Spain. When expelled from Spain in 1492, and later from Portugal, most Sephardi Jews settled along the shores of the Mediterranean, establishing large, influential, and flourishing communities in Morocco, Italy, Greece, Turkey, Egypt, and the Levant [q.v.]. From the 16th century onward, differences between Sephardim and Ashkenazim [q.v.] became sharper. These pertained to synagogue [q.v.] architecture and rites (of Babylonian origin for Sephardim, Palestinian origin for Ashkenazim); their pronunciation of Hebrew [q.v.]; and their social customs. The mother tongue of Sephardim was Judeo-Spanish or Ladino [q.v.].

As inhabitants of Palestine [*q.v.*] since the late 15th century under the Ottomans, Sephardim claim the longest residency in Israel [*q.v.*], where they have had their own chief rabbi. After the founding of Israel in 1948, the immigrating Oriental Jews [*q.v.*]—originating in the Arab countries away from the Mediterranean and in Iran and India, where their rites were neither Sephardic nor Ashkenazi—were classified Sephardic. With a large influx of Jewish immigrants from the Arab states, the percentage of Sephardim rose sharply. Due to this, and a higher birth rate among them, they became a majority in the mid-1960s. Three decades later they lost that position due to a large influx of Ashkenazim from former Soviet Union. Sephardim are about one-fifth of the world Jewry.

Seveners: *see* Ismailis.

al-Shaabi, Qahtan Muhammad (1920–81): *South Yemeni politician; president, 1967–69* Born into a notable family in the Lahej principality of the Aden Protectorate, Shaabi received secular education before joining the Lahej land department. He became its director in 1955. Three years later he joined the nationalist South Arabian League. He escaped to North Yemen in 1960 and, after the republican coup of September 1962, co-founded South Yemen's National Liberation Front (NLF) [*q.v.*] there. Following the NLF's declaration of an armed struggle against the British in October 1963, he became its leader. He also directed its fight against the moderate Front for the Liberation of South Yemen (FLOSY). Within three years the NLF had occupied the Aden Protectorate and decimated FLOSY in the Aden Colony.

He negotiated South Yemen's independence with the British in Geneva in November 1967. Later that month he became president, prime minister, and chief of military staff of the People's Republic of South Yemen. When differences arose between NLF moderates favoring Nasserite [*q.v.*] socialism, and NLF radicals advocating Marxist-Leninist socialism, Shaabi sided with the former. Unwilling to split the ruling party then facing from its conservative neighbors, he sought accommodation with the rival camp. But, having tightened their control of the party machine and militia, the radical faction deposed Shaabi in June 1969. He was jailed in April 1970, and after his release he stayed away from public life.

Shabak (Hebrew: *acronym of* Sherut Betakhon Klali, *General Security Service*): *See* Shin Beth.

Shabuot (Hebrew: *Weeks*): *See* Pentecost. (Also spelled Shavuot)

Shafii Code: *Sunni Islamic school* This Sunni [*q.v.*] Islamic school was named after Muhammad bin Idris al-Shafii (767–820 A.D.). As a student of the Islamic law in Medina [*q.v.*] he was a contemporary of Malik bin Anas, the founder of the Maliki Code [*q.v.*]. He familiarized himself with the Hanafi Code [*q.v.*] by visiting Baghdad [*q.v.*]. Later, settling in Cairo [*q.v.*], he greatly influenced the legal-administrative apparatus of the Abbasid Empire (751–1258 A.D.). He founded the *fiqh* [*q.v.*]), religious jurisprudence, on four pillars: the Quran [*q.v.*], the Prophet Muhamad's *sunna* [*q.v.*] (later to be recorded in the Hadith [*q.v.*]), analogical reasoning (*qiyas* [*q.v.*]), and the consensus (*ijma* [*q.v.*]) of the community. So far, *ijma* had been construed as consensus of "ahl al-hall wal aqd" (Arabic: *those who loose and bind*), a term embracing various types of representatives of the community, including religious intellectuals, but Shafii enlarged it to include the whole community.

Analogical reasoning allowed the community to incorporate new situations into the Sharia [*q.v.*] (Islamic Law) without disturbing the primacy of the Quran and the *sunna*. It also permitted individual opinions and differences, as sanctioned by the Prophet Muhammad's statement in the Hadith: "The differences of opinion among the learned within my community are [signs of] God's grace." By pursuing this method the clergy could merge the Prophet Muhammad's teachings, Arab traditions, and non-Arab traditions into a single canonical system applicable to the life of all Muslims, Arab and non-Arab. Thus Shafii's systemization of the Sharia provided the foundation upon which a common identity of Muslims scattered around the world could be built.

The Shafii school, founded by his disciples and originating in Egypt, reached southern Arabia, and from there spread along the monsoon route to East Africa and Southeast Asia through Arab traders. Today it is particularly strong in Yemen.

Shafiq, Ahmed (1941–): *Egyptian military and political leader* Born to Muhammad Shafiq, a senior civil ser-

vant, and Naja Alwi, in Cairo [*q.v.*], Shafiq graduated from the Air Force Academy in 1961. He joined the air force and as a fighter pilot rose through the ranks to become an air force base commander. He served as a military attaché in the Egyptian Embassy in Rome (1984–86) before returning to active air force duties. In 1991 he was promoted to commander of the Air Operations Department. Five years later he became Commander of the Egyptian Air Force.

After his retirement from the military in 2002, he was named minister of civil aviation. He implemented a successful program of restructuring the state-owned EgyptAir, and improving the operation of airports. A fulsome admirer of Egyptian President Hosni Mubarak [*q.v.*], a former air force fighter pilot, he described Mubarak as a "father figure" and a "role model" in 2010.

When the pro-democracy demonstrations swelled in Cairo in January 2011, Mubarak appointed him prime minister on 31 January to placate the protestors. He survived Mubarak's ouster on 11 February but resigned on 3 March when he was accused of being a remnant of the Mubarak era. He ran in the residential poll in May 2012, and surprisingly came in second, with 23.3 percent of the vote.

After the second round on 16–17 June, the High Presidential Electoral Commission announced on 24 June that he had secured 48.3 percent of the vote. The next day prosecutors referred corruption charges against him to an investigative judge. Early on 26 June he fled to Abu Dhabi [*q.v.*] along with his family. In September the investigative judge charged him, along

the two sons of Hosni Mubarak [*q.v.*]
—Alaa and Gamal—with profiteering
and facilitating the seizure of public
funds to expedite the sale of land in
Ismailia province. The General Prosecutor asked Interpol to arrest him.

Shah, Muhammad Reza: *See* Pahlavi,
Muhammad Reza Shah.

Shah, Reza: *See* Pahlavi, Reza Shah.

Shamir, Yitzhak (1915–2011): *Israeli
politician; prime minister, 1983–84,
1986–92* Born Yitzhak Yazernitsky
into a religious family in Rozana,
Belarus, he attended a Hebrew [*q.v.*]
high school in the Polish town of Bi-
alystok where he joined the Revisionist Zionist [*q.v.*] youth
movement, *Betar*. He cut short his
studies at Warsaw University to migrate to Palestine [*q.v.*] in 1935. Two
years later he joined Irgun Zvai
Leumi [*q.v.*]. When Irgun split in
1940, with Avraham Stern [*q.v.*]
forming Lehi [*q.v.*], Shamir followed
Stern.

He was jailed by the British authorities in 1941, but escaped. Following
Stern's assassination in 1942, he
became one of the three commanders
of Lehi, in charge of operations. In
1944 two Lehi operators, Eliahou Bet
Zouri and Eliahou al-Hakim, assassinated Britain's resident-minister in
the Middle East [*q.v.*] in Cairo [*q.v.*].
Arrested by the British in 1946,
Shamir was dispatched to a detention
camp in Eritrea. Four months later he
escaped and found his way to Paris via
the French colony of Djibouti.

Soon after the founding of Israel in
May 1948, Shamir arrived in
Jerusalem [*q.v.*] and took charge of

Lehi. In September the assassination
in Jerusalem of Count Folke
Bernadotte, a Swedish diplomat acting
as the UN mediator between Arabs
[*q.v.*] and Jews [*q.v.*], was claimed by
Hazit HaMoledet (Hebrew: *The Homeland Front*), a sub-group of Lehi. Two
Lehi leaders, Nathan Yellin-Mor and
Matitiahu Schmulevitz were found
guilty and given eight and five years'
imprisonment, respectively.

After the disbanding of Lehi in
1949, Shamir turned to business. In
1955 he joined Mossad [*q.v.*] and
served in various senior positions until
1965. After running a mattress factory
for five years he reentered politics by
joining the Herut Party [*q.v.*]. Three
years later he became chairman of the
Herut Executive Committee, and in the
December 1973 election he won a seat
in the Knesset [*q.v.*]. Reelected in 1977
as a member of Likud [*q.v.*], he served
as speaker for the next three years. He
opposed the Camp David Accords
[*q.v.*] negotiated by Likud leader
Menachem Begin [*q.v.*]. In the Knesset
vote on the accords, he abstained. He
was named foreign minister in 1980.

Following Begin's retirement in
1983, he won the contest for party
leadership and became prime minister
while retaining the foreign affairs
portfolio. He inherited a military
imbroglio in Lebanon, along with
hyperinflation and the collapse of several banks. After the inconclusive result of the 1984 election, he reached a
rotation accord with Labor [*q.v.*]
leader Shimon Peres [*q.v.*] to form a
national unity government. He served
as deputy premier and foreign minister until 1986 and then became prime
minister. After the 1988 election he
managed to retain his leadership of a

coalition government which, until March 1990, included Labor and then survived without Labor's support for the next two years.

In October 1991 he participated in the Middle East Peace Conference in Madrid [*q.v.*] while insisting on expanding Jewish settlements in the Occupied Arab Territories [*q.v.*]. The bilateral negotiations between Israel and its Arab neighbors made no progress because, as he would reveal after losing the June 1992 election, he had planned to drag out the talks for 10 years. In 1993 he stepped down as Likud leader. He was reelected to the Knesset in 1996 and 1999.

He spent the last eight years of his life in a nursing home.

Sharett, Moshe (1894–1965): *Israeli politician; prime minister, 1953–55*
Born Moshe Shertok in Kherson, Ukraine, into a religious Zionist [*q.v.*] family that migrated to Palestine [*q.v.*] in 1906, he graduated from a Jewish school in Tel Aviv [*q.v.*]. During World War I he joined the Ottoman Turkish military and rose to become an officer. In 1922 he enrolled at the London School of Economics and Political Science and graduated three years later.

On his return to Palestine [*q.v.*] in 1925, he became a member of the editorial board of *Davar* (Hebrew: *Word*), the Histadrut [*q.v.*] newspaper. An activist of the Ahdut HaAvodah [*q.v.*], he joined Mapai [*q.v.*] on its formation in 1930. Three years later he succeeded Chaim Arlosoroff [*q.v.*] as chief of the Jewish Agency's [*q.v.*] political department. In that role, he campaigned against the 1939 British White paper, which restricted Jewish immigration into Palestine. During World War II he encouraged the Palestinian Jews [*q.v.*] to join the British army and helped to establish a Jewish brigade. After the war he led a Zionist political campaign that culminated in the United Nations resolving to partition Palestine in November 1947.

Following the founding of Israel six months later, Sharett was named foreign minister. He was elected to the Knesset [*q.v.*] in 1949 and retained a seat until his death. His pressure on Washington to sell arms to Israel led to the issuing of the Tripartite Declaration by the United States, Britain, and France [*q.v.*] in May 1950, which declared its opposition to any attempt to alter the truce boundaries fixed at the end of the 1948–49 Arab-Israeli War [*q.v.*] by force. He backed the U.S. when the Korean War started in June 1950. While Sharett and Prime Minister David Ben-Gurion [*q.v.*] agreed on the substance of foreign policy, his moderate, diplomatic style clashed with Ben-Gurion's hard, militarist style.

Sharett succeeded Ben-Gurion when he resigned his office in 1953. From January 1954 Sharett was also foreign minister. His attempts to seek a peaceful settlement with Egypt were fatally undermined by the sabotage carried out by the Egyptian Jews acting as Israeli agents, as planned by the defense ministry under Pinchas Lavon [*q.v.*], and Israel's reprisals against Egyptian-administered Gaza [*q.v.*] after the execution of the Israeli agents' leaders.

When the July 1955 election resulted in Ben-Gurion's leading the government, he put Sharret in charge of the foreign ministry. A year later, the differences between him and Ben-Gurion, as the prime minister planned an attack on Egypt, became so sharp that he resigned from the cabinet. He became the chief of Histadrut's publishing company. In 1960 he was elected chairman of the Jewish Agency's executive committee.

Sharia (Arabic: *way* or *road*): *Islamic law* Consisting of divine revelation in the form of the Quran [*q.v.*], and the Prophetic Muhammad's practice, *sunna* [*q.v.*] (as recorded in the Hadith [*q.v.*]), the Sharia completely governs the individual and social life of the believer. The Quran provides the principles and the Hadith the details of their application. The Sharia is the basis for judging actions as good or evil.

By the time the Hadith had been compiled into six canonical collections in the mid-10th century A.D., the religious jurisprudents had studied all human actions and categorized them as obligatory (performance is rewarded, omission punished), recommended (performance is rewarded, omission is not punished), indifferent (neither punished nor rewarded), undesirable (disapproved but not punished), and prohibited (punished, with the degree of punishment depending on the severity of the sin—grave, venial, or trespass). There were differences between Sunnis [*q.v.*] and Shias [*q.v.*] with regard to obligatory actions, the former prescribing five obligations and Shias enjoining more.

After categorizing human actions, jurisprudents graduated to prescribing exactly how the obligatory and recommended acts were to be performed.

They also minutely pondered all bodily functions—eating, drinking, breathing, washing, urinating, defecating, farting, copulating, vomiting, bleeding, shaving—and prescribed how these were to be performed or dealt with, stressing the need to keep the body pure. Along with this went a code of social behavior which too was all-encompassing. The twin codes were so demanding that, even with the best will in the world, a believer was unable to abide by them all the time. On the other hand, it was the introduction of these codes into the lives of those who embraced Islam that has led to common behavioral patterns among all Muslims, whether they lived in the Mauritanian desert or the Indonesian archipelago.

Shariati, Ali (1933–77): *Iranian Islamic thinker* Born into the family of an Islamic intellectual in Mazinan village near Mashhad [*q.v.*], Shariati grew up partly in Mazinan and partly in Mashhad. During the oil nationalization crisis of 1951–53 he backed Muhammad Mussadiq [*q.v.*] and was detained briefly. Trained as a teacher, he taught in elementary schools in rural areas. In 1956, after Mashhad University had set up a faculty of letters, he was able to pursue further studies in Arabic [*q.v.*] and French while working as a teacher.

Three years later he won a government scholarship to study sociology and Islamic studies at Paris University. He strove for a sociology that would interpret and analyze the realities of life in the Third World. In Paris he met many intellectuals, philosophers, and scholars on Islam [*q.v.*]. He was influenced by the Algerian anti-imperialist struggle, which triumphed in 1962, and its ideologue, Franz Fanon. However, while translating Fanon's *Wretched of the Earth* into Persian, he challenged his views on religion and revolution.

After receiving his doctorate in sociology and theology in 1964, he traveled home overland with his family and was arrested at the Turkish-Iranian frontier as a suspected subversive. Released six months later, he returned to his job as a teacher at a village school, then graduated to teaching at Mashhad University. After being dismissed from his post, he moved to Tehran [*q.v.*] in 1967, where he lectured at the Husseinyeh Ershad, a socio-religious institution run by the Liberation Movement of Iran [*q.v.*]. His lectures, later published in 50 volumes, proved popular with college and senior high school students. In 1972 the government closed down the Husseinyeh Ershad, arrested Shariati, and banned most of his works. Three years later it placed him under house arrest. In May 1977 he was allowed to travel abroad. He went to Britain and died in Southampton in June—of a heart attack, according to the coroner's report.

Bitterly opposed to the regime of Muhammad Reza Shah Pahlavi [*q.v.*], Shariati advocated participation in politics by the masses. He argued that Islam was not a conservative, fatalistic creed, but a revolutionary one, encompassing all aspects of life, particularly politics, that inspired the true believer to struggle against all forms of oppression, exploitation, and social injustice. Shariati found his inspiration in Shia Islam [*q.v.*] and his tools of analysis in Western social sciences. He did not want Twelver Shias [*q.v.*] to wait for the reappearance of the Hidden Iman, but to act forthwith to create a society based on equality. He was opposed to imperialism—political, economic, and cultural. In his *Intermediate School of Thought* (1973) he argued that Islam could be seen as an intermediate between socialism and capitalism, which adopted the advantages and positive aspects of other schools of thought while avoiding their negative aspects.

Shariatmadari, Muhammad Kazem

(1903–86): *Iranian Islamic leader* Born into a religious, Azeri-speaking [*q.v.*] family in Tabriz [*q.v.*], Shariatmadari went to Qom [*q.v.*] to undertake Islamic studies. After a decade in that city, he traveled to Najaf [*q.v.*] for further theological education. Returning to Tabriz in the late 1930s, he became a religious teacher. In 1950 he again moved to Qom, where he found himself in tune with the conservative Shia [*q.v.*] leader, Ayatollah Muhammad Hussein Borujerdi, and rose steadily in the clerical ranks. After Borujerdi's death in 1961, he was elevated to the rank of grand ayatollah, sharing this rare honor with two other clerics, Muhammad Reza Golpaygani [*q.v.*] and Shehab al-Din Marashi Najafi.

During the June 1963 protest against the government-sponsored White Revolution [*q.v.*], he was arrested, but the experience did not radicalize him. In June 1970, when Muhammad Reza Shah Pahlavi [*q.v.*] sent his condolences on the death of Ayatollah Muhsin Hakim, the seniormost Shia cleric based in Najaf, Shariatmadari reaffirmed his loyalty to the monarch, thus widening the gap between himself and radical Ayatollah Ruhollah Khomeini [*q.v.*], who had been expelled from Iran five years earlier.

In January 1978, after the security forces had broken into his theological college in Qom and killed two of his students, he voiced opposition and demanded the return to the 1906–07 constitution. But it was not until the massacre of unarmed civilians by the security forces on 8 September 1978 in Tehran [*q.v.*], that he hardened his stance. After the shah had installed a military government in November 1978, Shariatmadari joined his two fellow grand ayatollahs in Qom in their call for the dismantling of the political system. Nonetheless, when Shahpur Bakhtiar [*q.v.*] was appointed prime minister by the shah in early January 1979, Shariatmadari backed him.

After the revolution in February, Khomeini's leadership was balanced by Ayatollah Mahmoud Taleqani [*q.v.*] on the left, and Shariatmadari on the right. With Taleqani's death in September, the Islamic establishment became bipolar, with Shariatmadari leading the clerics, who advocated non-intervention by the clergy in the day-to-day running of the government, and Khomeini heading the interventionist camp. He lost. He abstained in the referendum on the Islamic constitution in December 1979, objecting to the excessive powers given to the Supreme Leader, Khomeini, and condemned the seizure of the American diplomats as hostages [*q.v.*]. Differences between him and Khomeini became irreconcilable, resulting in their respective followers clashing in the streets of Tabriz and Qom in January 1980. He emerged as the loser, and found himself placed under house arrest.

Secret documents retrieved from the United Embassy showed that he had accepted funds for promoting non-alcoholic American drinks in Iran, and that he had contacts in the U.S. Central Intelligence Agency (CIA). After the arrest of his son-in-law, Ahmad Abbasi, in April 1982 for coplotting a coup—to be led by Sadiq Qutbzadeh, foreign minister from 1979 to 1980—the police raided his house and seminary and publicized his clandestine links with the CIA. Four years later he died of natural causes.

Sharjah Emirate: *a constituent of the United Arab Emirates* Area 1,000 sq. mi./2,600 sq. km; population 946,000 (2010 est.). Sharjah, ruled by Shaikh Sultan bin Muhammad al-Qasimi (r. 1972–), is a founder member of the United Arab Emirates. Before the start of commercial extraction of oil in 1974, which reached 60,000 barrels a day two decades later, a large part of its income came from commemorative stamps, printed almost solely for philatelic purposes. Its gas reserves amount to 321.5 billion cu m, and the annual output is 4.1 billion a year.

Sharon, Ariel (1928–): *Israeli military officer and politician; prime minister, 2001–2006* Born Ariel Shinerman into a Zionist [*q.v.*] family in Kafr Malal, Palestine [*q.v.*], Sharon joined Haganah [*q.v.*] as a youth. He fought in the Arab-Israeli War (1948–49) [*q.v.*] and continued his military career, working as an intelligence officer. He established Unit 101, composed exclusively of volunteers, to carry out swift cross-border reprisal attacks—with one such operation against an Egyptian military camp in Gaza in

February 1955 resulting in 38 Egyptian deaths. When Unit 101 was incorporated into the paratroopers later in the year, he became a paratroop commander.

During the Suez War in 1956 [q.v.], Sharon, leading a brigade, exceeded his orders and engaged in a battle that ended in many casualties. This slowed down his promotion. Only when Yitzhak Rabin [q.v.] became chief of staff in 1965 was Sharon promoted to head the training department of the general staff. Two years later he became a brigadier-general.

In the June 1967 Arab-Israeli War [q.v.] he commanded a division on the southern front, capturing the Umm Katif range in the Sinai [q.v.]. In 1969 he was put in charge of the southern command. His iron-fist policy toward the Palestinian resistance to the Israeli occupation of the West Bank [q.v.] and Gaza [q.v.] proved controversial.

In mid-1973 he quit the army and entered politics by joining Gahal [q.v.]. He was instrumental in the creation of Likud [q.v.] out of the merger of Gahal, the Free Center, the State Party (a remnant of Rafi, a breakaway faction of Mapai [q.v.]), and the Eretz Yisrael [q.v.] movement. During the October 1973 Arab-Israeli War [q.v.], his conduct as the commander of a division proved controversial. Disregarding the strategy of his superiors to keep his division as a reserve force, he deployed it to establish a bridgehead over the Suez Canal [q.v.].

After being elected to the Knesset [q.v.] in December 1973, he resigned after some months to serve Labor Prime Minister Rabin as an adviser. In 1976 he formed his own group—Shlomzion (Hebrew: *Peaceful Zion*)—

which won two seats in the 1977 election. He merged his group with the Herut [q.v.] faction of Likud, and became minister of agriculture in the Likud-dominated government. He was also appointed chairman of the cabinet's (Jewish) settlement committee. Following the 1981 elections, he was named defense minister.

Once Israel had withdrawn its troops from the Sinai in April 1982, Sharon finalized his plans to attack Lebanon. Having launched the campaign with the ostensible aim of capturing a strip of Lebanese territory to rid it of Palestinian guerrillas, he expanded it into a fully fledged war, advancing to Beirut [q.v.], besieging it for 63 days and bombarding it mercilessly from land, air, and sea. After securing the departure of Syrian and Palestine Liberation Organization (PLO) [q.v.] troops from Beirut, he set out to become the kingmaker in the Lebanese politics by getting Bashir Gemayel [q.v.] elected president in September. He succeeded, only to see his protégé assassinated before he could take office.

Sharon allowed his Maronite [q.v.] allies a free hand to murder some 2,000 Palestinians [q.v.] in the refugee camps of Sabra and Shatila. A demonstration by 400,000 Israelis compelled the government to appoint a commission of inquiry, headed by the Supreme Court's chief judge, Yitzhak Kahan. Following a critical report by this commission, Sharon was forced to resign as defense minister in February 1983, although he retained his place in the cabinet as a minister without portfolio.

In the national unity government formed in September 1984, Prime

Minister Shimon Peres [*q.v.*] appointed him minister of trade and industry, and a member of the inner political cabinet. He held these jobs until January 1990. In the reconstituted cabinet led by Yitzhak Shamir [*q.v.*] in May 1990, he served as minister of housing and accelerated the building of Jewish settlements on the West Bank. After the Likud's defeat in the June 1992 election, Sharon lost his preeminence in Israeli politics.

However, in 1996, Prime Minister Benjamin Netanyahu [*q.v.*] put him in charge of a newly created ministry of infrastructure, elevating him to minister of foreign affairs in October 1998. After Netanyahu's defeat in the prime ministerial contest in 1999, followed by his withdrawal from politics, Sharon was elected leader of the Likud.

Escorted by 1,000 armed police, Sharon toured the Noble Sanctuary/ Table Mount [*q.v.*] in Jerusalem [*q.v.*] on 28 September 2000— a move designed to underscore Israeli sovereignty over Islam's third-holiest site. The Palestinian demonstration that followed after the Friday midday prayers at the Al Aqsa Mosque the next day was dispersed by the Israeli security forces with live ammunition, leaving seven protestors dead. This marked the start of the al-Aqsa Intifada [*q.v.*].

Sharon entered the February 2001 prime ministerial contest on a platform of continued expansion of Jewish settlements in the Palestinian Territories [*q.v.*], Israeli sovereignty over all of Jerusalem, and no talks with the Palestinians until there was complete cessation of terrorism. He secured 62.4 percent of the vote versus 37.6 percent for the incumbent, Ehud

Barak [*q.v.*]. His subsequent national unity government included Labor [*q.v.*], now led by Binyamin Ben-Elizier. Israeli-Palestinian violence escalated while the newly installed U.S. administration of President George W. Bush pursued a hands-off policy.

Following the terrorist attacks on the United States in September, Sharon attempted but failed to get the Palestinian resistance to Israeli military occupation equated to terrorism. He responded to periodic suicide bombings by the Palestinians with escalating force, pursuing his strategic aim of destroying the security and administrative infrastructure of the Palestinian Authority (PA) [*q.v.*] by deploying armed helicopters, fighter aircraft, and gunboats, and ordering assassinations of suspected terrorists. Retaliating for a particularly lethal Palestinian suicide bombing in Israel on 27 March 2002, Sharon ordered the reoccupation of all the towns under Palestinian Authority (except Hebron [*q.v.*] and Jericho [*q.v.*]), thus effectively abrogating the Oslo Accords [*q.v.*].

His defiance of President Bush's advice to vacate the occupied Palestinian towns was rewarded with an invitation to the White House and the sobriquet of "man of peace." He put PA President Yasser Arafat [*q.v.*] under house arrest in Ramallah.

In the Knesset election of January 2003, his Likud [*q.v.*] party improved its strength from 19 to 37. The next year, having realized that Israel's long-term survival rested on safeguarding its Jewish majority by preventing Palestinian Arabs [*q.v.*] from becoming the majority in the future if Israel incorporated the Occupied Territories [*q.v.*], he decided to vacate the Gaza

Strip. In September 2005, he withdrew the Israeli military from the Gaza Strip, but maintained control of its air space and territorial waters.

In December, he went into a coma after a series of heart attacks and was hospitalized. In 2011 he was moved to his home in the Negev, which was equipped with adequate medical facilities.

Shas (Hebrew: *abbreviation of* Shomere Torah, *Guardians of Torah*): *Israeli political party* Shas was formed in 1984 by the breakaway members of Agudat Israel [*q.v.*]. Its major backing came from Sephardic Jews [*q.v.*], many of them of Moroccan origin, who were critical of the Ashkenazi [*q.v.*] leadership of the existing religious political parties. Led by Moroccan-born Rabbi Arye Deri, it won four seats in the 1984 general election and six in 1988 and 1992. It joined the national unity governments formed in 1984 and 1988.

After the 1992 election it participated in the Labor-led coalition government, and went along with the Oslo Accords [*q.v.*], its spiritual leader Rabbi Ovaida Yosef declaring that peace was more important than territory. Despite the arrest of Deri on charges of corruption, Shas improved its size in the 1996 Knesset [*q.v.*] to 10 seats. It coalesced with Likud [*q.v.*]. In the 1999 general election, its strength rose to 17, and it joined the government led by Labor's Ehud Barak [*q.v.*]. When Barak lost office two years later, Shas joined the national unity government headed by Ariel Sharon [*q.v.*].

In his Passover [*q.v.*] sermon in 2001, Rabbi Yosef remarked that "enemies" had tried to hurt the Jewish people from the time of the exodus from Egypt. "It is forbidden to be merciful to Arabs. You must send missiles to them and annihilate them. They are evil and damnable." This statement earned Yosef nothing more than mild criticism from the Israeli minister of justice.

In the 2003 Knesset election, the strength of Shas declined to 11. By attacking the neo-liberal economic policies of the government it gained one more seat in the subsequent general election in 2006. It joined the coalition government led by Ehud Olmert [*q.v.*]. After securing 11 seats in the 2009 general election it joined the coalition administration led by Benjamin Netanyahu [*q.v.*], four of its members becoming ministers.

Along with the United Torah Judaism [*q.v.*], Shas continues to defend religious educational institutions and generous state benefits.

Shatt al-Arab (Arabic: *The Arab Stream*): (Called Arund Rud by Iranians) Beginning at Qurna, Iraq, with the confluence of the Euphrates [*q.v.*] and Tigris [*q.v.*] rivers, the Shatt al-Arab flows 120 mi./190 km southeast into the Gulf [*q.v.*], its width increasing from 150 ft./46 m at Basra [*q.v.*] to 2,000 ft./610 m at its mouth, and its discharge rising to 49,400 cu ft. per second or 1,400 cu m per second. For the last two-fifths of its length, it forms a fluvial border between Iran and Iraq. The demarcation of this frontier was a contentious issue between the two neighbors for a long time. The 1975 Algiers Accord [*q.v.*] settled the dispute for a while, but it was revived by Iraq five years later on the eve of its invasion of Iran, resulting in the Iran-Iraq War [*q.v.*]. In August 1990 Iraq stated its acceptance of the Algiers Accord, which divided the Shatt al-Arab between the two sides along the deepest channel.

Shazar, Shneor Zalman (1889–1974): *Israeli politician; president 1963–73* Born Shneor Rubashov of a religious family in Saint Petersburg, Russia, Shazar joined the Poale Zion [*q.v.*] as a youth and assisted the group's leader, Don Ber Borochov [*q.v.*], in editing the party periodical. During World War I he was a research student in Berlin, where he cofounded a branch of the Poale Zion.

In 1924 he migrated to Palestine [*q.v.*], where he participated actively in politics and journalism. He became a leader of Ahdut HaAvodah [*q.v.*] and from 1930 of Mapai [*q.v.*], as well as being a member of the Histadrut [*q.v.*] Executive Committee and one of the editors of the Histadrut daily, *Davar* (Hebrew: *Word*). In 1944 he was appointed editor-in-chief of the newspaper.

Elected to the First Knesset [*q.v.*] in 1949, he served as education minister from 1949 to 1950. After he had left the government he was elected to the Jewish Agency Executive Committee, becoming head of the department of education and culture in the diaspora [*q.v.*], and then acting chairman of the Jewish Agency Executive Committee from 1957 to 1961. Two years later he was elected president of Israel, and was reelected in 1968.

Shehab, Fouad: *See* Chehab, Fouad.

Shia (Arabic*: Partisan*): *Islamic sect* Shia or Shiat means Shia/Shiat Ali, Partisans of Ali, cousin and son-in-law of the Prophet Muhammad (570–632 A.D.). By advocating strict adherence to the Quran [*q.v.*] and the *sunna* [*q.v.*], Ali came to represent idealism in Islam [*q.v.*]. His camp drew most of its support from pious Muslims [*q.v.*] and non-Arab Muslim clients, who felt discriminated against by Arab [*q.v.*] Muslims. They were an important part of the coalition that engineered the Abbasid revolution in 751 A.D. against the Umayyad caliphs (661–750 A.D.) who, in their view, had deviated widely from the true Islamic path.

But it was not long before the Sunni [*q.v.*] Abbasid caliphs too began to slip away from the Quran and the *sunna*, thus allowing Shias to become the sole repositories of the vision of ideal Islam. The consequences were the subjugation of the Sunni caliph in Baghdad [*q.v.*] by a Shia king, Muizz al-Dawla al-Buyid, in 932 A.D., and the emergence of an Ismaili [*q.v.*] Shia caliphate, the Fatimids, in Cairo [*q.v.*] in 969 A.D. By then three branches of Shia Islam had crystallized: Zaidis [*q.v.*], Ismailis, and Imamis [*q.v.*].

During the Buyid hegemony in Baghdad (932–1055 A.D.), two collections of the Shia Hadith [*q.v.*] were codified. Shia domination lasted many generations, losing its grip first in Baghdad in 1055 and then in Cairo in 1171. Today Shias are a minority: 12–15 percent of the total global Muslim population of 1.62 billion. Of the 57 members of the Islamic Conference Organization (ICO) [*q.v.*] in 2011, only Bahrain, Iran, Iraq, and Azerbaijan were Shia-majority countries.

Shias differ from Sunnis [*q.v.*] in doctrine, ritual, law, theology, and religious organization. The Shia credo consists of five basic principles and 10 duties. While sharing three principles with Sunnis—monotheism, i.e., there is only one God; prophet-hood, which is a means of communication between God and humankind; and resurrection, i.e., the souls of dead human beings will be raised by God on their Day of Judgment and their deeds on earth judged—Shias have two more: *imamat* [*q.v.*] and *aadl* (justice), the just nature of Allah. Their duties include daily prayers, fasting during Ramadan [*q.v.*], *khums* (an Islamic tithe) [*q.v.*], *zakat* (alms tax) [*q.v.*], hajj (pilgrimage to Mecca [*q.v.*]), encouraging virtue, discouraging evil, and loving Shia Imams [*q.v.*] and their followers.

Shias believe that only those in the lineage of the Prophet Muhammad—and thus of his daughter, Fatima, and her husband, Ali—can govern Muslims on behalf of Allah, and that the Imams, being divinely inspired, are infallible. Shias insist that the ruler must be just, and that the Quran bears a pledge of sovereignty of the earth to the oppressed. Rooted in this pledge are the concepts of the return of the Hidden Imam—the arrival of the Mahdi [*q.v.*]—and the rehabilitation of society: that is, history is moving toward a predetermined goal and the forces of injustice will ultimately be defeated. This acts as a spur toward radical activism. (In contrast, Sunnis view Islamic history essentially as a drift away from the ideal community that existed under the rule of the first four Rightly Guided caliphs: Abu Bakr, Omar, Othman, and Ali.)

The Shia ethos is different from the Sunni. Shia emotionalism finds outlets in mourning Imams Ali (assassinated), Hassan (poisoned), and Hussein (killed in battle), and in the heart-rending entreaties offered at their shrines. Shias believe that through asceticism and suffering one can remove the ill effects of the humiliation and persecution inflicted on them. During the Ashura [*q.v.*], the annual enactment of passion plays about the martyrdom of Imam Hussein, along with self-flagellation by the faithful, provide outlets for expiating the guilt and pain originally felt by the inhabitants of Kufa [*q.v.*] for abandoning Imam Hussein after having invited him to their city to take charge. Sunni Islam offers no such outlets for its followers.

Finally, Shias and Sunnis organize religion and religious activities differently. Sunnis regard religious activities as the exclusive domain of the (Muslim) state. When the ulema [*q.v.*] act as judges or preachers or educators they do so under the aegis of the state. There is scant opportunity for the ulema to organize religion on their own. In contrast, in Shia Iran, free of the Sunni Ottoman or Christian European influence, the leading *mujtahids* [*q.v.*], being recipients of the *khums* from their followers, maintained theological colleges and social welfare activities independent of the state. Also, by adopting the custom of naming the most revered colleague as the *marja-e taqlid* (source of emulation) [*q.v.*], whose independent opinion on the compatibility of major state decisions with Islam had to be sought, the religious hierarchy underlined its independence. Unlike in the Sunni religious establishment, Shia clerics are ranked from *thiqatalislam* (trust of Islam) to *hojatalislam* (proof of Islam) to *ayatollah* (sign of Allah) to *ayatollah-ozma* (grand ayatollah).

Shiat Ali (Arabic: *Partisan of Ali*): *See* Shias.

Shiite: *See* Shia.

Shin Beth (Hebrew: *acronym of* Sherut Betakhon, *Security Service*): *Israeli domestic security service* When Israel was founded in 1948, Shin Beth, headed by Isser Harel (1948–52), was the only civilian intelligence agency and covered domestic and foreign fields.

After the formation of the foreign intelligence service, Mossad [*q.v.*], in 1951, Shin Beth's operations division was subdivided into three wings: Arab affairs department dealing with Palestinians [*q.v.*], Israeli Arabs [*q.v.*], and other Arabs, with an undercover detachment; non-Arab affairs department dealing with all non-Arab countries, including penetrating their foreign intelligence services and diplomatic missions in Israel, and surveillance of diplomats and foreign delegations, and counterintelligence; and protective security department, charged with safeguarding public buildings and embassies, high Israeli officials, defense industries, scientific installations, industrial plants, and the national airline.

In the early 1950s one of the Israeli groups that drew Shin Beth's attention was Mapam [*q.v.*], then a partner in the Mapai-led [*q.v.*] coalition, because of its warm relations with the Soviet Union.

After the June 1967 Arab-Israeli War [*q.v.*], Shin Beth started safe-guarding Israel from its opponents within the Occupied Arab Territories [*q.v.*]. To do this it set up a network of Palestinian informers, and made the local populace feel that they were everywhere. When, from later 1968, Palestinian groups started attacking Israeli aircraft on the ground or hijacking them, Shin Beth, then headed by Yosef Harmelin (1964–74), extended its operations abroad in pursuit of the terrorists. Following the assassination of Israeli athletes at the Olympics in Munich in September 1972 by the Black September Organization [*q.v.*], Shin Beth started running joint operations with Mossad in the hit-and-run campaign against the Palestinian terrorists.

During the directorship of Avraham Ahituv (1974–81) Shin Beth put under surveillance Kach [*q.v.*], founded by Rabbi Meir Kahane [*q.v.*]. It also found itself coping with terrorism by the Jewish extremists in the Occupied Territories [*q.v.*] and Jerusalem [*q.v.*], which led among other things to the maiming by car bomb of two West Bank [*q.v.*] mayors in June 1980. The problem continued under Ahituv's successor, Avraham Shalom (1981–86), with the Jewish terrorists killing four Arab students and injuring 33 in an attack on the Islamic College in Hebron [*q.v.*] in July 1983, and plotting to blow up the Dome of the Rock and al-Aqsa Mosque in the spring of 1984. The unearthing of a cell of 20 Jewish fanatics followed Shin Beth's discovery of 12 bombs attached to Arab buses in East Jerusalem [*q.v.*].

In order to weaken the Palestine Liberation Organization (PLO) [*q.v.*], Shin Beth actively fostered Islamic groups among Palestinians in the late 1970s and early 1980s, a policy that culminated in the rise of Hamas [*q.v.*] in the wake of the intifada [*q.v.*]. The United National Leadership of the Uprising (UNLU) [*q.v.*] resorted to targeting Israeli agents and informers, which numbered about 20,000 in a population of 1.6 million. This proved so effective that the Shin Beth chief, Yosef Harmelin (1986–88), privately conceded the virtual demise of the informer network built up over a generation.

Having failed to penetrate the UNLU, Shin Bet, then directed by Yaakov Peri (1988–94), cooperated with the Israeli military to train special units of Arabic-speaking Israeli soldiers in civilian dress and dispatch them to the Occupied Territories to mix with the local population. They were also used to carry out executions of suspected Palestinian terrorists.

With the signing of the Israeli-PLO Accord [*q.v.*] in September 1993, Shin Beth started protecting PLO Chairman Yasser Arafat [*q.v.*]. After the founding of the Palestinian Authority [*q.v.*] in July 1994, Shin Beth focused on penetrating its institutions. Its main area of recruitment shifted to those Palestinians who were allowed to work in Israel. The shrinking size of this pool against the background of a revival of the Israeli-Palestinian conflict after the assassination of Israeli Prime Minister Yitzhak Rabin [*q.v.*] in November 1995 proved no barrier to Shin Beth's success in recruiting Palestinian agents.

The launching of the Al Aqsa Intifada [*q.v.*] in September 2000 opened a new chapter in the history of Shin Beth, then led by Avi Ditcher (2000-2005). As the Israeli-Palestinian violence escalated, the number and frequency of Shin Beth's assassinations of suspected terrorists of all political hues, religious or secular, increased. Later it extended its policy of assassination to the leaders of Hamas [*q.v.*], claiming the lives of inter alia Ahmad Yasin [*q.v.*] and Abdul Aziz Rantisi in 2004. In its "targeted killings program," often involving the use of drones and helicopter gunships, it works closely with the air force.

In May 2011 Yoram Cohen succeeded Avi Dichter as director of Shin Beth. Five months later he was involved in the Egyptian-mediated deal for the freeing of Israeli soldier Gilad Shalit, captured by Hamas operatives inside Israel in June 2006, in exchange for the release of 1,027 Palestinian prisoners.

Shinui (Hebrew: *Change*): *Israeli political party* (Official title: *Shinui—Mifleget HaMerkaz* [Change—Party of the Center]) Shinui was formed by Amnon Rubinstein in 1974 as a protest group in the aftermath of the October 1973 Arab-Israeli War [*q.v.*]. It called for direct talks with Arab neighbors on the basis of territorial compromise and advocated liberalization of the Israeli economy. In 1978 it combined with the remnants of the Democratic Movement for Change. It won three Knesset [*q.v.*] seats in the 1984 election and joined the national unity government. In 1986 it absorbed the Center Liberal Party and the Independent Liberal Party, and quit the government in May 1987. It won two seats in the 1988 election.

Later it allied with Mapam [*q.v.*] and Ratz [*q.v.*] to form the Meretz [*q.v.*] alliance on a platform that included separation of religion and state. Of the 12 seats secured by Meretz in the 1992 election, two belonged to Shinui, which joined the Labor-led [*q.v.*] coalition. In the 1996 election it maintained its strength.

In the 1999 Knesset election, led by Yosef Lapid (aka, Tommy Lapid), Shinui entered the fray on its own on a strongly secular platform, strongly attacking the privileges enjoyed by the Orthodox [*q.v.*] and ultra-Orthodox Jews [*q.v.*]. It won six seats and refused to join a coalition that included any religious group. Its principled stand paid dividends in the 2003 election when, securing 15 seats, it emerged as the third-largest group in the Knesset, a position previously held by Shas [*q.v.*]. With the formation of Kadima [*q.v.*] in November 2005, it lost most if its constituency. It split into factions, none of which managed to pass the threshold of 2 percent of the ballots in the 2006 Knesset election.

Shiraz: *Iranian city* Population: 1.35 million (2011 est.). The recorded history of Shiraz dates back to the period of the conquests by Alexander of Macedonia (r. 336–323 B.C.). Part of the Fars region, it was a leading settlement during the reigns of the Seleucids (312–175 B.C.), Parthians (247 B.C.–226 A.D.), and Sassaniand (226–640 A.D.). After the defeat of the Sassanians by Muslim [*q.v.*] Arabs [*q.v.*], Shiraz entered the Islamic era. By the late 14th century, as the birthplace of Saadi (d. 1291) and Hafiz (d. 1389), outstanding Persian poets, and

the site of the Congregational Mosque (894 A.D.), the New Mosque (1215), the Great Library (1218), and the Shah Chiragh Shirne (1349), it competed with Baghdad [*q.v.*] as a center of learning and piety.

Its fame attracted Tamerlane (1336–1405), the Mongol conqueror, who occupied it in 1387 and 1393. The city was sacked by Afghan invaders in 1724. It became the capital of the Zand dynasty (1750–94), whose founder, Karim Khan Zand, endowed it with outstanding buildings, including his mausoleum and the citadel. It was here that in 1844 Ali Muhammad Shirazi declared that he was the *bab* (Arabic: *gate*) to the Hidden Imam, thus establishing the Babi movement [*q.v.*].

Besides the Islamic monuments and the garden tombs of Saadi and Hafiz, the city also offers as a tourist attraction the Church of Saint Simon the Zealot.

Shishkali, Adib (1901–64): *Syrian military leader and politician; president, 1953–54* Born into a middle-class Sunni [*q.v.*] family in Hama [*q.v.*], Shishkali pursued a military career by joining the Special Forces of the French Mandate. A nationalist officer, he backed Rashid Ali Gailani [*q.v.*] in his fight with the British in 1941. He participated in the May 1945 uprising against the French. After Syria's independence in 1946, he fought the Zionists [*q.v.*] in the 1948–49 Palestine War [*q.v.*]. He played an important role in the coup by Col. Hosni Zaim [*q.v.*] in March 1949, but lost his military post on suspicion of disloyalty. After Col. Sami Hinnawi had seized power from Zaim in mid-August, he reinstated Shishkali, only to see himself overthrown by Shishkali four months later.

Shishkali left intact the parliamentary regime established by Hinnawi, with Nur al-Din Attasi [*q.v.*] as president, and merely named himself deputy chief of staff. He was keen to reduce the influence of monarchical Iraq on Syrian politics. In late 1951 when Marouf Dwalibi, the pro-Iraqi leader of the People's Party, charged with forming the next government, refused to appoint his spokesman, General Fawzi Selu, as defense minister, he dissolved the parliament and dismissed President Attasi. He named Selu as president and prime minister.

After banning all political parties in 1952, he founded the Arab Liberation Movement. But it failed to strike roots, and the parliament dominated by it remained unrepresentative. In June 1953 he appointed himself prime minister, and then got elected president with wide powers in a referendum.

A soldier at heart, Shishkali lacked a socioeconomic ideology with which to shape his policies. His attempts at reform proved ill-conceived. His high-handedness toward the Alawi [*q.v.*] and Druze [*q.v.*] minorities created opposition to his rule in the Alawi and Druze regions. Hostile toward the Soviet Union but aware of the dangers of aligning with the United States or Britain, he sought the active cooperation of France.

A spate of strikes and demonstrations in Aleppo [*q.v.*] and elsewhere, caused by his mishandling of minor violence in the Druze Mountain, and the spreading of a mutiny by army officers in Aleppo in February 1954

to all garrisons except Damascus [*q.v.*], ended only after he had left the country.

Subsequently Shishkali lived in Lebanon, Saudi Arabia, and France. Charged with plotting a coup against the Syrian regime in 1957, he was tried in absentia and sentenced to death. In 1960 he migrated to Brazil. Four years later he was assassinated by Nawaf Ghazeleh, a Syrian Druze, whose parents were killed in the bombing of the Druze Mountain ordered by Shishkali.

Shuqairi, Ahmad (1908–80): *Palestinian politician* Born into an eminent religious-political family in Acre [*q.v.*], Shuqairi trained as a lawyer at the Jerusalem Law School and the American University in Beirut [*q.v.*]. In 1945 he became director of a Palestinian office in New York, and later in Jerusalem [*q.v.*]. He served as a member of the Arab Higher Committee [*q.v.*] from March to June 1946.

After the Palestine War (1948–49) [*q.v.*], he moved to Damascus [*q.v.*]. He was a member of the Syrian delegation to the United Nations (1949–50) and undersecretary for political affairs at the Arab League [*q.v.*] (1951–1957). He then served as Saudi Arabia's minister of state for United Nations affairs and then its ambassador to the UN (1957–62). During his years at the UN he espoused the cause of Palestinians, often with vehement verbal attacks on Israel.

In 1963 Syria and Iraq proposed at the Arab League that a Palestine National Council [*q.v.*] be elected, and its chief delegate should occupy the Palestinian seat at the Arab League. The First Arab League Summit [*q.v.*]

in January 1964 directed Shuqairi to consult his countrymen and present a plan for the creation of an organization to represent them. The result was the Palestinian National Charter [*q.v.*], which was adopted by a conference in East Jerusalem [*q.v.*], then under Jordanian jurisdiction, in May. It established the Palestine Liberation Organization (PLO) [*q.v.*]. Shuqairi was elected chairman of the PLO's executive committee.

Under Shuqairi, the PLO had the full backing of Egyptian President Gamal Abdul Nasser [*q.v.*], who allowed him to run a radio station from Cairo [*q.v.*]. His extremist and contradictory statements, advocating the extermination of Israeli Jews [*q.v.*], proved counterproductive since they played into the hands of Israel. On the eve of the June 1967 Arab-Israeli War [*q.v.*], Shuqairi, heading a small Palestinian militia, indulged in hyperbolic rhetoric, creating a war psychosis that was out of proportion to the force he commanded. After the Arab debacle in that war, he was forced to resign his chairmanship of the PLO in December 1967. He then fell into obscurity.

Sidon: *Lebanese city* Population: 200,000 (2011 est.). The history of Sidon, an ancient Mediterranean port, goes back to the third millennium B.C. As a thriving commercial center it appears in the Old Testament [*q.v.*] and later in the epic poems of the Greek poet Homer (born ca. eighth century B.C.). It was ruled by the Assyrians, Babylonians, Persians, Greeks, and Romans. King Herod (37–4 B.C.) and Jesus Christ (ca 6 B.C.–30 A.D.) found it attractive. Its prosperity stemmed from its glassware and purple dye industries.

In 637 A.D. Sidon fell to Muslim [*q.v.*] Arabs [*q.v.*]. During the Crusades (1095–1272) it was fiercely fought over by the two sides, and underwent repeated destruction and reconstruction. It then came under the successive rule of the Mamlukes (1250–1517) and the Ottomans (1517–1918). It became part of the Vilayat of Lebanon under Fakhr al-Din Maan (r. 1591–1633), and thrived as a port. It survived the disastrous earthquake of 1837. During the French Mandate its port facilities were improved. After the 1948–49 Palestine War [*q.v.*], Palestinian refugees set up two camps near it.

Besides being the commercial center of the region, it is the terminus of the Trans-Arabian Pipeline for Saudi oil, which was shut off during the 1975–90 Lebanese Civil War [*q.v.*]. Among its tourist offerings are the Temple of Ashmoon of the Phoenician era, and two Crusader forts.

Sinai Campaign (1956): This is the term used by Israelis for the Suez War (1956) [*q.v.*].

Sinai Peninsula: Area 23,500 sq. mi./61,000 sq. km. Sinai is a derivative of Sin, the ancient moon god, and has a recorded history dating back to the third millennium B.C. A triangular peninsula connecting Asia to Africa, the Sinai extends from its wide base on the Mediterranean to the Red Sea, whose two extended arms at the top bind it on the west (Gulf of Suez) and the east (Gulf of Aqaba). In the south lies *Jebel Musa* (Arabic: *Mount Moses*), known as Mount Sinai in English, the legendary site where Moses is believed to have received the divine Law inscribed on the tablets. On its slope is the renowned Greek Orthodox [*q.v.*] monastery of Saint Catherine, founded in ca 250 A.D., where the Codex Sinaiticus, one of the oldest manuscripts of the New Testament [*q.v.*], was discovered in the 19th century. The rest of the Sinai is a plateau sloping toward the Mediterranean Sea.

Oil, first struck in 1910, was not exploited until three years later. The site of fighting between Egypt and Israel during the Suez War [*q.v.*], the War of Attrition [*q.v.*], and the October 1973 Arab-Israeli War [*q.v.*], the Sinai Peninsula was occupied by Israel between November 1956 and March 1957, and again from June 1967 to April 1982.

Sinai I Agreement (Egypt-Israel, 1974): Instead of using the United Nations to make peace with the Arabs [*q.v.*] after the October 1973 Arab-Israeli War [*q.v.*], Israel approached U.S. Secretary of State Henry Kissinger to bring about an agreement with Egypt. Egyptian President Anwar Sadat [*q.v.*] went along with this. The result was the Sinai I agreement on 18 January 1974 on the disengagement of the two armies in the Sinai [*q.v.*], with Egypt making concessions, allowing Israel to control the Mitla and Gidi passes and limiting its own military presence east of the Suez [*q.v.*] to 7,000 troops and 30 tanks.

The agreement formally ended the wartime military alliance between Egypt and Syria, and enabled Kissinger to persuade the Arab oil states to end the oil embargo [*q.v.*]

against Israel's Western allies, imposed during the 1973 war.

Sinai II Agreement (Egypt-Israel, 1975): Consisting of three published and four secret documents, the Sinai II Agreement was signed by Israel and Egypt on 4 September 1975, with the United States playing a crucial mediating role. The disengagement in the Sinai [*q.v.*] required demilitarization of the Israeli-controlled Mitla and Giddi passes, an Israeli withdrawal of 12–24 mi./20–40 km to create a wider UN buffer zone, and the posting of 200 American technicians to supervise the Egyptian and Israeli early warning systems. Israel returned the Abu Rudais oilfield to Egypt. The signatories renounced the threat or use of force.

Of the four secret deals, three concerned Israel and one Egypt. The United States promised to assist Egypt to build an early warning system in Sinai, and to consult it in the event that Israel violated the agreement. Washington reaffirmed its earlier commitment to help Israel maintain military superiority over its Arab neighbors, pledged $2.5 billion aid to Israel in 1975–76, and guaranteed oil deliveries from Iran or the mainland America. It also promised not to recognize or negotiate with the Palestine Liberation Organization (PLO) [*q.v.*] until the organization recognized Israel's right to exist and accepted UN Security Council Resolutions 242 and 338 [*q.v.*]. This cramped U.S. policy-making in the region until the late 1980s.

Siniora, Fouad (1943–): *Lebanese politician, prime minister, 2005–09* Born into a Sunni [*q.v.*] family in Sidon [*q.v.*], Siniora obtained a master's degree in business administration from American University in Beirut [*q.v.*]. While working for Citibank he lectured at the AUB and Lebanese University. He joined the Central Bank in 1977. Five years later Rafiq Hariri [*q.v.*] recruited him to manage his burgeoning business interests.

When Hariri became the prime minister in 1992, he appointed Siniora finance minister. He held that position until 1998 and again from 2000 to 2004. During his tenure the national debt of Lebanon soared from $2 billion to $50 billion. An investigation into his mishandling of state funds initiated in 2000 cleared him of any wrongdoing in 2003. Once he ceased to be finance minister, Hariri hired him to become chairman of Groupe Méditerranée, which controlled four Hariri-owned banks.

Following the victory of the anti-Syrian 14 March Alliance [*q.v.*] in June 2005, Siniora became prime minister. His national unity cabinet included members of Hizbollah [*q.v.*]. During the Israeli-Hizbollah War [*q.v.*] in July–August 2006, his government did not join the conflict but described Hizbollah's fighting as "a natural and honest expression of the Lebanese people's rights to liberate their land and defend their honor against Israeli aggression and threats."

After the war, the unity cabinet split on the question of backing an international tribunal on Hariri's assassination. When, in November, all five Shia [*q.v.*] opposition ministers and their Christian [*q.v.*] ally resigned, Siniora rejected their resignations.

In December 2006 the opposition forces, led by 51 parliamentary deputies, started a sit-in in central Beirut [*q.v.*] to gain veto power over the government. These deputies refused to participate in the election of a new president after the term of Emile Lahoud [*q.v.*] expired. As a result, Siniora became acting president. He held that position until May 2008.

The nonviolent impasse in central Beirut turned violent on 6 May when Siniora ordered an investigation into Hizbollah's private telecommunications network and dismissed the airport security chief. Hizbollah and its allies attacked the airport and stormed Sunni streets and properties in central and west Beirut as well as the Government Palace housing the prime minister's office. Counterattacks followed. Fighting spread to other parts of Lebanon and altogether claimed 200 lives. To avert Lebanon's descent into full-fledged civil war, Qatar's ruler, Shaikh Hamad bin Khlaifa al-Thani [*q.v.*], invited the rivals to Doha [*q.v.*]. The concord reached there on 21 May invested the opposition 4 March Alliance [*q.v.*] with a veto in the government after Hizbollah had promised never to use arms for domestic political purposes in the future. It paved the way for the election of Michel Suleiman [*q.v.*] as president.

Sistani, Ali Husseini (1930–): *Iraqi religious leader* Born into a Shia [*q.v.*] religious family in the Iranian city of Mashhad [*q.v.*], Sistani pursued his theological studies in Qom [*q.v.*], where he became a student of Ayatollah Muhammad Hussein Borujerdi. In 1951, he traveled to Najaf [*q.v.*] where he studied under Ayatollah Abol Qasim Khoei [*q.v.*]. After obtaining a degree in *ijtihad* [*q.v.*], interpretative reasoning of the Sharia [q.v.], Islamic law, in 1960, he went back to Mashhad, only staying there for a year.

On his return to Najaf, he spent three more years on theological research, and then began to teach *fiqh* [q.v.], Islamic jurisprudence. Like his mentor Khoei, he belonged to the quietist school among Shia clerics, who wanted to focus exclusively on providing succor to the community in its spiritual life and social welfare—quite apart from those clergy who favored intervention in state affairs. This distinction became all the more important in the wake of the coup by the secular Baath Party [*q.v.*] in 1968, and the repression of the Shia religious establishment that followed after Saddam Hussein [*q.v.*] became vice president in 1975.

State repression of Shia clergy intensified in the aftermath of the Islamic revolution in Iran four years later. The Iranian-born Shia clerics came under further pressure during the early period of the Iran-Iraq War [q.v.]. This subsided when most Iraqi Shias proved loyal to their country and fought Iran. By the time the war ended in 1988, Sistani had acquired the status of an ayatollah and gained popularity due partly to his spartan way of life.

Following the death in 1992 of Khoei, whose funeral prayer was performed by Sistani, the mantle of the *marja-e taqlid* (Arabic: *source of emulation*) [q.v.] passed not to him, as had been widely expected, but to the younger Ayatollah Muhammad Sadiq al-Sadr, due to the intervention by Saddam Hussein.

But a breach opened between the Iraqi president and Grand Ayatollah al-Sadr in 1998 when he issued a religious decree calling on Shias to attend Friday prayers in mosques, a step disapproved by Saddam. In February 1999, al-Sadr and his two sons were shot dead as they left a mosque in Najaf. After blaming "foreign countries" for the assassinations, the government appointed Sistani as the marja-e taqlid, entitling him to the honorific of grand ayatollah.

After the deposition of Saddam Hussein in April 2003, the followers of al-Sadr's grandson, Muqtada al-Sadr, demanded that Sistani leave Najaf. This led his acolytes to take Sistani to a safe house. In the political administrative vacuum created by Saddam Hussein's ouster, the Najaf-based religious collective, dominated by Sistani, became the nerve center of the Shia network consisting of mosques nationwide to administer the neighborhoods in Iraq's urban centers, including providing armed vigilantes to maintain law and order.

While staying away from the day-to-day politics of Iraq during the Anglo-American occupation of Iraq from April 2003 to 30 June 2009, the National Sovereignty Day, Sistani intervened at crucial moments, calling on to all Iraqis to participate in the elections and referendums that were held. He gave his blessing to the formation of the United Iraqi Alliance (UIA), which brought almost all Shia groups under one umbrella, thus assuring its dominance in electoral politics.

When, in the aftermath of the December 2005 parliamentary election, a stalemate developed because of the opposition of U.S. President George W. Bush to the continuation of Ibrahim Jaafari [*q.v.*] as prime minister despite his majority support among UIA deputies, Sistani persuaded Jaafari to step down to make way for Nouri al-Maliki [*q.v.*].

Following the blowing up of the Shias' Al Askariya shrine in Samarra [*q.v.*] in February 2006, Sistani urged calm, arguing that the attack was the work of foreign Wahhabis [*q.v.*] and not of Iraqi Sunnis [*q.v.*]. A year later an alleged plot to assassinate him was foiled.

Six-Day War (1967): *See* Arab-Israeli War III (1967).

Sneh, Moshe (1909–72): *Israeli politician* Born Moshe Kleinbaum in Radzin, Poland, Sneh obtained a medical degree at Warsaw University. Active in Zionist politics, he was elected chairman of the Zionist Student Union in Warsaw in 1930, and then to the central committee of the Zionist Organization in Poland. In 1935 he was appointed political editor of a Yiddish [*q.v.*] daily newspaper, *Haint* (Today), and elected chairman of the Zionist Organization in Poland. He served as an officer in the Polish army when World War II erupted in September 1939.

He escaped to Palestine [*q.v.*] in 1940 and became head of Haganah's [*q.v.*] central command a year later. Elected to the Jewish Agency [*q.v.*] Executive Committee in 1945, he took charge of the political department of the Agency's European office. After his resignation from the Haganah central command in 1946, he was elected head of the illegal immigration department of the Jewish Agency. Impressed by the Soviet

backing for the partitioning of Palestine in November 1947, Sneh advocated an alliance with Moscow.

In January 1948 he joined the newly formed Mapam [*q.v.*], becoming a member of its executive committee and editor of its paper, *Al-HaMishmar* (Hebrew: *On the Guard*). He was elected to the Knesset [*q.v.*] in 1949 and retained a seat until 1965. Under his influence, Mapam moved leftwards, and this strained its relations with Mapai [*q.v.*]. In late 1952, the trial and conviction of Mordechai Oran, a Mapam leader arrested during his trip to Prague as a Zionist spy, created anti-Soviet feeling within Mapam ranks. This led to Sneh's expulsion from the party.

Sneh and his followers formed the Israeli Socialist Left Party, which merged into Maki [*q.v.*] in 1954. He became a leader of Maki and editor of its daily paper, *Kol Ha'Am* (Hebrew: *Voice of the People*). Within the party, Sneh led the pro-Jewish faction, which criticized Moscow's ban on the emigration of Soviet Jews and its Middle East policies. By mid-1965 a split in the party became inevitable, and the opponents of Sneh's faction left to form Rakah [*q.v.*]. Sneh supported the June 1967 Arab-Israeli War [*q.v.*] and opposed the unconditional withdrawal of Israel from the Occupied Arab Territories [*q.v.*]. A witty orator, he was respected even by his most vocal opponents.

Socialist Labor Party (Egypt): *Egyptian political party* After President Anwar Sadat [*q.v.*] had drained the Arab Socialist Party of Egypt [*q.v.*] of almost all its parliamentary deputies by forming his own National Democratic Party [*q.v.*] in August 1978, he tried to create "honest" opposition by encouraging the formation of another rightist group, the Socialist Labor Party (SLP) [*q.v.*], under the leadership of Ibrahim Shukri.

The SLP backed the Camp David Accords [*q.v.*] and the subsequent Egyptian-Israeli Peace Treaty [*q.v.*] in March 1979. In the June 1979 general election it won 26 seats in a house of 392 seats. When it retained only a fraction of these seats in the May 1984 election, President Hosni Mubarak [*q.v.*] bolstered its strength by appointing four SLP members as parliamentary deputies. In the 1987 election it joined the alliance led by the Muslim Brotherhood [*q.v.*] and won 13 seats. Along with all other opposition groups, except the National Progressive Unionist Alliance [*q.v.*], the SLP boycotted the December 1990 election, demanding that the state of emergency be repealed and that the election be supervised by a nongovernmental body. In 1995 it won one parliamentary seat. In 2000 the state-controlled Political Parties Committee suspended it and its weekly paper, *Al-Shaab* (Arabic: *The People*), which had been pre-eminent in exposing corruption in high places, for "exceeding its political mandate."

Socialist National Front (Lebanon):
Lebanese political party Composed of opposition groups, the Socialist National Front (SNF) was formed in 1952. It was led by Camille Chamoun [*q.v.*], Kamal Jumblat [*q.v.*], and others concerned mainly with domestic reform. After the resignation of President Bishara Khouri [*q.v.*] in September 1952 in the wake of charges of corruption, the SNF's nominee, Chamoun, was elected president by parliament. By pursuing a pro-Western foreign policy, which was at odds with rising Arab nationalism [*q.v.*], Chamoun alienated himself from the predominantly Muslim SNF, now led by Jumblat.

Chamoun's rigging of the 1957 general election further widened the gap between him and the SNF. Matters came to a head in May 1958 when fighting erupted between his supporters and the SNF, marking the start of the first Lebanese Civil War [*q.v.*]. The induction of U.S. Marines into the conflict by Chamoun enraged the SNF, which controlled about a third of Lebanon. The conflict ended in a compromise, with Chamoun stepping down at the end of his term after dropping his plans for a constitutional amendment that would have let him seek reelection. He was succeeded by General Fouad Chehab [*q.v.*]. During Chehab's presidency the SNF became dormant.

Society of Combatant Clerics (Iran):
(Official title, Persian: *Majma-e Ruhaniyoun-e Mobraz*) (Also translated as Assembly of Combatant Clerics) Popularly known as *Majma*, it was formed on 21 March 1988 with the tacit backing of Ayatollah Ruhollah Khomeini [*q.v.*] after the dissolution of the ruling Islamic Republican Party [*q.v.*]. It was composed of socioeconomic radicals and headed by Mahdi Karroubi. They broke away from the older Association of Combatant Clergy [*q.v.*].

Its members entered the 1988 parliamentary election and gained a majority, with the leftist camp, including moderates, claiming the loyalty of two-thirds of the deputies. In the 1989 presidential election, the Majma backed Ali Akbar Hashemi Rafsanjani [*q.v.*], then Majlis [*q.v.*] speaker, who won. Karroubi succeeded him as speaker for the rest of the tenure of the Third Majlis. When Majma members opposed Rafsanjani's economic liberalization program the president compromised by abandoning wholesale privatization and proceeding on a sector by sector basis. In the Fourth Majlis (1992–96), Majma members became a minority. In the 1993 presidential contest it backed Rafsanjani. In the Fifth Majlis (1996–2000) too, the Majma remained a minority.

In the 1997 presidential election, it supported Muhammad Khatami [*q.v.*], one of its leaders. On the eve of the parliamentary election in 2000, it formed an important part of the Second Khordad (23 May) Front, named after the date of Khatami's landslide victory. Karroubi was elected speaker by 186 votes to none in a Majlis dominated by leftist and left-of-center deputies, with 30 of them belonging to the Majma.

In the elections to the Seventh Majlis in 2004, conservatives pushed reformers down to 50. The following year Karroubi resigned as Majma's general secretary. He was succeeded by Muhammad Mousavi Khoeiniha, a former cabinet minister and prosecutor general.

After the disputed presidential election in June 2009, the Majma's application to hold a peaceful protest rally in Tehran [*q.v.*] was rejected. Karroubi, one of the two defeated candidates for the presidency, became a vocal critic of the government of the reelected Mahmoud Ahmadinejad [*q.v.*].

Solh, Riyad (1894–1951): *Lebanese politician; prime minister, 1943–45, 1946–51* (Also spelled Sulh) Born into a notable Sunni [*q.v.*] family in Beirut [*q.v.*], Solh joined the Arab nationalist movement as a youth. After studying law in Beirut he went to Istanbul for further studies. During World War I, he was condemned to death for his Arab nationalist activities, but was later pardoned and freed.

After the war he became one of the assistants of Faisal bin Hussein [*q.v.*] in Damascus [*q.v.*] and a cofounder of the nationalist Istiqlal Party. When Faisal was defeated, he fled from Syria. As a leader of the Syrian-Palestinian Congress, based first in Cairo [*q.v.*] and then in Geneva, Switzerland, he campaigned for the independence of Greater Syria [*q.v.*] from the French Mandate. Following the electoral victory of the leftist Popular Front in France in 1936, Solh returned home and became a leading Sunni leader of Lebanon.

During World War II, he was one of the two main architects of the 1943 National Pact [*q.v.*], the other being Bishara Khouri [*q.v.*], a Maronite [*q.v.*] leader. He became prime minister (1943–45) and played a leading role in the choice of Lebanon as a cofounder of the Arab League [*q.v.*]. After the war he again served as prime minister (1946–51). His government quelled an attempted coup by the leaders of the Syrian Social Nationalist Party (SSNP) [*q.v.*], and executed the party chief Antun Saadeh in mid-

1949. In retaliation SSNP militants assassinated Solh in July 1951 during his visit to Amman [*q.v.*].

South Lebanon Army: *Lebanese militia*
Formed by Israel during its occupation of southern Lebanon from March to June 1978, the South Lebanon Army (SLA), consisting mainly of Christian militiamen, was put under the command of Saad Haddad, a former (Christian) Lebanese army major. About 2,000 strong, it was armed, trained, and financed by Israel. It patrolled the border zone inside Lebanon, an area 2.5–7 mi./4–12 km wide and 50 mi./80 km long, running from the Mediterranean to Kafr Shuba and populated by 40,000 Christians [*q.v.*], mostly Maronite [*q.v.*], and 60,000 Muslims [*q.v.*], mostly Shia [*q.v.*]. The SLA kept the Lebanese army and the Arab League's [*q.v.*] peacekeeping force out of its area.

It acted as part of the Israel Defense Forces (IDF) when the latter invaded Lebanon [*q.v.*] in June 1982. When Haddad died in January 1984, Israel appointed Antoine Lahad, a retired (Christian) Lebanese army major, to succeed him.

When withdrawing from Lebanon in June 1985, Israel handed over its positions in the self-declared security zone to the 3,000-strong SLA, and left behind 1,000 Israeli troops as a backup force. With this, the SLA became as much of a target of the Lebanese resistance against Israeli occupation as IDF troops. When the end of Amin Gemayel's [*q.v.*] presidency in September 1988 led to Gen. Michel Aoun [*q.v.*] claiming monopoly of power, Lahad pledged his loyalty to him. But this had no practical impact on the situation. Equally, the end of the civil war in October 1990 changed little as far as the SLA was concerned.

During Gulf War II [*q.v.*] (January–February 1991) there were armed exchanges between pro-Iraqi Palestinian commandos and the IDF-SLA alliance. After the signing of the Lebanese-Syrian Treaty of Brotherhood, Cooperation and Coordination [*q.v.*] in May 1991, which was condemned by Israel, the IDF-SLA alliance hardened its stance. Israel responded to attacks on SLA or IDF patrols, mainly by Hizbollah [*q.v.*] partisans, by launching air raids and firing artillery shells at the Hizbollah positions outside the strip. Because most Lebanese viewed Hizbollah as a counterforce to the SLA, the government refrained from disarming Hizbollah.

On the eve of Israel's unconditional withdrawal from south Lebanon in May 2000, more than 6,000 current and past SLA troops escaped to Israel. The Lebanese government tried another 2,000 for serving in the SLA or for working inside Israel, and sentenced 800 former SLA soldiers to 25 years in jail.

South Yemen: Official title: People's Republic of South Yemen (1967–70); People's Democratic Republic of Yemen (1970–90). *See* Yemen: history.

South Yemeni-Soviet Friendship Treaty (1979): After several years of hesitation, often induced by the prospect of unity with North Yemen [*q.v.*], South Yemen signed a 20-year friendship and cooperation treaty with the Soviet Union in October 1979 during a visit by its president, Abdul Fattah Ismail [*q.v.*], to Moscow. The treaty assured South Yemen of its survival, a top priority for a country beleaguered since its independence in 1967 by hostile neighbors: Saudi Arabia, Oman, and North Yemen.

Southern Movement (Yemen): In 2009 various anti-government groups in southern Yemen formed an umbrella organization called the Southern Movement under the chairmanship of Hassan Baoum, a leader of the Yemeni Socialist Party [*q.v.*]. It called for equality with the north and honoring of the promises made at the time of unification in 1990. It highlighted the central government's discrimination in its distribution of resources. When President Ali Abdullah Saleh [*q.v.*] tried to repress the movement, it demanded independence for the south. It held demonstrations and appealed to the Arab League [*q.v.*] to supervise secession. The government arrested Baoum and other dissident leaders. When the protest did not end, it released them a year later. In 2011 it participated in the anti-Saleh protest and suspended its demand for secession.

Steadfastness Front (1977–87): *Front of radical Arab states* Formed in Tripoli, Libya, in December 1977, in the wake of a visit to Jerusalem [*q.v.*] by Egyptian President Anwar Sadat [*q.v.*], the Steadfastness Front consisted of Algeria, Libya, the Palestine Liberation Organization (PLO) [*q.v.*], Syria, and South Yemen. An Iraqi representative attended the plenary session but walked out, considering the

Front not radical enough. The Front upheld the official Arab League [*q.v.*] position of no negotiations with Israel until it had vacated all Occupied Arab Territories [*q.v.*]. Sadat reacted to its founding by severing diplomatic links with its constituents.

At its meeting in Damascus [*q.v.*] in September 1978, the Front supported the Omani people's struggle for liberation, and opposed the resolution passed by the Arab League [*q.v.*] by a majority vote, calling for an economic boycott of South Yemen, in July. At its behest, the subsequent Arab summit in November canceled the resolution against South Yemen.

Under the leadership of President Chadli Ben-Jedid (r. 1979–81), Algeria started to dissociate itself gradually from the Front, a trend accelerated by its economic decline following the collapse of oil prices in the spring of 1986. At about the same time Libya became the target of air attacks by the United States, and this considerably chastened its leader, Muammar Gaddafi. Syrian president Hafiz Assad [*q.v.*] was too preoccupied with the developments in the Lebanese Civil War [*q.v.*] to nurture the Front. It ceased to exit by 1987.

Stern, Avraham ("Yair") (1907–42): *Zionist guerrilla leader* Born in Suwalki, Poland, but brought up in different Russian towns after the outbreak of World War I in 1914, he migrated to Palestine [*q.v.*] in 1925. After graduating from a Jewish school in Jerusalem [*q.v.*] he studied philosophy at the Hebrew University.

A member of Haganah [*q.v.*], Stern played an active role during in the Arab-Jewish riots in 1929. Two years later he quit Haganah, and became one of the cofounders of the more militant Irgun B. When most of the Irgun B members returned to Haganah in 1937, Stern and his followers allied with Revisionist Zionists [*q.v.*] to set up *Irgun Zvai Leumi* [*q.v.*] (Hebrew: *National Military Organization*). He became one of its top commanders. Opposed to Irgun's subordination to the Revisionist leadership, he clashed with Vladimir Jabotinsky [*q.v.*].

He traveled to Poland in 1938 to test the feasibility of an Irgun plan to transport 40,000 Zionist partisans to Palestine to stage an anti-British uprising there. Due to the gathering war clouds in Central Europe, Irgun had to rethink its strategy. After Stern's return to Palestine and the outbreak of World War II in September 1939, his differences with the Revisionist leadership sharpened. Disagreeing with their decision to stop attacking the British and start cooperating with Haganah, Stern argued that with Britain at war, the time was right for the Zionists to pressure it to honor its promise to help the Jews [*q.v.*] to establish a Jewish homeland in Palestine.

He left Irgun in June 1940. Three months later he founded Lehi [*q.v.*]. It argued that, since the British were the number one enemy of the Jews, and since fighting them was the top Jewish priority, there was no harm in negotiating with the German Nazis to achieve this aim. Lehi contacted the German embassy in Ankara. This, and the terrorist attacks on British Mandate authorities, marginalized Lehi and Stern, who went underground. Discovered in a hideout during a British police raid in February 1942, Stern was shot dead. But Lehi, by now popularly known as the Stern Gang/Group [*q.v.*], survived.

Stern Gang/Group: *See* Lehi/Lehy.

Suez Canal: This Egyptian waterway—106 mi./170 km long, 197 ft./60 m wide and 42.5 ft./13 m deep—connects the Mediterranean Sea and the Gulf of Suez, and thus the Red Sea. Permission to construct the Suez Canal was granted by the Egyptian ruler, Said bin Abbas (r. 1854–1863) to Ferdinand de Lesseps, a French engineer. The construction of the canal, begun in 1859 by the Universal Suez Maritime Canal Company (USMCC), was completed 10 years later. Based in Paris, the USMCC, which was owned jointly by Britain and France, managed the Canal until its nationalization in July 1956, when Egypt set up the Egyptian Canal Authority (ECA) to run it. This also ended the British occupation of 3,000 sq. mi./7,790 sq. km in the Suez Canal Zone.

Egyptian President Gamal Abdul Nasser [*q.v.*] nationalized the Canal after the United States and Britain had humiliated him by withdrawing the World Bank loan for the construction of the Aswan High Dam [*q.v.*]. In 1958, compensation to the USMCC was agreed through the World Bank.

Closed during the June 1967 Arab-Israeli War [*q.v.*] due to the presence of sunken ships, and then due to the War of Attrition [*q.v.*], the Canal did not reopen until June 1975. In October, following the Sinai II Agreement [*q.v.*] between Israel and Egypt,

Israeli cargo ships were permitted to use it. After the 1979 Egyptian-Israeli Peace Treaty [*q.v.*] Israeli warships were also allowed passage. With the Canal's enlargement completed in 1980, larger ships with 53 ft./16 m draft were able to use it. Further modernization was completed in 2000. As a result, the canal became suitable for ships with the draft of 70 ft./21 m or 240,000 deadweight tons.

Suez War (1956): Anglo-French-Israeli Invasion of Egypt, 29 October–7 November 1956.

BACKGROUND: On 19 July 1956 the United States informed Egypt that it was withdrawing its offer of aid for the Aswan High Dam [*q.v.*], thus undermining the loan from the World Bank for Reconstruction and Development, which was predicated on U.S. assistance. A week later Egyptian President Gamal Abdul Nasser [*q.v.*] nationalized the Suez Canal [*q.v.*], which was jointly owned by Britain and France. After the debate on the subject at the UN Security Council, Egypt agreed on 11 October to the principles regarding running the Canal, including maintaining its status as an international waterway. On 24 October a secret Anglo-French-Israeli agreement on an invasion of Egypt was finalized.

OPERATIONS: On 29–30 October 1956 Israel invaded the Sinai [*q.v.*]. At 18:00 hours on 30 October Britain and France gave a 24-hour ultimatum to Egypt and Israel to cease hostilities and withdraw their troops 10 mi./16 km from the Suez Canal so as not to jeopardize freedom of shipping. As Israel's forces were some 30 mi./48 km from the canal, it accepted the ultimatum, but Egypt rejected it. Fighting between the two sides continued. When the deadline ended at 1800 hours on 31 October, Britain and France bombed Egypt's airfields, virtually destroying its air force, and continued attacking Egyptian military facilities for the next 36 hours. Cairo ordered its forces, sent earlier into the Sinai Peninsula [*q.v.*], to retreat and thus avoid being encircled by the enemy. They did so by 2 November. On that day the United States cooperated with the Soviet Union at the UN Security Council to sponsor a "Uniting for Peace" resolution, which condemned aggression against Egypt. The next day, while continuing to consolidate its position in the Sinai, Israel completed its occupation of the Gaza Strip [*q.v.*].

On 4 November the UN General Assembly voted to set up a UN Emergency Force (UNEF) [*q.v.*] to supervise the truce. On 5 November, British and French paratroopers landed at the northern (Port Said) and southern (Port Suez) ends of the Canal. Israel, advised by London and Paris, attached unrealistic conditions to its acceptance of the UN Security Council cease-fire resolution. Soviet Prime Minister Marshal Nikolai Bulganin, in a letter to his Israeli counterpart, David Ben-Gurion [*q.v.*], wrote: "It [the aggression] is sowing a hatred of the State of Israel among the peoples of the East such as cannot but make itself felt with regard to the future of Israel, and which puts in jeopardy the very existence of Israel as a state."

On the night of 5–6 November, British and French forces landed in the Port Said area, and, after seizing the town, started to move south along the Canal, which had been blocked by the Egyptians with sunken ships. In Washington, president-elect Dwight Eisenhower applied economic pressure on Britain, with the U.S. Federal Reserve Board selling large amounts of British pounds, thus weakening the exchange rate of the British pound. Yielding to the U.S.-Soviet pressure, the invading governments accepted a cease-fire from midnight on 6–7 November. By then Israel had occupied the Gaza Strip and most of the Sinai Peninsula, including its southeastern tip, Sharm el Shaikh, at the mouth of the Gulf of Aqaba.

LOSSES: Egypt: 1,650 killed, 215 aircraft; Israel: 190 killed, 15 aircraft; Britain: 16 killed, 4 aircraft; France: 10 killed, 1 aircraft.

AFTERMATH: UNEF, charged with supervising the truce, started arriving on 4 December. Britain and France completed their withdrawal by 23 December, handing over their positions to UNEF. Though Israel agreed to withdraw on 8 November it did not actually do so until 8 March 1957— and then only after the United States committed itself to standing by Israel's right of passage through the Gulf of Aqaba, ensuring that the Gaza Strip was not used again for launching guerrilla attacks against it, and assisting Israel, secretly, in its nuclear research program. On Israel's insistence, UNEF troops were posted exclusively in the Gaza Strip and the Gulf of Aqaba region to safeguard Israeli shipping. Egypt was allowed to return to the Gaza Strip to administer it.

Sufism (Arabic: *Sufi*, derivative of *suf*, *wool*; hence person wearing a woolen garment; ascetic): *mystical philosophy in Islam* Subscribing to the general theory of mysticism [*q.v.*] that direct knowledge of God is attainable through intuition or insight, Sufism is based on the doctrines and methods derived from the Quran [*q.v.*]. Some early Muslims undertook ascetic exercises, believing that this would bring them closer to God. They were inspired by the example of the Prophet Muhammad, who used to withdraw into a cave and undertake nightly vigils, and by the practices of Christian hermits. They stressed meditation and contemplation of God, and regarded involvement in worldly affairs, or pursuit of political power, as a distraction from the path of seeking Allah within. They came to be known as Sufis— from the word *suf* (wool)—because of the woolen garments the pioneers among them wore as a sign of asceticism.

Hassan al-Basri (d. 728 A.D.) was the first known Sufi personality. In time two types of Sufis emerged: ecstatic and sober. Among the latter, Abu Hamid Muhammad al-Ghazali (1058–1111) was the most prominent. He tried to integrate the whole Islamic legal system with a spiritual infrastructure originating in the Prophet Muhammad's mystic consciousness. His work became the living document for the Sufi orders/brotherhoods that sprang up soon after his death.

The first Sufi order was Qadiriya. Founded by Baghdad-based Abdul Qadir al-Gailani (1077–1166), it stressed piety and humanitarianism. A brotherhood consisted of aspirants (*murid*s), who took an oath of allegiance to the guide, known as shaikh, *pir*, or *murshid*. Women were admitted as associate aspirants. The shaikh headed a hierarchy within the order that was linked by a chain of inherited sanctity (*baraka*) or kinship to the founding saint. This chain went back to early Sufi founders such as Hassan al-Basri, and through them to the House of the Prophet or the Prophet Muhammad himself.

It was common for a Sufi order to establish its own convents. An example of a mainstream brotherhood was Naqshbandi, established by Yusuf al-Hamadani (d. 1140) but named after Baha al-Din Naqshband (1318–89), a mystic born in Tajikistan. Naqshbandis believed that there was no *tariqa* (road) outside the Sharia [*q.v.*], and followed the maxim, "The exterior is for the world, the interior for Allah." Believing that piety was best expressed through social activity, they opposed withdrawal from the world. They became noted for their silent remembrance (*dhikr*) in mosques, undertaken to induce a state of collective ecstasy.

Whereas Islamic rituals were generally austere, Sufi orders provided a framework within which rich and colorful liturgical practices were spawned in the form of devotional rituals by novices. Such ecstatic Sufi orders as the Rifaiiya brotherhood, originating in Iraq, are an example. Rifaiiya followers went into frenzies, during which they would ride dangerous animals, walk into fires, ravage venomous reptiles, or mutilate themselves by placing iron rings in their ears, necks, and hands to demonstrate the supremacy of mind over matter.

Sufism grew rapidly between 1250 and 1500, when the caliphate was based in Cairo [*q.v.*] under Mamluke sultans (1250–1517), and when Islam

penetrated central and western Africa and southern India and Southeast Asia along the land and sea routes used by Arab [*q.v.*] traders. Islam came into contact not only with paganism in Africa but also with the advanced religions and civilizations of Hinduism and Buddhism in Asia. It was through the rise of Sufism that Islam was often able to absorb the pre-Islamic beliefs and practices of the new converts. Today Sufi brotherhoods exist, overtly or covertly, in most Muslim communities.

suicide bombing: *Suicide committed by detonating explosives either strapped to the body of a person or carried in a vehicle, or by ramming a building with flying aircraft* A suicide bomber either triggers the detonator while in the midst of his/her potential targets or drives a vehicle loaded with explosives into the target, killing himself/herself along with many others— the latter method often called truck bombing. The destruction of the Twin Towers of the World Trade Center in New York City and part of the Pentagon in Washington, D.C., on 11 September 2001 by ramming flying passenger aircraft into the buildings, resulting in the death of 3,052 people, opened a new chapter in suicide bombing. As a rule, the suicide bomber is supported by an operational cell that provides accommodation, transport, food, clothing, and security until he/she reaches the target. This cell often consists of "sleepers," legal residents of a country with jobs and families. It was on 18 April 1983 that truck bombing was first deployed in the Middle East [*q.v.*], and the target was the American Embassy in Beirut [*q.v.*]. The driver rammed the embassy with his truck, loaded with explosives, at high speed, destroyed much of the building, and killed 63 people, including 17 Americans, of whom seven were Central Intelligence Agency officers. No group claimed responsibility, but the local Islamic Jihad was widely blamed.

Lebanon's Muslim [*q.v.*] terrorists did so in the course of the 1975–90 Civil War [*q.v.*] in which the United States, France, Britain, and Italy had intervened on behalf of the Lebanese Christians [*q.v.*]. They followed up the bombing of the American embassy with the truck-bombing of the U.S. and French military headquarters in West Beirut that left 300 dead.

The person who killed him/herself in the process was regarded by radical Islamists [*q.v.*] as a martyr in the path of God, described in the Quran [*q.v.*] (Chapter 3, Verse 164) thus:

"Count not those who were slain in God's way as dead,
but rather living with their Lord, by Him provided,
rejoicing in the bounty that God has given them,
and joyful in those who remain behind and have not joined them,
because no fear shall be on them, neither shall they sorrow,
joyful in blessing and bounty from God,
and that God leaves not to waste the wage of the believers."

The method of being killed in "God's way" has varied. During the Iran-Iraq War (1980-1988) [*q.v.*], Iranian leader Ayatollah Ruhollah Khomeini [*q.v.*] ruled that any Iranian who died in the war was a martyr. On the other side, Iraqi President Saddam Hussein [*q.v.*], hardly a scholar of

Islam [*q.v.*], issued similar statements. Since suicide bombing was a recent phenomenon, it led to controversy among Muslim scholars. Those who opposed it argued that it was un-Islamic to kill innocent civilians. Those in favor reasoned that suicide bombing enabled Muslims to overcome their general weakness vis-à-vis their enemies.

However, suicide bombing ceased to be the monopoly of Muslim fundamentalists [*q.v.*]. By 2001, it had been adopted by 10 organizations, both religious and secular, and used 160 times in 13 countries. Sri Lanka's Tamil rebels—Hindu by religion—fighting for an independent state, were the most frequent practitioners of suicide bombing.

Whether sanctioned by religion or not, suicide bombing has proved effective. The conventional concept of security rests on deterrence, where the terrorist is killed or apprehended by the authorities. But the certain death of the suicide terrorist(s) precludes the captors' extracting vital information, thereby enabling the terrorist group to undertake daring operations while protecting its cadres and organizational network.

In the case of the U.S. embassy bombings in Nairobi and Dar as Salam in August 1998, the authorities had rapid success in apprehending the conspirators because in each instance one of the terrorists chose not to commit suicide at the last moment. Conversely, when both terrorists died in the ramming of USS *Cole* in October 2000, the Yemeni authorities took more than a year to arrest their coconspirators.

Similarly, the black boxes saved from the crash of the fourth 9/11 aircraft in rural Pennsylvania—instead of ramming the targeted Capitol Hill in Washington—provided useful clues to the American authorities in identifying the 19 suicide hijackers of the four planes.

During the Al Aqsa Intifada [*q.v.*] (September 2001–December 2004), 96 Palestinians, including three women, carried out suicide bombings. Those claiming these attacks were not only Hamas [*q.v.*] and the Islamic Jihad [*q.v.*] but also the Tanzim, affiliated to secular Fatah [*q.v.*].

Suleiman, Michel (1948 –): *Lebanese military and political leader; president, 2008–* Born in a Maronite [*q.v.*] household in the town of Amsheet in Jbeil, he graduated from the Military Academy in 1970 as second lieutenant. He rose from being an infantry platoon leader to the army staff secretary-general in 1991. When he served as a brigade commander in southern Lebanon from 1993 to 1995, his force was involved in many skirmishes with the occupying Israeli troops. The next year he was put in charge of the vital Sixth Brigade. When General Emile Lahoud [*q.v.*] was elected president in 1998, Suleiman succeeded him as commander of the armed forces. After the Israeli pull-out from southern Lebanon in 2000, he supervised the army's deployment near the Israeli border.

He scrupulously kept his troops out of the domestic political fights that broke out after the assassination of Rafiq Hariri [*q.v.*] in 2005 and again in May 2008, arguing that such an involvement served the interests of Israel. He won national kudos in 2007 by flushing out Al Qaida [*q.v.*]-in-

spired militants from the Palestinian refugee camp of Nahr al-Bared in northern Lebanon after a four-month-long fight that claimed 420 lives, including 170 soldiers.

After the Israeli-Hizbollah War [*q.v.*] of 2006, he supervised the deployment of the army in the south as required by the United National Security Council Resolution 1701. In the impasse between Hizbollah [*q.v.*] and the Fouad Siniora [*q.v.*] government in 2008, he maintained strict neutrality. That in turn won him the backing of the opposing 8 March Alliance [*q.v.*] and 14 March Alliance [*q.v.*] for the presidency. He secured 118 votes out of 127.

Like his predecessors, he maintained cordial relations with Syria and refrained from commenting on the escalating protest movement there in 2011-2012.

sunna (Arabic: *custom, path*): In the pre-Islamic society of Arabia [*q.v.*] the term *sunna* applied to social practices based on ancestral precedents. After the rise of Islam [*q.v.*] under the Prophet Muhammad (570–632 A.D.), early converts took their cue either from the behavior of the Prophet's companions or the residents of Medina [*q.v.*], the capital of the Islamic realm. As for the later converts living away from Medina, codes based partly on local traditions and partly on the *sunna* evolved.

Though the Prophet Muhammad was an exemplar for Muslims, it was not until the eminent jurist Muhammad bin Idris al-Shafii (767–820 A.D.) had ruled that all legal decisions not stemming directly from the Quran [*q.v.*] must be based on a tradition going back to the Prophet Muhammad himself that a serious effort was made to compile the Prophet's sayings and doings—based on eyewitness accounts of his words, actions, and approbations. The *sunna* of the Prophet Muhammad was thus codified by Hadith [*q.v.*].

The authority of the *sunna* was reinforced when, reacting to the frequent fabrication of the Hadith by the adherents of different doctrinal, legal, and political schools, leading jurists developed *ilm al-hadith* (Arabic: *knowledge of the Hadith*)—to test the genuineness of an individual tradition. The *sunna* was then employed in the exposition of the Quran and in *fiqh* [*q.v.*], Islamic jurisprudence.

Sunnis (Persian: *derivative of* Ahl al-sunna, *Arabic, People of the path* [*of the Prophet Muhammad*]): *Islamic sect* Sunnis are the leading sect within Islam. They regard the first four caliphs—Abu Bakr, Omar, Othman, and Ali—as "Rightly Guided." They belong to one of the four schools of jurisprudence—Hanafi [*q.v.*], Maliki [*q.v.*], Shafii [*q.v.*], and Hanbali [*q.v.*]—and accept the six "authentic books" of the Hadith [*q.v.*], the first of which was compiled by Muhammad al-Bukhari (d. 870 A.D.).

They differ from the minority Shia [*q.v.*] sect in doctrine, ritual, law, theology, and religious organization. They share only three of the five doctrines of Shia Islam: monotheism, i.e., there is only one God; prophet-hood, which is a means of communications between God and humankind; and resurrection, i.e., the souls of dead humans are raised by God on the Day of Judgment and their deeds on earth

judged. Their five obligations—reciting the central Islamic precept ("There is no god but Allah, Muhammad is the Messenger of Allah"), daily prayers, fasting during Ramadan [*q.v.*], *zakat* (alms tax) [*q.v.*], and hajj (pilgrimage to Mecca) [*q.v.*]—are fewer than those required by Shias. Unlike Shias, Sunnis regard caliphs as fallible interpreters of the Quran [*q.v.*] and the *sunna* [*q.v.*]. Sunnis do not share the concept of Mahdi [*q.v.*] with Shias, and view Islamic history as essentially a drift away from the ideal community that existed under the rule of the first four Rightly Guided caliphs.

Sunnis and Shias also differ on the organization of religion and religious activities. Sunnis regard religious activities as the exclusive domain of the (Muslim) state. When the ulema [*q.v.*] act as judges or preachers or educators, they do so under the aegis of the state. There is little scope for the ulema to organize religion outside the confines of the Muslim state.

The Sunni ethos, too, is different from the Shia. There is no emotional outlet for mourning the martyrdom of early Islamic leaders, as in the Ashura [*q.v.*] celebrations of Shias. The only exception lies with the Sufi orders [*q.v.*] within Sunnism, where believers are provided with something emotional or heart-warming—the collectively performed rituals.

Finally, except for government-appointed religious officials such as *qadi* (judge), *mufti* (one who delivers *fatwas*, religious rulings), grand mufti, and shaikh-al-Islam (wise man of Islam), or professional theological teachers, called *maulawi* or *maulana* (learned man), Sunni clerics are not given the religious titles of their Shia counterparts.

Supreme Assembly of Islamic Revolution in Iraq: *See* Supreme Council of Islamic Revolution in Iraq.

Supreme Council of Islamic Revolution in Iraq (Arabic: *Majlis al-Aala lil Thawra al-Islamiya fi al-Iraq*): *Iraqi political organization* The Supreme Council of Islamic Revolution in Iraq (SCIRI) was formed in Tehran [*q.v.*] in November 1982 by three Iraqi Islamic organizations: al-Daawa al-Islamiya [*q.v.*], the Mujahedin Movement, and the Islamic Action Organization. Led by Ayatollah Muhammad Baqir al-Hakim, a Shia [*q.v.*] cleric with a history of resistance to the Iraqi Baath [*q.v.*] regime, SCIRI aimed to found an Islamic state in Iraq. It raised an armed force from among Iraqi exiles and prisoners of war, who then fought alongside the Iranians in the Iran-Iraq War [*q.v.*].

In late 1986 it participated in the Conference on Solidarity with the Iraqi People, held in Tehran and attended by the delegates of various Kurdish autonomist groups. But their decision to form a joint military committee was not implemented. After the Iran-Iraq War, its importance waned.

When Baghdad's control over the provinces weakened in the aftermath of Gulf War II [*q.v.*], SCIRI encouraged the Shias in southern Iraq to rebel against the regime. Its Iranian-based cadres crossed over into the rebel areas, unfurling its flag and the portraits of Ayatollahs al-Hakim and Ruhollah Khomeini [*q.v.*]. The move proved counterproductive. Having fought Iran for eight years, most Iraqis, irrespective of their sectarian affiliation, were loath to see Iranian interference in their affairs. After the failure of the rebellion, SCIRI once again became quiescent. Later it tried to focus international attention on the plight of the (Shia) residents of the marshes in southern Iraqi, which were being drained by the central government in order to develop the area economically and socially and to extract oil. But little came of it.

When Washington's Iraq Liberation Act, 1998, authorized the president to name Iraqi groups entitled to receiving military aid to topple the regime of Saddam Hussein [*q.v.*], President Bill Clinton named SCIRI as one such faction along with five others. But SCIRI, maintaining an army of 4,000 to 12,000 exiled Iraqis, rejected the entitlement, arguing that the American move made the Iraqi opposition appear to be U.S. agents. By then the Iranian government had resorted to using SCIRI to get even with the periodic pinprick attacks by the Baghdad [*q.v.*]-based Mujahedin-e Khalq along the Iranian-Iraqi border. In March 2000, when the Mujahedin activists inside Iran [*q.v.*] fired half a dozen mortars in central Tehran, SCIRI militants inside Iraq retaliated by firing mortars at a Baghdad neighborhood, killing four people.

In the spring of 2002, when the administration of U.S. President George W. Bush started making military plans to invade Iraq, it invited the six recognized Iraqi opposition factions to Washington. SCIRI representatives attended a meeting in August, thus reversing its previous stance with the tacit approval of Iran. Later it attended the Iraqi opposition conference in London.

After the overthrow of Saddam Hussein's [*q.v.*] regime in 2003 by the Anglo-American forces in April 2003, SCIRI cooperated with the occupying powers. Abdul Aziz al-Hakim, brother of SCIRI's founder, Muhammad Baqir al-Hakim, accepted a seat on the U.S.-appointed Interim Iraqi Governing Council. Following Muhammad Baqir's assassination in August 2003, Abdul Aziz became the leader of SCIRI.

As a major part of the Shia-dominated United Iraqi Alliance, SCIRI emerged as the strongest group in the Interim National Assembly in January 2005. Along with al-Daawa al Islamiya, it played an important role in giving the new constitution an Islamic orientation.

It did equally well in the parliamentary elections that followed in January 2006, and emerged as the largest single group. Its leading figure, Adil Abdul-Mahdi, was elected vice president, one of the two such officials. As a member of the presidential council, he had veto power over legislation.

In May 2007, the leadership of the quarter-century-old organization renamed it the Supreme Islamic Iraq Council [*q.v.*], arguing that, with the downfall of Saddam Hussein, a revolution had been accomplished in Iraq. It favored a decentralized Iraq state with an autonomous Shia zone in the south. *See also* Supreme Islamic Iraq Council.

Supreme Islamic Iraq Council (2007): This is the renamed Supreme Council of Islamic Revolution in Iraq [*q.v.*]. Due to the advancement of Abdul Aziz al-Hakim's cancer from the spring of 2007, the day-to-day running of the Supreme Islamic Iraq Council (SIIC) fell to his son, Ammar. Under his guidance the SIIC ran in the 2009 provincial elections on its own. On a popular vote of less than 7 percent it secured only 52 of the 440 seats. After the death of his father in August 2009, Ammar al-Hakim was formally elected leader of the SIIC.

It joined the Iraqi National Alliance (INA), led by Ibrahim Jaafari [*q.v.*], which also included the Sadrist Trend [*q.v.*], to enter the parliamentary election in March 2010. Of the 70 seats won by the INA, it got only 12. It thus became a minor player in Iraqi politics. In December it was the last group to back Nouri al-Maliki [*q.v.*] as the prime minister because, unlike Maliki, it favors a decentralized Iraq state with an autonomous Shia zone in the south.

Sur: *See* Tyre.

Sykes-Picot Pact (Anglo-French, 1916): A secret pact between London and Paris was signed in May 1916 by Sir Mark Sykes, senior British diplomat, and François Georges Picot, a former French consul in Beirut [*q.v.*], to carve up the Ottoman Empire among Britain, France, and Russia after their victory in World War I. Its provisions contradicted various British statements and declarations (one of them in conjunction with France) during the war, as well as the contents of the correspondence between Sir Henry McMahon, the British high commissioner in Cairo [*q.v.*], and Hussein bin Ali, the Arab governor of Hijaz [*q.v.*], which promised independence to the Arab territories of the Ottoman Empire after the victory of the Allies (Belgium, Britain, France, Greece, Italy, Japan, Montenegro, Russia, and Serbia) over the Central Powers (Austria-Hungary, Bulgaria, Germany, and the Ottoman Empire). An exchange of letters between Britain, France, and Russia in October 1916 finalized the pact. It was revealed in December 1917 by the Bolshevik regime in Russia, which published it in the official newspaper, *Izvestia* (Rusian: *News*).

The Sykes-Picot Pact covered the interests of Britain, France, and Russia. After the victory Russia was to acquire Constantinople (now Istanbul), a strip on each side of the Bosphorus Straits, and large parts of the four provinces of Turkey bordering Russia. As for the Ottoman Empire's Arab territory, in which Russia was uninterested, Britain and France made the following deal: British hegemony in the Baghdad and Basra provinces of Mesopotamia [*q.v.*]; French hegemony in Ottoman (Greater) Syria [*q.v.*] and Lesser Armenia (in Turkey); and an international zone in Palestine [*q.v.*], much smaller than the Palestine mandated to Britain in 1922. The rest was to be constituted into an independent Arab state or federation, divided into British and French spheres of influence.

synagogue (Greek: *assembly*): The terms for synagogue in Hebrew [*q.v.*] are: *beit ha-knesset* (house of the assembly), *beit ha-tefilla* (house of the prayer), and *beit ha-midrash* (house of the study). So a synagogue is a gathering place for prayer and religious study. Synagogues came into vogue after the razing of the First Temple

(of Solomon) in 586 B.C. and rose in significance after the demolition of the Second Temple in 70 A.D. They became the site of three daily services as well as special ceremonies on the Sabbath [*q.v.*] and other religious festivals.

Constructed with one end oriented toward Jerusalem [*q.v.*], synagogues tended to imitate basilicas in design, with a gallery. In time they came to be embellished with mosaics, frescoes, and carvings. After Roman Emperor Constantine (r. 306–337 A.D.) had adopted Christianity as the state religion in 313 A.D., old synagogues were demolished or converted to churches. Following the rise of Islam [*q.v.*] and an Islamic empire in the seventh century A.D., synagogues were allowed to be repaired in Muslim lands.

During the Middle Ages (476 A.D.–1492) synagogues emerged as the intellectual and social centers of Jewish life, the adjacent courtyards being used as law courts and for wedding ceremonies. Today a typical synagogue contains an ark (where the scrolls of the Torah [*q.v.*] are kept); an eternal light burning before the ark; two candelabra pews; and a raised platform, from which scriptural passages are read and, often, services conducted.

Segregation of the sexes, which is strictly observed by Orthodox and ultra-Orthodox Jews [*q.v.*], has been discontinued by Reform [*q.v.*] and Conservative [*q.v.*] Jewry. Among diaspora [*q.v.*] Jews, synagogues are often independent, reflecting the local community's wishes in its construction, maintenance, choice of priest, called rabbi (Hebrew: *teacher*), and officials.

Syria:

OFFICIAL NAME: Arabic Republic of Syria

CAPITAL: Damascus [*q.v.*]

AREA: 71,500 sq. mi./185,180 sq. km

POPULATION: 22.50 million (2011 est.)

GROSS DOMESTIC PRODUCT (nominal): $59.96 billion; per capita, $2,802 (2010 est.)

GROSS DOMESTIC PRODUCT (Purchasing Power Parity): $107.83 billion; per capita, $5,040 (2010 est.)

NATIONAL CURRENCY: Syrian Pound (SP); SP 100 = U.S. $2.13 = £1.36 = €1.64 (2010)

FORM OF GOVERNMENT: republic, president elected by voters

OFFICIAL LANGUAGE: Arabic [*q.v.*]

ADMINISTRATIVE SYSTEM: Syria consists of 14 governorates.

CONSTITUTION: The 1973 constitution, approved overwhelmingly in a referendum, described Syria as a democratic, popular, socialist state, and required that Islam [*q.v.*] should be the religion of the head of state. Article 8 stated "The Arab Baath Socialist Party [*q.v.*] leads the state and society." Executive power rests with the president with seven-year tenure. The National Assembly, elected directly, chooses the sole candidate for the presidency, who is then approved by voters in a referendum. The president has the authority to appoint or dismiss vice presidents, prime ministers, and individual ministers. He is also the commander-in-chief of the military. Legislative power lies with the 250-member People's Assembly, which is dominated by the Arab Baath Socialist Party-led National Progressive Front [*q.v.*]. Following the death of President Hafiz Assad

[*q.v.*] in 2000, the National Assembly lowered the age requirement for president from 40 to 34. The new constitution approved by 89.4 percent of the voters in February 2012 changed the minimum age for president to 40 years and limited his/her tenure to two seven-year terms. It ended the Baath Socialist Party's monopoly of power, but banned political parties based on ethnic, religious, regional, or tribal basis.

ETHNIC COMPOSITION (2011): Arabs [*q.v.*] 90 percent, Kurds [*q.v.*] 6 percent, Armenians [*q.v.*] and other 4 percent.

High officials:

Head of state: Bashar Assad [*q.v.*], 2000–

Vice presidents: (First) Farouoq al-Shaara (political and foreign affairs), 2006– ; (Second) Najah al-Attar (culture), 2006–

Prime minister: Wael Nader Halqi, 2012–

Speaker of the People's Assembly: Muhammad Jihad Laham, 2012–

HISTORY (since ca 1900): Following a collapse of the four-century-long Ottoman rule in 1918, Greater Syria [*q.v.*] enjoyed a brief spell of self-rule under Faisal I bin Hussein [*q.v.*] until his defeat by the French, the Mandate power, in mid-1920. After enlarging the Vilayat of Lebanon at the expense of Syria, the French divided the area into Latakia, Jebel Druze, Aleppo, and Damascus, combining the last two in 1924 to form the state of Syria.

It took France two years to quell the armed rebellion that erupted in Jebel Druze and spread elsewhere in 1925. The subsequent talks resulted in the convening of a national assembly in 1928. Dominated by the nationalist National Bloc, the assembly adopted a constitution that did not recognize the French Mandate. Paris dissolved the parliament and imposed its own constitution in 1930. The parliament elected under this constitution reached an impasse with the French high commissioner on the terms of a treaty to replace the mandate, and was suspended.

Popular protest reached a peak in early 1936 and shut down public services and markets for seven weeks. This compelled the French to negotiate with the National Bloc. Due to the installation of a leftist Popular Front government in Paris, these talks were successful. According to the Franco-Syrian Treaty [*q.v.*], initialed in September 1936, Paris agreed to grant independence to Syria in three years in exchange for long-term military, political and economic privileges. A National Bloc government, elected in November 1936, was in power on the eve of World War II, when France suspended both the 1930 constitution and the government, and imposed martial law.

After the occupation of northern France by Nazi Germany in 1940, and the subsequent establishment of a pro-German regime in Vichy in central France, control of the overseas French territories passed to the Vichy regime. It was defeated in Syria (and Lebanon) by British and Free French forces in June 1941, and Syria was granted (nominal) independence. When a general election was called in 1943 the National Bloc won handsomely. The next year Syria won the recognition of the United States and the Soviet Union. Because it declared war on Germany in February 1945,

Syria was invited to the founding conference of the United Nations. At the end of the war France tried to reassert its authority in Syria, but failed. France finally left in April 1946.

Syria's unsuccessful participation in the 1948–49 Palestine War [*q.v.*] led to rioting and paved the way for the army coup which occurred in March 1949. Military rule lasted for five years under different rulers, the last of them being Adib Shishkali [*q.v.*]. His overthrow was followed by the restoration of parliamentary democracy.

The first free election in the Middle East [*q.v.*] took place in Syria in September 1954, with women accorded suffrage. This led to the rise of radical groups, including the Baath Party [*q.v.*]. When faced with a choice of aligning either with traditional parties, such as the National Bloc, or radical ones such as the Communists [*q.v.*], the Baath chose a way out by proposing Syria's union with Egypt. The resulting United Arab Republic (UAR) [*q.v.*] lasted from early 1958 to September 1961.

A secret Military Committee formed by Baathist officers was the main force behind a coup in March 1963. Factional infighting within the Baath was settled in favor of the radicals, led by Salah Jadid [*q.v.*], in early 1966. The new government, with Hafiz Assad [*q.v.*] as defense minister, pursued radical socioeconomic policies at home and actively opposed the conservative Arab government in the region. Though it successfully withstood the loss in its popularity because of its defeat in the June 1967 Arab-Israeli War [*q.v.*], the regime became divided on apportioning blame. The nationalist wing, led by Assad, blamed the socialist wing, headed by Jadid. In the ensuing struggle, Assad's faction won in November 1970. He consolidated his presidency through a referendum in early 1971. By forming the Baathist-led National Progressive Front [q.v.] in 1972, he co-opted friendly parties.

The initial gains made by Syria on the Golan Heights [q.v.] front during the early phase of the October 1973 Arab-Israeli War [q.v.] were lost later. When, in the course of his intervention in the Lebanese Civil War [q.v.] in mid-1976, he sided with the Maronite Christian [q.v.] camp, there was an upsurge in support for the Muslim Brotherhood [q.v.]. It started a campaign of assassination and terrorism, which escalated into near-insurrection in Aleppo [q.v.] and Hama [q.v.] in March 1980, and reached a peak with an assassination attempt on Assad in June.

He went all out to crush the Islamists, and temporarily succeeded. The Brotherhood's violent activities resumed and culminated in an insurrection in Hama in February 1982. Assad hit back with unprecedented force, re-imposing control at the cost of 5,000 to 10,000 lives. When he suffered a heart attack in November 1983, his power was challenged, unsuccessfully, by his younger brother, Rifat.

Following the arrest and conviction in October 1986 of Nizar Hindawi (a Jordanian purportedly working in conjunction with the Syrian Embassy in London) for attempting to plant a bomb on an Israeli airliner in London, Britain broke off diplomatic relations with Syria. The United States recalled its ambassador from Damascus and placed Syria on the list of nations supporting international terrorism. The next year Syria closed down the training camps run by Abu Nidal [q.v.]. In September 1987 the U.S. ambassador returned to Damascus, but Washington retained Syria's name on its list of terrorist nations.

Meanwhile Assad justified his continuing involvement in the Lebanese civil strife on the ground that defection of Lebanon to the U.S.-Israel camp would present grave danger to Syrian security. He persevered, and in October 1990 the pro-Syrian side finally won in Lebanon. He was far less successful in dealing with the Palestine Liberation Organization (PLO) [q.v.], led by Yasser Arafat [q.v.]. After Egypt's defection from the Arab camp in 1979, Assad embarked upon a plan to achieve strategic parity with Israel, an ambitious proposition to be implemented with the active backing of the Soviet Union. Considering Palestinians an important part of an alliance to deal with Israel, he tried to bring Arafat under his wing. But Arafat, intent on maintaining the PLO's independence, resisted him. The subsequent Assad-inspired rebellion within Arafat's party, Fatah [q.v.], while weakening him made Arafat turn to moderate King Hussein [q.v.] of Jordan.

With the rapid decline of the Soviet Union as a superpower from 1989 onwards, Syria had to soften its strategy toward Israel. It took a realistic view of the leadership that the United States, now the sole superpower, provided in reversing Iraq's occupation of Kuwait after August 1990. When Syria's attempt to persuade Iraqi President Saddam Hussein [q.v.] to evacuate Kuwait failed, it joined the U.S.-led anti-Iraq coalition and sent 30,000 troops to reinforce Saudi Arabia's defenses.

In October 1991 Syria agreed to participate in the Middle East Peace Conference [q.v.]—which was intended to lead to bilateral talks between Israel and its Arab enemies—having been assured that the conference would be held on the basis of UN Security Council Resolutions 242 and 338, specifying Israel's return of the Arab lands captured in 1967 to secure peaceful coexistence. Syria disapproved of the Israeli-PLO Accord [q.v.] and the Jordanian-Israeli Peace Treaty [q.v.], but did nothing to undermine them. In its talks with Israel, it insisted on a clear Israeli commitment to vacate all of the Golan in return for total peace, and succeeded in getting the United States to play an active role in the negotiations.

Once Syria and Israel had agreed to a 10-point framework in late 1995, its representatives held talks at a venue in the United States in early 1996. But, when suicide bombings by radical Islamist Palestinians killed 50 Israelis in late February-early March, Israeli Prime Minister Shimon Peres [q.v.] demanded that Syria condemn the attacks. Assad replied that these had nothing to do with his country. Peres unilaterally terminated the negotiations with Damascus. The situation remained unchanged during the three years when Benjamin Netanyahu [q.v.] was Israel's prime minister. Talks resumed after the election of Ehud Barak [q.v.] as Netanyahu's successor. In September 1999, U.S. Secretary of State Madeleine Albright backed the Syrian demand for total

withdrawal from the Golan Heights. In December Barak met Syrian foreign minister Farouq al-Shaara in Washington. Three months later U.S. President Bill Clinton presented Barak's proposals to Assad in Geneva. These included Israel retaining sovereignty over a narrow strip on the northeastern shore of Lake Tiberias to safeguard its water resources. Assad agreed to give Israel access to the strip but not sovereignty. The talks broke down. Assad died in June.

Three years earlier Assad had begun mending fences with Iraq by resuming economic links with Baghdad which he had been broken in 1980 after Iraq's invasion of Iran. His successor, Bashar Assad continued this policy—with the reopened pipeline between the two neighbors providing Syria with 200,000 barrels of oil per day for domestic consumption, thus making an equivalent amount available for export—as well as sticking to the Syrian position that Israel had to withdraw from all of the Golan Heights in return for total peace and normalization of relations.

Soon after Bashar assumed supreme power in Syria, 99 leading intellectuals demanded an end to the martial law that had been in force since 1963. In response, the government announced that the emergency laws had been suspended. The release of 600 political prisoners on top of another 225, freed by Hafiz Assad in the last days of his rule, still left 1,500 politicians in jail. After the initial surge of liberalization, Bashar Assad slowed down the pace of political reform to placate the old guard in the Baath Party and the military and intelligence services. He maintained the Syrian force of 30,000 in Lebanon. He also continued to let radical Palestinian organizations maintain their head-offices in Damascus.

In the wake of the 11 September 2001 attacks on the United States by Al Qaida [*q.v.*], Syria, long opposed to Islamic fundamentalism [*q.v.*], offered actionable intelligence to Washington, thus thawing its relations with the sole superpower. But since Damascus continued to support Lebanon's Hizbollah [*q.v.*], America kept Syria on its list of the countries that sponsor international terrorism.

On 1 January 2002, Syria was elected a non-permanent member of the UN Security Council as a representative of the Arab member-states. It voted for the Security Council Resolution 1441 requiring Iraq to give unimpeded access to UN inspectors charged with locating and destroying Iraq's facilities for making weapons of mass destruction, thus making its adoption unanimous. It did so in order to avoid an invasion of Iraq by the United States which it opposed. The United States and Britain invaded Iraq, nonetheless.

Following the chaos and violence that erupted in postwar Iraq, many Iraqis took refuge in Syria. Their total reached 1.3 million by 2007, creating a huge burden on the government. By then Assad had strengthened further Syria's ties with Iran by signing a mutual defense pact with it in 2006. This became the backbone of the Iran-Syria-Hizbollah nexus, providing a regional counterforce to the United States-Egypt-Saudi Arabia alliance. As such when, in September 2007, Israeli jet fighters demolished a sus-

pected nuclear reactor under construction in northeastern Syria by North Korean technicians, neither Egypt nor Saudi Arabia or any other major Arab country protested.

Assad also forged strong links with Russia which became its chief arms supplier. In 2008 his government signed a deal to let Russia develop and enlarge the naval base in Tartus, with the first stage of modernization, completed within four years, to get the base ready to accommodate heavy Russian warships, including aircraft carriers.

In the region, on the eve of the presidential election in Lebanon in September 2004, the UN Security Council passed Resolution 1559 (by 9 notes to nil, with 6 abstentions) to express support for a free and fair presidential election in Lebanon, and called on all foreign troops to leave the country. Assad argued that these troops had been invited by the Arab League [*q.v.*] to pacify Lebanon in the midst of its long-running civil war.

After the assassination of former Lebanese Prime Minister Rafiq Hariri in Beirut [*q.v.*] in February 2005, the pro-West 14 March Alliance [*q.v.*] blamed Syria for the murder. It denied involvement. The UN Security Council set up a commission to investigate the assassination.

The pressure on Syria to withdraw its last soldier form Lebanon intensified. Syria did so in April 2005. A general election followed in Lebanon the next month. Two years later, once the National Assembly had chosen Assad as the sole presidential candidate, its decision was approved by 97.6 percent of the voters in a referendum.

Syria's relations with Lebanon improved. In 2008 the two neighbors established diplomatic relations, thereby according each other parity. The opening of the Syrian Embassy in December was followed by Lebanon reciprocating in March 2009. By paying Assad a visit in December the newly appointed Lebanese Prime Minister Saad Hariri [q.v.] implicitly recognized Syria's special role in his country. By then the U.S. administration of Barack Obama had reversed the policy of its predecessor to isolate and demonize Syria.

Steady improvement in Damascus-Washington relations came to a halt when the wave of Arab unrest reached Syria on 15 March 2011 with residents of the southern town of Deraa protesting the torture of youths who had sprayed anti-government graffiti. The demonstrators demanded release of political prisoners and lifting of the emergency laws dating back to 1963. The killing of three protestors in Deraa led to the protest spreading to other places. Assad ended the emergency rule in mid-April. But by then the anti-regime resistance had intensified in the Sunni-dominated cities of Hama and Homs [q.v.], with the calls for Assad's removal from office. The government resorted to sending tanks into restive areas as security forces and snipers opened fire on demonstrators. Those soldiers who refused to fire on civilians were executed summarily. Small scale defections followed.

On 29 July in a video uploaded on Internet a group of deserters in uniform, led by Colonel Riad Assad, announced the formation of the Free Syrian Army (FSA) with the aims of protecting civilians and overthrowing the Baathist regime. Almost a month later a group of exiled Syrian opposi-

tion leaders meeting in Istanbul announced the formation of the Syrian National Council (SNC)[q.v.]. Its funding came from Qatar, Saudi Arabia, and a few European countries, including France. It was formally launched on 2 October in Istanbul with its constitution describing toppling the Assad regime as its primary aim.

Two days later at the UN Security Council, a draft resolution strongly condemning "the continued grave and systematic human rights violations and the use of force against civilians by the Syrian authorities" was vetoed by Russia and China. They criticized the document as a preamble to changing the Syrian regime.

When after accepting an Arab League peace plan later that month, Assad stepped up attacks on protestors, the Arab League suspended Syria's membership. In the midst of this turmoil the Syrian government held local elections in December as planned.

In January 2012, by a majority vote, the Arab League urged Assad to step down and hand over power to a deputy to make way for a transition toward democracy. He rejected the call. On 4 February when 13 of the 15 UN Security Council members backed the Arab League plan, Russia and China vetoed it. Russia denounced the document because it made no mention of the killings of the security forces by armed extremists. On 16 February the UN General Assembly passed a non-binding resolution by 137 votes to 12 urging Assad to step down.

Stung by the killing of its 10 soldiers by the FSA in Homs on 3 February, the Syrian government intensified its efforts to seize the four city districts under partial or full control of the FSA. It directed artillery shells and mortars at these districts. After nearly three weeks of besieging the Bab al-Amr, controlled by a battalion of the FSA, on 10 February, the Syrian army launched a ground assault with infantry and recaptured the district which had been vacated by the FSA.

None of this interfered with the government's plan to hold a referendum on 26 February on the new constitution which abrogated the Baath Party's monopoly on power. On a voter turnout of 57 percent, it was approved by nearly 90 percent, according to the official sources. It also implemented its military plan to seize the control of the districts in Homs it had lost to the FSA. It succeeded.

On the first anniversary of the uprisings on 15 March 2012, the death toll of the protestors stood at 7,500 with the security forces having lost nearly 2,100 personnel at the hands of the FSA and other armed dissenters.

On 16 March Kofi Annan, acting as the UN-Arab League's special envoy to Syria, submitted a peace plan to the UN based on the principle of "an inclusive Syrian-led political process to address the legitimate aspirations and concerns of the Syrian people." Its main features were the UN-supervised "cessation of armed violence in all its forms by all parties"; timely provision of humanitarian assistance to the areas affected by the fighting; release of the arbitrarily detained persons; ensuring freedom of movement for journalists; and respecting he legally guaranteed freedom of association and peaceful demonstrations.

Once the Annan Plan was accepted by Assad, a cease-fire came into effect on 12 April. Monitors of the UN-supervised cease-fire started arriving in May. But the cease-fire started to unravel after about a month as the government tried to recover parts of some towns still controlled by the FSA and the FSA, now equipped with anti-tank missiles supplied by Saudi Arabia and Qatar with the active cooperation of Turkey, increased their attacks on the security forces. As Sunni militants, infiltrated by groups affiliated to Al Qaida [*q.v.*] resorted to attacking Alawi villages, the Alawi militia, commonly known as *Shabiha* (Arabic: *ghosts*), backed by the security forces, retaliated by massacring Sunni villagers, including women and children. In two such instances in the town of Houla near Homs and the hamlet of Mazraat al-Qubair near Hama in late May and early June, nearly 190 Sunnis lost their lives. They introduced the sectarian factor into the worsening crisis.

The situation worsened further in mid-July after the killing of the defense minister and his deputy during a meeting by a bomb triggered by remote control. In a concerted move, the rebels gained control of parts of Damascus and Aleppo. The International Committee of the Red Cross ruled that Syria was in the midst of a civil war. Backed by Russia and Iran, Assad reiterated his resolve to defeat the rebels. Due to lack of popular support in the city neighborhoods they captured, the rebels were often unable to consolidate their gains. The government mounted periodic offensives to regain the lost territory. The stalemate at the UN Security Council continued. Annan decided to step down as the UN-Arab League envoy for Syria at the end of August and was replaced by Lakhdar Ibrahimi.

As the size and importance of Syrian and foreign jihadists rose in the war, the Western powers and Turkey decided not to supply anti-aircraft missiles to the rebels, who continued to be vulnerable to the regime's air strikes. Western leaders feared that such weapons would end up with Islamist extremists and make Western aircraft vulnerable once Syria had gone off the boil. By early September, the conflict had claimed the lives of nearly 20,000 civilians and armed rebels and 8,000 members of the security forces. The ongoing battles between the two sides in Aleppo, Damascus, and Homs [q.v.] raised the death toll.

LEGISLATURE: The 250-member People's Assembly has a tenure of four years. They are elected in 15 multi-seat constituencies. In the chamber 169 seats are allocated to the National Progressive Front, consisting of several political parties, led by the Arab Baath Socialist Party, with the rest going to independents. The Assembly chooses the presidential candidate for the presidency, who is approved in a popular referendum. In the 2007 election the Baath Party won 134 seats. By the time the parliamentary poll was conducted under an amended constitution in May 2012, the PNF's membership had increased to 10. Altogether it won 168 seats, with the rest going to the 11 newly formed factions and independents. Among the PNF's constituents, the Baath Party led with 134 seats.

RELIGIOUS COMPOSITION: (2010) Muslim [q.v.], 90 percent, of which Sunni [q.v.] 73 percent, Alawi 12 percent, Druze [q.v.] 3 percent, Ismailis [q.v.] 2 percent; Christian, [q.v.] 9 percent; other, 1 percent.

Syrian Catholic Church: *Christian sect* As a Uniate Church [q.v.], the Syrian Catholic Church accepts the primacy of the Pope but has retained its Eastern rites and customs. Attempts at reconciling the Syrian Orthodox Church [q.v.] with the Western church, based in Rome, in the mid-13th century failed. But four centuries later some members began to convert to Catholicism [q.v.] while retaining their Liturgy of St. James in Syriac. The office of the Syrian Catholic Patriarch of Antioch was formalized in 1782. Since then the patriarch has been based in Deir Zafran, Sharfe, Aleppo [q.v.], Mardin (Turkey), and Beirut [q.v.].

Syrian National Council: In August 2011 the exiled leaders of the Syrian Muslim Brotherhood [q.v.] joined six opposition groups in Istanbul to announce the formation of the Syrian National Council (SNC). Its funding came from Qatar, Saudi Arabia, and a few European countries, including France. It was formally launched on 2 October in Istanbul with its constitution describing toppling the Assad regime as its primary aim.

The wide variety of its constituents—political groups, long time exiles living in Europe and North America, grass-roots organizers called Local Coordination Committees which advertised and coordinated demonstrations, and armed militants, divided along ideological, ethnic, or sectarian lines—militated against the

SNC devising and implementing a coherent policy and strategy. The fractious constituents elected Burhan Ghalioun, a Paris-based Syrian-French academic president on a monthly basis. His term was renewed with the crucial support of the Muslim Brotherhood [q.v.], the single largest group among the Council's 270 members, which was resolved to keep a low profile so as not to frighten the Western powers.

With many of its officials being Western-based exiles, the SNC had excellent contacts with European and American politicians. Therefore, the SNC quickly succeeded in persuading the United States and the European Union to impose sanctions on Syria. But their appeals for Western military intervention failed. They even had to discard the idea of humanitarian corridors inside Syria because no such resolution could be passed by the UN Security Council due to the opposition of Russia and China.

Serious differences arose among SNC leaders on the question of relationship with the Free Syrian Army. The largely secular, liberal, non-Islamic leaders of the SNC feared the FSA—an amorphous entity consisting of many small groups of army deserters and individual armed dissidents lacking unified command and control—getting Islamized. When SNC leaders refused to arm or fund the FSA, 20 leading Council members resigned in February to form the Syrian Patriotic Group.

After much wavering the SNC accepted the Kofi Annan peace plan, as did the FSA, with the cease-fire going into effect on 12 April 2012. Since then both sides were reported to have

violated the cease-fire but not too seriously. On the other hand, the FSA repudiated the cease-fire in late May.

In June, after the rotating presidency had passed to Abdulbaset Saida, a Kurd [q.v.] based in Sweden. He urged fresh defections from the security forces while reaching out to Kurds, Christians [q.v.], Alawis [q.v.], and Druzes [q.v.].

Noting the continued domination of the SNC by the Muslim Brotherhood, and its failure to link up with the rebel factions inside Syria, the United States and Britain discarded their earlier stance of encouraging all anti-regime groups to coalesce around the SNC.

Syrian Orthodox Church: *See* Orthodox Christians, Syrian.

Syrian Social Nationalist Party (Lebanon): *Lebanese political party* The Syrian Social Nationalist Party (SSNP) emerged in 1947 out of the Syrian Nationalist Party, founded in 1932 by Antun Saadeh [q.v.] with the aim of creating a Greater Syria [q.v.] that could accommodate all the people forming the Syrian nation, which Saadeh described as an ethnic fusion of Canaanites, Akkadians, Chaldeans, Assyrians, Arameans, Hittites, and Metannis.

The SSNP combined opposition to the French Mandate with secularism —including separation of church and state and removal of barriers between various sects and religions—and a state-directed program for modernizing society. The French banned the party in 1935, but it continued to function secretly. In 1938 Saadeh published *Nushu al-umam* (Arabic:

Rise of Nations), in which he argued the case for a unique Syrian identity.

The outbreak of World War II found Saadeh in Latin America on a mission to forge links with the Syrian settlers there. On his return to Lebanon in 1947 he reestablished control over the party, now renamed the Syrian Social Nationalist Party, which derived the majority of its support from the non-Maronite [*q.v.*] section of the Christian community. Due to his views on an all-embracing Syrian nationalism, he soon clashed with the Lebanese government. He went underground but was allowed to resurface after he had affirmed his acceptance of Lebanon as a sovereign state.

In June 1949 there was fighting in Beirut between the SSNP and the Phalange Party [*q.v.*], which, the SSNP alleged, had been provoked by the government of Riyadh Solh [*q.v.*]. The authorities described it as an attempted coup by the SSNP; they arrested 2,000 SSNP members and banned the party. Saadeh fled to Syria. Although received warmly by the Syrian leader Hosni Zaim [*q.v.*], he was extradited to Lebanon. Following a secret military trial he was executed; and in revenge SSNP militants assassinated Solh two years later. Though much weakened, the party continued to function semi-clandestinely until the lifting of the ban on transnational parties in 1970.

Led by Inaam Raad, the SSNP remained bitterly opposed to the Phalange. When the Lebanese Civil War [*q.v.*] broke out in April 1975 it allied with the Movement of the Disinherited, led by Musa al-Sadr [*q.v.*], to form the pro-Syrian

Nationalist Front. Habib Tanios Shartuni—who was responsible for blowing up the Phalange headquarters in Beirut in September 1982, killing the president-elect, Bashir Gemayel [*q.v.*]—was a member of the SSNP, which had by then emerged as a staunch ally of Syria in resisting Israel's ambitions in Lebanon. It became an important element in the anti-Israeli front, conducting guerilla actions against the Israeli troops and their surrogate, the South Lebanese Army (SLA) [*q.v.*], in southern Lebanon.

After the defeat of Gen. Michel Aoun [*q.v.*] in October 1990, the SSNP's fighters took over some of the offices of the Phalange, which had backed Aoun. In the national unity government formed two months later, Inaam Raad was appointed minister. The SSNP participated in the 1992 general election.

Later the party's leadership passed to Jibran Araiji. In the 2005 parliamentary election, it won two seats. As part of the 14 March Alliance [*q.v.*], it retained its two seats in the chamber four years later.

Syrian-Soviet Friendship Treaty

(1980): The following factors led Syrian President Hafiz Assad [*q.v.*] to conclude a 20-year Treaty of Friendship and Cooperation with the Soviet Union in Moscow in October 1980: the signing of the Egyptian-Israeli Peace Treaty [*q.v.*] in 1979, mounting domestic and regional pressures on his regime, and the outbreak of the Iran-Iraq War [*q.v.*] in September 1980.

It stipulated consultation "in the event of a situation jeopardizing the

peace and security of either party."
Later it was revealed that the treaty
contained a secret clause dealing with
the use of atomic weapons by a potential attacker, implying Israel. The
treaty boosted Syria's confidence.
Later there were unconfirmed reports
that Moscow had stockpiled heavy
weapons in Syria for use in the event
of war between Syria and Israel.
However, despite the treaty and
Syria's involvement in Lebanon, the
Soviet Union reacted passively to the
Israeli invasion of Lebanon [*q.v.*] in
June 1982, chiefly because of the rapidly deteriorating health of its leader,
Leonid Brezhnev. With the collapse
of the Soviet Union in 1991, the
treaty lapsed.

T

Tabriz: *Iranian city* Population: 1.6 million (2011 est.). Capital of East Azerbaijan province, Tabriz is Iran's
fourth-largest city. Known as Tauris in
ancient times, it was the capital of
Atropaten, named after Atropates, a
general of Alexander of Macedonia (r.
336–323 B.C.). Its present name, a
derivative of *tap riz*, meaning heat
flow, refers to the hot springs surrounding it. Capital of the Ghazni dynasty, founded by Khan Mahmoud
Ghazan (r. 1295–1304), from the late
13th century, Tabriz fell to Tamerlane
in 1392. Shah Ismail captured it from
the Ottoman Turks in 1501 and
founded the Safavid dynasty.

During the Second Russo-Iranian
War (1827–1828) it was occupied by
the Russians. They reoccupied it during World War I, and stayed until the
Bolshevik Revolution in October
1917. During World War II the Soviets occupied the city in 1941, when it
became an important link in the
transportation of American war materials from Iran's Gulf [*q.v.*] ports to
the Soviet Union by rail.

Tabriz was the capital of the Autonomous Government of Azerbaijan,
set up by the Democratic Party of
Azerbaijan in December 1945, which
lasted a year. It was at the forefront of
the revolutionary movement in 1977–
78, by which time it had emerged as
an important commercial, industrial,
and communications center, producing tractors, motor cycles, cement, tex-
tiles, and carpets.

Despite severe earthquakes, the last
one in 1780, several of its historical
monuments have survived. These include the early-14th-century citadel
and the mid-16th-century Blue
Mosque, so called because of its stunning blue tile decoration.

Taif Accord (Lebanese): *See* National
Reconciliation Charter 1989
(Lebanon).

Taimur bin Faisal (1885–1956): *Sultan
of Oman, 1913–32* Born in Muscat
[*q.v.*], Taimur succeeded his father,
Faisal, in 1913. He inherited a country
mired in a tribal revolt and heavy
debts. His attempt to buy peace failed.
In 1915 the rebellious tribal leader,
Shaikh Isa bin Salim al-Harthi, attacked the coastal region of Muscat-
Batinah. Aided by the military of
Britain's India government, he repelled the insurgents and regained the
coastal region, leaving the interior in
the hands of Shaikh Isa al-Harthi.

The subsequent uneasy peace allowed the British Political Agent in Muscat to initiate peace talks in 1918. The resulting Treaty of Sib [*q.v.*], signed in September 1920 between Taimur and "the people of Oman," recognized the authority of the sultan in external matters and guaranteed freedom of movement to the tribes and urban dwellers. Shaikh Isa al-Harthi, representing the tribal chiefs of the interior, promised not to break the peace or give refuge to wrongdoers from coastal towns. Taimur agreed not to raise taxes on coastal towns above 5 percent of the value of trade.

Since concluding a treaty with Shaikh Isa al-Harthi implied autonomy for the interior, Taimur was reluctant to do so. To overcome his resistance, Britain gave him a loan to repay the debts he had incurred from the coastal traders. However, he defaulted on his loan repayments and let the administrative machinery slacken. The efforts of British civil servants to salvage the situation failed, and in 1932 Britain forced him to abdicate in favor of his son, Said [*q.v.*].

al-Takfir wal Hijra (Egypt) (Arabic: *The Denunciation/Repentance and the Migration*): *Egyptian Islamic group* A clandestine group established in 1972, al-Takfir wal Hijra came to light during the January 1977 rioting that followed the withdrawal of subsidies on daily necessities, when its members attacked nightclubs and bars in Cairo [*q.v.*]. It was led by Shukri Ahmad Mustafa, an agricultural engineer, who, as a Muslim Brotherhood [*q.v.*] activist, had spent six years in jail (1965–71). Though his followers called themselves *al-Gamaat al-Mus-*

limin (Arabic: *The Muslim Groups*), the authorities pinned the title of *al-Takfir wal Hijra* on them to sum up their ideology and tactics.

In his manuscript, *Al-Tawassumat* (Arabic: *The Searching Looks*), Mustafa called on the faithful to avoid living among infidels, to spread their divine knowledge throughout the land, and to wage a jihad [*q.v.*] to establish an Islamic order. Arguing that atheists and their state, Egypt, would not be destroyed by Allah while the faithful lived among them, he advised Muslims to migrate and form a pure community along the lines of the Medinese polity of the Prophet Muhammad. Many of Mustafa's followers took to living in the caves and mountains of Minia in southern Egypt, where inter alia they underwent arms training. They were discovered by the security forces in September 1973, only to be pardoned by President Anwar Sadat [*q.v.*] after the Arab-Israeli War of October 1973 [*q.v.*].

Since Mustafa considered that religious functionaries were infidels, his followers boycotted prayers led by them, and instead prayed together in their homes. They married among themselves, withdrew their children from state schools, and refused to be drafted into the military. Organized into secret cells, they numbered 3,000 to 4,000 on the eve of the January 1977 riots. The government arrested 60. When the demand of al-Takfir wal Hijra activists to try them or free them was ignored, they forced the issue in July by kidnapping Shaikh Muhammad Hussein al-Dhahabi, a former minister of religious trusts, for writing a newspaper article against their party. When their demand was refused they killed Dhahabi. The subsequent repression led to the trial of 465 members by military courts. Of these, five, including Mustafa, were executed. Many of its members then joined the al-Gamaat al-Islamiya [*q.v.*]. However, in the mid-1990s, the party revived, and 245 of its members found themselves behind bars in 1996.

Later there were splits in the organization, and some Islamist extremist groups carried out terrorist acts outside of Egypt, particularly in Algeria and Sudan, while using its name.

Talabani, Jalal (1933–): *Iraqi Kurdish leader* Born into a landowning family in Koy Sanjak, Irbil province, Talabani obtained a law degree from Baghdad University and practiced as a lawyer. A member of the Kurdistan Democratic Party (KDP) [*q.v.*] since his late teens he rose to become a member of its politburo. Disagreeing with the accord that the KDP leader, Mustafa Barzani [*q.v.*], concluded with the Iraqi government in 1964, he quit the KDP and set up an "alternative" KDP in 1966.

After being defeated by Barzani's followers, he fled to Iran, and then to Baghdad [*q.v.*], where he sided with the government. When the KDP struck a deal with the Baathist [*q.v.*] regime in March 1970, he returned to its headquarters in Hajj Omran. But he fell out with Barzani again, and left for Beirut [*q.v.*], where he came under the influence of leftist Palestinian leaders, George Habash [*q.v.*] and Nayef Hawatmeh [*q.v.*]. He then moved to Damascus [*q.v.*] to serve as the KDP's envoy there.

Disagreeing with Barzani's decision to flee to Iran in the wake of the March 1975 Algiers Accord [*q.v.*], Talabani left the KDP to found the Kurdish Workers League. In mid-1976 it combined with the Social Democratic Movement to form the Patriotic Union of Kurdistan (PUK) [*q.v.*] under Talabani's leadership. It gained popular support in the southeast Kurdistan Autonomous Region (KAR) [*q.v.*], and became a rival to the KDP.

However, the outbreak of the Iran-Iraq War [*q.v.*] in September 1980 lessened hostility between the two parties as they concentrated on escalating their struggle against Baghdad. Talabani's agreement with the KDP in 1982 to open up all of the KAR to both parties helped the PUK to expand at the KDP's expense. Prodded by Iran, in May 1985 Talabani agreed to cooperate with the KDP. Two years after they sponsored the formation of the Iraqi Kurdistan Front (IKF) [*q.v.*].

The PUK set up liberated areas along Iraq's borders with Iran. But in the spring and summer of 1988 the Iraqi military recovered these areas, and Talabani and other PUK leaders fled to Syria. After Gulf War II [*q.v.*], Talabani helped trigger a Kurdish uprising against Baghdad in early March 1991. It was successful, but only briefly. Its crushing by the central government caused an exodus of some 1.5 million Kurdish refugees. The intervention by the Western powers created a safe haven in the KAR.

Following the general election for the KAR Legislative Council in May 1992, Talabani shared power equally with the KDP's Masoud Barzani [*q.v.*].

Yet the traditional rivalry between the urban-based PUK and the rural-based KDP was far from over. In May 1994 bloody clashes between the two left more than 1,000 people dead. In the seesaw struggle between the two parties, Talabani's PUK gained control of two-thirds of the 3.2 million inhabitants of Kurdistan, including those in Irbil [*q.v.*], by September 1995. But he lacked the resources to administer them. He turned to Iran for help. That upset Barzani as well as President Saddam Hussein [*q.v.*], and led to an alliance between the two erstwhile enemies in 1996. Barzani recovered most of the lost area, including Irbil.

The intra-Kurdish fighting undermined Washington's strategy of developing Kurdistan as the base for overthrowing Saddam. It withdrew its agents and funds from the area. Its efforts to conciliate Talabani with Barzani met with only partial success chiefly because Barzani refused to share the hefty customs duties he collected on the illicit export of Iraqi oil to Turkey. After the passage of the Iraq Liberation Act by U.S. Congress in 1998, Talabani found the PUK certified as a faction that was entitled to Washington's military aid. But he did not seek it.

When, after defeating the Taliban regime in Afghanistan in late 2001, the U.S. administration of President George W. Bush turned its attention to overthrowing Saddam's government by force, the importance of Talabani as well as Barzani rose. The high point came in August 2002 when he and the leaders of other five recognized Kurdish groups were received in Washington by Vice President Dick Cheney.

Talabani and his party cooperated fully with the Pentagon on the latter's plans to invade Iraq in March 2003. After the downfall of the Saddam Hussein regime, Paul Bremer of the Coalition Provisional Authority appointed Talabani as a member of the Interim Iraqi Governing Council.

In 2004 Talabani allied with the KDP to form the Democratic Patriotic Alliance of Kurdistan (DPAK). In the January 2005 general election, the DPAK won 75 seats in the 275-member Interim National Assembly and 104 places in the 111-member Kurdish Regional Assembly. In April Talabani was elected the interim president of Iraq. In that capacity he played an important role in the drafting of the new constitution.

After the parliamentary election under the new constitution in December 2006, he was elected president for a four-year term. He thus became the head of the presidency council of three, the other two members being a Shia [*q.v.*] and a Sunni [*q.v.*]. As such, he tried to act as an honest broker among the feuding factions in the parliament.

In December 2006 he criticized the report of the Iraq Study Group, led by James Baker, a former secretary of state, and Lee Hamilton, a former senior lawmaker, which recommended that the United States should withdraw its soldiers from combat role by 2009. His view prevailed at the White House, and President George W. Bush opted for a surge in U.S. troops in Iraq, raising it to 140,000.

Following the parliamentary elections in 2010, Talabani was reelected president of Iraq. In July 2011 he called a joint meeting of the cabinet and the presidential council to decide whether U.S. troops should stay in Iraq beyond the agreed date of December 2011. The participants decided against extending the presence of U.S. forces.

Talal bin Abdullah al-Hashem (1909–72): *King of Jordan, 1951–52* Born in Mecca [*q.v.*] to Abdullah bin Hussein al-Hashem [*q.v.*], Talal ascended the throne of Jordan in July 1951 following the assassination of his father. He issued a new constitution on 1 January 1952. It divided legislative power between the monarch and the parliament, consisting of a fully nominated senate and an elected chamber of deputies. His governing style deviated from the paternalism of his father. His rule was brief because he was diagnosed as mentally ill. He was forced to abdicate in favor of his son Hussein [*q.v.*], a minor, in August 1952 and was committed to a mental clinic in Istanbul, where he died 20 years later.

Taleqani, Mahmoud (1910–79): *Iranian Islamic leader* Born into a religious Shia [*q.v.*] family in Taleqan village, Mazandaran province, Taleqani went to Qom [*q.v.*] for his Islamic studies. After graduating in 1938, he taught at a theological school in Tehran [*q.v.*]. In 1939 he was jailed for six months for delivering antigovernment lectures—the first of many imprisonments that kept him behind bars for more than 15 years.

During the 1951–53 oil nationalization movement, he backed Premier Muhammad Mussadiq [*q.v.*]. After the 1953 countercoup by Muhammad Reza Shah Pahlavi [*q.v.*], he was arrested for having once sheltered Navab Safavi, the Fedai Khalq [*q.v.*] leader. In the early 1960s, in association with Mahdi Bazargan [*q.v.*], he founded the Liberation Movement of Iran [*q.v.*]. He was sentenced to 10 years' imprisonment in January 1964 for participating in the protest movement of June 1963.

Of his many books, *Labor and Property in Islam* was the best known. In it he argued that since God had created the world for all humankind, and had no intention of dividing up society into exploiting and exploited segments, a classless society is enjoined by Islam [*q.v.*]. This won him popularity among both Islamic and secular leftists. Known to be close to the Mujahedin-e Khalq [*q.v.*], he was arrested in June 1977 and charged with assisting an outlawed party. He was tortured. Mounting public pressure during the revolutionary turmoil compelled the shah to release him in November 1978.

With one son active with the Mujahedin-e Khalq and another with the Fedaiyan-e Islam [*q.v.*], he was well-placed to weld a revolutionary coalition of Islamic and secular opposition forces, and he did so. He was a member of the Islamic Revolutionary Council (IRC), appointed by Ayatollah Ruhollah Khomeini [*q.v.*] during his stay in Paris. After the revolution in February 1979 he became its chairman.

Following the arrest and torture of his two left-wing sons by the new regime in April, he left Tehran [*q.v.*] in protest at the return of despotism, but overcame his differences with Khomeini after a meeting with him a few days later. Khomeini appointed him the Friday prayer leader of Tehran, a great religious honor. He became Khomeini's chief trouble-shooter. Due to his intervention much bloodshed was avoided between the regime and the leftist forces, and also between the central government and Kurdish [*q.v.*] autonomists. He was at ease with both Prime Minister Bazargan and Khomeini, and he was also a bridge between the radical IRC and the moderate Bazargan government.

When it came to interpreting the Sharia [*q.v.*], he took a position midway between Ayatollah Muhammad Kazem Shariatmadari [*q.v.*], who forbade intervention by clerics in daily administration, and Khomeini, who wanted an activist role for the clergy in all walks of life. In the framing of the Islamic constitution, Taleqani insisted on a bill of rights for citizens, and stressed the importance of individual freedom. In terms of popular support, which spanned a wide political spectrum, he was second only to Khomeini, upon whom he was a moderating influence. His death in September 1979 deprived the Islamic regime of a much revered mediator and healer.

Talmud (Hebrew: *learning*) The Talmud is a multivolume compilation of Jewish Oral Law, codified and compiled in Hebrew by Judah HaNassi around 200 A.D., with added commentaries, written in Aramaic, during the next four centuries. Study in ancient academies was conducted orally, and it is not known when the Talmud was first written down.

There are two versions of it: the Palestinian (completed in 400 A.D.) and the Babylonian (completed in 500 A.D.). At 2.5 million words, the later version is three times as long the earlier one. The Babylonian Talmud is the authoritative version. It consists of the text of the Oral Law, Mishna [*q.v.*], and other collections, including Tosefta; and the Gemara [*q.v.*], the commentaries on the text. (Sometimes the term *Talmud* is used for Gemara alone.) When Rabbi Shlomo Yitzhaki, known as Rashi, a leading interpreter of the Hebrew Bible [*q.v.*] in the 11th century A.D., produced his commentary on the Talmud, the debates summarized in the Gemara became available to Jewish scholars at large. The comments of Rashi and his three grandsons were incorporated into the later versions of the Talmud.

The Babylonian Talmud was first published in Spain around 1482. The standard version, annotated in the 16th century, first appeared in Vilnius, Lithuania, in 1886, followed by 36-volume translations of the Babylonian Talmud into German and English in the 20th century.

The Mishna is divided into six orders and comprises 63 tractates, only 36 of which have commentaries. Though the main purpose of the Gemara was to summarize the rabbinical debates on the interpretation of the Mishna and judicial administration, it became a source of information on a variety of subjects, with its nonlegal text called the Haggada (Hebrew: *Narrative*). In a dialectical fashion, the Talmud presents a piece of legal text followed by various interpretations included in the Gemara and the works of Rashi and his three grandsons.

Devout Jews [*q.v.*] regard the opinions given by the judges in the Talmud as having the force of law. The Talmud is of major significance to Orthodox [*q.v.*] and ultra-Orthodox Jews [*q.v.*], and their rabbis consult it when considering any matter of importance. This is particularly true in Israel.

Tanua LeAhdut HaAvodah (Hebrew: *Movement for Labor Unity*): *Zionist group in Palestine* When, in early 1944, David Ben-Gurion [*q.v.*] proposed to the Histadrut [*q.v.*] Executive Committee that the delegates chosen for an international trade union conference in London should seek its support for an independent Jewish state in Palestine [*q.v.*], many leftists disagreed. Those in Mapai [*q.v.*] left to found the *Tanua LeAhdut HaAvoda*. Rejecting Mapai's demand for partitioning Palestine, and the HaShomer HaTzair's (Hebrew: *The Young Guards*) call for a single bi-national state, the new group opted for a socialist Jewish state in all of Palestine. In 1946 it allied with the left-wing Poale Zion [*q.v.*].

taqlid (Arabic: *to hang around the neck*) At first the term applied to the practice of designating a sacrificial animal with a sign around its neck; this was later extended to designating a public official with a badge or chain around his neck. Figuratively, it meant public acceptance, or the traditional way of doing things. In religion it is the opposite of *ijtihad* [*q.v.*]. It imitates or rests on the opinions and interpretations of the past clerics of the Quran [*q.v.*] and the Hadith [*q.v.*]. *See* marja-e taqlid.

Tashnak Party (Lebanon) (Armenian: *Federation*): *Lebanese political party* The Tashnak, the leading party of Armenian Orthodox Christians [*q.v.*] in Lebanon, is center-right in its policies. During the 1975–90 Lebanese Civil War [*q.v.*], while being close to the Phalange Party [*q.v.*], it insisted on maintaining "positive neutrality." Claiming that they wanted to eradicate gambling dens in the Armenian Orthodox districts in northeast Beirut [*q.v.*], the Phalangists attacked the area in 1979, but were repulsed by the Tashnak Party's militia. The party stuck to its neutrality, and after the civil war maintained a low profile in the Lebanese politics. It boycotted the parliamentary election in 2005, but joined the Hizbollah [*q.v.*]-led 8 March Alliance [*q.v.*] in the 2009 general election and won two seats.

Tehran: *capital of Iran* (Also spelled Teheran) Population: 8.54 million (2011 est.) Some 60 mi./100 km south of the Caspian Sea and situated at the foot of the Elbruz Mountains, Tehran is the most populous city in the Persian Gulf [*q.v.*] region. It is near the ancient settlement of Rages and the medieval Persian capital of Rey (now Reyshahar), which was razed by invading Mongols in 1220. It began to thrive during the Safavid rule (1501–1722), but it was not until three years after Aqa Muhammad Khan Qajar (r. 1779–1790), the founder of the Qajar dynasty, had consolidated his rule and conquered Tehran in 1785 that it became the national capital. Modernized by Reza Shah Pahlavi (r. 1925–41) [*q.v.*], who overthrew the Qajars, the city has expanded and absorbed a large number of migrants from the provinces.

In late 1943 Tehran was the venue for the Allied summit conference between U.S. President Franklin Roosevelt, British Prime Minister Winston Churchill, and Soviet Prime Minister Joseph Stalin, when they agreed on the scope and timing of military offensives against Germany and the creation of the United Nations to handle the problems of peace. The participants also declared their respect for the sovereignty and territorial integrity of Iran.

During the last quarter-century of the reign of Muhammad Reza Shah Pahlavi (r. 1941–79) [*q.v.*], the growth of the city, fueled by rising oil revenue, was dramatic. The contrast became sharper between the affluent districts of the north at the foot of the mountain, and the poor neighborhoods of the south.

Besides being the administrative center, Tehran is also the industrial hub of the country, producing nearly half of its many manufactured goods. Its tourist attractions include the Gulistan, Saadabad, and Maramar Palaces, which were turned into museums after the 1979 Islamic revolution [*q.v.*]; the Niavaran Palace, the former residence of the shah; the Baharstan Palace, housing the Majlis [*q.v.*]; and the Sepah-salar Mosque. The latest addition is the mausoleum of Ayatollah Ruhollah Khomeini [*q.v.*] on the southern outskirts of the city.

Tehiya (Hebrew: *renaissance*): *Israeli political party* Tehiya was formed in 1979 by Moshe Shamir after he had left Likud [*q.v.*] in protest at the Egyptian-Israeli Peace Treaty [*q.v.*], which involved returning all of Sinai [*q.v.*] to Egypt and uprooting the Jewish colonists there. Tehiya wanted Israel to assert its sovereignty over the Oc-

cupied Territories [*q.v.*] and accelerate the Jewish settlement program. In the 1984 election it won five seats, and in the 1988 election three. It joined the national unity administration that was formed in 1988, but withdrew in January 1992 in protest at the government's decision to continue to participate in the Middle East peace process [*q.v.*], initiated by the Middle East Peace Conference [*q.v.*] in Madrid three months earlier. In the June 1992 election it failed to win any seats.

Tel Aviv-Jaffa: *capital of Israel (internationally recognized)* Pop. 404,400 (2010 est.)

Jaffa: Claiming lineage from Japheth, son of Noah, Jaffa has over four millennia of history. Ruled in turn by Canaanites, Egyptians, Philistines, Israelites, Persians, Greeks, Assyrians, Maccabeans, and Romans, it was the see of a bishop in the Christian era. It fell to Muslim [*q.v.*] Arabs [*q.v.*] in 637 A.D., and remained under Muslim rule thereafter, except during 1126–1187 and 1191–1196, when it was held by the Crusaders. Fearing a fresh Crusade, the Cairo-based [*q.v.*] Mamluke ruler destroyed it. It was not until the late 17th century, under the Ottomans (r. 1516–1918), that Jaffa was revived as a thriving port.

It was captured by the British army during World War I in November 1917. After World War II there was sporadic fighting between the predominantly Arab Jaffa and its Jewish neighbor, Tel Aviv. Within a year of the founding of Israel in 1948, Jaffa was amalgamated with Tel Aviv, and the enlarged entity was called Tel

Aviv-Jaffa. With the inauguration of a modern port at Ashdod in 1965, the port of Jaffa, hitherto the second-largest in Israel, was closed.

TEL AVIV: Derivative of *Tel Havee* (Arabic: *Hill of Spring*). Established as a Jewish suburb of Jaffa in 1909, Tel Aviv was named after the Hebrew translation of Theodor Herzl's novel *Altneuland* (German: *New Old Land*). As the site of a Jewish secondary school opened in honor of Herzl, it started to attract more and more Jewish inhabitants. It became a separate town in 1921. After the Arab-Jewish riots of 1936, the town was provided with port facilities. On the eve of the establishment of Israel in May 1948 there was fighting between Jewish Tel Aviv and Arab Jaffa, which ended with the surrender of Jaffa and the flight of its Arab residents.

The State of Israel was declared in Tel Aviv on 14 May 1948, and the countries that recognized it opened their embassies there. These embassies stayed in Tel Aviv when the Israeli government, the parliament, and all the ministries except defense moved to West Jerusalem [*q.v.*]. Tel Aviv is the headquarters of almost all Israeli political parties and newspapers. It is the leading commercial and industrial center, employing a larger number of people in industry than any other Israeli city.

Temple Mount: *Jewish holy site See* Noble Sanctuary.

Terrorism: There is no universally accepted definition of terrorism. In the United States, three official definitions exist. According to the defense department: "Terrorism is the calculated use of violence or the threat of violence to inculcate fear, intended to coerce or intimidate governments or societies as to the pursuit of goals that are generally political, religious or ideological." According to the state department, "Terrorism is pre-meditated, politically motivated violence perpetrated against non-combatant targets by sub-national groups or clandestine agents, usually intended to influence an audience." Finally, according to the justice department, "Terrorism is the unlawful use of force or violence against persons or property to intimidate or coerce a government, the civilian population, or any segment thereof, in furtherance of political or social objectives." None of these match the definition used by the British government in its The Prevention of Terrorism Act, 2000: "The use or threat, for the purpose of advancing a political, religious or ideological cause of action which involves serious violence against any person or property, endangers the life of any person or creates a serious risk to the health or safety of the public or section of the public." The Uniting and Strengthening America by Providing Appropriate Tools Required to Intercept and Obstruct Terrorism (USA PATRIOT) Act, 2001, has two separate definitions of terrorism, both of them over-long and complicated.

Since terrorism is an international phenomenon, a globally accepted definition is essential. In the absence of it, the debate about the relationship, if any, between terrorism and resistance to military or colonial occupation remains unresolved. While the list of 22 terrorist groups published by Washington in November 2001 included Lebanon's Hizbollah [*q.v.*], thus resulting in its assets being frozen in the United States, Lebanon [*q.v.*] refused to follow its lead, arguing that it distinguished between those organizations which practiced terrorism and those which sought to liberate their occupied countries or territories by all means.

Another important factor in this case was whether a particular terrorist faction had a global reach—an essential pre-requisite used by America to make its list of banned organizations. In the view of the Lebanese government, Hizbollah lacked a global reach.

Not an ideology like fascism, capitalism, socialism, or Islamic fundamentalism [*q.v.*], terrorism is a method which is open for deployment not only by individuals or groups but also by governments. Indeed, the term entered political vocabulary two centuries ago as part of the "Reign of Terror" or just "The Terror" in 1793–1794, unleashed by the government of the Republic of France established a year earlier by the French revolutionaries, when some 12,000 people were executed as counterrevolutionaries.

In the Middle East [*q.v.*] the most dramatic example of state terrorism was in Syria. To crush the Islamist-inspired insurrection in Hama [*q.v.*] in February 1982, the government deployed thousands of troops to quell it. Before order was restored, between 5,000 and 10,000 people, including 1,000 soldiers, lay dead, and a quarter of the historic old city was razed. And the bombing of King David Hotel in Jerusalem [*q.v.*] by Irgun [*q.v.*], led by Menachem Begin [*q.v.*] in April 1946, which killed 96 civilians, including 15 Jews [*q.v.*], was the first mas-

sive terrorist political act of its kind in the Middle East of recent times.

al-Thani, Ahmad bin Ali (1911–78): *ruler of Qatar, 1960–72* Son of Shaikh Ali al-Thani [*q.v.*], Ahmad Thani was born in Doha [*q.v.*]. Though installed on the throne by the British, he tried to show some independence. In 1961 he led Qatar into the newly formed Organization for Petroleum Exporting Countries (OPEC) [*q.v.*]. Three years later, yielding to pressure by the National Unity Front [*q.v.*] and Britain, he appointed an advisory council with the power to issue laws and decrees for "the fundamental principles and basic rules of overall policy."

In April 1970 he promulgated an interim constitution, which, by specifying a largely elected consultative council, marked an important step toward a representative government. However, that left untouched the "rule of four quarters": the first quarter of revenues for the administration, the second for the ruler, the third for the al-Thani princes, and the fourth for economic development. Thani negotiated the ending of the 1916 Anglo-Qatari Treaty [*q.v.*] and declared Qatar independent in September 1971. Fueled by the proceeds of an oil output of 600,000 barrels per day, his extravagance reached unprecedented proportions. This, and his refusal to establish the advisory council specified by the 1970 constitution, paved the way for a bloodless coup by Prime Minister Khalifa bin Hamad al-Thani [*q.v.*] in early 1972.

al-Thani, Ali bin Abdullah (1894–1976): *ruler of Qatar, 1948–60* Son of Shaikh Abdullah bin Qasim, Thani was born in Doha [*q.v.*]. With the death in 1947 of his elder brother, Hamad, the heir apparent and deputy ruler, Thani was named to succeed him. His accession to the throne coincided with the extraction of oil on a commercial scale. This allowed him to develop public services and build up economic infrastructure. Being a Wahhabi [*q.v.*], he moved cautiously in economic and political spheres, while basing the legitimacy of his rule on Islam [*q.v.*] and refusing to share power. This was unsatisfactory to the British, who made him abdicate in 1960 in favor of his son, Ahmad [*q.v.*].

al-Thani, Hamad bin Khalifa (1950–): *ruler of Qatar, 1995–* Born in Doha [*q.v.*], Thani was educated there. After graduating from the Royal Military Academy in Sandhurst, Britain, in 1971, he joined the Qatari military as a major. Four years later he was promoted to major-general and appointed commander-in-chief of the armed forces. After being named crown prince in May 1977, he was put in charge of the defense ministry. He continued his program of modernizing the military; and in his additional role as president of the Higher Planning Council he started modernizing the state infrastructure. By the early 1990s he was involved in determining major domestic and foreign policies.

Under his leadership the Qatari military joined the Washington-led coalition against Iraq in Gulf War II [*q.v.*]. But in 1994 he reconciled Qatar with Iraq while Saudi Arabia, leader of the Gulf Cooperation Council [*q.v.*], was still hostile toward it. By reviving Qatar's border dispute with Riyadh, he tried to reassert his coun-

try's independence. In June 1995 while his father, Shaikh Khalifa bin Hamad al-Thani [*q.v.*], was in Geneva, Switzerland, he staged a bloodless coup and ascended the throne.

At home he ended censorship of the media, and communicated with the press, explaining government policies. In 1996 he sponsored the establishment of the partially state-funded Al-Jazeera television [*q.v.*], giving it as much editorial freedom as was accorded to the British Broadcasting Corporations by the British government.

In order partly to establish Qatar's individuality in the Arabian Peninsula [*q.v.*], dominated by Saudi Arabia, he pursued policies that differed radically from Saudi Arabia's. He established trade ties with Israel and improved relations with Iraq as well as Iran. He mediated successfully in Lebanon to reconcile opposing camps. He offered funds for the reconstruction of southern Lebanon after the Israeli-Hizbollah War of 2006 [*q.v.*].

Thani held the first direct election to the nationwide Municipal Council on the basis of universal franchise in 1999. The following year Qatar became chair of the Islamic Conference Organization [*q.v.*] but only after it had closed down the Israeli trade office in Doha.

In 2002, when popular sentiment in Saudi Arabia turned against the military presence of the United States, dating back to the 1991 Gulf War, in the Saudi kingdom, Shaikh Hamad al-Thani allowed the Pentagon to shift most of its military hardware and personnel to Qatar's al-Udaid air base. During the run-up to the Anglo-American invasion of Iraq in March

2003 [*q.v.*], he permitted the Pentagon's Central Command to set up a forward base at al-Saliyah Camp near Doha.

Buoyed by the ballooning income from natural gas and oil, he started playing an important role in regional affairs. After the Israeli-Hizbollah War [*q.v.*] in 2006, he stepped forward to help financially all those who had lost their homes and businesses. In May 2008 he mediated successfully between the rival camps in Lebanon and thus helped avert the possibility of full-scale civil war. When the Arab League [*q.v.*] headquarters refused to hold an emergency session of Arab leaders during the Israeli attack on the Gaza Strip [*q.v.*] in December 2008–January 2009, he hosted a meeting of 13 Arab leaders in Doha.

He resorted to using the hugely popular Al-Jazeera TV's Arabic channel to advance Qatar's foreign policy. During the 2011 Arab Spring [*q.v.*], he and his TV channel backed the popular uprisings, except in Bahrain. He became one of the vociferous supporters of the opposition to the regime of Syrian President Bashar Assad [*q.v.*].

In 2011, *Forbes* magazine put his personal net worth at $2.5 billion. Early the following year, as head of the Qatar Museums Authority, his daughter Sheikha Mayassa bint Hamad al-Thani paid a record-breaking $250 million for Paul Cézanne's painting *The Card Players*.

al-Thani, Khalifa bin Hamad (1930–): *ruler of Qatar, 1972–95* Son of Shaikh Hamad bin Abdullah, the heir apparent who died before his father, Thani was born in Doha [*q.v.*]. He started his administrative career as director of police and internal security, moved to education, and graduated to running the ministry of finance and petroleum affairs before being appointed prime minister and deputy ruler.

He staged a palace coup in February 1972 to seize the throne, fearing that his uncle, Shaikh Ahmad [*q.v.*], would nominate his son, Abdul Aziz, to succeed him. Thani appointed a fully nominated advisory council of 20 members, with the power to advise the cabinet only on matters referred to it by him. He abolished the practice of allocating a quarter of the state's revenue to the personal account of the ruler. But by giving 10 of the 15 ministries to his brothers and sons, he consolidated his power. He directed the process of modernization stimulated by the boom in oil production, which brought in revenue of $5.4 billion in 1980, making Qatar's per capita income one of the highest in the world. He backed Iraq in the 1980–88 Iran-Iraq War [*q.v.*] financially. He was a cofounder of the Gulf Cooperation Council [*q.v.*] in 1981. While continuing to rule by decree, he periodically expanded the advisory council. He joined the Washington-led coalition against Iraq in Gulf War II [*q.v.*].

In June 1995, during his trip to Switzerland, he was overthrown in a bloodless coup by his son, Hamad bin Khalifa [*q.v.*], whom he had appointed crown prince in 1977. He went into exile first in Abu Dhabi [*q.v.*] and then France. He was allowed to return to Qatar in 2004.

al-Thani dynasty: The progenitor of the al-Thani dynasty was Shaikh Thani bin Muhammad, who belonged to the Bani Tamim tribal confederation's Mudari tribe of Wahhabi [*q.v.*] persuasion, which had migrated to Qatar in the 18th century. After being under the authority of the al-Khalifas [*q.v.*] of Bahrain, the al-Thanis, led by Shaikh Qasim bin Muhammad, found themselves installed as the ruling family by the British in the 1860s. They maintained their preeminence during the Ottoman suzerainty (1872–1916). The collapse of the Ottoman Empire brought Qasim's son, Shaikh Abdullah al-Thani (1876–1948), closer to the British, who cosigned the 1916 Anglo-Qatari Agreement [*q.v.*]. He was succeeded by his son, Shaikh Ali al-Thani (1894–1976) [*q.v.*], who in 1960 abdicated in favor of his son, Shaikh Ahmad (1911–78) [*q.v.*]. In a bloodless coup in 1972 Shaikh Ahmad was replaced by his first cousin, Shaikh Khalifa bin Hamad al-Thani [*q.v.*]. The al-Thani clan was about 1,500-strong in the late 1990s.

Tigris River: Known in biblical times as Hiddekil, the Tigris River rises in the mountains of eastern Turkey and flows roughly 1,180 mi./1,900 km in a southeasterly direction through northern Syria and Iraq, where it joins the Euphrates River [*q.v.*] about 120 mi./190 km from the Persian Gulf [*q.v.*]. It provides irrigation for the fertile plain of Mesopotamia [*q.v.*], a cradle of civilization.

Tiran Strait: Situated between Egypt's Sinai Peninsula [*q.v.*] and Saudi Arabia, the Strait of Tiran lies at the mouth of the Gulf of Aqaba, at the end of which is the Israeli port of Eilat, the country's only opening to

the sea east of the Suez Canal [*q.v.*]. Following the 1956 Suez War [*q.v.*], a UN Emergency Force (UNEF) [*q.v.*] was stationed at Sharm el Shaikh at the mouth of the Strait to ensure its status as an international waterway. During the crisis preceding the June 1967 Arab-Israeli War [*q.v.*], Egypt asked the UN secretary-general to remove UNEF from Sharm el Shaikh. Once this was done, Egypt closed the straits to Israeli shipping. This escalated the crisis, which culminated in a war with devastating preemptive Israeli air attacks on Egypt, Syria, and Jordan.

Titles, Religious: (beginning with the highest rank)
  (1) CHRISTIANITY [*q.v.*]
  Catholic [*q.v.*]:
  Pope
  Cardinal
  Patriarch
  Archbishop/Primate
  Bishop
  Priest (often addressed as Father)
  Deacon (often addressed as Father)
  ORTHODOX [*q.v.*]:
  Armenian Orthodox [*q.v.*]:
  Patriarch
  Archbishop/Primate
  Bishop
  Priest
  Deacon
  Greek Orthodox [*q.v.*]:
  Ecumenical Patriarch
  Patriarch
  Metropolitan
  Archbishop
  Bishop
  Archimandrite
  Priest
  Other Orthodox denominations fall into one of the above hierarchies.

Protestant [*q.v.*]:
Archbishop/Primate
Bishop
Dean
Provost
Archdeacon
Canon
Priest (often addressed as Reverend)
Deacon (often addressed as Reverend)
(2) ISLAM [*q.v.*]
Shia [*q.v.*]:
Hazrat (Arabic: *Threshold*; a title accorded to a prophet)
Nabi (Arabic: *Apostle;* a title accorded to a prophet)
Marja-e taqlid (Arabic: *Source of emulation*)
Ayatollah Ozma (Arabic: *Grand sign of Allah*)
Ayatollah (Arabic: *Sign of Allah*)
Hojatalislam (Arabic: *Proof of Islam*)
Thiqatalislam (Arabic: *Trust of Islam*)
Mullah (derivation of Mawla; Arabic: *Master* or *learned man*)
Shaikh (Arabic: *old man*; a title accorded to a senior man of power)
Sayyid (Arabic: *Lord* or *Prince*; a hereditary title accorded to a male descendant of the Prophet Muhammad)
haajj/haji: (Arabic/Persian: *one who has performed the hajj* [q.v.])
These titles are not mutually exclusive.
Sufi [*q.v.*]:
Hazrat (Arabic: *Threshold*; a title accorded to a prophet)
Qutb (Arabic: *Pivot*)
Pir (Persian: *Guide*)
Ishan (Persian: a title of respect; accorded to a spiritual guide)

Murshid (Arabic: *Guide*)
Shaikh (Arabic: *old man*; a title accorded to a senior man of power)
These titles are not mutually exclusive.
Sunni [*q.v.*]:
Hazrat (Arabic: *Threshold*; a title accorded to a prophet)
Nabi (Arabic: *Apostle*; a title accorded to a prophet)
Mahdi (Arabic: *One who is guided by Allah*)
Mujtahid (Arabic: *One who practices interpretative reasoning*/equivalent to Ayatollah)
Shaikh-al-Islam (Arabic: *Wise man of Islam*)
Mufti al-Azam (Arabic: *Grand deliverer of fatwas*, religious rulings)
Mufti (Arabic: *One who delivers fatwas*, religious rulings)
Qadi (Arabic: *Religious judge*)
Shaikh (Arabic: *old man*; a title accorded to a senior man of power)
Maulana/Maulavi (derivation of Mawla; Arabic: *Master or learned man*)
Sayyid (Arabic: *Lord* or *Prince*; a hereditary title accorded to a male descendant of the Prophet Muhammad)
haajj/hajji: (Arabic: *One who has performed the hajj* [q.v.])
These titles are not mutually exclusive.

Titles, Secular: (in alphabetical order)
Emir (Arabic: *Commander or Prince*)
Emira (Arabic: *Princess*)
Fakhamah al-Rais (Arabic: *His Excellency*)
Jalalah al-Malik (Arabic: *His Majesty*)
Khan (Turkish: *Chieftain* or *Ruler*)
Malik (Arabic: *King*)
Malika (Arabic: *Queen*)

Mirza (Persian: *Son of Prince*; a title accorded to a noble man)

Pasha (Turkish: *Grandee* or *Governor*)

Shah (Persian: *King*)

Shaikh (Arabic: *old man*; a title accorded to a senior man of power)

Shaikha (Arabic: *old woman*; a title accorded to a senior woman of power)

Shahbanu (Persian: *Queen*)

Shah-en-Shah (Persian: *King of Kings*)

Sultan (Arabic: *Ruler*)

Torah (Hebrew: *law, precept*): Torah is the Hebrew name given to the first five books of the Old Testament [*q.v.*]: Genesis, Exodus, Leviticus, Numbers, and Deuteronomy. It is also known as the Written Law, the Law of Moses, and the Pentateuch (Greek: *Five Books*). Tradition has it that it was given by God to Moses on Mount Sinai during the wanderings of the Israelites in the Sinai Peninsula [*q.v.*] between ca 1290 B.C. and ca 1250 B.C. Strictly speaking, the Torah is the written text of the Pentateuch. Broadly speaking, though, it covers both the written text and the detailed oral exposition conveyed to Moses, known in Judaism [*q.v.*] as the Oral Law.

Torah Religious Front: *Israeli political party* The Torah Religious Front is the name given to the alliance formed periodically by Agudat Israel [*q.v.*] and Poale Agudat Israel [*q.v.*] on the eve of a general election. These parties did so in 1955 and again in 1973, winning respectively six and five seats in the Knesset [*q.v.*].

Despite its modest size, it ranked fourth in the 1973 Knesset, dominated by Labor Alignment [*q.v.*] and

Likud [*q.v.*]. After the split in the Front, the three-member Agudat Israel succeeded in bringing about the downfall of the Labor Alignment-led coalition in late 1976 by getting a no-confidence motion passed against it following the Israeli Air Force's breach of the Sabbath [*q.v.*].

Touma, Emile (1918–85): *Palestinian writer and politician* Born into a Greek Orthodox [*q.v.*] middle-class family in Haifa [*q.v.*], Touma moved to Jerusalem [*q.v.*] for his university education. He joined the Communist Party of Palestine (CPC) [*q.v.*] in 1939, then left it four years later for the Arab-dominated League of National Liberation (LNL), which spawned the Federation of Arab Trade Unions and Labor Societies. He founded the party journal *Al-Ittihad* (Arabic: *The Unity*). In line with the Soviet Union's decision to back partition of Palestine [*q.v.*] in late 1947, he remained in Israel after its establishment in May 1948.

In October when Maki [*q.v.*] was formed by a merger of the CPC and the remnants of the LNL, Touma became one of its leaders. He continued to edit *Al-Ittihad*. Following the publication in Arabic of his book *The March of the Arab Peoples and the Problems of Arab Unity*, he was awarded a doctorate in history by the Moscow Institute of Oriental Studies.

When Maki split in 1965, Touma joined Rakah [*q.v.*], which was recognized by the international department of the Communist Party of the Soviet Union two years later. He was often the party's chief representative at international gatherings. He was active, both as a journalist and an author, in promoting the national rights of Palestinians in Israel and abroad. His views on the subject were summarized in his *Sixty Years of the National Movement in Palestine* (in Arabic), published in 1978. As secretary of the Arab People's Conference in Support of the Palestine Revolution, he called a congress in December 1980, which was banned by the Israeli government.

His death five years later was widely mourned by Israeli Arabs [*q.v.*] irrespective of their party affiliations. The next year the Emile Touma Institute for Palestinian and Israeli Studies was established in Haifa in his memory.

Trablus: *See* Tripoli.

Transition Law, 1949 (Israel): In February 1949 the Constituent Assembly, resulting from an election held on 25 January by the provisional government of Israel, passed the Transition Law. It declared Israel a republic, to be headed by a president, elected by a simple majority for a five-year term by the Knesset [*q.v.*], a single-chamber house of 120 deputies. The Knesset was to be elected by adult franchise under a system of proportional representation, the leader of the largest group being invited by the president to become the prime minister and form the government, which would exercise full executive powers. Having passed the Transition Law, and having decided to postpone indefinitely a written constitution, the Constituent Assembly transformed itself into the Knesset.

Transjordan: Transjordan was the name given in July 1922 to the region east of the Jordan River [*q.v.*] in what had previously been southern Syria, now occu-

pied for more than a year by Abdullah bin Hussein al-Hashem [*q.v.*]. In May 1923, after Britain had recognized Emir Abdullah's rule and promised him an annual subsidy, it became the autonomous Emirate of Transjordan. He was required to establish a constitutional regime. He agreed, and declared Transjordan "independent." Almost five years passed before Abdullah had promulgated a constitution, which stipulated that legal and administrative authority should be exercised by the ruler through a legislative council. He then signed the Anglo-Transjordanian Treaty (1928), which required him to formulate a common foreign policy with Britain, and allow the stationing of British forces on its soil in exchange for a British guarantee to protect Transjordan against foreign attack. A British resident, by whose advice Abdullah agreed to be guided, was then appointed.

After Transjordan acquired independence in May 1946, Abdullah assumed the title of king and renamed his realm the Hashemite Kingdom of Jordan. *See also* Jordan.

Treaty of Frontier and Good Neighborly Relations (Iran-Iraq, 1975): On 6 March 1975 Iraq's vice president, Saddam Hussein [*q.v.*], and Iran's king, Muhammad Reza Shah Pahlavi [*q.v.*], signed an accord in Algiers, Algeria. They agreed to delimit their fluvial boundaries along the Shatt al-Arab [*q.v.*] according to the thalweg line (the median line of the deepest channel), and to end all infiltrations of a subversive nature. The latter provision applied chiefly to the Iranian-backed Kurdish insurgency against the Iraqi government. The

Treaty of Frontier and Good Neighborly Relations, based on the Algiers Accord, was signed in Baghdad on 13 June and ratified by both parties on 17 September 1975.

A joint commission was appointed to demarcate the new land border in Iran's Qasr-e Shirin area in the light of Iraq's claim that Iran retained territory in contravention of the 1913 Protocol of Constantinople [q.v.] and the concession Iraq had made on the Shatt al-Arab boundary, having so far claimed the full waterway as its territory. Overall, the treaty signified a victory for Iran as it incorporated the Iranian demand, made over 60 years before, that the thalweg principle should be applied to the Shatt al-Arab frontier. Harassed and exhausted by the Iranian-backed Kurdish insurgency, the Iraqi regime conceded the Iranian demand.

However, on 17 September 1980, accusing Iran of violating the 1975 treaty by intervening in Iraq's domestic affairs by backing and financing the leaders of the revived Kurdish insurgency, and by refusing to return to Iraq the border territories in the Qasr-e Shirin area it had retained in contravention of the 1913 Protocol of Constantinople, President Saddam Hussein abrogated the treaty forthwith. Tearing up Iraq's copy of the document on television, he claimed that Iraq had thereby regained full sovereignty over the Shatt al-Arab. He insisted that henceforth any Iranian ships using the waterway must engage Iraqi pilots and fly the Iraqi flag. Tehran refused. On 22 September 1980 Iraq invaded Iran, starting the Iran-Iraq War [q.v.], which lasted until August 1988.

During the talks that followed the truce, Iran blocked any United Nations moves to survey the Shatt al-Arab to assess the work needed to clear it of sunken vessels and unexploded mines, arguing that, according to the 1975 treaty, cleaning up the waterway was the joint responsibility of the signatories. Iraq said that the treaty contained four principles: non-interference in the internal affairs of the signatories; cessation of Iran's aid to the Iraqi Kurds [q.v.]; the return by Iran of the territory due to Iraq according to the 1913 Protocol; and delineation of the fluvial border along the mid-channel of the Shatt al-Arab. Violation of any one of these principles—such as the gross interference by Iran in Iraq's domestic affairs that, Iraq claimed, started soon after the 1979 Islamic revolution [q.v.]—invalidated the whole treaty. Iran argued that the treaty dealt primarily with boundaries, and could not be abrogated unilaterally. The matter remained unresolved until Iraq's occupation of Kuwait in early August 1990. In a letter to Iranian President Ali Akbar Hashemi Rafsanjani [q.v.] on 14 August, reversing his previous stand, Saddam Hussein agreed to abide by the 1975 treaty.

Treaty of Iran-Iraq Frontier (1937): Signed on 4 July 1937, the Treaty of Iran-Iraq Frontier confirmed the land boundaries as set out in the 1913 Protocol of Constantinople [q.v.], confirmed in 1914, but amended slightly the fluvial frontier along the Shatt al-Arab [q.v.]. Iraq conceded the thalweg—the median line of the deepest channel—principle for four miles opposite Abadan [q.v.], which housed an oil refinery of the Anglo-Persian Oil Company (APOC). The treaty stated that the Shatt al-Arab was open for navigation to all the countries of the world. Even though the treaty was between the sovereign states of Iran and Iraq, independent since 1932, it took ample note of the diplomatic and commercial interests of Britain, the leading foreign power in both countries, which dominated both APOC and the Iraq Petroleum Company, which had struck oil in northern Iraq in 1927.

Treaty of Good Neighborly Relations (Iran-Iraq, 1949): Following the conclusion of the Treaty of Good Neighborly Relations in 1949, a supplement to the Treaty of Iran-Iraq Frontier (1937) [*q.v.*], mutual ties were raised to ambassadorial level.

Treaty of Jeddah (Anglo-Saudi, 1927): The May 1927 Treaty of Jeddah formalized relations between Britain and Abdul Aziz bin Abdul Rahman al-Saud [*q.v.*] after he had declared himself King of Hijaz [*q.v.*] and Sultan of Najd [*q.v.*] and its Dependencies in 1926. London recognized Abdul Aziz al-Saud and his realm, and he in turn accepted Britain as the protector of Oman and the principalities in the Gulf [*q.v.*].

Treaty of Lausanne (1923): After the Turks under Mustafa Kemal had rejected the Treaty of Sèvres [*q.v.*] and defeated the Greeks in their attempt to conquer western Turkey, there were negotiations between Turkey and the Allies of World War I (Belgium, Britain, France, Greece, Italy, Japan, Romania, and the Kingdom of Serbs,

Croats, and Slovenes [later Yugoslavia]), resulting in the Treaty of Lausanne, signed on 23 July 1923. Turkey renounced its claims to the non-Turkish provinces of the Ottoman Empire, and the Allies confirmed Turkish sovereignty over Anatolia. A convention dealing with the interests of the powers in the Bosphorus Straits, including the Soviet Union, was signed on the same day, and added to the Treaty of Lausanne. It specified freedom of navigation for merchant ships of all nations in war and peace, and for warships of the powers in the straits in peace as well as the war, in which Turkey remained neutral.

Treaty of Muhammara (Najdi-Iraqi, 1922): The Treaty of Muhammara was signed in May 1922 to demarcate the border between Iraq and Najd [*q.v.*] (later Saudi Arabia). Later a neutral zone was created between the two countries according to the Protocol of Uqair [*q.v.*].

Treaty of Muslim Friendship and Arab Fraternity (Saudi-North Yemeni, 1934): After a six-week war in March-April 1934, North Yemen and Saudi Arabia signed the Treaty of Muslim Friendship and Arab Fraternity in May. The conflict had occurred in the wake of the failure of talks between the two sides in 1933 following attempts by North Yemen's Imam Yahya Hamid al-Din in 1931–32 to reassert his authority among the tribes around the fringes of his mountain heartland in the reigns of Najran, Asir, and Tihama. Having overpowered the North Yemenis and captured Hodeida port, the Saudis accepted a cease-fire mainly because British, French, and

Italian warships rushed to Hodeida, intent on curbing Saudi expansionism. The treaty, signed in Taif, Saudi Arabia, returned to Imam Yahya nearly half of the area he had lost in the war, including the southern part of the Tihama coastal plain, leaving the upland Najran and Asir in Saudi hands.

Treaty of Sèvres (1920): Signed on 10 August 1920 between Ottoman Sultan Muhammad VI's prime minister, Damad Ferid, and the victors of World War I, the Treaty of Sèvres— based on the 30 October 1918 Mudros Armistice, which was tantamount to an unconditional surrender on the part of the Ottomans—required the dismemberment not only of the Ottoman Empire but also of its nucleus, the Turkish heartland of Anatolia. The partitioning of Anatolia included turning the southeastern region, then containing the province of Mosul [*q.v.*], into an autonomous territory, with the prospect of full independence if recommended by the League of Nations, formed in January 1920. Rejected by the Turkish parliament, led by Mustafa Kemal, it was superseded by the Treaty of Lausanne [*q.v.*] on 23 July 1923.

Treaty of Sib (1920): The Treaty of Sib [*q.v.*], brokered by the British political agent in Muscat [*q.v.*] and signed in September 1920 between Sultan Taimur bin Faisal [*q.v.*] and "the people of Oman," who were represented by Shaikh Isa bin Salim al-Harthi, recognized the authority of the sultan in external matters and guaranteed freedom of movement to the tribes and urban dwellers. As leader of the tribal chiefs of the interior, Shaikh Isa

promised not to break the peace or give refuge to wrongdoers from coastal towns, and Sultan Taimur agreed not to raise taxes on coastal towns above 5 percent of the value of trade. The treaty implied autonomy for the interior, though its extent was not specified and became contentious in the 1950s.

tribalism: Based on common descent, a tribe (Arabic: *qabilah*) is a political organization above the levels of extended family (Arabic: *faghaz*) and clan (Arabic: *masheer*), and maintains its cohesiveness through blood solidarity. In the Arab world, tribes are often classified as noble or common. Tribes of the same category often combine to form federations or confederations. In Syria in the 1950s, the average size of a tribal federation, containing two to five tribes, was 30,000. Nationally, only one-seventh of the Syrian population was then organized along tribal lines. By contrast, most of the people in the Arabian Peninsula [*q.v.*] were thus organized. There were about 25 major tribal federations in the peninsula, including Anaiza [*q.v.*], Awazim, Harb, Mutair, Qahtan, Rashid, and Utaiba. Due to the migrations of the past, tribal relationships exist across present-day national boundaries.

There are today about 40 tribes or tribal federations in Saudi Arabia. The House of Saud [*q.v.*] belongs to the Ruwalla tribe (originally from Syria) of the Anaiza tribal federation of Najd [*q.v.*], Iraq, and Syria. The members of this federation are considered noble, due to their claim to lineal descent from Yaarab, the eponymous father of all Arabs [*q.v.*]. Common (or non-noble) tribal federations such as the Awazim, dating back to the 15th century in the Najd area, were only Arabized by intermarrying with noble lines. Tribal origins and loyalty are of great importance in recruitment to the National Guard [*q.v.*].

In Oman the struggle between the coast and the interior is rooted in tribalism. It basically revolves around two tribal confederations: one chiefly Ibadhi [*q.v.*], originally from Yemen and led by Bani Hina (also called Hinawi); the other largely Sunni [*q.v.*], originally from northern Arabia.

As monarchies, often with long-established ruling families, the six members of the Gulf Cooperation Council (GCC) [*q.v.*]—including the United Arab Emirates, composed of seven principalities—are strongly influenced by tribal considerations.

In North Yemen, the leading Hashid and Bakil confederations are the descendants of the Hamdan federation which embraced Islam [*q.v.*] soon after its inception. When the Hamid al-Din family, a branch of the original al-Rassi dynasty of the ninth century A.D., took over the reins of power in 1891, it largely succeeded in gaining the support of the Hashid and Bakil confederations. After Imam Ahmad bin Yahya [*q.v.*] failed to provide safe conduct for the leader of the Hashid confederation in 1960, he lost the support of the key tribes. This weakened his position and paved the way for the overthrow of the monarchy.

Following the establishment of the republic and the end of the civil war [*q.v.*] in 1970, the leaders of the Hashid and Bakil confederations, accounting for some 40 percent of the national population, continued to wield much power. Shaikh Abdullah Hussein al-Ahmar [*q.v.*], leader of the Hashid confederation, used his 50,000-strong militia to secure a position of authority in the central government. President Ahmad Hussein Ghashmi [*q.v.*] belonged to the Hashid confederation, as did his successor, Ali Abdullah Saleh (r. 1978–2012) [*q.v.*]. This enabled Saleh to mobilize the hitherto pro-Saudi Hashid tribal leaders against Riyadh when skirmishes took place between North Yemeni and Saudi troops in October 1979. When Hashid tribal leaders turned against Saleh during the Arab Spring [*q.v.*] of 2011, his fate was sealed.

In South Yemen the Marxist National Liberation Front [*q.v.*] and its successor, the Yemen Socialist Party [*q.v.*], mounted repeated campaigns against tribalism, which succeeded to some extent. But in the periodic internecine fighting among government and party leaders, tribal affiliations counted as much as ideology.

The Iraqi Baathist Party [*q.v.*] took detribalizing steps after assuming power in 1968. It outlawed the use of surnames in order to mask the tribal or geographical origins of citizens. Hence Saddam Hussein [*q.v.*] stopped using his surname, al-Tikriti, derived from the town of Tikrit. But under extreme pressure in the wake of Iraq's defeat in Gulf War II [*q.v.*], he successfully appealed to the loyalties of Sunni [*q.v.*] tribes, and survived.

After the Anglo-American invasion of Iraq [*q.v.*] in 2003, the importance of the Sunni tribal leaders rose. Angered and dispirited by the loss of power that Sunnis had enjoyed in Iraq since 1638 under the rule of Sunni Ottoman Turks, many of them allied with Al Qaida in Mesopotamia (AQM) [*q.v.*] to resist the Anglo-American occupiers. But, as the AQM started terrorizing those Sunnis who did not cooperate with it and mounted a series of lethal suicide attacks on large gatherings of Shias [*q.v.*], Sunni tribal chieftains became disillusioned with it. Encouraged and funded by the Pentagon, they set up Awakening Councils in the Sunni areas that worked in tandem with the U.S. forces from 2007 onward against the AQM. They also ended their earlier boycott of the electoral process and thus gained some bargaining power.

Tripartite Agreement (Anglo-Soviet-Iranian, 1942): This agreement was signed by Iran, Britain, and the Soviet Union in January 1942, following the occupation of Iran by British and Soviet troops in August 1941. It limited the Iranian army's role to one of maintaining internal security. It described the United States as an adjunct to Britain in the task of delivering supplies to the Soviet Union through Iran. It specified that the occupying troops would vacate Iran within seven months of the end of the war against the last member of the Axis Powers.

Tripartite Declaration (Anglo-American-French, 1950): The purpose of the Anglo-American-French declaration on the Middle East on 25 May 1950 was threefold: to help the United States coordinate its sale of weapons to Israel with Britain and France, the region's traditional arms suppliers, according to the treaties they had signed with the Arab states; to outline the basic stance of the three leading Western powers concerning the principal problems of the region; and to pave the way for a regional defense pact. The document proclaimed the signatories' resolve to uphold the armistice boundaries agreed by Israel and its Arab neighbors in 1949, and pledged to sell Israel and the Arab states enough arms to help them meet their "legitimate needs for self-defense," and allow them to play their part in the defense of the region "as a whole." It set the scene for the creation of a regional defense treaty led by the Western powers. The three cosignatories and Turkey put forward to Egypt a proposal for a Middle East Defense Command centered round the Suez Canal [*q.v.*] base. Egypt rejected the plan. But the Western powers persevered, and the concept finally emerged as the Baghdad Pact [*q.v.*] in February 1955.

Tripoli: *Lebanese city* Population: 500,000 (2011 est.). Known in Arabic as Trabulus al-Sham, Eastern Tripoli, in contradistinction to Trabulus al-Gharb, Western Tripoli, in Libya, Tripoli is Lebanon's second-largest city, with a recorded history of over two-and-a-half millennia.

Ruled in turn by the Persians, Greeks, and Romans, it fell to Muslim [*q.v.*] Arabs [*q.v.*] in 638 A.D. During the Crusades (1095–1272) it again changed hands and thrived as a seat of Christianity [*q.v.*] and learning, and as a trading center. It declined dramatically under the rule of the Cairo-based Mamlukes (1250–1517). Under the Ottomans (1517–1918) a new settlement, constructed a few miles inland, was linked to the old port. After the collapse of the Ottoman Empire, France, the mandate power in the region, incorporated it into Greater Lebanon (later the Republic of Lebanon) in 1920. During World War II it was liberated from the pro-German Vichy-based French government by the British and Free French forces in 1941.

Part of the Sunni Muslim [*q.v.*]-majority region of northern Lebanon, it was a leading center of the forces opposed to President Camille Chamoun [*q.v.*] in the brief Lebanese Civil War [*q.v.*] of 1958. In the long Civil War of 1975–90 [*q.v.*], it joined the pro-Syrian, predominantly Muslim camp. After the Palestine Liberation Organization (PLO) [*q.v.*] had been expelled from Beirut [*q.v.*] by the Israelis during their invasion of Lebanon in 1982 [*q.v.*], PLO leader Yasser Arafat [*q.v.*] tried to establish PLO headquarters in Tripoli, but failed due to the opposition of the Syrian forces occupying most of northern Lebanon.

Despite these political upheavals, the importance of Tripoli as the terminus of an oil pipeline from Iraq and as a leading commercial and industrial center, has remained unimpaired. Its tourist attractions include the ruins of an old cathedral and castle; the Great Mosque built to celebrate victory over the last of the Crusaders; the Teinal Mosque, completed in 1336; and the Tower of the Lions, erected in the late 15th century.

Trucial States: The Trucial States in the Lower Gulf [*q.v.*] included the principalities of Abu Dhabi [*q.v.*], Ajman, Dubai [*q.v.*], Fujaira, Ras al-Khaima [*q.v.*], Sharjah [*q.v.*], and Umm al-Qaiwan. By 1892, having signed exclusive agreements with London, the rulers of these emirates conducted their foreign affairs through Britain, which appointed a political officer to the capital of each of the emirates. In 1952 Britain established the Trucial States Council (TSC), consisting of the rulers of the seven emirates, with its Development Office acting as its executive. The next year Britain replaced the local political officers with a political agent based in Sharjah, and set up the Trucial Oman Scouts, a central military force charged with maintaining peace among the emirates. The TSC met regularly to discuss common problems.

With oil revenues beginning to grow in the 1960s, especially in Abu Dhabi, London's financial grants declined. In 1968 Britain initiated talks about the formation of an Arab Gulf Federation after its withdrawal in December 1971. At a TSC meeting in July 1971 it was announced that all the states except Ras al-Khaima had agreed to form a federation prior to the departure of the British from the region. This federation was named the United Arab Emirates.

Trumpeldor, Joseph/Yosef (1880–1920): *Zionist leader in Palestine* Born into a religious Jewish family in the southern Russia town of Pyatigorsk, Trumpeldor was drafted into the Tsarist military. He was severely injured at the Port Arthur front line in the 1904–05 Russo-Japanese War. When he had recuperated he returned to the front and was captured. After his release in 1906, he returned to

Russia, where he became the first Jewish commissioned officer in the army. During his law studies at St. Petersburg University he organized a Zionist [*q.v.*] student body.

In 1912 he migrated to Palestine [*q.v.*], and joined the Degania kibbutz. At the start of World War I in 1914, when he tried to leave for Russia, the Ottoman authorities deported him to Egypt. There he worked with Vladimir Jabotinsky [*q.v.*] to form Jewish battalions. In 1915 he served as second-in-command of the Zion Mule Corps, part of the British forces, on the Gallipoli front. After the dissolution of this corps, he traveled to London to form Jewish battalions in the British army.

After the February 1917 revolution in Russia he returned to his homeland, where he set up the HeHaltuz (Hebrew: *The Pioneer*) organization to prepare Jewish youth for migration to Palestine. In late 1919 he returned to Palestine. In January 1920 the Jewish settlements in Upper Galilee, then part of Syria and under French control, became embroiled in the anti-French campaign by local Arabs [*q.v.*]. The Zionist leaders advised the Jewish settlers to evacuate the area until order had been restored. Disregarding this, Trumpeldor and his followers traveled to Tel Hai, near present-day Kfar Giladi, to assist its settlers. In the subsequent bloodshed, on 1 March he was one of the first to die. The Labor battalions formed by fresh Jewish immigrants from southern Russia were named after him, as was the youth organization of the Revisionist Zionists [*q.v.*]—*Berit* (Hebrew: *Covenant*) Trumpeldor, *Betar*.

Tudeh Party of Iran: (Persian: *masses*) (Official name Tudeh Party of Iran: Party of Iranian Working Class) The Tudeh Party, formed in January 1942, evolved out of the Communist Party of Iran (established in June 1920), which had helped to found the Soviet Republic of Gilan along the Caspian Sea. When the Tehran government crushed the republic in November 1921, the Communist movement declined. However, its remnants managed to survive under the guise of local cultural and sports clubs. When the regime discovered this in 1931, it outlawed the formation of groups opposing constitutional monarchy or advocating Communist ideology or conduct. Fifty-eight members of the Marxist Circle were convicted in Tehran [*q.v.*] in 1937.

Following the occupation of Iran by Soviet and British troops in August 1941, and the deposition of Reza Shah Pahlavi [*q.v.*], all political prisoners were released. The Communist movement revived. But to respect the law and make the new organization more attractive to peasants, workers, and artisans, former Marxist Circle members decided to form a democratic front, naming it the Tudeh Party, under the leadership of Taqi Arani. It grew dramatically.

The demonstrations it sponsored in the autumn of 1944 toppled the conservative government of Prime Minister Muhammad Said. By staging a series of strikes in the oil industry, the pro-Tudeh trade union won concessions from the Anglo-Iranian Oil Company. In 1946 the party had 25,000 members and 75,000 sympathizers, and its trades union federation had 400,000 members. Its stress on modernism and progress in the socio-cultural field appealed especially to women and young people.

In November 1946, Prime Minister Ahmad Qavam Saltane arrested hundreds of Tudeh activists to forestall a threatened strike in Tehran. Claiming to restore normal conditions for parliamentary elections in Azerbaijan [q.v.], he sent troops to the province to overpower the year-old leftist National Government of Azerbaijan in Tabriz [q.v.], run by the Democratic Party of Azerbaijan.

The collapse of the government there as well as in Kurdistan [q.v.] was a setback to Iran's Communist movement as a whole. In protest, Tudeh leaders boycotted the 1947 election and concentrated on improving the party machine. In February 1949, claiming that his would-be assassin, an Islamist journalist, was a card-carrying member of a union affiliated to the pro-Tudeh Labor Federation, Muhammad Reza Shah Pahlavi [q.v.] suppressed the party.

But with the oil nationalization movement rising in 1951, conditions for its revival improved. In mid-1952, changing its view of Premier Muhammad Mussadiq [q.v.] as an ally of the United States, it cooperated with his National Front [q.v.]. The Tudeh was active up to and soon after the shah's flight from Iran on 16 August 1953. When he returned three days later his government repressed the party vengefully. It arrested 3,000 Tudeh activists, executing 54 and sentencing 200 to life imprisonment.

The party moved its headquarters to Eastern Europe, alternating between East Berlin and Prague. In 1960, having merged with the Demo-cratic Party of Azerbaijan, the organization acquired a longer name—the Tudeh Party of Iran: Party of Iranian Working Class. After a series of conferences during 1956–64, the party opted for peaceful means to bring about the downfall of the shah and establish a democratic republic. This led to the exit of radicals, and the party membership fell to 3,000. However, assisted by the Communist parties of the Soviet Union, East Germany, France, and Italy, the Tudeh engaged 50 full-time cadres to run a radio station, based in Bulgaria, and brought out two publications.

In Iran it was no longer the favorite of leftist militants, who gravitated toward the newly established Fedai Khalq [q.v.] and Mujahedin-e Khalq [q.v.]. To counter this, starting in 1972 the party began to set up secret cells in Tehran University, and in the oil and other major industries. Two years later it issued a call for the overthrow of the shah and the founding of a republic. Its membership in Europe and Iran grew to over 5,000.

In the autumn of 1977 it revived its clandestine cells in major Iranian cities, and in September 1978 its leadership decided to establish contacts with Islamic revolutionaries. A month later it instructed its followers in the oil industry—a crucial area of its traditional strength—to support Ayatollah Ruhollah Khomeini's [q.v.] call for a strike. More than any other development, this determined the shah's fall. In December 1978, Tudeh leaders instructed their followers to prepare for an armed uprising. They replaced Iraj Iskandri as first secretary with Nur al-Din Kianuri. Tudeh activists participated in the final battles with the shah's forces from 9 to 13 February 1979 in Tehran and elsewhere.

Kianouri and his aides returned from abroad to revive the party openly. In March the central committee met in Tehran, its first such meeting for a quarter of a century. In August the party described the political balance sheet of the regime of Ayatollah Khomeini as "positive": expelling the shah, declaring a republic, leaving the Western-dominated Central Treaty Organization [q.v.], breaking ties with Israel, and nationalizing banks and insurance companies. On the other hand, it criticized the religious content of the draft constitution. In the elections to the 1979 Assembly of Experts [q.v.], its candidates secured only 50,000 votes.

Despite its backing for the government in its defense of the Iranian territory when attacked by Iraq in September 1980, the authorities raided its office in Tehran and suspended its newspaper. But they took no further action since removal of President Abol Hassan Bani-Sadr [q.v.] from office took priority. Given the Tudeh's anti-Bani-Sadr stance, they tolerated its existence. But once they had resolved to get rid of Bani-Sadr, met the allied Mujahedin-e Khalq challenge head-on, and successfully held a presidential election in October 1981, they had no need for the support of nonviolent leftist parties such as the Tudeh.

When it came out against marching into Iraq in June 1982 during the Iran-Iraq War [q.v.], it angered the authorities. They accelerated the purge of Tudeh members from official institutions. In February 1983 they arrested

Kianouri and 70 other party leaders, charging them with spying for the Soviet bloc. In late April the Iranian television showed Kianouri admitting six major "misdeeds" by his party, including occasional espionage for the Soviet Union, not dissolving its secret sections, and not surrendering all the arms it had secured during the rise of the revolutionary movement. On 4 May the government dissolved the party and arrested about 1,000 of its 2,500 to 3,000 members. Most of the remainder crossed into Afghanistan, where they assisted the ruling leftist party to organize industrial workers and improve the state propaganda apparatus.

In December 1983, 87 members of the party's military section were found guilty of attempting to overthrow the regime and were sentenced to varying terms of imprisonment. Three months later there were further convictions, and 10 Tudeh leaders were executed.

The party continued to exist abroad, with a large contingent in Kabul, Afghanistan. Its central committee met in East Berlin in January 1984, when it decided to establish fraternal relations with the Mujahedin-e Khalq [q.v.], then based in Paris. But this arrangement ended when the Mujahedin-e Khalq headquarters moved to Baghdad [q.v.] in 1986. The party split, with the breakaway section basing itself in Paris and the main body continuing its activities from East Berlin.

With the merger of East and West Germany in 1990 and the reunification of East and West Berlin, the party lost its financial backing from Eastern European communist parties. The downfall of the leftist regime in Kabul in April 1992 destroyed its last bastion in the region. Committed to the secularization and democratization of Iran, it continued to publish a journal, *Nameh Mardom* (Persian: *People's Journal*), in Persian from Berlin.

Led by Ali Khavai, it backed the peaceful protest against the disputed presidential election in June 2009. At the same time it supports the Iranians' right to peaceful use of nuclear energy, and believes that the way to resolve the crisis between Iran and the West is for both sides to take confidence-building measures.

Tumb/Tunb Islands: While implementing its plan to withdraw from the Gulf [*q.v.*] by December 1971, Britain, in consultation with the United States, chose Iran under Muhammad Reza Shah Pahlavi [*q.v.*] to be the new guarantor of regional security and a bulwark against revolutionary change. Therefore, the shah decided to add the Lesser and Greater Tumbs belonging to Ras al-Khaima [*q.v.*], and Abu Musa [*q.v.*] belonging to Sharjah [*q.v.*], to Iran's Qeshm, Larak, and Hormuz Islands. Together, these six islands form a crescent, which guards the entrance to the strategic Hormuz Strait [*q.v.*]. On 30 November 1971, a day before the termination of the British treaty with Ras al-Khaima, Iran occupied the uninhabited Lesser Tumb Island and captured Greater Tumb Island after some fighting.

After the 1979 Islamic revolution [*q.v.*] in Iran, the ownership of these islands became a contentious issue between Iran and Iraq, the latter claiming to be the guardian of the interests of the Gulf's Arab states. In April 1980 Baghdad called on Iran to vacate the Tumb Islands and Abu Musa. Tehran ignored the demand. During its eight-year war with Iraq, the strategic importance of these islands became well established. In 1994 the Gulf Cooperation Council [*q.v.*] took up the matter on behalf of the United Arab Emirates and urged Iran to agree to refer the issue of its occupation of the Greater and Lesser Islands and Abu Musa Island to the International Court of Justice, but to no avail. The dispute continued to be a major barrier to cordial relations between Iran and the UAE.

Turkmen: (Also spelled Turcomen or Turkomen) The term Turkmen applies to those who speak Turkmen, a member of the south Turkic language group. Those living east of the Caspian Sea—in Iran, Turkmenistan, Uzbekistan, and Afghanistan—are known as Trans-Caspian Turkmen. A much smaller number of Turkmen are scattered in pockets in northern Iraq and Syria. They are almost invariably Muslim [*q.v.*].

Twelvers: *See* Twelver Shias.

Twelver Shias: The predominant category among Shias [*q.v.*], Twelvers or Twelver Shias are so called because they believe in 12 imams [*q.v.*]: Ali, Hassan, Hussein, Zain al-Abidin, Muhammad al-Baqir, Jaafar al-Sadiq, Musa al-Kazem, Ali al-Rida/Reza, Muhammad al-Taqi Javad, Ali al-Hadi, Hassan al-Askari, and Muhammad al-Qasim, also known as Muhammad al-Mahdi. They believe that Muhammad al-Qasim, the infant son of the 11th imam, went into occultation in Samarra [*q.v.*], Iraq, in 873 A.D., leaving behind four special assistants. As the last of them failed to name a successor, the line of divinely inspired imams became extinct in 940 A.D. Twelvers believe that the last imam will end his occultation at the end of time and institute justice and order in the world, as well as punishing the enemies of Allah.

Six of these Imams are buried in the Iraqi cities of Baghdad [*q.v.*], Karbala [*q.v.*], and Najaf; four in Medina [*q.v.*]; and one in the Iranian city of Mashhad [*q.v.*].

Tyre: *Lebanese city* Population: 318,000 (2011 est.). A thriving city of ancient times, originally built on an island, Tyre has a history dating back to the third millennium B.C. Its ruler, Hiram, is mentioned as a supplier of building materials for the First Temple, built by King Solomon (r. ca 970–930 B.C.). Ezekiel in the Book of Ezekiel is instructed to predict the fall of Tyre. By the ninth century B.C., Tyrians had set up colonies abroad, including Carthage (near modern Tunis). Tyre then came under the rule of the Assyrians and Achaemenians of Persia (550–330 B.C.). It withstood a siege by Alexander of Macedonia (r. 336–323 B.C.) for several months, and fell to his forces only after he had constructed a causeway to the island—his legacy to the city. In retribution, he killed or enslaved some 40,000 Tyrians. Tyre recovered from the trauma to regain its importance as a commercial center for purple dye and silk ware. After falling to the Egyptians, Greeks, and Romans, it emerged as a Christian [*q.v.*] center, and is mentioned several times in the New Testament [*q.v.*]. It

thrived under Muslim [*q.v.*] Arab [*q.v.*] rule from 638 A.D. Captured by the Crusaders in 1124 it became part of the Kingdom of Jerusalem and the burial place of Roman Emperor Frederick I Barbarossa (r. 1152–1190). It was conquered by the Mamlukes in 1291; fearing another Crusade, they razed it. Its port silted up, and it declined to insignificance during the Ottoman times (1517–1918). The subsequent French Mandate included it in Greater Lebanon (later the Republic of Lebanon). After the 1948–49 Palestine War [*q.v.*], Palestinian refugees set up a camp at nearby Rashidiya.

The title of one of William Shakespeare's play is derivative of ancient settlement: *Pericles, Prince of Tyre*. In more recent times, Oscar Wilde refers to "my Tyrian galley" in one of his poems.

U

ulama/ulema (Arabic: plural of *alim, possessor of ilm, knowledge*): Ulema is the term used collectively for religious-legal scholars of Islam [*q.v.*]. Since *ilm* in Islam means knowledge of the Quran [*q.v.*] and the *sunna* [*q.v.*], the ulema are theologians and canonists. They are the ultimate authority on the issues of law and theology, personifying the right of Muslims [*q.v.*] to self-governance. In modern times, however, in Sunni [*q.v.*] countries they have by and large become government functionaries, with only a minority among them acting as independent thinkers on theology and canon law.

ultra-Orthodox Jews (Hebrew: *Haredim*): The label *ultra-Orthodox* applies to those Jews [*q.v.*] who adhere to a strict interpretation of the Halakha [*q.v.*] Jewish Law. Full observance of the Halakha involves following all 613 religious prohibitions and obligations that regulate Jewish life, from trivial body functions to the organization of life in society—and separation between Jews and Gentiles. Because of their belief that only divine intervention could reestablish the Jewish state of Israel, they opposed the creation of Israel through human endeavor such as the one by the Zionist [*q.v.*] pioneers in Palestine [*q.v.*]. Later a majority cooperated with Zionists, arguing that Zionism [*q.v.*] could be put to the service of Judaism [*q.v.*] according to the Halakha.

There are two major schools and one minor within ultra-Orthodoxy: Hassidim (Hebrew: *pious*); Mitnagdim (Hebrew: *opponents*), and Bratslavic, named after the Ukrainian town of Bratslav.

Bearded adult males wear the garb of the Eastern European ghetto: black trousers, long black coats, and wide black hats, with their side-locks, shaped into ringlets, dangling. Women wear long-sleeved dresses, their skirts falling well below the knees; cover the upper part of their legs with heavy stockings; and shield their hair by a scarf or a wig. Television is off limits, as the viewer never knows when a semi-clad woman might appear on the screen. So too are newspapers and magazines. Therefore, the walls of the ultra-Orthodox neighborhoods are often plastered with news sheets without any offensive images. In Jerusalem [*q.v.*] ultra-Orthodox Jews live in Mea Shearim, Beit Israel, Geula, and Har Nof neighborhoods.

Ultra-Orthodox Jews are opposed to birth control. In Israel, one-third of all Jewish babies born in 2011 were ultra-Orthodox, even though as a community they made up less than 10 percent of the Jewish population of 5.85 million.

With most ultra-Orthodox youths enrolling at government-funded seminaries in Israel, whose students are exempted from compulsory service in the armed forces, the community enjoys exemption from conscription. But in February 2012 the Supreme Court ruled that this exemption must end within six months.

umm (Arabic: *mother*): It is customary among many Arabs to call a married woman the "umm" of her first-born son.

Umma: A derivative of either the Arabic umm, meaning *mother* or *source*; or a loan-word from Hebrew [*q.v.*] umma or Aramaic ummtha; *umma* appears many times in the Quran [*q.v.*], always alluding to ethnic, linguistic, or religious groups who were part of Allah's plan of salvation. As the Prophet Muhammad progressed from his unassuming origins to become the ruler of a territory, his definition of *umma* changed from the community of all Arabs, irrespective of their religious affiliation, to the community of all Muslims [*q.v.*]. Within a century of his death in 632 A.D., the *umma* spread far beyond Arabia and included different nations and races.

In modern times the *umma*, now meaning the worldwide Islamic community as a whole, has carried more of a communal connotation than the more legalistic Dar al-Islam (Arabic: *Domain of Islam*). On the other hand, the annual hajj [*q.v.*] is a dramatic illustration of the existence of *umma*.

umra: *small pilgrimage to Mecca* Umra involves the central ceremonies of the hajj [*q.v.*] for Muslims [*q.v.*]: circumambulating the Kaaba [*q.v.*] in Mecca [*q.v.*] and striding quickly between the Safa and Marwa hillocks. It can be performed at any time of the year, except during 8–10 Dhul Hijja, the days reserved for the hajj proper.

Uniate churches (Russian: derivative of *uniyat, union*): A group of Christian churches [*q.v.*] with Eastern rites that acknowledge the primacy of the pope of the Roman Catholic Church [*q.v.*] and accept the Roman Catholic Church in doctrine, but not in liturgy and customs. It includes the Armenian Catholic Church [*q.v.*], the Chaldean Catholic Church [*q.v.*], the Greek Catholic Church [*q.v.*], the Maronite Catholic Church [*q.v.*], and the Syrian Catholic Church [*q.v.*].

Union of the Peoples of Arabian Peninsula (Saudi Arabia): An organization of Nasserite [*q.v.*] persuasion, established in the late 1950s and led by Nasser Said, the Union of the People of Arabian Peninsula (UPAP) aimed to rid Saudi Arabia [*q.v.*] of the monarchy. Banned in the Saudi kingdom, it maintained an office in Beirut [*q.v.*]. In 1966 it claimed responsibility for bomb explosions in such places as the defense ministry in Riyadh [*q.v.*] and the state security office in Dammam in the eastern oil region. After the death of President Gamal Abdul Nasser [*q.v.*] in 1970, its appeal waned. Following the takeover of the Grand Mosque in Mecca [*q.v.*] in November 1979 by Islamic militants, it briefly became active before going into hibernation again.

United Arab Emirates:
    OFFICIAL NAME: United Arab Emirates
    CAPITAL: Abu Dhabi [*q.v.*]
    AREA: (including disputed land and island territories with neighboring states): 32,280 sq. mi./83,600 sq. km
    POPULATION: 6.327 million (2010 est.), with nationals being 12 percent of the total. (Abu Dhabi Emirate, 1.8 million; Ajman Emirate, 420,000; Dubai Emirate, 2.262 million; Fujairah Emirate, 165,000; Ras al-Khaimah Emirate, 300,000; Sharjah Emirate, 946,000; Umm al-Quwain, 76,000).
    GROSS DOMESTIC PRODUCT (nominal): $360 billion; per capita, $67,000 (2011 est.)
    GROSS DOMESTIC PRODUCT PER CAPITA (Purchasing Power Parity): $259 billion; per capita, $48,160 (2011 est.)
    NATIONAL CURRENCY: UAE Dirham (AED); AED 1 = $0.272 = £0.168 = € 0.21 (2011)
    FORM OF GOVERNMENT: monarchy; federation of seven emirates, each ruled by an emir, with the seven emirs constituting the highest federal authority: the Supreme Council of Emirs.
    OFFICIAL LANGUAGE: Arabic [*q.v.*]
    OFFICIAL RELIGION: Islam [*q.v.*]
    ADMINISTRATIVE SYSTEM: The United Arab Emirates consists of seven constituent emirates, each ruled by a hereditary emir.

CONSTITUTION: The interim constitution, which came into effect in December 1971, specified a federal system for the constituent emirates. The seven-member Supreme Council of Emirs (SCE) is the highest federal body, which elects the president and vice president of the UAE from among its members. The president appoints the prime minister and the cabinet. The SCE's decisions must be approved by five emirs, including those of Abu Dhabi and Dubai. The legislative authority lies with the Federal National Council, a fully nominated consultative assembly of 40 members, with two-year tenure. The provisional constitution was extended every five years until 1996 when it was made permanent. Following this, Shaikh Zaid ibn Sultan al-Nahyan [q.v.] was reelected president. After his death in 2004, his son Khalifa bin Zayid Al Nahyan [q.v.] was elected president.

ETHNIC COMPOSITION (2010): Arab [q.v.] 28 percent, including UAE Arab 12 percent; South Asian 60 percent; other 12 percent.

HIGH OFFICIALS:

President: Shaikh Khalifa bin Zayid al-Nahyan, 2004–

Vice president: Shaikh Muhammad bin Rashid al-Maktoum, 2006–

Prime Minister: Shaikh Muhammad bin Rashid al-Maktoum, 2006–

Members of the Supreme Council of Emirs (emirates in alphabetical order):

Shaikh Khalifa bin Zayid al-Nahyan (r. 2004–) of Abu Dhabi;

Shaikh Humaid ibn Rashid al-Nuaimi (r. 1981–) of Ajman;

Shaikh Muhammad bin Rashid al-Maktoum, (r. 2006–) of Dubai;

Shaikh Hamad ibn Muhammad al-Sharqi (r. 1974–) of Fujairah;

Shaikh Saud ibn Saqr al-Qasimi (r. 2010–) of Ras al-Khaimah;

Shaikh Sultan ibn Muhammad al-Qasimi (r. 1972–) of Sharjah;

Shaikh Saud ibn Rashid al-Mualla (r. 2009–) of Umm al-Quwain.

Speaker of the Federal National Council: Muhammad al-Murr al-Falasi: 2011–

HISTORY (since ca 1900): By 1892, having signed exclusive agreements with London, the rulers of the six emirates of the Lower Gulf [q.v.] (Abu Dhabi, Ajman, Dubai, Ras al-Khaimaa, Sharjahh, and Umm al-Quwain) were conducting their foreign affairs through Britain, which appointed a political officer to the capital of each of the emirates. In 1952, after upgrading the province of Fujairah to an emirate, Britain established the Trucial States Council (TSC), consisting of the rulers of the seven emirates, with its Development Office acting as its executive. The next year Britain replaced the local political officers with a political agent based in Sharjah and set up the Trucial Oman Scouts, a central military force changed with maintaining peace among the emirates. The TSC met regularly to discuss common problems.

With oil revenues beginning to build up from the early 1960s, especially in Abu Dhabi, which accounted for seven-eighths of the area covered by the TSC, London's financial grants declined. This was especially true after 1966, when Shaikh Shakbut ibn Hamdan al-Nahyan (r. 1928–66) was deposed by the British in favor of his younger brother, Shaikh Zaid, who was committed to economic development. When Dubai discovered offshore oil in 1966, the economic prospects of the TSC's constituents improved.

In 1968 Britain initiated talks about the formation of an Arab Gulf Federation after its withdrawal in 1971. At the TSC meeting in July 1971 it was announced that all the states except Ras al-Khaimaa had agreed to form a federation prior to the departure of the British from the region by December 1971. This federation was named the United Arab Emirates (UAE), with Shaikh Zaid al-Nahyan as president and Shaikh Rashid al-Maktoum [q.v.] of Dubai as vice president.

When a single federal council of ministers came into being in December 1973, Shaikh Zaid al-Nahyan abolished the Abu Dhabi cabinet and appointed a 50-member Consultative Council in his emirate. To the detriment of the UAE, the personal rivalry between him and Vice President Rashid al-Maktoum persisted for many years. Following the Islamic revolution [q.v.] in Iran in early 1979, the Federal National Council and the federal cabinet demanded parliamentary democracy and unitary statehood. This alarmed the president and the vice president, who sank their differences. Shaikh Rashid became prime minister of the UAE, replacing his son, Shaikh Maktoum al-Maktoum. In 1981 the UAE was one of the cofounders of the Gulf Cooperation Council [q.v.].

During the early phase of the Iran-Iraq War [q.v.] the UAE sided with Iraq, providing it with financial aid. But, as the conflict dragged on, with Iran gaining a stronger position than Iraq, the UAE took an increasingly neutral stance. During the spring of 1990 it allied with Kuwait in a strategy to harm the Iraqi economy by flooding the oil market and lowering the price of oil. After the death of Shaikh Rashid in October 1990, the ruler of Dubai, Shaikh Maktoum, succeeded him as vice president and prime minister of the UAE.

In the 1991 Gulf War [q.v.] the UAE joined the anti-Iraq coalition led by the United States and contributed $5 billion to the war chest. In 1994, when the UAE extended its defense agreement signed in the aftermath of the Gulf War, it tried to persuade Iran to open talks on the status of Abu Musa [q.v.] and the Greater and Lesser Tumb Islands [q.v.], but failed. The next year, Iran set up air defense systems on the islands. And in 1996 it inaugurated an electricity-generating plant on Greater Tunb. From 1995 onward, UAE President Shaikh Zayid appealed for the lifting of the UN sanctions on Iraq, but to no avail. The UAE sent food and medicine to Iraq in 1997 and 1998, which was allowed by the UN. It reopened its embassy in Baghdad [q.v.] in 2000.

Following the terrorist attacks on the United States in September 2001, the UAE severed its diplomatic links with the Taliban regime in Afghanistan. While supporting Washington's campaign to punish the perpetrators of 9/11, the UAE urged the resumption of the Arab-Israeli peace process, and cautioned against any U.S. military action targeting an Arab regime.

Prior to the Anglo-American invasion of Iraq in 2003 [q.v.], the UAE opposed it. In 2008 the UAE wrote off the $7 billion that Iraq under President Saddam Hussein [q.v.] owed it, and appointed an ambassador to Iraq. It signed a civil nuclear cooperation agreement with the United States in 2009 after agreeing not to enrich uranium or reprocess spent fuel. Then it inked a $20 billion contract for the first nuclear power reactors in the Arab Middle East with a South Korean-led consortium.

The global credit crunch of 2008–09, which led to a collapse in the real estate values in the UAE, severely slowed the economic boom the emirates had enjoyed over the past three decades. This was the background to the onset of the Arab Spring [*q.v.*] in early 2011. The government blocked a website popular with those UAE nationals who posted calls for a constitutional monarchy and a wholly elected parliament with full legislative powers, which culminated in a petition signed by 133 citizens in March. It disbanded the elected boards of the Jurists' Association and the Teachers' Association after their members signed a petition calling for reforms. It arrested five dissident intellectuals, charging them with committing acts "that pose a threat to state security, [by] undermining the public order, opposing the government system and insulting." When their requests for an open trial and cross-examination of witnesses were rejected, they went on hunger strike in mid-November. Two weeks later judges sentenced them to two years' imprisonment. But the next day, following a presidential pardon, they were released.

LEGISLATURE: The Federal National Council (FNC) is a quasi-legislative body, with a five-year tenure, that elects its speaker. Half of its 40 members are elected by a very small proportion of eligible citizens selected by the particular emirate's ruler, and the other half appointed by the emirs. Each emirate is accorded its quota on the basis of its population. The FNC debates the legislation proposed by the federal cabinet. It is authorized to question federal cabinet ministers. In the September 2011 election only 18 percent of the eligible UAE citizens were entitled to vote.

RELIGIOUS COMPOSITION (2010): Muslim [*q.v.*], 63 percent; Hindu, 22 percent; Christian [*q.v.*], 10 percent; other, 5 percent.

United Arab Republic (1958–61): In February 1958 Egypt and Syria merged to form the United Arab Republic (UAR). Part of the reason that the political and military leaders of Syria sought union with Egypt was to forestall the rise of leftists in their country. But, once Syria had been incorporated into the UAR, its president, Gamal Abdul Nasser [*q.v.*], extended to the Syrian region his policy of nationalizing banking, insurance, and major industries. He thus alienated an important social class in Syria. Likewise, his ban on all political parties in Syria alienated almost all Syrian politicians, and the creation of a unified military command, in which Syrian officers were relegated to secondary positions, created discontent in the officer corps. These factors created widespread disaffection in Syria and prepared the ground for its secession from the UAR, which came in September 1961 amid much rancor.

United National Leadership of the Uprising (West Bank and Gaza): Following the spontaneous outbreak of the intifada [*q.v.*] in the Gaza Strip [*q.v.*], leaders of the groups affiliated to the outlawed Palestine Liberation Organization [*q.v.*] and based in the occupied West Bank [*q.v.*] and Gaza Strip [*q.v.*] combined to form the United National Leadership of the Uprising (UNLU). It functioned clandestinely and guided the intifada, often through leaflets. Despite the disparate nature of its constituents, it remained effective, mainly because repeated efforts by Israel's Shin Beth [*q.v.*] to infiltrate it failed.

United Nations Disengagement Observer Force (1974–): After the disengagement agreement between the Syrian and Israeli forces on the Golan Heights [*q.v.*] on 31 May 1974, a UN Disengagement Observer Force (UNDOF) was posted to establish an area of separation and verify troop levels. UNDOF's 1,100 personnel were drawn from three European countries and Canada. In 2011, its operating budget was $50.5 million.

United Nations Emergency Force (1957–67): During the Suez War [*q.v.*], the UN General Assembly decided on 4 November 1956 to create a UN Emergency Force (UNEF)—composed of troops from countries not involved in the conflict—to supervise a cease-fire between the warring parties. With the truce taking effect on 7 November and UNEF units arriving in Egypt soon after, the British and French troops started to withdraw, completing the process by 23 December. At the insistence of Israel, which had completed its evacuation of Egypt by 8 March 1957, UNEF was stationed only on the Egyptian side of the Canal and in Egyptian-adminis-

tered Gaza [*q.v.*]. It was required to safeguard Israeli shipping through the Gulf of Aqaba.

Nine years later tension in the region escalated when Israel warned Syria—then militarily allied with Cairo—that it would retaliate vigorously if guerrilla attacks on it from Syria continued. In mid-May 1967, the Soviet, Syrian, and Egyptian intelligence agencies warned Egyptian President Gamal Abdul Nasser [*q.v.*] that an Israeli attack on Syria was imminent. On 18 May Nasser asked the UN secretary-general to withdraw UNEF from Egypt—which he was entitled to do, since UN forces are deployed in a country only so long as its government wishes. The secretary-general complied with Nasser's request. With UNEF units gone from Sharm el Shaikh at the mouth of the Gulf of Aqaba, Nasser closed the waterway to Israeli shipping.

United Nations General Assembly Resolution 194 (December 1948): It defines the role of the UN Conciliation Commission in the region of the British Mandate of Palestine [*q.v.*]. It calls for the return of Palestinian refugees, demilitarization and UN control of Jerusalem [*q.v.*], and protection of and free access to the Holy Places.

United Nations General Assembly Resolution 3236 (November 1974): At the end of a long debate on the "Question of Palestine" on 22 November 1974, the UN General Assembly reaffirmed the Palestinian people's right to self-determination, independence, and sovereignty, and their right to return to their homes and properties.

United Nations Interim Force in Lebanon (1978–): Following the Israeli invasion of southern Lebanon [q.v.] on 14 March 1978, UN Security Council Resolution 425 [q.v.] of 19 March called on Israel to cease fire, and authorized the formation of the UN Interim Force in Lebanon (UNIFIL) to confirm the Israeli evacuation and assist the Lebanese government to assume effective control in the area. But when Israel carried out its major withdrawal in mid-June it handed over its positions to a Christian militia, later called the South Lebanon Army (SLA) [q.v.], and did not allow the Lebanese government to deploy its troops alongside the 5,000-strong UNIFIL force, drawn from 10 countries and headquartered in Naqura.

With the second and larger Israeli invasion of Lebanon [q.v.] in June 1982, resulting in the occupation of southern Lebanon by Israel, UNIFIL's objective of helping the Lebanese government to assume effective control of southern Lebanon became more distant. Even though UN Security Council Resolution 425 pertained exclusively to Lebanon and had nothing to do with UN Security Council Resolution 242 of 1967 [q.v.], the basis of the Middle East peace process [q.v.] begun in October 1991, Israel insisted on interconnecting the two, linking Israel's evacuation of southern Lebanon to the conclusion of a Lebanese-Israeli peace treaty. Lebanon rebuffed Israel's attempt. Following the unilateral Israeli withdrawal from southern Lebanon in May 2000, UNIFIL confirmed the evacuation. But, with Israel refusing the Shaaba Farms contiguous with Syria, Hizbollah [q.v.] regarded the Israeli evacuation as incomplete and mounted periodic attacks on the Israeli positions on the Farms. Therefore, Israel insisted on UNIFIL's continuing its mission.

Its mandate is renewed annually, from August to the following July.

United Nations Iran-Iraq Military Observer Group (1988–91): After accepting the implementation procedure for UN Security Council Resolution 598 calling for a cease-fire in the Iran-Iraq War [q.v.], the UN secretary-general announced the formation of the United Nations Iran-Iraq Military Observer Group (UNIIMOG) to supervise the cease-fire from 20 August 1988. Its 350 troops and officers were to be drawn from 25 countries.

Later, facing military action by a 28–nation coalition to reverse Iraq's occupation of Kuwait in August 1990, Iraqi President Saddam Hussein [q.v.] hurriedly agreed that the Iraqi and Iranian forces should withdraw to the internationally recognized frontiers. This was done before the U.S.-led military campaign in January 1991. With that, the UN Security Council ended UNIIMOG's mandate in February.

United Nations Iraq-Kuwait Observer Mission (1991–2003): In line with UN Security Council Resolution 687 of 3 April 1991, concerning the cease-fire in Gulf War II [q.v.] between Iraq and the Washington-led coalition, the UN secretary-general selected a UN Iraq-Kuwait Military Observer Group (UNIKOM), composed of 320 military personnel from 35 countries, with the following mandate: to monitor the Khor Abdullah waterway and a demilitarized zone (DMZ) extending 10 km into Iraq and 5 km into Kuwait from the agreed boundary between the two countries, according to their agreement on 4 October 1963; and to deter violations of the boundary and observe hostile or potentially hostile actions. After a fresh demarcation of the international frontier by a UN committee at the expense of Iraq in 1993, and its acceptance by Baghdad in November 1994, UNIKOM started to function within the new boundaries.

At its peak, UNIKOM, based in Umm Qasr, Iraq, was nearly 1,200 strong in early 1995. After the Anglo-American invasion of Iraq in March 2003 [*q.v.*], UNIKOM lost its raison d'être. The UN Security Council disbanded it in September.

United Nations Monitoring, Verification, and Inspection Commission

(1999): According to the terms of paragraphs 1, 2, and 3 of UN Security Council Resolution 1284 (1999) on Iraq [*q.v.*], adopted on 17 December 1999, the UN secretary-general appointed the UN Monitoring, Verification, and Inspection Commission (UNMOVIC) to replace the UN Special Commission [*q.v.*] of 1991, and charged it to conduct on-site inspection of Iraq's biological, chemical, and missile facilities, and to cooperate with the International Atomic Energy Commission (IAEA) regarding on-site inspection of Iraq's nuclear capabilities, and together establish and operate current and future ongoing monitoring and verification regimes to verify Iraq's continued compliance of its undertakings in these areas. After

UN Secretary-General Kofi Annan had appointed Hans Blix executive chairman of UNMOVIC in 2000, UNSCOM was dissolved. UNMOVIC recruited and trained about 100 inspectors from more than 40 countries. It was not until late November 2002 that, following Iraq's acceptance of UN Security Council Resolution 1441, the UNMOVIC staff began performing their tasks.

During their inspections until 18 March, 2003, UNMOVIC inspectors found no evidence of weapons of mass destruction. But the whole UNMOVIC contingent had to leave so that the Anglo-American troops could invade Iraq, ostensibly to find the alleged weapons of mass destruction.

United Nations Relief and Work Agency for Palestinian Refugees in the Near East

(1949–): Following the UN General Assembly Resolution 302 (December 1949) to care for those Palestinians who had lost their homes and means of livelihood during the 1948–49 Palestine War [*q.v.*], the UN secretary-general established the UN Relief and Work Agency for Palestinian Refugees in the Near East (UNRWA) at the UN's offices in Vienna, Austria. That meant having to deal with 914,221 Palestinians, of whom some 500,000 qualified for UNRWA relief.

Israel's seizure of the West Bank [*q.v.*] and the Gaza Strip [*q.v.*] during the June 1967 Arab-Israeli War [*q.v.*], created a further 335,000 displaced Palestinians, of whom 193,600 were eligible for UNRWA support.

Financed by voluntary contributions of the member governments, UNRWA's mandate is renewed regularly to provide camps, food, clothing, schools, vocational training, and health clinics, often working in cooperation with the UN Educational, Scientific and Cultural Organization (UNESCO).

In 1980, of the 1,844,300 Palestinian refugees registered with UNRWA, about a third lived in 61 camps scattered throughout the West Bank (20), the Gaza Strip (8), Jordan (10), Syria (10), and Lebanon (13). By 2000, the total had risen to 3,806,055, divided among the Gaza Strip (837,750), Jordan (1,609,566), Lebanon (380,072), Syria (387,526), and the West Bank (591,141).

The escalated violence during the Al Aqsa Intifada [q.v.], resulting in Israel blockading the territories administered by the Palestinian Authority [q.v.], raised the number of Palestinians dependent on UNRWA's food rations 10-fold to 1.1 million in 2003.

In 2005, the number of Palestinian refugees registered in the region were: Jordan, 1.828 million; Gaza Strip, 986,000; West Bank, 700,000; Lebanon, 404,000; Saudi Arabia, 240,000; and Egypt 70,000.

The fate of the refugees and other Palestinians suffered when the Western governments boycotted the popularly elected Hamas [q.v.] government in 2006. Israel's siege of Gaza led to rising demand for UNRWA services, particularly when the cash-strapped Hamas government failed to pay its employees. Having raised $84 million in emergency funding, UNRWA provided food aid to 257,000 refugee families and supplemented the inadequate diet of 200,000 school pupils in Gaza.

Its normal services continued to play a vital role in the human develop-ment of the refugees by catering for their education, healthcare, and social services. In 2010, the number of Palestinian refugees registered with UNRWA stood at 4.7 million, up from 711,000 six decades earlier. In 2011 its regular budget, at $1.23 billion, was four times the figure for 2001.

United Nations Special Commission on Iraq (1991):

According to the terms of paragraph 9 of UN Security Council Resolution 687 (1991), adopted on 3 April 1991, the secretary-general appointed a Special Commission to carry out on-site inspection of Iraq's biological, chemical, and missile facilities, and to cooperate with the International Atomic Energy Commission (IAEA) regarding on-site inspection of Iraq's nuclear capabilities and in setting up a monitoring system to verify Iraq's continued compliance of its undertakings in these areas. The UN Special Commission (UNSCOM) on Iraq was headed by Rolfe Ekeus, a Swedish diplomat.

In early 1995, with UNSCOM having virtually accomplished its disarming missions in chemical weapons and missiles, Ekeus turned increasingly to biological warfare agents. Following top-level defections from Iraq in August 1995, the Iraqi government conceded that it had produced anthrax and botulinum in 1989–90. Later it admitted producing larger quantities of these agents than initially declared. On his part, at the behest of Scott Ritter, an American chief inspector, Ekeus set up a Concealment Investigation Unit under Ritter to conduct Special Information Collection Missions (SICMs). For this purpose Ritter requested and received assistance from the intelligence agencies of the United States and Israel.

For these SICMs to be successful, UNSCOM teams, headed by Ritter, initiated deliberately confrontational inspection exercises in order to make the Iraqi authorities activate its concealment mechanism so it could be detected by Ritter. The first such exercise in March 1996 failed to yield the desired result. In that month, while switching the monitoring system, installed at 300 sites countrywide, from collecting video images recorded by cameras onto a magnetic tape to transmitting video images using radio signals boosted by relays, the American signals-and-sensors technicians, working as UNSCOM staff, hid within the boosting stations antennas capable of intercepting microwave transmissions used by the Iraqi military. On the other hand, the second SICM in June linked to engineering an anti-Saddam Hussein [q.v.] coup—hatched by the U.S. Central Intelligence Agency, the British MI6, and Saudi and Jordanian intelligence agencies—also failed.

The covert cooperation between UNSCOM and the United States had deepened to the extent that Ritter gave regular briefings to the U.S. National Security Council before and after his inspection tours of Iraq. This relationship grew even stronger after Richard Butler, an Australian disarmament official, took over from Ekeus in July 1997. He pursued with greater vigor the strategy of using SICMs to lay bare Iraq's concealment mechanism.

In October Iraq's deputy prime minister Tariq Aziz [q.v.] told the UN Security Council that it would not accept American personnel in UNSCOM teams, as they had shown more loyalty to the United States than to the UN. He provided a team of visiting UN diplomats sent by the secretary-general, Kofi Annan, with evidence to back up his espionage charges against the Americans on UNSCOM. When Iraq expelled six American inspectors, Butler pulled out all of them. U.S. President Bill Clinton ordered a military buildup in the region. But an American attack on Iraq was averted by the intervention of Russian President Boris Yeltsin.

A crisis developed in early 1998 when Iraq refused inspections of eight presidential sites, describing them as being "sovereign." Following a visit to Baghdad [q.v.] by Annan, there was a seven-point agreement whereby Iraq undertook to accord UNSCOM "immediate, unconditional and unrestricted access," with inspection of the presidential sites to be conducted by a special group and Annan pledging to bring the subject of lifting sanctions on Iraq to the attention of the Security Council.

The inspection of presidential sites revealed nothing objectionable. Nor did intrusive, no-notice inspections of such other sensitive sites as the defense ministry yield anything incriminating. While, in his April 1998 report, Butler reported scant progress in disarmament because of the four-month-long crisis, Aziz alleged that UNSCOM's intrusive inspections were meant to provide intelligence to Washington—a charge substantiated by the targets hit by the Pentagon in its Operation Desert Fox [q.v.] in December, and the subsequent revelations made in the American press about the U.S. infiltration of UNSCOM.

In June Butler pointed out that Iraq had not accounted for 500 tons of missile rocket fuel and 1.7 tons of VX, a lethal nerve agent. Aziz claimed that Butler was deliberately focusing on minor issues in order to drag out the UNSCOM mission, as Washington wished. Saddam Hussein ordered that Iraq's cooperation with the inspection regimes of UNSCOM and the IAEA be suspended, while leaving their monitoring systems intact. At this point the Clinton administration said that the crisis was between Iraq and the UN. Privately, its officials stated that UNSCOM had outlived its usefulness, implying that it had achieved virtually all that it had set out to do. This view would later be echoed by Ritter, who would assert repeatedly that Iraq had been disarmed 90–95 percent.

Angered by the failure of the UN Security Council in October to mention anything about the lifting of sanctions following a debate on a comprehensive review of sanctions, Iraq stopped cooperating with UNSCOM and the IAEA in both inspecting and monitoring. It demanded a quick review of its compliance in disarmament linked to a timetable to lift sanctions. Annan intervened, saying that, if Iraq reversed its decision, the Council would settle the issue of a comprehensive review of Iraq's disarmament. Iraq agreed.

Butler worked closely with U.S. National Security Adviser Samuel Berger to carry out confrontational inspections during the second half of November. But given Iraq's cooperation, that ploy did not work.

While France, Russia, and China considered Iraq's disarmament practically finished, expecting the completion of the comprehensive review by Christmas, with the embargo on oil lifted, U.S. officials wanted a credible basis for bombing Iraq against the background of imminent impeachment proceedings against Clinton. Therefore, they advised Butler to stiffen his special report to the Security Council through Annan on 15 December.

In it Butler said that Iraq was not cooperating with UNSCOM. Advised by Peter Burleigh, the U.S. ambassador to the UN, Butler withdrew UNSCOM staff from Baghdad, without even informing the Council, so that the Pentagon could unleash its 100-hour blitzkrieg on Iraq.

The United States started Operation Desert Fox on the afternoon of 16 December Eastern Standard Time. By so doing, Butler and Clinton brought about the demise of UNSCOM, although it was officially disbanded in early 2000 after the adoption of UN Security Council Resolution 1284, which created the UN Monitoring, Verification, and Inspection Commission [q.v.].

During its existence, UNSCOM visited 700 sites and carried out 6,000 inspections. In biological warfare agents UNSCOM destroyed 8,400 liters (1,850 gallons) of anthrax; 19,000 liters (4,180 gallons) of botulinum; 3,400 liters (750 gallons) of clostridium (gangrene gas); 2,200 liters (485 gallons) of aflatoxin; and 10 liters (2 gallons) of ricin—as well as all the facilities for their research, development, and production. In chemical weapons, UNSCOM destroyed 500–

600 tons of mustard gas; 100–150 tons of nerve gases—sarin and tabun; 50–100 tons of VX nerve gas; 480,000 liters (105,600 gallons) of chemical weapons agents; more than 450,000 gallons of precursor chemicals; and 30 chemical warheads—as well as 38,537 filled and empty chemical weapons munitions—and all the facilities for their research, development, and production. In missiles and their delivery systems, UNSCOM destroyed eight types of delivery systems, 48 Scud missiles, six mobile launchers, eight fixed launch pads, and two fixed launch pads under construction.

United Nations Special Commission on Palestine (1947): On 15 May 1947 a special session of the UN General Assembly appointed an 11-member Special Commission on Palestine, consisting of Australia, Canada, Czechoslovakia, Guatemala, India, Iran, the Netherlands, Peru, Sweden, Uruguay, and Yugoslavia. While Arab Palestinians refused to cooperate with it, the Zionists [q.v.] took a contrary line. It submitted its report on 31 August 1947. Seven of its members proposed partitioning mandate Palestine into a Jewish state (53.5 percent of Palestine), an Arab state (45.4 percent), and Jerusalem [q.v.] and its suburbs (1.1 percent) under international trusteeship. India, Iran, and Yugoslavia proposed an independent federal state composed of Arab and Jewish segments. On 29 November 1947, the UN General Assembly adopted Resolution 181 on partitioning Palestine by 33 votes to 13, with 10 abstentions. With 72 percent of the voting members favoring partition, exceeding the required two-thirds majority, parti-

tioning Palestine became official UN policy. Challenging the UN's authority to partition a country against the wishes of its majority, the Arab members proposed that the matter be referred to the International Court of Justice for its verdict. Their motion was defeated by 21 votes to 20, with 15 members abstaining.

United Nations Truce Supervision Organization (1948–): To assist the UN Mediator and the Truce Commission in supervising the cease-fire in the 1948–49 Arab-Israeli War [q.v.], the UN Truce Supervision Organization (UNTSO) was created on 29 May 1948. After the formation of the UN Disengagement Observer Force in 1974 [q.v.] and the UN Interim Force in Lebanon in 1978 [q.v.], the UNTSO cooperated with them.

It continues to exist as an intermediary between the adversaries and provides a channel for stopping isolated incidents from turning into major armed confrontations. In 2012, its 384 military and civilian staff, drawn from 24 countries, were posted in Egypt, Israel, Jordan, Lebanon, and Syria. Its annual budget was $70.2 million.

It was the first peacekeeping operation by the United Nations. On the sixtieth anniversary of its establishment, the UN General Assembly declared 29 May as the International Day of United Nations Peacekeepers to pay them homage and remember those who had given their lives for keeping peace.

United Religious Front: *Israeli political alliance* On the eve of the first general election in Israel in 1949, Agudat Israel [q.v.] and Poale Agudat Israel [*q.v.*] combined with Mizrahi [*q.v.*] and Poale HaMizrahi [*q.v.*] to form the United Religious Front. Winning 16 seats (out of 120), the Front joined the government to run inter alia the ministry of religious affairs. This enabled its constituents to determine the funding of religious councils and religious courts, and to influence the composition and working of the Supreme Rabbinical Council, charged with supervising rabbis and synagogues [*q.v.*]. The Front's disagreement with Prime Minister David Ben-Gurion [*q.v.*] on the degree of control over religious education in schools brought down the first Israeli government in mid-1951. In the subsequent Knesset election later that year the Front's constituent parties ran in the election separately.

United States Middle East Force:

The U.S. Middle East Force based itself in Bahrain according to a secret agreement signed by Washington and the emirate on the eve of Britain's withdrawal from there in 1971. It included the United States's leasing of naval facilities previously used by the British for an annual rental of £300,000. Bahrain thus became the official headquarters of the U.S. Middle East Force, even though as early as 1949 the U.S. Navy had established a presence there. Because of its proximity to the oilfields of Saudi Arabia, Qatar, and the United Arab Emirates, Bahrain was ideal for naval reconnaissance missions in the Gulf.

During the October 1973 Arab-Israeli War [*q.v.*], angered at Washington's support for Israel, Bahrain's ruler, Isa II bin Salman al-Khalifa [*q.v.*], stated that he had abrogated the agreement with Washington. But what he had actually done was to cancel the provision about providing fuelling facilities to the U.S. Navy and raise the annual rental to £2 million. Later the Bahraini-U.S. military agreement, specifying naval and air facilities to the Pentagon, was secretly renewed beyond its expiry date of June 1977. The Bahraini-U.S. link was confirmed in April 1980 when, following their unsuccessful attempt to free American hostages in Tehran [*q.v.*], U.S. military planes refueled in Bahrain before taking off for Turkey.

Later the functions of the U.S. Middle East Force were assumed by the Central Command, with its jurisdiction covering all of the Middle East, southwest Asia, and East Africa.

United Torah Judaism: *Israeli political party* (Official title: *Yahadut HaTorah HaMeuhedet*) On the eve of the 1988 general election, Agudat Israel [*q.v.*] and Poale Agudat Israel [*q.v.*] merged with two smaller religious groups—Moria and Degel HaTorah—to form the United Torah Judaism (UTJ). It was opposed to negotiations with the Palestinians and the establishment of an independent Palestine, and favored expanding Jewish settlements in the occupied Palestinian territories [*q.v.*].

It won seven seats in that election and four in the 1992 election. In 1990 it joined the Likud-led [*q.v.*] government after Labor [*q.v.*] quit the national unity cabinet. It maintained its strength in the 1996 Knesset [*q.v.*] election, gaining one more seat in the 1999 election. Its score in the 2003 election was eight. It split into its two original factions when it joined Ariel Sharon's [*q.v.*] government in 2004.

But on the eve of the 2006 Knesset [*q.v.*] election, its constituents came together. It won six seats. Though its strength fell to five in the 2009 election, it was invited by Benjamin Netanyahu [*q.v.*] to join the Likud-led government to help him cobble together a slim majority in parliament, and it did so.

Universal Suez Maritime Canal Company: *See* Suez Canal.

ushr tax: A tax on harvest, it amounts to one-tenth of the produce if the land is irrigated naturally by rain or spring water, and one-twentieth if it is irrigated by artificial means such as a well or canal. It is derived from the following Quranic verses: "O Believers! Expend in Allah's way the best portion of the wealth you have earned and of what We have produced for you from the earth." (2: 267); and "And give away Allah's due at the harvest time" (6:141).

al-Utaiba, Juheiman ibn Saif (1939–80): *Saudi Arabian Islamic leader* Born in Sajir in Qasim province, Utaiba was a grandson of an Ikhwan [*q.v.*] militant who died in 1929 in a battle against Abdul Aziz al-Saud [*q.v.*]. At the age of 18 he joined the National Guard [*q.v.*], and rose to become a corporal. Military discipline frustrated his fierce piety and vocal opposition to the presence of non-Muslim Westerners in the Saudi kingdom's institutions, including the National Guard.

He left the National Guard in 1972 and enrolled at the Islamic University of Medina, where he became a student of Shaikh Abdul Aziz ibn Abdullah al-Baz [*q.v.*], who advocated a return

to the letter of the Quran [*q.v.*] and the *sunna* [*q.v.*]. Imbibing his teachings, Utaiba applied them to the actions of the Saudi dynasty, and concluded that it had deviated from the true path of Islam [*q.v.*]. This led to a clash with al-Baz and his expulsion from the university in 1974. On return to his native province, he started to preach along the lines of the founder of the Wahhabi [*q.v.*] doctrine, Shaikh Abdul Wahhab (1703–1787).

A popular poet and writer on Islam, Utaiba established cells in numerous bedouin settlements in Qasim. In 1976 he and his followers moved to Riyadh [*q.v.*]. There he published a pamphlet in which he attacked the Saudi rulers for their deviation from the Sharia [*q.v.*], their greed and corruption, misuse of laws for their own benefit, and socializing with atheists and unbelievers. In the summer of 1978 the government arrested him and 98 of his followers. But once al-Baz, now head of the Council of Senior Ulema [*q.v.*], had ruled that their ideas were not treasonable, they were released after they promised not to undertake subversive actions or propaganda. They were kept under surveillance but managed to slip away from Riyadh.

Resorting to clandestine preaching, Utaiba developed the concept of *mahdi* [*q.v.*] (messiah), which he allied to the traditional Wahhabi doctrine. In his brother-in-law, Muhammad bin Abdullah al-Qahtani, a former student of the Islamic University of Riyadh, he had found a mahdi with the name of the Prophet of Islam, and a surname that was a derivative of Qahtan, the legendary ancestor of Arabs [*q.v.*]. To this he tagged the notion widely held among Sunni Muslims [*q.v.*] that a *mujaddid* (Arabic: *reviver of faith*), appears once every (Islamic) century. The new Islamic century was to begin on 1 Muharram 1400 A.H./20 November 1979.

On New Year's Eve, hundreds of Utaiba's followers converged on the Grand Mosque in Mecca [*q.v.*], where they had concealed arms in the cellars and retreats of the vast complex. They planned to take hostage King Khalid al-Saud [*q.v.*], who was expected to join the faithful for the first prayer of the century. Despite Khalid's absence due to sudden illness, Utaiba and his armed followers took over the mosque. After condemning the Saudi regime, he introduced al-Qahtani as the mahdi/mujaddid. This was the most serious religious challenge to the Saudi kingdom since its establishment in 1932. It took King Khalid's government a fortnight, and the deployment of thousands of Saudi and Pakistani troops and the assistance of the French Special Forces, to regain the Grand Mosque. Al Qahtani was one of the 117 rebels killed in the operation. And in January 1980, Utaiba was decapitated along with 66 other rebels.

V

Vilayet-e Faqih: (Persian: *Rule of the Religious Jurisprudent*): *Islamic doctrine* Developed by Ayatollah Ruhollah Khomeini [*q.v.*] in his book *Hukumat-e Islam: Vilayet-e Faqih* (Persian: *Islamic government: Rule of the Faqih*) (1971), this doctrine specifies that an Islamic regime requires an Islamic ruler who is thoroughly conversant with the Sharia [*q.v.*] and is just in its application: a Just Faqih. He should be assisted by jurisprudents at various levels of legislative, executive, and judicial bodies.

The function of a popularly elected parliament, open to both lay believers and clerics, is to resolve the conflicts likely to arise in the implementation of Islamic doctrines. However, judicial functions are to be performed only by jurisprudents conversant with the Sharia. Such jurisprudents also oversee the actions of the legislative and executive branches. The overall supervision and guidance of parliament and judiciary rests with the Just Faqih, who must also ensure that the executive does not exceed its powers. After the establishment of the Islamic Republic of Iran in April 1979, the Vilayet-e Faqih doctrine became the backbone of the Islamic constitution adopted in December 1979.

W

Wafd: (Arabic: *Delegation*): *Egyptian political party* The Wafd was formed in 1919 under the leadership of Saad Zaghloul, a lawyer. It was a coalition of different social classes seeking independence from the occupying power, Britain. Its name derived from the delegation Zaghloul led two days after the end of World War I on 11 November 1918 to the British high commissioner in Cairo [*q.v.*], demanding that his delegation (*wafd*) be allowed to go to London to present its case for Egyptian independence. The British official refused. Over the next three years, demonstrations and riots ensued, interspersed with talks between the opposing parties. Wafdists demanded total independence for Egypt and Sudan.

A unilateral British declaration in November 1922 granted (nominal) independence to Egypt with stings attached. Britain was to retain responsibility for the communications system in Egypt, safeguard foreign interests and Egypt's national minorities (meaning Copts [*q.v.*]), and protect Sudan while defending Egypt against direct or indirect aggression. The British named Ahmad Fuad as king of Egypt. The constitution that he promulgated in 1923 incorporated the earlier British declaration.

The Wafd won the subsequent general election, and Zaghloul became prime minister. After his death in 1927 the nationalist camp split between the Wafd, led by Mustafa Nahas Pasha [*q.v.*], and King Fuad, with the monarch sacking Prime Minister Nahas Pasha in 1931 and suspending the constitution. Just before his death in early 1936 he reinstated the constitution.

The Wafd was returned to power with a large majority in the election of April 1936, when the Regency Council, headed by Nahas Pasha, reigned on behalf of 16-year-old King Farouq [*q.v.*]. In August 1936 the 20-year Anglo-Egyptian Treaty [*q.v.*], retaining all four provisions of the 1922 Declaration except British protection for foreign interests and national minorities, was signed.

When Farouq achieved adulthood in 1938, the tension between him and

the Wafd revived. Farouq dismissed Nahas Pasha. When Italy entered World War II in May 1940, it had an impact on Egypt, since Farouq was pro-Italian. The British demanded the dismissal of anti-British Prime Minister Ali Mahir and his replacement by Nahas Pasha, who was ready to cooperate with London. Farouq refused. In February 1942, while German troops were advancing on Egypt from Libya, and Farouq was on the verge of appointing a new premier known to be anti-British, the British ambassador compelled the monarch, at the pain of deposition, to choose Nahas Pasha for the post. Farouq complied. Nahas Pasha retained his office until October 1944 and ensured Egypt's affiliation to the Arab League [*q.v.*].

Following the Egyptian debacle in the 1948–49 Palestine War [*q.v.*], Farouq agreed to reconciliation with Wafd leaders on the understanding that each side would overlook the incompetence and corruption of the other. Farouq ordered a general election in January 1950, which put the Wafd firmly in power. To maintain popular support, the Wafd government pressed London to withdraw its troops from Egypt. When Britain stonewalled, the Egyptian unilaterally abrogated the 1936 Anglo-Egyptian Treaty (valid until 1956) in October 1951. It demanded immediate and unconditional British withdrawal from the Suez Canal [*q.v.*] zone. Guerrilla actions against British troops ensued, with leftist Wafdists participating.

After riots in Cairo in January 1952, Farouq dismissed the Wafd government. He lost his throne in the Free Officers' coup in July 1952. The new regime banned all parties, including the Wafd. A quarter-century later, following the promulgation of the Law of the System of Political Parties in June 1977, Fuad Serag al-Din, a veteran of the pre-1952 Wafd, secured a license to establish the Neo-Wafd Party [q.v.].

Wahhabism and Wahhabis: *Islamic sect* Wahhabism is an Islamic doctrine developed by Muhammad bin Abdul Wahhab (1703–1887), a native of Najd [q.v.], a bastion of Hanbalis [q.v.]. The name was coined by the opponents of Abdul Wahhab whose followers called themselves *Muwahidun* (Arabic: *Unitarians*), who accepted the Hanbali school as interpreted by Taqi al-Din bin Taimiya in the late 14th century. Abdul Wahhab condemned the medieval superstitions that had collected around the pristine teachings of Islam [q.v.]. Favoring *ijtihad* [q.v.] (reasoned interpretation of the Sharia [q.v.]), he opposed the codification of the Sharia into a comprehensive system of jurisprudence. He was especially opposed to the cult of saints, who were often beseeched by believers to intercede on their behalf with Allah. He and his followers resorted to destroying the tombs of saints.

Unlike Hanbali practices, Abdul Wahhab made attendance at public prayer obligatory and forbade minarets in the building of mosques. Later, in alliance with the followers of Muhammad bin Saud, who became the ruler of Najd in 1745 and founded the House of Saud [q.v.], Wahhabis mounted a campaign against idolatry, corruption, and adultery. Citing the Hadith [q.v.], they banned music, dancing, and even poetry, an integral part of Arab life. They prohibited the use of silk, gold, ornaments, and jewelery.

Regarding themselves to be true believers, Wahhabis launched a jihad [q.v.] against all others—whom they described as apostates. In 1802 they attacked and looted Karbala [q.v.], a holy city of the Shias [q.v.]. Under Saud bin Abdul Aziz (r. 1803–1814), Wahhabi rule spread to the Iraqi and Syrian borders, and included the Hijaz [q.v.] region containing the holy cities of Mecca [q.v.] and Medina [q.v.]. This led the Ottoman sultan to order the governor of Egypt, Muhammad Ali, to quell the movement. The result was the defeat and execution of Abdullah bin Saud in 1818.

The power of the Wahhabi House of Saud waxed and waned until 1881, when it was expelled from the Riyadh region. But with Abdul Aziz bin Abdul Rahman al-Saud [q.v.], Wahhabism rose again in the Arabian Peninsula [q.v.]. He propagated the creed using military and state power, and fostered the Ikhwan [q.v.] movement for the purpose. Considering themselves "the truly guided Islamic community," Wahhabis attacked polytheists, unbelievers, and hypocrites (i.e., those who claimed to be Muslim but whose behavior was un-Islamic). They labeled any deviation from the Sharia as innovation, and therefore un-Islamic.

With oil riches flowing into the coffers of the Wahhabi state of Saudi Arabia since the late 1930s, the sect has lost some of its earlier militancy. The final authority lies with the head of the Supreme Religious Council in Saudi Arabia. It has adherents in

Central Asia, Afghanistan, Pakistan, and India.

Wailing Wall: *The Western Wall of the Jewish temple in Jerusalem* Called Kotel Ma'aravi in Hebrew [*q.v.*], the Wailing Wall is part of the massive retaining wall, made up of stones, that the Roman king of Judaea/Judea, Herod the Great (37–4 B.C.), erected at the western, southern, and eastern borders of the Second Temple atop Mount Moriah in Jerusalem [*q.v.*] after extending the outer courtyard of the Temple. As the only remnant of the Second Temple, razed in 70 A.D., it is the most sacred site of Judaism [*q.v.*]. Since 70 A.D. Jews [*q.v.*] have visited it to grieve the destruction of the temple and pray. According to the Talmud [*q.v.*], divine presence has never departed from the Western Wall, and so the faithful say their prayers very close to the wall in the belief that the prayers will rise through the crevices to the Throne of Grace on Mount Moriah.

After the destruction of the Second Temple, Jews were permitted to enter Jerusalem only on the ninth of Av, the anniversary of the sacking of the temple. Since the pilgrims would ascend in silence and descend in tears, the wall acquired the epithet "Wailing." During the Muslim [*q.v.*] Arab [*q.v.*] rule from 638 A.D. onward, Jews were allowed to settle in Jerusalem and pray at the wall. The Ottoman Turks, who administered Jerusalem from 1516 for four centuries, formally recognized Jews' right to pray at the Wailing Wall.

In 1930, during the British Mandate over Palestine, a League of Nations Commission examined the contending ownership claims by Jews and Muslims over the Wailing Wall and the adjoining area, and declared Muslims the sole owners. The armistice agreement in April 1949 between Israel and Jordan, which controlled the Old City of Jerusalem containing the holy sites of Jews, Christians [*q.v.*], and Muslims, provided for free access to sacred sites. But in practice Jordan denied the Jews access to the Wailing Wall. The situation changed when the Israelis captured East Jerusalem [*q.v.*], including the Old City, in the June 1967 Arab-Israeli War [*q.v.*]. In the unsuccessful talks on final settlement of the Israel-Palestinian conflict between Israeli Prime Minister Ehud Barak [*q.v.*] and Palestine Liberation Organization [*q.v.*] Chairman Yasser Arafat [*q.v.*] in 2000, the latter agreed to Israel's having sovereignty over the Wailing Wall.

On Jewish holidays a large number of Jews pray at the Wailing Wall, divided by portable screens into prayer areas for women and men.

waqf (Arabic: *prevent*): In Islamic law, *waqf*, the term popularly used for a religious trust, means "prevent a thing from becoming the property of a third person." Though in practice it meant the legal process by which an endowment was created, in common parlance the term was applied to the endowment (*mawquf*) itself. Anas bin Malik (d. 796), founder of the Maliki school [*q.v.*], attributed the practice of religious trust to the *sunna* [*q.v.*]. The first major recorded example of waqf is that of Abu Bakr Muhammad bin Ali al-Madharai (d. 956 A.D.) in Egypt. He turned his agricultural land into a waqf for the holy cities of

Mecca [*q.v.*] and Medina [*q.v.*], and for other social purposes such as charities and religious education.

The waqfs, often administered by public officials, ameliorated poverty and advanced further education. On the other hand, the high concentration of landed property and inefficient management had an adverse economic effect. During the latter period of the Ottoman Empire (1517–1918) waqfs accounted for nearly three-quarters of agricultural land. In the mid-1930s the waqf estates comprised one-seventh of the cultivated land in Egypt and one-sixth in Iran.

The central administration of waqfs in Egypt, begun in 1851, was formalized with a ministry in 1913. The League of Nations mandates over Syria, Palestine, Transjordan [*q.v.*], and Iraq required that the mandatory powers should administer the waqfs in accordance with the Sharia [*q.v.*]. On independence, the governments of these states—all with a Sunni [*q.v.*] majority except Iraq—took over the function. In a Shia [*q.v.*]-majority country such as Iran this role was traditionally played by senior clergy, who used the income to run educational, social, and charitable institutions and theological colleges. The Civil Code of 1928 authorized the Waqf Organization of the ministry of education to approve or disapprove budgets of waqfs, transform a waqf into private property or prohibit such a change, or take over a waqf with unknown administrators. Following the 1979 Islamic revolution [*q.v.*], this code was abrogated.

War of Attrition (Egypt-Israel, 1969-70): Following the Arab defeat in the June 1967 Arab-Israeli War [*q.v.*], Egyptian President Gamal Abdul Nasser [*q.v.*] went through the stages of "standing firm," by resisting Israel's diplomatic and military pressures, and "active deterrence"—that is, keeping the conflict alive, thus preventing the status quo from congealing—to reach the final stage, the War of Attrition against the Israeli positions along the Suez Canal [*q.v.*] on 8 March 1969. By then, helped by the Soviet Union, he had re-equipped the Egyptian military to its pre-June 1967 level. Israel responded by saturation bombing of Egyptian targets and deep penetration raids into Egypt. This drove Nasser deeper into the Soviets' embrace. With a sophisticated Soviet-built air defense umbrella in operation in the spring of 1970, Egypt managed to curtail Israel's capacity for massive reprisals.

Against this background Egypt and Israel accepted the initiative of U.S. Secretary of State William Rogers for a temporary, renewable cease-fire in August 1970. By then, the Israeli army had lost 2,659 soldiers, and the Egyptian military almost 10,000 in this conflict. Also, some 500,000 Egyptians from the Suez Canal zone had been turned into refugees.

War of the Establishment, Israel: [Official title: *Milhemet HaKomemiyut* (Hebrew: *War of the Establishment*]) *See* War of Independence, Israel

War of Independence, Israel (1948–49): (Official title: *Milhemet HaKomemiyut* [Hebrew: *War of the Establishment*]) Since the war between the Zionists [*q.v.*] in Palestine [*q.v.*] and their Arab neighbors erupted *after*

the Declaration of the Establishment of the State of Israel by the People's Council of the Yishuv [*q.v.*] on 14 May 1948, it was called the War of the Establishment. Later, Israeli politicians and historians took to calling it the War of Independence, chiefly because it resonated well with the American people and government, thus mislabeling a seminal event in the history of Israel.

Washington Accord (1995): As required by the Oslo I Accord [q.v.], the Israeli and Palestinian teams, led respectively by Shimon Peres [q.v.] and Yasser Arafat [*q.v.*], negotiated a deal about the future of the West Bank [*q.v.*] and the advancement of Palestinian autonomy. Peres and Arafat initialed the final draft on 22 September 1995 in the Egyptian resort town of Taba. On 28 September they signed the agreement at the White House in Washington at a ceremony hosted by President Bill Clinton. It became known as the Washington Accord or Oslo II Accord [*q.v.*].

With 31 Articles, seven Annexes, and nine maps, the Accord was 314 pages long. It divided the West Bank into A, B, and C Areas, and provided for elections and responsibilities for the Palestinian Legislative Council and the Palestinian Authority [*q.v.*] presidency, a phased release of the Palestinian prisoners, and a timetable for implementation.

Palestinian jurisdiction would begin after the elections. In Area A, the PA was to exercise full control over civil affairs and security; in Area B, the PA was to exercise control over civil affairs and public order, with Israelis taking charge of overall security; and in Area

C, Israel [*q.v.*] was to exercise full control, including security, territorial jurisdiction, and Jewish settlers.

Area A consisted of seven Palestinian cities—Bethlehem [q.v.], Hebron [q.v.], Jenin, Nablus [q.v.], Qalqilya, Ramallah, and Tulkarm—and covered 2 percent of the West Bank. Here the PA was required to guarantee freedom of movement to Israeli civilians and settlers through these urban centers and provide joint Palestinian-Israeli escorts for their vehicles. Area B included 465 villages, 24 percent of the territory, and 63 percent of the population. Here the Israel Defense Forces (IDF) [*q.v.*] had the power to intervene at its own discretion to maintain overall security. The rest of the West Bank, taking up 73 percent of the land, was labeled Area C.

Finally, the Accord spelled out the powers of the PA presidency and the Legislative Council, both subject to review and final approval of Israel.

Full IDF evacuation of Area A cities, except Hebron, was scheduled for the end of 1995, followed by a partial withdrawal from Hebron by 28 March 1996.

The IDF's evacuation, starting with Jenin on 13 November, reached a climax with its withdrawal from Bethlehem on 21 December, leading to a four-day party there, combining the celebration of Palestinian nationalism with Christmas [*q.v.*].

Due to the impending Israeli elections, Arafat allowed the partial evacuation of Hebron to be postponed in order to help Peres beat his Likud [*q.v.*] rival Benjamin Netanyahu [q.v.] in the prime ministerial contest in May 1996. But Peres lost. Netanyahu forestalled further implementation of the Accord. It was not until October 1998, under the Wye River Memorandum [*q.v.*] brokered personally by Clinton, that he agreed to make some concessions to the Palestinians.

Wazir, Khalil (1935–88): *Palestinian political-military leader* Born into the household of a grocer in Ramla, Palestine [*q.v.*], Wazir and his family fled during the 1948–49 Palestine War [*q.v.*]. He grew up in al-Bureij refugee camp in the Gaza Strip [*q.v.*]. In 1954 he was selected by the Egyptian military, which administered Gaza, first for commando training, and then for further military instruction in Cairo [*q.v.*], where he met Yasser Arafat [*q.v.*]. He was commissioned as a lieutenant in the Gazan brigade of the Egyptian army.

Before Israel could capture Gaza in the 1956 Suez War [*q.v.*], he escaped to Cairo, where he became active in Palestinian student politics, dominated by Arafat. After spending a couple of years in Stuttgart, West Germany, along with Salah Khalaf [*q.v.*], he traveled to Kuwait in early 1959 to join Arafat, who was running a construction business there. Together they established Fatah [*q.v.*], and Wazir returned to Stuttgart to organize the Palestinian students in West Germany.

He was close to the National Liberation Front of Algeria, which won power in 1962. In December 1962 he and other leaders of Fatah went to Algiers, where the government authorized the opening of a Fatah office and training camps for Fatah activists. He visited Communist China in 1963. Arrested in January 1965 for sabotaging Israel's National Water Carrier from southern Lebanon, he was held in a Lebanese jail, where he acquired the *nom de guerre* of Abu Jihad, Father of Struggle. After his release in March, he and Arafat moved to Syria. From there they traveled together to the Palestinian refugee camps on the West Bank [*q.v.*], then part of Jordan, to enroll recruits for Fatah. The military wing of Fatah, called Assifa (Arabic: *Storm*), was headed by Wazir.

With Fatah becoming the leading constituent of the Palestine Liberation Organization (PLO) [*q.v.*] in 1968, the importance of Assifa and Wazir rose. In the 1970s, as Fatah and Assifa, now based in Beirut [*q.v.*], became more active, carrying out numerous guerrilla operations, he emerged as the right-hand man of Arafat, chairman of both Fatah and the PLO. He backed Arafat in his continuing endeavor to impose discipline and a centralized military command on the various PLO constituents without alienating any of them. After the expulsion of Fatah and the PLO from Beirut in 1982, he moved with the party headquarters to Tunis, Tunisia. With the Palestinian fighters scattered in seven Arab countries, his task became onerous. On the other hand his reputation as a conciliator remained unimpaired.

Following the outbreak of the intifada [*q.v.*] in December 1987, he worked closely with the PLO's Occupied Homeland Directorate to give direction to the uprising. He ensured the success of the United National Leadership of the Uprising [*q.v.*]. Therefore, he became a prime target for those in the Israeli government who felt that by eliminating him they would undermine the intifada, which

Israel had failed to achieve so far. He was assassinated by a Mossad [*q.v.*] hit team in April 1988 at his Tunis home. He was buried in Damascus [*q.v.*].

Weizmann, Ezer (1924–2005): *Israeli military leader and politician; president, 1993–2000* Born into a prominent Jewish family in Caesarea, Palestine [*q.v.*], Weizmann enrolled in the Royal Air Force during World War II and became a pilot. Soon after demobilization, he joined Irgun [*q.v.*]. During the 1948–49 Arab-Israeli War [*q.v.*], he was one of the first Israeli pilots. After the war he became an officer in the Israeli Air Force, rising to commander of the air force (1958–66). Under his command, the air force prepared its plan to destroy the air power of its Arab neighbors, which it implemented efficiently during the June 1967 Arab-Israeli War [*q.v.*]. He was promoted to chief of operations of the Israel Defense Forces.

When he realized in 1969 that there was no chance of his becoming chief of staff, he resigned and joined Gahal [*q.v.*]. Elected to the Knesset [*q.v.*], he served as transport minister in the national unity cabinet (1969–70). When Gahal left the government in August 1970 in protest at the majority decision to accept a cease-fire in the War of Attrition [*q.v.*], Weizmann followed suit. He was elected chairman of the executive committee of Gahal, a position he held until he fell out with the party leader, Menachem Begin [*q.v.*], in late 1972.

He was persuaded to return to politics in early 1977, when he was appointed head of the Likud [*q.v.*] election headquarters. Likud won, and he became defense minister (1977–

80). He played an important role in the peace talks with Egypt. When the Palestinian autonomy provisions in the Camp David Accords [*q.v.*] were not implemented by the deadline of May 1980, he resigned, hoping the government would fall. It did not.

In the 1984 election his group, Yahad (Hebrew: *Together*), won three seats. The stalemated election result gave him the chance to choose the next prime minister. He opted for Shimon Peres [*q.v.*], who headed the subsequent national unity government, in which Weizmann became minister without portfolio and a member of the inner political cabinet. Yahad joined Labor Party [*q.v.*].

Weizmann headed the Labor election headquarters in 1988, but failed to repeat his 1977 success for Likud. In the next national unity cabinet, he served as minister of science and a member of the inner political cabinet. In early 1990, following a revelation by Prime Minister Yitzhak Shamir [*q.v.*] that he had violated official policy and law by meeting a Palestine Liberation Organization (PLO) [*q.v.*] official in Geneva, he resigned.

Three years later, after the Labor-led government had lifted the ban on the PLO, Weizmann was elected president of Israel by 66 votes to 53. He was reelected in 1998 by 88 votes to 15. He resigned prematurely in 2000 after revelations that he had received $300,000 in undeclared cash gifts from two foreign businessmen during 1985–93.

West Bank (of the Jordan River): *Palestinian Territory* Area: 2,297 sq. mi./5,949 sq. km, including enlarged East Jerusalem (27 sq. mi./69 sq. km).

Population excluding enlarged East Jerusalem [*q.v.*]: 2.58 million Palestinians (2010 est.); 327,750 Jewish settlers in 121 officially recognized settlements (2010). In 2009, two-fifths of the West Bank was taken up by Israeli infrastructure of roads, water and electricity facilities, and security checkpoints.

In the 1948–49 Arab-Israeli War [*q.v.*] Jordan's army managed to retain an enclave on the west bank of the River Jordan [*q.v.*], including the eastern part of Jerusalem [*q.v.*]. Egypt's army held the semi-desert Gaza Strip [*q.v.*]. Together the two territories made up about half of the area allocated to the Palestinian Arabs [*q.v.*] by the UN partition plan of November 1947. Jordan annexed the West Bank, including East Jerusalem, in April 1950. In the June 1967 Arab-Israeli War [*q.v.*], Israel captured the West Bank and Gaza. The population figures, according to a census taken in September 1967, were: West Bank 589,000, Gaza 380,800. The military occupation of these territories was nominally changed in 1981 to "civil administration," working under military commanders. Jordan continued to pay its civil servants in the West Bank through the functioning Jordanian banks in Jordanian dinars.

In 1968 militant Jews established their presence in the center of Hebron [*q.v.*]. They won the approval of the Labor [*q.v.*] government two years later, when they set a colony, called Kiryat Arba, near Hebron. In August 1973 the ruling Labor Party formally reversed its policy of merely holding on to the Occupied Arab Territories [*q.v.*] until the Arab states were ready to negotiate peace with it directly. It

adopted the Galili Document, which allowed Jewish individuals and public bodies to purchase land in the Occupied Arab Territories, and permitted the government to supplement the hitherto privately funded settlement program.

Once Jordan had accepted the decision of the Arab League [*q.v.*] summit in October–November 1974 that the Palestine Liberation Organization (PLO) [*q.v.*] was the sole and legitimate representative of the Palestinian people, its legal position in the West Bank became tenuous. The local elections held in April 1976 in the territory showed that almost all the 24 mayors were supporters in varying degrees of the Palestine National Front, a front organization of the PLO, which was banned. By May 1977, when Labor was replaced by Likud [*q.v.*] as the leading member of a coalition government, there were 32 Jewish settlements, most of them authorized, in the West Bank.

The Camp David Accords between Israel and Egypt [*q.v.*] in September 1978 included an agreement for autonomy for the Palestinians in the West Bank and Gaza to be implemented by 26 May 1980. Since the PLO was not party to these talks and wanted nothing less than a Palestinian state, this plan proved stillborn.

Israel indefinitely postponed the local elections in the West Bank due in April 1980. The number of Jewish settlements continued to increase, and the existing ones grew more populous. The Palestinian intifada [*q.v.*], which started in Gaza in December 1987, spread to the West Bank. In July 1988 Jordan cut its ties with the territory. The seizure and/or purchase of land by

Israel and Jewish individuals and organizations continued. Neither the Oslo Accord I [*q.v.*], signed in September 1993, nor the Oslo Accord II [*q.v.*], signed in September 1995, mentioned a halt to new Jewish settlements or expansion of the existing ones. The Oslo Accord II specified Israeli troop withdrawal from seven cities, joint Palestinian-Israeli control of 450 Palestinian villages, and continued Israeli control of Jewish settlements. This was implemented in late 1995, except in Hebron [*q.v.*]. However, the existing 128 Jewish settlements were expanded and new ones established, the chief source of the Palestinian disaffection with the Oslo Accords.

Following the outbreak of the Al Aqsa Intifada [*q.v.*] in September 2000, relations between Israel and the Palestinians deteriorated. The situation worsened after the election of Ariel Sharon [*q.v.*] as Israeli prime minister in February 2001 on the platform of expanding Jewish settlement on the West Bank. As the number of the protesting Palestinians killed by the Israeli military rose and Islamist Palestinians resorted increasingly to suicide bombings, Israel reoccupied West Bank towns and cities in April 2002.

In June, the Israeli government started building a barrier between the West Bank and Israel—at the cost $2.2 million a km—inside the West Bank territory. In December the UN General Assembly called on the International Court of Justice (ICJ) to examine the barrier issue. In July 2004, the ICJ ruled that its construction contravened international law; that it was "tantamount to annexation" and impeded the Palestinian right to self-

determination; and that Israel must discontinue the project. By 150 votes to four, the UN General Assembly called on Israel to dismantle the barrier. Israel continued the construction.

By April 2006, it had authorized the building of 435 miles (700 km). Two-thirds had been built or was being built by then. When the barrier was constructed inside the West Bank territory, the space between it and the 1949 armistice line was declared "closed military zone" by Israel. That lopped off 9.5 percent of the original West Bank, turning the inhabitants of of the many villages there into displaced persons and depriving them of their property and livelihood.

The barrier consisted of a concrete base, most of it at the front of a 1-foot/4-meter-deep trench, and rolls of razor wire spread over 60 m/200ft., and the rest supporting 26-ft./8-meter-high concrete wall capped with high wire and mesh. The structure carried electronic sensors and had an earth-covered trace road running by its side where footprints of anybody crossing them could be noticed.

Palestinians saw the barrier as the last piece in an overarching Israeli plan to rob them of their land and contain them into disconnected enclaves on 42 percent of the West Bank. An earlier part of that strategy was to reserve all major roads in the West Bank, measuring 270 miles/700 km, for the Jewish settlers and bar Palestinians from using them. This measure was easy to enforce, since the vehicles of the Jewish settlers and Palestinians carried registration plates of different colors.

Israelis attributed the 90 percent reduction in terrorist acts between

2002 and 2005 to the erection of the barrier. They argued that the barrier was merely a temporary security measure that will become redundant once a negotiated final settlement was signed between Israel and the Palestinians.

By October 2011, the 472-mile/760-km-long barrier—roughly twice the length of the 1949 cease-fire line—was in place. Except for an 26-foot/8-meter-high concrete wall along its 30-km/24-mi. length, it consisted of an electric fence.

West Jerusalem: Area: 13 sq. mi./34 sq. km in 1948, 20 sq. mi./54 sq. km in 1993; population, 403,800 (2011 est.) West Jerusalem was captured by Israeli forces in the 1948–49 Arab-Israeli War [*q.v.*] and retained by Israel.

In December 1949 Israel moved its capital to West Jerusalem, a move not recognized by the international community. After its victory in the Six-Day War [*q.v.*], Israel added a vastly enlarged East Jerusalem [*q.v.*] to West Jerusalem on 28 June 1967 by extending its laws to the eastern sector. Additions in March 1985 and May 1993 expanded the area covered by West Jerusalem to 20 sq. mi./54 sq. km. Almost all its residents are Jewish.

West Syriac rite: *Christian rite* The West Syriac rite, initially called the Antiochene rite—the seminal system of liturgical practices and customs for almost all Eastern rites—originated in the patriarchate of Antioch, and is so called to distinguish it from the East Syriac rite [*q.v.*]. The liturgy of Saint James, a derivative of the Jerusalem-Antiochene rite, is the basis of the liturgy for Syrian Orthodox [*q.v.*],

Syrian Catholics [*q.v.*], and Maronite Catholics [*q.v.*].

Western hostages (in Lebanon): *See* Hostage-taking and hostages.

Western Wall: *See* Wailing Wall.

White Guard (Saudi Arabia): *See* National Guard (Saudi Arabia).

White Revolution (Iran): In early January 1963 Muhammad Reza Shah Pahlavi [*q.v.*] launched a six-point socioeconomic reform package called the White Revolution. It consisted of land redistribution, forest nationalization, the sale of public sector factories to pay compensation to landlords for land above the official ceiling, votes for women, profit-sharing in industry, and the eradication of illiteracy. According to official figures it was endorsed by 99.9 percent of those participating in a referendum on it on 25 January.

Opposition to the White Revolution, emanating primarily from hostility to the monarchical regime, came from both the secular National Front [*q.v.*] and militant Muslim clerics. The latter were incensed by the shah's threat to amend the 1962 Land Reform Act to include lands belonging to the religious trusts [*q.v.*], which were managed by the clergy. Street protest was encouraged by Ayatollah Ruhollah Khomeini [*q.v.*], who described the White Revolution as phony. The unrest reached a peak in early June 1963 and culminated in a nationwide uprising in which many thousands of people were said to have been killed by the security forces.

The Shah celebrated the 10th anniversary of the White Revolution in

January 1973 by announcing that the National Iranian Oil Company would take over the ownership and all operation of the Western oil consortium that had been running the petroleum industry since 1954.

Whitsunday: *See* Pentecost.

World Islamic Front for Jihad against Crusaders and Jews: (Official title: *Al-Jabah al-Islamiya al-Alamiyah li Qital al-Yahud wa al-Salibiyin*) At their base in Afghanistan, Osama bin Laden [*q.v.*] of Al Qaida [*q.v.*], Ayman Zawahiri [*q.v.*] of al-Jihad al-Islami [*q.v.*], Abu Yasser Rifia Ahmad Taha of al-Gamaat al-Islamiya [*q.v.*], Mir Hamza of Jamiat al-Ulama (Pakistan), and Fazl ul Rahman of Harkat al-Jihad (Bangladesh) announced the formation of the World Islamic Front for Jihad against Crusaders and Jews—or, for short, the World Islamic Front for Jihad (WIFFJ)—in February 1998.

In their communiqué they referred to America's continuing aggression against the Iraqi people—using the Arabian Peninsula [*q.v.*] as the staging post for the bombing of Iraq [*q.v.*]—as their evidence of the American occupation of the Peninsula since the 1991 Gulf War [*q.v.*]. Having caused the death of one million Iraqis through economic sanctions, Washington was intent on fragmenting and destroying Iraq, they argued. Its aims were to advance the interests of Israel [*q.v.*], divert attention away from Israel's occupation of Jerusalem [*q.v.*] and its murder of the Palestinians [*q.v.*], destroy Iraq, and fragment large Muslim countries like Saudi Arabia [*q.v.*], Egypt [*q.v.*], and Sudan into mini-states in order to ensure Israel's

survival and the continued American occupation of the Arabian Peninsula. The commission of such crimes and sins by the Americans were tantamount to a declaration of war on Allah, Prophet Muhammad, and Muslims [*q.v.*].

Therefore, the communiqué added, "The ruling to kill the Americans and their allies—civilians and military—is an individual duty for every Muslim who can do it in any country in which it is possible to do it, in order to liberate the Al Aqsa Mosque [in Jerusalem] and the Holy Mosque (in Mecca [*q.v.*]) from their grip, and for their armies to leave all the lands of Islam [*q.v.*], defeated, and unable to threaten any Muslim." It called upon Muslim ulema [*q.v.*], leaders, young believers, and soldiers to attack the American troops and their allies, and overthrow those Muslim regimes that were supporting them.

In March, the 40-member Council of Senior Ulema of Afghanistan met to debate the presence of the American troops in the Arabian Peninsula, and decided that the WIFFJ's call to jihad [*q.v.*] against America and Israel was in line with the Sharia [*q.v.*].

Its February 1998 statement was the primary document that the National Commission on Terrorist Attacks upon the United States—also known as 9/11 Commission—used to link Osama bin Laden, [*q.v.*], Ayman Zawahiri [*q.v.*], and Al Qaida [*q.v.*] to the aircraft suicide attacks in New York City and Metropolitan Washington, D.C., on 11 Sept, 2001.

World Muslim League: (Official title: Arabic: *Rabitat al-Alam al-Mussalmeen*) Propaganda issued by Egypt [*q.v.*]

under President Gamal Abdul Nasser [*q.v.*] against the Saudi royal family led Crown Prince Faisal bin Abdul Aziz [*q.v.*] to establish the World Muslim League (WML) in Geneva in 1962. Its function was to hold seminars and conferences on Islam [*q.v.*], and generally act as a mouthpiece of Saudi Arabia in its interpretation of Islam. Its charter stated that the allegiance of the Muslim [*q.v.*] should be to the Islamic doctrine and the overall interests of the Muslim *umma* [*q.v.*], and should override allegiance to nationalism or any other "ism". Faisal employed many exiled members of the Egyptian Muslim Brotherhood [*q.v.*] at the WML.

After the founding of the Islamic Conference Organization (ICO) [*q.v.*] in 1969, headquartered in Jeddah [*q.v.*], the WML was moved to Mecca [*q.v.*]. It remained tied to the House of Saud [*q.v.*] and reflected the official policies of Saudi Arabia.

When, during the 1990–91 Kuwait crisis, Iraq alleged that infidel troops in Saudi Arabia had defiled the holiest shrines of Islam in Mecca and Medina [*q.v.*], the WML pointed out that the conflict along the Saudi-Kuwaiti border was 900 mi./1500 km from the holy sanctuaries. The WML-sponsored conference of 350 Muslim ulema [*q.v.*] from 80 countries in Mecca stated that, since the Saudi government had invited foreign troops for self-defense, its action was in line with the Sharia [*q.v.*]. But its proposal to form an Islamic force under ICO supervision, to which its members could appeal in the event of armed conflict among them, was not implemented.

It becomes particularly active during the hajj [*q.v.*] season. It sponsors gatherings of Muslim intellectuals from different countries to help them grow strong ties among themselves and innovate ways of improving the living standards of Muslim masses.

It continues to be funded primarily by the Saudi government. It maintains offices of the Secretary-General and the Constituent Council of 120, with 60 countries represented on it. Its several departments manage the World Supreme Council for Mosques, the Fiqh [*q.v.*] Council, the Noble Sanctuary [*q.v.*] and Al Aqsa Mosque Foundation, and the International Islamic Relief Organization.

Since 2000 its Secretary-General has been Abdullah bin Abdul Mohsin al-Turki, a former minister of Islamic affairs and endowments in Saudi Arabia.

World Union of Zionist Revisionists: *See* Revisionist Zionists.

World Zionist Organization: Following the adoption of a new constitution in 1960, the Zionist Organization (ZO) [*q.v.*], established in 1897, became the World Zionist Organization (WZO). At its founding by the First Zionist Congress [*q.v.*] in Basle, Switzerland, the Zionist Organization adopted a program summarized thus: "Zionism [*q.v.*] strives to create for the Jewish people a home in Palestine [*q.v.*] secured by public law." It elected Theodor Herzl (1860–1904), chief ideologue of political Zionism, as president. Herzl based the organization in Vienna, Austria, where he lived. The 15-strong executive committee ran such departments as political (meaning external affairs), information, land and development (in Palestine), immigration and absorption (in Palestine), and Torah [*q.v.*] education and culture (in the diaspora [*q.v.*]).

The Fifth Zionist Congress in 1901 set up the Jewish National Fund (JNF) [*q.v.*] under the Zionist Organization's land and development section to finance the (communal) purchase of land in Palestine. Most of the Hovevei Zion (Hebrew: *Lovers of Zion*) societies, active in Russia, affiliated to it. When David Wolffsohn succeeded Herzl as president in 1905, he moved the headquarters to Cologne, Germany, his home base.

The Seventh Zionist Congress in 1905 rejected Britain's offer of land in Uganda for the Jewish homeland, and those who disagreed with the decision left the organization. The conflict between those who wanted to focus on securing a Jewish homeland through diplomatic means and those who wanted to concentrate on colonizing Palestine was resolved by deciding to work on both fronts simultaneously, with the Tenth Zionist Congress in 1911 electing Otto Warburg, an advocate of "synthetic Zionism." Its headquarters moved to Warburg's home base, Berlin. It opened a Palestine Office in Jaffa [*q.v.*]. In 1915, during World War I, the headquarters was moved to neutral Copenhagen in Denmark. In Palestine there was increasing cooperation between socialist pioneers and the Zionist Organization's financial institutions. With Chaim Weizmann's election as president in 1921, the headquarters moved to his base, London.

Following the 1922 British mandate, providing for a "Jewish agency" in Palestine to cooperate with the government of Palestine in establishing a Jewish national home there, Britain gave this role to the Zionist Organization, which appointed the Zionist Executive Committee in Palestine with its own chairman—Nahum Sokolow, based in Jerusalem [*q.v.*]. At Weizmann's initiative, the Sixteenth Zionist Congress in 1929 established a proper Jewish Agency for Palestine [*q.v.*] with its own executive committee consisting of an equal number of Zionists and non-Zionists—that is, those who supported the idea of a Jewish national home in Palestine but did not subscribe to political Zionism.

When the Eighteenth Zionist Congress in 1933 resolved that "in all Zionist matters discipline in regard of the Zionist Organization must take precedence over the discipline of any other body," the Revisionist Zionists [*q.v.*] left. They returned to the Zionist Organization at the Twenty-second Congress in December 1946 which—taking its cue from the resolution of the American Zionist Congress in May 1942 at the Biltmore Hotel, New York City—demanded the formation of an independent Jewish state in all of Palestine. When this Congress failed to reelect Weizmann president, the meetings of the Zionist Organization Executive Committee were cochaired by Nahum Goldmann and Berl Locker for the next 10 years.

In Palestine, with the resignation of the last remaining non-Zionist from the Jewish Agency Executive Committee in 1947, the distinction between the Zionist Executive Committee in Palestine and the Executive Committee of the Jewish Agency for Palestine disappeared, David Ben-Gurion [*q.v.*] being the chairman of both. His appointment as head of the London-based Zionist Organization's defense department enabled him to bring various armed Jewish factions in Palestine under a single command on the eve of the 1948–49 Arab-Israeli War [*q.v.*].

Following the Twenty-third Zionist Congress, held in Jerusalem in 1951, the headquarters was transferred from London to Jerusalem. The Zionist Organization continued to function as before, except that the heads of its departments now worked in conjunction with their counterparts in the Israeli civil service.

In between the congresses the Zionist General Council, reflecting the composition of the latest congress, functioned as a supervisory body. Its size increased from 25 in 1921 to 129 in 1968. It was the General Council that adopted a new constitution in 1960. Goldmann continued as president of the renamed Zionist Organization until 1968. After that the highest office of the WZO was held by the chairman of the Zionist Executive Committee, Louis Pincus. After the establishment of Israel the WZO's 500 delegates started meeting every four or five years in Jerusalem. They elected Aryeh Dolchin as chairman in 1978. He retained that position until 1987. His successors included Avaham Burg [*q.v.*], Zeev Bielski of the Kadima party [*q.v.*], and Natan Sharansky.

In 2009, a case before the Israeli Supreme Court revealed that, while acting as the Israeli state's agent, the WZO had taken private Palestinian land in the West Bank and passed it on to the Jewish settlers, thus defying the government's ruling that the property in question was not to be used for the settlement of the Jews.

Wye River Memorandum: Following mediation by U.S. President Bill Clinton, an agreement was hammered out by the Israeli and Palestinian delegations at a series of meetings at the Wye Plantation, Maryland. Israeli Prime Minister Benjamin Netanyahu [*q.v.*] and Palestinian leader Yasser Arafat [*q.v.*] signed a document—called the Wye Memorandum/Accord—on 15 October 1998 to facilitate the implementation of the Washington Accord/Oslo Accord II [*q.v.*] of September 1995. This involved Israel's transferral of a further 13 percent of the West Bank to the Palestinian Authority (PA) [*q.v.*] in two stages, and entering into immediate final status talks with the Palestinians with the aim of achieving an agreement by 4 May 1999. In return the PA agreed to combat terrorism and confiscate illegal weapons, and the Palestine Liberation Organization [*q.v.*] pledged to reaffirm the nullification of those provisions of the Palestine National Charter [*q.v.*] that were inconsistent with the provisions of the 1993 Oslo Accords [*q.v.*].

Y

Yamani, Ahmad Zaki (1930–): *Saudi oil expert and politician* Born into the family of a religious judge in Mecca [*q.v.*], Yamani studied law first at Cairo University and then at New York and Harvard Universities in the United States.

In 1958 Crown Prince Faisal bin Abdul Aziz [*q.v.*] appointed Yamani as adviser to the cabinet. Two years later he was promoted to minister of state, and in 1962 to minister of petroleum and mineral resources. In the mid-1960s he became chairman of the state-owned General Petroleum and Mineral Organization, and a director of the Arabian American Oil Company (Aramco).

As a pragmatist, he tried to persuade King Faisal, who was critical of Washington's staunchly pro-Israeli stance, to cooperate with it in formulating Saudi policies on oil output and pricing. His efforts were successful, and he became a close adviser of the monarch.

Yamani served as secretary-general of the Organization of Petroleum Exporting Countries (OPEC) [*q.v.*] during 1968–69. He backed Faisal's strategy to use the "oil weapon" during the October 1973 Arab-Israeli War [*q.v.*], thus endorsing the monarch's newly formed perception that petroleum could no longer be divorced from Middle Eastern politics. Equally, Yamani supported Faisal's decision to lift the Arab oil embargo [*q.v.*] against the United States in March 1974, even though the Saudi king's conditions, requiring Israel's evacuation of the Occupied Arab Territories [*q.v.*] and the granting of Palestinian rights, had not been met.

On 21 December 1975, when OPEC oil ministers, meeting in Vienna, were taken hostage by the commandos led by Ilich Ramirez Sanchez—alias "Carlos" Martinez—Yamani was one of their chief targets. He was freed two days later in Algiers after a clandestine deal involving the transfer of $5 million to $50 million by Saudi Arabia to Martinez.

He lobbied hard, and successfully, to maintain OPEC's share of global output, even if that resulted in lower oil prices. He thus became leader of the pro-Western camp within OPEC. He implemented the policy of Saudi Arabia, acting in tandem with Kuwait, to produce above its OPEC quota and thus depress the price of oil in order to impair Iran's ability to continue the Iran-Iraq War [*q.v.*]. This cut the price by nearly two-thirds between December 1985 and July 1986, to $10 a barrel. In August, yielding to pressure from other OPEC members, he agreed to reduced OPEC output, which raised the price to $14–16 a barrel. In early October 1986, after meeting the Iranian oil minister in Riyadh [*q.v.*], King Fahd bin Abdul Aziz [*q.v.*] backed the idea of a fixed price of $18 a barrel. When Yamani refused to endorse this, Fahd dismissed him on 29 October, thus ending his 24-year-long career as Saudi oil minister.

Yamani retired from public life and devoted himself to private business, including running the Center for Global Energy Studies, London, which specialized in offering analyses of energy markets. In the mid-1990s, with a political and financial crisis brewing in Saudi Arabia, Yamani, based in Jeddah [*q.v.*], became a center of attraction for disaffected businessmen and religious leaders.

Yasin, Ahmad (1936–2004) *Palestinian leader* Born into a land-owning household in Jora in Palestine [*q.v.*], a village near the northern border of what later became the Gaza Strip [*q.v.*], Yasin and his family sought shelter in a refugee camp in the Gaza Strip during the First Arab-Israeli War (1948–49) [*q.v.*]. He joined the clandestine Muslim Brotherhood (Egypt) [*q.v.*] in the mid-1950s a few years after suffering crippling injuries in a sporting accident that left him wheelchair-bound.

He worked as a schoolteacher in Gaza from 1957 to 1964, when he enrolled as a student of English at Ain Shams University, Cairo [*q.v.*]. He was jailed in 1966 when the Egyptian government cracked down on the Muslim Brotherhood in Egypt and Gaza. After the Strip was occupied by Israel in 1967, he was released. He resumed teaching as well as leading the reorganized Muslim Brotherhood. He urged his followers to purge society of social-moral ills, arguing that Islamization of society was a precondition for the establishment of an Islamic state in a liberated Palestine, thus skirting the contentious issue of resistance to the Israeli occupation.

In the autumn of 1973 the Israeli military authorities issued a license to Yasin to establish the Islamic Center to run social, religious, and welfare institutions, thus entitling it to receive zakat [*q.v.*], religious tax, from the believers. With the secular Palestine Liberation Organization [*q.v.*] emerging as a powerful force in the Occupied Territories [*q.v.*] from the mid-1970s, Israel decided to encourage the growth of the Islamic Center, with the military governor of the Gaza Strip, Brigadier General Yitzhak Segev, funding the mosques run by the Islamic Center.

In 1983 Israel reversed this policy, partly because the Islamic Jihad [*q.v.*], a recently established Islamist organization, had resorted to pursing a militantly anti-Israeli stance. In 1984 Israel arrested Yasin for illegal possession of arms and sentenced him to a 13-years jail term. But in 1985, as part of a prisoner exchange deal between Israel and the Popular Front for the Liberation of Palestine-General Command [*q.v.*], he was released. He resumed social work in Gaza.

But when the intifada [*q.v.*] erupted in late 1987, Yasin and his colleagues in the Islamic Center could no longer resist pressure from their nationalist grass roots to engage in a political struggle against their Israeli occupiers. The result was the founding of Hamas [*q.v.*] as the activist arm of the Islamic Center/Muslim Brotherhood. Yasin was arrested in 1989 and sentenced to 15 years' imprisonment for conspiring to abduct two Israeli soldiers. As a result of another prisoner exchange in the wake of the failed attempt by Mossad [*q.v.*] agents in Amman [*q.v.*] to assassinate Hamas leader Khaled Mashaal [*q.v.*] in 1997, Yasin was freed.

He resumed his leadership of Hamas, reiterating that the organization would continue to resist Israeli occupation by all means. He was put under house arrest after he had criticized the Palestinian Authority (PA) [*q.v.*] for signing the Wye River Memorandum [*q.v.*] in October 1998. But as the Wye Memorandum unraveled, relations between him and the PA thawed. With the outbreak of the Al Aqsa Intifada [*q.v.*] in September 2000 and the subsequent pulverizing of the PA by Israel, the differences between Yasin and the PA narrowed further. He mediated successfully between the PA and the more radical

Palestinians in Hamas and other organizations.

But when the recently appointed Prime Minister Mahmoud Abbas [*q.v.*] held a meeting with Israeli Prime Minister Ariel Sharon [*q.v.*], chaired by U.S. President George W. Bush, in June 2003, where the two leaders jointly referred to "the possibility" of establishing a "completely demilitarized" Palestinian state "within temporary borders," Yasin condemned the PA. In September, the Israeli air force dropped a bomb on a Gaza [*q.v.*] building where Hamas leaders had gathered, but Yasin was unhurt. In March 2004, a missile fired by an Israeli helicopter gunship killed Yasin as he was being wheeled out of a mosque, along with 11 others.

Yazidis: *A religious group* The origins of the Yazidi doctrine—an amalgam of pagan, Sabaean, Shamanistic, Manichaean, Zoroastrian [*q.v.*], Jewish [*q.v.*], Christian [*q.v.*], and Islamic [*q.v.*] elements—are unknown. Totaling about 100,000, Yazidis are to be found in northeastern Syria, northern Iraq, and the Trans-Caucasian republics. Though they often speak a Kurdish [*q.v.*] dialect, their scriptures are written in Arabic [*q.v.*].

Their principal divine figure is the Peacock Angel, the first of the seven angels who ruled the universe after it had been created by God. Violation of divine laws can be expiated by the transmigration of souls. Yazidis believe that their chief saint, Shaikh Adi, a Muslim mystic in the 12th century, acquired divine status through the transmigration of his soul. His tomb, situated north of Mosul [*q.v.*], is the site of an annual pilgrimage.

Though Yazidis do not believe in evil, sin, and the devil, they are often described as devil worshippers.

Yemen:

OFFICIAL NAME: Republic of Yemen

CAPITAL: Sanaa [*q.v.*]

AREA: 182,280 sq. mi./472,100 sq. km, excluding 23,070 sq. mi./59,770 sq. km claimed by North Yemen along the un-demarcated eastern frontier with Saudi Arabia. Claimed area totals 203,000 sq. mi./552,580 sq. km.

POPULATION: 25.1 million (2011 est.), with 79 percent in (old) North Yemen [*q.v.*] and 21 percent in (old) South Yemen [*q.v.*]

GROSS DOMESTIC PRODUCT (nominal): $33.68 billion; per capita, $1,340 (2011 est.)

GROSS DOMESTIC PRODUCT (Purchasing Power Parity): $57.97 billion; per capita $2,306 (2011 est.)

NATIONAL CURRENCIES: Yemeni Rial (YER); YER 100 = $0.467 = £0.288 = € 0.347 (2011)

FORM OF GOVERNMENT: republic, president elected by popular vote

OFFICIAL LANGUAGE: Arabic [*q.v.*]

OFFICIAL RELIGION: Islam [*q.v.*]

ADMINISTRATIVE SYSTEM: Yemen consists of 18 provinces.

CONSTITUTION: The Yemeni constitution, based on a document endorsed by North Yemen [*q.v.*] and South Yemen [*q.v.*] in 1981, was approved by a referendum in May 1991, a year after the proclamation of the united Republic of Yemen. Describing the republic as "an independent, indivisible state," it specifies Islam and Arabic as the state religion and state language respectively. The Sharia [*q.v.*] is the main source of legislation. Power rests with the people, who exercise it through elections and referendums. The state guarantees freedom of expression and assembly within the law. The republic's economy is founded on safeguarding private property and assuring Islamic social justice while striving to develop the state sector as the main means of production.

In September 1994, 29 articles were added to the constitution, with 52 of the previous document's 101 articles amended. Further changes, adopted by the lower house of parliament in November 2000, were approved by a referendum three months later. According to the revised document, the president is to be elected for seven years by universal suffrage. He is empowered to nominate the vice president. He first appoints the prime minister and then, advised by him, the rest of the cabinet. He is also head of the Supreme Judicial Council. The legislative power rests with the lower chamber of parliament, the Assembly of Representatives, elected for six years by universal suffrage. By contrast, the upper chamber, the Consultative Council, is nominated by the president. The revised constitution reaffirmed multiparty democracy.

ETHNIC COMPOSITION (2011): Arab [*q.v.*], including Afro-Arab, 99 percent; other, 1 percent.

HIGH OFFICIALS:

President: Abd Rabbu Mansour al-Hadi [*q.v.*], 2012–

Prime minister: Muhammad Basindawa, 2011–

Speaker of the Assembly of Representatives, Yahya al-Raee, 2010–

Chairman of Consultative (Shura) Council: Abdul Rahman Muhammad Ali Othman, 2011–

HISTORY (since ca 1900):

North Yemen: (Before the unification of North and South Yemen in 1990) Official name, Yemen Arab Republic; area, 77,220 sq. mi./200,000 sq. km; population, 9.274 million (1986 census).

At the turn of the 20th century North Yemen, under the nominal suzerainty of the Ottoman Turks, was ruled by Imam Yahya Hamid al-Din (1869–1948). By rebelling against the Ottoman Empire in 1911, he obtained wider powers. During World War I he was loyal to the Ottomans. With the collapse of the Ottoman Empire in 1918, North Yemen became fully independent, and Imam Yahya aspired to recreate the historic Greater Yemen. In 1925 he regained Hodeida port, which had been occupied in 1921 by the ruler of the neighboring Asir region with British connivance. The resulting dispute over Asir culminated in war in 1934 between North Yemen and Saudi Arabia, started by the latter. Having overpowered the North Yemenis and captured Hodeida, the Saudis accepted a cease-fire, mainly because British, French, and Italian warships rushed to Hodeida, intent on curbing Saudi expansionism. The Treaty of Muslim Friendship and Arab Fraternity [*q.v.*] returned to Imam Yahya nearly half the area he had lost in war, including the southern part of the Tihama coastal plain—leaving the upland Najran and Asir in Saudi hands.

Following an abortive coup in February 1948 that resulted in the murder of his father, Ahmad bin Yahya [*q.v.*] assumed supreme power. When his ambition to recreate Greater Yemen at the expense of the British Protectorate of Aden was frustrated by London, in

1956 he signed a mutual defense pact with Egypt, then ruled by President Gamal Abdul Nasser [*q.v.*]. In 1958 he formed a loose federation of North Yemen and the United Arab Republic (UAR) [*q.v.*], called the Union of Arab States. By then he had concluded friendship treaties with the Soviet Union, the People's Republic of China, and other Communist capitals. After the breakup of the UAR in September 1961, he cut his ties with Egypt and started attacking Nasser, who reciprocated. Soon after Imam Ahmad's death in September 1962, a military coup, led by Brigadier-General Abdullah Sallal [*q.v.*], ended the 1064-year rule of the al-Rassi dynasty.

A civil war [*q.v.*] ensued. The republicans, deriving their major support from the Shafii (Sunni [*q.v.*]) tribes inhabiting the coastal plain and the southern hills, were aided by Egypt, while the royalists, with a solid base among the Zaidi [*q.v.*] tribes in the north, were helped by the Saudis. In 1967 Sallal tried to regain the area lost in the war, but failed, partly because of the June 1967 Arab-Israeli War [*q.v.*], which diverted Egypt's resources. Cairo decided to withdraw its forces from North Yemen, and this weakened the position of Sallal. He was overthrown in November 1967, during his visit to Moscow, by forces led by Abdul Rahman al-Iryani [*q.v.*].

In March 1970, following complex negotiations, the civil war ended and an agreed-on governmental system—based on a presidential council and a nominated consultative council—emerged. The first post-civil war president, al-Iryani, was deposed in 1974; the second and third, Ibrahim Hamdi [*q.v.*] and Ahmad Hussein Ghashmi

[*q.v.*], were assassinated in October 1977 and June 1978, respectively. Ali Abdullah Saleh, deputy commander-in-chief, succeeded Ghashmi. He legitimized his power by gaining the backing of the Constituent People's Assembly (CPA). In October 1980 Saleh replaced Prime Minister Abdul Aziz Abdul Ghani with Abdul Karim Iryani to placate leftist opposition at home. In October 1981 he established a 1,000-member General People's Congress [*q.v.*], partly by appointment and partly by indirect elections, as an instrument for mass mobilization. Two months later he signed an agreement with South Yemen on unity.

Oil production, which began modestly in 1984, picked up rapidly. Saleh maintained friendly relations with Saudi Arabia, the chief paymaster of North Yemen, while cultivating the leftist South Yemen by periodically renewing the 1981 agreement on eventual unity between the two Yemens. After his reelection as president in 1988, he responded positively to the idea of an alliance of North Yemen with Egypt, Iraq, and Jordan, which materialized as the Arab Cooperation Council [*q.v.*] in early 1989.

South Yemen (Before the unification of North and South Yemen in 1990): Official name: People's Democratic Republic of Yemen; area 130,070 sq. mi./336,870 sq. km; population 2,121,000 (1986 est.).

At the turn of the 20th century, Britain ruled the Aden Colony through a governor attached to the India Office in London, and the Aden Protectorate, consisting of 23 provinces, through local rulers. After World War I, Britain frustrated Imam

Yahya's attempt to annex parts of the Aden protectorate. It split the Protectorate from the India Office in 1927 and from the Aden Colony 10 years later. In 1947 it introduced a fully nominated legislative assembly in the Aden Colony. In 1962 it offered a plan to knit together the Colony and the Protectorate into the Federation of South Arabia. This was opposed by, among others, the National Front for the Liberation of South Yemen [*q.v.*], popularly called the NLF. It achieved power in late 1967 by launching a successful armed struggle against the British.

After the founding of the People's Republic of South Yemen, differences between moderate and radical elements within the NLF surfaced in June 1969, resulting in the victory of hard-liners. A new, radical constitution was promulgated in November 1970. By the time the sixth congress of the NLF was held, in March 1975, the regime felt secure. In October the NLF decided to widen its base by forming the United Political Organization-National Front (UPO-NF), to be reconstituted in 1978. Following the assassination of North Yemeni President Ahmad Ghashmi in June 1978, there was fighting in Aden [*q.v.*], which President Salim Rubai Ali [*q.v.*] lost.

In October the UPO-NF was transformed into the Yemeni Socialist Party (YSP) [*q.v.*]. The radical policies of Abdul Fattah Ismail [*q.v.*], chairman of the Presidential Council, did not go down well with his erstwhile ally, Ali Nasser Muhammad [*q.v.*]. In April 1980 Ismail was forced to resign and go into exile in Moscow, leaving Muhammad as the sole leader.

Five years later Ismail returned thanks to the successful mediation by the Communist Party of the Soviet Union. He was appointed secretary-general of the YSP's central committee, a position without power. But the rapprochement broke down in January 1986. In the subsequent fighting Ismail lost his life, but his radical side won, and Ali Salim al-Beidh [*q.v.*] emerged as leader of the YSP.

While the presidency was placed in the hands of a technocrat, Haidar al-Attas, real power lay with al-Beidh. He started to moderate his radical stance and introduce economic and political reform—especially after Moscow cut its aid from $400 million in 1988 to $50 million in 1989. The steep decline in the Soviet Union's financial assistance accelerated the drive toward unification with North Yemen, which occurred the following year.

Republic of Yemen (After unification of North and South Yemen in 1990): On 22 May 1990, when the united Republic of Yemen was inaugurated, Saleh became its president and al-Beidh its vice president. The five-member Presidential Council consisted of three North Yemeni and two South Yemeni leaders. However, the two constituents maintained separate armed forces and broadcasting facilities. The political parties of the two Yemens were dissolved formally and then registered afresh to operate in all of the united Yemen. By September the Republic of Yemen had more than 30 political groups.

Since Yemen—the only Arab country on the UN Security Council—refused to follow Saudi Arabia into the Washington-led coalition against Iraq after its occupation of Kuwait in August 1990, the Saudi government retaliated by withdrawing the special treatment accorded to Yemeni nationals. The resulting exodus of 850,000 Yemenis from Saudi Arabia depressed the already weak Yemeni economy. Yemen voted against the UN Security Council Resolution 678, authorizing member states to use "all necessary means" to reverse Iraq's occupation evacuation of Kuwait) in November 1990. In early January 1991, Yemen's peace plan to avert a war against Iraq failed to prevent Gulf War II [*q.v.*].

At home, voters endorsed the new constitution in May 1991. But the multiparty general election based on universal suffrage, the first of its kind in the Arabian Peninsula [*q.v.*] and promised within a year of the new constitution, did not materialize until April 1993. Out of 301 parliamentary seats, the reconstituted General People's Congress (GPC) won over 40 percent, followed by the Yemeni Islah Group (YIG) [*q.v.*] and the Yemeni Socialist Party (YSP).

Al Beidh, leader of the YSP, which had so far shared power with the GPC, objected to Saleh's co-opting of the YIG into the new coalition government. Blaming Saleh for the lack of progress on unification, al-Beidh left Sanaa for Aden in August, setting the scene for a conflict that escalated into the Yemeni Civil War [*q.v.*] in April 1994, during which al-Beidh declared South Yemen independent. South Yemen's independence was not recognized by any other country, and al-Beidh's camp lost in July. The victorious Saleh and the GPC consolidated their power and Yemeni unity.

The next year, Saleh was elevated to chairman of the GPC, a new post. In

1997 the GPC improved its parliamentary strength by 64 seats partly due to the boycott of the polls by the YSP, which had 56 deputies in the dissolved legislature. But that did not lessen the problem the new government faced when trying to implement economic liberalization, prescribed by the International Monetary Fund, by phasing out subsidies on basic necessities and fuel. Also, the outlying mountainous regions under effective rule by the tribal chiefs remained out of the central government's control. Nonetheless, in the first popular election for the presidency, in 1999, Saleh secured more than 96 percent of the ballots. The following year he called the first-ever local elections. In April 2001 he promoted foreign minister Abdul Qadir Bajammal to the post of prime minister.

In foreign policy, Yemen strengthened its ties with the United States. It conducted its first joint military exercise with the U.S. forces in November 1998. But that did not inhibit it from condemning Washington's Operation Desert Fox [*q.v.*] against Iraq in December. However, its earlier agreement to let the U.S. Navy use Aden for refueling went ahead in 1999. On 12 October 2000 a harbor skiff, laden with explosives, piloted by two suicide bombers, struck the USS *Cole*, which was refueling in Aden, and killed 17 sailors. The attack, claimed by the Islamic Army of Aden-Abyan, was believed to be linked to the Al Qaida [*q.v.*] network. The Yemeni government cooperated fully with Washington to track down the culprits.

After the terrorist attacks on the United States in September 2001, cooperation between the two governments increased, with the American policy makers being aware that the mountainous terrain of Yemen, the homeland of the bin Laden clan, was ideal for setting up terrorist training camps.

In 2004, the government's attempt to arrest Hussein al-Houthi, a Zaidi Shia [q.v.] religious leader, sparked a rebellion in the northern border province of Saada. After he was killed in an offensive by the army, the leadership passed to his brother Abdul Malik. A truce was signed in 2007 but did not go into effect. In 2008, mediation by Qatar revived the peace agreement. But, claiming that the rebels were not adhering to it, Saleh announced a fresh campaign in August 2009 to crush the Houthi rebels [q.v.].

Earlier that year eastern Yemen became the base of Al Qaida in the Arabian Peninsula (AQAP) [q.v.], formed by the merger of Al Qaida in Saudi Arabia and Al Qaida in Yemen. The AQAP was blamed by U.S. President Barack Obama for attempting to blow up an American passenger plane over Detroit on Christmas Day in 2010 by training a young Nigerian, Umar Farouk Abdulmutallah, to carry out the operation. After this episode U.S. drones targeted several sites in Yemen suspected of being AQAP hideouts or training camps. The Yemeni government claimed these strikes as its own, a sign of further tightening of links between Sanaa and Washington.

In 2009 various anti-government groups in the South formed an umbrella organization called the Southern Movement [q.v.] under the chairmanship of Hassan Baoum, a leader of the YSP. It called for equality with the north and honoring of the

promises made at the time of unification. Most southerners complained of discrimination in the distribution of resources by the central government. When it resorted to repressing the Southern Movement, its leaders demanded independence for the south. They held pro-independence demonstrations and appealed to the Arab League [q.v.] to supervise secession. The government arrested the movement's leaders. But when the agitation did not end, it released them a year later.

With the onset of the Arab Spring [q.v.] in January 2011, the protesting demonstrators in Sanaa escalated their demands from ending unemployment and corruption to Saleh's resignation. Pro-Saleh supporters staged counter-demonstrations. More concerned about security and stability than democracy, the United States failed to sympathize with the protestors. Instead, it encouraged Saudi Arabia to mediate between the rival camps.

Saudi King Abdullah [q.v.] activated the Gulf Cooperation Council (GCC) [q.v.]. In late April, Saleh accepted the GCC's three-point plan, which required him to step down in favor of Vice President Abd Rabbu Mansour al-Hadi [q.v.] in exchange for immunity from prosecution for himself, his relatives, and senior members of his government. But when it came to signing the agreement, he balked three times. The GCC suspended its mediation on 22 May 2011. The next day, when Sadiq al-Ahmar, leader of the powerful Hashid tribal federation, declared his support for the opposition, the army split, followed by armed clashes involving artillery and mortars.

An explosive attack on the presidential palace's mosque during the Friday congregation on 3 June left Saleh and several others badly injured. Saleh flew to Riyadh [*q.v.*] for medical treatment after transferring his powers to al-Hadi. By broadcasting an address to the Yemeni people from Riyadh on 7 July, he underlined his presidential authority. But on 12 September he instructed al-Hadi to revive the GCC mediation. Then suddenly he returned to Sanaa on 23 September. Violent clashes between the opposing camps resumed. The GCC's revived peace efforts gained the support of the UN Security Council. On 23 November, Saleh signed the deal, agreeing to relinquish power within 30 days in favor of a transitional government headed by al-Hadi, while remaining president until fresh new elections in February 2012. After the election, he stepped down.

President al-Hadi undertook the task of reorganizing the high command of the military, which remained divided, a result of Saleh's continued presence in the capital. Both he and the U.S. administration considered a complete overhaul of the military as the first step to regaining full control of the three southern provinces where the AQAP's affiliate, the *Ansar al-Sharia* (Arabic: *Helpers of the Sharia*), had captured large swathes of the territory, including several towns and cities.

LEGISLATURE: From May 1990 to April 1993, legislative powers rested with the Assembly of Representatives, which consisted of North Yemen's People's Constituent Assembly (159 members), the Supreme People's Council of South Yemen (111 members), and 31 new members appointed by President Saleh. Fresh elections followed, based on universal suffrage, to the 301-member Assembly of Representatives. In 1997, Saleh established a fully nominated 59-member Consultative (Shura) Council and appointed Abdul Aziz Abdul Ghani as its chairman. In 2006, he raised its strength to 111.

The outcome of the April 2003 parliamentary election was General People's Congress, 238; Yemeni Islah Group, 46; Yemen Socialist Party, 8; other parties, 5; independents, 4. This parliament extended its term by two years to April 2011. Due to the political turmoil the parliamentary election was postponed.

RELIGIOUS COMPOSITION (2010): Muslim, 99 percent, with Sunni [*q.v.*] 52 percent, mostly Shafii [*q.v.*] but also Maliki [*q.v.*] and Hanbali [*q.v.*]; Shia [*q.v.*], 47 percent, mostly Zaidi [*q.v.*], but also Twelvers [*q.v.*] and Ismaili [*q.v.*]; other, 1 percent.

Yemen Arab Republic: *See* North Yemen under Yemen—history.

Yemeni Civil War (1962–70): *See* North Yemeni Civil War.

Yemeni Civil War (1994): The failure of the North-based General People's Congress [*q.v.*] and the South-based Yemeni Socialist Party (YSP) [*q.v.*] to win parliamentary seats across the old North-South border in the April 1993 election sowed the seeds of a conflict that culminated in a civil war within a year. The graduated process of unification had allowed President Ali Abdullah Saleh [*q.v.*] and Vice President Ali Salim al-Beidh [*q.v.*] to retain their authority over the respective armed forces of North and South Yemen. But as a gesture of unification, some units from each army were posted away from their native region.

The Northern forces' attack on the Southern units at Dhamar and Amran in former North Yemen on 27 April 1994 signaled the start of a civil war. It also illustrated the North's offensive strategy, both military and political. Efforts by the Arab League [q.v.], Egypt, and the UN Security Council to bring about a cease-fire failed as Saleh stuck rigidly to his slogan: "Unity or death!"

On 22 May 1994, the fourth anniversary of unification, al-Beidh declared South Yemen independent, calling it the Democratic Republic of Yemen (DRY). Al Beidh put his pro-Saudi vice president, Shaikh Abdul Rahman Jifri, in charge of defending Aden [q.v.] while retreating to Mukalla, 375 mi./600 km to the east. The southern leaders lobbied hard to win international recognition for the DRY, but failed. Even Saudi Arabia, which had backed their moves, equivocated, concentrating on securing a cease-fire through the UN Security Council, thus providing the DRY with breathing space. Saleh was adamant on keeping outsiders out of what he insisted was "an internal Yemeni affair."

On the ground the Southerners put up stiff resistance, but when the attacking Northerners cut off Aden's water and electricity supplies its fall became inevitable. The North's forces also captured Mukalla, and al-Beidh and his close aides fled to Saudi Arabia. The conflict ended on 4 July with more than 35,000 casualties, including some 10,000 fatalities, although the

government put the figure at 1,000.

One version of the events maintains that al-Beidh, acting in collusion with Saudi Arabia, started to escalate the political crisis in August 1993 as a preamble to a military coup against Saleh. The purported plan was to use the South's contingents posted in Dhamar and Amran, backed by the militia of the pro-Saudi Bakil tribal confederation, to besiege Sanaa [q.v.] on 5 May 1994 and overthrow Saleh. But intelligence sources loyal to Saleh got wind of the South's plans, and the Northern forces attacked the Southern units of Dhamar and Amran on 27 April.

Yemeni Islah Group (Official title: Arabic: *Al-Tajami al-Yamani lil Islah*, The Yemeni Group for Reform): *Yemeni political party* Following the legislation of political parties after the Yemeni unification in May 1990, the Islamic and Zaidi [q.v.] tribal forces combined to form the Yemeni Islah Group (YIG). It was led by Shaikh Abdullah Hussein al-Ahmar [q.v.] and Shaikh Abdul Wahhab al-Anisi. Objecting to the provision in the 1991 draft constitution that the Sharia [q.v.] was to be the main source of legislation, it demanded that the Sharia should be the sole source, and urged a boycott of the referendum on the constitution. However, it fought the general election held under that constitution in April 1993 and won 62 seats, more than the number gained by the Yemeni Socialist Party [q.v.].

President Ali Abdullah Saleh [q.v.] included the YIG in the new coalition government, and the position of parliamentary speaker went to its leader, al-Ahmar. In October Saleh gave up one of the three General People's Congress [q.v.] seats on the five-member Presidential Council to the YIG to maintain its support, which became crucial during the Yemeni Civil war [q.v.] the following spring.

During and after the conflict Islah members were active in attacking those aspects of life in former South Yemen they considered un-Islamic, including bars, women in jeans, and the government-owned brewery in Aden [q.v.]. In the 1997 parliamentary election, the YIG secured 53 seats, and its leader, al-Ahmar, was reelected speaker of the Assembly of Representatives. In the first-ever local elections in April 2001, the YIG presented a challenge to the ruling General People's Congress [q.v.], but won only 22 percent of the vote. Nonetheless, the government implemented a 1992 law requiring incorporation of religious educational centers, run by the YIG, into the state educational system. This further soured relations between the YIG and the governing party.

In the 2003 parliamentary election, the Islah's share fell to 46. After the death of al-Ahmar, its leadership passed to Muhammad Abdullah Yadumi. In 2006, along with other opposition parties, the Islah formed the Joint Parties Meeting alliance, which sponsored Faisal bin Shalman as its presidential candidate. He lost.

When the onset of the Arab Spring [q.v.] in January 2011 led to pro-democracy demonstrations and sit-ins at the Change Square in Sanaa [q.v.], thousands of Islah members arrived to provide security, food, and medical services. In fact, it was the jailing of journalist Tawakul Karman [q.v.], a member of the YIG, that triggered a

wider protest. She belonged to the moderate wing of the party with its conservative faction led by Shaikh Abdul Majid Zindani, the charismatic founder of the Iman University in Sanaa, who was named a "specially designated global terrorist" by the U.S. Treasury Department in 2004.

Following the acceptance of the Gulf Cooperation Council [q.v.] plan by Saleh to step down from the presidency in November 2011, YIG members participated in the presidential election three months later, and voted for Abd Rabbu Mansour al-Hadi [q.v.].

Yemeni Socialist Party (Official title: Arabic: *Al-Hizb al-Ishtiraki al-Yamaniya*): *Political party in South Yemen and Yemen* The unification conference sponsored by the National Liberation Front (NLF) [q.v.] in October 1975 decided to weld the NLF, the Vanguard Party (a Baathist group), and the Popular Democratic Union (a Communist group) into the United Political Organization-National Front as a transitional body to graduate into the Yemeni Socialist Party (YSP) in October 1978. It was a Marxist-Leninist vanguard party, committed to building scientific socialism in South Yemen.

Its first secretary-general was Abdul Fattah Ismail [q.v.]. After his exile to Moscow in April, the post went to Ali Nasser Muhammad [q.v.]. Muhammad lost the January 1986 internecine fighting and the party's top position went to Ali Salim al-Beidh [q.v.]. Under his leadership the YSP began to moderate its policies, a trend accelerated by the collapse of the Soviet Union-led socialist bloc in the wake of the demolition of the Berlin Wall in late 1989, resulting in the party's discarding of Marxism-Leninism and adopting a social-democratic program.

Following the unification of the two Yemens in May 1990, the YSP was allowed to function throughout the united Republic of Yemen. But it failed to gain support in former North Yemen. All the 56 parliamentary seats it won in the April 1993 election were from former South Yemen. During the civil war in the spring of 1994, the YSP, led by al-Beidh, was divided on the question of declaring former South Yemen independent. When al-Beidh did so, he failed to win it recognition by any country. After the defeat of al-Beidh and his partisans in the conflict, the party's standing suffered.

Objecting to the voter registration irregularities, the YSP, now led by Ali Saleh Obad, and several other opposition groups, boycotted the 1997 general election. It was not until 1998 that it was able to hold a national conference—after a gap of 10 years—in the southern city of Dali, when it elected a new politburo. And it was only in 2000 that it managed to convene a conference in Sanaa [*q.v.*]. In the 2003 parliamentary election it won only 8 seats. Its secretary-general was Yasin Said Numan, the last prime minister of South Yemen before its merger with North Yemen.

In 2006 it was one of the groups to found the Joint Parties Meeting alliance, which sponsored Faisal bin Shalman, a former oil minister, to challenge, unsuccessfully, Ali Abdullah Saleh in the presidential contest. Equally, it participated actively in the pro-democracy movement in 2011.

Yemeni War (1972): The emergence of a hard-line leftist government in South Yemen in mid-1969 alarmed North Yemen and Saudi Arabia. In cooperation with the South Yemeni émigrés in North Yemen and Saudi Arabia, the governments in Riyadh [*q.v.*] and Sanaa [*q.v.*] staged a series of border attacks on South Yemen in September 1972. South Yemen appealed to the Arab League [*q.v.*]. Its warning that the Soviet Union would not stand idly by if Saudi Arabia mounted a full-fledged invasion of South Yemen dissuaded the Saudi kingdom from intervening directly. With the Arab League's assistance, a truce went into effect on 28 October, with the warring sides announcing, astonishingly, that the two Yemens had agreed to work toward economic and political unification.

Yemeni War (1979): The victory of the leftist faction over its rival within the ruling National Liberation Front (NLF) in South Yemen [*q.v.*] in June 1978, and South Yemen's alleged complicity in the assassination of North Yemeni President Ahmad Hussein Ghashmi [*q.v.*], led North Yemen and Saudi Arabia to urge the Arab League [*q.v.*] to impose sanctions against South Yemen. It did so in July. Relations between Aden and Sanaa deteriorated.

The steady capture of North Yemen's territory along its border with South Yemen by the forces of the Yemeni National Democratic Front (NDF) [*q.v.*] of North Yemen, aided by Aden, led to the two Yemens going to war in February 1979. NDF fighters seized border towns and penetrated 12 mi./19 km inside North

Yemen on 22 February with the intention of cutting off the strategic Taiz-Sanaa [*q.v.*] highway. Saudi Arabia put its own forces on alert and paid $387 million to the United States to airlift heavy weapons to North Yemen. This slowed the NDF's advance. Syria and Iraq intervened and succeeded in arranging a cease-fire on 2 March.

Yemeni-British Treaty (1934): *See* Anglo-Yemeni Treaty (1934).

Yiddish language (German: *derivative of Judisch, Jewish*): A medieval German of the Middle Rhine region, developed under the influences of Hebrew [*q.v.*] and Slavic, Yiddish was spoken by most Ashkenazi [*q.v.*] Jews [*q.v.*]. Modern Yiddish, written in Hebrew characters and dating from about 1700, can be divided into Western Yiddish, now extinct, and Eastern Yiddish. The latter is subdivided into a northern dialect (Lithuania) and a southern one (from Poland to Rumania). Yiddish spelling was standardized by the Yiddish Scientific Institute, based in Vilnius, Lithuania, in 1937, when there were 10 to 12 million Yiddish speakers. As a result of the Holocaust during World War II, this number halved. Once predominant among West European and North American Jews, Yiddish is now rarely spoken by them outside of the Hassidic [*q.v.*] communities.

Yishuv (Hebrew: *Settlement*): The term Yishuv means the Jewish community in Palestine [*q.v.*], starting with the first wave of immigration in 1882 and ending with the founding of Israel in May 1948. Used in contrast to the term *diaspora* [*q.v.*], the Yishuv was viewed as the vanguard of world Jewry, laying the groundwork for the Jewish state in Palestine.

Yom Kippur (Hebrew: *Day of Atonement*): Observed on the 10th day of Tishri, the first month in the Jewish calendar [*q.v.*], and falling between early September and early October, Yom Kippur is the Sabbath [*q.v.*] of Sabbaths, a day of fasting and prayer for forgiveness of sins. Rabbinical tradition describes Yom Kippur as the day on which Moses came down from Mount Sinai with the second set of the tablets of the Law and declared divine pardon for the sins of the Golden Calf. In ancient times the high priest was allowed to enter the inner sanctum of the Temple on this day, dressed in white linen, signifying purity and humility. On Yom Kippur, Jews [*q.v.*] are required to confess their ethical lapses and other human failings. The evening service concludes with the declaration: "Next year in Jerusalem [*q.v.*]."

Yom Kippur War (1973): *See* Arab-Israeli War IV (1973).

Z

Zahal (Hebrew: acronym of *Zvai Haganah Le Israel*, Defense Force for Israel): *See* Military in Israel.

Zahedi, Fazlullah (1880–1963): *Iranian politician; prime minister, 1953–55* Born into a landlord family in Hamadan, Zahedi graduated from the Military Academy in Tehran [*q.v.*] in

1916. He joined the Cossack brigade, which participated in the successful campaign against the Soviet Republic of Gilan in 1921, and rose to the rank of major-general during the reign of Reza Shah Pahlavi [*q.v.*].

After Reza Shah's deposition in 1941 by Britain and the Soviet Union, and their occupation of Iran, the British arrested Zahedi for suspected pro-German activities in 1943. Elected senator in 1946, he undermined the coalition government of Premier Ahmad Qawam al-Saltane. He was so opposed to the pro-British Prime Minister Ali Razmara that he flirted with the National Front [*q.v.*], briefly becoming interior minister under the first government of Muhammad Mussadiq [*q.v.*] in 1951, before concluding that the monarchy and military would stand or fall together. He then turned against Mussadiq.

Under the guise of the Retired Officers Club, Zahidi organized the secret Committee to Save the Fatherland, consisting of the military officers retired by Mussadiq in 1952. By late July 1953 the Committee had become one of the two clandestine forces planning the overthrow of the Mussadiq government, the other being the U.S. Central Intelligence Agency (CIA). Before fleeing Iran on 16 August, Muhammad Reza Shah Pahlavi [*q.v.*] dismissed Mussadiq and appointed Zahedi prime minister even though he was in hiding. Three days later, as Mussadiq ordered the army and the police to restore order in Tehran, pro-shah troops arrived from Hamadan, a stronghold of Zahedi. He led an assault on Mussadiq's residence and captured him after a nine-hour battle.

When he formed the subsequent cabinet a third of his nominees were generals. Together with the shah, he followed a three-pronged policy toward the opposition: annihilation of the Tudeh Party [*q.v.*], repression of the National Front [*q.v.*], and surveillance of independent-minded clerics. His government reestablished relations with Britain, broken off by Mussadiq, and handed over the running of the country's petroleum industry to a Western oil consortium. He was dismissed from his office in April 1955, a sign of the shah's growing confidence

Zaidis: *Shia Muslim sect* Zaidis share the first four Imams of Twelver Shias [*q.v.*]—Ali, Hussein, Hassan, and Zain al-Abidin, a grandson of Imam Ali, a son-in-law of the Prophet Muhammad (570–632 A.D.)—but follow a different line with Zaid, son of Muhammad bin al-Hanafiya and half-brother of Imam Hussein bin Ali. According to Zaidis, any descendent of Ali can be an Imam [*q.v.*]. What he has to demonstrate is his ability to rule according to the Sharia [*q.v.*]. Since they do not claim infallibility for their Imams [*q.v.*], who are elected by notables of the Zaidi community, they are in least conflict with the Sunni doctrine [*q.v.*]. Zaidi principalities existed in northern Iran and Yemen in the ninth century A.D. The Zaidi state of Yemen, established by Imam Yahya bin Hussein al-Rassi in (North) Yemen in 898 A.D., continued, with some interruptions, until 1962.

Zaim, Hosni (1890–1949): *Syrian military leader and politician; president, 1949* Born into a Kurdish [*q.v.*] family in Aleppo [*q.v.*], Zaim was trained to become an officer in the Ottoman Turkish army. After World War I he was drafted into the Special Forces formed by the French Mandate authority. He stayed with the pro-German government of France, based in Vichy, during World War II. Following the defeat of the Vichy forces by the British and the Free French in 1941, he was jailed. After his release he was allowed to rejoin the Syrian army. He rose rapidly in rank. During the 1948–49 Palestine War [*q.v.*], he was promoted to brigadier and appointed chief of staff.

Working in conjunction with the American Embassy in Damascus [*q.v.*], intent on securing recognition of Israel by its Arab neighbors, Zaim mounted the country's first military coup on 30 March 1949. He deposed the popularly elected president, Shukri al-Quwatli [*q.v.*]; dissolved parliament; and established military rule. Following a rigged referendum in late June, he was elected president with wide powers.

On 20 July he signed an armistice agreement with Israel whereby he gave up the small enclave Syria held in Palestine [*q.v.*]. Pro-American in foreign policy, he backed Washington's proposal for a Middle East military pact. Through the United States he attempted to establish contact with Israeli leaders, indicating that he was interested in peace. This, and his partiality toward the Kurdish and Circassian [*q.v.*] units in the army, caused much disaffection among the officer corps. On 14 August a group of military officers, led by Col. Sami Hinnawi, staged a coup against Zaim. Following a summary trial by a military court, he was executed.

zakat (Arabic: derivative of *zakaa*, to be pure): The performing of *zakat*, mentioned in the Quran [*q.v.*] as the "free will offerings for the poor and needy…, the ransoming of slaves, debtors in God's way and the traveler," was later refined as obligatory charity by the believer and included in the five pillars of Islam [*q.v.*]. The underlying principle is that a Muslim [*q.v.*] should purify his/her wealth by paying his/her dues to the community, which spends the resources for social purposes. With the introduction of *fiqh* [*q.v.*] (Islamic jurisprudence), zakat was prescribed as a religious tax and regulated. The Shafii code [*q.v.*], for instance, prescribed zakat on cereal and fruit crops, livestock, gold and silver, and merchandise, the tax varying from 10 percent on crops to 2.5 percent on merchandise and gold and silver. In modern times *zakat* is paid either to the government of a Muslim country or to a Muslim religious-legal scholar, to be spent in ways prescribed by the Sharia [*q.v.*].

Zarqawi, Abu Mussab (1966–2006): *Jordanian jihadist and leader of Al-Qaida in Mesopotamia* [*q.v.*] Born Ahmad Fadil al-Khalalyle in Zarqa, Jordan, he was the seventh child of a Palestinian couple. A few years after he left school, he became interested in Islam [*q.v.*] and the jihad [*q.v.*] in Afghanistan. He arrived in Afghanistan in the spring of 1989 just after the Soviet troops had left. He became a reporter for *Al Bonian al-Marous* (Arabic: *The Strong Will*), an Islamist publication, interviewing those Arab [*q.v.*] mujahedin who had fought in Afghanistan. On returning to Jordan in 1992, he joined a group called *Bayat al-Imam* (Arabic: *Loyalty to the Imam*). In 1993 he was arrested for possessing rifles and bombs. In prison he started memorizing the Quran [*q.v.*], and his Islamist beliefs hardened. He was released in 1999 as part of an amnesty.

Early next year he took his dying mother to Peshawar, Pakistan, for medical treatment. In his absence the government accused him of a foiled terrorist plot against "a Christian pilgrimage place." When his mother died and his Pakistani visa expired, he crossed into the Taliban-ruled Afghanistan in June 2000. There he joined a training camp run by Al Qaida [*q.v.*]. After the fall of the Taliban in December 2001, he crossed into Iran and from there into an enclave of Iraqi Kurdistan [*q.v.*], then administered by the pro-American Patriotic Union of Kurdistan [*q.v.*].

After the fall of the regime of President Saddam Hussein [*q.v.*], Zarqawi's organization changed its name from *Ansar al-Islam* (Arabic: *Helpers of Islam*) to *Jamaat al-Tawihid wal Jihad* (Arabic: *Society of Divine Unity and Jihad*; JTJ). It offered resistance to the American occupation authority by attacking it and those Iraqis cooperating with it, as well as Iraqi Shias [*q.v.*].

Among the various Sunni [*q.v.*] groups resisting the American occupation, the JTJ emerged as the most lethal. It claimed responsibility for such dramatic acts as the bombing of the UN mission in Baghdad in 2003 and the assassination of the Iraqi Governing Council's president Izzeddine Salim 10 months later. The Pentagon raised the price on Zarqawi's head from $10 million to $25 million.

In 2004 the JTJ became an affiliate of Al Qaida and changed its name to Al Qaida in Mesopotamia (AQM) [*q.v.*] (Arabic: *Tanzim Qaidat al-Jihad fi Bilad al-Rafidayn*). It sent suicide bombers into Shia gatherings in Baghdad [*q.v.*] and Karbala [*q.v.*] to devastating effect. It took Westerners as hostages and beheaded some.

Arguing that the authority to legislate rested with Allah's word as revealed in the Quran [*q.v.*], the AQM opposed democracy and elections. It backed the decision of the Sunni tribal leaders to boycott the election for the Interim National Assembly in January 2005. It focused on high-profile and coordinated suicide attacks and created insecurity in the public at large. Because of its addiction to violence for violence's sake, and its intolerance of those who differed from it, the AQM began to lose whatever popular support it had gained earlier.

To reverse the trend, in January 2006, Zarqawi created the Islamic World Council to gather all Sunni resistance groups under one banner. His endeavor ended abruptly in June when he was killed in an operation mounted by the American and Iraqi forces.

Zawahiri, Ayman Muhammad (1951–): *Egyptian Islamist ideologue-politician, leader of Al-Qaida [q.v.] 2011–* (aka Abu Muhammad; Muhammad Ibrahim) Son of a Cairo University pharmacology professor, Muhammad Zawahiri, and grandson of Rabiaa Zawahiri, the Grand Shaikh of Al Azhar University [*q.v.*], he became politically active and was arrested as a member of the outlawed Muslim Brotherhood [*q.v.*] in 1965. He graduated as a surgeon from Cairo University's medical school in 1978.

He was a cofounder of Al Jihad al-Islami [*q.v.*], headed by Ismail Tantawi. When Tantawi moved to West Germany, Zawahiri became Al Jihad's leader. After the assassination of President Muhammad Anwar Sadat [*q.v.*] in 1981, he was jailed for three years for participating in the assassination plot. He was the author of the first manifest of Al Jihad, titled *The Philosophy of Confrontation*.

In 1986 Zawahiri traveled to Pakistan and joined the medical corps in Peshawar to serve the Islamist Mujahedin fighting the Soviets and the Soviet-backed regime in Afghanistan. There he met Osama bin Laden [*q.v.*]. He established a branch of Al Jihad in Peshawar as well as a monthly magazine, *Al-Ghazu* (Arabic: *The Conquest*). He stayed on in Peshawar after the Soviet military withdrawal from Afghanistan in 1989.

In 1992, he traveled to Sudan to join bin Laden. As leader of the Egyptian militant Islamist group, he wanted to focus on waging jihad in Egypt, whereas bin Laden advocated targeting America. The Islamic Jihad's unsuccessful attempts to assassinate the Egyptian prime minister and foreign minister, followed by the arrest of more than 1,000 of its activists, weakened the organization. The attempt to kill Egyptian president Hosni Mubarak [*q.v.*] during his visit to Addis Ababa in 1995, masterminded by the Islamic Jihad and al-Gamaat al-Islamiya [*q.v.*], failed.

Zawahiri scoured several European countries in 1996–97 in search of sanctuary and funds. When he tried to enter the Dagestan province of Russia without a visa in December 1996, he was arrested. His incarceration lasted six months.

On his release he traveled to Jalalabad in Afghanistan where bin Laden was then based. It was there that, in February 1998, Al Jihad, led by Zawahiri, allied with the Al Qaida network of bin Laden to form the World Islamic Front for Jihad against Crusaders and Jews [*q.v.*], with Al Jihad members concentrating on forging documents, transferring money, and arranging communications, and Zawahiri emerging as the ideologue of the World Islamic Front.

On 4 November 1998 a federal grand jury in the United States returned a 238-count indictment—covering 227 murders caused by the bombings of the American embassies in Nairobi and Dar as Salam in August 1998 and 11 other charges—against bin Laden and 16 others, including Zawahiri, and charging them with leading a terrorist conspiracy from 1989 to the present, working in concert with other terrorists to build weapons and attack American military installations.

In 1999 a court in Cairo [*q.v.*] sentenced Zawahiri to death in absentia for his leading role in the terrorist assaults in Egypt in the earlier years of the decade. Following the terrorist attacks in New York and Washington on 11 September 2001, Zawahiri was named as one of the leading conspirators by the United States, which offered a reward of $25 million for information leading to his capture. He was sitting next to bin Laden when the latter broadcast a 20-minute statement on Al-Jazeera TV on 7 October 2001 after the Pentagon started bombing Afghanistan.

After the collapse of the Taliban government in Afghanistan two months later, he is believed to have escaped into Pakistan's tribal areas adjoining the Afghan border.

The publication of his book *Knights under the Prophet's Banner: Meditations on the Jihadist Movement* in December 2001 established him as the leading ideologue of Al Qaida.

In the videotapes released by Al Qaida, he always appeared next to bin Laden—until 2003, when, evidently for safety reasons, the two leaders decided to operate from separate bases.

Since then, several attempts by the Central Intelligence Agency and the Pakistani military to kill him have failed. One well-publicized attempt was made in January 2006 in a village in Bajaur tribal agency of Pakistan. Later that year he advised Abu Mussab Zarqawu [*q.v.*] in Iraq to reconsider his strategy of targeting Shias [*q.v.*]. In 2007 Zawahiri is believed to have guided the two jihadist caretakers of the Red Mosque in Islamabad on how to resist the military siege that ended with the deaths of 112 people. In his video aired in August 2008, he appealed to Pakistani soldiers to reconsider their role in the fighting that had pitted them against fellow Pakistanis in the tribal region. The next month there was another failed attempt to kill or capture him in the Mohamand tribal Agency.

When pro-democracy demonstrations gathered pace in January 2011, Zawahiri took to releasing monthly recordings in which he linked the unrest in the Arab [*q.v.*] world to the jihadist inspiration behind the 9/11 attacks. After the killing of bin Laden on 2 May 2011 by U.S. Special Forces

in the Pakistani city of Abbottabad, Zawahiri was elected leader of Al Qaida. Five weeks later in his video recording he praised bin Laden. Dwelling on the uprisings in Syria and Yemen, he stressed that the post-Bashar Assad [*q.v.*] and post-Ali Abdullah Saleh [*q.v.*] regimes must transform themselves into Islamic states where Sharia [*q.v.*] has "the last word." In February 2012, he called on Muslims [*q.v.*] in Iraq, Jordan, Lebanon, and Turkey to join the fight against "the pernicious, cancerous regime" of Assad.

Zion: Zion is the Canaanite name of the hill upon which Jerusalem [*q.v.*] stood. In the Old Testament [*q.v.*] the name pertains to the easternmost hill of Jerusalem, which was the site of the royal palace—the center of Hebrew government and worship—built by King David (r. 1010–970 B.C.) of Israel. Following the destruction of Jerusalem by the Babylonians and the exile of the Jews [*q.v.*] in 586 B.C., Zion became embedded in the communal psyche. It was the site to which the Jews would be restored, where they would find Yahweh/Jehovah. Thus over the centuries Zion acquired the connotation of the Jewish homeland, and was adopted by those 19th-century Jews who wanted to set up a Jewish national center or state in Palestine [*q.v.*].

Zionism and Zionists: *A Jewish doctrine and movement* Zionism, the term named after Zion [*q.v.*], the hill in ancient Jerusalem [*q.v.*] upon which the royal palace of King David (r. 1010–970 B.C.) was built, was coined by Nathan Birnbaum in 1893. It was applied to the Jewish nationalist movement that aimed to create a Jewish state or national center in Ottoman Palestine [*q.v.*], the historic homeland of the ancestors of Jews [*q.v.*]. Until then the aspiration to return to Zion had been couched in religious terms and expressed in the liturgy. The movement gained ground among the Jews of Europe in the 19th century, when the political emancipation of the Jewish communities, and their assimilation into the mainstream culture, failed to secure them full acceptance.

In 1862 Moses Hess, a German Jew, published a book entitled *Rome and Jerusalem*, which advocated the return of Jews to Palestine and the creation of a spiritual center there for the Jewish diaspora [*q.v.*]. This was religious Zionism, which called on Jews to return to Zion for religious reasons. The idea was adopted by the *Hovevei Zion* (Hebrew: *Lovers of Zion*) societies that sprang up in Russia soon after the pogroms of 1881–1882 following the assassination of Tsar Alexander II. They organized the first immigration wave into Palestine. This was seen as part of an effort to create a spiritual center for Jewish civilization by such Jewish thinkers as Ahad HaAam (1875–1927), who stressed the significance of maintaining a Jewish national culture, including developing Hebrew [*q.v.*] as a modern language.

It was left to Theodor Herzl (1860–1904), an Austro-Hungarian Jewish journalist, to give a political dimension to the concept of Zionism. In his pamphlet *Der Judenstaat* (German: *The Jewish State*) (1896) he argued for a Jewish homeland to be set up— preferably, but not necessarily, in Ot-

toman Palestine—and that it should be secured through an international agreement. The next year Herzl convened the first Zionist Congress [*q.v.*] in Basle, Switzerland. It established the Zionist Organization [*q.v.*]—later called the World Zionist Organization (WZO) [*q.v.*]—which stated: "Zionism strives to create for the Jewish people a home in Palestine secured by public law." Most of the Hovevei Zion societies affiliated to the WZO, based in Vienna, Austria. The Ottoman sultan turned down Herzl's proposal for autonomy for Palestine, which was not a single administrative unit of the empire. Britain offered 6,000 sq. mi./15,550 sq. km of virgin land in Uganda to WZO in 1903, but the Seventh Zionist Congress in 1905 rejected the overture.

With the failure of the Russian revolution of 1905, and the subsequent repression and pogroms, the migration of Russian Jewish youths to Palestine increased, as did support for the Zionist movement among European Jews. Since many of the Russian settlers were socialists, Marxist, and non-Marxist, socialist Zionism found a home in Palestine, which by 1914 had some 90,000 Jews.

When World War I started, political Zionism became dominant, with the Russian Jews settled in Britain taking over its leadership. Two such figures, Chaim Weizmann and Nahum Sokolow, played a crucial role in securing the Balfour Declaration [*q.v.*] from the British government in late 1917. It pledged official backing for the creation of a Jewish national home in Palestine, and was incorporated into Britain's League of Nations mandate over Palestine in 1922. The mandate made a Jewish agency—the WZO until 1929 and then the Jewish Agency for Palestine [*q.v.*], working in coordination with the government in Palestine—responsible for Jewish immigration and settlement.

The 1920s and 1930s witnessed the development and consolidation of Jewish life in Palestine, funded by the WZO, which was financed mainly by American Jews. The Jewish community in Palestine was represented by an elected *Vaad Leumi* (Hebrew: *National Council*), a trade union federation, Histadrut [*q.v.*], and a militia, Haganah [*q.v.*].

The Jewish population increased from 108,000 in 1925 to 446,000 in 1939. Seeing their proportion in the national population rapidly decreasing, the Arabs [*q.v.*] protested, rioting in 1921 and 1926, and staging a revolt from 1936 to 1939. In 1939, Britain imposed a limit of 75,000 Jewish immigrants over the next five years. But illegal immigration grew.

In November 1947 the UN General Assembly, the successor to the League of Nations, recommended a swift end to the British mandate over Palestine, and partitioning of the country, giving Jews, then 30 percent of the population, 53.5 percent of Palestine, and internationalizing Jerusalem and its suburbs, covering a little over 1 percent of Palestine. The WZO accepted the UN plan; the Arabs rejected it. Civil conflict erupted.

The founding of the State of Israel on 14 May 1948 triggered the Arab-Israeli War [*q.v.*]. During this war, besides occupying the Jewish sector allocated to it by the UN, Israel annexed half of the area allotted to the Arabs—reducing their share to 23.4

percent of Palestine, including part of Jerusalem—and expelled some 760,000 Arabs, who became refugees. The affiliates to the WZO in 70 countries continued to provide financial backing to Israel and encourage Jews to settle there. In the June 1967 Arab-Israeli War [*q.v.*], Israel occupied the remainder of Palestine.

On 10 November 1975, the UN General Assembly passed Resolution 3379, which defined Zionism as "a form of racism and racial discrimination" by 72 votes to 35, with 32 abstentions. Sixteen years later, on 16 December 1991, the UN General Assembly revoked this resolution by 111 votes to 25, with 13 abstentions.

Unable to quell the intifada [*q.v.*] of the Palestinians [*q.v.*], which started in the Occupied Territories [*q.v.*] in 1987, Israel signed an accord on Palestinian autonomy with the Palestinian Liberation Organization (PLO) [*q.v.*], called the Oslo Accord I [*q.v.*], in 1993, thus recognizing the right Palestinians to their own state within the boundaries of the Palestine of the British Mandate.

Zionist Congresses: The first Zionist Congress was convened by Theodor Herzl (1860–1904) in Basle, Switzerland, in 1897. It established the Zionist Organization [*q.v.*]—later called the World Zionist Organization (WZO) [*q.v.*]—and stated: "Zionism [*q.v.*] strives to create for the Jewish people a home in Palestine [*q.v.*] secured by public law." It elected a 15-strong executive committee, headed by Herzl as president, and became the legislative body of the WZO.

The Fifth Zionist Congress in 1901 set up the Jewish National Fund

(JNF) [*q.v.*] under the WZO's land and development section to finance the (communal) purchase of land in Palestine. The Seventh Congress in 1905 rejected Britain's offer of land in Uganda for the Jewish homeland. The Tenth Congress in 1911 elected Otto Warburg as president of the WZO. He advocated working on both diplomatic and colonization fronts to achieve the Jewish homeland in Palestine. The Twelfth Congress in 1921 thanked Britain for the Balfour Declaration [*q.v.*]. The increase in registered Zionists (who elected delegates based on territorial unions and affiliated party unions) from 164,333 in 1907 to 855,590 in 1921 indicated the popularity of the movement.

At President Chaim Weizmann's behest, the Sixteenth Zionist Congress in 1929 established a proper Jewish Agency for Palestine [*q.v.*], with its own executive committee, consisting of an equal number of Zionists and non-Zionists—that is, those who supported the idea of a Jewish national home in Palestine but did not subscribe to political Zionism.

After the Eighteenth Zionist Congress in 1933 had resolved that "in all Zionist matters discipline in regard of the Zionist Organization must take precedence over the discipline of any other body," the Revisionist Zionists [*q.v.*] left. They returned to the WZO at the Twenty-second Congress in December 1946 (elected by 2,159,840 Zionists) which—taking its cue from the resolution of the American Zionist Congress in May 1942 at the Biltmore Hotel, New York City—demanded the formation of an independent Jewish state in all of Palestine.

The Twenty-third Congress, held in Jerusalem [*q.v.*] in 1951, formulated its objectives in the light of the founding of Israel: consolidation of Israel and the ingathering of the Jews [*q.v.*] in the diaspora [*q.v.*]. It resolved to move the WZO headquarters from London to Jerusalem. The Twenty-sixth Congress in 1964 endorsed the new constitution adopted in 1960 by the General Council which inter alia formalized the practice of holding a congress every four years.

The Thirty-sixth Congress was held in June 2010 in Jerusalem.

Zionist Organization: Founded in 1897, the Zionist Organization renamed itself the World Zionist Organization [*q.v.*] in 1960. *See* World Zionist Organization.

Zoroastrianism and Zoroastrians: *an ancient religion that is named after its founder, Zoroaster or Zarathustra* He is believed to have lived between 1750 B.C. and 1000 B.C. in a region that now covers eastern Iran and the southern part of Central Asia, The hymns attributed to him form the liturgical core of Zoroastrianism. In his era, society was divided into three castes: priests, warriors, and herdsmen and agriculturists. This is mirrored in Zoroastrianism, where particular *daivas* (heavenly ones) or gods, are associated with each caste. Above all these gods is Ahura Mazda (Old Persian: *Wise Lord*), who, according to the *gathas* (verses) attributed to Zoroaster, is the creator of heaven and earth and the supreme lawmaker. At the beginning of creation, his twin sons, Spenta Mainyu (Old Persian: *Generous Spirit*) and Angra Mainyu (Old Persian: *Destructive Spirit*), engaged in any ongoing struggle and threw the world into turmoil, which only the virtuous would survive to witness a new creation. A similar dualism runs through Zoroastrian cosmology, which divides the history of the universe into four ages of 3,000 years each, where the eternal struggle is between Ahura Mazda, who lives in the light, and Ahriman (derivative of Angra Mainyu, *Destructive Spirit*), who lives in the dark.

Zoroaster's teaching is based on the *Avesta*, the scripture in the ancient Persian language [*q.v.*] of Avestan, which includes various texts, such as the *Yasna* (Sacrifice), the *Yashts,* and the *Vendidad*. The *Yasna* includes verses attributed to Zoroaster, even though the text was not assembled in written form until about a millennium after Zoroaster's death. He stressed ethical and ritual purity, and retained the ancient cult of fire. During the fire ceremony the *Yasna* is recited, and haoma (an unfermented or intoxicating beverage) is consumed.

Since Ahura Mazda rules over all others, and is the father of all spirits, both good and evil, Zoroastrianism is considered monotheistic. It had an impact on Christianity [*q.v.*] and Islam [*q.v.*]. Each of the three castes in Persia regarded Zoroaster as a model. His doctrine spread to present-day Afghanistan and Tajikistan as well as Iran and Kurdistan [*q.v.*]. It flourished in the Achaemenian period (550–330 B.C.), suffered neglect during the Greek period that followed the conquest of this region by Alexander of Macedonia in 330 B.C., but revived at the end of the Parthian Empire (247 B.C.–226 A.D). It became the state religion during the Sassanian period (226–

640 A.D.). Under the Sassanian rule the *Avesta* was compiled and translated into the vernacular, Pahlavi [*q.v.*]. In addition, the dualistic doctrine, which had started to replace the monotheism of the gathas during the Achaemenian period, became the norm.

With the arrival of Islam [*q.v.*] in Persia and Afghanistan, the hold of Zoroastrianism began to wane. It survived until the 10th century, when diehard Zoroastrians migrated to the western coast of India, where they became known as Parsis. A small minority survived in Iran. The constitution of the Islamic Republic of Iran recognizes Zoroastrians, along with Christians and Jews [*q.v.*], as a religious minority, and allocates them one representative in a parliament of 270 members; in 2008, he represented a community of 21,000 Zoroastrians.

The Zoroastrian calendar, based on a solar cycle, consists of 12 months of 30 days each. The additional five or six days are kept for "remembering the dead."

Index

Index

Index

Index

Index

Index

Index

Index

Index

DATE DUE

GAYLORD		PRINTED IN U.S.A.